Gun Digest

33rd Anniversary

1979 Deluxe Edition

EDITED BY JOHN T. AMBER

DBI BOOKS, INC., NORTHFIELD, ILL.

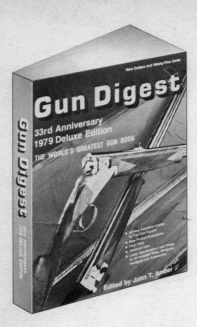

GUN DIGEST STAFF

EDITOR-IN-CHIEF

John T. Amber

ASSOCIATE EDITORS

Harold A. Murtz

Bob Anderson

ASSISTANT EDITOR

Lilo Anderson

CONTRIBUTING EDITORS

Roger Barlow

Bob Bell

Bob Hagel

Wallace Labisky

Maj. Geo. C. Nonte, Jr.

Larry S. Sterett

Kenneth L. Waters

A. M. Wynne, Jr.

EUROPEAN EDITOR

Raymond Caranta

GRAPHIC DESIGNS

James P. Billy

Casey Ziolkowski

ASSOCIATE PUBLISHER

Sheldon L. Factor

Our Covers

This year's covers, front and back, do honor to one of our oldest companies, Browning, now celebrating its Centennial Anniversary. On our front cover is a unique achievement in gunmaking history, for the Browning over-under double rifle, called the Continental, is the first ever manufactured in series production, here or abroad.

See our detailed article on this handsome rifle/shotgun set and other new Brownings further on in this issue.

Our back cover portrays Browning's Hi-Power 9mm auto-loading pistol, given special treatment for their 100th anniversary—special chrome-plating, oil-finished and hand-checkered walnut stocks, and the Centennial dates hand-engraved on the slide.

J.T.A.

Manuscripts, contributions and inquiries, including first class return postage, should be sent to the Gun Digest Editorial Offices, 540 Frontage Rd., Northfield, Ill. 60093. All material received will receive reasonable care, but we will not be responsible for its safe return. Material accepted is subject to our requirements for editing and revisions. Author payment covers all rights and title to the accepted material, including photos, drawings and other illustrations. Payment is made at our current rates.

ISBN-0-695-81200-9   Library of Congress Catalog #44-3588

IN THE BLACK ●

Townsend Whelen Award

Donald M. Simmons, Jr. is the recipient of our $500 award, its 13th presentation, for his deeply researched and authoritative article, "The Remington Model 51," for which he also did the splendid drawings and photographs.

This annual award is made to the writer who, in our judges' opinions, made the most outstanding contribution to arms literature, as published in GUN DIGEST.

Our sincere congratulations to Mr. Simmons, and our thanks.

NBRSA Gun Digest Heavy Varmint Trophy

Walt Berger, of Overland Park, Missouri, shot a grand aggregate of .2836 MOA to take the GUN DIGEST trophy for this match, his rifle a Hart-barreled 222 on a Stolle action. Berger made his own 51-gr. bullets, the dies by Rorschach.

Questions and Answers

Demands on the editors are such that not all letters can be answered, though we try. A stamped, addressed-to-oneself, envelope must be included. However, before writing to us for the location of suppliers, please see our Directory of the Arms Trade pages—you'll probably save a stamp.

An Offer You Can't Refuse!

Although some 500 Americans subscribe to the British weekly, *Shooting Times & Country Magazine,* thus receiving an entertaining and informative publication dealing with shooting matters, fishing, fox hunting and other field sports, the Editor feels that if more of us could read a few issues his U. S. circulation would increase.

To this end Editor Jackson is offering to send *free* a one month subscription to everyone here who sends him a postcard giving his name and address.

The pages of this unique magazine abound with superb writing. Indeed, many of us feel that the column by Gough Thomas, that erudite English authority on shooting matters, is alone worth the cost of a subscription.

Write: Mr. Tony Jackson, Editor, Shooting Times & Country Magazine, 10, Sheet Street, Windsor, SL4 1BG, England.

IBS Gun Digest Heavy Varmint Trophy

Pat McMillan of Phoenix, Arizona, who did all the gunsmithing/stocking of his 6mm PPC Remington 40X, won our GUN DIGEST trophy with a grand aggregate of .2799 MOA for the 100/200-yd. matches held at Mainville, Pennsylvania. He shot Broughton 70-gr. bullets.

Outdoorsman of the Year

Grits Gresham, shooting editor of *Sports Afield* magazine, and a long time ardent hunter/conservationist, was the winner of Winchester-Western's annual award for the year's outstanding outdoorsman—this signal honor was accorded Gresham by the votes of his colleguesin a nation-wide poll.

Bill Talley, Winchester senior vice president, made the presentation during the National Sporting Goods Assn. meeting last January at Houston, Texas. Accompanying the placque was a Winchester Model 101 over-under shotgun in Pigeon Grade.

Outstanding Handgunner Award

Pictured nearby is the winner of the 1977 Outstanding American Handgunner Award, Charles A. "Skeeter" Skelton. The presentation was made April 16, 1978 in Salt Lake City, Utah, during the NRA convention.

Best wishes and congratulations to Skeeter, a worthy recipient.

Jack O'Connor 1902-1978

While returning from a sea voyage to Hawaii aboard the SS Mariposa, Jack O'Connor died of a heart attack on January 19th, 1978. He would have been 76 the following Sunday.

Arms and ammunition editor of *Outdoor Life* for over 30 years, O'Connor became a world famous figure to million of readers. During his long editorship and after he received tens of thousands of letters asking for his advice and counsel.

A prolific writer, O'Connor produced a dozen or so books and hundreds of articles for periodical sporting publications, including the GUN DIGEST. His most popular work was *The Rifle Book,* first issued by A. A. Knopf in 1948, and offered in later years in revised and enlarged format. Other books by O'Connor still in print include *The Complete Book of Rifles and Shotguns, The Hunting Rifle* and *Sheep and Sheep Hunting*—a subject dear indeed to Jack's heart. He had made two "grand slams" on sheep—Desert, Big Horn, Dall and Stone.

Jack O'Connor, who had hunted the world over, won the coveted Weatherby Big Game Trophy in 1957.

Not an easy man to know, at times charming or irascible, Jack O'Connor and I became warm friends over the years. His death came as a great shock, and I'll miss his stentorian-voiced, often profane phone calls.

CONTENTS

DEPARTMENTS

The Remington

by DONALD M. SIMMONS, Jr.

Pair of consecutive serialized Model 51s—32 ACP, PA 65629 (above), PA 65630 (right). Both pistols are assembly-date coded but with different code.

IF ONE WERE ASKED to name milestones in the design of the pocket automatic pistol I believe the following outstanding guns must be mentioned: The Browning 1900 because it was the first successful one; the Walther PP and PPK of 1929 and 1931 respectively; the Mauser HSc of 1938 and the Sauer H (38) of 1938—all German. To this list of Who's Who I would add the Remington Model 51; each of the pistols mentioned owes something to the earlier Remington.

Remington Arms Company is the oldest of all U.S. firearms makers, having started in business in 1816. Though today we think of this great firm as a maker of shoulder arms only, Remington made handguns until 1930. Even today Remington makes a single shot high powered bolt action pistol, the XP-100. Two other Remington handguns were made in the 20th century. One is the venerable Model 95 double derringer in 41 rimfire, the other is the Remington Model 51 autoloading pistol.

The Designer

John Douglas Pedersen, born in Denmark, made his home for a time in Jackson's Hole, Wyoming. He licensed his firearms designs to Rem-

ington and acted as their consultant, starting in 1907 with a pump action repeating shotgun. The first such firearm made by Remington, it was named the Model 10. "JD," as Pedersen was called at Remington, next designed the Model 12, a pump action 22 rifle, in 1909. In 1912, Pedersen designed Remington's pump action high powered rifle, the Model 14, later called the 141 or "Gamemaster," which took the same cartridges as the Browning-designed Model 8 autoloading rifle. During World War I Pedersen designed a device to allow the foot soldier to convert his bolt action Springfield Model '03 (Mark I) to a semi-automatic rifle shooting a pistol cartridge from a 40-round magazine. Amazingly, the soldier could make this conversion without tools, in the field. The "Pedersen Device" came too late in the war to be used against the Germans. After the war these hush-hush conversions were scrapped by our government. On June 5, 1918, Remington offered a Pedersen-designed 45-cal. autoloading pistol to the U.S. Navy, the Model 53, big brother of the earlier-designed Model 51.

The trial of the M53 was held at Savage Arms Company's range in

Utica, New York, starting on June 5, 1918. The extensive test ran for three days, pitted against the standard Colt 1911 and the experimental Grant Hammond 45. Also tested at this trial was a Remington M51 in 380 caliber. Lawrence Goodstal, Remington design engineer and currently curator of their museum, has a copy of the test report which shows that the M51 was fired for velocity using Savage Arms chronographic equipment. Of the four trial pistols, the 380 gave a high average of 861.3 feet per second against the three 45s—Colt hit 791.9 fps, Remington 777.2, the Grant Hammond 805.6.

The Navy liked the M53 but Remington wanted so much money for development that the Navy decided to stick with the Colt 1911. There is no mention of whether the Navy was impressed with the performance of the Model 51 and if it fired the 5,250 round test performed by the other three pistols.

After the war "JD" was still with Remington. In 1921 he worked with the great one, John M. Browning, on the Remington Model 17, a 20-gauge pump shotgun. In 1923 Pedersen and Loomis designed for Remington the Model 25, a pared-down Model 14. It

Model 51

A definitive and deeply
detailed study of the U.S. arms
industry's highest quality and safest pocket
pistol ever made. Slim, flat and
beautifully balanced, this truly unique product
of John D. Pedersen's genius fitted
the palm like the hand of a friend.

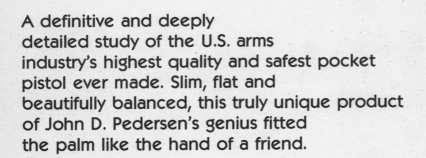

was the last Remington arm credited to J. D. Pedersen.

In 1923 John Pedersen began working for the U.S. government at Springfield Massachusetts Arsenal, designing a semi-automatic rifle for military use. Pedersen, then paid a munificent $10,000 a year, developed a new retarded-blowback rifle with a toggle action using its own special waxed cartridge* in 276 caliber. At the same time at Springfield, John C. Garand, receiving a paltry $3500 per year, was working on what would become our M-1 rifle of World War II fame, then also in 276 caliber. Both designs were looked on with favor but Gen. Douglas MacArthur, then Chief of Staff, decided to retain the 30-06 cartridge. The Garand rifle could function with the cartridge, the Pedersen could not.

John D. Pedersen, then living in Blandford, a suburb of Springfield, went on vacation to Sedona, Arizona in May of 1951, where he died of a heart attack. Pedersen, in a way,

worked in an unfortunate period—he was a younger man during the Browning era and an older one in the Garand period. His ideas, though great, were somewhat overshadowed by these inventive titans.

The Remington Model 51

In late 1914 or early 1915 Pedersen conceived the design of the Remington Model 51. The original U.S. Patent application was made in July of 1915. This application, renewed 4 years later, was granted on August 3, 1920 as patent number 1,348.733. It has an impressive 19 pages of drawings, among them 85 separate figures. The 52 pages of explanation are followed by 262 claims, bringing the total number of pages to 103. Also, on page 52, is the information that 11 additional patents were co-pending on other features of this well-documented pistol. A reading and studying of Pedersen's patent can be an education on astute small arms design, for Pedersen was always the professional engineer, never the backshed putterer. When all the various patents involved with the Model 51 are stacked together they're as thick as the Manhattan telephone directory.

The Action

The Pedersen Model 51 action design is truly unique among handguns, since it is neither a blowback nor a recoil system. In a typical blowback auto pistol the slide is driven backward, away from the barrel, by the rearward thrust of the cartridge, acting as a piston. The speed of movement or velocity of the slide is controlled only by its mass. The slide is usually made heavy enough to avoid the premature opening of the breech until the pressure in the chamber/barrel has dropped to a safe level. The residual pressure, acting through the cartridge case, pushes the slide to the fully open position. In a blowback pistol an extractor is unnecessary during normal cycling. Its only real function occurs during manual unloading, at which time it will draw an unfired round from the chamber. In a blowback system the barrel is not locked to the slide. Because of the limitations a too-heavy slide imposes on handgun design, there are very few successful high powered blowback automatic pistols.[†]

---

*This lubricated cartridge was required in Pedersen's retarded-blowback action because it helped extraction rather than having the cartridge rupture. This is a perennial problem with high powered blowback actions.

[†]Outstanding examples are the Astra 400 (9mm Bergmann Largo), the Astra 600 (9mm Luger) and the Beretta Models 1915 and 1923, both in 9mm Glisenti caliber.

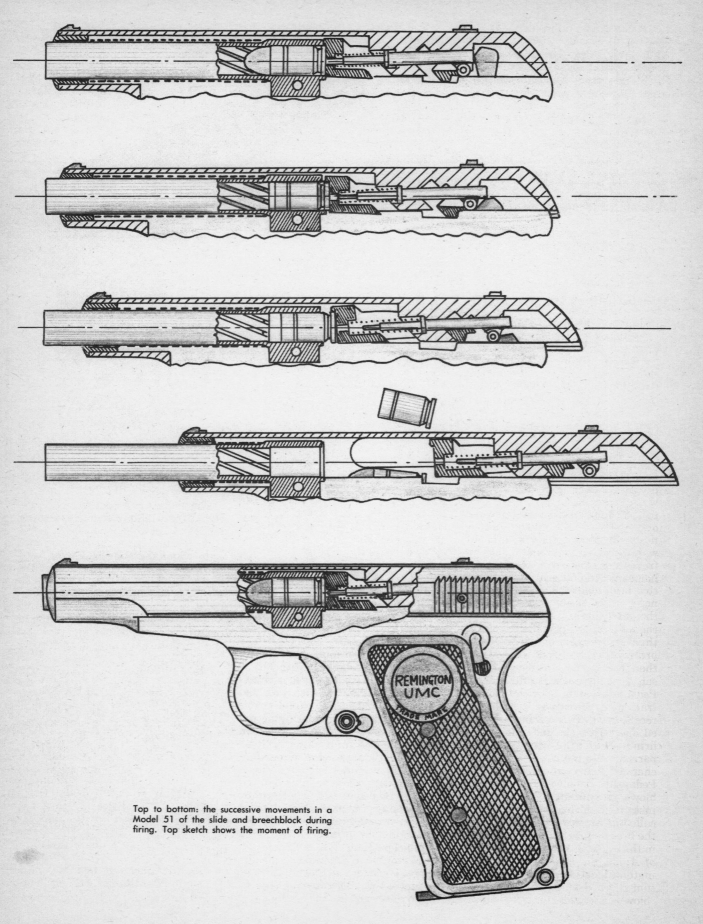

Top to bottom: the successive movements in a Model 51 of the slide and breechblock during firing. Top sketch shows the moment of firing.

In a typical recoil-operated pistol (we will consider here short-recoil types only) the slide is locked to the barrel at the moment of firing, and both units recoil a short distance (less than the length of a loaded cartridge), at which point the slide is unlocked from the barrel and, with its acquired momentum, continues to move rearward to the fully open position. The extractor, during the slide's movement, draws the empty cartridge from the now-arrested barrel. The extractor does, therefore, function during the regular firing cycle of the pistol.

In Pedersen's combination of these actions we have a blowback-recoil operation, as I'll call it. The slide is made in two pieces; the breechblock, which is relatively light, and the slide itself, which supports the breechblock, and is much heavier. At the instant of firing a Model 51 the breechblock is rapidly driven rearward (about .083"), at which point it locks in the frame. The slide also has been driven back by contact with the breechblock. The cartridge case has moved back from the breech the same .083" but, because of its strong walls near the base, has not burst or blown out even though unsupported by the chamber's wall. Because of the straight walls on this type of cartridge there is still a gas seal which prevents powder gases escaping rearward from the barrel breech. This period of the operation represents an obvious blowback stage. The slide now continues independently rearward with the momentum acquired from the locked breechblock. When it has moved an additional .200" it lifts the breechblock out of its locking notch in the frame and carries it and the extractor-gripped empty shell to the fully open slide position. It is in this 2/10th-inch travel, when the breechblock is still locked—even though slightly open—that represents the recoil-operated phase of the Pedersen system. Notice that an extractor is required in this blowback/recoil action. This can be demonstrated by removing the extractor and firing the pistol. The empty will stay partially withdrawn from the pistol's chamber, but it won't be ejected. The Pedersen action is not a "delayed blowback" since it is not locked at the instant of firing, neither can it be called a "retarded blowback" because the breechblock is locked at one point in the cycle. R. K. Wilson, in *Textbook of Automatic Pistols*, calls the Remington Model 51 action the "Momentum Block System," but I think that "blowback/recoil" describes it with

better lucidity and accuracy. Many users of the pistol are unaware that it is not a simple blowback-operated arm because, when the slide is manually pulled back, as in loading the pistol, the breechblock is drawn up and unlocked, thus there is no point when the operator will feel the locked phase. However, if a brass rod of suitable length is inserted into the barrel and pushed rearward to simulate the action of the cartridge, the breechblock will lock after .083" of movement is exerted on the brass rod. Now, with the pistol uncocked and

deep knowledge of its designer, John D. Pedersen, and the skill and devotion to quality of its manufacturer, the Remington Arms Company. Had Pedersen's pistol been made in Spain in those post-World War I days it would have been a disaster. On the other hand, a Spanish Ruby auto pistol made by Remington is a singularly unexciting idea. In the history of the Model 51 we find just the right ingredients, perfectly blended to produce a perfect product.

There is, too, another thing the Model 51 had going for it. With the

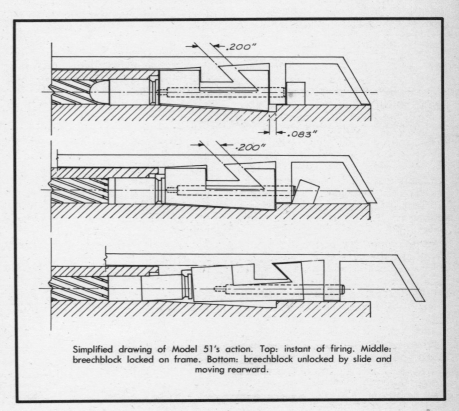

Simplified drawing of Model 51's action. Top: instant of firing. Middle: breechblock locked on frame. Bottom: breechblock unlocked by slide and moving rearward.

the grip safety depressed, hit the brass rod a sharp blow with a mallet. Even though you won't be able to see the additional slide and breechblock movement, you will find the hammer is cocked, indicating movement beyond the locked phase by the momentum of the slide.

The advantage of Pedersen's system is that it allows for a lighter slide than is usable in a pure blowback action. The fact that this system can be used in a high powered pistol was amply demonstrated by the Model 53 trial, during which it successfully fired the 45 ACP cartridge.

What made the Remington 51 so great and, if it was so great, why isn't it made today? I think the answer to both questions lies in two things—the

exception of the very limited production of Smith & Wesson's 32 pocket automatic pistol, the M51 was the last U.S. pocket automatic to appear, thus avoiding the mistakes and misconceptions made by Colt, S&W, H&R, Savage and, certainly, Warner's "Infallible." Remington and Pedersen, from this vantage point, produced the ultimate pocket automatic, one that was without peer until the products of the German triumverate—Walther, Mauser and Sauer—appeared on the market before World War II. The German firms, too, had the distinct advantage of a Nazi regime which encouraged gun production and eventually bought quantities of their pocket auto pistols.

The Pistol

Let us begin our discussion with the Remington 1923 catalog description of the Model 51:

Specifications: Hammerless, with side ejection. Magazine in 380 (9mm) cal., holds 7 cartridges and in 32 (7.65mm) cal., 8 cartridges an additional cartridge may be carried in the chamber, ready to fire instantly when the safety lever is forward. Each time the trigger is pulled one shot is fired, the empty shell is automatically ejected and a new cartridge is carried from the magazine to the chamber, ready for another shot. Length of barrel 3¼". Length over-all 6-⅝". Width or thickness ⁹/₁₀". Weight unloaded, 21 ounces. Flat matted sighting rib with low sights of the best design for accurate shooting. Furnished in black gun metal finish only. A wiping rod and bristle brush for cleaning are furnished with each pistol.

The Remington slogan, which would cause ad men to blush, was: *Fits in the palm like the hand of a friend.* This really was an apt saying, for during the design of the M51, hundreds of wax impressions of hands were used to get just the right and universal grip shape and angle. Further, the height of the barrel above the hand's grip was kept to a minimum. All these design concepts resulted in one of the most naturally pointing automatic pistols ever made. In addition, the sights were of the Patridge type, kept low so as not to catch on anything during the drawing of the pistol. The top of the slide was then matted to avoid the glare and reflections that can bother the aim under some light conditions. These refinements were most unusual in a pocket automatic pistol of those days.

The M51 is also one of the safest auto loading pistols ever made. Its multi-function grip safety serves primarily to lock the sear in a safe position at all times when the arm is cocked unless the gun is gripped in the firing position. Furthermore, when the grip safety is in its outward position, it tells the user that the pistol's concealed hammer is cocked. Finally, the grip safety, through its action on the disconnector, will lock the slide in the rearward position—retract the slide by hand and, when the slide is at the fully back position, the grip safety will snap out. The slide can be released by depressing the grip safety. If the slide's back position is to be maintained more positively, the manual safety lever can be set, which also locks the grip safety in its outward or safe position. The grip safety also locks the slide in its forward position when the pistol is cocked. This was claimed to be a safe-

ty feature that insures that the entire pistol is in the ready position and is locked at that position unless the grip safety is depressed as in firing or as would be done if a loaded cartridge were being ejected by hand.

Remington stressed that the pistol could be carried loaded and cocked with only the grip safety in operation, but those who wanted more safety could also apply the manual safety. The manual safety, also like the grip safety, serves as a hammer-position indicator. The manual safety can't be applied unless the hammer is in the cocked position and the grip safety is in the outward or "on" position.

The third safety is a magazine safety; a highly desirable feature in any automatic pistol. The magazine safety in the M51 locks the sear to the hammer when the magazine is removed from the pistol. This safety thus avoids the accident which can result when a shooter removes a magazine from a pistol and forgets to eject the loaded cartridge still in the gun's chamber. Also, pistols so equipped can have a round in the chamber with a loaded magazine stored elsewhere, being kept safely away from children or others who don't know where the "keylike" magazine is located.

The M51, from the very beginning,

had a magazine safety. Both major domestic producers of pocket automatics, Colt and Savage, did not have this feature initially. Colt added a magazine safety in 1926 but Savage never did.

Remington's advertisements on the M51 did not count the disconnector as a safety device, as did Colt. They did add, as a fourth safety feature, the fact that the hammer was completely covered. This acted to prevent accidents which might arise if a "hammered" pistol was dropped or struck by an object. In Remington's words: "The hammer cannot possibly be raised a particle by dropping the pistol or striking it against or with anything—the slide must be pulled back by hand."

The Many Patents

The "Patent Data" table shown lists the 32 U.S. patents known to be associated with the Model 51; of these, No. 1,348,733 is the basic patent, the other 31 extending and detailing those disclosures in the basic patent. Most of the U.S. patents are in John D. Pedersen's name and were not assigned to Remington Arms Company. On patent No. 1,466,749, on which Pedersen and Crawford C.

Patent Data

Subject	Patent No.	Date	Patentee	Use on Pistol
Barrel holding	1333570	Mar 9 1920*	Pedersen	Yes
Slide lock	1333571	Mar 9 1920*	Pedersen	No
Slide lock	1333572	Mar 9 1920*	Pedersen	No
Barrel bushing	1348284	Aug 3 1920*	Loomis	Yes
Basic patent	1348733	Aug 3 1920*	Pedersen	Yes
Slide lock	1355423	Oct 12 1920*	Pedersen	No
Grip safety	1355424	Oct 12 1920*	Pedersen	No
Grip safety	1355425	Oct 12 1920*	Pedersen	No
Barrel holding	1381291	Jun 14 1921*	Dygert	No
Grip safety	1387938	Aug 16 1921	Pedersen	No
Magazine safety	1389944	Sep 6 1921	Garrison	No
Grip safety	1390380	Sep 13 1921	Pedersen	No
Breechblock linked to slide	1391496	Sep 20 1921	Pedersen	No
Grip safety	1391497	Sep 20 1921	Pedersen	No
Grip safety	1391498	Sep 20 1921	Pedersen	No
Grip safety	1391499	Sep 20 1921	Pedersen	No
Grip safety	1395291	Nov 1 1921	Pedersen	No
Grip safety	1395292	Nov 1 1921	Pedersen	No
Magazine catch	1397109	Nov 15 1921	Pedersen	Yes
Extractor	1401552	Dec 27 1921	Pedersen	Yes
Trigger	1410265	Mar 21 1922	Pedersen	Yes
Method of holding grips	1410266	Mar 21 1922	Pedersen	Yes†
Grip safety	1410267	Mar 21 1922	Pedersen	No
Grip safety	1410268	Mar 21 1922	Pedersen	No
Grip safety	1410269	Mar 21 1922	Pedersen	No
Grip safety	1410270	Mar 21 1922	Pedersen	No
Barrel holding	1423358	Jul 18 1922	Pedersen	No
Machining barrel ramp	1461129	Jul 10 1923	Loomis	Yes
Magazine safety	1466749	Sep 4 1923	Pedersen & Loomis	Yes
Ejector	1518602	Dec 9 1924	Pedersen	Yes
Metal backed grip pieces	1531796	Mar 31 1925	Loomis	Yes
Cartridge pick-up 32 ACP	1571592	Feb 2 1926	Loomis	Yes

*These U.S. Patent dates are listed on the top of the slides on late manufactured 32 caliber pistols.
†Prototype only.

Remington Model 51 Auto Pistol
Sales and Serial Range*

Year	Total annual	380 ACP	32 ACP	380 ACP	32 ACP
1918	25	25	0	PA1-25	—
1919	22,966	22,966	0	PA26-22991	—
1920	12,263	12,263	0	PA22992-35254	—
1921	4,862	4,376	486	PA35255-41057	PA60801-61365
1922	5,164	2,617	2,547	PA41058-44527	PA61366-64326
Assembly Date Coding Begins					
1923	3,233	1,638	1,595	PA44528-46699	PA64327-66181
1924	2,334	1,216	1,118	PA46700-48313	PA66187-67481
1925	4,880	2,474	2,406	PA48314-51595	PA67482-70280
1926	6,034	4,617	1,417	PA51596-57717	PA90501-91917
1927	2,974	2,275	699	PA57718-60734	PA91918-92617
Shipments were made from stock or by assembling parts; all manufacturing had stopped					
1928	15	12	3	PA60735-60750	PA92618-92620
1929	39	33	6	PA60751-60794	PA92621-92626
1930	3	2	1	PA60795-60796	PA92627
1931	1	1	0	PA60797	—
1932	2	2	0	PA60798-60799	
1933	0	0	0		
1934	1	1	0	PA60800	
Totals	64,796	54,518	10,278		

*These numbers are based on "first gun in stock, first gun shipped," which is usually not the case. There are numbers for which no pistols were produced as this table shows.

Extractors used in the Model 51. Top: prototype. Middle: 380 ACP. Bottom: 32 ACP.

the withdrawal or insertion of the magazine an accidental pull on the trigger could fire the pistol. (George Garrison went on to become an important designer in his own right. He is credited with designing improvements on Remington Models 12 and 17 in 1925 and Model 14 and 141 in 1935 and, in collaboration with Loomis, on the Model 121 in 1936.)

Still, all this patent paper didn't make the M51 a market success. Though one of the safest auto pistols ever made, and probably the most instinctive-pointing handgun conceived, less than 65,000 were sold in both calibers. Colt and Savage, with earlier starts, had sold about 300,000 and 200,000 respectively by the time Remington began marketing the M51. The pistol started off well enough but sales after the first three years, or in 1921, fell off; from then on they were never in 5 figures again.

Sales of the M51 are shown in an accompanying table. The breakdown between the 380 ACP (Automatic Colt Pistol) and the 32 ACP was mathematically calculated via some known facts, but it's really no more than an educated guess on my part. The "sold per year" data comes from Remington's records.

Production of the 380 started in 1918 with an initial run of 25 pieces; the 32s began in 1921. Remington did not term these pistols 380s and 32s as we do today; the 380s were called the "Series of 1918" and all 32s were the "Series of 1921." The 380s went from serials PA 1 through PA 60,800, at

Loomis of the Ilion plant collaborated, Loomis' rights were assigned to Remington, as they usually were, but not so Pedersen's. Yet Loomis' rights on No. 1,461,129, strangely, were not assigned to Remington. Charles B. Dygert of the Ilion plant and George H. Garrison of the Bridgeport plant assigned their single patents to Remington.

There are 14 patents covering the grip safety, including the basic patent or 13 additional patents excluding the basic patent.

Interestingly, Dygert's patent shows a method of holding the barrel in the frame using only spring tension and friction. Though this patent date is listed on late 32-cal. M51s the method was never used; the older method (No. 1,333,570 of March 9, 1920) was always used.

Garrison's clever magazine safety, which required that the magazine be almost fully inserted in the pistol, was never used; the later Pedersen and Loomis device, much more complicated, was used. The Pedersen/Loomis safety was not activated until the magazine was as far as an inch and a half out of the pistol, which is not an entirely safe practice; during which point the series ended in September of 1926. The PA prefix found on every production gun's serial number stands for "Pedersen's Automatic." The 32s began in September of 1921 with serial PA 60,801, starting in the same range as the 380's terminal number. The first 32 shipped was PA 60,829. The 32s continued until they reached PA 70,280 and there they stopped for the moment. My guess is that this was intended to be the last sold, but when the stock of complete 32s were exhausted there were still some orders on hand and parts left over, so a new series was initiated, the serial number jumping to PA 90,501 and finally terminating with pistol PA 92,627. The 380 serials include many numbers for which no pistol was made. This is particularly true for the numbers from PA 50,000 on. There are also smaller blanks in the 32 block of numbers.

Why didn't the Model 51s sell? I think that, though they were very good, they were much too late. Shooters were still in love with the revolver, unconvinced of the autoloading pistol's much better qualities. Also the world depression which started in 1929 nailed down the coffin lid for the Remington as well as many other U.S.-made pocket automatics. The Colt auto was the only domestic pocket pistol to outlast this disaster, and even the Colt succumbed in the late 1940s.

Prototypes

I am lucky in owning a prototype of the Model 51, and thruout I've had the further good fortune of having closely examined the only two other known prototypes; one belongs to Mr. Sid Aberman of Pittsburgh, and the other is a cutaway version at Remington Arms Company. These pre-production pistols follow the patent drawings so closely that I'd guess they were made in 1915 or 1916. They differ from production pistols in the following points: Though the U.S. patent 1,348,733 does not show a manual safety, which all production pistols have, the prototypes also sport this feature. None of the prototypes have a magazine safety, yet this very desirable adjunct was added to all production pistols.

The grips on Mr. Aberman's prototype and Remington's cutaway are black baked rubber with the "Remington UMC" (Union Metallic Cartridge) logo but without the two-rivet-held backup plate which is found on all production 51s and on my prototype. Pedersen's original patent (1,410,266) called for these grips to be

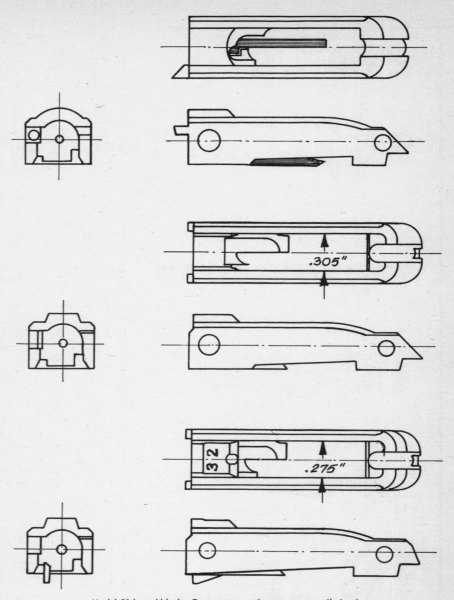

Model 51 breechblocks. Top: prototype (note separate tail piece). Middle: 380 ACP (thin walls and slanted rear section). Bottom: 32 ACP (thick walls and less slanted rear section).

held by dovetail grooves only—a pair of overhanging sections at front and rear of the grip. To remove them they were slid down and lifted off the frame. In production a spring plate was added to increase the holding ability of the grips; Loomis' U.S. patent 1,531,796. This added security made the M51s grips perhaps the most complicated of the world's automatic pistols.

The spring-backed production grips are held by one continuous overhanging section in the front of the frame and a pair of overhangs (like the prototypes) to the rear. In disassembly the grips are slid down and the rear edge is lifted outward, then the grips are removed from the still-engaged front overhang. Though

most production pistols have black grips, a few will be found in dark brown.

My prototype and Remington's cutaway have no ejector, and there is no cut in the frame for this necessary part. This is also the case in the original patent (1,348,733); the ejector is incorporated into the left lip of the magazine, as in a Webley & Scott pocket automatic. Unfortunately I don't have the original magazine for my prototype and Mr. Aberman's prototype has the conventional 51's pivoted ejector shown in Pedersen's patent 1,518,602.

The breechblock piece which characterizes the Pedersen design has a separate tailpiece in each prototype to prevent the bolt or slide snagging the topmost cartridge in the magazine or the disconnector during recoil. This separate piece was eliminated in production by incorporating it into the machining of the slide and breechblock. All prototypes have a cartridge-guide lug machined into the left face of the breechblock. There is a corresponding notch in the breech of the barrel. Interestingly, though production bolts never had the lug, the notch in the barrel will be found on all Model 51 380s below about serial PA 8,600. This helps to establish the authenticity of an early pistol's barrel and also shows how big a run of barrels was made by Remington before any production began. The extractor on the prototypes is just like that shown as the preferred type in the U.S. patent 1,401,552 and in the basic U.S. patent 1,348,733. This type of extractor has an integral pin section which snaps into corresponding grooves in the breechbolt. It is actuated by a spring and plunger. It does not, however, have the camming feature exhibited in U.S. patent 1,401,552. This camming system was used on all production pistols; as an integral flat-spring camming extractor in the 380s and as a springless pure cam extractor in the 32s. The prototype extractor was patent-claimed to act as a loaded-chamber indicator, being forced outward if holding a cartridge in its claw. However, to either feel or see this indication the slide had to be partially

pulled back; this really negates the value of the extractor as an indicator because, by a slight further retraction of the slide, the cartridge itself is visible. In practice a loaded-chamber indicator should require no action on the part of the user beyond sight or feel. The classic of such devices is on the Walther PP, PPk, HP and P-38. Their indicator protrudes noticeably from the rear of the slide, being both visible and touchable during sighting and in preparing to fire them.

The prototype barrels are held in the frame by teeth and grooves in the barrel and frame. These interlocking surfaces are cut on a helix, unlike most other pocket automatics of the Browning/Colt design. Production pistols have a boss on the barrel pierced by a hole and held in the frame by a semi-headed pin (not a split pin, as it has been erroneously called). The production pin is locked in the frame by notches at each of its ends. The semi-headed section aids in extracting the pin during takedown, using the thumbnail or the leading edge of the magazine's floorplate. Prototype barrels do not have the series of annular grooves just behind the muzzle because as with this method of barrel-to-frame retention these grooves would serve no purpose. Barrel muzzles and breech ends in prototypes and production models have a step, for about one quarter-inch, from the muzzle back to the grooves and just in front of the chamber boss.

These steps are of slightly greater diameter and finer finish than the rest of the barrel. The function of these surfaces is to give a very close fit with the barrel bushing of the slide and recoil spring-bushing when the slide is in the forward or firing position.

The prototype receivers have, of course, a square threaded section to secure the barrel and no hole for the production gun's semi-headed barrel lock pin. My prototype and Remington's have no cut for the ejector. The grip-retaining overhang sections are a pair, both front and rear, on all prototypes. Remington's highly interesting prototype has a hole drilled at the same position as shown in Dygert's patent (1,381,291) and it is my belief that this pistol (before it became a cutaway) was used by Dygert in experimenting with his friction-held barrel pin. None of the prototype receivers has a boss or hole in the rear grip area for the magazine safety.

The magazine catch on two prototypes has no concentric rings to give the finger a gripping surface, and none's locking section has a disassembly groove. Remington's prototype has concentric grooves on both sides of the magazine catch and even on the locking section. The first two catches look exactly like the pieces shown in U.S. patent 1,397,109. These two missing features exist on all production pistols, probably when it was found difficult to assemble and disassemble without them.

The slide has no cut on the left side for the semi-headed pin since it was not used on the prototypes. Although no prototypes have the characteristic matted top surface between sights, there is no marking in this area, as is found on all production pistols. The Remington cutaway has no matting but does carry a stamped logo on its top, reading thus:

Remington Arms Co.-Union Metallic Cartridge Co. Remington Works Ilion NY USA Pedersen's Patents Jan.5 1909, Oct.12 1909, Mar.8 1910, Nov.21 1911, Apr.16, 1912.

This is the stamping, in fact, found on a Model 12 Remington 22 pump rifle. This pistol, quite likely, must have been used to experiment with a stamp, just to see how it looked.

The prototype barrel bushing in the front of the slide is threaded into place by a special spanner wrench, corresponding to patent 1,348,733, but in production the bushing was swaged into place, making it a permanent part of the slide; this innovation was shown on Loomis' patent

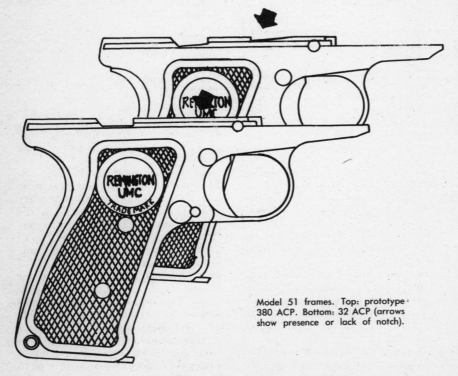

Model 51 frames. Top: prototype 380 ACP. Bottom: 32 ACP (arrows show presence or lack of notch).

1,348,284.

The prototype's grip safety was different in that the hammer spring and its two plungers were not pinned to the bottom on the grip safety. Production 51s had these parts captured by a pin, and they were considered as part of the grip safety and not normally disassembled by the user.

Major Types of Model 51 380s

There aren't many variations in the Model 51. This may be a testimonial to having spent so much time and energy on the initial design that, once production had started, there were very few bugs. There are two basic M51 types in 380 ACP. Early pistols have 9 U-shaped (in section) slide pulls for the fingers; no caliber indication on the barrel, as viewed through the slide's ejection port, and no Remington logo (later stamped on the right side of the frame, just above the trigger guard). The above is what I have chosen to call a Type I Variation.

The Type II has 15 sawtooth-section slide pulls, reveals the caliber stamping through the ejection port, and has a *Remington* over *Trade Mark* logo on the frame. Type Is go to about serial number PA 40,000; Type IIs from there to final serial number PA 60,800. These are the basic differences, but there are variations subdividing the types.

Variations in Model 51 380s

The earliest Type I variations have the previously-mentioned redundant second notch in the left-hand side of the barrel's chamber. This can be seen by locking the slide to the rear and looking at the barrel's breech through the ejection port. Pistols having the double notched barrel range from PA 1 to about PA 8,600.

The second variation has the barrel marked for caliber as viewed through the ejection port. This appears as *380 CAL* and will be found on pistols numbered as low as PA 23, but there is no consistency. PA 10,274, PA 11,077, PA 15,833 have marked barrels, but PA 17,434, PA 12,522, PA 13,290 and PA 14,315 do not. PA 23 probably has a replacement barrel. The 380 caliber marking must have been decided on when Remington determined to manufacture a 32-cal. Model 51, yet obviously they must have started the barrel marking long before the introduction of the new 32. The 32s appeared when the 380s had reached about PA 39,000. The caliber marking on the barrel had become standard by PA 25,000.

The third variation concerns the *Remington* over *Trade Mark* stamping on the right side of the frame. This new stamp started appearing on pistols in the PA 22,000 range and by PA 25,000 seems to have become standard from there on.

The 9 U-form slide pulls were replaced by 15 sawtooth cuts by PA 39,000, but there are also low-serial pistols having all the characteristics of a Type II pistol. I have a PA 25,012 which has the chamber marked 380 CAL, the right-side logo and the 15 slide pulls, but since two of these things can be altered without showing, there is no way to prove if this pistol came from the factory this way. Any M51 can have its barrel changed for another. Too, any 380 can have its slide swapped with another 380, but since these substitutable parts don't bear serial numbers, the change can go undetected. One of the difficult things about documenting any Model 51 is the fact that the pistol carries only one frame-located serial number. For many years the Model 51 collector had no problem because in the 1940-1950s the pistol sold for $25 to $30 and there were few buyers. Making a fake made no sense at all. But today Remingtons have become quite valuable, and it's just possible some unscrupulous people might doctor one.

The fourth and last variation has to do with very late pistols. On the left forward section of an M51 trigger guard will be found two stamped capital letters. An advanced collector and writer, Charles W. Walker, has found this to be a date code used on pistols made after regular production had ceased. Mr. Walker thinks this code gives the month and year of shipment from Remington. My guess is that with sales so low the pistols were assembled as ordered from finished parts and then stamped with the two coded initials, these representing both the assembly and approximate shipping dates. Whether the two letters have such meaning is still not completely determined, but there are very few "date-coded" 380s to be found. They are in the PA 50,000 to PA 60,800 range. I have also seen one Type II pistol (PA 5,663), not a Type I, which had the assembly date code of *LR*. This must have been a rejected frame which was reworked much later and then assembled. The frame even carried the late "Remington" logo. Occasionally, above the left trigger guard boss on the round part on M51 frames, some rather crude stampings will be found. These are not assembly date codes but represent instead a pistol returned to Reming-

ton for repairs, the stamping dating those repairs. It is possible to find an assembly date coded pistol which also has one or even several repair codes on it. Therefore, though it would appear that 60,800 Model 51s in 380 were made, my original estimate of 54,518 is probably a lot closer to the actual number made. The blanks don't appear in one block of numbers but are spread all the way from PA 40,000 to PA 60,800, which is the entire run of Type IIs.

Known Model 51s in 380 ACP

No.	Type	Marks
PA-23	I	380 CAL
PA-312	I	
PA-460	I	
PA-1265	I	
PA-1425	I	
PA-1653	I	Anchor ("U.S. Property")
PA-2994	I	
PA-5351	I	
PA-5663	II	LR/guard
PA-6385	I	
PA-7078	I	
PA-7373	I	
PA-8841	I	
PA-10274	I	380 CAL
PA-11077	I	380 CAL
PA-12522	I	
PA-13290	I	
PA-14315	I	
PA-15883	I	380 CAL
PA-16087	I	Repair KX3
PA-16658	I	380 CAL
PA-17434	I	No 380 CAL on mag.
PA-17505	I	
PA-18589	I	
PA-20721	I	380 CAL
PA-22298	I	RAC logo
PA-22319	I	380 CAL + logo
PA-25012	II	
PA-28001	I	380 CAL + logo
PA-30062	I	380 CAL + logo
PA-30433	I	380 CAL + logo + repair L30C
PA-30819	I	380 CAL + logo
PA-33868	I	380 CAL + logo
PA-35249	I	380 CAL + logo
PA-35577	II	
PA-35764	I	380 CAL + logo
PA-369011	II	British proofs
PA-37895	II	
PA-39223	II	
PA-39627	I	380 CAL + logo
PA-41338	II	
PA-42012	II	
PA-42173	II	
PA-47001	II	
PA-47459	II	
PA-50103	II	
PA-50823	II	P.U./guard
PA-53046	II	
PA-53311	II	
PA-59164	II	KU/guard
PA-60106	II	XT/guard

Major Types of Model 51 32s

All 380 slides carried under the top anti-glare matting:

THE REMINGTON ARMS, UNION METALLIC CARTRIDGE CO. INC. REMINGTON ILION WKS. N.Y. U.S.A. PEDERSEN'S PATENTS PENDING

This reference to UMC in the logo

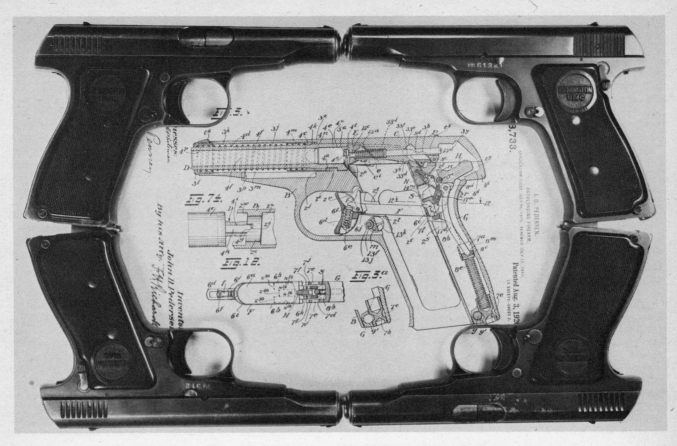

Upper left: prototype. Upper right: very early Type I 32 ACP. Lower right: prototype (Aberman's). Lower left: very early Type I 380 ACP. Background, the basic Pedersen patent cover sheet.

is strange, for from 1888 to 1918 UMC of Bridgeport owned Remington, but on firearms Remington was always mentioned first. By 1918 it had been decided to drop UMC entirely from the logo, yet here, on a pistol first marketed in 1918, we find UMC still being used. My guess is that the stamp, an expensive item, was made before the decision to drop UMC was made and, once made, they decided to use it.

The first Type 32s were stamped identically on the slide in the manner shown above. This will be found from PA 60,801 to at least PA 61,921. These pistols were also marked 32 CAL on the magazine and on the chamber. Next are the Type II variations, with the introduction of a new slide stamping:

REMINGTON ARMS COMPANY, INC.
ILION WKS. N.Y. U.S.A.
PEDERSEN PATENT/PAT'D. MAR.9 20,
AUG.3 20, OCT.12 20,
JUNE 14 21 OTHERS PENDING

This logo change took place somewhere in the early PA 62,000 range. At or near the same time the caliber designation on the chamber was changed to 32 CAL over 7.65 M/M. Adding the metric designation must have indicated anticipated overseas sales of the 32. The 380s never had "9 M/M Short" added to their barrels.

It is my opinion that, when the serial numbers of the 32s reached PA 70,280, it was decided to call it quits. This would have happened in December of 1925. Thus the Type IIs which are identified by serial number run from somewhere above PA 62,000 to PA 70,280. But there were sales for both calibers still coming into the factory and they must have been running out of serialized frames for the 32s. Rather than start where they had left off in the 32s they jumped ahead to serial PA 90,500, leaving space from PA 70,500 to PA 90,500 for 20,000 more 380s—which were never to be. Anyway, after PA 70,280 comes PA 90,501 and this second block of serial-numbered pistols went to PA 92,627, the highest number used by Remington. These form what I call the Type II Model 51 in 32 caliber. As in the 380s, some numbers were not assigned to any pistol, for 70,280 minus 60,801 leaves 9,479 and 92,627 minus 90,501 leaves 2,126 or a total of 11,605. However, my earlier-mentioned figure of 10,278 is probably closer to the truth.

Variations in Model 51 32s

The first variation is one that I don't feel is a legitimate factory variation. Sprinkled through the 380 block of serial numbers are a very few 32s. I have never been able to examine one of these hybrids, but there is a way they could have developed. First, by taking a 32-cal. barrel and magazine and assembling them to a 380, a 32 can be simply made. Remington sold the required parts—part 306, the barrel, for $3 and part 352, a magazine, for $1. I have done just this, and the gun fires and operates as a self-loader. However, when Remington made a 32 they changed the slide, breechblock and frame, and a 32 with such major changes doesn't, to my knowledge, exist in the 380 serial block. There, if you buy it, is Variation I.

The first legitimate variation, I feel, is the assembly-date coded 32s. These coded pistols will be found in Type I form, but such guns are rare. They would have to consist of a previously-serialized receiver which was dug up from the bottom of the pile and assembled into a gun later. Assembly-date coded 32s begin at about PA 65,000 in the Type IIs and continue right through Type IIIs to the terminal serial number. Therefore, code dated Type I and Type IIs are a variation, but all Type IIIs are code dated. There will also be code dated repaired 32s just as there were 380s, but they do not represent an original factory variation. Unlike the assembly-date coded 380s, the 32s carrying a code are more common than those not coded.

The Anchor and Sun Stamps

The last variation in the 32s are in the PA 65,500 range. The usual anchor stamp on the right-side trigger guard flat was replaced with a "sun" symbol. These inspection stamps were assigned to a group of inspectors for a period of time. Thus for a very short period in 1922-1923, the sun stamp was used to replace the anchor stamp. This makes a rather rare but exceedingly minor variation. They are found up to PA 66,800, but not all pistols within the number range are so stamped.

Known Models 51 in 32 ACP

No.	Type	Marks
PA-61221	I	
PA-61249	I	
PA-61520	I	
PA-61921	I	
PA-63039	II	
PA-63786	II	Repair L3CC◇3
PA-64952	II	
PA-65629	II	DR/guard
PA-65630	II	XR/guard
PA-65740	II	LN/guard
PA-66710	II	CR/guard
PA-67235	II	KS/guard
PA-67829	II	RP/guard
PA-68000	II	CR/guard
PA-70013	II	AT/guard + repair NY3
PA-90552	III	LT/guard
PA-92146	III	ET/guard
PA-92475	III	ET/guard
PA-92615	III	XT/guard

Note: Nos. 65,740 and 66,710 also show the sun stamp.

Summation of Types and Variations

Some original magazines have no caliber designation. One was found in 380 (PA 17,434), but this is not to my mind a characteristic of early pistols since they were the very ones which had no other caliber marking on them anywhere. It may be that when caliber marks were added to the barrel (there was no 32 yet) that 380 magazines without caliber identification

were tried, but with the advent of the 32, the caliber marking came back on the 380's magazine.

To identify a Model 51 type, look first through the ejection port. If the barrel is unmarked the pistol is a Type I 380. If it has "380 CAL" marked on the barrel, look at the number and type of slide grooves. If there are 9 U-sectioned pulls, it is also a Type I 380. On the other hand, if it has *380 CAL* but shows 15 sawtoothed grooves, it is a Type II 380. If the barrel breech is marked *32 CAL*, it is a Type I 32. If you see *32 CAL* over *7.65 M/M* look at the serial number. If it starts with 6 or 7, it is a Type II 32; if it starts with a 9 it is a Type III 32. That's it in a nutshell. The total numbers produced of each Type were about:

Type I/380	40,000
Type II/380	14,518
Type I/32	1,152
Type II/32	7,000
Type III/32	2,126
Total	64,796

Differences in 380s and 32s

Most M51 changes occur in the small breechblock. I believe the most basic change was required when the decision was made to make the 32. The breechblock mass had to be increased to give reliable action because the 32-cal. bullet was in the barrel for a little longer than the 380's bullet. To compensate for this the 32's heavier breechblock reduced its velocity, thus slowing the unlock-

ing of the block by the slide. This increase in weight was accomplished by adding $1/64''$ to the thickness of the breechblock legs and by reducing the cross-section of the rectangular center hole. This still wasn't enough so a little metal was added to the rear, which gave that section a more squarish appearance and may also have improved the vectoral forces transmitted to the slide. The regular 380 breechblock assembly plus extractor weighs 0.745 ounces, the block of the 32 going 0.845. The 32's extractor has no spring action at all; it is cammed on and off the cartridge's rim by the action of the independently-moving slide. It floats in a cut in the breechblock, locked against lateral movement but free to pivot, by the cam surface in the slide. The lower front side of the 32 breechblock has a cartridge pick-up finger, unlike the smoother 380 breechblock. This finger, shown in Loomis' patent (1,571,592), was needed because the 32 ACP cartridge is a semi-rimmed case, not rimless, as is the 380. The finger insured that the rim of the magazine's upper cartridge wouldn't catch in the ejection groove of the cartridge below during feeding. The firing-pin hole was reduced in size, as will be explained later. The little steps found on the front of the 380 breechblock, which locked into mating ones on the frame, were dropped on the 32. The extractor and gauging holes were reduced in diameter and depth to increase weight on the 32. Finally, to aid identification of this different breechblock, a *32* was stamped on its forward upper section. The 380 block never had such identi-

Prototype Model 51 cutaway from Remington Arms. Note the barrel locking threads and the cartridge guide lug, both prototype characteristics. (Photo by Remington Arms)

Prototype Model 51 (top) over Early Type I 380 ACP, serial number PA 312.

magazine are closer together and there is a notch for the breechblock finger at the rear of the magazine body. An empty 380-cal. magazine will keep the slide open on a 32-cal. M51 because the finger will catch on the unnotched magazine tube. All 32-cal. magazines are stamped with a *32 CAL* identification, but many late 32 magazines don't have the characteristic *U* acceptance stamp on the floorplate. Most 380 magazines are stamped *380 CAL*, but not all.

Barrels of 32-cal. M51s are stamped either *32 CAL* or *32 CAL* over *7.65 M/M*; the external dimensions are identical to those of the 380. Remington 51s are unique in that both calibers have 7-groove rifling. No other pocket automatic has so many.

These many differences between the 32 and the 380 have led me to think, as I've said, that any 32 in the 380 block of serial numbers was altered by the user, that it never left the factory that way. On the other hand, knowing Remington's apparent shipping policy of "last in, first out," old 380 frames already serial numbered could have been factory equipped with an all new 32-cal. slide/breechblock, barrel and magazine, to become a working 32. The only telltale feature would then be the little forward breechblock locking cuts in the 380's frame. Using the assembled 380 frame from PA 60,106 with the other parts from 32 PA 61, 520, a working autoloading 32 pistol was achieved. Since this hybrid pistol had the old "PATENT PENDING" slide markings it would have passed

fication.

The slides of all 32s have the later 15 sawtooth slide pulls. Types II and III will also have the later top stamping (with the patent dates). Internally, the thickness of the breechblock retaining lug has been reduced by $^{1}/_{32}''$ to fit the heavier 32 breechblock. This means that a 32's block will not fit into a 380's slide. To compensate for the lost cross-sectional strength of the lug, the firing-pin's hole was reduced in diameter. The angle of the breechblock/slide engaging section was also changed. Externally, then, the slides of a late 380 and a Type I 32 are identical but internally they are quite different.

The firing pin of a 32 (except its tip) was reduced .205″ on all diameters. Its spring also has a smaller diameter, required by the smaller hole in the breechblock lug of the slide. A 32's firing pin and spring will fit a 380 slide and breechblock but not vise versa.

The frame or receiver of a 32 does not have the little locking sections on each side of the magazine well for the mating pair of protrusions on the 380s breechblock. The large rear locking section of the 32 was apparently sufficient. Other than this, the frames are identical and carry no caliber marking whatsoever. All 32s have the *Remington/Trade Mark* stamping.

The 380 and 32 magazines are the same thickness, which allowed machining the magazine well the same for both calibers. The 32's magazine follower, which has a dual-purpose groove, allows clearance for the breechblock finger when the magazine is empty. More importantly, it staggers the 32-cal. cartridges as they are loaded into the magazine. This is required because of the greater width of the magazine, sized originally for the fatter 380 case. The lips of the 32

The only Model 53 Remington 45 ACP ever made reposes in the Remington Arms Museum. Note the hammer and the recessed magazine notch. (Photo by Remington Arms)

Remington Model 51, Type I, has the caliber marking "380 CAL" on the barrel. Serial number PA 15833, it still has the U-shaped slide pulls.

Walker can find no such purchase documented in U.S. Navy archives. The myth probably can be traced to two things. The Navy did test the M51's big brother in 1918—the Model 53 in 45 ACP. The other presumed tie-in to the U.S. Navy is the little anchor stamp found on most M51's trigger guards and grip safeties. In fact, this stamp identifies Remington's inspection team, and has no naval connotation. Spurred by those two myths, a few M51s have been sold with an additional bigger anchor stamp backed by a "U.S. Property" stamp sometimes at the same location on the frame where the Remington/Trade Mark stamp appeared later. I have seen two such pistols, one as described and the other stamped on the left side with the "U.S. Property" mark partially obliterating the serial number. The second pistol must be a fake; I think the first is also, but it

for a 32 in the 380 serial range.

Model 51 Faults and Myths

The first two problems were identified when the Model 51 was announced in *Arms and the Man* in the October 4, 1919 issue. The writer, Mr. Stephen Trask, found two points he didn't like among the 51's other very good features. The first was the difficulty in retracting the slide. This complaint was so taken to heart by Remington that the switch from 9 U-section slide pulls to 15 sawtooth cuts was probably a direct result. In measuring the amount of force required I found the average pull needed was 21 pounds for a group of 380s, with a low of 16.5 pounds in the prototype to a high of 25 pounds. The 32s averaged 19 pounds, the low 18, the high at 20.5. This compares favorably with Colt at $21^3/8$ and Savage at $23^3/4$ pounds. With the improved slide pulls a slippery hand could certainly retract the slide with greater ease. This complaint about the M51 was not voiced by any later writers as far as I know.

The next complaint Mr. Trask noted was the creep and heaviness of the trigger pull. This has been voiced by most other critics since Trask; Walter Smith and Dan Stern, to mention but two. In measuring trigger pull versus serial numbers, it seems that Remington made a serious effort to reduce the pull over the years the M51 was produced. The average of 380s measured was 8.6 pounds, the high 11, the low 6.75. The 32s averaged 5.6 pounds with a high of 7.5 and the low a respectable 4.12. As far as the long mushy pull is concerned (really part of Pedersen's design),

REMINGTON NO. 51 AUTO. PISTOL

Specifications: Capacity of magazine, caliber .380, 7 cartridges, caliber .32, 8 cartridges; hammerless; side ejection; fires one shot each time trigger is pulled; length 6⅝ inches; thickness 9-10 inch; weight unloaded 21 ounces; finish a dull black; stocks, hard-rubber; made only in one style and one finish..................Price, $19.50
Extra for Pearl Stocks.................Pair, 6.50

This page from a 1923-1924 H&D Folsom Arms Co. catalog mentions the two Model 51 calibers and the price. Note pearl grips were available.

no fix was possible. Too, since Pedersen was after an ultrasafe defense pistol, I think such a pull was justified.

The location of the annular rings on the barrel, which help disassembly, has been said by writer and M51 collector, Daniel K. Stern, to vary forward by $1/16''$ (.0625") on the 32s. I find little to substantiate this, after measuring 25 pistols in both calibers. The average distance from the barrel's muzzle to the ring is .256" on the 380s and .236" on the 32s. I believe that the operator who turned these rings was allowed to place them roughly $1/4''$ back, therefore they varied from tooling set-up to set-up. The greatest on a 380 was .266", the smallest .242"; in the 32s the maximum as .270", the minimum .193".

Allegedly, the U.S. Navy at one time bought some M51 pistols. This, I believe, is a pure myth. Charles W.

was well done and originally sold for little more than a comparable condition unmarked M51.

The final myth is that field stripping and total stripping of a Remington Model 51 is very difficult. I have heard and read this complaint often, but there seems to be no grounds for it except ignorance. The field strip rules follow:

Field Stripping the Model 51

1. Unload chamber, remove magazine.

2. Pull slide to rear, thus cocking the pistol. Hold pistol in left hand with the right-hand side up, muzzle toward your body. Left thumb is on the slide pulls and index finger is depressing the grip safety.

3. Push back slide with the right hand's thumb and forefinger until notch in slide and semi-headed barrel

locking pin are in line. Hold slide with left thumb's pressure. Lift out pin with the right thumbnail.

4. Push slide farther back, with thumb and forefinger of right hand at the barrel bushing on the slide. These two fingers can then grip the annular rings on the barrel's muzzle. Pull on barrel muzzle and remove the entire slide assembly, being sure to press the grip safety at the same time.

5. Looking at bottom of slide with barrel toward you, push barrel's lug to the left (counterclockwise) which will lock the barrel in the slide with the annular rings just sticking out of the barrel bushing. This is the step most often missed.

6. Put your thumb on the front face of the breechblock and pick up the rear edge with the nail of the forefinger. Lift the breechblock out of the slide and drop the firing pin and its spring down the barrel and out. On a 32 watch that the loose extractor doesn't fall and get lost. The barrel may now be lifted out of the slide by lifting its chamber end upward and backward. The recoil spring and its bushing can now be lifted out of the slide.

That is field stripping; I can do it in under 30 seconds and nothing is used but your hands—no tools at all. Reassembling will take me up to a minute but that's still not bad. When reassembling the entire slide, breechblock, barrel assembly to the frame, be sure the disconnector and ejector are in their *down* position and you'll have no trouble. The disconnector is kept down by depressing the grip safety just as during disassembly.

Complete disassembly of a Model 51 can be done by using the firing pin as a drift, and the barrel's chamber flats as a depressor for the hammer-spring plug. This full tool-less disassembly is well illustrated in the instructions shipped with each pistol. I have always contended that it is very desirable to be able to completely strip a firearm without tools so that field accidents, such as dropping the gun into water, don't prevent the use of the arm. Also, to fully strip an arm is to know that arm much better and to be able to repair it with the minimum of effort, should the necessity arise.

Conclusion

One can only wish that an updated Remington Model 51 was on today's pistol market. I feel sure that it would be a big seller, but if it were made with the same quality that Remington lavished on it during its 9 years of manufacture, it would cost well over $150, which is about the used price of a Model 51 today. One can wish, too, that the hammered Model 51 had been developed further and sold to the public. From there to a double action pistol would have been a reasonable step and such an arm could have rivalled the Walthers.

In the collector market there seems to be little price differential between the 380s and the 32s, probably because most dealers don't know there are five 380s to every 32. It is a buyer's situation which won't last long.

Collector Leonard Hunter started in 1976 to have the Remington Model 51 in both calibers classed as a curio and relic by the Alcohol, Tobacco, and Firearms Bureau (ATFB). That has now (1977) been done and today Model 51s can be much more readily acquired by the holder of a collector's license.

Here's my epitaph for the Remington Model 51—it had the right designer at the right company but not at the right time. •

Bibliography
Periodicals
Arms & The Man, Oct. 4, 1919, Stephen Trask.
Guns, Nov. 1958, D. M. Simmons, Jr.
American Rifleman, Sept. 1965, Daniel K. Stern.
Ordnance, May-June 1968, D. M. Simmons, Jr.
The Gun Report, Oct. 1969, (M-53), Charles W. Walker.
Guns, July 1970, Charles W. Walker.
Gun Digest, 1973/27th ed., D. M. Simmons, Jr.
American Rifleman, Dec. 1976, D. R. Lulling and E. R. Gerbsen.
Gun Digest, 1977/31st ed., D. M. Simmons, Jr.

Books
Pistols & Revolvers, Vol. I, W. H. B. Smith, NRA 1946 (now publ. by Stackpole Books, Harrisburg, PA).
Remington Arms (in American History). Alden Hatch, Rinehart & Co., N.Y. 1956.
Remington Handguns, Charles Lee Kerr et al. The Military Service Pub. Co. 1947. (out of print.)
Textbook of Automatic Pistols, R. K. Wilson, Small Arms Technical Pub. Co. 1943. Now publ. by Stackpole Books, Harrisburg, PA.
Firearms Identification, Vols. I & II, H. J. Mathews, Univ. of Wisconsin Press, 1962. Now publ. by C. C. Thomas, Springfield, IL.
Gun Digest Book of Exploded Firearms Drawings, H. A. Murtz, ed. Northfield, IL, 1973.
NRA Illustrated Firearms Assembly Handbook, Vol. I, NRA 5th printing, Washington, D.C.

Acknowledgements
Special thanks to Lawrence Goodstal, Remington Arms Co. and Charles W. Walker.

Thanks to Sidney Aberman, Leonard Arnold (U.S. Navy), Britt Brown, Don Crews, Len Hunter, Ernie Lang, Dan Stern, Ken Warner (NRA), Doris Simmons, and to many others who contributed serial numbers and data.

Alleged "U.S. Property" Model 51 in 380 ACP has navy anchor stamped above guard. Serial number PA 1653. Photo courtesy Mr. Britt Brown, Wichita, Kansas.

"The time and the place for a gunmaker just got together on this corner. And I happened along."

The firearm inventor's humble assessment of himself bears some validity. John Moses Browning was born at a place called Ogden in Utah Territory on January 23, 1855. The breech-loading cartridge was born about the same time, and by the time John would grow up, the gas-sealing metallic cartridge would be ready. The frontier, where a rifle was a household tool, was crying for a reliable repeating rifle. John's father, a black powder gunsmith, had tried to fill that necessity before John's birth with a slide action rifle and a cylinder repeating black powder rifle. Little did he know that what he struggled to sire in a rifle he sired in a son.

fully labelling his small shop "The largest arms factory between Omaha and the Pacific."

This rifle would make East meet West. For it impressed an Easterner by the name of T. G. Bennett so much that he travelled from Connecticut to Ogden in 1883 to meet the rifle's inventor. The Easterner left Ogden with the production rights to this rifle and an alliance with John M. Browning that was to last 19 years. T. G. Bennett was the General Manager of the Winchester Repeating Arms Co.

John M. Browning's first rifle became the famous Winchester Model 1885 High Wall. It would be followed by 43 more gun designs sold to Winchester. These would include many of the most famous Winchesters, such as the Model 86, 92, 94 and 95 lever

THE BROWNING

A close study of Browning's 100-year rifle/shotgun, the Mountain Carbine and the

For John M. Browning was to completely master the principles of repeating operation and manifest these principles in many forms. He would take practically every caliber of his day from the 22 short cartridge to the one-pound 37mm cannon projectile and adapt each to remarkably successful repeating and automatic arms. He would perfect lever actions and pump actions. He would give birth to semi-automatic and fully automatic actions utilizing varied methods of operation—gas operation, recoil operation and blowback operation.

There is no doubt where the spark came from that ignited his creative mind. His father's supply of broken gun parts provided intriguing toys. By his early teens, John was helping his father repair frontier guns, and he was only fourteen when he completely assembled a slide rifle from spare parts for his brother's birthday.

In 1878, at the age of 23, John M. Browning created his first gun, a single shot, lever-operated breech-loading rifle. With his brothers he commenced production in 1880, play-

action rifles and the Models 93 and 97 pump shotguns. Many were never produced but were bought by Winchester to keep their innovative design out of the hands of competitors.

But one of John Browning's designs was too innovative for Winchester. It precipitated John Browning's famous break with Winchester in 1902. T. G. Bennett, a conservative, was afraid of its revolutionary design. Bennett allowed the inventor to walk out of his office with the automatic shotgun under his arm.

This ended Winchester's monopoly on the genius of John M. Browning. His guns were now to be heard around the world. His automatic shotgun was quickly accepted by two prestigious arms producers—Fabrique Nationale of Belgium and Remington Arms Co. Other arms producers, military and sporting, were now to benefit from his genius.

He gave the U.S. armed forces the Government Colt 45, the BAR rifle, the 30 caliber and 50 caliber machine guns and the 37mm aircraft cannon. His military arms are credited (even by the enemy) with giving the U.S.

arms superiority through two World Wars and the Korean conflict. Of the 50 caliber machine gun the German Field Marshal Göring said, "If the German Air Force had had the Browning 50 caliber, the Battle of Britain would have turned out differently."

John M. Browning died in November, 1926 while working on his Superposed shotgun—still today's premier over and under shotgun. He had become a worldwide figure, decorated by many nations. His patriotism was commended by two U.S. Secretarys of War. He received Philadelphia's John Scott Legacy Medal and was knighted by the King of Belgium.

He walked with kings, yet he never lost the common touch. If his acclaim seemed to contradict his frontier ori-

CENTENNIALS

specials—the magnificent D.B. Rifle, the revived M92 9mm Hi-Power.

gins, he never disowned those origins. He was a modest, unassuming man, uncomfortable with publicity. His humility magnified his greatness. The epitome of every self-taught man, John M. Browning became "the greatest gun inventor the world has ever known."

Inventions

For four generations the inventions of John M. Browning have equipped the huntsmen and soldiers of the world. From 128 patents there have evolved more than 80 separate firearms, many of them the most successful the world has ever known. It is estimated that well over 30 million Browning designed firearms have been produced to this day.

Yet to millions of sportsmen, the name responsible for the guns they carry is almost unknown. For John M. Browning preferred to sell his inventions to established arms companies. He was directly responsible for many of the famous guns of Winchester, Remington, Colt, Fabrique Nationale and others. The inventions of John M. Browning that were put

into production by these arms companies include:

Winchester

Model 1885, Winchester "High Wall" Single Shot Rifle, invented 1878.
Model 1886, Lever action Rifle, invented 1883.
Model 1887, Lever Action Shotgun, invented 1885.
Model 1890 (later renamed Model 62) 22 caliber Pump, invented 1887.
Model 1893, Pump Shotgun, invented 1890.
Model 1892, Lever Action Rifle, invented 1891.
Model 1894, Lever Action Rifle, invented 1893.
Model 1895, Lever Action Rifle, invented 1894.
Model 1897, Pump Shotgun, invented 1897.
Model 1900 (later known as Models 1902, 1904, 58, 59, 60 and 68), Single Shot 22 Bolt Action, invented 1899.

Remington

Model 11, Semi-Automatic Shotgun, invented 1899-1900.
Model 8 and Model 81, Semi-Automatic High Powered Rifle, invented 1900.
Model 17, Bottom Ejecting Pump Shotgun, invented 1913.
Model 24 and Model 241, Semi-Automatic 22 Rifle, invented 1913.

Colt

Model 1900, 38 Cal. Semi-Auto Pistol, invented 1896.
Model 1903, "Pocket" 32 and 380 Cal. Semi-Auto Pistol, invented 1901.
Model 1911, 45 Cal. Semi-Auto Pistol, invented 1905.
Colt "Vest Pocket" 25 Cal. Semi-Auto Pistol, invented 1905.
Colt Woodsman, 22 Cal. Semi-Auto Pistol, invented 1914.

Fabrique Nationale & Browning

32 Cal. Semi-Auto Pistol, invented 1897 (FN only).
Auto-5, Semi-Automatic Shotgun, invented 1899-1900.
Model 1903, 9mm Semi-Auto Pistol, invented 1901 (FN only).
"Vest Pocket" 25 Cal. Semi-Auto Pistol, invented 1905.
Model 1910, 32 and 380 Cal. Semi-Auto Pistols, invented 1910.
Semi-automatic 22 Rifle, invented 1913.

22 Trombone (Pump) Rifle, invented 1919 (FN only).
Model 1935, 9mm Semi-Auto Pistol, invented 1923.
Superposed Shotgun, invented 1923-26.

Military

Model 1895, Automatic Machine Gun (nicknamed Browning Peacemaker), invented 1892.
Model 1911, Government 45 Cal. Semi-Auto Pistol, invented 1905.
Model 1917, 30 Cal. Machine Gun (air cooled and water cooled), invented 1910.
BAR, Model 1918A2, Automatic Rifle, invented 1917.
50 Cal. Machine Gun (air cooled and water cooled), invented 1919-1923.
37mm Aircraft Cannon, invented 1921.

Others

Savage—Semi-Automatic Shotgun, invented 1899-1900.
Stevens—Models 520 and 620, Side Ejecting Pump Shotgun, invented 1913.
Ithaca—Model 37, Bottom Ejecting Pump Shotgun, invented 1913.

It has been said that a study of John Browning's inventions is a study of the evolution of modern firearms. Among his credits are the first successful repeating and semi-automatic shotguns, the first successful autoloading high powered rifle, and the first successful semi-automatic pistol. He was the first to harness gas operation. He developed short- and long-recoil operation and perfected blowback semi-automatic operation.

He was often ahead of his time. He helped design the 25, 32, 380 and 45 caliber automatic pistol cartridges, so that cartridge design could catch up to his pending pistol designs.

He began work on his 50 caliber machine gun *before* 50 caliber cartridge design commenced. His 30 caliber machine gun was the first machine gun successfully mounted on pursuit aircraft and synchronized to fire between the revolving propeller blades. And yet he had worked out the basic principles of this machine gun 3 years before Orville Wright flew the first airplane. Shy and reserved, John M. Browning let his achievements speak for him.

Cradled in the same Wasatch mountains, where our founder drew his inspiration, Browning is still the largest arms company "between Omaha and the Pacific." Our corporate headquarters shares a 646 acre tract of canyon land with resident mule deer.

Superposed Continental

John M. Browning's genius was not purely mechanical. He was a design artist as well, and perhaps nowhere did he prove this as emphatically as he did with his last invention—the Browning Superposed. Few other sporting arms of any design achieve the economy of proportion and the complete harmony of components that the Superposed achieves. In testament to its esthetic composition the Superposed still stands as one of the most favored "canvases" of master gun engravers. The Superposed substantiates John M. Browning's complete dominance over form and function. The Superposed Continental issue is a unique blend of technology with art—an appropriate tribute to the "greatest gun inventor the world has ever known."

Unique in America the Superposed Continental brings the romance of the double rifle to America as part of a unique and limited 100th anniversary ensemble. The Continental is both an over and under shotgun and an over and under rifle. Two interchangeable and balanced sets of barrels are fitted to a specially constructed 20 gauge Superposed frame—one set of 20 gauge shotgun barrels with 3-inch chambers and one set of rifle barrels chambered for the 30-06 Springfield. The 20 gauge barrels are the popular 26½-inch length choked modified and full with engine turned ventilated rib. The 24-inch rifle barrels have a folding-leaf rear sight and a flat-faced gold bead front sight. To assure precise sight alignment and correct point of impact the front and rear sights are mounted on specially designed ramps. The rifle barrels have been carefully regulated and their performance confirmed in a shooting tunnel until convergence of the barrels produces the accepted accuracy and dispersion standards at 100 yards. The rifling twist is 1 turn in 10 inches and each rifle muzzle is carefully crowned.

The double rifle, whether in its traditional side-by-side barrel mode or in its over and under barrel configuration, is a legendary rifle. It's a rifle that possesses the fast instincts of a double shotgun and is, therefore, specially adapted for running game at short to medium ranges. Big bore double rifles are part of the African legend because of their quick-pointing characteristics and their ability to deliver two fast shots. But the advantages of the double rifle are not reserved for dangerous game. In the hands of an experienced hunter the double rifle is the best choice for hunting big game in timbered and brushy terrain where close in shots at running game are anticipated.

Gold Inlaid North American Game

The engraving motif was created by Louis Vrancken, one of the world's recognized master engravers. The engraving is executed by the premier engravers at Browning's Fabrique Nationale engraving facility—the largest assemblage of engravers in the world. A gold inlaid bob-white quail is frozen in flight and set in a bold fleur-de-lis frame on the right receiver side. On the opposite side a majestic, gold inlaid bull elk asserts the rifle personality of this unique arm. John M. Browning's profile, the inscription *Browning Centennial,* and the dates, *1878-1978* are engraved on the receiver bottom. Fine-line scrollwork and the satin-grey receiver finish serve to enhance the engraved and gold inlaid subjects.

The engraving is breathtaking. The masters of this rare art have fully developed the unique personality of this masterpiece. They have elevated it from a work of useful art to a work of fine art. The engraver of each Continental has signed his name in steel—inconspicuously on each gun's receiver.

Limited Centennial Issue

Only 500 ensembles are being produced to commemorate the Browning Centennial. Each bears its appropriate serial number—1878C-0001 through 1878C-0500—beneath the top lever. The Continental is one of those rare, uncommon possessions; its uniqueness and beauty assure timeless value.

A great deal of the Continental's appeal results from the straight grip stock and schnabel forearm styling. Only the very highest, select grade of American walnut with marked figure is chosen to stock the Continental. A traditional oil finish is hand rubbed into the walnut. After the final oil treatment the stock and forearm are checkered. The checkering, 25 lines to the inch, produces the fine diamond pattern that is traditional on firearms of stature. Both the rifle and shotgun barrels carry individual forearms. Stock dimensions conform to those conducive to proper gun mounting in both shotgun and rifle mode.

A walnut case joined and finished like a fine piece of furniture is provided for the Continental ensemble. Fitted with a full-length brass piano hinge, brass latches and brass corner guards, each case is lined with wine-red velvet to provide a regal environment for this unique possession.

In either the rifle or the shotgun mode the Continental offers the inherent advantages of Superposed design. Superbly fine balance brings the Superposed to the shoulder almost effortlessly and assures extremely

---

Superposed Continental Specifications

Action—Superposed 20 gauge action, specially engineered to function correctly with extra set of 30-06 over and under rifle barrels.

Shotgun Barrels—20 gauge, 26½". Choked modified and full with 3-inch chambers. Engine turned ventilated rib with medium raised German nickel-silver sight bead.

Rifle Barrels—30-06 Springfield caliber, 24". Right-hand rifling twist, 1 turn in 10 inches. Crowned muzzles. Folding-leaf rear sight finely calibrated for elevation. Flat-faced gold bead front sight mounted on matted ramp. Sight radius—16 $^{15}/_{16}$". Maximum distance between centers of impact of a 2 shot group from each barrel, using commercially available 150-grain 30-06 ammunition, is 1½ inches at 100 yards.

Hand Engraved Receiver—Gold inlaid bull elk head and bob-white quail in fleur-de-lis and scroll background on greyed steel receiver sides. Browning Centennial inscription and dates hand engraved on receiver bottom.

Trigger—Single, selective, inertia. Gold plated, fast and crisp. Let off about 4½ lbs.

Automatic Selective Ejectors—Fired shells ejected from chambers upon opening of action. Unfired shells elevated for easy removal.

Safety—Manual thumb safety on top tang incorporated with barrel-selector mechanism. Either barrel can be selected to fire first.

Stock and Forearm—Select high grade American walnut with deluxe oil finish. Straight grip stock and schnabel forearm with 25-line hand checkering.

	With Shotgun Barrels Installed	With Rifle Barrels Installed
Length of pull	14¼"	14¼"
Drop at comb	1½"	1$^{11}/_{16}$"
Drop at heel	2$^{7}/_{32}$"	2½"

Over-all Length—
With 20 gauge shotgun barrels—43½"
With 30-06 rifle barrels—41"
Average Weights—
With 20 gauge shotgun barrels—5 lbs. 14 oz.
With 30-06 rifle barrels—6 lbs. 14 oz.
Handsomely cased—furnished with deluxe walnut trunk type case lined with wine-red velvet. The assembled gun and extra set of barrels nest in form fitting cavities.

fast-pointing characteristics. A single, strongly defined sighting plane assists accurate placement of two instantly available shots. The tang-mounted safety is in convenient reach of the thumb. You can select the over or under barrel to fire first; a single trigger fires the first barrel on the first pull, the remaining barrel on the second pull. Ejection is automatic and selective. Only fired shells are ejected; unfired shells are elevated for easy removal.

Other Browning News

In addition to the strikingly handsome Superposed Continental rifle/shotgun described earlier—and which you saw pictured on our front cover—Browning has a number of other firearms to offer in this, their Centennial year. First and foremost is the Centennial Jonathan Browning Mountain Rifle, a 50-cal. caplock muzzle-loading rifle that is attractive indeed—and in its general form not unlike a Hawken!

The 30-inch octagonal barrel, 1-inch across the flats, is rifled 1-in-62 inches. A push-forward single set roller-bearing trigger lies in the scrolled guard—unset pull about 4-5 lbs., set weight (adjustable) down to 2 ozs. Good feeling—crisp and clean on two sample rifles examined.

The lockplate—browned in the old tradition, as are all other metal parts—carries a bust of Jonathan Browning that's excellently crafted, and there's an oval inscribed medallion on the stocks right side, both solid sterling silver.

The hand-rubbed select-grade American walnut halfstock has the curved steel buttplate of the preiod, its dimensions 13½″ by 2½″ at comb by 4″ at heel. The hooked-breech barrel is held in the fore-stock by two tinned wedges or keys, and the fore-end metal tip piece is also tinned.

Cased in alder wood, the lining is buckskin colored and wrinkled in simulation of age. Hinges and latches are of brass, the corners leather cov-

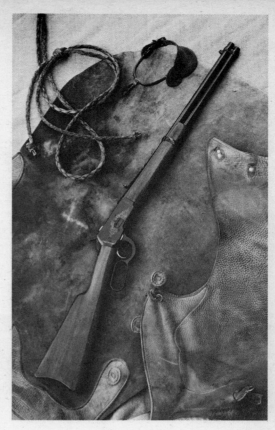

The Centennial Browning Model 92, caliber 44 Magnum.

ered. Included with the cased rifle are a nipple wrench, spare nipple, brass cleaning jag and patch retriever, plus a powder horn engraved with the rifle's serial number and, as well, this inscription on a medallion: *Jonathan Browning Mountain Rifle 1878-1978 One of One Thousand.* That is exactly how many will be made, and each rifle will bear a special serial number—1878A-0001 to 1878A-1000.

Weighing about 9⅝ lbs., the complete outfit is $650.

The same Mountain Rifle, but not in the Centennial grade and sold without a case, is also available, retail $319.50, blued steel or brass trimmed.

Centennial Browning 92

Second of Browning's 100th year commemoratives is a rebirth of the far-famed 1892 Winchester—which J.M.B. designed for that firm in 1891, and which sold over a million of them before the 1892's discontinuance in 1941. A faithful copy in all respects, except caliber, the new Browning carbine has a 20-inch round barrel, twin barrel bands, a round saddle ring (gold-plated, as is the trigger), rebated receiver walls and a modified-crescent steel buttplate. Hand cut scroll engraving appears on both receiver sides, the left carrying also: *Browning 1878-1978 Centennial,* gold filled.

Made of the strongest modern steels, this old design is chambered for the 44 Remington Magnum cartridge, the tubular magazine holding 11 cartridges. Light at about 5½ lbs., and 37½ inches long, the "new" 92 is a good looking, fast-handling rifle —metal-to-wood jointing, and finishing, are very well done, and there's

The Jonathan Browning Mountain Rifle

Browning's new bolt action centerfire rifle, the BBR.

much hand-fitting of internal parts, too—which isn't easily seen. Suggested retail price is just under $220.

Last among the commemorative Browning firearms this year is the 9mm Centennial Hi-Power, J. M. Browning's last pistol design. Identical otherwise to the standard Browning Hi-Power with fixed sights, this special is chrome-plated, and the select-grade walnut grips are hand checkered, 26 lines per inch. A Browning "B" is inset in each grip panel and the right side of the slide reads: *Browning Centennial/1878-1978*. A total of 3,500 of these special 9mm Hi-Powers will be made, their serial numbers starting with 1878D-0001 and ending at 1878D-3500.

Each pistol is furnished in a presentation walnut case, lined with velvet. Advertised retail price is $495.

Browning is offering three Centennial knives, too—all folding types, each of the three in the set having the same serial number, and the sets limited to 2,000 units. Made of highly polished 440C stainless steel, heat treated to a Rockwell hardness of C54-58, the scales are of genuine Sambar stag, the bolsters of polished solid brass.

German made, the Stalker II is a large single-blade hunting type, the Canoe is smaller and has two blades; the 3-blade pocket knife is in the well known Stockman pattern. Each blade carries an etched inscription: *1878/Browning Centennial/1978*.

Also new at Browning, though seemingly not part of the 100th-year theme, is their new bolt action rifle—it is, they say, a worthy successor to the departed FN Mauser recently in their line, and one offering significant improvements.

The new BBR has a hammer-forged

The Browning Centennial Hi-Power auto pistol.

barrel, and the detachable magazine box uses a patented "scissors" follower, a device that distributes pressure more uniformly against the follower for improved feeding and loading. The floorplate is hinged, too.

Nine forward-sited locking lugs are part of the short-throw (60°) bolt, and an anti-warp aluminum channel piece is inletted into the fore-end to prevent barrel contact with the fore-end, which can easily affect point of impact and accuracy.

The BBR has a top-tang safety, a red-colored cocking indicator and an adjustable trigger. Stocked in select American walnut (dimensions 13³⁄₈″ × 1⁵⁄₈″ × 2¹⁄₈″), with Monte Carlo comb, the wood shows a high-gloss durable polyurethane finish. Mag-

num calibers have a white-line rubber recoil pad installed, and low-profile sling-swivel studs are standard.

Offered only in 25-06, 270, 30-06, 7mm Rem. Mag. and 300 Win. Mag. at this time, catalog price is about $300.

A last note—I urge you to get a copy of the current Browning Centennial catalog. Beautifully printed and presented, its 152 pages hold scores of full color photos, and everything Browning markets is in it—from firearms of all kinds to leather goods, knives, clothing and boots, sleeping bags, archery and fishing tackle, you name it. An 8-page "Shooting Information" section is well worthwhile, as is one on fishing.   J.T.A.

New Armsport DB Rifle

First impressions of an over and under combination rifle/shotgun set received from Paul Bines of Armsport February 23rd, 1978.

The outfit reached me in a well done and handsome case of typical oak-and-leather style, dark green leather covered and with heavy cast brass corners. The case is lined and compartmented in the usual fashion, the padded head lining and the trim in general a very dark green Loden cloth—all nicely done, including the lockwork, etc.

This is an over-under gun/rifle, the 270-caliber rifle barrels 24 inches long, the shotgun barrels going 28 inches. The rifle barrels have a quarter-rib which holds the open rear sight, a widish V-type, with Suhler liftoff type scope mounts/bases. A scope is furnished, one of those marketed by Armsport, but I don't know yet what the power is—I can't find a mark on it, but 4x at a guess.

Introduction

As mentioned last year, there seems to be a trend among manufacturers to handle their own marketing arrangements in the U.S. Likewise, many U.S. gunmakers appear reluctant to introduce any radically new designs, which would require major retooling. Both trends possibly have the same roots—devaluation of the U.S. dollar on the world market and rising production costs everywhere.

Still, various firms, old and new, have introduced new products. Browning, for example, celebrates their Centennial in 1978 with a host of fresh models, including a bolt action rifle. Steyr-Daimler-Puch has added an excellent line of Italian-made shotguns to their inventory, and replica Sharps rifles are being introduced by almost everyone, in percussion and centerfire versions. Generally, the sporting arms picture looks good, but shotgunners will find more to enjoy than riflemen.

The 20-bore shotgun barrels have a low ventilated rib atop the upper barrel, and the side ribs are ventilated also, done to reduce weight, I should think. Quite attractive looking.

The buttstock is of a Monte Carlo type, with a low roll-over cheekpiece, of pistol grip form and carrying a Pachmayr-type ventilated one-inch thick rubber recoil pad.

The fore-end is of the semi-schnabel type, quite good looking, both fore-end and pistol grip extensively checkered, the very fine diamonds running about 30 lines to the inch. The checkering on the fore-end is a bit better done—they're of longer aspect—than the somewhat squarish diamonds on the pistol grip. The high glossy wood finish has also been put over the checkering, thus reducing the checkering's minimal grasping power further. As for run-outs, none at all that I could find—the execution of the checkering is excellent.

This over-under has a quite low-

Sporting Arms of the World

Our big annual review of the important new firearms, the unusual and, sometimes, unique products available this year to the shooting sportsman. The NSGA 1978 survey will be found elsewhere in this edition.

by LARRY S. STERETT and the editors

Custom Craftsmen at Salt Lake City

Here are some of the highly-talented men who made Joe Oakley's extensive displays at the NRA meeting a huge success. From left—Jay Frazier, Joe Oakley, Dick Hodgson, Tom Burgess, Thomas Wilson, Larry Amrine, Bob Winter, Gary Goudy, Duane Wiebe, Steve Billeb, Phil Pilkington, Joe Balickie, Herman Waldron, Bob Swartly, Al Biesen, Byrd Pearson. A report on the Salt Palace exhibits appears elsewhere in this issue.

profile frame, with double Kersten bolts protruding from the breech end of the barrels; lateral locking-lug recesses lie along either side of the lower barrel, a modified Boss system. The lockplate is of sideplate form, yet the action is essentially a trigger-plate type, not a true sidelock. The engraving is of nicely done scroll work, more or less in the English style. The sideplates and the rest of the receiver are finished in a silver gray.

Two gold-plated triggers are fitted, the front one a set type, if desired, this achieved by pushing the trigger forward. There is no pistol grip cap.

It's a top lever opener, of course, and the top tang sliding safety is of automatic type. There are no ejectors, a simple double extractor being fitted instead.

Each pair of barrels has its own fore-end, each virtually identical with the other. The top rib on the shotgun barrels is file cut its full length, making for very good glare reduction. The shotgun barrels carry a red plastic front sight, easily picked up in almost any light condition.

Here are the weights:

Rifle barrels attached, without scope or mount—7 lbs. 6 ozs.

Rifle barrels attached, scope mounted—8 lbs. 3 ozs.

Shotgun barrels attached—7 lbs. 2 ozs.

Handling with the shotgun barrels appears to be very good—most of the weight is between the hands, with the muzzles a bit on the light side. I like to have them this way for my own use.

The name, ARMSPORT, INC. is inlaid in gold on top of the rifle barrels, near the breech, and on both sides of the top shotgun barrel. The shotgun rib is $^3/_8$-inch wide at the rear, the width tapering only slightly from breech to muzzle.

All-in-all, a handsome and well-finished gun, the metal and wood components fitted perfectly, without any gaps noticeable to me. I would, of course, prefer to have seen a classic stock, but I'm equally sure that many of Armsport's potential customers will doubtless welcome the Monte Carlo type that is on it. I would also like to have seen something other than the one-inch ventilated recoil pad, for the 270 certainly doesn't recoil all that much. I think a plain rubber pad, non-ventilated, or a steel buttplate would have given the whole gun a better appearance.

Bines intended originally to offer only a double rifle, hence the Monte Carlo stock.

All popular calibers will be available from the 458 down. Stock styles and dimensions are to order, including the classic type for rifle and/or shotgun use. A rifle buttplate ($^1/_4$-$^3/_8$ inch in solid rubber colored black, brown or red) will be available, as will steel buttplates, I believe.

If extra pairs of shotgun barrels are not wanted, then deduct about $800 from the list price of $5,000. The $800 figure is tentative only; I think it may well be less, in fact.

If scope and mounts are not wanted (open sights only furnished) then deduct about $400. This figure is also tentative.

Regulating and targeting the double barreled rifle will now be done at 120 meters, not at 100 meters as before, and a 50mm group size is the norm if both shots are fired within 12 seconds. Groups will enlarge otherwise, that is, if fired more slowly.

In January 1979 Bines will have a side-by-side DB rifle ready, a full sidelock model a la Holland and Hol-

land, etc. A pair of 20 gauge barrels will be included (12 gauge in the larger rifle calibers) plus a case for all, scope and mount (any scope) at about $7,000. J.T.A.

Armsport D. B. Rifle

The weather at last relented, and on 23 April I got off two brief shooting tests, the temperature 50-some, the skies partly cloudy.

The first test covered the Armsport D. B. rifle (I'll get to the Brown rifle shooting later), so I set up the target frame at 60 meters from my garage's west window. First off, to condition the dried but still slightly oily barrels I fired some old 270 Remington

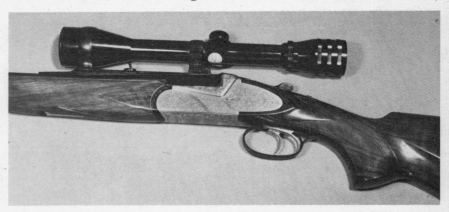

130-gr. soft points through them. I fired the 4 cartridges at a rapid rate—which is the approved technique with D. B. rifles—and they printed in about three-inches—using both barrels—two shots about on a level line with the other two, not spread vertically. Not very tight, I felt, but the shape was promising.

I used the Armsport scope, of course, which is carried in the Suhl-type hook-and-claw lift-off mount—which, I'd say, performed very well in light of the good group made.

Then using fresh RWS 130-gr. SPs, I got a pleasant and unexpected result. Six shots, 3 from each barrel, went into $1^9/_{16}$-inches, which I consider excellent with any double rifle. Again, I was shooting fast, the second shot of each pair fired within several seconds.

This good grouping appeared in spite of a very heavy front trigger, which my test scale showed to be $8^1/_2$-10 lbs., and not uniform. The front trigger has a setscrew, adjustable from the outside, but turning it both ways produced no change in the pull weight. The rear trigger (top barrel) was fine at about $4^1/_2$ lbs., crisp and clean. I had a problem releasing that front trigger without dis-

turbing my hold—and I'm not sure I fully succeeded.

Recoil from this rather heavy rifle was negligible, but snugging down onto a rollover Monte Carlo comb located for a righthanded shooter wasn't comfortable. As many of you know, I have to shoot from the left shoulder these days.

The Italian makers of this new D. B. rifle seem to know what they're doing—and I was sorry there wasn't time for extended testing.

Incidentally, Paul Bines is bringing into this country a variety of gun cases, a bottom price model running around $75 or so at retail, but these are more or less "universal" cases, designed to take barrels of various lengths (within reason) by the use of filler blocks, which Bines will supply.

The Armsport trunk gun case shown is the King model, genuine leather covered and compartmented to take barrels 26" to 32", may be had for one- or 2-barrel sets. They are lined throughout with Scottish loden cloth, plus pouches in the same wool material for the barrel sets and buttstock. Double combination brass locks are installed—set your own numbers. The King cases are $240-$265. There is a Prince line, too, priced $150-$172.50, these with twin snap-type brass locks but without the loden pouches.

Vincenzo Bernardelli

The V.B. shotgun line is distributed in the U.S. by Sloan's, but only one or two of the V.B. Model 110 over-under trap guns have arrived on these shores. Similar to other such target type guns, the 110 has a single selective trigger, separated barrels (no side ribs) and a 10mm wide ventilated top rib. The walnut stock is a Monte Carlo type, and the fore-end is a large beavertail. Available in 3 grades—trap, Skeet and pigeon—with various barrel lengths and chokes, it may be had with different finishes.   L.S.S.

This V.B. 110 has the "L" type of engraving.

Brown Precision's High Country Rifle

It was a rough winter this past season, and it was especially worrisome at Creedmoor Farm—you know how the snow builds up and stays on and on in the countryside, even though the highways and the town streets are fairly free of the white stuff. Anyway, though it reached me a while ago, my first chance to shoot the light 270 Brown rifle came only recently, as you'll read about later on.

The High Country is, as one might expect, meant for the mountain hunter, to whom every ounce counts, yet one who wants an adequate performance, at the least, from his rifle. The Brown rifle here certainly answers the weight requirement—it goes only $6^5/8$ lbs., including its Redfield 6x scope on alloy bases, also from Redfield. The crisp trigger pull was consistently $2^1/2$ lbs.

The tapered 20-inch barrel and the Remington 700 action are epoxy bedded in Brown's fiberglass, foam-filled simple stock—only a non-cheekpiece Monte Carlo is included. Otherwise it's a classic design, and I was surprised at its handling qualities, its pleasantly light feeling in the hands.

I wondered how well it might shoot, of course—matter of fact, I was skeptical about the ability of so light a rifle to group well—the short, thin barrel, the low weight, the muzzle blast and recoil, how could it do better than a couple of inches or so at 100 yards?

But I'd have to wait a bit to find out—it was too damn cold and the path to my targets was covered by some 15 inches of snow, more than that in the drifts.

As I've written elsewhere in this section, I set up 60-meter targets when I was about to shoot the Armsport D.B. rifle. After that trial I picked up the very light Brown 270 rifle and shot it at the same distance.

The sky was a bit more overcast by this time.

Using the 130-gr. Remington ammo again—an oldish lot—I put 5 rounds down range and got, this time, a pair of surprises. Despite the ultra-lightness of this fiberglassed, short barreled rifle, its felt recoil was easy to take and there was no cheek bruising at all. Moreover, I wore only a cotton shirt and light jacket, no recoil pad at the shoulder.

Mr. Brown, in fact, had asked me to let him know what I thought of the recoil, adding that he believed his stock design—no cheekpiece or high Monte Carlo comb, but the comb broad and nicely rounded, with a shallow rifle pad on the butt—lessened the recoil felt at the shoulder. He must, indeed, be doing something right.

The second revelation appeared when I walked down-range to measure the first 5 holes—the first shot, from the clean, cold barrel, had printed a trifle higher than the next 4, but even so the 5 went into $5/8$-inch; the 4 into $1/2$-inch. Certainly not match-winning quality, but these figures translate into 1.04 inches and .833 inches respectively at 100 yards, and the lateral measurement was less.

The second 5—all I had time for—went a little bigger, but the light was beginning to fail. This group measured $5/8$-inch vertically, but less than $1/2$-inch laterally. Holding the fine crosshairs on dead center wasn't easy now, but enough of excuses. I'll maintain that this was pretty good grouping for such a featherweight musket—perhaps I should say "carbine" because of the short barrel.

New Brown Stocks

Word has just reached us on 5 new fiberglass patterns C. H. Brown has now available—these in addition to the 6 types already obtainable from Brown Precision, Inc.

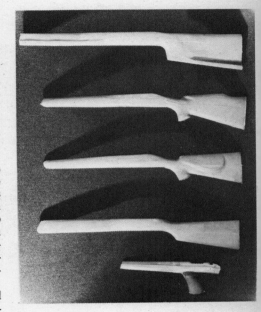

First of the latest is a Walt Berger Heavy Varmint design, inletted for Rem. 40X, Hart or Wichita actions. Fore-end and butt bottom are flat, and each 3" wide. Weight is 2 lbs., 4 ozs., price $75.

Next, a Hunter Bench pattern (or varmint) at 1 lb., 6 ozs. Made for the Rem. 700 short action, it will take up to an 1.25" barrel. $67.50. No. 3 is like the HB, but without Monte Carlo comb, and is intended for M70 actions, old or new. One lb., 4 ozs., cost $67.50.

Fourth—the Brown Pistol Gripless, a top choice among B.R. shooters, and made for Hart, Rem. 40X and Wichita actions. 1 lb., 8 ozs., $65.

Last, one for the Rem. XP-100 pistol/carbine which will take a bigger-than-standard barrel. A mere 12 ozs., price $65.

See our photo, top to bottom, and write Brown for full information on these and the older designs.   J.T.A.

Browning

Because the Browning Centennial firearms are described elsewhere in this edition, the notes that follow will be brief, meant chiefly for the record.

Leading off is the cased Continental 30-06/20 bore set, limited to 500 units, and furnished in a walnut case at $6500. The rifle barrels are 24″ long—the shotgun barrels 26½″.

Another Centennial longarm is the Jonathan Browning Mountain rifle in 50 caliber and limited to 1,000 examples. Delivered in an American alder wood case lined with suede fabric, and all necessary accessories, this halfstock rifle is stocked in select walnut with an inscribed medallion on the butt, plus a bust of Jonathan Browning on the lockplate, both sterling silver.

The Centennial Browning 92 is a recreation of the JMB-designed Winchester 92, but chambered for the 44 Magnum cartridge. Stocked in French walnut, the 92 has a highly polished blued receiver and barrel, gold plated saddle ring and trigger, and a small amount of engraved scrollwork.

Priced from $519.95 for a Grade I Sporter (12, 20, 28 or 410) to $1325 for a Grade V Sporter, there are 19 new versions of the Citori over-under. There is also a new Citori, the Grade I Combo Trap Set in 12 gauge for $939.95, plus Grade II and V versions, these last differing from the Grade I in greater amounts of engraving and stock quality. Most Citori stocks have a high gloss finish, but the new straight-stock Sporter has a satin oil finish.

Browning's Model 92 carbine (at top) and their straight-stocked Citori over-under shotgun, new for 1978.

The B-SS side-by-side shotgun is now offered in Standard Grade I and II versions in 12 or 20, and in a Grade II Sporter with straight stock. Priced from $389.95 to $725, the B-SS Sporter has a slimmed-down forearm, too.

The new Pigeon Grade Competition BT-99 trap gun has a deluxe American walnut stock with hand checkering, a greyed steel receiver with high relief hand-engraved pigeons, and a price tag of $1100. Barrel lengths and chokes are the same as for the Grade I BT-99 Competition shotgun.

Last year Browning introduced the BPS pump shotgun (see the full report elsewhere in this edition). It is now available in a Grade I Buck Special version with rifle sights, for $249.95.

A new Browning addition to the "initial" nomenclature is the BBR, or Browning Bolt Rifle. Its hammer-forged free-floating barrel is 24″ long,

weight is about 8 lbs., and it is 44½″ long. The fluted bolt design has 9 locking lugs, a 60° handle lift, a shrouded cocking piece and adjustable trigger, a cocking indicator, a tang-mounted slide safety, and a hinged floorplate with detachable box magazine. The Monte Carlo stock is of American walnut, urethane finished, has a grip cap, and checkered grip and forearm areas, plus flush, low-profile sling swivel studs. An unusual device is a special structural-aluminum barrel-channel insert in the forearm; about $1/8$″ thick and 8″ long, this insert helps strengthen the forearm and reduces forearm warpage, often a result of weather changes. Calibers—25-06, 270, 30-06, 7mm Rem. Mag. and 300 Win. Mag.

The rifles examined looked and felt good. Thus, for its Centennial year, to paraphrase a commercial, Browning has done itself proud. L.S.S.

Commercial Trading Imports

The Soviet-made Baikal shotguns, some formerly imported by Universal, are now distributed by a Minneapolis-based firm. CTI had 21 Baikal models on display at the 1978 NSGA show in Houston, including the MC models in side-by-side and over-under types, plus the MC-21, a modified copy of the Remington 11-48 Sportsman. Prices were not set as this is written (May 1978), but they will be at least competitive, I'm sure.

Many of the over-unders are a bit different from those U.S. shooters are used to seeing, these having deeper receivers and non-detachable (screw-attached) forearms. The barrels are detachable, of course, and many forearms are ventilated.

Most of the stocks seen were of European walnut, with an oil or glossy finish depending on the model.

The Baikal M27/27E

Trap and Skeet models have Monte Carlo stocks with pistol grip, but straight grip stocks are also available, and ventilated recoil pads were seen on all Baikal shotguns except field grades. Buttstock designs conformed to modern U.S. preferences generally, especially on target guns with a single trigger, but some of the side-by-side stocks seemed to be from another era.

The Baikal IJ-27/27E is available in three grades—Super, Deluxe and Silver—at least one of which has been

available in the U.S. for several years. The IJ-25 is similar to the IJ-27 but has a ventilated forearm and dimensions intended for trap or Skeet shooting.

The MC-7 is an over-under resembling the best of its type; the MC-8 and MC-109 are more ornate with different actions, and better quality walnut. The MC-8 has won many international trap matches. All 12-gauge models have 2¾″ chambers and other gauges are available. Most Baikals weigh around 7 lbs. L.S.S.

Aimpoint Electronic Sight

This sighting device, unusual to say the least, and probably unique, can be mounted on any firearm that accepts Weaver mounts—rifle, shotgun or muzzleloader. It does not have, note, any magnification, and the field of view is large at 100 yards.

Because it is not dependent on ambient light—it's powered by batteries—the Aimpoint is highly useful in early morning/late evening conditions, when the target is dimly seen.

An internal red-diode sighting dot, covering about 3 minutes of angle and fully adjustable for windage and elevation, is the only sighting element. Properly zeroed-in, putting the red dot where it's wanted will insure a hit, always assuming range estimation and hold-over, if any, are correct. As with a scope, there's only the one red dot to worry about—no aligning of rear and front sights, say.

Looking like a short telescope sight, the Aimpoint's red diode dot can be adjusted for intensity, comes with a removable polaroid rear filter (plus a semi-permanent front ditto), and is protected against dust and condensation.

Our sample Aimpoint (No. 14014) showed excellent construction. All parts appeared precisely machined and well fitted together, in general more like a fine optical instrument, which it is, certainly, than a mere sighting device. Mounting the Aimpoint took only a few minutes, plus a few more for getting its red-dot/aiming point roughly on the 50-yard target via bore sighting.

Two joined alloy tubes—roughly square in section—comprise the viewing system and the battery holder/rheostat, these lying atop and held to the steel upper part of the mount. This latter piece contains the screws for making elevation and windage changes, each click of either being worth about 15mm—about ³/₅th inch. A rotatable cap, covering the rear end of the battery tube, lets the user quickly adjust the light intensity of the red aiming point.

The Swedish makers of Aimpoint stress that the red dot follows, in effect, head or eye movement of the shooter—and that's quite true. There is a great amount of lateral leeway in using Aimpoint—even with the aiming eye well off center, a hit will be made as long as the red dot remains on the target. Just catching the dot at the extreme edge of the field of view works fine. Nor is eye relief critical—I'd say that 4-5 inches seems optimum, but the red dot remains visible out to arms length, in fact. At that distance the field of view is lessened, of course, but the Aimpoint could well be used on handguns, given an adequate mount system.

As I've said, placing the Aimpoint on a Winchester M70 rifle, in 30-06 caliber was quickly done. Bore sighting is rarely exact, of course, and my first shot at 55 yards landed some 3 inches high and a little left. Another two shots brought the point of impact about center, and I fired my first group of 5 shots. I found that, with care, I could hold the red dot centered with the black bull, and my second 5 shots improved on the first quintet— 2.1″ against 2.6″. The last 7 shots, emptying the box, went into 1.96″, but 6 of those measured 1.51″. A single flyer made the difference.

Aimpoint is a bit bulky—6 inches over-all, it's 2 inches wide and about that high above the receiver top. At 14 ozs. as received, it isn't a featherweight, and the Weaver bases would bring it to a pound. But it is certainly a fast aiming device, especially in poor light, and in those states where shotguns must be used on deer it should be the near-ideal answer.

An improved Aimpoint is in the works, which I expect to see soon. If time permits and the weather relents, I'll comment on the new version.

Retail price of the Aimpoint Electronic Sight is $149.95—write to Aimpoint USA, 29351 Stonecrest Rd., Rancho Palos Verdes, CA 90274.

J.T.A.

Aguirre y Aranzabal shotguns, among Spain's finest, are now available from two U.S. firms—Wm. L. Moore in Agoura, California, and IGI Domino in New York. Both firms import about the same models, although IGI also has several lower-priced boxlocks and sidelocks, plus the Matador II with single selective trigger, the Cosmos single barrel, and the Model 37 Super, a sidelock over-under. Moore's line includes several 20 bores and a few 28s and 410s plus the AYA Model XXV, a Churchill-like double with 25″ tubes. Moore also imports 6 Armas Garbi (Spain) models, all sidelock shotguns, of which 5 have hand-detachable locks.   L.S.S.

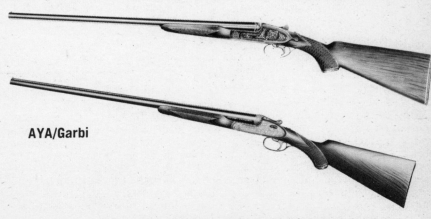

AYA/Garbi

Top, AYA's Model 53E, a sidelock double shotgun of high quality. The other AYA is the Model 117, another sidelock D.B. shotgun.

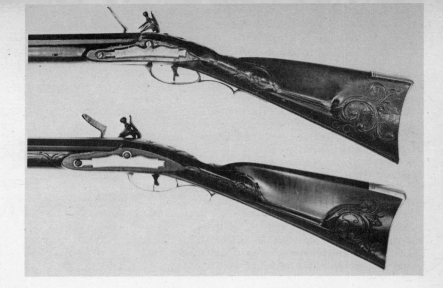

Homer L. Dangler

This dedicated longrifle maker is a critical, meticulous and tireless craftsman—he made the near-copy of a J. P. Beck rifle pictured nearby three times before he was satisfied—well, half satisfied! The upper rifle is an original J. P. Beck, the lower one Dangler's copy, the comb modified to suite a customer's idea.

Write for Dangler's brochure and price.   J.T.A.

Falling Block Works Single Shot Actions

This Troy, Michigan firm, makers in recent years of actions closely similar to the beloved Winchester High Wall (Models J and K, which accept 1"-14 and ³/₄"-16 TPI barrels respectively) have just announced their Model L, bigger and heavier than those just mentioned, and capable of taking a 1¹/₈"-12 TPI barrel. This big action, called by FBW "The Express Model," has side walls 0.175" thick and is 1.47" wide over-all. Weighing about 2¹/₂ lbs., the Model L accepts big cartridges, certainly anything makable from RCBS basic brass or, for that matter, Jim Bell's like cases. The Model L retails for $170.

Another single shot action, different in profile and in design, is the FBW Model H, their "Plains Pattern"—it is 1.375" wide, has side walls 0.187" thick, and accepts a 1"-14 TPI barrel shank. This action sells for $140, the Model J is the same price, and the Model K is $115.

All of the FBW actions have full, non-rebated side walls, center-hung hammers and a plain but adjustable trigger. There are no rear tangs, top or bottom, and the rear action face is recessed to accept a tenoned section of the buttstock, assuring rigidity of assembly. Through bolts for holding the buttstock to the action are standard on all models. All types but the Model

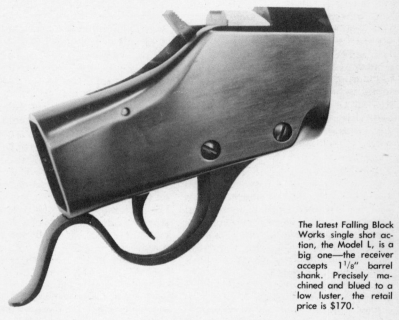

The latest Falling Block Works single shot action, the Model L, is a big one—the receiver accepts 1¹/₈" barrel shank. Precisely machined and blued to a low luster, the retail price is $170.

H have bushed (removable for repair) gas-proof firing pins. Schuetzen and closed-loop levers are available for Models J and L, these prices $22 to $27 extra or at $12 over action prices if ordered at time of purchase.

I've examined two FBW late-production actions recently, the Model K and L, and I'm pleased to see that Leo Fix—who owns the company—continues to improve the quality and design elements of his actions. Both actions show smooth finishing and polishing, the action sides and octagon receiver tops carefully flatted; the rounded areas are uniformly radiussed. A rich, low-luster blue completes the job. I'm impressed by these latest FBW specimens.

A new brochure is offered by FBW, free for the asking.   J.T.A.

MTM Big Box

MTM's new Case-Gard Silhouette 100 case holds 100 rifle rounds in perfect security. Though designed for the metallic silhouette competitor, it will also be welcomed by ballistics experimenters, varmint hunters, benchresters and big bore fans. The Silhouette 100 accommodates all calibers from 222 to 375 H&H Magnum. Loaded rounds can be carried bullet-

up or bulletdown. Made of durable polypropylene, the new container is scuff resistant and its integral hinge is guaranteed for 1,000,000 open-close sequences. Its generously proportioned handle is also recessed into the top, making the Silhouette 100 stackable, too.

The Silhouette 100 measures 7¹/₂"×8"×4³/₈", with the handle down, and it's available in green or red at $3.95 each.

Green Electric Trigger

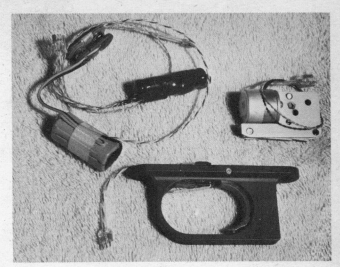

Frank Green started to develop electric triggers in the early 1960s, and some time after that he installed a well-working prototype in a 6mm Remington rifle. However, it had a fault which turned off some of the then top competitors—it had a lot of movement, about like a very light 2-stage system, though it was highly consistent in let-off.

At around this time the transistors appeared, solving what had been serious problems using straight battery power, solenoids and resultant arcing contact points—with such components consistent letoff and reliability suffered severely. Using silicon-controlled rectifiers (SCR) for switching solved all the switching problems.

His new SCR switching system proved fully satisfactory in free pistols, and Green developed the Electroarm, a free pistol which currently holds *all* U.S. free pistol records. The installation of his electric trigger in the Electroarm, done by him and unified with the pistol's design, precluded failure—it *couldn't* be tampered with or modified. In fact, if repair were needed, the sealed system had to be cut open!

On the other hand, his currently-available Electronic Trigger System Kit is vulnerable, its dependability relying on the carefulness of the installation—or on the installer. If the owner/buyer is a tinkerer, unwilling to follow instruction or exercise reasonable care, damage to the unit can result—and probably will! Green will, of course, do the installation himself, as he did in my case—I wasn't about to attempt that job with my inexpertise, though his instructions are clear and ample.

The Remington 40X rifle I sent to Frank Green was returned to me in short order, after about a week or so. That was in mid-winter, cold and the snow deep. I had to try it, of course, so I set the rifle up in my basement shop area, fixing it in simulated bench shooting position. Opening and closing the bolt, I then armed the system by pushing upward on the small lever at the top of the guard. On my first letoff I goofed—it got away from me, the extreme lightness of the release almost impossible to believe. After a few more trials, during which I gradually gained a degree of control, I was achieving a release when I wanted it—but the finger effort involved—or rather the non-effort—remained consistently the same, utterly light. There was, for me, no apparent motion, but as Frank Green says, his electric trigger does move, the amount an infinitesimal 0.0015"–0.002", but there is no "feel of the motion at the switch closure." He also points out that his "trigger is free to move a few additional thousandths after (switch) contact," but this motion "does not normally occur because finger pressure and spring tension are balanced at the time of switch closure," thus there's nothing to indicate or signal to the shooter that the sear is released. The letoff weight is about 1½ oz., but it is readily adjusted.

Frank Green's electric trigger is remarkable, no less—ever uniform and without perceptible movement, at least in my hands. I only wish I were able to take better advantage of it, as I could have, say, 10 years ago.

The Green Electronic Trigger System Kit sells for about $92, and is made for Remington 700 and 40x actions, Shilen, Wichita and, later perhaps, for Remington 788 and Mauser actions. For installation by Frank Green add about $25.00. J.T.A.

Golden Eagle 2000

To round out their sporting arms line, Golden Eagle has now introduced the Series 2000 line of rimfire rifles—4 rifles, all in 22 LR chambering. There's a bolt action with a 15-round tubular magazine or a 10-round detachable box magazine; a semi-automatic with the same magazine choices. All have 23″ barrels, ramp bead front sight and a fold-down open rear sight; the receivers are grooved to accept most tip-off scope mounts. The walnut stock, with fluted comb and pistol grip cap, has a non-slip rubber buttpad but no checkering. All 4 rifles have bolt sleeves similar to that found on the Golden Eagle 7000 centerfire rifle, plus the same sliding tang safety. L.S.S.

Griffin & Howe

Fine rifle makers since the 1920s, and for some years associated with the defunct Abercrombie & Fitch, G&H continues to offer top notch custom gunsmithing and gunmaking.

Now they're into metallic cartridge case manufacturing, using a production technique reported to be a lot more simple than conventional methods, according to William A. Ward, who heads G&H. Orders for as few as 1,000 cases will be a practicability, he said, though admittedly such relatively small lots will be more costly per unit than larger batches would run.

For further information, address G&H Ammo Sales, Inc., 589 Broadway, New York, 10012. J.T.A.

Marvin Huey
Custom Casemaker

The case shown here, holding the 270 singleshot break-open rife made for me by Renato Gamba—plus the Zeiss scope and other fittings—was hand crafted especially for me by Marvin Huey of Reed's Spring, Mo.

In most respects it is a faithful copy of a best-quality British gun case—oak-and-genuine-leather construction, the polished wood fence or wainscot inside correctly formed and cut, the lining made of tournament-grade billiard table green felt. The exterior departs from tradition in that the corners, top and bottom, are without the heavy cast-brass pieces usually fitted. Instead, Huey placed separate and sturdy leather covers over each already leather-covered end, both lid and lower sections, these about 6-inches wide and gracefully shaped.

All in all, a very well built case, put together with skill and care, the interior compartments made an exact fit

for the fittings I supplied. This high craftsmanship has its price, of course—the case shown cost me $390.21, which isn't excessive for

such quality.

Marvin Huey offers a colorful brochure, his prices listed, for a stamped, self-addressed envelope.   J.T.A.

Interarms

Mauser has a new bolt action rifle, the Model 77—so far seen only in pictures—which Interarms will have to offer in small numbers this year. Production is limited. A new locking safety is fitted, the trigger is usable set or unset, the metallic sights are readily removable (for scope mounting), and a 3-round steel magazine box is detachable using one hand.

The new-design bolt carries 3 rear-mounted lugs for a 60° lift, and the bolt sleeve is easily removed without tools. Chamberings, U.S. and metric, start with 6.5×57 and go to the 458.

The oil-finished stock, with Bavarian cheekpiece/Monte Carlo comb, is of European walnut, recoil pad equipped. Rosewood tips at fore-end and grip cap, as well as white-line spacers at both points, are standard, as is a palm swell on the grip's right side. Retail price is $1200.

The Model 66 Mauser, the double-shuffle bolt type that so enhanced Mauser's world reputation, is back in new guise. Now it's a sniper rifle, with muzzle flash hider, a thumb-hole, adjustable cheekpiece match-type stock, and offered with 3 scopes—a conventional Zeiss variable-power or one of two battery-powered light-gathering scopes for night use.

Interarms now has, at long last, the Commemorative Parabellum pistols (otherwise known as L*g*rs). Made by Mauser, natürlich, the Bulgarian version is in 7.65mm caliber with 4¾" barrel. The Russian model, in 9mmP, has a 4" barrel. Both come

with presentation cases, have appropriate national crests and gold-filled lettering, and will retail at $1800 each. Total production won't exceed 250, of which Interarms may get a third. Some few matching-serial numbered specimens will be available, both listing for $3800.

That's a damned shame. Whether at $1800 or $3800, those special P-08 pistols will sell like the proverbial hotcakes, I'm certain. Pity the poor collector unable to get up the dough or too late to get in the queue. J.T.A.

Interarms offers some of the sporting arms once distributed by Garcia, including the various Rossi shotguns and rifles. The M11 Overland hammer shotguns and the hammerless M14 Squire are available in 12, 20 or 410. These doubles have two triggers, beavertail forearms, pistol grip

stocks, and come with assorted barrel lengths and chokes. The Overland, as the Coach Gun, is available in 12 or 20 gauge with 20" barrels.

Rossi rifles include the 6-lb. M92 Saddle Ring Carbine in 357 Magnum, and the 62SA and 62SAC slide-action rifle and carbine in 22 rimfire. The M92 has a 20" barrel. The 5½-lb. 62SA has a 23" barrel, and is offered in blued or nickel finish; the 4¾-lb. 62SAC has a 16½" barrel.

The several Mark X rifles include the Classic, Viscount and Cavalier models, with or without sights, the Alaskan, Mannlicher and the new 20" barreled Continental Carbine. This latest Mark X has an European-Style Mannlicher stock with sculptured cheekpiece, single or double-set triggers, detachable sling swivels, and a "butter-knife" bolt handle.   L.S.S.

Rossi's Gallery Model 22 (top) and the Mark X Mannlicher-styled Carbine, both from Interarms.

Lyman Plains Rifle/Ditto Kit

Both of these muzzle-loading items are available in calibers from 45 to 58. The Assembly Kit can be finished into a rifle identical to Lyman's factory-built caplock Plains Rifle with only a few common household tools and a weekend or two of the builder's time.

All needed drilling, tapping and threading has been done, leaving only the final fitting, polishing and finishing to do.

The kit features:
- walnut stock—90% inletted and shaped.
- precision rifled 28″ barrel with 1/48″ twist in all calibers—drilled, tapped and dovetailed.
- lock—fully assembled and color case-hardened lock has durable coil mainspring, and fly on tumbler, essential for set-trigger system.
- assembled and blued adjustable double-set triggers.
- all needed screws and brass parts; the latter, including patchbox, require final filing and polishing.
- complete assembly/shooting instructions.

Cost retail is $224.95 for the Plains Rifle; $169.95 for the Assembly Kit.

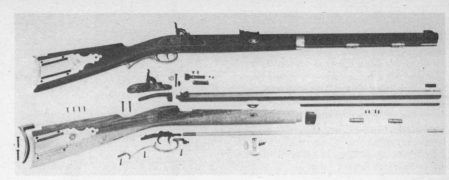

J. J. Jenkins

I doubt that the double barreled shotgun pictured here will reproduce well enough to show the beautiful case-hardening in color that Jenkins does, but you can see a portion of the superb stock and fore-end work, the smoothly-flowing lines of this sidelock by W. and C. Scott.

But here's proof that Jenkins' metal coloring efforts are highly appreciated—custom gunmakers all over the U.S. are sending such jobs to him, and I've heard nothing but glowing praise for him.

As J.J.J. says, "...we offer top grade work on (fine) sporting arms, from front sight to buttplate," and virtually all "...restorations are done in the house." Write for Jenkins' brochure.   J.T.A.

J.J. Jenkins

Hoppe's 1978 Catalog

There's a bunch of new stuff in this fresh publication, now 28 big pages—black powder accessories, NRA targets, Starstrobe distress lights (for boating use), and the improved "Sta-Put" claybird machine. Plus the usual wide array of Hoppe's products for hunters and shooters. See your dealer or write to Penguin Industries, Box 97, Parkesburg, PA 19365.   J.T.A.

Lightload

Lightload

This interesting and well-made device will help you get more accuracy from your revolver if you'll practice properly—and such practice can take place in your home at 10-14 foot ranges. In fact, because a battery-powered light beam is projected through the handgun's barrel, you'll see the flash of the light spot better in a darkened room.

Supplied by Jafin Products are a replacement cylinder (which holds the two small type N 1.5V batteries required, a lens tube for the barrel, a reflecting target, and a substitute crane. Our sample kit is intended for use in S&W J-, K- or N-frame revolvers, and it took only a few minutes to make the installation, using the highly adequate Instruction Manual furnished.

Using the 4-color plastic combat-type target (11½″×24″), hung on a wall, and a 2-hand hold on a new S&W Model 66 with 6″ barrel, practice did indeed improve hits and scores—relearning to watch the sight picture more carefully, successive light splashes began to register in the 10- and 9-rings. I'll have to keep this up!

Light Load sets are also made for most revolvers and the Colt 45 ACP models, all priced at $92.50, without batteries. Write to Jafin Products, P. O. Box 547, Clinton, AL 35045 for full information.   J.T.A.

Michaels of Oregon

Michaels of Oregon, maker of the many "Uncle Mike" shooting accessories, now offers several Presentation Grade carrying straps to complement its wide array of sling swivels. All made from specially-tanned latigo leathers and with linings of white shearling lambswool, the new straps are colored a deep mahogany, and all hardware is brass-plated. All straps fit 1" or 1¼" swivel loops.

The Eagle Cap, No. 2658 (far right), has a sheepskin-lined shoulder pad, the latter showing deeply-tooled basketweave design. A slide-to-adjust buckle permits ample adjustment for length. Retail, $16.95.

The Chief Joseph, No. 2656, is a cobra-type, with a figure-8 pattern stitched into the upper portion. Sheepskin lined with an adjusting buckle, the strap retails at $15.50.

The Mt. Hood, No. 2657, named for Oregon's tallest mountain, has a sheepskin-lined sliding shoulder pad, with no tooling, and an infinitely-adjustable sliding buckle. Retail, $15.95.

The Three Fingered Jack, No. 2655, is a deluxe cobra style with deeply tooled basketweave design and a soft sheepskin lining. Retail, $15.50.

Michaels offers three other slings and straps—an unlined cobra, a military-type sling and a tote strap,

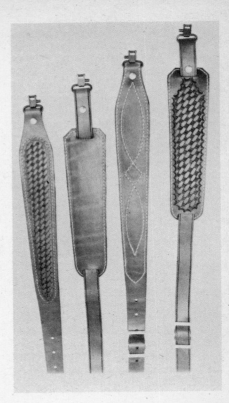

plain or basketweave design optional.

Need to replace your CVA muzzle-loader's nipple? Michaels now has one in stainless steel, threaded 6x1mm, cost $1.15 each, and designed to take No. 11 caps. This latest nipple makes

7 in the line, the others for black powder rifles, shotguns and handguns.

Send for the free and well-filled catalog to Michaels of Oregon, P. O. Box 13010, Portland, OR 97213.

Sharon Barrel for T/C Hawken

A 32-inch replacment barrel for Thompson/Center Hawken-type rifles is available from Sharon Rifle Barrel Co., well-known for their own muzzle-loading rifles, shotguns, kits and barrels.

The new octagonal barrel, completely finished and ready for installation, replaces the standard 28" barrel on the T/C rifle. Front and rear sights, breechplug, underlug, underrib, ramrod ferrules and nipple are included, and only minor modification to the T/C rifle is necessary to install the Sharon barrel, which is blued to match the original barrel.

The ¹⁵/₁₆" diameter replacement barrel, bored and machined from a special steel, is cut rifled to provide 8 grooves, .011" to .012" deep. This precision process produces a highly accurate and uniform barrel bore, important in achieving a tight gas seal. Such precision rifling won't cut the patches, either, thus letting gas escape and reduce muzzle velocity.

Made in 45, 50 and 54 caliber, the new Sharon barrels sell for $67.95.

Sharon Rifle Barrels offers a Hawken-style rifle kit, this one with full-length stock for a 34" barrel, calibers 50, 54, 58 and 62, the wood hard eastern maple, with detailed instructions for assembly. Cost, $295 or, finished complete (limited quantity) $530.

Sharps Rifle Co.

This is the third firm to offer replica Sharps rifles (Shiloh and Sile the others) but all SRC models are on the 1874 action, sporters to Mid-Range to Creedmoor. Five versions are

offered—the 45-70 caliber "Business" rifle at $395 is the least costly. The top of the line is the Creedmoor No. 1 (spelled Credemoor in their ads) at $795. The firm address is 3428 Shakertown Rd., Dayton, OH 45430.

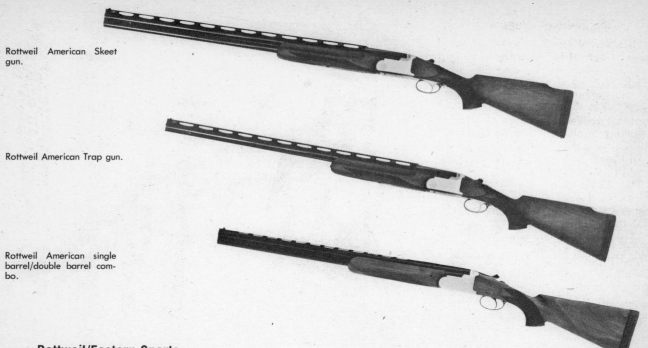

Rottweil American Skeet gun.

Rottweil American Trap gun.

Rottweil American single barrel/double barrel combo.

Rottweil/Eastern Sports

The '72 Super Trap Combo is still available for shotgunners wanting one of the best, but a couple of other over-unders have been added. The Rottweil 650 Field gun, 12 gauge only, has 28″ barrels and sells for well under $700. The 650 can be had with a single selective trigger or double triggers, and ejectors are standard. Except for lacking the slight schnabel fore-end, the 650 resembles the '72 Field Supreme over-under.

With a suggested list price of $1895.00, The American Skeet Gun, especially designed for insert-tube use by Robert Paxton, has the same basic action and finish as the '72 Olympia Skeet model, but comes with a single selective mechanical trigger, an 11mm vent rib topping the 26³/₄″ barrels, and conventional Skeet choking in place of the Retro Skeet chokes. Workmanship on the shotgun examined was excellent. Interchangeable trigger units and stock assemblies are available, including an unfinished one for the do-it-yourselfer; the walnut is oil-finished and hand checkered, pull length is 14¹/₂″ to the middle of the recoil pad, the drops at comb and heel 1³/₈″ and 1⁵/₈″ respectively.

Two more interchangeable trigger units are available, making a total of 6 such. Intended for trap guns, the new ones are: single selective, with a choice of "release-release" or "release-pull" triggers. Although $300 may sound like a steep price for a trigger assembly, both units, examined and tried, functioned like a fine watch mechanism.   L.S.S.

Marble Cleaning Kits

I commented on Marble's "Universal" kit in Handloader's Digest 8, but that was written before I had one in my hands—of which more later.

The kit shown here is a new durable plastic packaging for the Universal gun cleaning materials, which includes a 36″ rod (aluminum or brass), their gun oil and solvent, patches, etc.

The Universal I've seen has the same small-diameter rod (in 3 pieces, and sturdily-jointed), but because of its slenderness I can't consider it highly useful or efficient in, say, a 12-gauge shotgun. Sure, it could work well enough for ordinary, light-effort big-bore scrubbing, but one would have to guard against wobble and, perhaps, ultimate breakage.

Cleaning rods work best when they're close to bore diameter, rifles or shotguns. Rigidity or stiffness is what's needed, *especially* in the larger calibers/gauges, particularly when any heavy effort is called for—as it often is.

The Universal Gun Cleaning Kit is $7.95 with a light-alloy rod, $8.95, if the brass rod is wanted.   J.T.A.

Hoenig & Rodman

Well known for some years for their stock duplications work—plus the custom gunsmithing also offered—this Boise, Idaho shop has decided to market their stock-turning precision pantograph machines.

The Standard Model, on 42″ centers and furnished with one spindle and two rotary clamps, is $10,000. A like machine, but with 60″ centers and supplied with three rotary clamps, is $11,000. A Rotary Power Feed is optional at $1,000, and extra spindles cost $2,000 each.

H&R can accurately duplicate any stock provided the customer furnishes the original to act as a model (which can be altered externally as desired) or if H&R have a master stock on hand. Prices for their work start at $110, including outside shaping (M70s, Rugers, Sakos, Remington 700) and run to $185-$225 for sidelock shotgun buttstocks. These prices do not include cost of the wood (H&R prefer that the customer supply the wood), and if *outside shaping* is not desired, the prices mentioned are reduced by 20%.   J.T.A.

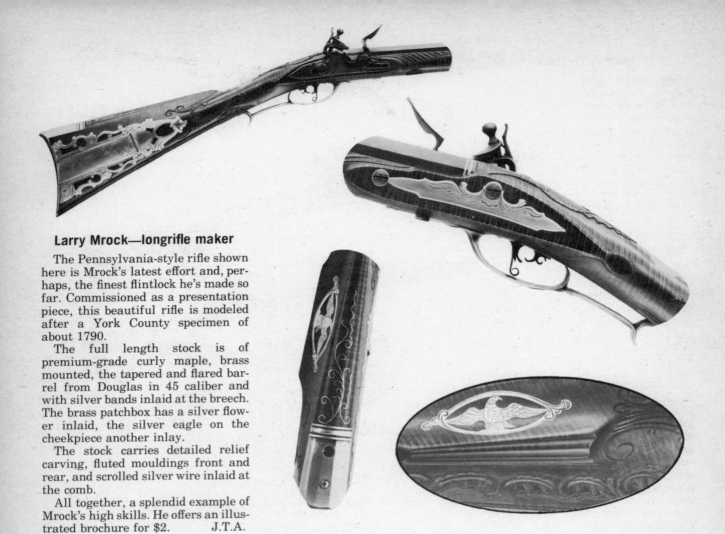

Larry Mrock—longrifle maker

The Pennsylvania-style rifle shown here is Mrock's latest effort and, perhaps, the finest flintlock he's made so far. Commissioned as a presentation piece, this beautiful rifle is modeled after a York County specimen of about 1790.

The full length stock is of premium-grade curly maple, brass mounted, the tapered and flared barrel from Douglas in 45 caliber and with silver bands inlaid at the breech. The brass patchbox has a silver flower inlaid, the silver eagle on the cheekpiece another inlay.

The stock carries detailed relief carving, fluted mouldings front and rear, and scrolled silver wire inlaid at the comb.

All together, a splendid example of Mrock's high skills. He offers an illustrated brochure for $2.   J.T.A.

Stoeger/Franchi/Sako

The Sako rifles, actions and barreled actions formerly distributed by Garcia are now offered by Stoeger. The line remains about the same, except for some changes in model designations; the 3 action lengths are now called the AI (short), AII (medium), and AIII (long), as are the rifles in Standard and Deluxe grades. In addition the Model 78, Carbine and Varmint rifles are available.

The Franchi 530 Trap Automatic shotgun should be on sale before you read this. Production guns are a bit different from the prototypes first shown in 1976. At $499.95 and weighing about 8³/₈ lbs., this gun has a 30″ barrel with "Hi-Loft" ventilated rib, matte metal finish, and 3 interchangeable choke tubes. The receiver is of forged steel, the gas system is specially tuned, and there's a "snap-in" shell catcher for singles and a deflector for doubles. A Skeet version of the 530 is scheduled for later.

Next year should see the Franchi 12-gauge Undergun ready. Resembling their 2004 single barrel trap gun, the Undergun has only a single lower barrel topped by an extended-height ventilated rib—the super "Hi-Loft" trestle rib. The low barrel position supposedly reduces recoil and muzzle lift; the new rib, which has a bright red line down the center, is said to dissipate heat and mirage faster than conventional ribs.

The Franchi 520 autoloader in 12 gauge can now be had in an Eldorado Gold grade at $1000, with 26″ or 28″ barrels. The Peregrine Series of Franchi over-unders now includes a $1195 Limited Edition Diamond De-luxe grade, with 26″ or 28″ barrels and special finish and engraving, as does the Eldorado.

Two other Franchi shotguns—the Imperial Monte Carlo side-by-side and the Grand Prix over-under—are obtainable on special order only, delivery time about one year. These two shotguns are handmade, with stock measurements, barrel lengths and choke combinations to the customer specifications. The O-U has a boxlock action, the side-by-side is a fully engraved sidelock. A single trigger is standard on both models, but double triggers can be had.   L.S.S.

Smith & Wesson

The Model 1000 Magnum auto-loading shotgun is now available in two 20-gauge steel-receiver versions chambered for 3″ shells. Barrel lengths include 28″ modified or 28″ full, each with vent rib and double sighting beads. Priced $307.95 (extra barrels $101.95), the latest 1000 models have walnut stocks and recoil pads. There are also new 20-gauge M916 and M916T magnum shotguns, with 3″ chamber length/choke combinations. Priced from $136.75 for the plain-barrel 916 to $169.45 for the 916T with vent rib, the new 20-gauge pumps have steel receivers, a new extractor design, and a new cam-operated cartridge cut-off. Extra barrels are available; $38.60 and $71.50 for the plain and vent-rib models respectively.　　　　L.S.S.

T. F. White—Powder Horns

Tom, to his many friends, is a master powder horn maker, and a carver as well of Kentucky long rifles. Tom supplies John Bivins, among others, with horns to accompany the muzzleloaders these other craftsmen make.

White makes small, medium or large horns, with his own scrimshawing in almost any style one might want—hunting scenes, map horns, ships, symbols, and any of these with plain or embellished end plugs. His prices range from a mere $5.50 to $225, and a brochure on them is available at $1.

Pictured is a small bag horn and one priming horn for flintlocks, both ends handsomely decorated with an inlay and scrolls of silver.

Tom's address is: 5801 Westchester Ct., Worthington, OH 43085.　J.T.A.

Powder horns handcrafted and scrimshawed by Tom White, the wood butts handsomely inlaid with silver.

Wichita Varmint Rifle

Wichita Engineering has added a varmint rifle to their line of long guns. The new rifle's action is based on the Wichita Model 1375, popular with benchrest shooters. The large diameter bolt, 7/8″, is ground to a perfect fit with the receiver, and we're told, the bolt face is recessed. The cocking block and firing pin are housed within the bolt and shroud. A loading ramp is machined into the bottom of the receiver of single shot models. In the event of a ruptured case, or a perforated primer, the gases are harmlessly vented via three pressure ports in the bolt.

The trigger is a fully adjustable Canjar, and the 20⅛″ chrome-moly barrel is precision fitted to assure perfect alignment with the receiver.

The barreled action is glass bedded in a stock of AAA fancy American walnut, given a hand-rubbed finish, and the checkering hand cut 20 lines to the inch.

All popular varmint calibers are offered, as well as special order chamberings, and reloading dies matched exactly to the individual rifle's chamber are available. Serially numbered to match the rifle, they're designed for use in conventional reloading presses or as hand tools.

Wichita Precision Rifle Rest

This long-popular rifle support is now offered in two versions—a lightweight aluminum/steel model going 6 lbs., the other an iron/steel rest of 11 lbs. and priced at $49.95. The alloy type is $10 less.

Both, of course, are of the same proved design that has made Wichita rests a top choice—baked wrinkled finish plus chromed hardware, entirely hand-adjustable, contoured and non-rotating bag rest, hardened-point leveling screws, etc.

As you probably know, Wichita Engineering & Supply (Box 11371, Wichita, KS 67211) is now producing several rifles and actions, among the latter a light shell-holder design Mini-Action for benchresters and their Model WBR 1375, a slightly heavier action, also for the stoolshooters, that is offered in 4 variants—right-hand bolt with right- or left-side loading ports, and a left-hand bolt form with the same choice of loading ports, right or left. J.T.A.

Friedrich Wilhelm Heym

a return to excellence

A history of the famed gunmaking firm and its re-emergence as a prime producer today of the high quality firearms it proudly offered before World War II.

by TOM TURPIN

This is Herr Peter Bang, Managing Director of the Heym factory. The rack behind his desk contains some of Heym's finest products.

THE LONG, U-shaped two-story building provides no external hint as to what's inside—it could easily be a dress or furniture factory, even a pickle plant. The outside is absolutely undistinguished.

The only clue as to what might be going on inside is its location. The town holding this rather drab building is Münnerstadt—which most West German shooting enthusiasts know is a gunmaking center.

Walking around the building, one finally comes to a rather nondescript entryway with a small sign, perhaps 8 by 18 inches, that reads: *Fr. W. Heym, Waffenfabrik, Gegr. 1865/ Suhl.* Translated, the sign denotes that this is the Friedrich Wilhelm Heym Arms Factory, founded in 1865 in Suhl.

Most sporting arms devotees around the world are well aware that the heart of the German armsmaking industry, before WWII, was in Suhl—about 30 miles from Münnerstadt, but today Suhl is on the other side of the Iron Curtain in East Germany.

The Heym people, perceptive enough to see the handwriting on the wall, clandestinely crossed the border into what was to become West Germany, in 1948.

A Time at Ostheim

The Heym operation settled briefly in the small town of Ostheim, almost on the border. At that time the manufacture of sporting firearms was not allowed by the victorious Allied Forces, so Heym re-started its efforts by making air guns.

By 1952 the Heym management felt that its location in Ostheim was too close to the border for comfort and was too far removed from lines of communication and transportation to regain its former productivity. A search for a new and more suitable location was begun.

They found in Münnerstadt what they were looking for. The town had constructed an industrial building, hoping to attract industry, and that building was ready for occupancy. In addition, the town was located on

Some of the fine Heyms behind Herr Bang's desk. The 4 examples in the middle are the finest of the gunmaker's art. All are sidelock models, all are engraved with exhibition quality patterns and inlaid with gold and silver, and represent the very top quality of Heym's production.

Highway 19, leading straight into the centers of Schweinfurt and Würzburg. Heym moved to Münnerstadt that same year, 1952, since which time they've been operating full-bore.

Once inside the modest building there is no doubt about its purpose. Naturally, one sees machinery of differing types—milling machines, drill presses, metal-turning lathes, etc. More notably, however, at least in this day and age, is that on practically every workbench one sees files, files, and more files. They're ready to hand in all sizes, shapes, and cuts. Obviously this is not just an ordinary manufacturing effort, but rather one that uses a machine as just another tool, for Heym relies heavily on hand work. As one observes the workers, busy at various tasks, it is unusual to see one without a file of some type in his hand.

Under One Roof

Heym, a small operation compared to the giants of the industry, employs about 130 factory workers. All parts of their several models are manufactured entirely in the Heym factory, except for such things as springs and screws. From hammer forging their own barrels to the final polishing and blueing of the completed firearm, it's all done under one roof. For some of the exhibition engraving the talents of Germany's best independent engravers are used, but much engraving is done by and at the factory. All engraving on Heym arms, by the way, is of the hand cut variety—there is no machine engraving on a Heym.

Heym's basic production today consists of five types of arms, heavily weighted in favor of combination guns. They produce a drilling (double shotgun with a rifle barrel underneath), an over-under shotgun, or rifle, or combo, a "safety" model o-u combination gun, a slick bolt-action repeater and, last, a Germanized single shot rifle based on Bill Ruger's great Number One action. The drilling and the o-u types can be had in boxlock or sidelock varieties.

According to Herr Peter Bang, Heym's managing director, the factory produces about 300 firearms a month, some 65% of which are exported. Most go to France and Scandinavia, with a smattering to Belgium, Austria, South America, Canada, and the Middle East. Heym is just beginning to export to the United States.

For the past two years Heym has exhibited at the NSGA show, and the beginnings of a dealership network have been developed. It will take some time yet, however, before Heym's sporting arms are readily available in America. In the interim, if the reader cannot locate a Heym dealer in his area, he should write to the factory at the address given below. The name and address of the nearest dealer will be forwarded shortly thereafter.

Pre-War Days

I had been aware of the Heym name for a number of years. One sometimes sees an advertisement in the various arms publications, or an occasional Heym firearm turns up at gun shows. By and large, these are pre-WW II guns, for Heym exported numerous sporting arms to the U.S. in the 1920s and '30s. They also exported a few in the early '60s. Some, too, were probably brought back by returning GIs at the end of the war. However, I've never seen an ad for, nor an example of, Heym's current production in the United States.

Having spent three military tours in Germany, I became somewhat familiar with their current sporting arms. I saw a few Heym examples while on hunts, at range sessions, and the like. I had never shot or closely examined a Heym gun, however, until my second German military tour, 1969 to 1971.

It was during those years that I met and became a close friend of Erich Boessler, one of Germany's—and the world's—finest engravers. It was through Erich that I became more familiar with Heym's products. First, he is a former employee of Heym and has a great number of dealings with them, professionally and socially. Second, Erich lives in Münnerstadt, largely because the Heym factory is located there. It was through him that I took my first tour of the factory and, through those examples of Heym arms that had been provided to him for engraving, that I formed my early opinion of Heym products.

Quite frankly, I wasn't overly impressed. At the time they were using investment castings for their actions. This, in itself, was OK, but some of the finish work was not done as well as it could have been. Small details, to be sure, but I'm very particular when it comes to firearms. I want my shooting irons to be as near to perfection as possible.

A New Broom

Recently, however, I have seen enough to change my opinion. About three years ago, Heym changed the top operational management of the firm. Herr Peter Bang, holder of a graduate degree in management, was hired to head the Heym operation. He had little experience with firearms but he was an experienced manager. He undertook to improve operations at the factory and head it back on the road to pre-war quality. From what I have seen, he is well on the way to doing just that. In addition, I can't think of a more appropriate name for the manager of a firearms factory than Bang!

I recently spent most of a day in Peter Bang's office. During our lengthy discussions I frankly told him my honest opinion of Heym products in the past. He agreed essentially with my comments, and told me of his actions to improve the operation. By and large, the biggest changes instituted by him were in the area of quality control and scheduling. Additionally, Heym has gone back to machining actions from solid steel instead of using investment castings.

Heym has now returned to the high quality of those few pre-war pieces I've had the opportunity to handle. Herr Bang is very proud of the current Heym line, and rightly so. He even offered to provide me with one of his current products to test. I was really itching to try one of their side-lock over-under shotguns, but unfortunately one was not available at the moment.

I was given instead their boxlock model 77F over-under. It was selected at random, off the rack, not a special gun just for testing.

My First Sample

This basic model comes in 12 bore with 2¾ inch chambers or, as the Model 55F, in 16- and 20 bore. The 20 may be had with 3 inch chambers. This model can be had in o-u rifle, o-u shotgun, or in a combination of both. Naturally interchangeable barrels can also be bought.

The 12 bore 77F furnished me came with an extra set of 9.3x74R rifle barrels, these with selective ejectors, Suhler claw mounts, and a Zeiss 1½ to 6 power Diavari Z scope.

The 9.3x74R, seldom seen in the U.S., is well known in Europe. It is similar in looks and performance to the 375 H&H Magnum. More on that aspect of the gun later.

Upon my return from Münnerstadt, the Heym o-u in my clutches, I had to bide my time awaiting a suitable opportunity to put a few rounds through the gun. In the meantime, I disassembled it and took a close look. I was, very frankly, looking for flaws. I looked it over from stem to stern and didn't find any. The Krupp steel barrels, 28¼ inches long, were choked Modified and Full. It had a vent rib, selective ejectors, cocking indicators, double triggers, and was hand engraved with hunting scenes. Factory literature on the Model 77 lists its weight at about 7.7 pounds, and the gun in my possession weighed exactly that.

The action is a modified Anson type

Heym's resident "meister," Rudi Henneberger, shows a youngster how it is done. Herr Henneberger does a great deal of design work for Heym, and is responsible in large measure for the technical excellence of their sidelock models.

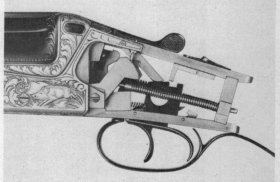

The Heym O-U boxlock mechanism includes coil springs and cocking indicators. Photo courtesy of Heym.

and, as noted earlier, is machined from a solid block of chrome-molybdenum steel. Its multiple locking lugs include double Greener type cross-bolts. The safety is non-automatic, which I personally much prefer. The stock was fashioned from a piece of very dark European walnut with a bit of a figure and hand checkered in a skip-line pattern. Its plastic buttplate and grip cap have white spacers. Peter Bang tells me that future production guns will have conventional checkering, and that the white spacers will be eliminated. Both desirable moves, in my opinion! The oil finished stock has a pull length of 14½ inches to the front trigger, drop at the comb of 1½ inches, drop at the heel 2½ inches. All in all, the gun seemed to be very well made indeed. The only faults I found were not of the technical variety but rather of the personal preference sort.

From left—30-06, 338 Winchester, 375 H&H and the 9.3x74R—bullet is 9.3mm in diameter, the case is 74mm long and rimmed.

Critique

First of all, the stock finish, for American tastes, was not good. It was well sanded, for no scratches were evident, and the wood was quite smooth. In the Suhl tradition, however, the stock had evidently been dunked in a vat of oil until it would absorb no more, then rubbed down. The pores were not adequately filled and what might have been an attractive piece of walnut was turned so dark that the figure could hardly be seen. Also, as I've indicated, the plastic buttplate and grip cap were hardly in keeping with the over-all quality of the piece otherwise. I would have much preferred a solid rubber recoil pad and a steel grip cap. The stock comes with a cheekpiece, which I could live without but in all fairness this gun is a Continental model, and such stocks are found on virtually all German guns I have seen in Europe. Commenting on these points Herr Bang told me that furnishing stocks in conformance with American tastes would be no problem, and would be done.

The proof of any gun is in the shooting and I was anxious to get on with that part of the test. I had planned a trip to the patterning board before unleashing the 77 on feathered game. I always try to do that with any new shotgun before taking it afield.

In the case of the Heym, however, the first opportunity that presented itself left me with a decision to make. I could spend the day at the range or go afield after ringnecks, hare and huns. As an avid hunter who hadn't had much free time during the year for hunting, I decided on the latter (it must have taken all of a second or two to decide).

Initial Test

My patterning consisted of one shot from each barrel at a paper the size of a shoe box. From this I was able to determine that: it shot where it looked and the shot pattern, as best I could tell from the very small target, looked evenly spread and in keeping with its indicated Full and Modified choking. With that done I headed for the beet fields, hoping to find a few ringnecks.

One of Heym's stocking experts is Herr E. Ries. Here he is fitting a forearm to an O-U shotgun.

Boxes of actions with the initial machining cuts made. These blocks of steel will become Heym's Model 22 O-U competition gun.

The first field we walked into produced a fine cock that flushed rather wild at about 30 yards. I was, admittedly, a bit slow mounting the heavier Heym, being used to my lightning fast 20 bore Merkel o-u. I shot behind, not touching a feather and, because I hadn't used a double trigger gun in years, I had difficulty finding the second trigger. By the time I hit it the bird was a good 50 yards away and moving fast. My second shot (which shouldn't have been taken) also ended up with the bird continuing merrily on his way.

After this miserable beginning things got considerably better. In brief, I downed the next 8 straight pheasants with a shot apiece. After switching from 6s used on the ring-

necks to 4s I even managed to roll a *hase* (European hare) with a single shot. The first day afield with the Heym ended with a score sheet of 9 for 11 shots.

Pattern Tests

The next test was at the 40-yard patterning board. The Heym shot where it looked, using 4s and 6s, both shooting very even patterns with no gaping holes in them. The gun did, however, seem to prefer the larger shot. Five patterns with each barrel, using 4s, averaged 58% from the Modified barrel and a surprising 75% from the Full choke tube. With 6s the patterns were a bit less dense, 55% and 70%, but still very evenly spread over the 30-inch circle.

After the patterning I shot a couple of rounds of straight trap, the Heym continuing its excellent performance. I did as well from 16 yards as I normally do with my Ithaca 4E single barrel trap model. Although my performance offered no challenge to competitive trapshooters, the 22 and 23 scores I shot are about as good as I ever do.

The final task before reluctantly returning the Heym was to switch to the rifle barrels and head for the range. Unfortunately, I'd been unable to try the gun on game.

Shooting the 9.3x74R

All testing was done on the Heidelberg Rod and Gun Club 100-meter range. The RWS factory ammo was loaded with 258-gr. H-Mantle bullets. The weather was a cool 41 degrees, the day reasonably clear for January in Germany.

Until this time I had never shot a double rifle of any type. I had, however, read a lot about them, including the difficulty in regulating the double tubes to shoot reasonably close together. I was fully prepared for 5 to 6 inch groups, which from my reading seemed to be acceptable accuracy.

The optically excellent Zeiss 1.5-6x variable scope had the usual and typical European reticle—a broad, pointed vertical and horizontal posts on either side. Europeans simply won't have any other. Supposedly very good for poor light situations but not so hot for precision bench shooting.

With the Zeiss inadvertently set at 2.4x, I loaded both barrels. The target was a standard 50-yard slow-fire pistol target, but even with its 8-inch black I couldn't see well enough for a center hold. Reverting to my military rifle team days I shifted to a 6 o'clock hold and fired the bottom barrel. The

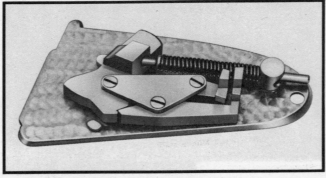

The inner workings of a Heym sidelock. Photo courtesy of Heym.

Herr Reinhold Reuscher, a young but accomplished gunmaker, hand filing an action part. The wooden jaws in the vise protect the parts being filed. The manner in which the wood is fitted to the vise is a Suhl tradition.

shot struck about an inch low and right of my aiming point. The next shot, with the top barrel, struck low also, about two inches from the first hole.

Then, noticing the low scope setting, I jacked the power to 6x. At that power, despite the wide post, I could see amply well for a center hold. I then fired 3 shots from the bottom barrel and two from the top. The results are shown in the accompanying photo.

The three bottom barrel shots are in an almost perfect triangle, the group a hair over $7/8$th-inch, center-to-center. The other two shots landed within $1 1/4$ inches of each other. Total spread for the 5 is $2 3/4$ inches. Later shooting with this Heym o-u rifle proved it to be as accurate as most sporters, a truly surprising discovery as far as I was concerned.

Though I can't comment on Heym's other firearms, this one, the only Heym that I have ever used, is one fine shooting gun. I wouldn't hesitate to head out after any game that North America offers (or most anywhere else for that matter) with this 9.3x74R Heym o-u.

The rifle weighs, with scope, sling and two rounds, $10 1/4$ pounds. That's a bit on the heavy side for lugging through the alders all day, but with those 25″ tubes I don't see how it could be made significantly lighter. One big plus for that weight, however, is reduced recoil. The big Heym is a pleasant gun to shoot, even from the bench, the felt recoil about like that of a 300 magnum.

Costs and Customizing

As noted earlier, Heym guns are essentially custom, hand-made products. This hand work is, unfortunately, reflected in the price of their guns, as it must be. The price of the Model 77 I shot, including extra barrels, claw mounts, and Zeiss variable scope, is about $5,500 from your dealer. If you don't want the claw mounts and Zeiss scope, a whopping $800 could be subtracted from that price.

One can order pretty much anything desired on a Heym gun—special wood, stock carving, deluxe engraving, special dimensions, etc., are all available. One option I like is a new trigger mechanism—the front trigger functions as a single, non-selective trigger, the first pull firing the bottom barrel. A second pull on the same trigger fires the top barrel. If selective firing is desired one simply uses the double triggers normally. When this special trigger is installed anoth-

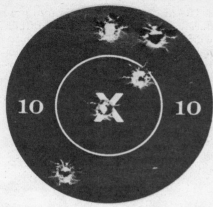

Five shots at 100 meters with the 9.3x74R O-U double rifle by Heym. The top three shots are from the bottom barrel, measure $7/8$th-inch, center-to-center; the 5 shots just under $2 3/4$ inches.

er mechanism is added to positively prevent doubling.

Expensive? Yes, no doubt about it. But a better question, is it worth it? Naturally, each reader must decide that on his own. I can only answer for myself. I feel that the Heym is well worth its price. I can't afford one on my budget (the Model 77F, with extras that is), but I'd buy the 77F in a moment if it were within my comfortable financial reach.

Today I can unhesitatingly recommend Heym firearms. I base this recommendation not only on my experience with the Model 77, but also on my discussions with Herr Bang and my tour of the Heym facilities. I like what I saw!

For more information, write to Peter Bang, Friedrich Wilh. Heym, 8732 Münnerstadt, West Germany. Good Shooting! •

Heym's Model 77 with shotgun tubes attached, after a day in the field. The results are obvious.

THE DEMAND for handguns has been dropping a bit, I'm told. True, possibly, but certainly I have seen no diminishing interest in acquisition or use. Many factors today are responsible for what was, at least, an ever-increasing interest in the one-hand firearm, not the least of which is the development in recent years of several new types of competitive shooting. What used to be called "west-coast style shooting" has now spread across the country under the auspices of the

HANDGUNS

by GEORGE C. NONTE, JR.

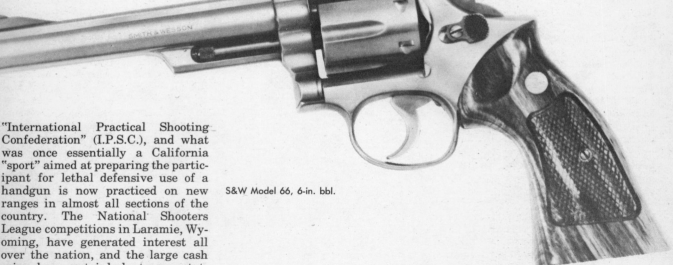

S&W Model 66, 6-in. bbl.

"International Practical Shooting Confederation" (I.P.S.C.), and what was once essentially a California "sport" aimed at preparing the participant for lethal defensive use of a handgun is now practiced on new ranges in almost all sections of the country. The National Shooters League competitions in Laramie, Wyoming, have generated interest all over the nation, and the large cash prizes have certainly lent a new stature to handgun competition as well as livened the interest of many pistoleros who would like to see their shooting *make* money instead of consuming it. The so-called "bowling-pin shoot," which originated in Michigan, has likewise stirred up interest, and the perfectionist long-range shooters participating in metallic silhouette matches around the country have put a good many rifle shooters to shame.

All of these shooting games are aimed at optimizing speed and accuracy to suit particular real-life uses of handguns. That all but the silhouette shooting emphasize defensive gun work (whether admittedly so or not) is a predictable commentary on our times, when well-armed criminals

In spite of prices that are high, and rising almost weekly, the demand for handguns continues unabated. Here's a report on the reasons therefore, in good part because of our troubled economy, and a review of what's being offered and what isn't, plus a preview of things to come.

NOW!

Wildey gas-operated auto-loading pistol, in 9mm Mag. or 45 Mag. cals.

Rising Costs

There's another factor—one of great importance to most of us—that is certainly reducing the ability if not the urge to buy a new handgun. Before writing this dissertation I pulled some old GUN DIGEST copies off the shelf to compare prices. The 1957 11th edition listed the Colt Official Police Model at $64.50. This now-discontinued revolver was a plain, fixed-sight 38 Special double-action with a great reputation for durability, reliability and accuracy; it was among the lowest-priced Colt revolvers then offered. The same gun in the 1967 GUN DIGEST had risen a bit over 16%, up to an even $75. Well, I thought, barely over a dollar a year increase in price for a full decade isn't really bad. It happened so slowly that I doubt any of us noticed it; I certainly wasn't conscious of any significant cost increase. Then (sob!) I looked at our 1978 issue, published a few years after the OP had been discontinued, replaced by the Colt Lawman Mark III. Therein I found this new and quite modern, fixed-sight service revolver priced at $199.95! From a 16% increase over the previous decade, the second 10 years produced a phenomenal 166% cost jump. Now, I know that my income went up a good bit during those years, and I think most people enjoyed the same experience, but there's no way that my spendable income rose $1^2/_3$ds during that period. Worse yet, as if that isn't enough, by the time you read this that last price will show yet another significant increase.

I don't mean to imply that the handgun manufacturers have been giving shooters the shaft any more than usual in recent times, but it *has* been a sellers market for the past dozen years or so. One can't help but think that if the makers had been required to work a bit harder to sell those *2½ million* handguns per year, perhaps the prices, at least for domestic makes, might not have risen quite so rapidly or so high.

Foreign gun prices have changed even more drastically. For example,

prey far and wide upon the citizenry, seemingly little deterred by a tremendous population of law-enforcement officers. They're seldom taken out of circulation by the courts on those rare occasions when they are caught and (more seldom) tried and convicted.

Older competitive programs are no less popular: the NRA "Standard American" type epitomized in the annual National Championship Matches traditionally held at Camp Perry, Ohio; the highly-developed Police Matches which reach their zenith when law officers from all over the country congregate at Jackson, Mississippi, for the annual national championships. Handgun plinking is about as strong as it ever was, but as shopping centers, housing developments, and the general urban sprawl proliferate, more and more shooters are denied this type of casual practice—the areas where it may be safely engaged in are now at an unreasonable distance. The days of taking the streetcar or driving to the edge of town and shooting undisturbed into a convenient creek bank or hillside are long gone for most of us. Certainly a lack of places to shoot is having an effect on handgun demand, not to mention long guns.

Wildey gas-operated auto-loading pistol, in 9mm Mag. or 45 Mag. cals.

Here's the new 6-inch Diamondback Colt, which won't be with us long—all D-frame Colt revolvers (Detective Special, Agent, Cobra, et al) are scheduled for oblivion!

the 1967 GUN DIGEST listed the excellent Walther P.38 9mm auto pistol at only $99.50; the 1978 book shows it at the nice round figure of $400—an increase of more than 300%, and it has gone up again in the meantime. Of course, international financial manipulations and currency fluctuations alone are responsible for a good deal of this horrendous increase.

So, it becomes obvious that across the board—from the plain bread-and-butter domestics to the more exotic imports—the cost of acquiring a new handgun is spiraling out of sight, which cannot help but reduce sales. The guy with the money to burn will still buy what he wants, without conscious concern for the price; the working stiff to whom a gun may be absolutely essential will also still buy, but he is by no means happy with the tremendous bite the purchase takes out of his pocket. In between, the casual pistolero can no longer drop into the corner gunshop and buy a

new sixgun or auto out of his lunch/cigarette/booze money without feeling the pinch. Of course, as new guns rise in price, good used guns follow close behind. Our same Colt OP example, if bought new a decade ago for $75 and carefully maintained in the meantime, can easily bring today $50 more—as a *used* gun—than it cost. It'd be foolish to sell, of course, in view of what a new replacement costs these days.

They Come and Go

Though we have new guns in plenty coming along, it is also interesting that more and more old models are being discontinued. The latest story we get from **Colt** is that before long the D-frame models will be discontinued, including the New Viper and Police Positive models, these last introduced only a short time ago. If all of these models are in fact discontinued (Cobra, Detective Special, Agent, Diamond Back) then Colt will be left

with exactly two basic double-action sixguns; the very expensive Python on the original Official Police frame and lockwork, and the Mark III Series introduced in the late 1960s. Further, this means that Colt will be offering nothing in the double-action line except pure service and service/target guns, nothing at all in the "hideout" or "belly gun" range. Considering the popularity of the two-inch D-frame guns in the law enforcement field I find it hard to understand their discontinuance. Of course, the question of the Colt M71 big-bore autoloader developed years ago and given some publicity from time to time usually comes up—but we are told that Colt has no specific plans for marketing this gun in the near future.

It seems odd that though Colt plans to discontinue the D-frame series by the end of 1978, at the beginning of the year it introduced a new 6-inch barrel version of the Diamondback. Actually, those who liked the Diamondback have asked for a longer barrel for some time and will welcome this addition to the line—but apparently it won't be around for long. Another model introduced early in '78 should be with us for a long time; at least it would appear so since the basic frame and design is one we cannot conceive being discontinued. This is the "new" Colt Ace 22 LR auto, built upon the Gov't Model (Model O) frame. This is reminiscent of the 22 Ace made by Colt many years ago, when 22 autos were not so plentiful, and there was considerable demand for a small-caliber, low-ammunition-cost practice gun to pair with the big 45 auto. The new Ace is like the old one, using the original floating-chamber design, in essence being merely a factory assembly of the well-known "22-45 Conversion Unit" marketed for the basic GM frame.

Colt continues its lucrative commemorative line, the latest being the "U.S. Cavalry Commemorative" edition of the 44 caliber 1860 Army percussion revolver. This outfit comprises a matched pair of consecutively-numbered guns, cased with a flask, bullet mould, nipple wrench, cap box and a detachable shoulder stock in the original style.

One very nice gun that disappeared temporarily is now back. The **Budischowsky TP-70,** introduced several years ago and supplied in small quantities by Norton Armament Corp., vanished some time back with the failure of that company. Now, though, this fine little gun is again in production as the "Norton TP-70." Production began only a few months ago, so it isn't plentiful yet. In this scribe's opinion the TP-70 is the best of the very small 22 LR autoloaders, and it's also offered in 25 ACP.

Last year **Browning** introduced its BDA, a double-action big-bore autoloader and, though early availability was limited to 9mm, the more desirable 45 ACP is now becoming generally available. As most gunbuffs know, this pistol is simply the Swiss SIG P.220 design (made by Sauer & Sohn of West Germany), and marketed otherwise as the Sig/Sauer P.220. A most excellent gun, and probably representing the latest in autoloading pistol technology. This year, though, Browning introduces a companion pistol of lesser size and power, the "BDA 380." Though the designation might lead one to expect this gun to be quite similar to the big BDA, that isn't the case. Instead, the BDA 380 is a small, compact, double-action pocket-type (but not really pocket size) autoloading pistol with a double-column magazine holding 12 rounds (plus, of course, one in the chamber when fully loaded). Weighing 23 ounces, the gun is 6³/₄ inches long by 4³/₄ inches high, with a barrel length of 3¹³/₁₆ inches. It is of unlocked-breech, tubular-slide design with a fixed barrel and magazine safety. The slide-mounted manual safety is of the hammer-dropping/hammer-blocking type which, when engaged, drops the hammer from full-cock to an intercept notch. Thus the gun cannot be carried cocked and locked, but must be carried with the hammer down, from which condition

New Colt Service Ace 22 LR auto pistol, revived in 1978.

Colt's U.S. Cavalry Commemorative M1860 Army includes, among other things, a detachable shoulder stock.

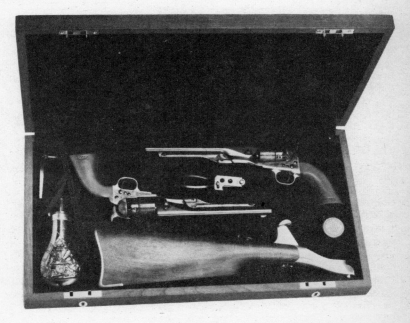

This is the Browning "BDA 380," made with an ambidextrous safety, and with a magazine holding 12 cartridges.

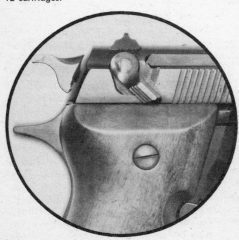

Stoeger's Llama, shown here in 380 version.

it may be fired double-action on the draw or manually cocked during the draw for deliberate single-action fire. The frame is light alloy, with all other parts of appropriate types of steel; grips are smooth walnut, and the rather wide trigger is serrated. The BDA 380 magazine catch is much more appropriately located than on the big BDA, being in the usual Browning location to the left rear of the trigger. This greatly facilitates speedy reloading.

Around $220, the BDA 380 is a modified version of the Beretta M81/84 series introduced here a couple of years back. The slide has been redesigned and the hammer-dropping safety is an addition. This takes away the characteristic Beretta look with its cutaway slide. We've had no chance to shoot a BDA 380, but from experience with the Beretta counterpart, we expect it to perform quite well.

There has been much talk about a new **Llama** 44 Magnum revolver and a double-action big-bore autoloading pistol. We've worked with prototypes of the revolver, and approve generally of the design, but it is still in final development stages. We don't know exactly what the production guns will be like, and Stoeger Industries, the importers, indicate that it will be another year before production examples of this massive gun are ready. As usual, this new target date is farther in the future than had originally been reported.

As for the new Llama D.A. auto-

loader, its development is behind that of the 44 Magnum. So far there's been no opportunity to shoot even prototypes. Optimistic estimates of its arrival date are two years hence.

The Stinger in Foreign Pistols

For many years Llama has supplied an excellent small-frame auto in 22 LR, 32 and 380 calibers; the first two are of blowback design, the latter using the Browning locked breech. The 22 version has been criticized since the advent of CCI "Stinger" ammunition, with reports of burst cartridge cases occurring with this new ammunition. This problem has now been corrected at the Llama plant, and all shipment of 22 autoloaders now have a modified barrel to eliminate the complaints. This doesn't mean the original barrel design was defective, but rather that when the gun was first placed in production it was deliberately manufactured with a bore somewhat *undersized* by domestic (SAAMI) standards. This was done to insure reliable functioning with some European-made cartridges whose chamber pressure was a bit low; the slightly tighter bore boosted pressure, and thereby velocity and recoil impulse, to obtain reliability. This slightly smaller bore gave no problems whatever with standard U.S.-made ammunition until the Stingers came along. With them the smaller bore *occasionally* raised pressures enough to cause a blown case head.

A complete stock of repair parts is maintained by Stoeger, and owners wanting to replace the original barrel may buy the new type. So far we haven't obtained the serial-number division point, which number would enable users to learn whether they have the older or the new barrel. You may safely assume, however, any Llama 22 LR pistol bought before the spring of 1978 will most likely have a barrel of the original design and dimensions, that is, the tighter barrel.

For many years the Stoeger 22 Luger was made by the Stanley Tool Company in Connecticut. Now, to slow down cost increases, Stoeger has switched manufacture to a New Jersey company. The gun won't be changed, we're told, but Stoeger is working on a locked-breech modification of this design chambered for the 9mm Parabellum cartridge—and has progressed to the point that shooting prototypes are being tested. This sets up an interesting probability (but not a certainty) that this gun may be offered to the shooting public within the next few years.

SIA to the Wall?

Last year **Security Industries** showed us an interesting and needed improvement in the lockwork of its small-frame 357/38 Special 5-shot revolvers. The proposed changes would certainly improve the gun functionally, and we were looking forward to working with improved samples. However, since then, the company seems to have dropped out of sight. We, and others we know, have been unable to make contact with the company. We've also had reports from SIA gun owners who were unable to reach the company for service and repairs.

Flash—SIA has new lease on life apparently. See my notes further on under Mossberg.

High Standard was much in the news the past couple of years with the development of its Crusader, a big-bore double-action revolver. Well, our latest report says that tooling is complete and that the first production guns will come off the line in May of this year (this is being written in March) and that initial production will be devoted to the commemorative versions. Delivery of standard models won't begin until year's end, perhaps not until early '79.

High Standard's 22 rimfire autos have been refined (?) a bit; the Sharpshooter and Sport King models will now be assembled on the basic Supermatic Military Model frame. This makes these two models different, but not new—this is a production economy measure whereby the separate frame used until now for these two models is abandoned; matter of fact, I think the guns will be improved by this change.

After a long dry spell and considerable confusion High Standard has moved into its new plant, and production has resumed. Their 22 rimfire autoloaders and derringers should once again become readily available. Good news, certainly, because last year Colt discontinued its entire Woodsman 22 RF auto pistol line. That's a shame, incidentally, because the Colt Woodsman was for many years the *only* 22 autoloader made in this country, and for a very large portion of its 60-odd years of production life it was considered the best available.

Navy Arms is noted primarily for its muzzle-loading products and activities. However, starting with an imported replica cartridge revolver a few years back, it is now getting into the modern handgun field with a will. Under the able guidance of its originator and current honcho, Val Forgett, it has introduced its "Mamba" double-action, 9mm service-type, stainless-steel autoloader—manufactured in its entirety at the Navy Arms plant in New Jersey. As this is written, only a few tool-room guns exist, but tooling is quite well advanced. Though Forgett won't set a specific delivery (he doesn't want to make a promise he might not be able to keep), we anticipate at least a trickle of standard production Mambas before the end of 1978.

The Mamba gets its name from the country of its origin, the Republic of South Africa. The Mamba, a very deadly and venomous snake, is lightning fast and more than ordinarily aggressive. The Mamba, designed by U.S. and West German engineers in response to an RSA military requirement, is currently made there to equip South African military forces. If you wonder why RSA felt compelled to manufacture its own military sidearm, you'll find the answer in what we consider the totally unjustified and, in fact, discriminatory embargo placed upon arms shipments to that country. They would gladly buy Colts and Smith & Wessons—and in considerable quantity—were it not for this ridiculous embargo, imposed for many years by our government.

Forgett obtained manufacturing and sales rights in the U.S.A. Made of

High Standard's Supermatic Citation, here in 22 LR cal.

The new Mamba 9mm double action auto from Navy Arms is made of stainless steel, is sturdy and well made.

stainless steel, the Mamba has a magazine capacity of 14 rounds (plus one up the spout), and is rather hefty at 38 ounces. It has an ambidextrous manual safety at the upper rear of the frame, and a "hooked" trigger guard for two-hand shooting. Double-action trigger reach is a bit long for small hands, but when cocked and fired in the single-action mode the reach is short enough for any adult. Sights are of conventional fixed service type, and the magazine catch is in our preferred position at the rear of the trigger on the left side.

The Mamba's top half is essentially a slightly modified copy of the Browning High-Power—which has long been a popular sidearm in South Africa. The frame also resembles the Browning a good deal, but the lockwork is considerably different, being a basic, second-generation, double-action system somewhat similar to the S&W M39, but adapted to a Browning-type manual safety.

Smith & Wesson has long been noted for a fairly conservative approach to new products, and thus, aside from such rare exceptions as the

M39 and M61, most new items are logical and carefully-developed evolutions of existing products. Those new products are also, usually, direct responses to consumer demand. Consequently, this year S&W has introduced a 6-inch barrel version of the stainless steel M66, a sixgun that has become popular in its 4-inch tube among law-enforcement officers. In addition, maintaining its tremendous lead in the production of stainless steel handguns, S&W has also announced the Model 63; this is nothing more or less than the much-revered "22 Kit Gun," but made in stainless steel with a 4-inch barrel. When I was a youngster, all of my pistol-packing acquaintances of the Iver-Johnson set aspired to ownership of a 22 Kit Gun. This new stainless version cannot help but make this model more popular than ever.

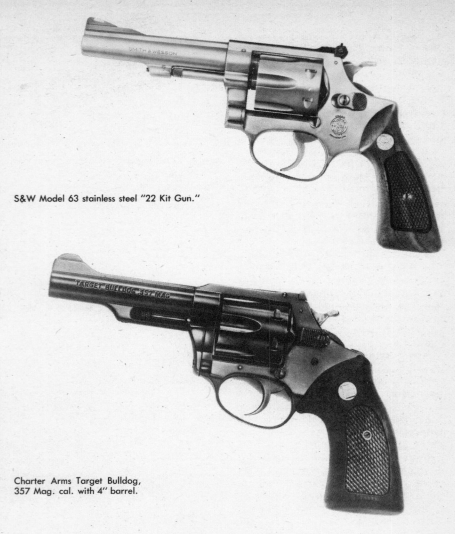

S&W Model 63 stainless steel "22 Kit Gun."

Charter Arms Target Bulldog, 357 Mag. cal. with 4" barrel.

S&W Kit Gun in Stainless Steel

Though even a stainless steel handgun requires care and maintenance, it resists corrosion better than blued steel. Thus it's more likely to be ready when you need it.

The new Model 63 continues the desirable features of the regular model—it has a 1/8th-inch red ramp front sight, the rear sight S&W's black stainless steel micrometer-click with square-notch, adjustable for windage and elevation.

Offered with a 4-inch barrel and square butt only, the Model 63 weighs 24 1/2 ounces not loaded. Retail cost, $173, availability mid-1978.

S&W Modifications

S&W also has taken a significant step in customer relations and product improvement by offering to modify existing M59 pistols (by parts replacement) to improve feeding and reliability with modern high-performance ammunition; likewise, a modification is available to reduce chamber mouth/barrel breech "spitting" in various models. These factory modifications (actually done at service centers) are not entirely free of charge, but their cost is so low that the shooter can hardly afford to pass them up.

Aside from that, the S&W handgun line remains essentially the same except, of course, for the inevitable price increases we all must live with.

Earlier handgun reports have mentioned the **Wildey** gas-operated auto-loading pistol that is under development. In January of this year, for the first time, we were able to examine working prototypes in both of the proprietary calibers—the Wildey 9mm Magnum and 45 Magnum. As noted here before, the two cartridges are based on the 9mm Parabellum/Luger and 45 ACP cases, lengthened and loaded to pressure in the 40,000 CUP range to produce ballistic performance comparable to the 357 Magnum and 44 Magnum. The gun itself, unique in its gas-operation and made entirely of stainless steel, is massive and heavy. The samples examined were a good many ounces over the intended weight because of excess metal in the frames, which excess will not be present in production guns. The design weight is 48-49 ounces with a 6-inch barrel, and barrel lengths of 5 to 10 inches will be available.

Though there's some hope that production guns will be available before the end of 1978, it is this scribe's considered opinion—taking into consideration the pitfalls of achieving real production of any new handgun—that it's unlikely you'll be able to buy one quite that soon. The Wildey auto appears to be aimed at the autoloading pistol fan, the handgun hunter or long-range shooting enthusiast. Its bulk and weight preclude great all-round utility, and it's unlikely to be considered suitable for law-enforcement or defensive purposes by most people. However, for hunting big game and for metallic silhouette shooting it should perform quite well. This is especially true of the longer barrel lengths, which will exploit the maximum potential of the hot cartridges.

Wildey will have their new autoloaders at the NRA meeting in Salt Lake City. If we get a chance to shoot one or more of these, there may be time for an add report here.

Charter Arms has been working with a single basic revolver design ever since the beginning. In the past couple of years it has introduced numerous variations to adapt that design to a much broader range of uses. Last year saw several such variations introduced, but thus far this year we have nothing new to report. Apparently the company is quite busy meeting demand for its "Target Bulldog" models in 44 Special, 38 Special and 357 Magnum, and hasn't had the time to go any farther. Knowing the key figures at Charter Arms rather well, we can expect them to make up for the current lack next year.

Several years ago **Indian Arms** introduced its slightly modified stainless steel copy of the Walther PPK pistol in 380 ACP caliber. After a few years of modest production the gun vanished. However, the latest report from Indian Arms (March) indicated that production is again in full swing and that shipments are being made. By no means cheap at the new price of $275, the comparable Walther PPKS (the PPK is no longer imported, thanks to GCA 68) costs about the same. I've always been more than a bit fond of this autoloader, and most others who have tried it also like it.

A few years back we noted here the advent of the **F.I. Model D 380** ACP pistol, a slightly modified copy of the well-known Star "Starfire." This is an especially nice pocket-size single-action 380 with exposed hammer, which we hate to see disappear, but manufacture has been suspended, and we cannot say whether it will be resumed in the future. However, some Model Ds are still in the pipeline, and if you're interested in having the smallest gun of its caliber and type available, pick one up before they disappear forever.

Dan Wesson Arms is well known as the producer of the *only* interchangeable-barrel, big-bore revolver. The basic gun, now widely accepted, needs little further comment. However, recent improvements have been made in the lockwork, the goal being smoother, lighter and more consistent single- and DA trigger pulls without extensive (read "expensive") hand-fitting in final assembly. This is simply a continuation of the product-improvement program in effect at the Wesson plant since its beginning. Dan Wesson is also developing some interesting features for inclusion in the basic design, but these aren't ready to talk about yet. There are also rumors of impressive new models in the near future, but nothing is anticipated for this year.

Formerly the Colt Pony and F.I. Model D, this excellent little 380 auto is now being made by Iver Johnson as their X300 Pony.

Dan Wesson 1502 with all its various barrels.

Astra 6-inch barrel 357, imported by Interarms.

Interarms, long an importer of fine handguns, notably Walther and Mauser, entered the manufacturing field last year with the excellent "Virginian," a big-bore single-action revolver in the Colt image. Once this model gets off the ground we may well see something else manufactured at the same plant, but that's speculation. The most interesting handgun news at Interarms this year is that it has assumed exclusive distributorship of the Spanish Star pistols, which were imported for many years by the now-defunct Firearms Division of Garcia. This includes the entire current Star line—the big-frame Browning-type autos in 9mm, 38 Super, and 45 ACP; the small-frame 9mm "Starlight" auto, and the successful and highly regarded Star Model PD 45 auto. In addition, Interarms is the exclusive distributor for Astra Spanish pistols and revolvers, notably the Astra double-action pocket-size auto in 22, 32 ACP and 380 ACP, plus the Astra 357 Magnum revolver. Well known now, these Astras have good reputations.

Thompson/Center's pistol has been prominent in metallic silhouette shooting from the beginning. As a consequence it has introduced a new long-range model, its heavy 14-inch barrel specifically meant for such shooting. This increases its sighting radius and holding capabilities, making it even more suitable for knocking down those steel-plate game targets. It also gives the neophyte or low-budget shooter a production single-shot pistol, one superior to even the best production revolvers for silhouette matches.

F.I.E. (Firearms Import and Export) has introduced the "Titan Model 380," an exposed-hammer pocket-size autoloading pistol. To the best of my knowledge it costs less at this writing than any other 380 pistol available— about $85. Relatively heavy at 25 ounces, it's made entirely from steel, mostly from investment castings. The barrel is 3.870 inches long and the magazine holds 7 rounds. Looking like a cross between the older Beretta and the Bernardelli, it has a cutaway slide with the barrel pinned rigidly and permanently to the frame. In view of the price, the mechanism is simple, without such frills as a slide stop or hold-open. An elementary hammer-blocking manual safety, mounted on the slide, permits the hammer to be dropped by pulling the trigger at any time, but prevents it from driving the firing pin forward when the safety is engaged. On su-

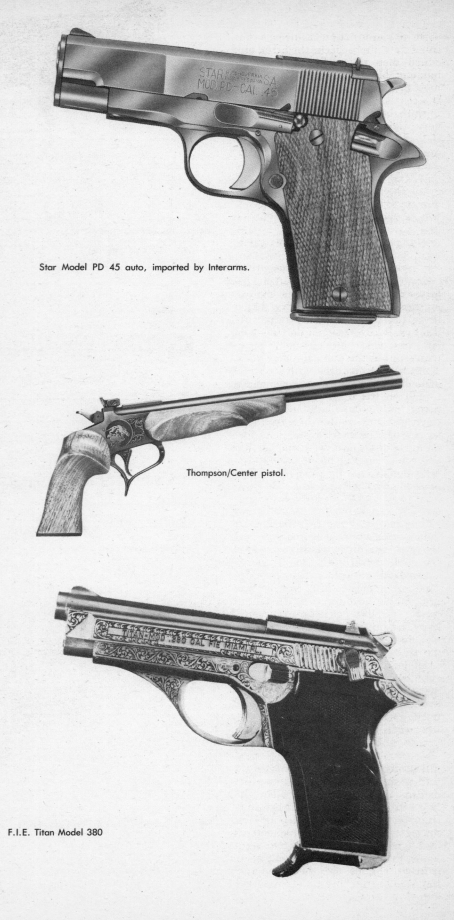

Star Model PD 45 auto, imported by Interarms.

Thompson/Center pistol.

F.I.E. Titan Model 380

perficial examination it appears that this safety simply locks the firing pin, which then takes the brunt of the hammer blow—but this is not true; most of the hammer blow is taken by the rear surface of the slide, the firing pin being free to move forward very slightly before being blocked by the safety. A simple but effective magazine safety is also incorporated, which is especially valuable inasmuch as the slide cannot be locked open. Disassembly is by means of a Beretta-type lever above the trigger which, when pointing directly to the rear halts the slide short of the dismount position; pointed directly forward, it permits the slide to be drawn far enough to the rear to be lifted clear of the frame and then moved forward off the barrel. This lever is marked as if it were a safety, which in fact it is, for in the disassembly position it covers a red dot (marked "F") and also blocks trigger movement so that the gun cannot be fired. This prevents firing the gun when the dismount lever has been inadvertently left in the dismount position; if firing could occur under those conditions, the slide would travel rearward to its own dismount position, and might bound upward to jam, though this could cause no harm to the shooter or bystanders. At $88.95 the Titan 380 can hardly be expected to compare in fit and finish with a Walther or S&W, but in our experience it is a safe, functional gun. We need such guns in all price ranges, regardless of the way the anti-gun forces equate criminal use with low price.

Sterling Arms has shown prototypes of a most interesting service type double-action 45 autoloader for a couple of years. Though we don't know when you'll see this gun displayed for sale, Sterling has just moved into a new and larger plant at Lockport, NY. The old factory was too small for large-scale production. All development is done and tooling is nearly complete (it's now March). Gene Sauls, president of Sterling, told us he'll begin shipping production guns well before 1978 draws to a close.

Sterling has also upgraded its double-action pocket-size 380 autoloaders, the new series called the Mark II. Though no significant mechanical or design changes were made, the guns have been slenderized and lightened. Also, a new rear sight adjustable for windage and elevation is fitted. The rest of the Sterling line, the M300 series of 22 and 25 pocket autos, remains the same.

F.I.E. Titan II, cal. 32 auto.

Sterling Arms Model 400 MK II 380 DA in nickel finish.

Sterling Arms Model 450 DA 45 autoloader.

We've been aware for some time that the old-line firm of **O. F. Mossberg** has been working on a 45 autoloading pistol design, but it wasn't until most of the material for this section had already been sent off that we obtained worthwhile details of the project. The gun, incidentally, scheduled for deliveries before the end of this year, will have a retail price of $349.50. Or should this read " . . . a mere $349.50?"

Having examined one prototype Mossberg "Combat Model" 45 pistol, here's what it looks like: all stainless-steel construction; typical Browning-type, locked-breech mechanism; screw-in barrel bushing; recoil spring captive on a full-length guide; rounded hammer spur; ambidextrous slide-mounted safety which blocks the hammer (through the sear) *and* firing pin; a conventional butt-housed box magazine which *may* have a removable floor plate for ease of maintenance; a spurred trigger guard for two-hand shooting; and a combat-type, rearward-extending slide stop. Grips are of moulded and checkered black plastic. The front and rear sights are separate and removable, which allows them to be finished black and thus provide better definition than is possible with the "white" sights found on so many stainless steel guns today. The front sight is dovetailed into the slide from front to rear and secured by two transverse pins; the rear element moves laterally for windage (only) adjustment in a slot in a high boss integral with the slide to protect it from damage. The slide appearance is a bit unusual in that all longitudinal surfaces are flat; the sides are polished parallel flats, the top is another but rising flat narrowing from rear to front, and merging with the sides by flats narrowing to the rear. The top flat curves upward sharply to form the rear-sight boss. The appearance is unusual and, to my eyes at least, pleasing. The threaded barrel bushing is notched in front to accept a spanner wrench to ease removal; the entire slide/barrel/recoil spring assembly comes forward off the frame as a unit when the slide stop is withdrawn. With the exception of the slide's side flats, which are polished bright, the entire gun carries a soft matte finish in the natural color of stainless steel, a sort of silvery-grey.

Though this gun looks much like the Colt Combat Commander in size and configuration, its weight feels a bit less. The prototype examined was a single-action type with a threaded

Government Model pistol from Crown City.

stop in the trigger face to bear upon the typical Browning/Colt magazine catch. Early production guns will be single-action, too, but the design allows for double-action types as well, which Mossberg intends to offer later on.

Traditionalists in the crowd may scratch their heads and mutter at the mere thought of a modern DA 45 auto from a company known almost exclusively for its low-to-medium-price rifles and shotguns, but I rather like the idea. Further, from what could be determined by looking over the one specimen displayed at the NRA show, I believe I'll like the gun.

Another New Mossberg

But wait a moment—that's not the only Mossberg entry into the handgun field. Earlier in this report I mentioned that Security Industries of America, makers of a small-frame, 5-shot 357 Magnum revolver, had apparently dissolved into the woodwork, had folded. Well, Mossberg has obtained manufacturing rights to the SIA gun and will be producing it shortly. We can't say at this point whether Mossberg will provide service and warranty action on existing SIA guns, but from past experience we know that service on the new ones will be up to Mossberg's usual excellent standards.

Throughout its history Mossberg has produced but one other pistol, the diminutive "Brownie" 4-shot 22 rimfire of nearly 60 years ago. Anything but a howling success, it soon disappeared from the scene. Today it's a lesser collector's item. This time Mossberg seems to have taken a much more likely tack and we expect to see a good shooter response to these two guns.

Crown City

Crown City Arms has been supplying all sorts of parts for 45 Government Model pistols for some years, including stainless-steel frames and slides, aluminum-alloy frames, and parts kits to assemble your own gun. As owner Terry Hudson told me a few days ago, "It seemed almost foolish not to assemble and sell complete guns since we carry all the parts." As a result, Crown City Arms is now offering fully assembled and test-fired GM-type pistols of pre-1970 Colt configuration in at least 8 variations, including calibers 9mm Parabellum and 38 Super, as well as the traditional 45 ACP. A mix of lengths and frame materials includes the full-length gun on both steel and aluminum frames, the Commander length likewise, and stainless guns in both lengths. I'd also guess that if one asked he could have any other mix of carbon steel, stainless and aluminum. The basic price is just under $200, which is less than I've seen ex-military M1911-A1 guns sell for in recent times. Crown City Arms is at Box 1126, Cortland, NY 13045. ●

Crosswind Deflections

a Cast Bullet Anomaly

by KENNETH L. WALTERS

A curious phenomenon occurs when bullets — cast or jacketed — are propelled at muzzle velocities in the 1000-2000 foot second range. The author shows cause and effect, with graphic charts that reveal the extent of such bullet drift — and how to combat it.

A PARTICULARLY interesting aspect of exterior ballistics is the lateral deflection effect created by crosswinds. Numerous controlled experiments have clearly proven that crosswind velocities multiplied by a quantity called *lag time** are the cause of such deflection.

Surprisingly—at least to those unfamiliar with the subject—is the fact that any bullet having a muzzle velocity (MV) of about 1000 to 2000 foot seconds (fs) is particularly susceptible to a given wind velocity.

Various reloading manuals show the formula for determining crosswind deflections. Here's the one found in the *Sierra Reloading Manual*:

$z - v/cw$ $(t - x/v_0)$.
where z = crossrange deflection.
v/cw = crosswind velocity.
t = bullet's time of flight in air.
x = range.
v_0 = muzzle velocity.

The quantity $(t-x/v_0)$, called the lag time, is the difference between t and the corresponding time of flight in a vacuum, x/v_0.

(The crosswind velocities noted here, and shown in the figures, are to be considered constant over the ranges indicated.)

For a constant crosswind bullet deflection is large only if the lag time is large. As MVs increase from a value of 300 fs to around 3000 the changes in lag time are such that the wind deflections caused by a 10-mph crosswind are as illustrated in Fig. 1. You'll notice that as MV increases past 1000 fs, the corresponding deflections increase rather rapidly. At about 1400 fs a maximum occurs, making this the worst possible MV for wind deflection susceptibility, apart from extremely low velocities.

The oddly-shaped curve in Fig. 1 can be explained in several ways. Homer Powley presents an argument, somewhat mathematical in nature, concerning the mean velocity of air molecules.† Cummings *(op cit)* discusses it from the viewpoint of the irregular shape of the air-resistance function.

Basically the underlying fact is this: As a bullet travels faster and faster, the *differences* between the time of flight it would have in a vacuum (x/v_0) and its actually observed time of flight (t) become smaller and smaller until the bullet's MV starts to approach the speed of sound. Thus the beginning portion of the Fig. 1 curve shows a steadily *decreasing* crosswind deflection. Then, as the speed of sound is neared, the actually observed time of flight becomes longer than expected, hence the sudden upswing in the graph.

Below the speed of sound the shock wave created by the bullet easily moves ahead of it. As the speed of sound is approached, however, the bullet starts catching up with its shock wave, and after the speed of sound has been passed, the bullet must divert some of its energy in carrying the shock wave along with it. Since this corresponds to an increase in air resistance, the bullet loses a little of its velocity. Once this transitional region has been passed by the bullet, an increase in muzzle velocity *decreases* the crosswind deflection.

Fig. 1 deserves a little additional attention. Consider a bullet with a ballistic coefficient (BC) of 0.354 and a MV of 2400 fs. By locating the MV value—at the bottom of the graph—and the assigned BC value, and then going across to the vertical axis at left, we see that the total lateral bullet deflection caused by a 10-mph crosswind over a 100-yard range is 1.2 inches. Note that *only* the MV is used in determining these figures. (Rough estimates of BC curves for values between those shown could easily be sketched in. A BC of 0.320 would be almost exactly between the 0.289 and 0.354 curves, for instance.)

*A detailed explanation of this phenomenon is in Charles Cummings' book *Everyday Ballistics*, Chapter X (1950, Stackpole & Heck, Inc., Harrisburg, Pa).

†See Homer Powley's book *Ballistic Notes by Powley*, page 124, printed in 1976 at Frankford Arsenal, Philadelphia, Pa.

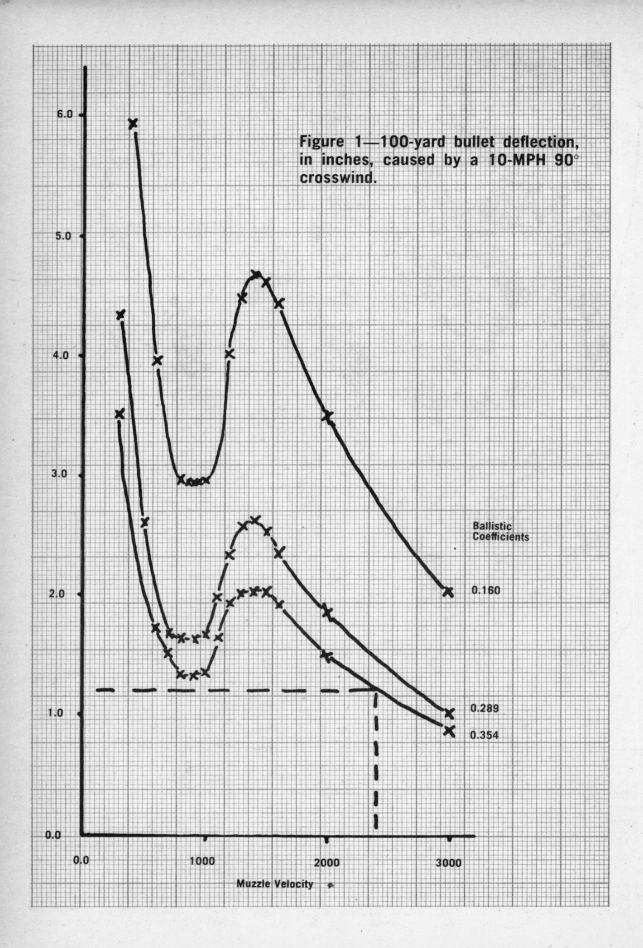

Figure 1—100-yard bullet deflection, in inches, caused by a 10-MPH 90° crosswind.

Ballistic Coefficients

0.160

0.289

0.354

Muzzle Velocity

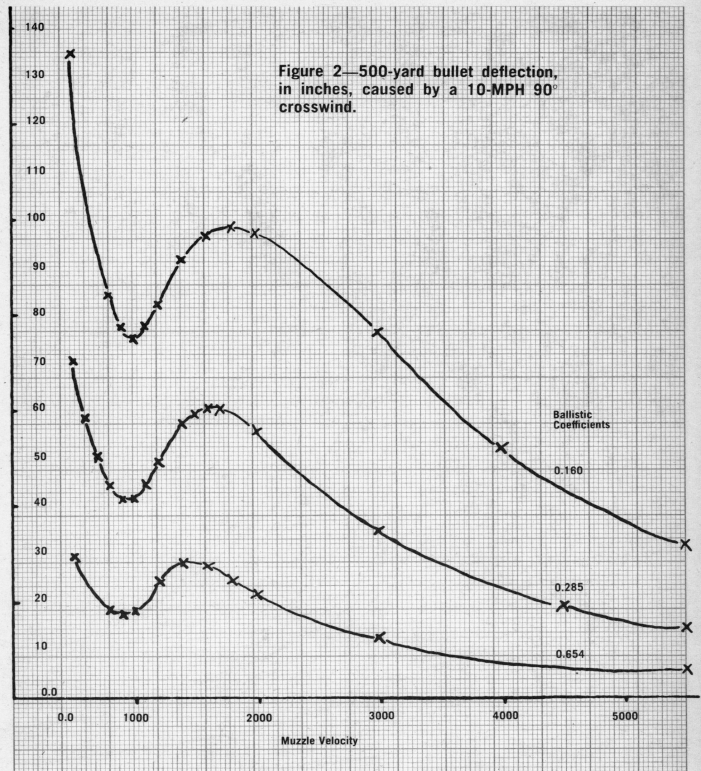

Figure 2—500-yard bullet deflection, in inches, caused by a 10-MPH 90° crosswind.

Ballistic Coefficients

0.160

0.285

0.654

Muzzle Velocity

Velocity Critical

Those loading manuals showing handgun loads list various bullets launched with MVs close to the critical 1400 fs noted earlier. Examples include the 30 M1 Carbine pistol, 9mm Luger, 38 Super, 357 Magnum, and others. The saving grace here, however, is the normally short range involved. To see the positive benefit that short ranges offer, note the differences in deflection for the BC = 0.160 bullets in Figs. 1 and 2. In the latter the deflection is 97 inches at 500 yards. Similar decreases would occur at even shorter distances.

Long range handgunners, of course, face larger wind deflections, as do shooters of cast bullets in many rifles. The *Lyman Cast Bullet Handbook* lists many calibers that are loadable in the important 1400 fs region, among them such cartridges

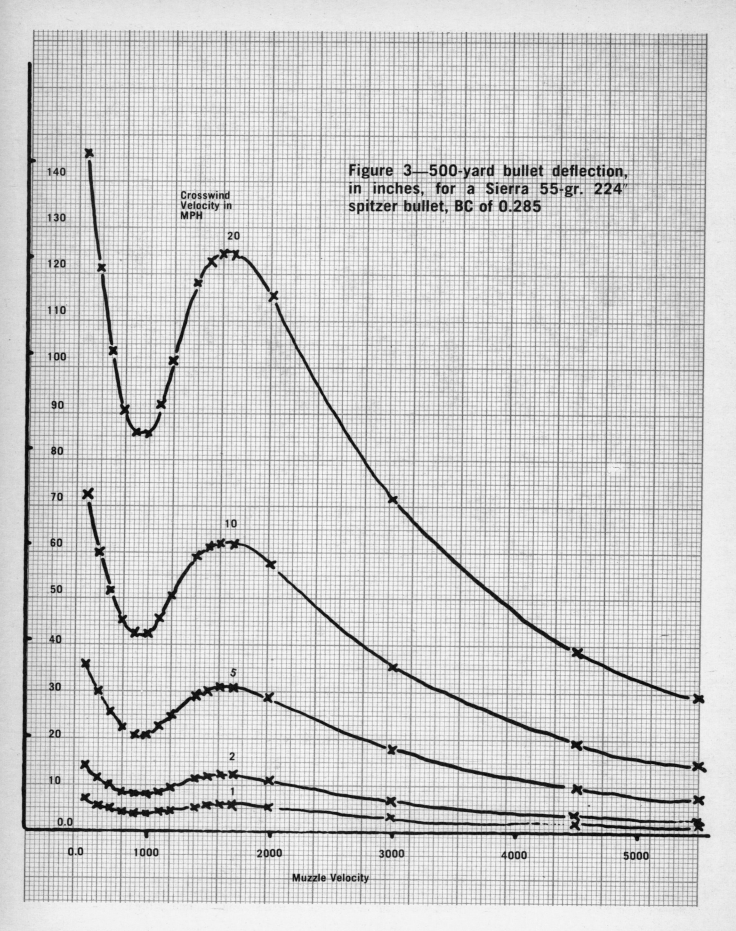

Figure 3—500-yard bullet deflection, in inches, for a Sierra 55-gr. 224" spitzer bullet, BC of 0.285

Crosswind Velocity in MPH

20

10

5

2

1

Muzzle Velocity

as the 22 Hornet, 6mm Remington, 250 Savage, 30-30 Winchester and the 308 Winchester.

Defeating Deflection

If you must load cast bullets in this 1000-2000 MV range, handgun or rifle, there are at least a couple of things you can do to minimize the effect. The most fruitful approach is to pick bullets with the highest possible BC, as Fig. 1 illustrates. Although BC numbers aren't readily available for cast bullets, they can be estimated from tables in, among other places, *Hatcher's Notebook*.* It may also be possible to gain a little velocity with no change in bullet or powder weight by using a filler which keeps the powder adjacent to the primer. To quote from John Wootters' excellent book†, *The Complete Book of Practical Handloading:*

> The procedure is quite simple. After charging cases, the reloader plucks a tuft of Dacron from his supply, balls it lightly by rolling between his fingers and stuffs it into the case, using a dowel to poke it firmly down atop the powder.

However, *don't* do this without first reading Wootters' comments in full, because not all of the argument is presented here.

(Wootters also presents many other interesting ideas for the cast bullet user. Incidentally, Wootters' book and *The ABC's of Reloading*** by Dean Grennell are, in my opinion, two references any serious reloader should have.)

The best way to minimize wind deflection problems with any type of bullet lies in reaching MVs high enough to take you out of the trouble region. (Too, within reason, a lower MV may help.) Although this isn't always easy to achieve, the door was recently opened to minimizing the deflection problem, at least for cast rifle bullets. The March 1977 *American Rifleman* contained an article called "Paper Patched Bullets Come of Age." The technique related—which I couldn't do justice to by abstracting—allows cast rifle bullet MVs as high as 2750 fs. To illustrate the positive effect this higher MV has, the BCs for the two Lyman bullets noted in the E. H. Harrison article were used for calculating the two lower curves in Fig. 1.

These 30-cal. bullets are Nos. 301618, of 160 grains, and 301620, 196 grains. I'm not sure the custom

*Harrisburg, Pa., 1952-1957.
†New York, 1976.

**Northfield, Ill., 1974.

mould blocks are available.

The cited work noted that these bullets were very accurate, and it is possible that a major contributing factor to this accuracy was a muzzle velocity high enough to give these two bullets excellent crosswind-bucking properties. My 10-mph crosswind figures were also derived from this same *American Rifleman* piece.

Range *versus* BC

Fig. 2 shows another interesting but expected phenomenon—as range increases wind deflection becomes greater, which seems reasonable and obvious. Although the curves illustrated are correct for any bullet with the given BC, these three examples were picked with some care. The 0.654 figure represents, among other things, the 175-gr. Sierra Remington 7mm Magnum bullet—the highest BC, to my knowledge, for any readily available bullet. Hence this bullet has the best ability to retain its velocity—the usual significance placed on a high BC figure—but it also has the lowest wind-deflection susceptibility of any bullets currently available, regardless of its MV.

The .285 BC curve shown in Fig. 2 applies to the Sierra 55-gr. .224" spitzer bullet, which can be used in many 22 centerfire rifles. It is also the bullet weight used in the new Remington 30-06/22 Accelerator cartridge. I don't mean to suggest that Remington is using Sierra bullets, but rather that the Sierra bullet is enough like Remington's to be a good example of the Accelerator's wind-deflection properties.

It follows from Fig. 2 that most 22 centerfire rifles have high enough MVs to reduce significantly their wind deflection susceptibility. Obviously, however, it does not eliminate it or even reduce it as much as might be desired. Fig. 2 also shows that the new Remington 30-06/22 round, with a MV of over 4000 fs, is minimally affected by crosswinds simply because of its high MV. This, to me at least, wouldn't be readily obvious.

The top curve on Fig. 2 relates to a 150-gr. round nose 30-cal. bullet, which is interesting to compare to the .224" Accelerator example. This curve, as well as my others, are representative of any bullet with the stated BC.

Fig. 3 shows how bullet displacement is affected by changes in crosswind velocity. Our basic equation indicates that crosswind velocity directly multiplies the lag time to yield the bullet's displacement. Thus in going from one to 20 mph the whole curve

simply increases in size. Note, however, even at one mph and very high muzzle velocities, the deflection isn't entirely gone.

Oddly enough, if the only available information were the wind deflection formula, this interesting dependence on lag time might have been overlooked or ignored. It would be quite reasonable to write this phenomenon off as a fluke caused, perhaps, by trying to over-interpret a simple equation.

Credit to Cummings

Cummings' book, in addition to deriving the wind deflection formula, offers the following insight:

> Although the windage effects discussed above have been experimentally verified, perhaps no other ballistic formula arouses as much skepticism on the part of the shooter as the formula that gives the deflection of a bullet due to the wind.

Cummings' book is interesting for several other reasons. He predicted the 30-06/22 Accelerator round, for instance, a quarter-century before it was marketed. The same book shows plots similar to the three found here except that he graphed 22 rimfire data. Interestingly, normal high speed 22 rimfire loads and the new CCI Stinger rounds are in a MV range that assures rather large wind deflections.

Summary

It is clear that any bullet, cast or otherwise, leaving the muzzle at speeds between 1000 and 2000 fs is especially affected by crosswinds. The muzzle velocity that maximizes this situation appears to occur at around 1400 fs. To reduce this condition two approaches are possible. First, bullets with higher BCs show less lateral wind deflection in flight. Where practicable, then, deflection can be lessened by changing to bullets with greater BCs. Second, increasing bullet muzzle velocity above 1400 fs helps; the greater the MV the bigger the assistance. This can be aided—as noted above—by using a filler to hold the powder next to the primer, or by using the paper-patched bullets described by Col. Harrison. The latter approach seems far more fruitful and one certainly worth every serious consideration.

In looking over the cast rifle bullets I've used in the past, it appears I've been singularly successful in picking those that had *maximum* wind deflection susceptibility! I hope, after reading this report, that the lead bullet shooters among you can avoid my unfortunate choices. ●

WITH ONE notable exception—the United States of America—all major nations producing such sporting firearms as rifles, shotguns and handguns employ a government sanctioned facility for "proving" such small arms. Such proofing today subjects the guns received to far more stringent and complete trials then was the case in the past, when a single black powder test usually sufficed.

The oldest proof houses came into being centuries ago—at Liége (Belgium) in 1622, at London in 1637 and at St. Etienne in France in 1741. Gun proof, of a sort, also took place at Gardone Valtrompia, in northern Italy, during the days of the Venetian domination. *Sales d'Armi* existed there, though proving firearms was not then compulsory as it is today.

Italy became a unified nation only a hundred years ago. Before that it had consisted of a loose federation of small states, and during the days of Austrian control (1848-1870) the art of gunmaking was all but destroyed.

Yet, as Lee Kennett reported,* an English sportsman and writer (one Edward Davies) told his readers in 1617 that " . . . he that loves the safetie of his own person should get his gun abroad, preferably in Italy."

That advice serves to confirm the fact that the safety and strength of firearms have always been highly considered in Italy, though an official Proof House was first established only recently as time goes in such establishments.

Proof of firearms at Gardone VT was inaugurated by a royal decree *(Regio Decreto No. 20)* on January 13th in 1910–one Proof House was to

*Gun Digest, 31st ed. p. 161.

be located in Gardone itself, with another one at Brescia—close by today but some distance off in 1910 when transport was chiefly by horse.

As usual, bureaucracy's inertia, abetted by World War I, prevented the two proof houses from officially opening until 1920. In the beginning the proof testing was optional, but almost immediately the better gunmakers realized that the prestige and reputation of their firearms would be enhanced if they could point to their having been government proved. Moreover, their sale abroad would be facilitated if their arms had received impartial, official proof, tests conforming to the regulations existing at other (foreign) proof houses.

On December 20th, 1923, another royal decree (No. 351) made gun proof of Italian firearms mandatory within a year of the decree date, yet it was

Gardone Valtrompia
and the proof of Italian firearms

by MARIO ABBIATICO

Ing. Domenico Salza, Director of the Gardone proof house, watches an assistant, Pietro Benedetti, fire a rifle.

not until February 9th, 1925, that the order became fully effective. From that date forward all firearms had to be submitted for proof testing to the *Banco di Prova Nazionale per le Armi Portattili*. The now-operative proof houses were given two directives:

1. To guarantee the safety of the firearm user.

2. To improve the quality of Italian firearms by acquiring and operating special test equipment, tools the individual gunmaker could rarely afford.

I believe that both of those goals have been achieved in good part, particularly user safety, though the acquisition of more and more sophisticated equipment continues, of course.

As a federal institution, please note, the Italian proof houses operate on a non-profit basis. The gunmakers pay only a nominal amount of money for each firearm submitted for proof, these fees designated to cover only expenses—salaries, materials, amortization of equipment, and so on.

The Italian proof facilities work closely with their counterparts in other countries, and conform to the regulations affecting proof laid down by the Permanent International Commission (C.I.P.), with headquarters in Brussels, Belgium. The C.I.P. formulates and unifies standards of fabrication, dimensions, rules of proof, and so on, one important aim being to have firearms produced that will handle, interchangeably, the ammunition produced in the several countries signatory to the international convention. These countries now include Italy, France, England, Belgium, West Germany, East Germany, Jugoslavia, Czechoslovakia, Austria, Hungary and Chile.

At a meeting of the C.I.P. on September 3, 1971, a decision was made to extend the activities of the group—in light of the successes obtained in gunmaking—to the subject of ammunition. A subcommittee, under the direction of Ing. Domenico Salza, director of the Gardone Valtrompia proof house, was charged with looking into the fabrication of cartridges and their characteristics. "If the primary purpose of the proof houses is to insure safe firearms," Mr. Salza said, "then certainly the ammunition used in those guns must be equally safe and reliable." The subcommittee has been working since then to set up the rules and regulations for implementing this new program. When this system will become compulsory cannot be said now, but some of the goals can be described:

A. The largest ammunition makers will be required to install modern

The proof house at Gardone Valtrompia as it looks today, the mountains rising behind it.

The room of long guns at the Gardone proof house.

Putting the proof marks on.

test equipment, which tools will be inspected and tested by proof house technicians periodically to insure their proper functioning. The smaller cartridge manufacturers will send their products to the official proof house(s).

B. Ammunition which passes the test program satisfactorily will carry a special label, thus permitting its exportation to those countries affiliated with the C.I.P. At a later date ammunition for domestic consumption will also require the "passed" label.

How does the gun world regard the proof of firearms in Gardone Valtrompia today? As an Italian I'm proud of the fact that our proof practices and techniques are admired and honored by our colleagues in other countries, despite the relative youth of our system. Various proof equipment created and developed at Gardone Valtrompia has been bought by the St. Etienne and West German

proof houses, and by the French firm of Gevelot.

The Sporting Arms and Ammunition Manufacturing Institute (S.A.A. M.I.), of which most American makers of guns and cartridges are members, has been cooperating with the Italian proof authorities in an exchange of information and test procedures, apparently having recognized the advanced state of technology prevailing in Italy these days. Some of the equipment currently in use is shown nearby.

In addition to the main proof house at Gardone Valtrompia, branch facilities have been set up at the Beretta and Franchi factories as a convenience for those large firms, but the Gardone house has full and final authority over all firearms proving, including the affixing of proof marks.

As a practicing gunmaker myself, I'm a frequent visitor at the proof house, and I'm freshly impressed during these trips with the continuing

studies and scientific experiments carried on there by the dedicated Ing. Salza and his corps of competent assistants. Their work has, indeed, become a way of life for them. Already they have made important contributions to the science of interior and exterior ballistics, to the steady improvement in the quality and reliability of Italian portable firearms. At the moment new test equipment is under development which, when completed and put into operation, will undoubtedly advance the state of the art considerably, benefitting gunmakers and their guns everywhere.

Test Equipment at Gardone Valtrompia

Smoothbore guns: Pattern tests, coincidence of patterns for double-barrel models, breech pressure, choke performance, free recoil.

Rifled arms: Machine rests for rifles and handguns. Determination of grouping ability to 100 metres. Breech pressures.

Shotshells: Pressure barrels in all gauges, readings recorded at 17mm and at 162mm, using both crusher gauges and piezo-electric strain gauges. Chronographing at 10 metres. Time of flight measurements. Humidity (10% to 95%) and temperature tests (10° to 80° Celsius).

Metallic cartridges: Velocity tests, 0 to 100 metres. Pressure and velocity tests (simultaneously) in pressure barrels, otherwise as above.

Other test devices include: profilometers, primer drop-test, ultra high-speed cine cameras, barographs, hygrometers, bullet recovery boxes, residual energy test media, etc. Much of the proof test ammunition, shotshell and metallic, is formulated and assembled at the proof house.

Italian Firearms Production

In the past 8 years (1970-1977 inclusive) 5,209,400 firearms of all types passed proof at the Gardone Valtrompia proof houses. This number includes 237,700 side-by-side shotguns; 1,067,450 over-under shotguns; 1,065,750 autoloading shotguns; 335,700 single-barrel (one shot) shotguns; 483,700 muzzle-loading replicas, rimfire rifles, etc. Handguns passing proof totaled 2,019,100.

Because *all* firearms made in Italy must be submitted to proof, the numbers shown here represent Italy's total small arms production for the 8-year period covered. •

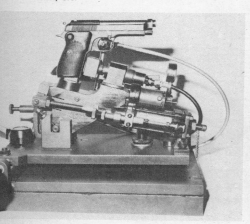

This highly developed machine rest for handguns is used at Gardone to make a variety of tests—velocity, recoil, grouping ability of ammunition, etc.

This special chronograph/target, designed at the Gardone proof house, records the average instrument velocity of shotshells, using piezo electric transducers.

Some of the test equipment used today at the Gardone Valtrompia proof house. From left—temperature and humidity controls, two oscilloscopes and chamber pressure test instruments.

Match Air Pistols

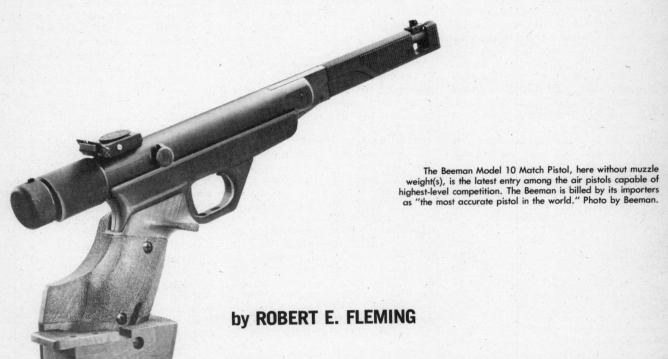

The Beeman Model 10 Match Pistol, here without muzzle weight(s), is the latest entry among the air pistols capable of highest-level competition. The Beeman is billed by its importers as "the most accurate pistol in the world." Photo by Beeman.

by ROBERT E. FLEMING

Many shooters who rarely enter a formal pistol match are buying precision models. This report covers the leading makers—Daisy's Feinwerkbaus, the Beeman Diana Model 10 and the Walthers imported by Interarms.

ONE OF THE MOST dramatic developments in competitive pistol shooting over the past 10 years has been the proliferation of match quality air pistols, most of them imported from West Germany.

The U.S. International Championships at Black Canyon, Arizona, draw so many competitors in air pistol shooting that elimination matches have to be fired for two days before the actual championship, and only the best air pistol marksmen even make it to Black Canyon.

Throughout the nation international programs are including air pistol events. Special air pistol and air rifle matches have also been set up, often attracting a good turnout of junior shooters as well as adults.

But a lot of shooters who never even enter a regular air pistol match buy precision air pistols—for backyard practice during off season, for competition in inexpensive N.R.A. postal matches, for training new shooters, or just for informal shooting.

The four very best air pistols currently available, capable of firing per-fect scores in the hands of the right shooter, are (in alphabetical order) the Beeman Model 10, also offered as the Hy-Score 819M by another company, the Feinwerkbau 65 and 80 models; plus, the recently redesigned Walther LP3 Match. Over the past 18 months I've been testing these 4 fine guns, comparing their characteristics and performances.

It's hard to give a short answer to the question, "Which is best?" but I hope I can relate enough information about the 4 so that the reader can make an intelligent choice.

The Beeman Model 10

The Beeman, modestly billed by its importer as, "The Most Accurate Pistol in the World," is the largest and heaviest of those to be reviewed here. At 16.5″ long and 53.5 ozs., it was designed, it seems, to fall just within the limits prescribed by the I.S.U. (International Shooting Union). Basically, this is correct; the engineers at Dianawerk, the German company which produces the Beeman, set out to give shooters who choose their pistol every advantage they are legally entitled to.

Besides length and weight, this meant designing a grip which encloses more of the hand than any other precision air pistol on the market. The other pistols under discussion have palm shelves at the bottom of their adjustable grips, too, but the Beeman/Hy-Score has an extra little shelf that slides out to the rear, thus supporting more of the heel of the hand than the Feinwerkbau or the Walther. In addition, the receiver extends far back over the *top* of the shooter's hand, so that it's squeezed between palm shelf and receiver. Needless to say this gives a great deal of contact between pistol and hand, resulting in a very secure grip.

As with the other 3 pistols in its class the Beeman has no sensed recoil; a second piston inside the gun duplicates the movement of the piston that compresses the air which launches the pellet, and the gun stays precisely aligned just where you had it pointed when the shot broke—or it does if the shooter is adept!

Much planning went into the Beeman trigger design. It can easily be adjusted to 500 grams (17.6 ozs.) for the lightest allowable trigger pull for formal competition, or it can be made as heavy as 1000 grams (35.2 ozs.). The range of adjustment through which the trigger can be put—length of pull, slack, and width of the surface your trigger finger contacts—is remarkable. It should accommodate shooters with virtually any size or shape of hands.

The micrometer rear sight, lying quite close to the shooter's hand, is precise in its movements. Three different sight plates come with the gun, letting the individual choose a sight notch of 2.5, 3.0, or 3.5mm; the front sight pivots vertically so that its apparent width varies from 2.5 to 4.0mm. Sight radius can be varied from 12.4″ to 14″ by installing the rear sight in different holes in the receiver.

Cocking the Beeman is done by twisting a barrel jacket around, to protect the hand from the front sight, and then simply breaking the barrel downward as with the more inexpensive air pistols and rifles. This method allows you to look through the barrel and to clean it from the breech, but it is theoretically less desirable than Feinwerkbau's rigidly-mounted barrel or Walther's barrel, which also drops for loading but is secured by a manual barrel catch.

In general the gun feels good and solid in the hand, especially with the new 2.8 oz. barrel weight in place. It's packed in an attractive attache case and comes with a machine-rest group that will amaze you.

The Feinwerkbau 65

The Feinwerkbau 65 has been king of the hill in competitive circles since air pistol match shooting hit the U.S.A. It holds all the world class records in international competition, and even at the smaller matches in the U.S. it is unusual to see really serious competitors using any other. Beeman and Walther, of course, would like to change all that.

Like the Beeman, the F'bau 65 is a good-sized pistol. Almost 15″ long, it weighs 42 ozs. and has a sight radius of 14″. This long sight radius is disturbing to the beginner, or even to an experienced shooter who has never fired a free pistol extensively. However, once you get used to it, more precise aiming is possible when you have this much distance between the sights.

The FWB is designed to have no appreciable recoil when it is used in competition, but the engineering approach differs from that used at Dianawerk. The F'bau is made in two sections; the upper one, containing barrel, spring, compression chamber and sights, is allowed to recoil freely for about ¹/₂″ when the spring pushes the piston forward to compress air behind the pellet. Again the feeling is about the same; little spring surge is felt, if any, but if you practice careful follow-through after trigger release you will be able to note the movement of the sights.

Another difference between the FWB 65 and the other 3 is in the provision that's made for using the pistol as a trainer. The Beeman and the Walther are truly recoilless guns. The FWB 65, because of the way the recoil is tamed, can be readily converted to give a distinct feeling of recoil. Just attaching a small accessory plate to the front of the upper section with a single bolt will stop the independent movement of the barrel section and cause the entire gun to jump, very much like a firearm.

The FWB optional adjustable grips, which are used by most of the better shooters, are comfortable and secure, but they don't enclose the hand as completely as the grip of the Beeman. A movable shelf slides up under the shooter's hand and can then be locked in place to be sure that he assumes the same grip, shot after shot.

The adjustable trigger on the FWB can be set very precisely to suit the preference of the shooter, and the trigger is wide enough so that it's not necessary to add a trigger shoe. A major plus for the FWB is a feature that allows you to flip an internal lever, using a special little spanner furnished with the gun, and convert it instantly from the legal minimum of 500 grams to 1500 grams, or about 2 lbs., 10 ozs. Thus, both heavy and light trigger pulls can be finely adjusted, and the gun can be used as a trainer one day and instantly readied for competition the next, all without going through a lot of fine tuning.

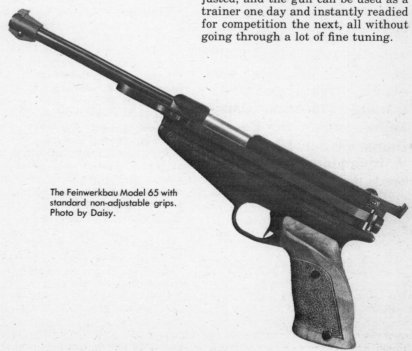

The Feinwerkbau Model 65 with standard non-adjustable grips. Photo by Daisy.

The Feinwerkbau 65 with adjustable grips, which Daisy designates the Model 67. However, it's the same gun except for the grips. Photo by Daisy.

The Walther LP3 Match. Barrel shown has recently been replaced with a heavier, improved version. Photo by Interarms.

The rear sight moves the pellet impact in increments of about $1/16''$ per click at 10 meters, allowing the shooter to make highly exact adjustments. In place of the interchangeable rear sight blades of the Beeman, the FWB rear sight notch can be adjusted to any width from 2.0 to 2.8mm by turning a screw to give more or less light on each side of the front sight, useful when different lighting conditions are encountered. The rear sight does ride a bit higher over the hand than I like because of the sandwich design of the gun, and the rear sight extends back over the web of the hand. Some American shooters find this distracting, since an attempt to move the pistol to correct the sight picture causes the rear sight to move one way and the front sight in the other. The purpose, to give the greatest possible sight radius, does pay off in the end, though, and you'll find this type of sight on free pistols.

Cocking the FWB is done by pulling a right-side lever out from beside the compression chamber and all the way to the rear. It takes the least force of any of the three guns tested. There is also an advantage, at least in theory, because the sights are mounted rigidly—on the barrel, which is screwed into the receiver, and on the rear of the compression chamber housing. Unlike the other pistols, there is no fear that a hinged barrel will not go back to precisely the same position for shot after shot.

In place of the O-ring that seals the Beeman and Walther breeches, the FWB has a beveled breech seal that encloses a conical extension of the barrel. It is the most positive seal used on any airgun and will prevent the leaking of any air at all unless the seal becomes damaged.

The gun is obviously another fine, precisely made piece of equipment and because of the almost effortless cocking it can be fired for a great many shots before fatigue sets in. I have often fired two 40-shot international courses in a row with the gun without an appreciable dropping off of my scores.

The FWB Model 80

Not wanting to rest on their past achievements, Feinwerkbau designers came up with a couple of improvements in the 1977 version of the Model 65—a new double mainspring and a slightly redesigned sight. The real news at Feinwerkbau, though, is a completely new target pistol, the Model 80.

Though it looks much like the Model 65 from a distance, and is loaded and fired in exactly the same

manner, the M80 goes beyond the earlier gun in several respects. The metal grip frame has been reduced in size to allow more customizing of the wooden grip, and the tang that extends above the hand has been lengthened so that, as on the Beeman, the shooter's hand is firmly squeezed between the top tang and the shelf at the bottom of the adjustable grip.

The trigger was redesigned along the lines of that on the F"bau match rifles. It can be moved back and forth for about .65", letting it fit the individual needs of shooters.

The most obvious change is the provision for adding a variety of weights to the forward end of the receiver. Three weights, of 15, 60, and 85 grams, come with the gun, and one or more may be attached beneath, but not touching, the barrel. To some shooters the FWB 65 always seems a bit muzzle light, but the only available barrel weight could not be installed without removing the front sight, a lengthy process if you wanted to experiment. Now shooters can easily vary the M80's weights and find the best combination for their individual preferences.

Like the latest M65, the M80 has a double mainspring and a wider rear sight. Unlike the M65, however, the

M80 is purely a match gun. It cannot be adjusted to recoil, nor can its trigger be instantly switched to a heavier weight for training purposes.

According to my tests, the M80 is no more accurate than the old Model 65. However, the superior handling and balance qualities made possible by the new trigger and weights probably mean that the pistol will compile an even better record in competition than the M65 did, and that will indeed be an enviable record.

The Walther LP3 Match

The last precision air pistol to be considered here bears a name that will be familiar to more American shooters than the others—Walther. As early as 1952 Walther designed a training pistol that would handle about the same as their famous Olympia match pistol. The LP52 (LP standing for *Luft Pistole* and 52 for the year the gun was developed) was replaced the next year by an improved design, the LP53. Still marketed as a trainer, the LP53 is an excellent choice for that purpose, but it has spring recoil deliberately built in to accustom the shooter to the feel.

The latest descendant of the LP53, the LP3 Match, is a highly sophisticated piece of equipment, suitable for matches on the highest level of competition. It is also completely recoilless, but achieves this goal through a third system, which needs a bit of explanation.

All the other guns described are spring-air pistols. When the trigger activates the sear, an airtight piston is released to build air pressure in a chamber which has a small vent hole leading to the pellet in the breech. When enough pressure builds up behind the pellet, it begins to move down the barrel. The Beeman keeps the shooter from feeling the movement of the piston by using a second dummy piston to cancel out the movement, and the FWB allows the whole top assembly of the gun to move with the recoil. So much for review.

Walther opted for an entirely different system, the pneumatic. Any shooter familiar with Benjamin, Crosman, or Sheridan pump air guns knows that the pneumatic works by pumping air into the compression chamber by using a pump lever on the gun. Instead of a moving piston, a pneumatic has a small hammer which strikes a valve, opens it, and lets the trapped air out into the breech behind the pellet. Recoil doesn't have to be canceled out because none exists in the first place. The Walther gets rid of one of the objectionable variables found in pneumatic guns by making just one pump per shot feasible. In such conventional pneumatics as the American guns mentioned the speed and manner of pumping as well as the number of pumps can make velocity vary; with a match gun this will make groups unacceptably large.

The FWB Model 80 with all three weights in place, giving it a total weight of 50 ounces, just under the legal limit. Note the new sliding trigger. Photo by Beeman.

For Walther this one-stroke pneumatic system works. Not only does the LP3 use it, but the LGR, Walther's latest top of the line air rifle, has begun to make a record for itself in world competition.

Of the 4 guns tested the LP3 will probably feel most familiar to the American shooter when he first picks it up. In the first place, it's the shortest of the four at 14″. Secondly, it has a grip angle much closer to that of the Government Model 45 or other standard American target pistols, as compared to the free pistol grip style of the other guns, which force the shooter to hold them in the "broken" or relaxed-wrist position. Third, the sight radius is an inch shorter than the Beeman's and almost 3″ shorter than that of either FWB. At 11.25″ the sights are still farther apart than they are allowed to be on any gun designed for standard American shooting games, but the relatively shorter radius makes the shooter feel steadier, may keep him from jerking shots. At 48 ozs. it is in the middle of the guns tested.

The LP3 grip, like those of the other pistols, has an adjustable shelf that can be locked into the optimum position to support the lower edge of the shooter's hand. Unfortunately, the shelf itself is not contoured as well as the shelves of the others—it has a flat surface rather than a con-

cave one. Shooters can remedy this problem with a little work, of course. The grip itself, because it must fit around the pneumatic chamber, is bulkier than the grips of the other 3 guns, and only a limited amount of wood can be removed. People with very small hands could find this a disadvantage.

The receiver of the latest model LP3 has now been cut out so that the shooter's hand rests very high, close to the sights and about on a line with the bore. This gives the Walther a particularly good feel and is in line with experiments tried out by a number of rapid fire shooters on the international scene.

Trigger action on the LP3 is excellent, as it is on any of those already mentioned. It comes set at the standard international minimum of 500 grams, but it can be adjusted to a somewhat heavier pull. The sample I got from Interarms was adjusted perfectly except for the slightest amount of backlash, which I easily removed by adjusting the trigger stop. The gun does lack the instant switch feature of the FWB 65, which allows easy transition from light to heavy pull.

As with the Beeman, three rear sight blades are furnished, allowing the shooter to set up for different light conditions or to suit his own preference. Notches come in 3.2, 3.5, or 3.8mm.

To cock the Walther, the shooter pulls down on a cocking lever that extends from the lower part of the grip to just ahead of the trigger guard. This is pulled down as far as it will go, about to where it is pointing straight down. Then it is pushed quickly up into its original position.

Until you develop a technique, this can be hard work, but as gun and shooter get broken in, it becomes easy.

Like the Beeman, the Walther breaks for loading, so that same question arises—does the barrel return to the exact same position every time? If it doesn't the sights can be slightly out of line and the breech may not seal completely. Walther puts a manual catch on the pistol, up near the barrel hinge, to lock the barrel in place. From the size of the groups the gun will shoot I'm confident the system works.

I found the gun pleasant to shoot and accurate. Several other shooters at the local club tried it and were also very impressed with the way it felt and shot.

Which of these sophisticated pistols would be the best for you to buy? That's a question you'll have to answer yourself. After all, you're the one who will be putting up some $200 to $400 to buy one. (See our catalog pages for the lastest prices.) But a few comparisons can be made.

Comparisons

As far as reliability and maintenance are concerned, all 4 are about equal from what I've been able to learn. Sure, things can go wrong with any piece of mechanical equipment, but any of the guns tested should last you a lifetime if you treat them with care.

Air Rifle Headquarters used to imply in their catalog that the Walther was less sturdy than a spring-air gun, but the test specimen I've been shooting has digested over 3500 rounds with no sign of a problem. About the only thing I would advise, besides always using the highest quality pellets from H&N, RWS, or Bimoco, is to have one or two extra breech seals on hand. These cheap and easily changed parts are probably the only ones you'll ever have to replace.

As for accuracy, the test groups that come with any of these pistols are machine-rest one-hole groups. The Beeman will often produce a group that is just .04", center-to-center. However, the Walther and the FWB pistols I tested also included test groups that were .08" center-to-center for each gun. But machine rests aren't allowed in pistol matches!

When it came to firing the guns over a rest, some surprises came up. The Walther turned in the smallest groups, as small as .38" on centers.

The FWB requires less energy to cock than either of the other two match pistols. Photo by E. M. Fleming.

The FWB guns readily turned in groups just over the half-inch mark, with an average of .56". The Beeman groups simply would not go under .63" for me. Any of these groups will make

"possibles" on the 10-meter target, but naturally the smaller the group the better. Robert Beeman later told me that the pistol I tested had an abnormal breech seal, but I wasn't able to test fire another Model 10.

Ease of cocking could be a factor. If the shooter does not have a great deal of strength, he or she should probably go with one of the FWB models. They are by far the least fatiguing of the 4 to cock. The other two are a toss-up. Neither bothered me personally, but women I asked to try them found both guns hard to cock.

Price should not really be a factor. From time to time the various distributors offer special deals, and if you shop around or wait for a promotional special, you can probably have the gun you want, rather than the one that's cheapest. For a gun that you shoot in your home or yard every day, even $300 is not as big an investment as it would be if you knew you'd use the gun only three or four times a year.

For the American pistol shooter with no interest in match pistol shooting, the Walther may be a logical choice. Anyone used to free pistol shooting or planning to acquire one will probably find the other three guns fully acceptable.

One final note: for the past 10 years or so Feinwerkbau has been piling up the medals. If you want to shoot what the winners of the big matches have been shooting, pick an FWB. But remember, both Diana and Walther are going to be doing their best to take that crown away from FWB, and either of these pistols has the potential to start winning its share of the matches over the next decade. •

The Walther LP 53. This is the old standby which the LP2 and the LP3 replaced in the highest level of competition. As a trainer, it's still useful. Photo by Beeman.

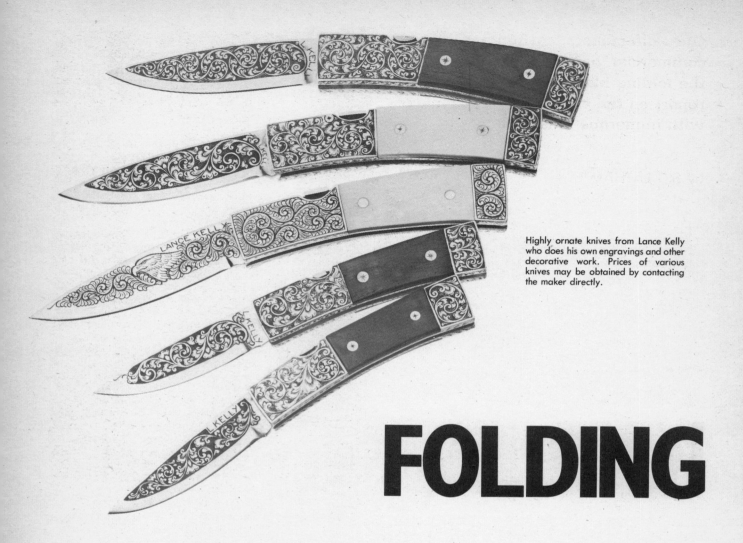

Highly ornate knives from Lance Kelly who does his own engravings and other decorative work. Prices of various knives may be obtained by contacting the maker directly.

FOLDING

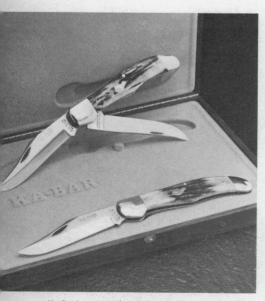

Ka-Bar's reintroduced Dog's Head folders are offered as a matched-serial number set—only 1,000 units will be made of a knife first offered in the 1920s.

IN THE PAST few years the custom knifemen have raised their sights to even more involved and intricate cutlery; the folding knives. At the last Knifemaker's Guild show in the summer of 1977 few knifemakers failed to display folders on their tables, along with their straight-bladed sheath knives. There were some nifty knives on view, too, make no mistake about that. Aside from the usual high standard of Henry Frank's magnificent (and expensive) pieces of art work, there were also examples of the cutler's craft from such talents as Bob Ogg, Wayne Goddard or Woody Naifeh. Knives from any of the latter craftsmen could be had from $45 to around $85 and a fellow might even find a gut-hook folder, the first ever made, by Bill Cheatham of Phoenix, Arizona.

Why the Folder?

What caused the rush to folders is pretty obvious if you just think about

it for a moment. For the past 10 years or so sheath knives have just about reached the peak of perfection in design, imagination and applied skill. Added to that is the fact some customers don't favor the Buffalo Bill look when going hunting and don't eye with much enthusiasm a knife swinging from their belt. Conversely, many craftsmen wanted the challenge of doing something different or, if you will, something even more difficult. Certainly it isn't easy crafting a folding knife with all those tiny bits and pieces being fitted into a small area. It also takes double and sometimes triple the man hours making springs, locking bars, bolsters, liners, shaping covers and, least of all, a well fitting blade. Next you've got to put all those pieces together into a finely finished knife that walks and talks with authority. In addition, if a craftsman adds a bit of fancy file work to decorate a blade, engraves the bolsters and even works over the

Our knifemakers, custom and commercial, have warmly embraced the folding blade. Here's a concise report on the current trend, coupled with numerous illustrations.

by SID LATHAM

KNIVES

A pair of elaborately executed folding knives by Harvey McBurnette, both having the convenient forward locking device.

liners, he has a fairly time-consuming and expensive package to deliver to his customer.

Factory Folders

Representatives of the major commercial cutlery firms have begun to attend the knife shows around the country, paying great attention to what is being shown, and then hurrying home with tales of all those expensive and ornate knives. It didn't take long for the factory heads to cast an eye over their lines and issue an order for some modern-working, good looking cutlery in a hurry.

Just last year Harvey Platts of Western Cutlery in Boulder, Colorado, took me on a tour of their modern plant, where I saw some fine, solidly built lock-back folders of a new and unusual design. One Western knife had a covered spring to protect the inner workings of the 3¾-inch blade. The knife had rose-

Folders from top makers. From left—a Lloyd Hale model with stag slabs, a George Herron with African blackwood, a Paul-type knife in all stainless steel, a small Barrett folder, one from Hayes with cocobolo covers and a Billy Mace Imel blade with ivory covers. About $250 to $1000.

From left—a handsome folder from old-timer Harvey Draper, another by Bill Moran, a stag handle blade by Frank Centofante and a well-engraved model by Will Wilbur.

wood covers and nickel-silver bolsters. Potential customers can be assured there are almost as many hand operations on this new Western model as you'll find in any custom shop. Platts is understandably proud of his latest creation, and anyone who lays out $30 will be getting a lot of knife for his money.

Incidentally, you can save $3.50 if you order it without the belt pouch.

Smith & Wesson, the venerable firearms firm, seeing the direction good knives were taking a few years ago, had knife expert Blackie Collins design a complete line of knives, among them a fine folder. Called the Model 6060, it has a 3½-inch drop-point blade, a notched tang locking

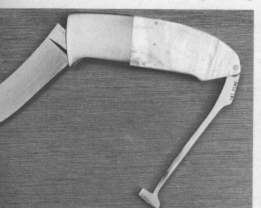

An unusual folder by Leon Pittman. Called the "Worm," it locks open and closed via the locking bar shown. Nickel silver bolster and mother of pearl covers. $250 to $500.

the blade firmly in place. Made of 440C steel and with Wessonwood (an impregnated material) plates, this handsome folder sells for $65. It's a good value.

Browning, one of the most famous names in firearms, has been adding to their line of knives, and now has a complete array of sporting blades, including 10 folders and 11 smaller pocket knives. Many are made in their own factory in Utah, others in Germany and some by those wonderful folks who brought you Sony television, Nikon cameras and Citori shotguns. These very good Browning knives sell for about $35. In today's knife market they can be considered an excellent buy.

New Designs

In the past few years some interesting developments in the cutlery field haven't had much publicity. One of these interesting but time-consuming projects is the RS-1 Survival Knife, the result of much research by Mark Reveaux of New Haven, Conn. Reveaux has come up with a true survival knife that is a bit of marvelous ingenuity in concept and design. Although a folder, it is a pretty hefty number for the pocket, being better suited for use in light aircraft, a snowmobile or a 4-wheel drive vehicle. As Reveaux says, "The RS-1 is not intended for the backyard camper nor is it a showpiece. It is built strictly for hard use under extreme conditions in

remote wilderness areas."

The RS-1 blade is of 440C stainless steel, a mighty ¼" thick, and is heat-treated to a Rockwell C of 58-60. The handle slabs are cast from No. 319 corrosion-resistant aluminum and coated with ebony-colored Armor-hide. The interior of the covers have storage compartments for such additional survival equipment as fish hooks, line, spare saws and blowgun darts. A roll-out 16" wire saw will cut through bone, ice and non-ferrous materials. The saw pull bar can be used as a combination screwdriver, pry bar, flint striker, and for field stripping the knife. Lengths of steel tubing will soon be available which can be used as a suction device for snake bite and, with the inner winding spool, as a blow gun mouth piece. The RS-1 sells for $50, and may be ordered directly from the manufacturer: The Remote Survival Co., P. O. Box 523, New Haven, CT 06503.

The second knife that has caused a great deal of interest is a Barry Wood variation devised by Carl Addis of the Wyoming Knife Corp. These are the same folks who wrought the strange looking brass knuckle kind of knife with a couple of razor sharp blades jutting out at odd angles. This one, named the Powder River, differs from the Wood knife in that both steel handle covers and the blade may be taken completely apart with a couple of dimes. The retail price is $30 with belt pouch, extra blades $3.50 each.

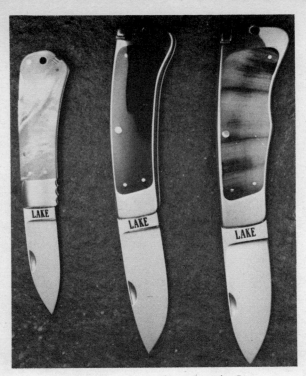

Three folders by master craftsman Ron Lake. From left—mother of pearl, Cape buffalo and Big Horn sheep. Value $850 and up.

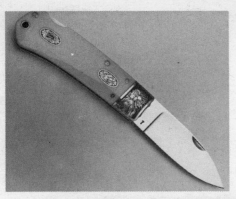

Perhaps the ultimate in folders is Ron Lake's elegant blade, the engraving by the great Winston Churchill.

Folders from top makers—the Imel at top has ossik covers, the Barry Wood folder below is of titanium with ivory slabs. $600 and $1200.

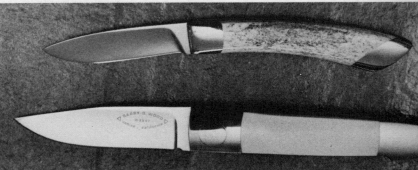

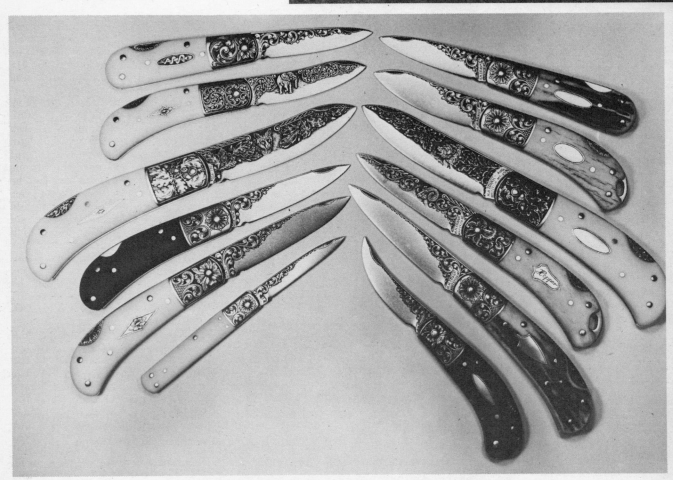

No article on folding knives could be considered complete without showing the superb work of Henry Frank. Feast your eyes on these, no two exactly alike, no one less than excellent, all hand made and engraved by the master.

Three lock-open folders by Melvin M. Pardue, who makes also a good variety of sheath knives, Bowies, fighters, etc.

Four popular and well-made factory folders—at top is a used Track blade, one of the author's favorites, selling for $65; the Western Cutley's lockback at $30; Wyoming Knife Co. made this variation on the Wood folder, with interchangeable blades at $30, and Ka-Bar's new Khybar knife, $12 to $20 depending on blade length.

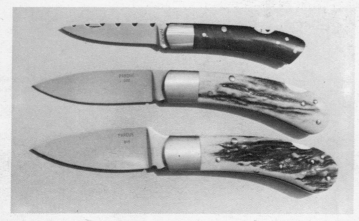

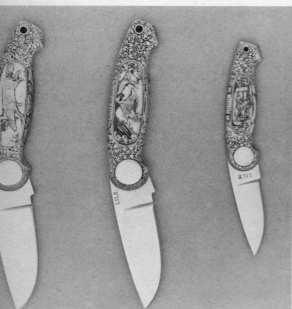

Jimmy Lile's latest—folding hunters with an unusual device that locks the blade open and closed. Limited edition only.

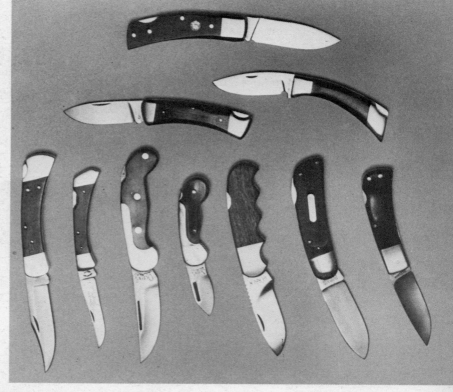

A selection of the finest commercial folders. Top, a Smith & Wesson by Blackie Collins; next two are Brownings. Below, from left—Buck, Double Eagle by Imperial, two Olsen knives, Gerber, Schrade and Morseth. About $10 to $85.

Fancy knives seem to be the rule among some custom craftsmen, as these attest. From left—two made by S. R. Jobs, using ivory and mother of pearl, a gentleman's steak knife by Wayne Goddard, and an unusual folder by Californian Bob Hayes.

The Khybars

One of the oldest names in the commercial cutlery field is Ka-Bar. They recently introduced a line of folders that they call the Khybar line. Developed under Ka-Bar's direction these are produced in Japan. They're said to be the first folders from Japan with Micarta-like covers, a linen-base material (used by many custom cutlers). This makes an exceptionally sturdy handle for a factory knife. Among the least expensive of the new knives, they sell for $11 to $24 depending on blade length.

Schrade Cutlery offers new models almost yearly. Although I'm not particularly keen on Staglon as a handle material—more a matter of esthetics than practicality, I can't deny that Henry Baer keeps on top of trends. The Old Timer lockback (#510T) is a rugged folder with a 3½-inch blade of high carbon tool steel, nickel-silver bolsters and brass scales. For $30 it would be difficult to go wrong. The new Frontier series, produced by the Imperial Knife division of Schrade, has a couple of folders of merit. A few of the man-size lockback models have pretty hefty blades, but the heftiness is offset by fine construction, brass bolsters and hand-rubbed laminated wood covers. The simple locking device has been around for years; a small brass tab springs sideways when the blade is opened and prevents an accidental closure. There is also a lock-back Sportsman model with a handy blade length of 3⅛ inches. All of these knives are priced at $8 to $25.

Unique Folder

As always, I like to save the best news 'till last, and Pete Gerber has come up a winner once again. To digress a bit: in the spring of 1976, at the Dallas Knife Expo, a young engineer and aerospace designer named Paul Poehlmann showed up with some knives that were unique, to say the least. That these were hand-made models selling for $300 to $750 made little difference to those knife collectors clamoring for one of Paul's knives. What made these knives so desirable, even at such high prices? Since the advent of the Barry Wood and Ron Lake folders these Poehlmann blades were probably the most unusual opening-and-closing knives devised to that time. Fingers never touch the blade—instead an unusual axial locking mechanism consisting of two buttons, are pressed to open and close the blade and lock it in place. With orders piling up Paul knew he could never turn out enough

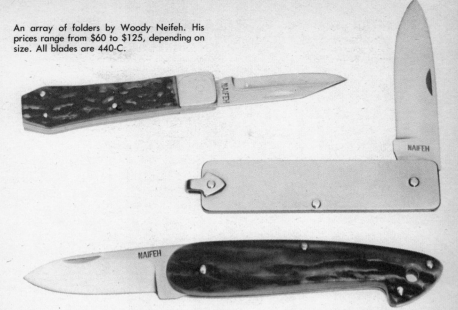

An array of folders by Woody Neifeh. His prices range from $60 to $125, depending on size. All blades are 440-C.

An array of excellent folders by Bill Thomason, the handle slabs varying and optional.

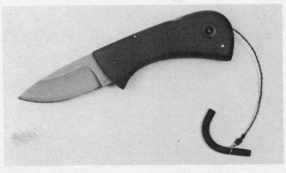

The RS-1 Survival knife designed by Mark Reveaux of New Haven, Conn. This is a hefty and genuine survival knife of 440-C steel. Note the flexible saw that pulls out from the butt. A bargain at $50.

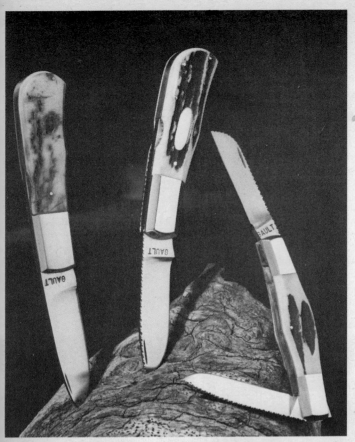

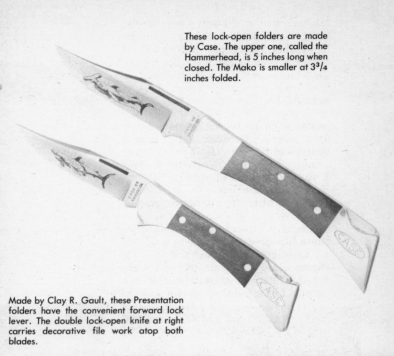

These lock-open folders are made by Case. The upper one, called the Hammerhead, is 5 inches long when closed. The Mako is smaller at 3³/₄ inches folded.

Made by Clay R. Gault, these Presentation folders have the convenient forward lock lever. The double lock-open knife at right carries decorative file work atop both blades.

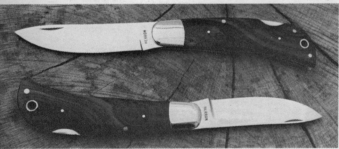

Two handsome folders from George Herron. Prices run about $200, plus $100 for African blackwood or the rare African pink ivory.

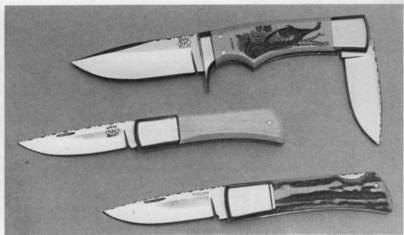

Custom folders by Doyal Nolen including a sheath knife with two folding blades.

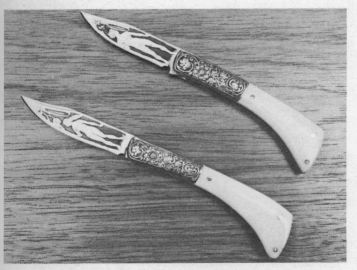

Two beautifully crafted folders by Bob Ogg, the etching by Shaw-Leibowitz, the bolsters engraved by Henry Frank. Priced at around $1000 each.

A Jim Small folder, the scrimshaw by Michael Collins on ivory covers and engraving by Lance Kelly. Around $750.

knives, so he cast about for a manufacturer who could and would maintain his own high standards of quality. Gerber Legendary Blades joined forces with Poehlmann to bring out the knife in mid-1978. From the original high price the Paul knife can now be had for $55 with stainless steel covers, or at $60 for a deluxe model with hardwood or ivory Micarta covers. The Paul folder, a welcome addition to the Gerber line, complements the Classic, Sportsman I, the Skookum and others. All Gerber folders are made of 440C steel and use sturdy tropical hardwoods for covers.

I don't want to imply that none of these fine new factory folders wouldn't have seen the light of day without the pressure of the custom craftsmen, yet the flurry of activity among the factory folks and their continuing attendance at the custom knife shows says something.

Scrimshanders

Many of the newer custom knifemen are sticking with folders (no pun intended) and selling all they can make. Tommy Lee and Ron Hewitt, both southern craftsmen, do a fine job, and Lee offers scrimshaw work by Don Haynes of Gardner City, SC. Hewitt knives feature art work by Ray Mellen, a top scrimshander and engraver who is becoming popular with knifemakers. Of course a Damascus folder by Bill Moran costs a fair bundle, and a George Herron folder with pink ivory or a rare African wood could set a fella back about $300. It is not impossible for a man to spend more on a folder than on a sheath knife and, sometimes, even more than that. Though Jess Horn or Billy Mace Imel will turn out some pretty fancy work, Rendon Griffin will hand a man a knife for around $85 that will be a damn fine piece of work, too. I've been told that Frank Centofante sells practically every folder he makes, which means he's putting in many long hours aside from his regular job.

Folders are becoming more popular then ever and, whether a man wants a hunter, skinner or even a boot knife, they're all available in the pocket knife. It just depends how long you want to wait for delivery and how much you want to pay. There is a vast array of first-class cutlery available today in sport shops and local hardware stores. Too, in case a fellow wants the best of all worlds he can still buy an excellent factory knife while he's waiting for an order to be filled for something more fancy. ●

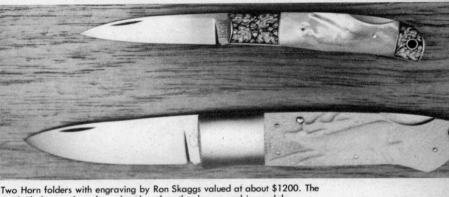

Two Horn folders with engraving by Ron Skaggs valued at about $1200. The top knife has mother of pearl scales, the other has carved ivory slabs.

Four fine folders from George Stone. Prices depend on material used—write for further information.

Rendon Griffin's "Circle G" knives come in a variety of blade lengths and are usually finished with stag covers. Prices range from around $80 to about $150.

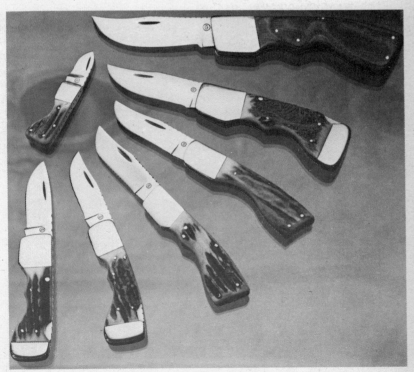

Alex Henry

and his falling block rifles

ON APRIL 17TH, 1865, Alexander Henry of Edinburgh (Scotland) petitioned for British patent protection and was granted patent No. 1071 on an outside hammer, underlever, falling-block rifle. There is little doubt that Henry's action design was patterned after the earlier American Sharps system, Henry borrowing the basic falling-block and underlever; but the rest of Henry's action was such a total redesign and improvement that it bore little resemblance to the Sharps.

Many variations were produced, the early rifles closely following the patent drawings, but improvements followed until the design settled down to become the rifle so familiar to collectors and shooters today.

His final design used a large and graceful outside hammer, with a typical back-action lockplate let into the buttstock. The breechblock, at right angles to the bore, is connected by a short link to the finger lever. Before the action can be opened the hammer must be drawn to half-cock. A locking catch on the end of the finger lever is pressed and the finger lever is pushed forward and down. This lowers the breechblock until it contacts a short extended arm on the Martini-type extractor, which withdraws the fired case. The extractor, spring loaded, reseats itself when pressure on the finger lever is released. A flat spring does the reseating.

Early production rifles followed the extractor shown in the patent drawings. A plate was soldered to the underside of the barrel and an extractor fitted that slid in line with the barrel. The finger lever was extended ahead of its pivot pin and provided with a short arm. As the action opened fully this short arm was raised to contact the extractor's front end. Final pressure on the finger lever forced the fired case from the chamber, the extractor extending over the top of the breechblock ³/₈"— much farther than the usual falling-block extractor travelled. Many other rifle designs barely started the case from the chamber.

Henry had trouble with this extractor, however, when his rifle was rejected from the British Army trials. These trials were set up to find a successor to the 577 Snider, then the standard British service arm. One

Fig. 1—This quite plain Alex Henry is without the bolting lever, and its caliber is 577/500, a scarce chambering. Serial No. 1672.

complaint concerned the soldered plate holding the extractor to the barrel, another was made because a cartridge could be seated ahead of the extractor, thus jamming the piece. Modifications of the sliding extractor quickly followed, and Henry finally settled for the Martini extractor type, which has its own pivot pin with a flat spring provided to reseat it.

While we are on extractors, most Henrys show cartridge rims rebated into the barrel, but a few have the rim rebate in the breechblock face.

Three Locking Systems

Patent drawings show three lock systems that could be used with the falling block. Apart from the familiar back action lock, Henry's patent covered a front action lock with the lockplate and working parts within the buttstock, extending through the action body and into the fore-end. The

patent drawing also shows a shotgun using a horizontal firing pin within the standing breech. The interesting point is that the standard back action lockplate is shown, but with a completely enclosed hammer fitted onto the usual back action pivot. This variation could, of course, have been used with his falling block action, and Henry thought enough of it to improve on it in patent No. 511 of February 1869, four years later.

Henry was granted many patents for falling block rifles, hammerless and hammered. I've seen one other variation of this 1869 patent. One wonders how many of each were made and in what numbers they exist today.

Much confusion exists over the back action lock used by Henry. Some collectors have contended that all sporting rifles had right-side locks and that all military rifles had left-

A detailed and fully documented
report on the beautifully built
single shot cartridge rifles made
by the great Scottish gunmaker.

by WAL WINFER

Fig.2—This untypical Alex Henry, caliber 360 Nitro, was built (probably) on
the thin-trigger Jeffery action which, in fact, looks much like a Farquharson
action, at least externally. Serial No. 7197.

the hammer at half-cock. This was considered a safety feature when carrying the rifle at half-cock in the bush. A trailing vine or branch could catch the unbolted hammer, draw it slightly out of the half-cock notch until it slipped, broke out the notch on its return, and continued on to fire the cartridge. The serial-number study showed that the bolt change occurred between number 3,800 and 4,100, roughly, or about half-way through total production. There are few exceptions to this rule.

Now consider the thought that went into the hammered back-action design. This hammer, quite heavy and powered by a strong V-type mainspring, is arranged to increase the power of its blow as the hammer falls, through its hook up to the hammer. At the moment the hammer nose strikes the firing pin the hammer's heavily-constructed flat underside comes to rest on the long action top, thus the blow delivered (more than is needed to fire the cartridge) is absorbed along the action top, eliminating the battering of firing pin, bush or hammer nose—quite neatly done.

Only two action sizes are known to me. The small-frame type could, perhaps, be called rook size but, in the 10 or so I've seen, all were chambered for the 360/2¹⁄₄″ black powder cartridge.

side locks. Others feel that the right-side action is much rarer on a rifle that was basically a left-side hammer type. A serial-number study, together with the rifles on hand, shows that most early rifles had left-side hammers, safety bolted behind. Later rifles had right-side hammers, front bolted. Why the change was made I don't know. Nothing is certain and nothing can be taken for granted with British rifles, for there was no real standard. You could order what you wanted—and get it. A few right-side hammer types will be found among early rifles, and by the same token, a few left-side ones occurred in later production. Henry also supplied barreled actions to the trade, firms which stocked them and fitted their own locks; some had safety bolts, some none.

All of the bolted-hammer Henrys I have seen could only be bolted with

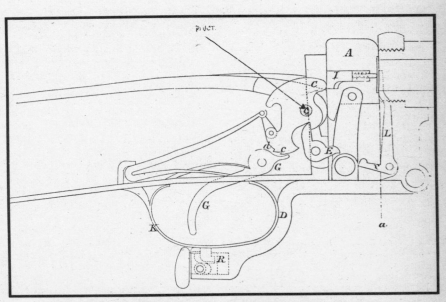

This is Alex Henry's 1869 patent, No. 511. See text for details of this system,
which appeared well before the John Farquharson patent.

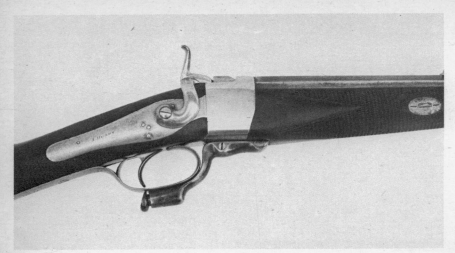

Fig. 3—Another plain-grade Alex Henry—caliber 360, built on the light-frame action, and made without hammer locking lever or bolt. Serial No. 4120.

Fig. 4—This Alex Henry rifle, chambered for the 450/3¹/₄-inch cartridge, is fully engraved in floriate/scroll designs, and has the safety bolt ahead of the hammer breast. Serial No. 4327.

This cartridge, of about 30-30 head size, was loaded with 150-gr. bullets ahead of about 60 grains of black powder; later the bullet weight was increased to 190 grains and, later again, it carried a 300-gr. jacketed bullet ahead of smokeless Cordite powder. (Do not use smokeless loads in such rifles, even though they will fit the chamber, unless the rifle is proved and so-marked for the much more powerful nitro load.)

Small Frame Henrys

The small action, quite light and neat, is essentially a scaled-down version of the larger action. All small-frame rifles I've seen have been rather plainly finished, had straight grip stocks and border-line engraved at most. Most of them have a 26″ gradually-tapered full octagon barrel—a few will be round—with a matted or cross-hatched top flat. Rifling will be typically Henry type—7 flats and a small ridge between each pair of flats. The front sight, put in from the muzzle end, slides in a narrow front-to-rear slot. Some may be secured with a tiny screw. The rear sight is dovetailed in the usual manner, across the barrel. It will ordinarily have a fixed standard leaf marked for 100 yards, and a folding leaf marked for 200 yards. Both leaves usually have a platinum line inletted vertically below the wide and shallow V, a common British usage. The barrel should show Henry's name and address, behind the rear sight and ahead of the receiver ring; and, most times, his patent and a number—this is not the patent number, note, but the usage-number of a barrel with Henry's patented rifling. All early rifles will have such a barrel number, also an action number engraved on a small flat atop the receiver ring, and the rifle's serial number on the lower

tang. Later barrels don't usually carry the barrel number, perhaps because the patent(s) had expired.

These small-frame rifles were quite light, about 5-6 lbs. on average. Recoil, even with a heavy black powder load, is mild, though more weight would be needed if one found a rifle handling the 300-gr. bullet and its Cordite powder charge.

The small-frame rifles were not, it seems, made with the safety-bolted hammer. I have been able to disassemble only one small-frame action. The lock was unmarked inside and did not have a fly fitted at the half-cock position. The lock and action inside finish was every bit as good as the most elaborate specimen examined to date, however.

The buttstock and fore-end are generally of finely-grained walnut, without cheekpiece. Henry liked checkering, and much of it will be found on the grip and fore-end, extending unbroken on both sides and bottom of the latter. Very well done, too. The fore-ends do not have the typical

Henry tip shape found on his bigger rifles, being rounded and usually not capped. Buttplates are of steel or horn, most of them steel. Fore-ends will be cross-bolted (or keyed), as are all Henrys I have seen except the take-down models.

Large-Frame Henrys

The large action—by far the most common of the two sizes, if either could be called common—will generally, but not always, carry the finest of stock wood, finished to perfection with faultless inletting. The lock, action, barrel and furniture look as if they have been nailed to a tree and the wood grew around them, so expert is the fit. Many are superbly engraved in the very best manner, but a few rifles by Henry were unadorned, as were quite a lot of those fitted up by other markers using Henry's action.

Alex Henry was certainly one of the best—if not *the* best—gunmakers in the British Isles in the late 1800s. He built many of the highest quality single and double barrel rifles of his day. Everything he made was handsomely crafted; even his plainly-finished rifles received as much handwork and attention to detail as the most elaborately engraved specimens. The balance of Henry rifles is near perfection, even though they vary in stock length, shape, barrel diameter and weight. All Henry's I've had the pleasure of handling swung, pointed and balanced almost as if alive.

Henry was, apparently, particularly fond of cheekpieces, as time wore on, and most of his later-period pistol grip models on the large-frame action have them, well placed and undercut in the best manner, with a neat fillet behind the back edge of the grip. Early rifles—for the most part—lacked cheekpieces, but about midway through production, 1880 or so, saw them gaining in favor.

A few straight-grip stock rifles were also made, generally unengraved, and having much plainer stock wood. Cheekpieces were absent on these and they were generally plainly finished. Nevertheless, the same degree of skilled handwork went into them, for quality was always a watchword with Henry.

Recoil and Castoff

The British learned early that to save one's face from the recoil of a heavy-caliber rifle or gun called for a stock with castoff—meaning that the vertical centerline of the buttplate was offset to the right about $1/4''$ to $3/8''$—for a right-handed shooter. That allowed the rifle to slide away from

Left-hand hammer Alex Henry rifle, cal. 450/3^1/4". Its 28" barrel has broad file-cut full length rib. Receiver sides, hammer, lockplate, etc., fine scroll engraved, receiver top reads "PATENT NO. 756," and the rifle number, 2774, appears on the lower tang.

the face in recoil, and the buttplate to fit more neatly—depending on the individual—into the hollow between shoulder and arm, not on the muscles of the arm. The heavy-cheeked shooter benefitted most from castoff. A final touch often seen on British firearms is the placement of the stock's toe a little farther to the right than the heel. This also helps place the buttplate in an area best able to absorb recoil with the least discomfort to the shooter.

Apart from the straight-grip military rifles, most large-frame Henry's seem to have been pistol-grip stocked; these grips will be capped in horn or in steel, the latter often having a trap or small hinged-lid compartment. The neatly-fitted hinged cover lifts up, revealing space for a spare front sight, firing pins or other small parts or springs, items one could have ordered with the original rifle. These

steel trapped gripcaps are often so well made that in a couple of engraved specimens I have seen it is impossible to detect the seams unless they're pointed out.

Fore-ends carry the well-known Henry shape—so well liked by Bill Ruger that he adopted it for his sporting No. 1 single shot rifle. Forearms are cross bolted (keyed or pinned) and, together with the pistol grip, carry profuse and finely-executed checkering.

Round barrels, nicely tapered and made with the top flatted at the breech, seem to be standard—if anything can be called "standard" on early British falling-block rifles. Some round barrel rifles have a full-length matted rib, hand filed to a cross-grooved appearance and thereby reducing glares. These ribbed barrels will have sights put on the same way as do the small-frame octagon-barrel rifles. Non-ribbed round barrel rifles have sights on small and neat ramps at breech and muzzle via the same methods of fitting. Engraved on the small ovalled flat atop the receiver ring will be found "PATENT" and a number; early rifles may carry "HENRY'S PATENT" followed by the *action* number. The serial number, as before, is found on the lower tang. Yet earlier barrels have barrel number and action number engraved following Henry's address. Later barrels carried only the barrel number and, still later, this barrel number was left off, presumably when his patent expired. However, this action number, in the receiver top, was used to the end of production.

The typical Henry military rifle, full length or carbine style, is unmarked as to barrel, action or serial numbers, so we don't know if these rifles were included in Henry's numbering system. If they were included and *not* numbered it would mean that far fewer sporting rifles are around

Fig. 5—The same 450/3^1/4-inch rifle pictured in Fig. 4, here with operating lever fully open and hammer cocked.

than the numbering system would indicate.

Henry supplied rifle actions and barrels to the trade, too. I have seen Henry hammered-action rifles carrying such names as Purdey, Holland & Holland, S. Alport, Dickson, et al—again the question, were these actions—without his number—included in Henry's numbering system or did he number only his own production? The only exception I've seen was a 450 BP rifle by E. M. Reilly which had "HENRY'S PATENT" stamped on the *rounded* receiver ring—no flat—and an indistinct number. Its left-side lock was unbolted, the hammer large and ungraceful, the work generally not up to Henry's standards.

It is not generally known that Henry made take-down rifles on a unique system, using the large frame action. He might also have made them on the small-frame system, but I don't know of any.

The barrel shank is unthreaded and is made with a taper of about 6°; a corresponding taper is formed within the receiver ring. The underside of the barrel is milled out fore-and-aft for about 1¼" and a heavy lug is inserted and silver soldered or brazed in place. The action body has a large integral bracket extending about 2" forward from the action face. This extension is milled out to take the barrel lug just noted. All three sides of the barrel lug are sloped outward, away from its leading edge; the recess

in the receiver or action bracket is similarly treated and shaped to match. The front quarter or so of the receiver extension tapers in slightly, in line with the barrel. On one side there's a pivoted latch and, being fitted on the slope, it has some camming power. Similarly a slight cam surface is formed on the back edge of the barrel lug. To seat the barrel it is pushed into its mating seat within the receiver ring and then rotated downward until the barrel lug enters the bracket extension. At this point the barrel is seated on two tapers and, to hold the rifle together, the lever latch is rotated upward until its short end overlaps the barrel lug and cams it tightly within the seat. The system is sturdy and solid. I cannot vouch for its durability after much shooting, but because the mating surfaces are large I see no reason to suspect that oft-repeated assembly/disassembly could wear the parts appreciably.

This take-down rifle has a rounded-tip fore-end, not of the typical Henry shape, and attaches to the barrel via a side-swinging lever pivoted a few inches back from the tip. This lever operates an internal cam surface mating with a slotted lug formed on the underside of the barrel. The forearm is detached by swinging the small neat lever to the right; returning it to straight ahead effectively cams and locks the forearm tightly to the barrel. A tiny stud, formed on the metal seat below the lever, mates in a hole provided in the

underside of the spring-tempered lever.

All large-action barrels seen have Henry's typical rifling—7 or more flats with a sharp ridge raised in the corner of each pair of flats, the 7-flat type giving a 14-point bearing surface to the bullet. Larger bores had more—my 577 has 11 sets. Some Henry rifles had gain-twist rifling; these start at the breech end with a slow twist, or pitch, the pitch gradually becoming faster. Many barrels were also slightly choke bored, being about .002" smaller internally at the muzzle. Both ideas, it was argued, increased accuracy. This may have been true (Harry Pope did it also) but when the British Government adopted the Henry barrel and Martini action in 1871 a standard or steady twist was used. However, such barrels were still choke bored and used Henry's form of rifling.

Big Action Marks

Various markings appear on early Henry barrels—and also on barrels by other makers who used Henry's patented rifling system—amongst them Westley Richards, Soper, Holland & Holland and a host of smaller makers. "Henry's Patent" will be found stamped or engraved close to the proof marks as will the letters A & T with a winged spear surrounded by two coiled snakes. There may be numbers present also. All of these marks will be found on the left-hand side of the barrel just above the fore-

Fig.6—A relatively early Alex Henry rifle, this specimen is chambered for the 2-inch 577 cartridge. Note the quite different profile of lockplate (a bar action rather than a back action), breechblock and operating lever, and the half-cock safety bolt behind the hammer. Serial No. 1437.

Fig.7—The same 577/2-inch Henry rifle seen in Fig.6 to show different form of the opened lever and the hammer profile.

end. (Someone out there may know what all of these markings mean; if so I'd like to hear from him.) I have no concrete evidence, but I'd guess that the letters and numbers belong to the barrel maker. I am assured that Henry did not actually make barrels at this time, which would in no way be unusual. Many British gunmakers, even large ones, bought their barrels, mostly from Birmingham. This was also true with locks, for very few makers of rifles or shotguns made their own locks, preferring to buy them from such as the famed J. Brazier (The Ashes, Wolverhampton) who specialized in such work. Though the rifle builder's name appeared on the outside of the lockplate, the inside of the plate will often show a different name.

I pulled the locks from 4 Henrys to check this. A small-frame 360 rifle was unmarked inside, nor was a 500/3¼″ straight numbered 6128, hence a quite late production piece. The small-action rifle is numbered 4120, thus made about 10 years before. Both 450/3¼″ straight rifles were marked "J. BRAZIER" on the inside. All locks had "ALEX. HENRY" engraved on the outside. The three large locks were identical internally as to pin placement, parts, shape, finish and general expertise. These three had large-bolted locks and a swinging hammer-fly at the half-cock position. The small rifle lacked fly or bolt.

Buying barrels and lockwork, even

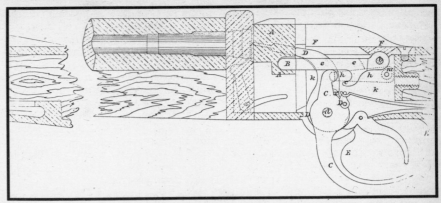

Shown here is one view of Alex Henry's patent of 1870, No. 2769, and illustrating a very early hammerless design.

sidelocks, is still practiced in Britain today. I think few British gunmakers ever made a *complete* rifle or shotgun.

Getting back to Henry and the winged-spear device, which seems confined to early production, other numbers and letters will be found stamped on action parts, the front face of the receiver and the underside of the barrel. Some of these are inspection marks or assembly numbers.

Three proof marks will usually be found on Henry BP rifles, these appearing on the left side of the barrel just in front of the action. A single proof mark will be found on the action body adjacent to the barrel proof and also one on the breechblock. This is no place for a study of proof marks but it should be pointed out that the number stamped between the barrel

proof marks is the gauge or bore size in round balls. If the number is 52 (balls to the pound) it will be of 450 caliber. For the 360 gauge figure is 105; the 577 is 25 gauge; 39 is the 500 bore.

A study of the serial numbers, action numbers and barrel numbers makes collecting Henrys an even more interesting undertaking. (Gibbs and Fraser each had a similar numbering system.) By cross-checking these various numbers it is possible to get at least a rough idea of when these rifles were made. Also, assuming Henry did indeed make barrels, any that did not go into falling blocks must have gone into double barrel rifles or were sold to the trade. Thirdly, a number of British rifles were made up for presentation, most of these having a dated presentation plate in or on the stock. Such dates give us an almost certain year of manufacture and, using this and other numbers, the year(s) of production of fall-block rifles can be approximated. I know it is dangerous to stick my neck out, but it seems clear from my study of action and serial numbers that about 32% to 38% of Henry's production was falling-block rifles.

The Production Years

Henry made these from about 1865 to the late 1890s, perhaps to about 1905 at the latest, judging from the serial numbers of his hammered falling-block rifles. Around 1900-1905 he made some rifles on the Jeffrey Farquharson action and on a later, larger Farquharson action said to have been made in Belgium for the British gun trade—it is a near Jeffrey-action copy with a top tang safety.

For many years Henry had been

Fig. 8—This Alex Henry rifle, otherwise conventional, is a rare take-down version. See fig. 9 for details.

trying to get his hammerless action accepted by the shooting public and, from 1869 to 1873, he obtained patents on more than 24 action designs. Several of these actions reached limited production, but he never managed to capture more than a quite small portion of the market.

Henry persisted with his hammer action, though, and some 2,500 were produced between 1865 and 1900 or so. Toward the end of production Henry was making about 100 of these fine sporting rifles per year. This might seem low to the general collector but it was considerably more than Gibbs made; he managed less than

found by the courts to be the inventor and an embittered Henry licked his wounds. There is today considerable doubt about Farquharson being the inventor of such a highly ingenious mechanism due to his total non-mechanical upbringing, and more doubt arises when Alex Henry's inventive genius is considered in developing falling-block designs before and after the legal suit. Be that as it may, Henry started to build rifles to the Farquharson design, since the patent had expired.

When one measures the success of Henry's hammered falling block against the hammerless actions of his

that a successful hammerless action was evolved; it had a reasonably short life (about 35 years) and it was made when 95% of the rifles offered had a large exposed hammer. Shooters of that age were slow to see any advantage in concealed-hammer rifles; they required a safety of some kind, hence there were additional parts, some rather complicated, so more could go wrong. Shooters were long familiar with a large outside hammer, they could see at a glance if the rifle was cocked, and thus it appeared safer to them. These points, coupled with a high workmanship Henry bestowed on his rifles, left little reason to make the change.

Henry's Patents

Evidence of this reluctance to change is seen in the patents taken out by Henry in the late 1860s and early 1870s for various improvements, designs that were only accepted much later (and used by other makers when the patents had expired). Henry's detachable-barrel patent (2158 of 1873) used two lugs formed on the barrel, these mating with matching recesses formed within the breech. Only a quarter-turn was needed to detach the barrel. This system was copied and used by Westley Richards as late as 1912, perhaps later, on rifles in 577, 425 and 600 Nitro built on their underlever falling-block action.

Henry patented the round breechblock (2158 of 1873) later used by Webley in their small-frame rook rifles of about 1902 and in calibers at least up to 32-40. Patent No. 2540 of 1872 covered, in part, a spring-loaded catch to hold an underlever closed. Later on Field used this same system on his side-lever falling block patented in 1877, No. 1927.

Perhaps Henry's most interesting patents covered an improvement to the back-position rifle. This 1877 patent (number unknown) used an extended trigger situated halfway along the fore-arm, at which point a seperate pistol grip was formed on much the same lines as the grip on a submachine gun.

The regular pistol grip and trigger were kept, the grip much deepened. The buttstock, behind the grip and between the buttplate, was deeply hollowed to fit over the shooters shoulder thus the stock would fit well and the extended rear pistol grip would take the recoil. The forward grip and trigger allowed the right arm to stretch out fully, allowing the rifle to be shot in the back position,

This is an Alex Henry double rifle, cal. 450-400/3¹/₄", in hammerless underlever form. Each lockplate has "COCKED" inlaid in gold ahead of the cocking indicator levers. Ahead of the tang safety is "SAFE," also inlaid in gold. All action area metal is profusely engraved in fine scroll work. The 26" barrels carry a broad file-cut rib.

The receiver top shows "HENRY'S PATENT NO. 173" and the rifle's serial number, 6334, appears on the lower tang. This rifle is cased (oak-and-leather, red felt lined) and among the usual fittings are a case sizing die with ram and knockout rod, a powder measure (not a flask), etc. Several tools are missing, however.

1,000 rifles on the Farquharson patent, but he made many other guns, of course. These hammered Henry rifles seem to have been made into the high 6,000 serial range at least, and perhaps beyond. The Jeffrey and Belgian Farquharson actions start showing up in the 7,000 serial range and it looked—at this stage—that Henry had given in on the popular Farquharson action.

In 1872 Henry and Farquharson went to court over the Farquharson action, which both men claimed to have invented. Farquharson was

competitors one may be forgiven for wondering why all the fuss was made over the need for a hammerless action. The hammerless action, of course, was the coming thing and none of the many makers busily perfecting the falling block could see the bolt-action rifle just around the corner. If the turn-bolt rifle had been delayed just 10 more years the question of a hammerless falling block would have been vital to Henry.

The success of Henry's falling block hammer rifle is not hard to understand. It was not until the early 1870s

Fig.9—The same rifle seen in Fig.8. Note tapered barrel breech (inverted) and barrel lug that mates with matching recess in action extension. Pivoted lever on extension moves upward to lock barrel. See text for further data.

yet not cramped or uncomfortable.

Many Henry falling blocks were cased outfits, usually furnished with loading details, such reloading tools as case sizers, neck reamers, steel bullet moulds (numbered to match the rifle and including an ebony-handled hollow-nose plug to fit the mould). Powder measures were also supplied, again with ebony handles as were the set of screwdrivers—or turnscrews as the British call them—and a special key to take out the firing pin. Spare firing pins, a bridle (or link) and small springs were often included as were full sets of cleaning gear, rods, special non-spill white metal oil bottles, in fact everything needed to keep the hunter shooting, down to the jointed cleaning rods and leather wallets to hold the brass brushes used.

These Henry cases were usually of oak and leather, lined with red or green felt or baize, the better ones covered in pig skin. Walled compartments around the rifle permitted the proper stowing of each piece of reloading and cleaning gear.

Besides giving a superb rifle, the best it was possible to build, we owe Henry thanks for cutting his chambers to take the standard cartridges of the day—nothing special or 'way out in case sizes or bullet diameters, so that today we can obtain brass cases and shoot our Henrys again.

Shooting the Henrys

The 450 straight is nothing but the earlier black powder version of the 450 Nitro Express; the 500 straight preceded the 500 Nitro and the 577 BP can be made from the 577 Nitro. Cases for the 450/400 can also be made from 450 Nitro. The 360/2¼" can be formed from 30-30 brass but as it will be a little short it is better to use the 9.3x72R, a case ideal as to head size; only trimming to length is needed.

Please note—in all of Henrys I've tried the 450 N.E. will fit the 450 B.P. chamber, the 500 N.E. fits the 500 B.P., and the 577/3" Nitro will fit 577/3" chambers made for black powder only, and in some cases will even fit 577s with 2¾" chambers. *Under no circumstances,* however, should nitro rounds be fired in black powder rifles. This is a highly dangerous way to get empty cases, and it could result in a blown-up rifle and perhaps, loss of life. At best it will be quickly shorten the life of a good rifle, for the steels of 1870 were not like those of nitro express days. Most actions of that black powder period were made completely of wrought iron in one form or another.

The best bullet I have found for the 450/3" and 3¼" B.P. rifles is Winchester's 300-gr. 45/90 bullet, Lyman number 456/191. The 500/3" and 3¼"

B.P. uses the 360-gr. Lyman 509/134. Bullets for the 577/2¾" and 3" can be about 530 grains.

All of the early B.P. loads used a deeply hollow-pointed bullet that was light in weight for its bore size. Thus high velocity was obtained—1700 to 1900 fps—and flat trajectory out to about 200 yards, the maximum useful range for these fast-stepping rifles. Beyond 200 yards the light bullet lost most if not all of its moderate accuracy.

We needn't worry about hollow point bullets for our needs. The tigers are long gone, and we don't need the smashing blow such bullets delivered. Solid bullets of the weight suggested will work well, and we use a caseful of black powder, which was the standard charge. Use FG only, nothing finer. It is important to "slug" barrels to ascertain actual bore-groove size, for many old rifles have varying dimensions. There was little standardization as we know it today. As noted before, many rifles were put out with bullet moulds that fitted such variant bores. No rifles will shoot well with undersize bullets and it should be noted that many old rifles have over-size bores. I have one 577 that slugs .585", a 360 that is .375" and a second that is .385". As the latter is a rook, break-open rifle, and by a maker not well known, it worries me a little. Bullets should be cast rather soft, using a little tin to help the melt flow better—about 1 to 40 or 30 would do. Harder bullets can be used but there is not much point unless one has worked up light loads of smokeless powder—such loads don't do so well in large cases. There is too much air space, wads and fillers do not help much and I am loath to use larger charges of slower powder for fear of damaging the many fine bores found in these rifles. The point is not how much the action will safely stand but rather how much damage hot smokeless powder gases in large doses do to fine rifling in soft steel barrels.

Henry rifles command large prices these days, the better ones selling for more than the famous Farquharson. At times justly so, too, for most Henrys exhibit fine fitting, magnificent stock wood, and simply superb engraving—nothing could better them. A cased Henry lying surrounded by its full set of tools and accessories is a sight not easily forgotten by any real rifleman. •

Fig.10—This view shows an Alex Henry hammerless single shot, falling-block design, probably made after Henry's patent 2769 of 1870.

A History of Proof Marks

Gun Proof in India

This new "History of Proof Marks," begun in our 22nd edition has been deeply researched by the author. With this issue we present our 12th installment, "Gun Proof in India," an interesting and instructive account.

by Lee Kennett

INDIA

SINCE INDIA offered some of the finest hunting in the world, firearms have, of course, figured in her history. When the nation was a colony, the English hunters imported their guns from London or Birmingham. There were, however, local craftsmen of varying degrees of skill who made arms for the local population. These guns were generally muzzle-loaders. The British Army also created numerous ordnance installations, including the Dum Dum Arsenal, which gave its name to the expanding bullet produced there. Manufacture of military rifles began at Ishapore in 1905.

When India proclaimed her independence in 1950, she retained many ties with her former mother country. So when the manufacture of breechloading shotguns began in 1951, they were proved at the Ishapore Rifle Factory according to the British Rules of 1925. In July, 1957, the Indian government issued its own proof rules, based upon the British ones of 1954.

In most of its text, the Indian law is identical with British 1954 rules (q.v.). Certain differences should be noted, however. There are only three classes in Indian proof: 1. breechloading shotguns, 2. breechloading rifles, and 3. all other types of arms, including black powder guns and muzzle-loaders. (There is no class for revolvers and automatic pistols, since these do not figure currently in the gun trade.) In addition to the powders prescribed in British proof, the Indian system uses two others—"G-20" and Ballistite B-16. These are surplus military powders of which large stocks are available. The G-20 is permitted for provisional proof of smoothbores and a duplex loading of the two powders is used for definitive proof.

Sizeable quantities of muzzle-loaders are still produced in India. While proof of these arms is left to the discretion of the proof master in England, the Indian rules are more explicit. Proof is according to fixed scales, these being taken from the table of charges for muzzleloaders under the British Rules of 1925.

Proof facilities are authorized in the cities of Ishapore, Kirkee, and Armapore. Two distinctive proof marks have been devised, the *Dharma* wheel (mark no.1) and the Lions of Ashoka (mark no. 2); both of these symbols are drawn from Indian history. All distinctive marks are given in the accompanying table; for others see under the British Rules of 1954.

GUN PROOF IN INDIA

Rules of 1957 Mark no.	Mark	Significance
1	 P	Provisional proof of smoothbore barrels.
2	 BP	Definitive black powder proof

GUN PROOF IN INDIA

Rules of 1957 Mark no.	Mark	Significance
3	NP	Definitive nitro proof
4	SP	Special definitive proof
5	R	Reproof of a barrel or arm

Marks in use from 1953 to 1957

6	V	View mark
7	P	Definitive proof mark
8	CHOKE	Supplementary mark for choke barrels

Gun Proof in India

An Historical Account

This portion of our "History of Proof Marks" was researched
and written by the former Proof Master at the
Rifle Factory Proof House, Ishapore, India. His comments
on his experiences there make most interesting reading.

by A. G. HARRISON

Historical Retrospect

Proof testing of military sporting rifles, shotguns and
revolvers is carried out at the Rifle Factory at Ishapore,
West Bengal, 17 miles north of Calcutta. A broad gauge
railway line connects the Ishapore station to the factory.

It is generally believed that Ishapore got its name from
one Isha Khan who was one of the twelve landlords of
Bengal during the reign of the Mogul emperor, Akbar,
circa 1572. The word "pore" means village.

In 1722 Ishapore was the site of the Ostend Company,
formed under a charter granted that same year by the
Emperor of Austria, whose flag was flown there. During
1722-1733 two bungalows were built at Ishapore as resi-
dential quarters for Ostend officers.

Today these quarters are known as No. 8 and No. 4, the
Park.

The Ostend Co. met with bitter resistance from the
British, Dutch and French settlements, lying across the
Hugli river. The British settled around Calcutta, their
main stronghold Fort William. The Dutch settled at
Serampore and Bandel, the French at Chandernagore.
These place names are still with us today.

In 1733 the Moslem ruler of the Hugli district, contigu-
ous to and north of Bandel, besieged Ishapore and the
European settlement was abandoned.

In 1756 Diraj-ud-Dowlah, Moslem ruler of Bengal, was
granted bivouac facilities at Ishapore. From there he
launched an attack on Fort William by road and river.
This assualt resulted in the infamous Black Hole of
Calcutta.

In 1757 Robert Clive defeated Siraj-ud-Dowlah at the
battle of Plassey, and the eastern bank of the river Hugli
from Murshidabad to Dum Dum fell into British hands.
Ishapore was part of this tract.

The East India Co. had from the early 18th century
established gunpowder mills at Fort William, Akra and
Perrin Gardens, all within the precincts of Calcutta city.
In 1788 The East India Co. planned to open another
gunpowder mill at Ishapore. Construction commenced in
1789. Completed in 1791, work started there that same
year. The first Gunpowder Agent was John Farquhar, who
served from 1789 to 1814.

Mr. John Farquhar first resided in the building now
known as No. 8, the Park. Sometime in 1800 Mr. Farquhar took residence at the building now known as No. 4,
the Park.

There were several explosions at the Ishapore mills; the
records show one each in 1795, 1796, 1799 and 1800, plus
two in 1802 and 1809.

In 1832 Lord William Bentick, Governor-General of
Bengal, suspended gunpowder manufacture at Ishapore,
but records show that gunpowder continued to be made at
Ishapore after 1832. These records indicate that the
Ishapore Gunpowder Manufactory commenced work on
January 1, 1791, as noted above, was closed from 1829 to
1832, but recommenced work in 1832. It did not cease
operation until June 1, 1902,

In 1901 the British Government in India proposed to
erect a factory for the production of small arms and for the
overhaul and repair of machine guns. The erection of the
Rifle Factory was started in 1903 on the site of the old
Gunpowder Factory, Ishapore.

Lt. Col. H. B. Foote, Royal Artillery, was the first
Superintendent of the Rifle Factory, serving from July
1903 to 22 May, 1914.

A page from Colonel Foote's diary reads:

Erection commenced	22-8-1903
First shaft erected	22-4-1904
Power turned on	26-9-1905
First rifle proved	22-9-1907
Production commenced	March 1908

Before 1917 the wood for rifle stocks was imported, but
from then on local walnut and maple were used. Between
1918 and 1919 the factory manufactured 36,037 rifles of
S.M.L.E. Mk. III pattern and converted 22,636 rifles for
Mk. 7 ammunition. Also made were 9,200 bayonets of Mk.
II pattern for S.M.L.E. rifles.

Military Proof Marks and Tests of India

Before 1908 proof-tested military small arms were
imported into India from England.

During the regime of the East India Co. all small arms
brought into India by them were impressed with the East
India Co. marks of ownership, and in some cases a
Rampant Lion was used. However, this Lion mark does
not necessarily accompany the East India mark.

 The East India Co. mark.

 A flintlock musket barrel marking.

 The Lion mark.

On the breech screw strap this mark appeared: G.R. 3

This would clearly indicate a George the Third musket, which musket is positively the India Pattern Musket, proved at the London Proof House.

An early 19th century Brown Bess musket was found with the following marks:

   DAVID

    REA 1801 ◁

A Victorian caplock musket had the following marks:

Lockplate

 1864 Enfield

 Proof mark on barrel

You will notice that this caplock musket lacks the East India Co. mark; the administration in India was taken over by the British Crown circa 1864. However, there are exceptions to the rules! I have found another form of East India Co. mark on a B.S.A.-made 1877 Snider Mk. II .577 rifle.

 This mark is found on the lockplate, back of the hammers.

Whether the East India Co. was allowed to use the Crown with their own monogram by design or default I don't know, but there it is.

Another Victorian Snider with the following marks was found:

 1864 ENFIELD

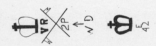 **Receiver ring**

 **Barrel**

 On strap

You will notice that this arm was subjected to two proofs, both blackpowder. 1. Provisional Proof or 1st Proof, to which the barrel only is subject; 2. Definitive Proof or 2nd Proof for barrel and receiver. The other marks are War Department ownership and viewer marks, that is, Crown, E (Enfield) and 10 or 42, the examiner's number.

The earliest rifles made at Ishapore were of the SMLE Mk. III pattern. The proof marks impressed on the barrel rounds and receivers were:

 This means Edward Rex Imperator, that is, King Edward VII.

 On bolt head claws and bolt handles appear the crossed flags.

In this arm the lockplate is 1802 and barrel 1801.

 East India mark **Lion mark**

During the reigns of George V and George VI the barrel and receivers of the SMLE Mk. III* rifles made and proof tested in India were struck thus:

 The bolt head claws and bolt handles continued to be impressed with the crossed flags only.

The GRI and Crown proof marks continued to be used until June 1953, though India became a republic on 26 January 1950. From June 1953 the Indian national proof stamps replaced the King George marks. This stamp is a stylized form of the Lion mount of the Ashok Pillar including an abacus. The mount surmounts crossed flags and the letter P thus:

 On receivers and barrels.

 On bolt handles and bolt head claws the crossed flags appear.

This Ashoka Lion stamp is impressed on barrels and receivers after passing proof test. The crossed flags (only) are still impressed on bolt handles, bolt head claws, breechblocks, etc. On hardened surfaces of such components the crossed flags were etched.

From 1908 to 1950 all military bolt action rifles made at Ishapore were proof-tested with a dry proof round followed by an oiled proof round. The proof cartridge was loaded to 24 tons psi breech pressure, or 25% higher than the service pressure. In 1950 the material for rifle bodies was altered from an EN steel to SWES 48 steel (not heat treated) except for the recoil shoulder and cam recess in the receiver. With this change rifle receivers distorted when oiled proof cartridges were fired. This was discovered when hard and sometimes impossible bolt retraction was experienced. Large quantities of rifles were rejected. To avoid rejections the authorities ordered discontinuance of the oiled proof. Therefore, from 1950 to the end of SMLE rifle production (June 1965) rifles made at Ishapore were proof tested with one dry proof only, although the specification called for both dry and oiled proof. All bolts and bolt heads issued as spares were always proofed with a dry proof round only.

Machine guns were never mass produced at Ishapore, but LMG Brens were repaired and Bren barrels for these repared LMGs were manufactured at Ishapore. These barrels were proof tested with the dry proof round and marked with the crossed flags only.

It may be mentioned a self-loading rifle similar to the British L1A1 was more or less mass produced at Ishapore since November 1962. These rifles are first proof tested with a dry proof round and followed with an oiled proof round. The receiver and barrels are marked with the Indian national proof Mark. The breechblocks and slides are etched with the crossed flags only.

A bolt action rifle similar to the SMLE Mk. III*, modified to fire the 7.62mm NATO cartridge, was produced at Ishapore, first in February 1965. Their receivers were made of SWES 48 steel, un-heat-treated, and with the NATO proof cartridge receivers were found to distort with the oiled or the dry proof round! The material was changed to an EN steel so now the rifles stand up better to dry and oiled proof. After passing proof the receivers and barrels are impressed with the Indian national proof stamp. The bolt handles and bolt head claws are struck with the crossed flags only.

Proof Tests and Proof Marks of Sporting Arms in India

The manufacture of sporting arms in India began in October or November of 1952. At the time Mr. M. N. Walton, an Englishman, was superintendent of the Rifle Factory, Ishapore.

Due to restrictions on importing foreign sporting arms into India, and to satisfy native demand, Mr. Walton suggested that an English-made double barrel shotgun be copied. A 25-year old B.S.A. shotgun was drawn from the Rifle Factory museum and used as a model. The sample gun was disassembled for compiling component drawings.

By February 1953 the first lot of guns and barrel tubes were completed and sent to the London Proof House. However, the guns and tubes were promptly rejected because they were considered "not in a fit state for proof test." The following comments were offered by the London Proof Master.

a) The barrels are "rivelled," meaning that the bores are very wavy, thus impossible for the viewer in pre-proof

and after-proof views to determine changes in the bores, if any.

b) Chambers not to gauge; they do not accept the Proof House chamber gauges.

c) Action "off the face" more than .002". Since guns are rejected if a .002" gap appears *after* proof, obviously a gap larger than .002" cannot be accepted before proof.

d) Looseness in action. There is perceptible shake between barrels and action body.

e) The tubes sent for provisional proof were not accepted because they were chambered, hence making it impossible to fit a plug.

When the guns and tubes came back to Ishapore they were altered according to the advice of the London Proof Master. The guns were then sent to the Rifle Factory Proof House, where I was Proof Master. I was asked to accept the guns as 12 bore barrels. I rejected them because the bore diameters were less than .729". The bores were then lapped out to accept the .729" plug gauge and returned to the proof house. The first Indian-made shotguns passed proof in March 1953.

The system of proofing, charge weights and markings was based on the English Proof Rules of 1925.

There were two proof tests for shotguns: 1) Provisional and 2) Definitive. In provisional proof gun tubes with plugs were fired off in a series of 5 tubes at a time with the aid of low-tension electric fuzes and a 6-volt battery. For Definitive proof the semi-completed guns were submitted in the white but without stocks. The guns were tested in a proof carriage. These methods are still used at Ishapore.

The proof charges were same as those tabulated for breech-loading shotguns in the English Proof Rules of 1925. T.P.P.H. and T.S.P. gunpowders are imported from the U.K. through Imperial Chemical Industries. The Rifle Factory at Ishapore manufactures only 12-ga. shotguns with 2½" and 2¾" chambers. No other gauge of shotgun is made in India just now.

The proof marks used from 1953 to June 1957 follow:

a) Provisional Proof: The Dharma (fate) wheel, surmounting the letter P, is struck on each barrel forward of the flats. This wheel appears on the abacus below the lion's paws, in the Lion Mount shown on the next page.

b) Definitive Proof: The Ashoka Lion mount surmounting the letter P. Struck on the barrel flats.

c) View: The Ashoka Lion Mount surmounting the letter V.

d) Nitro Proof: The Ashoka Lion Mount surmounting the letters NP.

e) Gauge of gun in diamond:

f) Chamber length in inches, that is, 2½" or 2¾".

g) Smokeless powder proof and shot load: NITRO PROOF 1⅛ oz. or NITRO PROOF 1¼ oz.

The word CHOKE is impressed only if the barrel is choke bored.

The Rifle Factory's double barrel shotguns were bored left barrel full choke, right barrel cylinder. Single barrel shotguns have full choke barrels. In the case of single barrel shotguns the marks from b) to g) are struck on the right side of the barrel breech just above the action line when action and barrel are assembled. The mark a) is struck ahead of the lug or on the barrel steel. Below is a drawing showing placement of marks on double barrel shotguns.

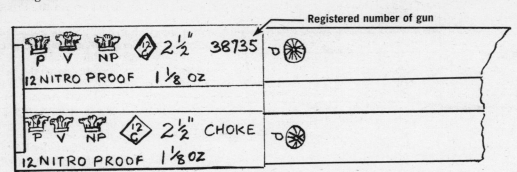

Registered number of gun

12 NITRO PROOF 1⅛ OZ

12 NITRO PROOF 1⅛ OZ

Right barrel is marked with gun number. Left barrel is choke marked.

In 1965 Col. R. Williams, working at the Kirkee Ammunition Factory, suggested to the Government of India that the large stocks of Ballistite-B16, usually used for grenade cartridges, could be used for the definitive proof of shotguns. He suggested the following duplex loads of Ballistite B16 and blackpowder for 12-ga. shotguns:

Gauge	Chamber	B'stite B16	Blackpowder	#6 soft shot
12	2½"	14 grs.	145 grs.	1¹¹⁄₁₆ 0 .
12	2¾"	14 "	175 "	2 oz.

The Ballistite was loaded first, followed by a .005"-thick celluloid cup. Over this went the blackpowder, followed by a ½" felt wad. Loaded thus the cartridge cases were inserted into the chambers, the shot charges then poured into the barrels from the muzzles and one ½" felt wad was rammed down in each barrel.

I protested this duplex loading, commenting that the burning and loading characteristics of Ballistite and blackpowder are so dissimilar that they are not conducive to duplex loading. However, the Government of India, gulled, accepted the Colonel's suggestion and this shotgun proof charge became law in India, being incorporated into the rules of proof.

As I've said, only 12-gauge shotguns are made in India. Adequate knowledge and skills with regard to other gauges and their respective cartridges is woefully lacking. However, between January and May 1958 private gunmakers did send shotguns of 14, 16 and 20 gauge to the Proof House. At this time I was away on duty at Kirkee, and when I returned I found that these shotguns were being altered in the chambers to accept 12 gauge cartridges, the only size available. These guns of 14, 16 and 20 gauge were being accepted for proof and were being "proved" and marked as 12 gauge guns!

I was on the Board of Inquiry to investigate this mess. It came out that the officers and staff had ordered the alteration of the gun chambers because only 12-gauge cartridges were available in the Proof House. The people

This is the Ashoka Lion Mount in stylized form, the proof mark used on all Indian-made guns and rifles. There are, in fact, four lions, and at the feet of each is a Dharma (fate) wheel. Between each wheel is an animal, there being four in all: bull, horse, rhinoceros and goat. The Dharma wheel derives from Bhuddism, not Hinduism.

involved informed the Board that they were not aware that shotguns of different gauges had different dimensioned changes. Over one thousand of the dangerous guns were released for sale before the error was discovered.

In June 1957 the first written Indian Proof Rules were published and became statutory law. These were a near-Chinese copy of the British Proof Rules of 1954 (effective from 1st February 1955). Hence the proof scales, chamber sizes and dimensions and other dimensional data given in the British Proof Rules Appendixes have been copied into the Indian Proof Rules of 1957. Again, the classification of arms and other parts of the British 1954 Proof Rules have been dutifully copied in the Indian Proof Rules of 1957. These rules are now current.

There is, however, a slight difference in marks on Indian-made muzzle-loading shotguns versus British marks. The Ashoka Lion mount surmounts the letters BP and the words NOT NITRO. In the British Proof Rules BP stands for Birmingham Proof, and NOT NITRO is used as the London blackpowder stamp. These letters and words are combined to indicate blackpowder proof in India.

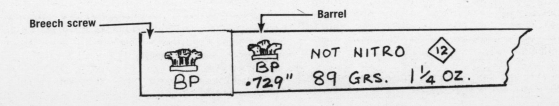

Breech screw

Barrel

BP

BP .729" NOT NITRO 89 GRS. 1¼ OZ. ⑫

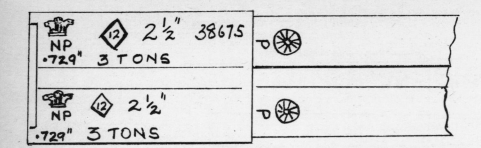

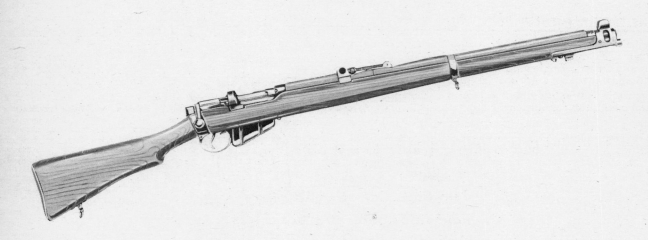

One of the many types of rifles made at Ishapore was the SMLE Mk. III*, a common pattern and well made. Enfield collectors consider Ishapur-made rifles necessary items to fill out their collections. Text gives details of the various marks applied to the guns.

Here I should like to add some remarks on Indian methods and proof rules—these comments may sound caustic, but as we are the searchers for the truth, there is nothing like telling it.

1. Although it is provided in the Indian Proof Rules of 1957 that proof loads should be adjusted and established by firing 5 service loads (see British rules 1954, Part IV), in the Indian Proof House there is no apparatus to determine the charge pressure. Nevertheless, sporting rifles and shotguns are marked with the service pressures, that is, for 12 gauge shotguns, 3 TONS and 3¼ TONS respectively.

2. No Indian ammunition factory appears capable of manufacturing cartridges except 9mm Parabellum, 380 Webley, 22 rimfire, 7.62mm NATO and 303 British Mk. VII. However, these are not the variety found in commercial manufacture. The cartridges mentioned are currently made for military arms.

Why were the Indian Rules, Regulations and Scales copied from the British system? Well, perhaps to show those concerned knew much—like flaunting an ability one does not have.

Sometime in 1958 during a duty absence another mess was discovered. Muzzle-loading shotguns were being stamped with the Nitro Proof stamp but proofed with the blackpowder service load. On my return from duty, while passing through the Final View room, I discovered the stamper striking the following stamps on a 12-gauge muzzle-loading shotgun:

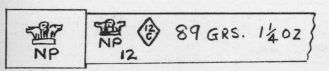

When I quizzed the man he showed me an instructional blueprint indicating this form of stamping. I approached the authorities, who challenged me to prove that muzzle-loading shotguns should not be proof tested for nitro powders. It took me over two days to get the information to penetrate their skulls. At last there was an awakening and the stamps and instructions were altered. Over 1500 guns were accepted and passed to the public before the alteration.

In 1962 an Indian officer at the Chief Inspectorate of Armaments, Kirkee, came up with a boner which was accepted by the Indian Government. This officer suggested that the Ballistite B16 and blackpowder charges (duplex load) for the Definitive Proof of 12-gauge breech-loading shotguns be reversed. That is, the black powder be poured into the capped case first, followed by a celluloid cup .005″ thick; then the Ballistite B16 was to be poured in, followed by an over-powder ½″ thick felt wad. Thus the black powder would be next to the cap, the Ballistite on top, under the overpowder wad. The powder charges were altered as follows:

Gauge	Chamber	B'stite B16	Blackpowder	#6 soft shot
12	2½″	30 grs.	130 grs.	1¹¹⁄₁₆ 0 .
12	2¾″	33 ″	100 ″	2 oz.

Notice the 30-grain Ballistite load for a 2¼″ chamber and the higher 33 grains of Ballistite for a 2¾″ chamber; then note the higher blackpowder charge weight for the smaller chamber! What can one make of this?

These loadings are incorporated in the India Proof Rules of 1957.

●

THE 6TH RUNNING of this big annual affair, held in London March 12-14, was a much-improved session, certainly from the standpoint of spaciousness, general lighting and so on. Held in the Alexandra Palace (about which more later), some 9 miles north of London's East End, roughly, the cavernous interior offered much better facilities than the Hotel Nikko had in 1977. The aisles were wide, the booths larger, there was no sense of crowding.

Situated on a low hill top—the countryside in good weather is visible for miles—the Alexandra Palace is an unbelievably ugly building, a jumbled, awkward mass of brick and stone in a decaying condition. In the circumstances—having to find space for some 350 exhibitors, the largest number in the Exhibition's history—

Christian de Moffarts had to find a big enough hall, and this was it.

With 350-odd exhibitors there was no way I could adequately cover them all, but with Roger Barlow's able help we did pretty well. Not that there were any strikingly new products, that is, items of new and original design. There were, of course, several upgradings or improved versions of this and that.

The growing importance of the European Hunting and Shooting Exhibitions held in a different European capitol each year is attested to by the growing number of American firms that participate. The 6th such annual trade show was held in London during March of 1978.

Winchester, Remington, Federal, Hornady, Sturm-Ruger and 25 other U.S. firms were there. Only the Ital-

ians with 49 exhibitors and France with 36 had greater representation. In all there were 16 nations and over 300 companies participating in this year's Exhibition arranged by Christian de Moffarts, of Belgium.

Firearms, ammunition, fishing gear, outdoor clothing, knives, trap and Skeet equipment, reloading supplies and equipment, scopes and binoculars, decoys, stock blanks and hunting and fishing magazines were only part of the items on display—not for the public—to enable manufacturers, importers, exporters and wholesalers to arrange their commercial contracts for the coming year.

Some of the new items we saw there may be on the market here in the U.S. soon after this appears in print. Our photographic coverage of this Exhibition will, perhaps, serve as a sort of personally conducted tour:

European Hunting & Shooting Exhibition 1978

The 6th running of this great event, held in London this time, was easily the biggest and best—over 300 exhibitors displayed their wares to the throngs of buyers.

by JOHN T. AMBER

Famars (Abbiatico & Salvinelli) showed their latest small-bore shotguns, two well worth examining closely, and both firsts for the firm. Both are over-unders with low-profile Boss-system frames, very trim looking and with superb handling qualities. The 410 frame is *not* the same size as the 28-gauge—which might well have been the case had another maker produced these—but smaller. Mario A. also had a sample of his latest fore-end "iron," this one of easy-opening design and which he'll be using soon on various models. Not least, certainly, was a magnificent piece of Fracassi's inimitable engraving, mounted under a magnifying glass. This master of the *bulino* technique—extremely fine-lined portraiture—had cut a wondrously delicate and beautifully rendered cloud effect in the background. The sun's rays, breaking through the billowing cloud formation, made a scene that must be seen to be fully appreciated. I've never seen better work.

London Show Report

Your Editor and Christian de Moffarts, organizer of this big trade show, have a visit on opening day.

Pictured nearby, I hope, is a prototype rifle (one of 3) that Mario will be offering in about two years. However, I have a hunch he could cut that time if he heard from enough serious customers. The side-by-side express double rifle shown is chambered for the 9.3×74R—very popular in Europe—but it will also be offered in 375 H&H and 458 Winchester. A new receiver, extra strong, was designed in Mario's shop, along with special lockplates of back-spring type. Without scope or mounts the new D.B. rifle weighs about 7½ lbs.; with a Zeiss Diavari variable in Suhl-style mounts the weight is about 9 lbs.

The prototype 9.3 was shot 40 times in one test, the extreme spread at 60 meters going about 3½ inches. That's a fine performance for that many rounds, and some 4-shot groups (with the Zeiss scope attached) ran around 2½ inches.

Mario was reluctant to fix prices now, for fear of what inflation might do in the next 24 months, but he thought the cost then might be $5,000-$6,000 for the single, unadorned D.B. rifle pictured.

Renato Gamba had a most impressive double booth, with many examples of fine handmade guns on view. His extensive line runs the gamut now—side-by-sides predominate, naturally, but over-unders, drillings and single barrels (including his revived Mustang single shot break-open rifle) are included, all handsomely made and clasically styled. One of his latest, the London, is appropriately named—stocked in the tradition of best British double guns, the engraving restrained and tasteful. It should do well in the British Isles.

Don Allen, custom gunmaker/ stocker of Northfield, Minn., and some of his fellow craftsmen, were the only Americans exhibiting their high skills at Alexandra Palace. For some time before the show opened, Don and I had talked about several more stock artists getting together to exhibit at London, but that wasn't to be. However, Al Lind, himself a fine stockmaker, and Mark Lee, a very much first class metalsmith were on hand, and Don had brought over several flitches of the attractive stock blanks he imports, most of them from New Zealand. Don's stock-carving machine, probably the best of such tools now available, attracted considerable interest too.

M. Chapuis, the French gunmaker whose low-priced double rifles I've described elsewhere in this issue (he exhibited at the NSGA Houston show), showed his attractive rifles at London, but he had lost no time in raising his prices! His base cost at Houston for his standard boxlock D.B. rifle was $1,054, FOB the factory, but he'd upped that some 20% for London. I'm sure his costs have not jumped that much, but I suspect his Houston prices were hastily arrived at. All who viewed his D.B. rifles thought the earlier price unrealistic. I'd asked M. Chapuis for a test rifle at Houston, but it hasn't arrived as of now (late March), and I fear it won't reach me in time for a shooting report.

I'm happy to report, from a personal-use standpoint, that I found a new claybird trap machine on display that is exactly what I've been after for years. Being alone here at Creedmoor Farm, with rarely a helper to give me a hand, I've searched for years for an automated trap, one with a magazine for, say, 25 to 50 birds, and one which would be self-loading and self-cocking.

M. Chapuis (left), a French gunmaker, makes a gratifyingly inexpensive double rifle—about $1275 delivered in France.

Two stages in the making of a new low-profile 28 or 410 over-under shotgun receiver designed by Abbiatico & Salvinelli—a solid steel billet was the beginning.

An example of Renato Gamba's English-styled double 12 bore is profusely engraved on its rounded frame.

This is Armi Famars' latest design, a double express rifle elegant in its simplicity, and built on a new stock frame. See text for details.

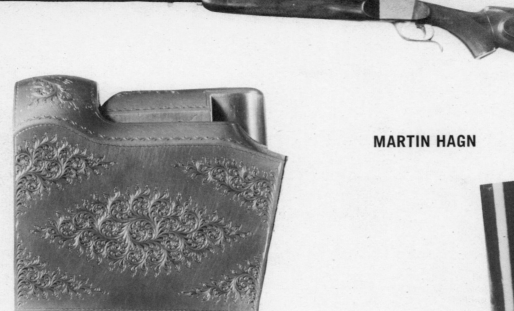

MARTIN HAGN

Martin Hagn, a gunmaker in the best sense of the term, might be called, perhaps, a footloose craftsman—he's worked here in the U.S., Alaska included, on one or more occasions, though he's now settled down in Kochel a. See, West Germany. Hagn, a free spirit and a creative gun designer, has been granted several German patents on a single shot action developed by him.

Hagn informed me that a complete rifle, using his next-to-latest action design, had been sent to me, but so far it's not here. I'd hoped to give a first-hand report on it, but . . . I saw several years ago at a Houston NSGA show about as compact a single shot action as I'd ever seen—the receiver was less than two inches long, its height under that, but attempts to get details from the man showing it were fruitless. Then, last year, Hagn wrote to me, describing the same action I'd seen at Houston and sending photos of it. As before, I was impressed with its ultra compactness, the more so when Hagn said that the rifle seen here was in 300 Winchester Magnum.

Hagn's action, though showing some external similarities to the Heeren action in the curvature of the receiver-ring top and in the breech-block, differs completely from the Heeren internally. Hagn's action is a falling or dropping block type, actuated by a more or less conventional center underlever—the Heeren action uses a rear-pivoted trigger guard to open and close the action, and the internal parts differ materially from the Hagn design in form and function. I've wondered for years why most single shot actions were so bulky and, thereby, heavy. What need was there for all that mass of metal, as in the Winchester High Wall, and in the modern copies of it? Surely not for strength as such—many earlier single shot actions have more "lug" area support than do most bolt actions. Too, what valid reason is there for the excessive length of such earlier S.S. actions, particularly the falling-block types, in which access to the chamber for loading/unloading is unimpeded? Why the long tangs, top or bottom or both? Such rifles cannot be handsomely stocked—the comb nose is, unavoidably, too far back.

The light, compact Hagn action, amply adequate to withstand high gas pressures, tang free or nearly so, stiffened and secured by a bolt running through the buttstock, seems to answer all requirements, I believe. The Hagn action fits this bill of particulars, as I see it. (Aside from their bulk and weight, the two FBW actions, large and small, made without tangs, answer well, too. Both use adequately strong through bolts.)

Unfortunately, the Hagn rifle is not yet here, so I can't particularize, but you'll get the idea from the picture(s) we'll show. It was shipped Air Mail, and attempts to trace it have produced nothing.

This is the one-man-operable claybird trap made by MCM (Mathalienne de Construction Mecanique) of France. The magazine holds 35 targets, loaded and released automatically via a 12V motor.

The new **MCM** (Mathalienne de Construction Mecanique) device, made in France, is exactly as I'd have it, and as far as I can learn no one else anywhere offers the type. The centrally-located magazine holds 35 clays, these fed one at a time (doubles are not feasible) to the throwing arm. The latter is power cocked via a 12-volt DC powered motor and, once cocked and loaded, may be released by actuating a 25-meter long cable, ending in a hand- or foot-powered release switch. Target speeds are normally set for International Shooting Union velocities, which means that's a fast bird going away.

The machine is well and sturdily built, many of its working components thick steel castings or heavy-gauge sheet metal. Ordinarily, that is, in manual operation (which is a mode instantly available), a loader sits behind the throwing section in a tractor-type seat, cocking the release arm by hand and, at will, varying the lateral angle of throw within about 80 degrees. A curved steel section controls this, as it does elevation as well. A similar curved segment is optional, but this one is cut to allow a wide range of elevation throws, the operator lifting the throwing section into or out of a series of notches.

This is the only defect, if that's the right word, in the MCM machine from a one-man use of it. In my use I'll place the trap forward of my shooting position, as is the case in standard trapshooting, anywhere from a few yards to 25 yards, maximum distance limited only by the 25-meter cable. Shooting thus I'll be unable to alter lateral and/or vertical departure of the targets unless I walk forward now and then to re-set the controls. Well, I can't have everything, and I'm amply pleased with the MCM machine as offered.

Now for the so-called bad news—the MCM machine, as described and with the optional elevation segment, plus a handful of spare parts, sells for about $1100 in France, FOB some designated port or airfield. What U.S. Customs and shipping charges will be I don't know yet, but the machine is semi-portable, having two wheels forward and a lifting handle behind the seat. I'd guess its shipping weight at about 250 lbs., not including a 12-volt car battery, of course. I think I'll want to rig up a 110V-12V DC converter to offset battery drain—which must be fairly heavy—or use a 12V charger during operation. The latter would be simpler and cheaper if it kept the battery charged up adequately. One of the MCM machines is being sent to us for trial, and I'll report further if time permits.

On hand at the Famars stand was Firmo Fracassi, one of the world's truly great gun engravers, with examples of recently engraved guns as well as some partially completed lockplates and frames.

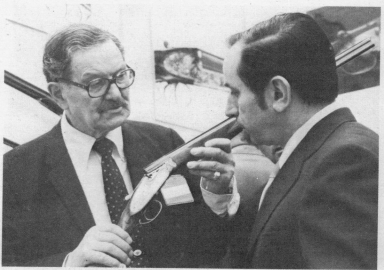

First call was on old friends at the Famars stand to see Mario Abbiatico's delightful new small sidelock O-U, which will be available only in 410 bore or 28 gauge, at least for a while.

Friedrich Wilhelm **Heym** had a representative group of their sporting firearms at London, though certainly not every variation in their extensive line. Herr Peter Bang, whom I've known for a couple of years now, was in charge of the display, and Bill Ruger managed to visit Heym's booth to examine the Heym/Ruger No. 1 single shot rifle—restocked in the German fashion—and sometimes rebarreled for certain metric cartridges. Bill liked the work, he told me later, and intends to add one to the Sturm, Ruger study collection.

Col. Tom Turpin, a member of the U.S. Armed Forces in Germany, came over to London to give Herr Bang a hand. Elsewhere in this edition you'll find Col. Turpin's article on the Heym operation, with photographs of various models included.

The **Ferlach** (Austria) Genossenschaft's large stand held a brilliant array of best quality sporting arms—virtually every piece profusely engraved, many of them rich with gold or silver inlaying, and fancy to ultra-fancy walnut found in the buttstocks and fore-ends. Dr. Lauren **Kortz,** an old Ferlach native who now lives and works in Belgium, was on hand to greet me and to tell me about his latest wildcat, a 459 Magnum! On view at the Ferlach booth were three bergstutzen rifles, a favorite style of mine—over-under double rifles chambered for two unlike calibers, one for game season, the other a smaller caliber for off-season or varmint shooting. **Franz Sodia,** the well-known Ferlach gunmaker, did not attend, but a few of his handsomely prepared guns were on view.

Hartmann & Weiss operate a custom gunshop in Hamburg, West Germany. I had been introduced to their work via a letter from Martin Hagn, another German gunmaker who I'll comment on later. I'd corresponded with Mr. Weiss before going to London, and he'd sent me good color photos of their work. Most impressive, believe me, and done in typically English or American styling, not at all Germanic or Austrian—no hogback comb lines, no tightly curling pistol grips. Instead, clean and elegant classic forms. Though H&W wouldn't have a stand at M. de Moffarts' show, Mr. Weiss would come over with a couple of their rifles, which I was invited to examine.

In spite of the fine color views, I wasn't quite prepared for what I saw! The first rifle was based on a 98 Mauser action, the stock a terrific piece of French walnut. The entire receiver area was covered with low-

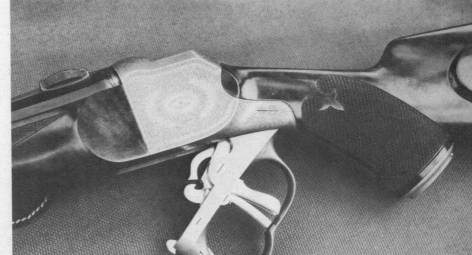

This is Heym's special treatment of the Ruger No. 1 single shot rifle, offered in numerous metric and U.S. calibers up to the 375 H&H. A full-length stock version is an option, as are octagon barrels, etc. Hand engraved game animals, plus scroll work are standard, as is a Canjar set trigger. Prices, from $1225.

The Heym 33N drilling (3-bbl. gun-rifle) is similar to their Models 55/77. Made in 12, 16 or 20 gauge plus a rifle barrel, calibers to 375 H&H. The boxlock sells for $2785; the sidelock $3475 to $4035. A double-rifle drilling is $4830 to $5480.

Heym's 55 BFSS over-under rifle-shotgun. The rifle calibers range from the 5.6x50R to the 375 H&H. A boxlock version is also available. Prices are slightly higher than the O-U shotguns—$2235 to $3765.

This Heym over-under rifle is handsomely engraved in the German tradition.

The unique Heeren action is a favorite of Hartmann & Weiss. This specimen is superbly fashioned in every respect.

relief engraving of the highest quality, plus areas of scroll and floriation, and much gold line work strategically positioned. The receiver, floorplate, guard and bolt were case-colored in brilliant fashion, the flowing, variegated colors bright and gleaming. That all sounds pretty gaudy, doesn't it? Yet it was not—the various elements were blended together in a subtle pattern, the effect of the whole striking without being offensive. I don't think I've seen a better example of bolt action rifle treatment. Cost? About $6,000, yet Mr. Weiss said they couldn't keep up with their orders!

The several Hartmann & Weiss firearms examined here were of the highest quality and their stocks, which had a very high gloss, were in fact oil finished! The case shown here holds a 12-bore sidelock double, the lockplates and other action areas beautifully engraved and case colored. Various accessories are in the case, including several horn-handled screwdrivers.

Louis Vrancken created this striking masterpiece as a special-order design on a Browning over-under double with the inlaid false sideplates. Magnificent work, perfectly laid out.

A handsome side-by-side double rifle, styled in the English tradition, the maker Casartelli & Son of Italy. Excellent workmanship, but small production. Over-under express rifles are also made.

Inflation and the dollar/Deutsche mark situation have done us in.

The other rifle was built around one of the world's oldest single shot rifles, the Heeren, first produced about 1880, I think, at Strasbourg-and-Baden, Germany, by or for the designer, Arturo Heeren y Massa (I have an original specimen, an 11mm,, and so marked). Not as elaborately embellished as the 98 Mauser I'd just handed back to Mr. Weiss, the Heeren was without the gold inlay work. It was, however, profusely and excellently engraved—game scenes, scroll, floriate designs—the stock and fore-end beautifully figured and colored a rich, warm reddish. Not as costly as the other, the Heeren would sell for a paltry $3,000. Does that sound like a putdown? I don't mean it that way—I consider $3,000 an attractive price, indeed paltry. What will it bring, say, 5 or 10 years hence?

Hartmann & Weiss will celebrate their 5th (or may be their 3d) anniversary this year, and I've been invited to attend the soiree. Granted the time—and the money—I hope to attend.

Peter Dyson runs a gunshop and factory at Honley in England. We'd corresponded about the very wide assortment of accessories and tools he makes for use with 19th century cap-lock firearms—turnscrews of many styles and sizes, cap magazines in several forms, nipples in several sizes, and much more—too many to detail here, but a letter to him at 29-31 Church Street, Honley, Huddersfield, Yorkshire HD7 2AH, England, along with $1 for return air mail postage will bring you his brochures or catalog. Don't send U.S. stamps.

Mr. Dyson was at the London show briefly, as was his lovely wife, and I saw at first hand the very wide range of attractive products he makes and markets.

My old friends from Spain, **Victor Sarasqueta,** were at London, displaying their attractive—and attractively priced—line of sporting rifles and shotguns. I'd hoped to bring to London my Model 13 over-under 375 H&H double rifle for new sights and adjustment, but I got scared off! I was told that if I brought it in via normal channels that the rifle would have to go to the Palace in "bond" or whatever, and I'd have to pay about $200 just for the official transfer from the airport to Alexandra Palace. True enough, too—for example, Peter Bang of Heym told me that their bill was over $400. Ripoffs everywhere.

I've mentioned **Ken Steggles** and his beautifully hand-made products in recent issues, and at last I met him at the London show, which he and Mrs. Steggles visited for a day. A charming and interesting man, I found, and a dedicated one, too. The high quality of his products—replicas of 19th century muzzle-loading tools and implements, in the main—continues as before, despite his having added several things to the array and in spite of increasing sales.

He brought with him a near-full assortment of his things, a number of which I saw for the first time, and I was further impressed by their superb craftsmanship. I say "further" because I had bought from him in recent years several things—his copy of a Whitworth muzzle-loading rifle combination nipple wrench; a 6-flint leather wallet, which holds a very well made double turnscrew with touch-hole pricker, and a set of his ebony handled turnscrews, three in different lengths and blade dimensions, all housed in a leather wallet also.

Among Mr. Steggle's new items—or new to me—was a handsome copy of a Hawksley pistol flask, a bar-type cap dispenser and a full-scale replica of an oak case originally made (circa 1863) for Whitworth Military Target Rifles—his largest product by far!

Other Steggles items include: ebony pistol mallets, the type found often in cased sets, brass mounted, and made in 35, 45 or 50 caliber; an ebony loading-cleaning rod of a type found in Adams and Tranter revolver cases (36 or 45 caliber or to order), furnished with a worm, jag and ball-seating attachment.

To show what Mr. Steggles can and will do to supply a need, I had asked if he could locate a high-quality cleaning rod to go with the beautiful break-open 270 single shot rifle **Renato Gamba** had made for me. I'd also asked about a bullet-starter for a Gibbs-Metford muzzle-loading target rifle I have made for Sir Henry Halford, Wm. Metford's friend and co-researcher. I was and am without exact information on how long cylindrical bullets were started into the muzzles of such rifles. I've never seen one in any form, and I'd doubt they were made like American piston starters.

On meeting Mr. Steggles in London he opened his kit and handed me two items—he had modified his ebony-and-brass pistol mallet, turning a gracefully-cut swell 8 inches from the

This copper-bodied flask accurately copies an old Hawksley. The solid brass patent rifleman's top has a double cut-off and is adjustable from 60 to 110 grains (one side) and from 2¼ to 4¼ drams on the other; about $75. With common nozzles (adjustable), about $50. Spare common nozzles are about $10 to $16, depending on capacity. Postage is extra, air or sea mail.

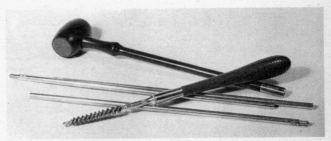

Here are the items Ken Steggles custom made for your Editor—the ebony, brass-mounted mallet/starter and the brass cleaning rod with wood handle. Excellent craftsmanship.

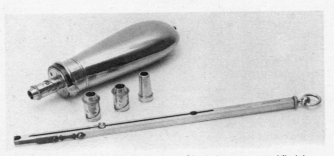

Closely copying an original Hawksley, this 4¼"-long copper pistol flask has a top of solid brass. Holding about 2 ozs., a standard charger is included at $40. Extra chargers, about $3.50 to $9. Postage is extra. The percussion cap dispenser, made from a drawn square brass tube, takes 27 small caps. This capper is useful with most revolvers, including original Remingtons.

This solid oak case closely copies an original Whitworth made for their Military Target Prize rifle and the various accessories shown—which Steggles also makes. About $140, plus shipping.

bullet-seating brass ferrule, the rod diameter .450-inch. A lovely piece of work. The swell will serve as a stopper and as a means of seating the bullets uniformly.

The other item was a 3-piece all-brass cleaning rod, topped by an elegantly turned rosewood handle of a form popular years ago. The three rod sections are threaded uniformly for Parker-Hale jags and brushes, so

there's none of the usual trouble in finding which section mates with another. A perfect rod indeed for the Gamba SS 270, and I am delighted with it.

Ken Steggles (77 Lower Eastern Green Lane, Coventry CV5 7DT, England) will gladly furnish details and prices of all his excellent products for $1 (no U.S. stamps), refundable on your first order.

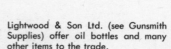

My old Belgian friends from **Ernest Dumoulin & Deleye** came to London with a quite extensive array of their numerous rifle and shotgun models—double-barreled shotguns and rifles, bolt actions, too, and all very well engraved, including several styles ranging from delicate scroll work to deeply cut game scenes. Some of the latter were gold inlaid as well. I regret not having enough space to show all of them!

My gracious hunting-party hosts from Czechoslovakia—the men who helped me obtain a great moufflon—were at London showing the wide variety of **BRNO** firearms. Mssrs. Kotek and Slouk greeted me warmly, and we explored the sporting arms situation in their country.

I was a bit surprised that the new-design centerfire bolt actions I'd heard about in Prague were not yet ready for full production—the ZKK rifles at London were the long-standard types, their extractor system still based on the well-proven '98 Mauser form. I only wish they would retain it!

Prominent at the Czech booth was the BRNO Super Express, a true sidelock express rifle in over-under style. Made in 7x65R, 9.3x74R and 375 H&H calibers, this handsome and good handling rifle has twin triggers (setable at will), ejectors, and comes with a factory-fitted scope mount.

I also examined their BRNO Super, an over-under rifle-shotgun combination in sidelock form also, but offered only, so far, in 7x65R. A pair of 12-gauge barrels are optional, too.

I also looked over their handguns—a couple of versions of the Drulov target pistols, both single shots, and the new 9mm Parabellum double-action auto pistol. As with the Czech long guns, the workmanship and assembly of these pistols was excellent.

Merkel had a fine display at London, and the old pre-war quality seems to be back in full force—wood and metal work was excellent, as was finishing, and the engraving was something else! I'll try to show a photo or two here, space permitting.

Lightwood & Son Ltd. (see Gunsmith Supplies) offer oil bottles and many other items to the trade.

This is the wheel-lock made by MENDI of Spain and seen at London. Sold in kit form at $66 (FOB Box 48, Eibar), there is also a like carbine, kit price $103.

Holland & Holland held rifle and shotgun matches at their shooting school, in collaboration with Zeiss, during the London show, their old muzzle-loading cannon and a piper opening the events.

Chamois on this side, red deer on opposite side, this rifle is an over-under double by Merkel.

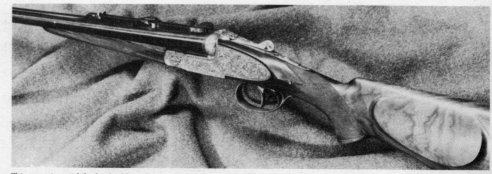

This genuine sidelock double rifle by Dumoulin-Deleye is their best quality. The quarter-rib carries Suhl-type scope mounts.

Raznoexport, worldwide distributors for the sporting firearms made in the Soviet Union, had an extensive and colorful display at the London show. A very wide range of firearms are made, from low-priced single guns to elaborately-done sidelock doubles, and I think samples of every type and grade were on view. Barlow

John Amber talks with Ms. V. L. Saveljeva at the Raznoexport display of Russian sporting arms in London.

and I had an interesting talk with Ms. V. I. Saveljeva, Senior Interpreter for Raznoexport. I was a little surprised to learn from her that she was fully familiar with the discussions I'd had at Houston with the Raznoexport representatives about various matters, including a hunt in Russia later this year, perhaps for fallow deer. Nothing firm yet, to be sure, but Ms. Saveljeva said it was being looked into at Moscow.

Press Coverage

I must say I'm surprised that the American firearms/sporting press doesn't cover this important show to any extent—apart from Roger Barlow (who I'd asked to help out with pictures and information gathering) and me, I saw no U.S. reporters. There were some British and European scribes present—Geoffrey Brown of *Guns Review* and our own Raymond Caranta, notably, and perhaps a few others I didn't meet.

I've called it an "important" exhibition, which term I suppose could be argued, but it cannot be denied that M. de Moffarts' annual gathering is important enough to attract some 25 U.S.-based firms, and their number grows each year—as does the total number of stand holders.

Well, the GUN DIGEST has led the way before, in this or that area, and we'll continue to do so, never mind the parochial-minded publications here. Still, it'd be good to see a familiar face or two—it can get a little lonely over there.

I had expected to meet Gough Thomas, the noted English writer on shooting matters, in London during the Exhibition but an injured foot prevented him from making the trip from Devonshire, where he lives.

Fortunately, one of Roger Barlow's friends, Emil Rosner, a London car dealer and gun collector, had ar-

ranged for us to test drive one of the latest SAABs. After the Show closed we headed west on the M4 highway. Because England is a smallish country, and traffic in the fast lane of their superb motorways really moves (75-80 mph), it didn't take long to get to Exeter. We clearly demonstrated that it is quite possible to drive at the speeds for which motorways were designed without using much fuel. At 80 mph our highly stable and comfortable SAAB hatchback coupe (with an outstandingly good automatic transmission) was averaging just over 20 miles per U.S. gallon! A 2-ton V8 with automatic will hardly do that well idling at a stop light and not get within 4 miles of that even if driven at 55—which rarely happens. If we're going to save gas it has to be done with smaller cars.

Anyway, 3 hours after leaving London we were in Silverton being greeted by Gough and Mildred Garwood (and Susie, their Springer spaniel who is one of my favorite dogs).

Even at the start of the trip I'd felt awful and, by the time we reached Gough's house I was sick. I went to bed about 6 P.M., and stayed there until Sunday—over three days. A doctor came to see me, his tentative diagnosis "a touch of the flu," and his remedy an anti-biotic. Still feeling rough, I boarded the plane for home, and I've been slowly recovering since.

I'd meant to stay several more days, visiting such provincial gunmakers as Albert Brown of Birmingham, Ian Crudgington of Bath, the John Dickson works at Edinburgh, et al, but that wasn't to be.

Anyway, as I think I've said, a truly good show, instructive and enjoyable, and I hope to make Christian de Moffarts' next Exhibition, set for mid-March of 1979, and again in Paris, as it was in 1977.

John Amber bids the Garwoods goodby—Gough, Mildred and Susie, their lovable and lovely Springer spaniel. Gough was kind enough, thank God, to bed down the stricken traveler.

Two Inches of Pleasure and Problems

by PETER BARRETT

Getting the ultra lightweight Holland & Holland double gun to shoot safely and effectively with homemade shotshells wasn't easy, but teamwork and perseverance paid off.

The 2-inch chambered Holland & Holland in its original oak-and-leather case.

EVERY GROUSE AND WOODCOCK hunter enamored of fine double guns dreams of acquiring the perfect shotgun—one that flies to the shoulder effortlessly, swings like a dream and seems to point by a special instinct of its own. Of course, there is no perfect shotgun because there is always some little thing wrong or that displeases. Nevertheless, we search. And one wintry day in 1974 I picked up a dream gun, swung it a few times, hefted it and fell in love.

The place was Gary T. Herman's Safari Outfitters, on Route 7 north of Ridgefield, Conn.—a barn-red old house with white trim whose lower floor is crammed with handguns, rifles and shotguns. There's every grade of firearm at Herman's, but the emphasis is on top-of-the-line guns in good to fine condition.

The gun I'd picked up and swung was a 12 bore Holland & Holland side-by-side with its original lightweight leather case and accessories. Most of the casehardening colors on the full-sidelock plates remained, and there was minimal blue wear. The stock had been expertly refinished and, I'm sure, the checkering recut. The gun closed with an elegant *thunk!* and was absolutely tight.

I was not happy that there were two black spacers at the butt instead of one. Yet the Holland fitted me so well it nearly brought tears to my eyes.

We put it on Gary's scale and I could hardly believe the reading of 5½ pounds, for this was a 12 bore with 28-inch barrels. It was then that I took a hard look at the rib and read: "Centenary—For 2 Inch Cases Only."

This brought me up sharp. "What kind of a load does the gun shoot?" I asked. Herman wasn't sure but thought 1 ounce, maybe 1¹/₁₆ ounces. I considered this information. If I were to shoot 1-ounce loads I'd be practically using a 20 gauge, though the patterns and shot string might be a bit better. But 1¹/₁₆ ounces is only about 25 pellets below 1¹/₈ ounces in 7½ shot.

Quandary

You can see how my mind was working. I *wanted* the gun and want-

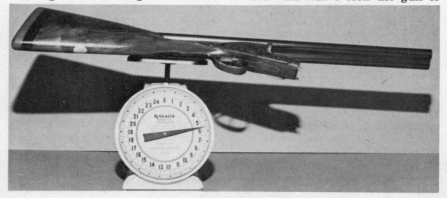

H&H 2-inch chambered shotgun weighs just over 5½ lbs.

ed to justify getting it. I recalled that when I'd shot driven grouse in Scotland for one glorious week, those of us with 12 gauges shot British ammo loaded to 1¹/₁₆ ounces, which was very effective when the gun was pointed right.

Then I got to musing about some WW2 experiences in England. I'd bought a used field-grade Jeffery 12 gauge for an amazingly low $65. This gun had 2½-inch chambers, and we in the Air Force had nothing but 2³/₄-inch Skeet shells loaded with 8s. Regardless, I bought the gun, tied it to a table and shot 10 rounds through it, pulling the triggers with a long string. The gun didn't burst and I was to shoot some hundreds of 2³/₄-inch paper shells through it.

After the war I took the gun to

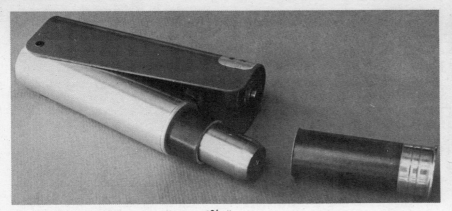

The Lyman hand trimmer was adjusted to cut a $2^3/_{16}$". Severed cut case sections are on mandrel.

Finished $2^3/_{16}$-inch shell sits beside same-length case in P-W shortened shell holder.

Judson S. Darrow, my gunsmith at Woodbury, Conn., and asked if he could lengthen the chambers to $2^3/_4$". "No problem," he said. "There's plenty of metal and I've done this several times."

So, I thought, *Maybe Jud can stretch these 2-inch chambers a bit.*

Now I asked Gary Herman to measure the chokes. "About improved cylinder," he announced. "The left barrel could be a hair tighter."

Later that day, after telling my wife at lunch that I was going to swap some guns for one that cost as much as a new car (in 1974, remember), I parted with a pair of 12 gauge over-under S03 EL Berettas which I'd come to consider a bit on the heavy side, and an exquisite 28 gauge top-grade Zoli. I'll regret losing the latter till my dying day. But at the time I reflected I was out of pocket for only half the price of the Holland.

Now the problems began.

I couldn't find any 2-inch cartridges in the New York area. A salesman in Abercrombie & Fitch called the Chicago branch, then shook his head. "The Eley factory in England blew up recently," he remarked. "There's no telling when they'll be back in business."

I called Gary Herman. Yes, he had a shipment of British ammunition but it was tied up in a dock strike.

In desperation I wrote to Malcolm Lyell, Director of Holland's in London and a friend. My gun was made in 1936, he wrote me, and continued: "The shot load for 2-inch cartridges is $^7/_8$-ounce. It would certainly not be safe to have this gun chambered for $2^1/_2$-inch cartridges."

What had I done?

My next move was to take the gun to Jud Darrow who made a cast of one of the chambers. To our mutual surprise this proved to be $2^1/_8$ inches long. After doing some careful measuring Darrow finally decided he could lengthen the chamber by $^1/_{16}$-inch only, and ease the angle of the forcing cone which he said was rather steep.

Cartridge at Last

In the interim Gary Herman's British ammo arrived and I picked up 10 boxes. Nowhere on Eley's boxes was there mention of the weight of the shot charge, though in the fine print on the back there was an obscure reference to proofing at $^7/_8$-ounce. Back home, I cut open a shell and weighed its No. 6 pellets (about the size of our $7^1/_2$s)—$^7/_8$-ounce on the nose. Sonofabitch!

I knew in my heart when I decided to have the chambers lengthened that I was going to have to take up shotshell loading, and the Eley loads (only ordered by Herman in 6s) reinforced this. I took a box of them to Darrow's when the gun was ready and we fired two shots in his yard, then measured the paper hulls. They were $2^1/_8$-inches long.

Jud was looking hard at the mouth of the fired case and smiling. "Notice how thick the wall is?" he said. "Well, the Federal paper case is only about half as thick so there'll be more room for shot. I'm sure we can load $1^1/_{16}$ and maybe $1^1/_8$."

So I took the plunge and ordered a Ponsness-Warren Model 375 Du-O-Matic loader with 20 and 12 gauge tooling. I'd long been a reloader of centerfire cartridges and could now look forward to making conventional-length shells with loads unobtainable from the arms companies— such as 12 gauge 3-$1^1/_4$-$8^1/_2$s for early-season woodcock—as well as $2^3/_{16}$-inch minis.

The Du-O-Matic, an expensive outfit, would be easy to adapt for short shells, Darrow felt. We ordered an extra 12 gauge shell holder to shorten, and two 6-point crimp starters, one to lengthen and reach down to $2^3/_{16}$-inches. A 6-point crimp starter is usual for paper shells, 8 points for plastic.

Right from the start we decided against using a roll crimp and card atop the shot for fear of ruined patterns. The 2-inch Eleys have a roll crimp and their 6s patterned well, I was to find. Still I don't regret using a folded crimp and doubt there is much difference in shot capacity between the two systems.

We ordered Federal paper shells because paper is much easier to trim by hand than plastic. For this operation Darrow altered a Lyman shotshell trimmer to cut exactly at $2^3/_{16}$. I was to find the trimming job surprisingly fast.

After Jud Darrow had altered my loader, he set about assembling a $1^1/_8$ ounce load after finding room for the shot above modest wadding. An experienced shotshell loader himself, he checked several individuals and sources, including the first edition of the excellent Lyman Shotshell Handbook.

First Handloads

"Aren't they neat?" he said when I arrived. Jud was holding some newly made minis. "And believe it or not, it wasn't hard to get $1^1/_8$ ounces of shot in there."

He showed me how to work the loader and I built several shells right there. It was downright easy. I bought some bags of shot in different sizes from Jud and went home.

Here's the load Darrow had worked up:

Federal paper shells with Federal 209 primers.

Alcan P.G.S. overpowder wad and Winchester $^1/_4$-inch fiber wad.

An alternate load substituted the Federal 12SC100 plastic shot cup for the $^1/_4$-inch fiber wad. This shot protector is nothing more than a flat-based shot cup with side cuts, by the way, and no cushioning of any sort at its base. The protector sits atop the P.G.S. (for plastic gas seal) wad. There is no room for even a slim card wad inside or outside the shot protector unless the shot load is reduced, which I was against.

It was now the middle of August, 1974. I loaded some shells with 8s (since this is what I'd use first come fall) in both styles—with and without the shot protector. Then I patterned the gun at 40 yards and at some closer distances.

There were two surprises. The 5½-pound Holland was quite comfortable to shoot in shirtsleeves with the 1⅛ load and was, of course, even milder with the Eley shells. The unprotected-shot patterns were the tightest. Here's how the gun patterned at 40 yards:

Protected shot	Unprotected shot
Right—32%	Right—38.3%
Left—34.4%	Left—41.1%

The Eley patterns were exceptionally even but, since I wasn't planning to hunt with these shells much, I did not figure their patterns. As to the patterns being more open with shot-cup shells, I figured the culprit had to be the lack of cushioning—many soft-lead pellets deformed inside the cup at the instant of firing.

At this point you may well think: *He got away with stuffing 1⅛ -ounces into those little shells. No need to read further.* Wait! This was only the beginning.

I loaded some 8½s in protected loads (the widest shooting) for use in the right barrel for early woodcock, plus a good supply of 8, 7½ and 6 unprotected-shot (tighter shooting) shells.

The gun proved a delight to shoot and I downed the first ruffed grouse I fired at. Somehow the 28-inch barrels did not prove cumbersome in woods and brush. At a preserve shoot, using 6s, the gun did well for me on pheasants and helped me perform beyond my normal ability on flighted ducks.

Seasons passed and about half a case of my minis went through the Holland. Last winter I prepared to write this article and John Amber said, "We must have pressure and velocity figures on the Eley and your shells. Would you mind sending a box of each to Mike Bussard of Federal who has kindly offered to help?"

The Bad News

In time I had a call from Mike, who is director of public relations for Federal Cartridge Corp. in Minneapolis. "We tested the shells," he told me,

Comparing crimps—Eley roll on left, author's 6-point pie at right.

From left—Eley 2-inch, W-W 2¾-inch and author's handload.

"and the Eleys are about normal—1280 fps and 7100 LUPs."

There was a pause, LUP is the abbreviation for lead units of pressure and the recommended safe average limit is 10,500.

Mike Bussard went on, "Are you sitting down?"

I said I was.

"The velocity of your handloads is 1153 fps, but you are getting 15,600 LUPs average. Some went over 16,000."

Mother of God! More than 50 percent above the safe limit!

I would like to have called Jud Darrow about this but he has gone to that wonderful place where a gunsmith never drops anything, screw heads don't get buggered and where all parts fit the first time. Instead I asked Mike Bussard for advice.

In essence, he felt I was overly ambitious in trying to cram 1⅛ ounces into such little shells and also hope for acceptable pressure and a desirable velocity. "Go to a cooler primer, say the Remington 97*," he advised, "and try Green Dot, a slower-burning powder." He recommended a charge of no more than 19 grains. Finally he added, "That PGS overpowder wad in your particular load is probably a big factor in your pressure problem."

That weekend I frantically searched Connecticut for fiber wads of different thicknesses, and card wads. There were none! One-piece plastic wads had made cardboard and fiber combinations obsolete. Winchester had quit making such, but I learned that Federal still made components.

Next I cut open an Eley shell to check its makeup, which consists of two overpowder .085″ card wads and one ½-inch brown felt wad. I noticed that the shell wall was not nearly twice as thick as Federal's, as Jud had thought. The *mouth* of a fired Eley fluffs out, giving the false impression that the wall is thicker than it is. So I now found I didn't have as much volumetric room to play with as I'd thought I had.

Luckily Jud had made for me a

1¹⁄₁₆-ounce shot bushing by slightly boring out a 1-ounce bushing and I decided to use this. Following Mike Bussard's suggestion, I made some Green Dot loads using two ¼-inch Winchester wads and 1¹⁄₁₆-ounces of shot, which just fitted. The pressure checked out at a mere 6900 LUPs, but the velocity was only 1000 fps., too low.

I also modified the original 15,600 LUPs load, substituting for the PGS wad a ¼-inch Winchester wad (now there were two), and dropping from 1⅛-ounces of shot to 1¹⁄₁₆. Pressure was now 9900 LUPS average, velocity 1166 fps. Perfect!

Meanwhile, I've acquired some Federal ½-inch wads—the discontinued brown fiber cushions and the current gray counterparts. I also learned about a specialist in hard-to-find components—Ballistic Products, Inc., 17610 19th Avenue N., Wayzata, Minn. 55391. Phone 612/473-1550.

All's Well

In the interest of presenting a load with available components, here's how one checked out: Federal paper shells with Remington 97* primers, 20¼ grains Green Dot, Federal ½-inch gray fiber cushion wad, 1¹⁄₁₆-ounces shot—9800 LUPs, 1079 fps. The velocity is a touch low, and there were considerable swings in pressure, from 8900 to 11,800, not exactly ideal. A different wad might smooth out the pressure swings, so I'll try again.

I'll also try some ½-inch wads in the 700-X load, against the day when I run out of ¼-inch Winchester fiber wads.

Meanwhile, thanks to John Amber's insistence on pressure and velocity figures, I'll not be shooting proof loads through the Holland this fall. As for the shot reduction from 1⅛ to 1¹⁄₁₆-ounces, there are nevertheless 383 No. 7½ pellets average in my new mini shells (a magnum loading by British standards). I'm sure they'll do the job when my Holland points itself for me in my grouse and woodcock covers. ●

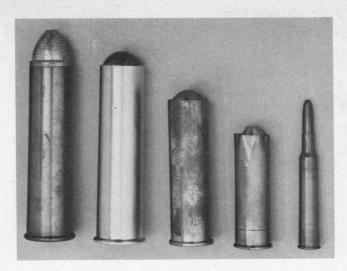

From left—8-bore brass case with 1250-gr. conical bullet; another 8-gauge with 875-gr. round ball; 10-bore brass holding 700-gr. round ball; 12-bore brass case with 750-gr. conical Paradox bullet, and a 7mm Flanged cartridge for comparison.

H4831 for a velocity of 2430 fps. Since both the case and the .323″ 8mm bullet is fairly close to the 318's .329″ bullet and case, I thought the same weight bullet for the 318 would shoot with the same powder. I decided to begin with 60 grains, which I estimated should produce something near the standard 2400 fps of the 318's 250-gr. bullet. I could scarcely credit my eyes when my first 4 cartridges, left and right, produced a 100 yard group, high and central, of 1.25 inches. I then tried 59 grains and got several 4-shot left and right groups under one inch at 100 yards. Later, after obtaining the former owner's supply of Kynoch 250-gr. non-

no loss of convergence or tendency to cross.

Crimping is important for heavy caliber nitro-expresses to prevent the bullet from loosening or receding into the case, but a too-heavy crimp on thin necks will cause neck telescoping. I made a case-indenting device but found that the indentations created a work-hardening condition, which made the dimples break through after a while.

Such indenting tools were often supplied to the rifle buyer, particularly for straight-taper cases. One type put a small rounded depression into the case just below the bullet's base, usually 3 dimples. Another type made a shallow half-moon depression in either side of the case, these tools usually found with the big bore (8, 10, 20 or so) Paradox or Fauneta double rifles, the latter name a Westley Richards term. Factory loaded Kynoch or Eley cartridges often have small indentations below the bullet's base.

Loading a 318 H&H

My experience in loading for my H&H 318 Modele de Luxe (made for the Rajah of Sailana) with a 3x Voigtlander scope may be interesting. The man from whom I bought it was disgusted with its cross-firing and primer flattening developed by his Kynoch 250-gr. non-corrosive cartridges— which ammo I did not get with the rifle. I found some late corrosive-primer Kynoch loads which also cross-fired, plus some head separations and blown primers. I decided to pull the bullets and replace the hot double-based Nobel powder with our cooler, slower-burning IMR powder. I located a load for the 8mm-06, one using a 250-gr. bullet of 63 grains of

Above—sidelock over-under double rifle by Karl Hauptmann of Ferlach (Austria), made with two sets of barrels—7mm Remington Magnum and 243 Winchester. The 12-bore below is by the same maker.

The Hauptmann 2-caliber O-U rifle in its case. Two scopes are included, plus various accessories.

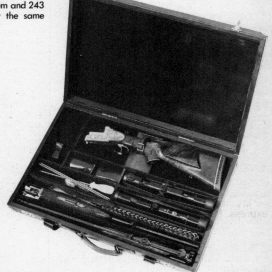

NRA REPORT 1978

The custom craftsmen—stockmakers,
metalsmiths, engravers—were the
big attraction at Salt Lake City.
The teeming throngs were well rewarded,
too, for magnificence was the rule.

by JOHN T. AMBER

A Waldron Special

I think I've attended every annual meeting of the National Rifle Assn. since the late 1940s with one exception—I missed one a few years ago when I was hospitalized. This most recent convention, held at Salt Lake City, Utah, was the best ever from the standpoint of the exhibition-visiting members interested in custom gun work. He—and she—got their full measure this time.

Joe Oakley, Oakley & Merkley, stock blank purveyors of Sacramento, CA, had assembled an extensive display of the best quality custom stocked and metalsmithed rifles and shotguns ever seen at one time, I believe. This multiple-booth setup, 4 of them side-by-side, exhibited some 100-plus pieces, I think. Just about every great name in gun craftsmanship, past and present, appeared on Joe's well-lit display boards—far too many for listing all of them here.

The Salt Palace, which housed all the exhibits, is a very large hall, the aisles between the booths wide. Despite this, the crowds thronged to the O&M booths during every hour the hall was open to visitors—there were many times when it was almost impossible to get through the jam of people. In addition, and deeply gratifying to the surging crowds, was the presence at Joe's display—and elsewhere—of numerous stock and metal artists themselves, ready and willing to talk with their visitors, to answer the streams of questions.

Among the gun engravers present at the O&M location were two of the greats, Winston Churchill and Robert Swartley, both with several examples of their outstanding work. Churchill had a newly done work, in the *bulino* school or very close to it, that was superb—the delicately cut sky scene, above a brilliantly executed hunting dog, was beautiful. Two bolt action rifles, each having specially-made *brass* floorplates, guards and buttplates (I thought at first they'd been gold plated in satin finish), had been embellished by Swartley in grand

fashion. Two or three aspiring young engravers were also on hand, their work showing good promise.

Another engraver, who was unknown to me until recently, was Brian Bridges, also a young man, who is doing great work. He has been cutting relief medallion work for one or other of the limited-edition firms, among other more conventional techniques. The several samples of his efforts I looked over were handsomely done indeed.

The craftsmen listed below—stockmakers, metalsmiths, engravers—were present at Oakley's stand, as were samples of their work:

Larry Amrine	Monte Kennedy
Joe Balickie	Maynard Lambert
Al Biesen	Phil Letiecq
Roger Biesen	Franz Marktl
Steve Billeb	Dan Martin
John Bivins	Bill McGuire
Ted Blackburn	C. D. Miller
Len Brownell	Earl Milliron
Tom Burgess	Maurice Ottmar
Kevin Campbell	Byrd Pearson
Winston Churchill	Phil Pilkington
Bob Emmons	Keith Stegall
Jerry Fisher	Bob Swartley
Jay Frazier	Gordon Tibbitts
Dale Goens	Herman Waldron
Gary Goudy	Duane Wiebe
Hubert Hecht	Tom Wilson
Dick Hodgson	Bob Winter
Dave Huntington	

The works of Bill English, Lynton McKenzie, Leonard Mews, Clayton Nelson and Alvin White were also displayed, although these men were not present. On view, too, were guns by several now dead—Gale Bartlett, Aaron Gates, Alvin Linden and Tom Shelhamer.

Joe had a lot of help in setting up his booths, which must have been a big job, and he wants to thank Byrd Pearson and his son, Joe, for making the display. He also thanks the ". . . great gang of guys who showed up a day early to set up the booths, and then stayed over a day to help take it down."

Joe said he also is thankful to Lou Leonard, who brought along various original engraved Winchesters.

Herman Waldron, one of our best metalsmiths and a creative one, too, had brought to Salt Lake City a pre-'64 M70 action I'd sent to him, including a Dave Huntington 280 barrel. Herman had fitted a new and hand-made one-piece straddle guard and floorplate, he'd created a custom scope mount base to take his own two-piece lever rings and, a crowning touch, he had installed a new form of floorplate release.

Well, not really brand new, for Herman had modified an old design—one I had examined many years ago. That early form had been a small rectangle of checkered steel set into the rear of the floorplate; spring loaded, a finger push depressed the small plate, letting the plate pop open.

I had never been fully satisfied with the various floorplate releases used in the past—the fairly standard guard-button type, often hard to get open or, conversely, too easy, inviting disaster; the several under-plate levers, among them the Mauser sporting style, and others, including the Mauser military form. I had described the push-in system to several gunsmiths over the years, none of whom tried it, as far as I know.

I was, then, a bit surprised when Waldron showed me the release he'd fitted. Instead of using the type I'd once seen he had recessed the rear of the straddle-type floorplate to make a rounded or domed depression. In that lay a checkered, like-shaped sliding steel piece, double-spring locked, a bit shorter than its recess. Pushing this piece forward releases the floorplate. The floorplate, slightly rounded, yet hardly above the level of the release is invisible in profile, there is nothing foreign in the guard to mar its simple form and, highly important to the hunter, this release is not vulnerable to accidental release—it must be manually and firmly pushed before it unlatches.

Herman was rather reluctant to try this unusual release, he told me, fearing that other customers might not accept it. He needn't have worried—on the second day of the exhibition he told me several customers had stopped by, saw the new design and changed their orders. They wanted it!

Other Craftsmen

Not all of the custom craftsmen were at Joe Oakley's place—Len Brownell's booth was next to Joe's display, and at it Len had a half-dozen or so of his custom rifles, all work his including the metal-smithing, which was extensive on some rifles. Len learned the metal arts years ago, finding the turn-around time insupportable often enough, and the returned work not just as he'd have preferred.

Len had examples of his side-lever scope mounts on view, many of these now used by his colleagues in the field. He does full custom installation of these rings/bases, too, modifying and fitting them to double rifle ribs, for example. Len also continues to supply his handles for rifle bolts, finished form or otherwise, and he had a new item at the show, too. This is a coiling spring, emergency type bore-cleaning tool, stiff enough when inserted into the barrel to push out snow or mud usually. One end holds a threaded loop for patch use, too. Coiled into a circle, this useful device can be placed into the opening underneath a trapped buttplate or carried in the pocket.

Don Allen is a custom stockmaker who has the assistance of a top metal-smith, Mark Lee, in his shop at Northfield, Minn. Don had some excellent examples of handsome stock work on hand, as did his old friend and fellow Northwest Airlines pilot, Al Lind. Don and Al are doing excellent stockmaking nowadays, and I intend to send the Waldron-worked M70 action to Don for stocking.

Don had a big lot of his stock blanks at the booth—most of the best were soon sold—as did a friend from New Zealand, Ted Stone, whose walnut was more on the lighter English type, being rather light colored.

Al Lind was showing a very nicely done sidelock double gun he'd stocked, and a quite young fellow named Eric Meitzner, who works for Don Allen, had a handsome Ruger No. 1 at the booth which he'd stocked in first class fashion. Yet Eric has been doing stock work for only a few months, and this rifle job was the 7th or 8th he'd completed.

My pre-'64 Model 70 action was worked over in and out by Waldron—new guard/floorplate, custom scope rings/bases, new floorplate release (see picture at top of preceding page).

This little Winchester Low Wall, made as a 22 Hornet for Don Allen, the winging woodsman, is ready for the engraver. Len made the ¼-rib, the double-lever scope rings/bases and the open express sights, as well as the full-fancy stock and fore-end.

The pantograph or copying machine that Don Allen builds and markets, which does very precise inletting and exterior stock forming on a one-to-one ratio, has been a great help to those craftsmen using it. The machine eliminates much of the drudgery work in readying a stock blank for the final hand scraping and cutting. I believe that Hoenig and Rodman of Boise, Idaho, were the first to develop and use such copying devices, which they still do and quite successfully.

Longrifle Makers

John Bivins, Monte Mandarino and Lew Sanchez, all top flight practitioners in building muzzle-loading long-rifles, occupied a booth next to Don Allen's. Several of their handsomely-crafted rifles were displayed, and Bivins showed me a short section of a recently-made barrel by Robert Griffith of Tuscaloosa, Ala., done in the old Damascus technique—the multiple strands of iron and steel twisted and coiled around a mandrel while hot, then welded together. The figure or pattern typical of such barrels showed clearly. John Bivins will be getting a full length barrel in this Damascus form quite soon, which he'll fit to a wheel-lock rifle he's building, the lockworks a replica of

Al Lind stocked this AYA (Aguirre y Aranzabel) 12-gauge double gun using colorful California English walnut in typical English style. A Biesen steel buttplate, cut in two, made heel and toe plates, the wood between checkered.

A delectable example of the great craftsmanship at John Bivins' command is this flintlock longrifle—a beauty in every aspect.

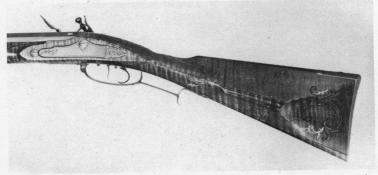

An attractive flintlock longrifle made by Monte Mandarino in 1780 style, with steel mounts and a 50-cal. swamped barrel by Getz. The relief-carved curly maple full stock is silver-wire inlaid. Monty's rifles start at $1800.

This is the Jerry Fisher rifle described below.

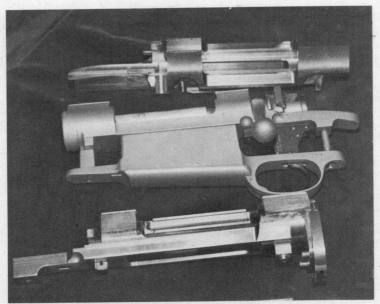

Some of the Fred Wells-made bolt actions—a left-hander is second from the top.

an early wheel-lock I supplied to John. Helmut Zeit did this difficult job.

As you may not have heard, John Bivins has been charged by the Internal Revenue Service with evading the Federal Excise Tax (11%) assessed against firearms manufacturers for many years now. This appears to be a "test" case or suit which, if the IRS successfully presses and wins, would establish a precedent and make *all* custom gunmakers/gunsmiths/craftsmen liable to the same FET. Bivins courageously elected to fight this ill-advised assault on him (and potentially on thousands of other custom workers), and over the past year or two his legal defense costs have reached nearly $10,000. I think this is an outrageous money grab by the IRS, as does everyone I've talked to about it. Larry Mrock of Orchard Lake, Michigan, is being harassed by the IRS for the same reasons, and there may well be others in the same fix unknown to me.

A number of us have contributed to Bivins' defense fund, and if you want to help defeat this attack on craftsmen, send a check to John Baird, Box 885, Big Timber, Montana 59011.

Jerry Fisher

Can you imagine a bolt action sporting rifle that would look any better than this superbly-crafted example of Jerry Fisher's high skills. Every aspect of this rifle is exactly right—let me call your attention to the graceful yet functional sweep of the pistol grip, the perfect angle that the grip-cap end makes with the stock's toe line, the comb and height and shape.

Built on a '98 Mauser action, the metalsmithing was done by Tom Burgess, then engraved by John Warren of Cape Cod—one of our greatest engravers. This rifle is one of a matched pair.

Dick Hodgson had a magnificent Ruger No. 1 single shot rifle on view, profusely engraved by Lynton McKenzie, and housed in an equally splendid case. The case, I daresay, would cost as much as the rifle to duplicate—beautiful.

Speaking of custom gun cases, Joe Balickie of Raleigh, NC, exhibited a beautifully done rifle, another Ruger No. 1, in a full-length leather-covered wood case made by Marvin Huey and lined in red ultrasuede—very attractive and nicely done indeed.

Balickie's Ruger had been beautifully and fully engraved by Robert Swartley, the stock and fore-end made from a piece of exhibition grade walnut.

(For some reason Huey doesn't like the traditional cast-brass corners for cases, a form in use since the early 19th century at least. Why have they persisted? Durability and longevity, for such sturdy corners will outlast the case leather many times, whereas leather corners will, as time goes by, scuff and wear, the stitches eventually breaking down to an irreparable degree. As it happened, hence these notes, I looked over an oak-and-leather cased rifle the other day, the case holding an early John Dickson (Edinburgh) hammerless double rifle, probably made in the 1880s or so. The leather cover is in sad shape, but the stout brass corner pieces are, apart from a few scratches, unworn.)

Hubert Hecht, who learned his trade in Germany, had an unusual double rifle to show, hence of big interest to me! Surprisingly, the action, stock and fore-end were a standard Winchester Model 101 in 20 gauge, to which had been fitted a pair of rifle barrels. Hubert's brother, a gunsmith still in Germany, sends the fully prepared and officially German-proved barrel sets to Hubert, who does the final action fitting, polishing and blueing. The sample Hubert had was well set up and balanced, the wood and metal finish excellent. As described, Hecht has priced these M101 D.B. rifles at $2300. That isn't exactly cheap, of course, but as double rifles go these days, his price is about as low as can be found, apart from Victor Sarasqueta's price of around $2,000 for his Spanish-made D.B. rifles—which will easily cost $2,300 by the time one were delivered here.

Hecht can furnish these over-under rifles in many calibers—243, 270, 30-30, 308 and 30-06, plus such metrics as 6.5×57R, 7×57R, 7×65R, 8×57R, 9.3×62 and 9.3×74R. The 375 H&H *(Cont'd. on next page)*

Keith Stegall

Keith Stegall

One of the old master's latest custom rifles is pictured here, made for four-year old R. W. Schafer of Bixby, Okla., but he won't get it until he's 18. I can't help but think that his father will have fired a few shots through it before then.

Made on a pre-64 M70 action barreled in 280 Remington by Bill Atkinson of Prescott, Ariz., the wood is a top piece of French walnut, the point-pattern checkering 24 lines per inch, and running over the grip top. Al Biesen supplied the grip cap and buttplate, and a Canjar trigger is fitted.

The handsome engraving of grip cap, trigger guard and floor plate was done in Austria. J.T.A.

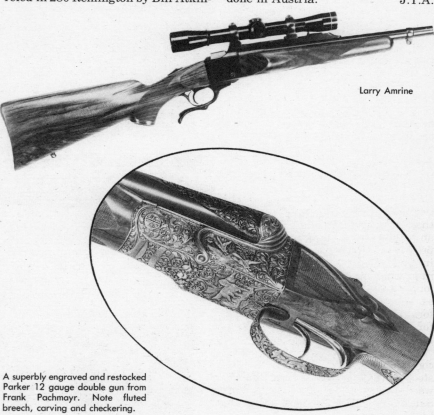

Larry Amrine

A superbly engraved and restocked Parker 12 gauge double gun from Frank Pachmayr. Note fluted breech, carving and checkering.

Larry Amrine

This elegant Ruger No. 1 single shot, caliber 30-06, is stocked in French walnut from Oakley & Merkley, has a Brownell grip cap, a Biesen buttplate, and the 1/4-rib, mounts, sights and safety are by Brownell also. The 24 lpi checkering wraps fully around the fore-end, an ebony diamond centered and holding the fore-end screw.

Old friend **Frank Pachmayr**—who I'm sure needs no introduction at all—had a big display at the Salt Palace, and as always it was jammed with fine firearms of all kinds. Almost every one of the rifles and shotguns on view was of deluxe or better quality—exotic woods from all over, engraving in many styles and including gold-inlaid specimens, eye-catching all.

will be offered soon. Both barrels, fired in quick succession and depending on caliber, will shoot 4-shot or 6-shot groups at 60 meters of about 3 inches or less. Hecht will also supply fully custom stocks or semi-finished stocks, and if you have a 101 in 20 gauge that you'd like to convert to a double rifle, he'll do the conversion for $1300. You won't, note, get your 20-gauge barrels back—they're part of the conversion.

Hecht had a useful small item on hand, too—a ⅛-inch thick buttplate, the hinge at the heel virtually invisible, that is mounted between the stock end and any recoil pad, rifle or shotgun type. Lifting the assembly, which is spring-loaded to stay closed, revealed a pre-cut trap or opening large enough, if desired, to accept 5 rifle cartridges or 4 shotshells—or whatever small emergency items one might want to store therein. These sell for $45 singly, not including fitting or recoil pad; they're available to the gunsmith at a discount in lots of 10.

Fred Wells of Prescott, Arizona, had several of his meticulously machined and highly polished Mauser-derived actions on display—short ones, medium length and magnum, with or without flat tops, right-hand specimens and left-handers, some with *integral* scope bases, more or less like the left-side attached Griffin & Howe mounts. Fred had another action, also with an integral scope base, that was considerably less obtrusive and thus more pleasing than the prominent G&H type. Made entirely in Wells' shop, not many are produced in a twelve months span, so there's a long waiting list, even at Fred's prices. One version I looked at, a small form and a left-hander, I think, sells for $3,500! What can I add? Only that I envy the guy who can afford one.

Bill Dowtin, with whom I've corresponded—and bought some stock blanks from, good fancy wood—had a separate booth at the Salt Palace. I'd seen some photos of his stock work, which looked very nicely done, but I'd not met him nor seen his stocks to handle. Bill proved to be a big young man, with less years than I'd thought, and standing about 6 foot 3 inches. His custom stocks were in no way a disappointment—he's doing first class work now, yet he's been doing such work for only a short time, two or 3 years, I think, perhaps less. He had some excellently done stocks on view, and I was and am tempted to order a stock from him. I need another rifle, don't I, besides the one Don Allen will make

(Cont'd. on next page)

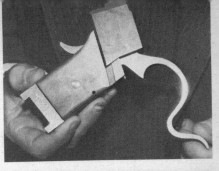

Here is something new—a single shot action, designed by John P. Foote, which drops the rear section away from the forepart as the underlever is operated. Readily interchangeable barrels could result.

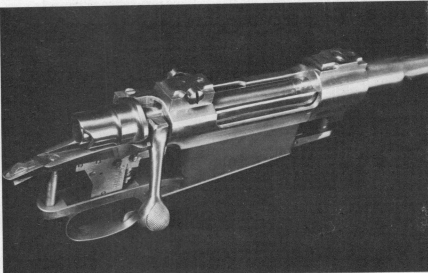

Mark Lee—Metalsmith

This still quite young man is, already, one of our finest workers in the demanding art of metal forming and shaping, not to mention his creative skills in the design area. The left-hand Mauser 98 action pictured nearby, originally a crude military type and one of several imported by P.O. Ackley years ago from Japan, has been reworked completely by Lee to make it the gleaming specimen you see now.

Lee's work included fitting a Titus (Huntington) 270 barrel and a Canjar trigger, installing a tang safety, adding a new 2-panel checkered bolt knob and a straddle-type hinged floorplate and guard. He also modified the Leupold scope bases.

Mark Lee, a colleague of Don Allen's, is at Rt. 1, Timberlane, Northfield, MN 55057.

From left—Fred Wells, noted Mauser-action maker; Ralph Bone, master of various skills in gunmaking, and Bill Dowtin, a young and very good custom stockmaker.

for me?

An old and warm friend, a fine custom stockmaker of long standing, appeared at the Salt Palace—Keith Stegall, with whom I'd hunted years ago for elk, and his charming wife. We had an all-too-short visit, and I was pleased to see how kind the long years had been to both of them—they looked far younger than they should have. I was envious.

All the custom stock men I've listed earlier had one or more examples of their high craftsmanship on display but, apart from those workers I've specifically written about, I don't have space to describe their efforts in detail. However, many of them will find their rifles or shotguns pictured in this 33d edition, if not most of them.

In closing I want to make a well-deserved tribute to Joe Oakley. He's been showing the works of custom craftsmen in the firearms world for many years, with all of the strenuous efforts entailed in setting up the displays and, at the end, tearing them down. As I've said, the Salt Lake City presentation was easily his best ever, but the cumulative showcase he's provided over the years for these gentlemen has been of incalculable value to them. In many cases, in the past, many of these dedicated men couldn't have afforded to rent the space for a one-man or even, perhaps, two-men show.

Joe Oakley has done a great job, and I applaude him for his own dedication to high skills and creative abilities. Long may he flourish.   J.T.A.

NRA Members Meeting

In spite of the clearly-expressed wishes of the voting NRA members at the 1977 Cincinnati meeting that the Raton project be abandoned—all 37,000 acres of it—and no more money be spent on it, it was voted at Salt Lake City that this costly boondoggle be given a new lease of life, that a study be made to determine its ultimate fate.

The vote didn't take place until after midnight, when certainly a fair number of voting members must have left. The meeting had started at about 7.00 PM, and during the first several hours the vast crowd was subjected to a great spate of rhetoric and rodomontade by various NRA officers, notably by a gentleman in a fetching pink pants suit, Mr. Howard Pollock. The voting procedure was, I felt, disgraceful—the Arthur H. Anderson company had been hired to supervise the voting, and they had furnished all members qualified to vote with a large booklet of tickets marked "Yes" and "No." There were, I think, some 90 of these tickets (180 in all), and the motions as they came up and were duly seconded, were to be voted on via these tickets. Ballot boxes were to be passed among the voters and the tickets deposited therein.

Yet, from beginning to end, only *two* votes were decided by using the tickets—the many other votes were by show of hands (voters were supposed to raise their ticket booklets aloft) or by voice vote. How many votes were cast illegally, I wonder? During my stay—until about 1:00 AM—I saw scores of people waving newspapers or other papers.

Certainly the money spent on hiring Anderson's service was completely wasted. So far I haven't learned just what that fee was, for a call to the NRA revealed Anderson had not yet sent in a bill. $5,000, perhaps?

During the meeting, and throughout the six hours I spent in the great hall, several men manned the aisles, most of them carrying large, easily visible cards, these lettered YES and NO—as had also been done at Cincinnati. I can only assume that these cards were meant to be held up high when one motion or another was about to be voted on, the object being to sway the members for or against. I'd equate this with inviting partisan precinct captains into the polling place, there to do their electioneering.

Now we'll have the better part of a year to wait and watch—to see what happens at Raton, to see what the new "study" reveals (a similar study, to have been implemented in 1977, never took place), to learn next April how much more money was spent in 1978 at Raton. This much seems clear—if the projected facilities at Raton are ordered built or, in fact, actually built or near-completed, the NRA membership will be faced with a *fait accompli*—a situation virtually impossible to reverse.   J.T.A.

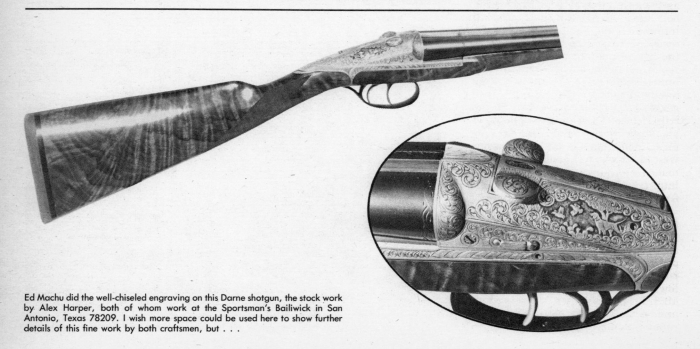

Ed Machu did the well-chiseled engraving on this Darne shotgun, the stock work by Alex Harper, both of whom work at the Sportsman's Bailiwick in San Antonio, Texas 78209. I wish more space could be used here to show further details of this fine work by both craftsmen, but . . .

by LARRY S. STERETT

Benelli 12 Gauge Autoloader

This Italian-made autoloading 12 bore, distributed here by Heckler & Koch, is a bit unusual in design but it is a quality shotgun. Most of today's autoloading shotguns are operated by a long-recoil system or they're gas-operated; the Benelli is neither. It is classed as a "forward inertia unlocking system," in which the barrel is fixed, a separate bolt head moving to start the unlocking.

The Benelli has a couple of other unusual features. Single shells can be loaded directly into the chamber through the ejection port, then chambered by pushing the bolt-release button on the right side of the frame; shells *cannot* be fed directly from the magazine manually, but do feed during the firing cycle. It's a nice safety feature, since the magazine can be kept full without any worry about a live round being accidentally fed into the chamber.

The other novelty is the black crackle frame finish, in place of anodizing or bluing. The barrel is blued, as is the steel receiver housing the bolt assembly, but the alloy frame into which the receiver fits is black crackle. The bottom of the frame and the trigger guard are a flat black, the receiver having a black chrome-like finish. The bolt body and charging handle are bright chromed; the trigger and crossbolt safety, behind the trigger guard, are satin chromed.

The test gun, a Model SL-121V, is 47$\frac{1}{2}$" long with the 27$\frac{3}{4}$" barrel, the weight an even 7 lbs. The barrel, made by Manufrance, carries a ventilated rib .264" wide, an alloy bead up front.

The buttstock and forearm are of Italian walnut, well-finished but without much figure. The forearm, almost 12" long, appears longer because of its slimness. Finger grooves run almost the entire length, the lower half hand checkered at about 18 lines-per-inch, without a border and with few runouts. The well-rounded comb is fluted on both sides.

A black plastic buttplate is standard, but there is no pistol-grip cap. The test gun had a rear swivel and one on the forearm cap, both non-detachable and designed for a $\frac{3}{4}$" sling—hard to find here but common in Europe. Stock dimensions are 1$\frac{5}{8}$" and 2$\frac{1}{2}$" at comb and heel, pull 14$\frac{3}{8}$".

Takedown is simple: Unscrew and remove forearm cap and spring, followed by the forearm. Then, grasping the barrel in one hand and the buttstock assembly in the other, pull the barrel and receiver forward off the frame. The bolt can now be removed by pulling the retaining pin which holds the firing pin in place; this pin is visible when the bolt assembly is projecting from the rear of the receiver. No further stripping is necessary, although the trigger guard assembly can be removed by pushing out the roll-steel crosspin, lying in the frame directly above the safety (no external screws are visible in the Benelli, other than the two attaching the buttplate).

Before trying the Benelli on clay pigeons it was patterned using the new Peters Blue Magic light target loads (2$\frac{3}{4}$-1$\frac{1}{8}$-8) and Federal's 3$\frac{1}{4}$-1$\frac{1}{4}$-7$\frac{1}{2}$ Premium field load. Five rounds of each load were fired at the standard 40-yard distance. The barrel was not marked as to what choke it was supposed to have, but the Peters load shot a 73.9% 5-shot average into the 30" circle; the Federal load averaged 67.1% for 5 shots, indicating the choke to be in the improved-modified to full region. Pattern centers were right at the point-of-aim, when cheeked loosely, and distribution was fairly even.

The Benelli functioned reliably at straight trap but it has a slightly odd feel in the hands, perhaps because the underside of the frame is flat, as is the front of the pistol grip. The result is a bulkiness not found on most shotguns. Another oddity is the shape of the cast trigger guard; the sides are parallel, the surfaces of the bow perfectly flat. (A bulge in the front of the guard houses the hammer spring.) The trigger shape is excellent, although the 6$\frac{1}{2}$-lb. pull weight is a bit heavy.

When cheeked tightly only the sloped rear of the Benelli frame is visible; cheeked loosely, the muzzle bead and a short section of the ventilated rib are visible; targets shot using the latter method, and just covered, were dead birds.

The Benelli is well made. Alloy castings and several stamped steel parts are used internally, but they function as intended. The Benelli is currently priced around $400, hence still more costly than other currently imported autoloading shotguns.

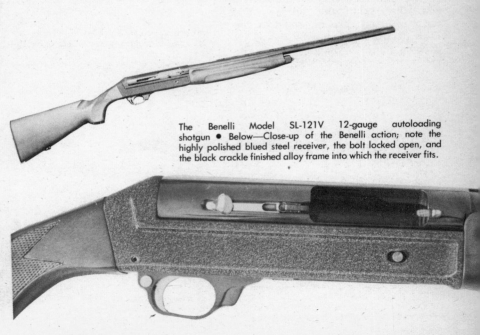

The Benelli Model SL-121V 12-gauge autoloading shotgun ● Below—Close-up of the Benelli action; note the highly polished blued steel receiver, the bolt locked open, and the black crackle finished alloy frame into which the receiver fits.

Golden Eagle 7000 Rifle

Golden Eagle rifles and shotguns are now distributed out of Houston, Texas, the company having moved there from Illinois. The firm name is new, too—Golden Eagle Firearms, Inc.

The test rifle, in 7mm Rem. Mag. caliber, weighs just under 9½ lbs., including a scope—a touch heavy. Total length is 44″ with its 4-groove, tapered 24⅛″ barrel.

At first glance the 7000 resembles a Weatherby, the well-figured walnut stock having a streamlined rosewood forearm tip, and a forward-sloping Monte Carlo comb/cheekpiece. There's skip-line checkering fore and aft, a ventilated recoil pad and a black pistol grip cap with a Golden Eagle head encased therein.

The action of the 7000 (made in Japan by Nikko), is the outstanding feature. The recoil lug is attached between the barrel and cylindrical receiver in the same manner used on the 700 Remington; the trigger unit, housed in steel, attaches to the receiver bottom. A separate top-tang sliding safety dovetails onto the back of the trigger unit. The checkered gold-plated trigger, .305″ wide, has a 3-lb. letoff. When the safety is "on" (back) a green-colored indicator appears, and when "off" a red-colored indicator is seen.

The bolt is a cylinder .745″ in diameter, with 5 rear-locking large lugs grouped in a set of two and a set of 3, the latter 120° apart. The pair of lugs lie 4″ back of the bolt face, the trio .372″ behind the rear of the first group. The modernized bolt sleeve, somewhat triangular shaped, but with rounded corners, encloses the rear of the bolt; only a tip of its cocking piece is visible beneath the sleeve to serve as a cocking indicator.

The bolt face holds a plunger ejector and a short-length pinned-in .250″ wide extractor is fitted. The bolt body has 3 gas-vent holes, each .100″ in diameter, in case of a ruptured primer; venting is to the right, via the loading port.

The bolt handle, raked to the rear, has a M70 style knob; when locked in place it serves as a 6th locking lug. To remove the bolt the safety is put on "off" and, holding the trigger back, pull the opened bolt straight back.

The magazine well and its spacer are steel stampings. In keeping with some modern manufacturing techniques, the follower and floorplate are each made from sheet steel parts spot-welded together. The trigger guard is made from a light alloy, streamlined fore and aft. The grooved floorplate-release button is in the guard forepart. Unlike early production rifles, the current 7000 has a conventional Mauser-type box magazine with hinged floorplate; early rifles had a detachable box magazine concealed by a hinged floorplate.

Metal finish on the 7000 was a highly polished blue-black, except for the bright engine-turned bolt body, the gold-plated trigger and the anodized guard; all parts appear well polished before finishing.

Wood-to-metal fit is very good, particularly around the receiver, but the tangs have clearance where necessary; the barrel is not free-floating. The high gloss stock finish was assumed to be a plastic or epoxy; even the inletted areas are sealed against moisture to reduce warping.

The sliding tang safety is visible here, as is the rear of the receiver bridge, shaped to receive the bolt sleeve.

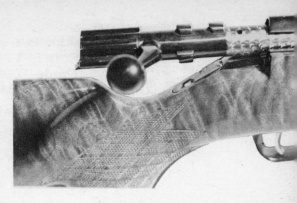

Note 3 of the 5 rear locking lugs on the bolt of the 7000 rifle. The tip of the cocking piece is also visible at the lower rear edge of the bolt sleeve to serve as a cocking indicator.

The test rifle came with a Golden Eagle 3-9× wide-angle scope in Burris mounts, but other mounts, such as the Conetrol, are usable. The scope has duplex crosshairs.

Accuracy

The 7000 was bench fired at 100 yards using an assortment of bullet weights—from Winchester's 125-gr. soft points to and including Herter's 175-gr. round nose Banana Peel de-

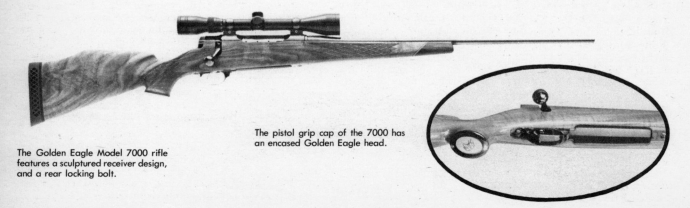

The Golden Eagle Model 7000 rifle features a sculptured receiver design, and a rear locking bolt.

The pistol grip cap of the 7000 has an encased Golden Eagle head.

sign. With the scope set at 9×, 3-shot groups were fired. The rather light-weight barrel tended to heat rapidly so firing was timed to let it cool. The smallest group, 1⅜″ center-to-center, was with Federal's 150-gr. Hi-Shok load; most groups fired with this load stayed around 1½″, but other loads grouped closer to 2″. With handloads, perhaps other factory loads, the 7000 might group below an inch, which would be good for a hunting rifle.

There were no problems. Fired cases were extracted and ejected easi-ly, and the trigger pull was excellent. Recoil with this rather heavy rifle wasn't uncomfortable. Considering workmanship, its accuracy and func-tioning, the 7000—made in a dozen calibers from 22-250 to 458—is a rifle many shooters would like to own.

H&R 700 22 WRM Autoloader

The 22 WRM cartridge was devel-oped and introduced by Winchester before they had a rifle chambered for it, but over the years since several firms have made such rifles. Most were bolt rifles but a few were lever or pump actions, even some autoloaders. At least two autoloaders were made in Germany, but only the H&K sur-vives. The one U.S.–made 22 WRM went out of production nearly a dec-ade ago—the Kodiak. Now there's a new autoloader for the 22 WRM, the Harrington & Richardson 700. Though introduced in early 1976 the 700 was not readily available until last year.

Our M700 test rifle weighs 6⅝ lbs., its tapered barrel 22″ long. The tubu-lar steel receiver is 9½″ long, only an inch more than autoloaders chamber-ing the 22 L.R. cartridge. Because the action is of blowback design, the addi-tional springwork necessary to han-dle the greater recoil of the 22 WMR is located beneath the barrel, func-tioning via twin action bars. The re-sult is a trim action without any bulky projections at the rear. A single-hook extractor lies on the bolt's right side, the ejector tossing fired cases nearly 8 feet to the shooter's right. The right-side charging handle is ⅞″ long and knurled for non-slip grasping. The pivoting thumb safety, also on the right side, is grooved for the same reason. Though without a last-shot hold-open device, the bolt can be locked open manually by pull-ing the charging handle fully to the rear, then rotating it slightly to catch in the takedown hole.

The gracefully-tapered barrel car-ries a ramp-mounted post front sight and a fold-down square-notch rear sight adjustable for elevation; sight radius is 16¹¹/₁₆″.

The walnut pistol grip stock,

The H&R 700 barreled action is held to the stock by two bolts running through the magazine-guide plate (foreground).

uncheckered, does have a Monte Carlo comb and a slim forearm; wood finish was very good, and wood-to-metal was satisfactory. The barrel is not free-floating.

The trigger guard is big enough to take a gloved finger, the trigger long and non-slip grooved. Letoff was a bit heavy at 6 lbs., and with some creep.

A detachable 5-round box magazine is standard; a 10-round version is an extra-cost option. The magazine is easily released using either hand via a release lever.

Open sights on the 700 are fine, but shooting a 22 WRM calls for a scope, and the receiver is tapped for regular scope mounts. No mounts were avail-able for early-production rifles, but Weaver soon came through; their one-piece No. 87 base accepts all Weaver-type rings. Now several other firms make mounts for the 700.

After its examination the 700 was fitted with Weaver bases and a Tasco 6×40 scope mounted and collimated. Five-shot groups were fired from the bench at 25 yards, the ammo CCI. No ejection problems arose during the firing of 250 rounds, but one feed problem occurred when FMJ car-tridges were used. The bullet nose of the first round from the magazine would catch on the junction between the feed ramp and the barrel, exactly where the rim of the cartridge would be located when a cartridge was chambered. Soft point bullets fed well enough, the nose deforming to let the bullet slip into the chamber. During the firing, several FMJ bullets were jammed back into the case on hitting the step, so FMJ first rounds were loaded manually. After this hand feeding, few jams occurred during the firing cycle, probably because of the more rapid slam-bang movement of the bolt.

Accuracy at 25 yards ranged from ⅝″, center-to-center, to just over an inch. At 100 yards groups averaged over two inches, still small enough for the larger predators—fox, coyote, even groundhogs.

In general, the H&R 700 is a well-designed, well-constructed rifle that shoots a good but neglected varmint cartridge. Reasonably priced at $159.50 (lowest price for a rifle of its design and caliber today) it's as accu-rate as many other sporters available. Also, for those who desire, there's a 700DL grade at $225, which includes a roll-over Monte Carlo comb, a rub-ber buttpad with white spacer, check-ering on grip and forearm, plus a mounted 4× scope but minus open sights.   LSS

The H&R 700 rifle in 22 WMR caliber is the least expensive of its type on the market today.

Mossberg Model 377 Plinkster Rifle

This rifle, though introduced last year, could not be field tested until recently. Only 40″ long with its 20″ Ac-Kro-Gruv rifled barrel, the test Plinkster weighed one ounce over 6 lbs., including a Tasco 4×15 scope. The autoloading action is not essentially new, being almost identical to that used on the Mossberg M353; there is a different magazine system. New is the moulded polystyrene stock, with thumbhole, and moulded-in checkering on the forearm. The stock is made in two halves and then joined down the center—the seam on the stock's underside is hidden by 5 narrow grooves. This is not a bit distracting, as might have been expected—the stock is wood grained so that even the pores can be felt. A roll-over cheekpiece and full pistol grip make the rifle comfortable to hold, and the size and position of the thumbhole should be OK for all but big-handed shooters.

The butt is black plastic, and in the lower half (sunk below the plate surface) is the magazine locking knob. Loading is done through a port on the right side of the buttstock. Unlocking the brass magazine tube and withdrawing it 15 inches permits loading 15 cartridges in 22 Long Rifle caliber. An orange-colored nylon magazine follower could serve as an empty magazine indicator, except it is not readily visible through the ejection port because of the clip-on fired-case deflector—which deflects all empties downward, to the right.

The 377 comes with quick-detachable swivel studs and a Tasco 4x scope with mount, plus a special extruded-aluminum scope-mount riser. These must be installed by the buyer, the work of a few minutes.

The author shooting the Plinkster, on which he's installed a carrying strap.

With the scope mounted, a collimator was used to align the crosshairs with the bore, but it took nearly all of the scope's windage adjustment to achieve a nominal alignment. Maybe it would be satisfactory!

Five-shot groups were fired at 25 yards from the bench, the first 5 off to the right nearly 3 inches and slightly low. Adjustments were made, but successive groups still shot to the right. Moving the windage knob as far as possible, the last group was still nearly an inch right. That was that—the rest of the groups were fired for size only.

After shooting 500 rounds of assorted target, standard, and HV loads by CCI, CIL, Eley, Federal, Herter's, Remington and Winchester, the point of impact had not changed, and groups ranged from 3/4″ down to several under 3/16″, center-to-center. The 377 was loaded to its 15-shot capacity always, and cartridge feeding was perfect. Ejection was positive except

for a few rounds which jammed in the ejection port; these failures almost always occurred on the last shot, never with the magazine full. They happened with all ammo brands, including some W-W Xpediter 22s tried later. Though such cases were well crushed, turning the rifle on its side and retracting the bolt cleared the bent case each time. There seemed to be plenty of follower clearance, so drag between follower and bolt was not the cause of the problem.

Using the NRA offhand position is not recommended with the 377, for the hot brass will drop right into your open palm!

The safety functioned reliably, and the trigger pull was a rather long 5½ lbs.; the investment-cast trigger ought to have a rounded surface for more comfort than the flat surfaced, sharp-edged design offers. However, these are minor complaints on a rifle at under $80, including scope and mount.

The Mossberg Model 377 Plinkster rimfire autoloading rifle.

Mossberg's Hi-Rib Trap Gun

This version of the Model 500, priced at $249.95 and specially designed for trap, weighs 7⅞ lbs., its Accu-Choke barrel 28½ inches long. (Only a modified choke tube was furnished, but Full and Improved-Modified tubes will be provided.)

Since the M500 action and Accu-Choke barrel are the same as before, only the special features of the new trap gun will be covered here. The ventilated Hi-Rib (.315″ wide and

topped by a .160″ white bead and an .065″ brass center bead) is the free-floating Simmons Olympic type and is installed by them. To compensate for the higher sighting plane the buttstock has a high Monte Carlo, with a slight forward slope. Drop at the flut-

The Mossberg 500 AHTD Hi-Rib Trap Gun has an Olympic Rib by Simmons and Accu-Choke tubes are standard.

ed comb is $^7/_8''$ and drop at the heel of the Monte Carlo is $^3/_4''$. Drop at the heel proper is $1^3/_4''$, the length of pull $14^1/_2''$. The high gloss stock has a ventilated rubber recoil pad, plus a black plastic pistol grip cap. The buttstock is considerably darker than the beavertail forearm, and the wood projects slightly above the metal where the buttstock and receiver join.

Checkering on the pistol grip and the forearm runs 20 lines per inch, with only a few runouts. Checkering on the pistol grip is more decorative than functional, since the stock finish was applied after the checkering was done. Checkering on the forearm wraps completely around, making it

highly functional, and there were only a few flat diamonds located near the upper edge of the pattern, which has a wide border.

At the pattern board only the new Peters Blue Magic light target load $(2^3/_4$-$1^1/_8$-8$)$ was shot; the 5-shot average at 40 yards gave 63.0% in the 30" circle—about right for the modified choke tube. The patterns centered just above the front bead, and average distribution was well balanced. There were few holes, and only a slight tendency toward dense centers.

The 500 Hi-Rib was an excellent fit, the center of balance at the front edge of the receiver. At the shoulder

only the receiver top and elevated rib were visible, the center bead directly in line with the front bead. My trap targets were "dead" if centered just above the front bead as it rose. Only a few hundred shells went through the 500 Hi-Rib, but those were enough to indicate Mossberg has a good thing going in this gun. When you consider the cost of having a regular Simmons Olympic Rib installed on your own shotgun barrel, you can buy the complete Mossberg shotgun for only a bit more. Too, if desired, you could switch barrels and buttstock to produce a shotgun suitable for trap, Skeet, or field use.

Remington Classic Bolt Action Rifle

Along with such nostalgic items as old gun catalogs, some of today's shooters are discovering what others have long admired—the classic rifle stock. The current popularity of those centerfire rifles having a stock with a Monte Carlo comb and cheek-piece, rollover or otherwise, and a fore-end cap with or without spacers, dates from post-World War II. Roy Weatherby was one of the greatest promoters of this style, and the trend caught on everywhere. Even our largest manufacturers went the same route, if to a slightly lesser degree.

Then, after nearly three decades of Monte Carlos, forward-sloping, rollover, dished-out, streamlined stocks and other features, Ruger introduced the Model 77 rifle with a beautifully plain stock of the style popular back in more peaceful times; the Model 77 had no Monte Carlo, no cheekpiece, no fore-arm cap, no spacers, only the good clean lines of what has been termed the "classic" rifle stock.

Many new shooters, and a lot of older ones, discovered they liked this

styling. Now Remington has introduced their Model 700 rifle in classic form. The test rifle, in the ever-popular 30-06 caliber, weighed $6^7/_8$ lbs., and is $42^3/_8$ inches over-all with its 22-inch barrel. It is identical in all respects to the 700 BDL, even the cut checkering pattern of 20 lines-per-inch being the same. Only the stock differs.

The walnut stock has no grip cap or spacer, no Monte Carlo or cheekpiece, only a straight line from the rounded comb, fluted on both sides, to the heel; the butt has a thin brown-colored solid rubber pad, with a *black* spacer. The slim, well-rounded fore-end is without a contrasting cap or tip. The buttstock, rather straight, has a comb drop of $1^3/_{16}''$ and $1^3/_4''$ at the comb and heel, no doubt a compromise for scope use, lacking a Monte Carlo. As a result the front and rear sights (easily removable) are higher than they would have been 40 years ago. The receiver is tapped for regular scope mounts. The high sights are not unhandy, at least for this writer, for the front bead aligned perfectly in the U-shaped rear sight when the rifle was shouldered rapidly.

Since the Classic 700 (this word does not appear anywhere on the rifle) is not a major new design, only a model modification, it was bench shot using the open sights, with Federal, Frontier, Remington and Winchester cartridges. Bullet weights ranged from 125-gr. to 220-gr., including soft point and HP designs. Firing was from 100 yards, and several 3-shot groups were shot with each bullet weight. Groups ran from about two inches to nearly 5, the 180-gr. bullets generally best. No problems arose but the recoil sensation seemed more pronounced than that felt using a 7mm Remington Magnum rifle of a different design being tested at the same time. Recoil under such static conditions sometimes seems greater than it actually is.

The new Remington Classic 700 rifle rates a near excellent mark. The wood-to-metal fit is up to the Remington standards, if not equal to custom work of the best quality, the stock and metal finishing very good. Available in 5 other chamberings, from the 22-250 to the 7mm Remington Magnum, the retail price is the same as for the regular Model 700 BDL rifles.

The Remington Model 700 Classic rifle is a BDL with a simple uncluttered stock. It's slim, trim, and a joy to behold.

LET THE GUN TALK

J. M. Pyne was aware of more than his friends and helpers knew, that a sinister attempt might be made to steal his new rifle design. But, as he said, let the gun talk.

JOE HILL backed his battered roadster up to the store-room and asked for a case of Government 30-caliber ammunition.

"Okay, Mr. Hill," the boy said.

Joe noticed the "Mr." He had been a mechanic ever since he was big enough to say he was 16. He had become a toolmaker, trusted with nice work. He had made good with J.M. Pyne. But he had never been a boss until he came to Gaylord Arms. He wasn't used to being mistered.

The boy would have put the case aboard, but it weighed a hundred pounds and he was a skinny kid. Joe hoisted it into the rumble seat and drove across the factory yard to what they called the Water Shop, because in the beginning it had got power from a dam several hundred yards up the river. They hadn't used it since the 1890s, so they had given it to the old man.

The gun was lying on the bench. J.M. Pyne was wearing his Sunday clothes, and his beard had been freshly trimmed. He was rummaging in a case that looked like the bag family doctors carry on their rounds. He spread the contents out on the bench—screw drivers, two kinds of pliers, a dozen shapes of needle files, and spare action springs. He had carried that kit to rifle matches for 40 years, because his rivals expected him to stop shooting and fix their

rifles when anything went wrong with them, while his own gun got cold and the wind shifted and the light changed. He had made world's records just the same.

The old man looked at Joe over the top of his glasses. "You're feeling pretty good."

Joe knew what he meant. It was his way of saying, "You think you're going to get somewhere with the gun this afternoon."

"It's a nice day," Joe said.

It was a nice day, clear and bright and warm.

The old man stared out of the iron-barred window at the river rushing by below them. The river was at flood after a week of rain. But now the sun was shining on the dark water.

"Yes," he said, "it's a nice day. I hope you still think it's a nice day when we get back here."

He had been like that about the gun ever since the first time Joe had seen it, two months back. They had been packing up the stuff in the Jersey City shop, getting it ready to ship to Gaylord Arms, when Joe had found the box, with a card tacked on the lid addressing it to an Army officer at the Aberdeen Proving Ground, and asked what was in it. The old man had put him off. Joe had bothered him until he had opened the box and pulled out the wadded newspapers, dated July, 1929, and there it was—a semiauto-

matic military rifle, ugly after its kind, but beautiful in its simplicity.

J.M. Pyne said he had changed his mind about sending it in for trial when he had heard that the Army was working on its own semiautomatic rifle. He had decided it wasn't any use. He didn't much care. He had satisfied himself that he had solved the problem. Why try to convince men who knew less about it than he did? He'd had enough of trying to tell the Army something about small arms.

J.M. Pyne bent his head over the tools on the bench. "You don't know what you're getting into, Joe," he said.

"The gun is good."

"What's that got to do with it?"

"I'd like to put it over."

The old man growled something about having been young once himself.

"It's a quarter of two," Joe said. "You ready?"

"In ten minutes."

Joe picked up the gun. The old man turned his head. He glared at the gun in Joe's hands as he spoke. "I don't like semiautomatic rifles. They won't shoot."

He knew how the old man felt. J.M. Pyne had given his whole life to making rifles that were more accurate than any others. He was famous for his knowledge and for his precise workmanship. He couldn't get the results he demanded from a semiautomatic rifle. The tolerances had to be bigger. Besides, being a military arm, it couldn't weigh more than 10 pounds. He couldn't put enough weight in the barrel for fine shooting.

"You can't compare it with one of your 300 magnum bull guns," Joe said.

"Of course it isn't as good as they are."

"What's the use of it, then!"

Joe wanted to remind him that his semiautomatic rifle had shot as well as other military rifles. But he knew

by LUCIAN CARY

it was better not to argue. He put the gun in the car. He guessed he had time to walk through the barrel shop and make sure that everything was going all right. He had 200 men under him. He would soon have 400—maybe a thousand. Gaylord Arms had been dying for 20 years. Now it was alive again. Joe was, though he still didn't quite believe it, superintendent of the works. He was 28 years old.

He looked into the reception room as he was passing the door. The girl at the information desk was known to have ignored—with a cool, contemptuous stare—all attempts to kid her along. But she had a way of giving Joe a long, slow, sidewise look, as if they shared a secret. It was a year since he'd had a date with a girl. Betty had made it plain, without a word, that he had only to ask. But she wasn't there at the moment.

A girl with gorgeous red hair, slim and smart in a blue-gray dress, was standing at the information desk. Joe paused, without thinking what he was doing, to get a better look at her, and she turned and caught him staring at her. He could have walked on down the hall toward the barrel shop as if their eyes had never met.

"Is there anything I can do for you?" he asked.

"Yes," she said, "I came to see Mr. Pyne."

Her voice was the kind he liked, low-pitched, and her smile was pretty swell. But Joe felt that her manner took it for granted that if she wanted to see the old man, somebody would go running to fetch him.

"Mr. Pyne is busy right now," he said. "Is it a personal matter?"

"Yes," she said. "I mean it always is with him, isn't it? I want him to make me one of his target rifles."

Joe shook his head and smiled at the absurdity of it. She was, of course, the daughter of some rich man and so spoiled that she thought she could

LET THE GUN TALK

The article to be presented here in two parts was first published in four successive issues of The Saturday Evening Post in 1941—August 9, 16, 23 and 30. The second World War was raging in Europe, its rumbles and impact felt in the United States as the Allies and other nations, desperately and in haste, sought to obtain firearms in large numbers and various types.

Let the Gun Talk is the longest piece that the late Lucian Cary wrote about J.M. Pyne, the great rifle barrelmaker who, in reality, was Harry M. Pope. The thin disguise, in fact, had not deceived many in the 1930s and '40s—when the several J.M. Pyne stories were first in print—certainly not those with some knowledge of high accuracy rifles and the men who made barrels for them. Harry Pope, who died October 11, 1950, at the age of 89, had become a legend in his own

time, well before the publication of the J.M. Pyne stories, but Cary did much indeed to foster and enlarge the reputation that Pope had attained over the many decades of his working years. Pope had been a great barrel maker well before 1900, his name a byword among schützen—or offhand—riflemen even then.

The Gun Digest was happy to arrange with Lucian Cary in 1963 for reprinting of our first J.M. Pyne story. That was *Forty-Rod Gun,* to be found in our 18th/1964 edition. Since that time we have published others in the J.M. Pyne series—*Madman of Gaylord's Corner,* 21st ed./1967; *Johnny Gets His Gun,* 26th ed./1972; *J.M. Pyne Shoots Twice,* 27th ed./1973; *The Secret of the Old Master,* 29th ed./1975; *Center Shot to Win,* 31st ed./1977 and *The Old Man Who Fixes the Guns,* 32nd ed./1978.

have anything that struck her fancy, whether she had any use for it or not. She needed to learn that there were some things she couldn't have just because she was nice to look at.

"Do you have to be so rude?" She said it without raising her voice, so it irritated him more than if she'd got mad.

"You don't understand. J.M. Pyne doesn't make rifles for everybody. He hasn't time. He only makes them for men who are good enough shots to need them."

"How interesting." She looked straight into his eyes. "Is it true?"

Joe hesitated. It wasn't strictly true. The old man would do anything for a friend, even if he couldn't shoot.

"It doesn't matter," she said. "I'm a good shot."

Joe smiled again. Half the people he met said that about themselves and believed it. Rifle shooting was neither fashionable nor spectacular, so most people never saw any good shooting. They picked up a boy's rifle in the country and hit tin cans at 50 feet and thought they knew how to shoot. Their choice of so big a target proved they didn't know what rifles were for.

He had to get rid of the girl. He had been trying to get J.M. Pyne to make more models of his semiautomatic rifle. He had stayed up nights milling out two new receivers, which housed the working parts of the gun, from solid blocks of tough alloy steel, to save the old man as much work as he could. If this crazy girl barged in on him she might persuade him to make a rifle for her, and that would mean another delay of a week or a month.

"I'm sure you are a good shot," Joe said, trying to be diplomatic.

"You mean you're sure I'm not."

"That's right," he said, letting her have it straight.

If she was surprised, she didn't show it. "Last weekend," she said, "I broke five pop bottles in succession."

She thrust her chin out at him as if daring him to say that wasn't good shooting.

He didn't laugh. But she guessed what he thought.

"You aren't impressed."

"No," Joe said.

"What would you call good shooting?"

"Nowadays, the 22 rimfire shooters use a target at a hundred yards that has a 10 ring two inches in diameter. The top men in a prone match will have all their shots in the 10 ring. They call that a possible, or clean score."

"Then who wins?"

"They had to put a one-inch ring inside the 10 ring to decide that. They call it the X ring. The man who has a clean score and the most Xs wins."

"That makes pop bottles just funny, doesn't it?" She dropped her eyelashes in confusion. He saw how soft her skin was, with freckles faintly showing on either side of her slightly turned-up nose. Her cheeks were delicately flushed. "And," she added, "they weren't a hundred yards. They weren't anything like that."

Joe thought it was sweet of her to admit that she was wrong. It would be easy enough now to persuade her not to bother the old man about the barrel. His irritation left him. He wanted to be kind and helpful.

"Anyway," she said, looking up at him, "it was fun."

"Of course it was."

"But you think I don't rate a Pyne rifle."

"You don't need it. You'd find it much too heavy. You can buy a perfectly good light rifle for $10 in a hardware store."

"Thank you ever so much," the redheaded girl said. "You've been so—so educational. I mustn't take any more of your time. But may I ask one question?"

"Yes, of course."

It was only then that he saw how scornful she was.

"Can you speak for J.M. Pyne?" she asked.

"No one can speak for J.M. Pyne."

"That's what I thought."

Betty came in and sat down behind the information desk. The redheaded girl asked her for a sheet of paper.

"Take my chair," Betty said.

The girl wrote rapidly. Joe stood staring at her bent head. Her hair was a marvelous red, and so thick and soft and curly it made you want to run your hand through it. She folded the note and held it out to him.

"Will you be so good as to give that to Mr. Pyne?"

"If you insist," Joe said, trying not to show how angry he was.

The old man was trying the door of his shop to make sure it was locked. He had two bandoleers of ammunition over his shoulder.

"What have you got there?"

"Some 1938 National Match stuff."

Joe remembered that lot. They had shot several hundred rounds of it, testing the semiautomatic rifle. It was loaded with the boat-tail bullet that had so greatly increased the range of the service rifle. The old man must have some pride in his gun, no matter what he said, or else he wouldn't have taken the trouble to bring along the more powerful ammunition the Army had given up when they adopted the Garand rifle. He wanted to show that his gun could handle the load that had done so well at long range in the 1903 Springfield.

He smiled as he read the note the redheaded girl had written. "It's from Frieda Guerdner. She's Fritz Guerdner's daughter. I used to shoot with Fritz at the old Schutzen club here in Waterford. I lost track of him years ago when I moved my shop to Jersey City. I heard he'd gone out West."

"If you want to see the girl," Joe said, "I'll tell her to come back tomorrow."

"What for? I'd like to see her now."

Joe knew it wasn't any use. You couldn't force the old man. You had to get around him. And this girl was doing it. Somebody had told her how to manage J.M. Pyne, or else she just knew, without being told.

"All right," he said. "I'll get her."

She was sitting in the reception room. She looked up, ever so innocent.

"Mr. Pyne will see you," Joe said.

"Oh," she said, "I was sure he would."

Joe was too sore to say anything.

J.M. Pyne took both her hands in his. Joe had noticed before that the old man liked pretty girls. He might be 75, but he was just as susceptible as anybody else. He told Frieda Guerdner that she must go with them to Reuben Gaylord's farm and see the gun shoot.

"I've got my car," she said. "But I could leave it here."

"Joe will put your car in the yard," J.M. Pyne said. "You ride with us."

He handed her into the roadster with an old man's gallantry.

She gave Joe her key. Her car was a convertible coupe, of the same year as his roadster, and looked as if it had taken the same kind of beating.

When he got back, she and J.M. Pyne were old friends. Joe squeezed in behind the wheel. There was so little room that the girl was pressed against him. It didn't seem to bother her, but it bothered him. He stared straight ahead, as if she wasn't there. But he could hear everything that she said, and he could imagine how she was looking at the old man when she told him she had heard about him all her life and longed to meet him and dreamed of someday having a Pyne rifle.

"I'll make you a rifle," J.M. Pyne said.

Joe knew by the tone of his voice that the old man was flattered. He had heard that kind of thing from gun cranks. It only made him crustier

than usual.

But when a girl with lovely brown eyes said it, he fell for it as if he were a college boy and she'd been telling him that he was so big and strong she was afraid of him.

"I've got a barrel nearly finished," he went on. "I intended it for Joe here. But he can wait. If it shoots when I put it in the machine rest, it's yours."

Joe thought if she had any sense of decency she'd offer to do the waiting. The old man had been promising him that barrel for a year.

"Oh," she said, "how nice of you!" But it's only fair to tell you that Mr. Hill thinks I'm not a good enough shot to need a Pyne rifle."

"What has Joe got to say about it?" the old man demanded.

Joe wondered where the girl had got her fixed idea. Did she think a Pyne rifle was something to hang on the wall and brag to her friends about? It wouldn't get her much. A Pyne rifle looked like other rifles, except on the inside. And you had to know what to look for to see what was there to see. Not one man in 50,000 could appreciate the perfection with which the grooves were cut. She certainly couldn't. To let her have a Pyne rifle was like letting a baby have a chronometer to play with.

The road bore south, sometimes close to the river, sometimes half a mile from it, through a country of small fields enclosed by stone walls, with wooded hills rising tier on tier in the distance. Joe turned off the concrete highway into a dirt road and then into the long, winding drive, with a row of elm trees on either side, that led to the Gaylord place. The house, half hidden by trees and shrubbery, had once been a plain, rectangular one with four chimneys. The wings on either side were plainly of a later date. It looked big and shabby and comfortable.

J.M. Pyne pointed to a long, low wooden building, with many small-paned windows, off to the right. "That," he said to Frieda Guerdner, "is where the first Reuben Gaylord made carbines for the Union Armies before he built the Water Shop in Waterford. When I started making rifles 50 years ago, I used to buy my barrel steel from the old gentleman, and it was smooth-cutting stuff. Yonder is the big meadow where he had his rifle range."

The meadow sloped gently to the river, where there was a homemade footbridge suspended on wire cables well above the water. On the far side the meadow extended northeast for a good half-mile, until it met a steep wooded ridge that made a natural backstop for bullets.

Joe saw, at the firing point, the things he had asked for—a table and a spotting scope, a tub of water, and a wheelbarrow load of garden dirt with a spade sticking in it. The driveway ahead was full of cars. He had to stop.

The old man got stiffly down and gave his hand to the girl.

"Joe," he said, "don't claim too much. Let the gun talk."

II

They had to meet a lot of people on the east terrace. Some of them were friends of the Gaylords, country-club people in sports clothes who didn't matter. Joe guessed that most of the others were the sort of chiselers, disguised as businessmen, who swarmed whenever arms or ammunition could be made, in the hope of running a shoestring into a bank roll while no one was looking.

He saw one man he couldn't place—a tall man with graying hair and a proud unsmiling face who carried himself as if he had been a soldier or an athlete. He had a scar across his cheek, almost from his mouth to his ear, that might have been a saber cut. What made Joe look again was the dog that stood at the

man's heel, obedient, but trembling with eagerness. The dog was big, with the short black coat and tan markings of a Doberman pinscher, only taller at the shoulder and more powerful.

Joe started back to the car to get the gun, and guessed he'd better check first with the Gaylords. Reuben Gaylord, looking more like a nice college boy than a man in his middle 30s should, was busy at the table where the whisky had been set out. Mrs. Gaylord was talking to a little group of chiselers.

He waited for her, admiring the way she did it. She knew what they were as well as he did. She was being a good hostess. He did not like the kind of make-up she chose—dark tan, with the lips and fingernails a purplish red. But he knew her artificiality was only color deep.

"Do you see anybody who counts?" he asked when she got away.

She shook her head, "Reuben did the best he could. It seems all the purchasing commissions are at New Haven looking over the new submachine gun. There isn't a single person here who rates anything. But the newspapers have all sent reporters and photographers. And"—she made a face—"Winthrop Harris said he'd be here."

He did not feel free to ask Mrs. Gaylord what Winthrop Harris rated at Gaylord Arms. The story around the plant was that Harris represented new money in the company, but that Reuben Gaylord was still president in fact as well as on the letterhead.

"And," Connie Gaylord went on, "Harris is bringing an Army officer—a major or a major general or something."

Joe smiled. She understood as well as he did how it was with Army officers. The Army had adopted the Garand rifle in 1936. The choice had been so strongly criticized that the Army was touchy on the subject.

"Who," Joe asked, "is the fierce man with the big dog?"

"Oh," she said, "you mean Winkler. I suppose Reuben asked him because he has money. But he's only interested in his dogs. He breeds them and trains them to capture criminals."

Joe found J.M. Pyne beside the roadster with the rifle in his hands.

"Let's get started," he said.

"Mrs. Gaylord says there isn't anybody in the whole crowd who knows anything about guns."

"Mrs. Gaylord is mistaken," the old man retorted, and went off toward the firing point with the rifle.

Joe followed, lugging the case of ammunition. The old man sent two

boys off to the two-hundred-yard butts with a sheaf of targets, and orders to stay in the pit until they had pulled the targets down and raised a red flag as a signal to cease firing.

"What did you mean?" Joe asked. The old man did not answer.

"You said she was mistaken."

The old man grumbled something. Joe saw that the boys had to wade to reach the footbridge. The river was over its banks. He turned toward the terrace. Reuben Gaylord had started his guests toward the firing point. Joe braced himself. The hardest thing he had to do was to speak his piece about the gun. He wondered if he ought to begin by saying, "Ladies and gentlemen." He guessed that would sound too stiff.

"We should have had Reuben string a rope to keep them away," the old man said. He sat down on the camp stool behind the spotting scope, within reach of the field telephone on the table that connected with the target pit. The crowd stood in a semicircle, two or three deep. Joe picked up the rifle and faced them.

"Ladies and gentlemen." he said, "the rifle I have here was made, lock, stock and barrel, by J.M. Pyne. You all know who he is. The gun is a recoil-operated semi-automatic rifle. In other words, it fires each time you press the trigger."

He saw Winthrop Harris coming across the grass with the Army officer. He couldn't think of what to say next. He stood there sweating. Winthrop Harris and the officer joined the semi-circle. It was getting unbearable, when he remembered a sentence from the speech he had started to write that morning.

"The gun has certain advantages over any other semi-automatic rifle. It is loaded from standard Army clips. It takes two 5-shot clips at a time, so it is good for 10 shots without recharging—in fact, for 11 shots if you put one cartridge in the chamber. Thanks to its design, the gun does not heat up as fast in rapid fire as others. It is more accurate than other semi-automatic rifles. In our tests on this range it has proved as accurate as the Springfield service rifle with the same ammunition."

"Just a minute, Joe," J.M. Pyne interrupted. "The gun shot as well as the two service Springfields we had. We are not certain those two were up to standard."

Joe saw several people smiling at the old man's insistence on the pre-cise truth.

"I stand corrected," he said. "But all these are minor points, compared with the fundamental superiority of the gun. You all understand that modern mass production can go into high gear only when the product is designed to be built by mass-production methods. The Pyne rifle is the only semi-automatic rifle ever designed to take full advantage of such methods.

"It will not take 18 months or a year, or even 6 months to tool up for it. At most, it will be a 90-day job. And when you have tooled up for it you can make it three times as fast as you can make any other gun of its speed of fire. It overcomes the only serious objections to supplying every private in an army with a semi-automatic rifle—the slow-motion manufacture and the high cost. You may have wondered why the armies now fighting in Europe and Asia are not armed with semi-automatic rifles. The answer is, no country in the world, except the United States, can afford to wait for or to pay for the kind of semi-automatic rifles now being made."

Joe found himself out of words. He took a quick look over his shoulder. The targets were up. He saw Reuben Gaylord handing out cotton.

"Before I shoot the gun," he went on, "and while Mr. Gaylord makes sure you all have cotton to put in your ears, I want to tell you that the targets down there at two hundred are Army targets with a 10-inch bull. It is no trick to stay in the bull from the prone position when you take your time. I am going to see how many I can keep in there while shooting rapid fire. The Army says the ordinary soldier can fire 40 aimed shots in 60 seconds with the Garand. I'm going to shoot her at that speed . . . Reuben, will you hold a stop watch on me?"

He stripped two clips of cartridges into the gun and put a dozen more clips on the grass and lay down in the military prone position. He felt the sling go tight as the weight of his head and shoulders went into it, felt the wood of the stock warm and friendly against his cheek, felt the earth solid under his belly and his legs, saw the bull sitting on top of the sight, and all his nervousness was gone. He was home again. He was no talker. But this gun could talk.

"Fire," Reuben Gaylord said.

Joe broke the shot dead on, without conscious effort, and the front sight leaped up across the bull at twelve o'clock the way it should, and he had the good feeling with which the gun sat back against his shoulder and he heard the sharp clean blast from the muzzle ringing in his ears as he pulled the front sight down to 6 o'clock and again the gun sat back. He was in the groove, getting them off fast and clean, when the gun misfired.

He reached out for the bolt handle. He yanked the bolt back. But no cartridge came flying out. The gun had failed to feed. It had never happened before. It couldn't happen. But it had happened. The next cartridge just hadn't come out of the magazine to be picked up by the bolt as it went forward.

The old man leaned toward him. "Put in another clip."

Joe stripped a fresh clip into the magazine and the gun worked perfectly for 5 shots. He had to go on that way, putting in a fresh clip every 5 shots on top of the 5 cartridges that refused to come out of the magazine until he had fired his 40 shots.

"They're pretty well bunched," J.M. Pyne said, studying the target through the spotting scope.

"The time," Reuben Gaylord said, "was one minute and fifty-eight seconds."

Joe got off the ground. He saw the grin on the Army officer's face. He felt he had to say something, to admit that the gun had failed to do what the Garand would do.

"That was twice as long as I intended," he said.

The gun was pretty hot to handle, but he got the magazine out, meaning to see what was the matter with it.

"Let it alone," J.M. Pyne said. "You can't fix it now."

Joe put the magazine back. There wasn't anything else to do. He turned to the crowd again.

"We'll have that target up here in a few minutes," he said. "While we're waiting, I'll give the gun a mud test."

He spread out the pile of garden dirt, making a hollow, and dumped the tub of water into it. He puddled the mud and laid the gun in it. When he thought it was cool he picked it up and wiped it off on the grass.

"Before I shoot the gun again," he said, "I am going to take one precaution that would be difficult with any other semiautomatic rifle. I am going to look through the barrel to make sure that there isn't enough mud inside it so that the first shot will blow the muzzle off."

He took the barrel out, saw that it was clear, and put it back again. The gun fired 5 shots in spite of the mud in the action when he worked the bolt

by hand, but quit on the 6th shot as it had before.

The boy had come back with his 40-shot target. Joe saw that he had all but three of his shots in the black and gave the target to Reuben Gaylord to pass around.

He did most of the things he had planned to do. He took the gun completely apart with no tools but a loaded cartridge, and put it together again. He fired two successive 10-shot groups, taking his time, to show what the gun would do at 200 yards, and both times he kept the spread of the shots under 5 inches.

But he knew the show was a flop. The gun had balked. And nothing else mattered.

He asked if anyone would care to shoot the gun. Two news photographers came forward.

"We want a picture of a girl shooting the gun," one of them said. "How about that redheaded one?"

"It's up to her," Joe said.

They brought Frieda Guerdner over. Joe loaded the gun with the National Match ammo. It would kick more. He hoped she'd feel it.

"I'll need the sling shortened," she said.

Joe was afraid then that she knew what she was doing. She was taller than most girls and wider in the shoulders. But she would need the sling a good deal shorter than he did. He took up three holes.

She got down into the prone position. He could see that she was used to it. She had the loop of the sling high on her left arm, her left elbow under the gun, her left arm stretched far out, her right thumb around the grip, her legs at the proper angle to her body and spread wide apart as she hugged the ground.

"Lend me your hat, will you?" she said to J.M. Pyne. "The sun is in my eye."

The old man gave her his hat and she jammed it down over her eyes. Joe wondered if she was nervous. The sun couldn't possibly bother her.

"I want one sighter," she said as she settled again into the sling. "Will you tell me where this one goes?"

Joe knew that was what he would have asked in her place. A rifle sighted in for one person was right for another only if their eyes and their ways of aiming and holding were the same.

He watched her finger on the trigger. He could see her taking up on the pull. She did not flinch as she got the shot off, and he could see no sign that the recoil surprised her.

"You're in the black between one and two o'clock," the old man said. "About four inches from center each way."

"That was a good hold," she said. "I'll take a chance on it." She reached for the rear sight. "How much do I give it?"

"They're half-minute clicks," Joe said, hoping she didn't know what a half-minute of angle meant.

She knew. She gave the elevation screw four clicks down and the windage screw four clicks over.

He watched her as she shot. The recoil lifted that red hair of hers each time, but it did not disturb her rhythm. She got her first 5 shots off at regular intervals. He knelt down and loaded another clip into the gun.

When she had fired her 10 shots, J.M. Pyne turned to Joe. "I thought you said she couldn't shoot. Take a look."

Joe looked through the spotting scope. Her sight correction hadn't been quite enough. You really couldn't correct a sight on the strength of one shot. But her group was better than either of his 10-shot groups. He guessed it wasn't over four inches.

He knew how to take being beaten in a match with other men. But to be beaten by this girl was maddening. How had she learned to shoot like that? And what for? Why should a girl want to shoot? This one had deliberately deceived him with her story about hitting pop bottles, knowing that it would convince him she didn't know anything about shooting.

"I was wrong." Joe said to the old man.

The photographers asked Frieda Guerdner to pose for them standing up. They said the pictures of her they had got would be nothing to look at. The hat had hidden most of her face and the prone position was not graceful.

"I'm sorry," she said, "but I won't pose."

Joe looked at her. He would have guessed that she would like to see her picture in the papers. But it was plain she meant what she said. The photographers were astonished and indignant. They argued and cajoled. But it didn't do them any good.

III

Connie Gaylord asked Frieda Guerdner and J.M. Pyne and Joe to come in when the crowd had gone. Joe let the others go into the house ahead of him. He wanted a look at that magazine.

The Gaylords were in the gun room. One wall was lined with cases displaying examples of all the rifles Gaylord Arms had made, beginning with the Civil War carbines and counting through a series of buffalo rifles and long-range match rifles, and ending with the current model, a well-made single shot that had no sale to a public that demanded repeating rifles.

Over the fireplace was a large portrait of Reuben Gaylord the first, looking a good deal like U.S. Grant. On a stand at one side of the room was the first Gaylord power plant—a little 5-horse steam engine, all polished brass and steel, that the founder had built himself.

The room was, Joe felt, a museum that told the story of the rise and fall of Gaylord Arms. He looked at Reuben Gaylord, glass in hand, leaning carelessly against the mantel under the portrait of his grandfather, and the contrast saddend him. Everybody liked Reuben Gaylord, but no one took him seriously. He had inherited Gaylord Arms. It hadn't paid a dividend since.

"Joe," Reuben said, "what was the matter with the gun?"

"Somebody tampered with it."

"What?" Reuben said.

Joe saw that they were all leaning forward, startled and curious—all of them except J.M. Pyne.

"The magazine spring is a flat ribbon of steel," Joe said. "It is shaped like three v's in succession. Somebody cut off one whole v. That made the spring too short. It was only long enough to feed the first 5 cartridges."

"Who would do a thing like that." Reuben asked.

"Who had a chance to do it?"

"I did," J.M. Pyne said.

"But what for?" Reuben Gaylord demanded.

"I saw too many strangers when I got here this afternoon."

They all looked at the old man as if they thought he was a little cracked.

"I decided it was better," he added, "if the gun didn't do too well. The word will go out now that the gun is no good, and no one will bother about it."

"You mean," Reuben said, "that no one will buy it."

"No one would buy it anyway," the old man retorted. "It's too different from the others. And the Army isn't interested, or the Marine Corps. They've adopted the Garand. They won't look at any other gun. But I'd just as soon no one stole the idea."

Reuben started to say something,

and thought better of it. No one said anything. It was not easy to tell J.M. Pyne he had taken care against an imaginary danger. Joe felt sore and puzzled. He remembered bitterly the moment when the gun had balked for the first time. It wouldn't have been so bad if he hadn't said he was going to shoot 40 shots in 60 seconds. He could still see the self-satisfied grin on that Army officer's face. The old man had let him down. It wasn't like him. It wasn't like him to be so fearful, either.

faster to produce by producing it faster.

"Pyne is right," Joe said. "There's no chance to sell the gun to the Army, and as long as it's just an idea there isn't any chance to sell it to anybody else either. The market is full of buyers, but they aren't buying ideas. They want rifles. Springfield Armory and the big arms companies are making all they can for the Government. They will be for years to come. The purchasing commissions from the Dutch East Indies and the South

maybe $200,000."

"So what? I'm not talking arms factory production. I'm talking about the way the automobile people do things. Suppose we brought a man on here from Detroit like that fellow Bostwick you went to M.I.T. with. He'd make an engineering study and lay out the West Shop for real mass production. It would be a small unit by Detroit standards. But we'd show what could be done by using modern methods to make a gun like Pyne's. We'd produce guns three or four times

But Joe saw now that it hadn't done any good to demonstrate the gun to a crowd, and that it wouldn't have done any good, no matter who had been there or how well the gun had performed. He had taken it for granted that when you had a good thing, all you needed to do was to show it. Pyne target rifles had never needed any selling. His friends shot them and found out how good they were and talked about them, and other men wanted them. The old man had never been able to keep up with the demand.

But a semi-automatic rifle was different. It wasn't something handmade to suit an expert. It was a mass-production job. The superiority of Pyne's design was of a kind that only a man who was both a mechanic and an engineer could appreciate. And if he was a mechanic and engineer who had grown up in an old-fashioned factory—and all firearms factories were old-fashioned—he probably wouldn't see it. You'd have to prove to him that the Pyne gun was

American countries don't know where to turn. The State Department is glad to license sales to them. The Government wants them to have rifles. But where are they going to buy?"

"I know," Reuben Gaylord said. "But what can we do about it?"

"There's the whole West Shop," Joe said. "It's full of lathes and milling machines and drill presses. They're old, but they're good. All they need is jigs and fixtures. We could have the forgings delivered by the time we were tooled up."

"It would take $100,000 to start," Reuben said.

"What's $100,000?" Joe asked.

"A lot of money," Reuben Gaylord said.

"Not in times like these. Not when you're tooling up to make millions of dollars worth of stuff. You'd get your money back with one million-dollar order and make a profit besides."

"Maybe," Reuben Gaylord said. "Maybe you would. But somebody's got to stick his neck out first. Somebody's got to put up the $100,000,

as fast as they've ever been produced before. We'd get all the orders we could fill. And the time is coming when the Army is going to take anything it can get. The Army will give us orders if we're in production. And that's the only way we'll ever have a chance to prove that Pyne's gun is better than the Garand."

Reuben Gaylord smiled at Joe. "Have you any idea what George Bostwick gets for making engineering studies. His fee would be at least $5,000."

"I'm not surprised."

"It's too bad you're talking to me, Joe," Reuben Gaylord said, "instead of to my grandfather." He looked up at the portrait of Reuben Gaylord the first. "You might get somewhere with him. If you could sell him on your proposition, he would go out and get the money even if he had to hock everything he owned."

He poured himself another drink. Joe thought he'd had enough.

"The trouble is, Joe," he went on, "I'm a grandson. Did it ever occur to

you that there's the whole trouble with New England? The grandsons have got all the fine old factories and all the fine old names. And they're a timid lot. Their only ambition is to hang on to what they have."

"You can see how it is with me. I own this old house and the 700 acres that used to be a good farm. I own almost half the stock in Gaylord Arms, and if it goes to pot, as it will as soon as this little boom is over, I'll still have enough money to live here. Maybe I could raise $100,000. But why should I risk it? Why should I let myself in for all the grief that sort of thing means? I'm just not that kind of guy, Joe." He looked down at the tall glass in his hand. "I don't really care."

Joe felt there wasn't anything to say. He looked at J.M. Pyne to see if he was ready to go. The old man was sitting with his hands clasped around one knee and staring up at the portrait of Reuben's grandfather. Frieda Guerdner was sitting on the sofa beside him with her chin in her hand. She hadn't said a word, but Joe could see how interested she was.

Connie Gaylord stood up and started to leave the room. "I want to talk to Joe," she said.

He followed her out into the hall. She walked into the dining room and kicked the door shut.

"I like men who have no illusions about themselves, don't you? Who never let you down because they never promise anything. Who haven't got much on the ball and admit it. Who haven't any ambition and don't pretend to have."

"Yes," Joe said, because that seemed to be the thing to say.

"So," she said, "you really are dumb. You believe anything you hear, and never think."

Joe waited.

"Don't you know that's only his alibi?" she went on. "He says he doesn't care, and he cares so much he can't go to sleep at night. All his pride is in Gaylord Arms. Do you think he wants Winthrop Harris to take it away from him? Do you?"

"No," Joe said, "I don't suppose he does."

"Why do you think he went out to Jersey City to get you and J.M. Pyne? Because he doesn't care?"

"No," Joe said. "But he didn't seem much interested in tooling up to make the gun."

"He thought you were just talking, and maybe you were."

"No," Joe said, "I wasn't just talking. And he knew it."

She looked up at him, and he saw that her eyes were full of tears.

"I've got to save him," she said. "Don't you see I've got to save him? You can help. You can break through that pose of his. You go to work on him."

"All right," Joe said, "I will."

"If it was anybody else, I'd think you were yessing me. But there's something convincing about you, Joe."

She started for the door of the dining room. Joe took her arm and pulled her back.

"Listen," he said. "The first thing to do is to get George Bostwick."

"Consider it done," Connie Gaylord said. "What next?"

"Ask those South Americans up here and make them believe we are going to build the Pyne gun, and high pressure them into giving us a letter of intention, so we can get a clearance from the State Department."

"I can do something about that, too," she said. "You'd be surprised. But you understand, don't you? Please understand. Nothing matters except Reuben. He's sunk now, but if this thing goes through, he won't be."

"I understand," Joe said. "All I care about is the gun. We've got to make the gun."

The traffic was bad, driving back to Waterford at the hour when the day shifts from the big airplane factory and the machine-tool plants were coming out and the night shifts were going in.

Joe found a kind of relief in the difficulty of getting into town. He did not hear what Frieda Guerdner and the old man were saying. He was busy with his own thoughts.

He had come a long way since the day, a year ago, when he had appeared at Pyne's shop in Jersey City, hoping to persuade the old man to teach him how to make fine shooting rifles. Until then, his only tough problems had been those of a toolmaker. You didn't solve those with your hands alone. You had to think. But you worked with things you had learned how to control. You might have to make something to a tolerance of nothing minus and a half a thousandth plus. When you did you knew where you were. You could prove it with a micrometer caliper.

But if he was going to put the gun over, he would have to work with people. You couldn't change them to suit your purpose—heating them to a cherry red, quenching in oil, and drawing to the right color. You had to take them as they came, even if they were as crotchety as the old man, or as badly licked as Reuben Gaylord, or as hard to take as the redheaded girl beside him.

IV

They went to a place called Brick's for dinner—a large square room with a bar across one end that looked as if it had not changed for 50 years. Frieda noticed that Joe Hill carried the gun in with him and laid it on a chair beside him, and the waiter showed no surprise.

"I used to come here with your father," J.M. Pyne said to Frieda, "before you were born. The steaks are just as good now as they were in those days."

Frieda said she hadn't had any lunch, so steak appealed to her. The old man ordered a steak for three.

She looked across the table at Joe Hill and wished she had resisted the temptation to take him for a ride when he had told her that J.M. Pyne only made rifles for men who shot well enough to need them. Her impression of him at the moment had been that he was a big dumb young man who needed to be taken down, and she was the girl who knew how to do it. Now that she had seen him in action, she knew she had made a bad mistake. He wasn't dumb. He was merely not given to bright chatter, after the manner of the young men she knew in New York. And if he was arrogant, he had some right to be. He wasn't handsome—unless you counted his long, lean, hard build—but he was increasingly impressive. She wanted to make him talk. She had always found it too easy to get men to talk about themselves. But she was afraid she had alienated this one so completely that he would never tell her anything. The calm with which he ignored her was apparently final.

She saw that he had a cartridge he was turning back and forth in his fingers.

The cartridge wasn't the usual color. It was nickeled or tinned.

"Why the color?" she asked.

"It's a blue pill," he said. He rolled the cartridge across the tablecloth to her.

"I don't know what that means," she said.

"It's loaded to heavy pressure for use as a proof test on a rifle. The color is to prevent it being mixed with regular cartridges. I meant to fire that one this afternoon to show that the Pyne gun would stand it."

"The gun would take it," J.M. Pyne said. "But I don't hold with firing blue pills from the shoulder. You run too big a chance of getting your head blown off. At Springfield Armory they put the gun in a rest with steel plates

around it, so if anything lets go no one gets hurt. Joe, you put that where you won't pick it up by mistake."

Joe Hill obediently put the blue pill in the watch pocket of his trousers.

That was that, so Frieda tried again to make Joe Hill talk.

"I feel guilty," she said, "taking a barrel that J.M. Pyne intended for you."

The old man chuckled. "You needn't. If Joe wants a barrel, he can make it himself as well as I can."

"It wouldn't be a Pyne barrel," Frieda said.

"No one could tell the difference if he used my tools," the old man said. "At least I couldn't."

The steak came then. The old man grew reminiscent as they ate, telling them about the days when he had shot offhand at 200 yards against men like Fred Ross and Michael Dorrler and Doctor Hudson. But over his coffee he remembered the semiautomatic rifle.

"I'm sorry about this afternoon, Joe," J.M. Pyne said. "Maybe I should have told you that I had cut off that spring."

"I wish you had," Joe Hill said. "I wouldn't have made such a fool of myself in front of that Army officer."

"I know that came hard, Joe. But I thought it would look better if you were suprised when the gun balked. And I had to do something when I saw Winkler there."

"Why?" Joe Hill asked. "What about Winkler?"

"You saw him, didn't you, Frieda?" the old man said. "The man with the scar across his face who had the big dog."

"Yes, I did," Frieda Guerdner said, remembering how the man had stared at her.

"He's made a hobby all his life of rifle actions, and he's the most successful thief of rifle actions in the world."

"Connie Gaylord told me he had no interest in guns," Joe Hill said.

"I wouldn't know any more about him than she does if it hadn't been for a German gunsmith I went to New Haven with 10 years ago," J.M. Pyne said. "My friend saw Winkler on the street and pointed him out to me. He told me some things about Winkler. I told him that when I was working on the Bennett semiautomatic pistol in 1917, one pistol disappeared. In the '20s a copy of that pistol was patented all over Europe. They even sold it here. Bennett was dead by that time and his heirs didn't have any money to fight with. My friend said he had no doubt Winkler had the pistol stol-

en and sent it over."

"You think he's working for somebody over there?" Frieda said.

The old man shrugged his shoulders. "From what I've heard, he's working for Winkler. That's why he's rich."

"What good did it do to cut off the spring?" Frieda asked. "He'll try to steal your gun just the same, won't he?"

"In the long run, there's no way to stop the theft of military arms. The moment a thing goes into production it can be stolen, and it is. I don't doubt that Winkler has a Garand of the latest model."

"But what if he stole your gun now?"

J.M. Pyne smiled. "He won't—not after what he saw today. He thinks it's got a bug in it, and he'll wait until we get the bug out. They always like to wait until a gun is perfected before they take it. That's why I say Winkler probably has the latest Garand. He wouldn't want one of the first 40,000, before they changed it so it would shoot decently."

"You speak of it as if it were all a matter of course," Frieda said.

"In my experience," J.M. Pyne said, "stealing is a matter of course. There's nothing romantic or exciting about it. You can bet Winkler never takes any chances. He hires somebody for a few dollars to steal something he expects to make thousands out of. Perhaps sometimes it's just a case of adding to his collection. I understand he takes great pride in having the best collection of modern military small arms. But mostly he's out to make money."

"Why can't something be done about him?" Frieda asked.

"What?" J.M. Pyne asked.

"I thought there was a law forbidding individuals to possess machine guns unless they were registered."

"Including sawed-off shotguns and 22 caliber pistols with shoulder stocks," J.M. Pyne said. "But like most laws about guns, it's only obeyed by honest men. If you wanted to get out a search warrant against Winkler, you'd have to get evidence. He's got money and he's got position. He's probably a director of the First National Bank, if not of Waterford Aircraft, so it would have to be good evidence. And if you did get a warrant, you wouldn't find anything."

The old man talked of other things after that. When he said he was tired, they walked with him around the corner to the place where he and Joe Hill had found rooms over a second-hand store.

"Frieda," the old man said, "I'll be seeing you at the shop in the morning."

"You truly don't mind my watching you work?"

"I'll be glad to have you," he said. He turned to Joe. "I'd put the gun in the safe."

Frieda walked with Joe Hill to his roadster. He was driving her back to Gaylord Arms to get her car.

"You're sore," she said, as they started off.

"You could have told me you knew how to shoot."

"I did."

"No, you didn't. You told me that pop-bottle story because you knew it would make me think you didn't know what rifle shooting was about."

"You had it coming. You were so superior when I said I wanted a Pyne rifle. You might as well have laughed out loud."

"I didn't mean to high-hat you," he said. "I was trying to keep you away from the old man."

"You're bound to make him do what you want," she said, hoping to sting him out of his matter-of-factness. "You don't care what he wants."

"He should be making another model of the gun," Joe Hill said. "So far, he hasn't even got working drawings. He made this one by cut and try."

"I am sure you can make him do whatever you want him to."

"He'll go to work on the gun just as soon as you get out of here," Joe Hill said.

"At least he'll have a few days of doing what he loves to do before he has to work on something that doesn't interest him."

"I am not so sure as you are that the semiautomatic rifle doesn't interest him. You don't know how important it is. He does. He knows he's got something the whole world has been trying for ever since 1918. Longer than that, of course. But especially since then."

Frieda did not try again to get under his skin until the watchman in the shanty at the gate to Gaylord Arms had let them in and Joe Hill had stopped alongside her car.

"I think it's stupid of you to worry about what J.M. Pyne does," she said when she had got out. "What you need to worry about is how you're going to make the gun."

He was opening up the rear deck of his car. He paused and looked her up and down as if he were appraising a rifle he had to make up his mind about.

"Maybe," he said—"maybe you

aren't the dumb little rich girl I picked you for."

For a moment she wanted to yell at him that she was not dumb, not little, and not rich—especially not rich. But she recovered herself in time.

"I earn my own living," she said.

"As a model?"

"No!" She realized she had spoken hotly when there was no reason to. She had modeled clothes for photographers when she first came to New York. She could do it then because she hadn't had enough to eat while she was at the art school in Chicago. She was still slim by ordinary standards, but she no longer had the paperdoll flatness of a model. "I'm a commercial artist," she said.

V

She spent 10 hours a day with J.M. Pyne, watching the painstaking way in which he did things and listening to his talk of rifles and riflemen, and marveling at the passion for his chosen work that still burned in him. She knew, from what he said, that Joe Hill came into the shop after they left and worked until two o'clock in the morning on some kind of gadget to be used in making the Pyne gun, but she did not see him until toward the end of the third day.

J.M. Pyne had her new rifle in the vise. He was turning in the last of the screws that held the telescope blocks.

Joe Hill stood watching. He must have noticed that the old man had chosen a Gaylord action with fine English scroll engraving and found a stock made from a beautiful piece of crotch walnut, with a full feather figure running the length of it.

"I thought," he said, "that you didn't care how the outside of a rifle looked."

J.M. Pyne acted as if he'd been caught in something he didn't want to admit.

"I don't usually," he said. He glanced at Joe Hill over the top of his glasses. "Why not go to dinner with us, and come back here afterward and see how this gun shoots?"

Joe Hill said he would have to leave early, because he had a date.

At dinner, he told the old man how hopeful he was about the semiautomatic rifle. Reuben Gaylord had actually wired Bostwick, who would be in from Detroit in time for lunch the next day, which was Saturday; and he had a promise from the South American crowd that they would be in Waterford on Monday.

"One other thing," Joe Hill said as he was leaving. "I've asked Reuben to have the Water Shop wired for the watchmen's clocks. The electricians start tomorrow, and hereafter a watchman will go through every hour seven days a week, just as he goes through the rest of the plant."

Frieda saw that J.M. Pyne was eager to get back to the rifle. They followed Joe Hill out. She saw his car ahead. He stopped beside the curb and a girl got in. J.M. Pyne didn't notice, so she said nothing. But presently she remembered where she had seen the girl before. It was at the information desk in the offices of Gaylord Arms.

She remembered the narrow, slanting Slavic eyes that gave the girl a slightly exotic look, and the rounded feminine figure, positively luscious, and, finally, the red hair. It wasn't exceptional red hair, Frieda thought. It didn't approach her own. But perhaps a man like Joe Hill couldn't see the difference.

"There's going to be a thunderstorm," J.M. Pyne said. "Have you got a raincoat?"

She knew better than to argue with him. She stopped at the hotel and got her raincoat.

The old man put the rifle in the machine rest and gave her a little telescope with which to watch the target, and began to shoot. When he had fired 10 shots, she saw that he was smiling. When he had fired 50 shots, she saw that he was happy at the way the gun was shooting.

He went on and on for hours, while the storm broke outside and the thunder rolled and the lightening flashed and the rain drove against the window-panes, trying one make of match ammunition after another. It was 11 o'clock when he took the gun out of the rest and cleaned it.

"Tell me," Frieda said, "how do you feel about the semiautomatic rifle? Do you care whether they make it?"

He did not answer in words. He went to the big old-fashioned safe against the wall and turned the combination. He came back to the bench with the breech action and stock of the semiautomatic rifle in one hand and the barrel in the other. He put the gun together and held it in the pool of bright light from the big bulb over the bench.

Then he took it apart, stripping it down quickly, until all the parts lay on the bench.

"I hope I'll be remembered as a maker of fine shooting rifles," he said. "But"—he made a gesture with his hand at the parts on the bench top—"that took more brains than anything else I ever did. Of course I want it made."

He picked up the barrel as if he were going to fit it back in place, and then he looked at Frieda over his glasses.

"It's good," he said. "It's as good as Joe thinks it is."

She was looking straight at him, thinking what a fine old man he was, so patient and so knowing and so gentle, when a harsh voice spoke out of the darkness behind him. "Be quiet and you won't get hurt."

The old man whirled, the rifle barrel in his hands, and struck hard and low. The intruder groaned as the iron bar hit his shin, and he went down. The next instant J.M. Pyne slumped to the floor as someone struck him from behind, and Frieda saw that there was a second man behind the first—a short and heavy man, with little eyes peering out from folds of flesh above the handkerchief he was wearing as a mask. •

LET THE GUN TALK

VI

"MADAME," he said to Frieda, "I am Henry." For a moment she could only stare at him in panic, and then the meaning of his words came to her. He was addressing her with a deference that could only mean he regarded her as his superior, and friendly to his purpose.

He took off the handkerchief he was wearing as a mask, revealing as ugly a face as Frieda had ever seen, with thick, protruding lips and a nose that looked as if it had been smashed flat, except for the big nostrils. He was short, for a man, no taller than she was, but wide, thick and powerful. She felt that a gorilla, wishing to make friends with her, would smile as he was smiling now.

She knew it would do no good to scream. She couldn't possibly scream loud enough to be heard outside the Water Shop; and the watchman was either in his shanty at the factory gate, a hundred yards away, or making his rounds of the other buildings. He never came into this place.

She did the thing she had to do. She knelt down beside J.M. Pyne and put her hand over his heart. His body seemed quite lifeless. A bruise on the side of his head was swelling fast. But his heart was beating.

Her mind leaped ahead. She told herself that this thug who had knocked out the man from behind with a blow so quick and cruel, and then said to her "I am Henry," thought she was somebody else. He had addressed her as "madame." He didn't know the name of the woman he supposed she was, or he would have used it. His manner said that she was his superior, and that he wanted to please her, and that they were both there on the same errand. Until he found out how mistaken he was, she had power over him. And if she was guessing right, the bolder she was the better. She took one quick breath and assumed the role he so innocently suggested.

"At least," she said as she stood up, "you were not clumsy enough to kill him."

"I have been taught how to hit with this." He held out in his hand what looked like a long leather pouch containing something heavy. "They go to sleep for a time. That is all that happens. I know how to do it."

"You know nothing," Frieda said. "You are stupid and careless." She pointed to the tall man, who still sat on the floor holding his shin with both hands. The handkerchief had slipped down and she saw that he was a boy of nineteen or twenty, with a nice face. He had blue eyes and close cropped blond hair, and his mouth was drawn with pain. "Look at him!"

"Please," Henry said, and his tone was abject, "how could we know that a man so old would do such a thing?"

She was secretly delighted.

He was a tough criminal, probably a murderer, but he was no more proof against a woman's words than gentler men.

"Why didn't you wait until I had gone?" Frieda demanded. "How do you think I can get away now?"

"Please do not be angry," Henry begged, and she saw that he was fearful of her anger, and she guessed he was afraid that she might make a bad report of him to somebody higher up. "We will take you with us."

The idea, which he seemed to take as a matter of course, was so startling to her that she had to have time to think about it.

"If you had waited, everything would have been so simple."

"But, madame, you had him open the safe. I thought you meant us to come in while the gun was out. What if he had put the gun back while we waited?"

"You do not know how to open an old safe like that?"

"I know how, yes. I have the tools. But it takes time. It makes a noise. It is late. We have a long way to go."

She looked straight at him. He dropped his eyes before hers and she made her decision. He was afraid of her, and because he was afraid, she might somehow save the Pyne gun.

"Very well," she said, shrugging her shoulders to let him know how impatient she was with his excuses. "I will go with you because you have made it impossible for me to do anything else. Do your job."

Henry stood behind the boy and put one hand under each of his arms and lifted him to his feet.

"How bad is it, Louis?" he asked.

"It feels as if it were broken" the boy said, holding one foot off the floor.

"Here, rest against the bench."

The boy supported his weight on the bench while Henry leaned down and felt of the injured shin. The boy shut his teeth.

"No," Henry said, "it is not broken."

He took a long narrow bag, like a sail bag, from his belt. He picked up the rifle barrel with which J.M. Pyne had struck the boy and stuffed it in the bag, then the stock and the other parts lying on the bench. He tied the drawstring and hung the loop around his neck so the bag hung down his back, and took a flashlight out of his pocket.

"Come, Louis," he said, "rest one hand on my shoulder . . . gracious lady, will you be so kind as to follow us?"

Frieda picked up her raincoat and her purse and followed them into the next room. She saw a pistol butt sticking out of Henry's back pocket and knew it for a Luger. She noticed for the first time that both men had taken off their shoes and were wearing heavy knitted socks. Henry opened the door into the next room, which was dark. His flashlight showed that it was half full of empty packing cases. Frieda guessed that they had waited here, perhaps for hours. The partition was of rough wood, with cracks between the boards, so they could have heard everything in J.M. Pyne's shop and probably have seen everything too.

Henry opened another door. She felt a draft, damp and cool, as if a window were open on the river. Then, as he swung his flashlight, she saw the window. There was a long, light ladder on the floor. Louis sat on a packing case and Henry turned off his flash. She heard the ladder scraping across the floor.

Then he turned the flashlight on and laid it on the floor, so the light did not shine out of the window.

He found two pairs of heavy workman's shoes against the wall. He gave one pair to Louis and put on the other pair.

"I will go down first," Henry said, turning off the light, "and lash the ladder."

She heard him climbing over the sill. She stood in the dark, unable to see anything and hearing nothing but the rain outside and the boy's breathing close beside her, for what seemed a long time. Then she heard Henry climbing back through the window.

124   THE GUN DIGEST

His feet struck the floor heavily.

He turned the flash on, keeping it low, until he found a heavy canvas bag with a light line fastened to the leather handles. She guessed that the bag held the tools he had bought in case he had to break open the safe. His flash went out as he lowered the bag out of the window.

"Madame," he said, "I will go first because I will have to help Louis. When I get him down, you come. You will have to do it by the feel. But do not be afraid. I will be below you on the ladder, ready to catch you. It is only 12 feet to the boat. If you are

to do something. Henry had said they had a long way to go. They must have a car parked across the river. Once they were in the car, she could tell them to stop at a gas station while she telephoned. She could telephone the police.

She buttoned her raincoat and swung one leg over the window sill, feeling with her foot in the dark for a rung of the ladder. Her foot found a rung. She could feel, as she let her weight rest on the rung, that the ladder was not solid. She remembered that it stood in a boat. Of course it wasn't solid.

ladder and then the big splash as he tossed the ladder overboard.

"Here, Louis," he said, "cut the bow line."

Henry leaned so close his shoulder touched hers as he cast off another line. She heard an oar scrape against the stone foundation of the building. He dropped the oars in the locks and she felt the boat jump ahead as he pulled. He swung the bow downstream. Frieda felt the current take hold of the boat.

The rain lashed her face, forcing her to keep her eyes almost closed. There was water in the bottom of the

L. REEDSTROM.

careful there will be no danger. You are not afraid?"

"Of course not," Frieda said, and put her hand hard against her mouth, so he could not hear her teeth chattering.

The boy groaned once as he climbed through the window. Frieda could hear Henry's words of encouragement. She walked to the window and put her hand on the sill and found the ladder. The ladder creaked with the weight of the two men down there in the dark. She could hear the river rushing by, and the rain.

"Come now," Henry called to her.

Frieda took hold of the ladder. She had only to give it a quick hard push outward and run back into the shop and on into the factory yard. They could not follow her. But J.M. Pyne's gun would be gone. If she went with these men, she would have a chance

Her breath came short. She told herself not to be frightened. What was there to be afraid of? Henry was afraid of her. And then she heard him speak.

"Take it easy," he said.

She swung the other foot over the window sill, holding tightly to the ladder. She reached down into the dark for another rung. The she felt Henry's weight on the ladder below her. She took another step down. His big hand grasped her ankle and guided her foot down to the next rung. She went on down quickly and he helped her to find the broad seat in the stern of the boat.

His flashlight went on, and she saw how neatly the ladder was lashed to the thwart in the middle. Louis was up forward. Henry had a knife in his hand as he turned off his flash. Frieda heard him cutting the lashings of the

boat; she could feel it soaking through her light pumps.

"Gracious lady," Henry said, "would you be so kind as to hold the gun? It is in my way and I cannot put it on the bottom of the boat because of the water."

She took the gun in its cloth bag and laid it across her lap. He picked up his oars again, rowing with quick short strokes.

Frieda did not dare ask any questions, for fear she would ask something to which she was supposed to know the answer. She could only wait for whatever might happen. She felt her hair. It was so wet she could squeeze water out of it. A trickle of water ran down behind one ear and on down her neck.

"I am sorry it is so wet," Henry said. "But if it were not raining, it would be moonlight. The rain is bet-

ter for us."

"I do not mind getting wet," Frieda said.

She asked herself how long it would be before someone would find J.M. Pyne. It was close to one o'clock by now. No one would go into the Water Shop except Joe Hill. When he got home and found that the old man hadn't come in, he would be worried about him. He'd drive to Gaylord Arms to look for him. But Joe Hill had gone places with the girl from the information desk. It might be daylight before he got home.

The boat suddenly struck hard aground, so hard that she was thrown forward on her knees. She heard Louis groan. Henry turned on his flash, and she saw that they were on a narrow sand bar around which the current swept. Henry stepped overboard into shallow water and shoved the boat off, and climbed in again.

"If you would be so kind, take the flash," he said to Frieda. "Turn it on every once in a while, and if I am going ashore tell me."

Frieda stole a glance at her watch the first time she used the flash. It was five minutes past one. She was aware of a strange roaring sound in the distance.

"What is that?" she asked.

"A dam," Henry said. "Keep the light on. I want to go as close as I can but it would be bad if we went over."

He ran the boat aground a few yards above the dam, and got overboard and helped Louis ashore.

"You sit here," he said to Louis, and I will come back after you." He turned to Frieda. "If you will hold the light I will drag the boat around."

He dragged the boat 10 or 15 feet before he stopped to rest and asked her to turn off the flash. She could hear his heavy breathing.

"It is hard," he said. "But it is better this way. They will send out an alarm over I do not know how many states to look for us. They will be stopping cars on all the roads from New York to Canada, but we will not be in a car. We will be safe in our little house by the pond."

He hauled the boat 50 or 60 yards before he got it close to the water below the dam. "I made a mistake," he said, as he straightened up. "I should have killed the old man."

"Do you really think so?" she asked, trying to sound as matter of fact as she felt he would expect her to be.

"The old man knows too much. It would have been better. But it is too late now. If you will sit here in the boat, I will go back for Louis."

VII

Frieda watched the spot of light from the flash flickering ahead of him. The news he had so casually given her about the house by the pond meant the end of her hope. She couldn't say she had to telephone. She couldn't scream at a passing policeman. She could only go with these men down the river in the dark. When they found out who she was, they would certainly feel that she knew too much.

She tried pushing the boat. If she could get it into the water before Henry came back, she could go on with the gun. She tried again, lifting until she thought her heart would burst. But it was no use.

She sat down on the gunwale of the boat. The gun was lying on the thwart. She could throw it into the boil of water just below the dam and run. Only she couldn't run in the black dark. She couldn't help making tracks in the mud and Henry could travel a lot faster with a light than she could without one. He would find her with the light, and he would shoot.

She looked back. Henry was coming with Louis. It couldn't be long before she was exposed. These men had a boss. They thought she was a friend of his. Her pose was good only until the moment when he saw her.

She loosened the drawstrings of the bag that held the gun and reached in. She felt the barrel and stock. She reached down to the bottom of the bag and found the bolt. But if she took the bolt it would be noticed the minute they got the gun out of the bag. She wanted something special, something that would not be noticed at once, and that would not be easy to replace. She felt the trigger guard. But it was like a Springfield trigger guard. She found the hammer. She knew that was something special. Most bolt-action guns had no hammer, but the Pyne gun had one. Its design was something of which J.M. Pyne was proud.

She took the hammer and put it in the pocket of her raincoat, an oddly shaped piece of steel, thicker than a silver dollar, but not so big around, and no heavier. She pulled the strings of the bag tight again and calculated her chances. They wouldn't discover that the hammer was missing until they tried to put the gun together; they wouldn't discover it then unless they knew about it. But without it you couldn't fire the gun. She wondered if a gunsmith who had never seen the hammer could figure out the shape of the missing part.

Henry and Louis were within a few yards now. If she tossed it into the river, they would never know. She would run no risk. But if something happened so that Pyne got his gun back he would want the hammer. Joe Hill had said he had no working drawings. He would have to cut and try to replace the hammer. It might take him a week.

Henry picked up the bow of the boat, which she had been unable to lift, and pulled it forward. Then he got behind the stern, his legs bent. With a heave and a grunt, he shoved the boat into the water. He helped Louis into the bow. Frieda sat down in the stern.

Henry rowed steadily for an hour. "I think," he said, "we have come almost far enough. Now I will have to keep close to the bank to find the place."

He swung the boat over to the right bank and let it drift with the current.

They ran along the bank for half an hour, until they came to a rocky cliff that rose almost straight up from the water and higher than the light of the flash would reach.

"Soon we will be there," Henry said.

After a few minutes Frieda saw a break in the cliff. Henry swung the boat toward it. She had a glimpse of a small brook boiling down over boulders into the river. Henry got overboard.

"We walk from here," he said, holding out his hand to her.

Frieda stepped into water that swirled up over her skirts, pulling at her legs. She started for the shore, hoping that her pumps would stay on until she got there.

"No, no," Henry said, "Do not step on the bank. We must not leave footprints. We must walk in the stream."

Frieda sat on a boulder that stuck out of the water. Henry helped Louis out of the boat and to another boulder. He handed the gun to Frieda and the bag of tools to Louis.

In the light of the flash, the leaves of the trees, washed by the rain, were a strange pale green. Henry picked up stones from the bottom of the brook, some of them as big as he could lift, and dropped them in the boat.

When the stones had sunk the boat so low the gunwales were only a few inches above the water he reached in and pulled a plug in the bottom of the boat. Then he walked back to the boulder where Louis sat and slung the bag of tools over his shoulder. He took the gun from Frieda and slung it

on top of the tools.

"Now," he said to her, "if you will walk ahead holding the light, I will help Louis."

"I can't walk in the water," Frieda said, "My shoes will come off."

"I will fix them," Henry said.

He cut long pieces of the light braided line with which he had lowered the bag of tools from the window of the Water Shop to the boat.

"Please to hold up your foot."

Frieda managed, sitting on the boulder, to hold one foot at a time clear of the water. He tied her pumps on, putting the cord around several times, making sure it was not too tight for comfort, and tying the ends with a knot she had never seen before.

"Now," he said, "we go."

Frieda staggered upstream, holding the flashlight. One foot went down in the crack between two big stones grinding the ankle bone so hard that tears came to her eyes. She looked back. The boy was tall. He looked a foot taller than Henry. He had one arm around Henry's neck and Henry had one arm around his waist as he hopped forward on one leg.

It seemed impossible for them to travel a hundred yards that way up the boulder-strewn bed of the brook. But they were coming on. Frieda shut her teeth. Once she stumbled and fell to her knees. But she kept on until she came to a tight barbed-wire fence, stretched between trees on either bank. The water was flush with the lowest strand.

Henry lifted the wire while she ducked under it. He had to lift it higher for Louis. He put one hand on the bottom of the brook, his chin in the water, and shoved the wire high with the other hand. They sat down to rest after that, each on a separate boulder.

"Come," Henry said, "we go."

They came to an old stone dam, five or six feet high, with one end broken out where the brook tumbled down over a pile of rocks. They climbed up the rocks in the rushing water on their hands and knees. For a few yards they walked on a smooth, sandy bottom. And then they were in the boulders again.

"Henry," the boy said, "I can go no more. Leave me here."

"Come, Louis," Henry said. "It is only a little way to the road."

"I can go no more," the boy said. "Let me sleep."

"You can sleep all you want when we get home. You can sleep until Sunday—when he comes," Henry said, dragging the boy relentlessly forward.

So, Frieda thought. *The boss is not coming until Sunday.*

They trusted her. It would be simple to run away as soon as it was light, and find a house and a telephone. It must be nearly daylight now. She'd go as soon as they were asleep.

She guessed that they walked a good quarter of a mile farther up the brook before they came to a bridge of logs with rotting planks on top, a bridge that had sagged so low the flooded brook was running over it inches deep.

"From here it is easy," Henry said. Frieda stepped on a rock and was raising one knee to the bridge when her foot slipped and she went down, turning her ankle. The pain was sickening. She scrambled up again, determined to ignore the ankle, and found she couldn't put any weight on her right foot. It hurt too much.

"What is the matter?" Henry asked.

"I've sprained my ankle." He got down into the water to help her. "It is nothing," she added, wanting to believe it.

He lifted her up and sat her on the bridge. "Wait," he said. "First I will get Louis ashore where it is not so wet, and then I will help you. It is only a little way from here."

Henry got Louis over to the bank and came back with the flash. He lifted her to her feet and put his arm around her.

"It is only a few meters," he said. "Lean on me."

Frieda hopped forward across the bridge into a woods road. It had not been used for years. It was hardly wider than a footpath.

"I've got to rest," she said at last. She managed, with his help, to sit down.

"You had better let me carry you," he said.

"No," she said, "I can go on."

"It is only a little way now," he said.

This time he was telling the truth. After 50 yards the flashlight showed a low cabin with an addition on either side and windows with heavy board shutters.

"We will go around to the front," Henry said.

They passed between the cabin and an open shed, with a half-built boat upside down on wooden horses under it, and, beyond, Frieda saw the gleam of water. That must be the pond Henry had spoken of.

She sat down on the step while Henry unlocked the front door and lit a large oil lamp that hung from the ceiling. He came back and helped her across the porch and into a chair.

"This," he said, with pride, "is our home."

Frieda saw a small room with a rough stone fireplace, a few chairs, a phonograph, and a portable radio on a shelf against the wall. An alarm clock that hung from a nail above the fireplace said half past four.

"In here," he said, opening a door, "is your room."

Frieda had a glimpse of a small room with a white iron bed on either side and a chest of drawers at the end with a mirror over it.

"Over here," Henry said, opening the opposite door, "is our room." He opened a door to a third room and went in and lighted a lamp hung from the wall on a bracket, with what looked like a round concave mirror behind it. "And this is the kitchen."

She saw a room hardly bigger than a yacht's galley, with an oil stove on one side and a sink with the pump at the end. She heard him pumping water. Then she saw him put a teakettle on the stove and light a flame under it.

"I am heating water for your ankle." he said, "It is best to soak it in hot water. Then I'll bandage it. I am good at bandages."

He knelt down in front of her and lifted the injured ankle gently. She gave a sigh of relief when he pulled the free end of the knot and took the cord off.

"Go back and get Louis," she said.

"First I will get your ankle into the warm water," Henry said.

"Do what I tell you. The ankle can wait."

He stood up and bowed, with a little jerk of his head. "I am here to do whatever you ask."

Henry went into the kitchen and got a bottle of whisky and glasses and a pitcher of water. He poured whisky.

"Drink," he said. "You are shivering. You were in the water too long."

"It is true," she said, glad that he did not guess why she was shaking.

The fear of what might happen to her had gripped her again, but she managed to raise the glass without spilling any.

"Go and get Louis," she said.

VIII

Frieda heard the screen door shut behind him. She waited a full minute before she stood up. By pushing a chair along and supporting herself with her hand on the back of it, she

reached the radio. She turned the switch, and presently a light began to glow, so she knew it was working. She turned it off again.

She was afraid that Henry and Louis would listen to a news broadcast from the Waterford station. There was one at noon every day. The story of the burglary at Gaylord Arms would be on by noon. Henry and Louis would learn that she wasn't the person they thought she was. If she could get inside the box she could loosen the connections.

The back of the box was fastened with screws. She hadn't time to hunt for something that would turn the screws. She did not dare push the box off the shelf and let it fall on the floor. That would be harder to explain than the news.

She went back to the chair at the table where Henry had left her. Then she saw that her clothes were still dripping water on the floor. She had left a trail of water wherever she had gone. But it didn't matter so long as she hadn't knocked the radio off its shelf. She took off her other pump and what was left of her stockings. She felt in the pocket of her raincoat for the gun hammer. It did not seem a safe place for it. She put it in her brassiere.

She heard Henry and Louis coming. Henry half carried Louis across the porch and to a chair. The boy's wet face was white and set. Frieda knew by now what it was like to hop along on one foot. She wondered how the boy had lasted through that trip up the brook. She looked down and saw that his shoe was oozing blood.

Henry brought a small galvanized-iron tub half full of cold water and put it down in front of her and poured boiling water into it from the teakettle while he tested the mixture with his hand.

"Try that, please," he said.

Frieda tried the water. It was very hot. But she managed gradually to get her foot down in it. She looked again at Louis. His teeth were clenched, the muscles of his jaws were standing out with the effort he was making to avoid groaning with pain. He was as tall and broad-shouldered and lean and hard as Joe Hill. But he was a boy and he was hurt. She remembered things she had heard about injuries to a bone and how serious they could be.

"Let us see how bad his leg is," she said.

Henry pulled Louis' chair under the overhead lamp and raised the injured leg up on the seat of another chair and took off the shoe and the blood-soaked sock. He was about to roll up the leg of the boy's heavy denim trousers when Frieda stopped him.

"Use your knife," she said.

Henry obediently took out his knife and cut away the heavy cloth, and shook his head at what he saw. Frieda knew that if infection set in, the boy might loose his leg.

"Get some warm water," she said. "Have you any absorbent cotton?"

Henry shook his head.

"Clean towels, then."

He went into the kitchen and

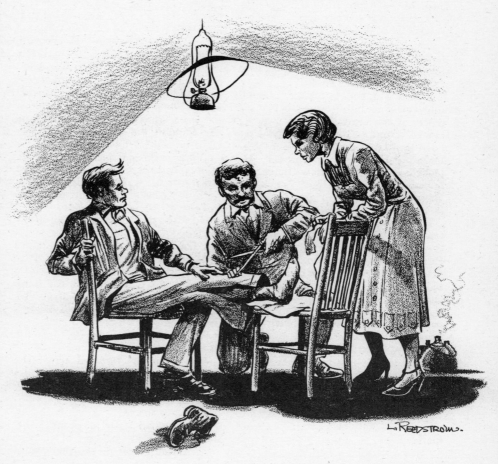

brought a tin washbasin half full of water, and several towels. Frieda picked out the oldest and softest towel and dipped it in the basin.

"I will do it," Henry said.

"No," she said, "pull my chair around so I can reach."

She bathed the wound as gently as she could and washed away the blood that covered the leg and the ankle below it. Then she poured whisky over the whole surface and began to make bandages by tearing a towel in strips.

"I can do that," Henry said. "I know how."

Frieda gave him the strips, and he bound up the wound with the same skill he had shown in tying on her pumps.

"The bandage must be kept wet," she said. "And he must not put his weight on that foot. I know that much."

Henry picked the boy up in his arms and carried him into the bedroom. He came back and got the whisky and a glass.

"I will now give him a big drink so he can go to sleep," he said.

Frieda could hear them talking about their night's work.

"You are badly hurt, Louis," Henry said, "But at least we have done a good job. We have the gun."

"Do you think he will be angry because of his girl?" Louis asked.

So that was what they thought— that she was the boss' girl. But why did they think that?

Henry came back into the room to ask her if she would like food. "I have

rye bread and Swiss cheese and sausage."

Frieda shook her head. He went into the kitchen. Presently he came back with two enormous sandwiches, made of thick slices of bread with cheese and liver sausage between, and bottles of beer.

"I am hungry," he said, "and so is Louis."

With an effort, Frieda spoke in her normal voice, "I am going to bed."

"Let me bandage your ankle first."

"No," she said, "it will not do any good to bandage it. But you can help me."

He put down his sandwiches and beer and got a roll of adhesive tape.

"Please," he said, "this will help. I have done it before."

He took her foot on his knee, passed the adhesive tape under the arch of her foot and, pulling it tight, crossed it over the top of her instep. Freida had to admit to herself that the ankle felt better.

He got a tin candlestick and lit the candle and put it on the chest of drawers between the two iron beds in the room he had said was hers. Then he got matches and a clean towel and helped her into the room. She sat down on the one chair.

"Louis must have a doctor," she said.

"It is impossible until he comes tomorrow. I cannot leave here to get a doctor until he has come for the gun."

"You mean not until Sunday?"

He nodded. "But do not be afraid. We rented this place a long time ago. We are known to be workmen in the big Waterford machine shop. We drive to work every day except Saturday and Sunday. Our car is parked at the end of the good road half a mile from here. We have no neighbors. As long as no one sees you, nothing can happen."

"What about the gun?"

"That I will hide, so if anyone did come, he would not find it."

"Very well," she said.

He said good night and closed the door behind him as he went out. Frieda saw that the only fastening to the door was a wooden button. She supported herself on the chair, pushed it to the door, and turned the button. Then she looked at the bed. The pillowcase and the sheets were fresh.

She saw herself in the mirror. Her short-sleeved cotton dress, which she had chosen because it was such a lovely green and so becoming to her red hair, hung on her like a wet rag.

She hung her clothes on the chair and tucked the hammer in her purse and dried her hair with the towel. She put the candle on the seat of the chair where she could reach it.

She could hear Henry and Louis talking. She crawled to the door and listened. They sounded as if they were a little drunk and talking louder than they knew.

"Is it really true, Henry," Louis asked, "that redheaded women are warmer in love than the others?"

"I have never known but one," Henry said, "and she tried to kill me with an ax. Maybe they are all like that, I do not know. But he likes them. He will have no other kind."

Frieda crawled back to the bed.

IX

When she awoke, the sun was shining on the floor, and from somewhere outside came the sound of a cheerful hammer. It was five minutes of eleven by the watch on her wrist.

She sat on the edge of the bed and reached for her clothes. They were still damp as she put them on. Her hair was dry and so tightly curled that she could hardly get her pocket comb through it. Her ankle seemed less swollen than it had been the night before, but she still couldn't put her weight on it without cringing. She hung on to the furniture to save it as she got the door open.

"Good morning, gracious lady," Louis called out.

She made her way, with the aid of a chair, to the doorway of his room.

"How is the leg, Louis?" she asked.

"It aches like a tooth," he said. "But it is no worse. Please call Henry. He will get you coffee."

She hobbled to the door and looked out.

Henry was busy at his workbench in the shed beside the half-built boat. When he saw her he took something out of the vise and came toward her.

"Good morning, gracious lady. I have been making crutches for you. But I have to measure them."

He came in, bearing two lengths of peeled sapling. He had inletted a crosspiece at one end of each of them. He placed the crosspieces under her arms, his thick lips pursed in thought.

"Please let your arms hang," he said, taking a pencil from behind his ear, "so I can mark where the handles will go."

He marked the place and went into the kitchen and heated coffee and gave her a hand to a chair at the livingroom table.

"If you will excuse me," he said, "I will have them done in 10 minutes. Then I will make breakfast."

Frieda sat at the table, looking out at the pond shimmering in the sun. She guessed it was a quarter of a mile across and a good deal longer than it was wide. She couldn't see either end of it. On the other side the land rose steeply to a high ridge.

"Madam," Louis called out, "can you play checkers?"

"A little," she answered.

"After breakfast I will beat you," he said. "I am a good checker player."

Frieda wanted to laugh. Louis was so obviously the child who is lonely because he has to stay in bed and wants someone to amuse him. Henry was happily making work for himself on a Saturday, like any good suburban father of a family.

This, she thought, *is what life with two murderers is really like.*

Henry came in with the crutches for her approval. She told him they were marvelous, because it would have hurt his feelings if she had said anything less.

"First," he said, "I must pad them."

He hunted out a torn pillowcase, thriftily saved for emergency, and tore it into strips, which he wrapped around the crosspieces of the crutches.

"Now," he said.

Frieda took the crutches and propelled herself out across the porch and into the bright summers sunlight.

"Oh," she said, "what a beautiful day to sit in the sun."

"It is a beautiful day," Henry said, "but—"

He looked out at the pond, frowning unhappily.

"But what?" Frieda asked.

"Sometimes men fish on the pond, on Saturday afternoon especially," Henry said. "It is forbidden, but they do it. Someone might see you."

"You don't think anyone would recognize me from the pond, do you, Henry."

"Hair like yours can be seen a long way. The police have, of course, sent out word to look for a beautiful red-haired lady."

"Very well, Henry. I will try to keep out of sight of the pond. But I must sit in the sun."

"First I will make breakfast," he said.

Frieda went into the house and he followed her.

"Ah," he said, "it is nearly 12 o'clock already. Then is the broadcast."

He turned the radio on and went into the kitchen. Frieda could hear him getting out pots and pans. She sat down at the table and tried to

brace herself for what was coming. She told herself that if she thought fast enough, she could explain anything the broadcast said about her.

The voice that came out of the machine was so loud that Henry hurried across the room to turn down the volume.

"It is now 12 o'clock, Waterford watch time," the voice said, and went on to give the weather report, which promised fair and warmer after the two inches of rain that had fallen the night before.

"Early this morning," the voice continued, "masked men entered the Water Shop of Gaylord Arms from the river, blackjacked J.M. Pyne, the most famous riflemaker in this country, and stole the model of his semi-automatic rifle. Before he went down, Mr. Pyne, who is a man of 75, struck one of the intruders with an iron bar. Mr. Pyne is under the care of a physician, but his injuries are not believed to be serious. He saw only one of his assailants, who, he said, was a tall man, before he was knocked out. When Mr. Pyne recovered consciousness he found the night watchman and notified the police. An alarm was sent out over the teletype system to 5 states. Mr. Pyne said the gun would be of little value to an ordinary criminal, but would be priceless to a foreign government, because it could be manufactured so much more cheaply than any other military weapon of its kind. The police suspect that the crime was the work of foreign agents, and 14 suspicious persons were rounded up this morning. It is understood the FBI is actively interested."

The broadcaster went on to something else. Henry turned to Frieda. She saw suspicion in his little, fat-enfolded eyes.

"Why did they say nothing of you?"

"I can't imagine," Frieda said, "Perhaps you hit the old man so hard he doesn't remember I was there."

"No," Henry said, "He remembered hitting Louis. For some reason he did not tell the police about you."

"I think the police are not telling all they know."

Henry nodded. "That is what I think too," he said.

Frieda thought he was satisfied with that explanation, but she wanted to change the subject as quickly as possible before he did any heavy thinking. This was the moment to let him know that the gun he was keeping hidden somewhere outside lacked one of its essential parts.

"Get the gun," she said. "I'd like to make sure it isn't rusted after last

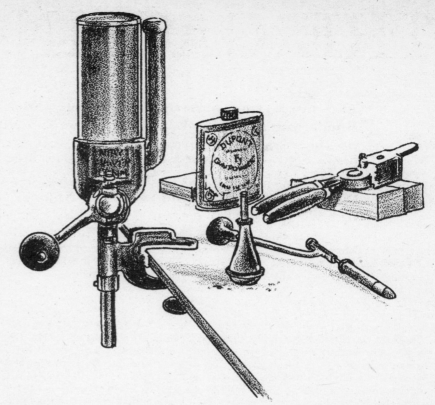

night."

"I dried everything and put grease on it last night before I went to sleep," Henry said. "The gun is not rusted. But I would like to put it together. I do not wish to give it to him in pieces. But first I will make breakfast."

He helped Louis out of bed and into a chair at the table and boiled eggs and toast and got sausage and cheese and beer. When they had eaten, he cleared the table and went out to get the gun. Frieda noticed that it took him 10 minutes to get it.

He laid the parts out on the table as he took them from the bag. Frieda realized that she was leaning on her elbow with her chin in her hand, so her arms concealed the spot where she had hidden the piece of polished steel in her bra when she put on her clothes.

Henry pursed his lips as he looked at the parts. "I do not know what to do first."

"I think I remember," Frieda said. She put the longest coil spring in the buttstock, put the action rod in place, and fitted the bolt into the receiver.

"I need a cartridge. That is what the old man used."

Henry gave her a Luger pistol cartridge, but it was not long enough.

"Get me an ice pick or a screwdriver or something."

Henry got a screwdriver and she pushed the plunger down and put the barrel into the receiver. She looked at the few remaining parts on the table. She felt the moment had come. She pushed the parts about as if she were looking for something.

"Give me the bag," she said sharply. Henry handed her the bag. She turned it upside down over the table. Nothing came out. She reached down into the bag, but there was nothing left in it.

"What is the matter?" Henry asked.

"The hammer," she said. She turned on him furiously. "You did not bring the hammer!"

"It is a bolt gun. Why would it have a hammer?"

"But it has," Frieda said, holding the gun upside down. "Look. Don't you see that there is nothing to connect the sear to the firing pin?" That is where the hammer goes—on this pin. Otherwise when you pull the trigger nothing happens."

"Good God!" Henry said. "He will kill us!"

He walked back and forth across the room, his long arms swinging, his lips muttering.

"I will have to go back and get it," he said. "There is no other way."

"How would you get in again?" Frieda asked. "And how would you find it if you did?"

He stopped short. "You are a woman. You do not know what he is like when he is angry." ●

THE GATLING GUN

The interesting material presented here is from Ernest L. Reedstrom's new book, *Bugles, Banners and War Bonnets*, reproduced with the permission of the author and publisher. This large volume, published in 1977, was edited by Don Russell. Published by the Caxton Printers, Ltd., of Caldwell, Idaho, the big book was among the top three finalists in the annual Spur Awards for Best Western Nonfiction books, this competition held by the Western Writers of America, Inc.

Military historians and armchair Indian War buffs have never quite forgiven Custer for refusing the 3 Gatling guns offered by General Alfred Terry, commander of the Department of Dakota, or the additional force of the Second Cavalry battalion prior to the march to the Little Big Horn. Custer refused the Gatling guns, it is said, because they were drawn by condemned horses, and would slow and impede his march.[48] More likely, Custer's refusal was not because the Gatling guns were hauled by condemned horses, but because of the terrain which he confronted. Second Lieutenant W. H. Low, 20th Infantry, had problems with the Gatlings upsetting several times on the march. Custer sought and obtained permission to have the battery of Gatling guns detached from his regiment and the battery was accordingly ordered to join General Gibbon on the north bank of the Yellowstone.[49]

The Gatling gun had proved itself and played a decisive part in a fight against Comanches and Kiowas on August 30, 1874 at Mulberry Creek in El Llano Estacado, the "Staked Plains" of West Texas. From ambush, some 200 Indians charged Brevet Major General Nelson A. Miles' Indian Territory Expedition, almost destroying an advanced party of scouts in the first assault. Lieutenant James W. Pope, commanding a Gatling gun battery, moved into action swiftly, scattering the attacking warriors. On other occasions, the Gatlings were reported to "have done splendidly" in brief encounters with Indians.

The Little Big Horn terrain was quite different. Much of the area shown on maps studied by Custer was unsuited for wagons, or for wheeled Gatlings pulled by condemned cavalry horses and their ammunition limbers. The ground was hilly and the trail was undetermined. Like wagons, the Gatlings might straggle behind, placing the command in a dangerous position. Every seasoned officer knew that mobility was the key to Indian warfare. In order to fight Indians, you had to find them. One of the main reasons Custer ordered pack trains instead of wagons to carry food and ammunition was because of the fast pace needed. He proved his point by arriving at the Little Big Horn on June 25 instead of the proposed June 26.

General Terry's confidential telegram to General Sheridan, July 2, 1876, reads in part:

"The plan adopted was the only one that promised to bring the infantry into action and I desired to make sure of things by getting up every available man. I offered Custer the battery of Gatling guns but he declined it saying that it might embarrass him;

Gatling Gun at Washington Arsenal viewed from the rear, May 26, 1866. *Courtesy National Archives.*

Custer in parley with some Indians. *Art by E. L. Reedstrom.*

that he was strong enough without it."[50]

Custer's attitude toward Gatlings was different in 1874, when he commanded the expedition into the Black Hills. In a letter to a friend, Custer wrote:

Fort Lincoln Dakota, May 19th, 1874.
My Dear Laurence . . .
. . . I will have ten full companies of the best Cavalry in Uncle Sam's service, a detachment of Indian scouts taken from (sic) friendly to the whites and hostile to the Sioux, and a section of Gatling guns, the latter capable of being fired fifty times a minute.[51] I will tell you candidly that we will have contests with the noble red man but my friend Laurence need feel no anxiety on that score as he can remain an impartial witness of the battle and be exposed to no danger whatever.[52]

Many officers had objections to the Gatling gun, even though its firepower was that of two companies of infantry while it took the services of only four infantrymen to operate it. However, training of gun crews was often inadequate. During the late 1860's and early 1870's, target practice was infrequent because of objections to extra expenditures for ammunition. It was said that the weapon was clumsy and hard to conceal. The operators were exposed to enemy fire,[53] in a stationary position, and the weapon would soon lose its effectiveness with several men wounded.[54] Officers cautioned the operators to keep their heads down when firing, but, towering above the men was the Gatling's gravity-fed ammunition case. A stray bullet might slam into the feed case, rendering it useless or exploding several cartridges within it.[55]

In swinging the gun about to change firing positions, two men were exposed, one at each wheel; one man would push one wheel forward, the other pull back on the opposite wheel. This lateral roll gave the Gatling a wider field of fire power, but exposed the men operating it.

It has commonly been assumed that the Gatling guns of the Little Big Horn expedition were of 45-70 caliber, the standard carbine and rifle ammunition of 1876. Unimportant as this might seem, it has confused the subject. Dr. Gatling had made various improvements and a new patent was awarded in 1865. After a number of tests and inspections, the battery was approved and 100 guns were distributed to various commands.[56] Gatlings were shipped by rail to Fort Sully, Fort Rice and Fort Randall.[57] These weapons were of the modified model of 1866, and in both .50-, and 1-inch calibers. The report of the War Department, 1876 (Vol. 2, Part 3, p. 700) refers to "A battery of three half inch Gatling guns, (.50 caliber)[58] commanded by Second Lieutenant W. H. Low, Twentieth Infantry," substantiating that the .50-caliber was in use instead of the 45-70 caliber.

Dr. Richard Jordan Gatling did not have an opportunity to see his "battery gun" in action during the Civil War. It was introduced too late to be used in many campaigns. However, it had been put to many practical tests by officers of the Ordnance Corps, who spoke of its performance in high terms. At the beginning, Gatling's gun was called a "novel engine of war" that would prove useful in guarding bridges, fords and roadways. There was little recoil to affect the accuracy of its aim, and, once

sighted on a target, it can be fired day or night from an aimed position. Lieutenant Maclay, U.S. Ordnance, reported: "The advantages claimed for this gun are: 1st. There is no escape of gas at the breech. 2d. There is no recoil, which can destroy its accuracy. 3rd. It performs the operations of loading, firing, and extracting the case, by simply revolving the crank. 4th. Accuracy. 5th. Rapidity of fire." The report concludes, "All parts of the gun work well."[59]

Army plans placed the Gatling in the artillery arm. It was contemplated that in campaigns against the Indians the gun could be used to advantage as a "flank defense gun."

Two sizes of Gatlings were manufactured by the Colt's Arms Company, Hartford, Connecticut, one of 1-inch caliber, capable of being fired 100 times a minute, and one of .50 caliber, which could be fired 200 times a minute. Copper-case primed cartridges were used in both guns. Each gun had 6 steel rotating barrels. The reason the Gatling had little recoil is that gun and carriage were of sufficient weight to overcome the recoil of each discharge without movement and therefore no time was lost in sighting after each fire. If an operator other than the one who was cranking moved a wheel forward or backward, the gun was given a lateral movement while firing, to sweep a sector of any circle within its range.

An order for 100 Gatling guns was issued to Talbot, Jones & Company of Indianapolis, Indiana, August 24, 1866. Fifty .50-caliber, or half-inch guns, and 50 1-inch caliber guns were ordered by General A. B. Dyer. Each weapon had 6 steel barrels, all rifled. The wooden field gun carriages were to be of seasoned white oak, with all iron or steel parts blued, with the exception of the gun barrels which were to be browned, a blue-black rusting process.

The weapons that Custer declined were of the 1866 improved models, chambered for the 50-70-450 center-fire infantry cartridge, interchangeable for rifle. The weight of the machine, not including the carriage and limber, was 224 pounds. Total weight of carriage, omitting the gun, was 202 pounds. The limber (empty) weighed 200 pounds. The smaller sized gun had a range up to one mile, while the larger gun had a range up to two miles. Of course, the extreme ranges would seldom produce accurate hits.[60] Open sights were located centrally upon the breech housing; when the sights were not used, they could be

At the Washington trials, May 8, 1866, three Gatling guns are posed on the banks of the Potomac; the 50-cal. and 1-inch guns have all passed severe tests. *Courtesy National Archives Records Group, Wash. D.C.*

retracted into the case. Elevation was attained by use of a jackscrew in the trail.

The mobility of the Gatling gun had not been criticized by other commands. The gun and its carriage, compared to other artillery, was light in weight and could be drawn by two horses.[61] Four horses or six were required for field guns. The lives of three or four men at the most need only be exposed; and the results attained can only be measured by the exposure of as many as a hundred men armed with ordinary rifles.

The men of the Seventh U.S. Cavalry had already found uses for the Gatling gun. One company, returning from the Hancock Expedition in 1867, ran into a large herd of buffalo while escorting a wagon train on the Smoky Hill route. When the buffalo threatened to stampede the wagon train, two companies of cavalry dismounted, knelt and fired volleys into the oncoming herd. This only frightened the animals and they headed straight for the train. Two Gatling guns then came into position and began firing. After a number of buffalo were killed, the rest of the herd broke around the wagon train. A detailed group of soldiers went forward to cut the hind quarters of the dead buffalo, loading them into the wagons for garrison consumption.[62]

The Gatling gun manual and firing tactics in battery formation are as follows:

The New Battery Manual
of the Gatling Gun
Positions of the Cannoneers in Battery
Figure One

Nos. 1 and 2 on the right flank of the piece, No. 1 opposite the cascabel, No. 2 opposite the rear end of the hand spike, and both facing towards the piece, 18 inches outside of the face of the nave of the wheel, Nos. 3 and 4 on the left flank piece, No. 3 opposite the cascabel, No. 4 opposite the rear end of the hand spike, both facing toward the piece, 18 inches outside of the face of the nave of the wheel.

A feed-drum has been placed on the piece, the crank and traversing apparatus has been placed in action, and the hand spike has been placed at the end of trail.

At the command PREPARE TO FIRE, No. 1 places himself in position to turn the crank with his right hand, No. 2 directs the piece and seats himself on the trail seat, prepared to elevate or depress the piece. No. 3 goes to the feed-drum, and attends it, No. 4 goes to the limber, and gets a second feed-drum all ready to relieve No. 3. At the command FIRE, No. 1

Footnotes

48. Custer would have known these horses were condemned because of their brands "I.C.," which means "Inspected and Condemned," E. B. Custer microfilm, Roll 6, No. 6427, Custer Battlefield.
49. Narrative of First Sergeant Hugh A. Hynds, Sergeant of the Gatling gun battery which General Terry offered Custer and he declined. Hynds mentions four Gatlings, two .50 calibers or 1/2-inch guns and two .100 or one-inch guns. On file at the Custer Battlefield Museum Library. Also see Research Review, Little Big Horn Associates, Vol. VI, Winter, Number 4.
50. For full text see: The Custer Tragedy, by Fred Dustin, privately printed by Edwards Bros. Inc., Ann Arbor, Mich., 1936, p. 197.
51. The Gatling Gun, by Paul Wahl & D. R. Toppel, p. 30, includes a report by T. G. Baylor, Captain of Ordnance, Ft. Monroe Arsenal, Virginia, July 14, 1866, "I had the oil rubbed off this gun, drenched it with water, and then exposed it for two nights and a day to rain and weather, but though it was quite rusty, it was fired 97 times in a minute and a half, one man turning at the crank."
A short time after the Gatlings were delivered to the Army, it was noted that, when cranking at top speed to attempt the firing power of two hundred shots in one minute, shots occasionally struck the front cross bar of the frame, throwing lead and parts of metal back into the crew. This could very well be the reason for Custer's mention of 50 shots per minute. See "The Gatling Gun," p. 32.
52. From the collections of the Manuscript Division, Library of Congress (AC. 11700), Ghent Collection.
53. Infantry Uniforms, Book No. 2, 1855-1939, p. 210, Robert and Christopher Wilkinson-Latham; MacMillan Co.
54. See this chapter for "The Gatling Gun Battery Manual" for duties of each man.
55. Army and Navy Journal, Feb. 21, 1874, p. 443.
56. Army and Navy Journal, Aug. 20, 1870, p. 6.
57. Ibid., Aug. 3, 1872, p. 813.
58. Author's note. See reference No. 49 in this chapter: Narrative of First Sergeant H. A. Hynds who states two Gatlings were .50 calibers, and two were one-inch. I am more inclined to take the War Department's word of three Gatlings in the .50-caliber; the fourth in the one-inch caliber.
59. Army and Navy Journal, July 13, 1867, p. 741.
60. Author's Note: A good example of this particular model can be found in Francis Bannerman Sons, Military Goods Catalog, Illustrated and Descriptive, 1931, "Cannons . . . p. 134 . . ." Gatling Rapid-Fire Guns, Cal. 50; the breech mechanism was encased in a bronzed jacket with four-foot wheels.
61. General E. S. Godfrey had four Gatlings hauled by two mules during the fall of 1867. Guns were receipted to Godfrey from Ft. Harker. Winners of the West, March 30, 1930.
62. Elizabeth Custer microfilm, Roll 6, No. 6402, Custer Battlefield.
63. Army and Navy Journal, June 15, 1872.
64. Narrative of First Sergeant Hugh A. Hynds, on file at Custer Battlefield Museum.
65. Ibid.
66. Ibid.
67. Records of U.S. Army Continental Commands, 1821-1920, Fort Abraham Lincoln, Special Orders, Vol. 83; Special Orders 48, 1876, Record Group No. 393.
68. Record Group No. 156, Records of the Office of the Chief of Ordnance, Letters Received, 1875.
69. Records of the Office of the Chief of Ordnance, Letters Received No. 2520, 1876, Record Group No. 156.
70. Record Group No. 156, Records of the Office of the Chief of Ordnance, Letters Received, No. 2520, 1876.

turns the crank, No. 3 attends the feed-drum, seeing that the cartridges are fed regularly, No. 2 sees that the piece is properly aimed. When the feed-drum is nearly exhausted, No. 3 warns No. 4 by calling out, "Drum," when No. 4 brings up a loaded feed-drum, and when the first drum is exhausted, No. 3 lifts it off, takes it to the limber chest, and gets another loaded feed-drum ready. No. 4 at the same time takes his feed-drum on the piece, and takes the duties previously performed by No. 3. He is in turn relieved by No. 3, and so on. At the command CEASE FIRING, No. 3 or No. 4, as the case may be, keeps the feed-drum stationary. No. 1 turns the crank until the loose cartridges are fired. All then take the positions "in battery."

When feed-cases are used instead of feed-drums, the duties of the cannoneers No. 1 and No. 2 are not changed. The duties of the cannoneers No. 3 and 4 are to supply the piece with the feed-cases. At the command PREPARE TO FIRE, No. 3 inserts the lower end of the feed-case in the hopper, and No. 4 stands by ready to insert a filled case when the first is exhausted. At the command FIRE, No. 3 sees that the cartridges feed regularly, withdraws the case when it is empty, and No. 4 inserts at once a filled case, and is in turn relieved by No. 3, and they too keep up a constant supply of cartridges. At the command CEASE FIRING, Nos. 3 and 4 remove the feed-cases to the limber, and place them in the chest. At the command LIMBER TO THE FRONT, No. 1 fastens the crank, ungears the traversing apparatus, and goes to the end of the trail. No. 3 and No. 4, as the case may be, takes off the feed-drum and places it in the limber chest, where the other feed-drums, ready for use, are also placed. No. 2 unships the hand spike, keys it in its place on the trail, and places himself at the end of the trail opposite No. 1.

The limber is brought to the front of the piece, passing it on the right, and No. 1 and No. 2 bring the piece to the right about, limber up and key the pintle. All then take the positions "in battery," except that Nos. 1 and 3 are opposite the naves of the wheels of the piece, and Nos. 2 and 4 opposite the naves of the limber wheels. At the command LIMBER TO THE REAR, the actions of the cannoneers are the same as in the last command, except that the limber is brought to the rear of the piece and is brought to the left about, and the piece is limbered and keyed, but not brought to the right about. On the march, the cannoneers march in the places indicated in the last two commands. At the command CANNONEERS-MOUNT, Nos. 1 and 3 mount on the rear side of the limber, Nos. 2 and 4 on the front side. The piece being limbered, and on the march, at the command IN BATTERY, the piece halts, the cannoneers, if mounted, dismount. Nos. 1 and 2 unlimber the piece and bring it to the right about. The limber is brought to the left about, is taken 20 paces to the rear, and is again brought to the left about. No. 1 frees the crank and gears in the traversing apparatus. No. 2 detaches the hand spike, places

it on the trail, and gives the general direction to the piece, and notes whether the traversing apparatus works properly. Nos. 3 and 4 go to the limber and get out two loaded feed-drums. No. 3 takes one to the piece, places it on the pintle, and gets it ready for feeding. Then all take the positions of the cannoneers "in battery". The foregoing instructions apply to pieces of ordinary musket caliber, and mounted as small field-pieces.

For the large calibers, the feed-drums are so heavy that two men will be required to handle them. An additional man must therefore belong to each piece, who may be called No. 5, and whose position "in battery" will be in the rear of the limber box, and on the march midway between Nos. 3 and 4. His duty will be to assist Nos. 3 and 4 in getting the feed-drums in readiness, and in carrying them to and fro between the limber and the piece, and in packing them in the limber chest. He must be mounted with the other cannoneers on the front of the limber chest or on a caisson if there be one.

With the guns of musket caliber disposed for transportation on animals' backs (camel guns), the number of cannoneers will be the same as that given above for small field-pieces. Any intelligent officer can make the modifications that the case requires, thus No. 2 should arrange the tripod for field-carriage and keep the gun accurately pointed. No. 1 should adjust the crank and traversing apparatus, and Nos. 3 and 4 should see that the supply of cartridges is kept up. Nos. 1 and 2 will remove the gun from the back of the animal and adjust it on the carriage. With guns of caliber larger than that of the musket, it will be advisable to have a sixth cannoneer, whose duty it shall be to relieve No. 1 at the crank.

In drilling at the school of the cannoneer in garrison or camp, it will be well to remove the locks, to prevent the unnecessary snapping of the springs, and the

cartridges can then be run through the hopper at will, familiarizing the men with the use of the gun without waste of ammunition or injury to the locks.[63]

Second Lieutenant William Hale Low and Second Lieutenant Frank X. Kinzie arrived at Bismarck, Dakota Territory, March 20, 1876 with 32 half-frozen men from the 20th Infantry[64] with orders to report to the commanding officer of Fort Abraham Lincoln and organize a Gatling battery for an expedition against hostile Indians. Some of the men remembered seeing General Custer driven in an ambulance to a railway terminal at Bismarck, en route to Washington, D.C., to give evidence in the Belknap case.[65] The snow had drifted into huge banks, swept by the winds, making travel difficult by foot or wagon. After reaching the fort, Low began to train his men with the Gatling guns awaiting them. Within 6 weeks they would be ready to march. May 10, the command moved to Cannon Ball Creek, 3 miles south of the fort on the west bank of the Missouri River. Here organization of the expedition was completed and troops were put under canvas until the march began on May 17.[66]

Orders to Lieutenant Low were:

Headquarters, Fort Abraham Lincoln, D. T., March 18, 1876.
Special Orders No. 48[67]
Article 8. Upon the arrival at this post of the detachment of the 20th Infantry under command of Second Lieutenant Low of that regiment the officers and men of the Detachment will be provided with quarters at Infantry Barracks and under the direction of Lieutenant Low will be organized and drilled for service in the field with a Gatling gun battery consisting of four pieces.

As soon as the weather will permit horses to be kept on the picket line at night the Post Quartermaster will turn over to Lieutenant Low for services with the Gatling

At Fort McKean, North Dakota, in 1877, members of the 20th Infantry stand at ease next to caissons and 1-inch Gatling guns. *Courtesy Custer Battlefield Museum.*

CUSTER'S LAST SHOT

BY

ERNEST L. REEDSTROM

"Tom Custer and his brother George—at the final hour."
Courtesy Dr. Larry Frost/art by E. L. Reedstrom.

gun battery such numbers of horses as may be suitable and may be required to supply the battery, not including mounts for the cannoneers. Two horses will be supplied for use of officers serving with the Battery. The officers and men composing the Gatling gun detachment will not be required to perform any duty at this post which will conflict or interfere with their organization and preparation for the field.

Lieutenant Low will fully instruct his men in the duties pertaining to the Gatling Gun service in the field and render them as familiar as practicable in the proper care and management of horses.

By order of
Brevet Major General Custer
(Signature) W. W. Cooke
1st Lt. & Adjt. 7 Cavy.
Post Adjutant.

The lighter 45-70 Gatling guns could have been available for the Little Big Horn campaign, had not it been for a delay in communications among department headquarters in Chicago and Washington Ordnance offices, which held up requisitions for the distribution of the weapons for 5 months. We would have to wade through a tide of letters, telegrams and second- and third-endorsements to pin down the responsibility.

On November 17, 1875, Brigadier General S. V. Benet, Chief of Ordnance, Washington, D. C., announced that 45-70 Gatling guns at various arsenals were available, and asked what disposition the Lieutenant General wished to make of the guns. The weapons could be requisitioned by commanding officers of posts needing them most. There were 10 Gatlings at the San Antonio Arsenal to be issued to posts in the Department of Texas, 5 guns at Fort Union Arsenal for the Department of the Missouri, and 17 guns at Rock Island Arsenal, of which 8 were to be allotted to posts in the Department of Dakota and 9 to the Department of the Platte. With each

weapon, a sufficient supply of ammunition would be furnished with harness for 2 horses. It was noted that these guns were much lighter than the 1-inch caliber and ½ inch, or .50 caliber, already serving garrisons in many departments.[68]

Five months dragged by before communications from officers reached General Benet's desk in Washington; meanwhile, Benet sent a second communication:[69]

Ordnance Office
War Department
Washington, May 5th, 1876

Captain J. W. Reilly, Chief Ordnance Officer Military Division of the Missouri, Chicago, Illinois
Sir:
Referring to my letter of November 17, 1875 (copy enclosed) directing you to advise to this office, what distribution the Lieutenant General of the Army desired to make of the 17 Gatling guns Cal. 45, on hand at the Rock Island Arsenal, I infer that as this information has not yet been furnished, it may have been overlooked.
Respectfully
Your obedient servant,
(Signed) S. V. Benet
Chief of Ordnance

Captain Reilly had reported:

Headquarters Military Division of the Missouri, Office of Chief Ordnance Officer

Chicago, Illinois,
April 6th, 1876

Chief of Ordnance U.S.A.
Washington, D. C.

Sir,
I have the honor to inform you that your communication of November 17th, 1875, relative to the distribution to Troops in this Division of certain Gatling Guns in the possession of the Ordnance Department, was referred by me with an Endorsement to the Lieutenant General November 20, 1875. I recommended that the 10 at San Antonio Arsenal be issued to Posts and Troops in Department of Texas. Five at Fort Union Arsenal be issued to Posts and Troops in Department of Missouri. Nine at Rock Island Arsenal to Posts and Troops in Department of the Platte. Eight at Rock Island Arsenal to Posts and Troops in Department of Dakota. The Commanding Generals of the Departments were instructed by the Lieutenant General, if they desired these Guns to designate, their disposition in the proportion I recommended. Reports have been received from Generals Terry and Crook; and Generals Pope and Ord have today been directed to forward reports at once.

The delay in returning the complete papers to your office, has been caused by the failure of the latter named officers to answer the communication. The matter will now however be pushed to a conclusion . . .
Very respectfully
Your obedient Servant,
(Signed) J. W. Reilly
Captain of Ordnance
Chief Ord. Off. Mil. Div. Mo.

Eventually, all department commanders replied. General Terry designated the companies to receive the 8 guns allotted to his department. General Crook stated that he did not wish the guns. General Pope designated posts to receive the 5 guns at Fort Union Arsenal and requested 3 additional guns. They were allotted from those apportioned to the Department of the Platte. General Ord designed the disposition of 8 guns at San Antonio Arsenal, but asked that 2 remain there for emergencies. The 6 guns remaining at Rock Island Arsenal were retained there for possible use in the Department of the Platte.[70]

Although Custer favored the early Gatlings on a previous expedition he refused to have the battery accompany him to the Little Big Horn.

Steel Shot Update

An up-to-date report on what's going on among the big three shotshell producers this year, plus a tabular breakdown of the available steel-shot loads and their performance at the pattern board. They're beginning to look a bit better, but . . .

by WALLACE LABISKY

THE FEDERAL POSSE is still pounding leather, still raising a cloud of dust in its determination to head 'em off at the pass. Steel-shot loads for waterfowl shooting will become mandatory throughout the nation during the 1978-79 gunning season. Previously the ban on lead-shot loads included only the Atlantic and Mississippi flyways and was confined to certain high-risk areas, as will continue to be the case in the immediate future.

This same hot-spot implementation will be followed this year in the Central and Pacific flyways in an attempt to further curb lead-poisoning mortality that occurs when feeding ducks and geese ingest lead pellets that accumulate on marsh bottoms. However, several western states, where the bulk of the shooting is routinely done over dry land (field and pass shooting as opposed to wetland decoying), will probably be affected only to a very limited extent. A few states may actually be exempted altogeth- er—at least temporarily.

Last year in these columns we reported on what was available in steel-shot loads and outlined what was in store for load improvement. As was predicted in that report, the ongoing efforts have been toward heavier shot charges in both 2³/₄" and 3" 12-ga. shells.

Throughout all this the smaller gauge shells have been totally neglected, and our hunch is that this situation will undergo no change. The 3¹/₂" 10-ga. shell, on the other hand, offers great potential for use with steel shot. This largest of legal bores

Steel shot loads from W-W now include a 12-ga. 2³/₄" shell with a 1¹/₄-oz. shot load and a 3-incher with 1¹/₂ ozs. of shot. Both are fold-crimp loads available in shot sizes 1, 2 and 4. The earlier 1¹/₄-oz. shell with a roll-crimp closure and the "Flyaway" overshot wad has been discontinued. W-W had no plans for other new steel loads in the immediate future.

will be able to handle heavy shot loads at much higher velocities than the 12-bore, thus combining extra dense patterns with high pellet energies. Once the 12-ga. steel loads have reached their ultimate development, we should be seeing some activity on the 10-ga. side. Certainly this would be the next most logical move.

As for handloading, suitable components (mainly the proper wadding and the steel shot itself) are not yet on the market. But this situation is likely to change in the near future, for rumor has it that some of the smaller firms specializing in wad manufacture have 10-ga. shotcup wads of extra-tough, high-density polyethylene almost ready to go. Once those few lingering kinks are ironed out, the last remaining hurdle will be to pry loose the steel pellets—and to work up and disseminate safe, reliable loading data.

Among factory loads, here is what you can expect to find on dealer's shelves for the upcoming 1978 gunning season:

Federal Cartridge Corporation

FCC lists two new 12-ga. steel-shot loads in its 1978 catalog, but as this is written (March 1978) neither one has quite reached the production stage. Federal is aiming for the highest possible MV (muzzle velocity) without exceeding normal chamber pressure. The W148 load will be in a $2^3/4''$ shell holding $1^1/4$ ozs. of shot that will exit the muzzle at close to 1300 fps. The W149 is a 3" magnum package with a $1^3/8$-oz. load, the MV goal being somewhat in excess of 1200 fps. Both of these new loads will be offered in shot sizes 1, 2 and 4. Additionally, steel BBs will be available in the 3" load only.

Both loads will be put together in the familiar Hi-Power plastic shell with a brass-plated steel head. Both will also be fold-crimp loads with a one-piece plastic shot-pouch wad of high-density polyethylene.

Federal will continue to offer the $2^3/4''$ 12-ga. W147 load with $1^1/8$ ozs. of steel shot in sizes 1, 2 and 4. Incidentally, several years ago the writer gunned pheasants, barnyard pigeons and jackrabbits with this "light duty" load (MV about 1365 fps) and it did a good job so long as I kept a critical eye on the yardage.

Remington Arms Company

There was very little firm information that Remington could give us about its steel shot program for the 1978 season. However, it's a safe bet that a new $2^3/4''$ 12-ga. load containing $1^1/4$ ozs. of shot will be rolling out of Bridgeport before the leaves are touched by frost.

In fact, such a load was used experimentally last fall at Remington Farms, and with highly encouraging results. There are reports of some geese (Canada honkers) being killed out as far as 60 yards! No. 1 shot, of course. According to Remington spokesman Dick Dietz, this particular load may or may not be the one to go into full-scale production. It is still under nitpicking scrutiny in Remington's R&D section.

We can report this: The forthcoming $1^1/4$-oz. load will have a new one-piece, high-density plastic wad complete with shot pouch, and a fold-crimp closure. The shot sizes will be Nos. 1, 2 and 4. The MV, it is hoped, will be close to 1300 fps—the desired goal being to keep pellet energy high by pouring on as much speed as safe chamber pressure will allow.

A 3" 12-ga. load? Yes—and soon, we hope. Remington has had this project on the back burner for about three years. Our guess is that when this load finally does appear it will contain either $1^3/8$ or $1^1/2$ ozs. of shot, and that it will have the necessary ballistics to reliably function gas-operated magnum autoloaders, such as the Remington Model 1100—which the current $1^1/4$-oz. steel-shot loads won't do.

Winchester-Western's current 12-ga. steel-shot loads use a one-piece plastic wad column that is virtually a carbon copy of the design used in previous loads. At left is the $1^1/4$-oz. wad used in $2^3/4''$ shells, at right the $1^1/2$-oz. version for 3" magnum shells. The shot pouches are divided into four segments by fine-line slits, and the very tough high-density polyethylene is highly effective in preventing pellet contact with the gun's bore.

Winchester-Western

W-W has been pushing its steel shot program at a somewhat faster pace than either of its two competitors. A pair of 12-ga. loads appeared following our report in GUN DIGEST No. 32. In production since mid-1977, the $2^3/4''$ shell carries $1^1/4$ ozs. of shot, and the 3" offering holds $1^1/2$-oz. Shot sizes are Nos. 1, 2 and 4.

The preceding $1^1/4$-oz. steel-shot load from W-W had a roll crimp in conjunction with a specially designed "Flyaway" overshot card of plastic construction. This closure has been superseded by a 6-point fold crimp on both loads. The plastic shells have a smooth exterior and at first glance appear to be of the Double A or compression-formed type, but are actually of built-up construction (Reifenhauser type) with a paper base-wad. The one-piece plastic wads with heavy-duty shot pouches show no design change from what was used previously and are very similar, basically, to the wads used in Federal's steel-shot loads.

MV for the $2^3/4''$ load is 1275 fps (a slight increase over the preceding $1^1/4$-oz. offering at 1265 fps), and 1200 fps for the 3" shell. W-W says that individual energy for the No. 4 steel pellet at 40 yards is 2.5 ft. lbs. for the $1^1/4$-oz. loading, and 2.0 ft. lbs. for the slower 3" shell. Opinions vary, but most authorities feel that a minimum pellet energy of 1.5 to 2.0 ft. lbs. is necessary for adequate penetration on ducks. At this writing, W-W was unable to supply us with downrange energy figures for the larger-sized steel pellets.

Several rounds of the $2^3/4''$ and 3" loads were broken down for a check on the details of loading. For the $1^1/4$-oz. loads, the shot charges averaged only a few grains light for the 4s and 2s, but the No. 1 loads were considerably under, these running only a few grains heavier than $1^3/16$ ozs. The $1^1/2$-oz. loads in the 3" shells were very close to being full weight with No. 4 shot, but averaged 16.0 grains short for the No. 1 and 2 sizes.

Steel shot is only about two-thirds as dense as lead shot, which means that a matching charge weight of steel will eat up a great deal more space in the shell. Thus there is no room for a fiber or felt wad in the shot pouch for cushioning purposes and to yield expansion space for the initial build-up of powder gases. This is one of the reasons why the chamber pressure/velocity situation is so tricky with steel shot and why special powders with a very slow burning rate

are so necessary.

Very dense Ball-type propellants are used in the W-W steel-shot loads, of course. Charge weights ranged from 33.0 to 34.0 grains for both the 1¼- and 1½-oz. loads. About 100 grains of powder taken from the 1¼-oz. loads was spread on the ground in a 1″ × 6″ train and one end was ignited with a match. The time required for complete burning was close to ten seconds. That's slow! Try this with such a propellant as 452AA or 473AA and you'll see a dramatic difference.

Test Results

Both of the new W-W steel-shot loads were tested for pattern at 40- and 45-yd. distances using a Winchester Model 1200 Magnum pump gun with a 30″ full-choke barrel (see appended table for complete details). In all instances the average efficiency for 5 shots was 75% or higher at 40 yards. A performance level of this magnitude is not at all unusual for steel-shot loads, for the extremely hard pellets suffer practically no deformation during their passage through the gun's bore. Pellets that retain a large measure of sphericity are better equipped to cope with air resistance, and dense patterns are the result. Theoretically, when in flight the shot cloud should also string out less than lead shot does, and all pellets comprising the cloud should be very nearly equal in terms of retained energy.

But despite the steel pellets' ability to withstand pattern-robbing deformation, the author feels that if it were possible to incorporate some means of cushioning within the wad column, pattern efficiency would tend to climb. At the same time, however, we would very likely see an even stronger imbalance in pellet distribution—that is, an increase in the core density at the expense of thin pellet coverage in the annular portion of the pattern. All existing steel shot loads already lean quite heavily in this direction (as our photos and pattern summary table show). At a distance of 40 yards, the shooter using a full-choke barrel must do a pretty precise job of gun pointing if he is to center the charge and avoid a lightly hit—and crippled—bird.

In light of this it would appear that a modified choke would be much the better choice for shots in the 35 to 40-yd. bracket, particularly when gunning ducks with the heavier loads of steel 4s. Such a combination would strike a highly acceptable balance

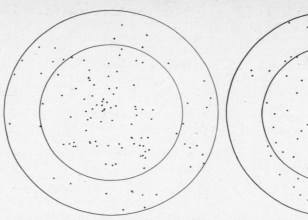
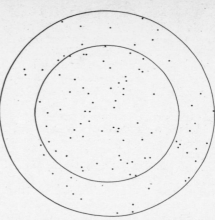

This 40-yd. pattern with W-W's new 3″ 12-ga. load containing 1½ ozs. of No. 1 steel shot shows the very strong center density that can be expected when using a max-choke barrel. Here the 20″ core contains 77 pellets, but the 5″ annular area has only 34 hits, less than half as many. If the pattern is not perfectly centered, this sort of pellet distribution can easily result in a lightly hit or crippled bird. This is a 75% pattern (111 hits in the 30″ circle), the gun a Winchester Model 1200 Magnum with a 30″ Full-choke barrel.

Based on a 5-shot average, W-W's 1½-oz. load of No. 1 steel shot suffered an efficiency loss of 12% between 40 and 45 yards. As this 98-count (66.2%) pattern reveals, pellet distribution was much improved over the 40-yard results. However, the 5″ annular area still has several pellet-free "holes" that would produce crippling with a less-than-perfect hold. Assuming a 15% density loss over the next 5 yards, the pattern count would drop to 75 hits, which would still provide more than adequate coverage on even a small 5-pound goose—and pellet energy at 50 yards will certainly be high enough to give adequate penetration.

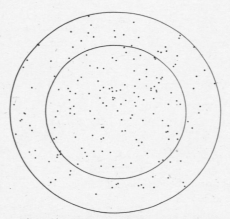
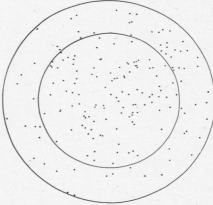

W-W's 2¾″ load with 1¼ ozs. of No. 4 steel shot printed this 181-count (72.6%) pattern at 40 yards using the Winchester Model 1200 Magnum. At a MV of 1275 fps the 40-yd. energy is 2.5 ft. lbs. per pellet, thus total delivered energy in the 30″ circle is 452 ft. lbs. In comparison, a 72% pattern with a high-velocity load of lead 6s (MV 1330 fps) delivers only 428 ft. lbs. of energy at this distance. From a Full-choke barrel all sizes of steel shot tend to strong center density at 40 yards. The breakdown here for steel 4s amounts to 110/71 pellets for the 20″ core/5″ annular area.

Density of the 1½-oz. load of steel 4s at 45 yards (seen here) was equal to the 1¼-oz. load at 40 yards. The heavier 3″ load, however, has a lower MV and thus delivers less energy per pellet—the actual difference being 0.5 ft. lb. at 40 yards. Probably due to the lower MV the 1½-oz. load of steel 4s suffered only an 11% efficiency loss between 40 and 45 yards, in contrast to a nearly 16% loss for the lighter, faster load. This 45-yd. 181-count (63.5%) pattern, which is typical, exhibits very strong center density with a 114/67 breakdown in pellet distribution.

between pattern density and penetration. A 60% pattern at 40 yards with 1¼ ozs. of steel 4s, for example, would mean close to 150 pellet hits in a 30″ circle. Assuming balanced distribution (and certainly it would be improved over full-choke distribution), we could expect to score about 7 pellet hits on a 2½-lb. duck (based on

Burrard's formula that 88% of a bird's weight in ounces represents the vulnerable target area in square inches). Thus the total delivered energy on target in this instance would be 17.5 ft. lbs., amply adequate for a clean kill.

Returning, briefly, to our pattern tests, the one puzzling aspect was the

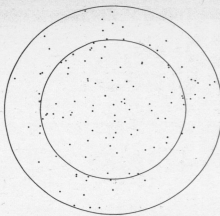

The new W-W 2³/₄" fold-crimp load with 1¹/₄ ozs. of No. 2 steel shot averaged nearly 80% at 40 yards from the Model 1200 Magnum. If well centered, this 118-count pattern would certainly crumple a large duck in a no-nonsense way, for steel 2s starting at 1275 fps arrive at 40 yards with far more individual pellet energy than is necessary for adequate penetration on ducks. At this distance, and if fired from a Full-choke barrel, the load would very likely have enough authority to effectively handle small geese. The pellet distribution breakdown is 72/46 for this 79.1% pattern.

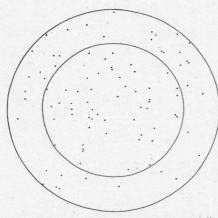

Moving back to the 45-yd. marker, average efficiency with the 1¹/₄-oz. load of No. 2 steel dropped nearly 20%. This 61% pattern, with 91 pellets registering in the 30" circle, has enough density to score 4.5 pellet hits on a 2¹/₂-pound duck and certainly steel 2s won't be short on penetration. But pellet distribution could be better with a 52/39 breakdown between the 20" core and the 5" annular area, there are some "thin" spots around the edges that would result in crippling.

unusually high loss in efficiency between 40 and 45 yards with the 1¹/₄-oz. loads containing Nos. 2 and 4 shot. This amounted to nearly 16% and 20%, respectively. Puzzling, because with No. 1 shot the loss amounted to only 8.3%, which compares favorably with what can be expected when using lead pellet loads. Further, the

Winchester-Western 12-Gauge Steel Shot Loads

Load	Ounces Shot	Shot Size	Pellet Count	Actual Charge Weight	Muzzle Velocity	40-Yard Pellet Energy
Super-X 3³/₄"	1¹/₄	4	249	544.6 grs.	1275 fps	2.5 ft. lbs.
	1¹/₄	2	149	541.2 grs.	1275 fps	NR
	1¹/₄	1	121	526.0 grs.	1275 fps	NR
Super-X 3"	1¹/₂	4	285	654.1 grs.	1200 fps	2.0 ft. lbs.
	1¹/₂	2	178	639.9 grs.	1200 fps	NR
	1¹/₂	1	148	640.6 grs.	1200 fps	NR

Comments: The "pellet counts" and the "actual shot charge weights" listed represent an average of 3 rounds.
NR = Pellet energies at 40 yards for these shot sizes and muzzle velocities have not been released by W-W. 1¹/₄ ozs. = 546.9 grs. 2¹/₂ ozs. = 656.3 grs.

3" loads holding 4s and 1s were likewise within the norm for lead shot loads. Unfortunately, our sample 3" loads with 1¹/₂ ozs. of steel 2s did not arrive in time to be included in the pattern testing.

Insofar as pattern density alone is concerned, there are some interesting parallels to note. For No. 4 steel the 1¹/₂-oz. loading delivered the same density at 45 yards as the 1¹/₄-oz. loading produced at 40 yards. With No. 1 steel it was the same story—the heavier load at 45 yards equaled the lighter load at 40 yards. Chances are this same pattern will likewise hold true with No. 2 shot. Another parallel that the pattern summary table reveals is that density runs very much the same at both 40 and 45 yards for 1¹/₄ ozs. of 2s and 1¹/₂ ozs. of 1s.

The Economic Side

If you find yourself planning a hunt in a steel-shot zone, better brace yourself, for these loads are anything but bargain priced. A current listing for the W-W loads shows a cost of $11.80 per box for the 1¹/₄-oz. loads, and $14.85 for the heavier 3" pack-age. That's about $5 per box over what you're now paying for 12-ga. "duck" loads containing the same weights of lead shot.

Why the large difference? Although lead shot can no longer be considered cheap, it is certainly cheap compared to steel pellets. And it is largely the manufacturing process that accounts for the vast spread in cost between lead and steel factory loads. Lead shot can be produced for only a few cents more per pound than the cost of the pig lead from which it is made. Making steel pellets is a much more involved process. According to a reliable source the various steps include forming the steel into a rod, drawing it into wire, cutting the wire into slugs, forming the slugs into spherical pellets on special machines, then polishing the pellets and coating them to prevent rusting.

Perhaps a less costly process will evolve in time, but until that day arrives waterfowlers will have no choice. They'll be paying a pretty penny for shells that are, undeniably, much less energy efficient than their lead shot counterparts. •

STEEL SHOT PATTERN TESTS
Winchester 1200 12-Gauge Magnum
30-Inch Full-Choke Barrel Bore .731"—Choke .037"

Load	Shot Charge	Yards	20-Inch Density	30-Inch Density	30-Inch Efficiency	Extreme Density Variation	Imbalance
W-W Super-X 2³/₄"	1¹/₄-4 (249)	40	114	188	75.8 %	10.9 %	+ 40
		45	89	149	60.0 %	5.2 %	+ 29
W-W Super-X 2³/₄"	1¹/₄-2 (149)	40	80	119	79.8 %	4.7 %	+ 40
		45	53	90	60.5 %	14.1 %	+ 17
W-W Super-X 2³/₄"	1¹/₄-1 (121)	40	57	93	77.3 %	9.9 %	+ 22
		45	49	83	69.0 %	19.0 %	+ 15
W-W Super-X 3" Mag.	1¹/₂-4 (285)	40	139	217	76.2 %	13.0 %	+ 61
		45	113	186	65.2 %	5.9 %	+ 41
W-W Super-X 3" Mag.	1¹/₂-1 (148)	40	78	114	77.2 %	14.9 %	+ 43
		45	60	96	65.2 %	8.7 %	+ 23

Comments: All loads with 6-point fold crimp. These results represent the average performance for 5 shots with each load listed. The "plus" figure shown in the imbalance column is the actual number of pellets by which the 20" density exceeds that of the 5" annular area of the 30" pattern. A "zero" imbalance rating would signify near-ideal pellet distribution. Ambient range temperature at time of firing, 60° to 70° F.

The Model 77 Ruger Rifle

It wasn't easy, deciding to buck the prevailing trend in gaudy rifles, but Bill Ruger acted with courage and boldness in styling and designing his first bolt action rifle. The dangerous gamble paid off, and the rest, as they say, is history.

IN 1968 STURM, RUGER & Co. introduced a new rifle—basically on a Mauser-type turnbolt action with two forward locking lugs. At that time it hardly seemed likely that the gun world was breathlessly awaiting yet another bolt rifle. Besides the three long-time American favorites—the Winchester M70, Remington's M700 and the Savage 110, there was a host of other commercial bolt actions available from foreign shores, plus thousands of military Mausers, Springfields and Enfields. It was obvious that a newly-hatched bolt rifle had to have a lot going for it to compete successfully. From the start, however, it was apparent to many riflemen/hunters that Ruger's new rifle had desirable design aspects that set it apart from most of the others.

Like many other young gun nuts, I was devoted to the writings of Jack O'Connor. Anytime an article appeared in *Outdoor Life* about bolt actions you could be sure it would show pictures of and carry comments on those beautifully classic rifles made by Biesen, Milliron, Brownell and others. Most anything made by these craftsmen had the typical classic looks; straight and elegant stocks without Monte Carlo combs or roll-over cheekpieces, gracefully sweeping bolt handles and hand checkering in multi-point or fleur-de-lis patterns.

Author with a morning's bag of crows taken with a Ruger 77 in caliber 22-250 Rem.

Seeing such rifles made my head swim. I longed for the day I'd own one of them, but I might as well have wished I could fly. I feel sure that such articles by O'Connor and other writers had a certain salutary effect on many riflemen as to what the bolt-action sporter should be, what it should look like.

The Brownell Touch

As popular as the Remington and Winchester bolt actions were at this time, both had "checkered" stocks which, in fact, were not truly checkered—instead the pattern revealed diamonds pressed in *reverse*, the design sunk into the wood by a system of heat and pressure.* Such stocks were compromises, near-classics, perhaps, if one stretches a point, yet not far from the California school of design. They contained elements not really needed on a stock— Monte Carlo combs, white line spacers at butt, grip and fore-end, the latter plastic tipped, as was the butt-plate usually.

Winchester, since 1965, has produced at least 6 different Model 70 buttstocks, none very attractive to the rifleman wanting a classic handle. The old M70 had gained its reputation as the "Rifleman's Rifle" with a simple-lined, well-designed stock, especially in the years before WW II.

The Ruger stock, however, was designed by Lenard Brownell, the famed Wyoming gunmaker, which displayed the epitome of the classic style.

The Ruger Model 77 stock has nothing that isn't needed on a hunting rifle, but no more than that. It is hand checkered in a simple, borderless point pattern which looks and feels good. The finish is of a warm, semi-oil type that was welcomed by the conservative minded rifleman who had been used to seeing the hard, cold, California style supposedly "in" at that time. In addition the M77 had

---

*Frank Pachmayr, head of the Los Angeles shop that bears his name, commented to me in the 1960s that this press-in technique could just as well have used dies that produced raised diamonds, thus closely simulating handcut checkering. Frank was long familiar with such die work, his factory using a wide variety of them in making Pachmayr recoil pads and handgun grips.   J.T.A.

Ruger 77 rifle here has round top, standard barrel form. Trim, graceful lines proclaim the classicism of this outstanding Brownell design.

by DANIEL PETERSON

many features that had previously been available only on true custom rifles. Among these desirable aspects were a (hinged) floorplate-release latch inside the trigger guard bow, a top tang safety, and a barrel—if desired—free of sights or plugged screw holes. The M77's weight, too, was a factor in its appeal. For years the more astute rifleman/hunter had been searching for a handy, lightweight rifle, hefting with scope about 8 pounds. The M77, with scope, could just wriggle under the wire in this department. In total, the M77 resembles, as closely as any production rifle can, costs considered, the style and the mechanics of those eye-appealing custom jobs.

Mauser Extractor

However, another design factor, I believe, helped increase the acceptance of the M77 when it was introduced. When Winchester designed the post-1964 M70 one of the features abandoned—which many writers criticized—was the sturdy Mauser-type wide-claw extractor. Many riflemen, myself included, believe that the broad-arc Mauser extractor is stronger and more reliable than the newer, cheaper-to-manufacture bolt-head type now in use. I know of several such extractors that failed to work. Ruger wisely retained the Mauser extractor in the M77.

All of these factors, then, were a decided plus for the new Ruger bolt rifle. However, I also think that the Ruger came along at precisely the right time to give additional impetus to its popularity.

Initially the M77 was offered in a medium length action only (2.925″ magazine length), designed to handle the popular 308-length family of cartridges. The first four cartridges offered were the 22-250, 243, 6mm and 308. These were followed in 1969 by the 284 Win., the 6.5 Rem. Mag. and the 350 Rem. Mag., though these last three have been since dropped.

(They're being sought out by collectors already.) I feel that the idea behind the short action was to put Ruger in something of a monopolistic position, bearing in mind that short actions have always had a dedicated following, as well as the fact that everyone made the standard-length action. However, because of demand, in late 1970 Ruger brought out the long action M77, (3.380″ magazine length) calling it the M77 Magnum. It was not a true magnum action, of course, if one compares the Mauser extra-length action, but one designed for 30-06-length cartridges and the belted short magnums. This normal-length action was first offered in 30-06, 25-06, 270 and 7mm Rem. Mag. From time to time other cartridges have been offered in both action lengths, as we shall see.

One of the few things disliked aesthetically about the new M77 was its odd-shaped bolt handle. The 1917 Springfield (Enfield) had a similar one. Some writers even compared its form to a dog's hind leg. Functionally it was satisfactory. However, a new style bolt handle was offered in 1970. A marked improvement, it bore a great resemblance to the old M70's bolt style, having a similar rearward slant and a pear-shaped hollowed-out knob. This is the rarest of M77 bolt handle types. The third and current style, identical to the second type but without the hollow knob, has been used for the past 4 or 5 years. However, in checking with the factory I was told that the old crooked handle is still in production, but I haven't seen a new rifle with this bolt handle in several years.

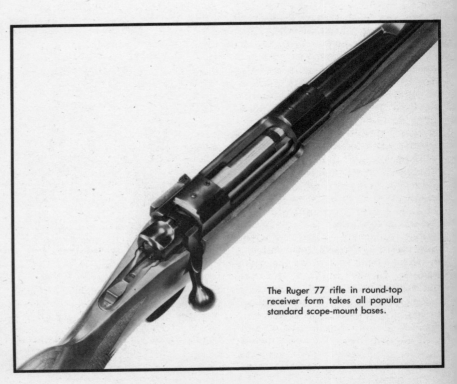

The Ruger 77 rifle in round-top receiver form takes all popular standard scope-mount bases.

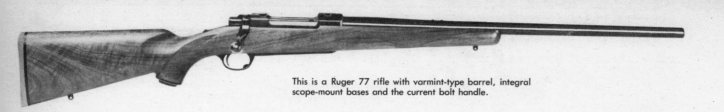

This is a Ruger 77 rifle with varmint-type barrel, integral scope-mount bases and the current bolt handle.

Varmint Type Appears

In 1971 the varmint type M77 appeared. First offered in 22-250, the M77V had a heavy barrel tapped for varmint-target scope bases. Several other popular varmint calibers appeared in subsequent years.

In 1972 Ruger began the most startling resurrection of supposedly dead cartridges ever recorded in the annals of firearms production. The gun magazines were filled with the announcements of these reintroduced cartridges. Short production runs were made of the 220 Swift, 257 Roberts, and 7x57 Mauser at various times during 1972 and '73 to test the market. These short runs were grabbed off the dealer shelves immediately. Ultimately the Swift, 257 Roberts, 250 Savage, and 7x57 became regular cataloged offerings. Not only were these all excellent, time-tested cartridges, they had all been offered in the pre-64 M70s, another similarity between the two rifles. This quick success clearly demonstrated, I think, that there were many people who desired a commercial 220 Swift or 257 Roberts but were unwilling to pay the steep collector's price for an old M70. Offering the 250 Savage in the M77 was probably the most ideal mating ever made commercially, especially since the short action was used. The 257 Roberts was chambered in the long action, which allowed for shallow seating of the bullet, given adequate throating.

When the M77 first came out one could order (from Ruger) a steel floorplate and trigger guard, but only as separate parts. These have never been offered on 77s from the factory with one exception. In 1976 Ruger offered the M77 in a 458 Win. Mag. made with a "Circassian" walnut stock—actually French walnut. This stock, somewhat fuller than the regular stock, I understand, comes with the steel floorplate and trigger guard as standard. These parts, beautifully finished and blued, enhance the beauty of the entire rifle. There is a weight difference, of course—the steel components (minus the guard screws)

weigh about 7 ounces as opposed to 3 for the alloy units. As nice as it would be if these were standard items on all M77s, the price would go up, as would the weight. Incidentally, these parts are available from time to time, in long action form only, at about $20 for both. However, you may have to wait quite a while since production is quite low on the rifle using them. They are *not* shown on the parts list in the M77 owner's manual.

Trigger Pulls

Perhaps the greatest complaint against the M77 concerns the trigger pull. Though nominally adjustable for weight of pull, the criticism has been that this adjustment still leaves something to be desired. For a hunting rifle I feel that no complaint whatsoever is justified. At the bench and on varmints, where optimum trigger control is necessary, it is something else. Currently my M77s have Ruger triggers, which I've worked down to 3-3½ lbs. In correspondence with Jim Carmichel he wrote that he'd talked several times with Bill (Ruger) about the quality of the triggers. Jim added, ". . . I must admit that with a little tinkering the triggers can be adjusted quite nicely.

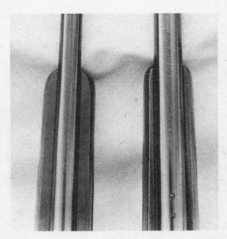

Fore-end at right is the old style with narrow top compared with new style at left. Author feels these top ledges would be more functional with less flat surface exposed.

I have heard that some of them resist adjusting but of the three or four I own, all have been adjusted down to about a 2-2½ lb. letoff." However, for those that must have something better, Canjar makes set-type and single-stage replacement triggers.

An unusual design aspect of the original M77, and still incorporated, is the integral-base system for scope mounting. Using the pair of rings supplied by Ruger, no other bases are needed. This not only saves money but eliminates one step, that of mating mount with receiver—which often enough introduces problems. Although this system in different forms had been offered on Czech Brno actions and on the Finnish Sakos, it was a first for an American made production action. I believe it is a most excellent system. The ring bottoms clamp onto the receiver bases via grooves milled into each side. The ring tops attach to the lower rings by using two 6-40 screws on each.* Two ring heights are available—the standard sets that come with the rifle (Cat. No. D71), and a set ⅛" higher (Cat. No. D71H). I would like a set even lower than standard, for use with straight-tube scopes. Even with the standard rings some scope objective housings touch the barrel, necessitating shims or the use of the higher rings.

In 1972 the M77 appeared with another receiver profile, this one called the "round top," tapped for all popular commercial mounts, but offered only in the longer action. However, I still prefer the integral-base receiver because I believe it secures the scope in the most positive way. Sales of the two receiver types reflect the same preference by the buying public.

The other important design feature of the M77 is the patented diagonal (slanted) front guard screw. This an-

---

*Early-production scope rings were split vertically, unlike the horizontally-divided halves now in use. These original rings were criticized, too, hence the change. I like the older type—I think they're better looking and I've had no trouble with them. J.T.A.

gled screw not only pulls the barrel-receiver assembly together, it also pulls the recoil lug firmly back against the recoil shoulders of the stock—assuming correct dimensioning. The M77 action is flat bottomed, and I've found the bedding of the action and barrel to be excellent, especially in the action area. In fact, some notable gun authorities feel that the M77 actions are bedded so well that it is one of the few actions that cannot be improved by glass bedding. However, it isn't unusual to find some high spots in the barrel channel, which causes some binding, especially along the sides. This can easily be corrected, though, with some light sanding. I have also found that the wood-to-metal fit along the edges of the action has, in some rifles, been rather poor. This is especially true at the rear of the tang.

The fore-end's last inch or so beds tightly against the barrel. In examining many M77s I have found their fore-ends exerting, sometimes, as much as 12-15 lbs. of pressure. I regard this as somewhat excessive, but in my experience many such rifles, though untuned, shoot quite well. Of course the accuracy seeker will certainly want to examine the barrel and action for any excessive rubbing. Of the several sporter weight M77s I own and use, all can be relied upon to shoot careful handloads with the right bullet into 1-1½″ groups at 100 yards if I do my part.

Varmint weight M77s have achieved a high reputation for accuracy. I've read many reports of M77s in 220 Swifts giving exceptional accuracy. Although my experience has been limited to only one Ruger Swift, it certainly lives up to those findings. My Ruger 22-250 consistently delivers 5 shots at 100 yards into groups of ½- to ¾-MOA. Interestingly, perhaps, my most temperamental M77 is a late model 257 Roberts. After trying nearly every usable powder/bullet combination, this rifle seems to prefer IMR 4350 teamed with 100-gr. Hor-

The longer bolt, from a Ruger 77 in caliber 458, has the current bolt handle style. The other bolt shows the earlier type of handle.

nadys.

As in any rifle, we now know, much can be done to maintain high accuracy by judiciously cleaning the barrel regularly and frequently, and by not shooting so fast as to heat the barrel excessively.

In my long-time association with the M77 I have examined and shot many of them. They generally are found with quite straight-grained walnut, but it's quite common to find some nice figure in at least part of the stock. I have, in fact, seen quite a few M77 stocks with rather exceptional wood figure. One of mine, a 25-06, shows a handsome figure in the butt-stock. Checkering is generally very good, with few runovers, the diamonds sharp and well formed. However, from time to time I've seen checkering that looks as though the checkering tool had dulled, causing the diamonds to be less than sharp and the grooves somewhat cluttered with wood shavings. Blueing has been very good, the polishing really excellent; in fact the metal finish has been as good as that on many much

more expensive rifles. The bolts sometimes operate a bit roughly as they come out of the box, but usually they slick up quickly with use. Several of mine were improved by hand stoning until now they snick in and out delightfully, as well as feeding and ejecting more smoothly.

The M77 has been offered in 3 different barrel weights and lengths. The 22″ lightweight or sporter weight is standard except for those calibers needing longer barrels for ballistic reasons. Those cartridges with 24″ barrels, other than the varmint models, include the 25-06, 7mm Mag., 300 Mag., 338 Mag. and the 458 Mag. The original short run of 257 Roberts rifles had a 24″ tube. I would call the 24″ barrel a "medium" weight, since it is far more husky, especially back toward the receiver, than the 22″. The varmint weight barrels have all been 24″ except for the 26″ Swift. Recently Ruger offered a "sporter weight" Swift, with the 24″ medium-weight barrel.

One caliber, the 308, was originally offered in sporter weight, then reintroduced in 1976 in the varmint version for silhouette shooting. It is now being made again (1977) in the 22″ sporter weight.

Changes Desired

If I could change the M77 there are several things I'd do. Though there is little fault with the stock, I feel it could be slimmed or narrowed down in the action section and in the fore-end. Older M77 fore-ends were narrower at the top, a treatment that was superior, in my judgment, to the pre-

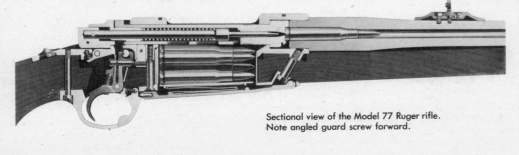

Sectional view of the Model 77 Ruger rifle. Note angled guard screw forward.

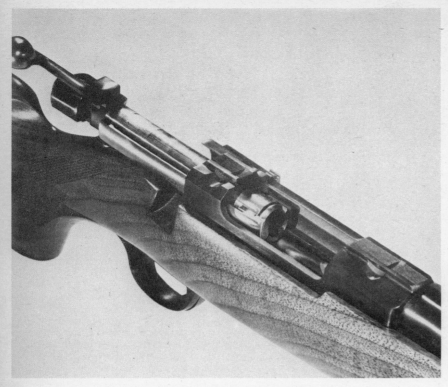

Ruger 77 rifle, here with integral scope-mount bases.

of course, but interesting for the Ruger collector.

Collecting Ruger 77s? Don't laugh. Some discontinued calibers are sky-rocketing in price, notably the 358 Win., a non-cataloged caliber. A recent issue of *Shotgun News* advertised one "as new" for $350. I expect that now, with the 257 Roberts and 250 Savage out of production, their prices will quickly increase as well.

Conclusions

Since the Ruger M77 was introduced in 1968, it has offered the rifleman much that is good. It is, in my opinion, the finest-stocked commercial production rifle ever offered. It gave the conservative, classic-minded rifleman something to cheer about. It combined the proven old with the proven new—plunger ejector and recessed bolt face. It was, I feel, at least partly responsible for the move from pressed checkering to cut checkering on some rifles. Ruger proved that well done hand checkering could be offered on a rifle that was competitively priced. It became a rifle that offered

sent style. I would also like to see, regardless of cost, the steel floorplate and trigger guard offered on the complete rifle in any caliber and on short and long actions. Finally, I am sure that if Super Grade M77s were offered there'd be many buyers standing in line, money in hand. Perhaps these could have a larger and fancier checkering pattern, steel floorplates and trigger guards, a steel grip cap replacing the plastic one, and some time spent on slicking up the action. In talking with the Ruger people in New Hampshire, where the M77 is made, they say there has always been difficulty in keeping up production on the M77 as it is now, that being one of the main reasons why a Super Grade has never been offered.

Variations

A few minor variations in M77s, through the years, have not been design changes. For example, during the early life of the rifle, the rubber butt pads used had rounded edges; the square-cornered type has been used since then. The dimensions of the checkering pattern have varied slightly, although the pattern itself has not changed. The Ruger people tell me that the size changes minutely when bad runovers occur, a few

additional lines being put in to eliminate these errors. The easiest variation to spot is on the fore-ends, as previously mentioned. Originally the top of the fore-end was about $3/16''$ wide on each side, whereas the newer style is wider, some $5/16''$ wide. This wider type suffers, to my way of thinking, in appearance and in practical terms. This wide platform allows snow and rain to accumulate, to run perhaps into the barrel channel. A better treatment would be to show an outside downward curve, letting water/snow run down the stock exterior.

There have also been slight differences in the circumference of the pistol grip; not noticeable to the eye but obvious to the feel and the tape. I have also noticed that earlier M77 extractors were drilled to match up with the hole in the right side of the receiver ring, meant to vent escaping powder gases in the event of a case failure. These holed extractors have not been seen for several years.

Finally, there have been differences in what I call the "ribbing" or the grooves that run lengthwise on receivers with integral scope bases. Sometimes this ribbing is larger and coarser, a result of different mould dimensions, I've heard. A small thing,

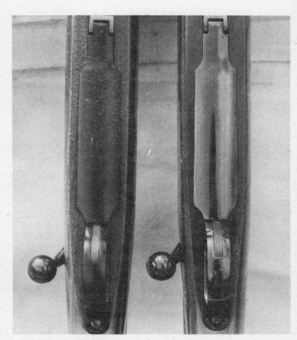

Ruger 77 at right has steel trigger guard and floorplate (sometimes factory available at extra cost), the rifle at left has standard alloy types.

At left, the original Ruger telescope ring; the other is the current style.

The three barrel weights offered in M77s. From left—medium, varmint and lightweight.

new-generation riflemen calibers, some with superior ballistics, considered dead by the larger companies. Most of all, Bill Ruger had the courage to bring out a rifle that was, many felt, behind the times. It was without white-line spacers, had no Monte Carlo combs, no "plastic finish." One of Ruger's old M77 advertisements noted that "not a penny is spent on meaningless ornamentation." I heartily agree.

Perhaps you wonder what we conservative-minded shooters mean when we refer to a "classic" rifle? According to Mr. Webster "classic" means "of the highest order, correct, refined." As far as bolt-action rifles are concerned, that definition fits the Ruger M77 perfectly. •

(Late in 1977, at Remington's seminar for writers and editors, a variant of their M700 centerfire rifle was introduced—the Classic. Simply and functionally designed, the new rifle has no cheekpiece, no Monte Carlo comb, no white spacers, no fore-end tip. There's no grip cap, either, and the bottom of the pistol grip lies close to the stock's toe line, as it should. I don't know what prompted this step, but the Classic 700 is a handsome sporter—and welcome. *J.T.A.*)

Notes on Ruger M77 Bolt Action Rifles

The following calibers were once offered in the M77 (some were reintroductions), but all have now been discontinued except the 220 Swift and the 280 Remington.

220 Swift	280 Remington
250-3000 Savage	284 Winchester
257 Roberts	350 Remington Magnum
6.5 Remington Magnum	

This list shows the calibers that have been or were commercially offered in M77s. Barrel lengths are in inches.

Calibers	77R	77RS	77V	77ST
22-250 Rem.	22	22	24	
220 Swift	24		26	
243 Win.	22	22	24	
6mm Rem.	22	22	24	
250 Sav.	22	22		
257 Rob.	22&24	22&24		24
25-06 Rem.	24	24	24	24
6.5 Rem.	22	22		
270 Win.	22	22		22
7.57	22&24	22&24		24
280 Rem.	22	22		
7mm Rem. Mag.	24	24		24
284 Win.	22	22		
308 Win.	22	22	24	
30-06 Spfg.	22	22		22
300 Win. Mag.	24	24		24
338 Win. Mag.	24	24		24
350 Rem. Mag.	22	22		
358 Win.*	22			
458 Win. Mag.		24		

*non-cataloged. Ruger factory officials said that one short run of nearly 1000 rifles were assembled in 358 Win.

Electronic Night Sight

BY JAMES D. MASON

At last there's an illuminated handgun sight set that works well in darkness, thanks to that little wonder, the LED or Light-Emitting Diode. Shooting performance in dim light is greatly improved, confidence is enhanced and safety aspects are strengthened.

WITH ALL THE emphasis given to daylight marksmanship, night shooting techniques have been sorely neglected in most police training programs. In recent years some of the more progressive law enforcement agencies have put in night firing courses to prepare peace officers for the most likely conditions of a shootout. Well over 90% of such shootings take place after dark or in very dim-lit surroundings.

The moment-of-truth in night firing is when the handgun discharges. First shot hits are imperative for the officer's safety and to avoid a wild exchange of fire from an armed felon. Training with the Night Sight gives the best hit probability of any similar device available.

A new illuminated gun sight installation available from Triple-K Manufacturing Company (568 Sixth Ave., San Diego, CA 92101), provides unparalleled performance for low-light shooting. The Night Sight, as it is called, is installed in the shooter's Colt, Smith & Wesson, or Ruger revolver for a suggested retail price of $69.50, with discounts to police and dealers. This includes parts, installation, battery charger, return postage,

and a three-year warranty. The increased effectiveness afforded by this sight will amaze any marksman who has trained in night shooting. Out to 25 yards, with a little knowledge and practice, scores will nearly match those of comparable daylight conditions.

Nighttime combat shooting courses have been devised in the past that depend on target illumination and/or point shooting* techniques to register hits. Scoring standards for many of these courses are, of necessity, con-

throwing of a lot of lead with no hits registered on either side. Elliott knew that a special sight was needed and began to research for a solution.

Over the years various reflective or phosphorescent materials and paints have been applied to standard gun sights with mixed results. Elliott, wanting a truly illuminated sight, experimented with various light bulb and fiber optic installations before settling on light emitting diodes (LEDs) as the illuminating source. His work with Cap Cresap, an elec-

tions are made on S&W, Colt, and Ruger revolvers on both fixed and adjustable sight frames. Basic price is $69.50, with discounts to police and dealers. Cresap will offer autopistol kit installations later.

Secret of Success

Light emitting diodes (LEDs) are commonly found, among other applications, on numerical displays of pocket calculators. LEDs are solid state devices that emit light energy when a small electrical current pass-

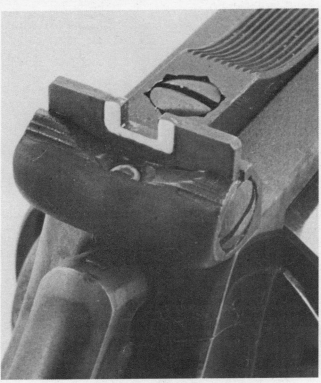

The rear sight is illuminated by an LED mounted in the micrometer sight body. The white epoxy outline of the sight notch reflects red light from the LED.

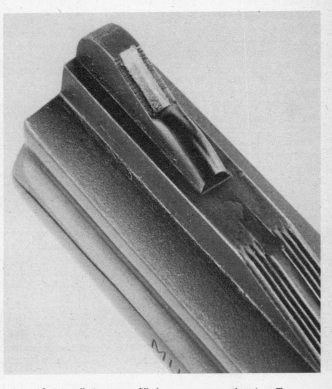

After installation epoxy-filled grooves are unobtrusive. The front sight blade is hollowed out to install a light-emitting diode, which provides an illuminated post sight.

siderably lower than for similar daytime shooting. However, artificial target illumination may not be possible or even desirable under field conditions. Too, nighttime point shooting is not reliable or practical for average untrained shooters at distances beyond 15-20 feet.

During his career with the LAPD, John Elliott, co-inventor of the Night Sight, examined closely reports on shootings from the Rampart Division, scene of many nighttime gun duels. A typical case history involved the

---

*"Point shooting" implies firing the handgun without aligning the sights visually; its effectiveness depends on well-developed feedback from the muscles to tell the shooter that the gun is pointed at the spot where his eyes and concentration are focused. The gun can be in any firing position—from the hip on up to eye-level.

tronics specialist and co-inventor of the sight, resulted in a design that earned a patent for this compact, reliable unit, which can be fitted unobtrusively to a revolver having a ribbed barrel and adjustable sights.

Installation of this sight is also available from Cresap, too (21422 Rosedell Dr., Saugus, CA 91350). Cresap's installation differs from the Triple-K version in several ways. Cresap drills deep holes in the frame and barrel rib as conduits for sight wiring. He also provides a hidden switch installation at extra cost. The standard Cresap installation uses yellow LED light on the rear sight with red illumination in the front blade to provide separation of elements in the sight picture. Installa-

es through them. Electrical current running across the semi-conductor material (gallium arsenide) drops electrons into molecular "holes," releasing free photons that are seen as visible light. No filament is used, as is the case in regular resistance-type light bulbs. These LEDs are small, use little power, produce negligible heat, and last almost forever. They are ideal light sources for installation into a gun frame.

The current Triple-K Night Sight design includes two LEDs, one each mounted behind the front and rear sights. Wiring is inletted into the frame, sideplate, and barrel ribs through small milled slots. After wiring these channels are sealed with black epoxy resin. (Cresap's version,

called the L-tronic, channels wiring via small holes drilled through the barrel rib and frame, leaving virtually no evidence of its presence.) The front sight is hollowed out to accept clear epoxy material after painting the bottom of the channel with reflective red-orange paint. When the front LED glows, the whole sight post is illuminated to the shooter's eye. The rear sight blade notch is outlined with reflective white epoxy enamel. The rear LED is imbedded into the micrometer sight housing at an angle so that the notch is illuminated without projecting light into the shooting eye.

A pressure-sensitive microswitch is inletted into the right grip panel (the palm position for right-handed shooters), unless the shooter specifies finger-tip control (on the left side) by the master hand. This sensitive switch actuates the LEDs as the gun handle is gripped. For left-hand shooting the switch can be situated so the fingertips of the left hand depress it as the gun is grasped.

An optional miniature potentiometer (rheostat) is available ($10), so the light intensity of the LEDs can be regulated to suit individual needs and special conditions. Design of the sight allows no light to be seen from the front or sides of the gun. Some visibility is apparent about 45° to each side of the rear end of the gun. Red-light LEDs (the most popular installation) are slightly visible only about 5-10 feet or closer from the rear of the gun. No glow radiates back to the shooter's face, although a faint shadow can be cast on light colored wall surfaces of a hallway or room if the gun is held close to the wall.

Yellow and green colored LEDs were tested by Elliott but found unsatisfactory. These colors, no more visible to the eye than red, may tend to "burn" sight images onto critical areas of the eye's retina. This phenomenon may drain visual purple from the retina, after prolonged viewing, temporarily reducing night vision sensitivity. Red light, on the other hand, stimulates visual purple in the retina, thus it doesn't interfere with night vision. Red light is more difficult for the eye to focus sharply, however, and may cause sights to appear fuzzy for the near-sighted shooters. Cresap's L-tronic version of the sight uses low intensity yellow light in the rear aperture to avoid merging of the front/rear sights.

LEDs draw so little current that a single charge of the nickel-cadmium batteries will run both LEDs continu-

Various milling cuts are made in the barrel rib, frame, and side plate of the revolver to install and conceal Triple-K Night Sight wiring. Here a .055" deep slot is milled in the rib to install the front sight blade.

ously for about 8 hours. Batteries should receive an overnight recharge once every six months to maintain 100% sure, reliable performance. Recharging too often can reduce battery capacity to hold a charge. A recharging accessory, included with the Night Sight installation, consists of a plug, lead wires, and a 9-volt battery.

Test Results

Tests with the Night Sight showed conclusive evidence that the device does its job well. For comparison a S&W Model 15 equipped with the Night Sight was shot along with a Model 10 Heavy Barrel with standard sights. Firing was done at 15 yards, normally considered the longest effective range for night shooting. Starting at twilight, firing was done every 15 minutes until well into total darkness. "E" series silhouettes were used for targets. No light meter was available to record precise illumination levels, but estimates were related to $3/4$, $1/2$, or $1/4$ light conditions.

No discernible differences were detected between the two guns in group size or shot placements on the targets until less than half-light conditions were encountered; as soon as regular sights became difficult to see clearly, the Night Sight came into its own. Also, the Night Sight demonstrated no deficiencies over regular sights during normal, expected daylight shooting conditions, although some shooters may prefer a narrow line of

black outlining the notch for daytime shooting. This treatment is now available on all Night Sights.

For aimed fire, the basic problem in night shooting is not so much in seeing the target clearly, but being able to align sights precisely—as in aimed daylight shooting—and the ability to focus clearly on the front sight blade. The target itself is relatively easy to see: it only needs to be barely discernible in the darkness to assure killzone hits. This discernibility develops only with practice, however. The Night Sight is uncanny in its ability to maintain precise alignment, but group-size reduction and shot placement are a matter of practice and the individual's general capacity. Achieving a narrow cone of shot-pattern dispersion will enhance effectiveness in nighttime as well as daylight shooting. Basic daylight skills transfer easily to night shooting when the Night Sight is used to maintain precise alignment.

In testing done at 15 yards the Night Sight meant the whole difference between consistent K-zone hits and erratic dispersions. The Model 10, predictably, failed to register hits as $3/4$ darkness conditions ($1/4$ light) approached. In half-light regular sight pictures are a strain to maintain without high target contrast. With diminished visibility even point-shooting techniques become ineffective beyond 10-12 feet. Conversely, the Model 15, with the Night Sight equipped, shot virtually as well as it

TRIPLE K
NIGHT SIGHT

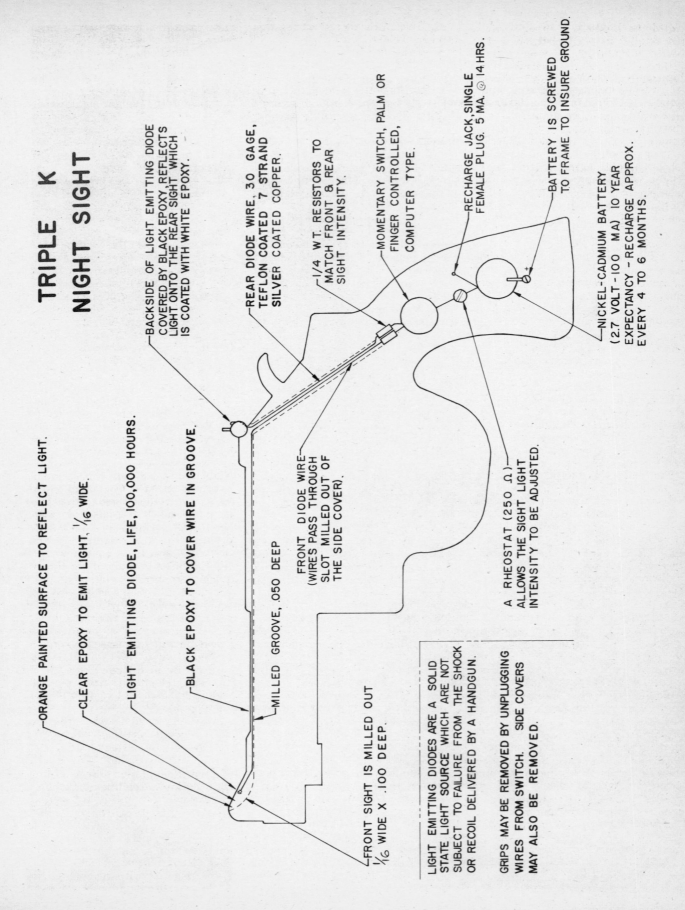

ORANGE PAINTED SURFACE TO REFLECT LIGHT.

CLEAR EPOXY TO EMIT LIGHT, 1/16 WIDE.

LIGHT EMITTING DIODE, LIFE, 100,000 HOURS.

BLACK EPOXY TO COVER WIRE IN GROOVE.

MILLED GROOVE, .050 DEEP

FRONT DIODE WIRE (WIRES PASS THROUGH SLOT MILLED OUT OF THE SIDE COVER).

FRONT SIGHT IS MILLED OUT 1/16 WIDE X .100 DEEP.

BACKSIDE OF LIGHT EMITTING DIODE COVERED BY BLACK EPOXY, REFLECTS LIGHT ONTO THE REAR SIGHT WHICH IS COATED WITH WHITE EPOXY.

REAR DIODE WIRE, 30 GAGE, TEFLON COATED 7 STRAND SILVER COATED COPPER.

1/4 WT. RESISTORS TO MATCH FRONT & REAR SIGHT INTENSITY.

MOMENTARY SWITCH, PALM OR FINGER CONTROLLED, COMPUTER TYPE.

RECHARGE JACK, SINGLE FEMALE PLUG. 5 MA. @ 14 HRS.

BATTERY IS SCREWED TO FRAME TO INSURE GROUND.

NICKEL-CADMIUM BATTERY (2.7 VOLT-100 MA) 10 YEAR EXPECTANCY - RECHARGE APPROX. EVERY 4 TO 6 MONTHS.

A RHEOSTAT (250 Ω) ALLOWS THE SIGHT LIGHT INTENSITY TO BE ADJUSTED.

LIGHT EMITTING DIODES ARE A SOLID STATE LIGHT SOURCE WHICH ARE NOT SUBJECT TO FAILURE FROM THE SHOCK OR RECOIL DELIVERED BY A HANDGUN.

GRIPS MAY BE REMOVED BY UNPLUGGING WIRES FROM SWITCH. SIDE COVERS MAY ALSO BE REMOVED.

had under daylight or twilight conditions. One 4-inch, 6-shot group was made, centered in the chest area of the silhouette target. Skeptical of this unusually good result, second and third trials produced slightly smaller groups, both fired in virtual darkness. However, the author is a trained combat marksman capable of relatively small groups; it should not be inferred that all Night Sight users will shoot 3-4-inch groups. The Night Sight won't improve one's daylight shooting capacity, but it will allow night shooting with very nearly the same results.

Techniques

After several trials it was possible to see silhouettes with only part of the outlined figure visible. It was also possible to bracket a silhouette between two other visible objects when no part of the actual target could be seen. These are all techniques that can be developed with applied use. It is a good idea to have one's vision checked clinically, if target visibility in darkness is a problem.

With silhouettes defined against a relatively light background, accurate 25-yard shooting is entirely possible, using the Night Sight. Shooting prone at 50 yards resulted in consistent torso hits on the "E"-style silhouettes. This, of course, takes some practice, and the ability to hit 50-yard silhouettes well during daylight hours.

The Los Angeles Police Dept. tested the Night Sight extensively before authorizing its installation on officers' handguns. Comments from 67 police officers who participated in the tests produced 52% "excellent" ratings, with only 3% dissenting. The remainder thought the Night Sight was "good" to "very good" in performance, expressing only minor criticisms. This test was the first experience of these officers with the Night Sight, nor was any previous training given. No comparison was run between given Night Sight performance ratings and the regular-sights shooting ability of each officer. A composite of comments indicated ease of sight alignment, higher scores and improved confidence as major contributions of the Night Sight.

The LAPD approves both versions, but the LA County Sheriffs and Phoenix City police approve only the Cresap system, chiefly for serviceability reasons. No outside cuts in rib or frame are made in the Cresap installation, and Cresap's sideplate removes without problems. The Elliott sideplate has a wire attached.

Shooting with standard sights in dim light produces high-centered groups with erratic dispersion. The muzzle is elevated, usually, to locate the front sight in darkness; aligning the sights under these conditions results in high shooting. When no light can be seen between the blade and the rear notch, wrist instability causes horizontal dispersion. The resulting shooter tension and confusion produces flinching and mental lapses, with a further deterioration of scores.

For close-range application the Night Sight can all but eliminate horizontal group dispersion caused by sight alignment problems. Even if the shooter does not make a precise sight picture (not needed at 7 yards), the illuminated blade and notch can be center-aligned by holding the gun slightly below the eye level. This is a quick, consistent, repeatable technique that enhances point shooting for most combat pistoleers when used

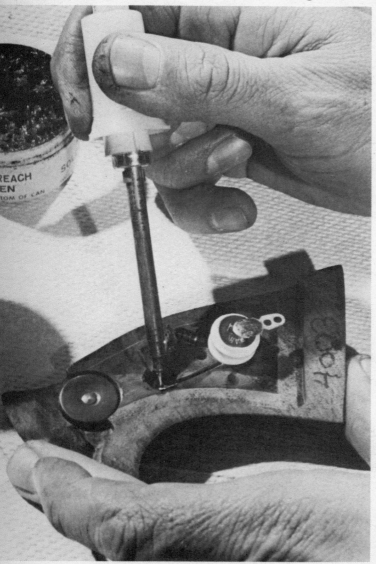

All switches, batteries, and electronic components are contained in the grip panels of the revolver. Miniaturization makes all this possible.

This microswitch turns on the LEDs. It can be set for fingertip control (which must be specified by the customer) as shown here, or a palm pressure switch can be installed.

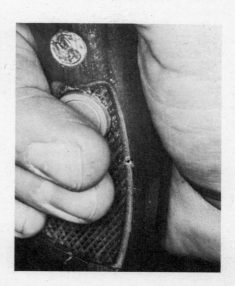

with the two-hand hold.

Confidence Level

The confidence instilled by use of the Night Sight helps in picking up multiple targets in rapid fire. Again, at 15 yards, performance was outstanding in firing two shots on each of three targets; the frustration of having no sight picture is eliminated with the Night Sight, so concentration on picking up and squaring the target is greatly improved. No daytime distractions are present, so sight alignment becomes easy and natural after a bit of practice. This kind of confidence and assurance will be contagious within any law enforcement group.

While darkness is a cloak for the psychopathic law breaker, a reputation for fast and deadly night shooting by the local enforcement officers will be a deterrent for felonious acts. Any second story man is going to think twice before shooting back or running from an officer's challenge if he is operating in a city noted for police night shooting excellence.

The public safety aspect is also strong. Since with the Night Sight disabling hits are registered quickly, fewer stray bullets from both police and felons add up to improved public safety. Also, since the greatest danger to the policeman is during nighttime patrols, the Night Sight can surely be considered part of his safety equipment.

45 Auto Next

The latest development for these illuminated sights concerns the 45 ACP. Cap Cresap has perfected the means for mounting all the components and getting them to work on the big self-loader.

Diodes are mounted in the slide and connected by wiring that runs through holes and cuts inside the slide walls. Nothing appears outside but the sliding electrical connection that interfaces with a corresponding set of stationary contacts mounted on the top end of the right hand grip panel. A printed circuit is inletted into the underside of the grip panel that mounts and houses the palm switch and battery. Otherwise, the unit functions the same as a revolver installation; nothing interferes with normal pistol operation.

After seeing several gimmick-type sighting devices introduced over the years, all either fragile and/or ineffective, it is refreshing to have such a satisfactory sight illuminating device. The Night Sight deficiencies are small, but its benefits are very real. •

Adaptation of the Cresap L-Tronic night sight to the 45 ACP (here a Colt Combat Commander) requires a special sliding switch that interfaces just above the right grip handle. Palm switch and batteries are mounted under the hollowed-out grip panel; the sliding connection carries electricity to the diodes mounted in the sights on the slide.

An optional potentiometer (rheostat) adjusts the light intensity of the LEDs. Adjustment is easily made with a small screwdriver without disassembling the gun.

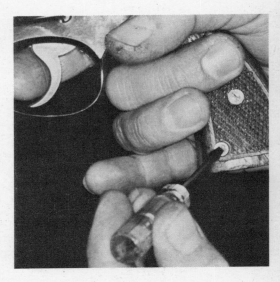

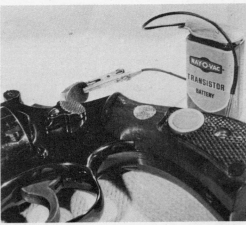

Night Sight batteries supply energy for 6-months use. An overnight charge every 4 to 6 months will keep the batteries reliable. NiCad batteries can last virtually forever, taking many thousands of recharges. Battery charger comes with the Night Sight installation.

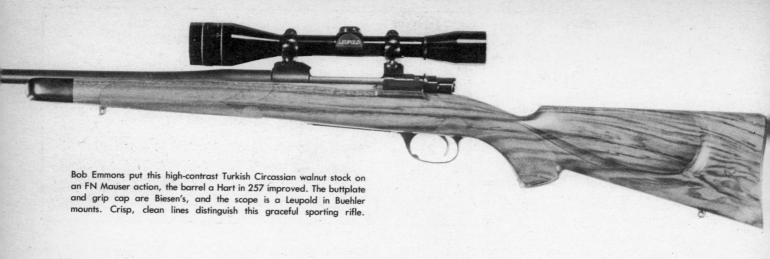

Bob Emmons put this high-contrast Turkish Circassian walnut stock on an FN Mauser action, the barrel a Hart in 257 improved. The buttplate and grip cap are Biesen's, and the scope is a Leupold in Buehler mounts. Crisp, clean lines distinguish this graceful sporting rifle.

Bob Emmons–Stockmaker

DISCOVERING a real artisan—the painstaking sort having the skill and patience needed to produce near-perfect jobs—is a most rewarding experience. When such a craftsman is a stockmaker whose work challenges the best of the old masters, he's a find indeed. Bob Emmons of 238 Robson Road, Grafton, Ohio (44044), fully merits this description.

Our mutual friend, J. Hall Sharon of the Sharon Rifle Barrel Co., introduced me to Mr. Emmons, and of course I asked a number of questions. The responses of this quiet-spoken, modest man proved as interesting as the superlative specimens of stock artistry he displayed. A man's motivating philosophies can be indicative of his dedication.

A native Ohioan, Bob Emmons came up the hard way, forced at the start to make his own inletting and bottoming chisels, scrapers and checkering tools. James V. Howe's writings on gunsmithing were his guide. Never content to do work just "good enough," Emmons devoted the intervening years to perfecting his workmanship and techniques until today they're as precisely sharp as his chisels.

A specialist in stocking fine sporting rifles, shotguns, double rifles and drillings, Emmons does his own hand-polishing and bluing but, like many of today's master stockmakers, he doesn't do major metalwork or general gunsmithing. He is also fully capable of reproducing the stocks of great old pieces, restoring them to

their original pristine condition—an undertaking best reserved for someone with plenty of experience in this field. I wouldn't hesitate to entrust such a job to Bob Emmons.

I asked Bob if he would work to customers' designs and tastes, or did he insist on using his own style? His reply struck me as most practical. He said: "I try to get them pointed in the right direction, but other than that it's the customer's decision. The reason he goes custom is to get what he wants, so I do my best to comply with his ideas."

That question inevitably led to another. Would he characterize his stockwork as being Classical or Contemporary, and would he do either on request?

Though preferring the Classic styling, he would attempt to accomodate a customer within reason, discouraging the use of colored spacers, 45-degree fore-end tips and sharply hooked pistol grips. However, he added, he wasn't always successful! Rubber recoil pads have no place on a fine sporting rifle, he maintains.

I then wanted to know whether his work is patterned after that of one of the "old masters" and, if so, which one? Emmons replied that though he respected such old craftsmen as Linden and Owen, he had never consciously copied their style, preferring to develop and perfect his own.

I was curious as to his choice of actions to use in building a fine custom sporter. Not in the least surprising, the nod went to the old flat-

bottom basic Mauser design and the old Model 70 Winchester.

Finally our discussion turned to woods and stockmaking. This being Emmons' primary field, he has some pretty definite ideas, as exemplified by his comment that, "Pretty wood is not necessarily good, and good wood is not necessarily pretty." Usually he prefers to work with hard, dense, tight-grained woods. "The more a tree struggles to survive, the better the wood," he said.

"To which school," I asked, "do you subscribe regarding the bedding of a sporting rifle stock?"

"Anything we do in bedding a barrel," I was told, "is merely an attempt to control or damp barrel vibrations." Though free-floating the barrel may have some theoretical merit, he feels that method has no place on a custom sporter, preferring to fully bed his barrels.

My closing query concerned waiting time. Most shooters don't like to wait months or years for a gun to be completed, hence his response was encouraging. Generally it has been possible for him to get started on a job within three or four months, after which a stock can be finished in a few weeks. Complete rifles involving much metalwork and/or special order items understandably require more time.

Judging from the Bob Emmons work I've seen, he's already making what the English refer to as a "Best" gun, thus they'll be well worth waiting for.

Ken Waters

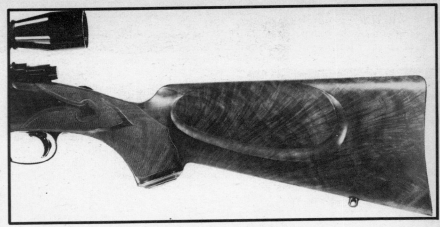

This close-up shot of the butt section of an Emmons-stocked Mark X Mauser in 358 Norma Magnum shows the crisp styling and flawless execution this stockmaker is capable of. A Biesen buttplate provides a graceful termination.

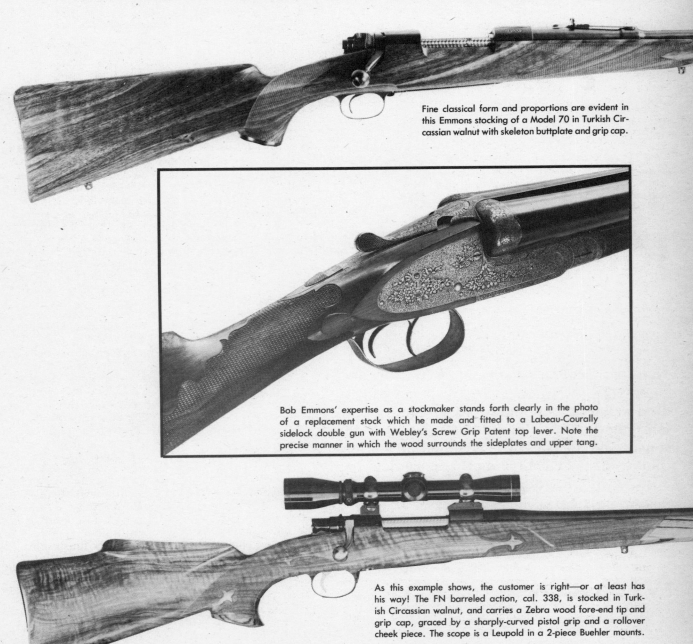

Fine classical form and proportions are evident in this Emmons stocking of a Model 70 in Turkish Circassian walnut with skeleton buttplate and grip cap.

Bob Emmons' expertise as a stockmaker stands forth clearly in the photo of a replacement stock which he made and fitted to a Labeau-Courally sidelock double gun with Webley's Screw Grip Patent top lever. Note the precise manner in which the wood surrounds the sideplates and upper tang.

As this example shows, the customer is right—or at least has his way! The FN barreled action, cal. 338, is stocked in Turkish Circassian walnut, and carries a Zebra wood fore-end tip and grip cap, graced by a sharply-curved pistol grip and a rollover cheek piece. The scope is a Leupold in a 2-piece Buehler mounts.

No WRITER, regardless of his shooting and hunting experience, can tell another hunter exactly what stock design and dimensions will be the best for him and be correct every time. Neither can he know how the tastes of the other fellow will run as to the figure and color of the wood in the stock are concerned, or the checkering design that turns him or her on. Many hunters have pretty strong notions along these lines, and are not backward in letting any writer who steps on their toes know about it.

Then, too, you have to consider the stockmaker—though most stockers do custom work, which is supposed to mean "made according to the customer's order," many of them have their own ideas of how a custom stock should be made and finished, and what it should look like, nor are their minds easily changed by the wishes or whims of the customer. In some cases this is probably as it should be

because of their long experience in stockmaking, but only a few stockmakers spend much time in hunting country, so they really don't know very much about the requirements of stocks for hunting rifles.

For this reason, someone who has spent the big end of a lifetime hunting big game under a wide range of hunting conditions, and who has also made stocks for the rifles he used, as well as custom work for other hunters now and then, should have learned a few things about hunting stocks, and perhaps can offer some helpful advice. I'll try.

Wood Selection

To start at the beginning let's take a look at wood. There are a great many species and colors of wood suitable for gun stocks, and individual tastes will certainly enter the picture here. There is little doubt that plain straight-grained wood makes the

The Hunting Rifle Stock

Many aspects of stockmaking for the big game rifle are often overlooked or mishandled or both. The author—a veteran hunter who has made numerous custom rifle stocks—offers cogent but sometimes unorthodox ideas on achieving the near-ideal in a hunting rifle handle.

by BOB HAGEL

most stable hunting stock, but few hunters who want a custom stock will settle for that—they usually love beautiful wood and will want it in a custom stock. I admit to being one of them. But the right kind of wood, laid out properly, will make a beautiful and stable stock.

To cover the wood angle fully would take more space than is available to me, so we'll brush over it lightly. Perhaps the best wood from the point of stability, beauty and workability comes from the European varieties of walnut—the Circassians, French, English—there is little difference except for the area where they are grown. Some very good English walnut, by the way, grows in California.

For the greatest stability the wood forward of the grip should be straight grained, the grain slanting slightly upward. If good color and contrast are present in the action/fore-end section,

advance just how stable a given piece of wood will be; however, several things can be done to help prevent a change in group size and impact.

Bedding Systems

Starting with the barrel channel, there are various ways of bedding the barrel in it, and it is here where many top-rated stockmakers stub their toes when making hunting rifle stocks. Good stockmakers always strive to do precise wood-to-metal fitting as a symbol of their inletting ability, but that's a mistake when inletting and bedding the barrel of a hunting rifle. Some stockmakers try to fit the whole barrel channel tightly to the barrel, others leave space except along the top edges. Either way is wrong if you want that rifle to shoot the same place day after day in all kinds of weather. I have yet to see a piece of wood that will not move at least a little during

maybe enlarge groups. The main reason for this is that when the bullet passes through the bore the barrel vibrates in more or less of a circle, and when the pressure is changed from one point of contact to another, the point of bullet impact will almost certainly change.

Some barrels require different bedding techniques than do others, and certain barrels will do their best with some upward pressure being exerted by the stock near the tip of the fore-end. This damps the vibrations, often giving tighter grouping, but if the wood warps up or down, or badly to one side or the other so that this pressure is changed, so will the point of bullet impact move. Only experimenting will prove how the individual barrel should be bedded to give the tightest groups it is capable of; if it won't shoot acceptable groups without up-pressure, it will have to be

Left—the modified Monte Carlo comb will fit most shooters well and it works in all shooting positions; it also handles heavy recoil without banging the cheekbone. Though it may not please the tastes of some shooters, it still makes a reasonably attractive stock. Note radius and relative closeness of pistol grip.

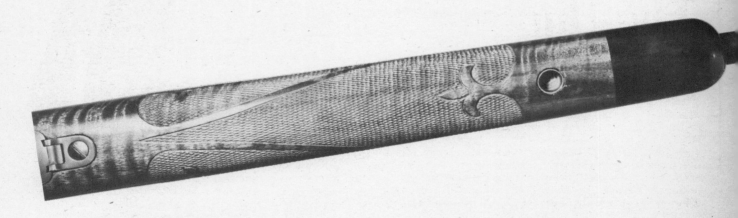

it will enchance the beauty of the stock and has no effect on stability. Keep the fancy grain structure in the buttstock or to the rear of the grip, and if such wood wanders a bit now and then it won't change group size or point of impact usually.

By "stability" I mean wood that stays in one place after the stock is finished, that it does not warp and twist when subjected to various atmospheric conditions. Without stability the point of group impact will not only change from Monday to Friday, but if the pressure comes in the right spot groups may double in size.

Though even straight-grained wood is not immune to moving when it takes up moisture or dries out, there is no way I know of for determining in

It doesn't make sense to seal the inside and outside of a stock and leave the checkering bare to sop up moisture like a sponge. This 22 line-per-inch checkering was sealed with a couple of coats of Lin-Speed, the surplus brushed out with a stiff toothbrush. This rifle had seen several years of hard use when the photo was taken. Checkering is still clean and fairly sharp.

severe weather changes; and the barrel channel that is tight all-round, or only at the top edges, will exert pressures at different places on the barrel. This will change the point of impact,

bedded that way, with the hope that the wood doesn't walk much in use.

Floated Barrels

After a great deal of experimental bedding I find that most barrels shoot just as well or better if they are floated completely from about $1\frac{1}{2}''$ forward of the receiver ring; that way the fore-end is free to move a little without affecting accuracy or point of impact. Even if a barrel gives slightly better accuracy with up-pressure near the fore-end tip, say $1''$ groups as opposed to $1\frac{1}{2}''$ for the same barrel floated, I'll float it every time for a big game rifle. I much prefer knowing that it will consistently shoot the larger groups to the same point of

impact, than the smaller clusters that move from here to there every time the sun is swallowed by a cloud.

By "floating" a barrel I don't mean that it must have a gap along the fore-end wide enough to stow your lunch in. With a good stable piece of wood, one properly sealed inside and out, the clearance doesn't have to be unsightly; just enough space so that that particular piece of wood will not make contact with the barrel when the weather goes sour. Some old school riflemen still contend that a floating barrel won't shoot as well as one that is skin tight in the wood, or with pressure out in front. I don't think I have to argue that point; groups fired with benchrest rifles and their floating tubes should be proof enough.

Action Bedding

Some stockmakers also bed an action just as tight as they can get it while still being able to remove it from the stock—and I mean *all* of the receiver. Again this is a mistake because weather conditions are likely to move the wood slightly. In the worst cases the pressure can be so severe that the action is actually bent. I've seen this happen to the point where the bolt would bind in the receiver, but if one or both guard screws were loosened the bolt was completely free. To avoid this the action should be bedded tightly from the forward end of the receiver ring to the magazine well, then make no contact from there to the tang area, where it is again bedded tightly. There should be no movement whatever in barrel or action when the guard screws are tightened. If a third (center) guard screw is present, the receiver should make tight contact with the stock at this point to avoid a bending action between stock and action. This does not mean that the top edges of the stock should not be bedded to fit the metal of the receiver with an even full contact, which is desirable for obvious reasons, and which will not affect accuracy.

Few hunters are aware of the effect poor action bedding can have on accuracy, and that warping of the wood here through taking and losing moisture will cause a rifle to go completely sour during a hunt. This is more likely to cause poor grouping rather than change of group impact, but may work either way or both.

There is also much difference of opinion whether it is better to bed the barreled action directly into the wood or to use one of the epoxy bedding compounds. An old friend, of long

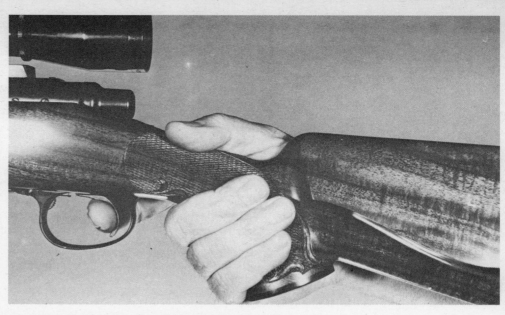

With properly shaped pistol grip the hand is held in correct position for good trigger control. An important point for shooting from quickly taken, often makeshift hunting positions.

hunting experience but none in stockmaking, maintains that the only purpose of bedding compounds is to cover up sloppy inletting. Then there are those who think that if the barrel and action are bedded solidly and completely in bedding material, all grouping and change of impact problems will be eliminated. Both points of view are in error.

As for bedding in the wood being better, I have stocks bedded that way, and they shoot tight groups and maintain point of impact well, but they are made of exceptionally stable wood, and have been rebedded whenever they showed the least bit of movement. But let's face the fact that no stockmaker, no matter how good he is, can mate metal and wood as evenly in the right spots as a good job with bedding compound will. And I've looked inside the stocks of some of those stockmakers considered the best.

On the other hand, those who believe that bedding the full length of the inletting with glass or other bedding compound will cure all stock warping problems are in for a sur-

prise if they pack the rifle very long in country where the weather changes twice a day. I much prefer epoxy bedding to wood bedding, but it is successful only if it is done right. The method is the same as for bedding in the wood, only better and easier—relieve the barrel channel as for wood, and bed the action solidly only in the places described earlier.

Sealing the Wood

If the hunting stock is to remain stable under hunting conditions it must be thoroughly sealed to eliminate taking on moisture as much as possible. This means that it must be sealed *inside and out.* Obviously, if it is bedded in a compound, those portions of the inletting will be completely sealed, but that is not enough. The *whole* inside should be sealed. This can be done with whatever finish is used on the outside, but I find that the best sealer is an epoxy treatment. I use Brownell's Acraglas, mixed without adding floc, and warmed to at least 70°. Rub it into all surfaces of the inletting with the fingers, then wash your fingers with raw

vinegar to remove the material before it dries. This treatment will effectively seal the inletting with a single coat for all time. Give the area under the buttplate and pistol grip cap the same treatment.

As for the outside finish there are many products that work about equally well. A hard epoxy finish such as that found on Weatherby rifles is excellent for sealing the stock and shielding it from moisture, but it does reflect light like a mirror—something that is hardly desirable for hunting. Many hunters prefer a dull oil finish (sometimes called a London finish) because it does not reflect light badly, but it, too, has disadvantages. Unless a stock with a straight oil finish is kept saturated with oil it will absorb water like a paper towel when exposed to rain for long periods—like

hunting in Southeast Alaska. And if you use too much oil the wood will warp anyway, and it will also become spongy and soft.

Finishing and Checkering

My personal preference is for Lin-Speed or the like. Given many very light coats, each completely rubbed into the wood by hand, the finish will be built up *within* the wood to form a hard waterproof surface without giving an extremely high gloss.

Also, if the stock is to be fully sealed against moisture, the checkering too should have a couple of coats of finish. I know that a lot of stockmakers will scream over that statement, because they say it fills the checkering, dulls the points, and spoils the esthetic appeal. They are right if it is done wrong, but wrong if

it is done right. If applied with a stiff toothbrush and brushed until only a very thin coating is left on the wood, it will enhance the wood by bringing out the color, while sealing the area against absorbing moisture. It just doesn't make sense to seal all other parts of the stock and leave an open checkering pattern that, by its very nature, will soak up water like a sponge.

While we're on checkering, let's give some thought to what's best for a hunting stock as far as lines per inch are concerned. Here is another place where I feel that many of our best stockers are in error. Very fine checkering, of 28 to 32 lines per inch, is considered the criterion of top-drawer workmanship if it is perfectly executed. Now I have no quarrel with that line of thought, but is it best for a hunting stock? The answer is no, for two reasons. First, very fine checkering is also very shallow, and it takes very little grease, dirt or whatever to fill it. Second, the points of the tiny diamonds dull rapidly, and such checkering doesn't offer a very good grip even when sharp. After all, the main function of checkering on a hunting rifle is to give a slip-proof grip, and for that use 20-22 lines per inch is about as fine as it should be. I have made several stocks for my old hunting partner Jake Jacobson, who lives and hunts in Southeast Alaska, and he likes 16-line checkering on his hunting rifles for that rain-drenched land where the rifle stock is nearly always wet and slick.

Stock Design

When we look at design and dimensions of the hunting rifle stock, taste and esthetics often overshadow usefulness. Which isn't to say that a stock can't be beautiful, graceful and useful all at the same time. Perhaps the greatest controversy here centers around the Classic and Monte Carlo stock designs. Both have good and bad features as far as the individual hunter is concerned. There are those

Four different types of butt covers. The plate at left is of hard rubber, next is factory steel plate, then a custom steel plate with trap door, and last a rubber recoil pad. Hard rubber and plastic are both slick, break easily. Steel is non-breakable, but slick on some surfaces, hard on the shoulder, especially with light clothing. Recoil pads are better on all counts.

No stockmaker, no matter how good he is, can fit metal to wood at critical points as closely as it can be done with good bedding compound. Note that this stock is bedded tightly in Acraglas from forward end of magazine cut to a couple of inches forward of receiver ring, and also in the tang area. Other parts of the action and barrel channel (except top edges of action) are relieved to prevent contact with metal, but are coated with Acraglas as mentioned in the text.

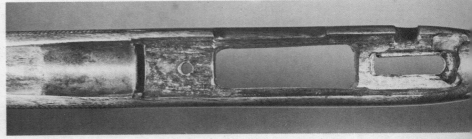

who feel that the Monte Carlo design is a complete disaster in both looks and usefulness. I'll agree it is not the most beautiful design ever dreamed up, but it is useful for many individuals and for many hunting situations. Properly done, it gives adequate heel drop for any shooting position, while holding the line of the comb under the cheek straight, or slightly higher at the rear, so that it does not bump the cheekbone under recoil. And it does very well in both departments. If made correctly it will slide under the cheekbone without bumping it, and it has enough drop for fast offhand shooting.

Its critics claim it gives much more felt recoil than a very straight classic design that has no more drop at heel than at the point of the comb, and that anyone can shoot the straight classic stock just as well from all positions. I agree with the felt recoil part, and I shoot a straight stock quite well with reasonable speed from the offhand position, but this doesn't mean that everyone can. Sure, most shooters can eventually learn to use a stock of any design with almost any reasonable dimensions fairly well, if they use it long enough, but they may never be very good with it. If this were not true, there would be no difference in stock dimensions on shotguns for use in the field, or on those intended for trap or Skeet. Nor would claybird shooters have stocks made to the dimensions they shoot the highest scores with.

The point to consider here is that nearly anyone can shoot a very straight rifle stock well from prone, sitting, or from a rest when there is plenty of time, but not everyone can use the same stock well for fast offhand shooting in the brush. It is usually better to compromise on a hunting stock, giving it about 1″ more drop at heel than at the comb point. Such a stock, Classic or Monte Carlo, will handle recoil nicely and be well suited to fast offhand work for most hunters of assorted shapes and sizes.

Length of Pull

One of the more critical dimensions of a hunting rifle stock is its length of pull. People of different sizes and proportions require stocks of different lengths, and the way they hold a rifle also makes a difference. There is no way I can suggest what stock length anyone should use without seeing him shoot, but I can give one piece of advice. Remember that most big game hunting is done during cool or cold weather, and that clothing will be thick. A stock that is too long may hang up when you can least afford it.

The pistol grip shape is also important for a firm grip at the same point every time, which is what the pistol grip was designed for. The distance from trigger to grip cap will vary with the size and shape of the hand, but a reasonably close grip, say 3¼″-3½″, will be about right for most people, and if it has a rather tight curve it will hold the hand in position better. It will also hold the hand up where it belongs better if it is slim in the tang-to-comb area and flares outward slightly toward the cap. A grip that is tapered smaller toward the cap will allow the hand to slip downward, changing the angle and leverage of

A pistol grip that is about 3¼″-3½″ from trigger to forward edge of cap will fit most hands if it has a rather tight curve. The 20 lines-per-inch checkering on this Classic-stocked grip may not be as esthetically appealing as 28-32 lines, but affords a much better grip on a hunting rifle stock. Diamonds stay sharp longer, do not fill with grease and dirt as easily. This rifle had been used a good deal when photo was taken.

the trigger finger.

The fore-end doesn't need to be bulky, but it should be big enough to fill the hand for a good grip. Neither should it be flat on the sides and bottom—I can't recall ever seeing a hand that fit that fore-end design—but rounded and a little wider than it is deep toward the tip.

Slings and Swivels

A sling is a near must on a hunting rifle, and of a design that can be used for shooting if the hunter knows how to use it. Swivels should be detachable so the sling can easily be removed when the rifle is cased. If the sling is to be used as a shooting sling, the front swivel should be mounted on the fore-end, not on the barrel. Though the tension of a tight fore-end mounted sling will have no effect on point of bullet impact, the barrel-located swivel will lower impact when the sling is pulled tight. I like the sling attached to the barrel only on rifles with very heavy recoil, which position will avoid bruising the hand against the swivel.

Cheekpiece design is largely a matter of personal taste, but there is no practical reason for it to be long and bulky. The cheek is never placed at the rear of a cheekpiece, and excessive length only serves to add unnecessary weight.

Buttplates and Pads

The type of buttplate used is highly important on a hunting rifle, and the hunter should never let his taste and visions of beauty override function. Skeleton buttplates are elegant examples of the gunmaker's art, but are far from practical on a hunting rifle. Steel and plastic buttplates are somewhat more useful, but are not ideal for a number of reasons.

Obviously the beautiful skeleton plate, with the attendant bare wood that goes with it, will soon be defaced in hard hunting use, as it is impossible to avoid setting the rifle butt on the ground at times. Any kind of plastic or hard rubber not only breaks quite easily, but they're slick and the cause of many rifles and sights being damaged when the rifle is leaned against something. Solid steel buttplates are tough and can be roughened enough so that they're not prone to slipping on the shoulder or when the rifle is set down on a smooth surface, but they do stick to and pick up snow and dirt during cold weather. Also, any and all of these buttplates are tough on the shoulder when attached to rifles of heavy recoil.

Even though it may not be the most beautiful, the rubber recoil pad is by far the most practical type for a hunting rifle. It holds well on nearly any surface, making it safe to set the rifle down without fear that it will fall, yet it does not pick up dirt and snow like cold steel does. Moreover, it will take a great deal of the jar out of heavy recoiling rifles. The rubber pad need not be of the open or ventilated type, nor overly thick and bulky.

There are those who will not agree with these suggestions, but they are based on long experience, not on theory, and it is hoped they will prove of value in choosing your next hunting rifle stock. •

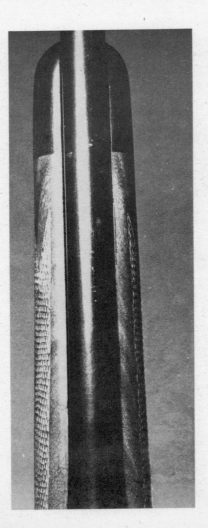

If a floated barrel (left) shoots well (and most do), it will be much less likely to change point of bullet impact due to atmospheric conditions. As this photo shows, the space between wood and metal along the top edge does not have to be so wide that it is unsightly.

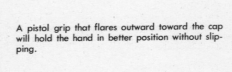

A pistol grip that flares outward toward the cap will hold the hand in better position without slipping.

GLOW PLUG GUNS

There's little enough that is really new, we're often reminded. True, but how about electric ignition muzzle-loaders? The author made a couple of them that work well.

by ROBERT W. METZE

MATCHLOCK, FLINTLOCK, percussion, electric: Yes, *electric ignition*. Although the idea is not entirely new, its application to handguns and rifles is rather unusual, to say the least. Navy guns and artillery pieces have been fired this way in the past years, and recently there has been some progress in small arms using electric ignition with caseless ammunition.

But I'm going to report here on black powder muzzle-loading guns using electric ignition. Electric ignition (EI) has several advantages: First, there is no direct mechanical linkage between trigger and barrel. Second, a very light trigger pull results from using a micro-switch. Third, the feasibility of interchangeable barrels and, I feel, better reliability of ignition than other systems offer.

For my initial effort EI was obtained by using a glow plug of the type fitted to model airplane engines. Various glow plugs are available, and my choice was the Fox, a long, heavy-duty, 1.5-volt type. Powering this glow plug in a 22-caliber handgun are two AA size alkali batteries placed in the handle, the two wired in series to produce 3 volts. This makes the plug light up rapidly — a condition I wanted — but be warned, if the trigger is held too long the plug filament will burn out. Behind the trigger there's a micro-switch, actuated with very light pressure on the trigger — about the same light pull usually found with a set trigger. In the 30-caliber carbine the trigger is the switch itself, pow-

ered by 4 penlight batteries contained in the stock. These are connected in paralled-series to again get 3 volts, but the hookup gives longer battery life. There are electronic circuits which would prevent the burn out of the plug but I have not explored this area.

Because the current usage is brief, the battery is good for about 200 shots in the pistol, starting with fresh batteries. All other components are identical with any other firearm except for the safety — that's a second switch that interrupts the electrical circuit.

The Pistol

For the handgun I used a heavy barrel from a 22 Hornet rifle, turning it on my lathe to .750″ diameter for the full length, 8 inches. Both sights are dovetailed into the barrel. The breech end of the barrel was threaded for a 5/16″x24 hardened breech plug, both lathe jobs done in my shop. The glow plug goes into the barrel at about 2 o'clock (see photo) just ahead of the breech plug, and is so seated as to be flush with the bore surface. The glow plug comes from the factory with a ¼″x32 thread, but I could not find a tap of that size, so I ran a ¼″x28 die over the plug to rethread it. The barrel is mounted on the ⅜″ thick aluminum frame with two 8x32 Allen-head bolts, these entering the barrel from below, front and rear.

I made the frame in the style, roughly, of Daisy's CO₂ pistol. A ¼″

Batteries inside handle are grounded to frame. Wiring then ran through micro switch to glow plug.

Circuit wire is soldered to brass clip attached to glow plug. Note tempered bolt (rear) used as breech plug.

Fox brand 1.5V heavy duty glow plug was used in 22 muzzle-loading pistol made by author.

slot milled into the top of the frame made a snug fit for the trigger and the micro switch. The micro switch, picked up in a surplus store, is an Acro, made in Columbus, Ohio, but various other switches would work as well, depending on the frame design. Two aluminum brackets—threaded into the frame's right side—hold a piece of ³/₁₆″ nickel-plated brass tubing (available in hobby shops). Into this tube the ramrod slides snugly. The walnut grips, linseed oil finished, are also styled a la Daisy.

I also made an aluminum bullet mould to cast a .210″ round ball which, when patched, fits the 22 pistol bore perfectly. I load with a scoop of triple F black powder, using a measure made from a 22 rimfire case, Long or Short, depending on how much powder I want to load. Accuracy is excellent—even my 12-year old son shoots into the black at 50 feet.

Before cleaning the barrel I remove the glow plug first, hold it under a warm water faucet, then shake it vigorously several times. If a cleaning patch is run into the barrel with the plug in place the nichrome filament could be snagged and ruined.

The Carbine

I made the carbine barrel from a 1917 Enfield, 30-06 caliber, of course, cutting it off to 20 inches. Using a piece of rosewood some two inches wide, I routed a channel for the barrel, using two bolts from below, as with the pistol, to attach the barrel. I made a breech plug, much as before, and used a brass guard and trigger from Dixie Gun Works. I fitted a nickeled brass fore-end cap, drilling a hole through it and the wood to hold the ramrod of brass.

As with the muzzle-loading pistol, I cut dovetails in the barrel for the metallic sights—an old Redfield peep

Author's muzzle-loading carbine has name plate on right side. Circuit wire from glow plug goes into top of redwood stock.

Underside of carbine buttstock was opened to hold 4 C- or D-type batteries. Cover below was made to conceal storage area.

Sliding safety is installed in left side of carbine. With switch to rear (Safe) green-painted area shows; when switch is moved forward (On) a red-colored area appears.

rear and a god bead Marble front. I cut a recess into the underside of the butt for the 4 penlite cells, running the connecting wire through the grip area, and letting it emerge from the right side of the fore-end top to join the glow plug.

I mounted the sliding safety switch on the left side of the stock. A rearward motion of the knob opens the electrical circuit—and vice versa.

No micro switch is used on the rifle. Instead, the trigger touches a contact screw at the rear of its travel, thus completing the circuity to the glow plug and firing the rifle.

The carbine shoots a .295″ patched ball and performs nicely—at 50 yards it will put 5 balls into two inches, often less. That's with a charge of 20-22 grains of 3F, and I've thought a slower-twist barrel might help. It would be easy to have interchangeable barrels.

The carbine glow plug is also on the upper right side of the chamber, about where a percussion nipple would be. If a blow-out on either plug should occur, it will not be toward the shooter.

Strength—Reliability

The reliability of glow-plug electric ignition is excellent. On one occasion, in my garage, I fired the 22 pistol 40 consecutive shots without a misfire. I had to quit because the black powder smoke was getting too thick.

These glow plugs appear to withstand the reasonable pressures developed by black powder. I tested the 22 pistol with 30 grains of FFFg powder behind two patched balls with complete safety and with no signs of trouble. The carbine was test-fired with 48 grains of the same powder and two patched balls. These represent quite an overload, but there was no damage to either glow plug. ●

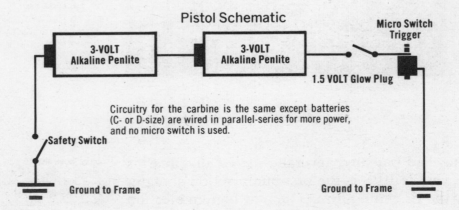

Pistol Schematic

3-VOLT Alkaline Penlite — 3-VOLT Alkaline Penlite

Micro Switch Trigger

1.5 VOLT Glow Plug

Circuitry for the carbine is the same except batteries (C- or D-size) are wired in parallel-series for more power, and no micro switch is used.

Safety Switch

Ground to Frame

Ground to Frame

BROWNING'S New Pump Shotgun

THE WINCHESTER Model 1897 .... the Stevens Model 520 .... the Remington Model 17. Even though these three slide-action scatterguns were miles apart in terms of mechanical design, they all had one thing in common. They were fathered by John M. Browning, probably the most prolific designer of sporting arms the world has ever known.

This trio comprised only a part of JMB's efforts on the slide-action side. His list of credits include patents on a half-dozen others, among these a pair of 10 gauges, all of which were grabbed up by Winchester but never placed in production. The Remington Model 17, which subsequently became the current Ithaca Model 37, represented JMB's final fling at pump gun design, having been patented in 1915 but not introduced by the crew at Ilion until 1921.

This brief look at yesteryear may cause one to wonder why the Browning firm waited so long before coming out with a slide-action repeater under its own banner. Don't look this way for an explanation, because I don't have one handy, and I'm not about to speculate. I do know that Browning's new BPS (which stands for Browning Pump Shotgun), introduced to U.S. shooters early in 1977, promises to give all existing trombone actions a strong run for their money.

Made by Miroku

It will come as no surprise to learn that the BPS is being manufactured in Japan by Miroku, the same firm that builds the B-SS double, the Citori O-U and several other guns in the current Browning line-up. Right now the new pump is offered only in 12 gauge and, according to Browning, there are no plans to come out with a

J. M. Browning had patented several slide-action firearms over the years, yet the BPS is the first pump-action shotgun ever offered by the Browning firm. The new bottom ejection gun gets good marks from a critical observer.

by WALLACE LABISKY

Labisky gave the 12-gauge BPS test gun a good workout in the field on pheasants, sharp-tailed grouse and Hungarian partridge. No malfunctions were experienced, and he found the gun to be a natural pointer that came on target with a high degree of precision. On the aesthetic side, the gun is handsomely finished and has very appealing lines.

20. The two 12-bore models are a field gun at near $240 and a trap gun at $20 more. The trap gun handles only 2 ³/₄″ shells, but the field gun is chambered for 3″ magnum loads. Extra barrels (no fitting required) are available in 26″, 28″ and 30″ lengths—full, modified and improved cylinder chokes. Don't look for a BPS Skeet gun; Browning says there won't be one.

There has been some talk bandied around that the new BPS is simply a copy of the old Remington M-17 and its close kin, the Ithaca M-37. Wrong! There are basic similarities, of course. One is that the BPS has a solid-walled receiver with bottom ejection, and another is that the combination shell carrier/ejector is of much the same design. But beyond this, the BPS is largely an all-new gun. I won't be continually making design comparisons, for there isn't space for that here, but as we go along many of the differences will become apparent to those of you who are familiar with the M-17 and M-37 guns.

Beyond doubt, the most eye-catching feature of the BPS is its distinctive high-profile ventilated rib, which has a maximum above-barrel height of fully ³/₈″ near the magazine cap and a minimum height of just under ¼″ at the muzzle. The width is a nominal ⁵/₁₆″, and the flat surface (including a 2⁷/₈″ ramp-type extension on the receiver) carries cross-hatched lines to scatter reflected light. There are no design differences between ribs on the field and trap models. However, the trap gun has ivory beads located front and center, the field-gun rib having only a white-metal bead of .152″ diameter up front.

Recoil Reduced

In addition to a speedy dissipation of heat waves, this high-loft rib offers what is surely an even greater advantage. By elevating the line of sight relative to the axis of the bore, the forces of recoil are placed more directly in line with the shooter's shoulder and, in turn, there is a lessening of felt recoil at the comb of the stock.

The BPS rib is of the "floating" type, being dovetailed to its support posts and anchored only at one point—about 4 ¼″ behind the muzzle. This method of rib fastening aids in maintaining a constant point of pattern impact when the barrel heats up with rapid and continuous firing.

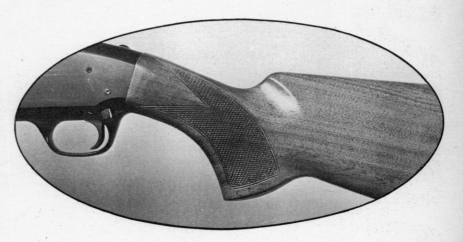

A select grade of walnut is used for BPS buttstocks—no fancy figure, just straight-grained quality wood that wears Browning's high-gloss, weather-resistant finish. A recoil pad with white-line spacer is standard. The too-thick stock comb's fluting angles downward a bit much, could be bettered. The pistol grip is left uncapped.

Trapshooters will probably appreciate this feature more than hunters, though there are times when a hunting-gun barrel will warm up considerably—an example being a fast-action dove shoot in summery weather.

The BPS is distinctive in being the very first pump-action shotgun ever to be fitted with a magazine cutoff. This exclusive Browning feature permits switching the shell in the chamber without disturbing the shells in the magazine. The cutoff mechanism consists of a rotating half-collar that surrounds the magazine tube immediately forward of the receiver, and there are two settings—"S" for single shot and "R" for repeater.

Using the Cutoff

To change the chambered shell the cutoff selector is rotated to the "S" position. This "freezes" the left-hand cartridge stop and prevents the shells in the magazine from feeding when the action is opened. The shell carrier is simultaneously rendered inopera-tive and the load being extracted from the chamber will simply fall of its own weight from the bottom-side ejector port, rather than being kicked out with force. The replacement load can then be dropped into the open receiver and closing the action will chamber it.

The gun can be fired, of course, with the cutoff selector on the "S" setting and this mode of operation will likely be preferred by trapshooters for 16-yard and handicap targets, because it does simplify single-round loading. Also, the "S" setting makes it easier to save those reloadable emp-

Browning's new BPS slide-action shotgun—a bottom-ejecting gun with a high-profile ventilated rib. *Photo courtesy Browning*

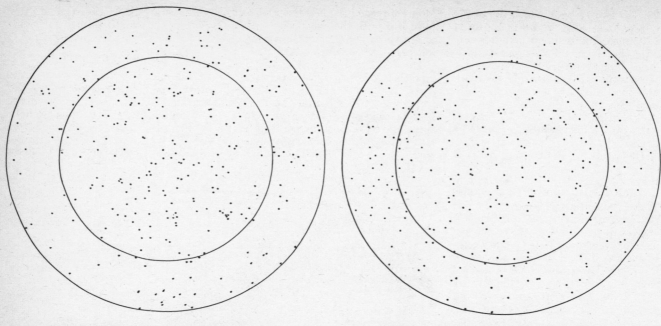

When the BPS was teamed with Winchester's Upland load (1¼ ozs. No. 7½ chilled) the patterns opened to roughly 48″ at 40 yards, but still averaged 62.5% for good, solid, modified-choke performance. This pattern went 65.4%, the center density exceeding that of the 5″ annular area by 45 pellets. This barrel/load combo proved to be a good field choice for sharp-tailed grouse and Huns.

Of the 5 different loads patterned, the BPS modified-choke barrel gave its lowest efficiency with the Federal Premium Field load—1⅛ ozs. of copper-plated 8s. This 56.5% pattern with a slightly dense center (the core and annular difference amounting to 21 pellets) exceeds the average density by only 5 pellets. Weak modified— or quarter-choke performance.

ties, for with the carrier "neutralized" it's a free fall from the receiver on extraction. With a bit of practice, the hulls can be neatly caught by the trigger hand for transfer to jacket pocket or belt pouch.

The cutoff on my test gun worked very smoothly and was easy to manipulate even when wearing gloves. Going from one setting to the other calls for about a one-eighth turn of the selector collar, and ball detents that produce an audible click serve to lock the setting and prevent accidental movement. The index line on the selector itself is inlaid in white and it would be an improvement, I think, if the "S" and "R" markings on the receiver were given the same treatment, for in poor light they're rather hard to see.

Working the Slide

The BPS forearm is linked to the bolt slide via twin action bars and the full pump stroke is 3¹¹/₁₆″. This length of travel rates pretty much middle-of-the-road, for in checking out a few other pump guns which also handle the 3″ shell I found both longer and shorter action strokes.

You will probably notice, when pumping the BPS, that a tad more effort is required to close the action than to open it. The fact that a shell is being chambered on the closing stroke has little to do with this. Rather, it is because the breech bolt, in being returned to battery position, must pass between the two arms of the forked shell carrier and spread them apart. This extra drag begins shortly after the bolt starts to move forward and is limited to about ½″ of travel, at which point the carrier arms are snugged up against the receiver walls. This bolt/carrier drag becomes much less noticeable, of course, if the forearm is moved forward very smartly.

Yet even when this bolt/carrier friction is totally discounted, the BPS still doesn't measure up as the slickest-operating pump gun to come down the pike—at least my test gun doesn't. This is not to imply that the action stroke is actually rough, nor that it calls for an extra amount of muscle. What seems to be missing is a certain "freeness," and maybe it's entirely a matter of Browning holding the parts relationship to very close tolerances. At any rate, I do look for some improvement as the various working surfaces "wear in" with continued use. In fact, my test gun is

already showing promise of this.

A few pump-gun purists may cluck their tongues at the location of the BPS safety, but placing it at the top rear of the receiver, as Browning has done, provides the ultimate in convenience for both right-handers and southpaws. And with its low profile it does not detract one iota from the gun's sleek lines. The action-release lever has a serrated end and is located at the rear of the trigger guard on the receiver's left side where it is also convenient for most shooters. The release operates so smoothly that there is no fumbling around, not even when wearing gloves.

The BPS' magazine holds four 2 ¾″ shells or three 3″ shells. A lightweight plug is furnished to limit the capacity to two rounds in compliance with certain federal/state hunting regulations. Loading the magazine is a breeze, what with the shell carrier hidden away in the upper part of the receiver and the bottom-side ejection port wide open. The procedure for unloading, as suggested by Browning, is to turn the gun upside-down and depress the right-side cartridge stop, which will allow the shells in the magazine to pop out one at a time. But my test gun balked when this

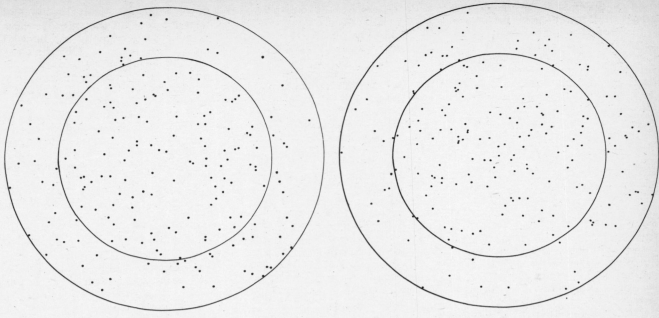

The BPS's 28" modified-choke barrel (.021" constriction) threw 40-yard patterns that averaged 77.5% using Federal's 3" Premium Magnum load with 1⁷/₈ ozs. of copper-plated 4s buffered with granulated polyethylene. At 79.6% this pattern rates as super-choke performance and is representative in terms of pellet distribution. Here the 20" core contains 112 pellet hits, with only 80 registering in the 5" annular area.

Tight-cored, full-choke patterns ranging from 71.8% to 80% resulted when Federal's Hi-Power Premium load with 1¹/₄ ozs. of coppered 6s was tried in the BPS modified-choke barrel. The pellet-distribution breakdown for this 72.9% pattern is 120 hits for the core, 74 for the annular area. Recoil sensation with this high-velocity loading was mild out of the 7³/₄-lb. BPS.

was tried. The shell rims persisted in hanging up on the front edge of the bolt slide. "Cracking" the action open about ³/₁₆" solved the problem by providing the necessary clearance.

Disconnector Fitted

With some pump guns an unwanted double discharge can occur if the trigger is held back as a fresh round is being chambered. But this cannot happen with the BPS because of a disconnector in the trigger unit. The trigger must be released following each shot in order for it to return to a fully operative state.

Speaking of the trigger, the pull weight for my test gun isn't the 7, 8, or 9-pound sort that is all too often found on a production-line gun. Rather, let-off occurs at an easy-to-live with 4 ¹/₄ pounds and the pull is quite crisp.

Breech lock-up for the BPS is quite conventional. Cammed by the bolt slide, a locking piece pivots vertically through the center of the breech bolt and engages a mortise in the barrel extension.

In addition to the pivoting locking piece, the bolt body contains only two other primary parts. There is a spring-loaded, claw-type extractor centered at the bottom of the bolt face. This quite massive extractor takes a wide, positive bite on the shell rim. The other part is a floating firing pin of the non-inertial type, and the parts relationship is such that its forward movement is blocked until after the locking piece elevates to engage the barrel extension. The remainder of the bolt-body parts are retaining pins—one each for the locking piece, extractor and firing pin.

Takedown

Many shotgunners are a little short on mechanical aptitude and, knowing this, Browning suggests that disassembly of the BPS be limited to removal of the barrel only—a simple matter of unscrewing the magazine cap and easing the barrel forward off the magazine tube. However, a college degree in mechanical engineering isn't necessary to strip the BPS receiver for a thorough cleaning of its component parts. This should be done at least once a year, and more frequently if the gun is subjected to wet or gritty weather. Briefly, here's the drill:

With the barrel removed from the action tap out the lower crosspin at the rear of the receiver to free the trigger unit. Do not disassemble the trigger; it can be sloshed around in a solvent bath as a unit.

Removal of the trigger group frees both cartridge stops, which can now be lifted out of the receiver. The stops are not identical, so take note as to which side each belongs.

Next, move the forearm rearward until the bolt slide begins to cam the shell carrier, at which point there will be clearance for the slide and bolt to be lifted off the action bars and out of the receiver. The forearm and the attached action bars are now free to slide forward off the magazine tube.

The only part now remaining in the receiver is the shell carrier. Removal of the carrier is not necessary in order to flush out the receiver interior with a solvent, but it can be done by simply drifting out the crosspin on which it pivots.

Reassembly is in reverse order, of course, and the only halfway tricky part involves the cartridge stops—that is, keeping them seated in the proper position while reinstalling the trigger unit.

The BPS receiver, by the way, is made in the good, old-fashioned way by machining a solid block of forged steel. In fact, the only non-steel metal

used in this gun is for the trigger guard and its integral fire-control framework. The guard carries an anodized finish that blends most harmoniously with the well-polished, deeply-blued receiver and barrel. The receiver walls, however, are as naked as a new-born babe, but surely this total lack of ornamentation is far better than a plastering of *el cheapo* curlycues.

Stock and Fore-end

The BPS is stocked with a select grade of straight-grained walnut of "medium" color, which the fore-end wood matches up nicely. The finish is Browning's high-gloss, weather-resistant formula. Checkering on both the uncapped pistol grip and the fluted forearm is hand cut in a double-border style running 18 lines per inch. This work shows an occasional miscue here and there along the edges, but is otherwise well done. A ventilated recoil pad with a white spacer is standard on all BPS models,

with generous butt dimensions of 1 3/4" by 5 1/8".

Stock measurements for the test gun checked out at 14 1/4" by 1 7/16" by 2 3/8". With a 28" barrel, the down-pitch is 1 3/4". No cast-off could be detected at the stock heel. Total length runs 48 3/4" from muzzle to stock toe.

The Browning catalog lists the weight of the BPS at 7 3/4 pounds for a 28" barrel, and the test gun is in very close agreement with this—chamber and magazine empty, of course. Adding three shells boosts the weight to roughly 8 pounds, and if those loads happen to be 3-inchers, the total heft will run a bit higher. For an empty 28" barreled gun, the balance point occurs about 6 1/2" forward of the trigger, with weight distribution that promotes a smooth swing and yet avoids a too muzzle-heavy feeling.

The Barrel

Like all Browning barrels I've ever squinted through, the test gun's bore

finish is superb—baby smooth and mirror bright all the way. The bore diameter, according to my internal dial caliper gauge, is .726" at a point 5" behind the muzzle and also just forward of the forcing cone. Muzzle constriction for the modified choke is .021".

Browning still favors the conical-parallel type of choke, and for the test gun the length of the tapered or conical section is 1 1/8", while the parallel at the muzzle is one inch long. The forcing cone is of conventional length, about 1/2". Barrel-wall thickness at the muzzle is close to .070", which should provide enough strength for the BPS to take steel-shot loads in stride.

Pattern testing with the BPS involved small, medium and large-sized shot with 5 different factory loads at 40 yards. As will be noted on reading the appended table, the barrel not only lived up to its choke marking, but with some loads it delivered patterns that were much tighter than modified. For both the Federal Hi-Power Premium 6s and the Premium 3" Magnum 4s, the 5-shot averages slightly exceeded the extra-full-choke rating of 75 percent. I also found that the test barrel shot very flat—which is to say that the patterns printed dead-on with a level, down-the-rib sight picture.

The BPS Afield

When mid-September rolled around I took the BPS to the steep-hilled prairies of western South Dakota where it was blooded on sharp-tailed grouse and Hungarian partridge. Later, in October, it was given a workout on pheasants in coverts closer to home. Under the gray, chill skies of November it accounted for a double handful of mallards taken over harvested corn. There were no malfunctions.

One fact that surfaced quickly during these back-country jaunts is that

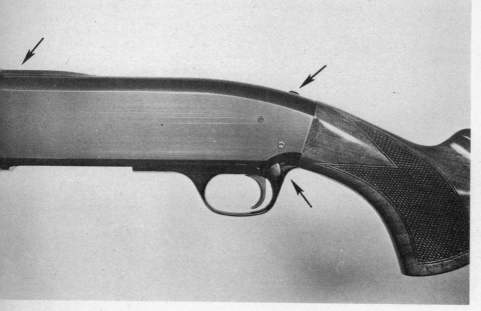

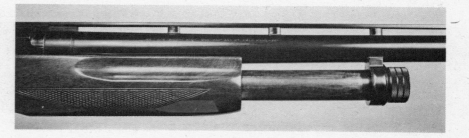

The sides of the BPS all-steel receiver lack any ornamentation. Visible here are the 2 7/8" ramp-type rib extension, atop the receiver; the top tang safety and the action-release button abaft the trigger guard; the magazine cutoff selector is just forward of the receiver. Decorative and functional, the hand-cut checkering on the BPS runs 18 lines per inch. The only non-steel part is the trigger guard, an alloy finished to closely match the deeply blued receiver/barrel.

The BPS high-profile floating rib has a maximum above-barrel height of nearly 3/8". Deep finger flutes over the forward 5" of the fore-end serve to keep the shooter's hand well forward so as to not interfere with shell ejection. A premature loss of blueing on the magazine tube (as this photo shows) was experienced with guns from the initial production run. Browning has since taken steps to correct this cosmetic problem.

the BPS rates in spades on the handling side. Despite a weight of right around 8 pounds when loaded, it is, in this shooter's opinion, a dynamic gun. It responds in a lively way during mounting and it comes on target with a large measure of precision—all this being a matter of favorable weight distribution combined with a low center of gravity that stems from the high-loft rib.

Those sessions in the field also served to reaffirm some conclusions I had reached earlier regarding various BPS features. For sheer convenience, the topside safety stands head and shoulders above the conventional crossbolt type in the trigger guard. The magazine cutoff will be of little import on upland shooting, but it should prove highly useful on the waterfowling and trapshooting scenes. With the BPS ejecting fired shells downward and directly in front of the shooter, practically all of the "search" is eliminated in retrieving those precious hulls for handloading. Certainly not least, that high-profile rib is every bit as functional as it is attractive, for it does, indeed, serve to diminish felt recoil at the comb of the stock—a fact that readily came to light when touching off 1 7/8-oz. magnum loads.

Notes and Comments

Most shooters will probably find the stock drop at the comb and heel quite

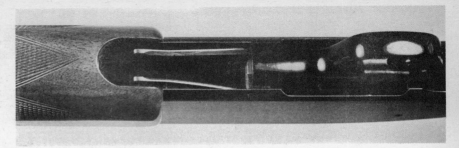

This underside view of Browning's pump repeater shows the U-shaped opening in the rear of the fore-end, necessary to provide clearance for the bottom-ejected shells. Also visible is the forked shell carrier, seen here in the full eject position. As the fore-end is moved forward the carrier elevates a fresh round to chamber level and then comes to rest against the receiver's ceiling as the breechbolt closes.

easy to adapt to. There is, however, one thing that displeases me about the BPS buttstock and this is its configuration at the nose of the comb. The width here is very close to 1/2", which is excessively broad for my facial structure. I find that unless I cheek the stock with more-than-normal force, I end up with my eye aligned along the left edge of the rib. I cannot recall having ever had this problem with an as-issued field-gun stock (trap-gun stocks, yes), and in light of this I believe it would be a smart move for Browning to slightly reduce the comb width on future pro-

duction runs. Perhaps they are already doing so.

One other thing about the BPS distresses me—the very rapid loss of blueing that occurs on the magazine tube. Some loss was already in evidence when my test gun was received, so apparently it had seen prior use. My pattern testing and limited hunting added only about 75 rounds to whatever the amount of previous shooting, yet all told it was enough to scrub away about 40 percent of the color. Bright spots also appeared on both sides of the barrel ring where it was scuffed by the fore-end wood.

Not surprisingly, Browning is highly displeased with this situation and corrective steps are being taken. Early on it was thought that the installation of a nylon bushing in the forearm would be the solution, but that idea has been scrapped, according to a company spokesman. The cosmetic "surgery," I've been told, will involve a new forearm ring which will have three small protruding ridges on the inside. These ridges will glide on the surface of the magazine tube. Chances are this small design change will not completely eliminate the blueing wear, but henceforth it will be limited to three narrow streaks rather than occurring over the entire surface of the magazine tube. And a possible fringe benefit that may result will be an action stroke that may be a bit more free of friction.

It is fitting, I think, that the BPS appeared, as it did, on the eve of Browning's centennial year. Only time will tell, but if qualified craftsmanship, reliability, classy appearance and first-rate handling count for anything, this new pump gun should travel far. ●

40-Yard Pattern Tests
Browning BPS 12-Gauge Pump Gun
28″ Modified-Choke Barrel–3″ Chamber
Bore .726″—Choke Constriction .021″

Load	20″ Density	30″ Density	30″ Efficiency	EDV	Pellet Distribution Imbalance
Federal Premium Field 2 3/4″ 3 1/4-1 1/8-8 copper-plated (476 pellets)	148	264	55.5%	12.2%	+ 32
Winchester Mark-5 Upland 2 3/4″ 3 1/4-1 1/4-7 1/2 chilled (414 pellets)	144	258	62.5%	7.0%	+ 29
Federal Premium Hi-Power 2 3/4″ 3 3/4-1 1/4-6 copper-plated (266 pellets)	121	201	75.8%	8.2%	+ 40
S&W High-Velocity 2 3/4″ 3 3/4-1 1/4-6 chilled (264 pellets)	97	163	61.8%	7.2%	+ 30
Federal Premium Magnum 3″ 4-1 7/8-4 copper-plated (241 pellets)	108	187	77.5%	8.3%	+ 28

The performance figures represent an average for 5 shots. Ambient temperature 70° F.

Imbalance: The average difference in pellet count between the 20″ pattern core and the 5″ annular area. A "plus" prefix indicates that core density was greater by the number of hits shown.

EDV: Extreme variation in pellet density between low- and high-count patterns.

Scopes and Mounts

An up-to-date survey and critical appraisal of the glassware and related equipment available today for the shooting sportsmen.

by BOB BELL

Bob Bell with M788 Remington 223, 16x Siebert Conversion of 8x Lyman AA scope and Anderson chuck rest.

I GOT MY FIRST scope, a little Weaver 29S, in 1938. That's 40 years ago, which is a right good piece in terms of a human's life, and it seems I've been using glass sights almost daily ever since. There are worse things a fella could do, I suppose. I don't know if I've improved any during the past four decades, but scopes sure have. (This is not meant as a slur on my old 29S. I bought that small-tube scope on the advice of the late Col. Townsend Whelen, one of the true gentlemen of the gun writing field. It made me aware of the possibilities inherent in a rifled barrel and gave me more fun-filled days than any scope I've owned since. I still have it and wouldn't trade it for the most expensive rifle scope in the world. Yet there's no denying that countless advances have been made in the intervening years.) Let's look at some of the current crop of scopes and mounts.

Armsport, Inc., Miami, Fla., offers a full line of big game scopes and a pair of rimfire models. Called the "Forever" series, the centerfire models come in all normal powers with either CH or Duplex reticle, the 4x and 3-9x being available with either 32mm or 40mm objective. Wide-angle models are also offered in 4x, 6x or 3-9x. They are listed waterproof, with Multi-Koted lenses, which are said to have unusually high transmission values.

B-Square makes a number of useful items for shooters, including a rather extensive line of scope mounts. All are made of a strong aluminum alloy and use heat-treated hex-head socket screws. Adjustable models are available for the 94 Winchester, Ruger Mini-14, Colt AR-15 and various Remingtons, Rugers, Weatherbys, Winchesters and Shilens, while one-piece base mounts with dovetail rings are made for even more rifles plus the Ruger Blackhawk and Thompson-Center Contender. Most units weigh only 2½ oz., the Colt AR-15 going to 4 oz. though the ring set that fits grooved receiver is only 1½ oz. Prices range from $6.95 to $24.95.

Windage in the adjustable units is obtained by changing half-moon metal shims from one side of the base to the other, while elevation is via a sloping tapered slot in the mounting plate. These are intended only for rough zeroing, to get you reasonably near center before making final adjustments within the scope. Thus they are simple and sturdy.

We had a new model, the Lightweight Silhouette-Benchrest, for ex-

B-Square's LWS/LSB scope.

AR-7 mount by B-Square.

B-Square scope mount on Ruger Blackhawk.

amination. It's unusually interesting because the rings straddle a vertical projection of each base in such a way that they can adapt to minute misalignments between the scope and rifle action, thus provide stress-free mounting. This is a good feature, as it's quite common to bend a scope tube when snugging things tight in a solid mount. The practicalities of manufacturing rifle actions and mounts just don't permit perfect matching in all cases, and under normal circumstances if anything has to give when all mounting screws are pulled tight, it's the scope-tube. This B-Square mount solves that problem. Its design also allows considerable freedom in positioning the scope for proper eye relief.

Buehler, Inc., has added several new mounts this year, making its extensive line of excellent models even greater. For the Dan Wesson revolver, a one-piece base is now available. It's installed on the barrel shroud with screws. Shrouds can be changed without removing the mount (Code DW). A one-piece base (Code VH) is also made for the Hi-Standard Victor autoloader, to be installed on the ramp with three screws.

For riflemen, a one-piece base with 4-inch ring centers to accommodate short-tube scopes such as the Leupold Vari-X III is offered for Browning's new BBR bolt action (Code BR); two-piece bases with metric screws to fit most models of the Steyr-Mannlicher and Mannlicher-Schoenauer M72 (various Codes; check with Buehler literature); and short one-piece bases for the Ruger Mini-14 (for either rifles which have the bridge 1/16″ higher than the receiver ring or those which are level).

Burris, the comparatively new Greeley, Colo., company, has added five new scopes to their already extensive line. Apparently feeling they had the conventional powers and sizes blanketed with Fullfield models ranging from 2.7x to 12x and variables from 1.7-5x to 4-12x, Burris this year looked to the small end of the spectrum and came up with three Mini scopes and two Long Eye Relief (LER) designs.

The Mini models are intended for carbines and compact rifles. In 4x, 6x and 8x, all are built on one-inch tubes with round, 1.375″ eyepieces. Only the 8x has an enlarged objective lens (1.52″ OD). The 4x is just over 8″ long and weighs 7.8 oz., the 6x is 9″ and the same weight, while the 8x is under 10″ and 9 oz. Fields of view are 24, 17 and 13 feet, and eye relief in each is 3.75″—enough for safe use on a magnum if properly mounted. Adjustments are internal, of course, and there's a choice of Plex, Post-Crosswire or 3 MOA Center Dot ($10 extra). The 4x sells for $79.95, the 6x $84.95 and the 8x $89.95.

Seems to me that the 4x should be right at home on a rig like the M660 Remington 350 Magnum, if you're lucky enough to have one, or any of the short bolt action timber rifles, but the higher powers will be excellent on any high-grade 22 rimfire hunting rifle, for instance.

The LER scopes come in 2x and 3x. Also on straight one-inch tubes, they weigh less than 7 oz. and are under 9″ in length. Designed primarily as handgun glasses, eye relief is 10″-24″ in the 2x, 10″-20″ in the 3x, with fields of 21 and 17 feet. These scopes also can be mounted ahead of the action on top-ejection lever guns, for good service in the woods. Prices are $79.95 and $84.95.

Mount bases ($10.95) which accept Burris Universal, Redfield and Leupold rings, are available for the Interarms Virginian, Ruger Blackhawk (or similar Rugers with adjustable rear sight), Thompson-Center Contender, and the Winchester 94 carbines.

In addition to their strong bridge-type mounts, Burris now supplies Sight-Thru mounts machined from aluminum extrusions. These lift the scope high enough to permit use of iron sights beneath. The front ring is enlarged so it is not seen through the rear one, eliminating some distraction and field reduction. $14.95.

See our catalog section for specs and current prices on scopes and mounts.

Bushnell has for decades been a leading scope manufacturer, and over the years has put together two lines of rifle scopes—the Scopechiefs and the Banners—which pretty much cover all hunting situations. All have the popular Multi-X reticle (4 posts with crosswire intersection), Neoprene Eye Guard to reduce the chance of a cut brow when firing from an unorthodox position, and Bullet-Drop Compensator, which lets you immediately adjust for ranges up to 500 yards, after calibrating a yardage dial.

The current Scopechief VI line includes a 4x and three variables—1.5-

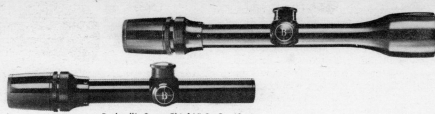

Bushnell's ScopeChief VI 3x-9x 40mm (top) and 1.5x-4.5x 20mm (above), both with Bullet Drop Compensator (BDC) and Multi-X reticle.

4.5x, 2.5-8x and 3-9x, prices $85.50 to $129.50. There are 11 Banners—5 straight powers and 6 variables. These once were thought of as inexpensive models, but the current crop tops out at $112.95, so maybe that old impression needs revising. This is not to suggest they aren't worth their cost. The Bushnell users I've known are happy hunters.

Clear View "See Through" mounts are made to fit many centerfire and rimfire rifles, a number of shotguns and even muzzleloaders. As the name suggests, they raise the scope up to permit use of iron sights through the tunnel-like bottom section of the rings. Scopes as large as 3-9x variable can be accomodated by the centerfire model. New this year is the SM-94, a side mount for the Winchester carbine, priced at $19.95.

Clearview's new SM-94.

Clearview's Model 336 See-Through mount.

Conetrol now has two-piece bases for the presitgious Shilen DGA rifle, in Huntur, Gunnur and Custum grades ($9.95, $11.95 and $14.95 respectively), and new side-mount base designs for the M94 Winchester, Ruger Mini-14, old-style split-bridge Mannlicher-Schoenauer, Krag, Lee-Enfield, and M1 Garand. By the time this appears in print, other rifles will also be accommodated, I'm sure, as Conetrol has for years been aggressively producing designs for centerfire rifles.

Nor are the handgunners forgotten. A recent addition is a 3-ring unit for the Thompson-Center Contender. Two-ring Conetrols have long been made for this handgun, but as everhotter loads have been chambered in this strong single shot, it seemed some extra insurance would be welcomed by shooters, so the third ring is George Miller's answer. The 3-ring base comes in all Conetrol grades, at the same price as a conventional base—i.e., $10.98, $12.98 and $14.97.

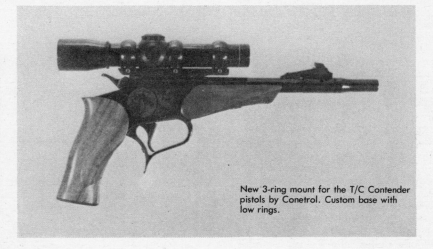

New 3-ring mount for the T/C Contender pistols by Conetrol. Custom base with low rings.

Davis Optical Co. has for many years been supplying attachments to increase the magnification of hunting scopes to make them suitable for most varmint shooting. In years past several friends and I used these on small-tube Weaver scopes, with more than satisfactory results. These come in several powers and objective diameters, at prices from $20 to $32.50, which is considerably less than the cost of a new varmint scope. For handgunners, Davis installs an attachment on the ocular lens rather than the objective, reducing the magnification but greatly increasing the eye relief. $16.50.

Kris Mounts has a new model for the 94 Winchester—a Side-Saddle base which uses the factory-drilled holes in 94s made after 1946 (SN 1,400,000 and higher). Earlier 94s can be adapted to the Side-Saddle by drilling and tapping two 6-48 holes. Weaver-type rings can be installed to provide two spacings, which permits adjustment for eye relief. Bases are machined from hardened aluminum alloy. Price, $9.98.

Pachmayr Low-Swing mounts are made for practically all hunting rifles. By the time you read this, one is expected to be available for Ruger's Mini-14, a little hellcat of a rifle which is gaining followers every day.

Kris Mounts' 2-piece See-Through mount on Model 70 Winchester.

Leupold & Stevens

A new and attractive scope was unveiled at the Houston show by L&S—the M8-2.5x Compact, meant for mounting on the smaller, lighter rifles, rimfire or centerfire. On such trim rifles the usual 4x or 6x scope overwhelms the piece, and that's even more true of the bigger variables.

As our illustration shows, the newest L&S glass has a straight 1-inch tube forward; it weighs only 7½ ozs. and total length is 8½ inches. A Compact indeed, its field of view at 100 yards is 26.5 feet and, especially noteworthy for those hunters who'll put the new scope on big bore rifles, the eye relief is a big 4.3 inches.

Cost is $96.50—for more information on the L&S "Golden Ring" scopes—including a projected 4x Compact, send for the current L&S catalog.   J.T.A.

Leopold M8-4x Extended Eye Relief scope on S&W revolver with Leupold "STD" mount.

Leupold M8-4x Compact.

Leupold M8-2.5x scope.

Lyman has done considerable revamping of its line this year, dropping three scopes and adding one. Missing are the 3x, the 6x-P and—somewhat surprisingly and certainly sadly—the Super Targetspot. Nobody who ever used a Targetspot would deny it was a great glass; it has always held a special place in the affections of serious shooters. But the appearance a few years back of the internally adjustable 20x and 25x Light Weight Bench Rest models apparently reduced its sales to the point that it had to be dropped.

Lyman also has discontinued the use of the "All-American" designation for their hunting scopes, now

Lyman's 6x, 8x, 10x Metallic Silhouette scopes.

calling the 2¹/₂x, 4x and 6x the "Hunter." According to Ken Ramage, this change was made because Lyman will soon be phasing in Japanese-built hunting scopes in these three powers, thus the AA name would not be accurate. Commendable honesty, I feel, and I like the new name better. Though it still lacks the magic of their old "Alaskan" monicker, it avoids the grid-iron connotation and gets things back in the woods.

Lyman's new entry this year is a 2-7x variable, which fills the gap between their previously announced 1.7-5x and 3-9x models. It looks like an excellent choice for any big game hunting. Its power spread covers any reasonable need, it weighs under 11 oz., has half-minute click adjustments and—importantly—has an adjustment range of 70 inches at 100 yards. Some variables don't approach this amount and as a result can be

Lyman's 25x LWBR (top) and new 2-7x variable scope (above).

difficult to get zeroed. Field varies from 49-19 feet, CH or Center Range* reticle. Price, $129.95.

———————

*This, of course, is the understandably ubiquitous four-posts-with-crosswire-intersection design popularized by Leupold in modern times (though available in Zeiss and probably Hensoldt scopes before I was born). It's a good reticle; probably the best choice for general big game hunting. But why in hell does each manufacturer think he has to have a proprietary name for it? Consider these which come readily to mind in addition to Lyman's Center Range: Burris— Plex; Bushnell—Multi-X; Leupold—Duplex; Redfield—4-Plex; Swift—Quadraplex; Tasco— 30-30; Weaver—Dual-X; Williams—TNT (Thick-N-Thin). Doubtless there are others, but you get the idea. All refer to the same design so it seems reasonable that all should have the same name. It also seems reasonable to me that since Leupold was the first to popularize it in this country, their Duplex tag should do the job. So from now on that's what I'm calling 'em. Wish I'd thought of this years ago!

———

Redfield is another manufacturer with so many scopes that it's hard to keep up with them. If I count correctly, there are 22 at the moment, including 5 fixed-power Traditional (round eyepiece) models, five Traditional variables, three fixed-power Low Profile Widefields, four LPW variables, three Metallic Silhouette/Varmint models, the M3200 target scope, and the M6400 target/varmint. Powers range from 1.75x (in a small variable) to 24x; prices from $47.30 to $282.20. It should be obvious that one or another of these Redfields will fill the bill for any kind of shooting requiring a magnifying sight. Over the years we've used a lot of them, always

with great satisfaction. Maybe I'm old-fashioned, but I still prefer the round eyepiece design of the Traditionals, yet I have been using a 1.7-5x Widefield variable with good results. I know a lot of hunters who prefer this design.

New this year is a 3-9x LPW called the Accu-Trac. It combines the older Accu-Range system (which indicates the range by bracketing a game animal with a pair of horizontal wires) with the Accu-Trac compensator. The Accu-Trac is a unit in the elevation adjustment which is calibrated in yards. Once you know the yardage from the Accu-Range you simply dial it on the Accu-Trac, hold right on, and

squeeze. This scope comes with three dials, one of which will closely match the trajectory of your factory loads. For handloaders, a blank dial which can be marked to correspond to your reloads is available. Price, $216.10.

Redfield also has a new collimator with tapered spuds which are designed to always align the collimator exactly with the bore. Collimators are useful not only for bore sighting, to get you on the paper quickly without waste of ammo, but also for checking zero on a hunt, if radical weather changes or a tumble make you think your scope is out of alignment. It is priced at $39.80, spuds (14 calibers from 17 to 458) $6.80 each.

Redfield's optical collimator.

Redfield's 3x-9x Accu-Trac.

Wally Siebert's power-boosting conversions, particularly of the Lyman AA action-mounted scopes, continued to find favor with bench shooters during the past year. Among the NBRSA's Top Twenty in the Sporter Class in 1977, fourteen used Siebert conversions, while eleven chose them in the Light Varmint Class and thirteen in the Heavy Varmint. That's a clear majority in each class, which should give some indication of the feelings of these shooters—probably the most perfectionist-minded bunch in captivity.

Wally currently is converting the Lyman All American and Lightweight Benchrest scopes to 16x-36x, Leupold Varmint and BR to 15x-30x, and the Unertl BV-20, Ultra Varmint and 2″ target to 25x-30x ($35). He no longer converts Weavers. Fine crosshairs (choice of three diameters) or small center dot can be installed ($15). For handgunners, Siebert converts various Leupold and Redfield models to long eye relief jobs (12-15 inches), cutting magnification in half in the process. Price, $30.

I've been using a Lyman AA 8x boosted to 16x for varmints for several years now, with excellent results.

Butler Creek lens caps.

Despite what some of the earlier writers said, it's been my experience that for long range chucks and crows, reasonably high power (14x-20x) works better than the 6x-10x so often advised.

Stoeger Arms recently sent along a set of Sako mounts designed for the popular Sako actions which have integral tapered dovetail blocks—a highly admirable design, the way I see it. Years ago, in these review pages, I commented that these Finnish-made mounts, though beautifully designed and finished externally, were rough inside the rings. The maker said this was intentional, to prevent scope slippage, and I responded that this seemed unnecessary in view of the solidity which Redfield, Buehler and other makes held scopes on hard-recoiling rifles.

At any rate, the current rings, if our sample is representative, are as nicely finished inside as out and, with 4 screws per ring, I'm sure they will not permit slippage if snugged up tightly.

These Sako rings, which are made in three heights, are quick detachable by means of a large-headed screw, and have windage adjustment via a spring-loaded screw on the opposite side. The bottom of the rear ring has a projection to fit an indent in the action dovetail, to further lock things together. All in all, these are handsome, efficient mounts.

Swift markets an extensive line of optical equipment—binoculars, spotters, etc., as well as their Mark I Riflescopes. Besides conventional 4x, 6x, 1.5-4.5x and 3-9x big game scopes, Swift has wide angle models in 4x (choice of 32mm or 40mm objectives), and 3-9x. These are round-eyepiece scopes, giving extra field at top and bottom as well as horizontally. Prices range from $49.50 to $75.

Tasco has several new items this year. The "Tascorama" is an optical sighting unit that mounts on the action of a rifle, shotgun or grooved-receiver 22. Battery-operated, it creates a bright red dot which appears to be superimposed on your target. It is zeroed via internal adjustments and, because of a very large exit pupil, non-critical eye relief and large field, is fast and easy to use, especially on big game at woods ranges or for pass shooting on waterfowl.

Tasco also is offering a 3-9x variable with a trajectory-compensating system designed to allow rapid in-the-field sight changes so you can hold right on target rather than high to allow for bullet drop. To use, the scope is zeroed conventionally at a known distance and the calibrated elevation drum is set accordingly. Then the cap is tightened into place. Turning the drum to any of the ranges indicated on it automatically adjusts the reticle, permitting a dead-on hold. This assumes, of course, that

your estimate of distance is accurate. The drum's calibrations are color coded to allow adaptation to different load characteristics.

A new mount from Tasco uses a bridge-type base with QD rings which lock to it much as the long-popular Weaver units do. Raised "tunnel" rings called Quick Peeps also are available for those who want instant access to iron sights. All these rings are made to fit grooved rimfire rifle receivers too.

Weaver's Model T scopes, developed primarily for metallic silhouette shooting, were described in these pages last year, but deserve further mention for a couple of reasons. First, because we've had a year to use one of the 10x models, and that adds up to considerable shooting. Not on *siluetas*—there's no such range hereabouts—but on a couple of varmint rifles and several target outfits. Most of the latter shooting was by Cliff Hocker, a highly skilled long range shooter. He'd seen the scope

when we were chuck hunting one day and was interested in giving it a workout, so I loaned it to him. Seemed like a good way to get additional comment, for there's never enough time to do all the shooting these items deserve. Anyway, he ended up with it on a Hart-barreled M70 308 Hunter Class rifle, and after months of use his conclusion was that it's a highly dependable high-grade glass. That's the way I felt about it as a varmint outfit. Occasionally I wished for a bit more power, but the 16x would han-

dle that aspect for anyone of similar feelings.

The second reason for mentioning the T models is that their Micro-Trac adjustment system (a highly accurate design which uses four tiny carbide balls as contact points with the inverter tube; see GUN DIGEST 32 for more complete description), now is incorporated into all Weaver scopes having one-inch tubes—the Ks, the KWs, the Vs and the VWs. This means the guy who buys a Weaver hunting scope to put on his old '06 will be getting the same high quality adjustment system the metallic silhouette shooters get. Even if his need isn't as critical, it'll make zeroing easier and cheaper.

For the deer hunters who prefer rifled slugs from a smoothbore, or who must use them to comply with local regulations, Weaver now has a package deal—scope and mount—that can be installed in minutes on the Remington 1100 or 870 shotguns. The system comes pre-assembled with a choice of K1.5 or K2.5 scope mounted on a conventional base which positions the glass low and centered over the action. The difference is that the base is not fastened to the top of the action (there's precious little thickness of metal there to accept drilling and tapping for screws); rather, it's assembled onto a plate that snugs against the side of the action and is held solidly in place by two bolts which replace the existing trigger plate pins. It's a slick sturdy solution to the problem of mounting a scope on a smoothbore . . . if your smoothbore happens to be one of these Remingtons. The chances of that are pretty good, though, for the 1100 and 870 sell by the boxcar load.

Weaver's Qwik-Point unit, which projects a red aiming point to infinity, is also available with the same mounting system for these two shotguns, as well as other mounts for numerous other smoothbores or rifles. For M94 Winchester fans a new mount base, the 3B, can be attached with a screwdriver, using the top three screw holes that already exist. Scope is offset on this carbine, of course. ●

Chuck Fergus with M700 Remington 22-250, 12x Leupold scope with Redfield Jr. mounts.

BLIND

one you can easily build to bag more

DUCKS

by PAUL T. HENNIG

A good morning's shooting. The twin-post blind poles designed by Hennig (left) lie to port, the tennis net-weeds system rest forward.

THE CHANCES of success on your next duck hunting excursion—and all subsequent ones—can be greatly increased with an easily constructed and readily transported duck blind.

In these days of rapidly increasing population, participation in what should be a relaxing and enjoyable sport makes it imperative that you get away from the throng of other would-be hunters and their clamors and irritations. One of the most annoying of their habits is "sky busting."

With the idea that I'm about to unfold, being able to *select* a desirable location—and not being forced to follow the crowd, which must perforce take its sport and location site at random—is easily accomplished.

The great majority of duck hunters are compelled, because of many factors, to situate themselves along the shores of a body of water, some place where the vegetation is dense enough to offer some concealment.

Using the type of blind I'll describe here, you can be highly selective in your choice of location. You can set up this portable blind along the very fringe of the sparser vegetation, farther from shore and in deeper water. You'll be fully concealed, well away from most—if not all—of the other hunters, men who are forced to remain where the vegetation is more dense.

The blind I've designed can be built in a few hours or less. The materials required to make this blind are inexpensive and readily obtained from your nearest lumber yard and hardware store.

The stakes and hardware required for its erection are illustrated in the accompanying drawing. The twin stakes, each about 6 feet long, can be bolted together to make their total length almost 12 feet—or less, of course.

These extendable wooden stakes are driven upright into the water bottom, around which a netting with vegetation interwoven into it is draped, providing a place for skiff or boat. I use three such pairs of posts, locating them in the water as conditions demand. These are capped with iron pipe fittings screwed onto them for longer life; I use a short-handled sledge to drive the posts, but a hefty mallet would work as well.

Threading the 1-inch pipe caps on to the posts is the only time-consuming chore. I use a coarse wood rasp to rough shape the post ends into circular form, leaving just enough wood to take the cap threads tightly.

The blind proper is made of tennis netting with weeds woven into it. One

I've used for many years was made of such netting. It was first dyed with Rit to a dead grass color, then dipped in linseed oil as a preservative. When rolled up for storage or transport, including the 6 poles, this blind makes a very compact bundle. It served me well for many seasons, requiring only the periodic replacement of the weeds. This interval can be lengthened by tying the weeds in place at the bottom, thereby preventing their loss through handling. My first blind of this type, incidentally, was constructed with chicken wire, but the tennis netting makes for a more compact, more easily handled system.

Use the weeds rather sparingly when you're interweaving them into the net openings, taking care not to

make too dense or thick a mat; you'll want to be able to peer through those weeds, not over them, otherwise you'll lose the full camouflage effect.

This portable blind is especially useful when you're hunting such deep water diving ducks as canvasbacks, redheads, bluebills and the like. However, it is also fully effective as a supplemental blind for the shallow water dipper ducks, such as mallard, pintail, widgeon, etc.

The depth of the water or the consistency of the bottom is easily compensated for by varying the paired-stake length. It requires little effort and less time to erect this blind, and doing so will pay dividends every time.

Equipped with this blind I found myself enjoying duck hunting much more fully. I was enabled to get away from all distractions and annoyances but, even more importantly, perhaps, I came home with game where others came back empty handed!

Compared to the cost of such other indispensable and essential equipment as a gun, ammunition, skiff, transportation, etc., this inexpensive blind will return its investment, many times over, in greater total enjoyment.

Bill of Materials

6 poles, 1½" square, 6' long. 6 bolts, ½" dia. by 4". 12 washers for above bolts. 6 iron pipe caps, 1" inside dia. threaded.

Galvanized or chromed hardware is suggested to defer corrosion.

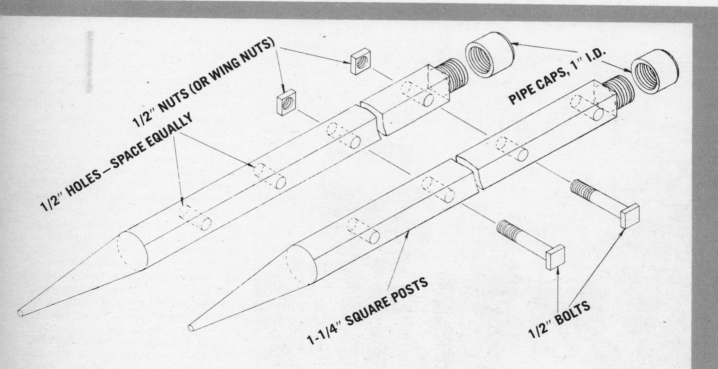

1/2" NUTS (OR WING NUTS)

1/2" HOLES—SPACE EQUALLY

PIPE CAPS, 1" I.D.

1-1/4" SQUARE POSTS

1/2" BOLTS

SCALE: 2" = 1 FOOT

Hennig's blind posts are designed to be used in sets of 2, as pairs, around which the blind material is wrapped and/or woven. Depending on depth of water and bottom conditions, the 6-foot (approx.) posts of each pair may be bolted together to form a unit 6 to 10 feet or so long. The pipe caps are threaded onto the post tops after these have been roughly rounded slightly over internal cap-thread diameter.

The 444/308—
another 94 Winchester Wildcat

Whether the increased velocities obtainable with the 444/308 are worth the trouble is a matter of opinion, but the case forming and action alterations are fairly simple and inexpensive. You be the judge.

by MYRON ROCKETT

Photography by Vic Post

A CASUAL GLANCE AT the sporting arms field shows that many gun nuts are fully satisfied with factory-produced rifles and cartridges. The number of wildcat cartridges on record to date is impressive, though admittedly there aren't the number in use now that there were some years back. I, too, was struck by the desire to stuff a bigger case into a standard production rifle. This is an account of my wildcatting efforts.

The base of this project was a Winchester 94 rifle. I wanted a Win 94 with greater performance than the standard 30-30 cartridge could deliver. Equally important, the conversion had to be practicable and inexpensive.

This project really began many years ago after I acquired my first 94, a 30-30. As had many people before me I liked the neat and trim little rifle, but I soon became dissatisfied with the performance of the humble 30-30. Then I came upon a series of articles concerned with improving the 94, notably *Turpentining the 30-30* by H.V. Stent, a fellow Canadian, which appeared in the 4th edition HANDLOADER'S DIGEST. The article outlines load development for the 30-30 as well as two 30-caliber wildcats. One of these wildcats was quite feasible, requiring only a rechambering job. The cases were made by fire-forming but special reloading dies were required. This cartridge, the 30-30 Ackley Improved was, I felt, limited by its mere 5% greater powder capacity. The other Stent wildcat was the 30-30 Lever Power. This case holds considerably

more powder, but for most of us, including me, the conversion is a little too troublesome. Rechambering and action modifications are necessary and, to make matters a little worse, the new cases must be made from 30-40 Krag brass. That'd be a difficult job for people, yet the only alternative —having them custom built—would add considerable cost.

For several years thereafter the idea of a 94 wildcat haunted me. The big problem was finding a suitable case, one with greater capacity than the 30-30, but at the same time one calling for minimal modification to the rifle. The ease of obtaining brass

also had to be considered. After exhaustive research I concluded that no cartridge answering this description existed. There was one solution...I must design one!

At last, on October 9, 1973, I discovered my Holy Grail! Out at the local rifle range that day I stumbled across a single discarded 444 Marlin case. Having an eye for measurements I soon concluded that the 444 could be made to run through the 94 action with only a few changes to action and cartridge. The rim of the 444 Marlin is only few thousandths of an inch larger than the 30-30 rim, and its body diameter is almost identical to the rim diameter of the 308 Winchester.

The rimless 308 case can be quite easily made to run through the 94 action—its only drawback being that the 94 requires a rimmed case for proper extraction. All right, I thought, I need a 308 with a rim and here's the 444 Marlin—almost as if it were made specially for my wildcatting needs.

As I've said, the new wildcat was useless to me unless it could be made with great ease. The new cartridge fulfilled all my expectations. To form the new cases a bench press (I used the standard RCBS Junior press) and a set of reforming dies are required. I used the standard two-piece 308 full length sizing dies. If any of you inspired 94 owners can't afford the $45 or so this equipment costs you had better forget any such conversions, but such tools are standard equipment with most handloaders so I don't consider them part of the cost of this project. You'll need a 444 Marlin shell

This Model 1894 breechblock face has been altered to accept the wider-rimmed 444 Marlin case. See text for details of operation.

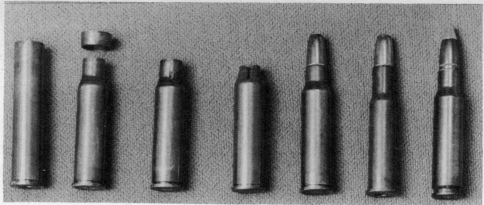

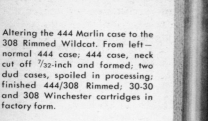
Altering the 444 Marlin case to the 308 Rimmed Wildcat. From left— normal 444 case; 444 case, neck cut off 7/32-inch and formed; two dud cases, spoiled in processing; finished 444/308 Rimmed; 30-30 and 308 Winchester cartridges in factory form.

holder, of course.

The first step in making the new case is to cut 7/32-inch from the neck of the 444 Marlin. This must be done with care, for a crooked cut or a dent in the case will result in a collapsed case at a later stage. For best results use a ½" pipe cutter. A hacksaw can be used, but that's pretty primitive. Next, chamfer the case mouth in the standard fashion, inside and out. For safety sake remove the primer punch and expander from your sizing die; these could be damaged if a case collapses in the die. Slip the 444 Marlin shell holder in place and lock the sizing die. Apply case lube sparingly, for an excess will usually cause folds or indentations in the neck and shoulder of the newly formed case. Now feed the case into the die and gradually apply pressure to the handle. The press had better be well anchored as considerable pressure must be applied to force the shell all the way home. Withdraw the case and, if everything was done correctly, you should have a perfectly formed and almost com-

pleted case. Now return the primer punch and expander ball to the die and feed the case into the die. Compare the length of the case with that of the 308. It should be the same length or slightly shorter. If it is too long trim it to size and re-chamfer. We'll call this new case the 308 Rimmed.

Altering the Rifle

Aside from the rechambering, altering of the action can be done in the home workshop. I paid a modest $20 to have my rifle rechambered. When taking the rifle to the gunshop for rechambering it is wise to include a 308 Rimmed case with the rifle. That way the gunsmith can be sure the job is done correctly. The 308 Rimmed must seat on the rim of the case, as with the 30-30, to enable the closing of the 94 action.

With the chambering complete, the action is ready to be altered. As mentioned earlier, the rim diameter of the 444 Marlin case is slightly larger than that of the 30-30. The 444 Marlin case

rim fits the breechblock counterbore perfectly. It is not a loose fit, as it is with the 30-30. As a result of this tight fit the rifle will occasionally fail to lock onto the 308 Rimmed case, therefore the counterbore circumference must be rounded or bevelled. This can be done with a ⅛" rattail file, the process simply a matter of trial and error. Round the perimeter to a small degree, then try locking the action with a 308R case in the chamber. If the action doesn't consistently lock up, without any stickiness, do a bit more work with the file. The bolt face is very hard, so the filing operation requires a bit of elbow grease. The important thing throughout this entire project is to have great patience, working slowly and carefully. Remember, if too much metal is removed it can't be replaced, so don't overdo it!

For the next two steps, as with the last, the action must be partially disassembled. The action will have to be reassembled several times throughout the procedure to check for correct fit-

The Model 1894 has two cartridge guides—left and right units, as shown here. Only the forward portions require metal removal—the left side guide (below) has been filed.

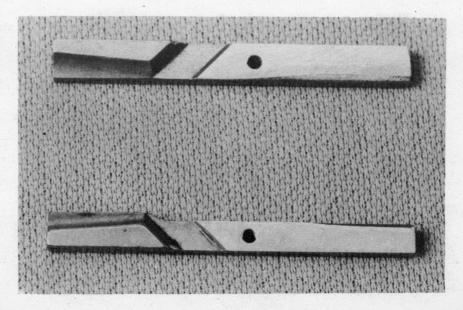

ting. For this reason time can be reduced by removing only the necessary parts for each phase. Total disassembly of the action is in no way necessary for any of the alterations.

When looking into the opened action two cartridge guides can be seen, about the color of stainless steel, one on either side of the action. Their purpose is to align cartridges as they are pushed by the bolt from the magazine into the chamber. Designed to guide the 30-30 cartridge, they naturally won't let the larger body diameter of the 308R pass through the action. These parts must be removed from the action and their forward segments planed down. These guides are not identical in shape, but the *same* thickness of metal must be removed from the inside face of each. If too much metal is removed from either or both parts they will fail to function properly. Using a file, the part held solidly in a vise, remove about 1/32" from each guide. Tape can be used as a marker when filing. It would be difficult to achieve a flat cut by any other method. Once again, don't overdo it! Remove a small amount of metal, assemble the action and test with a cartridge, repeating this until you've removed the desired amount. Now, that done, carefully file the two mounting screws (one for each guide) until they are flush with the new face of the guides.

With the rifle assembled, open the action slowly and watch the hinged carrier pop up as the action approaches the wide open position. There is a U-shaped notch cut into the end of this carrier. With a pencil push downward on the carrier and it will snap down into its lower position. When the carrier is in this position a lobe on

the link will fit into the U-notch of the ramp. Examine the lobe carefully, for it must be filed down 1/16" to let it clear the thicker body of the 308R round. As with the other parts that have been altered, this lobe will not fulfill its designed function if too much metal is filed off. As the action is opened, this lobe rises and prevents the magazine spring from pushing a cartridge into the action after the ramp has popped up into its upper position. If the lobe is filed down too much the shell will be pushed under the carrier and the rifle will jam. As you are looking at the lobe in the opened action it is the portion of the lobe which points directly upward which must be filed. Once again, trial and error is good practice. Because of production tolerances, different rifles will require different clearances.

There remains only one alteration to make the rifle field worthy. The magazine loading gate, properly known as the spring cover, does not open wide enough to permit 308R cartridges to enter without binding. Try feeding a cartridge into the gate and note where the binding occurs. The two areas where binding is likely to occur are the foremost end of the gate and the inside wall of the receiver, which is directly opposite the end of the gate. A 1/8" rattail file seems to work best on these parts. The gate can be removed for easier access, for most of the work must be done on the inside wall of the receiver. Quite a lot of filing must be done here, while the gate requires a small amount of rounding at its forward end. As these parts are filed, care must be taken to retain their smooth concave shape. There is little to worry about if too much metal is removed in this area.

Keep working on this area until a loaded cartridge will enter the magazine smoothly and with ease. It can be frustrating trying to fight cartridges into a rifle on a cold winter day.

After having completed these minor alterations the 94 rifle will function flawlessly with 308 Rimmed cartridges. I've been using them in my rifle for a full year, without malfunctions of any kind.

(These alterations can also be performed—and much faster—if a tool such as the Dremel Moto-Tool is used. Their latest models (370 and 380) offer variable speeds for better control. Use one or another of Dremel's silicon grinding points, but be sure to use it carefully, cutting only a minimum of metal as you go. Ed.)

Loads for the 308 Rimmed

It is a widely known fact that the Winchester 94 action is not particularly strong—a limiting factor to the performance of any cartridge to be used in this action. Too, the dimensions of the action require the deep seating of bullets, thereby reducing the volume available for powder. Furthermore round-nosed bullets must be used if the magazine will be filled, so 308 Winchester performance can't be expected in the 94 rifle. The 308 Rimmed has 28% more internal volume than the 30-30, so let's see what can be done with it.

As a guide I used the Homer Powley calculator to arrive at loads for the 308R case. To date I've tested 4 different weights—170-gr., 150-gr., 125-gr. and 100-gr. I haven't tested 190-gr. bullets, but the Powley calculator suggests that they could be quite worthwhile.

Forward section of Model 1894 link (Part No. 4694X). A lobe on this link (arrow) must be carefully filed down. About 1/16-inch of metal is removed, but the shape of the lobe is to be preserved. See text.

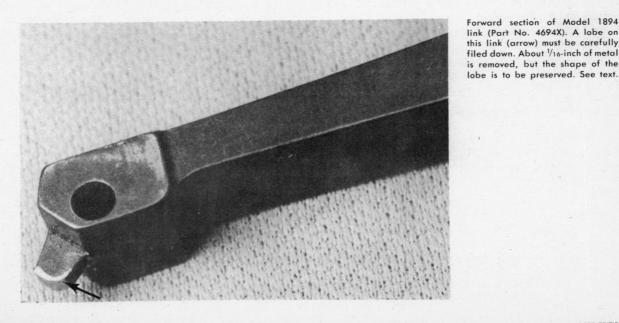

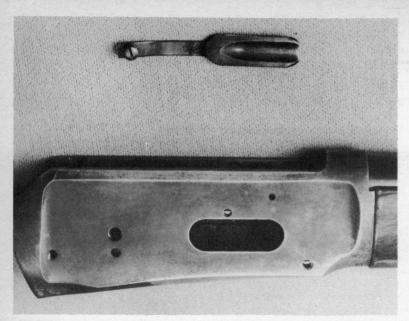

Loading gate (spring cover) is removed from Model 1894 receiver to permit alteration. Metal must be removed if 444/308 Rimmed case is to feed well. See text for details.

With the 100-gr. Hornady bullet properly seated there is room for about 50 grains of water. In this situation Powley suggests 43 grains of IMR 3031 and indicates velocity as 3170 fps for the 20″ barreled carbine. (I've been unable to do any chronographing so all MV figures are estimates.) I found I could load 44.5/3031 into my rifle without signs of excess pressure. Another load tried was 46/4895 with the same 100-gr. bullet, which proved surprisingly accurate for a lever-action carbine.

The next bullet tested was the 125-gr. Curry HP. As this is not a round-nosed bullet it should be loaded into the chamber by hand. Water capacity with this bullet is also 50 grains and, as before, the calculator recommended 43 grains of IMR 3031. I found 44 grains to be the right load for my rifle; anything more caused springing of the action. This time the calculator listed 2830 fps with 42/3031. Both 42- and 43 grains of 3031 gave good accuracy.

The 150-gr. round-nosed bullet leaves room for 48 grains of water, and the calculator indicated that 41/ IMR 4064 is the load to use. The calculator gives the velocity as 2590 fps, not bad at all considering that factory 30-30 ammunition gives a true velocity of some 2100 fps from the 20″ barrel. A load which gives me good accuracy is 42.5 grains of IMR 4895. For slightly better long-range ballistics a 150-gr. spire point bullet is the thing to use. Like the 125-gr. bullet, these 150-gr. bullets must not be run into the magazine. Feeding the cartridges into the chamber by hand permits seating of the bullet farther out, thus increasing powder capacity, but with this particular bullet only 1 grain of water capacity is gained. Therefore velocity gains over the standard 150-gr. round nose will be very slight. The advantage of the spire-point bullet will be in its greater ballistic coefficient. At 300 yards it will have some 30-40% more energy than will the round- or flat-nosed bullets. This is, of course, with the same initial velocity for both bullets. For this reason the spire-point bullet is superior for that occasional long range shot. The two different types of 150-gr. bullets require different sight settings in my rifle, so if both are to be used on a hunt a bit of serious target work is a must. If the shooter is not familiar with the different trajectories of the different bullets he'll end up with a very light game bag.

The final bullet I put to the test was the 170-gr. Hornady round nose, designed specially for the 30-30. Case capacity with this bullet is 46 grains of water. The calculator says 40 grains of IMR 4064 or IMR 4895 is best, velocity about 2410 fps. Although the trajectory is still far from being flat, this load is a good one. I hit a pail 3 out of 5 times at 400 yards with it—which isn't bad at all considering the standard iron sights and sitting position I was shooting from. However, wanting more velocity, I discovered that the rifle could handle 42 grains of 4895. Anything more caused a definite springing which could be felt in the lever. That was an ample warning, so I resigned myself to the 42-gr. load. For those who require a more devas-

tating load the 190-gr. bullet could be the answer. The W-W 190-gr. Silvertip (round nose) has the cannelure in the correct place. The Powley calculator indicates that 38 grains of IMR 4064 will produce 2240 fps.

Although these various loads may not seem particularly fast, they do represent a respectable gain. For example, the 150-gr., and 170-gr. loads show an increased velocity of 490 and 410 fps respectively. When comparing velocities, though, one must be careful. The factories claim that the 170-gr. bullet achieves 2200 fps from their cartridges, but independent chronographers have learned that about 2000 fps is more realistic from the carbine. If this is so the same bullet at well over 2410 fps is very nice indeed. At the least, the small cost of converting the rifle will not be a waste.

In loading for the 30-30 and the 308 Rimmed I found that full length sizing is a must. With the 308R it is often impossible to lock the action on a case that is not full length sized. As can be expected case life will not be great. I find that 308 Rimmed cases soon die after about 5 reloadings. This short case life is a result of the springing characteristics of the action, stretching the cases, making them brittle.

Much has been said with respect to reloading safety. All the safety rules apply to this rifle-cartridge combination. To ignore the precautions is to beg for disaster. At the top of the list of DONTS is any thought about using 308 Winchester ammunition in this rifle. The 308 will feed into the chamber, but if the 308 is chambered and fired, disaster is almost guaranteed. Standard 308 ammunition is designed for about 50,000 psi, whereas the Winchester 94 action can safely function with little more than 40,000 psi. When developing loads for the 308 Rimmed begin with light, safe loads and gradually work up. Never assume that your rifle has the strength of some others. Another suggestion, some indication that the rifle has been rechambered should be shown on the rifle itself. The rifle can be appropriately engraved or etched at low cost; it can be done in the home workshop.

This wildcatting project cannot be considered costly or highly impractical. It certainly gives the individual the opportunity to do a little tinkering and experimentation. Whether the increased velocities of the 308 Rimmed cartridge are worthwhile is a matter of opinion. One thing is certain—it will be difficult indeed to honestly make a further increase in velocity without major changes in the construction of the Winchester 94. ●

The Double Rifle
Its care and feeding

THE DOUBLE RIFLE has been with us for over 200 years and is still doing pretty well despite the magazine rifle's great price and accuracy advantages. In fact, there's been a recent upsurge of makes and models! The double rifle emerged to double the firepower of the single shot, a concept that survives today in a fair variety of types and calibers because of the undeniable appeal of fine doubles and a persistent belief by many that it is the most dependable rifle for dangerous game at close range. However, this typing of the double rifle as a *sine qua non* for dangerous game developed more in the cordite era since in blackpowder days the king of heavy dangerous game stoppers was the big single shot of from 8- to 4-bore until W. W. Greener and others popularized the double 8-bore with shorter barrels.

Most later blackpowder doubles of British make were made in 500-450/3¼″, 450/3¼″, 500/3″ and 3¼″,

Getting these rifles to group well with handloads isn't always easy—and sometimes it isn't possible. But most of them, if made by known, reliable gunmakers, will perform at least adequately. The author explains his methods and furnishes an extensive load table.

by JACK LOTT

This John Wilkes-made 450/3¼″ Nitro Express was purportedly John (Pondoro) Taylor's last double rifle, brought out of Mozambique by him in 1965, three years before his death.

and 577/2¾″ and 3″, all of which use the particular basic or actual case of the most popular large-bore nitro-expresses. For example, the 470, the 500/465, the 500/450 and the 500/3″ and 3¼″ nitro-expresses all use the basic 500/3¼″ case. This is a boon to the owner of such a blackpowder rifle since it means that he can keep on shooting his treasure with modern brass made for the nitro-expresses. A few cordite cases such as the 450 #2, the 475 #2 and the 400 Jeffery 3″ were purely cordite creations and have thicker rims and sidewalls. There is still, I'm sure, a good supply of Kynoch brass for most of the popular calibers around, but the availability to the new handloader of such cases is poor—they've been hoarded since Kynoch quit making them! Fortunately a new lease on life for some of these cases has been found in Jim Bell's Brass Extrusion Laboratories, Ltd. production of Boxer primer pocketed cases. Write him at 800 W.

Many, if not most, knowledgeable double rifle enthusiasts consider Holland & Holland the world's best makers—and with ample justification. This post-WW II Royal Ejector in 577 caliber upholds the long tradition. The craftsmanship, the finishing, the fitting—superb.

Maple Lane, Bensenville, IL 60106 or phone 312/595-2792.

Those with Kynoch cases can obtain a good Berdan decapper from RCBS (Box 1919, Oroville, CA 95965). I have found RCBS dies to be absolutely dependable for all my British case needs, including their special priming devices for the .254" Berdan primers.

Though they're often fancy engraved examples of the Victorian gunmaker's art, blackpowder doubles make fine woods rifles for deer, bear, moose and elk here, plus tiger, lion and leopard when and if available! They are not only cheaper than their nitro descendants but also easier to load for since they use cast lead bullets; some 450s shoot the 405-gr. jacketed 45-70 bullets nicely.

The most advanced category of handloading is for the nitro-expresses for dangerous game. These are the traditional stoppers of the "pukka sahib" and white hunter of the twilight of Empire. Another category is the small or medium bore double which, if British, is usually a side-by-side, but if German or Austrian is generally superimposed. Such rifles, quite popular today in Europe for woods and mountain game, are often scope sighted. Pressures for these are not only higher than for the large bores, but instead of being required to group both barrels together at 50 yards, these must be regulated for 200 yards or more. The ability of such doubles to group both barrels close together is not rare, and my old superimposed Merkel 9.3x74R and my present Holland 318, both scoped, would consist-

ently stay inside one to 1.5 MOA (minute of angle) to well over 100 yards. Those wanting to use any double for longer ranges can sight one barrel for 100 yards and use the second barrel for close shots.

Case Preparation

There are certain fundamentals involved in handloading for double rifles that should be strictly observed. All cartridges must fit the chambers so as to permit easy closure of the action. Case lengthening is common,

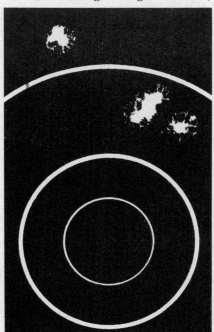

Four shots, lefts and rights, from a H&H 318 N.E. rifle carrying 3x scope, range 100 yards. The load was 58 grains of H4831, using Kynoch primed (corrosive) cases and Westley Richards 250-gr. capped bullets. 1⁵⁄₈" on centers.

and cases not trimmed periodically to minimum length can force the elongated necks against throat or the rifling's beginning, causing hard closing, perhaps pressure increases and certainly poorer shooting. Such continued forcing will stretch the locking areas, and we will soon have a loose rifle. Remember that a double rifle has much less leverage available for chambering and extraction than does a bolt action rifle. Full-length resizing—modified where indicated to match *your* chamber—is therefore a must for most double rifle cases, if not all. Be sure, too, that all case sizing lubricant is fully removed—if not, rearward thrust could be increased, and grouping might suffer.

Another vital rule is to keep pressures equal to or below those of the original loads. A double for the 375 H&H Magnum Flanged (rimmed) or the 300 H&H Magnum Flanged should not be loaded to pressure or velocity levels of U.S. belted rimless counterparts. There are many other cartridges chambered in doubles which are rimmed versions of rimless cases, such as the 275 H&H Magnum Flanged, the 280 Flanged version of the 280 Ross, the 7x65R Brenneke version of the 7x64, etc.

In recent years Holland & Holland has built many doubles for the 458 Winchester Magnum and the 375 H&H Belted Magnum. These rifles are now widely used, but I adhere to the time-tested British rule that rimmed cases are best for doubles. The reasons are germane to understanding the nature of doubles, regardless of what type one owns. Rim-

less cases, headspacing as they do on the shoulder, often show the equivalent of excessive headspace in doubles. This is not apparent in merely trying a round for fit or in headspace gauging, but occurs when a double is fired. The reasons are that a double rifle action must have clearance around its locking parts or it will be hard to open via the top or underlever, nor will it function properly if such clearances are absent. As a result of this and the hinged action, which causes clearance in the locking area lying lower down to increase via angulation, a few thousandths clearance at the bottom results in a considerable opening at the top under full pressure. Thus this opening tendency of doubles increases headspace as the barrels "go off the face" during full combustion. With a bolt action rifle all headspace clearance is in a direct line with thrust, but the hinging action of doubles works against tight headspace and for rimless cases a double should have minimum headspace. To avoid head separations I always adjust the full-length sizer to have the shoulder of a 318 case, say, barely clearing the chamber so that action closure is easy. This precludes incipient head separation caused by the firing pin driving the case forward until full pressure causes the sidewalls to grip the chamber while the head is forced back to the breech face.

Belted cases made years ago didn't work well in DB rifles because the area forward of the belt was thin, not part of the heavier-walled web as it is today. Such older belted brass expanded unduly as the gun was fired, and head separations could occur, especially if the cases were resized to factory dimensions before each loading.

With rimmed cases, of course, any

Jack Lott's Merkel 9.3x74R over-under and the steel scope mounts he made to replace the lost claw mount. Front trigger is a set type.

clearance in front of rim is well within the solid head area, and no risk of separation results from this alone. To detect incipient separations take a paper clip or other thin wire and straighten it out, leaving one end a short right-angle foot. Draw this sharpened feeler from the inside bottom of the case. If a slight groove is noted just above the solid head, and if there is a bright ring directly outside this groove, discard that case.

Extraction Problems

Extraction weakness is the other characteristic of the double rifle which makes it less suited to rimless cases or those which operate at high pressures. Extractors for rimmed cases are fixed, so to speak, with little or no side movement. They do not have to snap on and off as do those for rimless cases. Rimmed extractors usually have a larger area for purchase, and most rimmed cases have more rim to grab than rimless ones. Sometimes the snap-type rimless extractors snap off when the case sticks a bit or when rims are slightly undersize or worn or burred. This is one more reason to load such rimless cases for doubles with the lowest pressures consistent with normal grouping.

The dynamics of double rifles as opposed to single-barreled rifles are important for handloaders. Both barrels of a double rifle should shoot together at ranges normally used. For a heavy double this means 50 yards or so but 100 yards or more for the light to medium bore. Good quality doubles are closely regulated at the factory, but others are indifferently regulated, therefore cannot be made to shoot closely regardless of load. Many doubles, however, can be made to shoot better with good handloads than with factory ammo. For example, a 470 which places the right barrel's bullet 2 inches to the right of that of the left barrel at 50 yards can usually be made to print both barrels together with a handload. But if one barrel shoots high and right, say, and the other low and left, it may be a matter of inherently poor regulation, for which the remedy is re-regulation. As a rule of thumb, doubles shoot apart when the velocity is too low and cross fire when it is too high. The problem also occurs when heavier than original bullets are fired (causing shooting apart) and cross-firing with lighter

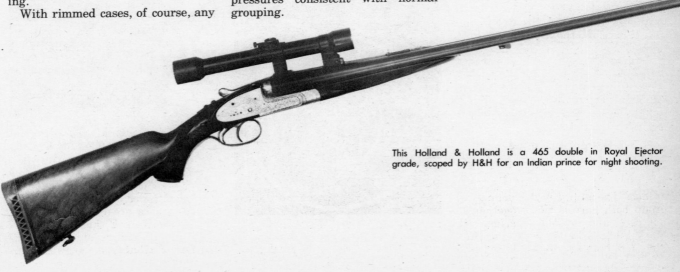

This Holland & Holland is a 465 double in Royal Ejector grade, scoped by H&H for an Indian prince for night shooting.

than original bullets. For example, I can use 500-gr. 458 bullets in my Rigby "best" sidelock ejector instead of the original 480-gr. Kynoch bullets, but they always shoot 2-2½ inches apart at 50 yards; the 480s shoot together.

Since superimposed barrels recoil in the same plane, backwards and upwards, the convergence built into them is less, and they are not usually as critical to regulate or load for as side-by-sides. I have also found side-by-sides with long heavy barrels easier to load for than shorter, muzzle light barrels. My Wm. Evans 27-inch barreled 500/3″ Nitro Express, weighing 12½ lbs., would group well with a much wider variation in loads than any of several Holland 10-lb. 24-inch barreled muzzle light 465 Royals.

When the right barrel of a double rifle is fired, it recoils sharply to the right, rearward and upward. The left barrel recoils to the left, back and up. Now if both barrels were attached with bores parallel, they would shoot far apart. Double rifle barrels, depending on caliber, barrel length, etc., are joined with various degrees of convergence to offset this tendency to shoot apart. When bullets shoot too far apart, it is from increased barrel time—from ignition to exit—and when they cross, the time up the barrel has been too short to permit the barrels to recoil to the point of proper convergence of bullet exit angle.

While writing this I learned from my friend and experienced hunter-handloader John Feyk of his successful Idaho elk hunt with a fine German boxlock double rifle in 9.3x74R. John was unable to bring 300- or 310-gr. bullets together at 100 yards with any load, but he got the rifle to group within 2 inches at 100 yards with 63 grains of IMR 4831, the Remington 9½ primer and the 250-gr. Bitterroot .358″ bullet.

John took his elk within 75 yards in dense forest while it ran broadside. Velocity was around 2250 fps, and we agreed that at that speed such a tough bullet was unneeded, but it certainly did the job.

Big Bore Loading

Two or three minute-of-angle grouping for heavy doubles at 50 yards is fine, but such groups with a smallbore or medium double could translate to 6 inches or more at 100 yards. A good rule of thumb for working up a load of nitro-cellulose for a cordite double is to begin with a charge of some nitro-cellulose equal

to the original cordite load, usually found stamped on the barrel flats of British rifles. Since cordite is a more efficient (though more erosive) powder than nitro-cellulose, it always takes more of an IMR powder to equal the grouping with cordite. For example, the 470 used 75 grains of cordite and the old 40 corrosive primer. I worked up from 75 grains of 3031 and the 40 Berdan primer to a fine grouping load of 79 grains of 3031. The additional percentage of nitro-cellulose required is usually from 5% to 10%. Try this—make up three test batches of 4 rounds each, starting with an amount of nitro-cellulose equal to that of the cordite load, then load four cases with two more grains and the last 4 cases with 4 more grains, which will usually come close to a proper load for the heavies. When both barrels shoot 2 inches apart at 50 yards one is at or within a grain or so of the right load. This system for the large bores works with 3031 using the old corrosive Kynoch 40 and the current R.W.S. equivalent non-corrosive Berdan primer 6507. If one

is using Kynoch's final 172 non-corrosive large rifle primers do *not* use 3031, 4895 or 4064 (except possibly with a straight-tapered case) because of the increased pressures generated by this more violent primer. I have not loaded any of the new B.E.L.L. Boxer-primed cases, but according to those who have, they work well with 3031 as well as 4895 and 4064. I cannot recommend any ball powders for double rifles because they are so compact in granulation, whereas what is needed for these big cases is a bulky, cool-burning powder, such as one of the larger-grained IMRs. Though cursed by many for making former favorite loads too violent, the 172 Kynoch primer enabled me to better fill the large cases by using 4350 and H4831, which paid off with the best groups I have ever obtained with double rifles. This was true for bottle-necked cases, but I also found that the 172 primer performed fine with 100 grains of 3031 and 750-gr. bullets in my 577/3-inch when two ⅛-inch thick cork wads were used. The ability of the 172 primer to pro-

This Rhodesian Cape buffalo bull was shot near the Chiredzi River by the author, using his H&H 577. His handload was 100/3031 and the Kynoch 750-gr. steel-jacketed Kynoch over 2 cork wads. The 172 NC primer was used.

duce loads with 4350 and 4831 is in the direction of that ideal of internal ballistics which says a load of powder which most nearly fills the case and produces full velocity at moderate pressures is best.

The new RWS primers—which replace the Kynoch 172—are excellent for large British cases; they're obtainable from the Old West Gun Room, 3509 Carlson Blvd., El Cerrito, CA 94530.

Du Pont IMR Powders

A recently-published information sheet on loads for doubles warns against using "IMRs of any type," meaning Du Pont tubular nitro-cellulose powders, "due to an occasional high pressure excursion." I am otherwise impressed by the information on this sheet but disagree with this sweeping rejection of some of the finest cool-burning progressive powders extant. I have loaded hundreds of rounds for doubles using Du Pont powders for over 20 years and have never had pressure problems unless I loaded them too heavily. It is clear from the information sheet that over-powder wads were not used, which may explain the "occasional pressure excursions." In such oversize cases the unused airspace can permit the powder to lie flat along the lower side of the case when the rifle is parallel to the ground, thus exposing too much of the powder surface to primer flash. This might ignite too much of the powder surface, possibly creating a semi-detonation occasionally. Perhaps the fact that I always use cork overpowder wads is the reason for my success with IMR powders, but in any case I advise this practice for accuracy's sake as well as for uniform pressures. Since Kynoch also used overpowder wads, that would seem ample precedent. If a load is worked up using cork gasket wads, pressures are always normal, not erratic, if the final load is carefully approached. Naturally, as this dope sheet says, no loads developed *without* overpowder wads should be used with them because of a corresponding increase in pressure. Though various materials have been recommended for overpowder wads, I prefer cork compositon gasket material about 1/8″ thick as noted above. These are easily cut with a hollow punch, they do not turn sideways in the barrel or remain intact, for they're quickly broken up and blown out. One or two such cork wads are all that is needed. I do not advise using such fillers as Kapok or

A recently-made (1969) 458 D.B. rifle by Holland & Holland in Royal grade. The sidelock plates carry 3-color raised gold coats of arms.

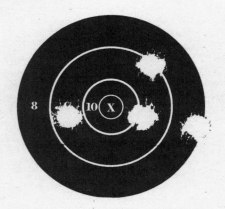

Four shots, rights and lefts, from a 500/3″ Wm. Evans Nitro Express at 50 yards, iron sights. The load was 84/3031 behind 570-gr. Kynoch bullets. 2″ on centers.

Dacron fibers or toilet paper, though some capable loaders do use such fillers.

Avoid Major Changes

Lengthening stocks, lightening or increasing weight by hollowing or adding lead, as well as putting recoil pads on rifles regulated without them will almost always cause changes in grouping. My 318 Holland double was regulated without a recoil pad, but I wanted a pad to avoid damaging the original checkered wood butt. That change promptly ruined the superb grouping I'd got earlier by opening up groups to 6 inches left and right at 100 yards. I tried to compensate by increasing the powder charge, but with three more grains it didn't help much. It dawned on me that I had been confronted by the law of double rifles which says that substantial changes in buttstock weight, or changing from a hard butt to a recoil pad, always alters grouping. I put the original walnut butt back in place and grouping promptly returned to the former excellence.

Despite what has been reported, double rifles don't change their points of impact with weather changes, although lengthy exposure of nitro cartridges or loaded barrels to the sun's rays can alter grouping quality. Blackpowder doubles are less affected by such pressure changes and load variations. Ultra-large bores, such as my 8-bore Rodda, will shoot well with round balls or conicals, and either projectile type with load variations of as much as two drams; there's little or

Smokeless-for-Black-Powder Loads

(Use with Steel-Barrel Black Powder Rifles Only.

Slug Bores and Size Bullets to Fit Grooves)

Cartridge	Bullet/grs.	Powder/grs.	Case	Primer	MV*	Notes
450/3¼″ B.P.E.	Ideal G.C./400	4198/53.5	Ky.	RWS 6507	1500	(2) 1/8″ cork OP wads.
	Rem. 45-70/405	3031/60	"	"	1500	(1) 1/8″ cork OP wad
500/3″ B.P.E.	Lead P.P./450	4198/60	"	"	1700	"
	G.C./465	4064/76	"	"	1700	(1) 1/8″ cork OP wad. E. Keith.
	"	3031/65	"	"	1600	
500/3¼″ B.P.E.	Lead/350	4198/65	Ky., B.E.L.L.	RWS 6507, Fed. 215	1800	(1) 1/8″ cork OP wad.
	Lead/440	4198/59.2	"	"	1775	"
	Lead/465	4198/56	"	"	1725	"
577/3″ B.P.E.	P.P./450	4198/58	"	"	1750	"
	P.P./500	4198/54.5	"	"	1650	"
	G.C./510	4198/54	"	"	1600	"
	Lead/630	4831/80	Ky.	Ky. 172 N.C.	1500	(2) 1/8″ cork OP wads. Keith bullet des. only.

*Estimated. B.P.—black powder; G.C.—gas check; N.C.—non-corrosive; O.P.—overpowder; P.P.—paper patch.

Note—These loads grouped both barrels well together in specific DB rifles. Do not use kapok or like fillers in these loads. Because of wide variations in rifles' condition we accept no responsibility for any negative results.

Black Powder Loads for British Double Rifles

Cartridge	Bullet/grs.	Bullet/dia.	Charge/grs.	MV*	ME†	Notes
360 B.P.E.	Lead HP/155	.367"	50	1700	1000	2⁷/₁₆" case.
	CT/190	"	50	1550	1015	"
	Lead/215	"	50	1450	1005	"
	CT/190	"	55	1700	1219	"
450/400	CT/230	.405"	80	1750	1563	2³/₈" case.
	Lead/255	"	80	1750	1610	"
450/400 Magnum	CT/230	.410"	110	2000	2045	Use 450/400/3¹/₄" or 450/3¹/₄" brass.
	Lead/255	"	110	1900	2045	"
450/3¹/₄" B.P.E.	CT/270	.458"	120	1975	2340	"
	Lead/310	"	120	1800	2240	"
	CT/325	"	120	1775	2280	"
	Lead/365	"	120	1700	2340	"
450/2³/₄" Long Range	Lead/480	"	125	1500 approx.	2400	
500/450 No. 1	CT/270	"	110	1900	2170	2³/₄" case.
	Lead/310	"	110	1825	2300	"
500/450 3¹/₄" Magnum	CT/325	"	140	1950	2745	Use 500/3¹/₄", 470, 465 or 500/450 brass.
	CT/365	"	140	1875	2850	
500/450 No. 2 Musket	Lead/480	"	76	1300	1805	
577/450 Martini-Henry	"	"	85	1350	1945	
	CT/325	"	90	1600	1850	
500/3" B.P.E.	CT/340	.510"	136	1925	2800	Use 500/3", 500/3¹/₄", 470, 465, 500/450 brass.
	Lead/380	"	136	1850	2890	
500/3" W.R.	Lead/570	"	120	1542	3005	"
500/3¹/₄" B.P.E.	CT/440	"	142	1775	3080	Use 500/3¹/₄", 470, 465 or 500/450 brass.
	Lead/480	"	142	1700	3080	
577/500 No. 2 B.P.E.	CT/340	"	130	1850	2590	2³/₁₆" case.
	Lead/380	"	130	1775	2660	"
577/500 Magnum	CT/440	"	164	1875	3440	3¹/₈" case.
	Lead/480	"	164	1800	3460	"
577 Solid Snider	"	.574"	70	1250	1660	
577/2³/₄" B.P.E.	CT/520	.584"	160	1725	3440	Can use 577/3" brass.
	Lead/560	"	160	1650	3380	"
577/3" B.P.E.	CT/570	"	167	1725	3770	"
	Lead/610	"	167	1650	3690	"
	Lead/648	"	164	1650 approx.	3913	Sir Samuel Baker's original 577/3" soft lead load.
12-bore, rifled	Rd. Lead/599	.725"	191	1584	3356	U.S. boxer-primed brass case available.
	Rd. Lead/585	"	191	1600 approx.	3323	"
	Lead Con./750	"	191	1550	4660	"
12-bore, Paradox, BC	Lead Con./735	"	123	1150	2150	"
10-bore, Paradox, BC	Lead Con./875	.775"	218	1550	4660	Brass cases hard to obtain.
8-bore, rifled, BC	Rd. Lead/875	.875"	328	1700 approx.	5617	
	Lead Con./1250	"	273	1500	6290	"
8-bore, rifled, Pap.	Rd. Lead/862	.835"	273	1654	5232	Rem. 8-ga. plastic "industrial" adaptable.
8-bore, Paradox, BC	Lead Con./1250	.875"	273	1500	6290	Brass cases hard to obtain.
4-bore, rifled, BC	Rd. Lead/1750	1.052"	382	1500 approx.	8750	Custom-made brass only option.
	Lead Con./1882	1.052"	328	1330	7400	"

*MV—muzzle velocity, fps. †ME—muzzle energy, foot lbs. HP—hollow pts. CT—copper tube. Con.—conical. B.P.E.—black powder express. BC—brass case. Pap.—Paper case.

Kynoch Nitro Express Cartridges for Double Rifles

Cartridge	Bullet/grs.	Bullet/dia.	Powder/grs.	MV*	ME†	Notes
240 H&H Apex Fl.	100 Semi-Ptd.	.245″	38.5 NC	2775	1711	.243″ bullets work in tight bores.
246 Purdey Fl.	100 Sptz.	.254″	40 NC	2950	1934	Swage .257″ bullets down.
7mm Rigby Mag.	140 Sptz.	.284″	40 NC	2675	2226	
275 H&H Fl. Mag.	160 S.N.	.284″	49 NC	2575	2357	
280 Fl.	160 Capped H.P.	.287″	52 NC	2600	2403	Bullets avail.
	140 H.P.	.287″	"	2800	2440	" "
	180 Sptz.	.287″	48 NC	2425	2353	" "
	150 Sptz.	.287″	49.5 NC	2675	2385	" "
300 H&H Fl. Mag.	150 S.N.	.308″	55 Cord.	2875	2755	Make cases from 375 H&H Fl. brass.
	180 S.N.	.308″	50 Cord.	2575	2653	" "
	220 S.N.	.308″	46 Cord.	2250	2475	" "
30 Purdey Fl. N.E.	150 S.N.	.308″		2700	2430	30-40 Krag brass is close.
303 British Mark VI	215 R.N.	.311″	31 Cord.	2050	2007	Suits most 303 D.B. rifles.
	192 CT	.311″	31.5 Cord.	2200	2065	" "
	210 WR Capped	.311″	31 Cord.	2070 approx.		" "
333 Jeffery Fl.	300 R.N.	.333″	65 NC	2200	3230	Bullets avail.
	250 Sptz.	.333″	70 NC	2500	3230	" "
400/350 Rigby Ex.	310 R.N.	.356″	43 NC	2000	2752	
360 N.E.	300 R.N.	.367″	30 Cord.	1650	1820	Norma, RWS, Speer 9.3 (.365″) bullets.
400/360 Purdey N.E.	300 R.N.	.367″	40 Cord.	1950	2537	" "
400/360 WR N.E.	314 R.N.	.367″	41 Cord.	1900	2520	" "
360 No. 2 N.E.	320 R.N.	.367″	55 Cord.	2200	3442	" "
369 Purdey	270 Semi-Ptd.	.375″	64.5 NC	2525	3815	Use standard .375″ bullets.
375 Fl. N.E.	270 R.N.	.375″	40 Cord.	1975	2340	" "
375 H&H Fl. Mag.	300 R.N.	.375″	56 Cord.	2425	3930	" "
	270 Semi-Ptd.	.375″	59 Cord.	2600	4060	" "
	235 Semi-Ptd.	.375″	60 Cord.	2750	3950	
400 Purdey 3″ N.E.	230 S.N.	.411″	47 Cord.	2050	2148	Bullets avail.
450/400/3″ N.E.	400 R.N.	.411″	60 Cord.	2125	4010	" "
450/400/3¼″ Mag. N.E.	400 R.N.	.411″	60 Cord.	2150	4110	" "
450/3¼″ N.E.	480 R.N.	.458″	70 Cord.	2150	4930	" "
500/450/3¼″ Mag. N.E.	480 R.N.	.458″	75 Cord.	2175	5050	" "
450 No. 2 N.E.	480	.458″	80 Cord.	2175	5050	475 No. 2 brass adapt.
500/465 N.E.	480	.468″	73 Cord.	2150	4930	470, 500/450, 500/3¼″ brass usable.
470 N.E.	500	.475″	75 Cord.	2125	5030	500/465, 500/450, 500/3¼″ brass usable.
475 N.E.	480	.483″	75 Cord.	2175	5050	450/3¼″,450/400/3¼″ brass usable.
475 No. 2 N.E.	480	.483″	85 Cord.	2200	5170	450 No. 2 brass also usable.
475 No. 2 Jeffery	500	.489″	85 Cord.	2120	5000	450 No. 2, standard 475 No. 2 brass usable.
476 WR	520	.476″	75 Cord.	2100	5090	470, 500/465, 500/450, 500/3″ and 3¼″ brass usable.
500/3″ N.E.	570	.510″	80 Cord.	2150	5850	500/3¼″, 470, 500/465, 500/450 brass usable.
500/3¼″ N.E.	570	.510″	80 Cord.	2125	5720	470, 500/465, 500/450 brass usable
577/2¾″ N.E.	650	.584″	90 Cord.	1950	5500	577/3″ brass usable.
	750	.584″	90 Cord.	1800	5400	" "
577/3″ N.E.	650	.584″	90 Cord.	1950	5500	In rifles proved for this load only.
	750	.584″	100 Cord.	2050	7010	" "
600 N.E.	900	.620″	100 Cord.	1850	6840	
600 N.E.	900	.620″	110 Cord.	1950	7600	

Sources: Kynoch (I.C.I.) 1954 Rules of Proof, bullets miked in most cases.
Fl.—flanged. S.N.—soft nose. H.P.—hollow pt. R.N.—round nose. NC—nitro-cellulose. Cord.—Cordite. *MV—muzzle velocity, fps.
†ME—muzzle energy, foot lbs. WR—Westley Richards.

Smokeless Powder Loads for Double Rifles
(Flanged or Rimmed Cartridges)

Cartridge	Bullet/grs.	Powder/grs.	Case	Primer	MV*	Notes
8×57JR	.318″ Nor. 196 RN	Nor. 203/44.8	Nor., RWS	Win. 120, Fed. 210, Rem. 9½	2362	Near max. O.A.L. 2.97″
8×57JRS	.323″ Nor., RWS/196	Nor. 203/45.5	"	"	2395	For modern "S" (.323″ groove dia.) barrels. O.A.L. 2.950″. Near max.
	"	3031/30.3	"	"	2300	O.A.L. 2.950″.
		Nor. 201/38	"	"	2000	Minimal load. O.A.L. 2.950″.
	.323″ Nor. 198 BT	Nor. 203/46.6	"	"	2461	Near max. O.A.L. 3.11″.
	.323″ Nor. 227 RN	Nor. 203/43	"	"	2200	O.A.L. 2.91″.
9.3×74R	.365″ Nor. 232 BT	Nor. 201/59.7	"	"	2624	O.A.L. 3.64″.
	.365″ Nor. RWS 286 RN	Nor. 201/56.5	"	"	2362	Standard Nor. ballistics for 286-gr. bullet. O.A.L. 3.70″.
	"	4064/57	"	"	2360	Cartridges of the World load.
	"	4064/55	"	"	2300	Grouped good at 100 yds. in my Merkel O-U. O.A.L. 3.632″.
	.366″ Speer 250 Sptz.	3031/54.5	"	"	2400	"
	.366″ RWS 293 TUG Brenneke	4895/53.5	"	"	2300	"
240 H&H "Apex" Fl.	.245″ Ky. 100	4350/42	Ky.	Ky. 81 N.C.	2900	Approxi. Ky. load. Cartridges of the World.
	"	4350/47	"	"	3100 Max.	Cartridges of the World.
280 Fl.	.287″ Ky. 140 Sptz.	Hi-Vel. 2/50	"	"	2800	"
	.287″ Ky. 160 H.P.	4350/55	"	"	2650	"
30 Purdey Fl.	.308″/150 SN	4320/45	"	"	2700	"
	.308″/180 SN	4350/48	"	"	2420	"
303 British	.311″ Rem. 215 RN	4350/46	Rem.	Rem. 9½	2290	Seating depth .26″, 38,480 psi.
400/350 Rigby	.357″/300 RN	4350/58	Ky.	Ky. 34	2180	Cartridges of the World.
	.357″/250 SN	3031/50	"	"	2300	"
360 2¼″ N.E.	.366″ Speer 250 Sptz.	4759/20	"	"	1700	"
360 No. 2 N.E.	.367″/320 Ky. or Barnes RN	3031/55	"	Ky. 172, RWS 6507	2200	Near max. Close to original Ky.
	"	4320/54	"	"	2200	Cartridges of the World. Close to original Ky.
369 Purdey N.E.	.375″/270	4320/70	"	RWS 6507	2530	
H&H 375 Fl. Mag.	.375″/270 Horn. RNSN	4350/79	Ky.	Ky. 81 N.C.	2600	26″ bbl. (1) Cork OP wad. Very accurate. Ross Seyfried load.
Jeffery 450/400/3″	.411″ Barnes or Ky. 400	4064/63-67	Ky.	RWS 6507 Ky. 40	2000-2150	Work up from 63 grs. (1) ⅛″ cork OP wad. Elmer Keith load.
	"	3031/63	"	"	2100	Cartridges of the World load.
"Magnum" 450/400/3¼″	"	3031/67	"	"	2175	(1) ⅛″ cork OP wad. E. Keith load.
450/3¼″ N.E.	.458″ Barnes or Ky. 480	H414/86	"	RWS 6507	2150	(1) ⅛″ cork OP wad. R. Seyfried load.
	"	3031/75	"	RWS 6507 Ky. 40		(2) ⅛″ cork OP wads. E. Keith load.
	"	4350/82	"	Ky. 172 N.C.	2100	(1)⅛″ cork OP wad.
	Win. .458″/500	4350/80	"	"	2050	2″-3″ spread in my Rigby. (1) ⅛″ cork OP wad.

Fl.—flanged. N.E.—Nitro Express. Ky.—Kynoch. OP—over-powder. N.C.—non-corrosive. W.E.—Westly Richards.

Cartridge	Bullet/grs.	Powder/grs.	Case	Primer	MV*	Notes
500/450/3¼″ N.E.	.458″ Barnes or Ky. 480	4350/81	″	″	2100	(1) ⅛″ cork OP wad.
450 No. 2 N.E.	″	3031/85	″	RWS 6507 Ky. 40	2150	″
500/465 N.E.	.468″ Barnes or Ky. .480	4350/83.5	″	Ky. 172 N.C.	2150	″
	″	3031/78	Ky. or B.E.L.L.	RWS 6507 Fed. 215	2150	″
470 N.E.	.475″ Barnes or Ky. 500	4350/81	″	Ky. 172 N.C.	2125	Light Kapok filler.
		3031/79	″	Ky. 40 RWS 6507 Fed. 215	2125	(1) ⅛″ cork OP wad.
	″	Hi-V. 2/81	B.E.L.L.	Fed. 215	2154	No wads or fillers. B.E.L.L. 28″ test bbl. only, may not group in double.
	″	Rel. 21/92	″	″	2184	″
	″	H414/95	″	″	2141	″
	″	748 BR/87	″	″	2109	″
	″	4064/85	″	″	2127	″
476 W.R.	.476″ Barnes or Ky. 520	3031/80	Ky.	RWS 6507 Ky. 40	2100	(1) ⅛″ cork OP wad. E. Keith load.
475 No. 2 N.E.	.483″ Barnes or Ky. 480	4064/90	″	″	2200	″
475 No. 2 Jeffery	.489″ Barnes or Ky. 500	″	″	″	2120	″
475 N.E.	.483″ Barnes or Ky. 480	3031/80	Make from Ky. 450/3¼″	″	2150	(2) ⅛″ cork OP wads.
500/3″ N.E.	.510″ Barnes or Ky. 570	4895/90	Ky.	RWS 6507	2150	(2) ⅛″ cork OP wads.
500/3″ N.E.	.510″ Barnes or Ky. 570	3031/84	″	Ky. 40 RWS 6507	2150	(1) ⅛″ cork OP wad.
577/3″ N.E.	.585″ Barnes or Ky. 750	4895/115	″	″	2050	(2) ⅛″ cork OP wads. E. Keith load.
	″	Hi-Vel 2/120	″	″	2050	(2) ⅛″ cork OP wads. Capt. Wadman.
	″	3031/100	″	Ky. 172 N.C.	2050	(2) ⅛″ cork OP wads. Author's H&H load.
	.585″ Barnes or Ky. 650	3031/85	″	Ky. 40 RWS 6507	1900	(2) ⅛″ cork OP wads.

Fl.—flanged. N.E.—Nitro Express. Ky.—Kynoch. OP—over-powder. N.C.—non-corrosive. W.E.—Westley Richards.

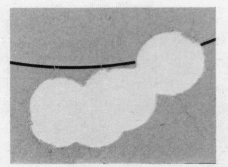

The author's Rodda 8-bore double rifle uses all-brass cases, has 22-inch barrels and weighs 17 lbs. Still tight and quite accurate, this early specimen has outside hammers, back-action locks and a side-swinging underlever.

Four lefts and rights from an Army & Navy 12-bore Paradox "Jungle Gun" at 25 yards. The 800-gr. conical bullets were fired by 5 drams of Fg black powder in the all-brass case.

for blackpowder doubles despite extra work in keeping the tubes clean. Remember that not all "nitro" doubles carry nitro proof if made before 1904. For example, many nitro doubles were made with underlevers and outside hammers which appeared exactly like blackpowder doubles.

If you own a BP double in 12-, 10-, 8- or 4-bore, slug the bore to find out if it was made for paper or brass cases. Brass case rifles have larger bores due to the thinness of brass cases; paper-case bores are smaller because of the thicker case walls. My 8-bore brass-case Rodda shoots .875″ bullets, whereas paper-case 8-bores shoot bullets of around .835″.

Those using Jim Bell's Boxer-primed cases will find the Federal 215 magnum primer unexcelled for the large nitro-express cases, and with these you can also use 3031, 4895 and 4064 powders, as with the old 40 Kynoch. Copper-jacketed bullets in soft-nosed or solid form for most British calibers can now be had from Barnes Bullets (Box 215, American Fork, Utah 84003), successor to Colorado Custom Bullets, Montrose, Colo. These Barnes-designed bullets with .049″ jackets work well on African game in "solid" form, but the copper jackets make them less effective for frontal shots on elephant skulls. They are, however, fine for buffalo and other shots on elephant.

Some writers say that doubles do well only if held in the hands—offhand, sitting or kneeling—and won't group from a bench, but this is

RIFLES AND CARTRIDGES
FOR DEER AND BIG GAME SHOOTING.

THE BEST DEERSTALKING RIFLES.

For Deer Stalking in Scotland the ·256 Mannlicher Schonauer Rifle is still very popular. It fires a 156 grain bullet with a muzzle velocity of 2,400 feet per second, and has a muzzle energy of 2,000 foot pounds.

THE JEFFERY ·300 MAUSER.

The ideal weapon for Deer Stalking in our opinion is a rifle firing the new Remington Hi-speed ·30-bore Springfield Cartridge, 1906 Model. This cartridge has a muzzle velocity of 3,000 feet per second, which gives a muzzle energy of over 3,000 foot pounds, thus making it a considerably more effective weapon than the ·256 rifle. The bullet is of the pointed expanding type and is extremely accurate. We are selling a large number of these rifles, and full particulars will be found on Page 13. This cartridge can also be supplied with a 110 grain bullet, giving a velocity of 3,500 feet per second.

THE BEST MEDIUM BORE RIFLES.

THE ·333 JEFFERY MAUSER.

This is a very powerful medium bore Rifle with a velocity nearly equal to the ·280 but shooting a much heavier bullet. With a 250 grain pointed expanding bullet it has a velocity of 2,500 feet per second, and has a striking force of about 3,500 foot lbs. It also shoots a 300 grain Solid or Soft Nose Bullet, and with these heavy bullets is very effective on almost any animal, hard or soft skinned.

Although theoretically the striking force of the ·333 is almost equal to that of the ·400 or ·404, yet we do not claim that it would be as effective against large and dangerous game as the ·400 or ·404. Against large animals a heavy bullet should be used, and it is important that the front of the bullet should not expand too much, otherwise its penetration power is lost, especially at short ranges. For head shots at elephant or bison the ·333 would exceed in penetration any other rifle obtainable when used with nickel covered bullets. Compared with the ·333 Government Bullet the ·333 is about twice as effective at short distances, and at 400 or 500 yards it is even more effective in proportion.

THE ·333 DOUBLE RIFLE.
REGULATED FOR 250 GRAIN BULLET ONLY.

Owing to the great demand for and popularity of the ·333 Jeffery Mauser, and numerous enquiries from sportsmen in all parts of the world for a Double Rifle taking this cartridge, we have for some time past been building Double Rifles for a ·333 rimmed cartridge. This rifle is beautifully balanced, and handles like a shot gun, as practically the whole weight is between the hands when being fired. The weight is about 9lbs., and it makes one of the most effective rifles on the market.

JEFFERY'S ·600 BORE
(Velocity, in India or Africa, 2,050 feet per second)

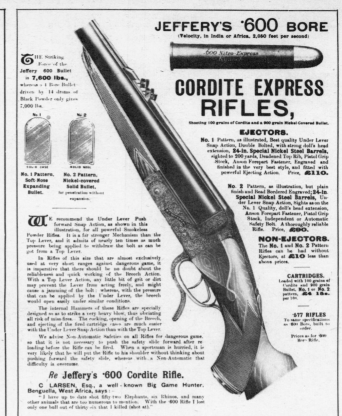

CORDITE EXPRESS RIFLES,
Shooting 100 grains of Cordite and a 900 grain Nickel Covered Bullet.

THE Striking Force of the Jeffery 600 Bullet is 7,600 lbs., whereas a 4 Bore Bullet driven by 14 drams of Black Powder only gives 7,000 lbs.

No. 1 Pattern. Soft-Nose Expanding Bullet.

No. 2 Pattern. SOLID CASE. SOLID NOSE. Nickel-covered Solid Bullet, for penetration without expansion.

WE recommend the Under Lever Push forward Snap Action, as shown in this illustration, for all powerful Smokeless Powder Rifles. It is a far stronger Mechanism than the Top Lever, and it admits of nearly ten times as much pressure being applied to withdraw the bolt as can be got from a Top Lever.

In Rifles of this size that are almost exclusively used at very short ranges against dangerous game, it is imperative that there should be no doubt about the reliableness and quick working of the Breech Action. With a Top Lever Action, any little bit of grit or dirt may prevent the Lever from acting freely, and might cause a jamming of the breech : whereas, with the pressure that can be applied by the Under Lever, the breech would open easily under similar conditions.

The internal Hammers of these Rifles are specially designed so as to strike a very heavy blow, thus obviating all risk of miss-fires. The cocking, opening of the Breech, and ejecting of the fired cartridge cases are much easier with the Under Lever Snap Action than with the Top Lever.

We advise Non-Automatic Safeties on all Rifles for dangerous game, so that it is not necessary to push the safety slide forward after re loading before the Rifle can be fired. When a sportsman is hurried, it is very likely that he will put the Rifle to his shoulder without thinking about pushing forward the safety slide, whereas with a Non-Automatic that difficulty is overcome.

EJECTORS.

No. 1 Pattern, as illustrated, Best quality Under Lever Snap Action, Double Bolted, with strong doll's head extension, 24-in. Special Nickel Steel Barrels, sighted to 200 yards, Deadened Top Rib, Pistol Grip Stock, Anson Forepart Fastener, Engraved and finished in the very best style, and fitted with powerful Ejecting Action. Price, **£110.**

No. 2 Pattern, as illustration, but plain finish and Bead Bordered Engraved ; 24-in. Special Nickel Steel Barrels, Under Lever Snap Action, Sights as on the No. 1 Quality, doll's head extension, Anson Forepart Fastener, Pistol Grip Stock, Independent or Automatic Safety Bolt. A thoroughly reliable Rifle. Price, **£90.**

NON-EJECTORS.

The No. 1 and No. 2 Pattern Rifles can be had without Ejectors, at **£10** less than above prices.

CARTRIDGES. Loaded with 100 grains of Cordite and 900 grain Bullet, No. 1 or No. 2 pattern, **£4 15s.** per 100.

·577 RIFLES. To same specifications as ·600 Bore, built to order.

Prices as for ·600 Bore Rifle.

Re **Jeffery's ·600 Cordite Rifle.**

C. LARSEN, Esq., a well-known Big Game Hunter, Benguella, West Africa, says : " I have up to date shot fifty two Elephants, six Rhinos, and many other animals that are too numerous to mention. With the ·600 Rifle I lost only one bull out of thirty six that I killed (shot at)."

JEFFERY'S
·333, ·375 Magnum, ·400, ·470, ·475 No. 2
BEST QUALITY
SIDE LOCK HAMMERLESS CORDITE EXPRESS RIFLES.

WE claim that our No. 1 Model Rifles are unsurpassed for finish, balance and accuracy, and that they will compare favourably with any double rifles in the World irrespective of their prices. These rifles have been most carefully designed, and balance and handle almost like shot guns, notwithstanding that they are so much heavier : a sportsman handling one of these rifles for the first time usually guesses the weight to be at least a couple of pounds less than it is.

The great failing with many Double Rifles, especially cheap ones, is that the two barrels are not adjusted to shoot together. We pay especial care to this particular point, and all weapons of our manufacture have to pass a most exacting test before being offered for sale.

Our Rifles have the metal in the place where it is wanted, viz., the Breech, and they are made as light as possible at the muzzle. Many makers maintain that it is necessary to have weight at the muzzle. Our barrels will easily shoot into a 3-inch square, on an average, whereas the others often cannot get their shots into a 5-inch square, at 100 yards.

We advise customers to have these Rifles with Non-Automatic Safeties, if they are intended for use against dangerous game.

No. 1 Model (as illustration). Top Lever Action, best quality Side Locks, with Intercepting Safeties, Specially Strong Ejecting Mechanism, best quality 24in. Nickel Steel Barrels, sighted to 300 or 500 yards with best quality Standard and Spring Leaf Backsight, Bead Foresight, Full Pistol Grip Stock, Anson Forepart, Iron Tips on Butt, Highly Scroll Engraved.

PRICE.

No. 1 Model Ejector ... **£110**
No. 1 Model Non-Ejector ... **£100**

Approximate Weights of Best Rifles.

·333	...	9¼ lbs.
·375 Magnum	...	9½ lbs.
·400	...	10 lbs.
·470	...	11¼ lbs.
·475	...	11¼ lbs.

Rifles can be built specially to order to take any selected cartridge without any extra charge.

These Rifles can be had with scroll engraving as illustrated, or with big game and scroll work combined.

JEFFERY'S
·333, ·375 Magnum, ·400, ·470 & ·475 No. 2
BEST QUALITY ANSON & DEELEY ACTION
CORDITE EXPRESS RIFLES
OTHER BORES BUILT TO ORDER.

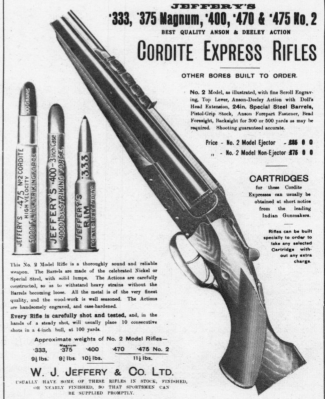

No. 2 Model, as illustrated, with fine Scroll Engraving, Top Lever, Anson-Deeley Action with Doll's Head Extension, 24in. Special Steel Barrels, Pistol-Grip Stock, Anson Forepart Fastener, Bead Foresight, Backsight for 300 or 500 yards as may be required. Shooting guaranteed accurate.

Price - No. 2 Model Ejector - **£85 0 0**
" - No. 2 Model Non-Ejector **£75 0 0**

CARTRIDGES
for these Cordite Expresses can usually be obtained at short notice from the leading Indian Gunmakers.

Rifles can be built specially to order to take any selected Cartridge without any extra charge.

This No. 2 Model Rifle is a thoroughly sound and reliable weapon. The Barrels are made of the celebrated Nickel or Special Steel, with solid lumps. The Actions are carefully constructed, so as to withstand heavy strains without the Barrels becoming loose. All the metal is of the very finest quality, and the wood-work is well seasoned. The Actions are handsomely engraved, and case-hardened.

Every Rifle is carefully shot and tested, and, in the hands of a steady shot, will usually place 10 consecutive shots in a 4-inch bull, at 100 yards.

Approximate weights of No. 2 Model Rifles—

·333,	·375 Magnum	·400	·470	·475 No. 2
9¼ lbs.	9½ lbs.	10¼ lbs.		11¼ lbs.

W. J. JEFFERY & CO. LTD.
USUALLY HAVE SOME OF THESE RIFLES IN STOCK, FINISHED, OR NEARLY FINISHED, SO THAT SPORTSMEN CAN BE SUPPLIED PROMPTLY.

Reproductions from an early W. J. Jeffery (England) catalog.

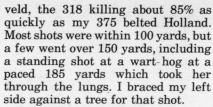
Lott downed this big Rhodesian Kudu—which had been hunted for months—using his H&H 318 Modele de Luxe. He used recharged Kynoch cases and their 250-gr. bullets.

veld, the 318 killing about 85% as quickly as my 375 belted Holland. Most shots were within 100 yards, but a few went over 150 yards, including a standing shot at a wart-hog at a paced 185 yards which took her through the lungs. I braced my left side against a tree for that shot.

For buffalo I used my H&H 577 double loaded with factory steel-jacketed solids and 100 grains of 3031 with two cork wads. I had no trouble in putting down these brutes with this load, including the stopping of one attempt to charge. This buff had gone a mile after a shot in the left flank ended in the right shoulder muscle. As he turned to charge my second shot took him in the right flank and smashed his left shoulder for the final count. Another shot for a finisher went bumping up the spine from base of tail to break his neck after nearly 6 feet of penetration!

Nitro for Black

Many owners of black powder doubles are interested in smokeless loads, and although I and others have successfully produced smokeless loads for blackpowder doubles with 3031 and other powders, I will not recommend such loads. This is because of the wide variation in condition of such rifles and their (usually) Damascus barrels which, if pitted or fissured, are prone to bursting. If you have enough confidence, skill and experience to make a start, plus a blackpowder double rifle in truly good condition, then there is no reason why you can't succeed in developing such smokeless loads, but use overpowder wads or lightweight fillers and proceed *cautiously*. Still, with blackpowder or the new blackpowder replica Pyrodex one is assured of safe loads

corrosive ammo I found this load wouldn't shoot, but substituting 54.5/4350 worked fine. I found no case capacity difference to account for this, which I attributed to a difference in the primers. Next, I reduced a supply of 250-gr. Winchester 338 Silvertips in my own dies to .3295" and, using RCBS dies, made cases out of Lake City 30-06 National Match brass, the strongest and heaviest cases I have ever used. However, with Federal 210 primers I found that none of my previous loads worked. I finally got good grouping with 49 grains of 4350, all three loads then shooting the same point of impact at 100 yards. I used these latter loads and the recharged Kynoch non-corrosive loads with 54.5 grains of 4350 on my 1974 Rhodesian and South African safari with great success on kudu, zebra, eland, wildebeest, waterbuck, impala, wart hog, reedbuck, duiker and hippo. The latter was brained with a 250-gr. Kynoch steel-jacketed solid at 75 yards in a pool of the Chiredzi River in Southeast Rhodesia near the Mozambique border.

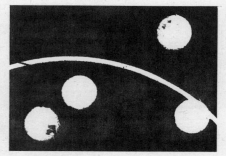
Four top and bottom shots at 100 yards from a scoped Merkel O-U in 9.3x74R. The DWM case held 293-gr. DWM H-Mantel bullet, the load 56/4895 with Fiocchi primers.

He was a lone bull with the habit of charging out of the water to drive humans and other hippos from his private lagoon. Chief Toan of the Shangaan tribe asked me to shoot him, the meat needed for a feast at a ceremony inducting 600 boys into manhood after circumcision.

I found the quick second shot and the crisp pulls excellent for the bush-

This oak-and-leather trunk case holds an 8-gauge Webley & Scott double rifle with back-action hammers and underlever.

contrary to my experience with many doubles over the years. One should rest the fore-end directly on the bags (not too firmly filled), or with the hand interposed between the fore-end and sandbag, at about point of balance, usually just forward of the hinge pin. Use padding under shirt or jacket to reduce felt kick. A *standing* rest (a system used by some British regulators) rocks the body in line with recoil and is less punishing, but it's unnecessary. If your double is loaded properly and kept clean and rust-free, it will last another hundred years. Handloads can keep your masterpiece in action, but you must supply the judgement and care essential to the performance and longevity that is the legacy of generations of the finest gunmakers in the world.

Shooting Double Rifles
Hints and Notes

Use fillers *only* when recommended. Safe fillers are Dacron, Kapok and toilet tissue. Author recommends 1/8" cork gasket material, obtainable at auto supply stores, for wads. *Do not use Cream of Wheat or other cereal fillers; they often increase pressures.*

In case of doubt as to chamber or cartridge, make a chamber/throat cast to determine exact dimensions. For black powder rifles use groove-diameter lubricated bullets, or, when using paper-patch bullets allow for paper thickness in casting or sizing.

Do *not* use IMR 3031, 4895, 4064 or Hi-Vel 2 or RelodeR 7 with Kynoch 172 non-corrosive primers for Cordite Nitro Express rifles having bottleneck chambers. Use Kynoch 40 corrosive, RWS 6507 or Federal 215 primers for these powders.

Do *not* mix loads or loading data for N.E. rifles with those for black powder expresses using identically-dimensioned cases and like numerical designations, such as the 450/3¼"

Nitro Express and the 450/3¼" black powder express.

The nitro-cellulose loads listed for Cordite calibers were developed for *specific* double rifles, and these grouped both barrels closely together. They may not shoot well in other doubles. It is better to work up a specific load for a specific rifle by using the original Cordite weight for a starting load of the appropriate nitro-cellulose powder.

Always clean barrels with boiling or very hot water after using Kynoch 40 or other corrosive primers.

Do *not* attempt to decap Berdan primers which show indentations but which did not fire. They often explode in decapping. Isolate them and discard.

Do *not* use old fired cases to make nitro express cartridges. They may have been weakened and corroded by the use of mercuric primers.

Though some high quality Damascus (twist) barrels in good condition will withstand mild smokeless-for-blackpowder loads, the practice is not recommended. Certainly any such barrels with deep pitting or fissures should not be fired, even with black powder.

Most black powder doubles were made to handle light bullets (for the caliber) at higher velocities and heavier bullets at lower velocities. Some, with a slow twist, shot only light bullets well. Check your rifle's rate of twist to let you select proper bullet weights. Light-bullet 450s, 500s, et al, will group apart when loaded with heavy-bullet cartridges.

When making shorter cases from longer ones, such as 500/3" from 500/3¼", make sure that neck-wall thickness is not so great that a loaded round enters the chamber too tightly. This will cause pressures to rise. Do not fire such tight-neck rounds. If this occurs get neck-reaming dies from RCBS. ●

Giles Whittome of East Surrey Firearms (England) fires a Greener 8-bore double rifle with 20-inch barrels. Note elbows lifting as recoil begins. The black Lab isn't gun shy.

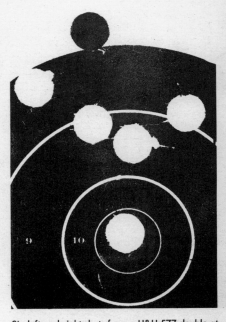

Six left and right shots from a H&H 577 double at 50 yards, iron sights. The load was 80/H4831 and 2 cork wads behind the 630-gr. Keith lead bullet, the primer Kynoch's No. 172. 3⅛" on centers vertical, 2⁵⁄₁₆" horizontal.

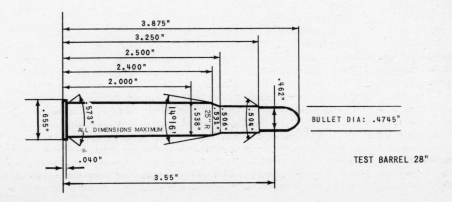

BULLET DIA: .4745"

TEST BARREL 28"

Jim Bell will soon offer new basic cases, among them to make 43 Mauser, 475 No. 2 Jeffery, 450/3½ No. 2, and 450/3½ Straight. He is also furnishing 416 cases/cartridges to Rigby. Write for the B.E.L.L. brochures, enclosing a stamped, self-addressed large envelope.

SLUG, MIKE, MATCH

This old 1909 Mauser Sherwood is shooting was used in his investigations of bullet diameters and varying bore and groove dimensions.

Old barrels generally, and earlier military barrels in particular, will frequently be found with abnormal bore/groove dimensions. Here's the way to check 'em out.

by ROBERT SHERWOOD

THE 7.65 Mauser cartridge has been among us for a long time, as have been the 1891 and 1909 Mauser rifles chambered for it. The cartridge is about on a par with other near-30s in the early smokeless military bracket; it is ballistically much like the 303 British or 7.7 Japanese loads. The rifles are something else, particularly the excellent 1909, which is a refined 1898 Mauser, made by Loewe and very well done indeed. Previously the 1909 wound up wearing a new barrel, but now that Norma brings us 7.65 Boxer-primed ammo, the 1891 is often modified and shot in the original, as is the 1909. It has an awkward 5-round straight feed magazine, much like a military Mannlicher, and the locking system is two lug, as on most pre-1898 Mausers. It is, however, a superbly finished action and very smooth; many like it, though hardly any of them well enough to rebarrel it to anything.

Occasionally both models get rechambered, this usually under-$30 operation being once a popular treatment. Some smiths touted the 300 Savage or even the 308 WCF for the 1891, and more of them counseled the 1909 owner to have his barrel reamed for the 30-06. Why not? The difference

between a 7.65 bore and a 308 is only .004/.005-inch, even sometimes only .003-inch. The late Phil Sharpe mentioned the occasional accuracy obtained by shooting 30-cal. bullets through 303 British and even through 8mm Mauser tubes. Ackley, too, recommends chambering 1909 Mausers to 30-06. Could anything be wrong with that?

My old partner Kelley would tell you there might be. He got a Belgian 91 in the days before Norma began selling 7.65 rounds on these shores. He lacked the dies to reform 8mms to 7.65s, but a smart Phoenix smith with an itchy reamer convinced Kelley that the 300 Savage case and reamer would solve all his problems. Kelley let loose on a running Galiuro Mountain buck with a fire pattern that would have let an elephant pass unscathed. That rifle would not hit a bedsheet with a dead-center hold 3 times out of 5! Kelley's first and only sighting shot had miraculously shot dead center, but never another followed it.

That was when the Earth was new, and I forgot the matter in pursuit of knowledge on cartridges more refined. But not long ago the owner of a 1909 told me about the cost of his re-

chambering job with a certain edge to his voice. He'd had it cut for the 06 case and, as he put it, the smith might just as well have pushed the reamer all the way through the barrel. Shooting factory ammunition, my friend was unable to get more than one out of 5 anywhere on a standard NRA 100-yard target. Curiosity on this matter of oversize bores began to tweak my mind, so I gathered a 1909 Argentine Mauser and a hatful of Speer bullets and set out to determine if it was the shooting or, indeed, if too wide a jacket-groove gap had let these deer and targets get away at that range.

Different Bullets Tested

My Mauser grooves miked .3133", found by careful slugging, with a land-to-land diameter of .3037". I obtained 100 each of Speer 180-gr. .308" bullets, 180-gr. .311" bullets for the 303 British and other 7.7 types, and Speer's excellent 175-gr. .313" bullets, designed specially for the 7.65 Mauser cartridge. Experience had shown me that powders of medium burning rate worked best in this case size and type of cartridge, so I used 4895, 4064 and Norma 203.

I found it fairly easy to get good groups with all three powders with the .313″ diameter 175-gr. Between 41 and 43 grains of any of them gave me groups of around 2-2.5 inches on centers at 100 yards. Using issue sights and issue barrel bedding, this is about as good as one could do.

The .311″ bullet was something else. By moving the target to 50 yards or so I could keep them all on it, but no charge weight in any of the 3 powders would keep them all in the black for me at this range; and I tried all of them, by half-grain increments from 41 to 45 grains. Conceivably, I could have killed a deer at very close range with this .311″ bullet in the 7.65, but the same could be said of an axe in hand.

With the .308″ bullets I got an 8-foot dispersal at 100 yards. Need more be said?

I tried seating the .308″ and .311″ bullets all the way out, in hopes of attaining a better and more direct seating in the lead and thereby correcting some of the wobble. It did not cut the spread of either. I tried slower- and faster-burning powders, not expecting much and not getting it.

It would appear that bullets closely matching groove diameter will give as good accuracy as throat and bore permit, and that those undersize by .002″ or more will not go in the same place twice.

I don't mean to give the impression that the .311″ bullet won't shoot in *any* 7.65. I advised my friend with the rechambered 1909 to switch to the Speer 180-gr. .311″ bullet, loading it in his '06 cases, and he reports excellent results. He also slugged the bore and came up with a groove diameter of .3123″.

Foreign military rifles and some of our own vary quite a bit in bore-groove diameter. For best results, slug and measure your barrel and keep your bullets within .001″ of groove diameter. ●

Measuring 5-Groove Barrels

Smith and Wesson handguns, many British and foreign guns and other occasional custom guns are made with five grooves and lands. Sometimes chambering reamers are made with five flutes to avoid chattering. In most cases the ordinary micrometer is not capable of accurately measuring them or slugs and casts from barrels. "Tri-mikes" are available for an odd number of points such as 3, 5 or 7. However, they are special and cost about five times as much as ordinarily.

Lead slugs shoved through barrels or casts made of the inside of barrels using chamber-cast metals may be easily measured in the V-block shown above. Make the block about ½″ wide, ⅜″ deep and about ¾″ in length. ⅜″ deep and about ¾″ in length. Dimension C should be carefully determined and then stamped on the block. To find this, place in the V a carefully measured round, such as a short section of drill rod. The diameter of the round is multiplied by 1.1180 to

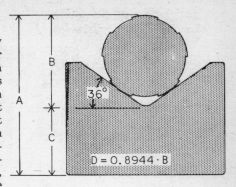

$$D = 0.8944 \cdot B$$

find dimension B for this setup. Use an ordinary micrometer to find A. A minus B is the required fixed dimension C for this block.

The diameter of any other round is found by measuring A and subtracting C to find B. As indicated in the drawing, multiplying B by 0.8944 gives the required diameter. The drawing shows a measurement for groove diameter but the bore diameter is also easily found by turning the slug in the block. Homer S. Powley

---

Slugging a Barrel

First, obtain a short cylinder or round ball of pure soft lead a little bigger than groove diameter, and a flat-ended brass or steel rod a bit longer than the barrel being checked. A short piece of brass rod, say 5″-6″ long, will also be needed, its flat end edges chamfered or radiussed.

Lightly lubricate the bore and the lead slug. Place the slug into the muzzle, then use a light hammer to tap the slug into the barrel for an inch or so. A ring of sheared lead left on the muzzle indicates that initial slug diameter was sufficient to insure getting the slug into intimate groove contact.

Now use the long rod to push the slug through the barrel, catching it on a piece of cloth or cotton to prevent its deformation. A refinement of this technique is to insert the long rod into the barrel from the breech after the slug is into the bore a short way. Hold the long rod firmly against the bottom of the slug, then tap the short brass rod against the slug. This insures complete upsettage or expansion of the slug.

Next, using a micrometer caliper, measure across the "lands," which will give groove dimensions. Use the mike with a gentle touch, for the soft lead slug can be easily compressed. Make several readings to strike an average, using each pair of "lands." This is a simple operation with barrels having an even number of grooves, but an odd-number barrel presents problems. Tri-Mikes can do it, but they're quite expensive. The V-block technique by Homer S. Powley, reproduced here, works well, and it measures bore diameters as well.

Lee military rifle

Diminutive But Deadly

by CLAIR F. REES

The 28 will kill ducks and geese, sure, but it's no wild-fowl gun in anybody's book. But on upland birds—pheasants, quail, woodcock, grouse and partridge—the 28 is just possibly the best gauge going!

Magnum IS A magic word that has captured the imagination of shotgunners and riflemen alike. Guns chambered for elongated shotshells or fat, belted rifle cartridges are the ones currently winning the praises of contemporary gun scribes.

I can't readily find fault with magnums, as two of my favorite upland scatterguns are regularly fed "magnum" shells—stuffed with a full *ounce* of shot. While this doesn't sound too impressive compared to 1¼-ounce 3-inch 20 gauge loads or the 1⅞ ounces of shot obtainable for the 12-gauge magnum, it's a real improvement over the ¾-ounce load that is (or was) standard 28-gauge fare.

However, I won't be able to feed my pet 28s factory shells with "magnum" stamped on their sides much longer, as Winchester-Western has, unfortunately, discontinued its one-ounce loading in this gauge. On the plus side, though, Federal has now standardized on a potent ⅞-ounce "hunting" load, and is now producing it in plastic cases.

Sound pretty tame to you "magnum" lovers? Stick around. You might

not know what you're missing.

I own a pretty fair-sized arsenal of scatterguns, these ranging from featherweight 28s through some twin-tubed 20s, and on up to an 8¼-pound 12 bore that is fed nothing but 3-inch magnums. In addition, I have a fair assortment of standard 12-gauge pumps and doubles, and I keep a couple of guns on hand that digest 410 shells. Even so, what are the guns that spend the most time *out* of the rack during hunting season? A full-choked Remington 11-48 autoloader and a Skeet-choked Hi-Standard pump—both in 28 gauge.

No, I'm not a crank that enjoys toting something different afield for the sheer pleasure of being different. Nor am I a gunshy featherweight (as my wife keeps telling me) who is allergic to recoil. Neither am I a supercrack shot who can drop every bird that gets up—feathered or clay—with a slingshot loaded with boiled rice.

No, I'm simply a slightly lazy scattergunner who likes to tote light, fasthandling guns afield, and who can cheerfully pass up those 50-yard-plus shots that some of my 12-bore-packing companions have trouble resisting.

When I first began experimenting with 28-gauge shotguns not too many years ago, my well-meaning friends

tried to kid me back to sanity. "What's wrong," they would chide, "do your mean, old 12 gauges kick too hard?" One gleeful buddy even offered me a shot at a sitting pintail with the gibe: "That might be your only chance to *kill* a duck this afternoon with that peashooter you're using."

Now these same friends have changed their tune. When I'm hunting pheasants with my Skeet-choked 28, they are more likely to grumble, "If you're going to carry that thing today, try to have the decency to let at least some birds get far enough out that we can shoot occasionally." (I, of course, answer, "But fellas, if I don't shoot fast they're out of range for me!")

My friends would be the last to concede that I am a better shot than they are, and they are right. Almost any of my hunting acquaintances can wipe my eye at Skeet or traps. But they *will* admit that a large percentage of birds that get up within 25 yards or so of my gun now have an excellent chance of ending up in a roasting pan.

Both I and my friends realize that my recently improved skill with a shotgun on upland game is more attributable to the gun than to the shooter. Where I once used a mod-

Author drops mourning doves with 28-gauge Remington 11-48 autoloader in Utah desert.

fied-choked 12-gauge pump for most of my upland work, the switch to an ultra-light open-bored 28 speeded my gun handling, and the wide pattern it throws greatly improved my ability to connect with close-flushing game.

Actually, many hunters have used standard ⅞-ounce and 1-ounce 20-gauge loads on pheasants, grouse and quail for years with excellent results. In fact, the 20 gauge has long been a favorite with upland gunners who recognized that the need for a fast-handling gun was more important than the need for a dense shot pattern at typical upland ranges.

Dropping from a lightweight 20 to an even lighter-weight 28-gauge carries this line of reasoning a step further. It is only logical to assume that a shooter who is fast with a 6½-pound 20 gauge will be even *faster* with a 6-pound 28. With modern factory loadings or hand-brewed fodder, the little-known 28 will perform right along with the best of the non-magnum 20s.

28-Gauge Loads

The following handloads, using Federal plastic cases and Federal 410 primers, have worked well for me in my 28-gauge guns:

10.3 grains of Hi-Skor 700X behind ⅞-oz. of No. 7½ shot in a Remington "Power Piston" plastic wad-cup. Even though the shot column extends past the end of the shot cup (which is designed for ¾-oz. loads), this load gives me even patterns that are deadly on pheasants and grouse. From a full choke, this load patterns approximately 68%, and produces 35-37% spreads from my Skeet-choked 28.

I have made up the same load with both 7½s and 6s, using two ¼-inch Federal felt wads and Federal plastic shot cups (not yet on the market for handloaders, unfortunately) with equally good results. In the "Honey" Bair press I'm using, wad pressures of up to 60 pounds are required to produce good crimps with either type of wad column, with somewhat more pressure required when loading 6s.

Another exceptionally good home-brewed hunting load for the 28 is 13.4 grains of Hercules "Herco" powder pushing a full ounce of 7½s. Again, Federal plastic cases and primers and either Remington "Power Piston" or the Federal felt wad—plastic shot cup combination described above are used. This 1-oz. load produces an exceptionally well-distributed pattern from either of my 28-gauge guns.

A note of warning: These are loads I have worked up for my own hunting needs and should be regarded as *maximum*. Exceeding these loads by only a few tenths of a grain resulted in signs of excessive pressure *when fired from my guns*. Anyone attempting to duplicate these loads (at his own risk!) should start out with something milder, and then work up cautiously.

A less potent handload that I have had good luck with in the field is ¾-oz. of No. 7½ shot in a Remington "Power Piston" one-piece shot cup ahead of 12.5 grains of Hi-Skor 700X. For this handload, I use Remington plastic cases exclusively, with Remington #69 primers.

My current favorite factory loads for my 28-gauge Hi-Standard are the no-longer-produced Winchester "magnums" throwing a full ounce of No. 7½ shot with 2¾ dram equivalents of powder, and the relatively new Federal ⅞-ounce load. I have used both 6s and 7½s in these two loads, but lean toward the latter for the more dense pattern this shot size provides (350 pellets, compared to the 225 6s in the one-ounce loading).

With the Winchester factory loads, the Skeet-choked pump puts an average of 298 No. 7½ pellets in a 30-inch circle at 20 yards, and 191 print in the same circle at 30 yards. A good, even, killing pattern is obtained at both these ranges.

On the other hand, Remington 28-gauge loads throwing ¾-ounce of 6s will give a fair killing pattern with this gun (169 pellets inside the circle) at 20 yards, but at 30 yards and beyond, sizeable holes appear. Obviously, this gun is at its best with the heavier loads, and should only be used at ranges on the shy side of 35 yards (hold it to 25 yards or less with ¾-ounce loads).

While this gun with either Federal or the now-unobtainable magnum Winchester shells is deadly on birds over dogs or in other close-shooting situations, not all upland hunting

These Idaho ringnecks fell to ⅞-ounce of 7½s in Federal's 28-gauge factory loading.

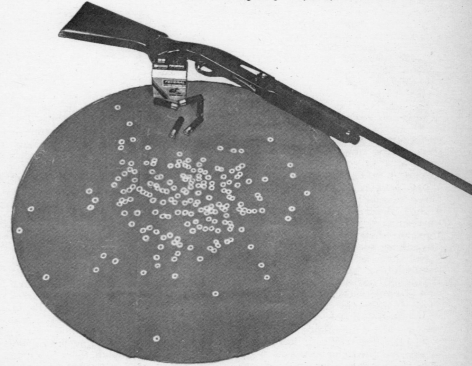

At 20 yards, author's full-choked 28-gauge Remington 11-48 throws pattern that is just beginning to open up with ⅞-ounce of 6s.

falls in that category. When I'm not sure that my shooting will be close to the gun, I uncase my other 28—a slim, trim Remington 11-48 sporting a full-choked 25-inch tube. (Remington now offers both the fine 1100 autoloader and the long-time favorite 870 in 28 gauge—or, if you like, either gun can be had in matched 410/28-gauge sets.)

This gun has done in ducks as well as heavy-bodied sage grouse, and is *the* gun I use for doves. It won't mangle a bird at 25 yards, and it will drop the toughest ringneck ever hatched at 40 yards or slightly beyond—provided I do my part. And as if that weren't enough, I can carry this perfectly balanced little arm by the grip, like a pistol, with the muzzle pointing safely skyward all day long without experiencing muscle fatigue (try *that* with your 7½-pound 12-gauge pumps!).

The 28 on Ducks

As I mentioned, while I regard the 28 gauge as primarily an upland gunner's tool, I have used it successfully on ducks. Loaded with 7/8- or a full ounce of 6s, my full-choked Remington is perfectly adequate on decoyed web-foots.

Until just recently, the 28 gauge had two primary drawbacks as far as the waterfowler was concerned—the first and most serious being its admitted inability to handle suitable concentrations of the heavier shot sizes (4s or larger) needed to make clean kills on geese and other tough species at ranges beyond 35-40 yards. While Remington did offer its 3/4-ounce standard 28-gauge load in size 4 shot, the pattern this ridiculous load prints at 40 yards has holes in it that an adult canvasback could fly through unscathed.

No, there is just no way to make the 28 into a long-range goose killer. If you get hooked on the 28 for ducks over decoys, and you think a stray goose might accidentally wander by, your only solution is to lug a second scattergun — preferably one stuffed with 1 7/8-ounce magnum loads of 2s or 4s—into the blind with you. Many waterfowlers (including me) regularly have such two-gun combinations on hand when hunting ducks near goose flyways.

The second drawback has been pretty well solved by the new Federal plastic hunting load. Until its introduction in late 1969 there was no suitable factory 28-gauge load available for waterfowl in anything but paper cases. (Remington has marketed plastic-hulled 28-gauge ammo for years, but only in the marginal 3/4-ounce loading.) Paper Winchester and Federal cases soaked up moisture like mad to the point that they wouldn't feed through the actions of pumps or autoloaders. I can remember at least two ocasions when I had to set damp shells aside for several weeks until they dried out enough to again assume their normal circumference.

But while the 28 may not be the best choice for the duck or honker hunter, it will give the other gauges a real run for the money where upland gunning is concerned.

Ideal Upland Gun

The great majority of all shotgunning in the U.S. is done with 12-gauge guns but, while there's no denying the versatility of the 12 bore for all-round use, it is not the best possible choice for the upland gunner.

In the first place, most 12s weigh some 7 pounds, with many models closer to 8 pounds loaded. While a 7- or 7½-pound scattergun may not seem heavy at daybreak, you're likely to wish it had wheels by the end of the day.

In contrast, 28-gauge guns are available at less than 6 pounds, carry like a feather all day long. Another advantage of these lighter guns is an almost inherently better balance and superfast handling characteristics. You'll find yourself getting on target 5 yards or so closer in, with better scores almost sure to result—if the choking is right.

Big-bore devotees are quick to point out that they can stuff their 12-gauge field pieces with anywhere from a mere ounce of shot on up to 1½ ounces, and more. True, but such heavier shot charges are not only unnecessary for most upland hunting, they actually handicap the gunner shooting over dogs or hunting in tight cover.

Even assuming that the hunter has chosen a relatively open choke, the dense pattern resulting from 1¼ or more ounces of shot is almost guaranteed to badly mangle a close-flushing bird centered at 20 yards or less. If you don't believe you ever shoot birds at that close range, try pacing off a few kills the next time you hunt pheasants or quail over dogs.

The 12 gauge (with 1¼-ounce Express loads) also falls down in another area. In addition to being overly tired from lugging his oversized gun over hill and dale all day, the 12-bore owner will have a tender spot at the junction of his right arm and shoulder that's going to turn a nice shade of purple by mid-afternoon. This is likely to result in much slower gun handling—and more misses—as the buf-

Top—Author"s full-choked Remington 11-48 autoloader in 28 gauge. Bottom—Skeet-choked Hi-Standard pump is also a 28.

feted nimrod becomes more and more solicitous of his bruised anatomy each time he mounts his gun.

It's true that a 12-gauge owner can tame his gun somewhat by using watered-down loads, thus enabling him to shoot comfortably and get the same kind of patterns that can be obtained with a similarly choked 20 or 28 gauge. But why tote that extra 1-1½ pounds of shooting iron afield unnecessarily?

The diminutive 28 makes no claims to the title of all-round shotgun—but this does not lessen its luster for those who want more than one lone bird-gun in their shooting cabinets. For any shotgun gauge that lays claim to that elusive title must, by necessity, be merely a compromise between the several gauges one would need to have in an ideal battery suitable for *all* types of scattergunning.

The 28 will kill ducks—but it really isn't a duck gun. Under the right circumstances it will kill geese—but it certainly couldn't be called a goose gun. However, it will kill pheasants, quail, woodcock, grouse and partridge —so well, in fact, that one could regard the 28 gauge as just possibly the *best* available choice for the upland gunner. I do! ●

I'VE NEVER SEEN it 50° below—or slept out in such temperature—and that's always saddened me a bit. I've wanted to ever since I was a kid fascinated by writers as different as Robert Service and Vilhjalmur Stefansson. One winter in the late '40s I camped out for a week when the mercury dropped to about minus 25 at night—no tent or heat, just my sleeping bag and an old quilt folded lengthwise for a mattress on the powdery snow, with a thick wool sweater (iced up solid in the morning) over the facehole of my mummy bag. You get satisfaction out of a stunt like that. Just to know you can take on one of Nature's most miserable conditions, and survive, is reassuring. When the action is technically unnecessary (as this was; I could have gone home at any time) the satisfaction is mostly mental and sometimes a trifle hard to maintain when crawling *out* of that bag into 50-some degrees of frost. Still, I did it and I enjoyed it, and the experience, plus many other similar if less extreme ones, is relevant to situations in which any hunter in our northern latitudes may find himself.

Survival under adverse fall and winter conditions has been made routine for many years now by one piece of equipment, the down-filled sleeping bag. There's something magic about a 5-lb. item which can be stuffed into a sack scarcely bigger than a bowling ball, then pulled out and fluffed up into a nearly weightless envelope which lets you dream your way through an Arctic blizzard in luxurious comfort.

No sleeping bag *produces* any heat, of course. The body itself does that by the metabolic use of food. By controlling the rate at which body heat is released to the atmosphere, a comfortable body temperature can be maintained.

*From *The Shooting of Dan McGrew* by Robert W. Service.

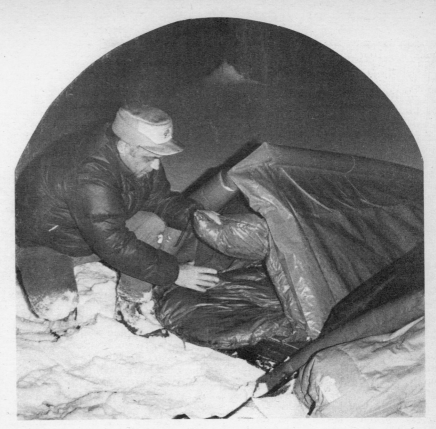

Sleeping warm in the cold and snow is no problem if the right bag is used.

THE SLEEPING BAG by BOB BELL

Survival under tough winter conditions was made possible—even enjoyable—many years ago with the advent of the down-filled sleeping bag. That's still the best material, but robes have changed in several ways—they're lighter, less bulky and more heat-efficient. Here's how bags are made, how they work, and tips on selecting one.

About three-fourths of the body's heat loss is via conduction, convection and radiation, the remainder through evaporation—sweating, insensate perspiration, and warmed water vapor lost through respiration. When sleeping outdoors in winter, sweating is rarely a problem, and nothing can be done to prevent the other two forms of evaporation; so most of our efforts are directed toward the first three causes of heat loss.

Conduction is reduced by removing the body from direct contact with a colder object. Convection is lessened through "deadening" the movement of air around the body by wrapping it in insulation. Air tends to cling to the body's surface in a layer about one-eighth inch thick; therefore any substance that breaks up its convection flow at that interval or less will serve as an insulator. In a practical sense, though, some insulators are better than others. Not only is dead air important, but also weight, adaptation to body movements, resistance to wetting (which increases conductivity and can alter the material's form itself), etc. Radiation is a less important problem, for the only heat which can be lost this way is that which escapes through the insulation.

Down Excels

The best insulation is the one which supplies the greater thickness of dead air with the lightest weight. High-grade goose or duck down best meets these requirements. Down is an incredibly light, fluffy, quill-less bundle of filaments which grows on the underside of geese and ducks. A magnified view of a down cluster resembles a light-colored octopus having a near-countless number of tentacles extending outward in all directions. It is cellular in structure, thus dispels moisture by "breathing." High resilience allows it to be compressed into a small volume, yet it quickly expands to its outer limits when released; at full expansion or "loft," an infinite number of tiny interstices trap dead air and thus insulate.

Down varies greatly in quality. The best comes from those mature birds that spend a lot of time in northern latitudes. Older birds have larger down clusters than young birds, thus have greater capacity for holding dead air. Most down comes from geese or ducks killed for food in northern Europe and Asia. The down is a by-product.

The best down nowadays has a lofting power of about 700 cubic inches

Lightweight, moderate weather backpackers' bag holds 1½-2 pounds of down, stuffs into small package.

per ounce. Some of it generates less than 400 cu. in./oz., and the average is probably 500-600, so the insulating power of one batch can be almost 100% better than another. Several decades ago, down with 800 cu. in. lofting power was available, but the current tendency to kill younger birds, making them more palatable, has resulted in poorer down.

Few regulations affect this industry. The Federal Trade Commission defines down as a substance being at least 80% down and down fiber, with up to 16% waterfowl feather fiber, 2% non-waterfowl feathers, and 2% miscellaneous. Some bag builders use down with as little as 8-10% feathers—usually termed "garment" grade—while others use the legal 20% of feathers. Such labels as "Prime," "Triple-A" or maybe "Super-Duper" down mean nothing in a legal sense.

Despite the unequaled performance of top quality down as an insulator, there are times when other materials should be considered. If the bag will often be exposed to wetness, down is not ideal. It clumps up when soaked, destroying its insulating qualities, and is extremely hard to dry. Here, one of the man-made polyesters is superior. None can match down's lofting quality, but the polyesters are less affected by wetness, they dry much faster and they're much less expensive. They are consistent in performance from lot to lot, rather than varying as down does. They're machine washable (down is not), and non-allergenic—a debatable point with down.

Dupont says that with equal pressure a Fiberfill II bag will compress about 90% as much as a goose down bag of equal weight (if the down bag stuffs to a 10" diameter for packing the Fiberfill II will go to 11"). Dupont

also says that 1.4 lbs. of Fiberfill II will give equal thickness of insulation to 1 lb. of goose down; thus, with equivalent construction and fabrics a bag containing 2 lbs. of down could be replaced by one with 2.8 lbs. of Fiberfill II.

The U.S. Army Quartermaster gives the following guide to insulation needed for sleeping comfort at various temperatures:

Temperature	Insulation
40 F	1.5"
20 F	2.0"
0 F	2.5"
−20 F	3.0"
−40 F	3.5"
−60 F	4.0"

These specifications are far from exact. To begin with they are for sleeping in still air, as in a tent. Wind reduces insulating efficiency by blowing away the thin layer of warm air which builds up around a heat-producing machine such as the body. Much also depends on the individual. Due to variations in metabolism, some persons "sleep warm," others "sleep cold." Despite these qualifications I'm dubious about the accuracy of this chart, particularly at the lower levels. A number of readily available bags have lofts exceeding 4", yet the comfort ranges claimed by their makers, based on testing, are usually in the −20 to −30 bracket.

Bag Construction

Ripstop nylon is used for the inner and outer shells of most down bags. It is available in light weights (1.9 oz./sq. yd. is most commonly used), it's durable and down proof, nearly windproof and water repellent, yet it permits the moisture (about 1½ pints per day, not including perspiration); which is constantly given off by the body, to pass through to the atmosphere. It is this insensate moisture which makes it impractical to use waterproof material for the sleeping bag cover. While that would be fine for keeping out rain and wet snow, it would at the same time keep in body moisture, and the bag's insulation would soon be soaked. (Some outdoorsmen have experimented with bags using the "thermos bottle" principle of the Korean insulated boot—insulation between two layers of waterproof material—but I've never tried it.)

Down is not simply stuffed between the inner and outer shells of a bag. It migrates quickly if unrestricted, moving away from weight or pressure and leaving uninsulated areas. The simplest control method is to sew the inner and outer shells together into tubes, each having its own filler. This prevents lateral movement, but most of the down is soon concentrated in the ends, leaving none beneath the body. Horizontal stitching at intervals, which converts the tubes to rectangles, reduces this movement, but is still inefficient because there is no insulation along the thread lines. Sewn-through bags, therefore, are suitable for summer-to-early-fall use only.

The next step, usually, is to use two sewn-up layers, offsetting them so that the seams of one bag overlay the thick portion of the other layer. Called "lamination," this efficient design was used in the GI double mummy bag, but the extra fabric layers increase weight.

Internal baffling is a more advanced approach—sections of material—nylon or nylon downproof netting are best—are sewn between the two shells, usually crosswise. This gives better down control; the baffles sewn in at 4"-6" intervals. If sewn in at right angles to the shell surfaces, the design is called "box" or "I-beam" baffling. The loft of the down keeps the shells separated but the vertical baffling seams provide no insulation so there are "cool" lines throughout.

Box baffling is improved by offsetting seams so that the top of each baffle, where it is sewn to the shell, aligns with down filler; this design, which is called a "slant wall" or "parallelogram" channel, is used in many top-grade bags, particularly if light weight is wanted.

Most efficient of all is the V-tube, originated by Woods for their Arctic-series bags years ago. This, viewed from the side, shows a series of interlocking triangles. This amount of baffling adds some weight and is diffi-

Sleeping Bag Construction

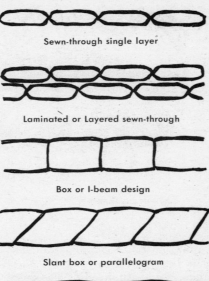

Sewn-through single layer

Laminated or Layered sewn-through

Box or I-beam design

Slant box or parallelogram

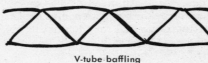

V-tube baffling

cult to install, but gives maximum control over the down. Some bags have a full length baffle, along the side opposite the zipper, to keep down from shifting between the top and bottom of the bag.

Thermos System

For decades both inner and outer shells were cut to the same dimension. Then someone applied the thermos-bottle principle and made the outer shell larger—a "differential" cut—asserting that this would avoid compression of the down, prevent cold spots if a knee or elbow pressed hard against the inner shell, etc. This design is popular with some, not liked by others. The main criticism is that differentially cut bags seem to "stand away" from the body rather than snuggling up to it, making more internal volume to be heated and not supplying that cozy feeling familiar to many. Anyone used to the original style should try a differential-cut bag before buying; it gives a decidedly different feel.

A method of opening the bag at the side is highly desirable, if not necessary. Without one you must wriggle in, snakelike, from the top, an impractical procedure even if lack of a closure does reduce weight and cost and adds warmth. Some bags open only for about a third of their length, but most have fasteners, usually zippers, extending the full length and perhaps across the bottom. Most of

today's zippers are nylon; it feels warmer than metal, weighs less, and is less destructive of fabric if snagged. Zippers should open from either end, to facilitate ventilation when the bag is too warm, and have grasping tabs inside, as well as outside, for convenience of operation.

If memory is correct the Woods 3-Star bag used to be offered with Lift-the-Dot fasteners as an optional closure; they're still used on the 4-Star's external zipper covering. At times I'm tempted to consider such a fastener, or even heavy duty snaps, in place of a zipper. When a zipper goes bad—and occasionally they do—you've got problems.

Zippers leak air so they should be backed up by a wide, insulated weather-sealing flap. Otherwise, whenever you move in the bag, you'll pump heated air out through the zipper teeth and cold air in.

Adding a hood to the bag was probably the most significant advance in basic design ever made. It makes an almost completely sealed unit out of the bag, eliminating the entrance of cold air which the body must heat, and it keeps the head warm. This is vitally important, for the head gets first call on the body's warm blood. If the head is exposed to cold the blood supply to the extremities will be reduced to keep the vital organs, particularly the brain, warm. If there is an excess of body heat, it is radiated off primarily via the head. Controlling the temperature of this part of the body thus is an important function of a sleeping bag, and the hood—which is adjustable by a drawstring to tightly enclose or leave the head fully exposed—makes this possible.

A further refinement is a down-filled "collar" sewn into the top of some bags. Enclosing the shoulders, it reduces drafts even when the hood is not used.

Stuffing Stuff

Many sleeping bag models are offered in several lengths and widths, to best fit prospective buyers who also come in assorted sizes. The more snugly a bag fits the easier it is to heat by body warmth, so the maker usually recommends a bag whose internal length is a few inches longer than the sleeper's height. However, there is one big advantage in having a longer bag: you can take stuff to bed with you and keep it from freezing. This might be a canteen (neophyte campers will be surprised at how hard it is to get a drink in real winter weather) or your boots (anyone who

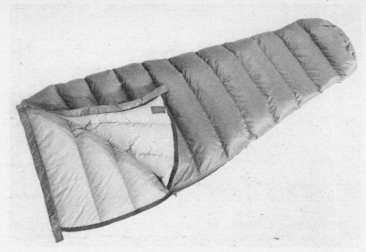

Eddie Bauer 16-oz. mummy bag.

has struggled to work his feet into brick-stiff leather boots on a below-zero morning will recognize the sense of dropping them into a plastic bag and shoving them to the bottom of his sleeper before going to bed). You also take stuff to bed to dry it out—socks and underwear, primarily. Sure, the moisture it gives off makes it harder for the bag to keep you warm, but most hunters have bags with a surplus of insulation anyway, so it might as well be used. After a few days in the bush I usually have an assortment of stuff in the sack with me. A bit smelly, perhaps, but what difference does that make?

Because the sleeper's weight compresses the filler in the bottom half of the bag, it loses insulating ability; therefore some kind of mattress is necessary to reduce heat transfer to the ground, which is often colder than the air. The balsam bough bed of Horace Kephart's day is an ecological no-no now, though there's never been a more delightful and aromatic experience than snoozing on a foot-thick, properly "shingled" mattress of evergreen tips. As with the sleeping bag, the trick is to get something that provides comfort under adverse conditions, yet not too heavy or bulky for transporting. For years the air mattress was the best answer. It was comfortable, when not over-inflated, but due to unrestricted air flow it was cold in winter. Too, there were always the problems of getting air into it and keeping it there.

Most of today's campers favor a foam pad—open-cell or closed-cell. The open-cell, of comparatively soft polyurethane, is non-waterproof and requires a cover to keep it from absorbing moisture. It's readily avail-

able in thicknesses from 1½" to 3" and is comfortable. The closed-cell, typified by the Ensolite pad, is another application of the thermos-bottle principle. A polyethylene foam from ⅛" to 9/16" thick, it's essentially non-compressible and is waterproof. It insulates as well as two or three times its thickness of open-cell foam, but it's not as comfortable.

Several years ago a fire destroyed much of my family camping equipment, including 4 down bags, so I had to start looking at currently-available items. It occurred to me that I might be able to borrow representative samples from different makers, use them under normal hunting conditions and report my findings.

I soon had an assorted dozen bags, and I could have had more. However, there's a point at which things become impractical.

I intended to use these various bags on as many hunting trips as possible, with winter conditions as adverse as I could get, the program to last a year. As it turns out, I've now wrapped up 4 winters with them—5 hunting trips to Canada and one to Alaska, with as many as 4 hunters using different models. (I wanted all the personal comment possible.) They've also been used on a number of hunts in the Rockies and in the worst weather we've had in central Pennsylvania in the last few winters. Admittedly, we didn't experience the extremes of the Yukon, but at different times it got down to minus 10 or so, with strong winds, and that's about as bad as most hunters face. In all of this a Woods Trail Bed of 1½" thickness was used; sometimes I had a shelter over me, sometimes I just put the foam pad down on the snow and went

to sleep looking at the stars.

Bauer Bags

I picked the warmest regular-length heavy duty Kara Koram available at the time. A mummy, its total weight of 7¼ lbs. includes 4½ lbs. of goose down in overlapping tubes, for 10" total loft (5" top and 5" bottom), its comfort rating of minus-20.

Since the U. S. Army Quartermaster lists 4" of insulation as enough for comfortable sleeping at −60 (a statement I view with a touch of doubt), I asked how Bauer determined comfort ratings. Here's their system: they test incoming down in their own lab, field test all models and also have sleeping bags tested at the University of Wisconsin in Green Bay, Wisconsin. Male and female students, chosen because they represent various types of sleepers (from "cold" to "warm"), use assorted Bauer bags under precisely controlled environmental conditions. Temperature measurements are recorded for 6 points on the body surface and for the mouth. From such testing, during which the bags are used as they would be normally, with some insulative protection beneath, an average comfort range for each is determined.

This is a far more scientific approach than I had the equipment to duplicate but, knowing outdoorsmen like to have personalized comments on equipment, I used the Kara Koram bag a lot. One moose hunt in Ontario was particularly miserable; it rained almost constantly. With no heat inside the tent everything eventually got quite damp, which in many ways is worse than cold. The Kara Koram was at times too warm, but the two-way zipper, located top center, made ventilation easy. By opening the foot end, I could expose my feet at will—a big help in cooling off. At other times the KK bag was more than comfortable at below-zero temps.

The Bauer Skyliner tested is a rectangular model, its slant-box tubes running lengthways, with zippers along each side. Its bottom extends beyond the top, at the upper end, the extension zipping into a

Gerry's Cascade Sleeper is all nylon fabrics, 100% white goose down filled with double quilt construction.

triangular hood when conditions necessitate. With 4½ lbs. of down (total weight of 7¾ lbs.), it is rated to minus 30. It hasn't got that cold in these parts lately, but I've slept in this Skyliner, without any other protection, in −8 temperature when the wind was blowing like the hammers of hell—the wind-chill factor may have made it 30 below or worse—and was perfectly comfortable. There was something awesome about this experience. I could feel the wind pressing hard against the bag, hear it howling through the trees—but inside the warmth seemed to curl around me in tendrils when I moved, sort of a toasty warmth that didn't seem reasonable under the conditions.

Wes Bower, a hunting pal, used this bag on that moose hunt mentioned, as did Lou Hoffman on a Colorado elk hunt, our camp just under 10,000 feet. Both men were snug as the proverbial bedbug in a buffalo

robe. After a quarter-century's use of the Army Arctic mummy bag I admit partiality for that basic design, but there's a lot to be said for a good rectangular model, one that gives you room to sprawl and turn at will.

The current Skyliner has a detachable hood and may be used as a bed comforter.

Bauer's 4-way Ultralight and 16-ounce Mummy were designed as liners for other bags. The Ultralight is a slightly tapered rectangle with a zipper that allows opening it into a comforter; with Mummy I have is a true bag—no zipper at all; you crawl into it via the top opening and, if desired, tighten that around your neck with a drawstring. (The current model has a short zipper.) Each, old or new, contains a pound of down and the shells are ripstop nylon. Either adds 20 degrees of warmth to any other bag.

Though meant to serve as cold weather

liners, they're also good summer-weight sleepers. With the 4-Way at 38 ozs., 31 for the Mummy, their utility for warm weather backpackers is obvious. I've used them a good bit. In conjunction with a foam pad the 4-Way was comfortable into the high 30s, the tighter-fitting slightly-thicker Mummy to about freezing.

Seattle Quilt (Comfy)

Seattle Quilt, founded by Charles and Jack Miller in 1915, made down-filled comforters and pillows. Five years later, in response to the needs of workmen building the Seward-to-Fairbanks railroad in Alaska, Charles Miller took a down comforter, covered it with canvas and attached harness snaps for fasteners. That was the first Comfy sleeping bag. Not very sophisticated, maybe, but it worked and, as time went on, designs improved until today's Comfy

This Comfy Quilt, a down-filled type, proved highly satisfactory on Bell's blizzard test.

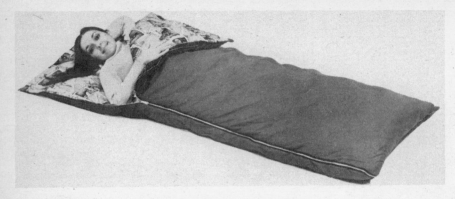

Wenzel's Yellowstone bag is a Dacron-filled type. These are less expensive than those carrying down insulation, yet offer good utility in moderate temperatures. The latest polyester fibers, as used in Wenzel bags, are much improved over earlier forms.

bags are considered top-quality by any standards. Seattle Quilt made many bags for the Quartermaster Corps during WW II and, like Bauer, has outfitted many expeditions.

Starting in 1947 Seattle Quilt had an independent research team conduct carefully-controlled tests of sleeping bag materials, such as those organized by Bauer. A test program continues today.

The Himalaya model I've been using, a long 5½-lb. mummy, holds 3¼ lb. of down, and an ACT (average comfort temperature) rating of −10. (The regular length weighs only 4¾ lbs., which should make it acceptable to any winter backpacker.)

I don't know whether I'm a "warm" sleeper or if these ACT ratings are conservative, but I'd guess this bag is warmer than specified. One night last winter I looked out at my backyard, where gale winds were blowing hard kernels of snow into opaque sheets. Almost a foot of snow already covered the ground. It wasn't a fit night for man nor beast, but Terry, being an understanding wife who thinks that Uncle John deserves the most from his writers, sweetly suggested, "Why don't you call Jim to come over and try out some sleeping bags with you?"

"Good idea," I said, knowing Bashline, outdoor editor of the *Philadelphia Inquirer,* would have too much sense for that.* "You gotta be kidding," he said when I called. I agreed, and a short time later was getting ready for bed—inside—when the phone rang. It was Jim. "I can't get up the hill," he said. "If you'll come get me in the Jeep, we'll do it."

Well, we did it. With a plastic tube tent for each of us, we crawled into the mummies. My only problem was that after awhile I was *too* warm. The Himalaya model is fairly slim at the foot end, which

means less space to heat, and despite the hard snow swirling around the open end of the plastic shelter, I had to keep the hood unsnugged. In the morning the thermometer on the sunny side of the garage registered +2 degrees. I'm not sure what it was during the night, but it was considerably colder than that, yet this Comfy Himalaya was warmer than necessary.

Gerry Bags

Friend Bashline, on the night just described, was comfortable in Gerry's best, their Expedition Sleeper—which seems to be Jim's favorite, maybe because it fits him well. He's a tall guy, and this is a long roomy bag.

Gerry has been, for many years, a recognized leader in the development of lightweight, efficient gear for outdoorsmen. The Expedition Sleeper exemplifies their design philosophy. Total weight is only 5 ¼ lbs., with 57 ozs. of goose down enclosed. That leaves just 27 ozs. for the two shells, baffling, 70″ zipper, draft tube and hood cord. No easy job when you're building a bag that will enclose a 6′ 7″ sleeper. Gerry says this bag is warm to −40, which should take in any circumstances a hunter will encounter.

Herter

Herter's Hudson Bay Ultralight Model Kodiak is recommended by them for use in the Arctic, at high altitude, and for outdoor winter sleeping. This 5-lb. mummy bag holds 3 lbs. of goose down in overlapping V tubes. A half-length zipper is installed atop the nylon shells.

When this bag arrived it was tightly compressed and apparently had been so for a long time. It took several days before it reached full loft but it's now okay. Except when it's necessary to stuff one tightly for a trip, I don't compress any bag for a long period—it is harmful.

I've never had a chance to use this bag in an Arctic situation, but I've slept in it at close to zero, and it performed well.

Woods

I had been corresponding with George Hill, manager of Woods Bag & Canvas Co.'s Ogdensburg, N.Y., plant and, when I told him Wes Bower and I would be passing through there on our way to a moose hunt in Quebec, he suggested we stop in. It was October 9, 1972, and late evening when we arrived, but that was no problem as far as George was concerned; he took us through the large frame building where the world-famed Woods sleeping bags are made, showing us the various operations, bales of raw down, different bags and clothing, etc. It was sort of spooky wandering through the shadowy old building at midnight, realizing that out of these rooms had come the Woods Arctic 3-Star bags used by such explorers as Admiral Richard E. Byrd, who spent months alone in the Antarctic; Roald Amundsen, the discoverer of the South Pole; Sir George Hubert Wilkins, Father Hubbard, Ernest Hemingway* and Will Rogers.

Hill had offered to lend me a bag for the moose hunt, a brand new design based on a friend's suggestion, suitable for varying temperatures. George had spent much time working out the complicated zipper arrangement. Basically a rectangular 3-layer bag, the user could sleep under one or two layers, according to the warmth needed. Viewed from the upper end, the edges of the layers have a Z appearance, with nylon zippers joining all edges and running across the bottom. The layout of the zippers—which made the design complicated—is such that the bag can be re-zipped into a conventional style for two persons. Drawstrings close the open ends when necessary. With a total down weight of 3½ lbs., the sleeper can have 2⅓ lbs. of down over him or as little as 1⅙ lbs. This makes it a chilly-to-cold-weather bag, a bit too warm for summer.

Naturally I couldn't pass up the chance to be the first hunter to use a bag so new it didn't even have a name. Tentatively called the Mount Rossi, it was finally cataloged as the Woods All-Star. It has a comfort rating of −15, a figure I feel is conservative.

I took that new design to moose country and used it for a week of wet-snowy weather. To come back after a day in the bush, soaked to the skin, ravenous, cold, and grab a belt of Scotch, devour a hot meal and crawl into that sack gave me a feeling of pure luxury that I've rarely encountered. One layer on top was plenty, and I just seemed to sink into the double layer beneath until I was engulfed in down so voluptuous it seemed sinful. That was the only trip I used that bag, but I remember it with fondness.

Two other Woods bags were used over a 4-year period. I'd asked for a 4-Star, want-

---

*This is typical Bell nonsense, putting the onus on his long-suffering wife for this hare-brained idea. Bob must have mesmerized Bashline, ordinarily a sensible fellow.   *Ed.*

*The Woods 3-Star, incidentally, is perhaps equally well known as the locale of one of the best known love scenes in American literature, the famous "sleeping bag" episode of Robert Jordan and Maria in Hemingway's *For Whom the Bell Tolls.*

Woods Arctic Series "All Season" robes come in a variety of sizes and down-weight fills, but aren't light weight.

Wenzel's Catskill bag carries a fill of Dacron.

Woods Pac-Lite bags are offered in 5 versions, holding from one pound of northern goose down to one having 2½ pounds.

ing to try the top of the line, and for a spring/fall model. The latter was their 1¾-lb. V-tube Mount Blanc. It's a modified mummy, plenty wide at the bottom for foot movement, with a full-length Delrin zipper for easy ventilation and a hood for cold weather. Total weight, 3¼ lbs.

Besides considerable use in Pennsylvania, I took this bag, plus the 16-oz. Bauer liner, to Alaska's southern coast in September and north of Blind River, Ontario, in October. (As it turned out, I slept on top of the liner, but it was good to know I had it.) A roomy, well-made unit, the Mt. Blanc is good for chilly fall temperatures.

The highly developed Arctic 4-Star is rated to −60, but I don't know how to test that. It's heavy and it's durable. Brad Angier told me he'd slept in a 3-Star almost every night for 30 years; the 4-Star is basically the same bag with another pound of down. This is the sort of outfit you buy when you move into the northern Canadian bush, build a cabin and plan to stay forever. It's not a backpacker's rig. The 34×78 size I used weighs 18½ lbs., the 40×84 size goes 21.

Besides the down (4¼ lbs. in the smaller bag, 5¼ in the big one, distributed through V tubes with Harwood patent equalizer to prevent shifting), the 4-Star has a virgin wool Kersey blanket zipped inside, an extension of which prevents shoulder drafts, a zipper-attached hood, full-length Delrin zipper backed by a down weather seal inside and covered by an external Lift-the-Dot fastened flap. The cover is polyester/cotton, treated to repel water. A nice touch is a zippered "personal pocket" inside, for wallet or whatever. There's a pocket for a mattress too—common in rectangular bags but missing in mummy models.

I haven't used this 4-Star as much as I'd like. It goes on most of my trips but so does my ol' hunting buddy/gunsmith Al Wardrop. He has sort of built up squatter's rights. The Woods 4-Star needs little to be said here. It's simply a great bag.

Dacron Bags

To be honest, I've used down bags too long (I got my first one from the Alaska Sleeping Bag Co. in 1939) to be completely sold on manmade fillers. Yet I know the new polyester fibers have many outstanding qualities and will improve even more as development continues.

Choosing a well-made polyester bag can also be complicated. Whereas down is made up of independent clusters which can be blown into tubes, the artificial fillers are fiber masses formed into battings. To keep them properly positioned around the sleeper, these batts are normally sewed to at least one of the shells. If sewed only along the edges the batts will eventually loosen and collect in the bottom of the bag when hung up to dry or whatever. Each sewn-through seam is a line of poor insulation, of course, so such bags are essentially summer weights. An improved system uses two layers of batting with offset seams, one layer sewn to the outer shell, the other to the inner.

A better system of installing manmade fillers is in overlapping or "shingled" batts which are sewn together to give a double layer of insulation. In the best bags the inner and outer shells are fastened together with nylon netting, to take strain off the filler.

Coleman

Some years ago, wanting a bag for spring and fall use, I decided to get a polyester model. Thayne Smith, then of Coleman, advised a rectangular one, suggesting I might as well have the extra room since maximum warmth wouldn't be necessary. It was good advice. The model I chose has 5 lbs. of Improved Dacron 88 polyester fiberfill, full-length baffled zipper, and a cotton flannel lining.

I've used this bag on one rainy spring bear hunt on the French River, Ontario, and for many chilly nights in my home state. Friends have borrowed it for elk hunts in Idaho, moose hunts in Quebec, and a young warm-blooded Boy Scout found it suitable for a Christmas campout. Everything considered, it's a good outfit.

Wenzel

When my teen-age daughter wanted to do some summer camping I got her Wenzel's Sierra model, a rectangular bag insulated with 3 lbs. of Improved Dacron 88. She's used it on many occasions and I've borrowed it several times. It has a full-length zipper, cotton poplin cover and cotton flannel liner, which makes a warm-feeling surface. Bags of this weight are essentially summer models. Wenzel uses their Bonded-Plus process on some bags, including this Sierra, to lock insulation in place without quilting.

Those who have several polyester "summer" bags may find it possible, and money saving, to combine two of them for winter use. This Wenzel, a few inches narrower than the Coleman, fits perfectly inside it, and putting the inner bag's zipper toward the closed side of the outer bag helps prevent air leakage. This particular combo is suitable to zero or so, which takes in most winter conditions the sportsman will face. Such rigs are especially useful in a permanent camp, where weight is no problem.

Cleaning the Bag

Like anything else, sleeping bags get soiled with extended use. Opinions vary, even among manufacturers, on the best way of cleaning them. Everyone agrees that so long as minor sponging will do the job, nothing more extensive should be carried out. Dry cleaning can completely ruin a down bag if the wrong chemical solvent is used. . . *and if the solvent isn't completely aired away before use, it can kill you in your sleep.* I suppose there are places which properly dry clean bags and air them till they're safe for sleeping, but I don't know who they are or what they use. If you want to dry clean yours, ask the maker for recommendations—but, and before you use the bag, air it yourself until there's no smell at all when your head is inside.

I wash my bags. This is a good way to ruin them if you're careless, but the smell of mild soap won't kill you. *Never wash a bag in a machine of any kind.* Water-soaked down is unbelievably heavy, and tumbling it in a machine will tear out the baffling, ruining the bag. Do it this way—put enough warm water in your bathtub to submerge the bag, then work up suds with a mild soap—*not a detergent,* which usually removes the natural oil from the down—and knead gently. You might have to drain, rinse and repeat the process several times, pressing the rinse water out gently.

When satisfied the bag is clean, and most of the water is pressed out, work your hands underneath and lift it out of the tub. Don't just grab it and jerk—that will tear out the baffling for sure. If the weather is sunny and you've got lots of time, air dry it on the lawn. It's quicker to use a large commercial tumble drier set at the lowest heat possible. Throw in a pair of clean, laceless sneakers to help break up any down that clumps.

For polyesters, follow the bag-maker's instruction. Many of these are machine-washable, but those with poorly fastened batting are not up to rough handling.

Close To Perfect

No sleeping bag is perfect; none ever will be. Conditions vary too much even when only one man on a single trip is involved. The trick is to choose the best compromise, the one that covers average conditions well and, if possible, can be adapted to extremes. The hunter, who for various reasons must often remain in the bush when a backpacker might call it quits, should err a bit on the side of warmth, so he can cope with unexpected temperature drops and go on functioning. My personal choice is a two-bag combination, a modern version of the WW II double featherdown unit that served so well (and which was the bag used in the opening scene of this article). Used with a 1½" foam pad, a current design mummy insulated with 2½ lbs. of top-quality down is comfortable to zero or a bit below. Inserting Bauer's 16-oz. Mummy liner takes it down to about −25. That's as good as the old GI outfit, but total weight is only 6½ lbs.—half of the GI double. Such a rig has complete versatility—the liner for summer use, the outer unit for fall and normal winter weather, both together for long trips or severe winters. ●

FIREARMS

"IDEAL"
BULL'S-EYE.

AND THE ENGLISH LANGUAGE

Millions of Americans know nothing about guns and shooting, yet their everyday speech is liberally larded with terms and phrases deriving from those fields.

by EDWARD DAMON

ANY ACTIVITY AS familiar as shooting invariably contributes colorful and highly descriptive terms to our common language. Without these easily-understood contributions our language would be much less interesting and direct. Some words and terms have already been made legitimate by dictionary acceptance; others will either die or be accepted and defended a half-century from now as the purest of English.

Some people will tell you that they know absolutely nothing about guns; they've never shot one and wouldn't know one gun from another. Their conversation, however, makes such frequent use of common gun terms that they sound like experts. The following glossary of gun terms is illustrative:

Aim Transposed now to our efforts to follow a single objective, keep a goal in sight, or have a purpose for action that we can understand.

Ammunition Whatever you have you need; words, arguments, power, or money.

Annie Oakley A free pass. A punched, free ticket, referring to Annie's bullet holes shot in a card.

Armed...with the facts...to the teeth, from the legendary knife-in-teeth pirate boarding party. To win arguments, try combining the two.

Arsenal Generally the repository for arms in large quantity; now, anything from two guns up. Also, anything you have a lot of—arguments, pitching curves, tricks—indicates variety.

Bad Shot Missed. Applies to pool, bowling, archery, or a losing argument.

Bag From game bag. To catch, sell, obtain.

Bang Off (Eng.) Go now.

Barker A gun. From circus barker, who makes loud noises.

Battle Lines A controversial lineup of forces. Used in court, around the bridge table, and traditionally in politics.

Big Gun The boss; anyone with power or authority at the top.

Big Shot Very important person. Sometimes derogatory.

Blunderbuss A stupid person. Misuse of the word, blunder, derived from (Dutch) *donderbus*—thunderbox.

Bombarded Today's use involves compliments or insults.

Both Barrels What you get on arriving home too late without a valid excuse. Works also after forgetting important birthdays, anniversaries, etc.

Bullet Head A derogatory term suggesting sectional density instead of external design.

Bullet Toed Applies to modern shoe design.

Caliber *High*—indicates accomplishment or good quality. *Low*—indicates poor quality or bad taste.

Cannonball Express Long used to denote speed in railroad and truck transportation.

Cannon Fodder If you are this, you are expendable. A common term for new military recruits.

Charcoal Burner A muzzle-loading gun using black powder.

Chokebore Pants Narrow, tapered trousers.

Cocked and Primed Ready.

Chiller A handgun.

Cooler A handgun.

Crossfire Not a good place to be caught, even in an argument.

Dead as a Duck Finished; no longer useful.

Dead Center Accomplishing something exactly as planned, including timing. Also shocked, e.g., the accusation hit him dead center.

Double Barreled Two approaches to a problem. Sneaky.

Drawing Fire Receiving criticism.

Dry Run Rehearsal. Practice.

Dud Nothing happened. It didn't work. Ineffective person.

Ear Back the Hammer A prelude to "letting him have it." In general, indicated preparation before action.

Easy on the Trigger Caution before action. Tactful, diplomatic.

Enforcer A handgun.

Equalizer A handgun.

Eraser A handgun. Sometimes machinegun.

Fair Game Something women think men are, and vice versa.

Fast on the Draw Acts quickly.

Fired Losing your job, sometimes accompanied by speed and loud noises.

Flash in the Pan Much fire and smoke but no action where it counts. An ineffectual person who started out well.

Gat A gun. From Gatling gun.

Getting the Drop Being there first. Having the advantage.

Giv'er the Gun Make it go—fast.

Goon One who depends on crude, brute force. From gun; the association is clear.

Great Guns An expletive indicating surprise. Blowing great guns indicates wind of great velocity.

Gun From *gunne, gonne*. (M.E.) Also from gin—engine. Enginery is the art of managing engines, or artillery.

Gun It Make it go—fast.

Gun Shy Reluctance, sometimes accompanied by fear of consequences.

Hair Trigger Temper, easily aroused.

Half-Cocked To go off half-cocked is to talk or act before being ready. Impulsive.

Hanging Fire Delayed while waiting for a decision or an action.

Hardware A gun, usually a handgun.

Held Up Action delayed.

Holdup Excessive price or unreasonable demand.

Hold Your Fire Wait. Temporarily cease action—or talk.

Heater A handgun. See "chiller."

Heeled Carrying a gun. If you are well-heeled you just have money.

Iron A gun, usually handgun.

Keep Your Powder Dry Indicates the need for patience—preserving your resources or arguments until needed.

Lead Poisoning Being killed or wounded with a bullet or shot.

Loaded for Bear Having plenty of whatever you need to accomplish what you want to do. A formidable adversary.

Lock, Stock, and Barrel Everything goes with the purchase, the works.

Looking Down the Muzzle Being at a disadvantage and unable to act. Forced capitulation to another's wishes or against your own.

Lower Your Sights Try for less. Drop the price.

Near Miss You almost won, got the job, or bought the property.

Not Worth the Powder...and Shot A load for a shotgun isn't worth much; neither is the individual.

...To Blow Him to Hell Hell is supposed to be downhill all the way; very little value is indicated.

Old...Any beloved gun acquires this prefix.

...*Reliable-Faithful*-meat in the pot. Later Sharps rifles so-marked, honoring Col. John Bodine.

...*Lightning.* Never hits the same place twice.

On the Mark Exactly where you wanted to go. Exactly on time. As far as you planned.

On Target Just the way you planned, including the time element.

Opening Gun The first argument. The beginning of the (social?) war.

Out of Ammunition You haven't any left—money, liquor, or arguments.

Peacemaker A handgun.

Pepperbox A gun. That's what one type of handgun looked like around 1830 and later. A peppershaker from the business end.

Persuader A handgun.

Petard A very short mortar, often a few inches in depth, used against doors or walls and often hung against them. The fuse was short, too, and sometimes "hoisted" the gunner before he could get away. "Hoist on his own petard" indicates being caught doing excessive bragging or by one's own bad plan.

Pigeon A sucker, a mark, a prospect. Also clay pigeon.

Plowhandle Said of grips used on Colt Peacemaker single action 6-guns.

Point Blank Without considering gravity or wind—in shooting. Now means a direct approach, usually face-to-face.

Popinjay A vain person. Originally a target in the form of a wooden bird on a pole.

Quick on the Trigger Tendency to act before thinking carefully.

Raise Your Sights Expand your personal horizons. Look forward to a bigger job or activity. Ask for more money.

Ram Home Present your arguments in a forceful, conclusive manner.

Rapid Fire Talking very fast. Presenting statements in quick succession.

Rifle To throw fast, as in baseball.

Rimfire A modern man's hat with narrow brim.

Rod A handgun.

Roscoe A handgun.

Scattergun An approach that uses all the arguments you can think of; one of them might work. Trying a little of everything in hope of results.

Set Your Sights High Don't be satisfied with mediocre aims.

Shell Shocked Visible sudden dismay or consternation. Extreme, numbing confusion.

Shoot Start talking. Go ahead. A mild expletive.

Shoot Off Your Mouth Talking too much. Excessive bragging.

Shoot the Bull From Bullseye, with overtones of baloney.

Shoot the Moon Go for broke. Moving at night to avoid paying the rent.

Shoot the Works Go all the way. Bet all you have.

Shoot your Cuffs From a previous generation. A sudden motion designed to expose starched shirt cuffs below the coat sleeve.

Shooting Trying, with a specified objective.

Shooting the Cat Vomiting.

Sharpshooter A clever operator. Now sometimes derogatory; one who is barely ethical or who operates just within the law.

Shot Tired. Pooped. Gone. Enough liquor for one drink. Many words and phrases include this term:

Call your Shot Say what you're going to do before trying to do it.

Gone Like a Shot Small boys can move this fast; so can frightened adults.

Half-shot Partially drunk.

Long Shot A slim chance. A bet against heavy odds.

Parting Shot Getting the last word, preferably just before leaving.

Pay the Shot Pay the bill.

Pot Shot Aiming in the general direction—more hope than planning.

Shot In The Dark Take a chance on scoring without knowing where the target (or objective) is. Unanticipated question.

Shot Out of the Door Leaving in a hurry.

Shot with Envy Deep, all-over envy.

Shots Left in the Locker Arguments or plans held in reserve.

Shotgun Prescription A little of everything, administered in hope that some ingredient works.

Shotgun Wedding Forced compliance under inescapable pressure. Is it still used for weddings?

Sitting Duck Vulnerable. Defenseless.

Smoke Clears Away Waiting for the end of confusion so you can see what to do next.

Smokepole A gun with black powder ancestry.

Snipe Hunt Effort that produces no results, often contrived by others.

Sniper One who takes oral shots at you, often without your knowledge.

Stick to Your Guns Stand firmly for what you think is right.

String Shot groupings were once measured by string length from the center of the bull, and a series of shots, usually 5 or 10, is called a string. If your string runs out, you are all through.

Sure as Shooting Certain. Without doubt.

Sure Fire Can't fail.

Target Date Planned time for completion.

Thumb Buster Handgun with big hammer and of large caliber, usually Colt single actions.

Touch Off To cause a reaction.

Touchy A sensitive disposition. Originally a sensitive trigger.

Two Dollar Pistol Something that you are hotter than. Those cheap guns must have warmed up easily.

Typewriter Machine gun or sub-machine gun.

Undergunned Without whatever you need at the moment.

Under the Gun Under forced pressure with involved penalties made known.

Whole Shooting Match Everything. The works.

Wild Shot Trying something without knowing just what you are trying to do.

Wad a Shotgun Not enough brains to... Wadding is the least valuable element in a shotgun load.

Wide of the Mark What was planned never came close to accomplishment.

Zero-In Getting to the point. Listing intently to the conversation of others.

●

NEW WHEELS FOR THE HUNTER

by ROGER BARLOW

A bevy of 4WD and other vehicles are briefly and critically reviewed —with good reason.

The new and larger Ford Bronco has full-time 4-wheel-drive and automatic transmission as standard. Conventional (part-time) 4-wheel drive with free-wheeling front hubs are optional.

FOR ONE THING, the too-big wagons are getting smaller and some of the too-small foreign wagons are getting usefully larger. Which is all to the good.

Probably the huge 120 in. wheelbase, over 2-ton wagons will have gone the way of all other dinosaurs in another year or so. We need not mourn their passing; such smaller replacements as the Malibu-size General Motors wagons, the Aspen/Volare and the Fairmont/Zepher wagons are far better handling, more economical, have about 85% as much cargo space, and are even more attractive looking vehicles.

I've recently used all three of the above "new size" 1978 wagons and, as both a hunter/outdoorsman and as a dedicated car nut, they have my whole hearted endorsement. It has often been said that all Detroit cars are alike. However, there is less truth in that statement today than there was only a couple of years ago.

Although each of the Malibu, Fairmont and Volare station wagons tested last winter filled the basic transportation needs of most hunters/outdoorsmen equally well, each offered other important qualities and characteristics which clearly set them apart from each other; the potential buyer could base his selection upon such other factors as steering and handling qualities, engineering differences, economy and performance, luxury items, even styling. A hunter's vehicle may be basically a work horse, but we might as well make certain that we enjoy driving it, or even just looking at it, for it represents a very considerable investment these days!

What sets these 3 wagons apart from each other? Let's see.

Ford Fairmont (Mercury Zepher)

This is a completely new project for Ford, except for the engines and transmissions, and it demonstrates what a good job can be done by Detroit engineers when they are given a chance. Their version of the European "strut" type front suspension, together with power assisted rack and pinion steering, results in an American car with the precise and responsive steering, together with much of the handling qualities, for which Jaguar, Mercedes and BMW have become renowned.

Sprung so that it clings firmly to the road, this lighter Fairmont wagon nevertheless absorbs bumps and potholes without the disturbing chassis and body flexing and shake so evident in virtually all older, full size wagons. No question, the Fairmont's rigid body cage is a distinct advancement over its big brothers—despite weighing 1200 lbs. less!

Crisp clean styling, superior handling and steering, without sacrificing comfort, make the Fairmont/Zepher wagons a logical choice for the enthusiastic driver. The only major fault are the front seats; the back rests are so badly angled as to make both driver and passenger sit too erect, almost as if actually leaning forward. This applies to both the split and the bench seats. Also, it must be said, the material used for seats and interior trim is distressingly shiny and cheap looking. How such a really

Modern styling and engineering have made the new Ford Fairmont wagon an instant success.

good car could come on the market with those terrible seats and ugly vinyl makes one wonder if the executives of the styling department at Ford ever drive their own products. Or maybe they're all golfers, not car men, and just don't know any better! I'd suggest more authority be given the engineering department heads who obviously know their jobs—and cars.

Chevrolet Malibu

This too, is one of the '78 cars with a completely brand-new computer-engineered body structure that is also commendably solid feeling and remarkably free of shake and flexing. Unfortunately the too-light power steering is completely devoid of any road feel, and the suspension allows an unexpected and disconcerting initial bit of roll when swerving or entering a curve. This primary roll never progresses much beyond that first little lurch so the Malibu wagon can actually be cornered pretty fast.

But passenger equanimity is adversely affected by that initial quick lurch, and so an enthusiastic driver, unless he is alone in the car, feels inhibited.

But in every other aspect of its design and manufacture Chevrolet has done an outstanding job. The Malibu is certainly the most handsome and elegant wagon on the market—its grill shape and its smaller size give it the edge over its corporate relatives, both larger and smaller. Indeed, the entire Malibu line makes many famous European cars look positively frumpy!

The interior of this Chevy wagon is surprisingly luxurious. Why is it that of all U.S. car makers only GM seems able to produce (or select) vinyl that doesn't have that dreadful "plasticky" look and feel. Even the several kinds of material used on the instrument panel and other trim areas of this wagon were a very close match in color and texture—something their competitors apparently don't worry about.

If a genuine sense of luxury and elegant styling are more important to you than "sporty" steering and handling, then the Malibu wagon is for you.

Plymouth Volare (Dodge Aspen)

Because this design is a couple of years older than the two other cars in this report, it suffers from not being based upon the latest in body-chassis engineering developments, thus it is not as rigid and rattle-free.

Yet the responsiveness and accuracy of its power steering is first rate and very nearly as good as that of the Fairmont. In roadholding and handling it is midway between the Ford product and the Malibu. And so offers another useful choice for the buyer.

The divided front seats are very well shaped and angled, but, again, are trimmed in "plasticky" material, the colors of which don't match very well. I've not mentioned so far the performance or fuel consumption of any of these wagons. Both can vary

The Chevy Malibu, a most handsome and well-appointed wagon. Its easy-lift up rear window and short, light tailgate is an excellent solution to rear-end loading problems.

The Plymouth Volare is a little larger than the other wagons in this new size classification. Its popularity has certainly accelerated the industry to move to this more efficient size.

widely because each is offered with 6-or 8-cylinder engines of different power (the Fairmont even offers a 4) and with manual or automatic transmissions. The Malibu with a V8 had excellent road performance—0-60 in 11-12 seconds. With the V6 zero to 60 took about 16 seconds, which was also what the 6-cylinder Fairmont with automatic did. Interstate cruising at 60-65 in the V6 Malibu resulted in just over 20 mpg.... about 18 with the V8 Volare.

The EPA ratings are reasonably useful indications of mileage *only* if you reduce their figures by about 20%. All of these wagons give 3 to 5 mpg better mileage than full-size wagons.

However, their gas mileage and performance would benefit greatly from a good modern 5-speed gearbox, with 5th being an overdrive. The market research types should know by now that nobody today wants a 3-speed manual box with column shift! That design went out with tail fins a decade ago, which the Japanese and European manufacturers realize.

The Smaller Get Larger

The '78 Dodge Colt wagon, now with a 2600cc or 1600cc engine, is an example of a too-small wagon that has usefully grown a bit. It is a completely new Colt with the same basic engine and chassis as the sporty new Dodge Challenger/Plymouth Sapporo coupes.

Having 4 doors it is a more practical wagon than are its 2 door competitors. Gone are the awkward "Japanese" styling touches of the past. Indeed, this new Colt wagon with its crisp lines looks more than anything like a slightly scaled-down Malibu!

It is endowed with the smoothest 4-cylinder engine yet seen—by virtue of its unique pair of counter-rotating balancing shafts, one in each side of the block and chain driven from the crankshaft. Though these balancing shafts don't affect the basic 4-cylinder flow of power impulses, they do cancel out most of the other vibrations and unbalanced forces to which a vertical 4 is subject.

Each cylinder of this engine also has a special very small diameter

auxiliary inlet valve and manifold that feeds a high speed jet of lean mixture into the combustion chamber; this sets up a swirling movement of the main mixture flow coming through the normal big inlet valve at much slower velocity so that, upon ignition, burning spreads throughout the combustion chamber more evenly and more rapidly. The net result of the balancing shafts and this high velocity jet of lean mixture is improved economy, reduced pollution and such a smooth idle that the engine simply cannot be felt. It seems to be every bit as unobtrusive as a well-tuned V8!

Although this Colt wagon is available with the excellent Chrysler-built TorqueFlite automatic, economy is appreciably improved by going with the manual box having a geared-up 5th—a proper overdrive which provides quiet and effortless cruising at the old Interstate speeds of 70-75 mph, with plenty of acceleration left for passing. Cruising at 60-65 mph, results in 27 mpg, local suburban driving around 21 mpg.

The all-new 1978 Dodge Colt wagon is a welcome break from previous, over-fussy Japanese styling. Small, but not too small, this is the wagon for the economy-minded outdoorsman who also appreciates innovative engineering.

MacPherson strut front suspension (coil, 4 link rear layout) provides handling in the Fairmont class, and the Chrysler-built power-assisted steering is even better—one of the best regardless of price class. It is not too light and has more road feel than most, despite not being of rack and pinion design.

Workmanship is excellent. This is a smallish car of real quality, marred only by a bad color match of the materials used for the facia—dash, that is—and trim.

The handsome and well finished single overhead cam engine provides good accessibility and the opportunity for the owner to do much of the basic maintenance.

A most attractive and enjoyable wagon with a happy amalgam of economy, performance, handling and comfort, together with ingenious and advanced engineering that can efficiently meet the transportation needs of many hunters, fishermen and outdoorsmen.

The Bronco Grows Up

There was a lot to be said in favor of the original Ford 4 wheel-drive Bronco. It was compact and able to make its way along narrow wooded trails with less damage to its bodywork than might be suffered by its later and larger competitors. Being smaller and lighter it used less fuel. It was every bit as comfortable and was certainly capable of going just about anywhere a Blazer or Ramcharger could. The one thing it never had was full time 4-wheel drive—which surely could have been added with little difficulty.

So why do we now have, instead, a *new* Bronco—fully as large and expensive and thirsty as a Blazer or Ramcharger? Apparently the paying customers made it unpleasantly clear to Ford that they were only interested in the larger Blazer-like units. Which is exactly what is now offered—a Ford "Blazer." Fortunately the new version retains the original Bronco type front suspension (this alone should give it a useful edge over its competitors) which is a genuinely superior bit of engineering.

Instead of depending upon the outmoded concept of stiff conventional leaf springs to locate the heavy front axle unit, the Ford Bronco obtains an appreciably better ride along with superior road-handling and much more precise steering through the use of relatively soft coil springs; locating the front axle with greater accuracy by means of torque arms.

This sturdy looking 4-cylinder engine is as quiet and vibrationless as any 6 and most V8s because of its unique vibration-damping balancing shafts. Accessibility is so good that owners will once again be able to carry out many basic maintenance operations.

This new Bronco, though not as comfortable in the rough as the new Range Rover, nevertheless, provides a better ride than the Blazer or Ramcharger. But equally, if not more important, the Bronco's front suspension eliminates the exasperating tendency to wander and weave at highway cruising speeds that is a characteristic of most 4-wheel drive vehicles. This factor alone is reason enough to select the Bronco if a substantial portion of your driving will be on hard surfaced roads.

The Bronco, now as large and heavy as the Blazer, is, of course, no more economical. Even in 2-wheel drive with the front hubs set in the "free" position, it was unable to better 10 mpg on the highway. With the front hubs locked and about 20% of my driving in 4-wheel the mileage was about 7-8 mpg. This vehicle had the 5.8 litre V8 and automatic.

(Incidentally, *all* 4-wheel drives, not just those with full time 4-wheel drive, should have an automatic transmission; for the fluid torque converter cushions and absorbs the considerable amount of free-play or backlash inherent in the driveline of all such vehicles. The life of all driveline components is extended, and the vehicle is more pleasant to drive.)

The new Bronco, so tough and capable of dealing with brutally rough conditions, surprisingly seems to have had its interior designed by the gay contingent at Ford, who apparently never even bothered to drive the unit around the proving grounds! On a bright day one can barely read the instruments for all the reflections

from the outrageous amount of chrome strips and trim on the instruments and panel. There is no place to stow even a map without buying the optional $86 Console Box, for the glove box is just that—it won't even hold a Nikon camera. Worse yet, there is no grab rail anywhere to help a passenger climb up into the high cab or to hang onto when the Bronco is bouncing around over the rough terrain it is meant to cope with (a shoulder belt doesn't help at all to keep you in your seat except in a frontal crash). Then there are those idiot-designed, unbelievably uncomfortable bucket seats made without adjustable backrests, even as an option. Here again driver and passenger are forced to sit so upright that they seem to be leaning forward, soon ending up with a crick in the neck. There is no way for a tired driver to catch some needed sleep, or even to really rest comfortably, in that ridiculous passenger seat. True, the Blazer and the Ramcharger have equally unsatisfactory seats, but why would Ford copy one of the worst faults of their competitors?

This new Bronco is too good an outdoorsman's vehicle to have been saddled with these styling stupidities. Some heads should roll and some changes should be made. Again, the engineers delivered the product, the stylists blew it.

The next issue of GUN DIGEST will carry an in-use evaluation of Diesel-engined vehicles of interest to hunters plus reports on some new and unusual 4-wheel-drive vehicles from abroad. •

Long Gun Report

by LARRY S. STERETT

The National Sporting Goods Assn. show at Houston was, this year as always, the big showcase for sporting arms of all types. Here's a first-hand review of all the shoulder arms, new or renewed.

At the annual NSGA shows the U.S. gun manufacturers and the importers introduce their new sporting arms, and the 1978 Houston meeting did see a few new arms—a 10-gauge shotgun from Savage Arms, a new centerfire rifle from Mossberg, and a new over-under smoothbore from Weatherby. Most other arms seemed to be modified or improved versions of previous models, such as a new finish, new chamberings, different checkering patterns or different barrel lengths. Whether new or renewed, you'll find them covered in the following update on what is available to U.S. shooters.

Armsport

There are 5 new over-under shotgun sets — 4 in 12-gauge and one 20, plus a new over-under rifle available, which last is commented on elsewhere in this edition. The shotguns have single selective triggers, ejectors and engraved (false) sideplates. The 12- and 20-gauge Skeet sets have 26-inch barrels, with extra 28-inch barrels choked modified and full. The three 12-gauge trap sets come in a deluxe luggage-style leather case, loden-cloth lined, as do the Skeet sets. The 3100 trap gun has 30-inch over-under barrels, plus a 32-inch single barrel; the 3101 and 3102 are the same except that a 32-inch over-under set with a 34-inch single barrel are optional. Basically the same as Angelo Zoli's Model Monte Carlo, the Armsport sets retail from just under $1100 for the Skeet sets to just under $1300 for the trap sets. The quality of the shotguns examined was excellent.

Beretta Arms

The Mark II Single Barrel Trap Gun is available again with a choice of 32- or 34-inch full choke barrel, and a special broad ventilated rib. Also new is the M-410 side by side in 10-gauge magnum, its weight about 10 lbs. This big 10 has 32-inch chrome-lined full-and-full barrels, a boxlock action, plain extractors and double triggers, the front trigger hinged. The frame is silver-gray finished, with light engraving, the other metal parts blued. (The contrast looks nice, but it could be glary in a goose blind.) The European walnut pistol grip buttstock carries a ventilated rubber recoil pad and the forearm is a beavertail type. Checkering is hand done and ample where needed.

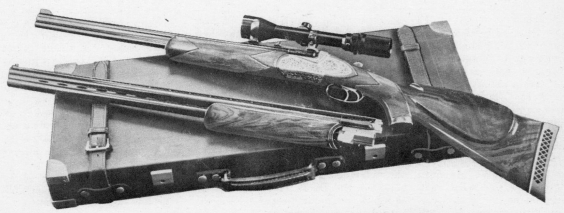

Dubbed "The Emperor" Model 4000, the Armsport over-under rifle also comes in a leather luggage-style case. The O-U shotgun barrels are in 12, 16 or 20 gauge.

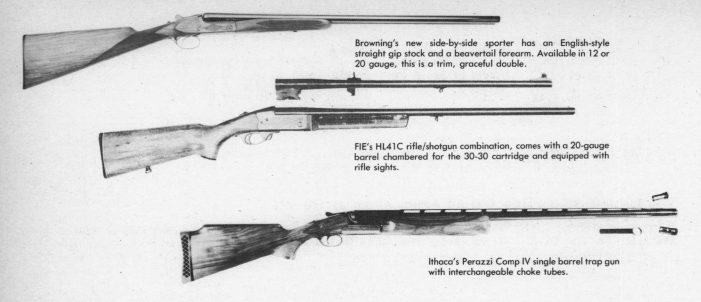

Browning's new side-by-side sporter has an English-style straight gip stock and a beavertail forearm. Available in 12 or 20 gauge, this is a trim, graceful double.

FIE's HL41C rifle/shotgun combination, comes with a 20-gauge barrel chambered for the 30-30 cartridge and equipped with rifle sights.

Ithaca's Perazzi Comp IV single barrel trap gun with interchangeable choke tubes.

Browning

This famous firm is celebrating its Centennial in 1978, and there are several new additions to the line, including 19 versions of the Citori over-under shotgun, a new bolt action rifle, a lever action copy of the excellent 92 Winchester, and some special Centennial models. The new items plus the over-under rifle/shotgun combination seen on our front cover will be covered elsewhere in this edition.

FIE

Several new shotguns, including a hammer gun in 20 gauge or 410, upgraded ERA single and double barrel models with 30-inch barrels and a youth-model CBC single barrel, are available. The big news is a hammerless CBC single barrel model offered as a shotgun or a rifle/shotgun combination. These have hardwood stocks and fore-ends, a tang-mounted slide safety, 1-inch sling swivels and a break-open action operated by a button ahead of the trigger guard. The new single barrel (the HL 40 in 12 gauge or the HL 41, a 20 bore) is chambered for 2³/₄-inch shells. The HL 41C comes with a regular 20-gauge barrel and an extra open-sighted rifle barrel in 30-30. Made in Brazil, the latest CBC retails for $61.50 with a shotgun barrel, or at $82.95 in the combination version

Harrington & Richardson

Their M176 single shot shotgun is now offered as the M176 Magnum series, designed for use with steel shot and magnum loads, in a choice of 10, 12, 16 or 20 gauge versions, all full choked. The 12 gauge can be had with a 36-inch barrel, the 10 and

other gauges with a 32-inch tube, if desired. The 12s and 20s have 3-inch chambers. Weights run from 8¹/₂ lbs. for the 20 to 10 lbs. for the 36-inch 10 gauge. All shotguns in this series have Monte Carlo-combed stocks and ventilated rubber recoil pads.

The H&R Model 162 is a 20 gauge with a rifle-sighted 24-inch cylinder-bore barrel. The three single-barrel "Greenwing" shotguns are offered to honor the Ducks Unlimited youth program. They're produced in 20- and 28-gauge, choked modified, or in a full choked 410. Gold plated triggers, plus a special gold inlaid inscription on the receiver, distinguish the Greenwings, which are Model 490 variations. Stocking is similar to that on the Model 176 Magnum series, as are the prices—$72.50. ($79.50 for the 10-gauge Model 176 with 36-inch barrel.)

Ithacagun

The time-tested Model 37 can now be had in a 12-gauge Magnum grade, chambered for 3-inch shells. Offered with 30-inch full or 28-inch modified vent rib barrels, the longer-receiver Magnum 37 has the standard M37 features, including an American walnut stock and forearm. Stock dimensions are the same as on the M37 Supreme Trap Gun. At less than $300 this newest 37 is a welcome addition to the line.

Also new is a M37 Deerslayer version with an 8-shot capacity and a 20-inch rifle-sighted barrel. Priced at $249.95, the Deerslayer comes with sling swivels and the rear sight base is grooved for mounting a long eye relief scope. In addition, a 28-inch modified-choke barrel can be special

ordered from the factory to exchange with the 20-inch barrel.

The Ithaca-Perazzi shotguns cost $500 more now, and a couple of versions have been discontinued. However, there are also some additions, such as the Comp IV Single, which comes with 32- or 34-inch barrel and 4 interchangeable choke tubes—full, extra full, improved modified, and modified. The MT-6 Combo, though introduced last year, is only now available. Its outstanding feature is the single barrel, which has a very high-rise ventilated rib of machined aluminum 1¹/₈ inches above the underbarrel to provide a sighting plane of regular height but with a more in-line recoil factor. The ³/₈-inch wide rib is anodized flat black for a glare-free top surface. Seven interchangeable choke tubes are included with the Combo.

Special High Grade versions of the MX-8 and single barrel Perazzi shotguns are available, starting with the $8000 single with 32-inch full choke barrel, and topped by the $10,000 MX-8 Combo. For the shooter wanting an expensive shotgun these may be the ticket, but the less expensive versions are said to shoot just as well.

The Ithaca Mag-10 has really caught on with waterfowlers since its introduction nearly 5 years ago, but there is now a short barrel version. Designed mainly for police use in a plain grade, the latest Mag-10 should do well on road blockades, but it would sure be rough on quail and rabbits.

Distribution of the Ithaca Hawken rifle has now been taken over by the Navy Arms firm. Quality will remain basically the same, as will the design, but availability should be better.

Marlin Firearms

The pump action 120 shotgun is now available in a plain Field Grade, with plain 28-inch modified choke barrel only. Priced at $184.95 in mid-1978, this 120 has the same steel receiver and walnut stock and forearm, minus grip cap and spacer, as the Magnum 120, and it will accept any of the regular 120 barrels.

Mossberg

The Model 500 shotgun is offered in several new grades, including a special trap gun, and there's a new Mossberg centerfire rifle with a rotary magazine, a 3-position safety (a la M70), and a classic-style stock. (See the report on the Model 500 AHTD Hi-Rib Trap Gun in our Testfire Report section of this edition.) The new rifle is labeled the RM-7, and the pre-production versions examined looked good. The classic stock is of American walnut with sling swivel studs, pistol grip with cap, rubber buttplate, and ample checkering on the grip and forearm. It's the action which is new, and it bears little resemblance to the 800 series. The rotary magazine is housed within the stock, and live cartridges can be removed through the ejection port by pushing down on a release in the right action rail. The 3-position safety locks the firing pin but permits bolt operation for safe ejection. The bolt handle, swept back for easy grasping, has a polished 4-lug body and blued flutes its entire length for reduced friction.

Scheduled for delivery before the '78 hunting season, the RM-7 will be chambered for 30-06 or 7mm Remington Magnum cartridges—and it will sell at a competitive price. A gold bead ramp-mounted front sight and an adjustable folding rear sight are standard, but both are removable, if desired, for use with a scope; the receiver is tapped for scope mounts.

The Model 500 Combo Pack is now available with a 28-inch Accu-Choke plain barrel, plus an extra 24-inch Slugster barrel with rifle sights, for $188.50, or at $204.50 with a vent rib barrel. In addition, the M500 Steel Shot Special Heavy Duck Gun is $179.95 with 30- or 32-inch barrels. Designed especially for use with steel shot, it has a vent rib and can be bought separately to fit regular Model 500 shotguns.

Mossberg is now into the black powder field. It will be distributing the Ozark Mountain Rifle manufactured in Missouri, one of the closer copies of the original Hawken design, which speaks well of Mossberg's choice. It will be competitively priced, and is a welcome addition to the Mossberg line of sporting arms.

Navy Arms

Val Forgett is a leader in the field of black powder sporting arms, and the most recent additions to the line include a couple of limited-production arms—the Smith carbine comes in 54 caliber, its total length 39 inches, its weight 7½ lbs. The frame is case-hardened in color, the barrel blued, and the American walnut stock has a brass buttplate. One of the earliest breechloaders used during the Civil War, the Smith replica is an excellent reproduction.

The Henry rifle, of which only 500 will be made, has a brass frame, a blued barrel chambered for the 44 rimfire or 44-40 centerfire cartridge, and an oil-finished American walnut stock. Yes, that's correct, it will be available in the original 44 rimfire chambering, the same cartridge used in the original forerunner of the Winchester line of lever-action repeaters.

Navy Arms also has the new and very well-done Parker-Hale Whitworth Military Target rifle, which has a 36-inch barrel with three bands, is 52½ inches long and weighs 9¼ lbs. It will be made in 45 caliber only.

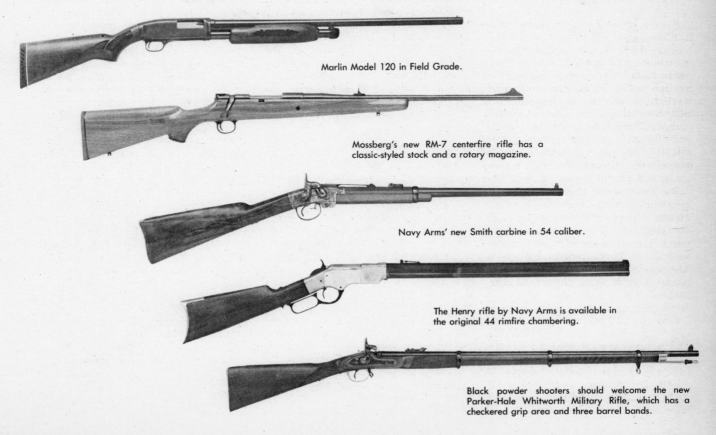

Marlin Model 120 in Field Grade.

Mossberg's new RM-7 centerfire rifle has a classic-styled stock and a rotary magazine.

Navy Arms' new Smith carbine in 54 caliber.

The Henry rifle by Navy Arms is available in the original 44 rimfire chambering.

Black powder shooters should welcome the new Parker-Hale Whitworth Military Rifle, which has a checkered grip area and three barrel bands.

Remington Arms

The 870 shotgun, which will have been around for three decades in 1979, is offered in 3 new trap versions—the 870TA, 870TB, and 870TC, which differ mainly in the quality of their American walnut stocks and the style and amount of checkering. Ventilated recoil pads are standard, as are vent ribs on the 30″ barrels. Prices range from $255.95 for the TA to $445 for the TC; the latter has select, highly-figured walnut with deluxe fine-line cut checkering.

The 870 and the 1100 lightweight 20-gauge shotguns are now available in deer-hunting versions with 20″ improved cylinder barrels, and adjustable rifle-type sights. (The 1100 stock is of American walnut, the 870 mahogany.) Prices for both are under $300, and each carries a ventilated recoil pad.

More complete coverage of the Remington line will be found elsewhere in this edition, including the new Classic 700 rifle in the Testfire Report section. Briefly, new items include a single shot adapter for the 581 rimfire bolt action rifle, permitting its use as a target or training arm; an improved checkering pattern on the 700 BDL centerfire rifles, and a redesigning of the 552 and 572 rimfire repeating rifles.

Ruger

The Red Label over-under 20 gauge, long awaited, is still not readily available. (The test gun promised us has not arrived.) However, in extenuation, the original design was slightly changed to produce a lighter gun. Production guns should be available by the time you read this, with the 26″ barrels available first; 28″ barrels will appear later. Production guns will weigh about 6 lbs., and toward year's end there may be some premium-quality grades offered. A standard 12-gauge version should arrive next year. The Red Label barrels are hammer-forged of 4130 chromemoly steel, the action and frame of 4140; a single trigger is standard, the barrel selector being part of the automatic safety mechanism. Coil springs are used throughout, and there are no screws in the working mechanism, or any visible pins or screws elsewhere. The American walnut stock and forearm are hand checkered at 20 lines-per-inch, the areas covered ample. At a $480 list, Ruger's Red Label represents a quality shotgun at a reasonable price.

Remington's Model 870 pump-action trap gun with regular stock.

Remington's Model 581 22-cal. rimfire rifle with single shot adapter.

Remington's Model 552 BDL deluxe autoloading rimfire rifle.

Remington's Model 572A pump-action 22 rimfire rifle in standard form. Barrel on the 572 and 552 rifles are now 21″ long.

Consult our Directory pages for the location of firms mentioned.

Ruger's 20-gauge over-under shotgun, the "Red Label."

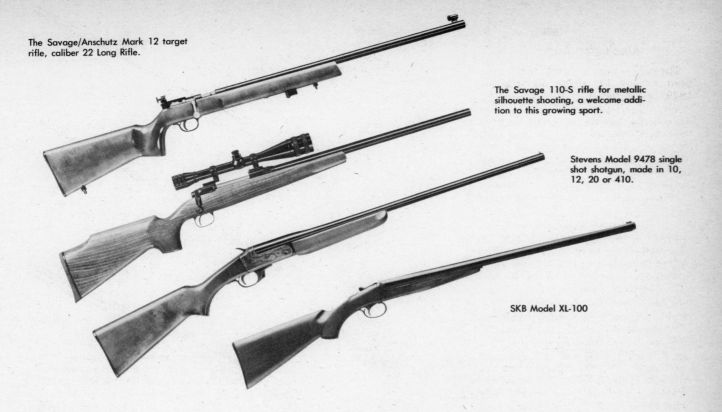

The Savage/Anschutz Mark 12 target rifle, caliber 22 Long Rifle.

The Savage 110-S rifle for metallic silhouette shooting, a welcome addition to this growing sport.

Stevens Model 9478 single shot shotgun, made in 10, 12, 20 or 410.

SKB Model XL-100

Savage Arms

In the rifle department the excellent 110 action has become the basis for a metallic silhouette rifle. A special 22″ tapered barrel, 7/8″ at the muzzle, is installed and, though without metallic sights, the receiver is tapped for scope mounts. The barrel is free-floated in the special silhouette-style stock of select walnut; this stock has a Monte Carlo comb, plus a hand-filling Wundhammer swell on the full pistol grip. The grip area and the underside of the forearm are stippled to prevent slippage. Currently available in a right-hand version only, chambered for the 308 cartridge, the 8 5/8-lb. 110-S lists at $215.

The second new rifle from Westfield is the Savage/Anschutz Mark 12 Junior Target Rifle in 22 LR. The Mark 12 (its action like that on the S-A Model 64) has a 26″ barrel of 7/8″ diameter, the total rifle weight about 8 lbs. The target type stock, of walnut-finish hardwood, has a full pistol grip with a deep flute for the thumb and a Wundhammer swell. Sling swivels are standard, and the forearm bottom has an adjustable hand stop.

Sights with the M12 include a globe front with 7 aperture and post inserts, and a micrometer rear peep with click adjustments for windage and elevation. Currently available only for right-handed shooters, the M12 lists at $105, a special target sling optional at $12.95.

The new Savage shotgun is the single shot Model 9478 in 10, 12, 20 or 410. Resembling the M94 with its outside hammer, the 9478 has a newly-designed opening lever ahead of the trigger guard, in place of a top lever. The 12, 20 and 410 shotguns are chambered for 3″ shells; the big 10 for 3 1/2″ magnums. Barrel lengths include 28″, 30″, 32″ or 36″ for the 12 gauge, 28″ for the 20, and 26″ for the 410; the 10 gauge is made only with a 36″ full choke barrel. The handles are of walnut-finished hardwood, the 9 1/2-lb. 10-gauge version having a rubber recoil pad and a grooved forearm for more positive gripping.

The Four-Tenner has been re-introduced in 12- and 20 gauge, permitting owners of any break-action shotgun in these gauges to use 410 shells. The Four-Tenner weighs only 5 ounces, comes with its own extractors, and sells for under $18.

SKB Sports

This Illinois-based firm has 4 new shotguns—three target grade over-unders and a no-frills 12-gauge slug gun—the XL 100. The last gun, which sells for $244.95, is based on the regular SKB gas-operated action. Weighing 7 lbs., the XL 100 has a plain walnut-stained hardwood stock and a large grooved forearm, sling swivels, a 20″ Duro-forged cylinder bore barrel with rifletype sights, and a non-glare black anodized, high-strength alloy receiver. Magazine capacity is 4 rounds, plus one in the chamber.

The three target guns, offered in trap or Skeet versions, differ mainly in the grade of walnut used, the finish and engraving. The Skeet guns weigh about 7 3/4 lbs., come with 26″ or 28″ barrels, and 12mm or 16mm raised vent ribs. Stock dimensions are 1 5/8″ and 2 1/4″ at comb and heel. Trap guns go about 8 1/4 lbs., are currently made only with 30″ barrels having a 16mm ventilated rib, and are choked improved modified and full; stock dimensions are 1 3/8″ and 1 3/4″ at comb and heel, and there are no Monte Carlos.

Priced from $860 (Model 5600) to $1900 (Model 5800) the new over-unders have selective ejectors, an enlarged locking lug on the barrels to prevent loosening despite years of heavy shooting, a new mechanical trigger mechanism so the second shot is always available regardless of the lightness of the load, and a new angled wood-to-metal union of the stock to absorb more recoil without added strain on the stock. In addition, the Skeet barrels are aligned so the bores are parallel; a concept based on the current International Skeet shooting theory that non-intersecting trajectories provide the same aiming point for either barrel.

Weatherby

The Regency over-under shotgun has a new companion o-u—the Olympian. Available in 12- or 20-gauge field or Skeet versions, or as a 12-gauge trap grade, the Japanese-made Olympian is without engraved sideplates. It has a machined one-piece steel receiver with chrome-moly steel barrels of monoblock construction. Locking and barrel selection are basically Browning, the vent-rib barrels pivoting on a full hinge pin. Side ribs on the trap guns are also ventilated.

All 20-gauge barrels are chambered for 3″ shells, as are the 30″ barrel field grade 12-gauge tubes. The 12-gauge trap gun comes with 30″ or 32″ barrels, and 26″ and 28″ lengths are available in the field and Skeet grades.

The Olympian is stocked in selected California walnut, hand checkered, has a rosewood pistol grip cap and a ventilated recoil pad. All forearms are finger grooved, and the finish is a durable high gloss like the Regency's. Pull ranges from $1^3/_{16}$″ on the field and Skeet guns to $1^3/_8$″ on the trap guns. Drops at the comb and heel are $1^1/_2$″ and $2^1/_2$″ for the Skeet and field guns, $1^7/_{16}$″, $1^{11}/_{16}$″ or $1^{15}/_{16}$″ on the trap guns, which have Monte Carlo combs.

The new Olympian sells for $525, and the examined guns appear to represent a lot of value for the money. Workmanship, wood-to-metal fit are excellent.

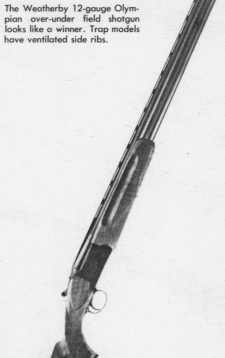

The Weatherby 12-gauge Olympian over-under field shotgun looks like a winner. Trap models have ventilated side ribs.

Winchester

More complete coverage of the Winchester line will be found elsewhere in this edition, but here are brief notes: several shotgun versions have been discontinued, and a few modified models introduced. The Pigeon Grade 101 is now made in 28 and 410 Skeet chamberings, and there's now a Pigeon Grade Skeet Set. The Super-X Model 1 Trap gun can now be had with an improved-modified choke and with a regular or Monte Carlo stock.

The big W-W news, however, is the introduction of the XTR series of shotguns and rifles—the 9422 XTR rimfires, the 70 and 70A centerfires, the 1300 XTR pump-action shotgun and the 1500 XTR autoloading shotgun. The XTR designation refers to an eXTRa deluxe stock and metal finish, at slightly higher prices, of course.

Rifle calibers are the same as for the regular models—no new cartridges—and the 1300 XTR and 1500 XTR shotguns are available in 12 or 20, with or without vent rib barrels, and with or without Winchoke tubes. Essentially the XTRs are upgraded versions of the 1200 and 1400 shotguns, with glossier finishes, additional checkering and white spacers. Only field grade XTRs will be offered for awhile. XTR prices range from $190.95 for the 1300 with plain barrel to $272.95 for the 1500 with a vent rib Winchoke barrel. ●

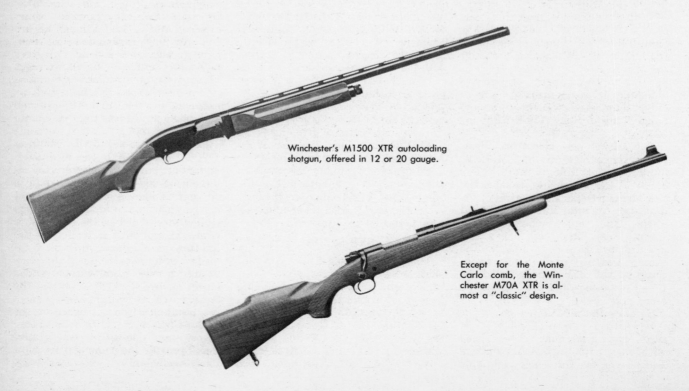

Winchester's M1500 XTR autoloading shotgun, offered in 12 or 20 gauge.

Except for the Monte Carlo comb, the Winchester M70A XTR is almost a "classic" design.

Blue Magic Shotshells

a brief report on Peters new long life easy loaders.

by JAMES NEILL

Peters Cartridge Division of Remington Arms has announced a new target load called Blue Magic. Blue is the color of the tube, but I'm not sure what "Magic" implies. Perhaps Peters hopes that this new load will take away some of the magic that Winchester-Western AA target loads have seemed to hold over reloaders; the AA case has been the most popular among hull fillers for some years.

Peters contends that the Blue Magic load will have a longer reloading life, hold extra hard shot (which means about 6%-6½% antimony), brass heads for easier resizing, a crimp offering easier loading, an improved primer and so on. I'll go into these claims a little later.

Late last year stories circulated that a new target load would soon hit the market, and at least one midwest jobber had these Blue Magics on hand well before the first of the year. That's rather unusual, for generally new products such as this don't appear until after the NSGA show held in January or February. In any case the Blue Magics were selling so well that Peters had a hard time supplying a big trapshoot in the southwest; they borrowed many cases from a jobber to

keep the shooters happy at this event. At this same shoot by the way, once-fired Blue Magic cases sold for 5¢ apiece which, here in the midwest, is at least 1¢ to 2¢ above the going price.

The Blue Magic target loads I have are stamped *Peters* and *Heavy 7½* just above the brass head and, though I haven't seen any, I would suppose that the 2¾ DE loads would be stamped *Light 7½*. The 2¾ DE loads come with 7½, 8, 8½ or 9 shot, the 3 DE loads in 7½, 8 or 9 only. Average weight of the shot charge in the Heavy 7½ load is 495.2 grains, a couple of pellets heavy. The powder averaged 18.1 grains weight with a few greenish-blue flakes scattered through the powder.

The Blue Magic tube or case body is extra smooth, almost slick, and has an 8 point crimp. The primer has an extra large flash hole, at least compared to Remington primers sold to reloaders, and it is doubtful that this primer will be sold as a component. Remington has never covered the primer flash hole with foil or paper, thus the use of these primers with Ball powders could result in ignition problems. The primer pocket appears newly designed for easier de- and

repriming and also for a better gas seal. It's also said that the powder used in the Blue Magics was specially formulated. The plastic wad is the regular RXP type, which I thought might result in a slightly sunken crimp because of the somewhat greater capacity of the Blue Magic case, which has a slightly lower base wad compared to the RXP tube. The case is of the one-piece moulded type, as is the RXP, AA and Champ II. The shot is extra hard (as noted 6%-6½% antimony), a hardness content more or less common to the other target loads and to National Lead's Magnum shot and to Remington's RXP shot, if you can find the latter brand anywhere. I've never seen RXP shot for sale, but it has supposedly been available for some time from Remington. The Blue Magic shot does look good, nice and round and, having a high antimony content, should and does make a smashing load, if you will pardon the small pun.

Are the Blue Magic cases easier to reload? Yes! In reloading on a MEC 600 Jr. and on Ponsness-Warren's 600 effort on the tool handle is much less, I felt, than with other target cases. One slight problem arose in seating primers initially because of the slightly lower base wad of the Blue Magic; primers were not seated fully. But a little bushing of the MEC priming rod and re-adjustment of the P-W priming post, soon cured the problem.

One case was reloaded 15 times, which meant it had been fired 16 times counting the factory load. The case was a little the worse for wear and tear, but it was in much better shape than I'd expected. There were several tears down from the case mouth, the first showing up after the 9th shot, but none so deep as to cause the base to bulge and create feeding problems. On the 7th loading of the case, during the start-crimp operation, the crimp mis-folded. Among other plastic cases, RXP included, each time the case is reloaded after mis-folding the crimp continues to mis-fold. However, the Blue Magic case crimped normally on the next or 8th loading and continued to crimp normally until the crimp had torn in three places. It will be interesting to see if this also occurs with other Blue Magic cases.

How do they shoot? Very well indeed, but testing was rather limited; the ammunition, which arrived late, was used at only one trapshoot, and J.T.A. wanted the story soonest because of early deadlines. In pattern tests the Blue Magic loads gave 76% at 40 yards, which is on a par with

RXPs and Champion IIs in the 32″ full choke barrel of my 3200 Competition trapgun. I'd liked to have tried these in a couple of other guns but time, deep snows and heavy winds prevented.

I didn't fire a full 100-target event with the Blue Magic loads; instead I shot 50 rounds with the factory loads and 50 with my reloads. I wanted to see how the two compared, although the results were loaded in favor of the factory loads. They held extra hard shot, whereas I had to put bagged shot in the reloads. Anyway, I was doing something right in the 16-yard event, for the Blue Magic loads gave me 49 ×50 both times and the targets were, for the most part, just puffs of black dust with very, very few pieces visible. Results with the reloads weren't nearly as good in the way the targets were broken or in the scoring, but I can't honestly lay the blame for the scores on the reloads—shooter stupidity was the culprit. At handicap, from 25½ yards, the results were about the same—although scores were much lower—but the clays were chopped to pieces, at least when I was on the target, with very few small pieces visible. Needless to say targets well hit with the reloads weren't nearly as well broken, but this was to be expected; they patterned only 63%.

From the top—97 Star primer (left) and the Blue Magic primer.

Blue Magic case (left) was reloaded 15 times; compare with once-fired case.

Blue Magic factory load (left) and MEC-reloaded Blue Magic next to it.

Base-wad heights of the Blue Magic case (left) and the RXP.

Some shooters have criticized RXP cases, but I can't agree; I've found RXP cases damned fine for reloading, though I must admit that until now my first choice was Federal's Champion II, followed closely by the RXP. I now expect that Blue Magics will take over first place. Though I did relatively little work with them, I haven't any doubt that Blue Magic cases will be highly popular with reloaders, especially target shooters.

The reloading data available calls for the Remington 97 Star primer, RXP-12 wads and 17.0 grains of Hi-Skor 700-X or Red Dot for a 2¾ DE load; for the 3DE load increase the powder charge to 18 grains.

Hornady's Frontier Ammo

IF YOU WERE A relatively small bullet maker catering strictly to reloaders, how would you go about getting the non-handloaders to use your product? Well, until those "store bought" guys become reloaders, the only way they can try your bullets is if they're offered as part of a package, that is, as factory cartridges.

That's what Joyce Hornady thought, too, so back in the late 60s he decided to go into the rifle ammunition business. Today, less than a decade later, Hornady's Frontier Cartridge division offers a diverse line of rifle and pistol ammo, and sells over 20 million rounds a year.

"It was just that simple," said young Steve Hornady in a recent interview. "Essentially, dad started out

From four cartridge offerings some 10 years ago to the current 43 different loads in 16 calibers is a big jump—and a sign of well-deserved success. Sundra tells how it happened.

by JON R. SUNDRA

by offering handloads to non-handloaders . . . and it grew into all this," he said, gesturing towards the neat rows of loading machines and the adjoining warehouse stacked high with cases of ready-to-ship Frontier cartridges.

"Of course," Steve added, "these decisions were all made before I entered the picture." Today, however, Steve is very much a part of the decision-making at Hornady Manufacturing. As Vice-President, Steve is involved in all phases of the business—even to the point of playing "tour guide" for me on my recent visit to Grand Island, Nebraska.

Frontier Cartridge, of course, is but one of the three divisions comprising Hornady Manufacturing; the others

The 270 is one of the four-only Frontier Cartridge calibers Joyce Hornady started with in the late 1960s; at left is his newest loading, the 22-250 topped with a match hollow point.

Hornady Manufacturing, Grand Island, Nebraska. Frontier Cartridge, Pacific Tool, and Hornady Bullet divisions are all housed in this modern facility.

are the bullet-making operation and Pacific Tool, which makes a full line of reloading presses, dies, and related handloading equipment.

Interestingly, by the way, Hornady is the only one of the four major component bullet makers which has not been absorbed by a conglomerate.

The Only Loner

"We enjoy being the 'last of the independents'" says Steve, "and we're going to stay that way."

As already noted, Frontier Cartridge was formed primarily to offer the non-handloader an opportunity to use a Hornady bullet. There was also another reason—economy. Joyce had no illusions that he would one day be competing with Remington or Winchester, and, therefore, felt he could make do with surplus loading machines, such as those used in making the tens of millions of rounds of small arms ammo used by American troops in WW II and the Korean conflict.

Joyce also figured that, by limiting the Frontier line to those sporting cartridges based on military brass, he could use once-fired 30-06 and 7.65 NATO (308 Winchester) cases. Since one trip through a sizing die will make a 270 from an '06 case and a 243 Winchester from a 308 hull, Joyce settled on those four cartridges as the entire Frontier offering.

For the first two years, then, Frontier ammunition consisted of 243, 270, 308 and 30-06 loadings based on once-fired cases topped with Hornady bullets. The actual loads were formulated using standard handloading techniques and the same canister powders available to the average reloader.

"In those days about the only difference between our ammo and the stuff turned out by the typical handloader was that our operation was capable of higher production," says Steve.

During those first couple of years Frontier ammo sold chiefly because it was priced substantially below the biggies, but after a while word got around that Hornady's cartridges didn't take a back seat to anybody's as far as accuracy was concerned. After a couple of years Frontier sales got to the point where Hornady couldn't get enough good surplus brass for his needs.

For that reason an important decision was made in mid-1971; henceforth, Frontier ammo would be assembled from new, virgin brass just like that used by the big three here. Federal Cartridge agreed to supply the primed brass.

New Worlds

Once the decision to make "new" ammunition was made, a grand new vista opened up at Frontier. No longer restricted to cartridges based on military brass or slightly altered versions thereof, Frontier's line was limited only by the selection of cases offered by Federal Cartridge. And by 1972, Federal began a tremendous expansion of their own cartridge line, loading most popular rifle and pistol calibers. Since they were tooled up to produce brass for their own ammo, it

was a simple matter of changing the headstamp to fill an order for Frontier. As for bullets, the Hornadys certainly had no problem there!

Since 1972 the Frontier line has grown from four rifle calibers and 8 loads to the current one—43 loadings among 10 rifle and 6 handgun calibers. In rifle chamberings there's the 222, 22-250, 223, 243, 270, 7mm, 30 Carbine, 30-30, 308 and 30-06. Fron-

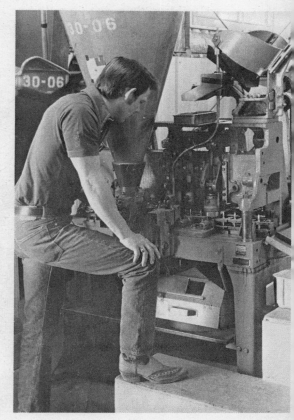

Each Frontier caliber is loaded on a machine permanently set up for that specific cartridge.

Frontier handgun cartridges are loaded on these several machines.

Steve Hornady waits for a prairie dog to show. Many Frontier cartridges are checked in the field in just this manner.

Steve Hornady records velocity and load data as ballistician Ed Heers shoots groups in underground test tunnel.

tier pistol and revolver cartridges can be had in 380, 9mm, 38 Special, 45 Auto, 357 Magnum and 44 Magnum.

Frontier's loading operations can best be described, perhaps, as somewhere between an efficient home handloading setup and the highly automated Winchester kind of operation. At Frontier there's a loading machine permanently set up to crank out each caliber; only the powder and bullets change according to the specific load.

If, for example, 130-gr. 270 ammo is needed, one of the operators goes over to that particular machine, adds the prescribed powder and bullets, makes whatever adjustments are necessary (based on the first few rounds), and that's it.

As informal as it sounds, the quality control used in the production of Frontier ammo is quite stringent. Random samples are continually taken next door to the bullet-making facility where they are checked for pressure, velocity, and accuracy in Hornady's ballistic lab/test range.

Speaking from my own experience, I've found Frontier ammo to be as accurate as any—and in some cases noticeably better. Here is an example—the 22-250, loaded with Hornady's 53-gr. match hollow-point, is consistently a half-MOA load in a Savage 112V I have. This same load proved itself further when Steve, his ballistician Ed Heers, and I went through about 10 boxes of the stuff shooting prairie dogs in western Nebraska. Shooting a Remington 700 sporter—not a varminter—we made some pretty impressive shots out to 300 yards and beyond. That's not bad at all for factory ammo! •

Steyr-Daimler-Puch

The rifle you'll read about here, a new bolt action tentatively called the Mannlicher Model 79, was one I used in SDP's great hunting grounds in 1976. That was a prototype, of course, but a rifle quite close to the production model in most if not all respects. I didn't do well with it at Donners bachwald on chamois, but that was my fault—as much as I hate to admit it! To recap briefly, I missed a shot at some 360-400 meters, my M79 in caliber 6.5×57R.

The new Mannlicher rifle was announced at the NSGA in Houston last January. From the comments I overheard from numerous visitors at the SDP booth, the new M79 showed a lot of appeal—which it has for me, too—and justly so.

Several unusual aspects of the M79 will, I think, intrigue U.S. hunter/riflemen—first, there's the quickly removable-replaceable magazine, the standard one holding 3 cartridges and reloadable in or out of the rifle. That last also applies to an optional 6-shot magazine, though this carrier necessarily protrudes below the stock line, thus hindering to a degree rifle handling and symmetry. Still, for those hunters who want, even demand, fire power, there it is. Incidentally, yet important, is the magazine's interior design—cartridges won't be point-damaged via recoil, which happens too frequently to those last one or 2 loads left lying in the bottom of the conventional magazine. These M79 magazines, note, are *steel,* not the plastic types used on some previous SDP rifles.

The new M79 continues the well-proven cold-hammered barrels that have enhanced the reputation of Steyr rifles for consistently good accuracy. Now these barrels are specially treated to produce a rust-resistant interior surface. Whether this modern bore-surface treatment will, in fact, preclude rusting I can't say now—it's too early to tell, but if it does many oft-neglected rifles would benefit indeed.

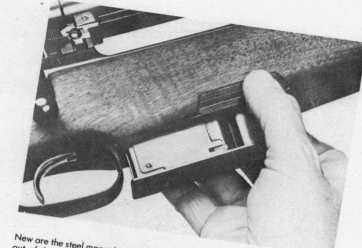

New are the steel magazines on the Model 79–3- or 6-shot, both loadable in or out of the rifle.

The Model 79 Mannlicher taken down. Note taper of barrel, trigger group, trigger guard and magazine. Latter can be loaded in or out of rifle.

Last, but notable, is a new-design trigger on the M79 Steyr rifle—a push-forward single-set type that, in the sample rifle I tried at Houston, worked well in both set and unset modes. Lacking a test scale, I'd guess the unset weight of pull was about 4 lbs. or less, the set letoff taking no more than an ounce or two of pressure. Both modes gave a firm, crisp release as factory adjusted, and the owner can readily alter the pull as desired, including travel and release weight.

The bridge and receiver ring of the Mannlicher M79 are tapped for scope mounting, of course, and virtually all scope bases can be attached in minutes. Steyr also offers its own quick-detachable scope mount system—a side-swinging type, the scope pivoting on the receiver a la Redfield.

A glare-free open rear sight is barrel mounted, as is a ramp front sight. The right-side silent safety, sited just behind the bolt handle, locks both firing pin and the bolt, and a rear-protruding pin—in the streamlined bolt sleeve—acts as an indicator to show when the rifle is cocked.

All in all, the latest Mannlicher bolt rifle is slim and trim, its average weight (unloaded) 7.7 lbs. Calibers offered include 270, 30-06, 6.5×57, 7×64, 6.5×55 and 7.5×55.

I'm anxious to try out the full-production version. My prototype, used in Austria, did not have the new trigger, and I'm a firm believer in light, crisp triggers, at the test bench or in the field.

The new Model 79 has a noiseless, easily-handled safety which locks the firing pin (note indicator showing the rifle is cocked) and the breechbolt.

What does the Mannlicher M79 rifle cost over here? Ouch—at $655 it can hardly be called inexpensive! But it is a truly high-quality, innovative-design sporting rifle, a cut well above some of the competition. Inflation and the falling dollar—as if you didn't know—are responsible for much of the current sales price, regrettably, but I suggest you examine the M79 closely before you decide that the price is too steep. In fact, of course, some of the others aren't far behind.

If a test specimen of the Mannlicher M79 reaches me in time I'll add a short shooting report to these notes, the deep snows and cold temperatures permitting.   J.T.A.

Steyr Daimler Puch/Renato Gamba

The handsome London side-by-side made by Renato Gamba and sold here by Steyr • Below—this is optional engraving on the Ambassador Executive shotguns, usually by Galeazzi or Fracassi.

There's a new detachable steel box magazine with single-column feeding available for a couple of the Steyr-Mannlicher centerfire rifles, but their biggest news is a line of side-by-side and over-under shotguns, these made in Italy by Armi Renato Gamba. Seven such Gamba shotguns are available, prices from $595 to $7310. Top of the line is a 12- or 20-gauge sidelock lateral double labeled the Ambassador, which has Holland & Holland-type locks with special patented double safeties, a choice of single or double triggers, ejectors, selected fancy walnut stock and extensive engraving. Barrel lengths are 27½″ or 28⅜″, with chokes as desired.

Side-by-side lovers will really go for the London models, these available in Field, Churchill or Competition grades, and differing mainly in barrel length, top-rib form, triggers, stock and forearm. In 12 or 20 gauge, with all the Ambassador features, but less costly engraving, the London is $2650 for the double trigger version, furnished in a handsome fitted leather case. A single trigger is $212 extra. The Churchill grade has 25″ barrels and a narrow Churchill-type rib. The Field grade has 26¾″ or 27½″ barrels, the Competition version 28⅜″ barrels.

Two Anson and Deeley boxlock side-by-side doubles—the Oxford and the Hunter—are priced at $1455 and

$595 respectively, these with double triggers, straight or pistol grip walnut stock, and the same barrel lengths as the London. The Oxford has ejectors, a hinged front trigger, and fine scroll engraving; the Hunter has plain extractors, double triggers and floral engraving.

Three boxlock over-unders, made in 12 gauge only, are offered by Steyr/Gamba—the 77/E has Purdey-type locking, a single trigger and ejectors, has a pistol grip stock and semi-beaver-tail fore-end, and chrome-lined barrels 26¾″ or 27½″ long. The greyed receiver carries hunting scene engraving, and the gun weighs 7¼ lbs. Retail cost is $680.

The Icaro comes with a single trigger and ejectors, and is basically the

same as the 77/E, but lacks the latter's chrome-lined barrels, BT forearm, recoil pad or pistol grip shape. The Icaro sells for $595, weighs under 6½ lbs. (The Icaro is available in three grades and two gauges in Italy.)

The Edinburgh, with 27½″ or 29″ chopper lump (demi-block) barrels, has a top ventilated rib as well as ventilated side ribs, and is considered Renato Gamba's best over-under offered here. (An over-under based on the Boss system and called the Commodore, is marketed in Italy, but is not now offered in the U.S.) Priced at $1545, the Edinburgh has a single trigger and ejectors, an oil-finished, hand-checkered walnut stocking and a hand-cut engraved receiver. It can also be had as a game gun.   L.S.S.

New Engraving Tool

by HARRY PHILLIPS

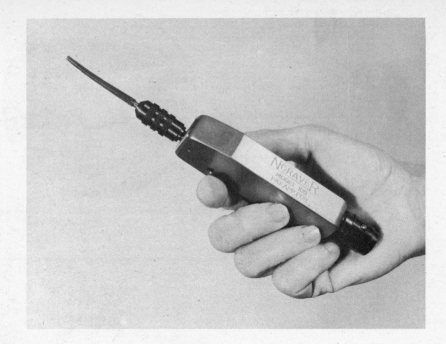

The new engraving machine pictured here is made by the NgraveR Co. of Oakdale, CT. This miniature impact tool, called the Model 100, is the brainchild of gunsmith R. J. Phillips. Four years ago he wanted an engraving machine, the well-known Gravermeister, but the $500 cost was more than he could afford. He decided to invent his own—and he did!

Today the M100 is used by all across the country. At under $100 it's one of the best tools available for the beginning engraver or amateur metalman.

Weighing only 5 ounces and well-machined, such quality parts as ball and needle bearings are used in its construction. Power is supplied by any flexible-shaft machine, this small jackhammer producing 300 to 1,500 impacts per minute.

Mechanically operated on a new patented principle (U.S. No. 4,030, 556, dated June 12, 1977), the flex-shaft machine selected rotates on an internal drive shaft, inside the M100, to which is attached a cam. This revolving cam causes a striker to retract against a plunger, which in turn compresses a spring, forcing the striker against the tool holder.

Even the beginner, we were told, can cut clean, bright lines effortlessly and without ever-present possibility of the graver accidentally skidding across the work.

With some practice, the amateur can chisel patterns in metal with the ease, accuracy and speed of a professional engraver. By using a foot-controlled rheostat, the craftsman can concentrate all his energy and efforts on the work before him.

The 39 different gravers offered are heat treated to an ultimate hardness of 61 on the Rockwell C scale.

According to the NgraveR Co., several professional engravers have tried the machine, all reporting that the M100 out-performs everything else similar to it on the market. ●

Stainless Steel Shotshells

Modern smokeless powder shotgun cartridges are a no-no for old shotguns made long ago—the outside hammer guns, with or without Damascus (twist) barrels, even many early hammerless guns—and factory loads powered by black powder are hard to find, impossible to locate in many areas.

Now there's a good solution—Conversion Arms, Inc. (P. O. Box 449, Yuba City, CA 95991) has just introduced all-stainless steel 12-ga. shotshells (2³/₄″ and 2¹/₂″) formed at the base to take standard No. 11 percussion caps. No loading or priming tools are needed—simply fill with black powder, 50 to 70 grains of FFG being suggested, add a card wad or plastic shotcap, pour in 1¹/₄ oz. of shot, place a card wad over the pellets and push the cap onto the integral nipple.

You can, of course, vary the shot load, too, but in any setup use a fair amount of pressure on the over-powder wad and on the over-shot wad

for best combustion and performance. A wood dowel or "short starter" works well, and snug-fitting cork or felt wads can be substituted if space permits.

CAI sells these S.S. shotshells for $7.95 each or 2 for $14.95, postpaid, and a detailed instruction pamphlet on their use is included. They're guaranteed for life.   J.T.A.

Handloading Report

The art and science of reloading ammunition, metallics or shotshells, continues to grow apace. In view of the soaring costs of fixed factory cartridges, that's hardly surprising. Here is a rundown on what's new and interesting.

by GEORGE C. NONTE, Jr. and the editors

Ponsness-Warren Mult-O-Matic

Well, it had to happen, I suppose. I've just learned that Posness-Warren, in designing their new Mult-O-Matic 600B shotshell press, hired time-and-motion experts to study the man-and-machine problem. Thus did P-W enter the realm of stop watches, sophisticated ergonomics, muscular motion, and the like.

The result? According to Charles Warren, P-W's president, the tool is capable of 500 finished shotshells per hour, *without fatigue,* and every shell perfect. Moreover, note, no rise in price!

The first thing learned, C.W. added, was that placing primers individually slowed down the loading process and also distracted the operator's attention, thereby spoiling good rhythm. Having made that surprising discovery, all was not lost—their primer-feed system used on the Size-O-Matic loader was used on the 600 B.

This primer-feed system takes a box of 100 primers, loadable without any hand touching, and a new feed tray cover prevents spilling or cocking of the primers. Operation of the press activates the gravity-vibration controlled primer unit, delivering them to the primer station automatically.

Operation of the new Mult-O-Matic is straightforward—the right hand pulls the angled lever and feeds in the empty cases, the left hand inserts wads into the tip-out guide and manually indexes the 8 stations.

Each shotshell is held throughout the loading cycle in its own full-length sizing die, avoiding distorsion that might otherwise occur during crimping, etc.

Other important points on the Mult-O-Matic are: extra capacity powder and shot containers, both with baffles for consistent charges; shutoff valves and drains for powder and pellets; a ball-bearing crimp starter; a spent-primer box, a chute to

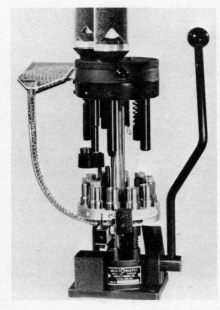

The Ponsness-Warren Mult-O-Matic shotshell press.

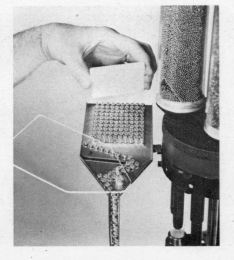

New P-W swing-away primer tray cover prevents cocking or tipping of primers.

control loaded rounds, and a twin-port construction for greater leverage, durability and rigidity.

Furnished usually in 12 gauge, other tooling sets in 16, 20, 28 and 410 are available, these interchanging in a few minutes. List price is $329.50.

P-W has several new items to improve or enhance performance of their shotshell loaders. A swing-away clear plastic primer tray cover is intended for use with the P-W Size-O-Matic 800B and Mult-O-Matic 600B shotshell tools. The patented auto primer system holds 100 primers and, after loading them and sliding the cover over, tipping or cocking of primers is prevented.

Extra long (24 inches) powder and shot tubes are now offered for the same P-W presses, meant for the high-production operators and costing $11 each.

Dust covers for P-W tools come in two sizes—one for the 800B/600B reloaders ($11.95 each), the other for the Du-O-Matic 375 and Magn-O-Matic 10, cost $9.95 each.

The powder bushing table in the 1978 P-W shotshell reloading catalog now includes powder drops for the heavier charges needed for reloading 10-gauge shotshells. The new figures dropped by the larger bushings cover DuPont IMR 4227, Winchester 540 and Winchester 571 powders.

The bushing chart lists powder drops for DuPont, Hercules, Winchester, Hodgdon, Alcan, C-I-L and Norma powers, using all Ponsness-Warren powder bushings. The chart also shows shot drops for 14 different P-W shot bushings from 1/2 to 2 1/4 ounces.   J.T.A.

New Sierra Bullet Board

Announced in late 1977, this new display shows Sierra's complete line of jacketed bullets, including their two latest—the 240-gr. 45 Colt (rimmed) and the 375 big game hunting bullet (300-gr.).

A handy and ready reference source, the board gives caliber, diameter, grain weight and design of each of the 84 precision-made Sierra bullets.

About 22″ wide by 15″ in its polished wood-tone frame, the Sierra Bullet Board makes a handsome wall decoration as well. Cost is $30—see your local Sierra dealer, or direct (postpaid) from Sierra Bullets, 10532 South Painter Ave., Santa Fe Springs, CA 90670.   J.T.A.

Universal Charge Bar

Multi-Scale Charge, Ltd., has an improved version available now of their popular device for accurately setting and throwing powder/shot loads for shotshells. The good basic qualities of the earlier type—which we've commented on before—have been retained in the Model B, a tool that takes the place of dozens of charge bushings. Adjustability runs from 4.5 to 71 grains of powder and from 1/2 to 1 3/4 ozs. of shot, the exact charges easily and quickly set via Vernier scales, and uniformly maintained from then on.

Made for most MEC shotshell presses and for the Texan LT, GT and FW models, the 5-year-guaranteed Universal Charge Bar is $17.95, including full calibration plus a powder and shot chart.   J.T.A.

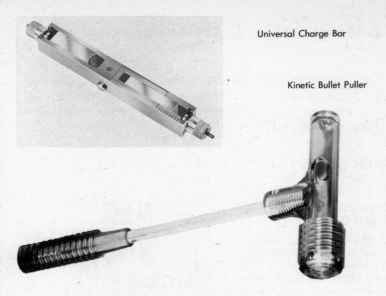

Universal Charge Bar

Kinetic Bullet Puller

Kinetic Bullet Puller and Shell Holder

I had owned and used one of these useful and effective tools for years, mine the original version. I'd used it on numerous occasions with no difficulty, and then one day I couldn't find it—I think I loaned it to someone who failed to return it.

I wrote to Quinetics, Inc. (Box 13237, San Antonio, TX 78213) and, soon thereafter, found the new version in my mailbox.

A pulling job was waiting so I put the revised and improved model to use immediately. It worked well, especially the redesigned chuck—rotating the cap to loosen it allows insertion of the cartridge (rimmed or rimless), then tightening the cap completes the loading. Next, a few sharp raps of the bottom end against a hard surface drops the bullet into the inside compartment.

To remove the pulled bullet and powder, the makers have provided a hole at the left side of the main body, but warn that the hole should be covered with a piece of tape to avoid accidental spilling of the powder during bullet extraction.

I found that technique tedious and awkward—removing the tape and replacing at every cycle was time-consuming, particularly because the hole was on the side. The curves near the hole made applying the tape inconvenient. I think it would be better to have the hole at the front of the plastic body, where tape application would be easier.

More than that, though. I found it easier to leave the tape on throughout the bullet-pulling session, removing the cap after each extraction and dumping bullet and powder out of the top end into a suitable container.

Cost, retail, of the KBP is $12.95.

Quinetics also sent me their newer product, the Multi-Caliber Shell-Holder. Usable on virtually all loading presses with removable shell-holder rams, this device holds its chuck jaws in the open position by magnetic action. No threading on or screws are needed to install the M-C holder, and it "automatically adjusts to receive and hold all popular cartridge cases—rimmed and rimless."

It didn't work out quite that way for me, but then I'm a fumble-fingered guy who has to stop and think when I tie my shoes. Mounting the unit on an RCBS press I rotated the knurled body ring to position the chuck finger in the open position, but it took a fair amount of twiddling and twirling to lock a case—more or less—into the chuck. Removing the case was a bit easier, but only a little. Nor did the case seem to become firmly locked, either. For that reason I've been using the Multi-Caliber shell-holder for bullet seating, not case sizing. This Quinetics device sells for $7.95.   J.T.A.

New Nosler Bullet Board

This latest projectile panel carries the complete line of Nosler bullets. Cutaways of both types—Solid Base and Partition—are encircled by over 50 bullets. Full-color illustrations of several game animals grace the new board, its walnut-stained wooden frame suitable for den or game room. Each board is consecutively serial numbered. The caliber and weight of each bullet appears next to each sample.

The boards, available at most dealers, may also be bought from the manufacturer, ($25 plus $2.50 for shipping), Nosler Bullets, Inc., P. O. Box 688, Beaverton, OR 97005.

Hornady Non-Fouling Bullet

Well, maybe not 100% non-fouling—that will depend on the particular gun being used, bullet velocity, and so on. Still, this latest 38-cal. bullet reduces barrel leading by about 70%, says Mr. Hornady.

Tests conducted at the company's ballistics lab, using the new knurled 158-gr. semi-wadcutter bullets showed a lead residue in the bore of only 1.2mg per bullet. Conventional bullets of the same type and weight left 4.3mg per bullet—almost 4 times as much.

Traditional bullets—again depending on their MV—lead the bore because the lube is dissipated long before the projectile reaches the muzzle. The new Hornady bullet has a *knurled* bearing surface instead of lubricating grooves. During manu-

facture the bullet is bathed in the lubricant, which penetrates the "pores" created by the knurling. Therefore the lube stays with the bullet throughout its trip down the barrel.

As if that weren't enough, plus the easier bore cleaning that results, Hornady reports a noticeable improvement in accuracy. Prices? About like those for standard bullets.

J.T.A.

Hornady 8mm Bullets

Early in 1977 Remington introduced a new cartridge, the 8mm Magnum. In mid-June of the same year, Hornady announced an 8mm bullet—a 220-gr. soft point—which is pretty fast work. Hornady's R&D department must have hustled.

The new flat-base bullet has Hornady's special Secant Ogive Spire Point form, internal jacket grooving for controlled expansion, and the jacket is extra heavy for deep penetration.

This new 8mm, one of 85 rifle bullets Hornady now offers the handloader, costs $8.95 per 100. Hornady will gladly supply complete information on all of their bullets, handgun types as included, on request.

New Hornady 45 ACP Bullet

This 230-gr. bullet has a heavy full metal jacket for deeper penetration and smoother, more reliable feeding. It's an accurate bullet, and its stopping power and dependability should make it a popular choice among handloaders. $7 per 100 is the retail price.

J.T.A.

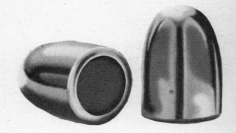

New Hodgdon Manuals

Two booklets, both released in mid-1977, are offered by the folks at Shawnee-Mission, Kansas (66202). One is their 44-page (plus covers) *Pyrodex/Black Powder Manual,* a most welcome paperback that relates the development of Pyrodex, plus articles on black powder shooting and hunting. Load data covers the propel-

lants in muzzle-loading and cartridge arms, and there's an excellent piece by George Nonte called "Basics of Black Powder Shooting." All this for $1, from your dealer or Hodgdon.

The other booklet (48 pp. plus covers) is a condensation of Hodgdon's *Data Manual,* presenting a good selection of loads—rifle, shotgun and handgun—that use, naturally, the numerous Hodgdon smokeless powders. However, there are some Pyro-

dex data also, and a valuable Pyrodex-Black Powder conversion table.

This Hodgdon publication is free.

New Hodgdon Catalog

This 255-page well-illustrated catalog—Hodgdon's 17th edition—offers shooters, hunters and reloaders a wider variety of products than ever before. The big book covers virtually every need of the gunning world. Want a copy? Write to B. E. Hodgdon, Inc., 7710 West 50 Highway, Shawnee Mission, KS 66202. J.T.A.

Hidalgo Bench Rest Stool

Like everyone else, BR shooters come in all sizes and hefts, not to mention lengths of legs and torsos. Obviously no fixed-height stool is going to serve such disparate human forms equally well—an adjustable-height *sitzbank* is the answer, of course, and Tony Hidalgo (6 Capp St., Carteret, NJ 07008), a benchrester himself, has come up with one that meets the requirements in basic form.

His sturdy and solid design is strong—three of his heaviest fellow

shooters, totaling some 775 lbs., stood on his stool at one time, and nothing dire happened. Good reason—the 4 legs supporting the 12″×19″ top (1/2″ exterior grade plywood) are made of 7/8″×2″ prime grade oak, as are the stretchers and rungs. The seat can be adjusted from 17″ to 21″ in 4 steps, which should be ample for most users. The stout hardware is of cadmium-plated steel.

The assembled stool, ready to use, is unfinished, the introductory price $19.95 (as of November 1977), but that may be—when you read this—

$24.75. Mr. Hidalgo will offer a finished stool, too, varnished and with a cushioned seat, for $29.95.

Our sample was all that it promised to be, strong and stable at any height. I found 17″ to be correct for my 6-foot frame, that elevation just right for my shooting bench when I'm using a high shooting position. It takes only a moment to re-adjust for any of the other 3 heights and, when desired, the Hidalgo stool can be readily folded into a compact, easily-stored package. Weight is 9 lbs.   J.T.A.

Griffith Cartridge Cases

The range of calibers offered by Dick Griffith (6000 Chandler, Bakersfield, CA 93307) is quite extensive, and he's adding to the list as demand dictates. Currently he can supply 62 varieties, from the 221 Fireball to the 50-110 Winchester—and with just about anything else in between. These are, of course, calibers *not* obtainable from the big factories.

Made from once-fired or new brass he has re-formed, he can also deliver the latest Basic Cases—those by RCBS, B.E.L.L. and Norma, including the latter's belted Magnum type, which is 2.835″ overall.

Dick's prices run from $3.75 for the 7.65 Belgian Mauser to a high of $30 for the 11.2×72 Schuler, all per box of 20, all unprimed. Most of his prices are well under $10 per 20, but a number exceed that figure slightly.

Send Dick a stamped, self-addressed envelope for his list, but note that he can actually ship *only* to holders of FFL licenses.   J.T.A.

Hoppe's Helps

In the dear dead past Hoppe's was well and favorably known—and it still is, these many years later—for one product, and only that one. Hoppe's No. 9, a bore-cleaning solvent whose unique and distinctive aroma (women generally call it a smell, and a noxious one at that, some of them insist), whenever sniffed, turns on the shooter, reminds him of days afield and afoot—the cool crisp days of fall, the acrid smoke of wood fires, the pungent fragrance of old No. 9, no matter what the ladies say!

Things are different today—Hoppe's is a division of Penguin Industries and the supplier of various products for the shooting world. (I sometimes wonder if we'll see, one day, a vast conglomerate that owns *everybody*.)

The latest Hoppe's items number two—both for the black powder fan, or for him using Pyrodex, too, I daresay. The Nipple Pick—a slender (0.025″) drill seated into a knurled handle for easy manipulation—is used for cleaning and clearing nipples or flintlock barrel flash holes. The length of the drill is 1¼ inches, so it could serve as an emergency punch for decapping short metallic cartridge cases. List, $1.49.

The other new piece is a lead ball or bullet retriever, meant for those sad occasions when you forgot to put the powder charge down the barrel first.

This Ball Puller has a knurled brass collar that holds a stud threaded for standard BP cleaning rods, the other end accepting one of two steel wood-type screws. Retail, $1.98.

However, this device is designed for 44 caliber (or larger) bores. To be most effective such devices should be a fairly close fit for the bore in use, otherwise there's too much wobble and the attendant danger of not being able to drive the screw into the ball's center—and damage to the bore could also result if the screw slipped.

See your M.L. dealer or write to Hoppe's—Parkesburg, PA 19365.
      J.T.A.

Hoppe's Lead Ball Puller

Gussert Bullet/Cartridge Co.

This enterprising firm has a number of useful products for the muzzle-loading shooter, as well as one for the cartridge handloader—this last is their Rx Lithi-Lube, said to eliminate leading and to improve rifle performance. Solid or hollow sticks are available, both designed to fit most lubricating-sizing presses, with cost $1 each.

Gussert's chief product is Rx Basic Lube (which is compatible with all other lubes and may be freely mixed with them) and is designed for black powder firearms. More shooting without cleaning is the claim, compared to conventional greases, and a plus factor is its ability to give greater shot-to-shot uniformity, tighter grouping and much less fouling.

The most unusual Gussert product is the Rx Minie-Matic, a holder for their detergent-formula lube that eliminates the problem of hand-greasing the Minie or similar bullets. The head or top of the lube container is sized to accept bullets of 44, 45, 50, 54, 56 and 58 caliber (your choice). Seat the bullet into the opening, squeeze the plastic container, and there's your lubed bullet, ready to be picked out and loaded. More shots without cleaning applies to this

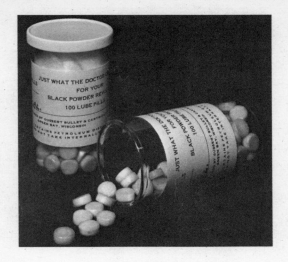

cuts down on loading time, and as before, the number of shots that can be fired without cleaning is increased. All popular calibers are available.

I have not found time to make a comparative test of these Gussert lubes—against greases of other makes or types—but I've used the handy Minié-Matic greasing device in 45 caliber, and it performed well. Removing the lubed bullet from the top opening does, in fact, put a mite of grease on the fingers, but not at all like the mess created when lubing Miniés by hand. The loads shot well, too, and I was able to get about 7-8 shots before having to clean the bore, whereas 3 or 4 firings were about the limit using another well-known BP grease.

I also used the Patch Pills, placing them over round balls in a Ruger Old Army. They were a lot faster to use, even though I placed *two* atop the balls, and there was a small but noticeable improvement in accuracy at the 25-yard range.   J.T.A.

Minié-Matic also.

The other Gussert items for the ML shooter are Rx Valley Forge, a black powder solvent and lube combined, which is said to permit lengthy shooting sessions without cleaning, and their Rx Patch Pills—those are wafer-like grease wads, round in form, that are placed over the seated balls in revolvers and pressed home. These "pills" consist of a superior lubricant, according to Gussert, which softens the BP fouling so that it is shot out of the barrel. Their use

---

Lyman Bullet Casting Kits

All three kits offer a choice of mould blocks from 20 of the most popular calibers, and they save you up to 20% of the separate component prices.

The Basic Contents include a single cavity mould with handles, a lead pot and dipper, a sizing die and punch, lube cutter, 4″ lube pan, Lyman's Ideal Lubricant, and Lyman's *Cast Bullet Handbook*. $39.95.

The Custom Offers the # 450 Lube/ Sizer, which prepares almost any cast bullet for high accuracy reloading, plus the Custom Kit offers an ingot mould, G-H&I dies, Lyman's *Cast Bullet Handbook* and Ideal lubricant, a single cavity mould with handles, and a lead pot with dipper. $89.95.

The Master Like the Custom Kit, but includes the new Mould Master XX casting furnace and a double-cavity mould with handles. The lead pot and dipper are excluded. $159.95.

MTM Products

MTM Molded Products (Dayton, Ohio 45414) has published their new catalog, yours for the asking. It offers complete information on MTM's line of high quality, plastic ammunition containers, tackle and fly boxes, and miscellaneous equipment for reloaders and shooters. Prices are shown for all products, and carry a 3-year guarantee.

New products include:
- 22 rimfire Match Ammo Box.
- 6- and 12-round Ammo Wallets for handgun cartridges.
- Magazine Wallets (clip carriers) for auto pistols.
- Slip-top ammo boxes for handgun rounds.
- 4″×3″×1″ pocket-size fly box.
- Lightweight tackle box.

MTM items are good stuff indeed,

Pro-Melt Lead Pot

It has long been a tenet of faith among handloaders—like for well over 100 years—that shooting lead balls or bullets was the way to go if component costs were to be reduced. Well, that's still true, though the numbers have changed for the worse, and there has always been the unreckoned cost, in time and money, of getting the lead alloy into shootable form, that is, casting the balls/bullets. That takes heat, mostly 110-volt these days, the lube, the gas-checks (if any), the cost of a lead pot and ladle, etc. In a word or two, and using the modern vogue phrase, there ain't no free lunch!

No indeed, and that brings me to the Pro-Melt machine—a rugged, excellently-designed and efficient lead pot, of bottom-pour style, that will cost the buyer a fair bit of money, an amount that will require a lot of bullet casting and shooting (anyway, casting) to amortize the initial outlay. I hasten to add—in view of what it is and how well it does its work—that the device seems worth its 3-figure cost.

Unlike other electric-powered, down-spout lead-mix melters, the Pro-Melt is truly thermostatically controlled and calibrated—you *know* what your particular mix temperature is, within a few degrees and, once the mix is fluid, a flashing red light demonstrates that the Pro-Melt is steadfastly maintaining the temperature selected within close limits. No separate thermometer is needed, whereas one is required with virtually all other lead pots if you're to be sure of getting the heat level you want.

Bullet casting, at best, is a pretty hot chore. If the heat generated isn't to escape and warm up the work area—which heat loss spells decreased efficiency, too—then good and adequate insulation is an emphatic requirement. The Pro-Melt is heavily insulated. In one test, with the mix temp at 800° F, the outside surface of the Pro-Melt measured 220° F. A competitive electric pot, its mix at 705° F, had a skin reading of 475° F —well over twice as high.

In other tests, including a 2,000-hour run and 900 test cycles without a hitch, the Pro-Melt showed a faster elapsed time to reach 800° F than other bottom-pour pots—25 minutes versus 29, 31 and 40 minutes—with its maximum 10-kilo (22 lbs.) load. Temperature variation with a full load was only plus or minus 9° F against almost twice that figure for

another brand.

My test of the Pro-Melt confirmed these claims, and only one small hitch developed. That soon fixed itself, as you'll see.

Assembly of the machine took about 10 minutes, and getting it to 650° F required about 35 minutes as lead scraps were placed in the reservoir. Start-up time is reduced considerably once the pot is well filled, for the thermostat—the heart of this modern device—is placed at the bottom of the pot, sensing the actual temperature in the pot. The user is warned—after the first use—to let at least a one-inch depth of lead mix *remain* in the pot unless the alloy is to be altered. With that much lead in the pot, or more, any temperature setting may be chosen when starting from cold. Adding the usual lead ingot (SAECO or Lyman type) after the mix is fluid drops the temperature for only a few minutes.

My small problem came after my lead mix reached the molten state—I could not get the mix to flow on lifting the lever-valve in spite of much jiggling, re-adjustment of the limit nuts

and mild cursing. Had I done something wrong in assembly or had I come across a fault? Suddenly—after another short lifting and dropping of the handle, here came the melted alloy, flowing smoothly and freely. I can only guess that some oxide of lead or dirt had entered the drop tube and temporarily impeded the discharge. An added bonus, I soon noticed, was a lack of leakage with the valve closed. Many bottom pour pots dribble a bit, when shut off, necessitating the placement of a container beneath the spout until the mix has cooled.

The Pro-Melt has a stainless steel non-rusting pot, comes with a roller-type adjustable mould guide, and may be set up for left- or right-hand operation. It carries a 1-year warranty against defects in material or workmanship, and is priced at $119.95, plus shipping charges. A similar pot, with like features but without bottom-pour ability, is $104.95—a saving for those casters who prefer the dip method.

The Pro-Melt pots are made by Ohio Thermal, 7030-A Huntley Rd., Columbus, OH 43229.   J.T.A.

RCBS

As most of you must know, Fred Huntington's big organization was taken over by Omark Industries a while back—as was Speer Bullets at about the same time—yet as far as I know all is still serene and untroubled in Oroville. That isn't always the case when a big fish gobbles up a smaller one—not infrequently new laws are laid down, new edicts from on high are issued and, sometimes, there's hell to pay.

As I've said, nothing drastic seems to have occured during the months since RCBS was absorbed or bought, but I can't help but wonder what happened to Alcan, once a flourishing concern, after its gathering in by Smith & Wesson? Alcan is out of business, of course, but why was it let die. Unprofitable? I suppose so, but it was, by all accounts, a going outfit when it was taken over several years ago—if the seven-figure sum paid for it, purportedly, is any evidence.

RCBS doesn't have much that's truly new or startling for the coming year unless they're holding out on me! Still, how could they have? RCBS already blankets the field—with a dozen blankets, that is—their offerings to the reloading clan comprising

RCBS Du-O-Measure, now redesigned, has multi-hole drum, allowing quick change from large- to small-cavity use. Built-in hopper baffle and cutoff plate are unique features. Price, $54.95 ● New

RCBS loading block has 80 stepped holes to accommodate most calibers except 22 Hornet, 380 ACP and 45-70. $2.25 each, and a 10-unit carton is available.

just about anything and everything I can think of apart from shotshell loading presses and the fringe gadgetry around that field. Best of all, to be sure, is the on-going high quality of the many things that RCBS offers—as anyone who has used their products knows. That quality is, I'm sure, the open secret of their great success; that and their cordial, under-standing relationship with their customers—a rapport, if you will, that far too many firms don't have, in or out of the reloading tool business.

The latest RCBS catalog is, as usual, filled with detailed information on the entire line, holds numerous illustrations and shows all prices. If you're getting into metallic cartridge loading, write for a copy—it's free. J.T.A.

Sinclair Inc.

Fred Sinclair operates this business, one devoted to making high-precision products for benchrest shooters—or for anyone interested in achieving greater accuracy. Among his several well-made tools are a small rack-and-pinion arbor press, a sensitive recapper and a conversion of the Lyman 310 tool into a handy case-neck sizer and decapper. The latter, made to handle any 222 case form via tool steel bushings, sells for $42.50 with one bushing. Extra bushings are $3 each.

Fred has several new tools for the reloader, he told me in a recent phone talk. Among these are a neck-turning tool, an improved deburrer for flash holes, a primer-pocket cleaner and a primer magazine for Lee's capper.

I've had no chance to use any of these new Sinclair items so far, but if time permits I'll try to show some pictures of them, plus their prices, and so on.

Sinclair offers moulds now in any bullet style, including gas check types. Those from 25- to 50-caliber cost $30, sizes over 50 and as large as 75, are $40 in regular form. Moulds for hollow-base or hollow-point bullets run $50. Fred is also offering

cut-rifled barrels, too—calibers from 25 to 72, rate of twist as desired (including gain-twist tubes), round or octagon, straight or tapered, and in outside diameters from 1¼" to 2½". False-muzzle barrels are also available, matching bullet starters, etc.

Sinclair markets a lot of stuff for the precision shooter, products other than his own make, too, and a catalog is available for $1. His address is 1200 Asbury Dr., New Haven, Ind. 46774.

I'm tempted to have Fred make me

a medium-heavy octagon barrel of 34 inches, chambered for the Sharps 40/3¼" Straight case, then fit it to a Sharps-Borchardt or High Wall action. Let's see—I'd need for it a 400-gr. mould, point pour type with a round-cavity base, a swage to bring the cast bullet to exact groove diameter, plus perhaps .001" to .0015" over groove size. Ah, if I were only 65 again, as Oliver Wendell Holmes once supposedly said as he watched some lissome damsel stroll along Pennsylvania Avenue. J.T.A.

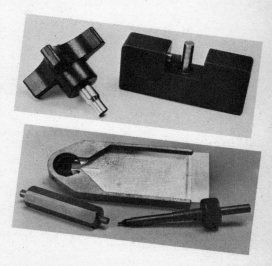

CUSTOM GUNS

AL LIND
Stocked in Russian Circassian, this 98 Mauser has a Titus 7x57 barrel, much custom metal work by Mark Lee and grip cap and buttplate engraved by Lynn Fliger.

JOE BALICKIE
Ultra-fancy English walnut stocks this pre-'64 M70 in 7x57mm. All metal work by Brownell except for Blackburn guard and Biesen buttplate. The 1/4-rib holds Brownell's double lever scope rings.

AL BIESEN
This M70 was stocked for the late Jack O'Connor some time ago, all metal work also by Biesen. A handsome job, typically Biesen, and now owned by Alex Schimek of Toronto, Canada.

EARL MILLIRON
One of Milliron's finest works is this classic 280 on a square-bridge *Mauserwerke* action. Metal work by Tom Burgess, the rifle owned by Alex Schimek of Toronto, Canada.

HAL HARTLEY
The Lenoir, NC, gunmaker created this colorful fiddleback maple stock for a Mark X Mauser-actioned rifle, the caliber 220 Swift—a favorite of his.

AL LIND

This rifle (and opposite) has a checkered bolt knob and M70 safety, by Mark Lee. A blind magazine was made and the stock hollowed out for a 6¾ lb. weight, including scope and mount.

DON ALLEN

A well-figured piece of Allen's own exotic walnut stocks this graceful '98 Mauser-actioned sporter. The scope is a Leupold and there's a floorplate release in the new guard.

AL BIESEN

A pre-64 M70 Winchester was used for this 375 H&H Magnum. The wood is French walnut, all work done by Al Biesen. Built for Alex Schimek of Toronto, Canada.

CHARLES E. GRACE

M70, its classic French walnut stock checkered in 24 lpi in a fleur de lis pattern completely encircling grip and fore-end. Trapped buttplate and grip cap by Al Biesen.

HAL HARTLEY

The Lenoir, NC, gunmaker created this colorful fiddleback maple stock for a Mark X Mauser-actioned rifle, the caliber 220 Swift—a favorite of his.

Consult our Directory of the Arms Trade pages for the location of firms or individuals mentioned.

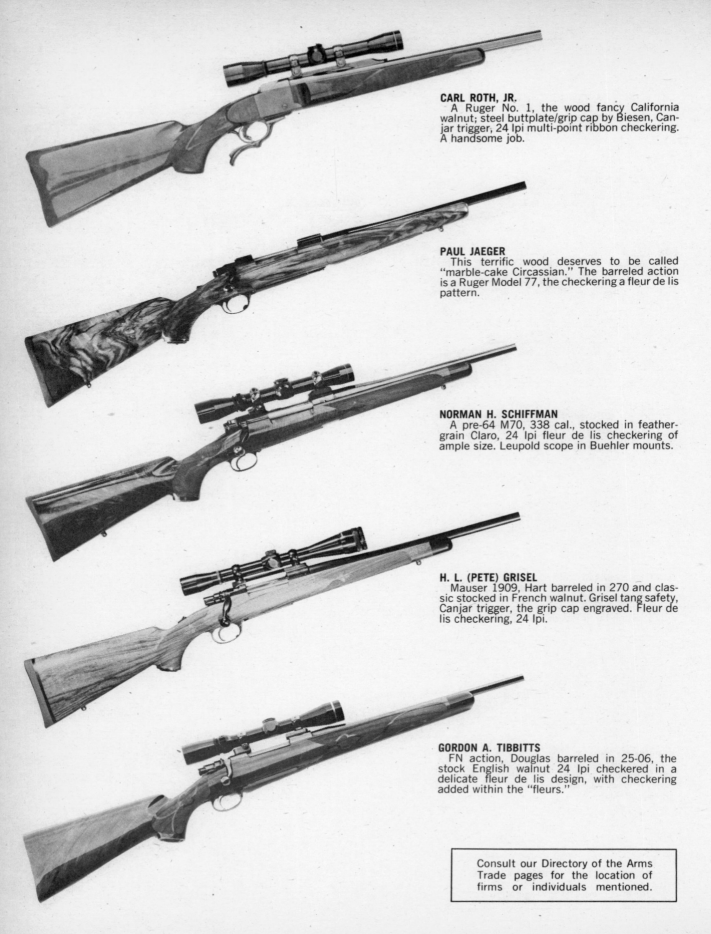

CARL ROTH, JR.
A Ruger No. 1, the wood fancy California walnut; steel buttplate/grip cap by Biesen, Canjar trigger, 24 lpi multi-point ribbon checkering. A handsome job.

PAUL JAEGER
This terrific wood deserves to be called "marble-cake Circassian." The barreled action is a Ruger Model 77, the checkering a fleur de lis pattern.

NORMAN H. SCHIFFMAN
A pre-64 M70, 338 cal., stocked in feather-grain Claro, 24 lpi fleur de lis checkering of ample size. Leupold scope in Buehler mounts.

H. L. (PETE) GRISEL
Mauser 1909, Hart barreled in 270 and classic stocked in French walnut. Grisel tang safety, Canjar trigger, the grip cap engraved. Fleur de lis checkering, 24 lpi.

GORDON A. TIBBITTS
FN action, Douglas barreled in 25-06, the stock English walnut 24 lpi checkered in a delicate fleur de lis design, with checkering added within the "fleurs."

Consult our Directory of the Arms Trade pages for the location of firms or individuals mentioned.

CARL ROTH, JR.
A Ruger No. 1, the wood fancy California walnut; steel buttplate/grip cap by Biesen, Canjar trigger, 24 lpi multi-point ribbon checkering. A handsome job.

PAUL JAEGER
This terrific wood deserves to be called "marble-cake Circassian." The barreled action is a Ruger Model 77, the checkering a fleur de lis pattern.

NORMAN H. SCHIFFMAN
A pre-64 M70, 338 cal., stocked in feather-grain Claro, 24 lpi fleur de lis checkering of ample size. Leupold scope in Buehler mounts.

H. L. (PETE) GRISEL
M42 Winchester stocked in Oregon walnut to conform with original fittings. Engraving and gold inlays by Eugene Koevenig, all metal work by Pete.

GORDON A. TIBBITTS
FN action, Douglas barreled in 25-06, the stock English walnut 24 lpi checkered in a delicate fleur de lis design, with checkering added within the "fleurs."

FRED D. SPEISER
This M70 action, with Shilen 25-06 barrel, is stocked in English walnut from Vic Miller, grip cap and fore-end of ebony. Photo by J. Frederikson.

ROBERT M. WINTER
A 700 Remington, Shilen barreled and stocked in fancy American walnut, a Pachmayr pad and Brownell grip cap fitted. Ted Blackburn made the trigger guard/floorplate.

DOMINIC DI STEFANO
Graceful stocking in the classic style of a pre-'64 Model 70-actioned rifle, the walnut showing a nice broken fiddleback grain.

DUANE WIEBE
A Mauser '98 shortened $^5/_8$", this 250-3000 stocked in French walnut, point checkered. Ted Blackburn guard/floorplate, a skeleton grip cap fitted. One of a near-pair.

BISHOP STOCKS
Custom fitted and hand finished at their Warsaw, MO, shop, this earlier drilling was stocked for a left-handed customer.

DAHL'S CUSTOM STOCKS
Unusual to see a restocked Mauser 660, here in 458! New Zealand walnut, fully checkered in a special pattern, fully around the fore-end and over the grip.

FRED D. SPEISER
A Ruger No. 1 in 243, stocked in fancy Claro walnut, Niedner steel buttplate and grip cap, fleur de lis/ribbon checkering. Photo by J. Frederikson.

ROBERT M. WINTER
M70 in 30-06, classic stocked in European walnut, 3-panel point checkered, a Pachmayr pad and skeleton grip cap fitted. Note grip radius.

DOMINIC DI STEFANO
Graceful stocking in the classic style of a pre-'64 Model 70-actioned rifle, the walnut showing a nice broken fiddleback grain.

FRED R. WELLS
A pre-64 M70 with Douglas 270 barrel, the French walnut stock ebony tipped, 26 lpi checkered and oil finished. Biesen trap buttplate and grip cap.

HUBERT HECHT
A Sauer & Sohn drilling restocked in dense French walnut, all metal parts fully reworked to as-new condition and refinished.

STEPHEN L. BILLEB
Classic and elegant stocking of a Mexican –98 action barreled by Hobaugh in 7x57mm, with metalsmithing also by Billeb, Biesen buttplate and grip cap. As shown, 6¾ lbs.

Double Action Auto Test

by KENNETH L. WALTERS

Four D.A. auto pistols were fired extensively to check reliability — 250 handloads and 50 factory rounds were put through each. There were problems.

DOUBLE ACTION big bore auto pistols have been available since the middle 1930s when Walther introduced the P38. Though such large-magazine-capacity single-action 9mms as the Browning were introduced about the same time, it was not until the early 1970s that a gun combining the D.A. mechanism and a high magazine capacity—the S&W M59—went into production. Since then other multi-shot pistols, the 9mm Beretta and Browning, plus the H&K 45 D.A. have also appeared. It is these two styles of automatics, large magazine capacity double action 9mm Luger and double action 45 ACP's, that are discussed and functionally tested herein.

For many years it was felt that a good single-action auto, say the Colt Commander or the 45 ACP, was all anyone really needed, and that such guns as the S&W M59 were, because of their more complex mechanisms, overly trouble prone. In the S&W case this criticism was valid until very

recently, as substantiated in at least one article.[1] (S&W recalled all of these M59s). However, my functional testing shows that the D.A. Beretta, the new or repaired S&W M59, the D.A. Browning and H&K 45s not only rival the functioning quality of the older Colts but, indeed, pass them.

To test these 4 pistols I decided, somewhat arbitrarily, to investigate their ability to handle cast bullet reloads, among others. Why? Well, for the average shooter to become proficient with a handgun requires more than casual practice, extensive shooting which few could afford to do with factory ammunition. Also, since the several 45 ACP guns I've owned

worked very well with factory ammunition but not at all well with cast bullets, the latter would provide a more severe test. Each gun was tested with 250 rounds of reloads and 50 factory cartridges.

Lyman bullet 356402 (truncated cone) was used for the 9mms and their 452374 (round nose) for the 45s because they're highly popular, at least of Lyman's offerings. New 9mm cases were used because those were all I had, but various old lots of GI brass were used in the Browning and H&K in the belief that they would increase the chances for trouble. Of course both 45s were fed equal quantities of cases of all types. A Star press was used to minimize unintentional variations in assembly.

1978 should see the introduction of Walther's new PP-Super pistol in 9mm Police, 380 and 32 calibers.

[1]"The S&W Model 59, Boon Or Bust," by J. Hillock, *Guns Illustrated*, 9th ed., 1976.

Walther's excellent P38 9mm Parabellum (Luger) double action automatic. Introduced in the 1930s and used throughout WW II, this was the first of its kind.

Smith & Wesson's M59 9mm Para. pistol was the first widely produced automatic to incorporate a double action mechanism with a large (14 shot) magazine capacity.

The Beretta 16-shot double action 9mm Para. pistol. No malfunctions occurred in firing 250 reloads and 50 factory cartridges.

The Browning D. A. 45, initially offered in 9mm Para. and 38 Colt Super, is no longer available in those calibers because of cost increases.

Magazine Performance

The first test observations concerned magazine functioning in the 9mms. These big-capacity magazines held the rounds almost in direct line with the bore. Thus when the slide comes forward and catches the cartridge it is very easy for the truncated-cone bullet to go straight into the chamber. The Walther P38s[2] and a Colt Commander, however, showed that these single-column magazines seem to hold the bullet just slightly lower. When the slide in these guns grabs the cartridge, the bullet nose usually drops a little, causing the bullet to hit the ramp too low for reliable feeding. Individual guns will vary, of course, so the functioning of any auto pistol should be repeatedly checked before serious use. Still, the large capacity 9mms do seem well suited to using Lyman's excellent bullet.

The Beretta and Browning took first honors with none and one malfunction respectively. Since the

Browning failed to chamber one of the cast bullet loads, its performance wasn't perfect, but certainly one failure in 300 tries is an impressive record. Both of these guns were felt to have passed these tests with no problems whatsoever.

Since the Beretta and Browning tied for first place, or almost so, what rating does the H&K get, which jammed only once but failed to extract the reloads three times? While I'm not capable of explaining how it came about, a statistician friend determined that in spite of the number of H&K failures, it *wasn't* exhibiting a lower reliability level.

The S&W M59 malfunctioned 12 times in the first 150 rounds, at which time its hammer broke. Clearly we have no problem, statistically or intuitively, calling this performance a failure.

Since the gun wasn't properly chambering cartridges because of what seemed to be a faulty extractor, which dragged on the case to the point where the slide couldn't go fully

forward,[3] and because the hammer notches were sheared off so that it would fire only in double action mode, the factory was called and new parts requested. A new hammer, drawbar, sear, extractor, extractor pin and extractor spring were supplied without charge. These parts clearly eliminated the hammer problem, which I'm sure was an unlikely fluke caused by a bad part,[4] but the failure to chamber remained. The gun was then returned to the factory.

Smith & Wesson Recall

While the gun was being repaired S&W announced "new product improvements to present owners of S&W Model 59 autoloaders." This total, no-cost recall was for alterations of the extractor, magazine follower, and slide-stop lever. Tested after its

[2]The Walther importer, Interarms, when told about this said they only recommend the use of round-nose bullets in their guns.

[3]This opinion was confirmed by two local gunsmiths.
[4]Several local gunsmiths and shooters could remember no other difficulty of this kind occurring.

The Heckler & Koch pistol, patterned after their similar 9mm gun, was the first mass-produced D. A. 45 ACP automatic.

The proposed H&K 18-shot capacity D.A.-only VP70Z. Import difficulties make sales of this auto pistol in the U.S. uncertain.

Walther's forthcoming models will consist of the P38 IV, the P5 and the P38 K (shown here), all having a new D. A. mechanism.

return showed it to be performing very well; it failed to chamber only twice, once while firing 250 reloads, and once with the 50 factory cartridges. Another M59, run as a control and which did not have the factory rework, also failed twice—once to eject and once to feed, both with reloads. It appears that those M59 troubles have now been overcome.

As an aside, the original S&W magazines supplied with my M59 hold 16 rounds easily. The one sent to the factory and returned with the pistol now holds only 14 cartridges, but both work equally well.

As far as I and some local gun store owners can determine, there is absolutely no way—other than perhaps by magazine capacity—to tell whether a used M59 has been back to the factory for repairs. It seems clearly a case of "buyer beware." The same people told me, incidentally, that S&W is lowering production on the M59 and other guns because of falling sales. Certainly the gunshops in this area face reduced demand for the pistol.

So, if we now consider these 4 guns equally serviceable, though differing in minor mechanical detail, the potential buyer could select any of them without worry.

Other Makes/Models

These 4 pistols, of course, don't represent all possible types offered, but simply all that were available to me at the time. LES, for instance, has been on the verge for some years of producing the Steyr-designed 9mm, and LES had a booth at the NRA meeting, a sample pistol on view.[5]

Too, it is well known that Colt has developed big bore prototypes. A source in the company told me that the firearms division has approved the design for full production but, alas, no decision has yet been made.

Also, though S&W categorically denies it, friends working there have seen prototypes of an 11-shot D.A. 45 which, they were told, would go into production in early '79. S&W prototypes in this caliber go back many years, so there is room for doubt about series production, but Colt sources confirm that S&W had recently hired several engineers who once worked on Colt's double action.

On a somewhat more promising note, the Thomas 45 D.A. (only) automatic is being produced, though in limited numbers. Dean Grennell has reported[6] that his test pistol had chambering problems, but Walter Rickell said he had no such difficulties.[7]

Finally, according to Hubert Zink, executive V.P. H&K, that firm will decide in '78 whether to produce their VP70Z. There are, I'm told, problems in getting it approved for importation, so its future is unclear.

Though many-shot D.A. pistols in 9mm Parabellum caliber were slow in arriving, and D.A. 45s have only recently appeared, I think the years ahead will see rapid growth in both of these areas. ●

[5]An LES spokesman, during a recent phone talk (mid-April, 1978) said that their gas pistol was being shipped to dealers, but could give no name of any Chicago area outlet which had been sent one, or more, nor was he willing to send us a sample gun for appraisal and testing. J.T.A

[6]"The i-Dotting Thomas 45," Dean Grennell in *Gun World,* January, 1978.
[7]"The Thomas 45," Walter Rickell in *The American Handgunner,* January/February, 1977.

Economy Double Guns
and how to buy one

A half-century ago this article wouldn't have been needed—just about everybody used a double gun and information on them was common enough. Not so today.

by WM. HOVEY SMITH

TWO GENERATIONS ago an article such as this one would have been unnecessary. Double guns were common. But about this time many shooters retired their dad's double in favor of the increased firepower provided by a pump or automatic. This was a mechanically minded age and, as the Tin Lizzy had revolutionized transportation, shooters adopted another invention of the age—a reliable repeating shotgun. The old Burgess, Spencer, and Winchester pumps worked after a fashion, but were delicate and easily sidelined by black powder fouling. It took the introduction of the 97 Winchester, the Browning auto and smokeless powders to demonstrate the practicality of repeating shotguns. After World War I, the tide had turned and sales of repeating shotguns increased. After World War II, repeating shotguns dominated sales, and manufacture of double-barreled shotguns practically ceased in the United States. Now, doubles that were put away are again appearing in the field and sales of new double guns are increasing.

Once a shooter has decided to buy a double, the used gun market becomes attractive because of the rapid price increase of many foreign doubles. This increase has been caused by the devaluation of the dollar, the demand for higher wages abroad, and the ef-

fects of world-wide inflation. These effects are felt here because almost all new doubles are imported from Japan, Italy, Belgium, and surprisingly, Russia.

Until quite recently, the only doubles manufactured in this country were a limited number of Winchester Model 21s, the Remington 3200

stack-barrels, the Savage-Stevens-Fox line. Now two newly announced doubles—an over-under Ruger and Winchester's side-by-side—will soon be seen. Prices are high indeed for the three Winchester 21 grades—a Grand American, the top of the line, sold lately for about $7500, including extra barrels. The Remington 3200

Some used double barreled shotguns. The right group includes an Ithaca Lefever Nitro Special priced at $140. At left is a standard grade Ithaca 16 gauge at $75, a Damascus-barreled Ithaca 16 at $50, and a Winchester 21 3-inch at $700.

A Parker Trojan. Later Trojans differ from the standard Parker in that the Trojans were not engraved and the curved shoulders on the frame of the standard gun were omitted.

over-under sells for $750 in field grade, the Savage-Stevens-Fox guns priced from $100 to $200. The Ruger Red Label 20 gauge will cost about $480 (no 12s ready yet), and the new Winchester 23 side-by-side, a near-copy, at least visually, of the M21, will, I'm told, sell for around $500.

The Choices

Let's assume that you have decided on a side-by-side with double triggers, cut checkering if at all possible, no ejectors, and have set a price limit of about $400. For this price a used American double can be bought that should appreciate in value. However, these criteria do restrict you to the field or economy grade guns by such

makers as Parker, L. C. Smith, Winchester or Ithaca. Each of these makers offered a variety of models that were originally priced from under $100 to well over $1,000. The higher grade guns, now highly prized, command from three to many times their original cost. L. C. Smith used the same gun design throughout, but in the higher grades single triggers, ejectors, better wood, engraving, precious metal inlays, and more careful finishing increased the price. Parker, Winchester and Ithaca offered as their economy guns revised designs that could be produced at less cost than their standard grade guns.

In order of desirability I would rate the Parker Trojan as the best of the group followed by the L. C. Smith

Field Grade, Winchester's Model 24 and the Ithacas. Parkers have the reputation of being the best American double, and the Trojan was designed so that it could be made to exacting standards and yet be competitively priced. Introduced in 1915, it was the best seller in the Parker line from its introduction until production ceased after World War II. Through the years the Trojan has been regarded as a reliable and good shooting gun. A Trojan in nearly new condition is a rarity, and Parker collectors are willing to pay up to $900 for one like that. A good clean Trojan probably has the best investment potential of any of the economy doubles.

The L. C. Smith Field Grade is the most common good quality sidelock

L. C. Smith Field Grade. A good looking, fine shooting, solid gun. Field Grade Smiths are not uncommon on used gun racks.

This is an Ithaca 16. Note split stock, behind tang, and loose fit of wood, general poor quality. Don't buy a used shotgun in this condition.

manufactured in this country. The separate locks are mounted on a sideplate, inletted into the wood behind the breech. I have shot L. C. Smiths that dated from the last century, yet I have never seen one shoot loose. L. C. Smiths do seem to suffer from broken stocks more often than boxlock guns, which is another reason I would rate the Trojan a cut above the Smith.

The Winchester 24, roughly similar to the Model 21, lacks many of the latter's refinements. The 24 is bulkier, less trim. The 24s omitted the fore-end latch, the checkering and fine fitting found on the 21. A 24 I have examined has the fore-end hanger welded to the barrel rib, and the welding beads were not removed before finishing. Ejectors were available at an extra cost on the field grade Smith, but were unavailable on 24s. Fancy walnut stocks, with or without checkering, were special order items, and a bit more care was taken with guns having these extra cost features. These are the best of the 24s.

Ithaca manufactured several economy guns. Among these were the Lefever Nitro Special and Western Long Range guns which might be compared to the basic models now offered by Savage-Stevens-Fox. They show rough fitting and poor if any checkering. In very good condition these guns can be had for about $200. The better grade Ithaca was a boxlock rotary-bolt gun with a locking mechanism similar to the L. C. Smith. However, the bolting on Ithaca doubles doesn't stand up as well as the Smith's, and often older Ithacas will be loose at the breech. It is a paradox that an Ithaca with checkering and ejectors may sell for less than a plain

but clean Trojan. The Ithaca does not have the buyer appeal of the Parker, Smith or Winchester.

Some of the guns I have described were made in the 1920s, and there are many potential problems that may arise when buying such a gun. Many of the older guns have Damascus barrels, generally considered unsafe with modern ammunition.* Some were chambered for shorter-length shells than is now standard. Others have much more drop in the stock than is customary today, and are almost impossible to shoot with the modern cheek-on-stock technique. Parts, which are mostly obtained by cannibalizing other guns, are in reasonably good supply for the more recent Parkers, Smiths, Winchesters and Ithacas; but are often unobtainable for the older guns.

Price Paradox

The price of used shotguns varies depending on the area of the country, the gauge, and gun condition. In the South side-by-side doubles are highly prized and prices are high. In the Southwest most shooters use pumps or autos, and it is often possible to buy doubles cheaper in Arizona than in Georgia. The less popular 16 gauge or a 2⅞-inch 10 gauge can be bought for about two-thirds the cost of an identical 12 gauge. The 10 gauge guns are creeping up in value, though.

Most lower priced doubles will show signs of use, of course. The bluing may be worn in spots, the

---

*True, yet Damascus-barreled guns often pass modern British proof tests.

stock scratched, and a few spots of rust may be seen on the metal. This "normal" wear does not detract from the usefulness of the gun, but does decrease its possible collectors' value. If the action is tight, the barrels of original length, and if the gun functions properly, it will probably give years of satisfactory service.

Making the Deal

After entering Ye Olde Gonne Shoppe and expressing interest in double barrel shotguns, the owner may let you look through his racks. Many doubles can be eliminated from further consideration, among them those with taped and wired stocks, those by such makers as Crescent Arms Company, those with Damascus or hand painted barrels, and those that rattle. You should be able to thin his total selection to a few possibilities by a brief external examination.

With a few of the better possibilities in front of you, detailed attention should be paid to the barrels, action and stock. The barrels should be smooth, have highly polished interiors, and be free from dimples. Even a very small dent not noticed on the barrel's outside will be easily visible as a bright dimple on the interior. Any indication of separation between the barrels and the ribs is a cause for the gun's rejection ordinarily.

Most shops will not remove the action from an old double, and one usually has to be content with an exterior examination. The action screws should not be marred. If they are, the gun was probably tinkered with and, if the gun has any other faults, you should probably choose another. The locking surfaces should

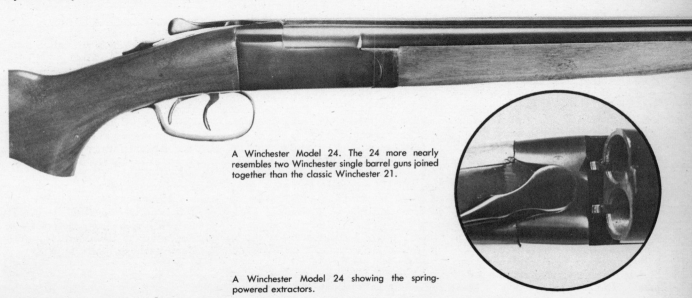

A Winchester Model 24. The 24 more nearly resembles two Winchester single barrel guns joined together than the classic Winchester 21.

A Winchester Model 24 showing the spring-powered extractors.

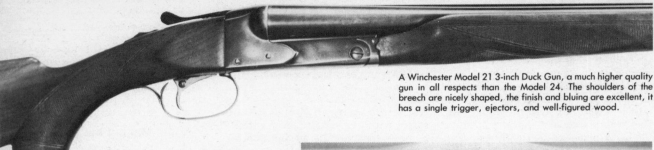

A Winchester Model 21 3-inch Duck Gun, a much higher quality gun in all respects than the Model 24. The shoulders of the breech are nicely shaped, the finish and bluing are excellent, it has a single trigger, ejectors, and well-figured wood.

be smooth and slightly polished where the parts have been sliding against each other. The safety should be checked out to see that it works freely in all its positions. The L. C. Smith has a three position safety. The central position is safe, the forward position is an automatic safety, and the rear position a non-automatic safety. When the barrels are joined with the action there should not be any looseness between the two components.

Testing the Action

The best way to test the action is by using a pair of snap caps. These caps may look something like a live round, but in place of a primer have a piece of resilient plastic to cushion the blow of the firing pin. With the caps in the gun first test the safety. If the safety works in all its positions, move it to the fire position and slowly pull one and then the other trigger. If there is a loud boom and a hole appears in the floor, you have not used a snap cap. The triggers should have a crisp 4-6 pound pull. A gun with a "hair trigger" should be avoided like the plague. The hammers should fall with a solid thunk-thunk. If one lock makes a markedly different sound than the other, one lock may have a weakened spring or a broken firing pin. The pins should be of the same length, their ends smoothly rounded.

Doubles are prone to stock breakage, so the buttstock and fore-end should be examined carefully. It is good practice to look at the wrist of the stock with a hand lens. The wood at the rear of the action will probably be slightly darker because of oil soaking. If soaking has been severe the wood will appear soft, and tiny fragments may be missing adjacent to the action and tang. Splits and cracks can be repaired with epoxy and concealed pins. When properly done epoxy

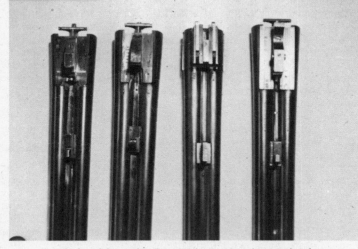

Barrels, from left to right—L. C. Smith 16 gauge, Ithaca-made Lefever 12 gauge, Winchester Model 24 showing spring-powered extractors, Winchester Model 21 with selective ejectors.

makes a strong repair, but should be combined with glass bedding to cure the original problem of poor action-to-stock fit.

Replacement Stocks

Replacement stocks are available for Parker, L. C. Smith, Winchester and Ithaca guns from E. C. Bishop, from Reinhart Fajen, plus a more limited selection from Dixie Gun Works. Because of the different stock dimensions used by such makers as Smith, it is difficult to determine if a stock for a particular gun is available. A letter should be sent detailing the make, grade, and serial number of the gun. Even so, it may be necessary to send the gun to insure getting a proper stock.

Good walnut is becoming increasingly difficult to obtain, and restocking costs are increasing almost monthly. The price can range from $80 for a semi-finished buttstock to well over $400 for a finished stock and forearm fitted to your shotgun. Costs increase dramatically when better wood and more labor is used on the stock. If you can do your own stock finishing and checkering, a considerable savings can be made. Re-

stocking, however, reduces the value of the gun to a collector because it is no longer in its original condition.

Shotgun Fit

This is the time to give attention to gun fit. Most doubles were designed for the mythical average man, a guy slightly overweight, 5 feet 10 inches tall, and with an arm reach of 32 inches. If you roughly fit these dimensions, the more modern production doubles will fit you fairly well. Stocks can be lengthened by using a slip-on recoil pad, but such other operations as shortening, reducing comb height and changing pitch require altering the stock. It is better to shop around and find a gun that nearly fits rather than alter an original stock.

Considerable patience is sometimes required to shop in the used gun market. You might find any number of Full and Full duck guns, but it may take a while to locate a Cylinder and Modified quail slayer. Almost without a doubt each trade is going to cost you money, and it is often better to hold out for a gun you really want.

By now the shop owner has decided you're a live one, and he moves in to show you some of his better guns. He

An Ithaca-made Lefever that is poorly finished but a good shooter. This double is unlike any gun made by Lefever, nor does it compare in finish with the standard Ithaca. Ithaca made very nice doubles, but this economy gun was not among them.

opens a cabinet with considerable ceremony and thrusts a Parker into your clammy hands. It is beautiful. The wood looks as if it had been hand rubbed for years with a finish so deep the richly figured wood appears almost alive. The action is engraved with figures of dogs and birds with such finesse that much other engraving looks scratchy by comparison. You don't dare open it and give it back before you drop it. As you hand it back, the owner casually remarks that he thinks he can let you have it for $5,000. You gulp, stammer, think about selling the T.V., your car, the wife's rings, and decline. Still half dazzled, you agree on a price for your double which is somewhat less than the sticker price, fill out the paperwork, fork over the money, and walk out.

The Pattern Board

Your next stop should be the pattern board. You should use your usual game load. After firing a round with each barrel, see if the pattern is around the point of aim. If it is slightly high that's fine, but if it centers consistently below, beside, or very high above the point of aim, it would be better to return the gun and try another. Many gunshops will let a customer try a double for a period of days, and permit him to return it if he can't shoot it. This is a valuable courtesy service, and should not be abused.

A Full choke barrel should put more than 65% of the counted shot charges in a 30-inch circle at 40 yards, a Modified 55% to 65%, and an Improved Cylinder from 45% to 55%. Older guns used with modern plastic-case ammunition will often shoot tighter than the indicated chok-

ing. Most doubles with 28-inch or longer barrels were choked Full and Full or Modified and Full, and those with 26-inch barrels Improved Cylinder and Modified. The amount of restriction varied with the maker, but a constriction from .030″ to .040″ for Full choke was often used in 12-gauge guns. Chokes can be measured with interior gauges, but the pattern the gun throws is the best indication of the actual amount of choke. I have seen so-called Improved Cylinder guns throw Full choke patterns.

If a double is throwing a tighter pattern than you need, the chokes can easily be relieved. I had a Modified and Full double recently rechoked to Improved Cylinder and Full by Jensen's Custom Ammunition in Tucson at a cost of $35, including test firing and pattern verification. I prefer this choke combination in a general purpose double. It enables me to take close-flushing quail or high flying ducks and make the best of any shots I might have.

Consult a Gunsmith

A trip to the gunsmith might now be considered. The stock should be removed and consideration given to glass bedding the action if it shows any signs of chipping or damage. The action may need to be disassembled and cleaned. I am often surprised at the amount of gunk that can accumulate in the action of a double that has not been cleaned in 20 years. This preventive maintenance should give you a trouble-free gun, one that should last for years.

Now you are eager to try your new gun but the hunting season is over. Take your gun to the local trap club and shoot some 16-yard targets. On a quiet day use $1\frac{1}{8}$ ounces of $8\frac{1}{2}$ or 9

shot fired from your more open barrel. Remember these are rising targets and you will have to cover the clay bird to hit it. After a few 10s or 14s out of 25 birds, you will start to get the hang of it and break an occasional 24 or 25. Field guns are seldom able to compete with specially stocked trap guns, but good off season practice can be had by an occasional visit to the trap range.

After shooting, the gun should be dismounted and cleaned with a slightly oily rag. If it has not been cleaned for a long time or after a season of use, a brass bristle brushing of the barrels will remove most of the stubborn lead fouling that accumulated around the choke. For normal cleaning, an oily patch is usually sufficient.

Because of the inherently closed action of the double, no further cleaning is needed unless the gun has been dropped from a boat, thoroughly soaked by rain, or exposed to salt water. The more often the gun is completely disassembled the less weather tight the locks become. I clean the internal parts of my duck gun every year, but thoroughly disassemble my upland guns only once every three years. When the locks are replaced, a little bee's wax applied to the action plate will help keep the gun weather tight.

Even though a gun is used every season, the value of even a field grade will increase over a 5-year period if the gun is well maintained. There is always a temptation to refinish the stock or reblue the barrels, but these "improvements" more often detract from the value of the gun than increase it. It is better to have a clean gun with no rust pits and 80% of its original finish than one that has been poorly refinished. Far better! ●

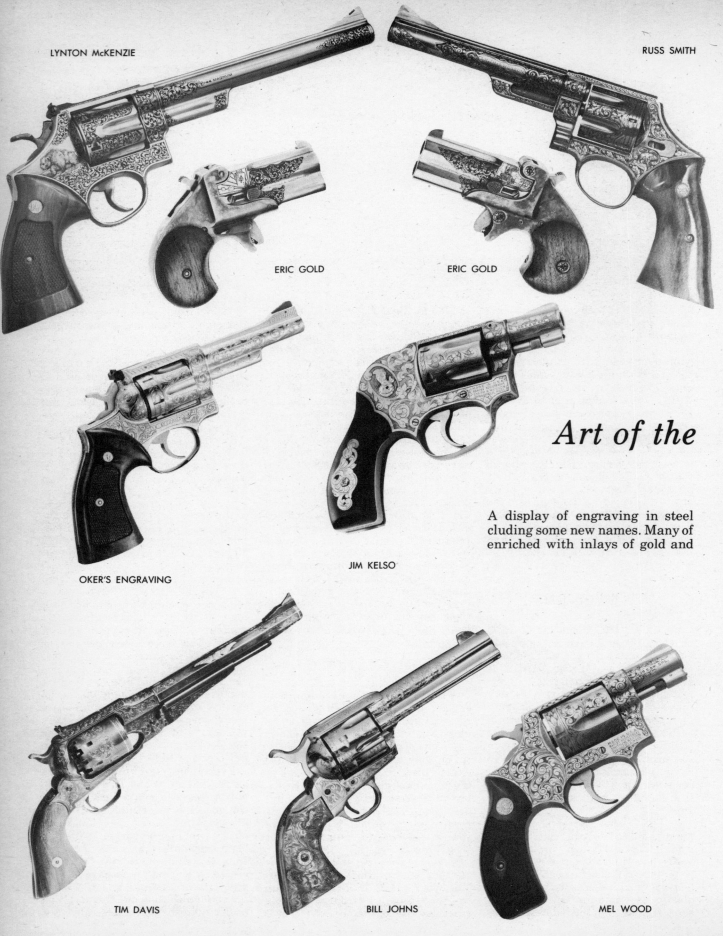

LYNTON McKENZIE

RUSS SMITH

ERIC GOLD

ERIC GOLD

OKER'S ENGRAVING

JIM KELSO

Art of the

A display of engraving in steel cluding some new names. Many of enriched with inlays of gold and

TIM DAVIS

BILL JOHNS

MEL WOOD

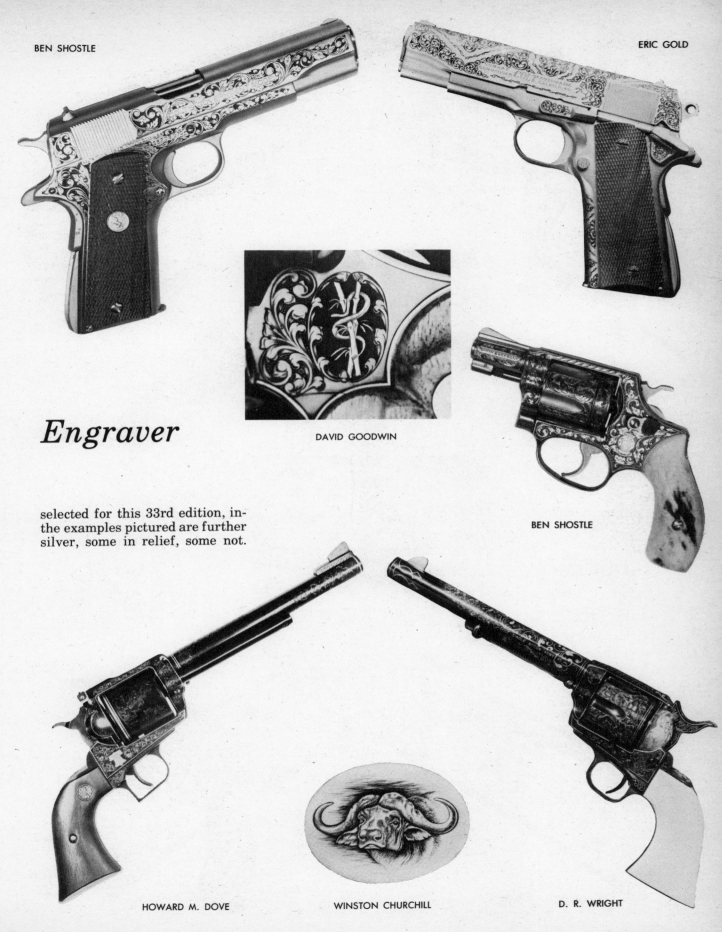

BEN SHOSTLE

ERIC GOLD

DAVID GOODWIN

Engraver

BEN SHOSTLE

selected for this 33rd edition, in-
the examples pictured are further
silver, some in relief, some not.

HOWARD M. DOVE

WINSTON CHURCHILL

D. R. WRIGHT

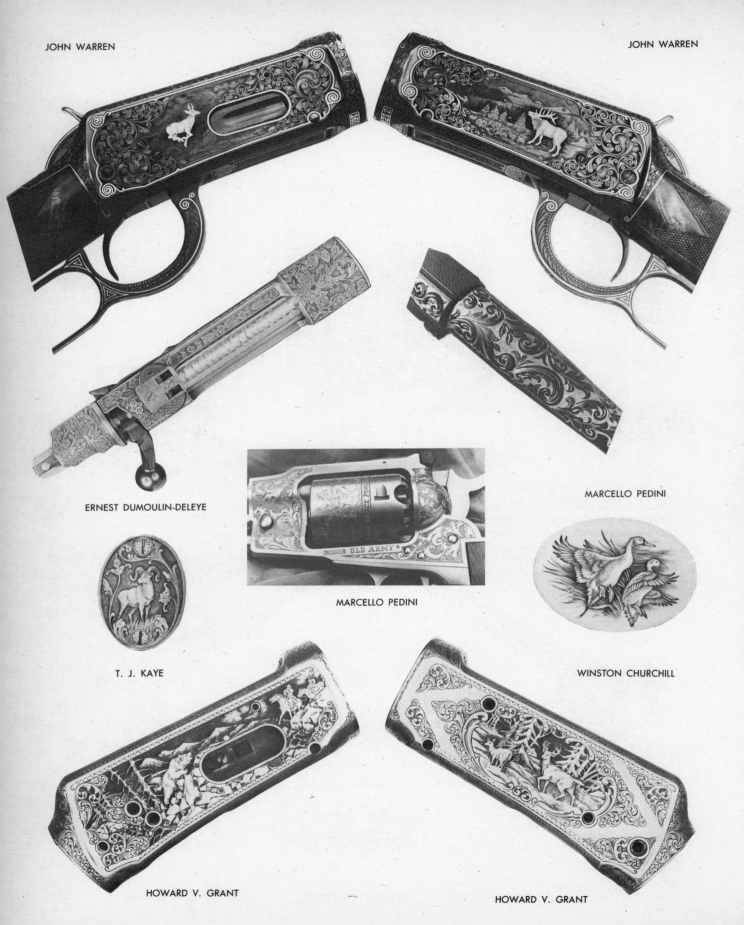

JOHN WARREN

JOHN WARREN

ERNEST DUMOULIN-DELEYE

MARCELLO PEDINI

MARCELLO PEDINI

T. J. KAYE

WINSTON CHURCHILL

HOWARD V. GRANT

HOWARD V. GRANT

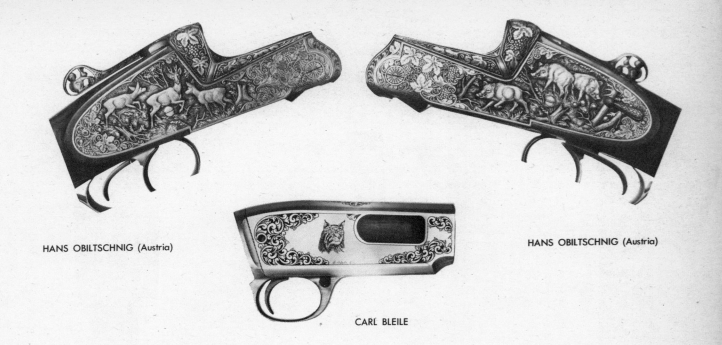

HANS OBILTSCHNIG (Austria)

HANS OBILTSCHNIG (Austria)

CARL BLEILE

HEIDE HIPTMAYER

Consult our Directory of the Arms Trade pages for the location of firms or individuals mentioned.

HEIDE HIPTMAYER

PACHMAYR GUN WORKS

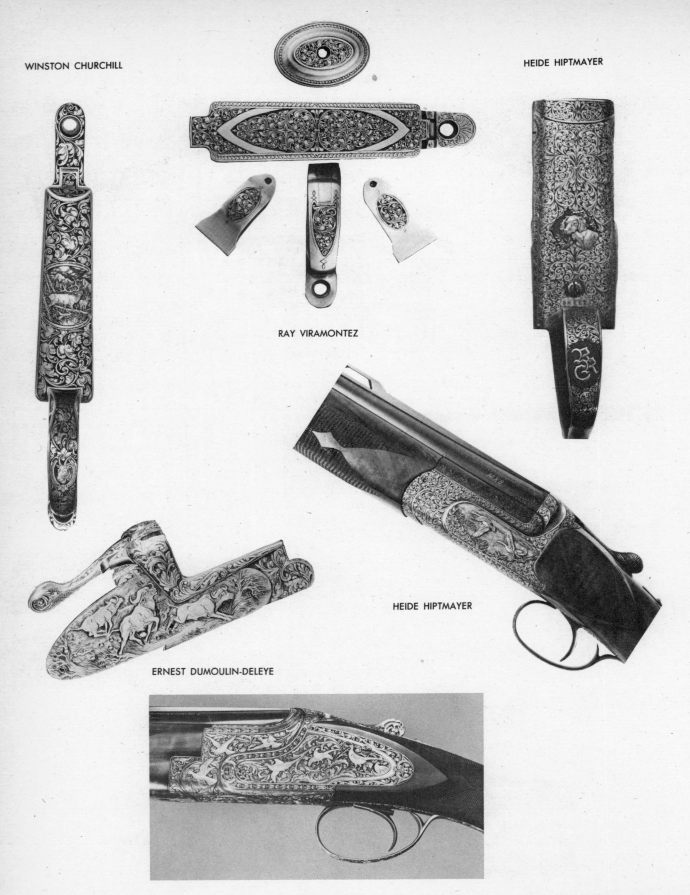

WINSTON CHURCHILL

RAY VIRAMONTEZ

HEIDE HIPTMAYER

HEIDE HIPTMAYER

ERNEST DUMOULIN-DELEYE

LOUIS VRANCKEN (Belgium)

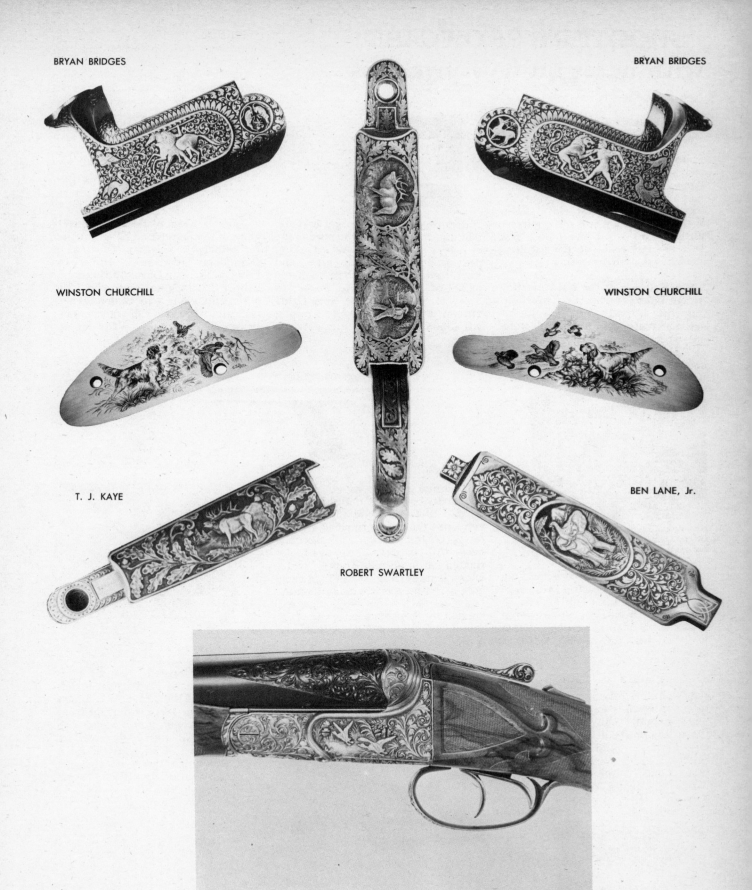

BRYAN BRIDGES

BRYAN BRIDGES

WINSTON CHURCHILL

WINSTON CHURCHILL

T. J. KAYE

BEN LANE, Jr.

ROBERT SWARTLEY

PACHMAYR GUN WORKS

SHOOTER'S SHOWCASE
with notes on new products

New Product Notes

Don Allen (Rt. 1, Timberlane, Northfield, MN 55057), the flying gunmaker and stock blank specialist, has a new brochure that's yours for the asking and a 1st class stamp. Well-illustrated, prices are quoted on virtually all wood and metal jobs. Don showed some of his excellent stocks at the NRA meeting.

Sid Bell was at the NRA meeting in Salt Lake City, his booth overflowing with literally hundreds of his artistic creations in men's and women's sporting jewelry, belt buckles, etc. He told me this was his best showing ever—he sold out many items in a day or so.

New designs by Sid Bell—grip plates for Gov't 45 auto pistols, in sterling silver and high-relief carved.

Bergamot Brass Works has a big new catalog of some 80 pages, every one showing several belt buckle designs plus numerous other metal products—pendants, conchos, watch and key fobs, too much to list or describe.

Brown Products offers rust and corrosion protection for firearms, tools, internal combustion engines and virtually any ferrous-metal items. Simple to use, the protection lasts for a year, and prices are low— $1.98 to $2.98. Write to Northern Instruments Corp., 6680 Highway North, Lino Lakes, MN 55014 for full details.

Reduce your paper target costs by making your own—all you need is one or more rubber stamps and an inking pad. Offered in various types and sizes, from 100-yd. bench rest squares to 200-yd. BR squares, etc., prices run $2.49 to $5.99 postpaid from **Craft Haven,** 20th and Vine St., Lincoln, NB 68505.

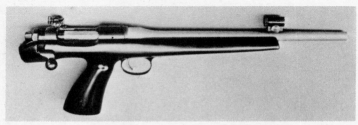

Durango gun rods, rapidly gaining popularity because of their high quality and usefulness, are offered in 10 versions—6 for modern rifled arms, 3 for BP shooters and one for shotgunners. All calibers are available, though not in all rods, from 22 to 62, and in lengths from 10″ to 44″. Mating accessory tips, too. All made of stainless steel, each rod has a "conical rod guide" to prevent bore wear. List prices—$11.95 to $17.95. A brochure is available.

Morton Cundy & Son, now at Box 315, Lakeside, Mont. 59922, have a new and large catalog/order book ready picturing, describing and pricing their various models of imported quality shotguns, all sidelocks and all built to order. Included are ready-for-delivery guns of standard stock dimensions.

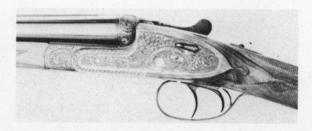

Edith G. Cooper's big 9″x12″ book, *The Kentucky Rifle and Me,* is a nostalgic tale of how Mrs. Cooper and her husband, the late T. J. Cooper, began collecting Pennsylvania rifles—in the early 1930s! The Coopers became famous dealers, and the book is profusely illustrated, including some dozen full-page plates by famous Ned Smith—these pencil sketches show component parts in detail.

The publisher is E. G. Cooper, Rte. l, Port Royal, PA 17087. $15.

Jack B. Dever offers two conversions of the Remington XP-100 action for Silhouette shooters. One has a thumb-hole wood stock, 12″ or 14″ Douglas barrel in Dever 30 Maxi-Mag caliber (222 Mag. case opened up), the other (illus.) has a 15″ Shilen SS barrel, cal. 7×250, and a fiberglass stock. Prices, $250 to $450. Write for details.

Ralph L. Carter had a most interesting display of his barrels at Salt Lake, most of them tapered octagons with or w/o rib —1/4 or full length, but some 1/2-octagon/round, some with vent ribs. All Carter barrels are draw-filed and hand polished for a satin blue finish. Prices start at $96.50, and his address is Rt. 1-Box 92, Fountain, Colo. 80817.

Norbert Ertel (Box 1150, Des Plaines, IL 60018) makes classic oak-and-leather trunk-type gun cases, all material of the finest quality—selected oak, top-grain cowhide, *all* metal of solid brass. Made only to order, prices start at $395 (one barrel set), go to $550 for a pair of guns. A leather-trimmed canvas cover is included, and such accessories as cleaning rods, oil bottles and snap caps are optional. I've examined an Ertel case very closely, and it is indeed handcrafted in the traditional manner. Most handsomely done.

Gussert Bullets, whose various lubes and cleaners for lead bullet and black powder shooters we've used and reported on, with good results, have added to and improved their several products in recent months. These are indeed satisfactory items—give 'em a try.

A new catalog is ready from **Golden Age Arms Co.,** their 10th ed., and its 160 pages, plus covers, loaded with the numerous things dear to the hearts of black powder shooters, and equally full of illustrations. A copy will cost you $2, and it's worth it.

George M. Fullmer, long and favorably known for his highly-precise chambering (all reamers by Francis or Elliott) of over 300 calibers, now offers pre-'64 M70 extractors in standard calibers—$15 to $20 each. Other M70 parts may soon be available, too—and superior to the originals, George says.

You may not have room for a locking gun cabinet, but you still can safeguard guns in a closet or on a wall rack. The No. 90 **Master** Gun Lock discourages theft and prevents accidental firing of stored firearms—rifles, shotguns and handguns.

The No. 90 clamps securely to both sides of the trigger guard, effectively blocking trigger action. To assure maximum security they're self adjusting to suit each firearm and have a key-operated pin tumbler locking mechanism. Cushioned pads protect the gun's finish. No. 90 Gun Locks are also available keyed-alike so a single key can control several guns. Cost, $6.29.

Lee Precision's latest powder measure kit now includes 15 such measures, these holding .3cc to 4.3cc and so marked. A sliding scale furnished quickly shows how many grains of powder each plastic measure holds for 88 powders, no less. Over 1300 charges are listed, but not all of them usable, of course—consult a reliable manual to determine *suitable, safe,* loads. Cost, $4.98.

The 1978 *Reloader's Guide for Hercules Smokeless Powder* is ready, its 32 pages full of valuable information on handloading for shotguns, rifles and handguns. Small complaint—the list of other reloading publications is woefully incomplete and out-of-date. See your dealer first.

You will surely want the latest well-illustrated **Green River Forge** catalog, plus their brochures and price list. Specialists in building black powder flint and caplock rifles, not to mention such related items as leather shirts and trousers, the rifle pictured is their halfstock Astorian, its 32″ octagon barrel in 45 or 50 caliber, its weight about 8½ lbs.

Jerry Fisher, one of our top stockmakers, offers the trade a new double-ended scraper intended for octagon-barrel or other straight-sided applications. Cost, $5.90, same price as his like but rounded-end scraper, described here a while back. Write to J.F. at 1244 Fourth Ave. West, Kalispell, MT 59901.

The I-Dent-A, made by **Edco,** serves to identify all centerfire and shotgun ammunition by stamping a number—preselected by the user—on the primer using a fast-drying ink. Perfectly safe, too, the pressure being very light. The tool includes stamping number 00 and 0 to 9 inclusive. Cost, $18.95. A Data Log book, designed to supplement the I-Dent-A tool, holds 50 charts for 1,000 load records, sells for $5.95. Edco is at Box 293, Boone, NC 28607.

I-Dent-A

Green River Forge

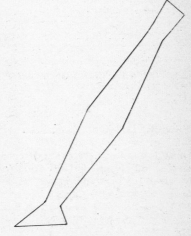

Jerry Fisher

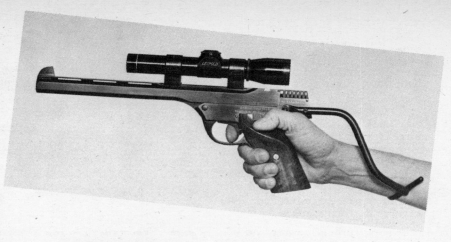

Rex Merrill's excellent single shot pistols have been improved recently—Micro rear sights are standard, and the barrel is grooved to now accept Weaver scope rings without drilling or tapping. A new positive-safety barrel lock is used, and all calibers—from 22 LR to 44 Magnum, including 30-30 Win. and the 30 and 35 Herrett chamberings—are available in either 9″ or 12″ barrels.

Prices have risen, inevitably, though not greatly. The 9″ barreled Merrill sells for $269.50; the 12″ model is $20 more. Readily interchangeable extra barrels, including the latest Micro sights, are $79.50 for the 9″, $99.50 for the 12″. The wrist attachment shown, a good steadying device, is $20.75.   J.T.A.

For the ultimate in handloading convenience, **Pacific's** new case-lube pad has a handy loading block in the easy-open lid. Heavy-duty felt pad provides just the right amount of lubricant; the durable loading block organizes your cases until they're ready for resizing. Cost, $6—see your dealer.

A red ramp insert can be added to your handgun's front sight in pretty short order, though some common tools are needed. Send for the Kit ($19.95) and detailed instructions to **Lee's Red Ramps,** 34220 Cheseborough Rd., Palmdale, CA 93550.

Consult our Directory pages for the location of firms mentioned.

Robt. H. Newell specializes in custom grips for handguns, offering these in many styles and various woods. Write for his fully-illustrated brochure, which includes a detailed order form. He prefers to have the gun itself on hand for a perfect fit, but a good fit can be managed otherwise. His address is 55 Coyote St., Los Alamos, NM 87544.

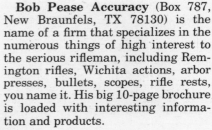

Ed Shilen, well-known custom barrel- and rifle maker, now has octagon barrels—octagonal on the *inside,* that is. Quite like the rifling design developed by Sir Joseph Whitworth in the 1850s, but modified to give a radius in the corners, Shilen says these barrels offer 30% longer peak-accuracy life and are just as accurate shooting as barrels with conventional rifling.

Bob Pease Accuracy (Box 787, New Braunfels, TX 78130) is the name of a firm that specializes in the numerous things of high interest to the serious rifleman, including Remington rifles, Wichita actions, arbor presses, bullets, scopes, rifle rests, you name it. His big 10-page brochure is loaded with interesting information and products.

Sport Style Associates make and market a great array of decorative/useful devices for sportsmen—tie-tacs and bars, lapel pins, belt buckles, all meticulously crafted and the designs well done indeed.

Telepacific's latest chronograph is the TPB-03, a compact instrument with rechargeable Ni-Cad batteries and the readout numbers a big 0.65″ high and showing foot seconds—no conversion tables required. A ballistic coefficient dial permits setting for the bullet in use, thus giving true MV, not instrumental velocity. With a pair of Electroscreen Detectors (photo-eye type), cost is $355. A detailed brochure is offered, no cost.

Johnny Stewart Game Calls, purveyors for many years of a large range of excellent calls (hand held, tapes and records), now have a new product—Skunk Musk. Mixing the 2 liquids downwind from the stand releases a powerful skunk odor, effectively masking the hunter/photographer. Price, $5.95.

Tamarack cast bullet lube, solid or hollow sticks, consists of half Alox and half A-1 beeswax—a proven formula for better accuracy, less leading. Furnished in capped plastic tubes for mess-free handling, cost is $1.50 each. See your dealer or write Tamarack Products, Box 224, Barrington, IL 60010.

Shiloh Products had a couple of sporting models of their single shot Sharps at Salt Lake City, these 1874 types with 28″ or 30″ octagon barrels, double set trigger, and offered in 45-70, 50-70, 45-90, 50-90, 45-120 and 50-140. A straight-hand or pistol grip stock is available.

Norm Schiffman, custom stockmaker, has revived his spare-cartridge trap, a steel compartment with hinged cover that holds four rounds. A useful, handy device that sets into the stock's toe line unobtrusively.

Dave Walters furnishes handguns given his "Akuriz" treatment, which means they're ready to shoot in top competition events. Prices run from $175 to $270 for these jobs done on the customer's gun, and $428.95 to $523.95 if Dave supplies the gun and does the "Akuriz" work. Also offered are various combat-pistol gunsmithing jobs, and he makes for the trade various handgun jigs and tools for achieving precise trigger/sear/hammer treatments. A brochure is available.

Rogers Combat Grips, finger-formed at front and usable right- or left handed, look and feel like fine walnut but they're not. My S&W K-frame pair, with dual palm swells, fit very well, and cost only $14.95. Write to Rogers Holster Co., 10601 Theresa Dr., Jacksonville, FL 32216. J.T.A.

Wet Notes This is a 100% waterproof notebook, $4\frac{1}{4}″ \times 7\frac{1}{4}″$, usable for pen or pencil notes wet or dry. Included is a pencil-in-loop, a 3-year calendar and a supply of pre-printed log sheets, etc., all for $4.95 from E. S. Ritchie & Sons, Oak St., Pembroke, MA 02359.

This recent addition to the famed-for-quality **Woods** line is a sleeveless garment that's covered with their 60/40 Sierra cloth and insulated with 6 ozs. of genuine northern goose down.

The heavy duty zipper is covered with an insulated storm flap, and there's an extra-high down collar for extra warmth. It has 3-way pockets in front—handwarmers plus two storage pockets on each side.

Machine washable or dry cleanable, No. 283 comes in beige, navy, ice blue, orange or camouflage, and in Medium (40-42), Large (44-46), X-Large (48-50) or XX-Large (52).

1978 Williams Catalog

Raised to 48 pages now, the new Williams line of custom designed accessories is amply covered, and there's a new section "How to Customize Sporting Rifles." Each year the section will be enlarged to cover all popular rifles—the 1978 list includes Winchester 70 and 94, Remington 700, 742 and 760, Interarms Mark X, Savage 99 and the T/C muzzleloaders.

New products for 1978 include single and double bladed "Guide Line" pocket knives, "Low-Sight Thru" scope mounts and a newly-designed FP micrometer receiver sight for the T/C Contender. This FP sight, with target knobs optional, may be had with a square-notch open sight blade or an aperture peep.

The 1978 catalog is $1—write to Williams Gun Sight Co., 7300 Lapeer Rd., Davison, MI 48423.

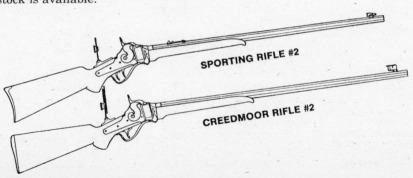

SPORTING RIFLE #2

CREEDMOOR RIFLE #2

AMERICAN BULLETED CARTRIDGES

by KENNETH L. WATERS

A thorough survey of new and interesting developments in metallic ammunition and components.

Last year the big news on metallic cartridges came from Remington-Peters. This year Winchester-Western and Federal share the spotlight. Read on and see if you don't agree.

Winchester-Western

Of all new developments, the one most outstanding—even amazing—is W-W's introduction of a new large-caliber rimmed cartridge for lever action rifles! With the single exception of the 444 Marlin, we haven't had a new factory-standard cartridge designed specifically for a lever rifle with tubular magazine in more than 40 years; not since the 348 Winchester appeared in 1936, to be exact.

Winchester calls it the "375 Big Bore," they're producing a beefed-up version of the old Model 94 carbine (with reinforced receiver) to go with it. Looking like the old 38-55, the new cartridge is entirely different ballistically. Two loads are offered: a 200-gr. bullet with muzzle velocity (MV) of 2200 fps, and a 250-gr. at 1900 fps. The first should be ideal for deer hunters in brush and timber; the second one provides moose- and bear-stopping power.

What about rechambering your old 38-55 Model 1894 for the 375 Big Bore? Take my advice, *forget* it. Chamber pressures are substantially higher in the new cartridge, as they must be to achieve the higher velocities, and the new bullets are a true .375″ diameter, hence would be inaccurate in a 38-55 barrel, most of which had groove diameters of .378″ or larger.

A look at the ballistics of this new round compared with a few old numbers is revealing. For instance, the 32 Winchester Special starts out faster but falls to the velocity of the 375 Big Bore 300-gr. bullet at 200 yards, and develops less energy at all ranges.

	Bullet grs.	Velocities MV	100 yds.	200 yds.	Energies ME	100 yds.	200 yds.
375 Big Bore	200	2200	1841	1526	2150	1506	1034
32 Win. Spcl.	170	2250	1870	1537	1911	1320	892
35 Remington	200	2080	1698	1376	1921	1280	841
44 Magnum	240	1760	1380	1114	1650	1015	661
375 Big Bore	250	1900	1647	1424	2005	1506	1126

Trajectory of the 200-gr. 375 BB load is about like that of the 32 Win. Spcl., hence if sighted in at 100 yards the bullet strike should be a trifle over 9 inches low at 200; if zeroed for 150 yards bullets will hit around 5 inches low at 200. The 250-gr. trajectory is close to that of the 303 Savage's despite its 60 grains heavier weight. Considering residual energy, velocity and trajectory, 200 yards appears to be the practical range limit for the 375 BB as a deer cartridge, and from 100 to 150 yards on moose.

Since most whitetail deer, black bear and moose are killed well within those ranges, the 375 BB should prove especially attractive to Northern U.S. and Canadian woods hunters, who prefer a light and handy lever action for ease of carrying, but would like to use the same rifle for bigger game.

W-W's other new item is at the opposite end of the line: a super high-speed 22 Long Rifle cartridge called the Super-X "Xpediter." Designed for the small game hunter and rimfire varminter, a lighter (29-gr.) Lubaloy hollow-point bullet has been paired with a slightly longer nickel-plated case and a powder (unspecified) charge producing a claimed muzzle velocity of 1680 fps from 24″ barrels. Over-all cartridge length matches that of a standard 22 Long Rifle.

The thinking here seems to have been to fill the gap between regular high-speed 22 LR rounds and the larger (and more costly) 22 Magnum Rimfire, accomplishing this in a cartridge fitting standard Long Rifle chambers. At a rated muzzle energy of 182 f.p., the new round is said to offer 25% greater energy and 30% higher velocity than regular Super-X 22 LR hollow points.

Our Oehler chronograph reports actual velocities (instrumental at 15 feet) averaging 1615 fps from our 24″ barrel Winchester 52 Sporter, 1610 from a 19¼″ Browning autoloader, and 1288 from a 6″ Colt revolver.

Regular 22 LR Super-X high-speed ammo fired in these same guns averaged 1308 fps from the M52 rifle and 1092 fps from the 6″ Colt.

Naturally this higher velocity affects trajectory, flattening it by around 30% also—2.5″ versus 3.6″ at 100 yards. I'm told that Xpediter pressures average 24,000 psi, so these cartridges should be used only in rifles and handguns chambered for 22 LR high-speed ammo—and in good condition!

Other W-W additions include: a new 9mm Luger (Parabellum) load with 95-gr. JSP bullet at 1355 fps MV from a 4″ barrel, and a 130-gr. FMC Super-X +P load in 38 Special at 950 fps from 4″ barrel.

Because many readers will be interested in pending discontinuances, I'm listing here those being dropped by W-W but of which there are still stocks on hand, subject to prior sale. In the past we've had no warnings; cartridges just disappeared from the catalog and that was that. Take advantage of this advance warning.

257 Robts.	87-gr. PSP (a fine varmint round)
30-40 Krag	220-gr. S'tip (sob!)
300 H&H Mag.	150-gr. S'tip
338 Win. Mag.	300-gr. P-P
358 Win.	250-gr. S'tip
9mm Para.	100-gr. PP

I wish W-W would reconsider. Since they'll still be making 87-gr. PSP bullets for the 250 Savage, why not continue loading them in 257 Roberts cases? Likewise, the 30-40 could use the same 220-gr. Silvertip as the '06, the 300 H&H the '06's 150-gr. ST without the need to make any additional components.

A final note: W-W is making one last lot of 38-55 unprimed brass as an accommodation to handloaders of this grand old caliber. This will be your last chance to get new brass, I'm told.

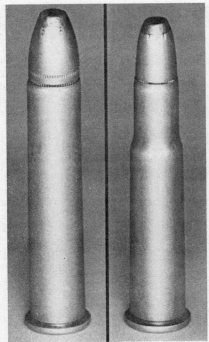

Jim Bell's steel-jacket copper-band .473″ bullet.

Winchester-Western's newest—the 375 Big Bore with 200-gr. SP bullet (left). A 30-30 with 170-gr. Power-Point is shown for comparison. See text for details.

Federal

As usual, FCC has come up with quite a list of metallic goodies, the star of which is a new 45-70. What makes this especially noteworthy is that it will be loaded with a 300-gr. jacketed HP, muzzle velocity 1810 fps.

Though this takes us back to the 'thirties, when a 300-gr. high-velocity SP load was last offered commercially, it has far more than nostalgic value. These faster-moving, quicker-expanding bullets will greatly improve the effectiveness of the 45-70 as a deer hunting round in such woods rifles as Marlin's 1895 lever gun. Handloaders have long known that, and now non-reloading hunters can also benefit. The hollow-point construction makes them even better for the smaller species of big game.

For some years now, our deer-hunting group has included two 45-70 Marlin users, these stoked with handloads containing 300-gr. JHPs chronographed at around 1900-2000 fps; *every* deer they've shot with those loads has been killed almost instantly. And those scoffers who think the 45-70 large for deer, meat destruction has usually been much less than in those animals shot with a 270 or 30-06.

The new Federal 45-70 load has a flatter trajectory to 200 yards than the old slow-moving 405-gr. bullets, re-

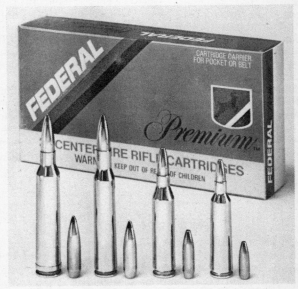

A year ago Federal introduced a line of Premium centerfire rifle cartridges with Sierra boat-tail soft point bullets in 8 calibers. In response to many requests 3 new lighter-weight bullets and one new caliber have been added to the Premium line for 1978. They are, from left—7mm Rem. Mag. with 150-gr. BTSP bullet; 270 with 130-gr. BTSP bullet; 243 with 85-gr. BTHP bullet, and 22-250 with 55-gr. BTHP bullet.

maining velocity at that range being nearly as high as the 405-gr. at 100 yards. Too, the lead required on running game is reduced, and these bullets *do* expand.

Another first for FCC is the 6mm Remington caliber, including an 80-gr. SP at 3470 fps MV, and a 100-gr. "Hi-Shok" SP at 3130. So far we haven't checked these factory-rated velocities. They'll be packaged in Federal's handy "Cartridge Carrier" 10-round plastic holders, for noiseless wear on the belt. I'm looking forward to trying these in my Sharon-barreled Mauser.

Devotees of the 44 Magnum (of which there are many, judging from those I see in the woods each fall), will want to try another new Federal offering—a 44 Mag loading with 180-gr. JHP bullet. Though primarily intended for use in revolvers, they should be suitable also for carbines—which Federal assures us they are.

MV is given as 1610 fps from only a 4″ barrel sixgun, with 1365 fps retained at 50 yards, from which I'd expect muzzle speeds to top 2000 fps from a 20″ carbine barrel.

Hunting with 44 Magnum ammo is growing in popularity, and I can attest to its game-killing potential in the hands of a hunter proficient in its use. I saw the results of a 44 Mag deer kill in rough mountainside cover last season, by a man who doesn't even bring a rifle to camp.

Another added Federal item is a high-velocity (+P) load for the 38 Special, its 158-gr. lead semi-wadcutter bullet driven at around 915 fps from a 4″ revolver barrel.

Federal's Law Enforcement Ammunition Division has also expanded, adding two new items for police long arms: a 30 Carbine load with 110-gr. FMJ bullet, and one for the 223 Remington with 55-gr. FMJ (or "Metal Case" as FCC calls them).

On special order only, Federal also offers a 308 Match cartridge with 168-gr. HP boat-tail bullet and their 210-M accuracy primer, MV 2630 fps. A minimum order is required, but the Federal brochure doesn't say what it is.

Last but by no means least, the success of their Premium rifle ammunition has prompted Federal to add 4 more rifle cartridges this year—a 22/250 with 55-gr. HPBT bullet at 3730 fps, a 243 with 85-gr. HPBT at 3320 fps, a 130-gr. SPBT at 3110 for the 270, and a 150-gr. SPBT also at 3110 fps for the 7mm Magnum.

These Premium cartridges, loaded with Sierra bullets noted for their accuracy and ballistic excellence, are subjected to more precise dimensional control, including case, primer and powder charge, for which you'll pay from 55¢ to 70¢ more per box. But it is truly "Premium" quality ammunition, its performance close to that of Match ammo in several of our test rifles.

Federal's new high performance 44 Rem. Magnum cartridge has a 180-gr. JHP bullet at 1610 fps MV from a 4″ vented test barrel.

An old favorite, the 45-70 Government, has been added to Federal's line of centerfire ammunition. Federal will offer only one load in this caliber, a 300-gr. JHP bullet at a muzzle velocity of 1810 fps.

Remington-Peters

Of greatest interest, it seems to me, is Remington's announcement of a pair of "factory wildcat" calibers. I say "calibers" rather than cartridges because, although they have designed two entirely new cartridges, they will *not* be produced as factory loaded rounds. Instead, Remington will offer straight untapered 308 WCF cases pocketed for No. 7½ Small Rifle primers, along with their proven-accurate 52-gr. 22-caliber Bench Rest bullets plus a new 6mm 68-gr. Bench Rest bullet.

The idea is for accuracy-conscious riflemen, especially bench rest shooters, to shorten these cases to 1.52″ length and neck them down with a 30° shoulder to 22 or 6mm, for which forming and loading dies are available (but not from Remington). With their short powder column and sharp shoulder, theory holds that the charge will ignite and burn more uniformly *in the case,* aided and abetted in the process by the smaller primer with its lesser brisance, the objective being to achieve a greater uniformity of velocity. There's something to the idea, for Remington's Jim Stekl made a new world's bench rest record with the 22 Remington BR cartridge and Remington bullets.

The same cylindrical case can also be necked to 6mm,

223 Remington cartridges are now available from Frontier with a choice of 55-gr. Spire Point or 55-gr. FMJ bullet, bringing to 10 the rifle calibers listed by this maker.

using the special 68-gr. bullet mentioned above and the same 30-degree case.

Remington's press release notes that they will chamber their 40-XBBR bench rest rifle for the 22 Remington BR cartridge, but nothing is said about chambering for the 6mm BR round. I think this should be done, and I further suggest that cases should be offered already *trimmed and formed,* which can be more readily performed at the R-P plant, saving handloaders considerable time and effort. If they can prove popular (as they well may), I'd like to see them produced as complete factory cartridges for the non-reloader.

The final R-P metallic cartridge news is a new load for the 380 Auto, its 88-gr. JHP bullet having a MV of 990 fps from 4″ barrels. R-P also has a discontinuance—the old 25-20 WCF having been dropped. Speaking for myself, I'd rather have seen them drop the lead bullet loading for the 32-20, retaining a single loading in each caliber.

Norma

This familiar Swedish-made line, imported by Norma-Precision of Lansing, NY, has added 6 cartridges: a 22/250 (new) loaded with 53-gr. SP Match spitzers, MV 3710 fps, and a 280 Remington round with 150-gr. semi-pointed SPBT bullet at 2900. This last is especially welcome, and I hope it will stimulate interest in this excellent but sadly neglected caliber.

New loadings in already-listed Norma calibers comprise a 222 Remington with 53-gr. SP Match spitzer with the surprising MV claim of 3115 fps; a 38 Special with 158-gr. FMJ semi-wadcutter rated 900 fps from 6″ barrels; a 357 Magnum with the same bullet at 1450 fps (from $8^{3}/_{8}$″ barrel), and a 44 Magnum carrying a 240-gr. bullet called the "Power Cavity," MV 1675 fps from an $18^{1}/_{2}$″ carbine barrel. This last cartridge replaces the Norma 236-gr. JHP load.

Dropped, and with quantities limited, are Norma's 25 ACP and 38 S&W cartridges, plus empty unprimed cases for the 358 Winchester—another nail in the coffin of that splendid timber load.

I'm particularly disappointed that Norma's 7×61 S&H cartridge (renamed the Super 7×61) will only be available until stocks are exhausted! This applies only to factory-loaded rounds; empty unprimed cases and bullets will continue to be available. Still, this news bodes ill for the future of a truly grand cartridge.

On the bright side, I'm cheered that Norma continues to offer loaded ammo for the 22 Savage High Power and the 220 Swift—something no American ammo factory has seen fit to do.

A final note: just as N-205 powder was replaced by MRP a few years ago, N-203 is now replaced by N-202, supposedly with much the same characteristics and burning rate. We're working with the new propellant now, but it's still too early for a meaningful report. My impression is that it's just slightly faster burning than N-203.

CCI-Speer

Big game hunters who've used the first 6 sizes of Grand Slam bullets have proclaimed them to be among our best controlled expanding types, and now Speer has added two more: a 250-gr. GS for the 338 and 340 Magnums, and a 285-gr. for the 375 H&H Magnum. If they perform as well as their smaller GS mates have, their reputation is made. Having described their unique construction in last year's GUN DIGEST I won't repeat it here.

Handgunners are likely to be equally enthused over Speer's new 45-cal. JHP bullet, described as being of "magnum type." That means, I suppose, that it will withstand being driven and impacting at higher velocities. This will take some doing, for the new bullet weighs 260 grains, making it the heaviest 45 pistol bullet of its type!

The jacket over the nose section is thinned with a dozen flutes to induce expansion when velocity has fallen off. The rear portion, enclosing a soft unalloyed lead core, is made uniformly thicker so as to hold together at higher velocities. This is, of course, precisely the bullet behavior sought by hunting handgunners, so they should be popular if and when their performance is verified by field testing. Advertised as being intended for use in 45 Auto and Auto Rim cases, as well as in the 45 Colt, I'm skeptical whether a bullet this heavy can attain high velocity from the short 45 ACP case. It should be a natural in the big 45 Colt hulls, however.

A new CCI product which hasn't been talked about much, but one which arouses my interest, is their Competition Green Tag 22 LR ammo—a premium match round with a distinctively shaped bullet listed as having a MV of 1138 fps from an $18^{1}/_{2}$″ test barrel, or 1027 from a 6″ barrel.

CCI has made great strides in developing rimfire ammunition, and even better accuracy is perhaps the most important goal for producers of rimfire cartridges.

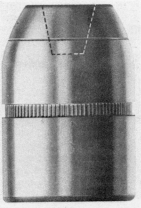

CCI-Speer's new 45-cal. 260-gr. JHP—heaviest jacketed pistol bullet available. Intended for use in 45 Colt, 45 ACP and 45 Auto Rim.

Sierra

Sierra has introduced 5 new bullets, the most significant of which is probably their 220-gr. .323″ diameter spitzer BT, obviously meant for the 8mm Remington Magnum, which appeared last year. I look forward to trying this new Sierra, not only in the 8mm Magnum, but in our 8×57 and 8×60 Mausers as well.

Sierra has long offered 30-cal. RN bullets with a favorable point form, that is, not too blunt. Considering their usefulness for brush and woods hunting, it's been a minor mystery why Sierra didn't make similar-shaped bullets in some of the other popular calibers. A few years ago they added one such in 35 caliber, but none in the smaller bore sizes, where they were needed. Now there are two more: a 150-gr. RN 270 and a 170-gr. RN in 7mm, both of which we're glad to see. One more is needed: a 150-gr. or 160-gr. RN in 6.5mm.

They've also added still another bullet to their ever-growing list of 30-cal. match bullets, this one a 220-gr. Match King HPBT, for use over really long yardages, I think.

Last, there's a rather strange new 38-cal. (.357″) FMJ bullet of 170 grains, identified as intended for the handgun silhouette game. I suppose its greater weight in combination with 357 Magnum velocities is designed to exert sufficient force to overturn the steel silhouette targets, where the additional momentum counts for more than increased velocity.

Sierra's latest bullet board doubles as a handy reference source, listing the caliber, diameter, weight and design of each of the 84 bullets mounted.

Hornady

Announced just too late for last year's ABC report was Hornady's 8mm 220-gr. SP for use in the 8mm Remington Magnum cartridge. Designed for big game at high velocities, these bullets have an exceptionally heavy jacket to insure deep penetration and avoid break-up, but they also have internal jacket scoring to assist expansion. Hornady's secant ogive Spire-Point shape, combined with their unusual length (1.350″), gives these bullets a high ballistic coefficient plus a sectional density of .301, qualifying them for long range efficiency. Accuracy has been excellent at speeds over 2800 fps.

Tests of Hornady's 185-gr. HP 45 ACP bullet, also introduced last year, reveal fine accuracy and jam-free feeding. Five-shot groups as small as 2″ at 50 yards were shot with our Colt Gold Cup auto. Jacket construction insures good expansion at low velocities, a real need in such bullets.

Two other new Hornady bullets have just been announced. One is a 38-cal. FMJ of 160 grains with a blunt round nose. Again we see the spreading influence of handgun silhouette shooting, this bullet having been designed especially for that purpose. I expect it to serve its intended use if loaded to 357 Magnum speeds, but I take exception to a claim made in the announcement that: " . . . its inherent full metal jacket design delivers greater impulse on the target." Whether you subscribe to the momentum or kinetic energy formula in determining the force of impact on a (silhouette) target, the governing factors are bullet weight and velocity. I fail to see how jacket material can affect the foot pounds of force impacting the targets, steel or not.

The other is just like the 357 bullet—a round-nose FMJ—but in 44 caliber (.430″ I make it) of 240 grains, and intended for the same silhouette handgun sport, I'm sure.

Hornady solid-jacket Silueta bullets, .358″ and .430″.

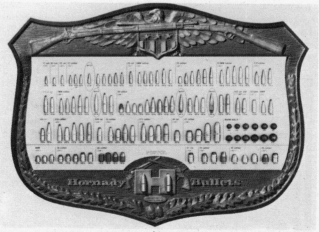

Hornady's 6th Edition bullet board, announced in January, 1978, shows their complete line of 106 rifle and pistol bullets, plus 12 round balls in different sizes.

Frontier Cartridge Co.

The continued growth of the Frontier cartridge line warrants an up-date in these columns. At last count the Frontier listing includes 10 rifle calibers in 26 loadings, plus 6 handgun calibers in 19 loadings, all carrying Hornady bullets in *new* brass cases. Included are: 222/223 Rem., 22-250 Rem., 243 Win., 270 Win., 7mm Rem. Mag., 30 M-1 Carbine, 30-30 Win., 308 Win. and 30-06, plus 380 Auto, 9mm Luger, 38 Spcl., 357/44 Magnum and 45 ACP.

I tested the first lots of Frontier cartridges in 308 and 30-06 many years ago, when salvaged military brass was used to hold down costs. That's still a prime aim at Frontier, but with the change to new commercial brass the line came of age. It can now be considered quality rather than just economy ammo.

In late 1977 Frontier added the 44 Magnum to their line of handgun cartridges, making available two loadings: a 200-gr. JHP and a 240-gr. JHP.

Lyman

This year Lyman celebrates their 100th Anniversary. William Lyman founded the Lyman Gun Sight Company in 1878 to design and make better rifle sights. Befitting their Centennial they have once again become a privately-owned firm aggressively engaged in product development.

Topping this program is a Lyman Commemorative called the 45-3¼″ Lyman, I believe. This, the old 45-120-3¼″ Sharps case, is to be chambered in a special edition of the Ruger No. 1 single-shot rifle, produced especially for Lyman. Only empty unprimed cases will be furnished, not loaded cartridges, I hear.

I'm already working up smokeless powder loads with jacketed and cast bullets for this revived cartridge, using an original Sharps-Borchardt action (with small bushed firing pin), barreled and chambered by B. W. Darr of the Saeco-Darr Rifle Co. in Carpinteria, CA. Darr is rightfully proud of his custom-grade barrels, and I'll have more to say about this big cartridge next year, and its performance.

Another bullet form dating to black powder days being revitalized by Lyman is a "composite" bullet for revolvers, these bullets cast in two parts separately, one hard and the other soft, then joined to permit higher velocities without barrel leading.

You'll have to make these 2-part bullets yourself. Lyman offers the two moulds, only three calibers now available: mould 358624 for the 357 Magnum; 429625 in 44 Magnum and 452626 for the 45 Colt.

Paper-patched bullets went out of style about the time metallic cartridges rifles took over. Their appearance is intended to allow the use of cast rifle bullets without leading at velocities heretofore considered impracticable.

I won't go into the complete details as to how these bullets are prepared. The only two paper-patch moulds available, to my knowledge, are 301618 (160/166-gr.), and 301620 (196/204-gr.), both 30 caliber. Directions for their preparation and use appeared in *The American Rifleman* issues of March and December 1977 and March, 1978. ●

Cross-section of Lyman's new composite (2-piece) cast handgun bullet. Hard alloy base withstands higher velocities without leading, it's said, the soft-lead front section providing increased expansion. Each section is cast separately, then both joined with epoxy.

Latest Hornady bullet is this 38-cal. 160-gr. round nose with full-metal-jacket, produced for handgun silhouette shooters. Note thicker nose area.

CENTERFIRE RIFLE CARTRIDGES—BALLISTICS AND PRICES

Winchester-Western, Remington-Peters, Federal and Speer-DWM

Most of these centerfire loads are available from Winchester-Western and Remington-Peters. Loads available from only one source are marked by a letter, thus: Winchester (a); Western (b); Remington (c); Peters (d); Federal (e). Those fewer cartridges also available are not necessarily uniform, hence prices are approximate.

Cartridge	Bullet Wt. Grs.	Bullet Type	Velocity (fps) Muzzle	Velocity (fps) 100 yds.	Velocity (fps) 200 yds.	Velocity (fps) 300 yds.	Energy (ft. lbs.) Muzzle	Energy (ft. lbs.) 100 yds.	Energy (ft. lbs.) 200 yds.	Energy (ft. lbs.) 300 yds.	Mid-Range Trajectory 100 yds.	Mid-Range Trajectory 200 yds.	Mid-Range Trajectory 300 yds.	Price for 20*
17 Remington	25	HP, PL	4020	3290	2630	2060	900	600	380	230	—	1.5	7.3	$ 7.75
218 Bee*	46	HP	2860	2160	1610	1200	835	475	265	145	0.7	3.8	11.5	17.25
22 Hornet*	45	PSP	2690	2030	1510	1150	720	410	230	130	0.8	4.3	13.0	13.95
22 Hornet*(c, d)	45	HP	2690	2030	1510	1150	720	410	230	130	0.8	4.3	13.0	14.25
22 Hornet*	46	HP	2690	2030	1510	1150	740	420	235	135	0.8	4.3	13.0	13.50
222 Remington (a, e)	50	PSP, MC, PL†	3200	2660	2170	1750	1140	785	520	340	0.5	2.5	7.0	6.40
222 Remington Magnum (c, d)	55	SP, PL†	3300	2800	2340	1930	1330	955	670	455	0.5	2.3	6.1	7.20
222 Remington Magnum (c, d)	55	HP, PL†	3300	2830	2400	2010	1330	975	700	490	0.5	2.3	6.1	7.75
223 Remington (a, c, d)	55	SP, PL†, PSP	3300	2800	2340	1930	1330	955	670	455	0.5	2.1	5.4	7.00
22-250 Remington (e)	55	PSP	3810	3270	2770	2320	1770	1300	935	655	0.3	1.6	4.4	7.00
22-250 Remington (c, d)	55	HP, PL†	3810	3330	2890	2490	1770	1360	1020	760	0.4	1.7	4.3	7.50
225 Winchester (a, b)	55	PSP	3650	3140	2680	2270	1630	1200	870	630	0.4	1.8	4.8	7.05
243 Winchester (e)	80	PSP, PL†	3420	3020	2620	2310	2180	1690	1320	1030	0.4	1.8	4.7	8.75
243 Winchester (c, d)	80	HP, PL†	3450	3050	2675	2330	2115	1650	1270	965	0.4	1.9	4.9	9.45
243 Winchester (e)	100	PP, CL, PSP	2960	2700	2450	2220	2090	1730	1430	1190	0.5	2.2	5.5	8.95
6mm Remington (a, c, d)	80	PSP, HP, PL†	3450	3130	2750	2400	2220	1740	1340	1018	0.4	1.8	4.7	8.70
6mm Remington (a, c, d)	100	PCL, PSP	3190	2920	2660	2420	2260	1890	1570	1300	0.5	2.1	5.1	8.70
6mm Remington (e)	80	SP	3450	3130	2756	2400	2220	1740	1340	1018	—	—	—	8.70
6mm Remington (e)	100	SP	3190	2920	2660	2420	2260	1890	1570	1300	—	—	—	8.70
244 Remington (c, d)	90	PSP	3200	2850	2530	2230	2050	1630	1280	995	0.5	2.1	5.5	7.55
25-06 Remington (c, d)	87	HP	3500	3070	2680	2310	2370	1820	1390	1030	0.4	2.0	5.1	9.45
25-06 Remington (c, d)	120	PSP, CL	3120	2850	2600	2360	2590	2160	1800	1480	0.5	2.2	5.6	9.75
25-20 Winchester*	86	L, Lu	1460	1180	1030	940	405	265	200	170	2.6	12.5	32.0	12.00
25-20 Winchester* (c)	86	SP	1460	1180	1030	940	405	265	200	170	2.6	12.5	32.0	12.95
25-35 Winchester	117	SP, CL	2300	1910	1600	1340	1370	945	665	465	1.0	4.6	12.5	8.85
250 Savage (a, b)	87	PSP, SP	3030	2660	2330	2060	1770	1370	1050	820	0.6	2.5	6.4	7.95
250 Savage	100	ST, CL, PSP	2820	2460	2140	1870	1760	1340	1020	775	0.6	2.9	7.4	8.45
256 Winchester Magnum*(b)	60	OPE	2800	2070	1570	1220	1040	570	330	200	0.8	4.0	12.0	14.50
257 Roberts (a, b)	87	PSP	3200	2840	2500	2190	1980	1560	1210	925	0.5	2.2	5.7	8.75
257 Roberts (a, b)	100	ST, CL	2900	2540	2210	1920	1870	1430	1080	820	0.6	2.7	7.0	8.75
257 Roberts	117	PP, CL	2650	2280	1950	1690	1820	1350	985	740	0.7	3.4	8.8	9.30
6.5mm Remington Magnum (c)	120	PSP, CL	3030	2750	2480	2230	2450	2010	1640	1330	0.5	2.3	5.7	13.50
264 Winchester Magnum	100	PSP, CL	3700	3260	2880	2550	3040	2360	1840	1440	0.4	1.6	4.2	12.20
264 Winchester Magnum	140	PP, CL	3200	2490	2700	2480	3180	2690	2270	1910	0.5	2.0	4.9	12.20
270 Winchester	100	PSP	3480	3070	2690	2340	2690	2090	1600	1215	0.4	1.8	4.8	9.45
270 Winchester (e)	130	PP, PSP	3110	2850	2600	2400	2850	2390	2000	1660	0.5	2.1	5.3	9.45
270 Winchester	130	ST, CL, BP, PP	3140	2850	2580	2320	2840	2340	1920	1550	0.5	2.1	5.3	10.00
270 Winchester (c, d)	150	CL	2800	2440	2140	1870	2610	1980	1520	1160	0.6	2.9	7.6	9.45
270 Winchester (a, b, e)	150	PP, SP	2900	2550	2230	1930	2800	2290	1890	1550	0.6	2.5	6.3	9.55
280 Remington (c, d)	150	PCL	2900	2670	2450	2220	2800	2370	2000	1640	0.6	2.5	6.1	9.85
280 Remington (c, d)	165	CL	2820	2510	2220	1970	2910	2310	1810	1420	0.6	2.8	7.2	9.85
284 Winchester (a, b)	125	PP	3200	2880	2590	2310	2840	2300	1860	1480	0.5	2.1	5.3	9.75
284 Winchester (a, b)	150	PP	2900	2630	2380	2160	2800	2300	1890	1550	0.6	2.5	6.3	9.85
7mm Mauser (e)	139	SP	2660	2400	2150	1910	2280	1850	1490	1190	0.7	3.0	7.8	9.85
7mm Mauser	175	SP	2470	2170	1880	1630	2410	1830	1400	1100	0.8	3.7	9.5	9.65
7mm Remington Magnum	125	CL	3430	3080	2750	2450	3260	2630	2100	1660	0.6	1.8	4.7	11.70
7mm Remington Magnum	150	PP, CL, SP	3110	2830	2570	2320	3540	2940	2430	1990	0.4	2.0	4.9	11.70
7mm Remington Magnum	175	SP	2860	2650	2440	2220	3660	2870	2240	1750	0.5	2.4	6.1	11.70
7mm Remington Magnum (c, d)	175	PCL	3070	2860	2660	2460	3660	3170	2740	2350	0.5	2.1	5.2	11.70
30 Carbine*	110	HSP, SP	1990	1570	1240	1040	950	575	370	260	1.4	7.5	21.7	15.20
30-30 Winchester (c, d)	150	CL	2410	1960	1620	1360	1930	1280	875	616	0.9	4.5	12.5	7.45
30-30 Winchester (e)	150	SP	2390	2020	1700	1430	1930	1360	960	680	0.9	4.2	11.0	7.50
30-30 Winchester (a, b)	150	PP, ST, OPE	2410	2020	1700	1430	1930	1360	960	680	0.9	4.2	11.0	7.50
30-30 Winchester	170	SP, HP, CL, ST, MC	2220	1890	1630	1410	1860	1350	1000	750	1.2	4.6	12.5	7.45
30 Remington	170	ST, CL	2120	1820	1560	1350	1700	1250	920	690	1.1	5.3	14.0	9.55
30-06 Accelerator	55	PSP	4080	3485	2965	2502	2033	1983	1074	764	1.0	0.0	5.0	10.50
30-06 Springfield (a, b)	110	PSP	3370	2830	2350	1920	2770	1960	1350	900	0.5	2.2	6.0	9.45
30-06 Springfield (e)	125	PSP	3140	2780	2450	2140	2840	2190	1710	1340	0.5	2.2	5.6	9.45
30-06 Springfield (c, d)	150	BP	2970	2710	2470	2240	2930	2440	2030	1670	0.5	2.4	6.0	10.00
30-06 Springfield (e)	150	SP	2910	2620	2340	2080	2930	2280	1760	1340	0.6	2.5	6.5	9.45
30-06 Springfield	150	ST, PCL, PSP	2970	2670	2400	2130	2930	2370	1920	1510	0.6	2.4	6.1	10.05
30-06 Springfield	180	PP, CL, PSP	2700	2330	2010	1740	2910	2170	1610	1210	0.7	3.1	8.3	9.45
30-06 Springfield	180	ST, BP, PCL, SP	2700	2470	2250	2040	2910	2440	2020	1660	0.7	2.9	7.0	10.00
30-06 Springfield	220	PP, CL	2410	2120	1870	1670	2830	2190	1710	1360	0.8	3.9	9.8	9.45
30-06 Springfield (a, b)	220	ST	2410	2180	1980	1790	2830	2320	1910	1560	0.8	3.7	9.2	9.45
30-40 Krag	180	PP, CL	2470	2120	1830	1590	2440	1790	1340	1010	0.8	3.8	9.9	9.95
30-40 Krag	180	ST, PCL	2470	2250	2040	1850	2440	2020	1660	1370	0.8	3.5	8.5	9.95
30-40 Krag (a, b)	220	ST	2200	1990	1800	1630	2360	1930	1580	1300	1.0	4.4	11.0	10.25
300 Winchester Magnum (a, c, e)	150	PP, PCL	3400	3050	2730	2430	3850	3100	2480	1970	0.4	1.9	4.8	12.35
300 Winchester Magnum (a, c, e)	180	PP, PCL	3070	2850	2640	2440	3770	3250	2790	2380	0.5	2.1	5.3	12.35
300 Winchester Magnum (a, b)	220	ST	2720	2490	2270	2060	3620	3030	2520	2070	0.6	2.9	6.9	12.50
300 H&H Magnum (a, b)	150	ST	3190	2870	2580	2300	3390	2740	2220	1760	0.5	2.1	5.2	12.45
300 H&H Magnum	180	ST, PCL	2920	2670	2440	2220	3400	2850	2380	1970	0.6	2.4	5.8	12.70
300 H&H Magnum (a, b)	220	ST, CL	2620	2370	2150	1940	3350	2740	2260	1840	0.7	3.1	7.7	12.90
300 Savage (e)	150	SP	2630	2350	2100	1850	2370	1840	1410	1080	0.7	3.2	8.0	9.55
300 Savage	150	ST, PCL	2670	2390	2130	1890	2370	1900	1510	1190	0.7	3.0	7.6	9.55
300 Savage (c, d)	150	CL	2670	2270	1930	1660	2370	1710	1240	916	0.7	3.3	9.3	9.55
300 Savage (e)	180	SP, CL	2350	2140	1940	1720	2240	1660	1240	920	0.9	4.1	10.5	10.00
300 Savage	180	ST, PCL	2370	2160	1960	1770	2240	1860	1530	1250	0.9	3.7	9.2	9.75
303 Savage (c, d)	180	CL	2140	1810	1550	1340	1830	1310	960	715	1.1	5.4	14.0	9.55
303 Savage (a, b)	190	ST	1980	1680	1440	1250	1650	1190	875	660	1.3	6.2	15.5	10.00
303 British (e)	180	PP, CL	2540	2300	2090	1900	2580	2120	1750	1440	0.7	3.3	8.2	9.70
303 British (c, d)	215	SP	2180	1900	1660	1460	2270	1720	1310	1020	1.1	4.9	12.5	9.70
308 Winchester (a, b)	110	PSP	3340	2810	2340	1920	2730	1930	1340	900	0.5	2.2	6.0	9.45
308 Winchester (a, b)	125	PSP	3100	2740	2430	2160	2670	2080	1640	1300	0.5	2.3	5.9	9.45
308 Winchester (e)	150	SP	2820	2530	2260	2010	2730	2120	1630	1240	0.6	2.7	7.0	9.45
308 Winchester	150	ST, PCL	2860	2570	2300	2050	2730	2200	1760	1400	0.6	2.6	6.5	9.45
308 Winchester (e)	180	PP, CL	2610	2250	1940	1680	2720	2020	1500	1130	0.7	3.4	8.9	9.45
308 Winchester	180	ST, PCL	2610	2390	2170	1970	2720	2280	1870	1540	0.8	3.1	7.4	9.45
308 Winchester (a, b)	200	ST	2450	2210	1980	1770	2770	2170	1750	1400	0.8	3.6	9.0	9.45
308 Match (e)	168	BTHP	2630	2440	2270	2100	2580	2230	1920	1640	—	—	—	11.50
32 Winchester Special (c, d, e)	170	HP, CL, SP	2250	1920	1630	1370	1960	1390	1000	750	1.0	4.8	12.5	7.90
32 Winchester Special	170	PP, ST	2280	1870	1560	1330	1960	1320	920	665	1.0	4.8	13.0	7.90
32 Remington (c, d)	170	CL	2120	1800	1540	1340	1700	1220	895	680	1.0	4.9	13.0	9.05
32 Remington (a, b)	170	ST	2120	1760	1460	1220	1700	1170	805	560	1.1	5.3	14.5	9.05
32-20 Winchester*	100	SP	1290	1060	940	840	370	250	195	155	3.3	15.5	38.0	13.25
32-20 Winchester*	100	SP, L, Lu	1290	1060	940	840	370	250	195	155	3.3	15.5	38.0	11.45
8mm Mauser	170	PP, CL	2510	2110	1740	1430	2380	1670	1140	770	0.8	7.0	25.7	9.75
8mm Remington Magnum	185	PSP	3080	2761	2464	2186	3896	3132	2494	1963	1.8	0.0	7.6	13.85
8mm Remington Magnum	220	PSP	2830	2581	2346	2123	3912	3255	2688	2201	2.2	0.0	8.5	13.85

CENTERFIRE RIFLE CARTRIDGES — BALLISTICS AND PRICES (continued)

Cartridge	Bullet Wt. Grs.	Bullet Type	Velocity (fps) Muzzle	100 yds.	200 yds.	300 yds.	Energy (ft. lbs.) Muzzle	100 yds.	200 yds.	300 yds.	Mid-Range Trajectory 100 yds.	200 yds.	300 yds.	Price for 20*
338 Winchester Magnum (a, b)	200	PP	3000	2690	2410	2170	4000	3210	2580	2090	0.5	2.4	6.0	$13.35
338 Winchester Magnum (a, b)	250	ST	2700	2430	2180	1940	4050	3280	2640	2090	0.7	3.0	7.4	13.35
338 Winchester Magnum (a, b)	300	PP	2450	2160	1910	1690	4000	3110	2430	1900	0.8	3.7	9.5	13.35
35 Remington (c, d)	150	CL	2400	1960	1580	1280	1920	1280	835	545	0.9	4.6	13.0	8.75
35 Remington (e)	200	PP, ST, CL	2080	1700	1380	1140	1950	1300	860	605	1.2	6.0	16.5	8.75
350 Remington Magnum (c, d)	200	PCL	2710	2410	2130	1870	3260	2570	2000	1550	0.7	3.0	7.7	13.65
350 Remington Magnum (c, d)	250	PCL	2410	2190	1980	1790	3220	2660	2180	1780	0.8	3.7	9.2	13.65
351 Winchester Self-Loading*	180	SP	1850	1560	1310	1140	1370	975	685	520	1.5	7.8	21.5	20.70
358 Winchester (a, b)	200	ST	2530	2210	1910	1640	2840	2160	1610	1190	0.8	3.6	9.4	11.35
358 Winchester (a, b)	250	ST	2250	2010	1780	1570	2810	2230	1760	1370	1.0	4.4	11.0	11.35
375 Big Bore (a)	200	FNPP	2200	1841	1526	—	2150	1506	1034	—	1.1	5.2	—	—
375 Big Bore (a)	250	FNPP	1900	1647	1424	—	2005	1506	1126	—	1.4	6.4	—	—
375 H&H Magnum	270	PP, SP	2740	2460	2210	1990	4500	3620	2920	2370	0.7	2.9	7.1	14.70
375 H&H Magnum	300	ST	2550	2280	2040	1830	4330	3460	2770	2230	0.7	3.3	8.3	14.70
375 H&H Magnum	300	MC	2550	2180	1860	1590	4330	3160	2300	1680	0.7	3.6	9.3	14.70
38-40 Winchester*	180	SP	1330	1070	960	850	705	455	370	290	3.2	15.0	36.5	17.10
44 Magnum* (c,d)	240	SP	1750	1360	1110	980	1630	985	655	510	1.6	8.4	—	7.00
44 Magnum (b, e)	240	HSP	1760	1360	1090	950	630	970	635	480	1.8	9.4	26.0	7.00
444 Marlin (c)	240	SP	2400	1845	1410	1125	3070	1815	1060	675	1.0	5.4	16.5	10.20
44-40 Winchester*	200	SP	1310	1050	940	830	760	490	390	305	3.3	15.0	36.5	18.90
45-70 Government (e)	300	HSP	1810	1410	1120	970	2180	1320	840	630	—	—	—	10.75
45-70 Government	405	SP	1320	1160	1050	990	1570	1210	990	880	2.9	13.0	32.5	10.75
458 Winchester Magnum	500	MC	2130	1910	1700	1520	5040	4050	3210	2570	1.1	4.8	12.0	30.05
458 Winchester Magnum	510	SP	2130	1840	1600	1400	5140	3830	2900	2220	1.1	5.1	13.5	19.85

*Price for 50   HP—Hollow Point   SP—Soft Point   PSP—Pointed Soft Point   PP—Power Point   L—Lead   Lu—Lubaloy   ST—Silvertip   HSP—Hollow Soft Point   MC—Metal Case   BT—Boat Tail   MAT—Match   BP—Bronze Point   CL—Core Lokt   PCL—Pointed Core Lokt   OPE—Open Point Expanding   FN—Flat Nose   †PL—Power-Lokt (slightly higher price).

WEATHERBY MAGNUM CARTRIDGES — BALLISTICS AND PRICES

Cartridge	Bullet Wt. Grs.	Bullet Type	Velocity (fps) Muzzle	100 yds.	200 yds.	300 yds.	Energy (ft. lbs.) Muzzle	100 yds.	200 yds.	300 yds.	Mid-Range Trajectory 100 yds.	200 yds.	300 yds.	Price for 20
224 Weatherby Varmintmaster	50	PE	3750	3160	2625	2140	1562	1109	765	508	0.7	3.6	9.0	$14.95
224 Weatherby Varmintmaster	55	PE	3650	3150	2685	2270	1627	1212	881	629	0.4	1.7	4.5	14.95
240 Weatherby	70	PE	3850	3395	2975	2585	2304	1788	1376	1038	0.3	1.5	3.9	14.95
240 Weatherby	90	PE	3500	3135	2795	2475	2444	1960	1559	1222	0.4	1.8	4.5	14.95
240 Weatherby	100	PE	3395	3115	2850	2595	2554	2150	1804	1495	0.4	1.8	4.4	15.95
257 Weatherby	87	PE	3825	3290	2835	2450	2828	2087	1553	1160	0.4	1.7	4.4	15.95
257 Weatherby	100	PE	3555	3150	2815	2500	2802	2199	1760	1338	0.4	1.7	4.4	15.95
257 Weatherby	117	SPE	3300	2900	2550	2250	2824	2184	1689	1315	0.4	2.4	6.8	15.95
270 Weatherby	100	PE	3760	3625	2825	2435	3140	2363	1773	1317	0.4	1.6	4.3	15.95
270 Weatherby	130	PE	3375	3050	2750	2480	3283	2685	2183	1776	0.4	1.8	4.5	15.95
270 Weatherby	150	PE	3245	2955	2675	2430	3501	2909	2385	1967	0.5	2.0	5.0	15.95
7mm Weatherby	139	PE	3300	2995	2715	2465	3355	2770	2275	1877	0.4	1.9	4.9	15.95
7mm Weatherby	154	PE	3160	2885	2640	2415	3406	2874	2384	1994	0.5	2.0	5.0	15.95
300 Weatherby	150	PE	3545	3195	2890	2615	4179	3393	2783	2279	0.4	1.5	3.9	15.95
300 Weatherby	180	PE	3245	2960	2705	2475	4201	3501	2925	2448	0.4	1.9	5.2	15.95
300 Weatherby	220	SPE	2905	2610	2385	2150	4123	3329	2757	2257	0.6	2.5	6.7	16.95
340 Weatherby	200	PE	3210	2905	2615	2345	4566	3748	3038	2442	0.5	2.1	5.3	25.50
340 Weatherby	210	Nosler	3165	2910	2665	2435	4660	3948	3312	2766	0.5	2.1	5.0	16.95
340 Weatherby	250	SPE	2850	2580	2325	2090	4510	3695	3000	2425	0.6	2.7	6.7	16.95
378 Weatherby	270	SPE	3180	2850	2600	2315	6051	4871	4053	3210	0.5	2.0	5.2	26.95
378 Weatherby	300	SPE, FMJ	2925	2610	2380	2125	5700	4539	3774	3009	0.6	2.5	6.2	30.95
460 Weatherby	500	RN, FMJ	2700	2330	2005	1730	8095	6025	4465	3320	0.7	3.3	10.0	34.95

Trajectory is given from scope height. Velocities chronographed using 26″ bbls. Available with Nosler bullets; add $2.00 per box.
SPE—Semi-Pointed Expanding   RN—Round Nose   PE—Pointed Expanding   FMJ—Full Metal Jacket.

RIMFIRE CARTRIDGES — BALLISTICS AND PRICES

Remington-Peters, Winchester-Western, Federal & Cascade Cartridge, Inc.

All loads available from all manufacturers except as indicated: R-P (a); W-W (b); Fed. (c); CCI (d). All prices are approximate.

Cartridge	Wt. Grs.	Bullet Type	Velocity Ft. Per Sec. Muzzle	100 Yds.	Energy Ft. Lbs. Muzzle	100 Yds.	Mid-Range Trajectory 100 Yds.	Handgun Barrel Length	Ballistics M.V. F.P.S.	M.E. F.P.	Price for 50
22 Short T22 (a, b)	29	C, L*	1045	810	70	42	5.6	6"	865	48	$1.37
22 Short Hi-Vel. (c)	29	C, L	1125	920	81	54	4.3	6"	1035	69	1.37
22 Short HP Hi-Vel. (a, b, c)	27	C,L	1155	920	80	51	4.2	—	—	—	1.45
22 Short (a, b)	29	D	1045	—	70	—	—	—	(per 500)	—	13.00
22 Short (a, b)	15	D	1710	—	97	—	—	—	(per 500)	—	12.15
22 Stinger	32	C, HP	1686	1047	202	78	2.61	—	—	—	1.95
22 Xpediter	29	HP	1680	—	182	—	2.5	—	—	—	2.11
22 Long Hi-Vel. (c)	29	C, L	1240	965	99	60	3.8	6"	1240	99	1.45
22 Long Rifle T22 (a, b)†-1	40	L*	1145	975	116	84	4.0	6"	950	80	1.55
22 Long Rifle (b)†-2	40	L*	1120	950	111	80	4.2	—	—	—	2.95
22 Long Rifle (b)†-3	40	L*	—	—	—	—	—	6¾"	1060	100	2.95
22 Long Rifle (d)†-4	40	C	1165	980	121	84	4.0	—	—	—	1.65
22 Long Rifle Hi-Vel.	40	C,L	1285	1025	147	93	3.4	6"	1125	112	1.45
22 Long Rifle HP Hi-Vel. (b, d)	37	C,L	1315	1020	142	85	3.4	—	1255	140	1.65
22 Long Rifle HP Hi-Vel. (a, c)	38	C, HP	1365	1040	149	86	3.4	—	1280	138	1.65
22 Long Rifle (b, c)	No.	12 Shot	—	—	—	—	—	—	—	—	3.05
22 WRF [Rem. Spl.] (a, b)	45	C,L	1450	1110	210	123	—	—	—	—	4.25
22 WRF Mag. (b)	40	JHP	2000	1390	355	170	1.6	6½"	1550	213	3.75
22 WRF Mag. (b)	40	MC	2000	1390	355	170	1.6	6½"	1550	213	3.75
22 Win. Auto Inside lub. (a, b)	45	C,L	1055	930	111	86	—	—	—	—	4.55
5mm Rem. RFM (a)	38	PLHP	2100	1605	372	217		Not Available			6.75

†—Target loads of these ballistics available in: (1) Rem. Match; (2) W-W LV EZXS, Super Match Mark III; (3) Super Match Mark IV and EZXS Pistol Match; (4) CCI Mini-Group.
C—Copper plated   L—Lead (Wax Coated)   L*—Lead, lubricated   D—Disintegrating   MC—Metal Case   HP—Hollow Point   JHP—Jacket Hollow Point
PLHP—Power-Lokt Hollow Point

NORMA C.F. RIFLE CARTRIDGES — BALLISTICS AND PRICES

Norma ammunition loaded to standard velocity and pressure is now available with Nosler bullets in the following loads: 270 Win., 130-, 150-gr.; Super 7x61 (S&H), 160-gr.; 308 Win., 180-gr.; 30-06, 150-, 180-gr., all at slightly higher prices. All ballistic figures are computed from a line of sight one inch above center of bore at muzzle. Write for their latest prices.

| Cartridge | Bullet Wt. Grs. | Type | Velocity, feet per sec. | | | | Energy, foot pounds | | | | Max. height of trajectory, Inches | | | Price for 20 |
			V Muzzle	V 100 yds.	V 200 yds.	V 300 yds.	E Muzzle	E 100 yds.	E 200 yds.	E 300 yds.	Tr. 100 yds.	Tr. 200 yds.	Tr. 300 yds.	
220 Swift	50	SP	4111	3611	3133	2681	1877	1448	1090	799	.2	.9	3.0	$11.50
222 Remington	50	SPSP, FMJ	3200	2660	2170	1750	1137	786	523	340	.0	2.0	6.2	7.15
22-250 Remington	53	SpPSP (Match Spitzer)	3710	—	—	—	—	—	—	—	—	—	—	9.70
22 Savage Hi-Power (5.6x52R)	71	SPSP, FMJ	2788	2296	1886	1558	1226	831	651	383	.0	4.8	18.06	14.45
243 Winchester	100	SPSP, FJSP	3070	2790	2540	2320	2093	1729	1433	1195	.1	1.8	5.0	9.45
6.5 Carcano	156	SPRN	2000	1810	1640	1485	1386	1135	932	764	Not Available			13.25
6.5 Japanese	139	SPSPBT	2428	2280	2130	1990	1820	1605	1401	1223	.3	2.8	7.7	13.25
	156	SPRN	2067	1871	1692	1529	1481	1213	992	810	.6	4.4	11.9	13.25
6.5x55	77	SPSP	2725	2362	2030	1811	1271	956	706	562	.0	4.8	18.1	13.25
	139	PPDC	2789	2630	2470	2320	2402	2136	1883	1662	.1	2.0	5.6	13.25
	156	SPSP	2493	2271	2062	1867	2153	1787	1473	1208	.3	2.9	7.9	13.25
270 Winchester	130	SPSPBT	3140	2884	2639	2404	2847	2401	2011	1669	.0	1.6	4.7	10.20
	150	SPSPBT	2802	2616	2436	2262	2616	2280	1977	1705	.1	2.0	5.7	10.20
7.5x55 Schmidt Rubin (7.5 Swiss)	180	SPSBT	2650	2450	2260	2060	2792	2350	1990	1665	Not Available			13.40
7x57	150	SPSPBT	2756	2539	2331	2133	2530	2148	1810	1516	.1	4.2	6.2	10.40
7x57R	150	SPSPBT, FJPBT	2690	2476	2270	2077	2411	2042	1717	1437	.0	5.2	15.2	14.55
7mm Remington Magnum	150	SPSBT	3260	2970	2700	2450	3540	2945	2435	1990	.4	2.0	4.9	12.45
7x61 S&H (26 in.)	150	SPBT	3100	2927	2757	2595	3415	3045	2701	2393	.0	1.5	4.3	14.80
7x64	150	SPSPBT	2890	2598	2329	2113	2779	2449	1807	1487	.0	3.3	12.5	14.50
280 Remington	150	SPSP	2900	2683	2475	2277	2802	2398	2041	1727	.0	3.4	12.4	10.40
30 U.S. Carbine	110	SPRN	1970	1595	1300	1090	948	622	413	290	.8	6.4	19.0	6.30
308 Winchester	130	SPSPBT	2900	2590	2300	2030	2428	1937	1527	1190	.1	2.1	6.2	10.20
	150	SPSPBT	2860	2570	2300	2050	2725	2200	1762	1400	.1	2.0	5.9	10.20
	180	PPDC	2610	2400	2210	2020	2725	2303	1952	1631	.2	2.5	6.6	10.20
7.62 Russian	180	SPSBT	2624	2415	2222	2030	2749	2326	1970	1644	.2	2.5	6.6	13.70
308 Norma Magnum	180	PPDC	3100	2881	2668	2464	3842	3318	2846	2427	.0	1.6	4.6	17.80
30-06	130	SPSBT	3281	2951	2636	2338	3108	2514	2006	1578	.1	1.5	4.6	10.20
	150	SPSBT	2972	2680	2402	2141	2943	2393	1922	1527	.0	1.9	5.7	10.20
	180	SPRN	2700	2494	2296	2109	2914	2487	2107	1778	.1	2.3	6.4	10.20
	180	PPDC	2700	2494	2296	2109	2914	2487	2107	1778	Not Available			10.20
30-30	150	SPFP	2410	2075	1790	1550	1934	1433	1066	799	.0	7.0	26.1	9.90
	170	SPFP	2220	1890	1630	1410	1860	1350	1000	750	.0	8.1	29.2	9.90
7.65 Argentine	150	SPSP	2920	2630	2355	2105	2841	2304	1848	1476	.1	2.0	5.8	13.15
303 British	150	SPSP	2720	2440	2170	1930	2465	1983	1596	1241	.1	2.2	6.5	10.45
	180	SPSPBT	2540	2340	2147	1965	2579	2189	1843	1544	.2	2.7	7.3	10.45
7.7 Japanese	130	SPSP	2950	2635	2340	2065	2513	2004	1581	1231	.1	2.0	5.9	13.50
	180	SPSPBT	2493	2292	2101	1922	2484	2100	1765	1477	.3	2.8	7.7	13.50
8x57J (.318 in.)	196	SPRN	2526	2195	1894	1627	2778	2077	1562	1152	.0	5.8	21.4	10.50
8mm Mauser (.323 in.)	196	SP	2526	2195	1894	1627	2778	2097	1562	1152	Not Available			10.50
358 Norma Magnum	250	SPSP	2790	2493	2231	2001	4322	3451	2764	2223	.2	2.4	6.6	17.15
9.3x57	286	PPDC	2067	1818	1595	1404	2714	2099	1616	1252	.0	9.1	32.0	17.00
9.3x62	286	PPDC	2362	2088	1815	1592	3544	2769	2092	1700	.0	6.5	23.5	17.00

P—Pointed SP—Soft Point HP—Hollow Point FP—Flat Point RN—Round Nose BT—Boat Tail MC—Metal Case DC—Dual Core SPSP—Soft Point Spire Point
SPSBT—Soft Point Semi Pointed Boat Tail FJPBT—Full Jacket Pointed Boat Tail SpPSP—Point Soft Point Spire PP—Plastic Point NA—Not announced *Price for 50

CENTERFIRE HANDGUN CARTRIDGES — BALLISTICS AND PRICES
Winchester-Western, Remington-Peters, Norma and Federal

Most loads are available from W-W and R-P. All available Norma loads are listed. Federal cartridges are marked with an asterisk. Other loads supplied by only one source are indicated by a letter, thus: Norma (a); R-P (b); W-W (c). Prices are approximate.

Cartridge	Bullet Gr.	Bullet Style	Muzzle Velocity	Muzzle Energy	Barrel Inches	Price Per 50
22 Jet (b)	40	SP	2100	390	8⅜	$14.95
221 Fireball (b)	50	SP	2650	780	10½	6.80
25 (6.35mm) Auto*	50	MC	810	73	2	9.15
256 Winchester Magnum (c)	60	HP	2350	735	8½	14.05
30 (7.65mm) Luger Auto	93	MC	1220	307	4½	14.00
32 S&W Blank (b,c)	No bullet	—	—	—	—	6.40
32 S&W Blank, BP (c)	No bullet	—	—	—	—	6.40
32 Short Colt	80	Lead	745	100	4	8.10
32 Long Colt IL (c)	82	Lub.	755	104	4	8.45
32 Colt New Police	100	Lead	680	100	4	10.75
32 (7.65mm) Auto*	71	MC	905	129	4	10.40
32 (7.65mm) Auto Pistol (a)	77	MC	900	162	4	9.95
32 S&W	88	Lead	680	90	3	8.15
32 S&W Long	98	Lead	705	115	4	8.45
32-20 Winchester	100	Lead	1030	271	6	11.15
32-20 Winchester	100	SP	1030	271	6	12.75
357 Magnum*	110	JHP	1295	410	4	13.70
357 Magnum*	125	JHP	1450	583	4	13.70
357 Magnum*	158	SWC	1235	535	4	13.70
357 Magnum (b)*	158	JSP	1550	845	8⅜	13.70
357 Magnum	158	MP	1410	695	8⅜	13.20
357 Magnum	158	Lead	1410	696	8⅜	11.60
357 Magnum	158	JHP	1450	735	8⅜	13.70
9mm Luger	115	MC	1165	349	4	12.95
9mm Luger	123	MC	1120	345	4	12.95
38 S&W Blank	No bullet	—	—	—	—	8.90
38 Smith & Wesson	146	Lead	685	150	4	9.95
38 S&W (a)	146	Lead	730	172	4	9.80
38 Special Blank	No bullet	—	—	—	—	9.40
38 Special, IL (c)	150	Lub.	1060	375	6	9.50
38 Special IL (c)	150	MP	1060	375	6	9.50
38 Special	158	Lead	855	256	6	10.10
38 Special	200	Lead	730	236	6	10.30
38 Special	158	MP	855	256	6	12.25
38 Special (b)	125	SJHP	Not available			12.25
38 Special	158	SJHP	Not available			11.95
38 Special WC (b)	148	Lead	770	195	6	10.10
38 Special Match, IL (c)	148	Lead	770	195	6	9.85
38 Special Match, IL (b, c)	158	Lead	855	256	6	9.95
38 Special Hi-Speed	158	Lead	1090	425	6	9.70
38 Special (a)	158	RN	900	320	6	6.40
38 Special*	158	SWC	755	200	4	10.10
38 Special Match*	148	WC	710	166	4	10.30
38 Special +P*	158	SWC	915	294	4	10.10
38 Special +P*	158	SWCHP	915	294	4	12.25
38 Special +P*	110	JHP	1020	254	4	12.25
38 Special +P*	125	JHP	945	248	4	12.25
38 Short Colt	125	Lead	730	150	6	9.20
38 Short Colt, Greased (c)	130	Lub.	730	155	6	9.45
38 Long Colt	150	Lead	730	175	6	12.70
38 Super Auto (b)	130	MC	1280	475	5	11.05
38 Auto, for Colt 38 Super (c)	130	MC	1280	475	5	10.80
38 Auto	130	MC	1040	312	4½	11.25
380 Auto*	95	MC	955	192	3¾	10.65
380 Auto	88	JHP	990	191	4	10.65
380 Auto*	90	JHP	1000	200	3¾	10.65
38-40 Winchester	180	SP	975	380	5	16.40
41 Remington Magnum (b)	210	Lead	1050	515	8¾	15.40
41 Remington Magnum (b)	210	SP	1500	1050	8¾	17.60
44 S&W Special	246	Lead	755	311	6½	13.80
44 Remington Magnum*	180	JHP	1610	1045	4	16.25
44 Remington Magnum	240	SP	1470	1150	6½	17.00
44 Remington Magnum	240	Lead	1470	1150	6½	17.50
44 Remington Magnum*	240	JHP	1180	741	4	16.25
44-40 Winchester	200	SP	975	420	7½	17.85
45 Colt	250	Lead	860	410	5½	13.70
45 Colt, IL (c)	255	Lub., L	860	410	5½	12.60
45 Auto	230	MC	850	369	5	13.95
45 Auto	230	JHP	850	370	5	14.00
45 ACP (a)	230	JHP	850	370	5	14.00
45 Auto WC*	185	MC	775	245	5	14.20
45 Auto*	185	JHP	950	370	5	14.75
45 Auto MC (a, b)	230	MC	850	369	5	14.00
45 Auto Match (c)	185	MC	775	247	5	14.75
45 Auto Match, IL (c)	210	Lead	710	235	5	14.90
45 Auto Match*	230	MC	850	370	5	14.75
45 Auto Rim (b)	230	Lead	810	335	5½	15.25

IL—Inside Lub. JSP—Jacketed Soft Point WC—Wad Cutter
RN—Round Nose HP—Hollow Point Lub—Lubricated
MC—Metal Case SP—Soft Point MP—Metal Point
LGC—Lead, Gas Check JHP—Jacketed Hollow Point
SWC—Semi Wad Cutter SJHP—Semi Jacketed Hollow Point

SHOTSHELL LOADS AND PRICES
Winchester-Western, Remington-Peters, Federal

In certain loadings one manufacturer may offer fewer or more shot sizes than another, but in general all makers offer equivalent loadings. Sources are indicated by letters, thus: W-W (a); R-P (b); Fed. (c). Prices are approximate.

GAUGE	Length Shell Ins.	Powder Equiv. Drams	Shot Ozs.	Shot Size	PRICE FOR 25
MAGNUM LOADS					
10 (a¹, b)	3½	Max	2	2	$14.70
12 (a, b, c)	3	4	1⅞	BB, 2, 4	10.55
12 (a¹, b)	3	4¼	1⅝	2, 4, 6	9.75
12 (a)	3	Max	1⅜	2, 4, 6	9.75
12 (a¹, b, c)	2¾	4	1½	2, 4, 5, 6	9.45
16 (a, b, c)	2¾	3¼	1¼	2, 4, 6	8.30
20 (a, b, c)	3	3	1¼	4, 6, 7½	7.95
20 (a¹)	3	Max	1³⁄₁₆	4	7.85
20 (a¹, b, c)	2¾	3	1⅛	2, 4, 6, 7½	7.05
LONG RANGE LOADS					
10 (a, b)	2⅞	4¾	1⅝	4	8.95
12 (a¹, b, c)	2¾	3¾	1¼	BB, 2, 4, 5, 6, 7½, 9	6.90
16 (a, b, c)	2¾	3¼	1⅛	4, 5, 6, 7½, 9	6.60
20 (a¹, b, c)	2¾	2¾	1	4, 5, 6, 7½, 9	6.60
28 (a, b)	2¾	2¼	1	6, 7½, 9	6.60
28 (c)	2¾	2¼	⅞	4, 6, 7½, 9	6.60
410 (b)	2½	Max	½	4, 6, 7½, 9	5.75
410 (b)	3	Max	¹¹⁄₁₆	4, 5, 6, 7½, 9	4.85
FIELD LOADS					
12 (a, b, c)	2¾	3¼	1¼	7½, 8	5.75
12 (a, b, c)	2¾	3¼	1⅛	4, 5, 6, 7½, 8, 9	5.75
12 (a, b, c)	2¾	3	1	4, 5, 6, 8	5.90
16 (a, b, c)	2¾	2¾	1⅛	4, 5, 6, 7½, 8, 9	5.90
16 (a, b, c)	2¾	2½	1	6, 8	5.25
20 (a, b, c)	2¾	2½	1	4, 5, 6, 7½, 8, 9	5.25
20 (a, b, c)	2¾	2¼	⅞	6, 8	5.30
SCATTER LOADS					
12 (a, b, c)	2¾	3	1⅛	8	6.15
TARGET LOADS					
12 (a, b, c)	2¾	3	1⅛	7½, 8	5.80
12 (a, b, c)	2¾	2¾	1⅛	7½, 8	5.10
16 (a, b, c)	2¾	2½	1	9	5.70
20 (a, b, c)	2¾	2½	⅞	9	4.80
28 (a, c)	2¾	2	¾	9	5.95
410 (a, b, c)	3	Max	¾	9	4.70
410 (a, b, c)	2½	Max	½	9	4.70
SKEET & TRAP					
12 (a, b, c)	2¾	3	1⅛	7½, 8, 9	5.70
12 (a, b, c)	2¾	2¾	1⅛	7½, 8, 9	5.70
16 (a, b, c)	2¾	2½	1	9	4.95
16 (c)	2¾	1⅛	1⅛	8, 9	4.80
20 (a, b, c)	2¾	2¼	⅞	9	4.70
BUCKSHOT					
12 (a, b, c)	3 Mag.	4½	—	00 Buck—15 pellets	12.50
12 (a, b, c)	3 Mag.	4½	—	4 Buck—41 pellets	12.65
12 (b)	2¾ Mag.	4	—	1 Buck—20 pellets	11.20
12 (a, b, c)	2¾ Mag.	4	—	00 Buck—12 pellets	11.20
12 (a, b, c)	2¾	3¾	—	00 Buck— 9 pellets	9.20
12 (a, b, c)	2¾	3¾	—	0 Buck—12 pellets	9.20
12 (a, b, c)	2¾	3¾	—	1 Buck—16 pellets	9.20
12 (a, b, c)	2¾	3¾	—	4 Buck—27 pellets	9.30
16 (a, b, c)	2¾	3	—	1 Buck—12 pellets	9.00
20 (a, b, c)	2¾	2¾	—	3 Buck—20 pellets	9.00
RIFLED SLUGS					
12 (a, b, c)	2¾	3¾	1	Slug	11.20
16 (a, b, c)	2¾	3	⅘	Slug	10.30
20 (a, b, c)	2¾	Max	⅝	Slug	10.00
410 (a, b, c)	2½	Max	⅕	Slug	9.75

W-W 410, 28 and 10-ga. Magnum shells available in paper cases only, as are their scatter and target loads; their skeet and trap loads come in both plastic and paper.

R-P shells are all of plastic with Power Piston wads except: 12 ga. scatter loads have Post Wad: all 10 ga., 410-3″ and rifled slug loads have standard wad columns.

Federal magnum, range, buckshot, slug and all 410 loads are made in plastic only. Field loads are available in both paper and plastic.

¹—These loads available from W-W with Lubaloy shot at higher price.

BERNARDELLI MODEL 100 PISTOL
Caliber: 22 LR only, 10-shot magazine.
Barrel: 5.9″.
Weight: 37¾ oz. **Length:** 9″ over-all.
Stocks: Checkered walnut with thumbrest.
Sights: Fixed front, rear adj. for w. and e.
Features: Target barrel weight included. Heavy sighting rib with interchangeable front sight. Accessories include cleaning equipment and assembly tools, case. Imported from Italy by Interarms.
Price: **$269.00**

BERETTA MODEL 76 PISTOL
Caliber: 22 LR, 10-shot magazine.
Barrel: 6″.
Weight: 33 ozs. (empty). **Length:** 8.8″ over-all.
Stocks: Checkered plastic.
Sights: Interchangable blade front (3 widths), rear is fully adj. for w. and e.
Features: Built-in, fixed counterweight, raised, matted slide rib, factory adjusted trigger pull from 3 lbs. 5 ozs. to 3 lbs. 12 ozs. Thumb safety. Blue-black finish. Wood grips available at extra cost. Introduced 1977. Imported by Beretta Arms Co.
Price: **$220.00**

CVA/UNIQUE D.E.S. 69 TARGET PISTOL
Caliber: 22 LR.
Barrel: 5.91″.
Weight: Approx. 35 oz. **Length:** 10.63″ over-all.
Stocks: French walnut target style with thumbrest and adjustable shelf; hand checkered panels.
Sights: Ramp front, micro. adj. rear mounted on frame; 8.66″ sight radius.
Features: Meets U.I.T. standards. Comes in a fitted hard case with spare magazine, barrel weight, cleaning rod, tools, proof certificate, test target and two year guarantee. Fully adjustable trigger; dry firing safety device. Imported from France by Connecticut Valley Arms.
Price: Right-hand **$375.00**
Price: Left-hand **$395.00**

COLT GOLD CUP NAT'L MATCH MK IV Series 70
Caliber: 45 ACP, 7-shot magazine.
Barrel: 5″, with new design bushing.
Length: 8⅜″. **Weight:** 38½ oz.
Stocks: Checkered walnut, gold plated medallion.
Sights: Ramp-style front, Colt-Elliason rear adj. for w. and e., sight radius 6¾″.
Features: Arched or flat housing; wide, grooved trigger with adj. stop; ribbed-top slide, hand fitted, with improved ejection port.
Price: Colt Royal Blue **$340.50**

DOMINO MODEL SP-602 MATCH PISTOL
Caliber: 22 LR, 5-shot.
Barrel: 5.5″.
Weight: 41 oz. **Length:** 11.02″ over-all.
Stocks: Full target stocks; adjustable, one-piece. Left hand style avail.
Sights: Match. Blade front, open notch rear fully adj. for w. and e. Sight radius is 8.66″.
Features: Line of sight is only ¹¹/₃₂″ above centerline of bore; magazine is inserted from top; adjustable and removable trigger mechanism; single lever takedown. Full 5 year warranty. Imported from Italy by Mandall Shooting Supplies.
Price: **$650.00**

DOMINO O.P. 601 MATCH PISTOL
Similar to S.P. 602 except has different match stocks with adj. palm shelf, 22 Short only, weighs 40 oz., 5.6″ bbl., has gas ports through top of barrel and slide to reduce recoil, slightly different trigger and sear mechanisms.
Price: **$650.00**

SIG P-210-6 AUTO PISTOL
Caliber: 9mm Para., 8-shot magazine.
Barrel: 4¾".
Weight: 37 oz. **Length:** 8½" over-all.
Stocks: Checkered black plastic.
Sights: Blade front, micro. adj. rear for w. & e.
Features: Adjustable trigger stop; ribbed front stap; sandblasted finish. Conversion unit for 22 LR consists of barrel, recoil spring, slide and magazine. Imported by Mandall Shooting Supplies.
Price: P-210-6 . . . . **$900.00**
Price: 22 Cal. Conversion unit **$450.00**

SIG/HAMMERLI P-240 TARGET PISTOL
Caliber: 38 Special Wadcutter, 5-shot.
Barrel: 6".
Weight: 4¼ oz. **Length:** 10" over-all.
Stocks: Walnut, target style, unfinished.
Sights: Match sights; ⅛" undercut front, ⅛" notch micro rear click adj. for w. and e.
Features: Semi-automatic, recoil operated; meets I.S.U. and N.R.A. specs for Center Fire Pistol competition; double pull trigger adj. from 2 lbs., 15 ozs. to 3 lbs., 9 ozs.; trigger stop. Comes with extra magazine, special screwdriver, carrying case. From Mandall Shooting Supplies.
Price: **$850.00**
Price: 22 cal. conversion unit **$575.00**

SIG P-210-1 AUTO PISTOL
Caliber: 22 LR, 7.65mm or 9mm P., 8-shot magazine.
Barrel: 4¾".
Weight: 31¾ oz. (9mm) **Length:** 8½" over-all.
Stocks: Checkered walnut.
Sights: Blade front, rear adjustable for windage.
Features: Lanyard loop; polished finish. Conversion unit for 22 LR available. Imported by Mandall Shooting Supplies.
Price: P-210-1 . . . . **$935.00**
Price: 22 Cal. Conversion unit **$450.00**

SMITH & WESSON 22 AUTO PISTOL Model 41
Caliber: 22 LR or 22 S, 10-shot clip.
Barrel: 7⅜", sight radius 9⁵⁄₁₆" (7⅜" bbl.).
Length: 12", incl. detachable muzzle brake, (7⅜" bbl. only).
Weight: 43½ oz. (7⅜" bbl.).
Stocks: Checkered walnut with thumbrest, usable with either hand.
Features: ⅜" wide, grooved trigger with adj. stop; wgts. available to make pistol up to 59 oz.
Sights: Front, ⅛" Patridge undercut; micro click rear adj. for w. and e.
Price: S&W Bright Blue, satin matted bbl., either caliber **$233.50**

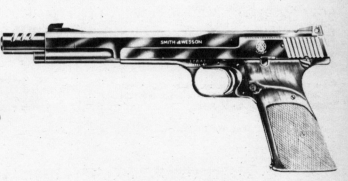

SMITH & WESSON 22 MATCH HEAVY BARREL M-41
Caliber: 22 LR, 10-shot clip.
Barrel: 5½" heavy, without muzzle brake. Sight radius, 8".
Length: 9". **Weight:** 44½ oz.
Stocks: Checkered walnut with modified thumbrest, usable with either hand.
Features: ⅜" wide, grooved trigger; adj. trigger stop.
Sights: ⅛" Patridge on ramp base. S&W micro click rear, adj. for w. and e.
Price: S&W Bright Blue, satin matted top area **$233.50**

SMITH & WESSON 38 MASTER Model 52 AUTO
Caliber: 38 Special (for Mid-range W.C. with flush-seated bullet only). 5-shot magazine.
Barrel: 5".
Length: 8⅝". **Weight:** 41 oz. with empty magazine.
Stocks: Checkered walnut.
Sights: ⅛" Partidge front, S&W micro click rear adj. for w. and e.
Features: Top sighting surfaces matte finished. Locked breech, moving barrel system; checked for 10-ring groups at 50 yards. Coin-adj. sight screws. Dry firing permissible if manual safety on.
Price: S&W Bright Blue **$381.00**

HAMMERLI MODEL 230 RAPID FIRE PISTOL
Caliber: 22 S.
Barrel: 6.3", 6-groove.
Weight: 43.8 oz. **Length:** 11.6".
Stocks: Walnut. Standard grip w/o thumbrest (230-1), 230-2 has adj. grip.
Sights: Match type sights. Sight radius 9.9". Micro rear, click adj. Interchangeable front sight blade.
Features: Semi-automatic. Recoil-operated, 6-shot clip. Gas escape in front of chamber to eliminate muzzle jump. Fully adj. trigger from 5¼ oz. to 10½ oz. with three different lengths available. Designed for International 25 meter Silhouette Program. Mandall Shooting Supplies, importer.
Price: Model 230-1 . . . . **$740.00**
Price: Model 230-2 . . . . **$790.00**

HAMMERLI STANDARD, MODELS 208 & 211
Caliber: 22 LR.
Barrel: 5.9", 6-groove.
Weight: 37.6 oz. (45 oz. with extra heavy barrel weight). **Length:** 10".
Stocks: Walnut. Adj. palm rest (208), 211 has thumbrest grip.
Sights: Match sights. fully adj. for w. and e. (click adj.). Interchangeable front and rear blades.
Features: Semi-automatic, recoil operated. 8-shot clip. Slide stop. Fully adj. trigger (2¼ lbs. and 3 lbs.). Extra barrel weight available. Mandall Shooting Supplies, importer.
Price: Model 208, approx. **$766.00**   Model 211 approx. **$737.00**

HI-STANDARD SUPERMATIC CITATION MILITARY
Caliber: 22 LR, 10-shot magazine.
Barrel: 5½" bull, 7¼" fluted.
Length: 9¾" (5½" bbl.). **Weight:** 46 oz.
Stocks: Checkered walnut with thumbrest, right or left.
Sights: Undercut ramp front; frame mounted rear, click adj.
Features: Adjustable trigger pull; over-travel trigger adjustment; double acting safety; rebounding firing pin; military style grip; stippled front- and backstraps; positive magazine latch.
Price: 5½" barrel **$184.00**
Price: 7¼" barrel **$194.00**

HI-STANDARD SUPERMATIC TROPHY MILITARY
Caliber: 22 LR, 10-shot magazine.
Barrel: 5½" heavy, 7¼" fluted.
Length: 9¾" (5½" bbl.). **Weight:** 44½ oz.
Stocks: Checkered walnut with thumbrest, right or left.
Features: Grip duplicates feel of military 45; positive action mag. latch; front- and backstraps stippled. Trigger adj. for pull, over-travel.
Sights: Undercut ramp front; frame mounted rear, click adj.
Price: 5½" barrel **$189.00**
Price: 7¼" barrel **$199.00**

HI-STANDARD VICTOR
Caliber: 22 LR, 10-shot magazine.
Barrel: 4½", 5½".
Length: 8¾" (4½" bbl.). **Weight:** 43½ oz. (4½" bbl., vent. rib), 46 oz. (5½" bbl., vent. rib).
Stocks: Checkered walnut.
Sights: Undercut ramp front, rib mounted click adj. rear.
Features: Vent. rib, interchangeable barrel, 2 - 2¼ lb. trigger pull, blue finish, back and front straps stippled.
Price: Either bbl. length **$223.00**

RUGER Mark 1 TARGET MODEL AUTO PISTOL
Caliber: 22 LR only, 9-shot magazine.
Barrel: 6⅞" or 5½" bull barrel (6-groove, 14" twist).
Length: 10⅞" (6⅞" bbl.). **Weight:** 42 oz. with 6⅞" bbl.
Stocks: Checkered hard rubber.
Features: Rear sight mounted on receiver, does not move with slide; wide, grooved trigger.
Sights: ⅛" blade front, micro click rear, adjustable for w. and e. Sight radius 9⅜" (with 6⅞" bbl.).
Price: Blued, either barrel length **$112.50**

HANDGUNS—TARGET AUTOLOADERS

WALTHER GSP MATCH PISTOL
Caliber: 22 LR, 32 S&W wadcutter (GSP-C), 5-shot.
Barrel: 5¾".
Weight: 44.8 oz. (22 LR), 49.4 oz. (32). **Length:** 11.8" over-all.
Stock: Walnut, special hand-fitting design.
Sights: Fixed front, rear adj. for w. & e.
Features: Available with either 2.2 lb. (1000 gm) or 3 lb. (1360 gm) trigger. Spare mag., bbl. weight, tools supplied in Match Pistol Kit. Imported from Germany by Interarms.
Price: GSP **$620.00**
Price: GSP-C **$775.00**
Price: 22 LR conversion unit for GSP-C **$430.00**
Price: 22 Short conversion unit for GSP-C **$450.00**

WALTHER OSP RAPID-FIRE PISTOL
Similar to Model GSP except 22 Short only, stock has adj. free-style hand rest.
Price: **$620.00**

HANDGUNS—TARGET REVOLVERS

COLT PYTHON REVOLVER
Caliber: 357 Magnum (handles all 38 Spec.), 6 shot.
Barrel: 2½", 4" or 6", with ventilated rib.
Length: 9¼"(4" bbl.). **Weight:** 38 oz. (4" bbl.).
Stocks: Checkered walnut, target type.
Sights: ⅛" ramp front, adj. notch rear.
Features: Ventilated rib; grooved, crisp trigger; swing-out cylinder; target hammer.
Price: Colt Blue .... **$382.50** Nickeled **$397.95**

SMITH & WESSON MASTERPIECE TARGET MODELS
Model: K-22 (M17).	K-22 (M48).
Caliber: 22 LR, 6 shot.	22 RF Magnum, 6 shot.
Barrel: 6", 8⅜".	4", 6" or 8⅜"
Length: 11⅛" (6" bbl.).	11⅛" (6" bbl.).
Weight: 38½ oz. (6" bbl.).	39 oz.(6" bbl.).
Model: K-32 (M16). (Illus.)	K-38 (M14).
Caliber: 32 S&W Long, 6 shot.	38 S&W Special, 6 shot.
Barrel: 6".	6", 8⅜".
Length: 11⅛".	11⅛". (6" bbl.)
Weight: 38½ oz. (loaded).	38½ oz. (6", loaded).

Features: All Masterpiece models have: checkered walnut, Magna stocks; grooved tang and trigger; ⅛" Patridge front sight, micro. adj. rear sights. Swing out cylinder revolver. For 8⅜" barrel add **$9.00**.
Price: Blued, all calibers M-17, 6" bbl. **$180.00**
Price: Blued, all calibers M-48, 4", 6" bbl. **$193.50**

SMITH & WESSON 1955 Model 25, 45 TARGET
Caliber: 45 ACP and 45 AR, 6 shot.
Barrel: 6½" (heavy target type).
Length: 11⅞". **Weight:** 45 oz.
Stocks: Checkered walnut target.
Sights: ⅛" Patridge front, micro click rear, adjustable for w. and e.
Features: Tangs and trigger grooved; target trigger and hammer standard, checkered target hammer. Swing-out cylinder revolver. Price includes presentation case.
Price: Blued **$313.50**

SMITH & WESSON COMBAT MASTERPIECE
Caliber: 38 Special (M15) or 22 LR (M18), 6 shot.
Barrel: 2" (M15) 4" (M18)
Length: 9⅛" (4" bbl.). **Weight:** Loaded, 22 36½ oz, 38 30 oz.
Stocks: Checkered walnut, Magna. Grooved tangs and trigger.
Sights: Front, ⅛" Baugham Quick Draw on ramp, micro click rear, adjustable for w. and e.
Price: Blued, M-15 .... **$144.50**
Price: Nickel M-15 .... **$155.50**
Price: Blued, M-18 .... **$172.50**

Smith & Wesson Accessories
Target hammers with low, broad, deeply-checkered spur, and wide-swaged, grooved target trigger. For all frame sizes, **$7.42** (target hammers not available for small frames). Target stocks: for large-frame guns, **$14.25** to **$16.00**; for med.-frame guns, **$12.00** to **$14.50**; for small-frame guns, **$10.75** to **$14.00**. These prices applicable only when specified on original order.
As separately-ordered parts: target hammers (**$15.75**) and triggers, **$13.55**; stocks, **$15.13-$26.40**.

Consult our Directory pages for the location of firms mentioned.

HANDGUNS—TARGET REVOLVERS

TAURUS MODEL 86 TARGET MASTER REVOLVER
Caliber: 38 Spec., 6-shot.
Barrel: 6" only.
Weight: 41 oz. **Length:** 11¼" over-all.
Stocks: Over size target-type, checkered Brazilian walnut.
Sights: Patridge front, micro. click rear adj. for w. and e.
Features: Blue finish with non-reflective finish on barrel. Imported from Brazil by International Distributors.
Price: **$110.00**
Price: Model 96 Scout Master, same except in 22 cal **$110.00**

HANDGUNS—AUTOLOADERS, SERVICE & SPORT

A.J. ORDNANCE "THOMAS" 45 D.A. AUTO
Caliber: 45 ACP, 6-shot magazine
Barrel: 3½".
Weight: 32 oz. (unloaded) **Length:** 6½" over-all.
Stocks: Checkered high impact plastic.
Sights: Fixed blade front; drift-adj. rear for w.
Features: Double action every shot, delayed blowback operation. Fixed stainless steel barrel, magazine disconnector safety. Matte finished top sighting surfaces.
Price: Blue **$375.00**
Price: Chrome **$425.00**

AMT 45 ACP HARDBALLER
Caliber: 45 ACP.
Barrel: 5".
Weight: 39 oz. **Length:** 8½" over-all.
Stocks: Checkered walnut.
Sights: Adjustable combat-type.
Features: Extended combat safety, serrated matte slide rib, loaded chamber indicator, long grip safety, beveled magazine well, grooved front and back straps, adjustable target trigger, custom-fitted barrel bushing. All stainless steel. From AMT.
Price: **$450.00**

AMT COMBAT GOVERNMENT
Caliber: 45 ACP.
Barrel: 5".
Weight: 38 oz. **Length:** 8½" over-all.
Stocks: Checkered walnut, diamond pattern.
Sights: Combat-style, fixed.
Features: All stainless steel; extended combat safety, loaded chamber indicator, beveled magazine well, adjustable target-type trigger, custom-fitted barrel bushing, flat mainspring housing. From AMT.
Price: **$395.00**

ASTRA CONSTABLE AUTO PISTOL
Caliber: 22 LR, 10-shot; 32 ACP, 8-shot; and 380 ACP, 7-shot.
Barrel: 3½".
Weight: 26 oz.
Stocks: Moulded plastic.
Sights: Adj. rear.
Features: Double action, quick no-tool takedown, non-glare rib on slide. 380 available in blue or chrome finish. Imported from Spain by Interarms.
Price: Blue **$198.00**
Price: Chrome **$208.00**

BAUER AUTOMATIC PISTOL
Caliber: 25 ACP, 6-shot, 22 LR, 5-shot.
Barrel: 2⅛″ (25 ACP), 2¼″ (22 LR).
Weight: 10 oz. **Length:** 4″ (25 ACP), 4⅛″ (22 LR).
Stocks: Plastic pearl or checkered walnut.
Sights: Recessed, fixed.
Features: Stainless steel construction, positive manual safety, magazine safety.
Price: Satin stainless steel, 25ACP $99.95
Price: Satin stainless steel, 22LR $99.95

BERETTA MODEL 70 PISTOL
Caliber: 22 LR, 32ACP, 380 ACP.
Barrel: 3.5″.
Weight: 23 ozs. (Steel) **Length:** 6.5″ over-all.
Stocks: Checkered black plastic.
Sights: Fixed front and rear.
Features: Steel frame in 32 and 380, light alloy in 22 (wgt. 18 ozs.). Safety lever blocks hammer. Side lever indicates empty magazine. Magazine capacity is 8 rounds (22 and 32), 7 rounds in 380. Introduced 1977. Imported by Beretta Arms Co.
Price: $169.00

BERETTA MODEL 81/84 DA PISTOLS
Caliber: 32 ACP (12-shot magazine), 380 ACP (13-shot magazine)
Barrel: 3¾″.
Weight: About 23 oz. **Length:** 6½″ over-all.
Stocks: Smooth black plastic (wood optional at extra cost).
Sights: Fixed front and rear.
Features: Double action, quick take-down, convenient magazine release. Introduced 1977. Imported by Beretta Arms. Co.
Price: M-81 (32 ACP) $245.00
Price: M-84 (380 ACP) $245.00

BERETTA MODEL 92 DA PISTOL
Caliber: 9mm Parabellum (15-shot magazine).
Barrel: 4.92″.
Weight: 33½ ozs. **Length:** 8.54″ over-all.
Stocks: Smooth black plastic.
Sights: Blade front, rear adj. for w.
Features: Double-action. Extractor acts as chamber loaded indicator, inertia firing pin. Finished in blue-black. Introduced 1977. Imported by Beretta Arms Co.
Price: $365.00

BERNARDELLI MODEL 60 AUTO PISTOL
Caliber: 22 LR, 10-shot; 32 ACP, 8-shot; and 380, 7-shot.
Barrel: 3½″.
Weight: 26 oz. **Length:** 6⅓″.
Stocks: Checkered plastic.
Sights: Post front, click adj. rear.
Features: Manual and magazine safeties. Optional thumb rest grips, $10.00. Imported from Italy by Liberty.
Price: $90.00

BERNARDELLI MODEL 80 AUTO PISTOL
Caliber: 22 LR (10-shot); 32 ACP (8-shot); 380 ACP (7-shot).
Barrel: 3½″.
Weight: 26½ oz. **Length:** 6½″ over-all.
Stocks: Checkered plastic with thumbrest.
Sights: Ramp front, white outline rear adj. for w. & e.
Features: Hammer block slide safety; loaded chamber indicator; dual recoil buffer springs; serrated trigger; inertia type firing pin. Imported from Italy by Interarms.
Price: Model 80 .... $139.00
Price: Model 90 (as above except 6″ bbl.) $154.00

Bernardelli Model 100 Target Pistol
Similar to Model 80 except has 5.9″ barrel and barrel weight; heavy sighting rib; checkered walnut thumbrest grips; 22 LR only (10-shot). Comes with case, cleaning equipment and tools. $269.00

BROWNING BDA AUTO PISTOL
Caliber: 45 ACP only (7-shot).
Barrel: 4$^{13}/_{32}$".
Weight: 29 ozs. (9mm) **Length:** 7$^{25}/_{32}$." over-all.
Stocks: Checkered black plastic
Sights: Blade front, drift adj. rear of w.
Features: Double action. De-cocking lever permits lowering hammer onto locked firing pin. Squared combat-type trigger guard. Slide stays open after last shot. Introduced 1977. Imported by Browning.
Price: 45 ACP **$349.95**

BROWNING BDA-380 D/A AUTO PISTOL
Caliber: 380 ACP, 12-shot magazine.
Barrel: 3$^{13}/_{16}$".
Weight: 23 ozs. **Length:** 6¾" over-all.
Stocks: Smooth walnut with inset Browning medallion.
Sights: Blade front, rear drift-adj. for w.
Features: Combination safety and de-cocking lever will automatically lower a cocked hammer to half-cock and can be operated by right or left-hand shooters. Inertia firing pin. Magazine safety. Introduced 1978.
Price: **$219.95**

Browning Renaissance Hi-Power 9mm Auto
Same as Browning Hi-Power 9mm Auto except: fully engraved, chrome plated, Narcolac pearl grips, with deluxe black vinyl case.
Price: With adj. sights **$975.00**
Price: With fixed sights **$955.00**

BROWNING HI-POWER 9mm AUTOMATIC PISTOL
Caliber: 9mm Parabellum (Luger), 13-shot magazine.
Barrel: 4$^{21}/_{32}$ inches.
Length: 7¾" over-all. **Weight:** 32 oz.
Stocks: Walnut, hand checkered.
Sights: ⅛" blade front; rear screw-adj. for w. and e. Also available with fixed rear (drift-adj. for w.).
Features: External hammer with half-cock safety, thumb and magazine safeties. A blow on the hammer cannot discharge a cartridge; cannot be fired with magazine removed. Fixed rear sight model available.
Price: Fixed sight model **$319.95**
Price: 9mm with rear sight adj. for w. and e. **$349.95**

Browning Centennial Hi-Power
Same as standard Hi-Power except has oil finished walnut stocks, hand checkered 26 l.p.i., with Browning medallion inset in both sides. All exposed metal surfaces, as well as the magazine are polished and deep chromed to a mirror finish. Centennial inscription with date hand engraved on slide. Gold plated trigger. Comes with fitted polished walnut case with red jeweler's velvet lining. Production limited to 3500 pistols, serial numbered 1878D-0001 through 1878D-3500.
Price: With fixed sights only **$495.00**

BROWNING CHALLENGER II AUTO PISTOL
Caliber: 22 LR, 10-shot magazine.
Barrel: 6¾".
Weight: 38 oz. **Length:** 10⅞" over-all.
Stocks: Smooth impregnated hardwood.
Sights: ⅛" blade front on ramp, rear screw adj. for e., drift adj. for w.
Features: All steel, blue finish. Wedge locking system prevents action from loosening. Wide gold-plated trigger; action hold-open. Standard grade only. From Browning.
Price: **$159.95**

COLT SERVICE MODEL ACE
Caliber: 22 LR, 10-shot magazine.
Barrel: 5".
Weight: 42 ozs. **Length:** 8⅜" over-all.
Stocks: Checkered walnut.
Sights: Blade front, fully adjustable rear.
Features: The 22-cal. version of the Government Model auto. Based on the Service Model Ace last produced in 1945. Patented floating chamber. Original Ace Markings rolled on left side of slide. Introduced 1978.
Price: Blue only **$263.95**

COLT COMMANDER AUTO PISTOL
Caliber: 45 ACP, 7 shot; 38 Super Auto, 9 shot; 9mm Luger, 9 shot.
Barrel: 4¼".
Length: 8". **Weight:** 36 oz.
Stocks: Sandblasted walnut.
Sights: Fixed, glare-proofed blade front, square notch rear.
Features: Grooved trigger and hammer spur; arched housing; grip and thumb
safeties.
Price: Blued $253.95

Colt Lightweight Combat Commander
Same as Commander except high strength aluminum alloy frame, wood
panel grips, weight 27 oz. 45 ACP only.
Price: Blue $246.50

Colt Conversion Unit
Permits the 45 and 38 Super Automatic pistols to use the economical 22 LR
cartridge. No tools needed. Adjustable rear sight; 10-shot magazine. Designed to give recoil effect of the larger calibers. Not adaptable to Commander models. Blue finish $140.50

COLT GOV'T MODEL MK IV/SERIES 70
Caliber: 9mm, 38 Super, 45 ACP, 7-shot.
Barrel: 5".
Weight: 40 oz. **Length:** 8⅜" over-all.
Stocks: Sandblasted walnut panels.
Sights: Ramp front, fixed square notch rear.
Features: Grip and thumb safeties, grooved trigger. Accurizor barrel and
bushing. Blue finish or nickel in 45 only.
Price: Blue $253.95
Price: Nickel $268.95

DETONICS 45 PISTOL
Caliber: 45 ACP, 6-shot clip.
Barrel: 3¼" (2½" of which is rifled).
Weight: 29 ozs. (empty). **Length:** 6¾" over-all, 4½" high.
Stocks: Checkered walnut.
Sights: Combat type, fixed
Features: Has a self-adjusting cone barrel centering system, beveled maga-
zine inlet, "full clip" indicator in base of magazine; standard 7-shot (or more)
clip can be used. Throated barrel and polished feed ramp. Introduced 1977.
From Detonics.
Price: $395.00

ERMA KGP22 AUTO PISTOL
Caliber: 22 LR, 8-shot magazine.
Barrel: 4".
Weight: 29 ozs. **Length:** 7¾" over-all.
Stocks: Checkered plastic.
Sights: Fixed.
Features: Has toggle action similar to original "Luger" pistol. Slide stays open
after last shot. Imported from West Germany by Excam. Introduced 1978.
Price: $165.00

ERMA KGP32, KGP38 AUTO PISTOLS
Caliber: 32 ACP (6-shot), 380 ACP (5-shot).
Barrel: 4".
Weight: 22½ ozs. **Length:** 7⅜" over-all.
Stocks: Checkered plastic. Wood optional.
Sights: Fixed.
Features: Toggle action similar to original "Luger" pistol. Slide stays open
after last shot. Has magazine and sear disconnect safety systems. Imported
from West Germany by Excam. Introduced 1978.
Price: Plastic grips $173.00

IVER JOHNSON MODEL X300 PONY
Caliber: 380 ACP, 6-shot magazine.
Barrel: 3".
Weight: 20 oz. **Length:** 6" over-all.
Stocks: Checkered walnut.
Sights: Blade front, rear adj. for w.
Features: Loaded chamber indicator, all steel construction. Inertia firing pin.
Thumb safety locks hammer. No magazine safety. Lanyard ring. From Iver
Johnson's.
Price: Blue $155.25
Price: Chrome $167.95
Price: Military (matte finish) $155.25

F.I.E. TITAN E32, E380 AUTOS
Caliber: 32 ACP, 380 ACP, 6-shot magazine.
Barrel: 3⅞".
Weight: 25¾ ozs. **Length:** 4" over-all.
Stocks: Checkered plastic, thumbrest-type. Walnut optional for $12.95.
Sights: Fixed.
Features: Magazine disconnector, firing pin block. Both calibers available in blue, chrome or engraved blue/chrome. Introduced 1978. From F.I.E.
Price: 32, blue $75.95
Price: 32, chrome $79.95
Price: 32, blue, engraved $90.95
Price: 32, engraved, chrome $95.95
Price: 380, blue $88.95
Price: 380, chrome $93.95
Price: 380, engraved, blue $105.95
Price: 380, engraved, chrome $109.95

F.I.E. E27 TITAN PISTOL
Caliber: 25 ACP, 6-shot magazine.
Barrel: 2⁷⁄₁₆".
Length: 4⅝" over-all. **Weight:** 12 oz.
Stocks: Checkered plastic.
Sights: Fixed.
Features: External hammer; fast simple takedown. Made in U.S.A. by F.I.E. Corp.
Price: Blued .... $39.95   Chromed: $46.95

F.I.E. G27 GUARDIAN PISTOL
Caliber: 25 ACP, 6-shot magazine.
Barrel: 2¼".
Weight: 13 oz. **Length:** 4¾" over all.
Stocks: Contoured plastic.
Sights: Fixed.
Features: Available in blue, gold or chrome finish. Made in U.S.A. by F.I.E.
Price: Blue .... $36.95   Chrome: $41.95
Price: Gold $46.95

F.I.E. "THE BEST" AUTO PISTOL
Caliber: 25 ACP, 6-shot magazine.
Barrel: 2½".
Weight: 13 ozs. **Length:** 4⅜" over-all.
Stocks: Checkered walnut.
Sights: Fixed.
Features: All steel construction. Has thumb and magazine safeties, exposed hammer. Blue finish only. Introduced 1978. From F.I.E.
Price: $88.95

FTL 22 AUTO NINE PISTOL
Caliber: 22 LR, 8-shot magazine.
Barrel: 2¼", 6-groove rifling.
Weight: 8¼ oz. **Length:** 4⅜" over-all.
Stocks: Checkered plastic.
Sights: U-notch in slide.
Features: Alloy frame, rest is ordnance steel. Has barrel support sleeve bushing for better accuracy. Finish is matte hard chrome. Introduced 1978. From FTL Marketing.
Price: $139.95

HAWES/SIG-SAUER D.A AUTO PISTOL
Caliber: 9mm, 38 Super or 45 ACP, (9-shot in 9mm, 7 in 45).
Barrel: 4⅜".
Weight: 28¼ oz. (9mm). **Length:** 7¾" over-all.
Stocks: Checkered walnut.
Sights: Blade front, drift adj. rear for w.
Features: Double action. De-cocking lever permits lowering hammer onto locked firing pin. Squared combat-type trigger guard. Slide stays open after last shot. Imported by Hawes Firearms.
Price: $349.95

HAWES/SIG-SAUER P-230 D.A. PISTOL
Caliber: 32 ACP (8-shot), 380 ACP, 9mm Police (7 shot).
Barrel: 3¾".
Weight: 16¼ oz. (32), 16 oz. (380), 18¾ oz. (9mm Police) **Length:** 6½" over-all.
Stocks: One piece black plastic.
Sights: Blade front, rear adj. for w.
Features: Double action. Same basic design as P-220. (9mm, 38 Super, 45 ACP). Blowback operation, stationary barrel. Introduced 1977. Imported by Hawes.
Price: 32 or 380 .... $299.95
Price: 9mm Police $349.95

HK P9S DOUBLE ACTION AUTO PISTOL

Caliber: 9mm Para., 9-shot magazine.
Barrel: 4".
Weight: 33½ oz. **Length:** 5½" over-all.
Stocks: Checkered black plastic.
Sights: Open combat type.
Features: Double action; polygonal rifling; sliding roller lock action with stationary barrel. Loaded chamber and cocking indicators; un-cocking lever relaxes springs. Imported from Germany by Heckler & Koch, Inc.
Price: P-9S $340.00
Price: P-9/P-9S Target Model (5½" bbl., target sights bbl. weight) $454.05
Price: P-9/P-9S Competition Model (similar to Target except comes with wrap around match grips, bbl. weight, 4" & 5½" bbl. $599.00

HECKLER & KOCH P9S DOUBLE ACTION 45

Caliber: 45 ACP, 7-shot magazine.
Barrel: 4¹⁄₃₂".
Weight: 32½ oz. **Length:** 7½" over-all.
Stocks: Checkered black plastic.
Sights: Open, combat type.
Features: Double action; polygonal rifling; delayed roller-locked bolt system. Imported by Heckler & Koch, Inc.
Price: $365.00
Price: With adj. trigger, trigger stop, adj. rear sight $425.00
Price: 8" hunting barrel $80.50

HECKLER & KOCH HK-4 DOUBLE ACTION PISTOL

Caliber: 22 LR, 25 ACP, 32 ACP, 380 ACP, 8-shot magazine (7 in 380).
Barrel: 3¹¹⁄₃₂".
Weight: 16½ oz. **Length:** 6⁹⁄₁₆" over-all.
Stocks: Black checkered plastic.
Sights: Fixed blade front, rear notched drift-adj. for w.
Features: Gun comes with all parts to shoot above four calibers; polygonal (hexagon) rifling; matte black finish. Imported by Heckler & Koch, Inc.
Price: HK-4 380 with 22 conversion kit $260.00
Price: HK-4 in 380 only $230.00
Price: HK-4 in four cals. $310.00
Price: Conversion units 22, 25 or 32 cal., each $60.00

HIGH STANDARD SPORT-KING AUTO PISTOL

Caliber: 22 LR, 10-shot.
Barrel: 4½" or 6¾".
Weight: 39 oz. (4½" bbl.). **Length:** 9" over-all (4½" bbl.).
Stocks: Checkered walnut.
Sights: Blade front, fixed rear.
Features: Takedown barrel. Blue only. Military frame.
Price: Either bbl. length, blue finish $134.75

HI-STANDARD SHARPSHOOTER AUTO PISTOL

Caliber: 22 LR, 10-shot magazine.
Barrel: 5½".
Length: 9" over-all. **Weight:** 45 oz.
Stocks: Checkered walnut.
Sights: Fixed, ramp front, square notch rear adj. for w. & e.
Features: Military frame. Wide, scored trigger; new hammer-sear design. Slide lock, push-button take down.
Price: Blued $143.50

L.E.S P-18 AUTO PISTOL

Caliber: 9mm Parabellum, 18-shot magazine.
Barrel: 5½", stationary; polygonal rifling.
Weight: About 36 oz.
Stocks: Checkered resin.
Sights: Post front, V-notch rear drift adj. for w.
Features: Gas-assisted action; all stainless steel; inertia firing pin. Made in U.S.A. Both single and double action models offered, in two finish grades. From L.E.S.
Price: Std. D.A. (matte finish) $289.95
Price: Deluxe D.A. (polished) $364.95
Price: Std. S.A. (matte finish) $269.95
Price: Deluxe S.A. (polished) $344.95

HECKLER & KOCH VP '7OZ DOUBLE ACTION AUTO

Caliber: 9mm Para., 18-shot magazine
Barrel: 4½".
Weight: 32½ oz. **Length:** 8" over-all.
Stocks: Black stippled plastic.
Sights: Ramp front, channeled slide rear.
Features: Recoil operated, double action. Only 4 moving parts. Double column magazine. Imported by Heckler & Koch, Inc.
Price: $248.00

> Consult our Directory pages for the location of firms mentioned.

LLAMA XI AUTO PISTOL

Caliber: 9mm Para.
Barrel: 5".
Weight: 38 oz. **Length:** 8½".
Stocks: Moulded plastic.
Sights: Fixed front, adj. rear.
Features: Also available with engraved, chrome engraved or gold damascened finish at extra cost. Imported from Spain by Stoeger Industries.
Price: $239.95

LLAMA MODELS XV, XA, IIIA AUTO PISTOLS
Caliber: 22 LR, 32 ACP and 380.
Barrel: 3¹¹/₁₆″.
Weight: 23 oz. **Length:** 6½″.
Stocks: Checkered plastic, thumb rest.
Sights: Fixed front, adj. notch rear.
Features: Ventilated rib, manual and grip safeties. Model XV is 22 LR, Model XA is 32 ACP, and Model IIIA is 380. Models XA and IIIA have loaded indicator; IIIA is locked breech. Imported from Spain by Stoeger Industries.
Price: **$158.95**

LLAMA MODELS VIII, IXA AUTO PISTOLS
Caliber: Super 38 (M. VIII), 45 ACP (M. IXA).
Barrel: 5″.
Weight: 30 oz. **Length:** 8½″.
Stocks: Checkered walnut.
Sights: Fixed.
Features: Grip and manual safeties, ventilated rib. Engraved, chrome engraved or gold damascened finish available at extra cost. Imported from Spain by Stoeger Industries.
Price: **$239.95**

MKE MODEL TPK AUTO PISTOL
Caliber: 32 ACP, 8-shot; 380, 7-shot.
Barrel: 4″.
Weight: 23 oz. **Length:** 6½″.
Stocks: Checkered black plastic.
Sights: Fixed front, adj. notch rear.
Features: Double action with exposed hammer; safety blocks firing pin and drops hammer. Chamber loaded indicator pin. Imported from Turkey by Firearms Center.
Price: **$259.95**

MAUSER HSc "ONE OF FIVE THOUSAND" PISTOL
Caliber: 32 ACP, 380 ACP, 7-shot.
Barrel: 3¾″.
Weight: 23 oz. **Length:** 6.05″.
Stocks: Checkered walnut.
Sights: Fixed.
Features: Double action, manual and magazine safeties. Matted non-glare sight channel. Inertia firing pin. Comes in fitted case with extra magazine, bore brush, test target. Final HSc production. Imported from Germany by Interarms.
Price: Bright blue only **$260.00**

MAUSER PARABELLUM SWISS MODEL PISTOL
Caliber: 30 Luger, 9mm Para., 8-shot.
Barrel: 4″ (9mm), 6″ (30 Luger).
Weight: 32 oz. **Length:** 8.66″ (4″ bbl.).
Stocks: Checkered walnut.
Sights: Fixed.
Features: Manual and grip safeties, American eagle over chamber and Mauser banner on toggle. Final production—guns offered until supply exhausted. Imported from Germany by Interarms.
Price: **$460.00**

PLAINFIELD MODEL 71
Caliber: 22 LR (10-shot) and 25 ACP (8-shot).
Barrel: 1″.
Length: 5⅛″ over-all. **Weight:** 25 oz.
Stocks: Checkered walnut.
Sights: Fixed.
Features: Easily converts from 22 cal. to 25 cal. by changing bolt, bbl. and magazine. Stainless steel frame and slide.
Price: With conversion kit. . **$99.95** M71 in 22 cal. only **$79.95**
Price: M71 in 25 cal. only **$79.95**

Plainfield Model 72
Same as Model 71 except: has 3½″ bbl. and aluminum slide.
Price: Model 72 & conversion kit **$99.95**
Price: 22 cal. only **$79.95**
Price: 25 cal. only **$79.95**

RG 26 AUTO PISTOL
Caliber: 25 ACP, 6-shot magazine.
Barrel: 2½".
Weight: 12 ozs. **Length:** 4¾" over-all.
Stocks: Checkered plastic.
Sights: Fixed.
Features: Blue finish. Thumb safety. Imported by RG Industries.
Price: $43.50

RAVEN AUTO PISTOL
Caliber: 25 ACP.
Barrel: 3".
Weight: 12 oz.
Stocks: Smooth walnut or Pearl-O-Lite.
Sights: Ramped front, fixed rear.
Features: Available in blue, nickel or satin nickel finish. From EMF Co.
Price: $49.95

RUGER STANDARD MODEL AUTO PISTOL
Caliber: 22 LR, 9-shot magazine.
Barrel: 4¾" or 6".
Length: 8¾" (4¾" bbl.). **Weight:** 36 oz. (4¾" bbl.).
Stocks: Checkered hard rubber.
Sights: Fixed, wide blade front, square notch rear adj. for w.
Price: Blued $87.50

SMITH & WESSON MODEL 59 DOUBLE ACTION
Caliber: 9mm Luger, 14-shot clip.
Barrel: 4".
Length: 7⁷/₁₆" over-all. **Weight:** 27½ oz., without clip.
Stocks: Checkered high impact moulded nylon.
Sights: ⅛" serrated ramp front, square notch rear adj. for w.
Features: Double action automatic. Furnished with two magazines. Blue finish.
Price: Blued $240.00
Price: Nickel $262.50

SMITH & WESSON 9mm MODEL 39 AUTO PISTOL
Caliber: 9mm Luger, 8-shot clip.
Barrel: 4".
Length: 7⁷/₁₆". **Weight:** 26½ oz., without magazine.
Stocks: Checkered walnut.
Sights: ⅛" serrated ramp front, adjustable rear.
Features: Magazine disconnector, positive firing pin lock and hammer-release safety; alloy frame with lanyard loop; locked-breech, short-recoil double action; slide locks open on last shot.
Price: Blued .... $200.50 Nickeled $221.00

STAR MODEL PD AUTO PISTOL
Caliber: 45 ACP, 7-shot magazine.
Barrel: 3.94".
Weight: 25 oz. **Length:** 7" over-all.
Stocks: Checkered walnut.
Sights: Ramp front, fully adjustable rear.
Features: Rear sight milled into slide; thumb safety; grooved non-slip front strap; nylon recoil buffer; inertia firing pin; no grip or magazine safeties. From Interarms.
Price: Blue $239.00

STAR BKM STARLIGHT AUTO PISTOL
Caliber: 9mm Para., 8-shot magazine.
Barrel: 3.9".
Weight: 25 oz.
Stocks: Checkered walnut.
Sights: Fixed.
Features: Blue or chrome finish. Magazine and manual safeties, external hammer. Imported from Spain by Interarms.
Price: Blue **$209.00**
Price: Chrome **$224.00**

STERLING MODEL 450 D.A. AUTO
Caliber: 45 ACP, 8-shot magazine.
Barrel: 4¼".
Weight: 35 ozs. **Length:** 7½" over-all.
Stocks: Checkered walnut.
Sights: Blade front, rear adj. for w. & e.
Features: All steel, reversible safety, inertia firing pin. Introduced 1977.
Price: Blue only **$269.95**

STERLING MODEL 302
Caliber: 22 LR, 6-shot.
Barrel: 2½".
Length: 4½" over-all. **Weight:** 13 oz.
Stocks: Cycolac, black or white.
Sights: Fixed.
Features: All steel construction.
Price: Blue **$79.95**
Price: Satin nickel **$86.95**
Price: Stainless steel **$98.95**

STERLING MODEL 300
Caliber: 25 ACP, 6-shot.
Barrel: 2½".
Length: 4½" over-all. **Weight:** 13 oz.
Stocks: Cycolac, black or white.
Sights: Fixed.
Features: All steel construction.
Price: Blued . . . . **$79.95**   Satin nickel **$86.95**
Price: Stainless steel **$98.95**

STERLING MODEL 400 MK II DOUBLE ACTION
Caliber: 380 ACP, 7-shot.
Barrel: 3¾".
Length: 6½" over-all. **Weight:** 18 oz.
Stocks: Checkered walnut.
Features: All steel construction. Double action.
Price: Blued . . . . **$158.95** Satin nickel **$165.95**
Price: Stainless steel **$204.95**

STOEGER LUGER 22 AUTO PISTOL
Caliber: 22 LR, 12-shot (11 in magazine, 1 in chamber).
Barrel: 4½" or 5½".
Weight: 30 oz.
Stocks: Checkered wood, identical to P-08.
Features: Action remains open after last shot and as magazine is removed. Grip and balance identical to original P-08 Luger.
Price: Either bbl. length **$99.95**
Price: Kit includes extra clip, charger, holster **$109.95**
Price: Adj. sight model **$129.95**

TDE "BACKUP" AUTO PISTOL
Caliber: 380 ACP, 5-shot magazine
Barrel: 2½".
Weight: 17 oz. **Length:** 5" over-all.
Stocks: Smooth wood.
Sights: Fixed, open, recessed.
Features: Concealed hammer, blowback operation; manual and grip safeties. All stainless steel construction. Smallest domestically-produced pistol in 380. From AMT.
Price: About $225.00

TARGA MODELS GT32, GT380 AUTO PISTOLS
Caliber: 32 ACP or 380 ACP, 7-shot magazine
Barrel: 4⅞".
Weight: 26 oz. **Length:** 7⅜" over-all.
Stocks: Checkered nylon with thumb rest. Walnut optional.
Sights: Fixed blade front; rear drift-adj. for w.
Features: Chrome or blue finish; magazine, thumb, and firing pin safeties; external hammer; safety lever take-down. Imported from Italy by Excam, Inc.
Price: 32 cal., blue $88.95
Price: 32 cal., chrome $93.40
Price: 380 cal., blue $104.00
Price: 380 cal., chrome $110.00
Price: 380 cal., chrome, engraved, wooden grips $145.00
Price: 380 cal., blue, engraved, wooden grips $139.00

TARGA MODEL GT27 AUTO PISTOL
Caliber: 25 ACP, 6-shot magazine
Barrel: 2⁷⁄₁₆".
Weight: 12 oz. **Length:** 4⅝" over-all.
Stocks: Checkered nylon.
Sights: Fixed.
Features: Safety lever take-down; external hammer with half-cock. Made in U.S. by Excam, Inc.
Price: Blue $46.25
Price: Chrome $51.00

WALTHER PP AUTO PISTOL
Caliber: 22 LR, 8-shot; 32 ACP, 380 ACP, 7-shot.
Barrel: 3.86".
Weight: 23½ oz. **Length:** 6.7".
Stocks: Checkered plastic.
Sights: Fixed, white markings.
Features: Double action, manual safety blocks firing pin and drops hammer, chamber loaded indicator on 32 and 380, extra finger rest magazine provided. Imported from Germany by Interarms.
Price: (22 LR) $370.00
Price: (32 and 380) $340.00
Price: Engraved models start at $925.00

Walther PPK/S Auto Pistol
Same as PP except bbl. 3.27", length 6.1" o.a.
Price: 22 LR $370.00
Price: 32 or 380 ACP $345.00
Price: Engraved models start at $925.00

WALTHER P-38 AUTO PISTOL
Caliber: 22 LR, 30 Luger or 9mm Luger, 8-shot.
Barrel: 4¹⁵⁄₁₆" (9mm and 30), 5¹⁄₁₆" (22 LR).
Weight: 28 oz. **Length:** 8½".
Stock: Checkered plastic.
Sights: Fixed.
Features: Double action, safety blocks firing pin and drops hammer, chamber loaded indicator. Matte finish standard, polished blue, engraving and/or plating available. Imported from Germany by Interarms.
Price: 22 LR $595.00
Price: 9mm or 30 Luger $545.00
Price: Engraved models start at $1,025.00

Walther P-38K Auto Pistol
Streamlined version of the P-38; 2¾" barrel, 6⅜" over-all, weight 26 ozs. Strengthened slide (no dust cover), recoil bearing cross-bolt. Rear sight adj. for windage, both front and rear sights have white accents. Hammer decocking lever. Non-reflective matte finish. Imported from Germany by Interarms. Introduced 1977.
Price: $555.00

Walther P-38IV Auto Pistol
Same as P-38K except has longer barrel (4½"); over-all length is 8", weight is 29 ozs. Sights are non-adjustable. Introduced 1977. Imported by Interarms.
Price: $555.00

HANDGUNS—AUTOLOADERS, SERVICE & SPORT

WILDEY AUTO PISTOL
Caliber: 9mm Win. Mag. (14 shots), 45 Win. Mag. (8 shots).
Barrel: 2", 6", 7", 8", or 10"; vent. rib.
Weight: About 49 oz. (6" bbl.).
Stocks: Select hardwood, target style optional.
Sights: Adjustable for windage and elevation; red or white inserts optional.
Features: Patented gas operation; selective single or autoloading capability; 5-lug rotary bolt; fixed barrel; stainless steel construction; double-action trigger mechanism. Has positive hammer block and magazine safety. From Wildey Firearms.
Price: 9mm Win. Mag., 5" bbl. $359.65
Price: 45 Win. Mag., 8" bbl. $369.65

WILKINSON "DIANE" AUTO PISTOL
Caliber: 25 ACP, 6-shot magazine.
Barrel: 2⅛".
Weight: 11½ oz. **Length:** 4¼" over-all.
Stock: Checkered styrene.
Sights: Fixed, integral with slide.
Features: Internal hammer; safety locks sear into hammer; separate ejector. Matte blue finish only. From Wilkinson Arms.
Price: $99.95

HANDGUNS—REVOLVERS, SERVICE & SPORT

A.I.G. POLICE MAGNUM, POLICE POCKET MAGNUM
Caliber: 357 Mag., 5 shot.
Barrel: 2", 2½", 4" or 6".
Weight: 18 oz. **Length:** 6⅛" over-all.
Stocks: Walnut, combat style.
Sights: ⅛" ramp front, grooved top strap rear.
Features: All stainless steel, brushed finish. Round butt, inertia firing pin; hammer drop block. From A.I.G. Corp.
Price: Any bbl. $225.00

A.I.G. POLICE POCKET SPECIAL
Caliber: 38 Spec., 5 shot.
Barrel: 2".
Weight: 18 oz. **Length:** 6½" over-all.
Stocks: Walnut Gunfighter style, round butt.
Sights: ⅛" serrated ramp front, fixed rear.
Features: All stainless steel, brushed finish; inertia firing pin, hammer drop block; ejector rod shroud. From A.I.G. Corp.
Price: $199.50

ARMINIUS REVOLVERS
Caliber: 38 Special, 357 Mag., 32 S&W Long (6-shot); 22 Magnum, 22 LR (8-shot).
Barrel: 4" (38 Spec., 357 Mag., 32 S&W, 22 LR); 6" (38 Spec., 22 LR/22 Mag., 357 Mag.); 8⅜" (357 Mag.).
Weight: 35 oz. (6" bbl.). **Length:** 11" (6" bbl. 38).
Stocks: Checkered plastic.
Sights: Ramp front, fixed rear on standard models, w. & e. adj. on target models.
Features: Ventilated rib, solid frame, swing-out cylinder. Interchangeable 22 Mag. cylinder available with 22 cal. versions. Also available in 357 Mag. 3", 4", 6" barrel, adj. sights. Imported from West Germany by F.I.E. Corp.
Price: .... $71.95 to $151.95

ASTRA 357 MAGNUM REVOLVER
Caliber: 357 Magnum, 6-shot.
Barrel: 3", 4", 6", 8½".
Weight: 40 oz. (6" bbl.). **Length:** 11¼" (6" bbl.).
Stocks: Checkered walnut.
Sights: Fixed front, rear adj. for w. and e.
Features: Swing-out cylinder with countersunk chambers, floating firing pin. Target-type hammer and trigger. Imported from Spain by Interarms.
Price: 3", 4", 6" $219.00
Price: 8½" $224.00
Price: 4" chrome $234.00

CHARTER TARGET BULLDOG
Caliber: 357 Mag., 44 Spec., 5-shot.
Barrel: 4″ or 6″.
Weight: 20½ oz. **Length:** 8½″ over-all.
Stocks: Checkered American walnut, square butt.
Sights: Full-length ramp front, fully adj., milled channel, square notch rear.
Features: Blue finish only. Enclosed ejector rod, full length ejection of fired cases.
Price: $156.00

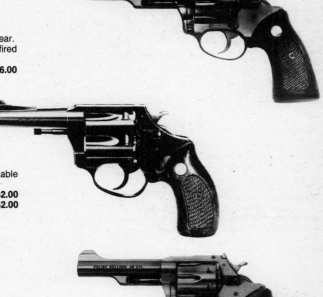

CHARTER ARMS BULLDOG
Caliber: 357 Mag., 44 Special, 5-shot.
Barrel: 3″, 6″.
Weight: 19 oz. **Length:** 7½″ over-all.
Stocks: Hand checkered walnut; Square butt.
Sights: Patridge type 9/64″ front, square notch rear.
Features: Wide trigger and hammer, chrome-moly steel frame, unbreakable firing pin, transfer bar ignition.
Price: 44 Spec., 3″ $142.00
Price: 357 Mag., 6″ $142.00

CHARTER ARMS POLICE BULLDOG
Caliber: 38 Special, 6-shot.
Barrel: 4″.
Weight: 20½ oz. **Length:** 8½″ over-all.
Stocks: Hand checkered American walnut; square butt.
Sights: Full length ramp front; fully adj. combat rear.
Features: Accepts both regular and high velocity ammunition; enclosed ejector rod; full length ejection of fired cases.
Price: Blue only, approx. $149.00

CHARTER ARMS UNDERCOVER REVOLVER
Caliber: 38 Special, 5 shot; 32 S & W Long, 6 shot.
Barrel: 2″, 3″.
Weight: 16 oz. (2″). **Length:** 6¼″ (2″).
Stocks: Smooth walnut or checkered square butt.
Sights: Patridge-type ramp front, notched rear.
Features: Wide trigger and hammer spur. Steel frame.
Price: Polished Blue . . . . . . **$120.00** Nickel $132.00
Price: With checkered square butt grips, blue, 3″ $129.00
Price: 32 S & W Long, blue, 2″ $120.00

Charter Arms Pathfinder
Same as Undercover but in 22 LR caliber, and has 3″ or 6″ bbl. Fitted with adjustable rear sight, ramp front. Weight 18½ oz.
Price: 22 LR, blue, 3″ **$134.00**
Price: 22 LR, square butt, 6″ **$146.00**
Price: 22 Mag., square butt, 3″ **$148.00**
Price: 22 Mag, square butt, 6″ **$151.00**

COLT DETECTIVE SPECIAL
Caliber: 38 Special, 6-shot.
Barrel: 2″.
Length: 6⅝″ over-all. **Weight:** 22 oz.
Stocks: Full, checkered walnut, round butt.
Sights: Fixed, ramp front, square notch rear.
Features: Glare-proofed sights, smooth trigger. Nickel finish, hammer shroud available as options.
Price: Blue $175.50
Price: Nickel $186.95

COLT AGENT REVOLVER
Caliber: 38 Special, 6 shot.
Barrel: 2″ (Twist, 1-16).
Length: 6⅝″ over-all. **Weight:** 16 oz.
Stocks: Checkered walnut, round butt. Grooved trigger.
Sights: Fixed, glare-proofed ramp front, square notch rear.
Price: Blued . . . . **$176.50** With a hammer shroud installed . . **$182.95**

COLT COBRA REVOLVER
Caliber: 38 Special, 6 shot.
Barrel: 2″.
Length: 6⅝″ over-all. **Weight:** 16½ oz.
Stocks: Checkered walnut, round butt. Grooved trigger.
Sights: Fixed, glare-proofed ramp front, square notch rear.
Price: Blued . . . . **$179.50** Nickeled **$197.50**

COLT DIAMONDBACK REVOLVER
Caliber: 22 S, L or LR, or 38 Special, 6 shot.
Barrel: 2½" or 4", or 6" (22-cal. only), with ventilated rib.
Length: 9" (4" bbl.). **Weight:** 24 oz. (2½" bbl.), 28½ oz. (4" bbl.).
Stocks: Checkered walnut, target type, square butt.
Sights: Ramp front, adj. notch rear.
Features: Ventilated rib; grooved, crisp trigger; swing-out cylinder; wide hammer spur.
Price: Blue, 2½" bbl., 38 Spec. $220.50
Price: Blue, 22 LR, 4" bbl. $222.95
Price: Blue, 4" bbl., 38 Spec. $222.95
Price: Nickel finish (38 Spl. only) $226.95
Price: Blue, 22-cal., 6" bbl. $226.95

COLT VIPER REVOLVER
Caliber: 38 Special, 6-shot.
Barrel: 4".
Weight: 20 oz.
Stocks: Checkered walnut, wrap-around.
Sights: Ramp-style front, fixed square notch rear.
Features: Lightweight aluminum alloy frame, smooth trigger, shrouded ejector rod. Uses Colt Cobra frame. Introduced 1977.
Price: Blue $179.50
Price: Nickel $197.50

Colt Police Positive Revolver
Same as Viper except has steel frame. Weight is 26½ oz.; 38 Spec. only. Introduced 1977.
Price: Blue $175.50
Price: Nickel $186.95

COLT LAWMAN MK III REVOLVER
Caliber: 357 Mag., 6 shot.
Barrel: 2" or 4", heavy.
Weight: 33 oz.
Length: 9⅜".
Stocks: Checkered walnut, service style.
Sights: Fixed, glare-proofed ramp front, square notch rear.
Price: Blued $215.95
Price: Nickel $229.95

COLT TROOPER MK III REVOLVER
Caliber: 357 Magnum, 6-shot.
Barrel: 4" 6".
Length: 9½" (4" bbl.). **Weight:** 39 oz. (4" bbl.), 42 oz, (6" bbl.).
Stocks: Checkered walnut, square butt. Grooved trigger.
Sights: Fixed ramp front with ⅛" blade, adj. notch rear.
Price: Blued with target hammer and target stocks $264.95
Price: Nickeled $280.95

F.I.E. MODEL F38 "Titan Tiger" REVOLVER
Caliber: 38 Special.
Barrel: 2" or 4".
Length: 6¼" over-all. (2" bbl.). **Weight:** 27 oz.
Stocks: Checkered plastic, Bulldog style. Walnut optional ($10.95).
Sights: Fixed.
Features: Swing-out cylinder, one stroke ejection. Made in U.S.A.
Price: Blued 2" or 4" ..... **$69.95** Nickel, 2" or 4" bbl. **$82.95**

HARRINGTON & RICHARDSON M622 REVOLVER
Caliber: 22 S, L or LR, 6 shot.
Barrel: 2½", 4", round bbl.
Weight: 20 oz. (2½" bbl.).
Stocks: Checkered black Cycolac.
Sights: Fixed, blade front, square notch rear.
Features: Solid steel, Bantamweight frame; snap-out safety rim cylinder; non-glare finish on frame; coil springs.
Price: Blued, 2½", 4", bbl. $59.50
Price: Model 632 (32 cal.) $64.50

HARRINGTON & RICHARDSON M732 GUARDSMAN
Caliber: 32 S&W or 32 S&W Long, 6 shot.
Barrel: 2½" or 4" round barrel.
Weight: 23½ oz. (2½" bbl.), 26 oz. (4" bbl.).
Stocks: Checkered, black Cycolac.
Sights: Blade front; adjustable rear on 4" model.
Features: Swing-out cylinder with auto. extractor return. Pat. safety rim cylinder. Grooved trigger.
Price: Blued, 2½" bbl. **$77.50** Nickel (Model 733), 2½" bbl. **$82.50**
Price: Blued, 4" bbl. . **$79.50** Nickel, 4" bbl. **$84.50**

H&R MODEL 940 ULTRA "SIDE-KICK" REVOLVER
Caliber: 22 S, L or LR, 9 shot.
Barrel: 6" target weight with ventilated rib.
Weight: 36 oz.
Stocks: Checkered walnut-finished hardwood with thumbrest.
Sights: Ramp front; rear adjustable for w. and e.
Features: Swing-out, safety rim cylinder.
Price: H&R Crown-Lustre Blue $92.50

H&R Model 939 Ultra "Side-Kick" Revolver
Like the Model 940 but with a flat-sided barrel.
Price: H&R Crown-Lustre Blue $96.50

HARRINGTON & RICHARDSON MODEL 666
Caliber: 22 LR/22 Mag., 6-shot.
Barrel: 6".
Weight: 28 oz.
Stocks: Checkered black Cycolac.
Sights: Blade front, fixed rear.
Features: Comes with two cylinders. Double action. H & R Crown Lustre blue finish.
Price: $69.50

Harrington & Richardson Model 649 Revolver
Similar to model 666 except has 5½" barrel, one piece wrap around walnut-finished hardwood grips, western-type blade front sight, adjustable rear. Loads and ejects from side. Weighs 32 oz.
Price: $84.50
Price: Model 650—as above except nickel finish $89.50

HARRINGTON & RICHARDSON M676 REVOLVER
Caliber: 22 LR/22 WMRF, 6-shot.
Barrel: 4½", 5½", 7½" or 12".
Weight: 31 oz. (4½"), 41 oz. (12").
Stocks: One piece smooth walnut-finished hardwood.
Sights: Western type blade front, adj. rear.
Features: Blue barrel and cylinder, "antique" color case-hardened frame, ejector tube and trigger. Comes with extra cylinder.
Price: 4½", 5½", 7½" bbl. $94.50
Price: 12" bbl. $110.00

HARRINGTON & RICHARDSON MODEL 922
Caliber: 22 S, L, LR, 9-shot.
Barrel: 2½", 4", 6".
Weight: 20 oz. (2½").
Stocks: Checkered black Cycolac.
Sights: Blade front, fixed rear.
Features: Double action. Cylinder is removed for ejection and loading. H & R Crown Lustre Blue cylinder and trigger guard.
Price: Blue $64.50

HARRINGTON & RICHARDSON M925 "DEFENDER"
Caliber: 38 S&W 5 shot.
Barrel: 2½".
Length: 7½" over-all. **Weight:** 22 oz.
Stocks: Smooth walnut-finished hardwood, birds-head style, one piece wrap-round.
Sights: Blade front, rear adj. for w.
Features: Top-break double action, push pin extractor.
Price: H&R Crown Lustre Blue $94.50

HARRINGTON & RICHARDSON M926 REVOLVER
Caliber: 22 S, L, or LR, 9-shot, 38 S&W 5-shot.
Barrel: 4". **Weight:** 31 oz.
Stocks: Checkered walnut-finished hardwood.
Sights: Adjustable front and rear.
Features: Top-break, double or single action
Price: Blued $99.50

HARRINGTON & RICHARDSON M929 "SIDE-KICK"
Caliber: 22 S, L or LR, 9 shot.
Barrel: 2½", 4" or 6".
Weight: 26 oz. (4" bbl.).
Stocks: Checkered, black Cycolac.
Sights: Blade front; adjustable rear on 4" and 6" models.
Features: Swing-out cylinder with auto. extractor return. Pat. safety rim cylinder. Grooved trigger. Round-grip frame.
Price: Blued, 2½", 4" or 6" bbl. $77.50
Price: Nickel (Model 930), 4" bbl. $82.50

HARRINGTON & RICHARDSON M949 FORTY-NINER
Caliber: 22 S, L or LR, 9 shot.
Barrel: 5½" round with ejector rod.
Weight: 31 oz.
Stocks: One-piece smooth walnut frontier style wrap-around walnut-finished hardwood.
Sights: estern-type blade front, rear adj. for w.
Features: Contoured loading gate; wide hmmer spur; single and double action. Western type ejector-housing.
Price: H&R Crown-Luster Blue 72.50
Price: Nickel (Model 950) $77.50

H&R SPORTSMAN MODEL 999 REVOLVER
Caliber: 22 S, L or LR, 9 shot.
Barrel: 6″ top-break (16″ twist), integral vent. rib.
Length: 10½″. **Weight:** 30 oz.
Stocks: Checkered walnut-finished hardwood, semi-thumbrest.
Sights: Front adjustable for elevation, rear for windage.
Features: Wide hammer spur; rest for second finger.
Price: Blued **$120.00**

HIGH STANDARD CRUSADER COMMEMORATIVE RE-VOLVER
Caliber: 44 Mag., 45 Long Colt.
Barrel: 4⅛″, 6½″, 8⅜″.
Weight: 48 oz. (4⅛″).
Stocks: Zebrawood, checkered on 45 LC, smooth on 44 Mag.
Sights: Blade front on ramp, fully adj. rear.
Features: Unique gear-segment mechanism. Cylinder release latch serves as a safety. Smooth, light double-action trigger pull. First production devoted to the commemorative; later (1979) guns will be of plain, standard configuration.
Price: .... **Not Available**

HI-STANDARD SENTINEL 9390 AND 9392
Caliber: 22 LR, 22 Mag., 9-shot.
Barrel: 2″ (9390), 4″ (9392).
Weight: 22 oz. (2″). **Length:** 6⅞″ over-all (2″ bbl.).
Stocks: Checkered walnut.
Sights: ⅛″ ramp front, fixed or adj. rear.
Features: Blue finish only. Steel frame. Dual swing-out cylinder.
Price: Fixed sights **$145.25**
Price: Adj. sights **$153.75**

Hi-Standard Camp Gun
Same as Sentinel 9390 except has 6″ barrel, adjustable sights, checkered walnut grips. Blue only.
Price: 22 LR/22 Mag. combo **$142.50**

HIGH STANDARD DOUBLE-NINE CONVERTIBLE
Caliber: 22 S, L or LR, 9-shot (22 WRM with extra cylinder).
Barrel: 5½″, dummy ejector rod fitted.
Length: 11″ over-all. **Weight:** 32 oz.
Stocks: Smooth walnut, frontier style with medallion
Sights: Fixed blade front, notched rear.
Features: Western styling; rebounding hammer with auto safety block; spring-loaded ejection. Swing-out cylinder.
Price: Blued **$152.00**
Price: With adjustable sights **$165.00**

High Standard Long Horn Convertible
Same as the Double-Nine convertible but with a 9½″ bbl., adjustable sights, blued only, Weight: 40 oz.
Price: With adjustable sights **$168.25**

HIGH STANDARD HIGH SIERRA DOUBLE ACTION
Caliber: 22 LR and 22 LR/22 Mag., 9-shot.
Barrel: 7″ octagonal.
Weight: 36 oz. **Length:** 12½″ over-all.
Stocks: Smooth walnut.
Sights: Blade front, adj. rear.
Features: Gold plated backstrap and trigger guard. Swing-out cylinder.
Price: Adj. sights, dual cyl. **$168.25**

IVER JOHNSON MODEL SIDEWINDER REVOLVER
Caliber: 22 S, L, LR, or 22/22 Mag., 8 shot.
Barrel: 4″ or 6″.
Length: 11¼″. **Weight:** 31 oz.
Stocks: Plastic Stag Horn.
Sights: Blade front, fixed or adj. rear.
Features: Wide spur hammer, half-cock safety, scored trigger, Flash Control cylinder, recessed shell head, push rod ejector.
Price: Blued, Model S-524 .... **$66.50**
Price: S-524C (walnut grips) **$69.95**
Price: S-524N (walnut grips, nickel) **$74.95**

IVER JOHNSON D.A. REVOLVER
Caliber: 22 LR, 22 Mag., 32 S&W Long, 38 Spec.
Barrel: 2″, 3″, 4″.
Stocks: Walnut.
Sights: Fixed or adj.
Features: Swing-out cylinder, hammer block safety. Blue or nickel finish. Introduced 1977. From Iver Johnson.
Price: 22, 32, 2″ and 3″, fixed sights **$96.50**
Price: 38 Spec., 2″ and 3″, fixed sights **$99.50**
Price: 22, 32, 38, 4″, fixed sights **$105.50**
Price: 22, 32, 38, 4″ vent. rib, adj. sights **$149.50**
Price: 22, 32, 38, 6″ vent. rib, adj. sights **$154.95**

> Consult our Directory pages for the location of firms mentioned.

Iver Johnson Cadet Revolver
Model C-222, similar to Double Action Revolver; fixed sights, with 2½″ barrel only, rounded tenite grips; weight 24 oz. In 22, 22 Mag., 32 or 38 S&W calibers.
Price: **$58.50**

KASSNAR/SQUIRES BINGHAM M-100D REVOLVER
Caliber: 22 LR/22 Mag.; 38 Spec.
Barrel: 3″, 4″ or 6″.
Weight: 44 to 48 oz.
Stocks: Checkered hardwood, target style.
Sights: Ramp front, open rear adj. for e.
Features: Double action; vent rib barrel. Imported by Kassnar.
Price: **$149.95**

KORTH REVOLVER
Caliber: 22 LR/22 Mag., 22 LR (only), 357 Mag.
Barrel: 3″, 6″ (357 only), 6″ (Target), vent. rib.
Weight: 40 oz.
Stocks: Checkered walnut, oil finish.
Sights: Blade front, micro. rear adj. for w. and e.
Features: Adjustable trigger. Cylinder automatically ejects cartridges when opened. Shrouded ejector rod. Imported from West Germany by Eastern Sports Int.
Price: 22 LR, 6″ **$1,125.00**
Price: 22 combo, 6″ **$1,325.00**
Price: 357 Mag., 3″ or 6″ **$1,190.00**

LLAMA COMANCHE REVOLVERS
Caliber: 22 LR, 38 Special.
Barrel: 6″, 4″ (except 22 LR, 6″ only).
Weight: 22 LR 24 oz., 38 Special 31 oz. **Length:** 9¼″ (4″ bbl.).
Stocks: Checkered walnut.
Sights: Fixed blade front, rear adj. for w. & e.
Features: Ventilated rib, wide spur hammer. Chrome plating, engraved finishes available. Imported from Spain by Stoeger Industries.
Price: 22 LR **$184.95**
Price: Comanche 357 Mag. **$199.95**

RG 14 REVOLVER
Caliber: 22 LR, 6-shot.
Barrel: 1¾" or 3".
Weight: 15 ozs. (1¾" bbl.) **Length:** 5½" over-all.
Stocks: Checkered plastic.
Sights: Fixed.
Features: Blue finish. Cylinder swings out when pin is removed. Imported by RG Industries.
Price: **$31.45**
Price: Model 23 (central ejector) **$40.25**

RG 31 REVOLVER
Caliber: 32 S & W (6-shot), 38 Spec. (5-shot).
Barrel: 2".
Weight: 24 ozs. **Length:** 6¾" over-all.
Stocks: Checkered plastic.
Sights: Fixed.
Features: Cylinder swings out when pin is removed. Blue finish. Imported by RG Industries.
Price: 32 cal. **$53.80**
Price: 38 cal. **$55.90**

RG 40 REVOLVER
Caliber: 38 Spec., 6-shot.
Barrel: 2".
Weight: 29 ozs. **Length:** 7¼" over-all.
Stocks: Checkered plastic.
Sights: Fixed.
Features: Swing-out cylinder with spring ejector. Imported by RG Industries.
Price: **$70.80**

RG 38S REVOLVER
Caliber: 38 Special, 6-shot.
Barrel: 3" and 4".
Weight: 3", 31 oz.; 4", 34 oz. **Length:** 3", 8½"; 4", 9¼".
Stocks: Checkered plastic.
Sights: Fixed front, rear adj. for w.
Features: Swing out cylinder with spring ejector. Imported from Germany by RG Industries.
Price: Blue **$71.45**

RG MODEL 88 REVOLVER
Caliber: 38 Spec., 357 Mag.
Barrel: 4".
Weight: 33 oz. **Length:** 9" over-all.
Stocks: Checkered walnut.
Sights: Fixed.
Features: Swing out cylinder, spring ejector. Wide spur hammer and trigger. Imported by RG Industries.
Price: **$170.80**

RUGER SECURITY-SIX Model 117
Caliber: 357 Mag. (also fires 38 Spec.), 6-shot.
Barrel: 2¾", 4" or 6", or 4" heavy barrel.
Weight: 33½ oz. (4" bbl.). **Length:** 9¼" (4" bbl.) over-all.
Stocks: Hand checkered American walnut, semi-target style.
Sights: Patridge-type front on ramp, rear adj. for w. and e.
Features: Music wire coil springs throughout. Hardened steel construction. Integral ejector rod shroud and sighting rib. Can be disassembled using only a coin.
Price: **$172.50**

RUGER STAINLESS SECURITY-SIX Model 717
Caliber: 357 Mag. (also fires 38 Spec.), 6-shot.
Barrel: 2¾", 4" or 6".
Weight: 33 oz. (4 bbl.). **Length:** 9¼" (4" bbl.) over-all.
Stocks: Hand checkered American walnut.
Sights: Patridge-type front, fully adj. rear.
Features: All metal parts except sights made of stainless steel. Sights are black alloy for maximum visibility. Same mechanism and features found in regular Security-Six.
Price: **$192.00**

RG 57 REVOLVER
Caliber: 357 Magnum, 41 Mag., 44 Mag., 45 Colt.
Barrel: 4".
Weight: 44 oz. **Length:** 9½".
Stocks: Checkered plastic.
Sights: Fixed rear.
Features: Swing out cylinder, spring ejector, steel frame. Imported from Germany by RG Industries.
Price: . . . . **$209.90 to $217.65**

ROSSI MODELS 68, 69 & 70 DA REVOLVERS
Caliber: 22 LR (M 70), 32 S & W (M 69), 38 Spec. (M 68).
Barrel: 3".
Weight: 22 oz.
Stocks: Checkered wood.
Sights: Ramp front, low profile adj. rear.
Features: All-steel frame. Thumb latch operated swing-out cylinder. Introduced 1978. Imported by Interarms.
Price: 22, 32 or 38, blue or nickel **$89.00**
Price: As above, 38 Spec. only with 4" bbl. as M 31 . . . . **$89.00**

RUGER POLICE SERVICE-SIX Models 107, 108 and 109
Caliber: 357 (Model 107), 38 Spec. (Model 108), 9mm (Model 109), 6-shot.
Barrel: 2¾" or 4".
Weight: 33½ oz (4" bbl.). **Length:** 9¼" (4 bbl.) over-all.
Stocks: Checkered American walnut, semi-target style.
Sights: Patridge-type front, square notch rear.
Features: Solid frame with barrel, rib and ejector rod housing combined in one unit. All steel construction. Field strips without tools.
Price: Model 107 (357) $140.00
Price: Model 108 (38) $118.00
Price: Mod. 707 (357), Stainless, 4" $154.00
Price: Mod. 708 (38), Stainless, 4" $140.00
Price: Model 109 (9mm), blue, 4" only $140.00

RUGER SPEED-SIX Models 207, 208 and 209
Caliber: 357 (Model 207), 38 Spec. (Model 208), 9mm (Model 209), 6-shot.
Barrel: 2¾" or 4".
Weight: 31½ oz. (2¾" bbl.). **Length:** 7¾" over-all (2¾" bbl.).
Stocks: Round butt design, diamond pattern checkered American walnut.
Sights: Patridge-type front, square-notch rear.
Features: Same basic mechanism as Security-Six. Hammer without spur available on special order. All steel construction. Music wire coil springs used throughout.
Price: Model 207 (357 Mag.) $140.00
Price: Model 208 (38 Spec. only) $118.00
Price: Mod. 737 (357), Stainless $154.00
Price: Mod. 738 (38), Stainless $140.00
Price: Model 209 (9mm), blue, 2¾" only $140.00

SMITH & WESSON M&P Model 10 REVOLVER
Caliber: 38 Special, 6 shot.
Barrel: 2", 4", 5" or 6".
Length: 9¼" (4" bbl.). **Weight:** 30½ oz. (4" bbl.).
Stocks: Checkered walnut, Magna. Round or square butt.
Sights: Fixed, ⅛" ramp front, square notch rear.
Price: Blued .... $119.50   Nickeled $130.50

Smith & Wesson 38 M&P Heavy Barrel Model 10
Same as regular M&P except: 4" ribbed bbl. with ⅛" ramp front sight, square rear, square butt, wgt. 34 oz.
Price: Blued .... $119.50   Nickeled $130.50

SMITH & WESSON 38 M&P AIRWEIGHT Model 12
Caliber: 38 Special, 6 shot.
Barrel: 2 or 4 inches.
Length: 6⅞" over-all. **Weight:** 18 oz. (2" bbl.).
Stocks: Checkered walnut, Magna. Round or square butt.
Sights: Fixed, ⅛" serrated ramp front, square notch rear.
Price: Blued .... $155.00   Nickeled $176.00

SMITH & WESSON Model 13 H.B. M&P
Caliber: 357 and 38 Special, 6 shot.
Barrel: 4".
Weight: 34 oz. **Length:** 9¼" over-all.
Stocks: Checkered walnut, service.
Sights: ⅛" serrated ramp front, fixed square notch rear.
Features: Heavy barrel, K-frame, square butt.
Price: Blue only, M-13 .... $132.50
Price: Nickel $144.50
Price: Model 65, as above in stainless steel ... $149.50

SMITH & WESSON Model 14 K-38 MASTERPIECE
Caliber: 38 Spec., 6-shot.
Barrel: 6", 8⅜".
Weight: 38½ oz. (6" bbl.). **Length:** 11⅛" over-all (6" bbl.)
Stock: Checkered walnut, service.
Sights: ⅛" Patridge front, micro click rear adj. for w. and e.
Price: 6" bbl. $181.00
Price: 8⅜" bbl. $190.00

SMITH & WESSON 357 COMBAT MAGNUM Model 19
Caliber: 357 Magnum and 38 Special, 6 shot.
Barrel: 2½", 4", 6".
Length: 9½" (4" bbl.). **Weight:** 35 oz.
Stocks: Checkered Goncala Alves, target. Grooved tangs and trigger.
Sights: Front, ⅛" Baughman Quick Draw on 2½" or 4" bbl., Patridge on 6" bbl., micro click rear adjustable for w. and e.
Price: S&W Bright Blue or Nickel $194.00

SMITH & WESSON 44 MAGNUM Model 29 REVOLVER
Caliber: 44 Magnum, 44 Special or 44 Russian, 6 shot.
Barrel: 4", 6½", 8⅜".
Length: 11⅞" (6½" bbl.). **Weight:** 47 oz. (6½" bbl.), 43 oz. (4" bbl.).
Stocks: Oversize target type, checkered Goncala Alves. Tangs and target trigger grooved, checkered target hammer.
Sights: ⅛" red ramp-front, micro. click rear, adjustable for w. and e.
Features: Includes presentation case.
Price: S&W Bright Blue or Nickel 4", 6½" $310.00
Price: 8⅜" bbl. $319.50

SMITH & WESSON HIGHWAY PATROLMAN Model 28
Caliber: 357 Magnum and 38 Special, 6 shot.
Barrel: 4", 6".
Length: 11¼" (6" bbl.). **Weight:** 44 oz. (6" bbl.).
Stocks: Checkered walnut, Magna. Grooved tangs and trigger.
Sights: Front, ⅛" Baughman Quick Draw, on plain ramp. micro click rear, adjustable for w. and e.
Price: S&W Satin Blue, sandblasted frame edging and barrel top . $176.50
Price: With target stocks $192.00

SMITH & WESSON 357 MAGNUM M-27 REVOLVER
Caliber: 357 Magnum and 38 Special, 6 shot.
Barrel: 3½", 5", 6", 8⅜".
Length: 11¼" (6" bbl.). **Weight:** 44 oz. (6" bbl.).
Stocks: Checkered walnut, Magna. Grooved tangs and trigger.
Sights: Any S&W target front, micro click rear, adjustable for w. and e.
Price: S&W Bright Blue or Nickel, 3½", 5", 6" $281.70
Price: 8⅜" bbl. $291.19

SMITH & WESSON 32 REGULATION POLICE Model 31
Caliber: 32 S&W Long, 6 shot.
Barrel: 2", 3", 4".
Length: 8½" (4" bbl.). **Weight:** 18¾ oz. (4" bbl.).
Stocks: Checkered walnut, Magna.
Sights: Fixed, ¹⁄₁₀" serrated ramp front, square notch rear.
Price: Blued .... $144.50   Nickeled $157.50

SMITH & WESSON 1953 Model 34, 22/32 KIT GUN
Caliber: 22 LR, 6 shot.
Barrel: 2", 4".
Length: 8" (4" bbl. and round butt). **Weight:** 22½ oz. (4" bbl.).
Stocks: Checkered walnut, round or square butt.
Sights: Front, ¹⁄₁₀" serrated ramp, micro. click rear, adjustable for w. & e.
Price: Blued .... $151.50   Nickeled $164.50
Price: Model 63, as above in stainless, 4" $173.00

SMITH & WESSON 38 CHIEFS SPECIAL & AIRWEIGHT
Caliber: 38 Special, 5 shot.
Barrel: 2", 3".
Length: 6½" (2" bbl. and round butt). **Weight:** 19 oz. (2" bbl.); 14 oz. (AIR-WEIGHT).
Stocks: Checkered walnut, Magna. Round or square butt.
Sights: Fixed, ¹⁄₁₀" serrated ramp front, square notch rear.
Price: Blued std. M-36 ... $139.00   Standard weight Nickel ... $151.00
Price: Blued AIR'W M-37 . $154.50   AIRWEIGHT Nickel $175.00

Smith & Wesson 60 Chiefs Special Stainless
Same as Model 36 except: 2" bbl. and round butt only.
Price: Stainless steel $168.00

SMITH & WESSON BODYGUARD MODEL 38 REVOLVER
Caliber: 38 Special; 5 shot, double action revolver.
Barrel: 2".
Length: 6⅜". **Weight:** 14½ oz.
Features: Alloy frame; integral hammer shroud.
Stocks: Checkered walnut, Magna.
Sights: Fixed ¹⁄₁₀" serrated ramp front, square notch rear.
Price: Blued .... $161.50   Nickeled $182.00

Smith & Wesson Bodyguard Model 49 Revolver
Same as Model 38 except steel construction. Weight 20½ oz.
Price: Blued .... $150.00   Nickeled $162.50

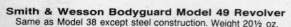

SMITH & WESSON 41 MAGNUM Model 57 REVOLVER

Caliber: 41 Magnum, 6 shot.
Barrel: 4", 6" or 8⅜".
Length: 11⅜" (6" bbl.). **Weight:** 48 oz. (6" bbl.).
Stocks: Oversize target type checkered Goncala Alves wood and target hammer. Tang and target trigger grooved.
Sights: ⅛" red ramp front, micro. click rear, adj. for w. and e.
Price: S&W Bright Blue or Nickel 4", 6" $310.00
Price: 8⅜" bbl. $319.50

SMITH & WESSON 41 M&P Model 58 REVOLVER

Caliber: 41 Magnum, 6 shot.
Barrel: 4".
Length: 9¼" over-all. **Weight:** 41 oz.
Stocks: Checkered walnut, Magna.
Sights: Fixed, ⅛" serrated ramp front, square notch rear.
Price: Blued .... $175.00   Nickeled $187.50

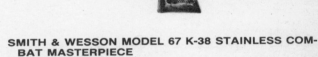

SMITH & WESSON MODEL 64 STAINLESS M&P

Caliber: 38 Special, 6-shot.
Barrel: 4".
Length: 9½" over-all. **Weight:** 30½ oz.
Stocks: Checkered walnut, service style.
Sights: Fixed, ⅛" serrated ramp front, square notch rear.
Features: Satin finished stainless steel, square butt.
Price: $140.50

SMITH & WESSON MODEL 66 STAINLESS COMBAT MAGNUM

Caliber: 357 Magnum and 38 Special, 6-shot.
Barrel: 2½", 4", 6".
Length: 9½" over-all. **Weight:** 35 oz.
Stocks: Checkered Goncala Alves target.
Sights: Front, ⅛" Baughman Quick Draw on plain ramp, micro click rear adj. for w. and e.
Features: Satin finish stainless steel, grooved trigger with adj. stop.
Price: $202.00

SMITH & WESSON MODEL 67 K-38 STAINLESS COMBAT MASTERPIECE

Caliber: 38 special, 6-shot.
Barrel: 4".
Length: 9⅛" over-all. **Weight:** 34 oz. (loaded).
Stocks: Checkered walnut, service style.
Sights: Front, ⅛" Baughman Quick Draw on ramp, micro click rear adj. for w. and e.
Features: Stainless steel. Square butt frame with grooved tangs, grooved trigger with adj. stop.
Price: $182.00

TAURUS MODEL 66 REVOLVER

Caliber: 357 Magnum, 6-shot.
Barrel: 4".
Weight: 35 ozs.
Stocks: Checkered walnut, target-type.
Sights: Serrated ramp front, micro click rear adjustable for w. and e.
Features: Wide target-type hammer spur, floating firing pin, heavy barrel with shrouded ejector rod. Introduced 1978. From International Distributors.
Price: Blue only, about $136.50
Price: Model 65 (as above except has fixed rear sight, ramp front), about $127.12

TAURUS MODEL 80 STANDARD REVOLVER

Caliber: 38 Spec., 6-shot.
Barrel: 3" or 4".
Weight: 31 oz. (4" bbl.). **Length:** 9¼" over-all (4" bbl.).
Stocks: Checkered Brazilian walnut.
Sights: Serrated ramp front, square notch rear.
Features: Imported from Brazil by International Distributors.
Price: Blue, about $78.00
Price: Nickel, about $82.00

TAURUS MODEL 83 REVOLVER
Caliber: 38 Spec., 6-shot.
Barrel: 4" only, heavy.
Weight: 34½ ozs.
Stocks: Over-size checkered walnut.
Sights: Ramp front, micro. click rear adj. for w. & e.
Features: Blue or nickel finish. Introduced 1977. From International Distributors.
Price: Blue, about $82.00
Price: Nickel, about 86.00

TAURUS MODEL 82 HEAVY BARREL REVOLVER
Caliber: 38 Spec., 6-shot.
Barrel: 3" or 4", heavy.
Weight: 33 oz. (4" bbl.). **Length:** 9¼" over-all (4" bbl.).
Stocks: Checkered Brazilian walnut.
Sights: Serrated ramp front, square notch rear.
Features: Imported from Brazil by International Distributors.
Price: Blue, about $80.00
Price: Nickel, about $84.00

TAURUS MODEL 74 SPORT REVOLVER
Caliber: 32 S&W Long, 6-shot.
Barrel: 3".
Weight: 22 oz. **Length:** 8¼" over-all.
Stocks: Oversize target-type, checkered Brazilian walnut.
Sights: Serrated ramp front, rear adj. for w. and e.
Features: Imported from Brazil by International Distributers.
Price: Blue, about $80.00
Price: Nickel, about $82.00

TAURUS MODEL 84 SPORT REVOLVER
Caliber: 38 Spec., 6-shot.
Barrel: 4".
Weight: 30 oz. **Length:** 9¼" over-all.
Stocks: Checkered Brazilian walnut.
Sights: Serrated ramp front, rear adj. for w. and e.
Features: Imported from Brazil by International Distributors.
Price: Blue, about $82.00
Price: Nickel, about $84.00

DAN WESSON MODEL 8-2 & MODEL 14-2
Caliber: 38 Special (Model 8-2); 357 (Model 14-2), both 6 shot.
Barrel: 2", 4", 6", 8". "Quickshift" interchangeable barrels.
Weight: 34 oz. (4" bbl.) **Length:** 9¼" over-all (4" bbl.).
Stocks: "Quickshift" checkered walnut. Interchangeable with three other styles.
Sights: ⅛" serrated ramp front, rear fixed.
Features: Interchangeable barrels; 4 interchangeable grips; few moving parts, easy disassembly.
Price: 2" barrel $164.50
Price: 4" barrel $170.55
Price: 6" barrel $176.55
Price: 8" barrel $182.75
Price: Pistol Pac (cased with all above bbls.) $383.80

DAN WESSON MODEL 9-2 & MODEL 15-2
Caliber: 38 Special (Model 9-2); 357 (Model 15-2), both 6 shot.
Barrel: 2", 4", 6", 8", 10", 12", 15". "Quickshift" interchangeable barrels.
Weight: 36 oz. (4" bbl.). **Length:** 9¼" over-all (4" bbl.).
Stocks: "Quickshift" checkered walnut. Interchangeable with three other styles.
Sights: ⅛" serrated blade front with red insert (Std.), white or yellow insert optional, as is Patridge. White outline, rear adj. for w. & e.
Features: Interchangeable barrels; four interchangeable grips; few moving parts, easy disassembly; Bright Blue finish only. Contact Dan Wesson for additional models not listed here. 10", 12" and 15" barrels also available with vent. rib.
Price: 9-2H, 15-2H (bull barrel shroud) 2" $230.90
Price: 9-2H, 15-2H, 6" bbl. $248.25
Price: 9-2V, 15-2V (vent. rib) 8" $260.45
Price: 9-2V, 15-2V, 10" $286.90
Price: 9-2VH, 15-2VH (heavy vent. shroud) 12" $334.60
Price: Pistol Pac, VH $620.05
Price: 9-2, 15-2 (Std. shroud) 2" $211.75
Price: 9-2, 15-2, 6" $227.45
Price: 9-2, 15-2, 8" $235.35
Price: 9-2, 15-2, 15" $308.25
Price: 9-2, 15-2, Pistol Pac $449.95

Consult our Directory pages for
the location of firms mentioned.

ABILENE SINGLE ACTION REVOLVER
Caliber: 357 Mag., 44 Mag., 6 shot.
Barrel: 4⅝", 5½", 6½", 7½", and 8½" (44 Mag. only).
Weight: About 48 oz.
Stocks: Smooth walnut.
Sights: Serrated ramp front, click adj. rear for w. and e.
Features: Transfer bar ignition, wide hammer spur. Blue or stainless steel. From United States Arms Corp.
Price: Blue, 357, 4⅝", 5½", 6½" **$192.45**
Price: Blue, 44 Mag., 7½", 8½" **$219.95**
Price: Stainless, 357, 4⅝", 5½", 6½" **$243.40**
Price: Stainless, 44 Mag., 7½", 8½" **$277.75**

BISON SINGLE ACTION REVOLVER
Caliber: 22 LR.
Barrel: 4¾".
Weight: 20 oz.
Stocks: Imitation stag.
Sights: Fixed front, adj. rear.
Features: 22 WRM cylinder also available ($9.00 additional). Imported from Germany by Jana.
Price: **$50.00**

DAKOTA SINGLE ACTION REVOLVERS
Caliber: 22 LR, 22 Mag., 30 Carbine, 357 Mag., 44-40, 45 LC.
Barrel: 4⅝", 5½" or 7½".
Weight: 44 oz.
Stocks: Smooth walnut.
Sights: Blade front, grooved backstrap fixed rear.
Features: From EMF Co.
Price: **$169.00**

COLT SINGLE ACTION ARMY REVOLVER
Caliber: 357 Magnum, 44 Spec. or 45 Colt, 6 shot.
Barrel: 4¾", 5½" or 7½".
Length: 10⅞" (5½" bbl.). **Weight:** 37 oz. (5½" bbl.).
Stocks: Black composite rubber with eagle and shield crest.
Sights: Fixed. Grooved top strap, blade front.
Price: Blued and case hardened 4¾", 5½" bbl. **$336.95**
Price: Nickel with walnut stocks **$396.50**
Price: With 7½" bbl. **$343.50**

Colt Single Action Army—New Frontier
Same specifications as standard Single Action Army except: flat-top frame; high polished finish, blue and case colored; ramp front sight and target rear adj. for windage and elevation; smooth walnut stocks with silver medallion.
Price: **$396.50**

FREEDOM ARMS MINI REVOLVER
Caliber: 22 Short, 22 LR, 5-shot.
Barrel: 1⅛".
Weight: 4 oz. **Length:** 3½" over-all; 4" 22 LR.
Stocks: Black ebonite.
Sights: Blade front, notch rear.
Features: Made of stainless steel, simple take down; half-cock safety; sheathed trigger; cartridge rims recessed in cylinder. Comes in presentation case.
Price: 22 Short **$95.00**
Price: 22 LR **$109.50**

F.I.E. "LEGEND" SINGLE ACTION REVOLVER
Caliber: 22 LR/22 Mag., 357, 44 Mag., 6-shot.
Barrel: 4¾" (22, 22 Mag.); 5½", 7½" (357, 44 Mag.).
Weight: 32 oz.
Stocks: Smooth walnut or black checkered plastic. Walnut optional ($10.95).
Sights: Fixed.
Features: Positive hammer block system. Brass backstrap and trigger guard. Case hardened steel frame. From F.I.E.
Price: 22 LR **$61.95**
Price: 22 combo **$71.95**
Price: 357 or 44 Mag., 5½", 7½" bbl. **$129.95**

FREEDOM ARMS 454 CASULL
Caliber: 454 Casull, 5-shot. Also fires 45 Long Colt.
Barrel: 7½".
Weight: 3 lbs., 2 oz. **Length:** 14" over-all.
Stocks: One piece hardwood.
Sights: Blade front, notched rear in top strap.
Features: Completely stainless steel, bright polish finish. New safety mechanism allows hammer-down carry on loaded chamber. Cylinder chambers counter bored to enclose case rim. Commercial ammunition will be available. From Freedom Arms.
Price: **$445.00**

HAWES FEDERAL MARSHAL REVOLVER
Caliber: 357, 44 Mag., 45 L.C.
Barrel: 6".
Weight: 44 oz. **Length:** 11¾" over-all.
Stock: Smooth walnut.
Sights: Blade front, fixed rear.
Features: Color case hardened frame, brass backstrap and trigger guard. Barrel, cylinder and frame are blued. Combo cylinder models avail. same cals. as Western Marshal (**$249.95**, **$260.45** resp.). Imported by Hawes Firearms.
Price: .... **$176.85** to **$211.40**

F.I.E. E15 BUFFALO SCOUT REVOLVER
Caliber: 22 LR/22 Mag., 6-shot.
Barrel: 4¾.
Length: 10" over-all. **Weight:** 30 oz.
Stocks: Smooth walnut (optional) or black checkered plastic.
Sights: Adjustable.
Features: Slide spring ejector.
Price: Blued, 22 LR **$39.95**
Price: Blue, 22 combo **$50.65**
Price: Chrome, 22 LR **$44.95**
Price: Chrome, combo **$54.95**
Price: Blue/brass, combo **$53.95**

HAWES CHIEF MARSHAL REVOLVER
Caliber: 357 Magnum, 44 Magnum, 45 Long Colt; 6-shot.
Barrel: 6".
Weight: 48 oz. **Length:** 11¾".
Stocks: Extra large smooth rosewood.
Sights: Ramp target front, rear adj. for w. & e.
Features: Single action. Combo cylinder models avail., same cals. as Western Marshal (**$193.75**, **$201.75** resp.). Extra heavy frame. Imported from West Germany by Hawes.
Price: .... **$174.70** to **$218.10**

HANDGUNS—SINGLE ACTION REVOLVERS

HAWES SAUER WESTERN MARSHAL REVOLVERS
Caliber: 357 Magnum, 44 Magnum, 45 Long Colt, 6-shot.
Barrel: 6″ (357 Mag., 44 Mag., 45).
Weight: 44 oz. **Length:** 11¾″.
Stocks: Rosewood.
Sight: Blade front.
Features: Single action. Interchangeable cyclinders available for 357/9mm Para., 45 LC/45 ACP (**$179.20**); 44 Mag./44-40 (**$186.30**). Imported from West Germany by Hawes.
Price: 357 Mag., 45 LC **$144.95**
Price: 44 Mag. **$151.75**

Hawes Montana Marshal Revolver
Same as Western Marshal except with solid brass backstrap and trigger guard.
Price: .... **$164.95** to **$207.70**

Hawes Texas Marshal Revolver
Same as Western Marshal except full nickel finish and white Pearlite grips.
Price: .... **$168.40** to **$220.05**

HAWES SILVER CITY MARSHAL REVOLVER
Caliber: 357, 44 Mag., 45 L.C.
Barrel: 6″ (357, 44, 45), 5½″ (22 cal.).
Weight: 44 oz. **Length:** 11¾″ over-all.
Stocks: White Pearlite.
Sights: Fixed.
Features: Nickel plated frame, brass backstrap and trigger guard, blue barrel and cylinder. Combo cyl. models available same as Western Marshal (**$194.75**, **$202.80** resp.). Imported by Hawes Firearms.
Price: .... **$175.75** to **$219.00**

HAWES DEPUTY MARSHAL REVOLVER
Caliber: 22 LR, 22 LR/22 WRM.
Barrel: 5½″.
Weight: 34 oz. **Length:** 11″ over-all.
Stocks: Black or white plastic.
Sights: Fixed.
Features: Available in std. blue finish with black grips, with brass backstrap and trigger guard and wood grips, with completely chromed finish and white grips, or with chrome frame, brass backstrap and trigger guard, blue cylinder and barrel and white grips. Imported by Hawes Firearms.
Price: .... **$59.95** to **$90.60**

IVER JOHNSON CATTLEMAN TRAILBLAZER
Caliber: 22 S, L, LR, 22 Mag.
Barrel: 5½″ or 6½″.
Weight: 2½ lbs.
Stocks: Smooth walnut.
Sights: Ramp front, rear adj. for w. and e.
Features: Comes with interchangeable magnum cylinder. Single action. Case-hardened frame, brass backstrap and trigger guard. Imported by Iver Johnson.
Price: **$142.95**

I. J. CATTLEMAN BUCKHORN MAGNUM
Caliber: 357, 38 Spec., 44 Mag., 45 LC.
Barrel: 6½″, 7½″ (44 Mag.), 5¾″ or 7½″ (357, 38, 45).
Weight: 2¾ lbs.
Stocks: Smooth walnut.
Sights: Ramp front, rear adj. for w. and e.
Features: Single action. Blued barrel, case-hardened frame, brass backstrap and trigger guard. Imported by Iver Johnson.
Price: 357, 38 Spec., 45 LC **$179.95**
Price: 44 Mag. **$205.95**

I. J. CATTLEMAN BUNTLINE BUCKHORN MAGNUM
Caliber: 357, 38 Spec., 44 Mag., 45 LC, 6-shot.
Barrel: 18″.
Weight: 3½ lbs.
Stocks: Smooth walnut.
Sights: Ramp front, rear adj. for w. and e.
Features: Single action. Blued barrel, case-hardened frame, brass trigger guard and backstrap. Comes with detachable shoulder stock. Imported by Iver Johnson.
Price: 357, 45 LC .... **$339.95**   44 Mag. **$359.95**

IVER JOHNSON CATTLEMAN MAGNUM
Caliber: 357, 44 Mag., 45 LC, 6-shot.
Barrel: 4¾", 5½" or 7½". 44 Mag. avail. with 6", 6¼" or 7½".
Weight: 2½ lbs.
Stocks: Smooth walnut.
Sights: Fixed.
Features: Case-hardened frame, single action, blued barrel, brass backstrap and trigger guard. Imported by Iver Johnson.
Price: 357, 45 LC .... **$163.75**   44 Mag. **$189.95**

LIBERTY MUSTANG
Caliber: 22 LR, 22 Mag. or combination, 8-shot.
Barrel: 5".
Weight: 34 oz. **Length:** 10¼" over-all.
Stocks: Smooth rosewood.
Sights: Blade front, adj. rear.
Features: Single action, slide ejector rod. Imported by Liberty.
Price: With one cylinder $34.95
Price: With two cylinders $42.95

RG 66 SUPER SINGLE ACTION REVOLVER
Caliber: 22 LR, 22 Mag., 6-shot.
Barrel: 4¾", 6" or 9".
Weight: 32 oz. **Length:** 10".
Stocks: Checkered plastic.
Sights: Fixed front, rear adj.
Features: Slide ejector rod, blue finish. Model 66M is combo set with both 22 LR and 22 mag. cylinders. Imported from Germany by R. G. Industries.
Price: Blue ....**$52.00**; (Model 66M) **$60.50**
Price: Blue (6") ....**$55.75**; Magnum **$65.50**
Price: Blue (9") ....**$59.00**; Magnum **$68.00**

RUGER NEW MODEL SUPER SINGLE-SIX CONVERTIBLE REVOLVER
Caliber: 22 S, L, LR, 6-shot. 22 WMR in extra cylinder.
Barrel: 4⅝", 5½", 6½" or 9½" (6-groove).
Weight: 34½ oz. (6½" bbl.) **Length:** 11¹³⁄₁₆" over-all (6½" bbl.).
Stocks: Smooth American walnut.
Sights: Improved patridge front on ramp, fully adj. rear protected by integral frame ribs.
Features: New Ruger "interlocked" mechanism, transfer bar ignition, gate-controlled loading, hardened chrome-moly steel frame, wide trigger, music wire springs throughout, independent firing pin.
Price: 4⅝", 5½", 6½", 9½" barrel **$124.00**
Price: 5½", 6½" bbl., stainless steel **$159.00**

RUGER NEW MODEL BLACKHAWK REVOLVER
Caliber: 357 or 41 Mag., 6-shot.
Barrel: 4⅝" or 6½", either caliber.
Weight: 42 oz. (6½" bbl.). **Length:** 12¼" over-all (6½" bbl.).
Stocks: American walnut.
Sights: ⅛" ramp front, micro click rear adj. for w. and e.
Features: New Ruger interlocked mechanism, independent firing pin, hardened chrome-moly steel frame, music wire springs throughout.
Price: Blued **$154.00**
Price: Stainless steel (357) **$178.00**

Ruger New Model 357/9mm Blackhawk
Same as the 357 Magnum except furnished with interchangeable cylinders for 9mm Parabellum and 357 Magnum cartridges **$168.00**
9mm cylinder, fitted to your 357 Blackhawk **$22.50**

RUGER NEW MODEL SUPER BLACKHAWK
Caliber: 44 Magnum, 6-shot. Also fires 44 Spec.
Barrel: 7½" (6-groove, 20" twist).
Weight: 48 oz. **Length:** 13⅜" over-all.
Stocks: Genuine American walnut.
Sights: ⅛" ramp front, micro click rear adj. for w. and e.
Features: New Ruger interlocked mechanism, non-fluted cylinder, steel grip and cylinder frame, square back trigger guard, wide serrated trigger and wide spur hammer. Deep Ruger blue.
Price: $180.00

RUGER NEW MODEL CONVERTIBLE BLACKHAWK
Caliber: 45 Colt or 45 Colt/45 ACP (extra cylinder).
Barrel: 4⅝" or 7½" (6-groove, 16" twist).
Weight: 40 oz. (7½" bbl.). **Length:** 13⅛" (7½" bbl.).
Stocks: Smooth American walnut.
Sights: ⅛" ramp front, micro click rear adj. for w. and e.
Features: Similar to Super Blackhawk, Ruger interlocked mechanism. Convertible furnished with interchangeable cylinder for 45 ACP.
Price: Blued, 45 Colt $154.00
Price: Convertible $168.00

Ruger New Model 30 Carbine Blackhawk
Specifications similar to 45 Blackhawk. Fluted cylinder, round-back trigger guard. Weight 44 oz., length 13⅛" over-all, 7½" barrel only.
Price: $154.00

Consult our Directory pages for the location of firms mentioned.

SMITH & WESSON K-38 S.A. M-14
Caliber: 38 Spec., 6-shot.
Barrel: 6", 8⅜".
Length: 11⅛" over-all (6" bbl.). **Weight:** 38½ oz. (6" bbl.).
Stocks: Checkered walnut, service type.
Sights: ⅛" Patridge front, micro click rear adj. for w. and e.
Features: Same as Model 14 except single action only, target hammer and trigger.
Price: 6" bbl. $221.00
Price: 8⅜" bbl. $230.00

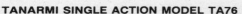

TANARMI S.A. REVOLVER MODEL TA22S
Caliber: 22 S, L, LR, 22 LR/22 Mag., 6-shot.
Barrel: 4¾".
Weight: 32 oz. **Length:** 10" over-all.
Stocks: Checkered nylon with thumb-rest. Walnut optional.
Sights: Blade front, rear drift-adj. for w.
Features: Manual hammer block safety; color hardened steel frame; brass backstrap and trigger guard. Imported from Italy by Excam.
Price: 22 LR only $63.70
Price: Combo $76.30
Price: 22 LR with walnut grips $75.60
Price: Combo with walnut grips $86.00

TANARMI SINGLE ACTION MODEL TA76
Same as TA22 models except blue backstrap and trigger guard.
Price: 22 LR, blue $42.60
Price: Combo, blue $53.98
Price: 22 LR, chrome $47.50
Price: Combo, chrome $58.99

THE VIRGINIAN DRAGOON REVOLVER
Caliber: 357 Mag., 44 Mag., 45 Colt.
Barrel: 44 Mag., 6", 7½", 8⅜"; 357 Mag. and 45 Colt, 5", 6", 7½".
Weight: 48 ozs. (6" barrel). **Length:** 11⅞" over-all (6" barrel).
Stocks: Smooth walnut.
Sights: Ramp-type Patridge front blade, micro. adj. target rear.
Features: Color case-hardened frame, spring-loaded floating firing pin, coil main spring. Firing pin is lock-fitted with a steel bushing. Introduced 1977. Made in the U.S. by Interarms Industries, Inc.
Price: 6", 7½", 8⅜" $209.00
Price: 12" Buntline (44 Mag. only) $269.00

HANDGUNS — MISCELLANEOUS

BUTLER DERRINGER
Caliber: 22 Short, single shot.
Barrel: 2½".
Weight: 8 oz.
Stocks: Smooth walnut or Pearl-O-Lite.
Sights: Blade front only.
Features: Spur trigger. Available in blue, gold or chrome finish. From EMF Co.
Price: From $44.95

F.I.E. MODEL D-38 DERRINGER
Caliber: 38 Special or 38 S&W.
Barrel: 3".
Weight: 14 oz.
Stocks: Checkered white plastic.
Sights: Fixed.
Features: Chrome finish. Spur trigger. Made in U.S.A.
Price: $44.95

HI-STANDARD 9194 AND 9306 DERRINGER
Caliber: 22 Rimfire Magnum. 2 shot.
Barrel: 3½", over and under, rifled.
Length: 5" over-all. **Weight:** 11 oz.
Stocks: Smooth plastic.
Sights: Fixed, open.
Features: Hammerless, integral safety hammerblock, all steel unit is encased in a black, anodized alloy housing. Recessed chamber. Dual extraction. Top break, double action.
Price: Blued (M9194) ...... **$81.50**   Nickel (M9306) **$95.00**

MERRILL SPORTSMAN'S SINGLE SHOT PISTOL
Caliber: 22 LR, 22 WMR, 22 Hornet, 22 Jet, 256 Win. Mag., 357 Mag., 357/44 B & D, 30-30 Win., 30 Herrett, 35 Herrett, 44 Mag.
Barrel: 9" or 12", semi-octagonal; .450" wide vent. rib, matted to prevent glare.
Weight: About 54 ozs. **Length:** 10½" over-all (9" bbl.)
Stocks: Smooth walnut with thumb and heel rest. Teakwood optional at extra cost.
Sights: Front .125" blade; rear "Micro Sight" adj. for w. and e.
Features: Polished blue finish. Barrel is grooved for scope mounting. Cocking indicator visible from rear of gun. Has spring-loaded barrel lock, positive thumb safety. Wrist rest attachment (optional) is adjustable, can be swung out of way for holster carry. Scope and mount shown are not included.
Price: 9" barrel $269.50
Price: 12" barrel $289.50
Price: Extra barrel, 9" .... **$79.50** 12" **$99.50**
Price: Wrist rest attachment $20.75

ROLLING BLOCK SINGLE SHOT PISTOL
Caliber: 22 LR, 357 mag.
Barrel: 8".
Weight: 2 lbs. **Length:** 12".
Stocks: Walnut.
Sights: Front adj. for w., buckhorn adj. for e.
Features: Polished brass trigger guard. Supplied with wooden display box. Imported by Navy Arms.
Price: $135.00

REMINGTON MODEL XP-100 Bolt Action Pistol

Caliber: 221 Fireball, single shot.
Barrel: 10½ inches, ventilated rib.
Length: 16¾ inches. **Weight:** 60 oz.
Stocks: Brown nylon one-piece, checkered grip with white spacers.
Features: Fits left or right hand, is shaped to fit fingers and heel of hand. Grooved trigger. Rotating thumb safety, cavity in fore-end permits insertion of up to five 38 cal., 130-gr. metal jacketed bullets to adjust weight and balance. Included is a black vinyl, zippered case.
Sights: Fixed front, rear adj. for w. and e. Tapped for scope mount.
Price: Including case **$209.95**

SEMMERLING LM-4 PISTOL

Caliber: 45 ACP.
Barrel: 3½″.
Weight: 24 ozs. **Length:** 5.2″ over-all.
Stocks: Checkered black plastic.
Sights: Ramp front, fixed rear.
Features: Manually operated repeater. Over-all dimensions are 5.2″ x 3.7″ x 1″. Has a four-shot magazine capacity. Comes with manual, leather carrying case, spare stock screw and wrench. From Semmerling Corp.
Price: Complete **$645.00**
Price: Thin Version (blue sideplate instead of grips) **$645.00**

TANARMI O/U DERRINGER

Caliber: 38 Special.
Barrel: 3″.
Weight: 14 oz. **Length:** 4¾″ over-all.
Stocks: Checkered white nylon.
Sights: Fixed.
Features: Blue finish; tip-up barrel. Made in U.S. by Excam, Inc.
Price: **$51.00**

THOMPSON-CENTER ARMS CONTENDER

Caliber: 218 Bee, 221 Rem., 25-35 Win., 30-30 Win., 22 S, L, LR, 22 WMR, 22 Rem. Jet, 22 Hornet, 22 K Hornet, 256 Win., 38 Spl., 357 Mag., also 222 Rem., 45 ACP, 44 Mag., 5mm Rem., 45 Long Colt.
Barrel: 8¾″, 10″, tapered octagon. Single shot.
Length: 13¼″ (10″ bbl.). **Weight:** 43 oz. (10″ bbl.).
Stocks: Select checkered walnut grip and fore-end, with thumb rest. Right or left hand.
Sights: Under cut blade ramp front, rear adj. for w. & e.
Features: Break open action with auto-safety. Single action only. Interchangeable bbls., both caliber (rim & center fire), and length. Drilled and tapped for scope. Engraved frame.
Price: Blued (rimfire cals.) **$165.00**
Price: Blued (centerfire cals.) **$165.00**
Price: Extra bbls. (standard octagon) **$67.00**
Price: 30 Herrett and 357 Herrett bull bbl. with fore-end, less sights **$62.00**
Price: As above except with sights **$67.00**
Price: Bushnell Phantom scope base **$7.50**
Price: Fitted walnut case **$39.50**
Price: 357 and 44 Mag. vent. rib, internal choke bbl. **$77.00**

Thompson-Center Super 14 Contender

Similar to regular Contender except has 14″ barrel with fully adjustable target-type sights. Available in 30 Herrett, 357 Herrett, 30-30 Win., 35 Rem., 41 and 44 Mag. only. Introduced 1978.
Price: **$185.00**
Price: Extra barrels **$75.00**

ARMALITE AR-180 SPORTER CARBINE
Caliber: 223 semi-automatic, gas operated carbine.
Barrel: 18¼" (12" twist).
Weight: 6½ lbs. **Length:** 38" over-all
Stock: Nylon folding stock, phenolic fiber-glass heat dissipating fore-end.
Sight: Flip-up "L" type sight adj. for w., post front adj. for e.
Features: Safety lever accessible from both sides. Flash hider slotted to prevent muzzle climb.
Price: $325.00
    3x (2.75 x 20mm) scope with quick detachable side-mount. $103.78
    Extra 5-round magazine $9.95

Auto-Ordnance 1927A-3
A 22 caliber version of the 27A-1. Exact look-alike with alloy receiver. Weight is about 7 lbs., 16" finned barrel, 10, 30- and 50-shot magazines and drum. Introduced 1977. From Auto-Ordnance Corp.
Price: $419.95

AUTO-ORDNANCE MODEL 27 A-1
Caliber: 45 ACP, 30-shot magazine.
Barrel: 16".
Weight: 11½ lbs. **Length:** About 39½" over-all (Deluxe).
Stock: Walnut stock and vertical fore-end.
Sights: Blade front, open rear adj. for w.
Features: Re-creation of Thompson Model 1927. Semi-auto only. Deluxe model has finned barrel, adj. rear sight and compensator; Standard model has plain barrel and military sights. From Auto-Ordnance Corp.
Price: Deluxe $419.95
Price: Standard $379.95
Price: 1927A5 Pistol (M27A1 without stock; wgt. 7 lbs.) $379.95

Browning Magnum Auto Rifle
Same as the standard caliber model, except weighs 8⅜ lbs., 45" over-all 24" bbl., 3-round mag., Cals. 7mm Mag., 300 Win. Mag.
Price: Grade I .... $449.95   Grade IV $1,225.00

BROWNING HIGH-POWER AUTO RIFLE
Caliber: 243, 270, 30-06, 308.
Barrel: 22" round tapered.
Weight: 7⅜ lbs. **Length:** 43" over-all.
Stock: French walnut p.g. stock (13⅝"x2"x1⅝") and fore-end, hand checkered.
Sights: Adj. folding-leaf rear, gold bead on hooded ramp front.
Features: Detachable 4-round magazine. Receiver tapped for scope mounts. Trigger pull 3½ lbs. Gold plated trigger on Grade IV.
Price: Grade I $399.95
Price: Grade IV $1,175.00

COLT AR-15 SPORTER
Caliber: 223 Rem.
Barrel: 20".
Weight: 7¼ lbs. **Length:** 38⅜" over-all.
Stock: Reinforced polycarbonate with buttstock stowage compartment.
Sights: Post front, rear adj. for w. and e.
Features: 5-round detachable box magazine, recoil pad, flash suppressor, sling swivels.
Price: $341.95

Colt AR-15 Collapsable Stock Model
Same as standard AR-15 except has telescoping nylon-coated aluminum buttstock and redesigned fore-end. Over-all length collapsed is 32", extended 39". Barrel length is 16", weight is 5.8 lbs. Has 14½" sight radius. Introduced 1978.
Price: $376.50

COMMANDO ARMS CARBINE
Caliber: 9mm P. or 45 ACP.
Barrel: 16½".
Weight: 8 lbs. **Length:** 37" over-all.
Stock: Walnut buttstock, walnut vertical or horizontal front grip.
Sights: Blade front, peep rear.
Features: Semi-auto only. Cocking handle on left side. Choice of magazines—5, 15, 30 or 90 shot. From Commando Arms.
Price: Mark 9 or Mark 45 .... $179.00

CENTERFIRE RIFLES—AUTOLOADING & SLIDE ACTION

HECKLER & KOCH HK770 AUTO RIFLE
Caliber: 308 Win., 3-shot magazine.
Barrel: 19.6".
Weight: 7½ lbs. **Length:** 42.8" over-all.
Stock: European walnut. Checkered p.g. and fore-end.
Sights: Vertically adjustable blade front, open, fold-down rear adj. for w.
Features: Has the delayed roller-locked bolt system and polygonal rifling. Magazine catch located at front of trigger guard. Receiver top is dovetailed to accept clamp-type scope mount. From Heckler & Koch, Inc.
Price: **$399.00**

HECKLER & KOCH HK-91 AUTO RIFLE
Caliber: 308 Win., 5- or 20-shot magazine.
Barrel: 19".
Weight: 9½ lbs. **Length:** 40¼" over-all.
Stock: Black high-impact plastic.
Sights: Post front, aperture rear adj. for w. and e.
Features: Delayed roller lock bolt action. Sporting version of West German service rifle. Takes special H&K clamp scope mount. Imported by Heckler & Koch, Inc.
Price: HK-91 with plastic stock **$389.00**
Price: HK-91 with retractable metal stock **$437.00**
Price: 22 cal. conversion unit **$268.00**
Price: Scope mount **$133.00**

HECKLER & KOCH HK-93 AUTO RIFLE
Similar to HK-93 except in 223 cal., 16.13" barrel, over-all length of 35½", weighs 7¾ lbs. Slight differences in stock, fore-end.
Price: HK-93 .... **$367.00**
Price: HK-93 with retractable metal stock **$418.00**
Price: Scope mount **$133.00**

Remington 742 BDL Woodsmaster
Same as 742 except: "stepped" receiver, Monte Carlo with cheekpiece (right or left), whiteline spacers, basket-weave checkering on p.g. and fore-end, black fore-end tip, RKW finish (13⁵/₁₆"x1⅝"x1¹³/₁₆"x2½"). Cals. 30-06, 308 .... **$301.95**

IVER JOHNSON'S PLAINFIELD CARBINE
Caliber: 30 U.S. Carbine.
Barrel: 18" four-groove.
Weight: 6½ lbs. **Length:** 35½" over-all.
Stock: Glossy finished hard wood.
Sights: Click adj. open rear.
Features: Gas operated semi-auto carbine. 15-shot detachable magazine.
Price: **$144.00**
Price: Paratrooper model—with telescoping wire stock, front vertical hand grip **$163.50**
Price: Super Enforcer (9" bbl., full p.g.) **$186.50**

Remington 742 Carbine
Same as M742 except: 18½" bbl., 38½" over-all, wgt. 6¾ lbs. Cals: 30-06, 308 Win. **$278.95**

Remington 760 BDL Gamemaster
Same as 760 except: "stepped receiver," Monte Carlo stock with cheekpiece (right or left), whiteline spacer, basket-weave checkering on p.g. and fore-end, black fore-end tip, RKW finish. (13⁵/₁₆"x1⅝"x1¹³/₁₆"x2½"). Cals. 270, 30-06, 308 .... **$267.95**
Also in Peerless (D) and Premier (F) grades ... **$1,200.00** and **$2,400.00**
(F), with gold inlay **$3,600.00**

REMINGTON 742 WOODSMASTER AUTO RIFLE
Caliber: 243 Win., 6mm Rem., 280 Rem., 308 Win. and 30-06.
Barrel: 22" round tapered.
Weight: 7½ lbs. **Length:** 42" over-all
Stock: Walnut (13¼"x1⅝"x2¼") deluxe checkered p.g. and fore-end.
Sights: Gold bead front sight on ramp; step rear sight with windage adj.
Features: Positive cross-bolt safety. Receiver tapped for scope mount. 4-shot clip mag.
Price: **$278.95**
Extra 4-shot clip magazine **$8.95**
Sling strap and swivels (installed) **$15.75**
Peerless (D) and Premier (F) grades .... **$1,200.00** and **$2,400.00**
Premier with gold inlays **$3,600.00**

Remington 760 Gamemaster Carbine
Same as M760 except has 18½" barrel. Wgt. 7¼ lbs., 38½" over-all. Cals: 308 Win. and 30-60 .... **$244.95**

REMINGTON 760 GAMEMASTER SLIDE ACTION
Caliber: 6mm Rem., 243, 270, 308 Win., 30-06.
Barrel: 22" round tapered.
Weight: 7½ lbs. **Length:** 42" over-all.
Stock: Checkered walnut p.g. and fore-end (13¼"x1⅝"x2⅛") RKW finish
Sights: Gold bead front sight on matted ramp, open step adj. sporting rear.
Features: Detachable 4-shot clip. Cross-bolt safety. Receiver tapped for scope mount.
Price: **$244.95**
Sling strap and swivels (installed) **$15.75**
Extra 4-shot clip **$8.25**

CENTERFIRE RIFLES—AUTOLOADING & SLIDE ACTION

RUGER MINI-14 223 CARBINE
Caliber: 223 Rem., 5-shot detachable box magazine.
Barrel: 18½".
Weight: 6.4 lbs. **Length:** 37¼" over-all.
Stock: American hardwood, steel reinforced.
Sights: Ramp front, fully adj. rear.
Features: Fixed piston gas-operated, positive primary extraction. 10 and 20-shot magazines available from Ruger dealers, 30-shot magazine available only to police departments and government agencies.
Price: **$200.00**
Price: As above except in stainless steel, about **$400.00**

RUGER 44 AUTOLOADING DELUXE CARBINE
Caliber: 44 Magnum, 4-shot tubular magazine.
Barrel: 18½" round tapered.
Weight: 5¾ lbs. **Length:** 36¾" over-all.
Stock: One piece American walnut with sling swivels.
Sights: Gold bead front, Ruger adj. peep rear.
Features: Automatic bolt hold-open after last shot, magazine unloading button. Drilled and tapped for scope mount.
Price: **$194.00**

RUGER 44 AUTOLOADING CARBINE
Caliber: 44 Magnum, 4-shot tubular magazine.
Barrel: 18½" round tapered.
Weight: 5¾ lbs. **Length:** 36¾" over-all.
Stock: One-piece walnut p.g. stock (13⅜"x1⅝"x2¼")
Sights: 1/16" front, folding leaf rear sight adj. for e.
Features: Wide, curved trigger. Sliding cross-bolt safety. Receiver tapped for scope mount, unloading button.
Price: **$189.00**

SIG-AMT AUTO RIFLE
Caliber: 308 Win., 20-shot detachable box magazine.
Barrel: 18¾".
Weight: 9½ lbs. **Length:** 39" over-all.
Stock: Walnut stock and fore-end, composition vertical p.g.
Sights: Adj. post front, adj. aperture rear.
Features: Roller-lock breech, gas-assisted action; right-side cocking handle; loaded chamber indicator; no-tool take-down. Winter trigger (optional) allows firing with mittens. Spare parts, magazine, etc. available. From Mandall Shooting Supplies.
Price: **$1,250.00**

SAVAGE MODEL 170 SLIDE ACTION
Caliber: 30-30 or 35 Rem., 3-shot mag.
Barrel: 22" round tapered.
Weight: 6¾ lbs. **Length:** 41½" over-all.
Stock: Walnut (14"x1½"x2½"), with checkered p.g. Hard rubber buttplate.
Sights: Gold bead ramp front, folding-leaf rear.
Features: Hammerless, solid frame tapped for scope mount. Top tang safety.
Price: **$149.95**

Savage Model 170-C Slide Action Rifle
Same as Model 170 except 30-30 only, has 18½" barrel, no Monte Carlo on stock. Silent-Lok feature eliminates slide handle rattle. **$139.50**

SPRINGFIELD ARMORY M1A RIFLE
Caliber: 7.62mm Nato (308), 10 or 20 round box magazine.
Barrel: 25¹/₁₆″ with flash suppressor, 22″ without suppressor.
Weight: 8¾ lbs. **Length:** 44¼″ over-all.
Stock: American walnut or birch with walnut colored heat-resistant fiberglass handguard.
Sights: Military, square blade front, full click-adjustable aperture rear.
Features: Commercial equivalent of the U.S. M-14 service rifle with no provision for automatic firing. From Springfield Armory. Military accessories available including 4X or 6X ART scope and mount.
Price: Standard M1A Rifle $377.78
Price: Match Grade $540.50
Price: Super Match (heavy Premium barrel) $599.95

UNIVERSAL ENFORCER MODEL 3000 AUTO CARBINE
Caliber: 30 M1 Carbine, 30-shot magazine.
Barrel: 10¼″ with 12-groove rifling.
Length: 17¾″. **Weight:** 4½ lbs.
Stocks: American walnut with handguard.
Sights: Gold bead ramp front. Peep rear adj. for w. and e. 14″ sight radius.
Features: Uses surplus 5- or 15-shot magazine. 4½-6 lb. trigger pull.
Price: Blue finish $199.90
Price: Nickel plated finish $224.90
Price: Gold plated finish $224.90

UNIVERSAL 1003 AUTOLOADING CARBINE
Caliber: 30 M1, 5-shot magazine.
Barrel: 18″
Weight: 5½ lbs. **Length:** 35½″ over-all
Stock: American hardwood stock inletted for "issue" sling and oiler, blued metal handguard.
Sights: Blade front aperture rear. With protective wings, adj.
Features: Gas operated, hammerless. Cross lock safety. Receiver tapped for scope mounts.
Price: $139.90
Price: Model 1011 nickel plated, M.C. stock $239.90
Price: Model 1016 gold plated, M.C. stock $248.90

Universal Model 1002 Carbine
Same as Model 1003 except: Military type with metal handguard and bayonet lug. Blue.
Price: $151.90

VALMET M-62/S RIFLE
Caliber: 7.62x39mm, 15- and 30-shot detachable box magazines.
Barrel: 16⅝″.
Weight: 8¾ lbs. **Length:** 36⅝″ over-all.
Stock: Fixed metal tube. Walnut optional.
Sights: Hooded post front adj. for w., tangent peep rear adj. for e.
Features: Finnish semi-automatic version of the AK-47. Basic Kalashnikov design (gas piston operating a rotating bolt assy.). Imported by Interarms.
Price: With metal stock $450.00

VALMET M-71S
Caliber: 223, 15- and 30-shot detachable magazines.
Barrel: 16⅝″.
Weight: 8¾ lbs. **Length:** 36⅝″ over-all.
Stock: Walnut (standard).
Sights: Open tangent rear sight adjustable for elevation. Post front sight with protectors, adjustable for windage.
Features: Finnish semi-automatic version of AK-47. Imported by Interarms.
Price: Walnut stock $475.00

WILKINSON "TERRY" CARBINE
Caliber: 9mm Para., 31-shot magazine.
Barrel: 16³/₁₆″.
Weight: 7 lbs. 2 ozs. **Length:** 28½″ over-all.
Stock: Black P.V.C. plastic stock, grip and fore-end.
Sights: Williams adjustable.
Features: Closed breech, blow-back action. Bolt-type safety and magazine catch. Ejection port has spring operated cover. Receiver dovetailed for scope mount. Semi-auto only. Introduced 1977. From Wilkinson Arms.
Price: $315.00
Price: Extra magazine $18.95

BROWNING CENTENNIAL 92 LEVER ACTION
Caliber: 44 Rem. Mag., 11-shot magazine.
Barrel: 20″ round.
Weight: 5 lbs., 8 oz. **Length:** 37½″ over-all.
Stock: Straight grip stock and classic fore-end in French walnut with high gloss finish. Steel, modified crescent buttplate. (12¾″ x 2″ x 2⅞″).
Sights: Post front, classic cloverleaf rear with notched elevation ramp. Sight radius 16⅝″.
Features: Tubular magazine. Hand-engraved scroll-work on both receiver sides. Centennial inscription with dates hand-engraved on left receiver flat with gold fill. Gold plated saddle ring. Only 6000 Centennial models produced, serial numbered 1878B-0001 through 1878B-6000.
Price: **$219.95**

BROWNING BLR LEVER ACTION RIFLE
Caliber: 243, 308 Win. or 358 Win. 4-shot detachable mag.
Barrel: 20″ round tapered.
Weight: 6 lbs. 15 oz. **Length:** 39¾″ over-all.
Stock: Checkered straight grip and fore-end, oil finished walnut (13¾″x1¾″x2⅜″).
Sights: Gold bead on hooded ramp front; low profile square notch adj. rear.
Features: Wide, grooved trigger; half-cock hammer safety. Receiver tapped for scope mount. Recoil pad installed.
Price: **$299.95**

DIXIE ENGRAVED MODEL 1873 RIFLE
Caliber: 44-40.
Barrel: 23½″, octagon.
Weight: 7¾ lbs. **Length:** 43″ over-all.
Stock: Walnut.
Sights: Blade front, adj. rear.
Features: Engraved and case hardened frame. Duplicate of Winchester 1873. Made in Italy. From Dixie Gun Works.
Price: **$295.00**
Price: Plain, blued **$250.00**

MARLIN 1894 LEVER ACTION CARBINE
Caliber: 44 Magnum, 10 shot tubular magazine
Barrel: 20″ Micro-Groove®.
Weight: 6 lbs. **Length:** 37½″
Stock: American black walnut, straight grip and fore-end. Mar-Shield® finish.
Sights: Hooded ramp front, semi-buckhorn folding rear adj. for w. & e.
Features: Gold plated trigger, receiver tapped for scope mount, offset hammer spur, solid top receiver sand blasted to prevent glare.
Price: **$149.95**

MARLIN 1894 CARBINE 357
Caliber: 357 Magnum, 9-shot tube magazine.
Barrel: 18″ Micro-Groove®.
Weight: 6 lbs. **Length:** 35½″ over-all.
Stock: American black walnut, straight grip and fore-end.
Sights: Bead front, adjustable semi-buckhorn folding rear.
Features: Solid top receiver tapped for scope mount or receiver sight; offset hammer spur. Gold plated steel trigger; receiver top sandblasted to prevent glare. **Available early 1979.**
Price: About **$160.00**

MARLIN 1895 LEVER ACTION RIFLE
Caliber: 45-70, 4-shot tubular magazine.
Barrel: 22″ round.
Weight: 7 lbs. **Length:** 40½″.
Stock: American black walnut, straight grip. Mar-Shield® finish.
Sights: Bead front, semi-buckhorn folding rear adj. for w. and e.
Features: Solid receiver tapped for scope mounts or receiver sights, offset hammer spur.
Price: **$215.95**

MARLIN 444 LEVER ACTION SPORTER
Caliber: 444 Marlin, 4-shot tubular magazine
Barrel: 22″ Micro-Groove®.
Weight: 7½ lbs. **Length:** 40½″
Stock: American black walnut, capped p.g. with white line spacers, recoil pad. Mar-Shield® finish.
Sights: Hooded ramp front, folding semi-buckhorn rear adj. for w. & e.
Features: Gold plated trigger, receiver tapped for scope mount, offset hammer spur; leather sling with detachable swivels.
Price: **$167.95**

MARLIN 336C LEVER ACTION CARBINE
Caliber: 30-30 or 35 Rem., 6-shot tubular magazine
Barrel: 20″ Micro-Groove®.
Weight: 7 lbs. **Length:** 38½″
Stock: Select American black walnut, capped p.g. with white line spacers. Mar-Shield® finish.
Sights: Ramp front with Wide-Scan™ hood, semi-buckhorn folding rear adj. for w. & e.
Features: Gold plated trigger, receiver tapped for scope mount, offset hammer spur, top of receiver sand blasted to prevent glare.
Price: Less scope **$149.95**

Marlin 336A
Same action as the 336C with 24″ round barrel, ½-magazine tube with 5-shot capacity. Blued fore-end cap and sling swivels. Available in 30-30 Win. only **$151.95**

Marlin 336T Lever Action Carbine
Same as the 336C except: straight stock; cal. 30-30 only. Squared finger lever. .... **$149.95.**

Marlin Glenfield 30A Lever Action Carbine
Same as the Marlin 336C except: checkered walnut finished hardwood p.g. stock, 30-30 only, 6-shot. **$136.95**

MOSSBERG MODEL 472 PC LEVER ACTION
Caliber: 30-30 or 35 Rem., 6-shot magazine.
Barrel: 20″.
Weight: 7½ lbs. **Length:** 38½″ over-all.
Stock: Walnut, fluted comb, p.g., rubber buttplate, white line spacers at p.g. cap and butt.
Sights: Ramp front, rear adj. for e.
Features: Trigger moves with lever on opening, hammer-block safety. Solid top receiver with side ejection. Also available with straight grip stock, either cal., same price
Price: **$154.50**

MOSSBERG 472 SC LEVER ACTION
Same as 472 PC except straight grip stock, curved steel buttplate, saddle ring on receiver, no sling swivels. **$154.50**

NAVY ARMS MODEL 66 LEVER ACTION RIFLE
Caliber: 38 Special, 44-40.
Barrel: 16½″, 19″, 24″.
Weight: 9¼ lbs. **Length:** 39½″.
Stock: Walnut.
Sights: Fixed front, folding rear.
Features: Replica of Winchester Model 1866 "Yellowboy." Available with three grades of engraving, selected stock and fore-end at additional cost. 22 LR also available with 16″ bbl. (Trapper's Model). Imported by Navy Arms.
Price: Trappers Carbine **$195.00**
Price: 24″ octagon bbl. (illus.) **$250.00**

NAVY ARMS "1873" MODEL RIFLE
Caliber: 44-40.
Barrel: 24″ (rifle, octagon); 20″ (carbine, round); 16½″ (trapper).
Weight: 9 lbs. (rifle); 7½ lbs. (carbine).
Stock: Walnut.
Sights: Blade front, step adj. rear.
Features: Available in blue, case-hardened or nickel (44-40 only) finish. Sliding dust cover, lever latch. Imported by Navy/Replica.
Price: Rifle **$275.00**
Price: Carbine **$235.00**
Price: Trapper **$235.00**

ROSSI SADDLE-RING CARBINE
Caliber: 38 Spec. (9 rounds), 357 Mag. (8 rounds).
Barrel: 20″.
Weight: 5¾ lbs. **Length:** 37″ over-all.
Stock: Walnut.
Sights: Blade front, Buckhorn rear.
Features: Re-creation of the famous lever-action carbine. Handles 38 and 357 interchangeably. Introduced 1978. Imported by Interarms.
Price: **$195.00**

SAVAGE 99E LEVER ACTION RIFLE
Caliber: 300 Savage, 243 or 308 Win., 5-shot rotary magazine.
Barrel: 22", chrome-moly steel.
Weight: 7 lbs. **Length:** 39¾" over-all.
Stock: Walnut finished with checkered p.g. and fore-end (13½x1½x2½).
Sights: Ramp front with folding leaf sporting rear. Tapped for scope mounts.
Features: Grooved trigger, slide safety locks trigger and lever.
Price: **$204.00**

Savage 99A Lever Action Rifle
Similar to the 99E except: straight-grip walnut stock with schnabel fore-end, top tang safety, no magazine window. Folding leaf rear sight. Available in 250-3000 (250 Savage), 243 or 308 Win. **$233.50**

Savage 99C Lever Action Clip Rifle
Similar to M99A except: Detachable staggered clip magazine with push-button ejection. Wgt. about 6¾ lbs., 41¾" over-all with 22" bbl. cals. 22-250 243, 308 . . . . **$239.95**

Savage 99 CD Lever Action Rifle
Similar to Model 99C except: removable bead ramp front; removable adjustable rear sight; white line recoil pad and p.g. cap; weight 7 lbs., Monte Carlo stock and grooved fore-end; hand checkered; q.d. sling with swivels. Comes in 250-3000, 243 or 308.
Price: **$267.50**

Savage Model 99-358 Lever Action Rifle
Similar to Model 99 CD except has straight-grip stock, no checkering, chambered for 358 Win., 6-shot rotary magazine with cartridge counter, no Monte Carlo, weight 7 lbs., removable ramp front sight, folding leaf rear. Has vent. recoil pad, swivel studs. Introduced 1977. . . . . **$241.00**

WESTERN FIELD 72 LEVER ACTION CARBINE
Caliber: 30-30, 6-shot magazine.
Barrel: 20".
Weight: 7½ lbs. **Length:** 38½" over-all.
Stock: Walnut finished hardwood.
Sights: Ramp front, adj. rear.
Features: Trigger moves with lever on opening, hammer-block safety. Solid top receiver with side ejection. Scope not included. Ward article No. 10772.
Price: Standard Model **$139.99**

WINCHESTER 94 LEVER ACTION CARBINE
Caliber: 30-30, (12" twist). 6-shot tubular mag.
Barrel: 20"
Weight: 6½ lbs. **Length:** 37¾" over-all
Stock: Walnut straight grip stock and fore-end (13"x1¾"x2½").
Sights: Bead front sight on ramp with removable cover; open rear. Tapped for receiver sights.
Features: Solid frame, top ejection, half-cock hammer safety.
Price: **$140.95**

Winchester 94 Antique Carbine
Same as M94 except: color case-hardened and scroll-engraved receiver, brass-plated loading gate and saddle ring. 30-30 only **$150.95**

CENTERFIRE RIFLES—LEVER ACTION

Winchester Antlered Game Model 94 Carbine

Similar to standard Model 94 except has antique gold plated receiver, lever, tang and barrel bands, and gold-colored medallion in stock. Medallion and receiver engraved with elk, moose, deer and caribou. Semi-fancy walnut stock and extended fore-end with high-luster finish. Fine cut checkering. Curved steel buttplate. Barrel is 20½".
Price: **$375.00**

Winchester Legendary Lawmen Commemorative

Similar to standard Model 94 except has engraved antique silver-finished receiver; on right side is a marshal's badge and a lawman astride his galloping mount. The left side shows a lawman riding back through town with an outlaw in tow. All scenes are surrounded by attractive scrollwork. The magazine tube runs the full length of the blued 16-inch Trapper barrel. Both barrel bands have antique silver finish; right barrel inscription reads: "Legendary Lawmen." Stock and fore-end are of semi-fancy American walnut with deep cut checkering, satin finish. Buttplate is blued. Buttstock has a special nickel-silver medallion. Introduced 1978.
Price: **$375.00**

WINCHESTER MODEL 94 BIG BORE XTR

Caliber: 375 Win., 6-shot magazine.
Barrel: 20".
Weight: 6⅛ lbs. **Length:** 37¾" over-all.
Stock: American walnut with fine cut checkering, warm rich color. Satin finish.
Sights: Hooded ramp front, semi-buckhorn rear adjustable for w. & e.
Features: All external metal parts have Winchester's new deep blue high polish finish. Stock measurements are: 13¼" x 1¾" x 2½". Rifling twist 1 in 12". Rubber recoil pad fitted to buttstock. Introduced 1978.
Price: .... **Not Available**

CENTERFIRE RIFLES—BOLT ACTION

ALPINE BOLT ACTION RIFLE

Caliber: 22-250, 243 Win., 264 Win., 270, 30-06, 308, 308 Norma Mag., 7mm Rem. Mag., 8mm, 300 Win. Mag., 5-shot magazine (3 for magnum).
Barrel: 23" (std. cals.), 24" (mag.).
Weight: 7½ lbs.
Stock: European walnut. Full p.g. and Monte Carlo; checkered p.g. and fore-end; rubber recoil pad; white line spacers; sling swivels.
Sights: Ramp front, open rear adj. for w. and e.
Features: Made by Firearms Co. Ltd. in England. Imported by Mandall Shooting Supplies.
Price: Custom Grade **$274.95**

BROWNING BBR BOLT ACTION RIFLE

Caliber: 25-06, 270, 30-06, 7mm Rem. Mag., 300 Win. Mag.
Barrel: 24" medium sporter weight with recessed muzzle.
Weight: 8 lbs. **Length:** 44½" over-all.
Stock: Select American walnut cut to lines of Monte Carlo sporter with full p.g. and high cheek piece; 18 l.p.i. checkering. Recoil pad on magnums.
Sights: None fitted. Drilled and tapped for scope mounts.
Features: Short throw (60°) bolt with fluted surface, 9 locking lugs, plunger-type ejector, adjustable trigger is grooved and gold plated. Hinged floorplate with detachable box magazine (4 rounds in standard cals, 3 in mags). Convenient slide safety on tang. Special anti-warp aluminum fore-end insert. Low profile swivel studs. Introduced 1978.
Price: **$299.95**

CHAMPLIN RIFLE

Caliber: All std. chamberings, including 458 Win. and 460 Wea. Many wildcats on request.
Barrel: Any length up to 26" for octagon. Choice of round, straight taper octagon, or octagon with integral quarter rib, front sight ramp and sling swivel stud.
Length: 45" over-all. **Weight:** About 8 lbs.
Stock: Hand inletted, shaped and finished. Checkered to customer specs. Select French, Circassian or claro walnut. Steel p.g. cap, trap buttplate or recoil pad.
Sights: Bead on ramp front, 3-leaf folding rear.
Features: Right or left hand Champlin action, tang safety or optional shroud safety, Canjar adj. trigger, hinged floorplate.
Price: From **$2,200.00**

CENTERFIRE RIFLES—BOLT ACTION

COLT SAUER RIFLE
Caliber: 25-06, 270, 30-06, (std.), 7mm Rem. Mag., 300 Wea. Mag., 300 Win. Mag. (Magnum).
Barrel: 24", round tapered.
Length: 43¾" over-all. **Weight:** 8 lbs. (std.).
Stock: American walnut, cast-off M.C. design with cheekpiece. Fore-end tip and p.g. cap rosewood with white spacers. Hand checkering.
Sights: None furnished. Specially designed scope mounts for any popular make scope furnished.
Features: Unique barrel/receiver union, non-rotating bolt with cam-actuated locking lugs, tang-type safety locks sear. Detachable 3- and 4-shot magazines.
Price: Standard cals. ...... $649.95   Magnum cals. $649.95

Colt Sauer Short Action Rifle
Same as standard rifle except chambered for 22-250, 243 and 308 Win. 24" bbl., 43" over-all. Weighs 7½ lbs. 3-shot magazine. $649.95

COLT SAUER GRAND AFRICAN
Caliber: 458 Win. Mag.
Barrel: 24", round tapered.
Length: 44½" over-all. **Weight:** 10½ lbs.
Stock: Solid African bubinga wood, cast-off M.C. with cheekpiece, contrasting rosewood fore-end and p.g. caps with white spacers. Checkered fore-end and p.g.
Sights: Ivory bead hooded ramp front, adj. sliding rear.
Price: $769.95

Du BIEL ARMS BOLT ACTION RIFLES
Caliber: Standard calibers 22-250 thru 458 Win. Mag. Selected wildcat calibers available.
Barrel: Selected weights and lengths. Douglas Premium.
Weight: About 9 lbs.
Stock: Five styles. Walnut, maple, laminates. Hand checkered.
Sights: None furnished. Receiver has integral milled bases.
Features: Basically a custom-made rifle. Left or right-hand models available. Five-lug locking mechanism; 36 degree bolt rotation; adjustable Canjar trigger; oil or epoxy stock finish; Presentation recoil pad; jeweled and chromed bolt body; sling swivel studs; lever latch or button floorplate release. All steel action and parts. Introduced 1978. From Du Biel Arms.
Price: Rollover Model, left or right-hand $1,750.00
Price: Thumbhole (illus.) $1,750.00
Price: Classic $1,750.00
Price: Modern Classic $1,750.00

DUMOULIN BOLT ACTION RIFLE
Caliber: All commercial calibers.
Barrel: 25".
Weight: 7 lbs. **Length:** 43".
Stock: French walnut with rosewood p.g. cap and fore-end tip, standard or skip line checkering, recoil pad.
Sights: Optional, available at extra cost.
Features: Made to customer requirements using Sako or FN action, with or without engraving (3 grades available). Imported from Belgium by Firearms Center.
Price: From $1,350.00

GOLDEN EAGLE MODEL 7000 RIFLE
Caliber: 22-250, 243, 25-06, 270 Win., 270 Wea. Mag., 7mm Rem. Mag., 30-06, 300 Win. Mag., 300 Wea. Mag., 338 Win. Mag., 375 H&H, 458 Win. Mag.
Barrel: 24" or 26".
Weight: 7¾ lbs. (8¾ lbs. in 338 and 375, 10½ lbs. in 458) **Length:** 43½" over-all (24" barrel).
Stock: American walnut, Monte Carlo, hand checkered p.g. and fore-end. Vent. recoil pad.
Sights: None furnished (except on 375 and 458). Drilled and tapped for scope mounting.
Features: Tang safety, five bolt locking lugs, grip cap with Golden Eagle head. Four-shot capacity in standard calibers, three-shot in magnums. From Golden Eagle Firearms.
Price: Std. cals. $399.00
Price: Mag. cals. $399.00
Price: African cals. $429.00

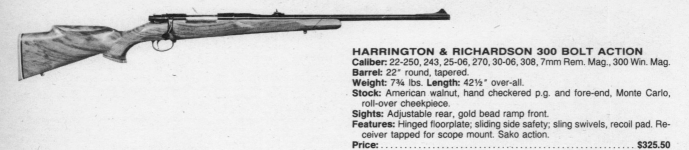

HARRINGTON & RICHARDSON 300 BOLT ACTION
Caliber: 22-250, 243, 25-06, 270, 30-06, 308, 7mm Rem. Mag., 300 Win. Mag.
Barrel: 22″ round, tapered.
Weight: 7¾ lbs. **Length:** 42½″ over-all.
Stock: American walnut, hand checkered p.g. and fore-end, Monte Carlo, roll-over cheekpiece.
Sights: Adjustable rear, gold bead ramp front.
Features: Hinged floorplate; sliding side safety; sling swivels, recoil pad. Receiver tapped for scope mount. Sako action.
Price: $325.50

Ithaca LSA-55 Deluxe Bolt Action
Same as the std. except rollover cheekpiece, fore-end tip and pistol grip cap of rosewood with white spacers. Scope mount rings supplied. Sling swivels installed.
Price: 222, 243, 308, 22-250 & 6mm $369.95

ITHACA LSA-55 STANDARD BOLT ACTION RIFLE
Caliber: 222, 243, 308, 22-250, 6mm Rem.
Barrel: 23″ round tapered, full-floating.
Weight: About 6½ lbs. **Length:** 41½″ over-all
Stock: Hand checkered walnut, Monte Carlo with built-in swell on p.g.
Sights: Removable rear adj. for w. & e. ramp front.
Features: Detachable 3-shot magazine, adj. trigger, top tang safety. Receiver tapped for scope mounts.
Price: 243, 308, 22-250, 6mm & 222 . . . . $329.95
Price: 270, 30-06 & 25-06, 7mm Rem. Mag., 300 Win. Mag. (LSA-65 Deluxe)
. . . . $369.95
Price: 222 heavy bbl. $399.95
Price: Heavy Bbl., 22-250 . . . . $399.95

KLEINGUENTHER K-15 INSTA-FIRE RIFLE
Caliber: 22-250, 243, 25-06, 270, 7x57, 7mm Rem. Mag., 30-06, 300 Win. Mag., 308 Win., 308 Norma, 375 H&H, 458 Win., 270-300 Wea. Mag.
Barrel: 24″, 26″.
Weight: 7⅛ lbs. **Length:** 43½″ over-all.
Stock: Available in light, medium or dark European walnut. Monte Carlo, hand checkered, cheekpiece, rosewood fore-end tip, rosewood p.g. cap with diamond inlay.
Sights: None furnished. Drilled and tapped for scope mounts. Iron sights optional.
Features: Ultra fast lock/ignition time. Rubber recoil pad, hidden clip, external trigger adj., recessed bolt face, 60° bolt lift. Lifetime warranty. Imported from Germany by Kleinguenther's.
Price: Std. cals. . . . . $549.00   Mag. cals. $549.00

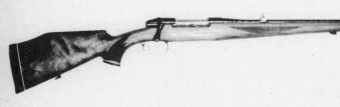

MANNLICHER MODEL SL
Caliber: 222, 222 Rem. Mag., 223, 5.6x50 Mag.
Barrel: 20″ (full stock), 23½″ (half stock).
Weight: 5½ lbs. **Length:** 38¼″ over-all (20″ bbl.).
Stock: Hand checkered walnut with Monte Carlo cheekpiece. Either full Mannlicher or half stock.
Sights: Ramp front, open U-notch rear.
Features: Choice of interchangeable single or double set triggers. Extra magazine included. Detachable "Makrolon" rotary magazine. 6 rear locking lugs. Drilled and tapped for scope mounts. Custom hand engraving and stock carving avail. Imported by Steyr-Daimler-Puch of America.
Price: $496.00
Price: Carbine $496.00
Price: Varmint (222 Rem. only) $496.00

MANNLICHER-SCHOENAUER M-72 MODEL L/M
Caliber: 22-250, 5.6x57, 6mm Rem. 243, 6.5x57, 270, 7x57, 7x64, 30-06, 308 Win.
Barrel: 20″ (full stock), 23½″ (half stock).
Weight: 7¼ lbs. (full stock). **Length:** 40″ over-all (full stock).
Stock: Full Mannlicher or standard half stock, oil or varnish finish. Rubber recoil pad, hand checkered walnut, Monte Carlo cheekpiece.
Sights: Ramp front, open U-notch rear.
Features: 6 forward locking lugs. 60° bolt throw, wing-type safety. Choice of interchangeable single or double set triggers. Drilled and tapped for scope mounting. Imported by Steyr-Daimler-Puch of America.
Price: Rifle $692.50
Price: Half-stock tropical (S/T) $840.00

Mannlicher Model S
Same as Model SL except available in 6.5x68, 257 Weatherby Mag., 264 Win. Mag., 7mm Rem. Mag., 300 H&H, 308 Norma Mag., 8x68S, 338 Win. Mag., 9.3x64, 375 H&H Mag. Avail. only with half-stock. Extra magazine fits in buttstock recess $644.95

MANNLICHER MODEL M
Caliber: 6.5x55, 270, 7x57, 7x64, 30-06, 8x57JS, 9.3x62, 5-shot.
Barrel: 20" (full stock).
Weight: 6½ lbs. (full stock). **Length:** 39" over-all (full stock).
Stock: Full Mannlicher or standard half stock. Rubber recoil pad, hand checkered walnut. Monte Carlo cheekpiece.
Sights: Ramp front, open U-notch rear.
Features: Extra magazine included. Choice of interchangeable double set or single trigger. Detachable 5-shot rotary magazine. 6 rear locking lugs. Drilled and tapped for scope mounting. Imported by Steyr-Daimler-Puch of America.
Price: **$551.25**
Price: Left-hand version **$588.00**
Price: Professional model (synthetic stock) **$419.95**

Mannlicher Model L Varmint
Same as Model M except available only in 22-250, 5.6x57, 6mm Rem., 243, 308 Win. Custom hand engraving and stock carving as well as heavy barrel varmint version available **$507.00**

MANNLICHER MODEL SSG MATCH
Caliber: 308 Win.
Barrel: 25½".
Weight: 8½ lbs. **Length:** 44½" over-all.
Stock: Walnut or synthetic.
Sights: Hooded blade front, folding leaf rear or Walther diopter match sight.
Features: Extra magazine included with rifle. 6 rear locking lugs, 60° bolt throw. Adj. trigger. Optional 10-shot magazine available. Imported by Steyr-Daimler-Puch of America.
Price: Synthetic stock **$690.00**
Price: Walnut **$741.50**
Price: Marksman, synthetic stock **$520.25**
Price: Marksman, wood stock **$571.25**

MANNLICHER-SCHOENAUER M-72 MODEL S
Caliber: 6.5x68, 7mm Rem. Mag., 8x68S, 9.3x64, 375 H&H Mag.
Barrel: 25½".
Weight: 8½ lbs. **Length:** 46" over-all.
Stock: Walnut half-stock style, varnished or oil finish. Rubber recoil pad, hand checkered. Monte Carlo cheekpiece.
Sights: Hooded ramp front, U-notch open rear.
Features: 6 forward locking lugs. 60° bolt throw. Wing-type safety. Choice of interchangeable single or double set triggers. Drilled and tapped for scope mounts. Custom engraving and stock carving avail. Imported by Steyr-Daimler-Puch of America.
Price: **$787.50**

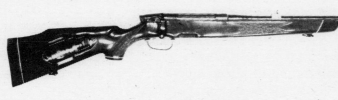

Mannlicher Model S/T
Same as Model S except available only in 9.3x64, 375 H&H, 458 Win. Mag., has 23½" barrel (458 has 23½"). Choice of interchangeable single or double set triggers. Detachable 4-shot Makrolon rotary magazine. Extra magazine (included) fits in recess in buttstock **$661.50**

MARK X MANNLICHER-STYLE CARBINE
Caliber: 270, 7x57, 30-06, 308 Win.
Barrel: 20".
Weight: 7½ lbs. **Length:** 40" over-all.
Stock: Hand checkered European walnut.
Sights: Ramp front with removable hood; open rear adj. for w. and e.
Features: Quick detachable sling swivels; fully adj. trigger; blue steel fore-end cap; white line spacers at p.g. cap and buttplate. Mark X Mauser action. Imported by Interarms.
Price: **$299.00**

MARK X VISCOUNT RIFLE
Caliber: 22-250; 243; 25-06; 270; 7x57; 7mm Rem. Mag.; 308 Win.; 30-06; 300 Win. Mag.
Barrel: 24".
Weight: 7½ lbs. **Length:** 44".
Stock: Genuine Walnut stock, hand checkered with 1" sling swivels.
Sights: Ramp front with removable hood, open rear sight ajustable for windage and elevation.
Features: One piece trigger guard with hinged floor plate, drilled and tapped for scope mounts and receiver sight, hammer-forged chrome vanadium steel barrel. Imported by Interarms.
Price: With adj. trigger, sights, from **$227.00**
Price: With adj. trigger, no sights, from **$215.00**

MARK X CAVALIER RIFLE
Caliber: 22-250; 243; 25-06; 270; 7x57; 7mm Rem. Mag.; 308 Win.; 30-06; 300 Win. Mag.
Barrel: 24".
Weight: 7½ lbs. **Length:** 44".
Stock: Checkered Walnut with Rosewood fore-end tip and pistol grip cap, Monte Carlo cheek piece and recoil pad.
Sights: Ramp front with removable hood, open rear adjustable for windage and elevation.
Features: Contemporary-styled stock with sculptured accents; roll over cheek piece and flat bottom fore-end. Adjustable trigger and quick detachable sling swivels, standard. Receiver drilled and tapped for receiver sights and scope mounts. Also available without sights. Imported by Interarms.
Price: From **$287.00**

CENTERFIRE RIFLES—BOLT ACTION

MARK X RIFLE
Caliber: 22-250; 243, 270, 308 Win.; 30-06; 25-06; 7×57; 7 mm Rem. Mag; 300 Win. Mag.
Barrel: 24".
Weight: 7½ lbs. **Length:** 44".
Stock: Hand checkered walnut, Monte Carlo, white line spacers on p.g. cap, buttplate and fore-end tip.
Sights: Ramp front with removable hood, open rear adj. for w. and e.
Features: Sliding safety, quick detachable sling swivels, hinged floorplate. Also available as actions or bbld. actions. Imported from Europe by Interarms.
Price: With adj. trigger and sights, from $249.00
Price: With adj. trigger, no sights, from $237.00

MARK X CONTINENTAL MANNLICHER-STYLE CARBINE
Caliber: 243, 270, 7x57, 308, 30-06.
Barrel: 20".
Weight: 7½ lbs. **Length:** 40" over-all.
Stock: Hand checkered European walnut. Straight European-style comb with sculptured cheekpiece.
Sights: Ramp front with removable hood; open rear adj. for w. and e.
Features: Similar to Mannlicher-Style except for stock differences noted above, single adjustable or double-set triggers, classic "butter-knife" bolt handle. Button release hinged floorplate. Imported by Interarms.
Price: Adj. trigger, with sights $319.00
Price: Double-set triggers, with sights $339.00

MARK X ALASKAN MAGNUM RIFLE
Caliber: 375 H&H, 458 Win. Mag.; 3-shot magazine.
Barrel: 24".
Weight: 8¼ lbs. **Length:** 32" over-all.
Stock: Select walnut with crossbolt; hand checkered p.g. and fore-end; Monte Carlo; sling swivels.
Sights: Hooded ramp front; open rear adj. for w. & e.
Features: Hinged floorplate; right-hand thumb (tang) safety; adj. trigger. From Interarms.
Price: $319.00

MOSSBERG MODEL RM-7A, B BOLT ACTION RIFLE
Caliber: 30-06, 7mm Rem. Mag.
Barrel: 22" (30-06), 24" (7mm Rem. Mag.), tapered, AC-KRO-GRUV.
Weight: 7½ lbs. **Length:** 44" over-all (30-06).
Stock: American walnut, classic-style, with checkered p. g. and fore-end. Decorative p.g. cap, non-slip rubber buttplate with black spacer.
Sights: Gold bead front on ramp, adjustable folding leaf rear.
Features: Rotary magazine; 3-position bolt safety; sling swivel studs. Receiver drilled and tapped for scope mounting. Introduced 1978.
Price: $217.95

MOSSBERG 800 SERIES BOLT ACTION RIFLE
Caliber: 22-250, 243 and 308. 4-shot magazine.
Barrel: 22" AC-KRO-GRUV round tapered.
Weight: 7½ lbs. **Length:** 42" over-all.
Stock: Walnut, Monte Carlo, checkered p.g. and fore-end.
Sights: Gold bead ramp front, adj. folding-leaf rear.
Features: Top tang safety, hinged floorplate, 1" sling swivels installed. Receiver tapped for scope mounts.
Price: $194.95

Mossberg 800 CVT Varmint Target Rifle
Model 800 with heavy 24" bbl, target scope bases, no iron sights. Cals. 243 and 22-250 only. 44" overall, wgt. about 9½ lbs. $204.95

MOSSBERG 810 AH BOLT ACTION RIFLE
Caliber: 30-06, 5-shot magazine.
Barrel: 22", straight taper.
Weight: 8 lbs. **Length:** 43½" over-all.
Stock: Walnut Monte Carlo with checkered fore-end and capped p.g. recoil pad and sling swivels installed.
Sights: Gold bead on ramp front, folding-leaf rear.
Features: Receiver tapped for metallic sight or scope mounts. Top tang safety. Hinged floorplate.
Price: $204.95
Price: 270 cal. is Model 810CH $204.95

Mossberg 810 BH Bolt Action Rifle
Same as 810AH except in 7mm Rem. Mag., 4-shot magazine, 24" barrel.
Price: $212.95

Consult our Directory pages for the location of firms mentioned.

PARKER-HALE SUPER 1200 BOLT ACTION RIFLE
Caliber: 22-250, 243 Win., 6mm Rem., 25-06, 270 Win., 30-06, 308 Win., 7mm Rem. Mag., 300 Win. Mag.
Barrel: 24".
Weight: 7¼ lbs. **Length:** 45".
Stock: 13.5" x 1.8" x 2.3". Hand checkered walnut, rosewood p.g. and fore-end caps, fitted rubber recoil pad with white line spacers.
Sights: Bead front, folding adj. rear. Receiver tapped for scope mounts.
Features: 3-way side safety, single-stage adj. trigger, hinged mag. floorplate. Varmint Model (1200V) has glass-bedded action, free-floating bbl., avail. in 22-250, 6mm Rem., 25-06, 243 Win., without sights. Imported from England by Jana.
Price: . . . . $274.95 ($289.95, mag. cals.)
Price: 1200V $289.95

REMINGTON 700 "CLASSIC" RIFLE

Caliber: 22-250, 6mm Rem., 243, 270, 30-06, 7mm Rem. Mag.
Barrel: 22" (6mm, 243, 270, 30-06), 24" (22-250, 7mm Rem. Mag.).
Weight: About 7 lbs. **Length:** 43½" over-all (22-250).
Stock: American walnut, 20 l.p.i. checkering on p.g. and fore-end. Classic styling. Satin finish.
Sights: Hooded ramp front with gold bead, sliding-ramp rear adjustable for w. & e.
Features: A "classic" version of the M700ADL with straight comb stock. Fitted with rubber butt pad on all but magnum calibers, which has a full recoil pad. Sling swivel studs installed.
Price: All cals. except 7mm Rem. Mag. **$279.95**
Price: 7mm Rem. Mag. **$294.95**

REMINGTON 700 ADL BOLT ACTION RIFLE

Caliber: 222, 22-250, 6mm Rem., 243, 25-06, 270, 308 and 30-06.
Barrel: 22" or 24" round tapered.
Weight: 7 lbs. **Length:** 41½" to 43½"
Stock: Walnut, RKW finished p.g. stock with impressed checkering, Monte Carlo (13⅜"x1⅝"x2⅜").
Sights: Gold bead ramp front; removable, step-adj. rear with windage screw.
Features: Side safety, receiver tapped for scope mounts.
Price: **$244.95**
Price: 7mm Rem. Mag. **$259.95**

Remington 700 Safari
Same as the 700 BDL except 375 H&H or 458 Win. Magnum calibers only. Hand checkered, oil finished stock with recoil pad installed. Delivery time is about five months. **$470.00**

Remington 700 BDL Bolt Action Rifle

Same as 700-ADL, except: skip-line checkering; black fore-end tip and p.g. cap, white line spacers. Matted receiver top, quick release floorplate. Hooded ramp front sight. Q.D. swivels and 1" sling **Price:** **$279.95**
Available also in 17 Rem., 7mm Rem. Mag. and 300 Win. Mag., 8mm Rem. Mag., caliber. 44½" over-all, weight 7½ lbs. **$294.95**
Peerless Grade .... **$950.00**   Premier Grade **$1,900.00**

Remington 700 BDL Varmint
Same as 700 BDL, except: 24" heavy bbl., 43½" over-all, wgt. 9 lbs. Cals. 222, 223, 22-250, 6mm Rem., 243, 25-06, and 308. No Sights. . **$294.95**

Remington 700 C Custom Rifle

Same as the 700 BDL except choice of 20", 22" or 24" bbl. with or without sights. Jewelled bolt, with or without hinged floor plate. Select American walnut stock is hand checkered, rosewood fore-end & grip cap. Hand lapped barrel. 16 weeks for delivery after placing order **$550.00**

Remington 700BDL Left Hand
Same as 700 BDL except: mirror-image left-hand action, stock. 270, 30-06 **$284.95;** 7mm Rem. Mag. **$299.95**

REMINGTON 788 BOLT ACTION RIFLE

Caliber: 222 (5-shot), 22-250, 223 Rem., 6mm Rem., 243, and 308 (4-shot).
Barrel: 22" round tapered (24" in 222, 223 and 22-250).
Weight: 7-7½ lbs. **Length:** 41⅝" over-all.
Stock: Walnut-finished hardwood with Monte Carlo and p.g. (13⅝"x1⅞"x2⅝").
Sights: Blade ramp front, open rear adj. for w. & e.
Features: Detachable box magazine, thumb safety, receiver tapped for scope mounts.
Price: **$174.95**
Sling strap and swivels, installed **$9.50**
Model 788 with Universal Model UE 4x scope, mounts and rings in cals. 6mm Rem., 243 Win., 308 and 22-250 .... **$199.95**

Remington 788 Left Hand Bolt Action
Same as 788 except cals. 6mm & 308 only and left hand stock and action.
Price: **$179.95**

CENTERFIRE RIFLES—BOLT ACTION

Ruger Model 77 Magnum Round Top
Same as Model 77 except: round top receiver, drilled and tapped for standard scope mounts. Open sights are standard equipment. Calibers 25-06, 270, 30-06, 7mm Rem. Mag., 300 Win. Mag.

Price: All cals. **$245.00**

RUGER 77 BOLT ACTION RIFLE
Caliber: 22-250, 220 Swift, 243, 6mm, 308, 358 Win. (5-shot).
Barrel: 22″ round tapered.
Weight: 6¾ lbs. **Length:** 42″ over-all.
Stock: Hand checkered American walnut (13¾″x1⅝″x2⅛″), p.g. cap, sling swivel studs and recoil pad.
Sights: Optional gold bead ramp front, folding leaf adj. rear, or scope rings.
Features: Integral scope mount bases, diagonal bedding system, hinged floorplate, adj. trigger, tang safety. Scope optional.
Price: With Ruger steel scope rings (77R) **$245.00**
Price: With rings and open sights (77RS) **$260.00**

Ruger Model 77 Magnum Rifle
Similar to Ruger 77 except: magnum-size action. Calibers 25-06, 270, 7x57, 30-06 (5-shot), 7mm Rem. Mag., 300 Win. Mag., 338 Win. Mag., 458 Win. Mag. (3-shot). 270 and 30-06 have 22″ bbl., all others have 24″. Weight and length vary with caliber.
Price: With rings only, 338 Win. Mag. **$260.00**
Price: With rings only, all cals. except 458 .... **$245.00**
Price: With rings and sights, 338 .... **$266.00**
Price: With rings and sights, 458 .... **$323.00**
Price: With rings and sights, other cals. **$260.00**
Price: With rings and sights, 458, Circassian walnut **$394.00**

RUGER MODEL 77 VARMINT
Caliber: 22-250, 220 Swift, 243, 6mm, 25-06, 308.
Barrel: 24″ heavy straight tapered, 26″ in 220 Swift.
Weight: Approx. 9 lbs. **Length:** Approx. 44″ over-all.
Stock: American walnut, similar in style to Magnum Rifle.
Sights: Barrel drilled and tapped for target scope blocks. Integral scope mount bases in receiver.
Features: Ruger diagonal bedding system, Ruger steel 1″ scope rings supplied. Fully adj. trigger. Barreled actions available in any of the standard calibers and barrel lengths.
Price: **$245.00**
Price: Barreled action only all cals. except 338, 458 .... **$184.00**
Price: Bbld. action, 338 .... **$197.00**
Price: Bbld. action, 458 .... **$253.00**

Sako Carbine
Same action as the Standard Sporter except has full "Mannlicher" style stock, 20″ barrel, weighs 7½ lbs. 30-06 only. Introduced 1977. From Stoeger.
Price: 30-06 only **$425.00**

SAKO MODEL 78 BOLT ACTION
Caliber: 22 LR or 22 Hornet.
Barrel: 22½″.
Weight: 6¾ lbs.
Stock: Hand checkered European walnut.
Sights: None furnished; receiver has rail-type scope mount bases.
Features: New action design with tapered sporter weight barrel, adjustable trigger, detachable box magazine (5 shots in 22 LR, 4 shots in Hornet). Shrouded bolt, silent sliding safety, low bolt uplift. Introduced 1977. Imported by Stoeger.
Price: 22 LR **$229.95**
Price: 22 Hornet **$274.95**

Sako Deluxe Sporter
Same action as Standard Sporter except has select wood, Rosewood p.g. cap and fore-end tip. Fine checkering on top surfaces of integral dovetail bases, bolt sleeve, bolt handle root and bolt knob. Vent. recoil pad, skip-line checkering, mirror finish bluing.
Price: 222 or 223 cals. **$495.00**
Price: 22-250, 243, 308 .... **$495.00**
Price: 270, 30-06 .... **$495.00**
Price: 7mm Rem. Mag. 375 H&H, 338 Mag. **$520.00**

SAKO STANDARD SPORTER
Caliber: 222, 22-250, 220 Swift, 223, (short action); 243, (medium action); 25-06, 270, 30-06, 7mm Mag., 300 Mag., 338 Mag., 375 H&H Mag. (long action).
Barrel: 23″ (222, 223, 243), 24″ (other cals.).
Weight: 6¾ lbs. (short); 6¾ lbs. (med.); 8 lbs. (long).
Stock: Hand-checkered European walnut.
Sights: None furnished.
Features: Adj. trigger, hinged floorplate. 222 and 223 have short action, 243 has medium action, others are long action. Imported from Finland by Stoeger.
Price: Short action **$369.95**
Price: Medium action **$369.95**
Price: Long action **$369.95**
Price: Magnum cals. **$395.00**

Sako Heavy Barrel
Same as std. Super Sporter except has beavertail fore-end; available in 222, 223 (short action), 22-250, 243, (medium action); 25-06, 7mm Mag. (long action). Weight from 8¼ to 8½ lbs. 5-shot magazine capacity.
Price: 222, 223 (short action) **$395.00**
Price: 22-250, 243 (medium action) **$395.00**
Price: 25-06, 7mm Mag. (long action) **$395.00**

Savage 110C Bolt Action Rifle

Same as the 110B except: Detachable box magazine. Cals. 243 (right-hand only), 270 and 30-06 (4-shot). Also in 7mm Rem. (3-shot).
Price: Right hand, std. cals. **$217.00** Left hand (110 CL), std. cals. **$225.00**
Price: Right hand, mag. cals. **$233.50** Left hand, mag. cals. **$240.75**

SAVAGE 110B, 110BL BOLT ACTION RIFLE
Caliber: 243, 270, 30-06, 5-shot.
Barrel: 22″.
Weight: 7 lbs. **Length:** 43″ over-all.
Stock: Select walnut with Monte Carlo, checkered p.g. and fore-end.
Sights: Removeable ramp front, folding leaf rear.
Features: Tapped for scope mounting, free floating barrel, top tang safety, internal box magazine, hard rubber buttplate.
Price: Right hand 110B **$210.00**
Price: Left hand 110BL **$214.50**

SAVAGE 110S, SILHOUETTE RIFLE
Caliber: 308 Win., 5-shot.
Barrel: 22″, heavy tapered.
Weight: 8 lbs., 10 ozs. **Length:** 43″ over-all.
Stock: Special Silhouette stock of select walnut. High fluted comb, Wundhammer swell, stippled p.g. and fore-end. Rubber recoil pad.
Sights: None. Receiver drilled and tapped for scope mounting.
Features: Receiver has satin blue finish to reduce glare. Barrel is free-floating. Top tang safety, internal magazine. Available in right-hand only. Introduced 1978.
Price: **$215.00**

SAVAGE MODEL 111 CHIEFTAIN BOLT ACTION RIFLE
Caliber: 30-06, 243, 270 (5-shot), 7mm Rem. Mag. (4-shot).
Barrel: 22″ (standard cals.), 24″ (mag. cals.). Free floating.
Weight: 7½ lbs. (std.), 8¼ (mag.) **Length:** 43″ over-all, 45″ for mag.
Stock: Walnut, Monte Carlo, hand checkered fore-end and p.g., p.g. cap, white spacers.
Sights: Removable hooded ramp front, open rear adj. for w. and e.
Features: Top tang safety, ejector clip magazine, teardrop design bolt handle. Drilled and tapped for scope mounts.
Price: Standard calibers **$255.50**
Price: Magnum calibers **$265.00**

SAVAGE 112-V BOLT ACTION RIFLE
Caliber: 222, 22-250, 220 Swift, 25-06, single shot.
Barrel: 26″ tapered, ¹³/₁₆″ at muzzle.
Weight: 9¼ lbs. **Length:** 47″ over-all.
Stock: Walnut. Free floating varmint stock with high, deeply fluted comb, Wundhammer swell at p.g., Hand checkered (20 l.p.i.). White spacer at recoil pad, 1¼″ q.d. swivels.
Sights: None. Drilled and tapped for scope mounting.
Features: Designed expressly for varmint shooting. Recessed bolt face; 2 gas ports; top tang safety; chrome moly steel barrel. Stock measures 13½″, drop at comb and heel ⁹/₁₆″ (measured from barrel centerline).
Price: **$262.50**

SAVAGE 340 CLIP REPEATER
Caliber: 22 Hornet, 222 Rem., 223 (4-shot) and 30-30 (3-shot).
Barrel: 24″ and 22″ respectively.
Weight: About 6½ lbs. **Length:** 40″-42″
Stock: Walnut, Monte Carlo, checkered p.g. and fore-end white line spacers.
Sights: Gold bead ramp front, folding-leaf rear.
Features: Detachable clip magazine, sliding thumb safety, receiver tapped for scope mounts.
Price: **$139.95**

SHILEN DGA BENCHREST SINGLE SHOT RIFLES

Caliber: 22, 22-250, 6x47, 308.
Barrel: Select/Match grade stainless. Choice of caliber, twist, chambering, contour or length shown in Shilen's catalog.
Weight: To customer specs.
Stock: Fiberglass. Choice of Classic or thumbhole pattern.
Sights: None furnished. Specify intended scope and mount.
Features: Fiberglass stocks are spray painted with acrylic enamel in choice of basic color. Comes with Benchrest trigger. Basically a custom-made rifle. From Shilen Rifles, Inc.
Price: DGA Benchrest Rifle $695.50
Price: Conetrol bases and rings $38.35
Price: Buehler bases and rings $32.50
Price: Redfield bases and rings $29.80

SHILEN DGA RIFLES

Caliber: 17 Rem., 222, 223, 22-250, 220 Swift, 6mm Rem., 243, 250 Savage, 257 Roberts, 284 Win., 308, 358 Win., 3-shot blind magazine.
Barrel: 24" (Sporter, #2 Weight), 25" (Varminter, #5 weight).
Weight: 7½ lbs. (Sporter), 9 lbs., (Varminter).
Stock: Selected Claro walnut. Barrel and action hand bedded to stock with free-floated barrel, bedded action. Swivel studs installed.
Sights: None furnished. Drilled and tapped for scope mounting.
Features: Shilen Model DGA action, fully adjustable trigger with side safety. Stock finish is satin sheen epoxy. Barrel and action non-glare blue-black. From Shilen Rifles, Inc.
Price: Sporter or Varminter rifle $596.75
Price: Target blocks installed on action $7.00
Price: Conetrol bases and rings $38.35
Price: Buehler bases and rings $32.50
Price: Redfield bases and rings $29.80

SHILEN DGA SILHOUETTE RIFLE

Caliber: 308 Win., 7x308 recommended. Others available. Single shot or magazine.
Barrel: 25", #5 contour.
Weight: 8 lbs., 11 ozs.
Stock: AA fancy Claro walnut. Competition-developed pattern for Silhouette shooting. Free-floated action, bedded action. Recoil pad installed with 13¾" pull.
Sights: None furnished. Drilled and tapped for scope mounting.
Features: Shilen DGA action. Fully adjustable trigger with side safety. Available with left-hand cheekpiece. Chrome-moly steel barrel with DGA rifling. Bore and chamber held to target tolerances. Available with Benchrest trigger (2-6 oz., $40.00) or Electric trigger ($150.00). Base and ring options same as Shilen Sporter and Varminter.
Price: Silhouette rifle $596.75

Consult our Directory pages for the location of firms mentioned.

STEVENS 110E BOLT ACTION RIFLE

Caliber: 30-06, 243, 4-shot.
Barrel: 22" round tapered.
Weight: 6¾ lbs. **Length:** 43" (22" barrel).
Stock: Walnut finished hardwood with Monte Carlo, checkered p.g. and fore-end, hard rubber buttplate.
Sights: Gold bead removable ramp front, step adj. rear.
Features: Top tang safety, receiver, tapped for peep or scope sights.
Price: About $149.95

TRADEWINDS HUSKY MODEL 5000 BOLT RIFLE

Caliber: 270, 30-06, 308, 243, 22-250.
Barrel: 23¾".
Weight: 6 lbs. 11 oz.
Stock: Hand checkered European walnut, Monte Carlo, white line spacers on p.g. cap, fore-end tip and butt plate.
Sights: Fixed hooded front, adj. rear.
Features: Removable mag., fully recessed bolt head, adj. trigger. Imported by Tradewinds.
Price: $295.00

WEATHERBY MARK V BOLT ACTION RIFLE

Caliber: All Weatherby cals., 22-250 and 30-06.
Barrel: 24" or 26" round tapered.
Weight: 6½-10½ lbs. **Length:** 43¼"-46½"
Stock: Walnut, Monte Carlo with cheekpiece, high luster finish, checkered p.g. and fore-end, recoil pad.
Sights: Optional (extra).
Features: Cocking indicator, adj. trigger, hinged floorplate, thumb safety, quick detachable sling swivels.
Price: Cals. 224 and 22-250, std. bbl. $529.50
With 26" semi-target bbl. $539.50
Cals. 240, 257, 270, 7mm, 30-06 and 300 (24" bbl.) $549.50
With 26" No. 2 contour bbl. $559.50
Cal. 340 (26" bbl.) $559.50
Cal. 378 (26" bbl.) $659.50
Cal. 460 (26" bbl.) $759.50

Weatherby Mark V Rifle Left Hand

Available in all Weatherby calibers except 224 and 22-250 (and 26" No. 2 contour 300WM). Complete left handed action; stock with cheekpiece on right side. Prices are $10 higher than right hand models except the 378 and 460WM are unchanged.

WEATHERBY VANGUARD BOLT ACTION RIFLE
Caliber: 25-06, 243, 270, and 30-06 (5-shot), 7mm Rem. and 300 Win. Mag. (3-shot).
Barrel: 24" hammer forged.
Weight: 7⅞ lbs. **Length:** 44½" over-all.
Stock: American walnut, p.g. cap and fore-end tip, hand inletted and checkered, 13½" pull.
Sights: Optional, available at extra cost.
Features: Side safety, adj. trigger, hinged floorplate, receiver tapped for scope mounts.
Price: **$349.50**

WESTERN FIELD MODEL 765 BOLT ACTION RIFLE
Caliber: 7mm (4-shot), 30-06 (5-shot).
Barrel: 22".
Weight: 8½ lbs. (30-06). **Length:** 43½" over-all.
Stock: Walnut-finished hardwood, Monte Carlo cheekpiece.
Sights: Ramp front, adj. folding leaf rear.
Features: Recessed bolt head; hinged floorplate. Receiver drilled and tapped for scope mounts. 1" sling swivels. Top receiver safety.
Price: 7mm **$179.99**
Price: 30-06 . . . . **$169.99**

WESTERN FIELD 767 BOLT ACTION RIFLE
Caliber: 243, 308, 5-shot mag.
Barrel: 22" round tapered.
Weight: 6½ lbs. **Length:** 42" over-all.
Stock: Walnut-finished hardwood; Monte Carlo.
Sights: Ramp bead front; rear adj. for e.
Features: Recessed bolt head, top tang safety, hinged magazine floorplate, Receiver tapped for scope mount. 1" sling swivels included.
Price: **$159.99**

WHITWORTH EXPRESS RIFLE
Caliber: 7mm Rem. Mag., 300 Win. Mag., 375 H&H; 458 Win. Mag.
Barrel: 24".
Weight: 7½-8 lbs. **Length:** 44".
Stock: Classic English Express rifle design of hand checkered, select European Walnut.
Sights: Three leaf open sight calibrated for 100, 200, 300 yards on ¼-rib, ramp front with removable hood.
Features: Solid rubber recoil pad, barrel mounted sling swivel, adjustable trigger, hinged floor plate, solid steel recoil cross bolt. Imported by Interarms.
Price: **$459.00**

WICHITA VARMINT RIFLE
Caliber: 17 Rem. thru 308 Win., including 22 and 6mm PPC.
Barrel: 20⅛", Atkinson chrome-moly.
Weight: 9 lbs. **Length:** 40⅛" over-all.
Stock: AAA Fancy American walnut. Hand-rubbed finish, hand-checkered, 20 l.p.i. pattern. Hand-inletted, glass bedded steel grip cap, Pachmayr rubber recoil pad.
Sights: None. Drilled and tapped for scope mounts.
Features: Right or left-hand Wichita action with three locking lugs. Checkered bolt handle. Bolt is hand fitted, lapped and jeweled. Side thumb safety. Firing pin fall is ³/₁₆". Non-glare blue finish. Shipped in hard Protecto case. From Wichita Engineering.
Price: **$765.00**

WICHITA CLASSIC RIFLE
Caliber: 17 Rem. thru 308 Win., including 22 and 6mm PPC.
Barrel: 21⅛", Atkinson chrome-moly.
Weight: 8 lbs., 2 oz. **Length:** 41" over-all.
Stock: AAA Fancy American walnut. Hand-rubbed and checkered (20 l.p.i.). Hand-inletted, glass bedded, steel grip cap. Pachmayr rubber recoil pad.
Sights: None. Drilled and tapped for scope mounting.
Features: Octagonal barrel and Wichita action, right or left-hand. Checkered bolt handle. Bolt is hand-fitted, lapped and jewelled. Adjustable Canjar trigger is set at 2 lbs. Side thumb safety. Firing pin fall is ³/₁₆". Non-glare blue finish. Shipped in hard Protector case. From Wichita Engineering.
Price: **$995.00**

CENTERFIRE RIFLES—BOLT ACTION

WINCHESTER 70 XTR STANDARD RIFLE
Caliber: 222, 22-250, 25-06, 243, 270, 308 and 30-06, 5-shot.
Barrel: 22" swaged, floating. 10" twist (222 & 22-250 have 14" twist, 308 is 12").
Weight: 7½ lbs. **Length:** 42½" over-all.
Stock: Walnut, Monte Carlo, (13½"x1¾"x1½"x2⅛") checkered p.g. and fore-end.
Sights: Removable hooded bead ramp front, fully adj. open rear flips down for scope mounting.
Features: Sling swivels installed, steel p.g. cap, hinged floorplate, receiver tapped for scope mounts. Has new streamlined rear sight base, new Winchester blue finish. Stock has new color and finish.
Price: **$277.95**

Winchester 70 XTR Magnum Rifle
Same as M70 Standard except with recoil pad and in these magnum cals.: 7 Rem., 264, 300, 338 Win., 375 H&H (not XTR), 3-round mag. capacity. Wgt. 7¾ lbs. (8½ lbs. in 375), 24" bbl., 44½" over-all. R.H. twist: 9" in 264, 9½" in 7mm, 10" in 300, 338. . . . . **$293.95**
Cal. 375 H&H (not XTR) **$430.95**

Winchester 70 African
Same as M70 Standard except: 458 Win. Mag. only, 3-shot. 22" non-floating heavy bbl. 14" twist. Stock measures 13½"x1⅜"x1¾"x2⅜", has ebony fore-end tip and grip cap; wgt. 8½ lbs., recoil pad and special rear sight.
Price: **$477.95**

Winchester 70 Target Rifle
Same as M70 except: heavy 24" barrel, contoured aluminum handstop that fits left and right hand shooter, high comb target stock. Tapped for micrometer sights, clip slot in receiver, cals. 308 and 30-06.
Price: **$467.95**
Price: 308 Int'l. Army Ultra Match **$582.95**

Winchester 70 XTR Varmint Rifle
Same as M70 Standard except: 222, 22-250, and 243 only, target scope blocks, no sights, 24" heavy bbl., 14" twist in 22-250, 10" twist in 243. 44½" over-all, 9¾ lbs. Stock measures 13½"x⁹⁄₁₆"x¹⁵⁄₁₆"x⅜" from bore line.
Price: **$293.95**

WINCHESTER 70A XTR BOLT ACTION RIFLE
Caliber: 222, 22-250, 243, 25-06, 270, 30-06, 308.
Barrel: 22" (25-06, has 24").
Weight: 7⅛ to 7½ lbs. **Length:** 42½" (22" bbl.).
Stock: Monte Carlo, checkering at p.g. and fore-end.
Sights: Removeable hooded ramp front, adj. open rear.
Features: Sling swivels installed, three position safety, deep cut checkering.
Price: **$245.95**

Winchester 70A XTR Magnum Rifle
Same as 70A except with black recoil pad and in these cals.: 264, 7mm Rem., 300 Win., 3-round mag. capacity. Wgt. 7¼ lbs. 24" bbl., 44" over-all. R. H. twist: 9" in 264, 9½" in 7mm Rem. 10" in 300 Win. **$261.95**

Winchester Model 70A Police
Same as Model 70A except: 30-06 or 308 only, stock is tung oil finished.
Special order only **$236.95**

WINSLOW BOLT ACTION RIFLE
Caliber: Most standard cartridges (magnum add $10).
Barrel: 24" Douglas premium. (Magnums 26")
Weight: 7-7½ lbs. **Length:** 43" over-all.
Stock: Hand rubbed black walnut, choice of two styles
Sights: None. Metallics available at extra cost.
Features: Receivers tapped for scope mounts, QD swivels and recoil pad installed. 4-shot blind mag. Mark X actions used for right-hand rifles, Remington 788, 700 for left-hand models. Basic rifle has Bushmaster stock of Grade A walnut, ivory diamond-shape inlay in p.g. cap, ivory trademark inlay in bottom of fore-end. Jeweled bolt and follower.
Price: Basic rifle **$550.00**
Price: Left-hand **$650.00**

CENTERFIRE RIFLES—SINGLE SHOT

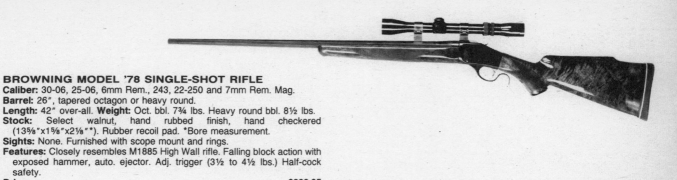

BROWNING MODEL '78 SINGLE-SHOT RIFLE
Caliber: 30-06, 25-06, 6mm Rem., 243, 22-250 and 7mm Rem. Mag.
Barrel: 26″, tapered octagon or heavy round.
Length: 42″ over-all. **Weight:** Oct. bbl. 7¾ lbs. Heavy round bbl. 8½ lbs.
Stock: Select walnut, hand rubbed finish, hand checkered (13⅝″x1⅝″x2⅛″*). Rubber recoil pad. *Bore measurement.
Sights: None. Furnished with scope mount and rings.
Features: Closely resembles M1885 High Wall rifle. Falling block action with exposed hammer, auto. ejector. Adj. trigger (3½ to 4½ lbs.) Half-cock safety.
Price: **$399.95**

BROWNING B-78 45-70 RIFLE
Caliber: 45-70.
Barrel: 24″ heavy octagon; 6-groove, 1-in-20″ twist.
Weight: About 8¾ lbs. **Length:** 40¾″ over-all.
Stock: Straight grip French walnut with semi-schnabel fore-end, hand checkered. Measures 13¼″x2″x2¾″.
Sights: Blade front, step-adj. rear. Drilled and tapped for scope mounts.
Features: Curved, blued steel buttplate; low profile recessed swivel studs (swivels provided).
Price: **$399.95**

HARRINGTON AND RICHARDSON 158 TOPPER RIFLE
Caliber: 30-30 and 22 Hornet.
Barrel: 22″ round tapered.
Weight: 6 lbs. **Length:** 37″.
Stock: Walnut finished hardwood stock and fore-end.
Sights: Blade front; folding adj. rear.
Features: Side lever break-open action with visible hammer. Easy takedown. Converts to 20 ga. Shotgun with accessory bbl.
Price: 22 Hornet or 30-30 .... **$76.50**

HARRINGTON & RICHARDSON Model 155 "SHIKARI"
Caliber: 44 Rem. Mag. or 45-70, single-shot.
Barrel: 24″ or 28″ 45-70, 24″ (44 Mag.).
Weight: 7-7½ lbs. **Length:** 39″ over-all (24″ bbl.).
Stock: Walnut finished hardwood.
Sights: Blade front, adj. folding leaf rear.
Features: Blue-black finish with color case hardened frame. Exposed hammer. Solid brass cleaning rod with hardwood handle included.
Price: Either caliber **$99.50**

HYPER-SINGLE RIFLE
Caliber: All calibers, standard and wildcat.
Barrel: Choice of maker, weight, length (std. twist and contours).
Length: To customer specs. **Weight:** To customer specs.
Stock: To customer specs. AA fancy American black walnut is standard.
Sights: None furnished. Drilled and tapped for scope mounts.
Features: Falling block action. Striker rotates on bronze bearing and is powered by dual coil springs. Trigger adj. for weight, pull and travel. Tang safety. Octagon receiver on special order (same price).
Price: Complete Rifle .....**$1,750.00**   Barreled action **$1,100.00**
Price: Action only (blank extractor) **$850.00**
Price: Stainless steel barrel (extra) **$75.00**
Price: Fluted or octagon barrel (extra) **$75.00**

RIEDL SINGLE SHOT RIFLE
Caliber: All calibers, standard and wildcat.
Barrel: Lengths from 22" to 30", weights from 2½ lbs to 12 lbs.
Weight: About 6 lbs. (Light Weight rifle).
Stock: Deluxe Calif. Claro walnut standard. Other woods available.
Sights: None. Furnished with bridge scope mount or target bases.
Features: Rack and pinion action operation. Choice of chrome moly or stainless steel. Fully adj. trigger. Basically a custom-made rifle made to customer specs. Base prices listed. From Riedl Rifle Co.
Price: Chrome moly rifle $439.00
Price: Stainless steel rifle $499.00

RUGER NUMBER ONE SINGLE SHOT
Caliber: 22-250, 243, 6mm Rem., 25-06, 270, 7x57mm, 30-06, 7mm Rem. Mag., 300 Win., 45-70, 458 Win. Mag., 375 H&H Mag.
Barrel: 26" round tapered with quarter-rib (also 22" and 24", depending upon model).
Weight: 8 lbs. **Length:** 42" over-all.
Stock: Walnut, two-piece, checkered p.g. and fore-end (either semi-beavertail or Henry style).
Sights: None, 1" scope rings supplied for integral mounts. 3 models have open sights.
Features: Under lever, hammerless falling block design has auto ejector, top tang safety. Standard Rifle 1B illus.
Price: $295.00
Available also as Light Sporter, Medium Sporter, Special Varminter or Tropical Rifle $295.00
Price: Barreled action, blued only $189.50

RUGER NO. 3 CARBINE SINGLE SHOT
Caliber: 22 Hornet, 223, 45-70.
Barrel: 22" round.
Weight: 6 lbs. **Length:** 38½".
Stock: American walnut, carbine-type.
Sights: Gold bead front, adj. folding leaf rear.
Features: Same action as No. 1 Rifle except different lever. Has auto ejector, top tang safety, adj. trigger.
Price: $215.00

WICKLIFFE '76 FALLING BLOCK RIFLE
Caliber: 22 Hornet, 223, 22-250, 243, 25-06, 270, 308, 30-06, 7mm Rem. Mag., 300 Win. Mag., 45-70; single-shot.
Barrel: 26", heavy sporter weight; 22" lightweight in, 243, 30-06, and 308 only.
Weight: 8½ lbs. (26" bbl.), 6¾ lbs. (22" bbl.).
Stock: Select American walnut, dull finish (Std. grade); fancy figured walnut, high-gloss finish (Deluxe grade). Monte Carlo buttstock with p.g., semi-beavertail fore-end.
Sights: Scope mounts on barrel, with extensions and 1" rings by Burris.
Features: Single-shot, falling block action. Adjustable extractor-ejector for extraction only or complete ejection; trigger adjustable for over-travel and sear engagement; diamond lapped 4140 chrome-moly barrel. Full 5 year warranty. Deluxe Grade has nickel silver grip cap, engine-turned breech block, better wood and metal finish. Magnum calibers available only in deluxe grade, standard calibers in either grade. Both left and right-hand versions offered. From Triple-S Development.
Price: Standard Grade $298.00
Price: Deluxe Grade $372.00
Price: Barreled action, (standard grade) $205.00
Price: Barreled action, (deluxe grade) $216.00

Consult our Directory pages for
the location of firms mentioned.

HARRINGTON & RICHARDSON L.B.H. Commemorative Carbine
Caliber: 45-70, single shot.
Barrel: 22".
Weight: 7 lbs., 4 oz. **Length:** 41".
Stock: American walnut with metal grip adapter.
Sights: Blade front, tang mounted aperature rear adj. for w. and e.
Features: Replica of the 1871 Springfield carbine. Engraved breech block, side lock and hammer. Action color case hardened. Each comes with book entitled "In the Valley of the Little Big Horn".
Price: **$265.00**

HARRINGTON & RICHARDSON Cavalry Model Carbine
Caliber: 45-70 single shot.
Barrel: 22".
Weight: 7 lbs. **Length:** 41".
Stock: American walnut with saddle ring and bridle.
Sights: Blade front, barrel mounted leaf rear adj. for e.
Features: Replica of the 1871 Springfield Carbine. Blue-black finish.
Price: **$225.00**
   Deluxe version shown has engraved breech block, side lock & hammer.
Price: **$265.00**
   Springfield Armory Museum silver plated carbine **$1,250.00**

HARRINGTON & RICHARDSON Officers Model 1873
Caliber: 45-70, single shot
Barrel: 26" round.
Weight: About 8 lbs. **Length:** 44" over-all
Stock: Oil finished walnut, checkered at wrist and fore-end white metal tipped.
Sights: Blade front, vernier tang rear adj. for w. & e.
Features: Replica of the 1873 Springfield has engraved breech block, side lock and hammer. comes with commemorative plaque.
Price: **$315.00**

NAVY ARMS MODEL 1875 REVOLVING RIFLE
Caliber: 357 Mag., 44-40, 45 L.C.
Barrel: 20".
Weight: 5 lbs. **Length:** 38".
Stock: Walnut, brass butt plate.
Sights: Front blade adj. for w., buckhorn rear adj. for e.
Features: Action resembles Remington Model 1875 revolver. Polished brass trigger guard. Imported by Navy/Replica.
Price: **$190.00**

ROLLING BLOCK BABY CARBINE
Caliber: 22 LR, 22 Hornet, 357 Mag.
Barrel: 20", octagon.
Weight: 4¾ lbs. **Length:** Approx. 35" over-all.
Stock: Walnut.
Sights: Blade front, rear adj. for e.
Features: Small rolling block action is color case hardened with blue barrel. Trigger guard and buttplate polished brass. Imported by Navy/Marietta Replica Arms.
Price: **$145.00**

NAVY ARMS ROLLING BLOCK RIFLE
Caliber: 45-70, 444 Marlin.
Barrels: 26½".
Stock: Walnut finished.
Sights: Fixed front, adj. rear.
Features: Reproduction of classic rolling block action. Available in Buffalo Rifle (octagonal bbl.) and Creedmore (half round, half octagonal bbl.) models. Imported by Navy Arms.
Price: **$165.00**
Price: Creedmore Model **$195.00**

ANSCHUTZ 1411 MATCH 54 RIFLE

Caliber: 22 LR. Single shot.
Barrel: 27½ round (¹⁵/₁₆″ dia.)
Weight: 11 lbs. **Length:** 46″ over-all.
Stock: French walnut, American prone style with Monte Carlo, cast-off cheek-piece, checkered p.g., beavertail fore-end with swivel rail and adj. swivel, adj. rubber buttplate.
Sights: None. Receiver grooved for Anschutz sights (extra). Scope blocks.
Features: Single stage adj. trigger, wing safety, short firing pin travel. Available from Savage Arms.
Price: Right hand, no sights $494.50
Price: Left hand stocked rifle, no sights $510.00
Price: Anschutz Int'l. sight set $108.75

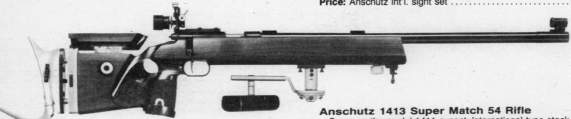

Anschutz 1413 Super Match 54 Rifle

Same as the model 1411 except: International type stock with adj. cheek-piece, adj. aluminum hook buttplate, weight 15½ lbs., 50″ over-all. Available from Savage Arms.
Price: Right hand, no sights $775.00
Price: Left hand stocked rifle, no sights $778.50

Anschutz 1407 Match 54 Rifle

Same as the model 1411 except: 26″ bbl. (⅞″ dia.), weight 10 lbs., 44½″ over-all to conform to ISU requirements and also suitable for NRA matches. Available from Savage Arms.
Price: Right hand, no sights $460.00
Price: Left hand stocked rifle, no sights $476.00
Price: Int'l sight set $108.75
Price: Match sight set $71.65

BSA MARTINI ISU MATCH RIFLE

Caliber: 22 LR, single shot.
Barrel: 28″.
Weight: 10¾ lbs. **Length:** 43-44″ over-all.
Stock: Match type French walnut butt and fore-end; flat cheekpiece, full p.g.; spacers are fitted to allow length adjustment to suit each shooting position; adj. buttplate.
Sights: Modified PH-1 Parker-Hale tunnel front, PH-25 aperture rear with aperture variations from .080″ to .030″.
Features: Fastest lock time of any commercial target rifle; designed to meet I.S.U. specs. for the Standard Rifle. Fully adjustable trigger (less than ½ lb. to 3½ lbs.). Mark V has heavier barrel, weighs 12¼ lbs. From Freelands Scope Stands.
Price: I.S.U., Standard weight $498.00
Price: Mark V heavy bbl. $505.00

FINNISH LION STANDARD TARGET RIFLE

Caliber: 22 LR, single-shot.
Barrel: 27⅝″.
Weight: 10½ lbs. **Length:** 44⁹/₁₆″ over-all.
Stock: French walnut, target style.
Sights: Globe front, International micrometer rear, p.g. or thumbhole style.
Features: Comes with sights and accessories (palm rest, hook buttplate, fore-end stop and swivel assembly, buttplate extension, 5 front sight aperture inserts, 3 rear sight apertures, allen wrench). Adjustable trigger. Imported from Finland by Mandall Shooting Supplies.
Price: $499.50
Price: Thumbhole stock model $535.00
Price: Heavy barrel model (either stock) $570.00

MOSSBERG MODEL 144 TARGET RIFLE
Caliber: 22 LR only. 7-shot clip.
Barrel: 27″ round ($^{15}/_{16}$″ dia.)
Weight: About 8 lbs. **Length:** 43″ over-all.
Stock: Target-style walnut with high thick comb, cheekpiece, p.g., beavertail fore-end, adj. handstop and sling swivels.
Sights: Lyman 17A hooded front with inserts, Mossberg S331 receiver peep with ¼-minute clicks.
Features: Wide grooved trigger adj. for wgt. of pull, thumb safety, receiver grooved for scope mounting.
Price: **$114.95**

REMINGTON 540-XR RIMFIRE POSITION RIFLE
Caliber: 22 LR, single-shot.
Barrel: 26″ medium weight target. Countersunk at muzzle.
Weight: 8 lbs., 13 oz. **Length:** Adj. from 43½″ to 46¾″.
Stock: Position-style with Monte Carlo, cheekpiece and thumb groove. 5-way adj. buttplate and full length guide rail.
Sights: None furnished. Drilled and tapped for target scope blocks. Fitted with front sight base.
Features: Extra-fast lock time. Specially designed p.g. to eliminate wrist twisting. Adj. match trigger. Match-style sling with adj. swivel block ($10.50) and sight set ($34.50) available.
Price: **$199.95**

Remington 540-XRJR Junior Rimfire Position Rifle
Same as 540-XR except fitted with 1¾″ shorter stock to fit the junior shooter, Over-all length adjustable from 41¾″ to 45″. Length of pull adjustable from 11″ to 14¼″.
Price: **$199.95**

REMINGTON MODEL 40XB-BR
Caliber: 222 Rem., 222 Rem. Mag., 223, 6mm x 47, 7.62 NATO (308 Win.).
Barrel: 20″ (light varmint class), 26″ (heavy varmint class).
Length: 38″ (20″ bbl.), 44″ (26″ bbl.). **Weight:** Light varmint class, 7¼ lbs., Heavy varmint class, 12 lbs.
Stock: Select walnut.
Sights: None. Supplied with scope blocks.
Features: Unblued stainless steel barrel, trigger adj. from 1½ lbs. to 3½ lbs. Special 2 oz. trigger at extra cost. Scope and mounts extra.
Price: **$530.00**

REMINGTON 40-XR RIMFIRE POSITION RIFLE
Caliber: 22 LR, single-shot.
Barrel: 24″, heavy target.
Weight: 10 lbs. **Length:** 43″ over-all.
Stock: Position-style with front swivel block on fore-end guide rail.
Sights: Drilled and tapped. Furnished with scope blocks.
Features: Meets all I.S.U. specifications. Deep fore-end, buttplate vertically adjustable, wide adjustable trigger. Redfield No. 75 rear, globe front. Match sight set available for **$40.00**.
Price: **$375.00**

REMINGTON 40-XB RANGEMASTER TARGET Centerfire
Caliber: 222 Rem., 222 Rem. Mag., 223 Rem., 22-250, 6mm x 47, 6mm Int., 6mm Rem., 243, 25-06, 7mm Rem. Mag., 30-338 (30-7mm Rem. Mag.), 300 Win. Mag., 7.62 NATO (308 Win.), 30-06. Single shot.
Barrel: 27¼″ round (Stand. dia.-¾″, Hvy. dia.-⅞″)
Weight: Std.—9¼ lbs., Hvy.—11¼ **Length:** 47″
Stock: American walnut with high comb and beavertail fore-end stop. Rubber non-slip buttplate.
Sights: None. Scope blocks installed.
Features: Adjustable trigger pull. Receiver drilled and tapped for sights.
Price: Standard s.s., stainless steel **$500.00**
Price: Repeating model **$537.00**
Price: Extra for 2 oz. trigger **$63.00**

REMINGTON 40-XC NAT'L MATCH COURSE RIFLE
Caliber: 7.62 NATO, 5-shot.
Barrel: 23¼″, stainless steel.
Weight: 10 lbs. without sights. **Length:** 42½″ over-all.
Stock: Walnut, position-style, with palm swell.
Sights: None furnished.
Features: Designed to meet the needs of competitive shooters firing the national match courses. Position-style stock, top loading clip slot magazine, anti-bind bolt and receiver, bright stainless steel barrel. Meets all I.S.U. Army Rifle specifications. Adjustable buttplate, adjustable trigger.
Price: **$550.00**

SAVAGE/ANSCHUTZ MARK 12 TARGET RIFLE
Caliber: 22 LR, single-shot.
Barrel: 26″, heavy. ⅞″ diameter.
Weight: 8 lbs. **Length:** 43″ over-all.
Stock: Walnut finished hardwood.
Sights: Globe front (insert-type), micro-click peep rear.
Features: Action similar to the Anschutz Model 64. Stock has thumb groove, Wundhammer swell p.g., adjustable hand stop and sling swivel.
Price: **$105.00**
Price: Mark 12 Target Sling **$12.95**

SAVAGE/ANSCHUTZ 64 MATCH RIFLE
Caliber: 22 LR only. Single shot.
Barrel: 26″ round (¹¹⁄₁₆″ dia.)
Weight: 7¾ lbs. **Length:** 44″ over-all.
Stock: Walnut finished hardwood, cheekpiece, checkered p.g., beavertail fore-end, adj. buttplate.
Sights: None (extra). Scope blocks.
Features: Sliding side safety, adj. single stage trigger, receiver grooved for Anschutz sights.
Price: .... **$221.00**   64L (Left hand) **$232.00**
As above but with Anschutz 6723 Match Sight Set.
Price: Model 64S (Right hand) **$292.65**
Price: 64SL (Left hand) **$303.65**
Price: Anschutz Match sight set **$71.65**

WALTHER MOVING TARGET MATCH RIFLE
Caliber: 22 LR.
Barrel: 23.6″.
Weight: 8 lbs. 5 oz. **Length:** 42″ over-all.
Stock: Walnut thumb-hole type. Fore-end and p.g. stippled.
Features: Especially designed for running boar competition. Receiver grooved to accept dovetail scope mounts. Adjustable cheekpiece and butt plate. 1.1 lb. trigger pull. Left hand stock available on special order. Imported by Interarms.
Price: **$540.00**

WALTHER U.I.T. SUPER
Caliber: 22 LR.
Barrel: 25½″.
Weight: 10 lbs., 3 oz. **Length:** 44¾″.
Stock: Walnut, adj. for length and drop; fore-end guide rail for sling or palm rest.
Sights: Globe-type front, fully adj. aperture rear.
Features: Conforms to both NRA and U.I.T. requirements. Fully adj. trigger. Left hand stock available on special order. Imported from Germany by Interarms.
Price: **$560.00**

Walther GX-1 Match Rifle
Same general specs as U.I.T. except has 25½″ barrel, over-all length of 44½″, weight of 15½ lbs. Stock is designed to provide every conceivable adjustment for individual preference and anatomical compatibility. Left-hand stock available on special order. From Interarms.
Price: **$850.00**

Walther U.I.T. Match

Same specifications and features as standard U.I.T. Super rifle but has scope mount bases. Fore-end has new tapered profile, fully stippled. From Interarms.

Price: **$620.00**

WINCHESTER 52 INTERNATIONAL PRONE RIFLE

Caliber: 22 LR, single shot.
Barrel: 28".
Weight: 11½ lbs. **Length:** 46" over-all.
Stock: Oil finished walnut. Designed for international prone position target shooting. Removable full roll-over cheekpiece for easy bore cleaning.
Sights: None. Receiver drilled and tapped for sights or scope.
Features: Same features as Model 52 International Match rifle except as noted above. **Special order only.**

Price: **$522.00**

WINCHESTER 52D BOLT ACTION TARGET RIFLE

Caliber: 22 LR only. Single shot.
Barrel: 28", standard or heavy weight.
Weight: 9¾ lbs. Std., 11 lbs. Hvy. **Length:** 46"
Stock: Marksman stock of choice walnut with full length accessory channel and adj. bedding device and non-slip butt pad.
Sights: None. Barrel tapped for front sight bases.
Features: Adjustable trigger.

Price: **$357.50**

WINCHESTER 70 INT'L ARMY MATCH RIFLE

Caliber: 308 (7.62mm NATO) 5-shot.
Barrel: 24" heavy-contour.
Weight: 11 lbs. **Length:** 43¼" over-all.
Stock: Oil finished walnut, (12" x 1¼" x 1¼") meets ISU requirements.
Sights: None. Receiver tapped for M70 sights (available at extra cost).
Features: Fore-end rail takes most std. accessories, vertically adj. buttplate, externally adj. trigger, glass bedded action.

Price: Match and Ultra Match **$582.95**

WINCHESTER 52 INTERNATIONAL MATCH RIFLE

Caliber: 22 LR. Single shot.
Barrel: 28" heavy bbl.
Weight: 13½ lbs. **Length:** 44½"
Stock: Laminated International-style, aluminum fore-end assembly, adj. palm rest.
Sights: Receiver tapped for sights and scope bases; scope blocks are included.
Features: Non-drag trigger. Lead-lapped barrel with Winchester muzzle counterbore. Options include Kenyon or ISU triggers. **Special Order Only.**

Price: **$645.00**
Price: With Kenyon or ISU trigger **$780.00**

DRILLINGS, COMBINATION GUNS, DOUBLE RIFLES

ARMSPORT "EMPEROR" DOUBLE RIFLE
Caliber: 243, 270, 284, 7.65, 308, 30-06, 7mm Rem. Mag., 9.3, 300 H & H, 375 H & H; Shotgun barrels in 12, 16 or 20-ga.
Barrel: Shotgun barrel length and chokes to customer specs.
Stock: Dimensions to customer specs. Stock and fore-end of root walnut.
Sights: Rifle barrels have blade front with bead, leaf rear adj. for w. Armsport scope and claw mounts included. Scope power to customer specs.
Features: Receiver and sideplates engraved. Gun comes with extra set of barrels fitted to action. Packaged in a hand-made, fitted luggage-type leather case lined with Scotch loden cloth. Introduced 1978. From Armsport.
Price: Complete **$5,000.00**

COLT SAUER DRILLING
Caliber: 12 ga., over 30-06, 12 ga. over 243.
Action: Top lever, cross bolt, box lock.
Barrel: 25" (Mod. & Full).
Weight: 8 lbs. **Length:** 41¾" over-all.
Stock: American walnut, oil finish. Checkered p.g. and fore-end. Black p.g., cap, recoil pad. 14¼"x2"x1½".
Sights: Blade front with brass bead, folding leaf rear.
Features: Cocking indicators, tang barrel selector, automatic sight positioner, set rifle trigger, side safety. Blue finish with bright receiver engraved with animal motifs and European-style scrollwork. Imported by Colt.
Price: **$2,075.00**

FERLACH DOUBLE RIFLE
Caliber: Any caliber desired; metric, English or American.
Action: Boxlock or sidelock, side-by-side or over-under.
Barrel: Any length desired.
Weight: To customer specs. **Length:** To customer specs.
Stock: Custom or standard dimensions.
Sights: Any desired, including folding, night sights and scopes.
Features: Any desired, including highly figured wood, auto ejection, folding sights, extra barrel sets, night sights. Imported by Ferlach (Austria) of North America.
Price: Base, boxlock action **$2,900.00**
Price: Base, sidelock action **$4,900.00**

HEYM MODEL 33 DRILLINGS
Caliber/Gauge: 5.6x50R Mag., 5.6x57R, 6.5x57R, 7x57R, 7x65R, 8x57JRS, 9.3x74R, 243, 270, 308, 30-06; 16x16 (2¾"), 20x20 (3").
Barrel: 25" (Full & Mod.).
Weight: about 6-8 lbs. **Length:** 42" over-all.
Stock: Dark European walnut, checkered p.g. and fore-end; oil finish.
Sights: Silver bead front, folding leaf rear. Automatic sight positioner. Available with scope and claw mounts.
Features: Greener-type crossbolt and safety double under-lugs. Double set triggers. Plastic or steel trigger guard. Sidelock model available. Engraving coverage varies with model. Contact Heym for more data.
Price: Model 33N (boxlock), from **$3,995.00**
Price: Model 33N (boxlock, with scope and mounts) **$4,450.00**

HEYM MODEL 55 O/U COMBINATION GUN
Caliber/Gauge: 5.6x50R Mag., 5.6x57R, 6.5x57R, 7x57R, 7x65R, 8x57JRS, 243 Win., 270 Win., 308 Win., 30-06, 9.3x74R, 375 H & H Mag., 12x12, 16x16, 20x20.
Barrel: 25" (combo.), 25" (O/U rifle), 28" (O/U shotgun).
Weight: 6.8 lbs. (combo.). **Length:** 42" over-all (combo.).
Stock: European walnut. Pistol grip, cheekpiece. Checkered p.g. and fore-end.
Sights: Bead on ramp front, open folding leaf rear. Available with scope and claw mounts.
Features: Shotgun has selective auto ejectors, combo. has extractor, O/U rifle can be had with extractors or ejectors. Interchangeable barrels for combo. not available. Contact Heym for more data.
Price: Model 55BF (combo., with scope, claw mounts) **$4,450.00**
Price: Model 55B (O/U rifle, with scope, claw mounts) **$4,450.00**
Price: Model 55F (O/U shotgun) **$3,995.00**
Price: Model 55F, 55BF, 55B, (without scope) **$3,995.00**

ITHACA TURKEYGUN
Caliber: 12 ga./222.
Barrel: 24½″ (Full).
Weight: 7½ lbs.
Stock: 14″x1⅝″x1⅞″x2¼″, walnut.
Sights: Ramp front, folding leaf rear.
Features: Detachable choke tubes (Full choke supplied, Mod., Imp. Cyl. available), rifle barrel, sling swivels, grooved for scope mounts. Imported by Ithaca.
Price: **$449.95**

KRIEGHOFF "TECK" DOUBLE RIFLE
Caliber: Most standard rimless and rimmed American and metric calibers, including 375 H & H and 458 Win. Mag.
Action: Kersten double cross bolt, double under-lug locking system.
Barrel: 25″.
Weight: From 8 lbs. **Length:** 42½″ over-all.
Stock: 14¼″x1¼″x2¼″, European walnut.
Sights: Sourdough front, express rear.
Features: Imported by Creighton & Warren.
Price: Teck, std. stock dimensions, 375, 458 ....**$2,800.00**
Price: Std. rifle with Lyman scope, German claw mounts **$2,750.00**
Special order rifles made to customer specs:
Price: Std. cals. **$2,464.00**
Price: Belted magnum cals. **$2,816.00**
Price: Model Ulm (sidelocks) **$3,695.00**
Price: Model Ulm (engraved, hand-detachable sidelocks) illus. ...**$4,495.00**
Price: Interchangeable o/u shotgun barrel **$695.00**
Price: Interchangeable o/u rifle barrel std. cals. **$1,450.00**
Price: Interchangeable o/u rifle barrel, magnum **$1,760.00**

KRIEGHOFF DRILLINGS
Caliber: 12 and 12 ga. (2¾″) and 30-06, 20 and 20 (3″) and 243 Win.
Action: Sidelock—Neptun; Boxlock—Trumpf.
Barrel: 25″, solid rib.
Weight: 7½ lbs. **Length:** 42″ over-all.
Stock: 14¼″x1¼″x2¼″, European walnut.
Sights: Sourdough front, express rear.
Features: Shot barrel locks cock on opening, rifle barrel cocked and rear sight raises by action of tang mounted slide. Split extractors. Free-floating rifle barrel avail. American scope can be mounted at factory with claw mounts $250.00. Imported by Creighton & Warren.
Price: Std. Trumpf with free-floating rifle bbl. **$2,500.00**
Price: Std. Trumpf with American Scope, claw mounts **$2,750.00**
Special order drillings made to customer specs.
Price: Boxlock action with optional engraving coverage and special stock features **$2,290.00**
Price: Sidelock version (Neptun) **$3,815.00**
Price: Deluxe Neptun (engraved) with hand-detachable locks, base **$4,840.00**

ROTTWEIL MODEL 85 O/U DOUBLE RIFLE
Caliber: 7x65R, 9.3x74R, 375 H&H Mag.
Barrel: 25″.
Weight: 8 lbs. **Length:** 42″ over-all.
Stock: European walnut, hand checkered and rubbed.
Sights: Square blade front, open V-notch rear.
Features: "Blitz" self-cocking action; front trigger has rebounding set trigger; lateral cocking indicator pins; wedge breech and Greener crossbolt locking. Engraved action. Can be had with or without ejectors. Imported by Eastern Sports Int.
Price: ....**$2,900.00** to **$3,596.00**

KRIEGHOFF RIFLE-SHOTGUN COMBO
Caliber: Top-12, 16, 20 (2¾″), 20 ga. 3″; lower-all popular U.S. and metric cartridges, rimless and rimmed.
Action: Sidelock—Ulm; Boxlock—Teck.
Barrel: 25″, solid rib.
Weight: 6¼ lbs. **Length:** 41″ over-all.
Stock: 14¼″x1¼″x2¼″, European walnut.
Sights: Sourdough front, express rear.
Features: Interchangeable rifle barrels in 22 Hornet, 222 Rem., 222 Rem. Mag. priced at $250.00. Scope optional. Imported by Creighton & Warren.
Price: 12 ga./30-06 or 222 Rem.—Teck **$2,115.00**
Price: Sidelock Ulm model **$3,170.00**
Price: Ulm Primus (deluxe) **$4,135.00**

DRILLINGS, COMBINATION GUNS, DOUBLE RIFLES

SAVAGE MODEL 2400 O/U
Caliber: Top barrel 12 ga. (2¾"), bottom barrel 222 or 308.
Barrel: 23½" separated barrels (Imp. Mod). Solid matted rib.
Weight: 7½ lbs. **Length:** 40½" over-all.
Stock: Walnut, cut checkered p.g. and semi-beavertail fore-end (14"x1½"x1¾"x2½").
Sights: Blade front, folding leaf rear.
Features: Action similar to Savage Models 333 and 330. White line rubber recoil pad, single selective trigger, sling swivels, Hand fitted action.
Price: $576.50

SAVAGE MODEL 24-C O/U
Caliber: Top bbl. 22 S, L, LR; bottom bbl. 20 gauge cyl. bore.
Action: Take-down, low rebounding visible hammer. Single trigger, barrel selector spur on hammer.
Barrel: 20" separate barrels.
Weight: 5¾ lbs. **Length:** 35" (taken down 20").
Stock: Walnut finished hardwood, straight grip.
Sight: Ramp front, rear open adj. for e.
Features: Trap door butt holds one shotshell and ten 22 cartridges, comes with special carrying case. Measures 5"x22" when in case.
Price: $115.00

Savage Model 24-D O/U
Caliber: Top bbl. 22 S, L, LR or 22 Mag.; bottom bbl. 20 or 410 gauge.
Action: Two-way top lever opening, low rebounding visible hammer, single trigger, barrel selector spur on hammer, separate extractors, color case-hardened frame.
Barrel: 24", separated barrels.
Weight: 6¾ lbs. **Length:** 40".
Stock: Walnut, checkered p.g. and fore-end (14"x1½"x2½").
Sights: Ramp front, rear open adj. for e.
Features: Receiver grooved for scope mounting.
Price: $123.00

SAVAGE MODEL 24-F.G. O/U
Same as Model 24-D except: color case hardened frame, stock is walnut finished hardwood, no checkering or M.C.
Price: $104.00

Savage Model 24-V
Similar to Model 24-D except: 222 Rem. or 30-30 and 20 ga. only; stronger receiver; color case-hardened frame; barrel; band; folding leaf rear sight; receiver tapped for scope $145.75

A. ZOLI RIFLE-SHOTGUN O/U COMBO
Caliber: 12 ga./308 Win.
Barrel: Combo—24"; shotgun—28" (Mod. & Full).
Weight: About 8 lbs. **Length:** 41" over-all (24" bbl.).
Stock: European walnut.
Sights: Blade front, flip-up rear.
Features: Available with German claw scope mounts on rifle/shotgun barrels. Comes with set of 12/12 (Mod. & Full) barrels. From Mandall Shooting Supplies.
Price: With two barrel sets, without claw mounts $1,295.00
Price: With two barrel sets, with claw mounts $1,495.00

RIMFIRE RIFLES — AUTOLOADING & SLIDE ACTION

AMERICAN 180 AUTO CARBINE
Caliber: 22 LR, 177-round magazine.
Barrel: 16½".
Weight: 5¾ lbs. (empty), 10 lbs. (loaded). **Length:** 36" over-all.
Stock: High impact plastic stock and fore-end.
Sights: Blade front, peep rear adj. for w. and e.
Features: Available in selective fire version for law enforcement or semi-auto only for civilians. Laser-Lok laser beam sight available at extra cost. Imported from Austria by American International.
Price: $350.00
Price: Laser-Lok sight system $495.00
Price: Extra magazine and winding mechanism $100.00

RIMFIRE RIFLES—AUTOLOADING & SLIDE ACTION

AP-74 AUTO RIFLE
Caliber: 22 LR, 15 shot magazine.
Barrel: 20″ including flash reducer.
Weight: 6½ lbs. **Length:** 38½″ over-all.
Stock: Black plastic.
Sights: Ramp front, adj. peep rear.
Features: Pivotal take-down, easy disassembly. AR-15 look-alike. Sling and sling swivels included. Imported by Navy Arms.
Price: **$114.95**
Price: With walnut stock and fore-end **$125.00**

BROWNING AUTOLOADING RIFLE
Caliber: 22 LR, 11-shot.
Barrel: 19¼ lbs.
Weight: 4¾ lbs. **Length:** 37″ over-all.
Stock: Checkered select walnut (13¾″x1¹³/₁₆″x2⅝″) with p.g. and semi-beavertail fore-end.
Sights: Gold bead front, folding leaf rear.
Features: Engraved receiver is grooved for tip-off scope mount; cross-bolt safety; tubular magazine in buttstock; easy take down for carrying or storage.
Price: Grade I .... **$189.95** Grade II .... **$284.95** Grade III **$699.95**
Also available in Grade I, 22 S (16-shot) **$197.95**

BROWNING BAR-22 AUTO RIFLE
Caliber: 22 LR only, 15-shot tube magazine.
Barrel: 20¼″.
Weight: About 6¼ lbs. **Length:** 38¼″ over-all.
Stock: French walnut. Cut checkering at p.g. and fore-end.
Sights: Gold bead front, folding leaf rear. Receiver grooved for scope mounting.
Features: Magazine tube latch locks closed from any position. Cross bolt safety in rear of trigger guard. Trigger pull about 5 lbs. Introduced 1977. From Browning.
Price: Grade I only **$179.95**

BROWNING BPR-22 PUMP RIFLE
Caliber: 22 LR, 22 Mag. (15 shots, 11 shots).
Barrel: 20¼″.
Weight: About 6¼ lbs. **Length:** 38¼″ over-all.
Stock: French walnut. Cut checkered p.g. and fore-end.
Sights: Gold bead front, folding leaf rear. Receiver grooved for scope mount.
Features: Short, positive pump stroke, side ejection. Magazine tube latches from any position. Cross bolt safety in rear of trigger guard. Introduced 1977. From Browning.
Price: 22 LR **$179.95**
Price: 22 Magnum **$189.95**

CHARTER AR-7 EXPLORER CARBINE
Caliber: 22 LR, 8-shot clip.
Barrel: 16″ alloy (steel-lined).
Weight: 2½ lbs. **Length:** 34½″/16½″ stowed.
Stock: Moulded grey Cycloac, snap-on rubber butt pad.
Sights: Square blade front, aperture rear adj. for e.
Features: Take-down design stores bbl. and action in hollow stock. Light enough to float.
Price: **$81.50**

ERMA ESG22 GAS-OPERATED CARBINE
Caliber: 22 WMR, 12-shot magazine.
Barrel: 18".
Weight: 6 lbs. **Length:** 35½" over-all.
Stock: Walnut-stained beech.
Sights: Military post front, peep rear adj. for w. & e.
Features: Locked breech, gas-operated action. Styled after M-1 Carbine. Also available as standard blowback action. Receiver grooved for scope mounting. Introduced 1978. From Excam.
Price: Gas **$255.00**
Price: Blowback **$158.00**

HARRINGTON & RICHARDSON Model 700 Auto Rifle
Caliber: 22 WMRF, 5-shot clip.
Barrel: 22".
Weight: 6½ lbs. **Length:** 43¼" over-all.
Stock: Walnut, Monte Carlo, full p.g., composition buttplate.
Sights: Blade front, folding leaf rear.
Features: Drilled and tapped for scope mounting. White spacer at buttplate. Made in U.S. by H&R.
Price: **$159.00**

HECKLER & KOCH HK270 AUTO RIFLE
Caliber: 22 LR, 5-shot magazine.
Barrel: 19¾".
Weight: 5.5 lbs. **Length:** 38.2" over-all.
Stock: European walnut with Monte Carlo cheek rest.
Sights: Post front adj. for elevation, V-notch rear adj. for windage.
Features: Straight blow-back action; 3½ lbs. trigger pull. Extra 20-shot magazine available. Receiver grooved for scope mount. Introduced 1978. From Heckler & Koch.
Price: **$205.00**

HECKLER & KOCH MODEL 300 AUTO RIFLE
Caliber: 22 Mag., 5-shot box mag.
Barrel: 19¾".
Weight: 5¾ lbs. **Length:** 39½" over-all.
Stock: European walnut, Monte Carlo with cheek rest; checkered p.g. and Schnabel fore-end.
Sights: Post front adj. for elevation, V-notch rear adj. for w.
Features: Hexagon (polygonal) rifling, comes with sling swivels; straight blowback inertia bolt action; single-stage trigger (3½-lb. pull). HK-05 clamp scope mount with 1" rings available at extra cost. Imported from Germany by Security Arms.
Price: HK300 .... **$230.00**
Price: Scope mount **$58.00**

MARLIN GLENFIELD 70 AUTO
Caliber: 22 LR, 7-shot clip magazine.
Barrel: 18" (16-groove rifling).
Weight: 5½ lbs. **Length:** 36¾" over-all.
Stock: Walnut-finished hardwood with Monte Carlo, full p.g., checkered p.g. and fore-end. Sling swivels included.
Sights: Ramp front, adj. open rear. Receiver grooved for scope mount.
Features: Receiver top has serrated, non-glare finish; chrome plated trigger; cross-bolt safety; bolt hold-open; chrome plated magazine. Scope shown not included. Introduced 1978.
Price: Less scope **$62.95**

MARLIN 99 M1 AUTOLOADING CARBINE
Caliber: 22 LR, 9-shot tubular magazine
Barrel: 18" Micro-Groove®.
Weight: 5 lbs. **Length:** 36¾" over-all.
Stock: Monte Carlo American black walnut with p.g. and handguard. White buttplate spacer, Mar-Shield® finish.
Sights: Ramp front, adj. open rear.
Features: Gold plated trigger, bolt hold-open, serrated receiver top is grooved for tip-off scope mount, sling swivels attached.
Price: **$73.95**

Marlin 989 M2 Autoloading Carbine
Same as the Marlin 99 M1 carbine except 7-shot detachable clip magazine.
Price: **$73.95**

Marlin 99C Autoloading Rifle
Same as the Marlin 49DL except: one piece American black walnut stock with checkered p.g. and fore-end.
Price: **$73.95**

MARLIN 49DL AUTOLOADING RIFLE
Caliber: 22 LR, 18-shot tubular magazine
Barrel: 22" Micro-Groove®.
Weight: 5½ lbs. **Length:** 40½"
Stock: American black walnut, Monte Carlo capped p.g., checkered fore-end and p.g., Mar-Shield® finish.
Sights: Ramp front, open rear adj. for w. & e.
Features: Gold plated trigger, bolt hold-open for safety and cleaning, scroll-engraved receiver grooved for tip-off scope mounts. Has new tube magazine closure system.
Price: **$82.95**

MARLIN GLENFIELD 60 AUTOLOADER
Caliber: 22 LR, 18-shot tubular mag.
Barrel: 22" round tapered.
Weight: About 5½ lbs. **Length:** 41" Over-all.
Stock: Walnut finished Monte Carlo, checkered p.g. and fore-end.
Sights: Ramp front, open adj. rear.
Features: Chrome plated trigger, matted receiver is grooved for tip-off mounts. Has new tube magazine closure system.
Price: Less scope **$62.95**

MOSSBERG MODEL 353 AUTOLOADING RIFLE
Caliber: 22 LR, 7-shot clip.
Barrel: 18" "AC-KRO-GRUV".
Weight: 5 lbs. **Length:** 38" over-all.
Stock: Walnut, checkered at p.g. and fore-end. Black Tenite two-position fold-down fore-end.
Sights: Open step adj. U-notch rear, bead front on ramp.
Features: Sling swivels and web strap on left of stock, extension fore-end folds down for steady firing from prone position. Receiver grooved for scope mounting.
Price: **$82.95**

MOSSBERG 377 PLINKSTER AUTO RIFLE
Caliber: 22 LR, 15-shot tube magazine
Barrel: 20" AC-KRO-GRUV.
Weight: 6¼ lbs. **Length:** 40" over-all.
Stock: Straight line, moulded one-piece thumbhole.
Sights: No iron sights. Comes with 4x scope.
Features: Walnut texture stock finish, checkered fore-end. Tube magazine loads through port in buttstock. Has bolt hold-open.
Price: With 4x scope **$72.50**

REMINGTON 572 FIELDMASTER PUMP RIFLE
Caliber: 22 S(20), L(17) or LR(14). Tubular mag.
Barrel: 21" round tapered.
Weight: 5½ lbs. **Length:** 42" over-all.
Stock: Walnut-finished hardwood with p.g. and grooved slide handle.
Sights: Blade ramp front; sliding ramp rear adj. for w. & e.
Features: Cross-bolt safety, removing inner mag. tube converts rifle to single shot, receiver grooved for tip-off scope mount.
Price: **$104.95**
Price: Sling and swivels installed **$13.25**

Remington Model 572 BDL Deluxe
Same as the 572 except: p.g. cap, walnut stock with RKW finish, checkered grip and fore-end, ramp front and fully adj. rear sights.
Price: **$119.95**
Price: Sling and swivels installed **$13.25**

Remington Model 572 SB
Similar to the 572, but has smoothbore bbl. choked for 22 LR shot cartridges.
Price: **$114.95**
Price: Sling and swivels installed **$13.25**

RIMFIRE RIFLES—AUTOLOADING & SLIDE ACTION

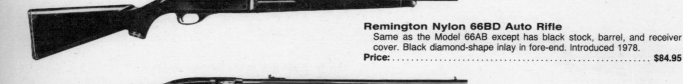

REMINGTON NYLON 66MB AUTO RIFLE
Caliber: 22 LR, 14-shot tubular mag.
Barrel: 19⅝" round tapered.
Weight: 4 lbs. **Length:** 38½" over-all.
Stock: Moulded Mohawk Brown Nylon, checkered p.g. and fore-end.
Sights: Blade ramp front, adj. open rear.
Features: Top tang safety, double extractors, receiver grooved for tip-off mounts.
Price: $84.95
Price: Model 66GS (22 Short only) $94.95
Price: With Universal UA 4x scope $89.95

Remington Nylon 66AB Auto Rifle
Same as the Model 66MB except: Apache Black Nylon stock, chrome plated receiver.
Price: $89.95

Remington Nylon 66BD Auto Rifle
Same as the Model 66AB except has black stock, barrel, and receiver cover. Black diamond-shape inlay in fore-end. Introduced 1978.
Price: $84.95

REMINGTON 552A AUTOLOADING RIFLE
Caliber: 22 S (20), L (17) or LR (15) tubular mag.
Barrel: 21" round tapered.
Weight: About 5¾ lbs. **Length:** 40" over-all.
Stock: Full-size, walnut-finished hardwood.
Sights: Bead front, step open rear adj. for w. & e.
Features: Positive cross-bolt safety, receiver grooved for tip-off mount.
Price: $99.95

Remington Model 552BDL Auto Rifle
Same as Model 552A except: Du Pont RKW finished walnut stock, checkered fore-end and capped p.g. stock. Blade ramp front and fully adj. rear sights.
Price: $114.95

ROSSI 62 SA PUMP RIFLE
Caliber: 22 S, L or LR.
Barrel: 23".
Weight: 5¾ lbs. **Length:** 39¼" over-all.
Stock: Walnut, straight grip, grooved fore-end.
Sights: Fixed front, adj. rear.
Features: Capacity 20 Short, 16 Long or 14 Long Rifle. Quick takedown. Imported from Brazil by Interarms.
Price: Blue $115.00
Price: Chrome $120.00

ROSSI 62 SAC CARBINE
Same as standard model except has 16¼" barrel. Magazine holds slightly fewer cartridges.
Price: Blue $115.00
Price: Chrome $120.00

RUGER 10/22 AUTOLOADING CARBINE
Caliber: 22 LR, 10-shot rotary mag.
Barrel: 18½" round tapered.
Weight: 5 lbs. **Length:** 37" over-all.
Stock: American walnut with p.g. and bbl. band.
Sights: Gold bead front, folding leaf rear adj. for e.
Features: Detachable rotary magazine fits flush into stock, cross-bolt safety, receiver tapped and grooved for scope blocks or tip-off mount. Scope base adapter furnished with each rifle.
Price: $79.50

Ruger 10/22 Auto Sporter
Same as 10/22 Carbine except: Hand checkered p.g. and fore-end with straight buttplate, no bbl. band, has sling swivels.
Price: $91.50

SAVAGE MODEL 80 AUTO RIFLE
Caliber: 22 LR, 15-shot tube magazine.
Barrel: 20".
Weight: 6 lbs. **Length:** 40" over-all.
Stock: Select walnut, checkered p.g. and fore-end.
Sights: Blade front, open rear adj. for w. & e.
Features: Adult-sized rifle. Monte Carlo stock with white spacers at p.g. and buttplate. Receiver grooved for scope mounting.
Price: $79.50

SQUIRES BINGHAM M16 SEMI AUTO RIFLE
Caliber: 22 LR, 15-shot clip.
Barrel: 16½".
Weight: 6 lbs. **Length:** 38½" over-all.
Stock: Black painted mahogany.
Sights: Post front, rear adj. for e.
Features: Box magazine, muzzle brake/flash suppressor. Imported by Kassnar Imports.
Price: $84.95

SQUIRES BINGHAM M20D SEMI AUTO RIFLE
Caliber: 22 LR, 15-shot clip.
Barrel: 19½".
Weight: 6 lbs. **Length:** 40½" over-all.
Stock: Pulong Dalaga wood with contrasting fore-end tip.
Sights: Blade front, V-notch rear adj. for e.
Features: Positive sliding thumb safety. Receiver grooved for tip-off scope mount. Imported by Kassnar Imports.
Price: $69.95

TRADEWINDS MODEL 260-A AUTO RIFLE
Caliber: 22 LR, 5-shot (10-shot mag. avail.).
Barrel: 22½".
Weight: 5¾ lbs. **Length:** 41½".
Stock: Walnut, with hand checkered p.g. and fore-end.
Sights: Ramp front with hood, 3-leaf folding rear, receiver grooved for scope mt.
Features: Double extractors, sliding safety. Imported by Tradewinds.
Price: $165.00

WEATHERBY MARK XXII AUTO RIFLE, CLIP MODEL
Caliber: 22 LR only, 5- or 10-shot clip loaded
Barrel: 24" round contoured.
Weight: 6 lbs. **Length:** 42¼" over-all.
Stock: Walnut, Monte Carlo comb and cheekpiece, rosewood p.g. cap and fore-end tip. Skip-line checkering.
Sights: Gold bead ramp front, 3-leaf folding rear.
Features: Thumb operated side safety also acts as single shot selector. Receiver grooved for tip-off scope mount. Single pin release for quick take-down.
Price: $219.50
Extra 5-shot clip .... $5.25   Extra 10-shot clip $5.95

Weatherby Mark XXII Tubular Model
Same as Mark XXII Clip Model except: 15-shot tubular magazine. **$229.50**

WINCHESTER 190 AUTOLOADING RIFLE
Caliber: 22 cal., L (17) or LR (15), tubular mag.
Barrel: 20½" round tapered (16" twist).
Weight: 5 lbs. **Length:** 39" over-all.
Stock: 2-piece walnut finished hardwood. checkered p.g. and fore-end, (13⅝"x1¾"x2¾").
Sights: Bead post front, step adj. rear.
Features: Cross-bolt safety, composition buttplate. Comes with Weaver 4X scope mounted.
Price: $78.95

RIMFIRE RIFLES — LEVER ACTION

BROWNING BL-22 LEVER ACTION RIFLE
Caliber: 22 S(22), L(17) or LR(15). Tubular mag.
Barrel: 20" round tapered.
Weight: 5 lbs. **Length:** 36¾" over-all.
Stock: Walnut, 2-piece straight grip western style.
Sights: Bead post front, folding-leaf rear.
Features: Short throw lever, ½-cock safety, receiver grooved for tip-off scope mounts.
Price: Grade I $149.95
Price: Grade II, engraved receiver, checkered grip and fore-end .. $169.95

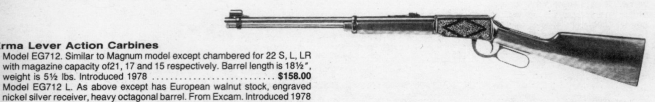

ERMA EG73 LEVER ACTION CARBINE
Caliber: 22 WRM, 12-shot magazine.
Barrel: 19¼".
Weight: 6 lbs. **Length:** 37⅜" over-all.
Stock: Walnut-stained beech.
Sights: Hooded ramp front, Buckhorn rear. Receiver grooved for scope
  mounting.
Features: Tubular magazine, side ejection. Introduced 1978. Imported by
  Excam.
Price: **$179.00**

Erma Lever Action Carbines
Model EG712. Similar to Magnum model except chambered for 22 S, L, LR
with magazine capacity of 21, 17 and 15 respectively. Barrel length is 18½",
weight is 5½ lbs. Introduced 1978 .... **$158.00**
Model EG712 L. As above except has European walnut stock, engraved
nickel silver receiver, heavy octagonal barrel. From Excam. Introduced 1978
.... **$279.00**

ITHACA MODEL 72 SADDLEGUN
Caliber: 22 LR, 15-shot magazine tube.
Barrel: 18½".
Weight: 5 lbs.
Stock: American walnut.
Sights: Hooded front, step-adj. rear.
Features: Half-cock safety, steel receiver grooved for scope mounts.
Price: Standard **$144.95**
Price: 22 WMR, std. grade **$159.95**

MARLIN GOLDEN 39A LEVER ACTION RIFLE
Caliber: 22 S(26), L(21), LR(19), tubular magazine.
Barrel: 24" Micro-Groove®.
Weight: 6½ lbs. **Length:** 40".
Stock: American black walnut with white line spacers at p.g. cap and buttplate.
Sights: Bead ramp front with detachable "Wide-Scan"™ hood, folding rear
  semi-buckhorn adj. for w. and e.
Features: Take-down action, receiver tapped for scope mount (supplied), gold
  plated trigger, sling swivels, offset hammer spur. Mar-Shield® stock finish.
Price: **$139.95**

MARLIN GOLDEN 39M CARBINE
Caliber: 22 S(21), L(16), LR(15), tubular magazine.
Barrel: 20" Micro-Grove®.
Weight: 6 lbs. **Length:** 36".
Stock: American black walnut, straight grip, white line buttplate spacer. Mar-
  Shield® finish.
Sights: "Wide-Scan"™ ramp front with hood, folding rear semi-buckhorn adj.
  for w. and e.
Features: Squared finger lever. Receiver tapped for scope mount (supplied)
  or receiver sight, gold plated trigger, offset hammer spur, sling swivels,
  take-down action.
Price: **$139.95**

NAVY ARMS MODEL 66 LEVER ACTION RIFLE
Caliber: 38 Special, 44-40.
Barrel: 16½", 19", 24".
Weight: 9¼ lbs. **Length:** 39½".
Stock: Walnut.
Sights: Fixed front, folding rear.
Features: Replica of Winchester Model 1866 "Yellowboy." Available with
  three grades of engraving, selected stock and fore-end at additional cost.
  22 LR also available with 16½" bbl. (Trapper's Model). Imported by Navy
  Arms.
Price: Trapper & Carbine **$195.00**
Price: 24" octagon bbl. **$250.00**

Winchester 9422M XTR Lever Action Rifle
Same as the 9422 except chambered for 22 WMR cartridge, has 11-round
mag. capacity **$190.95**

WINCHESTER 9422 XTR LEVER ACTION RIFLE
Caliber: 22 S(21), L(17), LR(15). Tubular mag.
Barrel: 20½" (16" twist).
Length: 37⅛" over-all. **Weight:** 6½ lbs.
Stock: American walnut, 2-piece, straight grip (no p.g.).
Sights: Hooded ramp front, adj. semi-buckhorn rear.
Features: Side ejection, receiver grooved for scope mounting, takedown ac-
  tion. Has new XTR wood and metal finish.
Price: **$184.95**

HARRINGTON & RICHARDSON 865 PLAINSMAN RIFLE
Caliber: 22 S, L or LR. 5-shot clip mag.
Barrel: 22″ round tapered.
Weight: 5 lbs. **Length:** 39″ over-all.
Stock: Walnut finished hardwood with Monte Carlo and p.g.
Sights: Blade front, step adj. open rear.
Features: Cocking indicator, sliding side safety, receiver grooved for tip-off scope mounts.
Price: **$62.00**

MARLIN 780 BOLT ACTION RIFLE
Caliber: 22 S, L, or LR; 7-shot clip magazine.
Barrel: 22″ Micro-Groove.
Weight: 5½ lbs. **Length:** 41″
Stock: Monte Carlo American black walnut with checkered p.g. White line spacer at buttplate. Mar-Shield® finish.
Sights: "Wide-Scan"™ ramp front, folding semi-buckhorn rear adj. for w. & e.
Features: Gold plated trigger receiver anti-glare serrated and grooved for tip-off scope mount.
Price: **$66.95**

Marlin 781 Bolt Action Rifle
Same as the Marlin 780 except: tubular magazine holds 25 Shorts, 19 Longs or 17 Long Rifle cartridges. Weight 6 lbs. **$70.95**

Marlin 782 Bolt Action Rifle
Same as the Marlin 783 except: 22 Rimfire Magnum cal. only, weight about 6 lbs. Sling and swivels attached. **$74.95**

Marlin 783 Bolt Action Rifle
Same as Marlin 782 except: Tubular magazine holds 13 rounds of 22 Rimfire Magnum ammunition. **$77.95**

Marlin Glenfield 20 Bolt Action Repeater
Similar to Marlin 780, except: Walnut finished checkered p.g. stock, without Monte Carlo, conventional rifling, bead front sight **$56.95**

MOSSBERG MODEL 321K
Caliber: 22 S, L, LR, single shot.
Barrel: 24″.
Length: 43½″ over-all. **Weight:** 6½ lbs.
Stock: Walnut finish, cheekpiece, checkered p.g. and fore-end.
Sights: Ramp front, adj. rear.
Features: Hammerless bolt action with drop-in loading platform and automatic safety, black buttplate. Model 321B has S330 peep sight with ¼-minute click adjustments.
Price: **$64.95**

MOSSBERG MODEL 341 RIFLE
Caliber: 22 S, L, LR, 7-shot clip.
Barrel: 24″ "AC-KRO-GRUV"
Weight: 6½ lbs. **Length:** 43½″ over-all.
Stock: Walnut, checkered p.g. and fore-end, Monte Carlo and cheek piece. Buttplate with white line spacer.
Sights: Bead front, U-notch rear adj. for w. and e.
Features: Sliding side safety, 8 groove rifling, "Magic 3-way" clip adjusts to Short, Long or Long Rifle cartridges.
Price: **$73.95**

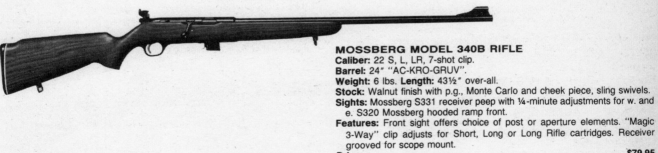

MOSSBERG MODEL 340B RIFLE
Caliber: 22 S, L, LR, 7-shot clip.
Barrel: 24″ "AC-KRO-GRUV".
Weight: 6 lbs. **Length:** 43½″ over-all.
Stock: Walnut finish with p.g., Monte Carlo and cheek piece, sling swivels.
Sights: Mossberg S331 receiver peep with ¼-minute adjustments for w. and e. S320 Mossberg hooded ramp front.
Features: Front sight offers choice of post or aperture elements. "Magic 3-Way" clip adjusts for Short, Long or Long Rifle cartridges. Receiver grooved for scope mount.
Price: **$79.95**

MOSSBERG MODEL 640K CHUCKSTER
Caliber: 22 WMR. 5-shot clip mag.
Barrel: 24″ AC-KRO-GRUV.
Weight: 6 lbs. **Length:** 44¾″ over-all.
Stock: Walnut, checkered p.g. and fore-end, Monte Carlo comb and cheek-piece.
Sights: Ramp front with bead, fully adj. leaf rear.
Features: Grooved trigger, sliding side safety, double extractors, receiver grooved for tip-off scope mounts and tapped for aperture rear sight.
Price: **$84.95**

REMINGTON MODEL 541-S
Caliber: 22 S, L, LR; 5-shot clip.
Barrel: 24″
Weight: 5½ lbs. **Length:** 42⅝″.
Stock: Walnut, checkered p.g. and fore end.
Sights: None. Drilled and tapped for scope mounts or receiver sights.
Features: Clip repeater. Thumb safety. Receiver and trigger guard scroll engraved.
Price: $225.00
Price: Extra 10-shot clip $5.50

Remington Model 582 Rifle
Same as M581 except: tubular magazine under bbl. holds 20 S, 15 L or 14 LR cartridges. Wgt. 5½ lbs.
Price: $99.95

REMINGTON MODEL 581 RIFLE
Caliber: 22 S, L or LR. 5-shot clip mag.
Barrel: 24″ round.
Weight: 4¾ lbs. **Length:** 42⅝″ over-all.
Stock: Walnut finished Monte Carlo with p.g.
Sights: Bead post front, screw adj. open rear.
Features: Sliding side safety, wide trigger, receiver grooved for tip-off scope mounts. Comes with single-shot adapter.
Price: $87.95
Price: Left hand action and stock $92.95

Savage/Anschutz Model 1432 Sporter
Same as Model 54 except chambered for 22 Hornet, 24″ barrel, 5-shot capacity, over-all length 43⅝″ $505.00

SAVAGE/ANSCHUTZ MODEL 54 SPORTER
Caliber: 22 LR. 5-shot clip mag.
Barrel: 23″ round tapered.
Weight: 6¾ lbs. **Length:** 42″ over-all.
Stock: French walnut, checkered p.g. and fore-end. Monte Carlo roll-over comb, schnabel fore-end tip.
Sights: Hooded ramp gold bead front, folding-leaf rear.
Features: Adj. single stage trigger, wing safety, receiver grooved for tip-off mount, tapped for scope blocks.
Price: $399.50
Price: Model 54M (22 WRM) $410.00

Savage/Anschutz Model 1418-1518 Sporters
Similar to Model 164 except has European Mannlicher stock with inlays, hand-cut skip-line checkering, double set or single stage trigger.
Price: 1418 (22 LR) $368.00
Price: 1518 (22 Mag.) $374.50

SAVAGE/ANSCHUTZ 164 BOLT ACTION RIFLE
Caliber: 22 LR. 5-shot clip mag.
Barrel: 24″ round tapered.
Weight: 6 lbs. **Length:** 40¾″ over-all.
Stock: Walnut, hand checkered p.g. and fore-end, Monte Carlo comb and cheekpiece, schnabel fore-end.
Sights: Hooded ramp gold bead front, folding-leaf rear.
Features: Fully adj. single stage trigger, sliding side safety, receiver grooved for tip-off mount.
Price: $259.50
Price: Model 164M in 22 WRM (4-shot) $264.50

Savage/Stevens Model 34 Rifle
Same as the Model 65-M except: 22 LR, walnut finished hardwood stock, bead post front sight.
Price: $62.50

SAVAGE MODEL 65-M RIFLE
Caliber: 22 WRM, 5-shot.
Barrel: 20″ lightweight, free floating.
Weight: 5 lbs. **Length:** 39″ over-all.
Stock: Walnut, Monte Carlo comb. checkered p.g. and fore-end.
Sights: Gold bead ramp front, step adj. open rear.
Features: Sliding side safety, double extractors, receiver grooved for tip-off scope mount.
Price: $76.50

RIMFIRE RIFLES—BOLT ACTION

SQUIRES BINGHAM M14D BOLT ACTION RIFLE
Caliber: 22 S, L, LR, 5-shot clip.
Barrel: 19½".
Weight: 6 lbs. **Length:** 41" over-all.
Stock: Nato wood with white line spacers. Monte Carlo comb.
Sights: Hooded ramp front, V-notch rear adjustable for e.
Features: Positive sliding thumb safety, receiver grooved for tip-off scope mount. Also available in 22 mag. as model 15. Imported by Kassnar Imports.
Price: Model 14D **$69.95**
Price: Model 15 (22 Mag.) **$74.95**

TRADEWINDS MODEL 311-A BOLT ACTION RIFLE
Caliber: 22 LR, 5-shot (10-shot mag. avail.).
Barrel: 22½".
Weight: 6 lbs. **Length:** 41¼".
Stock: Walnut, Monte Carlo with hand checkered p.g. and fore-end.
Sights: Ramp front with hood, folding leaf rear, receiver grooved for scope mt.
Features: Sliding safety locks trigger and bolt handle. Imported by Tradewinds.
Price: **$150.00**

WESTERN FIELD 852 BOLT ACTION RIFLE
Caliber: 22 S, L, LR; 7-shot clip.
Barrel: 24" round tapered.
Length: 43" over-all. **Weight:** 6½ lbs.
Stock: Walnut-finished hardwood.
Sights: Bead front, rear adj. for e.
Features: Thumb operated safety. Scope not included.
Price: **$59.99**
Price: Model 840 in 22 WRM (illus.) **$69.99**

RIMFIRE RIFLES—SINGLE SHOT

HARRINGTON & RICHARDSON MODEL 750 PIONEER
Caliber: 22 S, L or LR. Single-shot.
Barrel: 22" round tapered.
Weight: 5 lbs. **Length:** 39" over-all.
Stock: Walnut finished hardwood with Monte Carlo comb and p.g.
Sights: Blade front, step adj. open rear.
Features: Double extractors, feed platform, cocking indicator. sliding side safety, receiver grooved for tip-off scope mount, tapped for aperture sight.
Price: **$52.00**

ITHACA MODEL 49 SADDLEGUN
Caliber: 22 S, L or LR. Single-shot.
Barrel: 18" round.
Weight: About 5½ lbs. **Length:** 34½" over-all
Stock: Two-piece walnut, checkered straight grip, fore-end has bbl. band.
Sights: Bead post front, step adj. open rear.
Features: Rebounding hammer safety, Martini-type lever action. Rifle can be ordered with shorter (youth) stock at no extra cost.
Price: Standard and Youth models **$54.95**
Price: Chambered for 22 WRM only **$64.95**

MARLIN GLENFIELD 10 SINGLE SHOT RIFLE
Caliber: 22, S, L, LR.
Barrel: 22".
Weight: About 4½ lbs. **Length:** 40" overall.
Stock: Walnut-finished hardwood, checkered p.g.
Sights: Bead front, adjustable open rear. Receiver grooved for scope mount.
Features: Manually cocked action with T-shaped cocking knob. Chrome plated steel trigger. Introduced 1978.
Price: About **$41.95**

REMINGTON MODEL 580 SINGLE SHOT RIFLE
Caliber: 22 S, L or LR. Single-shot.
Barrel: 24″ round tapered.
Weight: 4¾ lbs. **Length:** 42⅜″ over-all.
Stock: Walnut finished hardwood, Monte Carlo comb and p.g., black composition buttplate.
Sights: Bead post front, screw-lock adj. rear.
Features: Single screw take-down, integral loading platform, sliding side safety, receiver grooved for tip-off mount, can be had with 1″ shorter (youth) stock.
Price: **$82.95**
Price: M580 Boy's Rifle **$82.95**

SAVAGE STEVENS MODEL 72 CRACKSHOT
Caliber: 22 S, L, LR.
Barrel: 22″ octagonal.
Weight: 4½ lbs. **Length:** 37″.
Stock: Walnut, straight grip and fore-end.
Sights: Blade front, step adj. rear.
Features: Falling block action, color case hardened frame.
Price: **$79.95**

> Consult our Directory pages for the location of firms mentioned.

SAVAGE STEVENS MODEL 73 SINGLE SHOT RIFLE
Caliber: 22 S, L or LR. Single-shot.
Barrel: 20″ round tapered.
Weight: 4¾ lbs. **Length:** 38½″ over-all.
Stock: Walnut finished hardwood.
Sights: Bead post front, step adj. open rear.
Features: Cocks on opening, automatic safety, key locks trigger against unauthorized use, may be had with 12½″ pull stock (youth model) at same cost.
Price: **$45.50**

SAVAGE-STEVENS MODEL 89
Caliber: 22 LR, single-shot.
Barrel: 18½″.
Weight: 5 lbs. **Length:** 35″ over-all.
Stock: Walnut finished hardwood.
Sights: Blade front, step adj. rear.
Features: Single-shot Martini-type breech block. Hammer must be cocked by hand independent of lever prior to firing. Automatic ejection. Satin black frame finish.
Price: **$55.50**

ULTRA-HI SINGLE SHOT RIFLE
Caliber: 22 S, L, LR. Single shot.
Barrel: 23″.
Weight: 5 lbs **Length:** 40″ over-all.
Stock: Cherrywood.
Sights: Blade front, adj. rear.
Features: Blue finish, receiver grooved for scope. From Ultra-Hi Products.
Price: **$39.95**

SHOTGUNS—AUTOLOADING

BENELLI AUTOLOADING SHOTGUN
Gauge: 12 ga. (5-shot, 3-shot plug furnished).
Barrel: 26″ (Skeet, Imp. Cyl., Mod.); 28″ (Spec., Full, Imp. Mod., Mod.). Vent. rib.
Weight: 6¾ lbs.
Stock: European walnut. 14″x1½″x2½″. Hand checkered p.g. and fore-end.
Sights: Metal bead front.
Features: Quick interchangeable barrels. Cross-bolt safety. Hand engraved on higher grades. Imported from Italy by Heckler & Koch, Inc.
Price: Standard model $354.00
Price: Engraved $399.50

BERETTA A-301 AUTO SHOTGUN
Gauge: 12 (2¾″ or 3″) or 20
Action: Gas operated.
Barrel: 12 ga.—22″ (slug); 26″ (Imp. Cyl.); 28″ (Mod., Full); 30″ (Full, 3″ chamber); 20 ga.—28″ (Full, Mod.); 26″ (Imp. Cyl.). Vent. rib except slug gun.
Weight: 6 lbs., 5 ozs. (20 ga., 28″).
Stock: 14⅛″x1⅜″x2⅜″, European walnut. Magnum guns have recoil pad.
Features: All gas system parts are of stainless steel. Alloy receiver decorated with scroll pattern engraving. Push button safety in trigger guard. Introduced 1977. Imported by The Beretta Arms Co.
Price: 12 or 20, 2¾″ $435.00
Price: 12 ga., 3″ Magnum $475.00
Price: Slug gun $450.00
Price: Extra barrels, from $125.00

Beretta A-301 Skeet and Trap
Same as standard A-301 except: Trap has M.C. stock (14¼″x1⅜″x 1⁹⁄₁₆″x1⅝″) with recoil pad, gold plated trigger, trap choke 30″ bbl. Skeet gun has Skeet choke, gold plated trigger, Skeet stock (14¼″x1⅜″x2⅜″x 2⁹⁄₁₆″) and 26″ barrel. Introduced 1977. Imported by Beretta Arms Co.
Price: Skeet $435.00
Price: Trap $435.00
Price: Extra barrels $130.00

BREDA AUTOLOADING SHOTGUN
Gauge: 12 only (5-shot, 3-shot plug furnished), 2¾″ chamber.
Action: Recoil operated.
Barrel: 26″ (Imp. Cyl., Mod., Full), vent. rib; interchangeable choke tubes.
Weight: 7 lbs.
Stock: Walnut finished hardwood; p.g. and fore-end checkered.
Features: Receiver made of lightweight aluminum alloy. Also available for 3″ shells (29″ vent. rib barrel). Imported by Diana Import Co.
Price: Standard Model $324.50
Price: Magnum $434.50
Price: Interchangeable choke tubes $21.60

BROWNING AUTO-5 LIGHT 12 and 20
Gauge: 12, 20; 5-shot; 3-shot plug furnished; 2¾″ chamber.
Action: Recoil operated autoloader; takedown.
Barrel: 26″ (Skeet boring in 12 & 20 ga., Cyl., Imp. Cyl., Mod. in 20 ga.); 28″ (Skeet in 12 ga., Mod., Full); 30″ (Full in 12 ga.).
Weight: 12 ga. 7¼ lbs., 20 ga. 6⅜ lbs.
Stock: French walnut, hand checkered half-p.g. and fore-end. 14¼″ x 1⅝″ x 2½″.
Features: Receiver hand engraved with scroll designs and border. Double extractors, extra bbls. interchangeable without factory fitting; mag. cut-off; cross-bolt safety.
Price: Vent. rib only $407.95

Browning Auto-5 Magnum 12
Same as Std. Auto-5 except: chambered for 3″ magnum shells (also handles 2¾″ magnum and 2¾″ HV loads). 28″ Mod., Full; 30″ and 32″ (Full) bbls. 14″x1⅝″x2½″ stock. Recoil pad. Wgt. 8¾ lbs.
Price: Vent. rib only $417.95

Browning Auto-5 Light Skeet
Same as Light Standard except: 12 and 20 ga. only, 26″ or 28″ bbl. (Skeet). With vent. rib. Wgt. 6⅜-7½ lbs. $407.95

Browning Auto-5 Magnum 20
Same as Magnum 12 except barrels 28″ Full or Mod., or 26″ Full, Mod. or Imp. Cyl. With ventilated rib, 7½ lbs. $417.95

Browning Auto-5 Light 12, 20, or 12 Buck Special
Same as A-5 Light model except: 24″ bbl. choked for slugs, gold bead front sight on contoured ramp, rear sight adj. for w.&e. Wgt. 12 ga., 7 lbs.; 20 ga., 6 lbs. 2 oz.; 3″ Mag. 12, 8¼ lbs. Illus.
Price: $417.95
Price: 12 ga. Magnum $427.95
All Buck Specials are available with carrying sling, detachable swivels and swivel attachments for $15.00 extra.

SHOTGUNS—AUTOLOADING

BROWNING B/2000 GAS OPERATED AUTO SHOTGUN

Gauge: 12 ga.; 5-shot, 4-shot in Magnum.
Barrel: 26", 28" or 30" in 2¾" Field Models, plain or vent. rib; 28", 30" or 32" in 3" Magnum models, vent. rib only.
Weight: 7½ lbs. (26" vent. rib) **Length:** 45⅜" (26" bbl.).
Stock: French walnut, hand checkered, full pistol grip, no recoil pad 14¼"x1⅝"x2½".
Sights: Medium raised bead, German nickel silver.
Features: Internal self-cleaning gas system, soft recoil, speed loading/unloading, extra bbls. interchangeable without factory fitting. No adjustment necessary to gas system for varying loads.
Price: Vent. rib $369.95
Price: Plain bbl. 12 ga. only $329.95
Price: Vent. rib, 3" Mag. $369.95
Price: Buck Special $384.95

Browning B-2000 20 Gauge

Same as 12 ga. B-2000 except: vent. rib barrel only; front and center ivory sight beads on Skeet barrel only; 24" Buck Special barrel 26" (Full, Mod., Imp. Cyl., Cyl., Skeet), 28" (Full or Mod.); extra barrels available, 2¾" or 3" chambers (3" not available in 26" Cyl. bore, 26" Skeet or 24" Buck Special). Weight is about 6¾ lbs, length with 26" barrel is 46½". Vent. rib barrel only $369.95

Browning B/2000 12 ga. Trap and Skeet Models

Similar to field grade B/2000 except has a special high post floating vent. rib mated to a special receiver rib; front and center ivory beads; special Skeet or trap recoil pads fitted. Trap model has Monte Carlo stock (14⅜"x1⅜"x1⅜"x2⅛"); Skeet has Skeet stock (14⅜"x1½"x2"). Checkered French walnut with semi-beavertail fore-end; 2¾" chamber.
Price: Trap $419.95
Price: Skeet $369.95

Browning B/2000 20 ga. Skeet Model

Similar to 12 ga. target guns except has conventional vent. rib with front and center ivory beads; does not have the special high post floating rib. Skeet stock and pad, semi-beavertail fore-end; 2¾" chamber.
Price: $369.95

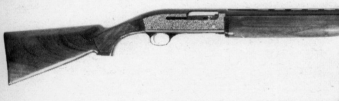

FRANCHI MODEL 500 GAS AUTO

Gauge: 12 only (2¾" chamber); 4-shot magazine, 2-shot plug furnished.
Barrel: 26" (Imp., Cyl., Mod.), 28" (Mod., Imp. Mod., Full).
Weight: About 7 lbs.
Stock: Select walnut, checkered p.g. and fore-end; semi-gloss finish.
Sights: Metal bead front.
Features: Gas operated, fixed barrel. Shell carrier need not be unlocked for loading. Ventilated rib with matted top surface; chrome lined barrel. Deluxe (Model 520) is identical except for full engraving on receiver sides. Imported by Stoeger Industries.
Price: Field Grade $279.95
Price: Model 520 Deluxe (engraved receiver) $349.95

FRANCHI MAGNUM AUTO SHOTGUN

Gauge: 12 or 20, 3-inch shells.
Action: Recoil-operated automatic.
Barrel: 32", 12 ga.; 28", 20 ga., both Full.
Weight: 12 ga. 8¼ lbs., 20 ga. 6 lbs.
Stock: Epoxy-finished walnut with recoil pad.
Features: Chrome-lined bbl., easy takedown. Available with ventilated rib barrel. Imported from Italy by Stoeger Industries.
Price: Vent. rib only $299.95

FRANCHI 530 AUTOMATIC TRAP

Gauge: 12 only, 2¾" chamber.
Barrel: 30" (Full or Imp. Mod.). Supplied with three interchangeable choke tubes.
Weight: 8 lbs. 6 ozs.
Stock: Select French walnut. Hand-applied oil finish, hand checkered p.g. and fore-end. Stock is interchangeable and drilled and tapped for recoil reducer. Choice of straight or M.C. stock in three sizes.
Features: Specially tuned gas system. Target grade trigger. Chrome lined bore and chamber. All stocks are cast-off for right-handed shooters—left-hand models available. Has Franchi's "Hi-Loft" vent. rib. Gun has matte blue to reduce light reflection. Comes with a snap-in shell catcher for singles, shell deflector for doubles. Introduced 1978. From Stoeger Industries.
Price: $499.95

Consult our Directory pages for the location of firms mentioned.

SHOTGUNS—AUTOLOADING

FRANCHI STANDARD AUTO SHOTGUN
Gauge: 12, 20 or 28, 5-shot. 2¾" or 3" chamber.
Action: Recoil-operated automatic.
Barrel: 24" (Imp. Cyl. or Cyl.); 26" (Imp. Cyl. or Mod.); 28" (Skeet, Mod. or Full); 30", 32". (Full).
Weight: 12 ga. 6¼ lbs., 20 ga. 5 lbs. 2 oz.
Stock: Epoxy-finished walnut.
Features: Chrome-lined bbl., easy takedown, 3-round plug provided. Available with plain round or ventilated rib barrel. Imported from Italy by Stoeger Industries.
Price: Vent. rib 12, 20 .... **$274.95**
Price: Hunter model (engraved, 12 or 20) **$339.95**

Franchi Slug Gun
Same as Standard automatic except 22" cylinder bored bbl., adj. rear sight, sling swivels.
Price: 12 or 20 ga. **$299.95**

ITHACA MODEL 51 DEERSLAYER
Gauge: 12 or 20 ga., 2¾" chamber.
Action: Gas-operated, semi-automatic.
Barrel: 24", special bore.
Weight: 7½ lbs. (12 ga.), 7¼ lbs. (20 ga.).
Stocks: 14"x1½"x2¼", American walnut. Checkered p.g. and fore-end.
Sights: Raybar front, open rear adj. for w. and e.
Features: Sight base grooved for scope mounts. Easy takedown, reversible safety. Scope optional.
Price: **$299.95**

ITHACA MAG 10 GAS OPERATED SHOTGUN
Gauge: 10, 3½" chamber, 3-shot.
Barrel: 32" only. Full choke.
Weight: 11¼ lbs.
Stock: American walnut, checkered p.g. and fore-end (14⅛"x2⅜"x1½"), p.g. cap, rubber recoil pad.
Sights: White Bradley.
Features: "Counterecoil" gas system. Piston, cylinder, bolt, charging lever, action release and carrier made of stainless steel. ⅜" vent. rib. Reversible cross-bolt safety. Low recoil force. Deluxe model has full fancy claro American black walnut.
Price: Standard, plain barrel **$429.95**
Price: Deluxe, vent. rib **$549.95**
Price: Standard, vent. rib **$469.95**
Price: Supreme, vent. rib **$649.95**

ITHACA MODEL 51 FEATHERLIGHT AUTOMATIC
Gauge: 12 ga. 2¾" chamber.
Action: Gas-operated, rotary bolt has three locking lugs. Takedown. Self-compensating for high or low base loads.
Barrel: Roto-Forged, 30" (Full), 28" (Full, Mod., or Skeet), 26" (Imp. Cyl. or Skeet). Extra barrels available. Raybar front sight. Vent. rib $25.00 extra.
Stock: 14"x1⅝"x2½". Hand checkered walnut, white spacers on p.g. and under recoil pad.
Weight: About 7½ lbs.
Features: Hand fitted, engraved receiver, 3 shot capacity, safety is reversible for left hand shooter.
Price: Standard **$274.95**
Price: With vent. rib **$307.95**

Ithaca Model 51 Featherlight Deluxe Trap
Same gun as standard Model 51 with fancy American walnut trap stock, 30" (Full or Imp. Cyl.) or 28" (Full or Imp. Mod.) barrel.
Price: .... **$384.95**   With Monte Carlo stock **$394.95**

Ithaca Model 51 Magnum
Same as Standard Model 51 except has 3" chambers.
Price: With vent rib **$329.95**

ITHACA MODEL 51 20 GAUGE
Gauge: 20 only, 2¾" or 3" chamber.
Action: Gas-operated rotary bolt.
Barrel: Standard Grade, 26" (Imp. Cyl.), 28" (Full, Mod.), Target Grade, 26" (Skeet).
Weight: 7½ to 8½ lbs.
Stock: 14"x1½"x2¼", American walnut.
Sights: Raybar front sight.
Features: Quick take-down, reversible safety, interchangeable barrels. Easily field stripped without tools.
Price: Standard model **$274.95**
Price: Standard model with vent. rib **$307.95**
Price: Vent. magnum **$329.95**
Price: Deluxe Skeet **$374.95**

LJUTIC BI MATIC AUTO SHOTGUN
Gauge: 12 ga. only.
Barrel: 30" (standard), 26" to 32"; choked to customer specs.
Weight: Approx. 10 lbs.
Stock: To customer specs. Oil finish, hand checkered.
Features: Two-shot, low recoil auto designed for trap and Skeet. One-piece actuating rod; pull or release trigger. Available with right- or left-hand ejector. From Ljutic Industries.
Price: **$1,995.00**
Price: Extra Barrel **$700.00**
Price: Release trigger **$250.00**

Ithaca Model 51 Featherlight Deluxe Skeet
Same gun as Model 51 Skeet with fancy American walnut stock, 28" or 29" (Skeet) barrel.
Price: **$374.95**

MANUFRANCE AUTO SHOTGUN
Gauge: 12 ga., (2¾" or 3"), 3-shot.
Action: Gas operated.
Barrel: 26" (Imp. Cyl.), 28" (Mod.), 30" (Full); vent. rib.
Weight: 6¾ lbs. **Length:** 48" over-all.
Stock: French walnut, hand checkered p.g. and fore-end.
Features: Magazine cut-off; black matte finish receiver; quick take-down; interchangeable barrels available. Imported by Interarms.
Price: $279.00

Remington 1100 Small Gauge
Same as 1100 except: 28 ga. 2¾" (5-shot) or 410, 3" (except Skeet, 2½" 4-shot). 45½" over-all. Available in 25" bbl. (Full, Mod., or Imp. Cyl.) only.
Price: Plain bbl. .... **$279.95**   With vent. rib **$312.95**

Remington 1100 SA Skeet
Same as the 1100 except: 26" bbl., special skeet boring, vent. rib, ivory bead front and metal bead middle sights. 14"x1½"x2½" stock. 20 and 12 ga. Wgt. 7½ lbs.
Price: $317.95
Price: 1100 SB (better grade walnut) $342.95
Left hand model with vent. rib $322.95
28 & 410 ga., 25" bbl. $322.95
20 ga. LT-20 Skeet SA $317.95
20 ga. LT-20 Skeet SB $342.95

REMINGTON MODEL 1100 AUTO
Gauge: 12, 16 (5-shot); 3-shot plug furnished.
Action: Gas-operated autoloader.
Barrel: 26" (Imp. Cyl.), 28" (Mod., Full), 30" Full in 12 ga. only.
Stock: 14"x1½"x2½" American Walnut, checkered p.g. and fore-end.
Weight: 12 ga. 7½ lbs., 16 ga. 7⅜ lbs.
Features: Quickly interchangeable barrels within gauge. Matted receiver top with scroll work on both sides of receiver. Crossbolt safety.
Price: .... **$274.95**   With vent. rib **$307.95**
Price: Left hand model with vent. rib **$312.95**

Remington 1100 LT-20
Basically the same design as Model 1100, but with special weight-saving features that retain strength and dependability of the standard Model 1100.
Barrel: 28" (Full, Mod.), 26" (Imp. Cyl.).
Weight: 6½ lbs.
Price: .... **$274.95**   With vent. rib **$307.95**
Price: LT-20 magnum (28" or 30" Full or Mod.) **$299.95**
Price: With vent. rib **$332.95**
Price: LT-20 Deer Gun (20" bbl.) **$296.95**

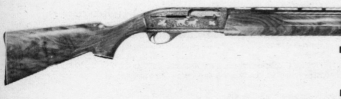

Remington 1100D Tournament Auto
Same as 1100 Standard except: vent. rib, better wood, more extensive engraving **$1,200.00**

Remington 1100F Premier Auto
Same as 1100D except: select wood, better engraving **$2,400.00**
With gold inlay **$3,600.00**

Remington 1100 Magnum
Same as 1100 except: chambered for 3" magnum loads. Available in 12 ga. (30") or 20 ga. (28") Mod. or Full, 14"x1½"x2½" stock with recoil pad, Wgt. 7¾ lbs. **$299.95**
Price: With vent. rib **$332.95**
Price: Left hand model with vent. rib **$332.95**

Remington 1100 TB Trap
Same as the 1100 except: better grade wood, recoil pad. 14⅜"x1⅜"x1¾" stock. Wgt. 8¼ lbs. 12 ga. only. 30" (Mod., Full) vent. rib bbl. Ivory bead front and white metal middle sight.
Price: .... **$352.95**   With Monte Carlo stock **$362.95**
Price: 1100TB Trap, left hand **$357.95**
Price: With Monte Carlo stock **$367.95**
Remington 1100 Extra bbls.: Plain **$68.95** (20, 28 & 410, **$71.95**). Vent. rib **$101.95** (20, 28 & 410, **$104.95**). Vent. rib Skeet **$109.95**. Vent. rib Trap **$106.95** Deer bbl. **$81.95**. Available in the same gauges and chokes as shown on guns.

Remington 1100 Deer Gun
Same as 1100 except: 12 ga. only, 22" bbl. (Imp. Cyl.), rifle sights adjustable for w. and e.; recoil pad with white spacer. Weight 7¼ lbs. **$296.95**

SHOTGUNS — AUTOLOADING

SKB MODEL XL 900
Gauge: 12 (2¾"), 20 (2¾", 3" chamber); 5 shot capacity.
Action: Gas-operated autoloader.
Barrel: 12 ga., Field Grade - 30" (Full), 28" (Full or Mod.), 26" (Imp. Cyl.); 20 ga., 28" (Full or Mod.,) 26" (Imp. Cyl.), Trap - 30" (Full or Imp. Mod.), Skeet - 26" (Skeet); 24" Slug Gun (Cyl.)
Weight: 6¾ lbs. **Length:** 48" overall.
Stock: 1½"x2½"x14" (Field Grade). Hand checkered French walnut.
Sights: Ventilated rib with Raybar front sight on field grades; Bradley-type on target grades.
Features: Self-compensating gas system, reversible safety, action release button. Silver game scene receiver, gold trigger, inlaid name plate. From SKB Arms.
Price: Ventilated rib ...... **$299.95**   Trap grade (12 ga. only) .. **$324.95**
Price: Skeet grade .... **$309.95**   Slug gun 12 or 20 .... **$294.95**
Price: Spare barrels (vent. rib), from **$104.95**

SKB XL 100 SLUG GUN
Gauge: 12 only, 2¾" chamber. 4-shot magazine.
Barrel: 20" (Cyl.).
Weight: 7 lbs. **Length:** 40⅜" over-all.
Stock: Walnut-finished hardwood.
Sights: Red ramp front with Ray-type blade, adjustable rear rifle sight.
Features: Gas-operated action. Reversible crossbolt safety. Deep vertical grooves in fore-end. Comes with sling swivels. Black anodized finish over high-strength aluminum alloy receiver reduces glare. Introduced 1978. From SKB Sports.
Price: **$244.95**

SKB MODEL XL 300
Gauge: 12 (2¾"), 20 (3" chamber).
Action: Gas-operated autoloader.
Barrel: 12 ga. Field Grade - 30" (Full), 28" (Full or Mod.), 26" (Imp. Cyl.). 20 ga. Field Grade - 28" (Full or Mod.) 26" (Imp. Cyl.).
Weight: 7½ lbs. **Length:** 48" over-all.
Stock: 1½"x2½"x14" (Field Grade). Hand checkered French walnut.
Sights: Raybar front sight on ventilated rib.
Features: Self-compensating gas system, reversible safety. From SKB Sports.
Price: Standard .... **$269.95**   Ventilated rib **$289.95**
Price: Spare barrels, from **$83.95**

Smith & Wesson Model 1000 20 Gauge & 20 Magnum
Similar to 12 ga. model except slimmed down to weigh only 6½ lbs. Has self-cleaning gas system. Choice of four interchangeable barrels (26", Imp. Cyl. or Skeet, 28" Mod. or Full).
Price: **$307.95**
Price: Extra barrels **$101.95**
Price: With 3" chamber **$329.35**

SMITH & WESSON MODEL 1000 AUTO
Gauge: 12, 2¾" or 3" chamber, 4-shot.
Action: Gas-operated autoloader.
Barrel: 26" (Skeet, Imp. Cyl.), 28" (Mod., Full), 30" (Mod. Full).
Length: 48" over-all (28" bbl.). **Weight:** 7½ lbs. (28" bbl.).
Stock: 14"x1½"x2⅜", American walnut.
Features: Interchangeable crossbolt safety, vent. rib with front and middle beads, engraved alloy receiver, pressure compensator and floating piston for light recoil.
Price: **$307.95**
Price: Extra barrels (as listed above) **$101.95**
Price: With 3" chamber, 30" (Mod., Full) barrel **$329.35**

TRADEWINDS H-170 AUTO SHOTGUN
Gauge: 12 only, 2¾" chamber.
Action: Recoil-operated automatic.
Barrel: 26", 28" (Mod.) and 28" (Full), chrome lined.
Weight: 7 lbs.
Stock: Select European walnut stock, p.g. and fore-end hand checkered.
Features: Light alloy receiver, 5-shot tubular magazine, ventilated rib. Imported by Tradewinds.
Price: **$259.50**

WEATHERBY CENTURION AUTO
Gauge: 12 only, 2¾" chamber.
Action: Gas operated autoloader with "Floating Piston."
Barrel: 26" (Mod., Imp. Cyl, Skeet), 28" (Full, Mod.), 30" (Full, Full Trap, Full 3" Mag.), Vent. Rib.
Weight: About 7½ lbs. **Length:** 48¼ (28").
Stock: Walnut, hand checkered p.g. and fore-end, rubber recoil pad with white line spacer.
Features: Cross bolt safety, fluted bolt, gold plated trigger. Extra interchangeable bbls. **$115.00**
Price: Field or Skeet grade . **$339.50** Trap grade **$369.50**

SHOTGUNS—AUTOLOADING

WINCHESTER SUPER-X MODEL 1 AUTO SHOTGUN
Gauge: 12, 4-shot.
Barrel: 26" (Imp. Cyl.), 28" (Mod., Full), 30" (Full).
Length: 46" over-all (26" bbl.)
Stock: American walnut with cut-checkered p.g. and fore-end, 14"x1½"x2½" (Field).
Sights: Metal bead front.
Features: Receiver and all metal parts made of machined steel. Straight-line, 3-piece bolt, short-stroke gas system, all steel trigger assembly, steel shell carrier.
Price: Vent. rib **$359.95**
Extra Barrels:
Price: Field, plain, 26", 28", 30" (Full, Mod., Imp. Cyl.) **$78.95**
Price: Field, vent. rib, 26", 28", 30" (Full, Mod., Imp. Cyl.) **$109.95**
Price: Trap or Skeet, 26", 30", (Full, Skeet) **$111.95**

Winchester Super-X Model 1 Trap and Skeet Models
Same as Field model except: Trap has 30" bbl., vent. rib (Full) and regular or Monte Carlo stock. Engraved receiver, red bead front sight, black rubber recoil pad with white spacer—**$473.95.** for regular stock, **$484.95** for Monte Carlo. Skeet model has 26" vent. rib barrel (Skeet), otherwise same as trap gun—**$473.95.**

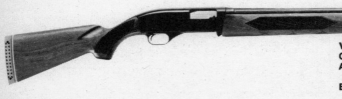

WINCHESTER 1400 AUTOMATIC MARK II
Gauge: 12, and 20 (3-shot).
Action: Gas operated autoloader. Front-locking 4-lug rotating bolt locks in bbl. Alloy receiver. Push button action release.
Barrel: Winchoke 28", Full, Mod. and Imp. Cyl. tubes only. Metal bead front sight. Available only with Winchoke.
Stock: 14"x1½"x2⅜". American walnut, new-design checkered p.g. and fore-end; fluted comb, p.g. cap, recoil pad.
Weight: With 26" bbl., 20 ga. 6½ lbs., 16, 12 ga. 6¾ lbs.; 46⅝" over-all.
Features: Self-compensating valve adjusts for std. or magnum loads. Bbls. interchangeable without fitting. Crossbolt safety in front of trigger guard.
Price: .... **$220.95**   With vent. rib **$239.95**

WINCHESTER 1500 XTR AUTO SHOTGUN
Gauge: 12 and 20, 2¾" chamber.
Barrel: 26" (Imp. Cyl.), 28" (Mod.), 28" (Full, 20 ga. only), 30" (Full, 12 ga. only). Plain or vent rib, with or without Winchoke tubes.
Weight: 6½ to 7¼ lbs. **Length:** 46⅝" to 50⅝" over-all.
Stock: American walnut, cut-checkered p.g. and fore-end. Field, vent. rib dimensions are 14"x1½"x2½".
Sights: Metal bead front.
Features: New Winchester XTR fit and finish. Gas-operated auto; self-adjusting system; front locking, rotating bolt. Interchangeable barrels in 3 standard lengths and chokes, or Winchoke system. Engine turned bolt, nickel plated carrier, cross-bolt safety. Introduced 1978.
Price: Plain barrel, 12 or 20 .... **$238.95**
Price: Vent. rib, 12 or 20 .... **$260.95**
Price: Plain barrel with Winchoke **$251.95**
Price: Vent. rib barrel with Winchoke **$272.95**

SHOTGUNS—SLIDE ACTION

BROWNING BPS PUMP SHOTGUN
Gauge: 12 only, 3" chamber (2¾" in target guns). 5-shot magazine.
Barrel: 26", 28", 30" (Imp. Cyl., Mod. or Full).
Weight: 7 lbs. 12 ozs. (28" barrel). **Length:** 48¾" over-all (28" barrel).
Stock: 14¼"x1½"x2½". Select walnut, semi-beavertail fore-end, full p.g. stock.
Features: Bottom feeding and ejection, receiver top safety, high post vent. rib. Double action bars eliminate binding. Vent. rib barrels only. Introduced 1977. From Browning.
Price: Grade I, Hunting **$239.95**
Price: Grade I, Trap **$259.95**
Price: Extra Trap barrel ... **$81.00**   Extra Hunting barrel **$74.00**
Price: Buck Special (no accessories) **$249.95**

HIGH STANDARD PPS-12 PUMP SHOTGUN
Gauge: 12, 6-shot magazine.
Barrel: 18" (Cyl.).
Weight: 17¼ lbs. **Length:** 38" over-all.
Stock: Walnut-stained birch.
Sights: Ramp front, rear adjustable for e., or available with bead only.
Features: Non-takedown police-type shotgun. Polished blue barrel and receiver. All steel.
Price: Plain barrel with bead **$186.50**
Price: With rifle sights **$197.50**

Ithaca Model 37 Ultra-Featherlight

Weighs five pounds. Same as standard Model 37 except comes only with 25″ vent. rib barrel choked Full, Mod. or Imp. Cyl. Has recoil pad, gold plated trigger, Sid Bell-designed grip cap. Also available as Ultra-Deerslayer with 20″ barrel.

Price: **$269.95**
Price: Ultra-Deerslayer **$254.95**

Ithaca Model 37 Deerslayer

Same as Model 37 except: 26″ or 20″ bbl. designed for rifled slugs; sporting rear sight, Raybar front sight; rear sight ramp grooved for Redfield long eye relief scope mount. 12, 16, or 20 gauge. With checkered stock, beavertail fore-end and recoil pad.

Price: **$244.95**
Price: As above with special select walnut stock **$269.95**

Ithaca Model 37 Supreme

Same as Model 37 except: hand checkered beavertail fore-end and p.g. stock, Ithaca recoil pad and vent. rib **$389.95**
37 Supreme also with Skeet (14″x1½″x2½″) or Trap (14½″x1½″x1⅞″) stocks at no extra charge. Other options available at extra charge.

ITHACA MODEL 37 FEATHERLIGHT

Gauge: 12, 16, 20 (5-shot; 3-shot plug furnished).
Action: Slide; takedown; bottom ejection.
Barrel: 26″, 28″, 30″ in 12 ga. 26″ or 28″ in 16 or 20 ga. (Full, Mod. or Imp. Cyl.).
Stock: 14″x1⅝″x2⅝″. Checkered walnut capped p.g. stock and fore-end.
Weight: 12 ga. 6½ lbs., 16 ga. 6 lbs., 20 ga. 5¾ lbs.
Features: Ithaca Raybar front sight; decorated receiver; crossbolt safety; action release for removing shells.
Price: **$219.95**
Price: With vent rib, stock (14″x1½″x2½″) **$254.95**

Ithaca Model 37 De Luxe Featherlight

Same as Model 37 except: checkered stock with p.g. cap; beavertail fore-end; recoil pad. Wgt. 12 ga. 6¾ lbs.
Price: With vent. rib **$259.95**

Ithaca Model 37 Magnum

Same as standard Model 37 except chambered for 3″ shells with resulting longer receiver. Stock dimensions are 14″x1⅞″x1½″. Grip cap has a Sid Bell-designed flying mallard on it. Has a recoil pad, vent. rib barrel with Raybar front sight. Available in 12 gauge only with 30″ (Full) or 28″ (Mod.) barrel. Weight about 7¼ lbs. Introduced 1978.
Price: **$277.95**

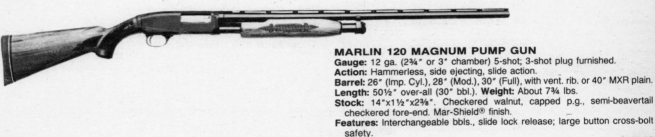

MARLIN 120 MAGNUM PUMP GUN

Gauge: 12 ga. (2¾″ or 3″ chamber) 5-shot; 3-shot plug furnished.
Action: Hammerless, side ejecting, slide action.
Barrel: 26″ (Imp. Cyl.), 28″ (Mod.), 30″ (Full), with vent. rib or 40″ MXR plain.
Length: 50½″ over-all (30″ bbl.) **Weight:** About 7¾ lbs.
Stock: 14″x1½″x2⅜″. Checkered walnut, capped p.g., semi-beavertail checkered fore-end. Mar-Shield® finish.
Features: Interchangeable bbls., slide lock release; large button cross-bolt safety.
Price: **$199.95**
Price: Extra barrels, about **$50.00**

Marlin 120 Field Grade Pump Gun

Similar to Deluxe Magnum except comes with 28″ plain barrel (Mod.), doesn't have fluted stock comb and p.g. cap. Weight is 7¾ lbs. Introduced 1978.
Price: About **$184.95**

MARLIN GLENFIELD 778 PUMP GUN

Gauge: 12 (2¾″ or 3″ chamber). 5-shot, 3-shot plug furnished.
Barrel: 28″ (Mod.), plain.
Weight: 7¾ lbs. **Length:** 48½″ over-all.
Stock: Walnut-finished hardwood. Semi-beavertail fore-end, vent. recoil pad, checkered p.g. and fore-end.
Features: Machined steel receiver, double action bars, engine-turned bolt, shell carrier and bolt slide. Interchangeable barrel. Introduced 1978.
Price: Plain barrel **$137.95**
Price: Vent. rib barrel **$156.36**
Price: Extra barrel, plain **$50.00**
Price: Extra barrel, vent. rib **$59.95**

Mossberg Model 500ALS Slugster
Same as standard Model 500 except has Slugster barrel with ramp front sight, open adj. folding-leaf rear, running deer scene etched on receiver. 12 ga.—18½", 24"; 20 ga.—24" bbl.
Price: **$162.95**

Mossberg Model 500AHT/AHTD
Same as Model 500 except 12 ga. only with extra-high Simmons Olympic-style free floating rib and built-up Monte Carlo trap-style stock. 30" barrel (Full), 28" ACCU-CHOKE with 3 interchangeable choke tubes (Mod., Imp. Mod., Full).
Price: Barrel **$244.95**
Price: ACCU-CHOKE barrel **$249.95**

Mossberg Model 500ALMR
Similar to Model 500ALDR with vent. rib 30" or 32" barrel. Chambered for 2¾" or 3" shells. Full choke only in 12 ga. Walnut-finish stock, checkered p.g. and fore-end; fluted comb; recoil pad (14"x1½"x2½"). Receiver has pintail and canvasback etched scenes.
Price: **$179.95**

NEW HAVEN BRAND MODEL 600 PUMP GUN
Gauge: 12, 410; 3" chamber.
Action: Takedown.
Barrel: 26" (Imp. Cyl.), 28" (Full, Mod.); 30", 32" (Full) 12 ga. only.
Weight: 6¾ lbs. (12-ga.). **Length:** 45¼" over-all (26" bbl.).
Stock: Walnut stock and fore-end, checkered. 13-oz. steel plug furnished for use with Magnum barrel.
Features: Easy interchangeability of barrels; side ejection; trigger disconnector. Introduced 1978. From Mossberg.
Price: Standard barrel with ACCU-CHOKE **$149.95**
Price: 3" Mag. **$153.95**
Price: Extra barrel, 2¾" chamber, from **$43.50**
Price: Extra Magnum barrel, from **$48.50**

MOSSBERG MODEL 500 ALD, CLD, ALDR, CLDR
Gauge: 12, 20, 3".
Action: Takedown.
Barrel: 28" ACCU-CHOKE (interchangeable tubes for Imp. Cyl., Mod., Full). Plain or vent. rib.
Weight: 6¾ lbs. (20-ga.), 7¼ lbs. (12-ga.) **Length:** 48" over-all.
Stock: Walnut-finished hardwood; checkered p.g. and fore-end; recoil pad. (14"x1½"x2½").
Features: Side ejection; top tang safety; trigger disconnector prevents doubles. Easily interchangeable barrels within gauge.
Price: Vent. rib **$174.95**
Price: Plain barrel **$158.95**
Price: Extra barrels, from **$44.95**

Mossberg Model 500EL
Similar to Model 500 except: 410 bore only, 26" bbl. (Full); 2½", 3" shells; holds six 2¾" or five 3" shells. Walnut-finished stock with checkered p.g. and fore-end, fluted comb and recoil pad (14"x1¼"x2½").
Weight: About 6 lbs., length over-all 45¾".
Price: With standard barrels **$153.95**
Price: With vent. rib barrel **$169.95**

Remington 870 Small Gauges
Exact copies of the large ga. Model 870, except that guns are offered in 20, 28 and 410 ga. 25" barrel (Full, Mod., Imp. Cyl.).
Plain barrel **$217.95**
D and F grade prices same as large ga. M870 prices.
Price: With vent. rib barrel **$250.95**
Price: Lightweight Magnum, 20 ga. plain bbl. (5¾ lbs.) **$239.95**
Price: Lightweight Magnum, 20 ga., vent. rib bbl. **$272.95**

Remington 870 Extra Barrels
Plain **$58.95**. Vent. rib **$86.95**. Vent. rib Skeet **$91.95**, Vent. rib Trap **$96.95**. 34" Trap **$106.95**. With rifle sights **$71.95**. Available in the same gauges and chokes as shown on guns.

Remington 870F Premier
Same as M870, except select walnut, better engraving **$2,400.00**
Price: With gold inlay **$3,600.00**

Remington 870 Magnum
Same as the M870 except 3" chamber, 12 ga. 30" bbl. (Mod. or Full), 20 ga. 28" bbl. (Mod. or Full). Recoil pad installed. Wgt., 12 ga. 8 lbs., 20 ga. 7½ lbs.
Price: Plain bbl. .... **$234.95**   Vent. rib bbl. **$267.95**
Price: Left hand model, vent. rib bbl. **$272.95**

Remington 870 SA Skeet
Same as the M870 except: 26" bbl. Skeet bored. Vent. rib with ivory front and white metal middle beads. 14"x1⅝"x2½" stock with rubber recoil pad, 12 or ga. only.
.... **$250.95**
Price: 28 and 410 ga., 25" bbl., no recoil pad **$255.95**

Remington 870D Tournament
Same as 870 except: better walnut, hand checkering, Engraved receiver & bbl. Vent.-rib. Stock dimensions to order **$1,200.00**

REMINGTON 870 WINGMASTER PUMP GUN
Gauge: 12, 16, 20, (5-shot; 3-shot wood plug).
Action: Takedown, slide action.
Barrel: 12, 16, 20, ga., 26" (Imp. Cyl.); 28" (Mod. or Full); 12 ga., 30" (Full).
Stock: 14"x1⅝"x2½". Checkered walnut, p.g.; fluted extension fore-end; fitted rubber recoil pad.
Weight: 7 lbs., 12 ga. (7¾ lbs. with Vari-Weight plug); 6¾ lbs., 16 ga.; 6½ lbs., 20 ga. 48½" over-all (28" bbl.).
Features: Double action bars, crossbolt safety. Receiver machined from solid steel. Hand fitted action.
Price: Plain bbl. .... **$212.95**   Vent. rib **$245.95**
Price: Riot gun, 18" or 20" Riot bore, (12 ga. only) **$197.95**
Price: Riot gun, 20" Imp. Cyl., rifle sights **$209.95**
Price: Left hand, vent. rib., 12 and 20 ga. **$250.95**

Remington Model 870 Brushmaster Deluxe
Carbine version of the M870 with 20" bbl. (Imp. Cyl.) for rifled slugs. 40½" over-all, wgt. 6½ lbs. Recoil pad. Adj. rear, ramp front sights. 12 or 20 ga.
Deluxe **$224.95**
Price: 20-ga. Lightweight version **$229.95**

> Consult our Directory pages for
> the location of firms mentioned.

SHOTGUNS—SLIDE ACTION

Remington 870 TB Trap
Same as the M870 except: 12 ga. only, 30" (Mod., Full) vent. rib. bbl., ivory front and white metal middle beads. Special sear, hammer and trigger assy. 14⅜"x1½"x1⅞" stock with recoil pad. Hand fitted action and parts. Wgt. 8 lbs. **$285.95**
Price: With Monte Carlo stock **$295.95**
Price: Add **$5.00** for left hand model

Remington 870 TC Trap
Same as 870 TB except has highly figured walnut stock and fore-end. New Monte Carlo stock dimensions of 14⅜"x1⅞"x1⅜"x1⅜". Weight 7¾ lbs.
Price: **$445.00**

SAVAGE MODEL 30-D PUMP GUN
Gauge: 12, 20, and 410, 5-shot (410, 4-shot) 3-shot plug furnished. All gauges chambered for 3" Magnum shells.
Action: Slide, hammerless, take-down; side ejection; top tang safety.
Barrel: Vent. rib. 12, 20 ga. 26" (Imp. Cyl.); 28" (Mod. or Full); 12 ga., 30" (Full); 410, 26" (Full).
Weight: 7 lbs. (410, 6¼ lbs.). Over-all 49½" (30" bbl.).
Stock: 14"x1½"x2½". Walnut, checkered p.g., grooved extension fore-end, recoil pad.
Features: Decorated steel receiver.
Price: **$179.95**

Savage Model 30 Field Grade
Same as Model 30 except plain bbl. and receiver, hard rubber buttplate.
Price: **$157.50**

Savage Model 30 Slug Gun
Same as the Model 30 Field Grade but with 22" bbl., 12 or 20 ga. only, with rifle sights **$160.00**

SMITH & WESSON Model 916 Pump Gun
Gauge: 12, 20 (3"), 6-shot (3-shot plug furnished).
Barrel: 20" (Cyl.), 26" (Imp. Cyl.) 28" (Mod., Full or adj. choke) 30" (Full), plain. Vent. rib 26", 28", 30".
Weight: 7¼ lbs. (28" plain bbl.).
Stock: 14"x2½"x1⅝", American walnut, fluted comb, finger-grooved fore-end.
Features: Vent. rib, vent. recoil pad, adj. choke available as options. Satin finish steel receiver with non-glare top.
Price: Plain bbl., no recoil pad **$136.75**
Price: Vent. rib and recoil pad (illus.) **$163.25**

Smith & Wesson Model 916T Takedown Shotgun
Same as standard Model 916 except has interchangeable barrel capability. Available in 12 or 20 ga. 26" (Imp. Cyl.), 28" (Mod., Full) 30" (Full). Extra barrels available in 20" (Cyl.) with rifle sights, 26" (Imp. Cyl.), 28" (Full or Mod.), 30" (Full), plain or vent. rib.
Price: 916T, plain barrel **$142.60**
Price: 916T, vent. rib barrel, recoil pad **$169.45**
Price: Extra barrel, plain **$38.60**
Price: Extra barrel, rifle sights **$48.50**
Price: Extra barrel, vent. rib **$71.50**

WEATHERBY PATRICIAN PUMP
Gauge: 12 only, 2¾" chamber.
Action: Short stroke slide action.
Barrel: 26" (Mod., Imp. Cyl, Skeet), 28" (Full, Mod.), 30" (Full, Full Trap, 3" Mag. Full). Vent. Rib.
Weight: About 7½ lbs. **Length:** 48⅛ (28" bbl.)
Stock: Walnut hand checkered p.g. and fore-end, white line spacers at p.g. cap and recoil pad.
Features: Short stroke action, hidden magazine cap, crossbolt safety.
Price: Extra interchangeable bbls. **$105.00**
Price: Field or Skeet grade **$289.50**   Trap grade **$319.50**

WESTERN FIELD 550 PUMP SHOTGUN
Gauge: 12 and 20.
Action: Slide action, takedown; top tang safety.
Barrel: 12 ga. 26″ (Variable); 28″ (Mod.); 30″ (Full); 20 ga. 26″ (Variable); 28″ (Mod., Full).
Stock: Walnut finished p.g. stock, molded buttplate, serrated fore-end.
Weight: 8½ lbs.
Features: Straight-line feed, interchangeable bbls., trigger disconnector prevents doubling.
Price: $109.99
   As above, but with variable choke in 12 or 20 ga. $119.99
   Slug gun with 24 bbl. without choke $149.99
   Deluxe Vent. rib models available, fixed or variable choke $169.99

WINCHESTER MODEL 12 TRAP
Gauge: 12 only, 2¾″; 6-shot (3-shot plug).
Barrel: 30″ (Full); vent. rib.
Weight: 7¾ lbs. **Length:** 49¾″ over-all.
Stock: Select walnut (14⅜″x1⅜″x1⅞″); Monte Carlo measures 14⅜″x1½″x2⅛″.
Features: Vent. rib; hand checkered stock; engine turned bolt.
Price: $775.00
Price: Monte Carlo stock $775.00

WINCHESTER 1200 FIELD PUMP GUN
Gauge: 12 and 20 (5-shot; 3-shot plug installed).
Action: Slide; front locking 4-lug rotating bolt locks into bbl. Alloy receiver, cross-bolt safety in front of trigger guard. Take-down.
Barrel: 26″ (Imp. Cyl.), 28″ (Mod., Full) and 30″ Full (12 ga. only). Metal bead front sight.
Stock: 14″x1⅜″x2⅜″. American walnut with new-design checkered p.g. and fore-end; fluted comb, recoil pad. Steel p.g. cap.
Weight: 12 ga. 6½ lbs. with 26″ bbl. 46⅝″ over-all.
Price: .... $171.95   With vent. rib $190.95

Winchester 1200 Field 3″ Magnum
   Same as 1200 except: 12 and 20 ga. only, 2¾″ or 3″ shells, 28″ and 30″ full choke bbls., 3 lbs. 48⅝″ over-all.
Price: .... $184.95   With vent. rib $204.95
Winchester 1200 Extra Barrels: Field w/o sights, 12, 20 ga. **$61.95.** Field with vent. rib, 12, 20 ga. **$81.95**
Winchester 1200 with interchangeable choke tubes which are screwed into the barrel and tightened with supplied wrench. Available in 12, and 20 ga. (28″) Mod. tube. **Price:** Field **$175.95** vent. rib **$195.95.** Extra tubes in Full, Mod. or Imp. Cyl. **$7.50.** Wrench **$1.95.**

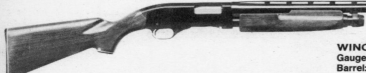

WINCHESTER 1300 XTR PUMP GUN
Gauge: 12 and 20, 3″ chamber, 5-shot.
Barrel: 26″ (Imp. Cyl.), 28″ (Mod.), 28″ (Full, 20-ga. only), 30″ (Full, 12-ga. only). Plain or vent. rib, with or without Winchoke.
Weight: 6½ to 7¼ lbs. **Length:** 46⅝″ to 50⅝″ over-all.
Stock: American walnut, cut-checkered p.g. and fore-end. Field, vent. rib dimensions are 14″x1½″x2½″.
Sights: Metal bead front.
Features: New Winchester XTR fit and finish. Has twin action bars, cross-bolt safety, Alloy receiver and trigger guard. Front-locking, rotating bolt. Nickel plated carrier, engine-turned bolt. Introduced 1978.
Price: Plain barrel $190.95
Price: Vent. rib $212.95
Price: Plain barrel with Winchoke $202.95
Price: Vent. rib with Winchoke $224.95

SHOTGUNS—OVER-UNDER

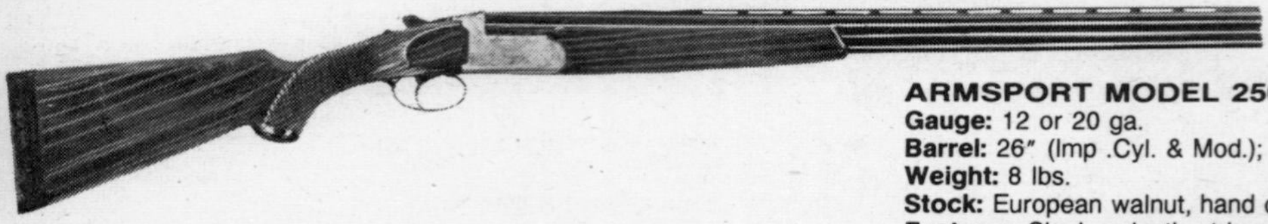

ARMSPORT MODEL 2500 O/U
Gauge: 12 or 20 ga.
Barrel: 26″ (Imp .Cyl. & Mod.); 28″ (Mod. & Full); vent. rib.
Weight: 8 lbs.
Stock: European walnut, hand checkered p.g. and fore-end.
Features: Single selective trigger, automatic ejectors, engraved receiver. Imported by Armsport.
Price: $550.00
Price: Deluxe field or Skeet $730.00
Price: With extractors only $450.00
Price: Deluxe Trap $775.00
Price: Trap Set (includes extra barrels, luggage-type leather case) $1,295.00
Price: Skeet Set (as above) $1,099.00

SHOTGUNS—OVER-UNDER

ARMSPORT 410-410 SPECIAL O/U
Gauge: 410/410 (3″ chambers).
Barrel: 26″ (Full & Full)
Weight: 7¼ lbs.
Stock: Walnut finished hardwood. Checkered p.g.
Sights: Front bead.
Features: Blued receiver and barrels, double triggers. Imported from France by Armsport.
Price: **$145.00**

Beretta S58 Skeet and Trap
Same as S55B/56E guns except stocked to Skeet or Trap dimensions. Trap guns have manual safety, 10mm vent. rib, Boehler steel barrels, light trigger pull. Both models have light scroll engraving on silver-gray receivers. Introduced 1977.
Price: Skeet or Trap **$780.00**

BERETTA 55B/56E O/U SHOTGUNS
Gauge: 12 (2¾″ or 3″) or 20 (3″).
Barrel: 12 ga.—26″ (Imp. Cyl. & Mod.); 28″ (Mod. & Full); 30″ (Mod. & Full, Full & Full, 3″ chambers) 20 ga.—26″ (Imp. Cyl. & Mod.); 28″ (Mod. & Full).
Weight: 6 lbs. 8 ozs. (20 ga)
Stock: 14⅛″x1⁷/₁₆″x2⅜″. Hand checkered European walnut. Recoil pad on 12 ga., 3″ Mag. guns. P.g. cap standard.
Features: Single selective trigger, plain extractors, automatic safety. Model S55B has light scroll engraving on receiver and selective auto ejectors. Introduced 1977. Imported by Beretta Arms Co.
Price: S56E **$640.00**
Price: S55B **$545.00**

BERRETTA SO-3 O/U SHOTGUN
Gauge: 12 ga. (2¾″ chambers).
Action: Back-action sidelock.
Barrel: 26″, 27″, 28″, 29″ or 30″, chokes to customer specs.
Stock: Standard measurements—14⅛″x1⁷/₁₆″x2⅜″. Straight "English" or p.g.-style. Hand checkered European walnut.
Features: SO-3—"English scroll" floral engraving on action body, sideplates and trigger guard. Stocked in select walnut. SO-3EL—as above, with full engraving coverage. Hand-detachable sideplates. SO-3EELL—as above with deluxe finish and finest full coverage engraving. Internal parts gold plated. Top lever is pierced and carved in relief with gold inlaid crown. Introduced 1977. Imported by Beretta Arms Co.
Price: SO-3 . . . . **$3,350.00**
Price: SO-3EL **$4,220.00**
Price: SO-3EELL **$5,695.00**

Beretta SO-4 Target Shotguns
Target guns derived from Model SO-3EL. Light engraving coverage. Single trigger. Skeet gun has 28″ (Skeet & Skeet) barrels, 10mm rib, p.g. stock (14⅛″x2⁹/₁₆″x1⅜″), fluted beavertail fore-end. "Skeet" is inlaid in gold into trigger guard. Weight is about 7 lbs. 10 ozs. Trap guns have 30″ (Imp. Mod. & Full or Mod. & Full) barrels, trap stock dimensions, fitted recoil pad, fluted beavertail fore-end. Weight is about 7 lbs. 12 ozs. "Trap" is inlaid in gold into trigger guard. Special dimensions and features, within limits, may be ordered. Introduced 1977. Imported by Beretta Arms Co.
Price: Skeet **$3,725.00**
Price: Trap **$3,725.00**

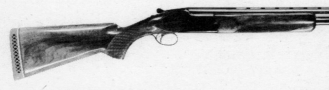

Browning Citori O/U Trap Models
Similar to standard Citori except: 12 gauge only; 30″, 32″ (Full & Full, Imp. Mod. & Full, Mod. Full, Mod. & Full), 34″ single barrel in Combo Set (Full, Imp. Mod., Mod.); Monte Carlo cheekpiece (14⅜″x1⅜″x1⅜″x2″); fitted with trap-style recoil pad; conventional target rib and high post target rib.
Price: Grade I, (conventional rib) **$499.95**
Price: Grade I, (high post rib) **$589.95**
Price: Grade II (high post rib) **$895.00**
Price: Grade V (high post rib) **$1,325.00**
Price: Grade I Combo (32″ O/U & 34″ single bbl., high post ribs) incl. luggage case **$939.95**

Browning Citori O/U Skeet Models
Similar to standard Citori except: 26″, 28″ (Skeet & Skeet) only; stock dimensions of 14⅜″x1½″x2″, fitted with Skeet-style recoil pad; conventional target rib and high post target rib.
Price: Grade I, 12 & 20 (high post rib) **$589.95**
Price: Grade I, 20 ga. (conventional rib) **$499.95**
Price: Grade I, 28 & 410 (high post rib) **$609.95**
Price: Grade II, all gauges (high post rib) **$895.00**
Price: Grade V, all gauges (high post rib) **$1,325.00**

BROWNING CITORI O/U SHOTGUN
Gauge: 12, 20, 28 and 410.
Barrel: 26″, 28″ (Mod. & Full, Imp. Cyl. & Mod.), in all gauges, 30″ (Mod. & Full, Full & Full) in 12-ga. only.
Weight: 6 lbs. 8 ozs. (26″ 410) to 7 lbs. 13 ozs. (30″ 12-ga.).
Length: 43″ over-all (26″ bbl.)
Stock: Dense walnut, hand checkered, full p.g., beavertail fore-end. Field-type recoil pad on 12-ga. models. on 12 ga. field guns and Trap and skeet models.
Sights: Medium raised beads, German nickel silver.
Features: Barrel selector integral with safety, auto ejectors, three-piece takedown.
Price: Grade I, 12 and 20 . . . . **$519.95**
Price: Grade I, 28 and 410 . . . . **$539.95**
Price: Grade II, all gauges **$895.00**
Price: Grade V, all gauges **$1,325.00**

Browning Citori O/U Sporter
Similar to standard Citori except; comes with 26″ (Mod. & Full, Imp. Cyl. & Mod.) only; straight grip stock with schnabel fore-end; satin oil finish.
Price: Grade I, 12 and 20 . . . . **$519.95**
Price: Grade I, 28 and 410 . . . . **$539.95**
Price: Grade II, all gauges **$895.00**
Price: Grade V, all gauges **$1,325.00**

BROWNING SUPERPOSED SUPER-LIGHT Presentation Series
Gauge: 12, & 20 2¾" chamber.
Action: Boxlock, top lever, single selective trigger. Bbl. selector combined with manual tang safety.
Barrels: 26½" (Mod. & Full, or Imp. Cyl. & Mod.)
Weight: 6⅜ lbs., average
Stock: Straight grip (14¼" x 1⅝" x 2½") hand checkered (fore-end and grip) select walnut.
Features: The Presentation Series is available in four grades and covers the Superposed line. Basically this gives the buyer a wide choice of engraving styles and designs and mechanical options which would place the gun in a "custom" bracket. Options are too numerous to list here and the reader is urged to obtain a copy of the latest Browning catalog for the complete listing. Series introduced 1977.
Price: From **$3,020.00**

Browning Presentation Superposed Lightning Skeet
Same as Standard Superposed except: 12 and 20 ga. only. Special Skeet stock, fore-end; center and front ivory bead sights. Wgt. 6½-7¾ lbs.
Price: From **$3,030.00**

Browning Presentation Superposed Magnum 12
Browning Superposed 3" chambers; 30" (Full and Full or Full and Mod.) barrels, Stock, 14¼"x1⅝"x2½" with factory fitted recoil pad. Weight 8 lbs.
Price: From **$2,990.00**

Browning Presentation Superposed Lightning
7-7¼ lbs. in 12 ga. 6-6¼ lbs. in 20 ga.
Price: From **$2,990.00**

Browning Presentation Superposed Combinations
Standard and Lightning models are available with these factory fitted extra barrels: 12 and 20 ga., same gauge bbls.; 12 ga., 20 ga. bbls.; 20 ga., extra sets 28 and/or 410 gauge; 28 ga., extra 410 bbls. Extra barrels may be had in Lightning weights with Standard models and vice versa. Prices range from **$4,100.00** (12, 20 ga., one set extra bbls. same gauge) for the Presentation 1 Standard to about **$11,600.00** for the Presentation 4 grade in a 4-barrel matched set (12, 20, 28 and 410 gauges).

Browning Presentation Superposed All-Gauge Skeet Set
Consists of four matched sets of barrels in 12, 20, 28 and 410 ga. Available in either 26½" or 28" length. Each bbl. set has a ¼" wide vent. rib with two ivory sight beads. Grade 1 receiver is hand engraved and stock and fore-end are checkered. Weight 7 lbs., 10 oz. (26½" bbls.), 7 lbs., 12 oz. (28" bbls.). Presentation 1 **$6,800.00**, Presentation 4 **$11,600.00**.

Superposed Presentation Broadway Trap 12
Same as Browning Lightning Superposed except: ⅝" wide vent. rib; stock, 14⅜"x1⁷/₁₆"x1⅝". 30" or 32" (Imp. Mod., Full; Mod., Full; Full, Full). 8 lbs. with 32" bbls.
Price: From **$3,090.00**

Browning Presentation Superposed Lightning Trap 12
Same as Browning Lightning Superposed except: semi-beavertail fore-end and ivory sights; stock, 14⅜"x1⁷/₁₆"x1⅝". 7¾ lbs. 30" (Full & Full, Full & Imp. Mod. or Full and Mod.)
Price: From **$3,030.00**

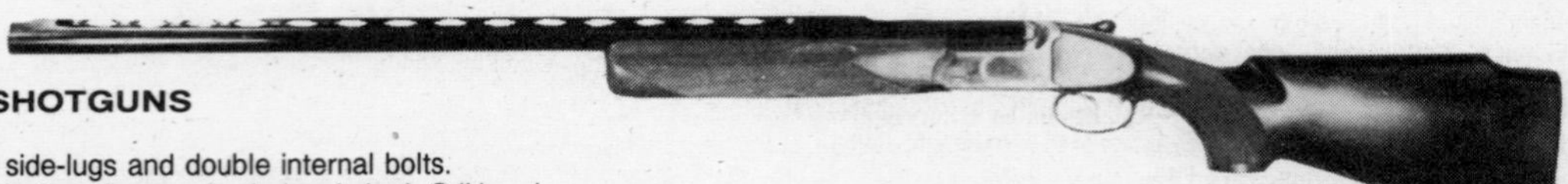

CONTENTO O/U TRAP SHOTGUNS
Gauge: 12 only.
Action: Boxlock, with Woodward side-lugs and double internal bolts.
Barrel: 32" (Mod. & Imp. Mod. or option of screw-in chokes in both O/U and single barrels. Has high "Mexico" sighting rib with vent. side ribs.
Stock: Hand checkered European walnut with Monte Carlo. 14½"x1⁵/₁₆". Recoil pad included for individual fitting.
Features: Single selective trigger, auto ejectors. MK3 model has fancy walnut and extensive Florentine engraving. Both MK3 and MK2 (shown) available with O/U and single interchangeable barrels with screw-in chokes. Combination sets are supplied in leather trunk case. Introduced 1978. From Ventura Imports.
Price: MK 2 O/U Trap **$815.00**
Price: MK 2 O/U and single bbl. **$1,165.00**
Price: MK 2 combination set **$1,495.00**
Price: MK 3 O/U Trap **$1,320.00**
Price: MK 3 O/U and single bbl. **$1,900.00**
Price: MK 3 combination set **$2,225.00**

> Consult our Directory pages for the location of firms mentioned.

ERA O/U SHOTGUN
Gauge: 12 or 20 ga., 2¾".
Barrel: 28" (Mod. & Full); vent. top and middle ribs.
Weight: 7¾ lbs.
Stock: Walnut-finished hardwood, hand checkered.
Features: Auto. safety; extractors; double triggers; engraved receiver. Imported from Brazil by F.I.E.
Price: **$224.95**
Price: Trap or Skeet versions **$249.95**

FRANCHI MODEL 2003 TRAP O/U
Gauge: 12 only (2¾" chambers).
Barrel: 30", 32" (Imp. Mod. & Full, Full & Full).
Weight: 8½ lbs.
Stock: 14½"x1⅞"x1½". Fancy French walnut; checkered p.g. and fore-end. Available in Monte Carlo or straight style; interchangeable. Different dimensions avail.
Features: "Ceiling-Swell" trap trigger with barrel selector; separated barrels; steel muzzle collar to maintain alignment; raised, vent. trap rib. Buttstock drilled and tapped for recoil reducer. Comes with hard luggage-type fitted case. From Stoeger Industries.
Price: **$1,095.00**

Franchi Model 2005 Trap Combo
Same as Model 2003/2004 except comes with two barrel sets—one single, one O/U in same lengths and chokes as specified for those models. Also comes with fitted case.
Price: **$1,595.00**

SHOTGUNS—OVER-UNDER

FRANCHI PEREGRINE O/U
Gauge: 12 only, 2¾" chambers.
Barrel: 26½" (Cyl. & Imp. Cyl., Imp. Cyl. & Mod., Mod. & Full), 28" (Mod. & Full). Vent rib.
Weight: 6 lbs. 1 oz. (M-451)
Stock: 14½"x1½"x2¼".
Features: Chrome lined barrels, single selective trigger, auto ejectors, non-auto safety. Model 451 has alloy receiver, Model 400 is steel. Both have silver-finish receivers with engraving. Selective auto ejectors. Introduced 1977. From Stoeger Industries.
Price: Model 400 .... $534.95
Price: Model 451 .... $469.95

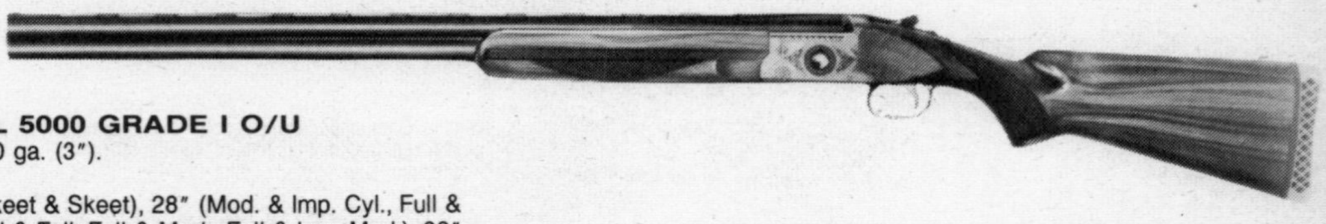

GOLDEN EAGLE MODEL 5000 GRADE I O/U
Gauge: 12 ga. (2¾" or 3") or 20 ga. (3").
Action: Boxlock.
Barrel: 26" (Mod. & Imp. Cyl., Skeet & Skeet), 28" (Mod. & Imp. Cyl., Full & Mod., Skeet & Skeet), 30" (Full & Full, Full & Mod., Full & Imp. Mod.), 32" (Full & Full, Full & Imp. Mod., Full & Mod.).
Weight: 6¼-8 lbs.
Stock: 14"x1½"x2½"x⅛" cast-off (Field; 14⅜"x1⅜"x1⅞"x¼" cast-off (Trap); select walnut.
Features: Single selective mechanical trigger; vent. top rib; selective ejectors; non-automatic tang safety/barrel selector; rubber recoil pad. Lifetime warranty to original owner. Imported by Golden Eagle Firearms.
Price: Grade I Field $749.00
Price: Grade I Trap $874.00
Price: Grade I Skeet $799.00

Golden Eagle Model 5000 Grade II O/U
Similar to Grade I except: Field only has gold colored mechanical trigger, others have gold inertia type; vent. side ribs; finer engraving and checkering; Trap model has wider rib; Field has brass beads, Skeet and Trap have ivory. Available in 12, 20, 28 and 410 gauge three barrel sets.
Price: Grade II Field $819.00
Price: Grade II Trap $999.00
Price: Grade II Skeet $899.00

Golden Eagle Model 5000 Grade III Grandee o/u
12 ga. only, 26" (Skeet & Skeet) or 30" (Full & Imp. Mod.); finer checkering and nearly full coverage receiver engraving; silver finish receiver. Comes with hard luggage-style case.
Price: Grade III Grandee Trap $2,999.00
Price: Grade III Grandee Skeet $2,999.00

Harrington & Richarson "Field Gun" o/u
Same as "Waterfowl" except has 2¾" chambers, 28" barrel (Imp. Cyl. & Imp. Mod.), no recoil pad.
Price: $350.00

HARRINGTON & RICHARDSON "WATERFOWL" O/U
Gauge: 12 ga. only (3" chambers).
Barrel: 30" (Full & Mod.).
Weight: 7½ lbs. **Length:** 46¾" over-all.
Stock: 14⅜"x1½"x2", hand checkered walnut.
Sights: Gold bead front on vent. rib.
Features: Vent. rib; single selective trigger; engraved action; rubber recoil pad. Imported from Spain by Harrington & Richardson.
Price: $365.00

ITHACA MIRAGE O/U
Gauge: 12 only (2¾" chambers).
Action: Boxlock type, interchangeable hammer-trigger group. Single selective trigger, specify choice of firing order.
Barrel: 28", 30", or 32" (Skeet and Skeet or Extra-Full and Mod.). Vent. rib.
Weight: 8¼ lbs. **Length:** 44" over-all.
Stock: Walnut, hand checkered with schnabel fore-end, (14"x1½"x2⅜"). Rubber recoil pad.
Price: Trap model $2,750.00
Price: Skeet model $2,750.00
Price: Live Bird Model $2,750.00

ITHACA MX-8 TRAP GUN
Gauge: 12 only (2¾" chambers).
Action: Boxlock type, single non-selective trigger; interchangeable trigger-hammer group offers choice of firing order.
Barrel: 30" or 32", especially bored for international clay target shooting. High concave vent rib has 5" ramp.
Stock: Custom, finely checkered (oiled or lacquer finish) European walnut, interchangeable with other models, 9 available including Monte Carlo.
Weight: About 8 lbs.
Features: Ventilated middle rib has additional vent ports for maximum heat dissipation, better balance and smoother swing.
Price: $2,750.00

Ithaca MX-8 Combination
Same as MX-8 Trap Gun except comes with interchangeable single barrel (32" or 34").
Price: $4,495.00

ITHACA PERAZZI MT-6 O/U

Gauge: 12 only (2¾" chambers).
Barrel: 30", 32". Five screw-in choke tubes are supplied. (Extra Full, Full, Imp. Mod., Mod., Imp. Cyl.) Vent. rib barrel.
Weight: 8¼ lbs.
Stock: European walnut, checkered p.g. and fore-end (24 l.p.i.) Dimensions to customer specs.
Features: Unique striped receiver design; wide target-style single selective trigger; wide target-style rib with self-aligning sighting ramp; special lacquer finished stock and fore-end; new fore-end latching system compensates for normal wood shrinkage and expansion. Barrels can be adjusted for point of impact. Comes with fitted hard case. Imported from Italy by Ithaca.
Price: $2,750.00
Price: Competition Trap single barrel $2,750.00
Price: MT-6 Combination Trap $4,495.00

IVER JOHNSON SILVER SHADOW O/U SHOTGUN

Gauge: 12 ga. only.
Barrel: 28" (Mod. & Full). Vent. rib.
Weight: 8¼ lbs.
Stock: Walnut. Checkered p.g. and fore-end.
Sights: Metal bead front.
Features: Single or double trigger. Imported from Italy by Iver Johnson.
Price: Single trigger $286.00
Price: Double trigger $265.50

KASSNAR/FIAS SK-1 O/U SHOTGUN

Gauge: 12 or 20 ga. (3" chambers).
Action: Top lever break open, boxlock, Greener cross bolt.
Barrel: 26" (Imp. Cyl. & Mod.), 28" (Mod. & Full), 30" (Mod. & Full), 32" (Full & Full).
Weight: 6-6½ lbs.
Stock: Select European walnut. 14"x2¼"x1¼".
Features: Double triggers and non-automatic extractors. Checkered p.g. and fore-end. Imported by Kassnar Imports.
Price: $310.00

Kassnar/Fias SK-3 O/U Shotgun
Same as SK-1 except has single selective trigger $335.00

Kassnar/Fias SK-4D O/U Shotgun
Same as SK-4 except has deluxe receiver engraving, sideplates, better wood $410.00

KLEINGUENTHER'S CONDOR O/U SHOTGUN

Gauge: 12 ga. only (2¾" chambers).
Action: Purdey type double lock.
Barrel: 28" (Full & Mod., I.M.& Mod.); chrome lined.
Weight: 6½ lbs. (26"20) to 7 lbs.3oz. (30"12).
Stock: 14"x1½"x2½" hand-checkered walnut, p.g. and fore-end, recoil pad.
Features: Single selective trigger, auto ejectors, manual tang safety, vent. rib. Skeet Grade has extra wide rib. Imported from Italy by Kleinguenther.
Price: $498.00

KRIEGHOFF "TECK" O/U SHOTGUN

Gauge: 12, 16, 20 (2¾"), 20 (3").
Action: Boxlock.
Barrel: 28½", vent. rib, choked to customer specs.
Weight: 7 lbs. **Length:** 44" over-all.
Stock: 14¼"x1¼"x2¼", European walnut.
Features: Kersten double crossbolt system. Interchangeable barrels. Imported from Germany by Creighton & Warren.
Price: With ejectors $2,115.00
Price: Interchangeable double rifle barrels up to 7mm Rem. Mag.$1,450.00
Price: Double rifle barrels, 7mm, 375, 458 Win. Mag. $1,760.00
Price: Interchangeable shotgun-rifle barrel combination $965.00
Price: Model Ulm with sidelocks $3,170.00
Price: Model Ulm with hand-detachable engraved sidelocks $4,135.00

LJUTIC BI GUN O/U SHOTGUN

Gauge: 12 ga only.
Barrel: 28" or 33", choked to customer specs.
Weight: To customers specs.
Stock: To customer specs. Oil finish, hand checkered.
Features: Hollow-milled rib, choice of pull or release trigger pushbutton opener in front of trigger guard. From Ljutic Industries.
Price: $3,500.00
Price: Matched set of barrels .... $750.00 to $1,200.00

SHOTGUNS—OVER-UNDER

MANUFRANCE "FALCOR" O/U SHOTGUN
Gauge: 12 ga. (2¾").
Barrel: 26" (Imp. Cyl. & Mod., Skeet), 28" (Mod. & Full); vent. rib.
Weight: 7¾ lbs. **Length:** 48" over-all.
Stock: Hand checkered walnut; white spacer at butt.
Features: Single selective trigger; automatic ejectors; chrome lined barrels. Imported by Interarms.
Price: **$579.00**

GEBRUDER MERKEL 201E O/U
Gauge: 12, 16, 20, 28, 3" chambers on request.
Action: Kersten double crossbolt.
Barrel: 26" (Mod. & Imp. Cyl., Cyl. & Imp. Cyl).
Weight: 6¾ lbs.
Stock: Walnut with p.g. or English style. 14¼"x1½"x2¼".
Features: Double, single or single selective trigger, cocking indicators. Fine hunting scene engraving. Imported by Champlin Firearms.
Price: With single selective trigger **$1,900.00**

Gebruder Merkel 200E O/U
Similar to 201E except: English arabesque engraving and color case-hardening.
Price: With single non-selective trigger **$1,300.00**

GEBRUDER MERKEL MODEL 203E O/U
Gauge: 12, 16, 20, 28, 3" chambers on request.
Action: Merkel H&H hand-detachable side locks with double sears. Double crossbolt breech.
Barrel: 26" (Mod. & Imp. Cyl.).
Weight: 7 lbs.
Stock: Deluxe walnut with p.g. or English style. 14¼"x1½"x2¼".
Features: Double, single or single selective trigger. Cocking indicators. Choice of arabesque or fine hunting scene engraving. Imported by Champlin Firearms.
Price: With single selective trigger **$3,845.00**

Gebruder Merkel Model 303E O/U
Similar to Model 203E except: double hook-bolting in conjunction with double crossbolt breech. Finer quality.
Price: **$5,500.00**

REMINGTON 3200 COMPETITION TRAP
Caliber: 12 ga. (2¾" chambers).
Barrel: 30" (Full & Full, Full & Imp. Mod., Full & Mod.), 32" (Full & Imp. Mod.).
Weight: 8¼ lbs. (30" bbl.). **Length:** 48" over-all (30" bbl.).
Stock: Fancy walnut checkered 20 l.p.i. Full beavertail fore-end. Satin finish. 14⅜"x2"x1½". Optional 1⅜" or 1½" drop on Monte Carlo stocks.
Features: Super-fast lock time, separated barrels, engraved receiver. Combination manual safety and barrel selector on top tang. Single selective trigger. Ivory bead front sight, white-metal middle.
Price: Special Trap **$925.00**
Price: Competition Trap with M.C. stock **$1,050.00**

Remington 3200 Competition Skeet
Same as Trap except: 26" or 28" (Skeet & Skeet) barrels, stock measures 14"x2⅛"x1½". Over-all length is 43" with 26" barrels, weight is 7¾ lbs.
Price: Skeet **$850.00**
Price: Competition Skeet **$1,050.00**

ROTTWEIL OLYMPIA '72 SKEET SHOTGUN
Gauge: 12 ga. only.
Action: Boxlock.
Barrel: 27" (special Skeet choke), vent. rib. Chromed lined bores, flared chokes.
Weight: 7¼ lbs. **Length:** 44½" over-all.
Stock: French walnut, hand checkered, modified beavertail fore-end. Oil finish.
Sights: Metal bead front.
Features: Inertia-type trigger, interchangeable for any system. Frame and lock milled from steel block. Retracting firing pins are spring mounted. All coil springs. Selective single trigger. Action engraved. Extra barrels are available. Introduced 1976. Imported from West Germany by Eastern Sports Int.
Price: **$1,995.00**
Price: Trap model (Montreal) is similar to above except has 30" (Imp. Mod. & Full) bbl., weighs 8 lbs., 48½" over-all **$1,995.00**

ROTTWEIL SUPREME FIELD O/U SHOTGUN
Gauge: 12 only.
Action: Boxlock.
Barrel: 28" (Mod. & Full, Imp. Cyl. & Imp. Mod., Mod. & Full), vent. rib.
Weight: 7¼ lbs. **Length:** 47" over-all.
Stock: Select French walnut, hand checkered and rubbed. Checkered p.g. and fore-end, plastic buttplate. Unfinished stocks available.
Sight: Metal bead front.
Features: Removable single trigger assembly with button selector (same trigger options as on American Trap Combo); retracting spring mounted firing pins; engraved action. Extra barrels available. Imported from West Germany by Eastern Sports Int.
Price: **$1,995.00**
Price: Live Pigeon (28" Mod. & Full) **$1,995.00**

ROTTWEIL 650 FIELD O/U
Gauge: 12 ga. only.
Action: Boxlock.
Barrel: 28″ (Mod. & Full); vent. rib.
Weight: 7½ lbs.
Stock: Select French walnut; satin oil finish; hand checkered p.g. and fore-end. Plastic buttplate. Fluted beavertail fore-end.
Sights: Plastic front in metal sleeve, center bead.
Features: Receiver milled from block steel. Introduced 1978. Imported by Eastern Sports Int.
Price:. **$650.00**

ROTTWEIL AMERICAN TRAP COMBO
Gauge: 12 ga. only.
Action: Boxlock
Barrel: Separated o/u, 32″ (Imp. Mod. & Full); single is 34″ (Full), both with high vent. rib.
Weight: 8½ lbs. (o/u and single)
Stock: Monte Carlo style, walnut, hand checkered and rubbed. Unfinished stocks available. Double vent. recoil pad. Choice of two dimensions.
Sights: Plastic front in metal sleeve, center bead.
Features: Interchangeable inertia-type trigger groups. Trigger groups available: single selective; double triggers;, release-pull; release-release selective. Receiver milled from block steel. Chokes are hand honed, test fired and reworked for flawless patterns. All coil springs, engraved action. Introduced 1977. Imported from West Germany by Eastern Sports Int'l.
Price:. **$3,495.00**
Price: American Trap O/U (as above except only with O/U bbls.)**$1,995.00**
Price: American Skeet O/U **$1,995.00**

RUGER "RED LABEL" O/U SHOTGUN
Gauge: 20 only, 3″ chambers.
Barrel: 26″, 28″ (Skeet & Skeet, Imp. Cyl. & Mod.).
Weight: About 7 lbs. **Length:** 43″ (26″ barrels).
Stock: 14″x1½″x2½″. Straight grain American walnut. Checkered p.g. and fore-end, rubber recoil pad.
Features: Initial production guns provided with 26″ barrels (28″ will be available in 1978). Premium grade 20 gauge models and 12 gauage guns will be offered later. Patented barrel side spacers may be removed if desired. Introduced 1977.
Price: About **$480.00**

SKB 600 Trap Grade O/U
Same as 500 Field Grade except 30″ bbl. (Imp. Mod., Full, or Full, Full), fine scroll engraved receiver; bead middle sight; Monte Carlo stock (14½″x1½″x1½″x2″), or standard stock, p.g. white line spacer and recoil pad.
Price:. **$644.00**
Price: Field Grade 600 . . . . **$620.00**
Price: Trap Grade 700, features select walnut, oil finished stock and engraved receiver **$834.00**

SKB 600 Skeet Grade O/U
Same as 600 Trap except: 12 or 20 ga., 26″ or 28″ bbls. (Skeet, Skeet), stock (14″x1½″x2⅝″), standard buttplate and whiteline spacer. Weight 7½ lbs.
Price:. **$634.00**
Price: 28 or 410 ga. **$655.00**
Price: Model 700 (Deluxe version of M600) **$834.00**

SKB 500 FIELD GRADE O/U
Gauge: 12 (2¾″ or 3″ chambers), 20 (3″).
Action: Top lever, hammerless, boxlock; gold-plated single selective trigger; automatic ejectors, non-auto safety.
Barrel: 26″ vent. rib (Imp. Cyl., Mod.); 28″ (Imp. Cyl., Mod. or Mod., Full); 30″ (Mod., Full); 12 ga., 2¾″ chambers. 26″ (Imp. Cyl., Mod.); 28″ (Mod., Full); 20 ga., 3″ chambers.
Stock: 14″x1½″x2⅝″. Walnut, checkered p.g. and fore-end, p.g. cap, fluted comb.
Weight: 7½ lbs. (12); 6½ lbs. (20).
Features: Border scroll engraved receiver. Chrome lined bbls. and action. Raybar front sight. From SKB Sports.
Price:. **$514.00**
Price: Magnum model **$524.00**
Price: Model 500, 28 or 410 ga. **$535.00**

SKB Model 600 Small Bore Skeet
Same as Model 600 Trap except: comes in 20, 28 (2¾″) and 410 (2½″) as a set (three barrels, one frame), choked Skeet & Skeet, 28″. Weight 7¼ lbs.
Price:. **$1,850.00**

SKB MODEL 5600 TARGET O/U
Gauge: 12 only, 2¾" chambers.
Barrel: 28", 30" (Imp. Mod. & Full), 26", 28" (Skeet & Skeet).
Weight: 7¾ to 8¼ lbs.
Stock: Walnut. Checkered p.g. & fore-end, white spacers at butt and p.g. cap. Trap—14½"x1⅜"x1¾". Skeet—14"x1⅝"x2¼".
Features: Hand polished and blued frame and barrels. Ventilated side ribs and top rib (16mm for trap, 12mm or 16mm for Skeet). Automatic selective ejectors. Mechanical single selective trigger. Many improvements made over previous target line.
Price: Model 5600 . . . . **$860.00**
Price: Model 5700 (Same as 5600 except better wood, checkering and color case-hardened receiver) **$1,300.00**
Price: Model 5800 (Same as 5700 except fully engraved receiver, barrel top; ivory grip cap) **$1,900.00**

SKB Model 680 English O/U
Gauge: 12 or 20 ga.
Action: Boxlock.
Barrel: 26" or 28" (Full & Mod., Mod. & I.C.).
Weight: 7 lbs.
Stock: 14"x1½"x2⅝", straight grip, walnut, wrap-around checkering.
Features: Auto, selective ejectors, Bradley-type sights on target grades. Single selective trigger, chrome lined barrels with black chrome exteriors. Introduced 1977. From SKB Sports.
Price: **$674.00**

SAVAGE MODEL 330 O/U
Gauge: 12 (2¾" chambers), 20 ga. (3" chambers).
Action: Top lever, break open. Selective single trigger, auto top tang safety locks trigger, coil springs.
Barrel: 26" (Mod. & Imp. Cyl.), 28" or 30" (Mod. & Full).
Stock: 14"x1½"x2½". Walnut, checkered p.g. and fore-end, hard rubber plate.
Weight: About 7 lbs., 46½" (30" bbl.) over-all.
Features: Monoblock locking rails are engaged by locking shield that snaps forward as gun is closed. This shield overlaps the breech for added strength.
Price: **$450.00**

SAVAGE 333-T
Same specifications as Model 330 except has trap specifications and features: 30" bbl. choked Imp. Mod. and Full, manually operated top tang safety (disconnects trigger from sears), stock measures 14½"x1½"x1½" at Monte Carlo, 2½" heel. Over-all length 47", taken down 30", weight 7¾ lbs. Has extra-wide ventilated rib, extractors, recoil pad.
Price: **$561.85**

SAVAGE 333 O/U
Gauge: 12 (2¾"), 20 (2¾" & 3" chambers).
Action: Top lever, break open.
Barrel: 26" (Skeet & Skeet or Imp. Cyl. & Mod.), 28" (Mod. & Full), 30" (Mod. & Full, 12 ga. only).
Weight: 6¼ to 7¼ lbs.
Stock: 14"x1½"x2½", French walnut. Fleur-de-lis checkering.
Features: Single selective trigger, auto. safety, ejectors, cocking indicators. Engraved steel receiver.
Price: **$576.50**

SAVAGE MODEL 242 O/U
Gauge: 410 (3" chambers).
Barrel: 24" (Full & Full).
Weight: 7 lbs. **Length:** 40" over-all
Stock: 14"x1¾"x2¾". Checkered walnut.
Sights: Bead front.
Features: Two-way opening top lever, barrel selector on hammer. Color case-hardened frame, blued barrels. Measures 24" when taken down. Introduced 1977.
Price: **$132.00**

VERNEY-CARRON SKEET O/U SHOTGUNS
Gauge: 12 only.
Action: Boxlock with side-lugs and double internal bolts.
Barrel: 28" (Skeet & Skeet). Wide vent. sighting rib.
Weight: 7 lbs., 3 ozs.
Stock: Select hand checkered French walnut. Full p.g. with large fore-end.
Features: Has all the features of the Field model except designed for Skeet. Available in four grades. Introduced 1978. From Ventura Imports.
Price: Skeet grade **$815.00**

VERNEY-CARRON O/U SHOTGUNS
Gauge: 12 only.
Action: Boxlock with side-lugs and double internal bolts.
Barrel: 26", 28", choked to customer specs. Vent. sighting rib.
Weight: 6 lbs., 7 ozs.
Stock: Select French walnut, hand checkered, English or full p.g.
Features: Self-opener; auto ejectors; single selective trigger. Extensive hand engraving and finishing. Three higher grades are available. From Ventura Imports. Introduced 1978.
Price: Field Grade **$775.00**

WEATHERBY OLYMPIAN O/U SHOTGUN
Gauge: 12 (2¾"; 3" for 30" barrel only), 20 (3").
Action: Boxlock (simulated side-lock).
Barrel: 12 ga. 30" (Full & Mod.), 28" (Full & Mod., Mod. & Imp. Cyl., Skeet & Skeet); 20 ga. 28", 26" (Full & Mod., Mod. & Imp. Cyl., Skeet & Skeet).
Weight: 7 lbs., 8 ozs. (12 ga. 26").
Stock: American walnut, checkered p.g. and fore-end. Rubber recoil pad. Dimensions for field and Skeet models, 20 ga. 14"x1½"x2½".
Features: Selective auto ejectors, single selective mechanical trigger. Top tang safety, Greener cross-bolt. Introduced 1978. From Weatherby.
Price: 12 or 20, Field and Skeet $525.00
Price: 12 ga. Trap $550.00

WEATHERBY REGENCY O/U SHOTGUN
Gauge: 12 ga. (2¾" chambers), 20 ga. (3" chambers).
Action: Boxlock (simulated side-lock) top lever break-open. Selective auto ejectors, single selective trigger (selector inside trigger guard).
Barrel: 28" with vent rib and bead front sight, Full & Mod., Mod. & Imp. Cyl. or Skeet & Skeet.
Weight: 12 ga. 7⅜ lbs., 20 ga. 6⅞ lbs.
Stock: American walnut, checkered p.g. and fore-end (14¼"x1½"x2½").
Features: Mechanically operated trigger. Top tang safety, Greener cross-bolt, fully engraved receiver, recoil pad installed.
Price: 12 or 20 ga. Field and Skeet $849.50
Price: 12 ga. Trap Model $899.50

WINCHESTER XPERT O/U SHOTGUN
Gauge: 12 and 20, 3" chambers.
Barrel: Field: 26" (Imp. Cyl. and Mod.) 28" (Mod. and Full), 30" (Full & Full); Skeet: 2¾" chambers, 27" (Skeet & Skeet); Trap: 12 only, 2¾" chambers, 30" (Full & Full). Vent. rib with metal bead front sight.
Weight: 6½ lbs. **Length:** 42¾" over-all (26" barrels).
Stock: 14"x1½"x2½". Walnut stock and fore-end, high-gloss finish.
Features: Plain blue receiver, no engraving. Single trigger, auto. ejectors, barrel selector safety. Trap gun avail. with either regular or Monte Carlo stock, with rubber recoil pad.
Price: Field (illus.) $525.00
Price: Skeet $540.00
Price: Trap (std. stock) $540.00
Price: Trap (Monte Carlo stock) $550.00

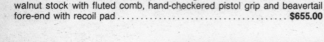

WINCHESTER 101 O/U FIELD GUN
Gauge: 12 and 28, 2¾"; 20 and 410, 3".
Action: Top lever, break open. Manual safety combined with bbl. selector at top of receiver tang.
Barrel: Vent. rib 26" 12, 26½", 20 and 410 (Imp. Cyl., Mod.), 28" (Mod & Full), 30" 12 only (Mod. & Full). Metal bead front sight. Chrome plated chambers and bores.
Stock: 14"x1½"x2½". Checkered walnut p.g. and fore-end; fluted comb.
Weight: 12 ga. 7¾ lbs. Others 6¼ lbs. **Length:** 44¾" over-all (28" bbls.).
Features: Single selective trigger, auto ejectors. Hand engraved receiver.
Price: 12 or 20 ga. $645.00
Price: 28 ga. (special order only) $675.00
Price: Standard Trap, Monte Carlo stock (special order only) ... $700.00

Winchester 101 Magnum Field Gun
Same as 101 Field Gun except: chambers 3" Magnum shells; 12 ga. only 30" (Full & Full or Mod. & Full); hand-engraved receiver, select French walnut stock with fluted comb, hand-checkered pistol grip and beavertail fore-end with recoil pad $655.00

Winchester Model 101 Pigeon Grade
Same as Model 101 Field except has new-design vent. rib with bead front and middle sights, hand-engraved satin finish receiver, knurled, non-slip trigger. Stock and fore-end of fancy French walnut, hand checkered p.g. and fore-end. 12, 20, 28 or 410 ga., 2¾" or 3" chambers. Barrels run from 26" through 32" with a full range of chokes. Weighs 8¼ lbs.
Price: Standard trap stock $795.00
Price: Monte Carlo stock $795.00
Price: Field grade $755.00
Price: 28,410 skeet $845.00

SHOTGUNS—OVER-UNDER

A. ZOLI DELFINO S.P. O/U
Gauge: 12 or 20 (3" chambers).
Barrel: 28" (Mod. and Full); vent. rib.
Weight: 5½ lbs.
Stock: Walnut. Hand checkered p.g. and fore-end; cheekpiece.
Features: Color case hardened receiver with light engraving; chrome lined
   barrels; automatic sliding safety; double triggers; ejectors. From Mandall
   Shooting Supplies.
Price: $499.50

ZOLI SILVER SNIPE O/U SHOTGUN
Gauge: 12, 20 (3" chambers).
Action: Purdey type double boxlock, crossbolt.
Barrel: 26" (I.C.& Mod.), 28" (Mod.&Full), 30", 12 only (Mod.& Full); 26" Skeet
   (Skeet & Skeet), 30" Trap (Full & Full).
Weight: 6½ lbs. (12 ga.).
Stock: Hand checkered European walnut, p.g. and fore-end.
Features: Auto safety (exc. Trap and Skeet), vent rib, single trigger, chrome
   bores. Imported from Italy by Galef.
Price: Field $416.75

Zoli Golden Snipe O/U Shotgun
   Same as Silver Snipe except selective auto ejectors.
Price: Field $489.00

SHOTGUNS—DOUBLE BARREL

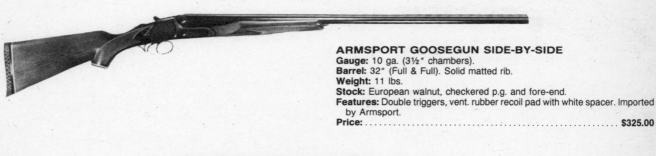

ARMSPORT GOOSEGUN SIDE-BY-SIDE
Gauge: 10 ga. (3½" chambers).
Barrel: 32" (Full & Full). Solid matted rib.
Weight: 11 lbs.
Stock: European walnut, checkered p.g. and fore-end.
Features: Double triggers, vent. rubber recoil pad with white spacer. Imported
   by Armsport.
Price: $325.00

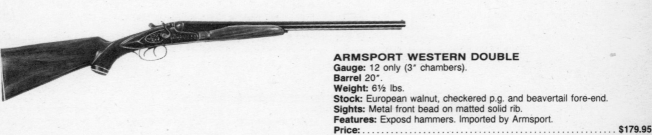

ARMSPORT WESTERN DOUBLE
Gauge: 12 only (3" chambers).
Barrel 20".
Weight: 6½ lbs.
Stock: European walnut, checkered p.g. and beavertail fore-end.
Sights: Metal front bead on matted solid rib.
Features: Exposd hammers. Imported by Armsport.
Price: $179.95

BERETTA M-424 SIDE-BY-SIDE
Gauge: 12 (2¾"), 20 (3").
Action: Beretta patent boxlock; double underlugs and bolts.
Barrel: 12 ga.—26" (Imp. Cyl. & Mod.), 28" (Mod. & Full); 20 ga.—26" (Imp.
   Cyl. & Mod.), 28" (Mod. & Full).
Weight: 6 lbs. 14 ozs. (20 ga.).
Stock: 14⅛"x1⁹⁄₁₆"x2⁹⁄₁₆". "English" straight-type; hand checkered Euro-
   pean walnut.
Features: Coil springs throughout action; double triggers (front is hinged);
   automatic safety; extractors. Hollow, matted barrel rib. Introduced 1977.
   Imported by Beretta Arms Co.
Price: $680.00

Beretta M-426E Side-By-Side
   Same as M-424 except action body is engraved; a silver pigeon is inlaid into
   top lever; single selective trigger; selective automatic ejectors. Introduced
   1977. Imported by Beretta Arms Co.
Price: $885.00

SHOTGUNS—DOUBLE BARREL

BERNARDELLI XXVSL DOUBLE

Gauge: 12.
Action: Holland & Holland-style sidelock with double sears.
Barrel: Demi-block (chopper lump), any length, choke.
Weight: About 6½ lbs. **Length:** To customer specs.
Stock: Best walnut with dimensions to customer specs.
Features: Firing pins removeable from face of standing breech; manual or auto safety; selective auto ejectors; classic or beavertail fore-end. Imported by Knight & Knight.
Price: With fitted luggage case $1,865.00

V. Bernardelli Roma No. 6 Double

Similar to Premier Game Cock except has double triggers (front one hinged), straight-grip or semi-pistol grip stock. Full fancy engraving covers action, has better wood. Same barrel lengths and gauges.
Price: $1,295.00

V. BERNARDELLI GAME COCK DOUBLES

Gauge: 12 ga. (2¾" chambers), 20 ga. (3" chambers).
Action: Boxlock.
Barrel: 25½" (Imp. Cyl. & Mod.), 27½" (Mod., Full).
Weight: 7 to 7¼ lbs. (12 ga.).
Stock: 14³⁄₁₆"x1⁹⁄₁₆"x2⅜". European walnut, straight grip, classic "English" style fore-end.
Features: Standard Game Cock: Double triggers, non-ejector, hard-chromed barrels, color hardened action with light engravings. Premier Game Cock: Selective auto ejectors, single trigger, color hardened sideplate action. Same Barrel lengths and chokes. From Sloan's Sporting Goods.
Price: Standard Game Cock $725.00
Price: Premier Game Cock (illus.) $990.00

V. BERNARDELLI ITALIA DOUBLE

Gauge: 12 ga. (2¾" chambers), 20 ga. (3" chambers).
Action: Sidelock with external hammers. Greener crossbolt.
Barrel: 25½" (Imp. Cyl. & Mod.), 27½" (Mod. & Full).
Weight: 7 lbs. (12 ga.).
Stock: 14³⁄₁₆"x1⁹⁄₁₆"x2⅜". European walnut, straight or semi-p.g., checkered.
Features: Outside rebounding hammers, double triggers, extractors, fully engraved silver-gray action. From Sloan's Sporting Goods.
Price: $935.00

V. BERNARDELLI V.B. HOLLAND DELUXE DOUBLE

Gauge: 12 only (2¾" chambers).
Action: Sidelock, Holland & Holland type.
Barrel: 25½" (Imp. Cyl. & Mod.), 27½" (Mod. & Full).
Weight: About 7 lbs.
Stock: 14³⁄₁₆"x1⁹⁄₁₆"x2⅜". Extra fancy European walnut.
Features: Action fully engraved to customer specs (deep relief, game scenes, etc.). Selective auto ejectors, double triggers, silver-gray finished action. From Sloan's Sporting Goods.
Price: Special order only $5,575.00

V. BERNADELLI ELIO LIGHTWEIGHT DOUBLE

Gauge: 12 ga. only (2¾" chambers).
Action: Boxlock.
Barrel: 25½" (Imp. Cyl. & Mod.), 27½" (Mod. & Full).
Weight: 6 lbs., 2 oz.
Stock: 14³⁄₁₆"x1⁹⁄₁₆"x2⅜". European walnut, checkered straight grip and fore-end.
Features: Silver-gray fully engraved action, double triggers (front one hinged), selective auto. ejectors. From Sloan's Sporting Goods.
Price: $1,055.00

BROWNING B-SS

Gauge: 12 (2¾"), 20 (3").
Action: Top lever break-open action, top tang safety, single trigger.
Barrel: 26" (Mod. and Full or Imp. Cyl. and Mod.), 28" (Mod. and Full), 30" (Full & Full or Mod & Full).
Weight: 6¾ lbs. (26" bbl., 20 ga.); 7½ lbs. (30" bbl., 12 ga.).
Stock: 14¼"x1⅝"x2½". French walnut, hand checkered. Full p.g., full beavertail fore-end.
Features: Automatic safety, automatic ejectors. Hand engraved receiver, mechanical single selective trigger with barrel selector in rear of trigger guard.
Price: Grade I, 12 or 20 ga. $389.95
Price: Grade II $725.00

Browning BSS 20-Ga. Sporter

Similar to standard BSS except has straight-grip stock and full beavertail fore-end with traditional oil finish. Introduced 1977.
Price: Grade I $399.95
Price: Grade II $725.00

SHOTGUNS—DOUBLE BARREL

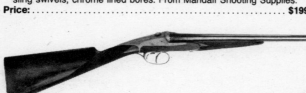

CRUCELEGUI HERMANOS MODEL 150 DOUBLE
Gauge: 12 or 20 (2¾" chambers).
Action: Greener triple crossbolt.
Barrel: 20", 26" 28", 30", 32" (Cyl. & Cyl., Full & Full, Mod. & Full, Mod. & Imp. Cyl., Imp. Cyl. & Full, Mod. & Mod.).
Weight: 5 to 7¼ lbs.
Stock: Hand checkerd walnut, beavertail fore-end.
Features: Exposed hammers; double triggers; color casehardened receiver; sling swivels; chrome lined bores. From Mandall Shooting Supplies.
Price: $199.95

DARNE SLIDING BREECH DOUBLE
Gauge: 12, 16, 20 or 28.
Action: Sliding breech.
Barrel: 25½" to 27½", choice of choking.
Weight: 5½ to 6½ lbs.
Stock: European walnut, hand checkered p.g., and fore-end. English style or semi-p.g.
Features: Double triggers, selective ejectors, plume or raised rib, case-hardened or engraved receiver. Available in 8 grades, stock or custom made. Imported from France by Firearms Center, Inc.
Price: from $800.00

DAVIDSON MODEL 63B DOUBLE BARREL SHOTGUN
Gauge: 12, 16, 20, 28 (2¾" chambers); 410 (3" chambers).
Action: Anson & Deeley with crossbolt (no crossbolt on 28 or 410).
Barrel: 30" 12 (Mod. & Full); 26" (I.C. & Mod.) and 28" (Mod. & Full) all except 410; 410, 25" (Full & Full) only.
Weight: 12 ga., 7 lbs.; 16, 20, 6½ lbs.; 28 and 410 ga., 5 lbs. 11 oz.
Stock: Hand finished checkered European walnut, white line spacers on p.g. cap and butt plate.
Features: Auto safety, manual extractors, gold-plated double triggers, engraved nickel-plated frame. Imported by Davidson.
Price: $200.00

DAVIDSON 63B MAGNUM DOUBLE SHOTGUN
Gauge: 10 (3½" chambers).
Barrel: 32" 10 (Full & Full).
Weight: 10 lbs., 10 oz.
Stock: Hand finished checkered European walnut, beavertail fore-end, white line spacers on p.g. cap and recoil pad.
Features: Auto safety, manual extractors, gold-plated double triggers (front hinged), engraved nickel-plated action. Imported from Europe by Davidson.
Price: 10 ga. $250.00

ERA DOUBLE BARREL SHOTGUN
Gauge: 12, 20, (2¾"), 410 (3").
Action: Boxlock.
Barrel: 12 (30"), 20 ga. 28" (Mod. & Full); 410 ga. 26" (Mod. & Full).
Stock: Hand checkered walnut, beavertail fore-end, white line spacers on p.g. cap and butt plate.
Features: Raised matted rib, double triggers, engraved receiver. Auto. safety. Extractors only. Imported from Brazil by F.I.E.
Price: $131.95
Price: 12, 16 or 20 ga. Riot Model, 18" bbl. $146.95
Price: 12, 16 or 20 ga. Quail Model, 20" bbl. $146.95

FRANCHI IMPERIALE MONTE CARLO EXTRA
Gauge: 12 only, 2¾" chambers.
Action: Holland & Holland type.
Barrel: Length and choking to customer specifications.
Weight: To customer specifications
Stock: Walnut root. To customer specs.
Features: Single or double trigger. Automatic wide profile hammer ejectors. Chrome lined Boehler steel barrels. A custom gun. Introduced 1977. From Stoeger Industries.
Price: Approx. $20,000.00

Consult our Directory pages for the location of firms mentioned.

GALEF'S DOUBLE BARREL SHOTGUN
Gauge: 10 (3½"); 12, 20, 410 (3"); 16, 20 (2¾").
Action: Modified Anson & Deeley boxlock, case hardened.
Barrel: 32" 10, 12 only (Full & Full); 30" 12 only (Mod.& Full); 28" all exc. 410 (Mod.& Full); 26" 12, 20, 28 (I.C.&Mod.); 26" 410 only (Mod.& Full); 22" 12 only (I.C.& I.C.).
Weight: 10½ lbs.(10), 7¾ lbs.(12) to 6 lbs.(410).
Stock: Hand checkered European walnut, p.g., beavertail fore-end, rubber recoil pad. Dimensions vary with gauge.
Features: Auto safety, plain extractors. Imported from Spain by Galef.
Price: 10 ga. . . . . $278.20   12 - 410 . . . . $209.95

SHOTGUNS—DOUBLE BARREL

GIB 10 GAUGE MAGNUM SHOTGUN
Gauge: 10 ga. (3½" chambers).
Action: Boxlock.
Barrel: 32" (Full).
Weight: 10 lbs.
Stock: 14½"x1½"x2⅝". European walnut, checkered at p.g. and fore-end.
Features: Double triggers; color hardened action, rest blued. Front and center metal beads on matted rib; ventilated rubber recoil pad. Fore-end release has positive Purdey-type mechanism. Imported by Mandall Shooting Supplies.
Price: $249.95

KLEINGUENTHER'S BRESCIA SHOTGUN
Gauge: 12 ga. (2¾" chambers).
Action: Anson & Deeley.
Barrel: 28" (Full & Mod.) chrome lined.
Weight: 6½ lbs.
Stock: Hand checkered walnut, p.g. or straight, recoil pad.
Features: Double triggers, engraved action. Imported from Italy by Kleingunther.
Price: $264.00

MERCURY MAGNUM DOUBLE BARREL SHOTGUN
Gauge: 10 (3½"), 12 or 20 (3") magnums.
Action: Triple-lock Anson & Deeley type.
Barrel: 28" (Full & Mod.), 12 and 20 ga.; 32" (Full & Full), 10 ga.
Weight: 7¼ lbs. (12 ga.); 6½ lbs. (20 ga.); 10⅛ lbs. (10 ga.). **Length:** 45" (28" bbls.).
Stock: 14" x 1⅝" x 2¼" walnut, checkered p.g. stock and beavertail fore-end, recoil pad.
Features: Double triggers, front hinged, auto safety, extractors; safety gas ports, engraved frame. Imported from Spain by Tradewinds.
Price: (12, 20 ga.) $198.50
Price: (10 ga.) $249.50

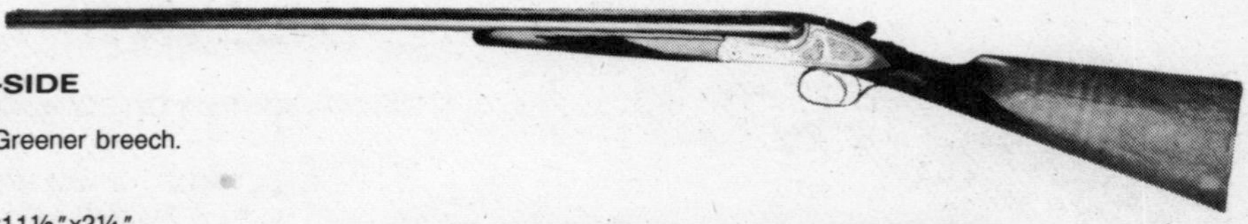

GEBRUDER MERKEL 47S SIDE-BY-SIDE
Gauge: 12, 16, 20, 3" chambers on request.
Action: Sidelock with double hook bolting and Greener breech.
Barrel: 26" (Mod. & Imp. Cyl.).
Weight: 6¼ to 6¾ lbs.
Stock: Walnut with p.g. or English style. 14¼"x11½"x2¼".
Features: Double, single or single selective trigger. Cocking indicators. English arabesque engraving. Imported by Champlin Firearms.
Price: With double trigger $1,435.00

GEBRUDER MERKEL 147S SIDE-BY-SIDE
Gauge: 12, 16, 20 ga. with 3" chambers on request.
Action: Sidelock with double hook bolting and Greener breech. Trigger catch bar.
Barrel: 26" (Mod. & Imp. Cyl., Cyl. & Imp. Cyl.).
Weight: 6½ to 6¾ lbs.
Stock: Walnut finish. English style or p.g., 14¼"x1½"x2¼".
Features: 30% faster trigger than conventional lock design. Hunting scene engraving. Highest grade side-by-side Merkel. Double, single or single selective trigger. Imported by Champlin Firearms.
Price: With double trigger $1,848.00

GEBRUDER MERKEL 147E SIDE-BY-SIDE
Gauge: 12, 16, 20, 3" chambers on request.
Action: Anson-Deeley with double hook bolting and Greener breech.
Barrel: 26" (Mod. & Imp. Cyl., Cyl. & Imp. Cyl.).
Weight: 6¼ to 6½ lbs.
Stock: Walnut. English style or p.g., 14¼"x1½"x2¼".
Features: Hunting scene engraving. Double, single or single selective trigger. Imported by Champlin Firearms.
Price: With double triggers $852.00
Price: Model 47E (as above except has scroll engraving) $694.00

Premier Continental Double Hammer Shotgun
Same as Ambassador except outside hammers, not avail. in 410.
Price: $278.15

PREMIER AMBASSADOR DOUBLE BARREL SHOTGUN
Gauge: 12, 16 (2¾"); 20, 410 (3").
Action: Triple Greener crossbolt, Purdey avail. on 410; side locks.
Barrels: 22" exc. 410; 26" all (Mod. & Full).
Weight: 7¼ lbs. (12) to 6¼ lbs. (410). **Length:** 44½".
Stock: 14" x 1⅝" x 2½" checkered walnut, p.g., beavertail fore-end.
Features: Cocking indicators, double triggers, auto safety. Imported from Europe by Premier.
Price: $306.00

SHOTGUNS—DOUBLE BARREL

Premier Brush King Double Barrel Shotgun
Same as Regent except 12 and 20 ga. only, 22" bbls. (I.C. & Mod.), weight 6¼ lbs. (12), 5¾ lbs. (20).
Price: $241.45

Premier Magnum Double Barrel Shotgun
Similar to Regent except 10 ga. (3½" chambers) 32" or 12 ga. (3" chambers) 30", both Full & Full. Recoil pad, beavertail fore-end.
Price: 12 ga. $251.00
Price: 10 ga. $280.00

Premier Presentation Double Barrel Shotgun
Same as Monarch except has gold and silver inlayed hunting scenes. Stock style and measurements to customer specs, as well as gauge, barrel length and choking.
Price: With one set of barrels $971.60
Price: Extra barrels $306.00

RICHLAND MODEL 200 DOUBLE BARREL SHOTGUN
Gauge: 12, 16, 20, 28 or 410 (12, 16 and 28 have 2¾" chambers, 20 and 410 3").
Barrel: 22" 20 ga. (Imp. Cyl. & Mod.) 26" (Imp. Cyl. & Mod., Mod. & Full 410 ga.), 28" (Mod. & Full).
Weight: 6¼ to 7¼ lbs.
Stock: 14½"x2⅜"x1½". Spanish walnut, checkered p.g. and fore-end; cheekpiece and rubber vent. recoil pad.
Sights: Metal bead front.
Features: Anson & Deely type action with double under-locking lugs; spring loaded firing pins removeable from front of action. Double triggers blue finish with light engraving. Imported by Richland Arms.
Price: $219.50

SKB 280 ENGLISH DOUBLE
Gauge: 12 ga. (2¾"), 20 ga. (3").
Barrel: 25", 26" (Mod. & I.C.), 28" (Full & Mod.).
Weight: 6½ to 7⅛ lbs.
Stock: English style straight grip. 14"x1½"x2⅝".
Features: Wrap-around checkering, semi-beavertail fore-end. Receiver hand engraved with quail and English scroll. Simulated oil finish stock. From SKB Sports.
Price: $529.95

PREMIER REGENT DOUBLE BARREL SHOTGUN
Gauge: 12, 16, 28 (2¾" chambers); 20, 410 (3" chambers).
Action: Triple Greener crossbolt; Purdey optional on 28, 410.
Barrels: 26" (I.C. & Mod.) exc. 28 and 410 only (Mod. & Full); 28" (Mod. & Full); 30" 12 only (Mod. & Full).
Weight: 7¼ lbs. (12) to 6⅛ lbs. (410). Length: 42½" (26" bbls.).
Stock: 14" x 1⅝" x 2½" checkered walnut, p.g. and fore-end.
Features: Matted tapered rib, double triggers, auto safety. Extra bbl. sets avail. Imported from Europe by Premier.
Price: $222.95
Price: With two sets of barrels, 12 ga. .... $423.00 20 ga. $386.75

PREMIER MONARCH DOUBLE BARREL SHOTGUN
Gauge: 12, 16 (2¾"), 20 (2¾" or 3").
Action: Triple Greener crossbolt.
Barrel: 26", 12 and 20 (Mod. & Imp. Cyl.), 28", 12, 16, 20 (Mod. & Full).
Weight: About 7 lbs. Length: 44½" over-all (28" barrels).
Stock: 14"x1⅝"x2½". Fancy French walnut, checkered p.g. and fore-end.
Sights: Metal bead, front and middle.
Features: Solid tapered rib; double triggers, auto. ejectors and safety, selective extractors; engraved action. Imported from Europe by Premier.
Price: $449.70

Richland Model 711 Magnum Shotgun
Similar to Model 200 except in 12 ga. (3") or 10 ga. (3½") magnums. Choked Full & Full, 12 ga. has 30" barrels, 10 ga. has 32". Weight is 7¾ lbs. (12), 11 lbs. (10.) Uses Purdey triple lock system, auto. safety with double triggers, raised full-length rib with metal beads at front and center.
Price: 12 ga. Magnum $245.00
Price: 10 ga. Magnum $280.00

ROSSI MODEL 11 OVERLAND DOUBLE BARREL
Gauge: 12, 20, 410 (3" chambers).
Action: Sidelock with external hammers; Greener crossbolt.
Barrel: 12 ga., 20" (Imp. Cyl., Mod.) 28" (Mod. & Full), 20 ga., 20" (Mod., Full), 410 ga., 26" (Full & Full).
Weight: 6½ to 7 lbs.
Stock: Walnut p.g. with beavertail fore-end.
Features: Solid raised matted rib. Exposed hammers. Imporderd by Interarms.
Price: 12 or 20 .... $165.00
Price: 410 ga. $170.00

ROSSI MODEL 14 "SQUIRE" DOUBLE
Gauge: 12, 20, 410 (3" chambers).
Barrel: 12 ga.—26" (Imp. Cyl. & Mod.), 28" (Mod. & Full); 20 ga.—28" (Mod. & Full); 410—26" (Full & Full).
Weight: About 7½ lbs.
Stock: Walnut finished hardwood.
Features: Double triggers, raised matted rib, beavertail fore-end. Massive twin underlugs mesh with synchronized sliding bolts. Introduced 1978. Imported by Interarms.
Price: 12 ga., 20 ga. $175.00
Price: 410 .... $185.00

SKB MODEL 280 QUAIL DOUBLE
Gauge: 20 only, 3" chambers.
Barrel: 25" (Imp. Cyl. & Imp. Cyl.).
Weight: 6½ lbs.
Stock: 14"x1½"x2⅝", English style.
Features: Designed for quail and upland game shooting. Straight stock, wrap-around checkering, scroll game scene on frame, semi-beavertail fore-end. Auto. selective ejectors, single trigger. From SKB Sports.
Price: $529.95

SKB 200E Field Grade Double

Same as 100 Field Grade except: automatic selective ejectors, bead middle sight and scroll engraving on receiver, beavertail fore-end. White line spacers. Gold plated trigger and nameplate **$514.00**

SKB 200E Skeet Grade

Same as 200E Deluxe Field Grade except: recoil pad, non-auto. safety. Bbls. 26″ 12 ga. or 25″ 20 ga. (Skeet, Skeet). Wgt. 7¼ and 6¼ lbs.
Price: **$519.95**

SKB 100 FIELD GRADE DOUBLE

Gauge: 12 (2¾″ chambers) and 20 (3″).
Action: Top lever, hammerless, boxlock, automatic safety, single selective trigger, non-automatic extractor.
Barrel: 12 ga. 26″ (Imp. Cyl., Mod.). 28⅛ or 30″ (Mod., Full). 20 ga. 28″ (Mod., Full). 25″ (Imp. Cyl., Mod.).
Weight: 7 lbs. (12 ga.); 6 lbs. (20 ga.)
Stock: 14″x1½″x2⅝″. Walnut, hand checkered p.g. and fore-end, p.g. cap, fluted comb.
Features: Automatic safety. Chrome lined action and barrels, hand engraved receiver. From SKB Sports.
Price: **$367.00**

SAVAGE-STEVENS MODEL 311 DOUBLE

Gauge: 12, 16, 20, 410 (12, 20 and 410, 3″ chambers).
Action: Top lever, hammerless; double triggers, auto top tang safety.
Barrel: 12, 16, 20 ga. 36″ (Imp. Cyl., Mod.); 12 ga. 28″ (Mod., Full); 12 ga. 30″ (Mod., Full); 410 ga. 26″ (Full, Full).
Length: 45¾″ over-all. **Weight:** 7-8 lbs. (30″ bbl.).
Stock: 14″x1½″x2½″. Walnut finish, p.g., fluted comb.
Features: Box type frame, case-hardened finish.
Price: **$163.00**

SAVAGE FOX MODEL B-SE DOUBLE

Gauge: 12, 20, 410 (20, 2¾″ and 3″; 410, 2½″ and 3″ shells).
Action: Hammerless, takedown; non-selective single trigger; auto. safety. Automatic ejectors.
Barrel: 12, 20 ga. 26″ (Imp. Cyl., Mod.); 12 ga. (Mod., Full); 410, 26″ (Full, Full). Vent. rib on all.
Stock: 14″x1½″x2½″. Walnut, checkered p.g. and beavertail fore-end.
Weight: 12 ga. 7 lbs., 16 ga. 6¾ lbs., 20 ga. 6½ lbs., 410 ga. 6¼ lbs.
Features: Decorated, case-hardened frame; white bead front and middle sights.
Price: **$245.50**
Also available with double triggers, case hardened frame, without white line spacers and auto. ejectors as Model B **$212.00**

VENTURA MODELS 51, 52 & 53 DOUBLES

Gauge: 10, 12, 20, 28, 410.
Action: Anson & Deeley boxlock, Purdey treble bolting.
Barrel: 26″, 28″, 30″, 32″, lengths and chokes according to gauge and use.
Stock: Select European walnut, hand checkered. Straight English or p.g. stock.
Features: Model 51 straight-frame with or without auto ejectors in 12, 20, 28 and 410; Model 52 in 10 gauge with two triggers only; Model 53 (shown) is deluxe gun with scalloped frame with auto ejectors in 12, 20, 28 and 410. All models have beavertail fore-ends and optional single triggers. Introduced 1978. From Ventura Imports.
Price: Model 51 . . . . **$295.00 to $395.00**
Price: Model 52 (10 ga.) **$425.00**
Price: Model 53 . . . . **$375.00 to $495.00**

VENTURA MODELS 61 & 65 DOUBLES

Gauge: 12 and 20.
Action: Holland & Holland sidelocks, Purdey treble bolting with intercepting safety sears.
Barrel: 26″, 27″, 28″, 30″, lengths and chokes according to gauge and use.
Stock: Select European walnut, hand checkered. Straight English or full p.g.
Features: Model 61 (shown) is deluxe grade, Model 65 is super deluxe with finest hand finishing and engraving. Both have beavertail fore-ends, auto ejectors, optional single selective trigger, file-cut sighting ribs, cocking indicators, and hand-detachable lock plates with floral engraving. Introduced 1978. From Ventura Imports.
Price: Model 61 . . . . **$695.00 to $815.00**
Price: Model 65 . . . . **$895.00 to $1,050.00**

Winchester 21 Pigeon Grade

Same as Custom grade except: 3″ chambers, available in 12 and 20 ga.; matted or vent. rib, leather covered pad (optional); style "A" stock carving and style "6" engraving (see Win. catalog); gold inlaid p.g. cap, gold nameplate or 3 gold initials in guard . . . . **Price on request from factory.**

WINCHESTER 21 CUSTOM DOUBLE GUN

12, 16 or 20 ga. Almost any choke or bbl. length combination. Matted rib, 2¾″ chambers, rounded frame, stock of AA-grade full fancy American walnut to customer's dimensions; straight or p.g., cheekpiece, Monte Carlo and/or offset; field. Skeet or trap fore-end. Full fancy checkering, engine-turned receiver parts, gold plated trigger and gold oval name plate (optional) with three initials . . . . **Price on request from factory.**

SHOTGUNS—DOUBLE BARREL

Winchester 21 Grand American
Same as Custom and Pigeon grades except: style "B" stock carving, with style "6" engraving, all figures gold inlaid; extra pair of bbls. with beavertail fore-end, engraved and carved to match rest of gun; full leather trunk case or all, with canvas cover . . . .**Price on request from factory.**

WINCHESTER MODEL 23 PIGEON GRADE DOUBLE
Gauge: 12, 3" chambers.
Barrel: 26", 28", 30" (Imp. Cyl. & Mod., Mod. & Full, Full & Full). Vent. rib.
Weight: 7 lbs. **Length:** 46¾" over-all (30" bbls.)
Stock: High grade American walnut, beavertail fore-end. Deep cut checkering, new warm, rich color, high-lustre finish. 14"x1½"x2½".
Features: Mechanical trigger; ventilated tapered rib; selective ejectors. A 20 gauge version will be introduced in 1979 with 26" or 28" (Imp. Cyl. & Mod. or Mod. & Full) barrels, weight of 6½ lbs. Receiver, top lever and trigger guard have silver gray satin finish and fine line scroll engraving. Introduced 1978.
Price: . . . .**Not available**

SHOTGUNS—BOLT ACTION

MARLIN SUPERGOOSE 10 M5510
Gauge: 10, 3½" Magnum or 2⅞" regular, 2-shot clip.
Barrel: 34" (Full), bead front sight.
Weight: About 10½ lbs. **Length:** 55½" over-all.
Stock: Extra long American black walnut with p.g., Pachmayr vent. pad., white butt spacer.
Features: Bolt action, removable 2-shot clip magazine. Gold plated trigger, positive thumb safety, red cocking indicator. Comes with quick-detachable swivels and leather carrying strap.
Price: **$163.95**

Marlin 55S Slug Gun
Same as Goose Gun except: 24" barrel, iron sights (rear adj.), drilled and tapped for scope mounting. Comes with carrying strap and swivels. Weight is 7½ lbs., over-all length 45". **$94.95**

MARLIN MODEL 55 GOOSE GUN BOLT ACTION
Gauge: 12 only, 2-shot (3" mag. or 2¾").
Action: Bolt action, thumb safety, detachable clip. Red cocking indicator.
Barrel: 36", Full choke.
Weight: 8 lbs., 57" over-all.
Stock: Walnut, p.g., recoil pad, leather strap & swivels. Mar-Shield® finish.
Features: Tapped for receiver sights. Swivels and leather carrying strap. Gold-plated trigger. Brass bead front sight.
Price: **$88.95**

MOSSBERG MODEL 395K BOLT ACTION
Gauge: 12, 3-shot (3" chamber).
Action: Bolt; takedown; detachable clip.
Barrel: 26" with C-Lect-Choke.
Weight: 7½ lbs. **Length:** 45¾" over-all.
Stock: Walnut finish, p.g. Monte Carlo comb; recoil pad.
Features: Streamlined action; top safety; grooved rear sight.
Price: **$85.95**
   Also available in 20 ga. 3" chamber 28" bbl. 6¼ lbs., as M385K **$80.95**

MOSSBERG MODEL 183K BOLT ACTION
Gauge: 410, 3-shot (3" chamber).
Action: Bolt; top-loading mag.; thumb safety.
Barrel: 25" with C-Lect-Choke.
Weight: 5¾ lbs. **Length:** 45¼" over-all.
Stock: Walnut finish, p.g., Monte Carlo comb., rubber recoil pad w/spacer.
Features: Moulded trigger guard with finger grooves, gold bead front sight.
Price: **$74.95**

SHOTGUNS—BOLT ACTION

NEW HAVEN BRAND MODEL 395K BOLT ACTION
Gauge: 12, 3-shot (3" chamber).
Action: Bolt; takedown.
Barrel: 26", C-Lect-Choke.
Weight: 7½ lbs. **Length:** 45¾" over-all.
Stock: Walnut-finished hardwood; p.g.; Monte Carlo comb; recoil pad.
Features: Top safety; grooved rear sight. From Mossberg.
Price: $85.95
Price: In 20 ga. (3" chamber), 28" barrel, wgt. 6¼ lbs. $80.95

NEW HAVEN BRAND MODEL 183K BOLT ACTION
Gauge: 410, 3-shot (3" chamber).
Action: Bolt; top-loading magazine.
Barrel: 25", C-Lect-Choke.
Weight: 5¾ lbs. **Length:** 45¼" over-all.
Stock: Walnut-finish hardwood; p.g.; Monte Carlo; rubber recoil pad with spacer.
Features: Moulded trigger guard with finger grooves; gold bead front sight. From Mossberg.
Price: $74.95

STEVENS SUPER VALUE 58 BOLT ACTION SHOTGUN
Gauge: 410 ga. (2½" and 3" chambers), 3-shot clip.
Action: Self-cocking bolt; double extractors; thumb safety.
Barrel: 24", Full choke.
Weight: 5½ lbs. **Length:** 43" over-all.
Stock: Walnut finish, checkered fore-end and p.g., recoil pad.
Features: Crisp trigger pull, Electro-Cote stock finish.
Price: About $66.95

WESTERN FIELD 150C BOLT ACTION SHOTGUN
Gauge: 20 or 410 (3" chamber).
Action: Self cocking, bolt action. Thumb safety. 3-shot magazine.
Barrel: 24", full choke.
Weight: 5½ lbs. **Length:** 44½" over-all.
Stock: Hardwood, Monte Carlo design.
Features: Top loading.
Price: $69.99

WESTERN FIELD 172 BOLT ACTION SHOTGUN
Gauge: 12 (3" chamber).
Action: Self-cocking bolt. Thumb safety, double locking lugs, detachable clip.
Barrel: 28" adj. choke, shoots rifled slugs.
Stock: Walnut, Monte Carlo design, p.g., recoil pad.
Features: Quick removable bolt with double extractors, grooved rear sight.
Price: $79.99
    M170 Similar to 172 except has patridge front sight, folding-leaf adj. rear, comes with sling and swivels $79.99

SHOTGUNS—SINGLE BARREL

BROWNING BT-99 COMPETITION TRAP SPECIAL
Gauge: 12 gauge only (2¾").
Action: Top lever break-open, hammerless.
Barrel: 32" or 34" (Mod., Imp. Mod. or Full) with $^{11}/_{32}$" wide high post floating vent. rib.
Weight: 8 lbs. (32" bbl.).
Stock: French walnut; hand checkered, full pistol grip, full beavertail fore-end; recoil pad. Trap dimensions with M.C. 14⅜"x1⅜"x1⅜"x2".
Sights: Ivory front and middle beads.
Features: Gold plated trigger with 3½-lb. pull, deluxe trap-style recoil pad, auto ejector, no safety. Also available in engraved Pigeon Grade.
Price: Grade I Competition $524.95
Price: Grade I Competition with extra bbl. $764.95
Price: Pigeon Grade Competition $1,100.00

CBC DELUXE SINGLE BARREL SHOTGUN
Gauge: 12, 20 (2¾"), 410 (3").
Barrel: 12 & 20 ga. 28" (Full); 410 ga. 26" (Full).
Weight: 6½ lbs.
Stock: Walnut stained hardwood.
Sights: Metal bead front.
Features: Button on front of trigger guard opens action. Exposed hammer. Automatic ejector. Imported from Brazil by F.I.E.
Price: $49.50
Price: 20 and 410, Youth Model $52.50
Price: Combo rifle-shotgun (20 ga. or 30-30 interchangeable bbls.) $82.95

ERA SINGLE BARREL SHOTGUN
Gauge: 12, 16, 20 (2¾″), 410 (3″).
Barrel: 12 ga. 30″ & 20 ga. 28″ (Full); 410 ga. (Full).
Weight: 6½ lbs.
Stock: Walnut stained hardwood, beavertail fore-end.
Sights: Metal bead front.
Features: Trigger guard is pulled to open action. Exposed hammer, auto extractor. Imported from Brazil by F.I.E.
Price: **$46.95**
Price: 20 and 410 ga. Youth Model **$48.95**

FRANCHI MODEL 2004 SINGLE BARREL TRAP
Gauge: 12 only (2¾″ chamber).
Barrel: 32″ or 34″ (Imp. Mod. or Full).
Weight: About 8 lbs.
Stock: 14½″x1⅞″x1½″. Fancy French walnut; checkered p.g. and fore-end. Available in Monte Carlo or straight style (interchangeble). Different dimensions avail.
Features: "Ceiling-Sell" trap trigger; raised competition, ventilated, trap rib. Buttstock drilled and tapped for recoil reducer. Comes with fitted luggage-type hard case. From Stoeger Industries.
Price: **$1,095.00**

GALEF COMPANION SINGLE BARREL SHOTGUN
Gauge: 12, 20, 410 (3″); 16, 28 (2¾″).
Action: Folding boxlock.
Barrel: 28″ exc. 12 (30″) and 410 (26″), all Full.
Weight: 5½ lbs. (12) to 4½ lbs. (410).
Stock: 14″x1½″x2⅝″ hand checkered walnut, p.g.
Features: Non-auto safety, folds. Vent. rib $5.00 additional. Imported from Italy by Galef.
Price: Plain bbl. .... **$72.95**   Vent. rib **$79.95**

H & R TOPPER MODELS 58 and 98
Gauge: 12, 20 and 410. (2¾″ or 3″ chamber), 16, 28 (2¾″ only).
Action: Takedown. Side lever opening. External hammer, auto ejection. Case hardened frame.
Barrel: 12 ga., 28″, 30″; 20 and 410 ga., 28″. (Full choke). 12, 16, 20 ga. available 28″ (Mod.), 28 and 410 ga., 26″ (Mod., Full).
Stock: Walnut finished hardwood; p.g., (14″x1¾″x2½″).
Weight: 5 to 6½ lbs., according to gauge and bbl. length.
Features: Self-adj. bbl. lock; coil springs throughout; auto. rebound hammer.
Price: M58 .... **$61.50**
  Model 98, Topper Deluxe Nickel frame, ebony finished stock. 20 ga. and 410, 28″ bbl. **$69.95**

H & R Topper Jr. Model 490
Like M58 except ideally proportioned stock for the smaller shooter. Can be cheaply changed to full size. 20 ga. (Mod.), 28 ga. (Mod.) or 410 (Full) 26″ bbl. Weight 5 lbs., 40½″ over-all **$64.50**

H & R Topper Buck Model 162
Same as M58 except 12 ga. 24″ cyl. bored bbl., adj. folding leaf rear sight, blade front, 5½ lbs.; over-all 40″. Cross bolt safety: push-button action release **$77.50**

H&R Topper Model 176
Same as Model 58 except in 10 gauge (3½″ chamber), 36″ barrel (Full), over-all length of 51″, weighs 10 lbs, recoil pad. **$79.50**

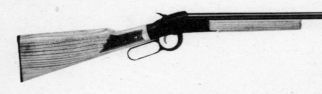

ITHACA MODEL 66 SUPERSINGLE
Gauge: 20 or 410 (3″ chamber).
Action: Non-takedown; under lever opening.
Barrel: 12, 20 ga. 28″ (Mod., Full); 12 ga., 30″ (Full), 410, 26″ (Full).
Stock: Straight grip walnut-finish stock and fore-end.
Weight: About 7 lbs.
Features: Rebounding hammer independent of the lever.
Price: Standard **$69.95**
Price: Buck Buster, 20 ga. **$79.95**

Ithaca Model 66 Supersingle Youth
Same as the 66 Standard except: 20 (26″ bbl., Mod.) and 410 ga. (26″ bbl., Full) shorter stock with recoil pad **$74.95**

ITHACA PERAZZI COMPETITION I SINGLE BARREL
Gauge: 12 (2¾" chamber)
Action: Top lever, break open, top tang safety.
Barrel: 32" or 34"; custom choking; ventilated rib.
Stock: Custom fitted European walnut in lacquered or oil finish.
Weight: About 8½ lbs.
Features: Hand-engraved receiver; interchangeable stocks available with some fitting.
Price: $1,995.00

ITHACA 5E GRADE SINGLE BARREL TRAP GUN
Gauge: 12 only.
Action: Top lever break open hammerless, dual locking lugs.
Barrel: 30" or 32", ramless vent. rib.
Stock: (14½"x1½"x1⅞"). Select walnut, checkered p.g. and beavertail fore-end, p.g. cap, recoil pad, Monte Carlo comb, cheekpiece, Cast-on, cast-off or extreme deviation from standard stock dimensions $100 extra. Reasonable deviation allowed without extra charge.
Features: Frame, top lever and trigger guard extensively engraved and gold inlaid. Gold name plate in stock.
Price: Custom made $4,000.00
Price: $5,000 Grade $5,000.00

Ithaca Perazzi Competition IV Single Barrel
Designed expressly for 16-yard and handicap shooting. Comes with four interchangable choke tubes—nine are available. Has wide crescent-patterned vent. rib, Bradley-type sights, wide target-style trigger, 24 line hand-cut checkering. Choke tube wrench, stock wrench for changing stocks, padded hard case. Introduced 1977. From Ithaca.
Price: With four choke tubes $2,195.00
Price: Extra choke tubes, each $29.95

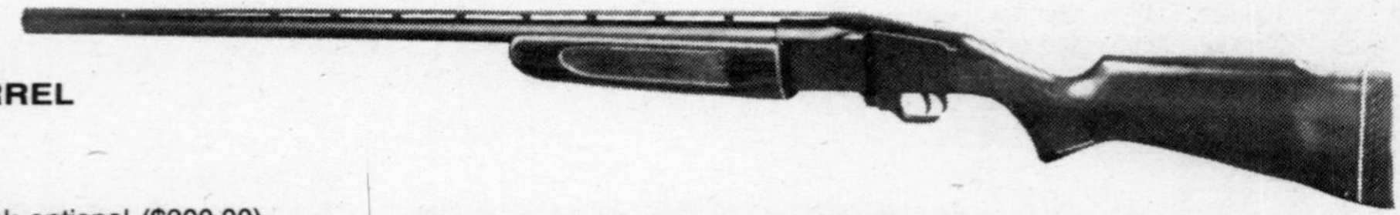

LJUTIC DYN-A-TRAP SINGLE BARREL
Gauge: 12 ga. only.
Barrel: 33" (Full).
Weight: Approx. 9 lbs.
Stock: Standard trap dimensions. Custom stock optional ($200.00).
Features: Regular pull trigger, release trigger optional ($75.00); extractor only; only 5 moving parts in action; Ljutic pushbutton opener. From Ljutic Industries.
Price: $1,100.00
Price: Release trigger $200.00
Price: Pull trigger $150.00

IVER JOHNSON CHAMPION
Gauge: 12, 20 or 410 (3" chamber).
Barrel: 12 gauge, 28" or 30"; 20 gauge, 28"; 410, 26"; full choke.
Stock: Walnut finish, trap style fore-end.
Features: Takedown action, automatic ejection.
Price: $55.00

LJUTIC MONO GUN SINGLE BARREL
Gauge: 12 ga. only.
Barrel: 34", choked to customer specs; hollow-milled rib, 35½" sight plane.
Weight: Approx. 9 lbs.
Stock: To customer specs. Oil finish, hand checkered.
Features: Pull or release trigger; removeable trigger guard contains trigger and hammer mechanism; Ljutic pushbutton opener on front of trigger guard. From Ljutic Industries.
Price: $2,195.00
Price: Extra barrel $700.00
Price: Release trigger $250.00

LJUTIC X-73 SINGLE BARREL SHOTGUN
Gauge: 12 ga. only.
Action: Push-button break-open.
Barrel: 33" (Full).
Weight: About 8½ lbs.
Stock: 14¾"x1⅜", straight or Monte Carlo; fancy walnut.
Features: Raised straight-taper rib; push-button action opener; pull or release trigger.
Price: $1,495.00
Price: Extra barrel $500.00
Price: Extra pull trigger assembly $200.00
Price: Release trigger $250.00

Ljutic Adjustable Barrel Mono Gun
Similar to standard Mono except has micrometer-adjustable choke (allows shooter to adj. the pattern from flat to an elevation of 4 feet), choice of Olympic, step-style or standard rib. Custom stock measurements, fancy wood, etc. $2,595.00

ROTTWEIL AMERICAN TRAP SINGLE
Gauge: 12 ga. only.
Action: Boxlock.
Barrel: 34" (Full); vent. rib. Chrome bore (except choke).
Weight: 8½ lbs.
Stock: Monte Carlo of select French walnut. Satin oil finish. Hand-checkered p.g. and fore-end. Two lengths available: 14¾"x1⅜"x1⅜"x1⅞" or 14½"x1⅜"x1⅜"x1⅞".
Sights: Plastic front in metal sleeve, center bead.
Features: Interchangeable trigger groups—special single covertible for O/U barrel use, or release-release single selective. Milled receiver. Choke is hand honed. All coil springs, engraved action. Introduced 1978. Imported by Eastern Sports Int.
Price: $1,995.00

MONTE CARLO SINGLE BARREL SHOTGUN
Gauge: 12 (2¾" chamber).
Action: Monte Carlo, bottom release.
Barrel: 32" (Trap).
Weight: 8¼ lbs.
Stock: 14½"x1⅛"x1⅝" hand checkered walnut, p.g., beavertail fore-end, recoil pad.
Features: Auto ejector, slide safety, gold plated trigger. Imported from Italy by Galef.
Price: $195.00

SKB CENTURY II SINGLE BARREL TRAP
Gauge: 12 only (2¾").
Barrel: 32" or 34" (Full).
Weight: 8 lbs.
Stock: 14½"x1½"x1⅞" (Trap). French walnut, hand checkered, curved pad, full beavertail fore-end. M.C. stock available.
Sights: Bradley-type front, middle bead.
Features: Improvements include wedge-shaped fore-end to reduce recoil, extra strength one-piece extractor, longer fore-end iron and latching system for tighter lock-up and easier removal. Stock dimension ⅛" higher, new firing pin retention system. From SKB Sports.
Price: **$599.95**
Price: Monte Carlo stock **$599.95**

Stevens M94-Y Youth's Gun
Same as Model 94-C except: 26" bbl., 20 ga. Mod. or 410 Full, 12½" stock with recoil pad. Wgt. about 5½ lbs. 40½" over-all. **$64.75**

SAVAGE-STEVENS MODEL 94-C Single Barrel Gun
Gauge: 12, 16, 20, 410 (12, 20 and 410, 3" chambers).
Action: Top lever break open; hammer; auto. ejector.
Barrel: 12 ga. 28", 30", 32", 36"; 16, 20 ga. 28"; 410 ga. 26". Full choke only.
Weight: About 6 lbs. **Length:** 42" over-all (26" bbl.).
Stock: 14"x1½"x2½". Walnut finish, checkered p.g. and fore-end.
Features: Color case-hardened frame, low rebounding hammer.
Price: 26" to 32" bbls. . . . . **$61.00**   36" bbl. **$64.75**

STEVENS "Super Value" 9478 SINGLE BARREL
Gauge: 10, 12, 20 or 410.
Barrel: 26" (Full, Mod.), 28" (Full), 30" (Full), 32" (Full), 36" (Full).
Weight: 6¼ lbs. (9½ lbs for 10 ga.) **Length:** 42" to 52" over-all.
Stock: Walnut finished hardwood. 14"x1½"x2½".
Features: Bottom opening action "lever", manually cocked hammer, auto. ejection. Color case-hardened frame. Youth Model available in 20 or 410, 26" (Mod.) barrel, 12½" pull stock, weighs 5½ lbs.
Price: 9478, about **$46.95**
Price: 9478-Y (Youth Model) about **$46.95**

"SNAKE CHARMER" SHOTGUN
Gauge: 410, 3" chamber.
Barrel: 18⅛" (Cyl.)
Weight: 3½ lbs. **Length:** 28⅛" over-all.
Stock: Moulded plastic, thumbhole type.
Sights: None.
Features: Measures 19" when taken apart. All stainless steel construction. Storage compartment in buttstock holds four spare rounds of 410. Introduced 1978. From Bob Meece Co.
Price: **$89.95**
Price: Vinyl carrying case **$5.95**

Winchester 37A Youth Model
Same as std. 37A except: shorter 26" bbl., youth-size stock (12½" pull), 40¾" over-all length. Rubber recoil pad. Available only in 20 ga. (Imp. Mod.) or 410 (Full). **$68.95**

WINCHESTER 37A SINGLE SHOT
Gauge: 12, 20, 410 (3" chamber), 16, 28 (2¾" chamber).
Action: Top lever break-open, exposed hammer.
Barrel: 26", 410 ga. (Full), 28", 20 & 28 ga. (Full), 30", 16 ga. (Full), 30", 32" 36", 12 ga. (Full).
Length: 42¼" over-all (26" bbl.). **Weight:** 5½ to 6¼ lbs.
Stock: 14"x1⅜"x2⅜", walnut finish.
Sights: Metal bead front.
Features: Checkered p.g. and fore-end bottom, gold plated trigger, engraved receiver, concave hammer spur. Grip cap and buttplate have white spacers. Auto. ejector. Top lever opens right or left.
Price: Standard Model, 12 ga. 26"-32" bbl. **$62.95**
Price: 16, 20, 28 410 ga. **$62.95**
Price: 12 ga., 36" bbl. **$68.95**

BLACK POWDER GUNS

The following pages catalog the black powder arms currently available to U.S. shooters. These range from quite precise replicas of historically significant arms to totally new designs created expressly to give the black powder shooter the benefits of modern technology.

Most of the replicas are imported, and many are available from more than one source. Thus examples of a given model such as the 1860 Army revolver or Zouave rifle purchased from different importers may vary in price, finish and fitting. Most of them bear proof marks, indicating that they have been test fired in the proof house of their country of origin.

A list of the importers and the retail price range are included with the description for each model. Many local dealers handle more than one importer's products, giving the prospective buyer an opportunity to make his own judgment in selecting a black powder gun. Most importers have catalogs available free or at

nominal cost, and some are well worth having for the useful information on black powder shooting they provide in addition to their detailed descriptions and specifications of the guns.

A number of special accessories are also available for the black powder shooter. These include replica powder flasks, bullet moulds, cappers and tools, as well as more modern devices to facilitate black powder cleaning and maintenance. Ornate presentation cases and even detachable shoulder stocks are also available for some black powder pistols from their importers. Again, dealers or the importers will have catalogs.

The black powder guns are arranged in four sections: Single Shot Pistols, Revolvers, Muskets & Rifles, and Shotguns. The guns within each section are arranged by date of the original, with the oldest first. Thus the 1847 Walker replica leads off the revolver section, and flintlocks precede percussion arms in the other sections.

BLACK POWDER SINGLE SHOT PISTOLS — FLINT & PERCUSSION

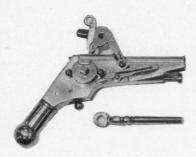

DIXIE WHEELOCK COURIER PISTOL
Caliber: 36.
Barrel: 4", half octagon, half round; flared muzzle.
Weight: 1¼ lbs. **Length:** 7" over-all.
Stock: Metal.
Sights: None.
Features: Replica of 1580 Courier Pistol. Frame and hammer of brass. Steel barrel. Comes complete with spanner. Imported from England by Dixie Gun Works.
Price: **$175.00**

CHARLEVILLE FLINTLOCK PISTOL
Caliber: 69.
Barrel: 7½".
Weight: 48 oz. **Length:** 13½" over-all.
Stock: Walnut.
Sights: None.
Features: Brass frame, polished steel barrel, brass buttcap and backstrap. Replica of original 1777 pistol. From Hopkins & Allen.
Price: **$125.00**

BLACK WATCH SCOTCH PISTOL
Caliber: 58.
Barrel: 7".
Weight: 1½ lbs. **Length:** 12" over-all.
Stock: Brass.
Sights: None.
Features: Faithful reproduction of this military flintlock. From Hopkins & Allen.
Price: **$86.95**

TOWER FLINTLOCK PISTOL
Caliber: 45, 69.
Barrel: 8¼".
Weight: 40 oz. **Length:** 14" over-all.
Stock: Walnut.
Sights: Fixed.
Features: Engraved lock, brass furniture. Specifications, including caliber, weight and length may vary with importers. Available as flint or percussion. Imported by The Armoury, F.I.E., CVA (only percussion in finished form), Dixie, Navy/Replica, Hopkins & Allen.
Price: ....**$23.00 to $59.95.**
Price: Kit form, flintlock (CVA, Dixie) ....**$43.95 to $46.95**
Price: Kit form, percussion (CVA) **$40.95**

COLONIAL PISTOL
Caliber: 45 (.451" bore).
Barrel: 6½", octagonal, rifled.
Length: 12" over-all.
Stock: Walnut.
Features: Case hardened lock, brass furniture, fixed sights. Available in either flint or percussion. Imported by CVA, Markwell.
Price: Percussion ....**$38.95 to $49.95**
Also available in kit form, either flint or percussion. Stock 95% inletted.
Price: ....**$28.95 or $34.95**

ENGLISH BELT PISTOL
Caliber: 44.
Barrel: 6½".
Weight: 2½ lbs. **Length:** 12" over-all.
Stock: Walnut-finished hardwood. Checkered p.g.
Sights: Fixed.
Features: A 44-cal. version of the English dueling pistol. Polished brass furniture, color case hardened lock, blued barrel. Comes as a kit or assembled. From Hopkins & Allen.
Price: **$69.95**

BLACK POWDER SINGLE SHOT PISTOLS—FLINT & PERCUSSION

HARPER'S FERRY 1806 PISTOL
Caliber: 54.
Barrel: 10".
Weight: 40 oz. **Length:** 16" over-all.
Stock: Walnut.
Sights: Fixed.
Features: Case hardened lock, brass mounted browned bbl. Replica of the first U.S. Gov't.-made flintlock pistol. Imported by Navy/Replica, Hawes.
Price: .... $95.00 to $100.00

KENTUCKY FLINTLOCK PISTOL
Caliber: 44, 45.
Barrel: 10⅛".
Weight: 32 oz. **Length:** 15½" over-all.
Stock: Walnut.
Sights: Fixed.
Features: Case hardened lock, blued bbl.; available also as brass bbl. flint Model 1821 ($110.00, Navy). Imported by Navy/Replica, The Armoury, Century, F.I.E., Dixie, CVA (kit only), Hawes, Kassnar, Euroarms, Hopkins & Allen.
Price: .... $40.95 to $95.00
Price: In kit form, from $24.95

Kentucky Percussion Pistol
Similar to above but percussion lock. Imported by Centennial, The Armoury, Navy/Replica, F.I.E., Hawes, CVA, Dixie, Century, Markwell, Armsport, Hopkins & Allen.
Price: .... $26.95 to $90.00
Price: Brass barrel (Navy) $100.00
Price: In kit form .... $35.95 to $55.95

CVA PERCUSSION MOUNTAIN PISTOL
Caliber: 45 or 50 cal.
Barrel: 9", octagon. ¹⁵/₁₆" across flats.
Weight: 43 oz. **Length:** 15" over-all.
Stock: American maple.
Sights: German silver blade front, fixed primitive rear.
Features: Engraved percussion-style lock. Adjustable sear engagement. Fly and bridle. Hooked breech. Browned steel on finished pistol. German silver wedge plates. Stainless steel nipples. Hardwood ramrod. Belt hook. Introduced 1978. From CVA.
Price: $78.95
Price: Kit form $49.95

KENTUCKY BELT PERCUSSION PISTOL
Caliber: 45.
Barrel: 7", rifled.
Weight: 29 oz. **Length:** 12" over-all.
Stock: Walnut.
Sights: Fixed.
Features: Engraved lock, brass furniture, steel ramrod. Available as flint or percussion. Imported by The Armoury, Hawes.
Price: .... $22.95 to $62.95.
Price: Kit form .... $27.95 to $44.95

DIXIE OVERCOAT PISTOL
Caliber: 39.
Barrel: 4", smoothbore.
Weight: 13 oz. **Length:** 8" over-all.
Stock: Walnut-finished hardwood. Checkered p.g.
Sights: Fixed.
Features: Shoots .380" balls. Breech plug and engraved lock are burnished steel finish; barrel and trigger guard blued.
Price: Plain model $26.95
Price: Engraved model $34.50

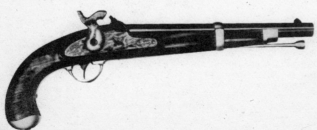

HARPER'S FERRY MODEL 1855 PERCUSSION PISTOL
Caliber: 58.
Barrel: 11¾", rifled.
Weight: 56 oz. **Length:** 18" over-all.
Stock: Walnut.
Sights: Fixed.
Features: Case hardened lock and hammer; brass furniture; blued bbl. Shoulder stock available, priced at $35.00. Imported by Navy/Replica.
Price: $95.00
Price: With detachable shoulder stock $125.00

BLACK POWDER SINGLE SHOT PISTOLS—FLINT & PERCUSSION

PHILADELPHIA DERRINGER PERCUSSION PISTOL
Caliber: 41, 45.
Barrel: 3⅛".
Weight: 14 oz. **Length:** 7" over-all.
Stock: Walnut, checkered grip.
Sights: Fixed.
Features: Engraved wedge holder and bbl. Also available in flintlock version (Armoury, $29.95). Imported by Hawes, CVA (not engraved), Markwell Arms, The Armoury, Hopkins & Allen.
Price: .... $18.37 to $39.95
Price: Kit form (Markwell) $26.95
Price: Kit form (CVA) $23.95

Richland "Mississippi Derringer"
Similar to Dixie Brass Frame Derringer except over-all length is 5⅜". Comes complete or as kit.
Price: Complete $29.95
Price: Kit form $23.95

BOUNTY HUNTER PERCUSSION PISTOL
Caliber: 44.
Barrel: 17".
Weight: 3½ lbs. **Length:** 22" over-all.
Stock: Oil stained walnut.
Sights: Fixed.
Features: A Kentucky-style pistol with long barrel. Polish brass furniture, blued barrel, color case hardened lock. Kit or complete. From Hopkins & Allen.
Price: $86.95

BUCCANEER DOUBLE BARREL PISTOL
Caliber: 36, 44 or 45 (Hawes).
Barrel: 9½".
Weight: 40 oz. **Length:** 15½" over-all.
Stock: Walnut, one piece.
Sights: Fixed.
Features: Case hardened and engraved lockplate, solid brass fittings. Percussion or flintlock. Imported by Hawes Firearms, The Armoury. Available as the "Corsair" from Armsport, Euroarms.
Price: Complete .... $73.95 to $82.95
Price: Kit form .... $61.95 to $65.95
Price: Corsair, complete .... $89.50 Kit $77.50

DIXIE LINCOLN DERRINGER
Caliber: 41.
Barrel: 2", 8 lands, 8 grooves.
Weight: 7 oz. **Length:** 5½" over-all.
Stock: Walnut finish, checkered.
Sights: Fixed.
Features: Authentic copy of the "Lincoln Derringer." Shoots .400" patched ball. German silver furniture includes trigger guard with pineapple finial, wedge plates, nose, wrist, side and teardrop inlays. All furniture, lockplate, hammer, and breech plug engraved. Imported from Italy by Dixie Gun Works.
Price: With wooden case $110.00
Price: Kit (Not engraved) $49.95

DIXIE PHILADELPHIA DERRINGER
Caliber: 41.
Barrel: 3½", octagon.
Weight: 8 oz. **Length:** 5½" over-all.
Stock: Walnut, checkered p.g.
Sights: Fixed.
Features: Barrel and lock are blued; brass furniture. From Dixie Gun Works.
Price: $39.95

DIXIE BRASS FRAME DERRINGER
Caliber: 41.
Barrel: 2½".
Weight: 7 oz. **Length:** 5½" over-all.
Stock: Walnut.
Features: Brass frame, color case hardened hammer and trigger. Shoots .395" round ball. Engraved model available. From Dixie Gun Works.
Price: Plain model $32.50
Price: Engraved model $37.50

Armsport New Orleans Derringer
Similar to Dixie Brass Frame Derringer shown nearby. Available either complete or in kit form. From Armsport.
Price: Complete $37.50
Price: Kit form $25.95

HOPKINS & ALLEN BOOT PISTOL
Caliber: 36 or 45.
Barrel: 6".
Weight: 42 oz. **Length:** 13" over-all.
Stock: Walnut.
Sights: Silver blade front; rear adj. for e.
Features: Under-hammer design. From Hopkins & Allen.
Price: $69.95

BLACK POWDER SINGLE SHOT PISTOLS—FLINT & PERCUSSION

Markwell "Loyalist" Target Pistol
Similar to the Thompson/Center Patriot pistol except has different lock. Available as complete gun or as kit, from Markwell Arms.
Price: Complete **$91.95**
Price: Kit form **$66.95**

THOMPSON/CENTER PATRIOT PERCUSSION PISTOL
Caliber: 45.
Barrel: 9¼".
Weight: 36 oz. **Length:** 16" over-all.
Stock: Walnut.
Sights: Patridge-type. Rear adj. for w. and e.
Features: Hook breech system; double set triggers; coil mainspring. From Thompson/Center Arms.
Price: **$135.00**
With accessory pack (bullet mould T/C patches, adj. powder measure, short starter, extra nipple and nipple wrench).
Price: **$164.00**

SINGLE SHOT PERCUSSION TARGET PISTOL
Caliber: 44.
Barrel: 10" octagonal.
Weight: 42 oz.
Stocks: Walnut.
Sights: Bead front, rear adj. for w. and e.
Features: Engraved scenes on frame sides; brass backstrap and trigger guard; case hardened frame and hammer. Imported by Dixie.
Price: **$79.95**
Price: Optional 28-ga. shotgun barrel, 10" long **$12.95**

BLACK POWDER REVOLVERS

WALKER 1847 PERCUSSION REVOLVER
Caliber: 44, 6-shot.
Barrel: 9".
Weight: 72 oz. **Length:** 15½" over-all.
Stocks: Walnut.
Sights: Fixed.
Features: Case hardened frame, loading lever and hammer; iron backstrap; brass trigger guard; engraved cylinder. Imported by Navy/Replica.
Price: .... **$100.00** to **$130.00**

SECOND MODEL DRAGOON 1848 REVOLVER
Caliber: 44, 6-shot.
Barrel: 7½".
Weight: 64 oz. **Length:** 14" over-all.
Stocks: One piece walnut.
Sights: Fixed.
Features: Case hardened frame, loading lever and hammer; engraved cylinder scene; safety notches on hammer, safety pin in cylinder. Imported by Navy/Replica. First and Third Models also available.
Price: **$125.00**
Price: Third Model **$130.00**

POCKET MODEL 1849 PERCUSSION REVOLVER
Caliber: 31, 5-shot.
Barrel: 4", 6".
Weight: 26 oz.
Stocks: Walnut finish.
Sights: Fixed.
Features: Round trigger guard; Colt stagecoach hold-up scene on cylinder. Imported by Hopkins & Allen.
Price: **$113.95**

BABY DRAGOON 1848 PERCUSSION REVOLVER
Caliber: 31, 5-shot.
Barrel: 4", 5", 6".
Weight: 24 oz. (6" bbl.). **Length:** 10½" (6" bbl.).
Stocks: Walnut.
Sights: Fixed.
Features: Case hardened frame; safety notches on hammer and safety pin in cylinder; engraved cylinder scene; octagonal bbl. Imported by F.I.E., Hawes.
Price: .... **$38.15** to **$46.95**
Price: Kit form **$94.95**

1850 WELLS FARGO PERCUSSION REVOLVER

Caliber: 31, 5-shot.
Barrel: 3″, 4″, 5″, 6″.
Weight: 22 oz.
Stocks: Walnut.
Sights: Fixed.
Features: No loading lever; square-back trigger guard; case hardened frame and hammer; engraved cylinder; brass trigger guard and back-strap. Imported by Hawes.
Price: **$95.00**
Price: Kit form **$91.95**

1851 SHERIFF MODEL PERCUSSION REVOLVER

Caliber: 36, 44, 6-shot.
Barrel: 5″.
Weight: 40 oz. **Length:** 10½″ over-all.
Stocks: Walnut.
Sights: Fixed.
Features: Brass back strap and trigger guard; engraved navy scene; case hardened frame, hammer, loading lever. Available with brass frame from some importers at slightly lower prices. Imported by The Armoury, Navy/Replica, Hawes, Richland.
Price: Steel frame .... **$41.95 to $100.65**
Price: Brass frame .... **$34.95 to $54.95**
Price: Kit, brass or steel frame (Hawes) .... **$44.95 to $52.95**

1853 POCKET NAVY MODEL REVOLVER

Caliber: 36, 6-shot.
Barrel: 4½″, 5½″, 6½″.
Weight: 26 oz. **Length:** 12″ over-all (6½″ bbl.).
Stocks: Smooth walnut.
Sights: Fixed.
Features: Shortened version of std. Navy model. Case hardened frame, hammer and loading lever; brass backstrap and trigger guard. Imported by Navy/Replica Arms, Armoury.
Price: **$95.00**

> Consult our Directory pages for the location of firms mentioned.

NAVY MODEL 1851 PERCUSSION REVOLVER

Caliber: 36 or 44, 6-shot.
Barrel: 7½″.
Weight: 42 oz. **Length:** 13″ over-all.
Stocks: Walnut finish.
Sights: Fixed.
Features: Brass backstrap and trigger guard; some have engraved cylinder with navy battle scene; case hardened frame, hammer, loading lever. Imported by Centennial (36 cal. only), The Armoury, Navy/Replica, Hawes, Valor, Century, F.I.E., Dixie, (illus.) Richland, Euroarms, Armsport, Hopkins & Allen.
Price: Brass frame .... **$31.50 to $108.95**
Price: Steel frame .... **$40.95 to $100.00**
Price: Kit form .... **$30.95 to $52.95**
Price: Engraved model (F.I.E., Dixie) .... **$51.50 to $52.95**
Price: Also as "Hartford Pistol," Kit (Richland) ..**$59.95** Complete . **$79.95**
Price: Also as "Hartford Dragoon Buntline" (Hopkins & Allen) **$166.95**

1851 NAVY-SHERIFF

Same as 1851 Sheriff model except: 4″ barrel, fluted cylinder, belt ring in butt. Imported by Replica/Navy, Hawes, Richland, Armoury, Euroarms.
Price: .... **$50.00 to $114.95**
Price: Kit form (Hawes) **$44.95**

LYMAN 1851 NAVY

Same as standard model except 36 cal. only, has square-back trigger guard, nickel plated backstrap, color case hardened frame .....**$129.95.**
Price: Kit form **$84.95**

ARMY 1851 PERCUSSION REVOLVER

Caliber: 44, 6-shot.
Barrel: 7½″.
Weight: 45 oz. **Length:** 13″ over-all.
Stocks: Walnut finish.
Sights: Fixed.
Features: 44 caliber version of the 1851 Navy. Imported by Valor, The Armoury, Richland.
Price: .... **$33.50 to $65.00**

LYMAN 36 NEW MODEL NAVY REVOLVER

Caliber: 36, 6-shot.
Barrel: 6½″.
Weight: 42 oz. **Length:** 12¼″ over-all.
Stock: Walnut.
Sights: Fixed.
Features: Replica of 1860 Remington. Brass trigger guard and backstrap, case hardened trigger and hammer. Solid frame with top strap. Heavy duty nipples. From Lyman Products.
Price: **$134.95**

LYMAN 44 NEW MODEL ARMY REVOLVER

Caliber: 44, 6-shot.
Barrel: 8″.
Weight: 40 oz. **Length:** 13½″ over-all.
Stock: Walnut.
Sights: Fixed.
Features: Replica of 1858 Remington. Brass trigger guard and backstrap, case hardened hammer and trigger. Solid frame with top strap. Heavy duty nipples. From Lyman Products.
Price: **$134.95**
Price: Kit form **$94.95**

BLACK POWDER REVOLVERS

NEW MODEL 1858 ARMY PERCUSSION REVOLVER

Caliber: 36 or 44, 6-shot.
Barrel: 6½" or 8".
Weight: 40 oz. **Length:** 13½" over-all.
Stocks: Walnut.
Sights: Fixed.
Features: Replica of Remington Model 1858. Also available from some importers as Army Model Belt Revolver in 36 cal., shortened and lightened version of the 44. Target Model (Hawes, Iver Johnson, Navy/Replica) has fully adj. target rear sight, target front, 36 or 44 ($74.95-$152.45). Imported by Navy/Replica, Century, F.I.E., Hawes, Valor, Iver Johnson, The Armoury, Centennial (44 cal., 8" bbl. only), Markwell (brass frame), Richland, Euroarms (engraved and plain), Armsport, Hopkins & Allen.
Price: .... **$49.95 to $128.95**
Price: Kit form .... **$66.95 to $72.95**
Price: Nickel finish (Navy Arms) **$125.00**
Price: Stainless steel (Euroarms) **$165.00**
Price: Target model (Hawes, Euroarms, H & A) .... **$95.95 to $149.95**

1860 ARMY PERCUSSION REVOLVER

Caliber: 44, 6-shot.
Barrel: 8".
Weight: 40 oz. **Length:** 13⅝" over-all.
Stocks: Walnut.
Sights: Fixed.
Features: Engraved navy scene on cylinder; brass trigger guard; case hardened frame, loading lever and hammer. Some importers supply pistol cut for detachable shoulder stock, have accessory stock available. Imported by Navy/Replica, Centennial, The Armoury, Dixie, Lyman, Iver Johnson, Richland, Euroarms (engraved model), Armsport, Hopkins & Allen.
Price: .... **$44.95 to $134.95**
1861 Navy: Same as Army except 36 cal., 7½" bbl., wt. 41 oz., cut for stock; round cylinder (fluted avail.), from Navy/Replica **$100.00**
Price: Kit (Lyman) **$94.95**

1861 NAVY MODEL REVOLVER

Caliber: 36, 6-shot.
Barrel: 7½".
Weight: 2½ lbs. **Length:** 13" over-all.
Stocks: One piece smooth walnut.
Sights: Fixed.
Features: Shoots .380" ball. Case-hardened frame, loading lever and hammer. Cut for shoulder stock. Non-fluted cylinder. From Navy/Replica Arms, Iver Johnson, Euroarms.
Price: .... **$100.00 to $104.95**
Price: With full fluted cyl. .... **$100.00 to $104.95**

ROGERS & SPENCER PERCUSSION REVOLVER

Caliber: 44.
Barrel: 7½".
Weight: 47 oz. **Length:** 13¾" over-all.
Stocks: Walnut.
Sights: Cone front, integral groove in frame for rear.
Features: Accurate reproduction of a Civil War design. Solid frame; extra large nipple cut-out on rear of cylinder; loading lever and cylinder easily removed for cleaning. Comes with six spare nipples and wrench/screwdriver. From Euroarms.
Price: About **$115.00**

1862 POLICE MODEL PERCUSSION REVOLVER

Caliber: 36, 5-shot.
Barrel: 4½", 5½", 6½".
Weight: 26 oz. **Length:** 12" (6½" bbl.).
Stocks: Walnut.
Sights: Fixed.
Features: Half-fluted and rebated cylinder; case hardened frame, loading lever and hammer; brass trigger guard and back strap. Imported by Navy/Replica, Armoury, Euroarms.
Price: **$100.00**
Price: Cased with accessories **$125.00**

BLACK POWDER REVOLVERS

SPILLER & BURR REVOLVER
Caliber: 36.
Barrel: 7", octagon.
Weight: 2½ lbs. **Length:** 12½" over-all.
Stocks: Two-piece walnut.
Sights: Fixed.
Features: Reproduction of the C.S.A. revolver. Brass frame and trigger guard. Also available as a kit. From Dixie, Navy/Replica, Richland, Armsport.
Price: .... $69.95 to $75.00
Price: Kit form .... $39.95 to $44.95

GRISWOLD & GUNNISON PERCUSSION REVOLVER
Caliber: 36, 44, 6-shot.
Barrel: 7½".
Weight: 44 oz. (36 cal.). **Length:** 13" over-all.
Stocks: Walnut.
Sights: Fixed.
Features: Replica of famous Confederate pistol. Brass frame, backstrap and trigger guard; case hardened loading lever; rebated cylinder (44 cal. only). Imported by Navy/Replica, Markwell Arms.
Price: .... $60.00 to $74.95
Price: Kit form (Navy Arms, Markwell) .... $45.00 to $63.95

DIXIE "WYATT EARP" REVOLVER
Caliber: 44.
Barrel: 12" octagon.
Weight: 46 oz. **Length:** 18" over-all.
Stock: Two piece walnut.
Sights: Fixed.
Features: Highly polished brass frame, backstrap and trigger guard; blued barrel and cylinder; case hardened hammer, trigger and loading lever. Navy-size shoulder stock ($40.00) will fit with minor fitting. From Dixie Gun Works.
Price: $62.50

RICHLAND 44 BALLISTER REVOLVER
Caliber: 44, 6-shot.
Barrel: 12".
Weight: 2¾ lbs.
Stocks: Two-piece walnut.
Sights: Fixed.
Features: Barrel and cylinder blued, frame and trigger guard are brass; hammer and loading lever are color case hardened. From Richland Arms.
Price: $78.00

RUGER 44 OLD ARMY PERCUSSION REVOLVER
Caliber: 44, 6-shot. Uses .457" dia. lead bullets.
Barrel: 7½" (6-groove, 16" twist).
Weight: 46 oz. **Length:** 13½" over-all.
Stocks: Smooth walnut.
Sights: Ramp front, rear adj. for w. and e.
Features: Stainless steel standard size nipples, chrome-moly steel cylinder and frame, same lockwork as in original Super Blackhawk. Also available in stainless steel in very limited quantities. Made in USA. From Sturm, Ruger & Co.
Price: Stainless steel $175.00
Price: Blued steel $130.00

BLACK POWDER MUSKETS & RIFLES

FLINTLOCK BLUNDERBUSS
Caliber: 70.
Barrel: 15½".
Weight: 6¼ lbs. **Length:** 30".
Stock: Walnut finish, hand rubbed.
Sights: None.
Features: Brass barrel and fittings, steel lock from Navy; others have steel bbl., brass fittings. Imported by Hawes, The Armoury, Markwell Arms (kit only.)
Price: .... **$37.95 to $135.00**
Price: Percussion model, kit form **$72.95**
Price: Flintlock, kit form (Hawes) **$91.50**

CENTURY CHARLEVILLE FLINTLOCK MUSKET
Caliber: 69.
Barrel: 45½", smoothbore.
Weight: 8 lbs. **Length:** 43½" over-all.
Stock: Walnut finish hardwood.
Sights: Blade on front barrel band.
Features: Hand-fitted lock; brass trigger guard and barrel bands; polished steel barrel, buttplate and ramrod. From Century Arms.
Price: **$139.95**

DIXIE FIRST MODEL BROWN BESS
Caliber: 75.
Barrel: 46", smoothbore.
Weight: 10 lbs. **Length:** 62" over-all.
Stock: Walnut finished.
Sights: Fixed.
Features: Brass furniture with bright barrel, lock and ramrod. Lock marked "Grice 1762" with crown and "GR" underneath. Original Brown Bess bayonets $25.00. Imported from England by Dixie Gun Works.
Price: **$450.00**

BROWN BESS FLINTLOCK MUSKET
Caliber: 69, 70, 75.
Barrel: 42".
Weight: 10½ lbs. **Length:** 59" over-all.
Stock: Walnut.
Sights: Fixed.
Features: Replica of Revolutionary War period model. Imported by Hopkins & Allen.
Price: **$325.00**

DIXIE SECOND MODEL BROWN BESS
Caliber: 74.
Barrel: 41¾" smoothbore.
Weight: 9½ lbs. **Length:** 57¾".
Stock: Walnut-finished hardwood.
Sights: Fixed.
Features: All metal finished bright. Brass furniture. Lock marked "Tower" and has a crown with "GR" underneath. From Dixie Gun Works.
Price: **$250.00**

CENTURY STATE MILITIA MUSKET
Caliber: 56.
Barrel: 36".
Weight: 7¾ lbs. **Length:** 54" over-all.
Stock: Walnut finish hardwood.
Sights: Bead front only.
Features: Polished steel barrel and ramrod; 2-piece lock; buttplate, trigger guard and barrel brass plated. American eagle seal on lockplate.
Price: **$74.95**

DIXIE STANDARD KENTUCKY RIFLE
Caliber: 45.
Barrel: 40″, six land and grooves, 1 turn in 48″.
Weight: 10 lbs. **Length:** 56½″.
Stock: Chestnut colored maple.
Sights: Brass blade front, Kentucky-type rear.
Features: Trigger guard, buttplate, patchbox and thimbles are brass. Color case hardened lock. From Dixie Gun Works.
Price: Percussion $260.00
Price: Flintlock $282.50

CVA KENTUCKY RIFLE
Caliber: 45 (.451″ bore).
Barrel: 32″, rifled, octagon (⅞″ flats).
Length: 50″ over-all.
Stock: Dark polished walnut.
Sights: Brass Kentucky blade type front, dovetail open rear.
Features: Available in either flint or percussion. Stainless steel nipple included. Imported by CVA.
Price: Percussion $112.95
Price: Flint $119.95

KENTUCKY FLINTLOCK RIFLE
Caliber: 44 or 45.
Barrel: 35″.
Weight: 7 lbs. **Length:** 50″ over-all.
Stock: Walnut stained, brass fittings.
Sights: Fixed.
Features: Available in Carbine model also, 28″ bbl. Some variations in detail, finish. Kits also available from some importers. Imported by Navy/Replica, Centennial, The Armoury, Century, Dixie and Challenger, F.I.E., Hawes, Kassnar, CVA, Armsport, Hopkins & Allen.
Price: .... $59.95 to $185.00
Price: Kit form (CVA, Numrich, Hawes, F.I.E.) .... $72.95 to $134.50
Price: Deluxe model, flint or percussion (Navy Arms) $375.00

DIXIE FLINT SWIVEL BREECH RIFLE
Caliber: 45.
Barrel: 32″, octagon.
Weight: 11½ lbs. **Length:** 48½″ over-all.
Stock: Curly maple.
Sights: Fixed.
Features: Wood panelled barrels rotate for second shot. Single trigger. Brass furniture. From Dixie Gun Works.
Price: Flintlock $475.00
Price: Percussion $365.00

ULTRA-HI KENTUCKY PERCUSSION RIFLE
Caliber: 45 (.453″).
Barrel: 32½″, octagon.
Weight: 8 lbs. **Length:** 50″ over-all.
Stock: Walnut-stained hardwood.
Sights: Brass blade front, fixed iron rear.
Features: Hand engraved patch box, trigger guard and lock plate. From Ultra-Hi Products.
Price: $127.95

Kentucky Percussion Rifle
Similar to above except percussion lock. Finish and features vary with importer. Imported by Centennial, Navy/Replica, Firearms Import & Export, The Armoury, Challenger, Dixie, CVA, Valor, Hawes, Kassnar, Markwell Arms, Armsport (rifle-shotgun combo).
Price: .... $54.95 to $229.95
Price: Kit form .... $68.95 to $128.95
Price: Primitive Kentucky (Markwell) $71.50
Price: Armsport combo $210.00

PENNSYLVANIA LONG RIFLE
Caliber: 36 or 45.
Barrel: 39″ octagonal.
Weight: 10½ lbs. **Length:** 55″ over-all.
Stock: Full-length tiger striped maple, traditional Pennsylvania form.
Sights: Brass blade front, open notch rear.
Features: Solid brass engraved furniture (crescent buttplate, patch box, fore-end cap, etc.) From The Armoury.
Price: Flint or percussion form $179.95

ULTRA-HI MINUTEMAN MUSKET
Caliber: 67.
Barrel: 32″, round.
Weight: 8¼ lbs. **Length:** 49″ over-all.
Stock: Selected hardwood.
Sights: Bead front only.
Features: Polished steel barrel, brass patch box and nose cap. Flintlock only. From Ultra-Hi Products.
Price: $132.95

DIXIE PENNSYLVANIA PERCUSSION RIFLE
Caliber: 45.
Barrel: 40″, octagon.
Weight: 10 lbs. **Length:** 55″.
Stock: Maple, Roman nose comb.
Sights: Fixed, Kentucky open-type.
Features: Brass patchbox, wide buttplate, color case hardened lock, .blue barrel. From Dixie Gun Works.
Price: Flint $300.00
Price: Percussion $297.50
Price: Engraved model, flint or percussion (limited) $315.00

BLACK POWDER MUSKETS & RIFLES

KENTUCKIAN RIFLE & CARBINE
Caliber: 44.
Barrel: 35″ (Rifle), 27½″ (Carbine).
Weight: 7 lbs. (Rifle), 5½ lbs. (Carbine). **Length:** 51″ (Rifle) over-all, carbine 43″.
Stock: Walnut stain.
Sights: Brass blade front, steel V-Ramp rear.
Features: Octagon bbl., case hardened and engraved lock plate. Brass furniture. Imported by Dixie, Euroarms.
Price: Rifle or carbine, flint or percussion . . . . **$135.00 to $145.00**

PENNSYLVANIA HALF-STOCK PLAINS RIFLE
Caliber: 45 or 50.
Barrel: 32″, rifled or smooth.
Weight: 8½ lbs.
Stock Maple.
Sights: Fixed.
Features: Available in flint or percussion. Browned lock and barrel, brass furniture. Offered complete or in kit form. From Hopkins & Allen.
Price: Flint **$279.95**
Price: Percussion **$267.95**

CENTURY PERCUSSION MUSKET
Caliber: 69.
Barrel: 37″, part octagon, part round.
Weight: 7½ lbs. **Length:** 54″ over-all.
Stock: Walnut finish hardwood.
Sights: Bead front.
Features: Polished steel barrel, lock plate, hammer, barrel bands ramrod and trigger. From Century Arms.
Price: **$79.95**

DIXIE PERCUSSION MUSKET
Caliber: 66.
Barrel: 37″, smoothbore.
Weight: 8 lbs. **Length:** 54″ over-all.
Stock: Walnut-finish hardwood.
Sights: Fixed.
Features: Made from old original parts but with new Belgian-proofed barrels. Shoots shot or .650″ ball.
Price: **$93.00**

HOPKINS & ALLEN DELUXE BUGGY RIFLE
Caliber: 36 or 45.
Barrel: 20″, octagonal.
Weight: 6½ lbs. **Length:** 37″ over-all.
Stock: American walnut.
Features: A shortened version of the under-hammer Heritage rifle. Blued barrel and receiver, black plastic buttplate.
Price: **$199.95**

HOPKINS & ALLEN HERITAGE RIFLE
Caliber: 36 or 45.
Barrel: 32″, octagonal.
Weight: 8½ lbs. **Length:** 49″ over-all.
Stock: American walnut.
Features: Brass patch box, buttplate, finger rest, thimbles. Barrel and receiver left "white". Under-hammer design.
Price: **$199.95**

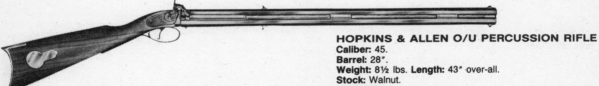

HOPKINS & ALLEN O/U PERCUSSION RIFLE
Caliber: 45.
Barrel: 28″.
Weight: 8½ lbs. **Length:** 43″ over-all.
Stock: Walnut.
Sights: Fixed.
Features: Barrels rotate for second shot. Each barrel has a set of sights. From Hopkins & Allen.
Price: **$199.95**

YORKSHIRE RIFLE
Caliber: 45.
Barrel: 36″, rifled, ⅞″ octagon.
Weight: 7½ lbs. **Length:** 51¾″ over-all.
Stock: Select maple.
Sights: Blade front, open U-notch rear.
Features: Adj. double set triggers. Brass front and rear sights, trigger guard, patch box, buttplate and fore-end. Case hardened lock plate. From Dixie and Richland.
Price: Percussion . . . . **$144.00 to $150.00**
Price: Flintlock . . . . **$153.00 to $159.95**

RICHLAND MICHIGAN CARBINE
Caliber: 45.
Barrel: 26″ octagon, ⅞″ flats.
Weight: 5¾ lbs. **Length:** 41⅜″ over-all.
Stock: Hand finished maple.
Sights: Blade front, open fixed rear drift adj. for w.
Features: Color case hardened lock plate; brass patch box, buttplate, trigger guard, fore-end tip and sights; adjustable double set triggers. From Richland Arms.
Price: Percussion **$158.00**
Price: Flintlock **$167.00**
Price: Kit form **$112.00**

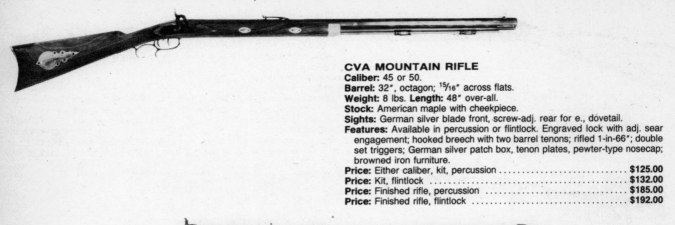

CVA MOUNTAIN RIFLE
Caliber: 45 or 50.
Barrel: 32″, octagon; $^{15}/_{16}$″ across flats.
Weight: 8 lbs. **Length:** 48″ over-all.
Stock: American maple with cheekpiece.
Sights: German silver blade front, screw-adj. rear for e., dovetail.
Features: Available in percussion or flintlock. Engraved lock with adj. sear engagement; hooked breech with two barrel tenons; rifled 1-in-66″; double set triggers; German silver patch box, tenon plates, pewter-type nosecap; browned iron furniture.
Price: Either caliber, kit, percussion $125.00
Price: Kit, flintlock $132.00
Price: Finished rifle, percussion $185.00
Price: Finished rifle, flintlock $192.00

JONATHAN BROWNING PERCUSSION MOUNTAIN RIFLE
Caliber: 45, 50 or 54.
Barrel: 30″, 1″ across flats.
Stock: Traditional half-stock with semi-cheekpiece.
Sights: Blade front, Buckhorn rear screw-adj. for e.
Features: Single set trigger; hooked breech. 45-cal. rifled 1 in 56″, 50-cal. rifled 1 in 62″, 54-cal. rifled 1 in 66″ twist. Offered in choice of browned steel or brass finish on buttplate, trigger guard and complimentary furniture. Hickory ramrod with brass ends. Spare nipple and cleaning jag included. Introduced 1977. From Browning.
Price: Brass or browned finish, 45, 50 or 54 cal. $319.50

Jonathan Browning Centennial Mountain Rifle
Similar to standard rifle except has sterling silver stock medallion with dates and inscription and sterling silver bust of Jonathan Browning on lock plate. Comes with powder horn with centennial inscription and matching serial number, nipple wrench, spare nipple, cleaning jag and patch remover. Comes in fitted Alder case lined with special suede buckskin-colored fabric. Only 1000 sets to be made; serial numbered 1878A-0001 through 1878A-1000.
Price: 50-cal. only $650.00

F.I.E. PERCUSSION BERDAN RIFLE
Caliber: 45.
Barrel: 25″, rifled, octagon.
Weight: 7 lbs. **Length:** 42¾″ over-all.
Stock: Walnut-finished hardwood.
Sights: Brass blade front, adj. open rear.
Features: Double-set triggers; brass trigger guard, patch box and buttplate. From F.I.E.
Price: $87.95

DIXIE PLAINSMAN RIFLE
Caliber: 45 or 50.
Barrel: 32″, octagon.
Weight: 8 lbs. **Length:** 47½″.
Stock: Cherry wood.
Sights: Brass blade front, buckhorn rear.
Features: Bolster-type breech plug with blow-out screw, brass stock furniture.
Price: $175.00

MARKWELL HAWKEN RIFLE
Caliber: 45.
Barrel: 28″.
Weight: 7 lbs. **Length:** 43½″ over-all.
Stock: Dark polished walnut.
Sights: Blade front, open read adj. for w.
Features: Brass patchbox, trigger guard, buttplate and furniture; color case hardened lock, rest blued. From Markwell Arms.
Price: $124.95
Price: Kit form $91.95

Markwell Super Hawken
Similar to the Lyman Plains Rifle except in 50-cal. only, different lock and patch box. Available complete or as kit. From Markwell Arms.
Price: Complete $166.50
Price: Kit $116.50

HAWKEN HURRICANE & HUNTER
Caliber: 45 or 50.
Barrel: 28″, octagon.
Weight: 6 lbs. **Length:** 44¾″ over-all.
Stock: American walnut.
Sights: Blade front, open fixed rear.
Features: American made. Curved buttplate, brass stock furniture. From Navy/Replica.
Price: 45 or 50 cal. $195.00
Price: Hawken Hunter (58 cal.) $195.00
Price: Hawken kit $125.00

ULTRA-HI HAWKEN RIFLE
Caliber: 50, (.503″).
Barrel: 28″, octagon with $^{15}/_{16}$″ flats; hooked breech.
Weight: 8½ lbs. **Length:** 46″ over-all.
Stock: Walnut stained cherrywood.
Sights: Blade front, read adj. for w. and e.
Features: Engraved lock plate. Coil mainspring. Brass furniture, single trigger. Available in percussion or flintlock. From Ultra-Hi Products.
Price: $214.95

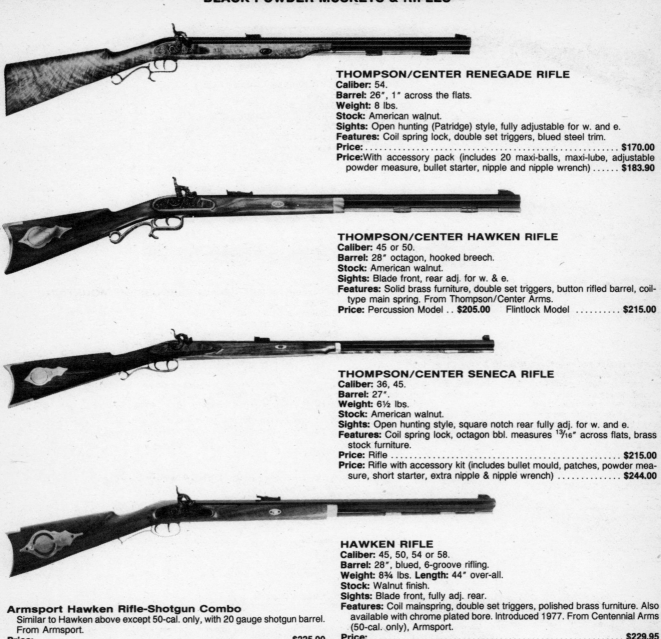

THOMPSON/CENTER RENEGADE RIFLE
Caliber: 54.
Barrel: 26", 1" across the flats.
Weight: 8 lbs.
Stock: American walnut.
Sights: Open hunting (Patridge) style, fully adjustable for w. and e.
Features: Coil spring lock, double set triggers, blued steel trim.
Price: **$170.00**
Price: With accessory pack (includes 20 maxi-balls, maxi-lube, adjustable powder measure, bullet starter, nipple and nipple wrench) **$183.90**

THOMPSON/CENTER HAWKEN RIFLE
Caliber: 45 or 50.
Barrel: 28" octagon, hooked breech.
Stock: American walnut.
Sights: Blade front, rear adj. for w. & e.
Features: Solid brass furniture, double set triggers, button rifled barrel, coil-type main spring. From Thompson/Center Arms.
Price: Percussion Model .. **$205.00**   Flintlock Model **$215.00**

THOMPSON/CENTER SENECA RIFLE
Caliber: 36, 45.
Barrel: 27".
Weight: 6½ lbs.
Stock: American walnut.
Sights: Open hunting style, square notch rear fully adj. for w. and e.
Features: Coil spring lock, octagon bbl. measures $^{13}/_{16}$" across flats, brass stock furniture.
Price: Rifle **$215.00**
Price: Rifle with accessory kit (includes bullet mould, patches, powder measure, short starter, extra nipple & nipple wrench) **$244.00**

HAWKEN RIFLE
Caliber: 45, 50, 54 or 58.
Barrel: 28", blued, 6-groove rifling.
Weight: 8¾ lbs. **Length:** 44" over-all.
Stock: Walnut finish.
Sights: Blade front, fully adj. rear.
Features: Coil mainspring, double set triggers, polished brass furniture. Also available with chrome plated bore. Introduced 1977. From Centennial Arms (50-cal. only), Armsport.
Price: **$229.95**
Price: Hard chrome bore Centennial **$238.95**

Armsport Hawken Rifle-Shotgun Combo
Similar to Hawken above except 50-cal. only, with 20 gauge shotgun barrel. From Armsport.
Price: **$225.00**

NUMRICH HALF-STOCK PLAINS RIFLE
Caliber: 31, 36, 45 or 50.
Barrel: 32".
Weight: 10 lbs.
Stock: Maple.
Sights: Blade front, fixed near.
Features: Hand-rubbed stock. Available with rifled or smooth bore. Brass stock furniture. From Numrich Arms.
Price: **$174.00**

BUFFALO HUNTER PERCUSSION RIFLE
Caliber: 58.
Barrel: 25½".
Weight: 8 lbs. **Length:** 41½" over-all.
Stock: Walnut finished, hand checkered, brass furniture.
Sights: Fixed.
Features: Designed for primitive weapons hunting. 20 ga. shotgun bbl. also available $45.00. Imported by Navy/Replica.
Price: **$160.00**

ITHACA-NAVY HAWKEN RIFLE
Caliber: 50.
Barrel: 32" octagonal, 1-inch dia.
Weight: About 9 lbs.
Stock: Black walnut.
Sights: Blade front, near adj. for w.
Features: Completely made in U.S. Hooked breech, 1⅞" throw percussion lock. Attached twin thimbles and under-rib. German silver barrel key inlays, Hawken-style toe and buttplates, lock bolt inlays, barrel wedges, entry thimble, trigger guard, ramrod and cleaning jag, nipple and nipple wrench. Introduced 1977. From Navy Arms.
Price: Complete .... **Price on request**
Price: Kit **$285.00**

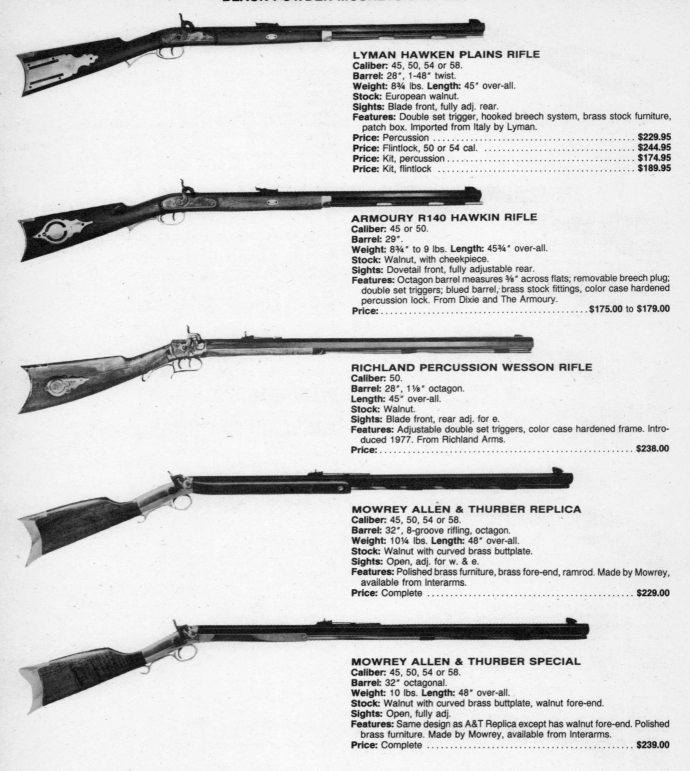

LYMAN HAWKEN PLAINS RIFLE
Caliber: 45, 50, 54 or 58.
Barrel: 28", 1-48" twist.
Weight: 8¾ lbs. **Length:** 45" over-all.
Stock: European walnut.
Sights: Blade front, fully adj. rear.
Features: Double set trigger, hooked breech system, brass stock furniture, patch box. Imported from Italy by Lyman.
Price: Percussion $229.95
Price: Flintlock, 50 or 54 cal. $244.95
Price: Kit, percussion $174.95
Price: Kit, flintlock $189.95

ARMOURY R140 HAWKIN RIFLE
Caliber: 45 or 50.
Barrel: 29".
Weight: 8¾" to 9 lbs. **Length:** 45¾" over-all.
Stock: Walnut, with cheekpiece.
Sights: Dovetail front, fully adjustable rear.
Features: Octagon barrel measures ⅜" across flats; removable breech plug; double set triggers; blued barrel, brass stock fittings, color case hardened percussion lock. From Dixie and The Armoury.
Price: .... $175.00 to $179.00

RICHLAND PERCUSSION WESSON RIFLE
Caliber: 50.
Barrel: 28", 1⅛" octagon.
Length: 45" over-all.
Stock: Walnut.
Sights: Blade front, rear adj. for e.
Features: Adjustable double set triggers, color case hardened frame. Introduced 1977. From Richland Arms.
Price: $238.00

MOWREY ALLEN & THURBER REPLICA
Caliber: 45, 50, 54 or 58.
Barrel: 32", 8-groove rifling, octagon.
Weight: 10¼ lbs. **Length:** 48" over-all.
Stock: Walnut with curved brass buttplate.
Sights: Open, adj. for w. & e.
Features: Polished brass furniture, brass fore-end, ramrod. Made by Mowrey, available from Interarms.
Price: Complete $229.00

MOWREY ALLEN & THURBER SPECIAL
Caliber: 45, 50, 54 or 58.
Barrel: 32" octagonal.
Weight: 10 lbs. **Length:** 48" over-all.
Stock: Walnut with curved brass buttplate, walnut fore-end.
Sights: Open, fully adj.
Features: Same design as A&T Replica except has walnut fore-end. Polished brass furniture. Made by Mowrey, available from Interarms.
Price: Complete $239.00

MOWREY GEORGIA TREE GUN
Caliber: 45, 50, 54, 58.
Barrel: 22".
Weight: 7¼ lbs. **Length:** 38" over-all.
Stock: Walnut.
Sights: Blade front, step adj. rear.
Features: Shortened version of Allen & Thurber Special rifle especially suited for tree stand shooting. Made by Mowrey, available from Interarms.
Price: Complete gun $239.00

MOWREY HAWK
Caliber: 45, 50, 54 or 58.
Barrel: 32".
Weight: 9½ lbs. **Length:** 49" over-all.
Stock: Walnut, sporter-type with cheek-piece, walnut fore-end.
Sights: Open, fully adj. for w. and e.
Features: Hawkins-type buttplate and action housing of brass. Adj. trigger. Made by Mowrey, available from Interarms.
Price: Complete $249.00

BLACK POWDER MUSKETS & RIFLES

"TEXAS CARBINE" Model 1 of 1000
Caliber: 58, takes .575" mini-ball or round ball.
Barrel: 24" octagon, 4-groove.
Weight: 8 lbs. **Length:** 39" over-all.
Stock: Walnut stock and fore-end, brass fore-end cap.
Sights: Adjustable front and rear.
Features: Model "1 of 1000". Saddle ring with leather thong and Texas seal imbedded in stock. Distributed by Trail Guns Armory.
Price: **$250.00**

MOWREY "ALLEN & THURBER" BENCH RIFLE
Caliber: 45, 50, 54 or 58.
Barrel: 36" over-all with false muzzle. 1½" octagon.
Weight: 24½ lbs. **Length:** 54" over-all.
Stock: Cherry wood with large cheekpiece, Schalk-type brass buttplate. Finished with 10 coats of hand-rubbed oil.
Sights: Available with target peep or non-magnifying tube sight.
Features: Polished solid brass furniture, browned iron. Introduced 1977. From Mowrey Gun Works.
Price: With peep sight **$415.00**
Price: With tube sight **$498.50**

REVOLVING PERCUSSION CARBINE
Caliber: 44, 6-shot.
Barrel: 18", 20".
Weight: 5 lbs. **Length:** 38" over-all.
Stock: Walnut, brass buttplate.
Sights: Blade front adj. for w., buckhorn rear adj. for e.
Features: Action based on 1858 Remington revolver. Brass trigger guard. Imported by Navy/Replica.
Price: **$175.00**

ZOUAVE PERCUSSION RIFLE
Caliber: 58, 59.
Barrel: 32½".
Weight: 9½ lbs. **Length:** 48½" over-all.
Stock: Walnut finish, brass patch box and buttplate.
Sights: Fixed front, rear adj. for e.
Features: Some small details may vary with importers. Also available from Navy Arms as carbine, with 22" bbl. Extra 20 ga. shotgun bbl. $45.00. Imported by Navy/Replica, Centennial (58-cal. only), The Armoury, Lyman, Ultra-Hi, F.I.E., Dixie, Hawes, Kassnar.
Price: .... **$87.95 to $189.95**
Price: Kit form (Hawes) **$114.95**
Price: Kit form (Lyman) **$154.95**

Mississippi Model 1841 Percussion Rifle
Similar to Zouave Rifle but patterned after U.S. Model 1841. Imported by Navy/Replica.
Price: **$160.00**

PARKER-HALE ENFIELD 1853 MUSKET
Caliber: .577".
Barrel: 39", 3-groove cold-forged rifling.
Weight: About 9 lbs. **Length:** 55" over-all.
Stock: Seasoned walnut.
Sights: Fixed front, rear step adj. for elevation.
Features: Three band musket made to original specs from original gauges. Solid brass stock furniture, color hardened lock plate, hammer; blued barrel, trigger. Imported from England by Jana.
Price: **$250.00**

DIXIE ENFIELD MUSKETOON
Caliber: 58 (.577").
Barrel: 24", 6 lands, 6 grooves.
Weight: 7 lbs. **Length:** 41" over-all.
Stock: Walnut with brass fittings.
Sights: Original style fixed front, adjustable rear.
Features: Uses standard .575" Minie ball or .570" round ball. Made in Italy. From Dixie Gun Works and the Armoury.
Price: .... **$179.95 to $186.00**

MORSE/NAVY RIFLE
Caliber: 45, 50 or 58.
Barrel: 26", octagonal.
Weight: 6 lbs. (45 cal.). **Length:** 41½" over-all.
Stock: American walnut, full p.g.
Sights: Blade front, open fixed rear.
Features: Brass action, trigger guard, ramrod pipes. From Navy/Replica.
Price: **$110.00**

PARKER-HALE ENFIELD PATTERN 1858 NAVAL RIFLE
Caliber: .577".
Barrel: 33".
Weight: 8½ lbs. **Length:** 48½" over-all.
Stock: European walnut.
Sights: Blade front, step adj. rear.
Features: Two-band Enfield percussion rifle with heavy barrel. 5-groove progressive depth rifling, solid brass furniture. All parts made exactly to original patterns. Imported from England by Jana.
Price: **$225.00**

BLACK POWDER MUSKETS & RIFLES

PARKER-HALE WHITWORTH MILITARY TARGET RIFLE
Caliber: 45.
Barrel: 36".
Weight: 9¼ lbs. **Length:** 52½" over-all.
Stock: Walnut. Checkered at wrist and fore-end.
Sights: Hooded post front, open step-adjustable rear.
Features: Faithful reproduction of the Whitworth rifle, only bored for 45-cal. Trigger has a detented lock, capable of being adjusted very finely without risk of the sear nose catching on the half-cock bent and damaging both parts. Introduced 1978. From Navy Arms.
Price: $475.00

PARKER-HALE ENFIELD 1861 CARBINE
Caliber: 577.
Barrel: 24".
Weight: 7½ lbs. **Length:** 40¼" over-all.
Stock: Walnut.
Sights: Fixed front, adj. rear.
Features: Percussion muzzle loader, made to original 1861 English patterns. Imported from England by Jana.
Price: $225.00

SMITH CARBINE
Caliber: 54.
Weight: 7½ lbs. **Length:** 39" over-all.
Stock: American walnut.
Sights: Post front, rear adj. for e.
Features: Re-creation of the Civil War Smith carbine. Has color case hardened frame, blued barrel, brass buttplate. Made in U.S.A. From Navy Arms.
Price: $250.00

GALLAGER 1860 CARBINE
Caliber: .54".
Barrel: 22½", 16-groove rifling.
Weight: 7¼ lbs. **Length:** 39" over-all.
Stock: Beechwood.
Sights: Fixed front, adj. V-notch Buckhorn rear.
Features: Reproduction of the breech-loading Civil War percussion carbine; loads using a brass cartridge. Comes with cleaning rod and attachments, spare nipple, one cartridge, nipple wrench. Imported by Jana.
Price: $199.95
Price: Extra cartridges, each $1.30

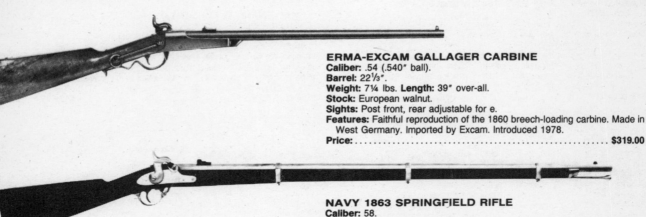

ERMA-EXCAM GALLAGER CARBINE
Caliber: .54 (.540" ball).
Barrel: 22⅓".
Weight: 7¼ lbs. **Length:** 39" over-all.
Stock: European walnut.
Sights: Post front, rear adjustable for e.
Features: Faithful reproduction of the 1860 breech-loading carbine. Made in West Germany. Imported by Excam. Introduced 1978.
Price: $319.00

NAVY 1863 SPRINGFIELD RIFLE
Caliber: 58.
Barrel: 40", rifled.
Weight: 8½ lbs. **Length:** 54¾" over-all.
Stock: American walnut.
Sights: Blade front, open step adj. rear.
Features: Full-size three-band musket reproduction. Imported by Navy/Replica.
Price: $190.00
Price: M1864 (as above except has color hardened lock) $200.00

BLACK POWDER MUSKETS & RIFLES

Shiloh New Model 1863 Sharps Carbine
Shortened, carbine version of the 1863 rifle. Has 22" barrel, black walnut stock without patch box, single barrel band. Weighs 7¾ lbs., over-all length is 39⅛". Made in U.S. by Shiloh Products.
Price: **$330.00**

SHILOH NEW MODEL 1863 SHARPS RIFLE
Caliber: 45, 50, 54.
Barrel: 30", 1-in 48".
Weight: 8¾ lbs. **Length:** 47" over-all.
Stock: Black walnut, oil finish.
Sights: Blade front, rear leaf adj. for e.
Features: Duplicate of original percussion rifle. Receiver sideplate, hammer, buttplate, patch box color hardened; barrel is blue-black. Made in U.S. by Shiloh Products.
Price: **$360.00**

H & R SPRINGFIELD STALKER
Caliber: 45 or 58.
Barrel: 28" round.
Weight: 8 lbs. (45 cal.), 7½ lbs. (58 cal.). **Length:** 43" over-all.
Stock: American walnut.
Sights: Blade front, rear open adj. for w. and e.
Features: Action similar to Civil War Springfield. Supplied with solid brass ramrod with hardwood handle and nipple wrench. Blue-black finish.
Price: **$210.00**

SILE SHARPS NEW MODEL 1863 CARBINE
Caliber: 54.
Barrel: 22".
Weight: 7¾ lbs. **Length:** 39" over-all.
Stock: Walnut.
Sights: Blade front, rear adj. for w. and e.
Features: Faithful reproduction of the original 1863 carbine. Receiver, sideplate, hammer and buttplate are color case hardened. Rifle model has 28" barrel, checkered p.g. and fore-end. Introduced 1977. From Sile Distributors and Centennial Arms.
Price: Carbine, about **$225.00**
Price: Rifle, about **$239.00**

H & R Deluxe Springfield Stalker
Same as standard model except has hand checkered p.g. and fore-end, better wood, hand polished American walnut stock.
Price: **$300.00**

Consult our Directory pages for the location of firms mentioned.

FRAZIER MATCHMATE PERCUSSION RIFLES
Caliber: 32, 36, 40, 45, 50 or 54.
Barrel: 26" to 38". Douglas Premium M/L. Octagon. Choice of diam.—$^{13}/_{16}$", ⅞", $^{15}/_{16}$", 1" or 1⅛".
Weight: 8 lbs. and up. Varies with size and wood. **Length:** 52½" over-all (32" bbl.).
Stock: Laminated of 5 layers of imported exotic high figure hardwoods. Thumbhole p.g., cheekpiece in line with bore. Satin finish. Adj. hooked buttplate.
Sights: Redfield Olympic front on detachable base (insert set included), Redfield #75 micro peep rear.
Features: A unique rifle designed for competition shooting. Underhammer action with Anschutz-Mauser set triggers. Comes with set of 8 weights to control balance, Lyman mould, short starter and rod. Adj. coil mainspring; stainless steel flashguard around nipple. Action housed in breech but removes easily for cleaning. Write for full specifics. From Frazier Matchmate Inc.
Price: Standard Offhand Rifle (illus.), from **$800.00**
Price: Custom Offhand Rifle, from **$900.00**
Price: "National Unlimited" bench rest rifle, from **$750.00**

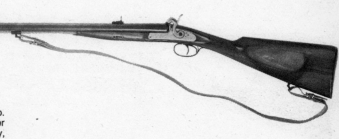

KODIAK DOUBLE RIFLE
Caliber: 58 (std.), 50 cal. and 50-cal./12 ga. optional.
Barrel: 28", 5 grooves, 1-in-48" twist.
Weight: 9½ lbs. **Length:** 43¼" over-all.
Stock: Czechoslovakian walnut, hand checkered.
Sights: Three leaf folding rear, adjustable gold bead front.
Features: Hooked breech allows interchangeability of barrels, matted rib. Comes with sling and swivels. Engraved lock plates, top tang and trigger guard. Locks and top tang polished, rest browned. From Trail Guns Armory, Inc.
Price: 58 cal. SxS **$399.50**
Price: 50 cal. SxS **$399.50**
Price: 50 cal. x 12 ga. **$399.50**
Price: Spare barrels, 58 cal. SxS, 50 cal. SxS **$215.00**
Price: Spare barrels, 50 cal. x 12 ga. **$215.00**
Price: Spare barrels, 12 ga. x 12 ga. **$140.00**

BLACK POWDER MUSKETS & RIFLES

H & R HUNTSMAN PERCUSSION RIFLE
Caliber: 45, 58, 12 gauge, single shot.
Barrel: 28", 32" (58 cal.).
Weight: 6¼ lbs. (12 ga.), 7¼ lbs. (58 cal.), 8 lbs. (45 cal.). **Length:** 43".
Stock: Walnut finished hardwood.
Sights: Open, rear adj. for w. and e., blade front, 45, 58 cal., 12 ga. have brass bead.
Features: Action similar to Model 158 Topper. Enclosed nipple (#11 size). Supplied with rifle are brass ramrod with wood handle and nipple wrench. Blue-black finish with color case hardened frame. From Harrington & Richardson.
Price: 12 ga. **$89.50**
Price: 45 and 58 cals. **$99.50**
Price: 58 cal. 32" bbl. **$115.00**

BLACK POWDER SHOTGUNS

MORSE/NAVY SINGLE BARREL SHOTGUN
Gauge: 12 ga.
Barrel: 26".
Weight: 5 lbs. **Length:** 41½" over-all.
Stock: American walnut, full p.g.
Sights: Front bead.
Features: Brass receiver, black buttplate. From Navy/Replica.
Price: **$125.00**

SINGLE BARREL PERCUSSION SHOTGUN
Gauge: 12, 20, 28.
Barrel: 28".
Weight: 4½ lbs. **Length:** 43" over-all.
Stock: Walnut finish, choice of half or full stock.
Features: Finish and features vary with importer. Imported by The Armoury, Dixie.
Price: .... **$32.95 to $59.95**

CENTURY "KENTUCKY" TYPE SHOTGUN
Gauge: 24.
Barrel: 29" (Cyl.).
Weight: 4¼ lbs. **Length:** 44" over-all.
Stock: European walnut, checkered at wrist.
Sights: Bead front only.
Features: English style stock, inletted patch box; steel ramrod. From Century Arms.
Price: Flintlock, full stock **$29.95**
Price: Flintlock, sporter **$29.95**

CENTURY SINGLE BARREL PERCUSSION SHOTGUN
Gauge: 28.
Barrel: 31" (Cyl.), part octagon.
Weight: 4¼ lbs. **Length:** 48½" over-all.
Stock: Walnut finish hardwood; checkered at small of butt.
Sights: Bead front only.
Features: Suitable for ball or shot; blue barrel; lock, buttplate, trigger guard, breech and patch box are case hardened; steel ramrod. From Century Arms.
Price: **$32.95**

DOUBLE BARREL PERCUSSION SHOTGUN
Gauge: 12.
Barrel: 30" (I.C.& Mod.).
Weight: 6¼ lbs. **Length:** 45" over-all.
Stock: Hand checkered walnut, 14" pull.
Features: Double triggers, light hand engraving. Details vary with importer. Imported by Navy/Replica, The Armoury, Dixie, Euroarms, Hopkins & Allen.
Price: .... **$125.00 to $194.95**
Price: Model 100 Mag. (Navy) **$225.00**

SINGLE BARREL FLINTLOCK SHOTGUN
Gauge: 28.
Barrel: 28".
Weight: 4½ lbs. **Length:** 43" over-all.
Stock: Walnut finish, choice of half or full stock. Imported by The Armoury.
Price: **$37.95**

MOWREY A. & T. 12 GAUGE SHOTGUN
Gauge: 12 ga. only.
Barrel: 32", octagon.
Weight: 7½ lbs. **Length:** 48" over-all.
Stock: Maple, oil finish, brass furniture.
Sights: Bead front.
Features: Available in percussion only. Uses standard 12 ga. wadding. Made by Mowrey.
Price: Complete **$229.00**
Price: Kit form **$154.00**

AIR GUNS—HANDGUNS

Guns in this section are powered by: A) disposable CO_2 cylinders, B) hand-pumped compressed air released by trigger action, C) air compressed by a spring-powered piston released by trigger action. Calibers are generally 177 (BB or pellet) and 22 (ball or pellet); a few guns are made in 20 or 25 caliber. Pellet guns are usually rifled, those made for BB's only are smoothbore.

BEEMAN'S "ORIGINAL" 6 TARGET PISTOL
Caliber: 177, single shot.
Barrel: 7", rifled steel.
Weight: 3.2 lbs. **Length:** 16" over-all.
Power: Spring, barrel cocking.
Stocks: Checkered plastic; walnut optional.
Sights: Hooded front with interchangeable inserts, micro click rear with 4 rotating notches.
Features: Velocity 420 fps MV. Advanced recoilless action. Shoulder stock and scope mount available. Imported by Beeman's.
Price: Plastic stocks $103.95
Price: Walnut stocks $153.90

BEEMAN'S "ORIGINAL" 5 TARGET PISTOL
Caliber: 177 or 22, single shot.
Barrel: 7", rifled steel.
Weight: 3.1 lbs. **Length:** 16" over-all.
Power: Spring, barrel cocking.
Stocks: Checkered plastic thumbrest. Walnut optional.
Sights: Hooded fixed front, micro-click rear with 4 rotating notches.
Features: Adjustable double-pull trigger. Shoulder stock and scope mount available. Velocity 420 fps MV. Imported by Beeman's.
Price: $68.95

BEEMAN'S "ORIGINAL" 10 MKI MATCH PISTOL
Caliber: 177, single shot.
Weight: 3.3 lbs. **Length:** 16" over-all.
Power: Barrel cocking spring.
Stocks: Walnut with adjustable palm rest and sliding support plate.
Sights: Adj. post front from 2.5mm to 4.0mm width; adj. rear with interchangeable notches.
Features: Recoilless action; trigger adj. for length of pull, area of contact, travel length, pre-travel weight, pressure point and weight; auto. cocking safety trigger stop; rear sight has three positions; new barrel weights. Comes with fitted case. Scope mount available. Imported by Beeman's.
Price: With case $299.50
Price: Without case $269.50

BEEMAN/WEBLEY "HURRICANE" PISTOL
Caliber: 177 or 22.
Barrel: 8", rifled.
Weight: 2.4 lbs. **Length:** 16³/₁₆" over-all.
Power: Spring.
Stocks: Thumbrest, checkered.
Sights: Hooded front, micro-click rear adj. for w. and e.
Features: Velocity of 530 fps (177-cal.). Single stroke cocking, adjustable trigger pull, manual safety. Scope base included; 1.5x scope **$29.95** extra. Introduced 1977. Imported by Beeman's.
Price: $84.95

BEEMAN/FEINWERKBAU MODEL 80 MATCH PISTOL
Caliber: 177, single shot.
Barrel: 7.5".
Weight: 2.8 to 3.2 lbs. (varies with weight selection). **Length:** 16.4" over-all.
Power: Spring piston, single-stroke sidelever cocking.
Stocks: Stippled walnut with adjustable palm shelf.
Sights: Interchangeable-blade front, rear notch micro. adj. for w. and e.
Features: Two-stage trigger adjustable for finger length. Recoilless operation. Interchangeable weights attach to frame, not barrel. Weights may be arranged to suit balance preference. Cocking effort 16 lbs. Muzzle velocity 475-525 fps. Introduced 1978. Imported by Beeman's.
Price: .... $399.95 to $429.95

BENJAMIN SUPER S. S. TARGET PISTOL SERIES 130
Caliber: BB, 22 and 177; single shot.
Barrel: 8"; BB smoothbore; 22 and 177, rifled.
Length: 11". **Weight:** 2 lbs.
Power: Hand pumped.
Features: Bolt action; fingertip safety; adj. power.
Price: M130, BB $50.70
Price: M132, 22 .... $50.70
Price: M137, 177 .... $50.70

CROSMAN MODEL 1322 AIR PISTOL
Caliber: 22, single shot.
Barrel: 8", button rifled.
Length: 11¾". **Weight:** 37 oz.
Power: Hand pumped.
Sights: Blade front, rear adj. for w. and e.
Features: Moulded plastic grip, hand size pump forearm. Cross bolt safety, self-cocking. Also available in 177 Cal. as **Model 1377.**
Price: About **$40.00**

CROSMAN 454 BB PISTOL
Caliber: BB, 16-shot.
Length: 11" over-all. **Weight:** 30 oz.
Power: Standard CO_2.
Stocks: Contoured with thumbrest.
Sights: Patridge-type front, fully adj. rear.
Features: Gives about 80 shots per powerlet, slide-action safety, steel barrel, die-cast receiver.
Price: About **$29.00**

CROSMAN MARK I TARGET PISTOL
Caliber: 22, single shot.
Barrel: 7¼", button rifled.
Length: 11". **Weight:** 42 oz.
Power: Crosman Powerlet CO_2 cylinder.
Features: New system provides same shot-to-shot velocity, adj. from 300- to 400 fps. Checkered thumbrest grips, right or left. Patridge front sight, rear adj. for w. & e. Adj. trigger.
Price: About **$43.00**

Crosman Mark II Target Pistol
Same as Mark I except 177 cal., about **$43.00**

CROSMAN 38T TARGET REVOLVER
Caliber: 177, 6-shot.
Barrel: 6", rifled.
Length: 11". **Weight:** 43 oz.
Power: CO_2 Powerlet cylinder.
Features: Double action, revolving cylinder. Adj. rear sight.
Price: About **$40.00**

Crosman 38C Combat Revolver
Same as 38 Target except 3½" BBL., 38 oz., about **$40.00**

CROSMAN PEACEMAKER "44"
Caliber: 177, 6 shot.
Barrel: 4¾", button rifled.
Length: 10⅜". **Weight:** 34 oz.
Power: Crosman CO_2 Powerlet
Features: Revolving cylinder; walnut finished grips. Positive valve design. Single-action.
Price: About **$24.00**

DAISY 179 SIX GUN
Caliber: BB, 12-shot.
Barrel: Steel lined, smoothbore.
Length: 11½". **Weight:** NA
Power: Spring.
Features: Forced feed from under-barrel magazine. Single action, molded wood grained grips.
Price: **$14.95**

DAISY 177 BB PISTOL
Caliber: BB, 150-shot.
Barrel: Formed steel, smoothbore.
Length: 11¼". **Weight:** NA.
Power: Spring.
Features: Gravity feed, adjustable rear sight, molded plastic thumbrest grips.
Price: About **$14.95**

FEINWERKBAU F-65 AIR PISTOL
Caliber: 177.
Barrel: 7½"; fixed bbl. wgt. avail.
Length: 14½" over-all. **Weight:** 42 oz.
Power: Spring, sidelever cocking.
Stocks: Walnut, stippled thumbrest.
Sights: Front, interchangeable post element system, open rear, click adj. for w. & e. and for sighting notch width. Scope mount avail.
Features: Cocking effort 9 lbs. 2-stage trigger, 4 adjustments. Programs instantly for recoil or recoilless operation. Permanently lubricated. Steel piston ring. Special switch converts trigger from 17.6 oz. pull to 42 oz. let-off. Imported by Air Rifle Hdq., Beeman's.
Price: ....$319.50 to $379.50

Feinwerkbau Model 65 International Match Pistol
Same as FWB 65 pistol except: new adj. wood grips to meet international regulations, optional 3 oz. barrel sleeve weight. Imported by A.R.H., Beeman's.
Price: ....$299.50 to $398.50

DAISY/FWB 65 TARGET PISTOL
Caliber: 177, single shot.
Barrel: 7½", rifled, fixed to receiver.
Length: 15½". **Weight:** 42 oz.
Power: Spring, cocked by left-side lever.
Features: Recoilless operation, may be set to give recoil; Micro. rear sight, 14" radius. Adj. trigger; normal 17.6 oz. pull can be raised to 48 oz. for training. Checkered, thumbrest target grips. From Air Rifle Hdqtrs. or Daisy.
Price: About $300.00

HAMMERLI "MASTER" CO_2 TARGET PISTOL
Caliber: 177 waisted pellets.
Barrel: 6.4", 12-groove.
Length: 16". **Weight:** 38.4 oz.
Power: 12 gram cylinder.
Stocks: Plastic with thumbrest and checkering.
Sights: Ramp front, micro rear, click adj. Adj. sight radius from 11.1" to 13.0".
Features: Single shot, manual loading. Residual gas vented automatically. 5-way adj. trigger. Imported by Beeman's.
Price: $169.95

HAMMERLI "SINGLE" CO_2 TARGET PISTOL
Caliber: .177 waisted pellets.
Barrel: 4.5", 12-groove.
Length: 12". **Weight:** 33 oz.
Power: 8 gram cylinder.
Stocks: Plastic with thumbrest and checkering.
Sights: Ramp front, micro-click rear. Adj. sight radius from 11.1" to 13.0".
Features: Single shot, easy manual loading, 4-way adj. trigger. Residual gas vented automatically.

HEALTHWAYS TOPSCORE 9100 AIR PISTOL
Caliber: 177, BB, 50-shot magazine.
Barrel: 6½".
Weight: 28 oz.
Power: Spring.
Stocks: Checkered, integral with frame.
Sights: Open, fixed.
Features: Quick, top-load magazine mass loads 50 BBs at a time. Cock by releasing a locking lever on left side of frame and lifting barrel.
Price: $22.95

HEALTHWAYS PLAINSMASTER CO_2 PISTOL
Caliber: 177 BB or 22
Barrel: 9⅜".
Weight: 40 oz.
Power: 8.5 or 12.5 CO_2 cylinders.
Stocks: Simulated walnut with thumbrest, and fore-end.
Sights: Open, fixed.
Features: Special vertical fore-grip (detachable), coin-slotted power control for 3 levels of power.
Price: $49.95
Price: Also avail. with short 3⅞" bbl., 22 cal. only $39.95

HEALTHWAYS 9401 CO_2 AUTOMATIC PISTOL
Caliber: BB, 100-shot repeater.
Barrel: 5⅞", smooth.
Length: 9½". **Weight:** 28 oz.
Stocks: Simulated walnut with thumbrest.
Power: 8.5 or 12.5 gram CO_2 cylinders.
Features: 3 position power switch. Auto. ammunition feed. Positive safety.
Price: **$32.95**

Healthways 9404 "Shorty" Automatic Pistol
Same action as M9401. Magazine capacity of 40+ BBs, 3⅞" barrel, 300 fps muzzle velocity, ramp blade front sight, adjustable notch rear.
Price: **$32.95**

ITHACA/BSA SCORPION AIR PISTOL
Caliber: 177 or 22, single shot.
Barrel: 5⅞".
Weight: 3½ lbs. **Length:** About 15½" over-all.
Power: Spring air, barrel cocking.
Stocks: Molded nylon, one piece, checkered grip panels.
Sights: Hooded ramp front, fully adj. open rear.
Features: Muzzle velocity of 510 fps. Adjustable trigger. Sight radius of 15¾". Same action as BSA Meteor air rifle. Receiver grooved for scope mount. Comes with barrel extender for easier cocking, pellets, targets, target holder, oil. From Ithacagun.
Price: **$94.95**

MARKSMAN #1010 REPEATER PISTOL
Caliber: 177, 20-shot repeater.
Barrel: 2½", smoothbore.
Length: 8¼". **Weight:** 24 oz.
Power: Spring.
Features: Thumb safety. Uses BBs, darts or pellets. Repeats with BBs only.
Price: Black finish **$13.50**

PRECISE/RO-72 BULLSEYE AIR PISTOL
Caliber: 177, single shot.
Barrel: 7¼", rifled.
Weight: 35 oz.
Power: Spring air, barrel cocking.
Stock: Molded plastic with thumbrest.
Sights: Hooded front, micro. adj. open rear for w. and e.
Features: Four interchangeable front sights—triangle, bead, narrow post, wide post. Rear sight rotates to give four distinct sight pictures. Muzzle velocity 325 fps. Precise, importer.
Price: **$35.00**

POWER LINE CO_2 1200 CUSTOM TARGET PISTOL
Caliber: BB, 177
Barrel: 10½", smooth
Weight: 30 oz. **Length:** 11¼" over-all.
Power: Daisy CO_2 cylinder.
Stocks: Contoured, checkered moulded wood-grain plastic.
Sights: Blade ramp front, fully adj. square notch rear.
Features: 60-shot BB reservoir, gravity feed. Cross bolt safety. Velocity of 420-450 fps for more than 100 shots.
Price: **$33.95**

POWERLINE MODEL 62 TARGET AIR
Caliber: 177 pellet, single shot.
Barrel: 7.2", rifled steel.
Weight: 46 oz. **Length:** 14⅞" over-all.
Power: Spring air.
Stock: Selected hardwood; contoured, articulated and adjustable to any shooting position.
Sights: Hooded ramp front, micro. adj. open rear.
Features: Crafted by Daisy. Long underlever for easy cocking.
Price: About **$69.95**

SMITH & WESSON MODELS 78G & 79G
Caliber: 22 cal. pellet (78G), 177 cal. pellet (79G), single-shot.
Barrel: 8½", rifled steel.
Weight: 42 oz.
Power: 12.5 gram CO_2 cartridge.
Stocks: Simulated walnut, checkered. Thumbrest. Left or right hand.
Sights: Patridge front, fully adj. rear with micro. click windage adjustment.
Features: Pull-bolt action, crossbolt safety. High-low power adjustment. Gun blue finish.
Price: **$44.75**

WALTHER MODEL LP-53 PISTOL
Caliber: 177, single shot.
Barrel: 9⅜".
Length: 12⅜" over-all. **Weight:** 40.5 oz.
Power: Spring air.
Features: Micrometer rear sight. Interchangeable rear sight blades. Target grips. Bbl. weight available at extra cost. Interarms, Alexandria, Va.
Price: **$150.00**

WEIHRAUCH HW-70 AIR PISTOL
Caliber: 177, single shot.
Barrel: 6¼", rifled.
Length: 12¾" over-all. **Weight:** 38 oz.
Sights: Hooded post front, square notch rear adj. for w. and e.
Power: Spring, barrel cocking.
Features: Adj. trigger. 24-lb. cocking effort, 365 f.p.s. M.V.; automatic barrel safety. Air Rifle HQ, Beeman's, importers.
Price: .... **$59.95** to **$64.50**

SHERIDAN MODEL E CO_2 PISTOL
Caliber: 20 (5mm).
Barrel: 6½", rifled, rust proof.
Weight: 27 ozs. **Length:** 9" over-all.
Power: 12 gram CO_2 cylinder.
Stocks: Checkered simulated walnut. Left- or right-handed.
Sights: Blade front, fully adjustable rear.
Features: Turn-bolt single-shot action. Gives about 40 shots at 400 fps per CO_2 cylinder.
Price: **$35.65**

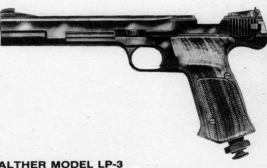

WALTHER MODEL LP-3
Caliber: 177, single shot.
Barrel: 9⅜", rifled.
Length: 13³/₁₆". **Weight:** 45½ oz.
Power: Compressed air, lever cocking.
Features: Recoilless operation, cocking in grip frame. Micro-click rear sight, adj. for w. & e., 4-way adj. trigger. Plastic thumbrest grips. Imported by Interarms.
Price: **$270.00**

Walther Model LP-3 Match Pistol
Same specifications as LP-3 except for grips, frame shape and weight. Has adjustable walnut grips to meet international shooting regulations. Imported by Interarms.
Price: **$325.00**

> Consult our Directory pages for the location of firms mentioned.

WEBLEY AIR PISTOLS

Model:	Junior MK II	Premier MK II
Caliber:	177	177 or 22
Barrel:	6⅛"	6½"
Weight:	23¼ oz.	31 oz.
Power:	Spring, barrel cocking	Same
Sights:	Adj. for w.	Adj. for w. & e.
Trigger:	Fixed	Adj.
ce:	**$47.95**	**$69.95** to **$94.50**

Features: Single stroke cocking, High-tensile aircraft alloy body; cylinder liner and all moving parts are steel. Walnut stocks avail. Imported by A.R.H., Fanta.

WISCHO BSF S-20 CUSTOM MATCH PISTOL
Caliber: 177, single shot.
Barrel: 7" rifled.
Length: 15.8" over-all. **Weight:** 45 oz.
Stocks: Walnut with thumbrest.
Sights: Bead front, rear adj. for e.
Power: Spring, barrel cocking.
Features: Cocking effort of 17 lbs.; M.V. 450 f.p.s.; adj. trigger. Optional scope and mount available. Detachable aluminum stock available from Beemans. Air Rifle HQ, Beeman's importers.
Price: .... **$76.95** to **$79.95**

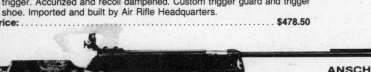

A.R.H. CUSTOM 120-X RIFLE
Caliber: 177 only.
Barrel: 18⅝".
Length: 44" over-all.
Power: Spring air, single stroke, barrel cocking.
Stock: Select American walnut with roll-over cheekpiece, Rosewood p.g. cap, white spacers, rubber buttplate, high gloss finish, detachable swivels.
Sights: Tunnel front with interchangeable inserts included, open rear. Match aperture or scope optional.
Features: Velocity 818 fps; cocking effort 16 lbs.; automatic safety; adjustable trigger. Accurized and recoil dampened. Custom trigger guard and trigger shoe. Imported and built by Air Rifle Headquarters.
Price: **$478.50**

ANSCHUTZ 250 TARGET RIFLE
Caliber: 177, single shot.
Barrel: 18½", rifled, one piece with receiver.
Length: 45". **Weight:** 11 lbs. with sights.
Power: Spring, side-lever cocking, 17 lb. pull.
Features: Recoilless operation. Two-stage adj. trigger. Checkered walnut p.g. stock with Monte Carlo comb & cheekpiece; adj. buttplate; accessory rail. Imported by Beeman's.
Price: **$530.00**

BSF 55, S-60, S-70 RIFLES

Model:	Bavaria 55	S-60 (illus.)	S-70
Caliber:	177 or 22	177 or 22	177
Barrel:	16"	19"	19"
Rifled:	Yes	Yes	Yes
Length:	40½"	43½"	43¾"
Weight:	6¼ lbs.	6½ lbs.	6½ lbs.
MV:	763, 580	763, 580	763
Sights:	Elev. only	w. & e.	w. & e.
Price:	$139.95	$124.95	$134.95
	to	to	to
	$114.95	$135.00	$158.00

Features: Spring piston powered, barrel cocking. Blued metal. Adj. 2-stage triggers. Beech stocks on B-55 and S-60, have checkered p.g. S-70 mechanically identical to S-60. Beech, checkered p.g. and fore-end. Raised cheek pad, curved rubber buttplate. Imported by Beeman's (Bavaria 55 only) and Fanta.

BEEMAN/WEBLEY OSPREY AIR RIFLE
Caliber: 177.
Barrel: 18½".
Weight: 7¾ lbs. **Length:** 43¼" over-all.
Power: Spring piston air; one stroke side-lever.
Stock: Walnut; sculptured cheekpiece, Monte Carlo comb, rubber buttplate.
Sights: Hooded front, micro. click rear adj. for w. & e. Receiver grooved for aperture sight or scope.
Features: Manual safety plus cocking lever safety to prevent accidental closing. Steel automotive-type piston rings. Trigger is adjustable from 3 to 8 lbs. Rifle in 22 cal. available on special order. Imported by Beeman's Precision Airguns.
Price: **$159.95**

Beeman/Webley Super Target Air Rifle
A special 177-cal. version of the Osprey rifle with slightly heavier weight, target front sight with interchangeable inserts, and an Anschutz match aperture rear sight. Imported by Beeman's Precision Airguns. **$299.95**

BEEMAN/WEBLEY HAWK MKIII AIR RIFLE
Caliber: 177 or 22.
Barrel: 17⅛", rifled steel.
Weight: 6½ lbs. **Length:** 42¼" over-all.
Power: Spring piston air; one stroke barrel cocking.
Stock: Walnut; cheekpiece, Monte Carlo, rubber buttplate.
Sights: Hooded front; micro. click rear adj. for w. & e.. Receiver grooved for scope.
Features: Velocity 725 fps. (177), 550 fps (22). Automatic thumb safety; self-lubricating piston rings; trigger adj. from 3 to 8 lbs. Imported by Beeman's Precision Airguns.
Price: **$99.95**

BEEMAN/FEINWERKBAU 127 SPORTER
Caliber: 22.
Barrel: 18.3″.
Weight: 6.2 lbs. **Length:** 43½″ over-all.
Power: Spring piston air; single stroke cocking.
Stock: Walnut finished hardwood.
Sights: Tunnel front; click-adj. rear for w., slide-adj. for e.
Features: Velocity over 600 fps, cocking effort of 19 lbs. Auto. safety, adj. trigger. Standard model has no checkering, cheekpiece, or swivels. Deluxe has hand-checkered p.g. and fore-end, high comb cheekpiece, ⅞″ sling swivels and buttplate with white spacer. Imported by Beeman's.
Price: Standard model **$154.95**
Price: Deluxe model **$184.95**
Price: Custom model **$354.95**

BEEMAN/FEINWERKBAU 300-S "UNIVERSAL" MATCH
Caliber: 177, single shot.
Barrel: 19.9″.
Weight: 10.2 lbs. (without barrel sleeve). **Length:** 43.3″ over-all.
Power: Spring piston, single stroke sidelever.
Stock: Walnut, stippled p.g. and fore-end. Detachable cheekpieces (one std., high for scope use). Adjustable buttplate, accessory rail. Buttplate and grip cap spacers included.
Sights: Two globe fronts with interchangeable inserts. Rear is match aperture with rubber eyecup and sight viser.
Features: Recoilless, vibration free. Grooved for cope mounts. Steel piston ring. Cocking effort about 9½ lbs. Barrel sleeve optional. Introduced 1978. Imported by Beeman's.
Price: . . . . **$546.00** to **$600.00**

BEEMAN/FEINWERKBAU 300-S "Junior" MATCH
Caliber: 177, single shot.
Barrel: 17⅛″.
Weight: 8.8 lbs. **Length:** 40″ over-all.
Power: Spring piston, single stroke sidelever cocking.
Stock: Walnut. Stippled grip, adjustable buttplate. Scaled-down for youthful or slightly built shooters.
Sights: Globe front with interchangeable inserts, micro. adjustable rear.
Features: Adjustable trigger, recoilless operation. Left-hand model available on special order. Introduced 1978. Imported by Beeman's.
Price: . . . . **$429.00** to **$456.00**

BEEMAN MODEL 75 RECOILLESS MATCH RIFLE
Caliber: 177, single shot.
Barrel: 18.9″.
Weight: 10.7 lbs. **Length:** 44½″ over-all.
Power: Spring-piston, single-stroke side lever cocking.
Stock: European walnut with full length fore-end accessory rail, curved adjustable rubber buttplate, stippled grip.
Sights: Globe front with adjustable aperture and optional standard inserts; rear aperture sight with micrometer adjustments for w. and e.
Features: Double-acting 2-piston recoilless action—receiver does not move. Cocking effort 9 lbs. Fully adjustable trigger including length of pull and lateral angle. Left-hand version with left-hand lever available. Detachable muzzle weight. Front aperture is unique neoprene O-ring with knurled ring to vary size. Non-reflective finish. Imported by Beeman's.
Price: **$379.00**
Price: Left-hand model **$479.00**

BEEMAN'S "ORIGINAL" 35 SPORTER RIFLE
Caliber: 177, single shot.
Barrel: 19″, rifled steel.
Weight: 7.1 lbs. **Length:** 44.3″ over-all.
Power: Spring, barrel cocking.
Stock: Adult-size walnut finished, soft rubber buttplate.
Sights: Hooded front with removable insert, steel rear adj. for w. & e.
Features: Scope and aperature sight ramp; adj. 2-stage trigger. Imported by Beeman's.
Price: **$107.95**

BEEMAN'S "ORIGINAL" 27 TARGET RIFLE
Caliber: 177, single shot.
Barrel: 18.7″, rifled.
Weight: 6 lbs. **Length:** 42″ over-all.
Power: Spring, barrel cocking.
Sights: Hooded front, 4-notch rotating rear micro. adj. for w. & e.
Features: Velocity 660 fps MV. Grooved for scope or peep sights; 17 lbs. single stroke cocking; adjustable trigger. Imported by Beeman's.
Price: **$88.98**

BENJAMIN SERIES 3100 SUPER REPEATER RIFLES
Caliber: BB, 100-shot; 22, 85-shot.
Barrel: 23″, rifled or smoothbore.
Length: 35″. **Weight:** 6¼ lbs.
Power: Hand pumped.
Features: Bolt action. Piggy back full view magazine. Bar V adj. rear sight. Walnut stock and pump handle.
Price: M3100, BB . . . . **$62.45** M3120, 22 rifled **$62.45**

BENJAMIN SERIES 340 AIR RIFLE
Caliber: 22 and 177 pellets or BB; single shot.
Barrel: 23″, rifled and smoothbore.
Length: 35″. **Weight:** 6 lbs.
Power: Hand pumped.
Features: Bolt action, walnut Monte Carlo stock and pump handle. Ramp-type front sight, adj. stepped leaf type rear. Push-pull safety.
Price: M340, BB **$62.45**
Price: M342, 22 . . . . **$62.45** M347, 177 . . . . **$62.45**

CROSMAN MODEL 2200 MAGNUM AIR RIFLE
Caliber: 22, single-shot.
Barrel: 19″, rifled steel.
Weight: 5 lbs. 6 ozs. **Length:** 39¾″ over-all.
Stock: Full-size, wood-grained plastic with checkered p.g. and fore-end.
Sights: Ramp front, open step-adjustable rear.
Features: Variable pump power—3 pumps give 395 fps, 6 pumps 530 fps, 10 pumps 620 fps (average). Full-size adult air rifle. Has white line spacers at pistol grip and buttplate, nickel plated receiver. Introduced 1978.
Price: About **$49.00**

CROSMAN MODEL 73 CO₂
Caliber: 177 pellets or BBs, 16-shot magazine.
Barrel: 18″, steel.
Weight: 3¼ lbs. **Length:** 34¾″ over-all.
Stock: Simulated wood.
Sights: Ramp front, rear adj. for e.
Features: Positive lever safety. Velocity is 425 fps (BBs).
Price: About **$24.00**

CROSMAN MODEL 788 BB SCOUT RIFLE
Caliber: 177, BB.
Barrel: 14″, steel.
Weight: 2 lbs. 3 ozs. **Length:** 31″ over-all.
Stock: Wood-grained ABS plastic.
Sights: Blade on ramp front, open adj. rear.
Features: Variable pump power—3 pumps give MV of 330 fps, 6 pumps 437 fps, 10 pumps 470 fps (BBs, average). Steel barrel, cross-bolt safety. Introduced 1978.
Price: About **$21.00**

CROSMAN 760XL PUMP RIFLE
Caliber: BB, 180-shot or 177 cal. pellet (single-shot).
Barrel: 19″, button rifled.
Length: 36″ over-all. **Weight:** 4¾ lbs.
Power: Hand pumped.
Stock: Full-size, wood-grained plastic with Monte Carlo.
Sights: Hooded front, step adj. rear for w. & e.
Features: Receiver grooved for scope mounting, gold-colored receiver, cross-bolt safety.
Price: About **$43.00**

CROSMAN MODEL 760 POWERMASTER
Caliber: BB, 180 shot.
Barrel: 19½″, smoothbore steel.
Length: 35″. **Weight:** 4⅛ lbs.
Power: High compression spring.
Features: Short stroke, power determined by number of strokes. Walnut finished plastic checkered stock and fore-end. Post front sight and adjustable rear sight. Cross-bolt safety. Scope and mount optional.
Price: About **$40.00**

CROSMAN MODEL 70 CO² BOLT ACTION RIFLE
Caliber: 177 pellet, single-shot.
Barrel: 23¾", rifled steel.
Length: 41" over-all. **Weight:** 5¾ lbs.
Stock: Full-size hardwood, walnut finish, Monte Carlo-style.
Sights: Blade front, rear adjustable for w. and e.
Features: Average velocity 650 fps. Full sized gun. Cross bolt safety. Each powerlet (12.5 grams) gives an average of 40 shots. Crosman 4X Super-scope and mounts available separately ($13.00).
Price: About **$52.00**

CROSMAN AMERICAN CLASSIC 766 AIR RIFLE
Caliber: 177 pellets or BBs, 15-shot magazine.
Barrel: 19" rifled.
Weight: About 5 lbs. **Length:** 39½" over-all.
Power: Pump-up, spring air.
Stock: Wood-grained checkered ABS plastic.
Features: Three pumps gives about 450 fps, 10 pumps about 700 fps. Cross-bolt safety; concealed reservoir holds over 100 BBs.
Price: About **$47.00**

DAISY/FWB 4301
Caliber: 177, single shot.
Barrel: 29¼", rifled.
Length: 45". **Weight:** 11 lbs.
Stock: Walnut, Monte Carlo cheekpiece, checkered palmswell p.g.
Sights: Globe front with inserts, micro. adj. peep rear.
Power: Spring, barrel cocking.
Features: Adj. trigger, adj. buttplate, patented recoil eliminator.
Price: About **$395.00**

DAISY 770
Caliber: BB only, 200-shot magazine
Barrel: 18¹³⁄₁₆", smoothbore.
Weight: 4 lbs. **Length:** 39⅛" over-all.
Power: Spring, lever cocking.
Stock: Fully contoured wood grain plastic with Monte Carlo.
Sights: Hooded ramp front, fully adj. open rear.
Features: Crafted by Daisy. Single stroke cocking system with automatic safety. With optional Model 808 4X scope as Model 1770 (**$49.95**).
Price: About **$31.95**

DAISY MODEL 840
Caliber: 177 pellet (single-shot) or BB (350-shot).
Barrel: 19", smoothbore, steel.
Weight: 3¼ lbs. **Length:** 37⅛" over-all.
Stock: Moulded wood-grain stock and fore-end.
Sights: Ramp front, open, adj. rear.
Features: Single pump pneumatic rifle. Muzzle velocity 310 fps (BB), 270 fps (pellet). Steel buttplate; straight pull bolt action; cross-bolt safety. Fore-end forms pump lever. Introduced 1978.
Price: About **$24.95**

DAISY 99 CHAMPION
Caliber: BB, 50-shot.
Barrel: 18", smoothbore.
Length: 36¼".
Power: Spring.
Features: Wood stock, beavertail fore-end; sling; hooded front sight with four insert apertures, adj. aperture rear, stock medallion.
Price: About **$32.95**

DAISY 1938 RED RYDER COMMEMORATIVE BB CARBINE

Caliber: BB, 700-shot repeating action.
Barrel: Sturdy steel, under-barrel loading port.
Length: 35" over-all. **Weight:** 3½ lbs.
Stock: Wood stock burned with Red Ryder lariat signature.
Sights: Post front, adjustable V-slot rear.
Features: Wood fore-end. Saddle ring with leather thong. Lever cocking. Gravity feed. Controlled velocity. Commemorates one of Daisy's most popular guns, the Red Ryder of the 1940s and 1950s.
Price: About **$25.95**

DAISY 1894 SPITTIN' IMAGE CARBINE

Caliber: BB, 40-shot.
Barrel: 17½", smoothbore.
Length: 38⅜".
Power: Spring.
Features: Cocks halfway on forward stroke of lever, halfway on return.
Price: About **$31.95**

DAISY 25 PUMP GUN

Caliber: BB, 50-shot.
Barrel: 18", smoothbore.
Length: 37¼". **Weight:** NA.
Power: Pump cocking spring.
Features: Ramp front and adj. rear sights. BBs are spring-force fed.
Price: About **$28.00**

DAISY MODEL 98 MONTE CARLO BB RIFLE

Caliber: BB only.
Barrel: Smooth bore.
Length: 36" over-all. **Weight:** 4 lbs.
Power: Spring air.
Stock: Wood grain moulded plastic with Monte Carlo cheekpiece.
Sights: Post ramp front, open rear adj. for e.
Features: Lever cocking, gravity feed. 700-shot magazine. Auto. trigger block safety.
Price: About **$28.95**

DAISY RIFLES

Model:	95	102	104	111
Caliber:	BB	BB	BB	BB
Barrel:	18"	13½"	13½"	18"
Length:	35"	30¼"	30½	35"
Power:	Spring	Spring	Spring	Spring
Capacity:	700	350	350	700
Price: About	$21.95	$14.95	$17.95	$19.95

Features: 95 stock is wood, fore-end plastic; 111 and 104 have plastic stocks; 102 has wood stock; 104 has sighting tube w/aperture and is gold finished.

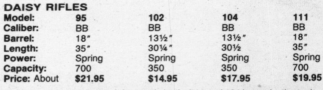

FEINWERKBAU 300-S TYROLEAN MATCH RIFLE

Caliber: 177, single shot.
Barrel: 19.9".
Length: 42.8" over-all. **Weight:** 9.5 lbs.
Power: Spring air, sidelever.
Stock: Walnut. High Tyrolean cheekpiece, medium weight fore-end.
Sights: Globe front with inserts, micro. adj. rear aperture.
Features: Barrel and receiver recoil together to eliminate felt recoil. 4-way adj. trigger. Muzzle velocity 640 fps. Optional 12 oz. bbl. sleeve. Imported by A.R.H. and Beeman's.
Price: . . . . **$532.00 to $548.50**

FEINWERKBAU 300-S SERIES MATCH RIFLE

Caliber: 177.
Barrel: 19.9", fixed solid with receiver.
Length: 42.8" over-all. **Weight:** Approx. 10 lbs. with optional bbl. sleeve.
Power: Single stroke sidelever, spring piston.
Stock: Match model—walnut, deep fore-end, adj. buttplate. Std. model—walnut finish, lighter weight, regular fore-end, lacks p.g. cap.
Sights: Globe front with interchangeable inserts. Click micro. adj. match aperture rear.
Features: Recoilless, vibration free. Grooved for scope mounts. Permanent lubrication, steel piston ring. Cocking effort 9 lbs. Optional 10 oz. bbl. sleeve. Imported by A.R.H., Beeman's.
Price: 300-S Match . . . . **$468.00 to $498.50**

FEINWERKBAU 124 SPORTER
Caliber: 177, 22.
Barrel: 18.3".
Length: 43.5" over-all. **Weight:** 6.3 lbs.
Power: Spring air; single stroke barrel cocking.
Stock: Walnut finished hardwood.
Sights: Tunnel front, fully adj. open rear.
Features: Velocity over 800 fps. Cocking effort 19 lbs. Automatic safety, adj. trigger. Standard model has no checkering or cheekpiece. Deluxe has checkered p.g. and fore-end, high comb cheekpiece, sling swivels and rubber buttplate with white line spacer. Grooved for peep sight or scope mount. A.R.H. has 177 cal. only, Beeman's both. Imported by A.R.H. and Beeman's.
Price: Standard model . . . . **$149.95 to $174.50**
Price: Deluxe model . . . . **$179.95 to $198.50**
Price: Deluxe left-hand . . . . **$194.95 to $214.50**

Beeman/Feinwerkbau 124 Custom Sporter
Same as Deluxe 124 except assembled in U.S. with select American walnut stock with cheekpiece, rosewood p.g. cap, white line spacers, rubber buttplate, oil finish. Velocity approx. 820 fps, cocking effort 16-18 lbs., q.d. swivels. Accurized version of 124. Options include trigger shoe and cast, checkered trigger guard, front sight with interchangeable inserts. Imported and assembled by Beeman's **$354.95**

Ithaca/BSA AIRSPORTER
Caliber: 177 or 22.
Barrel: 18½".
Weight: 8 lbs. **Length:** 44" over-all.
Stock: Walnut-finished hardwood.
Sights: Ramp front with interchangeable blade/bead, micro. adj. rear reversible to peep or U-notch.
Features: Under-lever cocking; adjustable trigger; recoil pad. Introduced 1978. From Ithaca.
Price: **$159.95**

ITHACA/BSA BUCCANEER AIR RIFLE
Caliber: 177 or 22.
Barrel: 18½".
Weight: 6 lbs. **Length:** 35½" over-all.
Stock: High impact polyurethane. Thumbhole-type.
Sights: Hooded front with bead or blade, aperture rear adj. for w. & e.
Features: Muzzle velocity of 510 fps (177), 400 fps (22); single-action cocking with separate cocking lever (included). Comes with lubricant, pellets, targets, steel target holder. From Ithaca. Introduced 1978.
Price: **$99.95**

ITHACA/BSA METEOR & MECURY RIFLES
Caliber: 177 or 22.
Barrel: 18½" rifled.
Length: 42" over-all. **Weight:** 6 lbs. (Meteor), 7 lbs. (Mercury)
Stock: European hardwood. Mecury has Monte Carlo.
Sights: Blade front, micro. adj. rear (Meteor). Mecury has hooded front.
Features: Meteor—barrel cocking action. Adjustable single stage trigger, 3-5 lb. pull. Receiver dovetailed for standard scope mounts. 650 fps (177 cal.); 500 fps (22 cal.). Mercury—700 fps (177), 550 fps (22), comes with pellets, target, target holder and lubricant. Imported by Ithaca.
Price: Meteor **$69.95**
Price: Mercury **$99.95**

MARKSMAN 740 AIR RIFLE
Caliber: 177, 100-shot.
Barrel: 15-½", smoothbore.
Length: 36½". **Weight:** 4 lbs., 2 oz.
Power: Spring, barrel cocking.
Stock: Moulded high-impact ABS plastic.
Sights: Ramp front, open rear adj. for e.
Features: Automatic safety; fixed front, adj. rear sights; shoots 177 cal. BB's pellets and darts. Velocity about 450 fps.
Price: **$25.95**
Price: M742 (same as 740 except stock is of lighter weight material, fixed rear sight, single spring power gives about 400 fps. **$21.00**

POWER LINE 880 PUMP-UP AIR GUN
Caliber: 177 pellets, BB.
Barrel: Smooth bore, steel.
Length: 37¾" over-all. **Weight:** 6 lbs.
Power: Spring air.
Stock: Wood grain moulded plastic.
Sights: Ramp front, open rear adj. for e.
Features: Crafted by Daisy. Variable power (velocity and range) increase with pump strokes. 10 strokes for maximum power. 100-shot BB magazine. Cross-bolt trigger safety. Positive cocking valve.
Price: About **$47.95**
Price: As Model 1880 with 4x scope, about **$65.95**

POWER LINE 881 PUMP-UP AIR GUN
Caliber: 177 pellets, BB.
Barrel: Decagon rifled.
Length: 37¾" over-all. **Weight:** 6 lbs.
Power: Spring air.
Stock: Wood grain moulded plastic with Monte Carlo cheekpiece.
Sights: Ramp front, step-adj. rear for e.
Features: Crafted by Daisy. Accurized version of Model 880. Checkered fore-end and p.g.
Price: About **$55.95**
Price: As Model 1881 with 4x scope, about **$73.95**

POWER LINE MODEL 922
Caliber: 22 pellets, 5-shot clip.
Barrel: 20.8". Decagon rifled brass barrel.
Weight: 5 lbs. **Length:** 37¾" over-all.
Stock: Molded wood-grained plastic with checkered p.g. and fore-end.
Sights: Ramp front, full adj. open rear.
Features: Muzzle velocity from 285 fps (two pumps) to 555 fps. (ten pumps). Straight pull bolt action. Separate buttplate and grip cap with white spacers. Introduced 1978.
Price: About **$55.95**

PRECISE MINUTEMAN MKI REPEATER AIR RIFLE
Caliber: 177.
Barrel: 17¼", 12-groove rifling.
Length: 41" over-all. **Weight:** 5¼ lbs.
Power: Spring, barrel cocking.
Stock: Walnut finish.
Sights: Hooded front, micro. adj. rear.
Features: 25-shot automatic pellet feed, m.v. 625 fps. Precise, importer.
Price: **$85.00**

Precise Minuteman Pistol Grip Rifle
Same as repeater version except: available in either 177 or 22 cal.; receiver grooved for scope mounting.
Price: **$85.00**

PRECISE MINUTEMAN TOURNAMENT AIR RIFLE
Caliber: 177, 22, single shot.
Barrel: 18". 12-groove rifling.
Length: 43" over-all. **Weight:** 6¾ lbs.
Power: Spring, barrel cocking.
Features: Muzzle velocty of 670 fps. Micro. adj. rear sight, hooded front. Walnut finish stock; Monte Carlo comb with cheek piece, recoil pad. Receiver grooved for scope mounting. Precise, importer.
Price: **$75.00**

PRECISE MINUTEMAN MK.II REPEATER AIR RIFLE
Caliber: 177, 25-shot.
Barrel: 17½", 12 groove rifling.
Length: 37½". **Weight:** 6½ lbs.
Power: Spring, barrel cocking.
Features: M.V. 675 fps. Micro, adj. target sights, adj. trigger; target type recoil pad, M.C. comb and cheekpiece. Precise, importer.
Price: **$100.00**

Precise Minuteman Carbine Air Rifle
Same as Tournament model except has plain stock without Monte Carlo comb, cheekpiece; over-all length 41", weight 5¼ lbs., M.V. 625 fps. **$60.00**

Consult our Directory pages for the location of firms mentioned.

SHERIDAN CO² AIR RIFLES
Caliber: 5mm (20 cal.), single shot.
Barrel: 18½", rifled.
Weight: 6 lbs. **Length:** 37" over-all.
Stock: Walnut sporter.
Power: Standard 12.5 gram CO_2 cylinder.
Sights: Open, adj. for w. and e. Optional Sheridan Williams 5D-SH receiver sight or Weaver D4 scope.
Features: Bolt action single shot, CO_2 powered. Velocity approx. 514 fps., manual thumb safety. Blue or Silver finish. Left-hand models avail. at same prices.
Price: CO_2 Blue Streak **$66.75**
Price: CO_2 Silver Streak **$69.75**
Price: CO_2 Blue Streak with receiver sight **$78.00**
Price: CO_2 Blue Streak with Weaver D4 scope **$93.95**

SHERIDAN BLUE AND SILVER STREAK RIFLES
Caliber: 5mm (20 cal.), single shot.
Barrel: 18½", rifled.
Length: 37". **Weight:** 5 lbs.
Power: Hand pumped (swinging fore-end).
Features: Rustproof barrel and piston tube. Takedown. Thumb safety. Mannlicher type walnut stock. Left-hand models same price.
Price: Blue Streak . . . . **$66.75** Silver Streak **$69.75**
Sheridan accessories: Intermount, a base for ⅜" Tip-Off scope mounts, **$7.75**; Sheridan-Williams 5DSH receiver sight, **$8.75** Sheridan Pelletrap, **$17.50**; Model 222 Targetrap **$69.50**; Model 333 Targetrap **$26.00**; Sheridan 5mm pellets, **$3.50** for 500. Weaver 4 x scope and Intermount installed **$24.70 (extra).**

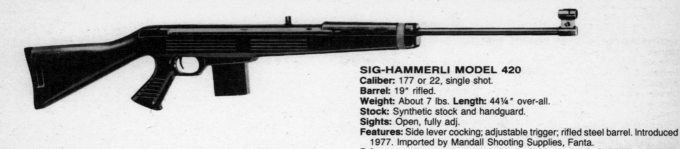

SIG-HAMMERLI MODEL 420
Caliber: 177 or 22, single shot.
Barrel: 19" rifled.
Weight: About 7 lbs. **Length:** 44¼" over-all.
Stock: Synthetic stock and handguard.
Sights: Open, fully adj.
Features: Side lever cocking; adjustable trigger; rifled steel barrel. Introduced 1977. Imported by Mandall Shooting Supplies, Fanta.
Price: . . . .$125.00 to $279.50

SMITH & WESSON MODEL 80 AUTO BB RIFLE
Caliber: BB, 50-shot tube magazine.
Barrel: 22".
Length: 39" over-all. **Weight:** 3¼ lbs.
Power: Standard CO_2 cylinder.
Stock: Walnut color, checkered, wood grain finish.
Sights: Ramp front, fully adj. rear.
Features: Top tang safety, receiver grooved for scope mounting, gas cut-off, fast CO_2 cartridge loading.
Price: $41.00

SMITH & WESSON MODEL 77A
Caliber: 22, single shot.
Barrel: 22", rifled.
Length: 40" over-all. **Weight:** 6½ lbs.
Power: Hand pumped, swinging fore-end.
Stock: Hardwood, p.g., M.C., walnut finish.
Sights: Blade front, adj. notch rear.
Features: Automatic safety, receiver grooved for scope mounting.
Price. $53.95

ULTRA-HI "KENTUCKY" BB RIFLE
Caliber: BB
Weight: 4 lbs. **Length:** 44" over-all.
Stock: Hardwood.
Sights: Blade front, left rear.
Features: Nose cap, buttplate, trigger guard and lock plate are plastic. Hammer cocks and serves as a safety. Introduced 1977. From Ultra-Hi Products.
Price: $39.95

WALTHER LGV SPECIAL
Caliber: 177, single shot.
Barrel: 16", rifled.
Length: 41⅜". **Weight:** 10¼ lbs.
Power: Spring air (barrel cocking).
Features: Micro. click adj. aperture receiver sight; Adj. trigger. Walnut match stock, adj. buttplate. Double piston provides vibration-free shooting. Easily operated bbl. latch. Removable heavy bbl. sleeve. 5-way adj. trigger. Imported by Interarms.
Price: $360.00

WALTHER LGR RIFLE
Caliber: 177, single-shot.
Barrel: 19½", rifled.
Length: 44¼" over-all. **Weight:** 10.2 lbs.
Power: Side lever cocking, compressed air.
Stock: French walnut.
Sights: Replaceable insert hooded front, Walther micro. adjustable rear.
Features: Recoilless operation. Trigger adj. for weight, pull and position. High comb stock with broad stippled fore-end and p.g. Imported by Interarms.
Price: $440.00

Walther LGR Match Air Rifle
Same basic specifications as standard LGR except has a high comb stock, sights are mounted on riser blocks. Introduced 1977.
Price: $490.00

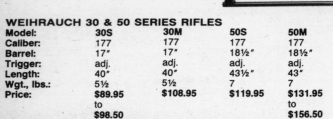

WEIHRAUCH 30 & 50 SERIES RIFLES

Model:	30S	30M	50S	50M
Caliber:	177	177	177	177
Barrel:	17″	17″	18½″	18½″
Trigger:	adj.	adj.	adj.	adj.
Length:	40″	40″	43½″	43″
Wgt., lbs.:	5½	5½	7	7
Price:	$89.95 to $98.50	$108.95	$119.95	$131.95 to $156.50

Features: All are rifled and spring-operated by single stroke cocking. Post and ramp front sights (50M has globe front with 4 inserts). Open click rear sights, adj. for w. & e. Walnut finished stocks. 50M has cheek-piece, wide fore-end, M.C. comb, ⅞″ sling swivels. MV of all 660-705 fps. Air Rifle Hdqtrs., Beeman's, importers. Also available from Fanta.

WEIHRAUCH 55 TARGET RIFLES

Model:	55SM	55MM	55T
Caliber:	177	177	177
Barrel:	18½″	18½″	18½″
Length:	43½″	43½″	43½″
Wgt. lbs.:	7.8	7.8	7.8
Rear sight:	All aperture		
Front sight:	All with globe and 4 interchangeable inserts.		
Power:	All springs (barrel cocking). 600 fps.		
Price:	$199.50 to $218.50	$246.00 to $248.50	$286.00 to $287.50

Features: Trigger fully adj. and removable. Micrometer rear sight adj. for w. and e. on all. P.g. high comb stock with beavertail fore-end, walnut finish stock on 55SM. Walnut stock on 55MM, (illus.) Tyrolean stock on 55T. Air Rifle Hdqtrs., Beeman's, importers. Also available from Fanta.

Consult our Directory pages for the location of firms mentioned.

WEIHRAUCH 35 SPORTER RIFLES

Model:	35/S	35L	35EB
Caliber:	177	177	177 or 22
Barrel:	19½″	19½″	19½″
Length:	45½″	43½″	45½″
Wgt. lbs.:	7.9	8	8
Rear sight:	open	open	Open
Front sight:	All with globe and 4 interchangeable inserts.		
Power:	All spring (barrel cocking).		
Price:	$139.95 to $144.50	$149.95 to $169.95	$169.50

Features: Trigger fully adj. and removable. Manual safety. Open rear sight click adj. for w. and e. P.g. high comb stock with beavertail fore-end, walnut finish, except 35E has checkered walnut with standard cheekpiece. Model 35L has Bavarian cheekpiece stock. Model 35EB available from Beeman's only. Air Rifle Hdqtrs., Beeman's, importers. Also available from Fanta.

WISCHO 70 SPORTING RIFLE

Caliber: 177 or 22, single shot.
Barrel: 16¼″, rifled.
Length: 41″. **Weight:** 6¼ lbs.
Power: Spring (barrel cocking).
Features: High velocity (750 fps in 177) and accuracy combined with rapid loading, can be reloaded in 5 seconds. Stock is walnut finished with checkered p.g. and buttplate. Open rear, bead front sights; receiver grooved for scope mounting. Trigger is adjustable. Air Rifle Headquarters, Beeman's, importers.
Price: .... $129.98 to $194.50

YEWHA TRIPLE B "DYNAMITE" SHOTGUN/RIFLE

Caliber: 25, single-shot.
Barrel: 23″, smoothbore.
Length: 41″ over-all. **Weight:** 6¾ lbs.
Power: Hand pumped, plunger.
Stock: Hardwood.
Sights: Post front, open rear.
Features: Use as rifle to fire lead balls or pellets (up to 950 fps. MV) or as unusually powerfull air shotgun with refillable plastic cartridges containing from 4 buckshot to 100 #9 birdshot. Patterns about 12″ at 50 feet with #8 shot. Imported by Beeman's.
Price: With accessory kit $99.95

Chokes & Brakes

Choke-Matic

Triple-S Development makes this choke in two models for 12 or 16 gauge. The first range goes from Cyl. to Imp. Cyl., the other from Mod. to Full. It is set for the more open pattern for the first shot, and when the gun is fired, the choke automatically advances to the next, or tighter position for the second, longer shot. Or, it can be locked into either position. Price is $34.95 with standard adaptor. "Screw-On" adaptor to fit Winchoke, Lyman Choke, Cutts or Poly-Choke is $4.95. Alternate inner choke sleeve, $6.95, gives a full range of settings. Factory installation is $8.50 for single barrel guns, $12.50 for ribbed barrels. Or, installation can be made by a gunsmith.

Contra-Jet Muzzle Brake

The steel tube on body of the C-J device has 48 intersecting slots that dissipate energy via the mutual interference of the emerging gases. Recoil energy is reduced nearly 38% (in cal. 308), accuracy is enhanced through lessened muzzle jump and flinching, yet no increase in muzzle blast occurs. Readily fitted by a competent gunsmith, the 3″ long, 3½ oz. Contra-Jet is available in 25, 28, 30, 35, 37 and 45 calibers. Cost is from $32.50 to $40.00. Installation is not included.

Cutts Compensator

The Cutts Compensator is one of the oldest variable choke devices available. Manufactured by Lyman Gunsight Corporation, it is available with either a steel or aluminum body. A series of vents allows gas to escape upward and downward, reducing recoil without directing muzzle blast toward nearby shooters. For the 12-ga. Comp body, six fixed-choke tubes are available: the Spreader—popular with Skeet shooters; Improved Cylinder; Modified; Full; Superfull, and Magnum Full. Full, Modified and Spreader tubes are available for 12, or 20, and an Adjustable Tube, giving Full through Improved Cylinder chokes, is offered in 12, or 20 gauges. Barrel adaptors in various internal diameters are available at $5.00 to permit exact fitting of Cutts Expansion Chambers. Cutts Compensator, complete with wrench and any single tube $37.00. All single choke tubes $10.00 each; adjustable tubes $25.00. No factory installation is available and stock is limited on gauges.

Dahl Muzzle Blast Controller

Only 1⅛″ long by ¾″ in diameter, this device is claimed to reduce recoil up to 30%. An outer sleeve, threaded onto the gun muzzle, is threaded on the inside to accept a machined plug which is bored through for bullet passage. Gas behind the bullet is bled off through slots in the plug, swirled through a number of tiny passages while contained by the sleeve, and then vented upward, this final action offsetting muzzle jump without discomfort to the shooter or bystanders. Price is $40.00, installed.

Emsco Choke

E. M. Schacht of Waseca, Minn., offers the Emsco, a small diameter choke which features a precision curve rather than a taper behind the 1½″ choking area. 9 settings are available in this 5 oz. attachment. Its removable recoil sleeve can be furnished in dural if desired. Choice of three sight heights. For 12, 16 or 20 gauge. Price installed, $22.95. Not installed, $17.50.

Vari-Choke

Herter's, Inc., supplies the Vari-Choke, which features a ball-bearing micro-click adjustment of the pattern sleeve, rather than the spring system used by others. This model has 8 choke settings, from Full to Improved Cylinder. With Recoil Eliminator, price is $18.95 installed; without Eliminator, $15.75.

Jet-Away Choke

Arms Ingenuity Corp., makers of the Jet-Away, say that this device controls patterns through partial venting of the powder gases which normally enlarge patterns. The Jet-Away has a series of three slots in the top of the tube and a sliding control sleeve. When the sleeve is in its rearward position, all slots are uncovered, the maximum of gas is vented and patterns are densest. To obtain more open patterns, the sleeve is moved to cover one or more slots. In 12, 16 or 20 gauge only, the Jet-Away is made of aluminum, weighs 3 ozs. $35.00 installed.

Lyman CHOKE

The Lyman CHOKE is similar to the Cutts Comp in that it comes with fixed-choke tubes or an adjustable tube, with or without recoil chamber. The adjustable tube version sells for $32.00 with recoil chamber, $27.00 without, in 12 or 20 gauge. Lyman also offers a Single-Choke Adaptor at $5.00. This device may be used with or without a recoil-reduction chamber; cost of the latter is $5.00 extra. Available in 12 or 20 gauge only, no factory installation offered.

Mag-Na-Port

EDM is the process to "install" this muzzle venting process on any firearm except those having shrouded barrels. EDM is a metal-erosion technique using carbon electrodes that control the area to be processed. The Mag-Na-Port venting process utilizes small trapezoidal openings that go into and through the barrel that direct powder gases upward and outward to reduce recoil.

The resultant opening made by the EDM process is smoothly and cleanly made, with no burring in or out. No effect is had on bluing or nickeling outside the Mag-Na-Port area so no refinishing is needed. Cost for the Mag-Na-Port treatment is $36.50 for handguns, $45.00 for rifles, plus transportation both ways, and $1.50 for handling.

Single barrel shotguns can be ported with four ports on both sides of the barrel for $45.00. Over-under shotguns are ported on both barrels, cost is $85.00.

Pendleton Dekicker

This Dekicker is unusual in that it is not a separate tube added onto a rifle muzzle but is machined into the barrel itself. Obviously, it cannot be installed by the customer. It must be sent to J. F. Mutter's Pendleton Gunshop, where a section of the bore a short distance behind the muzzle is relieved into an expansion chamber. Exit holes drilled at precise locations vent gas to lower apparent kick. Because metal is removed instead of being added, there is a small decrease in gun weight. Installation, including barrel polishing, is $50.00 for all calibers.

Poly-Choke

The Poly-Choke Co. manufacturers of the original adjustable shotgun choke now offers two models, the Deluxe Ventilated and the Deluxe Standard. Each provides 9 choke settings including Xtra-Full and Slug. The Ventilated model which will reduce approximately 20% of a shotguns recoil, is priced at $34.95. The Standard model is $32.95.

The Poly-Choke Co. is in its 48th year. Millions of Poly-Chokes are in use throughout the world. The Company also manufactures Ventilated Ribs for shotguns and handguns.

Micrometer Receiver Sights
Receiver Sights

LYMAN No. 57
¼-min. clicks. Target or Stayset knobs. Quick release slide, adjustable zero scales. Made for almost all modern rifles. Price **$24.00**

LYMAN No. 66
Fits close to the rear of flat-sided receivers, furnished with target or Stayset knobs. Quick release slide, ¼-min. adj. For most lever or slide action or flat-sided automatic rifles. Price **$24.00**

REDFIELD "PALMA" TARGET SIGHT
Windage and elevation adjustments are ¼-MOA and can be adjusted for "hard" or "soft" feel. Repeatability error limited to .001" per click. Windage latitude 36 MOA, elevation 60 MOA. Mounting arm has three positions, providing ample positioning latitude for other sighting aids such as variable diopter correction, adjustable filters. An insert in the sighting disc block accepts either the standard American sighting disc thread or the European 9.5mm × 1 metric thread. Elevation staff and the sighting disc block have dovetail construction for precise travel. Price **$131.00**

Redfield "Palma" Target Sight

WILLIAMS FP
Internal click adjustments. Positive locks. For virtually all rifles, plus Win., Rem. and Ithaca shotguns. Price **$19.90**
Extra shotgun aperture **$2.95**
With Twilight Aperture **$20.50**
With Target Knobs **$23.65**
With Target Knobs & Twilight Aperture **$24.25**
With Square Notched Blade **$20.90**
With Target Knobs & Square Notched Blade **$24.65**

B-SQUARE SMLE (LEE-ENFIELD)
For No. 4 and Jungle carbine. No drilling or tapping required. ³/₃₂" disc furnished. Price **$5.95**

BUEHLER
"Little Blue Peep" auxiliary rear sight used with Buehler scope mounts. Price **$3.35**
Mark IV front sight for above ....**.95**

FREELAND TUBE SIGHT
Uses Unertl 1" micrometer mounts. For 22-cal. target rifles, inc. 52 Win., 37, 40X Rem. and BSA Martini. Price **$80.00**

LYMAN No. 53
Shotgun receiver sight, mounts compactly near rear of receiver. For most Win., Rem., Sav., Marlin, Mossberg, J. C. Higgins and Ithaca shotguns. Limited quantities and selection. Price **$8.00**

WILLIAMS 5-D SIGHT
Low cost sight for shotguns, 22's and the more popular big game rifles. Adjustment for w. and e. Fits most guns without drilling or tapping. Also for Br. SMLE. Price **$11.30**
With Twilight Aperture **$11.90**
Extra Shotgun Aperture **$2.95**

WILLIAMS GUIDE
Receiver sight for .30 M1 Car., M1903A3 Springfield, Savage 24's, Savage-Anschutz rifles and Wby. XXII. Utilizes military dovetail; no drilling. Double-dovetail W. adj., sliding dovetail adj. for E. Price **$10.00**
With Twilight Aperture **$11.35**
With Open Sight Blade **$9.90**

Sporting Leaf and Tang Sights

BURRIS FIXED LEAF
Has windage and elevation adjustments; opposing screws for windage, sliding notch plate for elevation. Heights are .550" or .450" **$5.95**

BURRIS FOLDING LEAF
Two-way leaf rear sight with dovetail. Hefty spring holds sight in upright position. 2 heights—.450" to .575" (Model FLH), .350" to .475" (Model FLL). Price **$5.50**

BURRIS LEAF BASE
Screw-attaches with two screws into barrel. From bottom of dovetail to top of barrel measures .080". Use where there is no dovetail in barrel. Model FLBA has .562" hole span, FLBB has .625" span. Price **$3.98**

BURRIS SPORTING REAR SIGHT
Made of spring steel, supplied with multi-step elevator for coarse adjustments and notch plate with lock screw for finer adjustments. Price ..**$6.50**

HOPKINS & ALLEN NUMRICH MUSKET SIGHT
Three-way rear leaf sight designed for 58 cal. muzzle loading military rifles. Fixed V-notch for 50-yard range, flip-up aperture for 100 yards and V-notch for 200 yards. Particularly suited to Springfield and Zouave rifles. Price **$4.95**

LYMAN No. 16
Middle sight for barrel dovetail slot mounting. Folds flat when scope or peep sight is used. Sight notch plate adjustable for e. White triangle for quick aiming. 3 heights; A—.400" to .500", B—.345" to .445", C—.500" to .600". Price **$6.00**

MARBLE FALSE BASE
New screw-on base for most rifles replaces factory base. ⅜" dovetail slot permits installation of any Marble rear sight. Can be had in sweat-on models also. Price **$2.80**

MARBLE FOLDING LEAF
Flat-top or semi-buckhorn style. Folds down when scope or peep sights are used. Reversible plate gives choice of "U" or "V" notch. Adjustable for elevation. Price **$6.00**
Also available with both w. and e. adjustment **$7.00**

MARBLE SPORTING REAR
With white enamel diamond, gives choice of two "U" and two "V" notches of different sizes. Adjustment in height by means of double step elevator and sliding notch piece. For all rifles; screw or dovetail installation. Price **$6.20—$7.00**

MARBLE SPORTING REAR
Single step elevator. "U" notch with white triangle aiming aid. Lower priced version of double step model. Price **$3.00**

NUMRICH KENTUCKY STYLE SIGHT
Standard dovetail, traditional notched rear sight. ¼" high. For Kentucky and Hawken type rifles. Price **$2.75**

NUMRICH LONG RANGE REAR TARGET SIGHT
Adjustable for w. and e. with 3-size aperture target sight disc. Particularly suited for H&A Underhammer rifles. Price **$6.95**

WILLIAMS DOVETAIL OPEN SIGHT
Open rear sight with w. and e. adjustment. Furnished with "U" notch or choice of blades. Slips into dovetail and locks with gib lock. Heights from .281" to .531". Price with blade **$6.20**
Less Blade **$4.10**
Extra Blades **$2.10**

WILLIAMS GUIDE OPEN SIGHT
Open rear sight with w. and e. adjustment. Bases to fit most military and commercial barrels. Choice of square "U" or "V" notch blade, ³/₁₆", ¼", ⁵/₁₆", or ⅜" high. **$7.50**
Extra blades, each **$2.10**
Price, less blade **$5.40**

FREELAND SUPERIOR
Furnished with six 1" plastic apertures. Available in 4½"-6½" lengths. Made for any target rifle. Price with base **$27.00**
Price with 6 metal insert apertures **$29.50**
Price, front base **$5.00**

Globe Target Front Sights

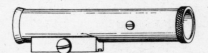

Redfield International Smallbore Front

FREELAND TWIN SET
Two Freeland Superior or Junior Globe Front Sights, long or short, allow switching from 50 yd. to 100 yd. ranges and back again without changing rear sight adjustment. Sight adjustment compensation is built into the set; just interchange and you're "on" at either range. Set includes 6 plastic apertures. Twin set (long or short) **$42.50**
Price with 6 metal apertures **$46.00**

FREELAND MILITARY
Short model for use with high-powered rifles where sight must not extend beyond muzzle. Screw-on base; six plastic apertures. Price **$27.00**
Price with 6 metal apertures **$29.50**
Price, front base **$5.00**

LYMAN No. 17A

7 interchangeable inserts which include 4 apertures, one transparent amber and two posts .50" and .100" in width. Price **$12.00**

REDFIELD Nos. 63 and 64

For rifles specially stocked for scopes where metallic sights must be same height as scopes. Instantly detachable to permit use of scope. Two styles and heights of bases. Interchangeable inserts. No. 64 is ¼" higher. With base, Price **$12.20**

REDFIELD No. 65

1" long, ⅝" diameter. Standard dovetail base with 7 aperture or post inserts which are not reversible. For any rifle having standard barrel slot. ¹³/₃₂" height from bottom of base to center of aperture. No. 65NB same as above with narrow base for Win. 64 N.R.A., 70, and Savage 40, 45, and 99 with ramp front sight base. Price **$9.20**

REDFIELD No. 66

Replaces entire removable front sight stud, locked in place by screw in front of barrel band. ¾" from bottom of base to center of aperture. For Spgfld. 1903. Price **$9.20**

REDFIELD No. 68

For Win. 52, heavy barrel, Sav. 19 and 33, and other rifles requiring high front sight. ¹⁷/₃₂" from bottom of base to center of aperture. Standard dovetail size only. Price **$9.20**

REDFIELD OLYMPIC FRONT

Detachable. 10 inserts—5 steel, sizes .090", .110", .120", .140", .150"; one post insert, size .100"; four celluloid, sizes .090", .110", .120", .140". Celluloid inserts in clear, green, or amber, with or without cross hairs. For practically all rifles and with any type rear sight. Fits all standard Redfield, Lyman, or Fecker scope blocks. With base, Price **$18.80**

REDFIELD INTERNATIONAL SMALLBORE FRONT

Similar to Olympic. Drop-in insertion of eared inserts. Outer sleeve prevents light leakage. Comes complete with 6 clear inserts and 6 skeleton inserts **$27.00**

REDFIELD INTERNATIONAL MILITARY BIG BORE

Same as International Match except tube only 2¼" long. For 30 cal. use. Price **$27.00**

Ramp Sights

BURRIS

Top ramps, screw- and sweat-on ramps with ⅜" dovetail. Accepts .250" width (N) front sight. 8 heights available from .200" to .500". Price **$5.95**
Hoods for above ramps **$1.20**

BURRIS BAND RAMPS

Tapered to slip over the barrel and be driven on until snug. Set screw locks ramp in place. 3 heights available, 3 barrel diameters. Price **$10.95**
Hoods for above ramps **$1.20**

LYMAN SCREW-ON RAMP AND SIGHT

Used with 8-40 screws but may also be brazed on. Heights from .10" to .350". Price with sight . . . . **$12.00** Price: Ramp without sight **$7.00**

Lyman Screw-On ramps.

MARBLE CONTOUR RAMP

For late model Rem. 725, 740, 760, 742. ⁹/₁₆" between mounting screws. Price **$6.80**

MARBLE RAMPS

Available in either screw-on or sweat-on style. 5 heights; ³/₁₆", ⁵/₁₆", ⅜", ⁷/₁₆", ⁹/₁₆". Standard ⅜" dovetail slot. Price **$6.30**
Hoods for above ramps **$1.50**

WILLIAMS SHORTY RAMP

Companion to "Streamlined" ramp, about ½" shorter. Screw-on or sweat-on. It is furnished in ⅛", ³/₁₆", ⁹/₃₂", and ⅜" heights without hood only. Price **$5.35**

WILLIAMS STREAMLINED RAMP

Hooded style in screw-on or sweat-on models. Furnished in ⁹/₁₆", ⁷/₁₆", ⅜", ⁵/₁₆", ³/₁₆" heights. Price with hood **$8.40**
Price without hood **$7.00**

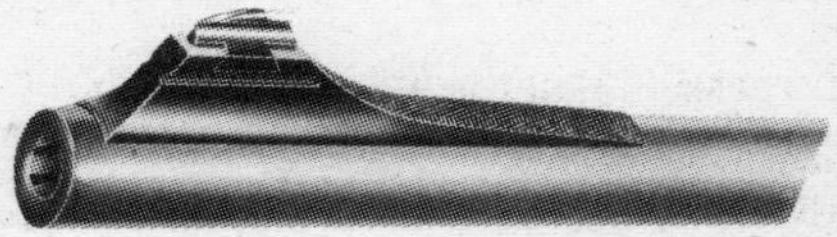

Williams Streamlined Ramp

WILLIAMS SHOTGUN RAMP

Designed to elevate the front bead for slug shooting or for guns that shoot high. Diameters to fit most 12, 16, 20 ga. guns. Fastens by screw-clamp, no drilling required. Price, with Williams gold bead **$5.10**
Price, without bead **$3.75**
Price, with Guide Bead **$6.00**

Front Sights

BURRIS FRONT SIGHTS

Two styles: Patridge, gold bead. Widths are .250", .340", .500" and Mauser .310". . . . . from **$3.50** to **$3.95**

Burris Patridge.

Burris Ivory Bead.

LYMAN BLADE & DOVETAIL SIGHTS

Made with gold or ivory beads ¹/₁₆" to ³/₃₂" wide and in varying heights for most military and commercial rifles. Price **$5.00**

Lyman hunting front sights.

MARBLE STANDARD

Ivory, red, or gold bead. For all American made rifles. ¹/₁₆" wide bead with semi-flat face which does not reflect light. Specify type of rifle when ordering. Price **$4.90**

MARBLE-SHEARD "GOLD"

Shows up well even in darkest timber. Shows same color on different colored objects; sturdily built. Medium bead. Various models for different makes of rifles so specify type of rifle when ordering. Also made for 30 or 9 mm Lugers, Colt's Single Action Army, Bisley Model, with plain sight or any other Colt's or S & W revolver with stationary front sight. Price **$4.90**

MARBLE CONTOURED

Same contour and shape as Marble-Sheard but uses standard ¹/₁₆" or ³/₃₂" bead, ivory, red or gold. Specify rifle type **$4.50**

NUMRICH MUSKET FRONT SIGHT

Traditional 58 cal. front sight. Can be used for 58 caliber Zouave replacement barrels., or '41 Mississippi barrel. Price **$2.95**
Springfield front sights **$2.25**

NUMRICH SILVER BLADE FRONT SIGHT
Same sight as used on H&A "Minuteman" rifle and Rolling Block "Buffalo Rifle." Suited for most ML and black powder cartridge guns. Price . . **$2.75**

WILLIAMS GUIDE BEAD SIGHT
Fits all shotguns. ⅛" ivory, red or gold bead. Screws into existing sight hole. Various thread sizes and shank lengths **$2.25**
Cultured Pearl Guide Bead **$5.00**

Handgun Sights

BO-MAR DE LUXE
Gives ⅜" w. and e. adjustment at 50 yards on Colt Gov't 45, sight radius under 7". For GM and Commander models only. Uses existing dovetail slot. Has shield-type rear blade. Price **$32.00**

Bo-Mar Deluxe sight.

BO-MAR LOW PROFILE RIB
Streamlined rib with front and rear sights; 7⅛" sight radius. Brings sight line closer to the bore than standard or extended sight and ramp. Weighs 4 oz. Made for Ruger Mark I Bull Barrel, Colt Gov't 45, Super 38, and Gold Cup 45 and 38. Price . . . . **$42.00** to **$48.00**
With extended sight and ramp, 8⅛" radius, 5¾ oz. Price **$48.00**
Rib & tuner—inserted in Low Profile Rib—accuracy tuner. Adjustable for barrel positioning. Price **$50.00**

BO-MAR FRONT SIGHTS
⅛" tapered post, made for Colt, Hi-Standard, Ruger and S&W autos. Price **$3.00**

BO-MAR COMBAT RIB
For S&W Model 19 revolver with 4" barrel. Sight radius 5¾"; weight 5½ oz. Price **$42.00**

BO-MAR FAST DRAW RIB
Streamlined full length rib with integral Bo-Mar micrometer sight and serrated fast draw sight. For Browning 9mm, S&W 39, Colt Commander 45, Super Auto and 9mm. Price **$42.00**

BO-MAR WINGED RIB
For S&W 4" and 6" length barrels—K-38 M10, HB 14 and 19. Weight for the 6" model is about 7¼ ozs. Price **$49.00**

BO-MAR COVER-UP RIB
Adj. rear sight, winged front guards. Fits right over revolver's original front sight. For S&W 4" M-10HB, M-13, M-58, M-64 & 65. Ruger 4" models SDA-34, SDA-84, SS-34, SS-84, GF-34, GF-84. Price **$49.00**

F.D.L. WONDERSIGHT
Micrometer rear sight for Colt and S&W revolvers. 1-min. clicks for windage. Sideplate screw controls elevation **$9.95**

MICRO
Click adjustable w. and e. rear with plain or undercut front sight in ¹⁄₁₀", ⅛", or ⁵⁄₃₂" widths. Standard model available for 45, Super 38 or Commander autos. Low model for above pistols plus Colt Service Ace. Also for Ruger with 4¾" or 6" barrel. Price for sets **$22.00**
Price with ramp front sight **$26.00**
Adjustable rear sight only **$18.00**
Front ramp only, with blade **$9.00**

MICRO
Fixed rear sight with blade front for 45 Govt. (⅛" or ¹⁄₁₀") . . **$12.50**

MICRO
All-steel replacement for Ruger single-action and double-action revolvers. Two styles: MR-44 for square front end of sight leaf; MR-35 for round front end **$14.00**

MMC COMBAT DESIGN
Available specifically for Colt M1911 and descendants, High Standard autos, Ruger standard autos. Adaptable to other pistols. Some gunsmithing required. Not necessary to replace front sight.
Price, less leaf **$16.10**
Plain leaf **$4.70**
White outline leaf **$7.00**
Extra for satin nickel finish (base only) **$5.60**

MMC NO. 5
Fully adjustable and replaces the factory sight for S&W M39 and M59. Supplied assembled, no gunsmithing required. ⅛" wide notch, white outline or plain. Not necessary to replace front sight.
Complete, plain **$41.70**
White outline **$44.00**
Extra for satin nickel finish (base only) **$5.60**

Shotgun Sights

FOR DOUBLE BARREL SHOTGUNS (PRESS FIT)
Marble 214—Ivory front bead, ¹¹⁄₆₄" . . . **$2.00;** 215—same with .080" rear bead and reamers . . . **$6.00.** Marble 220—Bi-color (gold and ivory) front bead, ¹¹⁄₆₄" and .080 rear bead, with reamers . . . **$7.00; Marble 221**—front bead only . . . **$3.00.** Marble 223—Ivory rear .080 . . . **$1.80. Marble 224**—Front sight reamer for 214-221 beads . . . **$1.50; Marble 226**—Rear sight reamer for 223 . . . . **$1.50**

FOR SINGLE OR DB SHOTGUNS (SCREW-ON FIT)
Marble 217—Ivory front bead ¹¹⁄₆₄" . . . **$2.20; Marble 216$4.40 Marble 218**—Bi-color front, ¹¹⁄₆₄" . . . **$3.20; Marble 219** . . . **$5.40 Marble 223T**—Ivory rear .080 . . . . **$3.00**
Marble Bradley type sights 223BT—⅛", ⁵⁄₆₄" and ¹¹⁄₆₄" long. Gold, Ivory or Red bead **$2.50**

SLUG SITE
A combination V-notch rear and bead front sight made of adhesive-backed formed metal approx. 7" over-all. May be mounted, removed and re-mounted as necessary, using new adhesive from the pack supplied **$7.95**

Sight Attachments

FREELAND LENS ADAPTER
Fits 1⅛" O.D. prescription ground lens to all standard tube and receiver sights for shooting without glasses. Price without lens **$35.50**
Price: Clear lens ground to prescription **$19.50**
Price: Yellow or green prescription lens **$19.50**

MERIT ADAPTER FOR GLOBE FRONT SIGHTS
An Iris Shutter Disc with a special adapter for mounting in Lyman or Redfield globe front sights. Price **$27.00**

MERIT IRIS SHUTTER DISC
Eleven clicks gives 12 different apertures. No. 3 and Master, primarily target types, .022" to .125"; No. 4, ½" dia. hunting type, .025" to .155". Available for all popular sights. The Master Disc, with flexible rubber light shield, is particularly adapted to extension, scope height, and tang sights. All Merit Deluxe models have internal click springs; are hand fitted to minimum tolerance. Price . . . . **$24.00—$30.00**
Std. Master . . . . **$30.00** Master Deluxe **$37.00**

MERIT LENS DISC
Similar to Merit Iris Shutter (Model 3 or Master) but incorporates provision for mounting prescription lens integrally. Lens may be obtained locally, or prescription sent to Merit. Sight disc is ⁷⁄₁₆" wide (Mod. 3), or ¾" wide (Master). Lens, ground to prescription,**$17.00** Standard tints, **$21.00.** Model 3 Deluxe. Price **$37.00**
Master Deluxe **$43.75**

REDFIELD SURE-X SIGHTING DISC
Eight hole selective aperture. Fits any Redfield target sight. Each click changes aperture .004". Price **$11.00**

REDFIELD SIGHTING DISCS
Fit all Redfield receiver sights. .046" to .093" aperture. ⅜", ½" and ⅞" O.D. Price, each **$2.40**

WILLIAMS APERTURES
Standard thread, fits most sights. Regular series ⅜" to ½" O.D., .050" to .125" hole. "Twilight" series has white reflector ring. .093" to .125" inner hole. Price, regular series . . . **$1.55.** Twilight series **$2.15**
New wide open ⁵⁄₁₆" aperture for shotguns fits 5-D and Foolproof sights. Price **$2.95**

MERIT OPTICAL ATTACHMENT
For revolver and pistol shooters. Instantly attached by rubber suction cup to regular or shooting glasses. Any aperture .020" to .156". Price, Deluxe (swings aside) **$28.00**

HUNTING, TARGET ▪ AND VARMINT ▪ SCOPES

Maker and Model	Magn.	Field at 100 Yds. (feet)	Relative Bright-ness	Eye Relief (in.)	Length (in.)	Tube Diam. (in.)	W&E Adjust-ments	Weight (ozs.)	Other Data	Price
American Import Co.										
Dickson R200	4	20	14.4	4	10	¾	Int.	5.8	Complete with mount for 22-cal. RF rifles.	$11.50
Dickson R218	2½	32	158	3	11.7	1	Int.	9.6		41.95
Dickson R220	4	28.5	64	3	11.7	1	Int.	9.6	Standard reticle 4 post fully coated lenses.	41.95
Dickson R226	6	18.5	43.5	3	12	1	Int.	10	Anodized finish.	46.50
Dickson R228	4	41	64	3	12	1	Int.	9.6	Wide angle.	57.95
Dickson R230	4	41	100	3	12	1	Int.	10.5	Wide angle.	61.00
Dickson R240	3-9	31.6-12.3	112-13	3	13.6	1	Int.	11.5		57.95
Dickson R242	3-9	31.6-12.3	177-19	3	13.3	1	Int.	12.2		61.00
Burris										
4x Fullfield	3.8	37	49	3¼	11¼	1	Int.	11	3″ dot $10.00 extra.	99.95
2x-7x Fullfield HiLume	2.5-6.8	50-19	81-22	3¼	11⅞	1	Int.	14	1″-3″ dot $10.00 extra.	141.95
3x-9x Fullfield HiLume	3.3-8.6	40-15	72-17.6	3¼	12¾	1	Int.	15	1″-3″dot $10.00 extra.	151.95
2¾ Fullfield	2.7	53	49	3¼	10½	1	Int.	9		94.95
6x Fullfield	5.8	24	36	3¼	13	1	Int.	12		104.95
1¾-5x Fullfield HiLume	2.5-6.8	70-27	121-25	3¼	10¾	1	Int.	13		129.95
4x-12x Fullfield	4.4-11.8	28-10½	—	3-3¼	15	1	Int.	18	Dot reticle $10.00 extra. Target knobs	179.95
10x Fullfield	9.8	12½	—	3¼	15	1	Int.	15	$15.00 extra. ½-minute dot $10.00 extra.	144.95
12x Fullfield	11.8	11	—	3¼	15	1	Int.	15	LER=Long Eye Relief. Ideal for forward	150.95
2x LER	1.7	21	—	10-24	8¾	1	Int.	6.8	mounting or on handguns. Plex or crosshair	79.95
3x LER	2.7	17	—	10-20	8⅞	1	Int.	6.8	only. Target knobs ($15.00 extra) available	84.50
4x Mini	3.6	24	—	3¾	8¼	1	Int.	7.8	for 3x.	79.95
6x Mini	5.5	17	—	3¾	9	1	Int.	7.8		84.95
8x Mini	7.6	13	—	3¾	9⅞	1	Int.	8.9		89.95
Bushnel										
ScopeChief VI	4	29	96	3½	12	1	Int.	9⅓	All ScopeChief, Banner and Custom models	85.50
ScopeChief VI	3-9	35-12.6	267-30	3½-3⅓	12.6	1	Int.	14.3	come with Multi-X MX reticle, with or without	129.50
ScopeChief VI	2½-8	45-14	247-96	3.7-3.3	11.2	1	Int.	12.1	BDC feature. Automatic bullet drop com-	113.50
ScopeChief VI	1½-4½	73.7-24.5	267-30	3.5-3.5	9.6	1	Int.	9.5	pensation that eliminates hold-over.	109.50
Custom 22	4	28¼	—	2½	10⁵⁄₁₆	⅞	Int.	5¼	Mount rail. Similar 4x at $29.95.	26.95
Custom 22	3-7	33-13.6	28-5	2¼-2½	10	⅞	Int.	6½	Similar 4x at $19.95.	32.95
Banner	2½	45	96	3½	10.9	1	Int.	8	BDC feature available in all Banner models,	54.95
Banner	4	29	96	3½	12	1	Int.	10	except 2.5x.	68.95
Banner	4	37⅓	150	3	12⅓	1	Int.	12	Wide angle.	89.95
Banner	6	19½	42	3	13½	1	Int.	10½		78.95
Banner	10	12	24	3	14½	1	Int.	14.6	Parallax focus adjustment.	95.95
Banner	1½-4	63-28	294-41	3½	10½	1	Int.	10.3		86.95
Banner	1¾-4½	71-27	216-33	3	10.2	1	Int.	11½	Wide angle.	94.95
Banner 32mm	3-9	39-13	171-19	3½	11.5	1	Int.	11	With 40mm obj. $92.95.	91.95
Banner 38mm	3-9	43-14.6	241-26½	2.9	12	1	Int.	14	Wide angle.	112.95
Banner 40mm	3-9	35-12½	267-30	3½	13	1	Int.	13		102.95
Banner	4-12	29-10	150-17	3.2	13½	1	Int.	15½	Parallax focus adjustment.	112.95
Magnum Phantom	1.3	17	441	7-21	7.8	¹⁵⁄₁₆	Int.	5½	Phantoms intended for handgun use.	48.50
Magnum Phantom	2½	9	100	8-21	9.7	¹⁵⁄₁₆	Int.	6½		52.50
Davis Optical										
Spot Shot 1½″	10,12 15,20, 25,30	10-4	—	2	25	.75	Ext.	—	Focus by moving non-rotating obj. lens unit. Ext. mounts included. Recoil spring $3.50 extra.	98.50
Spot Shot 1¼″	10,12, 15,20	10-6	—	2	25	.75	Ext.	—		76.50
Hutson										
▪ Handgunner	1	9	—	25	5¼	—	Ext.	5	CH ⅞″ obj. lens. Adj. in mount $16.95	45.00
	1.7	4.5	—	25	5½	—	Ext.	5		49.50
Hy-Score										
Gold Dot 471UV	2½	42	96	3¾	11	1	Int.	7¾		39.95
Gold Dot 475UV	4	27	96	3½	12	1	Int.	9½		44.95
Gold Dot 473UV	6	19½	50	3	13¼	1	Int.	10	Alloy tubes, rubber eyebrow guards, nitro-	49.95
Gold Dot 477UV	3-9	36-12	166-19	3	11½	1	Int.	11	gen filled. CH, dual CH or post and CH.	64.95
Gold Dot 476UV	3-9	33-12	265-29	3¼	12½	1	Int.	13¼		74.95
Red Dot 489UV	4	30	96	3¾	11½	1	Int.	10½		74.95
Red Dot 487UV	3-9	39-13	241-27	3½	12¼	1	Int.	12¼		109.95
Jana										
Economy 4x	4	28	—	3.5	11¾	1	Int.	9.5		27.50
Standard 4x	4	28	—	3.5	11¾	1	Int.	9.5		32.00
Deluxe 4x	4	26	—	3.5	13	1	Int.	12		53.00
Standard 3x9	3-9	35-14	—	3.2	12	1	Int.	11.5	All models equipped with DX reticle except	34.50
Deluxe 3x9	3-9	35-14	—	3.5	12½	1	Int.	13	for economy 4X & 4X .22 Scopes. Parker-	57.75
.22 Economy 4x	4	19	—	2.75	11½	¾	Int.	7	Hale models are wide-angle style.	10.00
.22 Deluxe 4x	4	23	—	2.3	12	⅞	Int.	8		17.25
.22 Deluxe 3x7	3-7	28-12	—	3	12	⅞	Int.	9		30.50
Parker-Hale 4x	4	36	—	3	11⅞	1	Int.	12		66.00
Parker-Hale 3x9	3-9	43.5-16.5	—	3.6	12½	1	Int.	12.5		96.00
Jason										
860	4	29	64	3	11.8	1	Int.	9.2		39.00
861	3-9	35-13	112-12	3	12.7	1	Int.	10.9		57.00
862	4	19	14	2	11	¾	Int.	5.5		12.50
864	6	19	28	3	11.8	1	Int.	12.2	Constantly centered reticles, ballbearing	41.00
865	3-9	35-13	177-19	3	13	1	Int.	12.2	click stops, nitrogen filled tubes, coated	60.00
869	4	19	25	2	11.4	¾	Int.	6	lenses. 4-Post crosshair about $3.50 extra	16.00
873	4	29	100	3	12.7	1	Int.	11.1	on models 860, 861, 864, 865, 873, 875,	46.00
875	3-9	35-13	177-19	3	13	1	Int.	12.2	877, 878.	61.00
877	4	37	100	3	11.6	1	Int.	11.6		56.00
878	3-9	42.5-13.6	112-12	2.7	12.7	1	Int.	12.7		66.00

SCOPES & MOUNTS

Maker and Model	Magn.	Field at 100 Yds. (feet)	Relative Bright-ness	Eye Relief (in.)	Length (in.)	Tube Diam. (in.)	W&E Adjust-ments	Weight (ozs.)	Other Data	Price
Kassnar										
4x15	4	13	31	3¼	11¼	¾	Int.	5½		11.95
4x20	4	25½	25	3½	11¼	¾, ⅞	Int.	5½	Most popular reticles available. Coated lenses, aluminum tubes, high gloss black anodized finish, waterproof, positive click stops. New binocular-style focus adj. Write Kassnar Imports for full line of scopes.	13.95
3-7x20	3-7	24½-11½	44-8	3	11	¾, ⅞	Int.	7½		28.95
2½x32	2½	32	164	3¼	11½	1	Int.	9½		39.95
4x32	4	29	64	3¼	11¼	1	Int.	9½		39.95
6x32	6	18	28	3½	12¾	1	Int.	11		45.00
3-9x32	3-9	36-13	112-12	3¼	12½	1	Int.	12		64.95
3-9x40	3-9	36-13	177-20	3¼	12½	1	Int.	12		74.95
Leupold										
M82x EER	1.8	22	—	10-24	8.1	1	Int.	6.8	Extended Eye Relief of from 10″ to 24″. For top ejecting arms, muzzleloaders. 50-ft. Focus Adapter for indoor target ranges, $29.50.	85.50
M8-4x EER	3.5	7.7	—	10-24	8.4	1	Int.	7.6		96.50
2.5 Compact	2.3	42	—	4.3	8.5	1	Int.	7.4		96.50
4x Compact	3.6	26.5	—	4.1	10.3	1	Int.	8.5	Constantly centered reticles; in addition to the crosshair reticle, the post, tapered (CPC), post and duplex, and duplex reticles are optional at no extra cost. Dot reticle $14.00 extra. 2x suitable for handgun and Win. 94.	96.50
M8	3	43	45	3.85	10.13	1	Int.	8.25		109.50
M8	4	30	50	3.85	11.50	1	Int.	9.00		109.50
M8	6	18	—	3.85	11.7	1	Int.	10.3		120.50
M8 Adj. Obj.	8	14	32	3.60	12.60	1	Int.	12.75		159.50
M8 Adj. Obj.	10	10	16	3½	13	1	Int.	13¾		159.50
M8 Adj. Obj.	12	9	11	3½	14½	1	Int.	14		165.50
M8 Adj. Obj.	16	6½	—	3½	15.2	1	Int.	16		235.50
M8-20X	20	5.4	—	3½	15¼	1	Int.	16.0		235.50
M8 Adj. Obj.	24	4½	—	3½	15¼	1	Int.	15½		235.50
Vari-X II	1-4	70-28	—	4¼-3½	9½	1	Int.	9½	Mounts solidly on action. ¼ MOA clicks. Crosshair or dot.	143.50
Vari-X II	2-7	42-18	144-17	3.7-4.12	11.00	1	Int.	10.75		157.50
Vari-X II	3-9	30.5-13	208-23	3.5-4.12	12.60	1	Int.	13.75		169.50
Vari-X III	1½-5	64-23	—	4½-3½	9¾	1	Int.	9¾	With adj. obj.—$189.50	169.50
Vari-X III	2½-8	36-12½	—	4¼-3½	11¾	1	Int.	11½		191.50
Vari-X III	3½-10	29½-10½	—	4-3½	12¾	1	Int.	12¾		219.50
Lyman										
All-American	2½	43	—	3¼	10½	1	Int.	8¾	2, 3, or 4 minute dot reticle $12.50 extra. Choice of standard CH, tapered post, or tapered post and CH reticles. All-weather reticle caps. All Lyman scopes have new Perma-Center reticle which remains in optical center regardless of changes in W. & E.	99.95
All-American	3	35	—	3¼	11	1	Int.	9		99.95
All-American	4	30	—	3¼	12	1	Int.	10		114.95
All-American	6	20	—	3¼	13⅞	1	Int.	12¼		119.95
■ All-American	8	14	—	3¼	14⅜	1	Int.	13		159.95
■ All-American	10	12	—	3¼	15½	1	Int.	13½	Adj. for parallax.	159.95
All-American	1¾-5	47-18	—	3	12¼	1	Int.	12¼		119.95
■ L.W.B.R.	20	5.5	—	2¼	17⅛	1	Int.	15¼	⅛ or ¼ MOA clicks.	259.95
■ All-American	3-9	39-13	—	3¾-3¼	10½	1	Int.	14	Non-rotating objective lens focusing. ¼ MOA click adjustments. Sunshade, $4.95 extra. Wood case, $29.95 extra. 5 different dot reticles, $12.50 extra.	139.95
2x-7x Var.	1.9-6.8	49-19	—	3¼	11⅝	1	Int.	10½		129.95
25x LWBR	25	4.8	—	3	17	1	Int.	19		269.95
Metallic Silhouette 6x-SL	6.2	20	—	3¼	13⅞	1	Int.	14¼	Standard crosswire, 4 Center-Range reticles.	159.95
Metallic Silhouette 8x-SL	8.1	14	—	3¼	14⅝	1	Int.	15¼	Std. Fine, Extra Fine, 1 Min. Dot, ½-Min. Dot, ¼-Min. Dot reticles. External adjustment knobs; hand lapped zero repeat w. and e. systems. Choice of 9 reticles.	169.95
Metallic Silhouette 10x-SL	10	12	—	3¼	15⅜	1	Int.	15¼		179.95
Nickel										
Supralyt	2½	42	64	3½	11½	1.024	Int.	7½		170.00
Supralyt	4	33	25	3½	11½	1.024	Int.	8		165.00
Supra	4	32	81	3½	11¼	1.024	Int.	9		180.00
Supra	6	21	36	3½	12½	1.024	Int.	9	¼ MOA click adjustments. Steel or alloy tubes. Weatherproof reticle caps. Crosshair, post and c.h. or post and crosshair reticles are standard. New "Diflex" coated lenses. Write Continental Arms Co. for details on other models.	185.00
■ Supra Varminter	6	24	49	3¼-5	12¼	1.024	Int.	11½		195.00
Supra Vari-Power	1-4	66.5-27.3	153-28	3½	10½	1.024	Int.	13.1		225.00
Supra Vari-Power	1½-6	60-21.6	176-36	3½	12	1.181	Int.	14.8		290.00
Supra Vari-Power	2½-7	38-21	125-36	3½	11¾	1.024	Int.	11		265.00
Supra Vari-Power	2½-9	42-15.6	—	3½	14½	1.181	Int.	17.3		300.00
Supra Vari-Power	3-10	30-12	100-18.5	3½	12½	1.024	Int.	12½		280.00
Precise										
20112	4-12	28-9	100-10.8	3.1-2.9	14.2	1	Int.	16	Parallax correction adj. from 25 yds. to infinity.	100.00
20241	4	23	13¾	3¾	10¾	¾	Int.	6.0	22 Scope with crosshair.	11.95
20244	4	29	64	3½	12	1	Int.	9.1	Luma-Glo crosshair.	39.95
20245	4	29	64	3½	12	1	Int.	9.1	Luma-Glo Post.	42.00
20251	3-9	35¾-12¾	112¼-12½	3	12¾	1	Int.	13.8	Luma-Glo crosshair.	58.00
20462	4	29	64	3½	12	1	Int.	9.1	Waterproof, Duplex Luma-Glo crosshair, Wideview. Amber-Glo Filter, Rubber Ring of Safety included.	47.00
20463	3-9	35¾-12¾	176¾-19½	3	12¾	1	Int.	15.2		70.00
20467	3-9	35¾-12¾	112½-12½	3	12¾	1	Int.	13.8		68.00
20562	4	37.3	64	3¼	11¾	1	Int.	10.5	Waterproof, Duplex Luma-Glo crosshair, Wideview. Amber-Glo Filter, Rubber Ring of Safety included.	58.00
20563	3-9	42½-13½	176¾-19½	3-2½	12¾	1	Int.	14.1		80.00
20567	3-9	42½-13½	112½-12½	3-2½	12¾	1	Int.	13.4		78.00
Redfield										
Traditional 4x¾″	4	24½	27	3½	9⅜	.75	Int.	—		47.30
Traditional 2½x	2½	43	64	3½	10¼	1	Int.	8½		75.00
Traditional 4x	4	28½	56	3½	11⅜	1	Int.	9¾		87.50
Traditional 6x	6	19	—	3½	12½	1	Int.	11½		100.00
Traditional 8x	8	15	—	3½	14⅛	1	Int.	13		144.70
Traditional 10x	10	11½	18	3½	14⅛	1	Int.	13		153.60
Traditional 3x-9xMS	3.3-8.4	10.6-4.2	—	3¾	12½	1	Int.	15½		186.50
Traditional 3x-9x Royal	3-9	34-11	—	3½-4¼	12½	1	Int.	13	Traditionals have round lenses. 4-Plex reticle is standard.	151.80
Traditional 2x-7x	2-7	42-14	207-23	3½	11¼	1	Int.	12		117.90
Traditional 3x-9x	3-9	34-11	163-18	3½	12½	1	Int.	13	Accu-Range Variable $166.10.	139.30
Traditional 6xMS	6	20.7	—	3¾	12⁷⁄₃₂	1	Int.	11½		125.00
Traditional 8xMS	8	16.6	—	3-3¾	14⅛	1	Int.	17⅕	Accu-Range reticle available on most variables at extra cost.	151.80
Traditional 10xMS	10	12.6	—	3-3¾	14⅛	1	Int.	17½		164.30
Traditional 12xMS	12.4	8.1	—	3-3¾	14⅛	1	Int.	17.5		176.80

SCOPES & MOUNTS

Hunting, Target and Varmint Scopes—Continued

Maker and Model	Magn.	Field at 100 Yds. (feet)	Relative Brightness	Eye Relief (in.)	Length (in.)	Tube Diam. (in.)	W&E Adjustments	Weight (ozs.)	Other Data	Price
Redfield (continued)										
Traditional 4x-12x	4-12	26-9	112-14	3½	13⅞	1	Int.	14		205.40
Traditional 6x-18x	6-18	18-6	50-6	3½	13¹⁵⁄₁₆	1	Int.	18		225.00
Low Profile Scopes										
Widefield 2¾xLP	2¾	55½	69	3½	10½	1	Int.	8	Dot about $12.00 extra in Widefields.	109.00
Widefield 4xLP	3.6	37½	84	3½	11½	1	Int.	10		123.20
Widefield 6x	6	24	—	3½	12¾	1	Int.	11		135.70
Widefield 1¾x-5xLP	1¾-5	70-27	136-21	3½	10¾	1	Int.	11½		136.60
Widefield 2x-7xLP	2-7	49-19	144-21	3½	11¾	1	Int.	13		163.40
Widefield 3x-9xLP	3-9	39-15	112-18	3½	12½	1	Int.	14	MS feature $16.10 extra.	180.20
3200 Target	12,16,20,24	6½, 5¼, 4, 3¾	9, 6, 3¼, 2¼	2½	23¼	1	Int.	21	Mounts solidly.	269.70
6400 Target	16,20,24	6½, 5, 4½	5¾, 3½, 3, 2½	17		1	Int.	18	Mounts on receiver. CH or dot. 20x—$259.00, 24x—$267.90	250.00
Accu-Trac	3-9	39-15	112-18	3½	12½	1	Int.	18.7		216.00
Sanders										
Bisley 2½x20	2½	42	64	3	10¾	1	Int.	8¼	Alum. alloy tubes, ¼" adj. coated lenses.	48.50
Bisley 4x33	4	28	64	3	12	1	Int.	9	Five other scopes are offered: 6x45 at	52.50
Bisley 6x40	6	19	45	3	12½	1	Int.	9½	$68.50, 8x45 at $70.50, 2½x7x at $69.50,	56.50
Bisley 8x40	8	18	25	3¼	12½	1	Int.	9½	3-9x33 at $72.50 and 3-9x40 at $78.50.	62.50
Bisley 10x40	10	12½	16	2½	12½	1	Int.	10¼	Rubber lens covers (clear plastic) are $3.50.	64.50
Bisley 5-13x40	5-13	29-10	64-9	3	14	1	Int.	14	Write to Sanders for details. Choice of reticles in CH, PCH, 3-post.	86.50
Southern Precision										
556	3-7	24.5-11.5	43.5-8.1	2.4	12	⅞	Int.	10.3		24.95
558	4	15.7	13.7	3.7	10.7	¾	Int.	6.1		8.95
564CW	4	30	64	3.7	12	1	Int.	9.1		29.95
567DW	6	23.5	44.7	3.1	12.5	1	Int.	10		37.95
576CW	3-9	35.8-12.7	112.4-13	3.1-2.9	12.8	1	Int.	13.8		45.00
579DWE	4-12	43-16	100-11.1	3.1-2.5	14.3	1	Int.	16		69.50
Swarovski										
Habicht S-D	4	30	64	3	11	26mm	Int.	13	Steel, double adj.	189.00
Habicht S-E	4	30	64	3	11	26mm	Int.	12½		179.00
Nova S-D	4	30	64	3	11	26mm	Int.	13	Steel, single adj.	225.00
Nova S-D	6	19	—	3¼	12¼	26mm	Int.	15½	Light alloy, single and double adj. 6x scopes avail. with spirit level ($29.00). Four reticles	250.00
Habicht S-D	6	19	—	3¼	12¼	26mm	Int.	15½	styles avail. All lenses double coated. Write	230.00
Habicht S-E	6	19	—	3¼	12¼	26mm	Int.	14½	the importer, Del-Sports, Inc., for details.	220.00
Swift										
Mark I 4x15	4	23	—	2	11	.75	Int.	6¾		16.00
Mark I 4x32	4	29	—	3½	12	1	Int.	9		49.50
Mark I 4x32 WA	4	37	—	3½	11¾	1	Int.	10½	All swift Mark I scopes, with the exception of	56.00
Mark I 4x40 WA	4	35½	—	3¾	12¼	1	Int.	12	the 4x15m have Quadraplex reticles and are	64.00
Mark I 3-9x32	3-9	35¾-12¾	—	3	12¾	1	Int.	13¾	fog-proof and waterproof. The 4x15 has	65.00
Mark I 3-9x40 WA	3-9	42½-13½	—	2¾	12¾	1	Int.	14	cross-hair reticle and is non-waterproof.	75.00
Mark I 6x40	6	18	—	3¾	13	1	Int.	10		58.00
Mark I 1½-4½x32	1½-4½	55-22	—	3½	12	1	Int.	13		70.00
Tasco										
611V Wide Angle	2-6	66-25	100-16	2¾	10	1	Int.	9.5	Lens covers furnished. Constantly centered reticles. Write the importer, Tasco, for data	84.95
627W	3-9	35-14	177-19	3½	12⅛	1	Int.	13	on complete line.	74.95
628V Wide Angle	3-9	43.5-15	177-19	3½	12	1	Int.	12¼	Brass tube for Hawkins, Plains, Pa.	99.95
1860 Tube Sight	4	12½	3.75	3	32½	¾	Ext.	25	½-stock, FIE, Zouave and Ky.	149.95
1903 Tube Sight	4	14	3.75	3¾	18½	¾	Ext.	17½	Brass tube. For Savage #72 and Gallagher.	99.95
United										
Golden Hawk	4	30	64	—	11⅞	—	Int.	9½		77.50
Golden Grizzly	6	18½	44	—	11⅞	1	Int.	11		105.00
Golden Falcon	4-9	29½-14	100-20	—	13½	1	Int.	12¾	Anodized tubes, nitrogen filled. Write United	111.50
Golden Plainsman	3-12	33-12½	169-11	—	13½	1	Int.	12¾	for data on complete line.	110.00
Unertl										
Falcon	2¾	40	75.5	4	11	1	Int.(1')	10	Black dural tube in hunting models. (2 oz.	77.00
Hawk	4	34	64	4	11¾	1	Int.(1')	10.5	more with steel tube.)	84.00
Condor	6	17	40	3-4	13½	1	Int.(1')	12		105.00
■ 1" Target	6,8,10	16-10	17.6-6.25	2	21½	.75	Ext.	21		111.00
■ 1¼" Target	8,10,12,14	12-6	15.2-5	2	25	.75	Ext.	25	Dural ¼ MOA click mounts. Hard coated lenses. Non-rotating objective lens focusing.	147.00
■ 1½" Target	8,10,12,14,16,18,20,24	11.5-3.2	—	2¼	25½	.75	Ext.	31		170.00
■ 2" Target	8,10,12,14,16,18,24,30,36	—	22.6-2.5	2¼	26¼	1	Ext.	44	¼ MOA dehorned mounts.	228.00
■ Varmint, 1¼"	6,8,10,12	14.1-7	28.7-1	2½	19½	.875	Ext.	26	With target mounts.	148.00
■ Ultra Varmint, 2"	8,10,12,15	12.6-7	39.7-11	2½	24	1	Ext.	34	With dehorned mount. With calibrated head.	191.00 / 214.00
■ Small Game	4, 6	25-17	19.4-8.4	2¼	18	.75	Ext.	16	Same as 1" Target but without objective lens focusing.	82.00
■ Vulture	8 / 10	11.2 / 10.9	29 / 18½	3-4	15⅝ / 16⅛	1	E or I	15½	Price with internal adj. Price with ¼ MOA click mounts.	137.00 / 171.00
■ Programer 200	8,10,12,14,16,18,20,24,30,36	11.3-4	39-1.9	—	26½	1	Ext.	45	With new Posa mounts. Range focus unit near rear of tube. Price is with Posa mounts. Magnum clamp. With	284.00
■ BV-20	20	8	4.4	4.4	17⅞	1	Ext.	21¼	standard mounts and clamp ring. $188.00.	198.00

SCOPES & MOUNTS

Maker and Model	Magn.	Field at 100 Yds. (feet)	Relative Brightness	Eye Relief (in.)	Length (in.)	Tube Diam. (in.)	W&E Adjustments	Weight (ozs.)	Other Data	Price
Universal										
UE-4	4	29	64	3½	12	1	Int.	9.1		28.95
UK-4*	3-9	36-13	112-13	3	12.8	1	Int.	13.8		43.95
UK*	3-9	36-13	112-13	3	12.8	1	Int.	13.8		42.95
UL-4	3-9	36-13	177-19	3	12.8	1	Int.	15.2	All scopes have alloy tubes, constantly centered reticles, coated lenses. Asterisk denotes quadraplex reticle is avail., otherwise standard crosshair is offered. Write to Universal Sporting Goods for details.	46.95
UE40-4	4	29	100	3½	12½	1	Int.	10		30.95
UD	4	23	25	2	12	⅞	Int.	12		21.95
UA	4	16	14	4	10.8	¾	Int.	10.8		9.95
UEW-4 Wide Angle*	4	35	64	3¼	12¼	1	Int.	12		28.95
Verano										
4-2520X	2½	45	—	3½	11½	1	Int.	8		37.80
4-432X	4	30	—	3½	11⅞	1	Int.	10	All models have Vari-X reticle.	40.30
4-3932X	3-9	40-13.5	—	3-3.6	12⅜	1	Int.	11		56.80
4-440X	4	37	—	3	12½	1	Int.	13	Models 4-440X and 4-3940X are wide angle. From Verano Corp.	54.40
4-3940X	3-9	35-12.5	—	3-3.5	13	1	Int.	13		66.70
Weatherby										
Mark XXII	4	25	50	2½-3½	11¾	⅞	Int.	9¼	Focuses in top turret.	44.50
Premier Standard	2¾	45	212	3½	11¾	1	Int.	12¼		99.50
Premier Standard	4	31	100	3½	12¾	1	Int.	12¼	Centered, non-magnifying reticles. Binocular focusing. Lumi-Plex or Open Dot, $5 extra.	109.50
Premier Standard	3-9	43½-14½	177-19	3	12	1	Int.	14¾		119.50
Premier Wide Angle	4	35¾	100	3	11¾	1	Int.	14		129.50
Premier Wide Angle	3-9	43½-14¾	177-19	3	12	1	Int.	14¾		139.50
Weaver										
K1.5	1½	56½	—	3-5¼	9⅜	1	Int.	10		52.50
K2.5	2½	40	—	3-4½	10⅜	1	Int.	10½		62.50
K3	3	34	—	3-4	10⅝	1	Int.	10½		67.50
K4	4	26	—	3-4	12	1	Int.	12		77.50
K6	6	20	—	3-3⅞	13½	1	Int.	13½		87.50
K8	8	15	—	3-3¾	16¾	1	Int.	16¾		99.95
K10	10	12	—	3-3⅝	17¾	1	Int.	17¾	Crosswires, post, rangefinder or Dual X reticle optional on all K and V scopes (except no RF in K1.5, K2.5, K3 and K3W; post in K8, 10, 12. No post in T models). Dot $12.00 extra in K and V models only. Objective lens on K8, K10, K12, V9, V12 and V9-W focuses for range.	104.95
K12	12	10	—	3-3⅝	18	1	Int.	18		114.95
K3-W	3	50	—	3⅝	11	1	Int.	11¼		87.50
K4-W	4	36	—	3⅝	11 13/16	1	Int.	13		97.50
K6-W	6	25	—	3⅝	13¼	1	Int.	14½		107.50
V4.5-W	1½-4½	75-29	—	4⅜-3¾	10⅜	1	Int.	15		112.50
V7-W	2½-7	45-18	—	3⅞	12⅜	1	Int.	17		122.50
V9-W	3-9	36-14	—	3⅝	13¾	1	Int.	21¼		132.50
V4.5	1½-4½	62-24	—	4¼-4⅜	10⅜	1	Int.	14¾		92.50
V7	2½-7	40-15	—	4¼-3⅞	12⅜	1	Int.	16¼		102.50
V9	3-9	33-12	—	3¾	13¾	1	Int.	20½		112.50
V12	4-12	24-9	—	3⅞-4¼	13¾	1	Int.	20¾		122.50
T6	6	19	—	3½	14¼	1	Int.	17¾		150.00
T10	10	11	—	3½	15	1	Int.	18		160.00
T16	16	7	—	3½	15¾	1	Int.	18¾		170.00
V22	3-6	31-16¼	—	1⅝-2¼	12⅜	.875	Int.	7¾	$2 extra for Dual X reticle on V22. D model prices include N or Tip-Off mount.	22.00
D4	4	29	—	2¼	11⅞	.875	Int.	6½		16.50
D6	6	19¾	—	2¼	12 5/16	.875	Int.	6¾	For rifles and shotguns. Projects red dot aiming point.	18.50
Qwik-Point	1	—	—	6	—	—	Int.	8		49.95
Accu-Point	—	—	—	—	—	—	—	—	Similar in principle to Quick-Point. For ribbed shotgun barrels only.	14.95
Williams										
Guide Line	4	29½	64	3¾	11¾	1	Int.	9½		93.25
Guide Line	1½-4½	78-26	196-22	4⅓-3¼	9½	1	Int.	7¾	Coated lenses, nitrogen filled tubes, ½ MOA adj. CH, dot, TNT or Guide reticle. Dot covers 3 MOA at 4x in all models.	124.75
Guide Line	2-6	60-20	169-18	3¼	10¼	1	Int.	10		124.75
Guide Line	3-9	39-13	161-18	3¾-3¼	12	1	Int.	14½		130.00
Twilight Crosshair	2½	32	64	3¾	11¼	1	Int.	8½	$6.50 more for TNT models.	53.00
Twilight Crosshair	4	29	64	3½	11¾	1	Int.	9½		58.50
Twilight Crosshair	2-6	45-17	256-28	3	11½	1	Int.	11½		81.75
Twilight Crosshair	3-9	36-13	161-18	3	12¾	1	Int.	13½		91.25
Wide Guide	4	35	64	3¼	12¼	1	Int.	14	CH, TNT or Guide reticle.	93.25

■Signifies target and/or varmint scope.

Hunting scopes in general are furnished with a choice of reticle—cross hairs, post with crosshairs, tapered or blunt post, or dot crosshairs, etc. The great majority of target and varmint scopes have medium or fine crosshairs but post or dot reticles may be ordered.

W—Windage E—Elevation MOA—Minute of angle or 1″ (approx.) at 100 yards, etc.

TELESCOPE MOUNTS

Maker, Model, Type	Adjust.	Scopes	Suitable for	Price
B-Square Co.				
Dovetail Rings	No	1″ scopes	All dovetail receivers such as Nylon 66. No drilling or tapping.	$11.95
M-94 Mono-Mount	No	1″, long eye relief such as Leupold M8-2X. Mounts ahead of action.	M-94 Winchester. No drilling or tapping.	15.95
M-94 Side Mount	W&E	All 1″ Scopes.	M-94 Winchester. No drilling or tapping.	19.95
AR-15 Base	No	Use any Weaver-type ring (not included)	Colt AR-15 Rifle. No drilling or tapping.	14.95
AR-15 Mount	W&E	All 1″ Scopes	Colt AR-15 Rifles. No drilling or tapping.	19.95
Mini-14 Mount	W&E	All 1″ Scopes.	Ruger Mini-14 (Mounts on top of receiver) (Gunsmith Drill Jig available for guns not drilled $34.95)	24.95
T-C Pistol Base	No	1″, long eye relief pistol scope. Use Weaver Tip-Off Rings.	Thompson-Center Contender Model Pistols.	6.95
Adj. Beam Mount	W&E	All 1″ Scopes.	All Popular Rifles.	19.95
One-Piece Base Mounts	W&E	1″ scopes	Most popular rifles.	17.95
LWS, LWB	E only	1″ scopes	Most popular rifles.	19.95
Remington Models	No	1″ scopes	Remington 600, 700, 788 and 1100 models.	19.95
Ruger Blackhawk	No	1″ scopes	Ruger Blackhawk revolver (has bolted rings).	21.95
T-C Contender	No	1″ scopes	T-C Contender, all calibers. Heavy Recoil Model $21.95.	14.95
Buehler				
One Piece (T)	W only	1″ split rings, 3 heights	Most popular models.	Complete 38.50
		1″ split rings, 3 heights	Fully engraved.	Rings only—51.75
		26mm, 26½mm, 28mm	Special.	Rings only—28.00
One Piece Micro Dial	W&E	1″ split rings, 3 heights	Most popular models.	Complete 48.25
Two Piece (T)	W only	1″ split rings, 3 heights	Most popular models	Complete 38.50
One Piece Pistol (T)	W only	1″ split rings, 3 heights	14 models.	Complete 38.50
Burris				
Supreme One Piece (T)	W only	1″ split rings, 3 heights	Most Popular Rifles. Universal rings, mounts fit Burris	17.95 / 1 piece base—11.50
Trumount Two Piece (T)	W only	1″ split rings, 3 heights	Universal, Redfield, Leupold and Browning bases. Comparable prices.	2 piece base—9.95
Browning Auto Mount	No	¾″, 1″ split rings	Browning Standard 22 Auto Rifle.	7.95
Sight-Thru Mount	No	1″ split rings	Most popular rifles.	14.50
Ring Mounts	No	¾″, 1″, split rings	Grooved receivers.	¾″ rings— 8.98 / 1″ rings—12.98
L.E.R. Mount Bases	No	1″ split rings	Universal dovetail; accept Burris, Universal, Redfield, Leupold rings. For Virginian, Ruger Blackhawk, Contender, Win. 94.	10.95
Bushnell				
Detachable (T) mounts only	W only	1″ split rings, uses Weaver bases.	Most popular rifles. Includes windage adj.	Rings—11.95
22 mount	No	1″ only		Rings— 4.95
All Purpose	No	Phantom	V-block bottoms lock to chrom-moly studs seated into two 6-48 holes. Rem. XP-100.	10.95
Rigid	No	Phantom	Heavy loads in Colt, S&W, Ruger revolvers, Ruger Hawkeye.	10.95
94 Win.	No	Phantom	M94 Win., center dovetail.	12.95
Clearview				
Universal Rings (T)	No	1″ split rings	All popular rifles. Uses Weaver Bases. Rings have a wide oval effect for use of open sights.	14.95
Mod. 101, & 336	No	1″ split rings		13.50
Model 104	No	1″ split rings	For 22-Rim Fired Rifles, with grooved receivers or bases.	7.95
SM-94	No	1″ split rings	Remington 14, 141, Sears 54, 100, Win. 94.	19.95
Conetrol				
One Piece (T)	W only	1″, 26mm, 26.5mm solid or split rings, 3 heights	All popular rifles, including metric-drilled foreign guns.	Huntur—19.92-24.96 / Bases only—10.98 / Solid Rings, ea.— 4.47 / Split Rings, ea.— 6.99
Two Piece (T)	W only	Same.	All rifles which will take conventional top mount low over receiver.	Gunnur—27.45-32.43 / Bases only—14.49 / Solid Rings, ea.— 6.48 / Split Rings, ea.— 8.97
One Piece (S)	W only	Same.	Win. 94, Krag, older split-bridge Mannlicher Schonauer, Ruger Mini-14, M-1 Garand, SMLE No. 1, etc.	
'DapTar' Bases (T) Pistol Bases (T) (write maker for details)	W only	Same.	All popular guns with integral mounting provision. (Sako, BSA, Ithacagun, Ruger flat-tops, Krico, LSA, BRNO, grooved-receiver rimfires, air rifles, etc.).	Custum—33.92-39.93 / Bases only—17.97 / Solid Rings, ea.— 7.98 / Split Rings, ea.—10.98
Griffin & Howe				
Standard Double Lever (S)	No	1″ or 26mm split rings.	All popular models (Garand $85.00; Win. 94 $75.00). High rings $37.50.	80.00
Holden				
Ironsighter (T)	No	1″ split rings.	Most popular rifles including Ruger Mini-14, and muzzleloaders. Rings have oval holes to permit use of iron sights.	14.95
Jaeger				
QD, with windage (S)	W only	1″, 26mm; 3 heights.	All popular models.	52.00
Jaguar				
QD Dovetail (T)	No	1″, 26mm and 26½mm rings.	For BSA Monarch rifle (Galef, importer).	23.30

TELESCOPE MOUNTS

Maker, Model, Type	Adjust.	Scopes	Suitable for	Price
Kesselring				
Standard QD (T)	W only	¾", ⅞", 1", 26mm split rings.	All popular rifles, one or two piece bases.	$24.50
See-Em-Under (T)	W only	Same.	Rem. 760, 740, Win. 100, 88, Marlin 336	29.50
Dovetail (T)	W only	1", 26mm.	Steyr 22, Sako, BRNO, Krico	29.50
Kris Mounts				
Side-Saddle	No	1", 26mm split rings.	One-piece mount for Win. 94	9.98
Two Piece (T)	No	1", 26mm split rings.	Most popular rifles and Ruger	6.98
One Piece (T)	No	1", 26mm split rings.	Blackhawk revolver. Mounts have oval hole to permit use of iron sights.	9.98
Kwik-site (T)	No	1" split rings.	Wider-View, $15.75. Mounts scope high to permit iron sight use. Offset base for 94 Win.	14.75 / 19.95
Leupold	W only	1" only, 3 heights. Interchange with Redfield Jr. and Sr. components.	Most popular rifles.	Rings—19.00 / Base—13.00
STD (T)				
45 ACP "Gold Cup" Mount	No	1" split rings.	For M8-2x or 4x EER mounting on a Colt Gold Cup N.M. 45.	28.00
Marlin				
One Piece QD (T)	No	1" split rings.	Most Marlin and Glenfield lever actions.	7.95
Numrich				
Side Mount	No	1" split rings.	M-1 carbine.	7.95
Pachmayr				
Lo-Swing (S)	Yes	¾", ⅞", 1", 26mm solid or split loops.	All popular rifles, including Ruger Mini-14. Scope swings aside for instant use of iron sights. Adjustable base. Win. 70, 88; Rem. 721, 722, 725,	30.00
Lo-Swing (T)	Yes	¾", ⅞", 1", 26mm split rings.	740, 760; Mar. 336; Sav. 99. New model for Colt Sauer.	35.00
Parker-Hale				
Roll-Off	No	1" and 26mm.	Most popular rifles.	15.55
Precise				
40421 (rings only)	No	1" tube; not over 32mm obj.	Fit Weaver bases.	7.50
40422 (rings only)	No	1" tube; 40mm obj. scopes.		7.50
Redfield				
JR-SR (T)	W only	¾", 1", 26mm.	Low, med. & high, split rings. Reversible extension front rings for 1". 2-piece bases for Mannlicher-Schoenauer and Sako. Colt Sauer bases $23.00.	Rings—19.00 / Bases—13.00-22.00 / Rings—36.00 / 12.00-13.90
Ring (T)	No	¾" and 1".	Split rings for grooved 22's.	
FR (T) bases	No	Takes ¾" or 1" rings. Widefield.	See-thru mounts $15.20; shotgun model $7.80 Rings $16.40.	3.90
IR	No	1" only.	Integral rings and mount.	15.20
S&K				
Insta-Mount (T) base only	No	Most take S&K or Weaver rings.	M1903, A3, M1 Carbine, Lee Enfield #3, #4, #5, P14, M1917, M98 Mauser, FN Auto, AR-15, AR-180, M-14, M-1. Bases—M94, 64.	11.00-20.00 / 10.00
Conventional rings and bases	No	1" split rings.	Most popular rifles. For "see through underneath" risers, add $4.15.	24.20
Sako				
QD Dovetail	W only	1" only.	Sako, or any rifle using Sako action. 3 heights available. Stoeger, importer.	39.95
Savage				
No. 40 (S)	No	1"	For Savage 340, 840 Springfield.	5.10
No. 70	No	1"	For Savage 170, 170-C rifles.	5.10
B-5	No	1"	For 24V, 222 or 30-30.	15.75
Tasco				
790 and 792 series	Yes	1" split rings, regular or high.	Many popular rifles.	7.95
M794	No	Split rings.	For 22s with grooved receivers.	7.95
795 Quick Peep	No	1" only.	Most popular rifles.	12.95
800L Series	No	1" only.	Most popular rifles.	9.95
Unertl				
Posa (T)	Yes	¾", ⅞", 1" scopes.	Unertl target or varmint scope.	41.00
¼ Click (T)	Yes	¾", 1" target scopes.	Any with regular dovetail scope bases.	37.00
Dehorned Varmint (T)	Yes	¾", ⅞", 1" scopes.	Add $3 for Posa.	29.00-32.00
Weaver				
Detachable Mount (T & S)	No	¾", ⅞", 1", 26mm.	Nearly all modern rifles. Extension rings, 1" $14.50.	12.50
Type N (S)	No	⅞" scopes only.	Same. High or low style mounts.	5.50
Pivot Mount (T)	No	¾", 1".	Most modern big bore rifles.	15.50
Tip-Off (T)	No	¾", ⅞".	22s with grooved receivers.	5.50
Tip-Off (T)	No	1", two-piece.	Same. Adapter for Lee Enfield—$3.50.	12.50
All Steel Rings	No	1" split rings.		17.00
All Steel Bases	No	Take 1" split rings.		11.00
See-Thru Mount	No	1" split rings and ⅞" tip-off. Fits all top mounts.	Snaps on, snaps off. ⅞"—$8.50	16.50
Williams				
Offset (S)	No	¾", ⅞", 1", 26mm solid, split or extension rings.	Most rifles (with over-bore rings, $23.35). Br. S.M.L.E. (round rec.) $3.20 extra.	23.70
QC (T)	No	Same.	Same.	22.00
QC (S)	No	Same.	Most rifles.	22.00
Low Sight-Thru	No	1", ⅞", sleeves $1.40.	Most rifles.	15.00
Sight-Thru	No	1", ⅞", sleeves $1.40.	Many modern rifles.	17.00
Streamline	No	1" (bases form rings)	Most popular rifles.	14.50

(S)—Side Mount   (T)—Top Mount   22mm=.866"   25.4mm=1"   26mm=1.024"   26.5mm=1.045"   30mm=1.181"

SPOTTING SCOPES

BAUSCH & LOMB DISCOVERER—60mm objective, 15X to 60X zoom. Constant focus throughout range. Field at 1000 yds. 40 ft. (60X), 156 ft. (15X). Comes with lens caps. Length 17½", wgt. 48½ oz. **$279.00**

Bausch & Lomb Discoverer

BUSHNELL SPACEMASTER—60mm objective. Field at 1000 yds., 158' to 37'. Relative brightness, 5.76. Wgt., 36 oz. Length closed, 11⅝". Prism focusing, without eyepiece **$160.00**
   15X, 20X, 25X, 40X and 60X eyepieces, each **$31.50**
   20X wide angle eyepiece **$39.50**
BUSHNELL SPACEMASTER 45°—Same as above except: Wgt., 43 oz., length closed 16¼". Eyepiece at 45°, sliding sunshade, without eyepiece.
   Price: **$190.00**
BUSHNELL SPACEMASTER—20X-45X zoom. 60mm objective. Field at 1000 yards 120'-72'. Relative brightness 9-1.7. Wgt. 36 oz., length 11⅝"
   Price: **$234.50**
BUSHNELL SENTRY—50mm objective. Field at 1000 yards 120'-45'. Relative brightness 6.25. Wgt., 25½ oz., length 12⅝", without eyepiece **$85.50**
   20X, 32X and 48X eyepieces, each **$28.00**
BUSHNELL ZOOM SPOTTER—40mm objective. 9X-30X var. power.
   Price: **$62.50**
BUSHNELL—10x30mm hand telescope. Field 183 ft. at 1000 yards. Weight 11 ozs.; 10" long. Tripod mount.................................. **$21.95**
DICKSON 270—20x to 60x variable, 60mm objective, achromatic coated objective lens, complete with metal table tripod with 5' vertical and horizontal adjustments. Turret type, 20x, 30x, 40x 60x.
   Price: **$175.00**
DICKSON 274A—20x to 60x variable zoom. 60mm achromatic coated objective lens, complete with adjustable metal table tripod.
   Price: **$95.00**
DICKSON 274B—As above but with addition of 4×16 Finder Scope.
   Price: **$100.00**
HUTSON CHROMATAR 60—63.4mm objective. 22.5X eyepiece at 45°. Wgt. 24 oz. 8" over-all. 10½ foot field at 100 yards. **$119.00**
   15X or 45X eyepieces, each............................. **$22.00**
HY-SCORE MODEL 460—60mm objective. 15X, 20X, 25X, 40X and 60X eyepieces included. Field at 100 yds. 15.8 to 3.2 ft. Length closed 11". Wgt., 35 oz. With tripod and case.................................. **$129.95**
   Zoom—20X to 40X **$144.95**
REDFIELD FIFTEEN-SIXTY—15X-60X zoom. 60mm objective. Field at 100 yards 15.6-3.7 ft. Relative brightness 16-1. Wgt. 48 oz., length 16¾"**$253.60**
   Tripod stand.. **$39.20**
   Bipod stand **$39.20**
   Carrying case **$53.40**
   Window mount **$8.00**
REDFIELD FIFTEEN-FORTY-FIVE—Similar to above but power range is 15X-45X **$205.70**
REDFIELD REGAL SPOTTING SCOPE—15X-45X, 15X-60X. Field at 100 yds. 16.1'-5.4' and 16.1'-4.0'. Separated focus and power rings. Wgt. 49 ozs., length 18". 15X-45X.. **$253.60**
   15X-60X **$289.30**
   Saddle head mount **$29.40**
   Sighting device **$4.90**
SOUTHERN PRECISION MODEL 550—60mm objective and 5 eyepieces from 15X to 60X; folding tripod. 14¾", Wgt., 4¼ lbs............ **$129.95**
SOUTHERN PRECISION ZOOM MODEL 543—60mm objective, 15X to 50X; folding tripod. 18", wgt. 4½ lbs. with tripod (included) **$119.95**
SOUTHERN PRECISION MODEL 552—80mm objective, 20X. Folding tripod. 13", wgt. 3 lbs. **$117.50**
SWIFT TELEMASTER M841—60mm objective. 15X to 60X variable power. Field at 100 yards 160 feet (15X) to 40 feet (60X). Wgt. 3.4 lbs. 17.6" over-all.
   Price: **$335.00**
   Tripod for above....................................... **$59.95**
   Photo adapter **$17.00**
   Case for above... **$48.00**
TASCO 18T ZOOM—60mm objective. 20X to 60X variable power. Field at 100 yards 158 feet (16X) to 40 feet (50X). Wgt. 4½ lbs. 18" overall**$199.95**
TASCO 28T ANGLEVIEW—60mm objective. 25X, resolves to 2 sec. at 100 yds. Rapid focus knob. Table top tripod with adj. elevation leg. Camera tripod adapter, extending sun shade. Wgt., 6 lbs., length 16½". Complete with lens covers... **$349.95**
TASCO 8T SPOTTING 60—60mm objective, 4 par-focal, variable power eye-lenses 15X, 30X, 40X and 60X. Resolves 2.8 sec. at 100 yds. Wgt., 4 lbs., length 16½" **$279.95**

UNERTL RIGHT ANGLE—63.5mm objective. 24X. Field at 100 yds., 7 ft. Relative brightness, 6.96. Eye relief, ½". Wgt., 41 oz. Length closed, 19". Push-pull and screw-focus eyepiece. 16X and 32X eyepieces $18 each.
   Price: **$176.00**
UNERTL STRAIGHT PRISMATIC—Same as Unertl Right Angle except: straight eyepiece and wgt. of 40 oz. **$151.00**
UNERTL 20X STRAIGHT PRISMATIC—54mm objective. 20X. Field at 100 yds., 8.5 ft. Relative brightness, 6.1. Eye relief, ½". Wgt., 36 oz. Length closed, 13½". Complete with lens covers..................... **$126.00**

Unertl 20x Straight Prismatic

UNERTL TEAM SCOPE—100mm objective. 15X, 24X. 32X eyepieces. Field at 100 yds. 13 to 7.5 ft. Relative brightness, 39.06 to 9.79. Eye relief, 2" to 1½". Weight, 13 lbs. 29⅞" overall. Metal tripod, yoke and wood carrying case furnished (total weight, 80 lbs.). **$575.00**
WEATHERBY—60mm objective, 20X-45X zoom................. **$206.50**
   Tripod for above....................................... **$43.50**

SCOPE ATTACHMENTS
DAVIS TARGETEER—Objective lens/tube units that attach to front of low power scopes, increase magnification to 8X. 1¼" lens, $27.50, 1½" lens $32.50
HERMANN DUST CAPS—Connected leather straps, hand made, natural color. For all popular scopes...................................... **$4.00**
LEE TACKHOLE DOTS—Various size dots for most scopes. Price**$15.00— $17.50**
PGS SCOPE SHIELDS—Flexible rubber, see-through. Protects lenses front and rear from rain or snow without removing for sighting. Sizes for most scopes. **$3.95**
W. H. SIEBERT—Converts Lyman, Leupold, Unertl and Weaver K model varmint scopes to 15X-36X............................... **$35.00**
STORM KING LENS CAPS—A hinged glass-and-rubber protector set (2), made in various sizes for all scopes. May be unhinged or sighted through. Anderson Mfg. Co. Per pair.................................. **$4.95**
   Price, with Haze Cutter............................... **$5.95**
SUPREME LENS COVERS—Hinged protectors for most scope models, front and rear lenses shielded. Butler Creek Corp. Per pair, postpaid.**$7.95**

Supreme lens covers

Storm King lens covers

Storm Queen lens covers

SPOTTING SCOPE STANDS
FREELAND ALL ANGLE—Tripod adjustable for elevation. Left or right side mount with worm drive clamp. Folding legs. Clamps available for any scope tube size. Gray crinkle finish. Price..................... **$34.00**
   Also 12" 18", 24" extensions.................... **$6.15, $8.00, $9.75**
FREELAND OLYMPIC—Bipod adjustable for elevation. All angle mount with padded worm drive clamp. Folding legs. Clamps available for any scope tube size. Gray crinkle finish. Price..................... **$38.00**
   Also 12", 18", 24" extensions.................... **$6.15, $8.00, $9.75**
   Zoom head for tripod or bipod......................... **$17.40**
FREELAND REGAL BIPOD—Choice of saddle or zoom head. All adjustment knobs are oversize for easy adjusting. Large "ball" carrying knob. Gray finish. **$40.00**
   Above with stability weight **$57.65**
   12", 18", 24" extensions **$6.15, $8.00, $9.75**
FREELAND GALLERY SPECIAL BIPOD—For all shooting positions. Zoom or saddle head. Adjustable for elevation. Comes with bipod base, gallery special head assembly and 12" extension. Gray finish, saddle head.**$40.00**
   As above with 18" extension **$41.50**
   Gallery Tripod (includes base, saddle head assembly and 12" extension) **$38.00**
   Zoom Gallery Bipod **$40.00**
   Zoom Gallery Tripod **$36.50**

The Arms Library for
COLLECTOR · HUNTER · SHOOTER · OUTDOORSMAN

A selection of books—old, new and forthcoming—for everyone
in the arms field, with a brief description by . . . JOE RILING

 ballistics *and* handloading

The ABC's of Reloading, by Dean A. Grennell, DBI Books, Inc., Northfield, IL. 1974. 8½"x11", 320 pp. Profusely illus. Paper bound. $6.95.
Written primarily for the novice, this book will also teach the pro a thing or two. A large amount of information on powder, primers, bullets, cases and shotshells.
The Air Gun from Trigger to Muzzle, by G. V. Cardew, G. M. Cardew, and E. R. Elsom, G. V. Cardew, Birmingham, England, 1976. 96 pp., illus. Paper covers. $8.95.
The internal ballistics of spring operated air weapons.
Ballistic Science for the Law Enforcement Officer, by Charles G. Wilber, Ph.D., Charles C. Thomas, Springfield, IL, 1977. 309 pp., illus. $23.00.
A scientific study of the ballistics of civilian firearms.
Ballistics & the Muzzle Loading Rifle, by Wm. C. Herring, Nat'l. Muzzle Loading Rifle Assn., Friendship, IN, 1974. 111 pp., illus. Paper covers. $5.95.
A manual of black powder reloading and ballistic data.
Ballistics in the Seventeenth Century, by A. R. Hall. 1st J. & J. Harper ed. 1969 [from the Cambridge University Press ed. of 1952]. 186 pp., illus., with tables and diagrams. $13.50.
A profound work for advanced scholars, this is a study in the relations of science and war, with reference principally to England.
The Bullet Swage Manual, by Ted Smith, Corbin Manufacturing & Supply, Inc., Phoenix, OR, limited second edition, 1976. 43 pp., illus. Paper covers. $3.50.
A good first swaging book, written by a master die-maker.
Cartridges of the World, by Frank C. Barnes, John T. Amber ed., Digest Books, Inc., Northfield, IL, 1972. 8½"x11", 384 pp. Profusely illus. Paper-bound. $8.95.
The third edition of a comprehensive reference for hunters, collectors, handloaders and ballisticians. Covering over 1000 cartridges, loads, components, etc., from all over the world.
The Complete Book of Practical Handloading, by John Wooters, Winchester Press, NY, 1976. 320 pp., illus. $12.50
An up-to-the-minute guide for the rifleman and shotgunner.
Computer for Handloaders, by Homer Powley. A slide rule plus 12 page instruction book for use in finding charge, most efficient powder and velocity for any modern centerfire rifle. $5.50
The Corbin Handbook & Catalog of Bullet Swaging No. III, compiled by Dave Corbin, Corbin Manufacturing & Supply, Inc., Phoenix, OR, 1977. 73 pp., illus. Paper covers. $2.50.
Information on Corbin products including reloading press dies, accessories, chemicals and the Mity Mite System of hand swaging.
Corbin Technical Bulletins, Volume I, compiled by Dave Corbin, Corbin Manufacturing & Supply Inc., Phoenix, OR, 1977. 66 pp., illus. Paper covers. $5.00.
Answers in depth the specific questions dealers and handloaders have about bullet swaging, plus new techniques.
A Digest of Cartridges for Small Arms Patented in the United States, England and France, by W. A. Bartlett and D. B. Gallatin, Museum Restoration Service, Ontario, Canada, 1977. 52 pp., illus. Paper covers. $4.95.
A facsimile reprint of the very scarce 1878 edition. A classic publication for the cartridge collector.
Discover Swaging, compiled by Dave Corbin, Corbin Manufacturing & Supply, Inc., Phoenix, OR, 1978. 200 pp., illus. $8.50.
Fills the need for a detailed, comprehensive book in the category of a major work, about bullet swaging.
Firearms Identification, by Dr. J. H. Mathews, Charles C. Thomas, Springfield, IL, 1973 3 vol. set. A massive, carefully researched, authoritative work published as:
Vol. I. **The Laboratory Examination of Small Arms.** . . . 400 pp., illus. $44.75.
Vol. II. **Original Photographs and Other Illustrations of Handguns.** 492 pp., illus. $44.75.
Vol. III. **Data on Rifling Characteristics of Handguns and Rifles.** 730 pp., illus. $69.50.
Firearms Investigation, Identification and Evidence, by J. S. Hatcher, Frank J. Jury and Jac Weller. Stackpole Books, Harrisburg, PA, 1977. 536 pp. illus. $22.50.
Reprint of the 1957 printing of this classic book on forensic ballistics. Indispensable for those interested in firearms identification and criminology.
Game Loads and Practical Ballistics For The American Hunter, by Bob Hagel, Alfred A. Knopf, NY, NY, 1978. 315 pp., illus., hardbound. $12.95.
Everything a hunter needs to know about ballistics and performance of commercial hunting loads.
Handbook for Shooters and Reloaders, by P. O. Ackley, Salt Lake City, UT, 1970. *Vol. I,* 567 pp., illus. $10.75. *Vol. II,* a new printing with specific new material. 495 pp., illus. $9.75. Both volumes. $20.50.
Handloader's Digest, 8th Edition, edited by John T. Amber, DBI Books Inc., Northfield, IL, 1978. 288 pp., illus. Paper covers. $7.95.
This completely new edition contains the latest data on ballistics, maximum loads, new tools, equipment, etc., plus a fully illus. catalog section, current prices and specifications.

Handloading for Handgunners, by Geo. C. Nonte, DBI Books, Inc., Northfield, IL, 1978. 288 pp., illus. Paper covers. $7.95.
An expert tells the ins and outs of this specialized facet of reloading.
Handloading for Hunters, by Don Zutz, Winchester Press, NY, 1977. 288 pp., illus. $12.50.
Precise mixes and loads for different types of game and for various hunting situations with rifle and shotgun.
Hazards and Problems of Handloading, by Fred Tucker, Fred Tucker, Moore, OK, 1963. 70 pp., illus., paper covers. $2.50.
Covers features of handloading which are not always mentioned in standard manuals.
Hodgdon "New" Data Manual No. 23, Hodgdon Powder Co., Shawnee Mission, KS, 1977. 192 pp., illus. $4.95.
New data on Pyrodex and black powder. New section on how to reload for beginners. Information on rifle, pistol, shotgun and lead bullet loads.
The Home Guide to Cartridge Conversions, by Maj. George C. Nonte, Jr., The Gun Room Press, Highland Park, NJ, 1976. 404 pp., illus. $12.95
Revised and updated version of Nonte's definitive work on the alteration of cartridge cases for use in guns for which they were not intended.
Hornady Handbook of Cartridge Reloading, Rifle-Pistol, Vol. 2, by J. W. Hornady, Hornady Mfg. Co., Inc., Grand Island, NB, 1973. 512 pp., illus. $5.95.
A comprehensive guide to handloading and shooting; nearly 100 rifle/pistol cartridge combinations. Thousands of loads.
The Identification of Firearms and Forensic Ballistics, by Major Sir Gerald Burrard, A. S. Barnes & Co., NY, 1964. $15.00.
The fundamentals of forensic ballistics in easy to understand language.
Lee Reloading Handbook, by R. Lee, Lee Custom Engineering, Hartford, WI. 98 pp., illus. Paper, 98¢.
Manual on reloading ammunition of various types.
Lyman Black Powder Handbook, ed. by C. Kenneth Ramage, Lyman Products for Shooters, Middlefield, CT, 1975. 239 pp., illus. Paper covers. $6.95.
The most comprehensive load information ever published for the modern black powder shooter.
Lyman Cast Bullet Handbook. Lyman Gunsight Corp., Middlefield, CT, 1973. 260 pp., illus. Paper covers. $6.95.
A long-awaited and fine reference for handloaders.
Lyman Handbook No. 45. Lyman Gunsight Corp., Middlefield, CT, 1967. $5.95.
Latest edition of a favorite reference for ammunition handloaders, whether novice or veteran.
Lyman Shotshell Handbook 2nd ed., edited by C. Kenneth Ramage, Lyman Gunsight Corp., Middlefield, CT, 1976. 288 pp., illus., paper covers. $6.95.
Devoted exclusively to shotshell reloading, this book considers: gauge, shell length, brand, case, loads, buckshot, etc. plus an excellent reference section. Some color illus.
Make Muzzle Loader Accessories, by R. H. McCrory, R. H. McCrory, Publ., 1971, 46 pp. Paper $2.50.
A revised 2nd ed. covering over 20 items from powderhorns to useful tools. Well illus.
Modern Handloading, by Maj. Geo. C. Nonte. Winchester Press, NY, 1972. 416 pp., illus. $10.00.
Covers all aspects of metallic and shotshell ammunition loading, plus more loads than any book in print; state and Federal laws, reloading tools, glossary.
Nosler Reloading Manual Number One, compiled and edited by Bob Nosler, Nosler Bullets, Inc., Bend, OR, 1976. 234 pp., illus. $5.95.
Provides thorough coverage of powder data, specifically tailored to the well-known Nosler partition and solid base bullet designs in all weights and calibers.
Pocket Manual for Shooters and Reloaders, by P. O. Ackley. publ. by author, Salt Lake City, UT, 1964. 176 pp., illus., spiral bound. $4.95.
Good coverage on standard and wildcat cartridges and related firearms in popular calibers.
Professional Loading of Rifle, Pistol and Shotgun Cartridges . . ., by G. L. Herter, Mitchell, SD, 1976. 430 pp., illus., paper covers. $5.95.
Technical load data on small arms ammunition, with related articles on firearms and their use.
The PSI Calculator, a slide rule designed by Homer Powley to add maximum chamber pressure to the velocity and powder charge computed. $4.00
Reloader's Guide, by R. A. Steindler, Stoeger Publ. Co., Hackensack, NJ, 1975. 223 pp., illus. Paper covers. $6.95.
Complete, fully illustrated step-by-step guide to handloading ammunition.
Shooter's Bible Black Powder Guide, by George Nonte, Shooter's Bible, Inc., S. Hackensack, NJ, 1976. 214 pp., well illus. $6.95.
Information on black powder weapons, ammunition, shooting, etc.
Shooter's Bible Reloader's Guide, 3rd Ed., by R. A. Steindler, Shooter's Bible, Inc., S. Hackensack, NJ, 1975. 256 pp., illus. Paper covers. $6.95.
A revised and up-dated ed. of the standard guide on the subject of reloading.
Sierra Bullets Reloading Manual, by Robert Hayden. Sierra Bullets, Santa Fe Springs, CA, 1971. 350 pp., illus. In loose-leaf binder. $5.95.
Reference manual on cartridge reloading, including ballistics and ammunition data on rifles and pistols.
Sierra Bullets Reloading Manual Supplement, by Robert Hayden, Sierra Bullets, Santa Fe Springs, CA, 1976. 204 pp., illus. Punched pages for inclusion with the *Sierra Manual.* $3.75.
Contains 21 additional rifle and pistol cartridges, including wildcats, plus added ballistics, wind deflection tables, etc.

Small Arms Ammunition Identification Guide. Anubus Press, Houston, TX, 1971. 151 pp., illus. Paper, $5.00.
A reprint of the guide originally published as FSTC-CW-07-02-66, revised.

Speer Manual for Reloading Ammunition No. 9, Speer, Inc., Lewiston, ID, 1974. 464 pp., illus. $5.50.
A popular manual on handloading, with authoritative articles on loading, ballistics, and related subjects. Revised and updated.

The .30-'06, by W. L. Godfrey, Elk Mountain Shooters Supply, Inc., Pasco, WA, 1975. 425 pp., illus. Spiral bound. $10.00
A valuable source book for the advanced handloader.

Why Not Load Your Own? by Col. T. Whelen. A. S. Barnes, New York, 1957, 4th ed., rev. 237 pp., illus, $7.95.
A basic reference on handloading, describing each step, materials and equipment. Loads for popular cartridges are given.

COLLECTORS

About Cannon in 1862, by Robert F. Hudson, American Archives Publ. Co., Topsfield, MA, 1971. 44 pp., illus. Paper, $4.00.
Reprint of an 18th century monograph on artillery pieces, with historical notes.

Accoutrement Plates, North and South, 1861-1865, by Wm. G. Gavin. Geo. Shumway, York, PA, 1975. 236 pp., 220 illus. Paper $14.00, Cloth $20.00.
The 1st detailed study of Civil War belt buckles and cartridge box insignia. Dimensions, materials, details of manufacture, relative and dollar values given.

Adams Revolvers 1851-1891, by W.H.J. Chamberlain and A.W.F. Taylerson, Herbert Jenkins, London, England, 1977. 256 pp., illus. $31.50.
Full story of the design, evolution and manufacture of the weapons produced by the chief rival of Sam Colt.

The Age of Firearms, by Robert Held. Digest Books, Inc., Northfield, IL, 1970. New, fully rev. and corrected ed., paper covers. 192 pp., fully illus. $4.95.
A popular review of firearms since 1475 with accent on their effects on social conditions, and the craft of making functional/artistic arms.

Air Guns, by Eldon G. Wolff. Milwaukee Public Museum, Milwaukee, WI, 1958. 198 pp., illus. Paper, $6.00.
A scholarly and comprehensive treatise, excellent for student and collectors' use, of air gun history. Every form of arm is described, and a list of 350 makers is included.

American Boys' Rifles 1890-1945, by Jim Perkins, RTP Publishers, Pittsburg, PA, 1976. 245 pp., illus. $17.50.
The history and products of the arms companies who made rifles for the American boy, 1890-1945.

American, British & Continental Pepperbox Firearms, by Jack Dunlap. H. J. Dunlap, Los Altos, CA, 1964. 279 pp., 665 illus. $15.00.
Comprehensive history of production pepperpots from early 18th cent. through the cartridge pepperbox. Variations are covered, with much data of value to the collector.

The American Cartridge, by Charles R. Suydam, Borden Publ. Co., Alhambra, CA, rev. ed., 1973. 184 pp., illus. $8.50.
An illus. study of the rimfire cartridge in the U.S.

American Engraved Powder Horns, by Stephen V. Grancsay. Originally published by The Metropolitan Museum of Art, at NYC, 1945. The 1st reprint publ. by Ray Riling Arms Books Co., Phila., PA, 1976. 96 pp. plus 47 full-page plates. $22.50.
A study based on the J. H. Grenville Gilbert collection of historic, rare and beautiful powder horns. A scholarly work by an eminent authority. Long out of print and offered now in a limited edition of 1000 copies.

The American Percussion Revolver, by F. M. Sellers and Sam E. Smith. Museum Restoration Service, Ottawa, Canada, 1970. 200 pp., illus. $15.00.
All inclusive from 1826 to 1870. Over 200 illus., with profuse coverage on lesser-known arms.

American Pistol and Revolver Patents 1800 to 1925, compiled by Jos. J. Macewicz, Museum Restoration Service, Ottawa, Canada, 1977. 52 pp., illus. Paper covers. $4.95.
A chronological listing of patents issued in the U.S.A. from 1800 to 1925. Cross indexed by inventor.

American Small Arms Research in W.W.II, Vol. I: Hand & Shoulder Weapons, Helmets & Body Armor, ed. by D. B. McLean, Normount Technical Publ., Wickenburg, AZ, 1975. 181 pp., illus. Paper covers. $8.95.
Describes and pictures nearly 300 experimental and developmental rifles, carbines, submachine guns, knives, helmets and armor.

American Sporting Arms of the 18th & 19th Century, compiled by Herbert G. Houze, Chicago Historical Society, Chicago, IL, 1975. 32 pp., illus. Paper covers. $3.75
A catalog of the Chicago Historical Society collection of antique sporting and martial firearms.

The American Sporting Collector's Handbook, by Allan J. Liu, Winchester Press, NY, 1976. 224 pp., illus. $10.00
A unique guide to sporting art and accoutrements, and their ever-increasing value. Covers rods, reels, guns, limited-edition books, prints, decoys, etc.

Antique European and American Firearms in the Hermitage Museum, by L. Tarassuk. Arco Pub. Co., NY, 1972. 224 pp., 130 pp. of illus., 54 pp. in full color. $20.00.
Selected from the museum's 2500 firearms dating from the 15th to 19th centuries, including the magnificently decorated Colt rifle and pistols presented by Samuel Colt to Tzars Nicholas 1st and Alexander II.

Antique Guns in Color 1250-1865, by Robert Wilkinson-Latham, Blanford Press, London, England, 1978. 211 pp., illus. $11.95.
Layman and collector will find this a fascinating survey of firearms. Illustrated in color.

Antique Pistols, by S. G. Alexander, illus. by Ronald Paton. Arco Publ. Co., New York, 1963. 56 pp., 12 color plates. $15.00.
The large 8-color plates show 14 examples of the pistol-maker's art in England and U.S.A., 1690-1900. Commentary on each by a knowledgeable English collector.

Antique Weapons for Pleasure and Investment, by R. Akehurst. Arco Pub. Co., N.Y., 1969. 174 pp., illus. $5.95.
Reprint of an English book covering an extensive variety of arms, including Japanese and Hindu edged weapons and firearms.

Les Armes Americaines 1870-1871 de las Defense Nationale, by P. Lorain and J. Boudriot. Librarie Pierre Petitot, Paris, France, 1970. French text, 96 pp., illus. $14.50.
Covers all U.S. weapons bought by the French government a century ago.

Armour & Weapons, by Charles ffoulkes, Museum Rest. Serv., Ottawa, Ont., Can., 1975. 112 pp., illus. $8.50.
A facsimile of the 1909 London ed. written by one of the leading scholars of arms and armor of his day.

Arms Archives, by H. B. Lockhoven, International Small Arms Publ., Cologne, W. Germany, 1969. Unpaginated but coded. Illus. English and German text, loose-leaf format. Available in 4 series; "A" Handguns, "B" Automatic Weapons, "C" Longarms, "D" Antique Arms. Each series in 4 installments at $15.00 per installment. Binders for each series $6.50.
A major breakthrough in arms literature. Scaled photographs of guns and their cartridges, fully described. Only 1st installment now available in series "D".

Arms and Armor Annual, Volume I, edited by Robert Held, Digest Books, Inc., Northfield, IL, 1973. 320 pp., illus., paper covers. $9.95.
Thirty outstanding articles by the leading arms and armor historians of the world.

Arms and Armor, by Vesey Norman. Putnam's N.Y.C., 1964. 128 pp., 129 illus. $3.98.
Authoritative, compact coverage of European armor and weapons prior to the age of firearms. Excellent illus., many in color.

Arms and Equipment of the Civil War, by Jack Coggins, Doubleday & Co., Inc, NY, 1962. 160 pp., $9.95.
Tools of war of the blue and the grey. Infantry, cavalry, artillery, and navy: guide to equipment, clothing, organization, and weapons. Over 500 illus.

Arms Makers of Maryland, by Daniel D. Hartzler, George Shumway, York, PA, 1975. 200 pp., illus. $29.95.
A thorough study of the gunsmiths of Maryland who worked during the late 18th and early 19th centuries.

Arms Through the Ages, by William Reid, Harper & Row, NY, 1976. 288 pp., illus. $35.
A handsome volume enchanced in impressive style with nearly 800 specially drawn color and black-and-white drawings.

Arms of the World—1911, ed. by Joseph J. Schroeder, Jr., Digest Books, Inc., Northfield, IL, 1972, 420 pp., profusely illus. $5.95.
Reprint of the Adolph Frank ALFA 21 catalog of 1911 in 4 languages—English, a German, French, Spanish.

Armsmear, ed. by Henry Barnard, Beinfeld Publ., Inc., North Hollywood, CA, 1976. 399 pp., illus. $24.95.
A reprint of the memorial to Samuel Colt and his work, including 100 pp. on Colt revolvers and the armory. Limited, numbered edition.

Artillery and Ammunition of the Civil War, by Warren Ripley. Van Nostrand Reinhold Co., New York, N.Y., 1st ed., 1970. 384 pp., well illus. with 662 black and white photos and line drawings. $22.50.
A fine survey covering both Union and Confederate cannon and projectiles, as well as those imported.

Artillery Through the Ages, by A. Manucy, Normount Armament Co., Wickenburg, AZ, 1971. 92 pp., illus. Paper, $2.50
A short history of cannon, emphasizing types used in America.

Australian Service Longarms, by Ian D. Skennerton, I. D. Skennerton, Margate, Australia, 1975. 213 pp., illus. $23.50.
A study of the firearms used in Australian service, from the first landing there (1788) to the present day.

Badges & Emblems of the British Forces 1940, Arms and Armour Press, London, 1968. 64 pp. Paper, $3.00.
Reprint of a comprehensive guide to badges and emblems worn by all British forces in 1940, including Welfare, Aux. Services, Nursing Units, etc. Over 350 illus.

Ballard Rifles in the H. J. Nunnemacher Coll., by Eldon G. Wolff. Milwaukee Public Museum, Milwaukee, Wisc., 2nd ed. 1961. Paper, 77 p. plus 4 pp. of charts and 27 plates. $3.50.
A thoroughly authoritative work on all phases of the famous rifles, their parts, patent and manufacturing history.

Basic Documents on U.S. Marital Arms, commentary by Col. B. R. Lewis, reissue by Ray Riling, Phila., Pa., 1956 and 1960.
Rifle Musket Model 1855. The first issue rifle of musket caliber, a muzzle loader equipped with the Maynard Primer, 32 pp. $2.50.
Rifle Musket Model 1863. The Typical Union muzzle-loader of the Civil War, 26 pp. $1.75.
Breech-Loading Rifle Musket Model 1866. The first of our 50 caliber breechloading rifles, 12 pp. $1.75.
Remington Navy Rifle Model 1870. A commercial type breech-loader made at Springfield, 16 pp. $1.75.
Lee Straight Pull Navy Rifle Model 1895. A magazine cartridge arm of 6mm caliber. 23 pp. $3.00.
Breech-Loading Rifle Musket Model 1868. The first 50-70 designed as such. 20 pp. $1.75.
Peabody Breech-Loading Arms (five models)—27 pp. $2.75.
Ward-Burton Rifle Musket 1871—16 pp. $2.50.
Springfield Rifle, Carbine & Army Revolvers (cal. 45) model 1873 including Colt and Smith & Wesson hand arms. 52 pp. $3.00.
U.S. Magazine Rifle and Carbine (cal. 30) Model 1892 (the Krag Rifle) 36 pp. $3.00.

The Bedford County Rifle and its Makers, by Calvin Hetrick, George Shumway, York, PA, 1973. 39 pp., illus., paper covers. $5.00.
Reprint of Hetrick's study of the graceful and distinctive muzzle-loading rifles made in Bedford County, PA.

The Bird Decoy; An American Art Form, edited by Paul A. Johnsgard, University of Nebraska Press, Lincoln, NB, 1976. 190 pp., illus. $17.95.
For decoy collectors, carvers, and anyone concerned with folk art or antiques in general.

Blunderbusses, by D. R. Baxter. Stackpole Books, Harrisburg, Pa., 1970. 80 pp., 60 illus. $5.50.
Traces blunderbuss development from the 16th century, covering basic designs, firing systems, the double blunderbuss and revolving pepperbox design.

The Book of the Continental Soldier, by Harold L. Peterson, Promontory Press, NY, 1974. 287 pp., illus. $6.98.
A complete account of the uniforms, weapons and equipment with which he lived and fought.

The Book of Winchester Engraving, by R. L. Wilson, Wallace Beinfeld Publ., Inc., Studio City, CA, 1975. Over 400 pp., illus. $39.95.
Over 700 photos (many in full color) of the great engraved Winchesters in the world.

The Boxer Cartridge in the British Service, by B. A. Temple, B. A. Temple, Burbank, Australia, 1977. 250 pp., illus. $30.
This work relates the history of the Boxer Cartridge as used by Britain and her colonies from 1866 to the 1930s.

The Breech-Loader in the Service, 1816-1917, by Claud E. Fuller, N. Flayderman, New Milford, Conn., 1965. 381 pp., illus. $14.50.
Revised ed. of a 1933 historical reference on U.S. standard and experimental military shoulder arms. Much patent data, drawings, and photographs of the arms.
A voluminous work that covers handloading—and other things—in

great detail. Replete with data for all cartridge forms.

A Brief History of Bullet Moulds, by Codman Parkerson, Pioneer Press, Union City, TN, 1975. 31 pp., illus. Paper covers. $1.75. Thoroughly examines the evolution of bullet moulds from their earliest forms to today's advanced types.

British and American Flintlocks, by Fred. Wilkinson. Country Life Books, London, 1971. 64 pp., illus. $2.95.
Historical and technical aspects of flintlock firearms, in military and civilian use.

British and American Infantry Weapons of World War II, by A. J. Barker. 1st ed., 1969, Arco Publishing Co., New York, N.Y. 76 pp., illus., $3.50.
A British officer's survey that includes numerous specialized weapons, all are illustrated and described.

British Military Longarms, 1715-1815 by D. W. Bailey. Stackpole Books, Harrisburg, PA, 1971. 80 pp., $5.95.
The Regulation service longarms of the British Army and Navy during a century of conflict in Europe, America and India, are fully described and illus.

British Military Longarms 1815-1865, by D. W. Bailey. Stackpole Books, Harrisburg, PA, 1972. 79 pp., illus. $5.95.
Concise account, covering muskets, carbines, rifles and their markings.

British Pistols and Guns, 1640-1940, by Ian Glendenning. Arco Publ. Co., NY, 1967. 194 pp., photos and drawings. $7.50.
Historical review of British firearms, with much data and illustration of furniture and decoration of fine weapons.

British Smooth-Bore Artillery, by Maj.-Gen. B. P. Hughes. Stackpole Books, Harrisburg, PA, 1969. 144 pp., illus. $14.95.
On the muzzle-loading artillery of the 18th and 19th centuries, covering dimensions, ammunition, and application.

California Gunsmiths 1846-1900, by Lawrence P. Sheldon, Far Far West Publ., Fair Oaks, CA, 1977. 289 pp., illus. $29.65.
A study of early California gunsmiths and the firearms they made.

The Canadian Gunsmiths 1608-1900, by S. James Gooding. Museum Restoration Service, Canada, 1962. 322 pp., illus. $17.50.
Comprehensive survey of the gunmakers of Canada and the products of their skill, from early settlement to the age of the breech-loader.

Cartology Savalog, by Gerald Bernstein, Gerald Bernstein, St. Louis, MO, 1976. 177 pp., illus. Paper covers. $8.95.
An infinite variations catalog of small arms ammunition stamps.

Cartridge Headstamp Guide, by H. P. White and B. D. Munhall. H. P. White Laboratory, Bel Air, MD, 1978. 263 pp., illus. $25.75.
An important reference on headstamping of small arms ammo, by manufacturers in many countries. Clear illus. of 1936 headstamps of every type.

Cartridges for Collectors, by Fred A. Datig. Borden Publishing Co., Alhambra, Calif, Vol. I (Centerfire), 1958; Vol. II (Rimfire and Misc.) Types, 1963; Vol. III (Additional Rimfire, Centerfire, and Plastic,) 1967. Each of the three volumes 176 pp., well illus. and each priced at $7.50.
Vol. III supplements the first two books and presents 300 additional specimens. All illus. are shown in full-scale line drawings.

Cast Iron Toy Pistols 1870-1940, by Charles W. Best, Rocky Mountain Arms & Antiques, Englewood, CO, 1973. 217 pp., illus. $15.00.
Provides photographs and descriptions of most of the iron toy pistols made, plus values and rarity guides.

A Century of Guns and Shooting, by H. J. Blanch, EP Publ., Ltd., London, England, 1976. 153. pp., illus. $10.00.
A reprint of the scarce 1909 London edition. A sketch of the leading types of sporting and military small arms, with over 150 illustrations of guns and rifles.

Chesapeake Bay Decoys: The Men Who Made and Used Them, by R. H. Richardson, Crow Haven Publishers, Cambridge, MD, 1973. 200 pp., illus. $12.00.
A comprehensive history of decoy making by decoy carvers of the Chesapeake Bay Area. Illus. with over 340 examples of their work.

Civil War Carbines, by A. F. Lustyik. World Wide Gun Report, Inc., Aledo, ILL, 1962. 63 pp., illus. paper covers, $2.00.
Accurate, interesting summary of most carbines of the Civil War period, in booklet form, with numerous good illus.

Civil War Collector's Encyclopedia, Volume I, by Francis R. Lord, Castle Books, NY, 1965. 384 pp., illus. $8.95.

Civil War Collector's Encyclopedia, Volume II, by Francis R. Lord, Lord American Research, Inc. West Columbia, SC, 1976. 224 pp., illus. $19.50.
A companion to Volume I. Over 300 illustrations. Covers insignia, guns, bayonets, swords, etc.

Civil War Guns, by William B. Edwards, Castle Books, NY, 1976. 438 pp., illus. $10.00
Describes and records the exciting and sometimes romantic history of forging weapons for war and heroism of the men who used them.

Civil War Weapons, by C. B. Colby, Coward, McCann & Geoghegan, NY, 1962. 48 pp., illus. $4.95.
Small arms and artillery of the Blue and Gray.

The Collecting of Guns, ed. by Jas. E. Serven. Stackpole Books, Harrisburg, PA, 1964. 272 pp., illus. $5.95.
A new and massive compendium of gun lore for serious collectors by recognized experts. Separate chapters cover major categories and aspects of collecting. Over 600 firearms illus. Handsomely designed, deluxe binding in slip case.

Collecting Military Antiques, by Frederick Wilkinson, Harper & Row, Publ., NY, 1976. 208 pp., illus. $14.95.
One of the most comprehensive surveys of military antiques ever published.

Collector's Guide to Luger Values 1972-73 Edition, by Michael Reese. Pelican Pub. Co., Gretna, LA, 1972. 10 pp., paper covers. $1.00.
Collector's guide to top prices.

The Collector's Handbook of U.S. Cartridge Revolvers, 1856 to 1899, by W. Barlow Fors, Adams Press, Chicago, IL, 1973. 96 pp., illus. $6.00.
Concise coverage of brand names, patent listings, makers' history, and essentials of collecting.

Collector's Illustrated Encyclopedia of the American Revolution, by Geo. C. Neumann and Frank J. Kravic, Stackpole Books, Harrisburg, PA, 1975. 288 pp., illus. $17.95.
Over 1,000 illus. show over 2,300 artifacts of the revolutionary period—from accoutrements to writing implements—with explanatory text for each.

Colonel Colt, London, by Joseph G. Rosa, Arms & Armour Press, London, England, 1976. 208 pp., illus. $26.50
The history of Colt's London Firearms 1851-1857. Details the arms produced in London armoury.

The Colt Collector Magazine Vol. I, ed. by Keith Cochran, Colt Collector Press, Rapid City, SD, 1975. 118 pp., illus. $22.75.
A limited and numbered bound edition of the first year of the magazine dedicated to Colt collectors everywhere.
Same, but 198 pp., Vol. II, $22.75.

Colt Commemorative Firearms, by R. L. Wilson, Robert E. P. Cherry, Geneseo, IL, 2nd ed., revised, 1973. 126 pp., illus. Paper only. $5.95

A valuable guide to the collector of Colt commemorative firearms. Lists all models to date.

Colt 1896 English Price List, a reprint by Americana Archives, Topsfield, MA, 1976. 16 pp., illus. Paper covers. $3.00.
Illustrates and prices (in English currency) the full Colt line of the period.

Colt Firearms Catalog, 1934, a reprint by Americana Archives, Topsfield, MA, 1976. 40 pp., illus. Paper covers. $4.00.
28 Colt revolvers and automatic pistols are described and illustrated.

Colt Firearms from 1836, by James E. Serven. New 7th ed. Foundation Press, La Habra, CA, 1973. 398 pp., illus. $19.95.
Excellent survey of the Colt company and its products. Updated with new SAA production chart and commemorative list.

Colt Peacemaker Dictionary & Encyclopedia Illustrated, by Keith A. Cochran, Colt Collectors Press, Rapid City, SD, 1976. 300 pp., illus. Paper covers, $12.95. Cloth, $15.95.
Over 1300 entries pertaining to everything there is to know about the Colt Peacemaker.

Colt Pistols, by R. L. Wilson and R. E. Hable, Taylor Publ. Co, Dallas, TX, 1977. 400 pp., illus. $100.00.
A non-technical book presenting a superb collection of Colt handguns in color.

Colt Tips, by E. Dixon Larson. Pioneer Press, Union City, TN, 1972. 140 pp., illus. Paper covers. $3.95.
Comprehensive, discriminating facts about Colt models from 1836 to 1898.

Colt's Variations of the Old Model Pocket Pistol, 1848 to 1872, by P. L. Shumaker. Borden Publishing Co., Alhambra, CA 1966, a reprint of the 1957 edition. 150 pp., illus. $6.00.
A useful tool for the Colt specialist and a welcome return of a popular source of information that had been long out-of-print.

Confederate Handguns, by Wm. A. Albaugh III. Hugh Benet Jr., and Edw. N. Simmons. Geo. Shumway, York, PA, 1963. 272 pp., 125 illus. $20.00.
Every known true Confederate pistol and revolver is described and illus., with the story of its maker and procurement by the C.S.A. Much new information includes listing of C. W. makers and dealers, information on replicas and fakes. Indispensable to the collector and student of these arms and their period.

Custer Battle Guns, by John S. du Mont, The Gunroom Press, Highland Park, NJ, 1977. 113 pp., illus. $10.00.
Complete story of the guns at the Little Big Horn.

Deanes' Manual of the History and Science of Fire-arms, by J. Deane. Standard Publications, Huntington, WV, 1946 facsimile reprint of the rare English original of 1858. 291 pp., three folding plates. $6.00.
A history of firearms, plus design and manufacture of military and sporting arms.

Decoy Collector's Guide 1963-1964-1965, ed. by H. D. Sorenson, Burlington, IA, 1971. Irregular pagination, illus. $16.00.
This volume includes all of the 12 booklets originally published as quarterlies.

Decoy Collector's Guide 1966-67 Annual, ed. by H. D. Sorenson, Burlington, IA, 1966. 125 pp., illus. $6.00.
Well-illustrated articles on American decoys.

Decoy Collector's Guide, 1968, ed. by H. D. Sorenson, 1967, Burlington, IA 128 pp, 75 photos. Spiral bound. $6.00.
History, decoy patents, carving, collecting, etc.

A Digest of Cartridges for Small Arms Patented in the United States, England and France, by W. A. Bartlett and D. B. Gallatin, Museum Restoration Service, Ottawa, Canada, 1977. 52 pp., illus. Paper covers. $4.95.
Reprint of the very scarce 1878 edition. A classic publication for the cartridge collector.

Digest of Patents Relating to Breech-Loading and Magazine Small Arms (1836-1873), by V. D. Stockbridge, WA, 1874. Reprinted 1963 by E. N. Flayderman, Greenwich, Conn. 18
An exhaustive compendium of patent documents on firearms, indexed and classified by breech mechanism types, valuable reference for students and collectors.

Dutch Muskets & Pistols, by J. B. Kist, J. P. Puype, and W. Van Der Mark, George Shumway, York, PA, 1974. 176 pp., illus. $24.00.
An illus. history of 17th Century gunmaking in the Low Countries.

The Samuel E. Dyke Collection of Kentucky Pistols, by Frank Klay, The Gun Room Press, Highland Park, NJ, 1974. 30 pp., illus. Paper covers. $1.75.
Reprint of a study of Kentucky pistols in the collection of the dean of Kentucky pistol collectors.

Early Indian Trade Guns—1625 to 1775, by T. M. Hamilton. Museum of the Great Plains, Lawton, Okla. 1969. 34 pp., well illus., paper covers. $3.50.
Detailed descriptions of subject arms, compiled from early records and from the study of remnants found in Indian country.

Early Loading Tools and Bullet Molds, by R. H. Chamberlain. The Farm Tribune, Porterville, GA, 1971. 75 pp., illus. Paper covers, $5.00.
An excellent aid to collectors.

English Pistols & Revolvers, by J. N. George. Arco Publ. Co., Inc., N.Y.C., 1962, 256 pp., 28 plates, $12.00.
The 2nd reprinting of a notable work first publ. in 1938. Treats of the historical development and design of English hand firearms from the 17th cent. to the present. A much better book than the former reprint, particularly as to clarity of the tipped-in plates.

Ethan Allen, Gunmaker, by Harold R. Mouillesseaux, Museum Rest. Serv., Ottawa, Ont., Can., 1973. 170 pp., illus. $19.95.
A complete history of Ethan Allen, his arms and his companies.

European Armour in the Tower of London by A. R. Dufty. H. M. Stationery Office, London, England, 1968. 17 pp. text, 164 plates, $12.60.
Pictorial record of almost 400 pieces of armor, helmets, and accouterments in the famous Tower of London collection.

European Arms & Armour, by Chas. H. Ashdown, Brussel & Brussel, NY, 1967. A reprint, 384 pp., illus. with 42 plates and 450 drawings. $5.95.
Historical survey of body armor up to the era of gunpowder, with some coverage on weapons and early firearms.

Famous Guns from the Smithsonian Collection, by H. W. Bowman. Arco Publ. Co., Inc., NY, 1967. 112 pp., illus. $3.50.
The finest of the "Famous Guns" series.

Famous Guns from the Winchester Collection, by H. W. Bowman. Arco Publ. Co., NYC, 1958 and later. 144 pp., illus. $3.50.
The gems of the hand and shoulder arms in the great collection at New Haven, CT.

Fifteen Years in the Hawken Lode, by John D. Baird, The Gun Room Press, Highland Park, NJ, 1976. 120 pp., illus. $12.95.
A collection of thoughts and observations gained from many years of intensive study of the guns from the shop of the Hawken brothers.

'51 Colt Navies, by N. L. Swayze. Gun Hill Publ. Co., Yazoo City, MS, 1967. 243 pp., well illus. $15.00.
The first major effort devoting its entire space to the 1851 Colt Navy revolver. There are 198 photos of models, sub-models, variations, parts,

markings, documentary material, etc. Fully indexed.

Firearms of the Confederacy, by Claud R. Fuller & Richard D. Steuart, Quarterman Publ., Inc., Lawrence, MA, 1977. 333 pp., illus. $25.00.
The shoulder arms, pistols and revolvers of the Confederate soldier, including the regular United States Models, the imported arms and those manufactured within the Confederacy.

Firearms Curiosa, by Lewis Winant, Ray Riling, Philadelphia, PA, 2nd and deluxe reissue 1961, 281 pp., well illus. $5.00.
Reissue publ. by Bonanza Books, N.Y.C., 1965. $2.98.
An important work for those with an interest in odd, distinctive and unusual forms and firing.

Firearms on the Frontier: Guns at Fort Michilimackinac 1715-1781, by T. M. Hamilton, Report No. 5 in the Reports in Mackinac History and Archaeology Series, Mackinac Island State Park Commission, Lansing, MI, 1976. 39 pp., illus. Paper covers. $3.00.
Report on the gun parts and related material recovered in the excavation of Fort Michilimackinac.

Firearms Past & Present, by Jaroslav Lugs, Grenville Publ. Co., Ltd., London, England, 1973. In two volumes, Vol. 1, text, 716 pp.; Vol. 2, plates, 429 pp. In slipcase. $50.00.
The English ed. of this extremely important work on firearm systems and their histories.

The Firearms Price Guide, by D. Byron, Crown Publ. Co., NY, 1978. 640 pp. Paper covers. $9.95.
A complete price guide to firearms. Over 20,000 prices, international in scope.

Firearms in the Prince Odescalchi Collection in Rome, by Nolfo de Carpegna, translated by Marcello Terenzi, Edizioni Marte, Rome, Italy, 1975. 201 pp., illus. $20.00.
English translation of the 1968 Italian edition describing and illustrating arms from this world famous collection.

Flayderman's Guide to Antique American Firearms,—by Norm Flayderman, DBI Books, Inc., Northfield, IL, 1977. 576 pp., illus. Paper covers. $12.95.
An invaluable guide for the serious collector by one of America's most astute firearms analysts.

Flintlock Guns and Rifles, by F. Wilkinson, Stackpole Books, Harrisburg, PA, 1971. 80 pp., $4.95.
Illus. reference guide for 1650-1850 period showing makers, mechanisms and users.

The Flintlock, Its Origin and Development, by Torsten Lenk; J. T. Hayward, Editor, Holland Press, London, 1964. 192 pp., 134 illus. $30.00.
First English-text version of the 1939 Swedish work termed "the most important book on the subject." Original illus. are reproduced, and a new index and bibliography complete this valuable book.

Flintlock Pistols, by F. Wilkinson, Arms & Armour Press, London, England, 1977. 76 pp., illus. Paper covers. $3.95.
An illustrated reference guide to flintlock pistols from the 17th to the 19th centuries.

For Fuhrer and Fatherland: Military Awards of the Third Reich, by John R. Angolia, R. James Bender Publ., San Jose, CA, 1976. 448 pp., illus. $17.95.
This massive presentation breaks down the highly complex system of Third Reich military decorations into easily understood segments.

Forsyth & Co.—Patent Gunmakers, by W. Keith Neal and D. H. L. Back. G. Bell & Sons, London, 1st ed., 1969, 280 pp., well illus. $12.95.
An excellent study of the invention and development of the percussion system by the Rev. Alexander Forsyth in the early 19th century. All Forsyth types are covered, plus a diary of events from 1768 to 1852.

.45-70 Rifles, by J. Behn, Rutgers Book Center, Highland Park, NJ, 1972. New ed., 150 pp., illus. $5.95.
Covers the official U.S. Army small arms cartridge and the weapons for its use.

The 45/70 Trapdoor Springfield Dixie Collection, compiled by Walter Crutcher and Paul Oglesby, Pioneer Press, Union City, TN, 1975. 600 pp., illus. Paper covers. $9.95.
An illustrated listing of the 45-70 Springfields in the Dixie Gun Works Collection. Little known details and technical information is given, plus current values.

Four Centuries of Liège Gunmaking, by Claude Gaier, English translation by F. J. Norris, Sotheby/Parke Bernet, London, England, 1976. 287 pp., illus. $80.
An essential reference work for all serious students of firearms, for specialist collectors and for everyone interested in gunmaking, engraving and the evolution of guns.

The French Army in America, by E. P. Hamilton. Museum Restoration Service, Ottawa, 1967. 108 pp., illus. $3.00.
Concise historical coverage, illus. with contemporary documents and manual-of-arms plates. Text in English and French. Paper wrappers.

French Pistols and Sporting Guns, by A. N. Kennard. Transatlantic Arts, Inc., Levittown, NY, 1972. 63 pp., illus. $2.95.
Traces the technical evolution of French pistols and sporting guns from matchlock to breechloader.

French Military Weapons, 1717-1938, by James E. Hicks. N. Flayderman & Co., New Milford, CT, 1964. 281 pp., profusely illus. $9.50.
A valuable reference work, first publ. 1938 as *Notes on French Ordnance*, this rev. ed. covers hand, shoulder, and edged weapons, ammunition and artillery, with history of various systems.

The Gatling Gun, by Paul Wahl & D. R. Toppel. Arco Publ., N.Y.C., 1971. 168 pp., illus. $5.95.
History of the famed rapid-fire weapon used by many of the world's armies and navies from 1861.

German Mauser Rifle—Model of 1898, by J. E. Coombes and J. L. Aney. A reprint in paper covers by Francis Bannerman Sons, New York, NY, of their 1921 publication. 20 pp., well illus. $1.50.
Data on the subject weapon and its W. W. I development. Bayonets and ammunition are also described and illus.

The German MP40 Submachine Gun, by Fred L. Rexer, Jr., Anubis Press, Highlands, TX, 1976. 27 pp., illus. Paper covers. $3.
The first English language manual on the German MP40 submachine gun used in most wars since 1945.

German Pistols and Holsters 1934-1945, by Maj. Robert D. Wittington III, The Gun Room Press, Highland Park, NJ, 1976. 224 pp., illus. $15.
A manual for collectors on subject items issued to military, police and NSDAP. Covers all models of various designs, including those of foreign manufacture.

A Glossary of the Construction, Decoration and Use of Arms and Armor in all Countries and in all Times, by Geo. C. Stone, Jack Brussel, NY, 2nd reprint, 1966, 694 pp., illus. $10.98.
The outstanding work on its subject, authoritative and accurate in detail. The major portion is on oriental arms.

Great British Gunmakers 1740-1790, by W. Keith Neal & D. H. L. Back, Sotheby Parke Bernet Publications, Los Angeles, CA, 1975. 196 pp., illus. $70.00
The history of John Twigg and the Packington Guns.

The Great Guns, by H. L. Peterson and Robt. Elman. Grosset & Dunlap, NY, 1972. $8.98.
Basic and general history with 70 full color illustrations and 140 photos of some of the finest guns from American collections. A well written text.

Great Sporting Posters of the Golden Age, by Sid Latham, Stackpole Books, Harrisburg, PA, 1978. 48 pp., illus. $8.95.
Over 20 nostalgic full-color reproductions of early 20th century calendars, posters, and other advertisements from sporting goods and firearms manufacturers.

Great Weapons of World War I, by Com. G. Dooly, Walker & Co., NY, 1969, 340 pp., illus. $14.50.
Describes all the important weapons and system developments used during WWI.

The Gun and its Development, by W. W. Greener. Bonanza Books, NY, 1967. A reprint. 804 pp., profusely illus. $8.95.
A facsimile of the famous 9th edition of 1910. Covers history and development of arms in general with emphasis on shotguns.

Gun Collector's Digest, Volume I, edited by Jos. J. Schroeder, Jr. Digest Books, Inc., Northfield, IL, 1974. 320 pp., illus. Paper covers. $6.95.
Articles on guns as an investment; rating gun condition; display and security; gun collecting and the law; building a collector's library; plus features on all sorts of collectors guns.

Gun Collector's Digest, Volume II, edited by Joseph J. Schroeder, Jr. DBI Books, Inc., Northfield, IL, 1976, 288 pp., illus. Paper covers $7.95.
Comprehensive coverage on guns, gun shows, bayonets, commemoratives, security, gun laws, current Treasury regulations. Includes updated collectors bibliography and gun show directory.

The Gun Collector's Fact Book, by Louis W. Steinwedel, Arco Publ. Co., NY, 1975. 256 pp., illus. Paper covers, $5.95; Cloth, $10.00.
An illus. introduction to "the gentle art of gun collecting"—where and how to buy antique guns, points that affect their value, and hints on restoration.

The Gun Collector's Handbook of Values 1977-1978, by C. E. Chapel, Coward, McCann & Geoghegan, Inc., NY, 1977. 462 pp., illus. $17.95.
Eleventh rev. ed. of the best-known price reference for collectors. Includes new chapters on Winchester and Smith & Wesson guns.

Gun Digest Book of Modern Gun Values, by Jack Lewis, DBI Books, Inc., Northfield, IL, 1975. 288 pp., illus. $7.95.
Invaluable guide for buying, selling, trading or identifying guns—handguns, rifles and shotguns are covered in separate sections. Feature articles relate to collecting and values.

Gunfighter Colts & Rigs, by Fred Warner, Colt Collector Press, Rapid City SD 1977. 100 pp., illus. Paper covers. $5.
The fast-draw rigs of the famous Western gunfighters.

Gunmakers of Indiana, by A. W. Lindert. Publ. by the author, Homewood, IL, 1968, 3rd ed. 284 pp., illus. Large format. $15.00.
An extensive and historical treatment, illus. with old photographs and drawings.

Guns and Gun Collecting, by De Witt Bailey; et al. Octopus Books, London, Eng., 1972. 128 pp., illus. $5.95.
A new look at the world of firearms, including not only the historical aspects but hunting and sporting guns and 19th and 20th century weapons of war. Nearly 180 photos, 78 in full color.

Guns of the World, edited by Hans Tanner, Bonanza Books, NY, 1977. 400 pp., illus. $5.98.
The complete collector's and trader's guide.

The Gunsmiths of Canada, by S. James Gooding, Museum Rest. Serv., Ottawa, Ont., Can., 1974. 32 pp., illus. Paper covers. $2.00.
Names, dates and locations for over 800 gunsmiths, plus bibliography.

Gunsmiths of Ohio—18th & 19th Centuries: Vol. I, Biographical Data, by Donald A. Hutslar, George Shumway, York, PA, 1973. 444 pp., illus. $29.50.
An important source book, full of information about the old-time gunsmiths of Ohio.

Hall System Military Firearms and Conversions in the Museum Collection. Veteran Association of the First Corps of Cadets Museum, Boston, MA, 1973. 20 pp., illus. Paper covers. $1.50
Illustrates and describes various models, including several Confederate conversions.

Hall's Breechloaders, by R. T. Huntington, Geo. Shumway, Publ. 1972. 369 pp., illus. Paper, $15.00.
Definitive treatise on John H. Hall and his inspectors. Shows all known models of the Hall rifle, appurtenances and pistol.

Handbook for the Canadian Service Rifle, Ross Mark III, reprinted by Marlowe Dev. Ltd., Port Moody, B.C., Canada, 1976. 32 pp., illus. Paper covers. $3.
Description and care of components for all models of the Ross service rifle.

Handbook of Identification Marks on Canadian Arms, by R. Barrie Manarey, Century Press, Alberta, Can., 1973. 82 pp., illus. Paper covers. $6.00.
Lists over 1000 translations of codes and initials which appear on Canadian arms.

Handfeuerwaffen System Vetterli, by Hugo Schneider; et al. Stocker-Schmid, A. G. Dietikon-Zurich, Switzerland, 1972. 143 pp., illus. $26.00.
Describes and illustrates the many models of Vetterli rifles and carbines, the bayonets and ammunition used with them. Many large clear illustrations. German text.

Hawken Rifles, The Mountain Man's Choice, by John D. Baird, The Gun Room Press, Highland Park, NJ, 1976. 95 pp., illus. $12.95.
Covers the rifles developed for the Western fur trade. Numerous specimens are described and shown in photographs.

Hints to Riflemen, by H. W. S. Cleveland. Distributor, Robert Halter, New Hope, PA, 286 pp., illustrated. $10.00.
A reprint of the original 1864 edition, to which *Practical Directions for the use of the Rifle* has been added.

Historical Hartford Hardware, by William W. Dalrymple, Colt Collector Press, Rapid City, SD, 1976. 42 pp., illus. Paper covers. $4.00.
Historically associated Colt revolvers.

A History of Firearms, by H. L. Peterson. Chas. Scribner's Sons, N.Y.C., 1961. 57 pp., profusely illus. $5.95.
From the origin of firearms through each ignition form and improvement to the M-14. Drawings by Daniel D. Feaser.

History of Modern U.S. Military Small Arms Ammunition, Vol. 2, 1940-1945, By F. W. Hackley, W. M. Woodin and E. L. Scranton, The Gun Room Press, Highland Park, NJ, 1976. 300 pp., illus. $25.00.
A unique book covering the entire field of small arms ammunition developed during the critical World War II years.

History of Smith & Wesson, by Roy G. Jinks, Beinfeld Publ., Inc., No. Hollywood, CA, 1977. 290 pp., illus. $15.95.
A record of 125 years of progress and excellence in producing fine products.

The History of Weapons of the American Revolution, by George C. Neuman, Outlet Books, NY, 1976. 373 pp., illus. $3.98.
A new printing of this important and timely work. Traces the history of

Revolutionary War weapons of all types.
The History of Winchester Firearms 1866-1975, 4th ed., ed. by George R. Watrous, James C. Rikhoff and Thomas H. Hall, Winchester Press, NY, 1975. 229 pp., illus. $15.00 in slipcase.
A comprehensive record of each model and the part it played in the establishment of Winchester's reputation for arms of the highest quality.
Hopkins & Allen Gun Guide and Catalog (ca. 1913). Wagle Publ., Lake Wales, FA, 1972. 32 pp., illus. Paper covers. $5.00.
Facsimile of the original catalog. Shows the firms rifles, shotguns and pistols, and includes prices. Full color cover painting by Dan Smith.
Identifying Old U.S. Muskets, Rifles and Carbines, by Arcadi Gluckman, Bonanza Books, NY, 1973. 489 pp., illus. $2.49.
A revision of Colonel Gluckman's *U.S. Muskets, Rifles and Carbines.*
Identifying Old U.S. Muskets, Rifles & Carbines, by Col. A. Gluckman. Stackpole Books, Harrisburg, PA, 1973. 487 pp., illus. $2.98.
Collector's guide to U.S. long arms, first publ. 1959. Numerous models of each type are described and shown, with histories of their makers.
Illustrated British Firearms Patents 1714-1853, comp. and ed. by Stephen V. Grancsay and Merrill Lindsay. Winchester Press. NY, 1969. Unpaginated. $20.00.
Facsimile of patent documents with a bibliography. Limited, numbered ed. of 1000, bound in ¾ leather and marbled boards.
An Illustrated History of Guns and Small Arms, by Joseph G. Rosa and Robin May, Castle Books, Secaucus, NJ, 1976. 96 pp., 135 color photographs. $7.98.
The story of the gun in all its forms from the invention of gunpowder to the rapid fire arms of today, and from tiny hand guns to machine guns.
Ingram M10 Submachine Gun Calibre .45 ACP and 9mm, by Fred L. Rexer, Jr., Anubis Press Ltd., Houston, TX, 1976. 44 pp., illus. Paper covers. $3.
A basic manual and guide to maintenance and operation of the subject weapons.
An Introduction to British Artillery in North America, by S. J. Gooding. Museum Rest. Serv., Ottawa, 1965. 54 pp., illus., Paperbound. $2.00.
Concise account of such equipment used in America 1750-1850.
Japanese Armour, by L. J. Anderson. Stackpole Books, Harrisburg, PA, 1968. 84 pp., illus. $4.95.
British reference on museum quality armor made by the Myochin and Saotome families between the 15th and 20th centuries.
Japanese Infantry Weapons of World War II, by George Markham, Arms & Armour Press, London, England, 1977. 96 pp., 80 plates and line drawings. $11.50.
Traces, section-by-section and gun-by-gun, the concise history and development of infantry equipment—pistols, rifles, sub-machine guns, machine guns, grenades, mortars, infantry artillery, etc.
The Kentucky Rifle, by J. G. W. Dillin. Geo. Shumway, York, PA, 1975. 6th Ed. 202 pp., illus. $20.00
A respected work on the long rifles developed in colonial days and carried by pioneers and soldiers. Much information of value to collectors and historians. Limited ed.
The Kentucky Rifle, by Merrill Lindsay. Arma Press, NY/The Historical Society of York County, York, PA, 1972. 100 pp., 81 large colored illustrations. $15.
Presents in precise detail and exact color 77 of the finest Kentucky rifles ever assembled in one place. Also describes the conditions which led to the development of this uniquely American arm.
Kentucky Rifle Patchboxes & Barrel Marks, by Roy F. Chandler, Valley View Offset, Duncannon, PA, 1971. 400 pp., $20.00.
Reference work illustrating hundreds of patchboxes, together with the mark or signature of the maker.
Kentucky Rifles and Pistols 1756-1850, compiled by members of the Kentucky Rifle Association, Wash., DC, Golden Age Arms Co., Delaware, OH, 1976. 275 pp., illus. $22.50
Profusely illustrated with more than 300 examples of rifles and pistols never before published.
The Leather Jacket Soldier, by O. B. Faulk. Socio-Technical Pub., Pasadena, CA, 1971, 80 pp., illus. $10.00.
History of such Spanish military equipment of the late 18th century as lances, horse accoutrements, guns, uniforms, etc.
Lever Action Magazine Rifles Derived from the Patents of Andrew Burgess, by Samuel L. Maxwell Sr., Samuel L. Maxwell, Bellevue, WA, 1976. 368 pp., illus. $29.95.
The complete story of a group of lever action magazine rifles collectively referred to as the Burgess/Morse, the Kennedy or the Whitney.
The Lewis Gun, by J. David Truby, Paladin Press, Boulder, CO, 1976. 203 pp., illus. $25.
A pictorial history of this famous gun.
The Lifesaving Guns of David Lyle, by J. P. Barnett, South Bend Replicas, Inc., South Bend, IN, 1976. 105 pp., illus. Paper covers. $6.95.
For students of firearms and maritime history; a useful and important corpus of information not available anywhere else.
J. P. Lovell Arms Co. 1890 Catalog of Guns and Hunting Supplies, The American Historical Catalog Collection, The Pyne Press, Princeton, NJ, 1971. 88 pp., illus. Stiff paper covers. $3.50.
Facsimile of the original catalog. Illus. with pictures of shotguns, rifles, pistols, revolvers, sights, and other firearms accessories.
Luger: An Illustrated History of the Handguns of Hugo Borchardt and Georg Luger, 1875-1975, by John Walter, Arms and Armour Press, London, England, 1977. 256 pp., illustrated with over 300 photographs. $27.50.
A full and comprehensive coverage of the world's most famous pistol.
Luger Tips, by Michael Reese II, Pioneer Press, Union City, TN, 1976. 96 pp., illus. Paper covers. $7.50
A compilation of the author's articles on the Luger which appeared in *Guns and Ammo* magazine.
The Lure of Antique Arms, by Merrill Lindsay, David McKay, Co., NY, 1975. Illus. with more than 50 photos. $9.95.
A beginning collectors book. Everything a novice needs to know to take up the exciting (and profitable) hobby of collecting antique arms.
Maine Made Guns and Their Makers, by Dwight B. Demeritt, Main State Museum, Hallowell, ME, 1973. 209 pp., illus. $22.00.
A fine reference work on Maine gunsmiths.
Manhattan Firearms, by Waldo E. Nutter, Stackpole Books, Harrisburg, PA, 1958. 250 pp., illus., in halftone. $10.00.
Complete history of the Manhattan Firearms Mfg. Co., and its products. Excellent specialized reference.
Manual of Rifling and Rifle Sights, by Lt.-Col. Viscount Bury, M.P., Ray Riling Arms Books Co., Phila., PA, 1971. 47 pp., Paper, $3.50.
Reprint of 1864 London edition done for the British National Rifle Ass'n. 141 illus., plus 3 folding plates.
The Manufacture of Armour and Helmets in 16th Century Japan, by Sakakibara Kozan. Holland Press, London, 1963. 156 pp., 32 pp. of illus. $20.00.
Important reference on styles and steps of making Japanese armor, first publ. Tokyo, 1800. Eng. trans., revised by H. R. Robinson of Tower of London Armouries.
Mauser Bolt Rifles, by Ludwig Olson, F. Brownell & Son, Inc., Montezuma, IA, 1976. 364 pp., illus. $24.95.
The most complete, detailed, authoritative and comprehensive work ever done on Mauser bolt rifles.
Metal Uniform Insignia of the US Army in the Southwest, 1846-1902, by S. B. Brinckerhoff, Arizona Pioneers Hist. Soc., Tucson, Ariz., 1972, 28 pp., illus. Paper covers. $2.50.
Monograph on buttons, badges, buckles, and other uniform insignia.
Metallic Cartridges, T. J. Treadwell, compiler. The Armoury, NYC, 1959. Unpaginated. 68 plates. Paper, $2.95.
A reduced-size reproduction of U.S. Ordnance Memoranda No. 14, originally publ. in 1873, on regulation and experimental cartridges manufactured and tested at Frankford Arsenal, Philadelphia, Pa.
Militaria, by Frederick Wilkinson. Hawthorn Books, New York, NY, 1969. 1st U.S. ed. 256 pp., well illus. in halftone. $5.95.
Introduction to military items of interest to collectors, including prints, medals, uniforms, military miniatures, weapons, badges, etc.
Military Arms of Canada, by Upper Canada Hist. Arms Soc. Museum Restoration Serv., West Hill, Ont., 1963. 43 pp., illus. $1.50.
Booklet cont. 6 authoritative articles on the principal models of Canadian mil. small arms. Gives characteristics of each, makers, quantities produced.
Military Breech-Loading Rifles, by V. D. Majendie and C. O. Browne, Fortress Publ., Inc., Stoney Creek, Ontario, Can., 1973. 129 pp. plus index, illus. $8.50.
A new ed. of the 1870 work dealing with the Snider, the Martini-Henry and Boxer ammunition.
Military Rifles of Japan, 1897-1945, by Fred L. Honeycutt, Jr. and F. Patt Anthony, published by the authors, Lake Park, FL, 1977. 212 pp., illus. $19.
A definitive work giving descriptions and serial number ranges of over 100 rifle variations.
Military Small Arms of the 20th Century, by Ian V. Hogg and John S. Weeks. Digest Books, Inc., Northfield, IL, 1973. 288 pp. Paper covers. $7.95.
Weapons from the world over are meticulously examined in this comprehensive encyclopedia of these military small arms issued since 1900. Over 600 illus.
Miniature Arms, by Merrill Lindsay. Winchester Press, New York, NY, 1970. 111 pp., illus. $5.95.
A concise study of small-scale replicas of firearms and other weapons of collector interest. Fine color photographs.
More Single Shot Rifles, by James C. Grant, The Gun Room Press, Highland Park, NJ, 1976. 324 pp., illus. $12.50
Details the guns made by Frank Wesson, Milt Farrow, Holden, Borchardt, Stevens, Remington, Winchester, Ballard and Peabody-Martini.
The NRA Collector's Series, Digest Books, Inc., Northfield, IL, 1971, 84 pp. paper covers $2.95.
Reprint of the three predecessors of *American Rifleman* magazine and the first edition of *American Rifleman.*
The NRA Gun Collectors Guide, by staff members of NRA. National Rifle Assn., Washington, D.C., 1972. 256 pp., well illus. $4.50.
A wealth of information on collecting and collectors arms, with 64 major and 41 short articles, selected from the last 18 years of "The American Rifleman."
Louis Napoleon on Artillery: The Development of Artillery from the 14th to the 17th Century, by W. Y. Carman, Arms and Armour Press, Middlesex, England, 1967. 24 pp., illus. Paper covers. $2.75.
A reprinting of rare original material—10 finely engraved plates, with 70 drawings, on the development of artillery, plus brief text.
Native American Bows, by T. M. Hamilton. George Shumway, York, PA, 1972. 148 pp., illus. $12.
Summary of the history and development of bows native to America, from early times to the present.
The New England Gun, by Merrill Lindsay, David McKay Co., NY, 1976. 155 pp., illus. Paper covers, $12.50. Cloth, $20.00
A study of more than 250 New England guns, powder horns, swords, and polearms in an exhibition by the New Haven Colony Historical Society.
The New Highland Military Discipline, by Geo. Grant. Museum Restoration Service, Ottawa, 1967. 32 pp., illus. $1.50
Reprint of a Scottish drill manual, regimental history, with illus. contemporary and modern. Paper wrappers.
The 9-pdr. Muzzle Loading Rifle, by J. D. Chown. Museum Restoration Service, Ottawa, 1967. 32 pp., illus. $1.50.
Reprint of an early Canadian artillery manual, with historical notes. Paper wrappers.
Simeon North: First Official Pistol Maker of the United States, by S. North and R. North, Rutgers Book Center, Highland Park, NJ, 1972. 207 pp., illus. $7.95.
Exact reprint of the original. Includes chapters on New England pioneer manufacturers and on various arms.
The Northwest Gun, by Charles E. Hanson, Jr., Nebraska State Historical Society, Lincoln, NB, 1976. 85 pp., illus., paper covers. $6.
Number 2 in the Society's "Publications in Anthropology." Historical survey of rifles which figured in the fur trade and settlement of the Northwest.
Notes on U.S. Ordnance, vol. II, 1776-1941, by James E. Hicks. Modern Books & Crafts, Greens Farms, Conn., 1971. 252 pp., illus. $8.00.
Updated version of a standard work on development of military weapons used by U.S. forces, from handguns to coast artillery and aerial bombs. This is not to be confused with Hicks 1940 United States Ordnance, referring mainly to Ordnance correspondence as Vol. II.
One Hundred Great Guns, by Merrill Lindsay, Walker & Co., NY, 1967. $35.00.
Here, in more than 200 superb full-color plates, is the flower of the gunmaker's art, perhaps the most famous and important of the world's firearms.
O.S.S. Special Weapons, Devices and Equipment, ed. by D. B. McLean, Normount Technical Publ. Co., Wickenburg, AZ, 1975. 114 pp., illus. Paper covers. $5.95.
Reproduction of the most fascinating materiel catalog ever issued, showing spy weapons of the legendary OSS.
An Outline of the History and Development of Hand Firearms, from the Earliest Period to About the End of the Fifteenth Century, by R. C. Clephan [Original ed., 1906]. A reprint in 1946 by Standard Publications, Inc., Huntington, W.Va. 60 pp., illus. $4.00.
A worthy facsimile of a very scarce, concise and scholarly work.
Peacemaker Evolutions & Variations, by Keith A. Cochran, Colt Collectors Press, Rapid City, SD, 1975. 47 pp., illus. Paper covers. $5.00.
Corrects many inaccuracies found in other books on the Peacemaker and gives much new information regarding this famous arm.
The Pennsylvania Kentucky Rifle, by Henry J. Kauffman, Bonanza Books, NY, 1977. 374 pp., illus. $6.98.
U.S. long rifles of collector interest. Makers, descriptions and manufacturing methods, etc.

Percussion Guns & Rifles, by D. W. Bailey. Stackpole Books, Harrisburg, PA, 1972. 79 pp., illus. $5.95.
A guide to the muzzle-loading percussion guns and rifles of the 19th century.
Pioneer Decoy Carvers, by Barry R. Berkey, Velma Berkey and Richard E. Berkey, Tidewater Publishers, Cambridge, MD, 1977. 161 pp., illus. $17.50.
A biography of Lemuel and Stephen Ward.
The Plains Rifle, by Charles E. Hanson, Jr., The Gun Room Press, Highland Park, NJ, 1977. 171 pp., illus. $11.95.
Historical survey of popular civilian arms used on the American frontiers, their makers, and their owners.
Plates & Buckles of the American Military 1795-1874, by Sydney C. Kerksis, The Gilgal Press, Kenesaw, GA, 1974. 567 pp., illus. $25.00.
Covers some 448 different belt and accoutrement plates from the post-revolution period to the "Hagner" plate of 1874.
The Pleasure of Guns, by Jos. G. Rosa and Robin May, Octopus Books, Ltd., London, 1974. 96 pp., illus. with 135 full color photographs. $4.98.
The intricate and beautiful work of famous gunsmiths.
A Price Guide to Antique Guns & Pistols, by Peter Hawkins, Director of Antique Arms Sales at Christie's, London, Antique Collector's Club, Suffolk (England), 1973. 380 pp., with over 1000 illustrations. $35.00.
A realistic valuation guide for over 1,000 antique long guns and pistols, foreign and American.
Price List of the U.S. Cartridge Company's Ammunition, A 1969 reprint of the 1891 original, publ. by J. C. Tillinghast, Marlow, N.H. 29 pp., illus., paper covers. $2.50.
Displays many of the now hard-to-find cartridges.
The Rampant Colt, by R. L. Wilson. Thomas Haas, Spencer, Ind., 1969. 107 pp., well illus. $15.00.
Study of Samuel Colt's coat-of-arms and the rampant colt figure used on Colt firearms and in advertising.
The Rappahannock Forge, by Nathan L. Swayze, The American Society of Arms Collectors, Gun Room Press, Highland Park, NJ, 1976. 40 pp., illus. Paper covers. $2.
The first in-depth research done on surviving Rapa Forge firearms as well as being an authoritative history of James Hunter.
Rare & Beautiful Guns, by De Witt Bailey, et al, Galahad Books, NY, 1975. 128 pp., 180 photographs, of which 78 are in color. $6.98.
A new look at the world of firearms, including not only the historical aspects but hunting and sporting guns and 19th and 20th century weapons of war.
Rare Selections from Old Gun Catalogs 1888-1919, edited by Joseph J. Schroeder, DBI Books, Inc., Northfield, IL, 1978. 96 pp., illus. Paper covers. $4.95.
Selections from rare old gun catalogs.
The Rare and Valuable Antique Arms, by James E. Serven, Pioneer Press, Union City, TN, 1976. 106 pp., illus. Paper covers. $4.95.
A guide to the collector in deciding which direction his collecting should go, investment value, historic interest, mechanical ingenuity, high art or personal preference.
Red Coat and Brown Bess, by Anthony D. Darling. Museum Restoration Service, Ottawa, Ontario, Can., 1970. Paper covers, 63 pp., very well illus., in line and halftone. $3.00.
An unusually excellent treatise on the British Army in 1774-1775. Includes detailed text and illus. of various models of the "Brown Bess," plus "Records of the Battles, Sieges and Skirmishes of the American Revolution."
Remington Arms in American History, by A. Hatch, Rinehart & Co., NY, 1956. 359 pp., illus. $6.50.
Collector's guide with appendix of all Remington arms, ballistics tables, etc.
Remington Catalog (Price List) of 1885, a reprint in facsimile, by The Rocky Mountain Investment and Antique Co., Cheyenne, WY, 1969. 48 pp., well illus., paper covers. $3.00.
All rifles, handguns, cane gun, sights, cartridges, shotguns, accessories etc. A priced catalog.
E. Remington & Sons, Reduced Price List for 1877, reprinted by Pioneer Press, Union City, TN, 1977. 42 pp., illus. Paper covers. $1.95.
A facsimile reprint showing all models of rifles, shotguns, pistols, etc. manufactured during this period by this firm.
Remington Rolling Block Firearms, by Konrad F. Schreier, Jr., Pioneer Press, Union City, TN, 1977. 65 pp., illus. Paper covers. $5.00.
A collectors listing of the famous rolling block action arms made by E. Remington & Sons.
Remington Tips, By E. Dixon Larson, Pioneer Press, Union City, TN, 1975. 99 pp., illus. Paper covers. $4.95.
Tips for collectors of Remington Handguns. Covers percussion, conversions, early cartridge models, etc.
The Revolver, Its Description, Management, and Use, by P. E. Dove. Arms and Armour Press, London, 1968. 57 pp., 6 engravings, stiff paper wrappers. $3.75.
A facsimile reprint of a rare classic, dealing principally with the Adams revolver compared to the qualities of the Colt.
Revolving Arms, by A. W. F. Taylerson, Walker and Co., New York, 1967. 123 pp., illus. $3.98.
A detailed history of mechanically-rotated cylinder firearms in Europe and the U.S. Primarily on handguns, but other types of revolving guns are included.
Rifled Infantry Arms, by J. Schon; trans. by Capt. J. Gorgas, USA. Dresden, 1855; facsimile reprint by W. E. Meuse, Schuylersville, NY, 1965. 54 pp., illus. $2.50.
Reprint of classic essay on European military small arms of the mid-19th century. Paper covers.
Ruger Blackhawk Revolvers in .357 and .44, by H. W. Ross, Jr., H. W. Ross, Jr., Bridgeville, PA, 1977. 54 pp., illus. Paper covers. $5.00.
Gives approximate production dates and numbers of guns produced.
Samuel Colt's New Model Pocket Pistols; The Story of the 1855 Root Model Revolver, by S. Gerald Keogh, S. G. Keogh, Ogden, UT, 1974. 31 pp., illus., paper covers. $3.50; hardbound $8.50.
Collector's reference on various types of the titled arms, with descriptions, illustrations, and historical data.
Savage Automatic Pistols, by James R. Carr. Publ. by the author, St. Charles, Ill., 1967. A reprint. 129 pp., illus. with numerous photos. $6.50.
Collector's guide to Savage pistols, models 1907-1922, with features, production data, and pictures of each. A reprint of the circa 1912 Savage promotional and instructive booklet titled *It Banishes Fear* is recommended to accompany the above. Paper wrappers, 32 pp. $1.50.
Schuyler, Hartley & Graham Catalog. publ. by Norm Flayderman, Greenwich, Conn., 1961. 176 pp., illus. $9.50.
A reprint of a rare 1864 catalog of firearms, military goods, uniforms, etc. An extensive source of information for Civil War collectors.
Scottish Arms Makers, by C. E. Whitelaw, ed. by Sarah Barter, Arms & Armour Press, London, England, 1977. Over 300 pp., illus. $25.
A bibliographical dictionary of firearms makers, edged weapons and armor working in Scotland from the 14th century to 1870.
Sears, Roebuck & Co. Catalogue No. 117, J. J. Schroeder, ed. A reprint of the 1908 work. Digest Books, Inc., Northfield, Ill., 1969, profusely illus., paper covers. $6.95.
This reprint of a famous catalog brings to all arms collectors a treasured replica of the collectibles and prices of yesteryear.
Sharps Firearms, by Frank Sellers, Beinfeld Publ., Inc., No. Hollywood, CA, 1977. Large format with over 500 photographs. $34.95.
The first complete review of the famous Sharps Firearms Co. and a detailed examination of every product made by them.
The following four items were published by the Americana Archives Publ. Co., Topsfield, MA.
Sharps Rifle: The Gun That Shaped American Destiny, by Martin Rywell, Pioneer Press, Union City, TN, 1977. 156 pp., illus. Paper covers. $2.95.
The role of Sharps guns in American history.
Sharps' Rifle Manufacturing Company Catalog, 1859, a facsimile reprint. 1976. 16 pp., illus. Paper covers. $3.
Shows the carbine and rifle, the forms for shot and powder tubes, plus cleaning directions.
Sharps' Rifle Manufacturing Company Catalog, 1864, a facsmilie reprint. 1976. 16 pp., illus. Paper covers. $3.
Illustrates the carbine, sporting rifle and army rifle with bayonet. Complete instructions on use, preparing charges and a manual of arms.
Sharps' Rifle Manufacturing Company Catalog, 1874, a facsimile reprint. 1976. 32 pp., illus. Paper covers. $3.
Six different rifles are illustrated, including the famous Creedmoor.
Shooter's Bible Gun Trader's Guide, 8th Ed., by Paul Wahl, Follet Publ., Co., Chicago, IL, 1978. 256 pp., illus. Paper covers. $7.95.
A fully illustrated and authoritative guide to identification of modern firearms with current market values.
Shotgun Shells: Identification, Manufacturers and Checklist for Collectors, by F. H. Steward. B. and P. Associates, St. Louis, Mo., 1969. 101 pp., illus., paper covers. $5.95.
Historical data for the collector.
Small Arms, by Frederick Wilkinson, Hawthorne Books, Inc., New York, 1966. 256 pp., illus. $4.95.
A history of small firearms, techniques of the gunsmith, equipment used by combatants, sportsmen and hunters.
Small Arms of the Sea Services, by Robt. H. Rankin. N. Flayderman & Co., New Milford, CT, 1972. 227 pp., illus. $14.50.
Encyclopedic reference to small arms of the U.S. Navy, Marines and Coast Guard. Covers edged weapons, handguns, long arms and others, from the beginnings.
Smith and Wesson 1857-1945, by Robert J. Neal and Roy J. Jenks. A. S. Barnes and Co., Inc., NYC, 1975. 500 pp., illus. with over 300 photos and 90 radiographs. $25.00.
A long-needed book, especially for knowledgeable enthusiasts and collectors. Covers an investigation of the series of handguns produced by the Smith and Wesson Company.
Southern Derringers of the Mississippi Valley, by Turner Kirkland. Pioneer Press, Tenn., 1971. 80 pp., illus., paper covers. $2.00.
A guide for the collector, and a much-needed study.
Spanish Military Weapons in Colonial America, 1700-1821, by S. B. Brinckerhoff & P. A. Chamberlain. Stackpole Books, Harrisburg, PA, 1972. 160 pp., illus. $14.95.
Spanish arms and armaments described and illustrated in 274 photographic plates. Includes firearms, accoutrements, swords, polearms and cannon.
The Standard Directory of Proof-Marks, ed. by R. A. Steindler, The John Olson Company, Paramus, NJ, 1976. 144 pp., illus. Paper covers. $5.95.
A comprehensive directory of the proof-marks of the world.
Starr Arms Co., 1864 Catalog, a reprint. 1976. 22 pp., illus. Paper covers. $3.
Contains operating and disassembly instructions, trial results and military testimonials.
Stevens Pistols and Pocket Rifles, by K. L. Cope, Museum Restoration Service, Ottawa, Can., 1971. 104 pp. $8.50.
All are shown, identified, detailed, variations, listings of dates, etc.
The Story of Firearms Ignition, by Edsall James, Pioneer Press, Union City, TN, 1975. 22 pp., illus. Paper covers. $3.50
Mechanical design and the firing contrivances for guns from early matchlocks to modern cartridge arms.
A Study of the Colt Single Action Army Revolver, by R. Graham, J. A. Kopec, and C. K. Moore, publ. by the authors, La Puente, CA, 1975. Over 500 pp., illus. $39.95.
A definitive work on the famous Colt Single Action revolver. Contains many new facts never before published.
Summary of D.C.M. Rifle Sales 1922-1942, compiled by Springfield Research Service, Silver Spring, MD, 1976. 80 pp. Paper covers. $4.
A compilation of individual serial numbers of rifles sold by the Ordnance Department between 1922 and 1942.
Swiss Handguns, by Fritz Hausler, publ. by the author, Frauenfeld, Switzerland, 1975. 140 pp., illus. $18.95.
Helvetian pistols and revolvers from 1817 to the present day in text and illustrations.
The 36 Calibers of the Colt Single Action Army, by David M. Brown. Publ. by the author at Albuquerque, NM, new reprint 1971. 222 pp., well-illus. $15.00.
Edited by Bev Mann of *Guns Magazine*. This is an unusual approach to the many details of the Colt S.A. Army revolver. Halftone and line drawings of the same models make this of especial interest.
30-06 Cartridges We Have Seen, Vol. 2, by Gerald F. Marcello, publ. by the author, San Diego, CA, 1975. 221 pp., illus. $$12.50.
A guide to the collecting of 30-06 cartridges. Illustrated with drawings of headstamps and photographs of box labels.
Thompson Guns: 1929 Commercial Price List and Catalog, published by Auto-Ordnance Corp., Ray Riling Arms Books Co., Phila., PA, 1976. A facsimile reprint. 18 pp., illus., paper covers. $5.
A limited, numbered reprint of the scarce 1929 Catalog on the Thompson Submachine Gun.
Those Other Colts, or Colt Conversions, by Albert Watson III, Colt Collector Press, Rapid City, SD, 1975. 32 pp., illus. Paper covers. $5.00.
Factory alterations to Colt holster pistols from the percussion cap to self-contained cartridge models.
Thoughts on the American Flintlock Pistol, by Samuel E. Dyke, George Shumway, York, PA, 1974. 61 pp., illus. Paper covers. $5.00.
Reprint of the "Kentucky Pistol" section from Dillin's book "The Kentucky Rifle."
Thoughts on the Kentucky Rifle in its Golden Age, by Joe Kindig, Jr. George Shumway, York, PA, 1975. A facsimile reprint of the 1960 original. 561 pp., replete with fine arms and data on many makers. $29.95.
Covers mainly the arms and their makers in the Lancaster area of

Pennsylvania. An authoritative work.
Toxophilus, by Roger Ascham. S. R. Pub. Ltd., Yorkshire, Eng., 1968. 230 pp., illus. $8.00.
A facsimile reprint of the 1788 ed. still regarded as the classic text on archery.
200 Years of American Firearms, by James E. Serven, DBI Books, Inc., Northfield, IL, 1975. 224 pp., illus. Paper covers. $7.95.
Covers the evolution of firearms in America from those carried by Spanish explorers to the M-16 rifle.
Underhammer Guns, by H. C. Logan. Stackpole Books, Harrisburg, PA, 1964. 250 pp. illus. $4.98.
A full account of an unusual form of firearm dating back to flintlock days. Both American and foreign specimens are included.
Uniforms of the American, British, French, and German Armies in the War of the American Revolution, 1775-1783, by Lt. Charles M. Lefferts, We Inc., Old Greenwich, CT, 1970. 292 pp., illus. $10.00.
Reprint of the original 1926 ed. and the only book on its subject today.
U.S. Army Weapons 1784-1791, by Wm. H. Guthman, The American Soc. of Arms Coll., 1975. 94 pp., illus. Paper covers. $6.50.
A detailed study of the surplus weapons and accoutrements stored in Federal arsenals after the Revolutionary War.
U.S. Cartridge Co. Collection of Firearms, We, Inc., Old Greenwich, CT., 1970. 142 pp., illus. $6.00.
Describes each arm in detail as to manufacture, action, period of use, function, markings, patents, makers, etc.
U.S. Cartridges and Their Handguns, by Charles R. Suydam, Beinfeld Publ., Inc., No. Hollywood, CA, 1977. 200 pp., illus. Paper covers. $9.95; hardbound. $14.95.
The first book ever showing which gun used what cartridge. A must for the gun and cartridge collector.
U.S. Firearms: The First Century, 1776-1875, by D. F. Butler. Winchester Press, NY, 1971. 320 pp., illus. $15.00.
A rich mine of carefully researched information and data on American firearms of this period. Illustrated with photos, schematics and historical documents.
United States Martial Pistols and Revolvers, by Arcadi Gluckman, Bonanza Books, NY, 1973. 249 pp. plus 29 plates. $2.98.
Covers all martial short arms made in the U.S. by the government or private makers from 1799 to 1917.
U.S. Martial and Semi-Martial Single-Shot Pistols, by C. E. Chapel, Coward-McCann Inc., NYC, 1962. 352 pp., over 150 illus. $7.50.
Describes in detail all single shot martial pistols used by the US armed forces and by military units of the states. A definitive guide.
U.S. Military Firearms, 1776-1956, by Maj. Jas. E. Hicks. J. E. Hicks & Son. La Canada, Calif., 216 pp., incl. 88 pages of fine plates. $12.50.
Covering 180 years of America's hand and shoulder weapons. The most authoritative book on this subject. Packed with official data.
U.S. Military Small Arms 1816-1865, by R. M. Reilly. The Eagle Press, Inc., Baton Rouge, La., 1970. 275 pp., illus. $22.50.
Describes and superbly illustrates every known type of primary and secondary martial firearm of the period 1816-1865. Limited, numbered ed.
U.S. Ordnance Manual 1862, compiled by T. T. S. Laidley, Bvt. Major, Capt. of Ordnance. Ordnance Park Corp., Lyons, CO, 1970. 559 pp., illus., 33 plates. A limited numbered ed. $15.40.
Facsimile of the 3rd ed. of the 1862 *Ordnance Manual for the Use of the Officers of the United States Army.*
A Universal Military Dictionary, by Captain George Smith. The rare original book was published at London in 1779. This facsimile reprint was released in 1969 by Museum Restoration Service, Ottawa, Ontario, Can. 336 pp., 16 fold-out plates. $27.50.
A most useful reference for mean of arms interest. Offered only in a numbered, limited issue of 700 copies.
The Virginia Manufactory of Arms, by Giles Cromwell, University Press of Virginia, Charlottesville, VA, 1975. 205 pp., illus. $24.00.
The only complete history of the Virginia Manufactory of Arms which produced muskets, pistols, swords, and cannon for the state's militia from 1802 through 1821.
Walther Volume II, Engraved, Presentation and Standard Models, by James L. Rankin, J. L. Rankin, Coral Galbes, FL 1977. 112 pp., illus. $17.50.
The new Walther book on embellished versions and standard models. Has 88 photographs, including many color plates.
The Webley Story, by Wm. C. Dowell, Skyrac Press, Leeds, Eng. 337 pp., profusely illus. $40.00.
Detailed study of Webley pistols and revolvers, covering over 250 specimens. This important reference also gives detailed listing of English small arms cartridge patents through 1880.
The Whitney Firearms, by Claud Fuller. Standard Publications, Huntington, W. Va., 1946. 334 pp., many plates and drawings. $20.00.
An authoritative history of all Whitney arms and their maker. Highly recommended. An exclusive with Ray Riling Arms Books Co.
The William M. Locke Collection, compiled by Robert B. Berryman, et al, The Antique Armory, Inc., East Point, GA, 1973. 541 pp., illus. $30.00.
A magnificently produced book illustrated with hundreds of photographs of guns from one of the finest collection of American firearms ever assembled.
Winchester Catalog of 1891, a facsimile reprint by the Rocky Mountain Investment and Antique Co., Cheyenne, WY, 1973. 84 pp., well illus., paper covers. $3.50.
All rifles, shotguns, reloading tools and ammunition of the time. A priced catalog.
Winchester—The Gun That Won the West, by H. F. Williamson. Combat Forces Press, Washington, D.C., 1952. Later eds. by Barnes, NY 494 pp., profusely illus. $7.98.
A scholarly and essential economic history of an honored arms company, but the early and modern arms introduced will satisfy all but the exacting collector.
The Winchester Book, by Geo. Madis. Art & Reference House, Lancaster, Texas. New revised 4th edition, 1978. 542 pp., illus. $35.00.
First release of 1,000 autographed deluxe copies at this special price.
World of Lugers: Proof Marks, Vol. I, by Sam Costanzo, Sam Costanzo, Mayfield Heights, OH, 1977. 432 pp., illus. $17.95.
Complete listing of different variations of proof marks on the Luger. A limited, signed edition.
World of Lugers: Volume I, Serial Numbers of Lugers Issued to German Agents in the U.S. 1913-16, by Sam Costanzo, Sam Costanzo, Wickliffe, OH, 1975. 79 pp., illus. Paper covers. $5.50.
The Lugers issued by Hans Tauscher to German espionage agents in the United States and Canada during the period 1913-1916. Also included is Government correspondence used as evidence in the Hans Tauscher court trial.
Wyatt Earp & the "Buntline Special" Myth, by William B. Shillingberg, Blaine Publ. Co., Tucson, AZ, 1976. 64 pp., illus. Paper covers. $3.95.
Much unpublished material on Earp, including the association with his later "biographer" Stuart N. Lake—himself the inventor of the Buntline presentation legend.

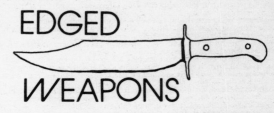

EDGED WEAPONS

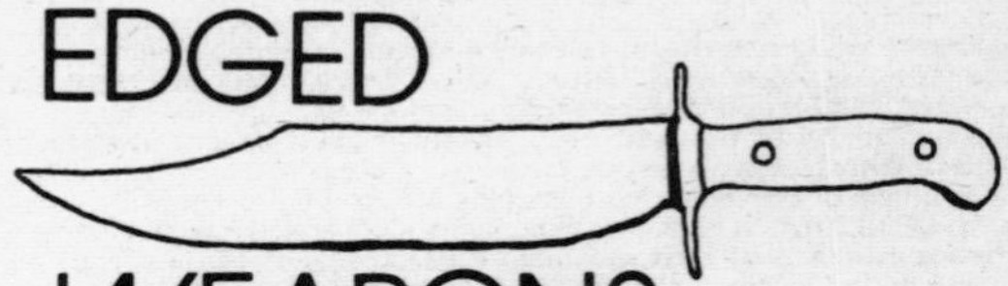

The Robert Abels Collection of Bowie Type Knives of American Interest, by Robert Abels, Robert Abels, Hopewell Junction, NY, 1974. 20 pp., illus. Paper covers. $1.95.
A selection of American Bowie-type knives from the collection of Robert Abels.
Allied Bayonets of World War 2, by J. Anthony Carter, Arco Publ., Co., NY, 1969. 80 pp., illus. $3.50.
Illustrates and describes all bayonets issued to the Allied armed forces between 1939 and 1946.
American Axes, by Henry Kauffman, The Stephen Greene Press, Brattleboro, VT, 1972. 200 pp., illus. $12.50.
A definitive work on the subject. Contains a roster of American axe makers, glossary and notes on the care and use of axes.
The American Bayonet 1176-1964, by Albert N. Hardin, Jr., Albert N. Hardin, Jr., Pennsauken, NJ, 1977. 234 pp., illus. $24.50.
Describes and illustrates over two hundred separate and distinct types of American bayonets from Colonial times to the present day.
American Handmade Knives of Today, by B. R. Hughes, Pioneer Press, Union City, TN, 1972. 56 pp., illus. Paper covers. $2.95.
A basic primer for novices who are just beginning to take an interest in handmade cutlery.
American Indian Tomahawks, by Harold L. Peterson, Museum of the American Indian, Heye Foundation, NY, 1965. 142 pp., illus. $10.00.
A brief description of various types and their makers.
American Knives: The First History and Collector's Guide, by Harold L. Peterson, Charles Scribner's Sons, NY, 1958. 178 pp., illus Paper covers. $4.95.
A landmark work and a book that will whet the appetite of knife collectors everywhere.
American Polearms 1526-1865, by Rodney Hilton Brown, N. Flayderman & Co., New Milford, CT, 1967. 198 pp., illus. $14.50.
The lance, halbred, spontoon, pike and naval boarding weapons used in the American military forces through the Civil War.
American Socket Bayonets 1717-1873, by Donald B. Webster, Jr., Museum Restoration Service, Ontario, Canada, 1964. 47 pp., illus. Paper covers. $2.50.
Helps identify the many variations of the triangular and angular bayonets used by the U.S. Army.
The American Sword, 1775-1945, by Harold L. Peterson, Ray Riling Arms Books, Co., Phila., PA, 1977. 286 pp. plus 60 pp. of illus. $18.50.
1977 reprint of a survey of swords worn by U.S. uniformed forces, plus the rare "American Silver Mounted Swords, (1700-1815)."
The Art of Blacksmithing, by Alex W. Bealer, Funk & Wagnalls, New York, NY, revised edition, 1976. 438 pp., illus. $11.95.
Required reading for anyone who makes knives or is seriously interested in the history of cutlery.
Australian Service Bayonets, by Ian D. Skennerton, Ian D. Skennerton, Margate, Australia, 1976. 134 pp., illus. $23.50.
Australian bayonets their production, proof and issue markings, experimental models, etc.
The Bayonet, by Anthony Carter and John Walter, Charles Scribner's Sons, NY, 1974. 124 pp., illus, $11.50.
A history of knife and sword bayonets 1850-1970.
The Bayonet Book, by John Watts and Peter White, John Watts, Birmingham, England, 1976. 504 pp., illus. $44.00.
Detailed guide to bayonets past and present used by the major countries of the world. Illus. with over 1052 photos.
Bayonet Fighting, by U.S. Dept. of the Army, reprinted by Normount Technical Publ., Wickenburg, AZ, 1973. 76 pp., illus. Paper covers. $1.50.
A facsimile reprint of FM23-25.
Bayonet Markings, by I. D. Davidson, I. D. Davidson, Brighton, England, revised edition, 1978. 21 pp., illus. Paper covers. $2.95.
Shows in detailed text and over 150 line drawings, all the types of markings commonly found on bayonets and other similar military weapons.
Bayonets Illustrated, by Bert Walsh, A Bashall Caves Publ., Dublin, Ireland, 1970. 49 pp., illus. $6.50.
162 detailed line drawings of bayonets from many countries and periods.
Bayonets of the World, Volume I, by Paul Kiesling, Military Collectors Service, Kedichem, Holland, 1973. 278 plates. $19.95.
Covers bayonets up to 515mm in length, includes scabbards, sockets, etc.
Bayonets of the World, Volume 2, by Paul Kiesling, Military Collectors Service, Kedichem, Holland, 1974. 131 pp., illus. $19.25.
Covers bayonets of all types and all countries. Arranged in size starting with 515mm and larger.
Bayonets of the World, Volume 3, by Paul Kiesling, Military Collectors Service, Kedichem, Holland, 1975. 130 pp., illus. $19.25.
Part 3 of this fine series on bayonets of all countries. Includes a cross index reference for all three volumes.
Bayonets of the World, Volume 4, by Paul Kiesling, Military Collectors Service, Kedichem, Holland, 1977. 190 pp., illus. $24.00.
The final volume in this monumental work on bayonets.
Blacksmithing for the Home Craftsman, by Joe Pehoski, Joe Pehoski, Washington, TX, 1973. 44 pp., illus. Paper covers. $2.50.
This informative book is chock-full of drawings and explains how to make your own forge.
Blades and Barrels, by H. Gordon Frost, Wallon Press, El Paso, TX, 1972. 298 pp., illus. $16.95.
The first full scale study about man's attempts to combine an edged weapon with a firearm.
Bowie Knives, by Robert Abels, Robert Abels, NY, 1960. 48 pp., illus. Paper covers. $3.00.
A booklet showing knives, tomahawks, related trade cards and advertisements.

British Cut and Thrust Weapons, by John Wilkinson Latham, Charles E. Tuttle Co., VT, 1971. 112 pp., illus. $7.50.
Well illustrated study tracing the development of edged weapons and their adoption by the British armed forces.
British Military Swords from 1800 to the Present Day, by John Wilkinson Latham, Crown Publ., Inc. NY, 1966. 79 pp., illus. $3.95.
Survey of British swords used by various branches of the army with data on their manufacture, specifications and procurement.
The Canadian Bayonet, by R. Barrie Manarey, Century Press, Alberta, Canada, 1971. 51 pp., illus. Paper covers $3.00.
An illustrated reference book on Canadian bayonets and their history.
Case Pocket Knives, by Allen P. Swayne, John M. Parker, Etowah, TN, 1975. 12 pp., illus. Paper covers. $2.50.
A listing of all known Case markings and dates with many illustrations.
Classic Bowie Knives, by Robert Abels, Robert Abels, NY, 1967. 96 pp., illus. $7.50.
A nostalgic story of the famous blades with trade advertisements on them, and photos of users.
Cold Steel, by John Styers, Paladin Press, Boulder, CO, 1974. 179 pp., illus. $9.95.
Reprint of the classic Marine bible on unarmed combat.
Collecting the Edged Weapons of the Third Reich, by Maj. Thomas M. Johnson, Maj. Thomas M. Johnson, Columbia, SC, 1975. $16.50.
The most comprehensive reference on Third Reich edged weapons published to date.
Collecting the Edged Weapons of the Third Reich Volume II, by LTC Thomas M. Johnson, LTC Thomas M. Johnson, Columbia, SC, 1976. 352 pp., illus. $18.50.
A companion volume to the author's first work on Nazi edged weapons. Limited edition.
Collector's Illustrated Price Guide to Pocket Knives, by William Schroeder, Collector Books, Paducah, KY, 1977. 64 pp., illus. Paper covers. $2.95.
Hundreds of knives are pictured with many more listings and prices.
The Collector's Pictorial Book of Bayonets, by Frederick J. Stephens, Hippocrene Books, Edison, NJ, 1977. 127 pp., illus. Paper covers. $3.95.
A photo reference to bayonets of over 20 countries with information pertaining to each.
A Collector's Reference Guide to Ka-Bar Knives, reprinted by Ka-Bar Knives, Olean, NY, 1976. 12 pp., illus. Paper covers. $3.00.
Facsimile reprint of an old catalog, **ca.** 1925, from the original Union Cutlery Co., Olean, NY.
A Compendium of British and German Regimental Markings, Compiled and edited by Gordon Hughes and Chris Fox, Gordon A. Hughes Publications, Sussex, England, 1975. 32 pp. Paper covers. $3.00.
A guide to identifying those intriguing marks stamped on the crossguards, pommels and scabbards of British and German bayonets.
The Complete Book of Knife Fighting, by William L. Cassidy, Paladin Press, Boulder, CO, 1975. 119 pp., illus. $10.95.
Most complete book of knife fighting technique and history with every facet covered.
Custom Knife . . . II, by John Davis Bates, Jr., and James Henry Schippers, Jr., Custom Knife Press, Memphis, TN, 1974. 112 pp., illus. $20.00.
The book of pocket knives and folding hunters. A guide to the 20th century makers' art.
The Cutlery Story: From Stone Age to Steel Age, by Lewis D. Bement, Custom Cutlery Co., Dalton, GA, 1972. 36 pp., illus. Paper covers. $3.50.
A classic booklet about the history, romance, and manufacture of cutlery from the earliest times to modern methods of manufacture.
A Directory of Sheffield: Including the Manufacturers of the Adjacent Villages, a facsimile reprint of the 1707 London edition, Da Capo Press, Inc., NY, 1969. Illus. $11.50.
With the several marks of the cutlers, scissor and edge-tool makers.
Do or Die, by Ltc. A. J. Drexel Biddle, U.S.M.C., Paladin Press, Boulder, CO, 1976. 74 pp., illus. $4.95.
A facsimile reprint of the classic book on individual combat. Contains chapters on bayonet and knife fighting.
The Duel: The History of Duelling, by Robert Baldick, Spring Books, London, England, 1970. 212 pp., illus. $4.98.
The romance and horror of duelling.
Early Japanese Sword Guards, by Masayuki Sasano, Japan Publ., Inc., San Francisco, CA, 1972. 284 pp., illus. $15.95.
220 of the finest open-work sword guards dating from a number of historical periods are illustrated in full size.
Edge of the Anvil, by Jack Andrews, Rodale Press, Emmaus, PA, 1978. 224 pp., illus. $9.95.
A basic blacksmith book.
Edged Weaponry of the Third Reich, by Maj. John R. Angolia, R. James Bender Publ. Co., Mountain View, CA, 1974. 256 pp., illus. $12.95.
A concise guide to all the edged weapons of Hitler's Germany.
Edged Weapons of the American Revolution 1775-1783, by Geo. C. Neumann, American Defense Preparedness Assoc., Wash., DC, 1975. 16 pp., illus. Paper covers. $2.00.
A monograph outlining the various types of swords, bayonets, knives and other edged weapons used by the Continental forces.
Edged Weapons, a Collectors Guide, by Frederick J. Stephens, Spur Books, London, England, 1978. 160 pp., illus. $14.95.
A comprehensive survey of the entire field of these weapons from all parts of the world.
Eickhorn Kundendienst 1938, reprinted by Jos. P. Curry, Anderson, SC, 1969. 80 pp., illus. Paper covers. $5.95.
Facsimile reprint of part of the 1938 sword catalog of Carl Eickhorn, Solingen, Germany.
An Encyclopedia of Knives, by Norman M. Strung, J. B. Lippincott Co., Phila., PA, 1977. 219 pp., illus. $12.50.
An illustrated consumer's guide to buying, using, sharpening, and caring for all over-the-counter knives.
European Edged Weapons, by Terrence Wise, Almark Publ. Co., Ltd., London, England, 1974. 96 pp., illus. Paper covers. $4.95; Cloth. $7.25.
The development of swords, axes, bayonets and other edged weapons in Europe.
The Fighting Knife, by W. D. Randall, Jr. and Col. Rex Applegate, W. D. Randall, Orlando, FL, 1975. 60 pp., illus. Paper covers. $2.75.
Manual for the use of Randall-made fighting knives and similar types.
The German Bayonet, by John Walter, Arms and Armour Press, London, England, 1976. 128 pp., illus. $12.50.
A comprehensive illustrated history of regulation patterns, 1871-1945.
German Ersatz Bayonets, by Anthony Carter, The Lyon Press, East Sussex, England, 1976. 64 pp., illus. $12.95.
A concise illustrated history of the emergency all-metal designs, 1914-18.
A Guide to Handmade Knives, edited by Mel Tappan, The Janus Press, Inc., Los Angeles, CA, 1977. Paper covers. $9.50; Deluxe hardbound. $19.50.
The official directory of the Knifemakers Guild.
Gun Digest Book of Folding Knives, by Jack Lewis and B. R. Hughes, DBI Books, Inc. Northfield, IL, 1977. 288 pp., illus. Paper covers. $7.95.
A cut above any other volume published on pocket or folding knives.
The Gun Digest Book of Knives, by B. R. Hughes and Jack Lewis, DBI Books, Inc., Northfield, IL, 1973. 228 pp., illus. Paper covers. $6.95.
How to collect, buy and care for knives.
Handbook for Pocket Knife Collectors, by D. Hanby, D. Hanby. Morgan City, AL, 1973. 23 pp., illus. Paper covers. $2.50.
Redbook of pocketknife values. Listing over 600 knives by name, manufacturer and value.
The History of the John Russell Cutlery Company, 1833-1936, by Robert L. Merriam et al, The Bete Press, Greenfield, MA, 1976. 120 pp., illus. $12.95.
A complete history of the people, places and events behind legendary American knives such as the Barlow, Green River Knife, Dadley and others.
The House of Wostenholm 1745-1945, by Harold Bexfield, George Wostenholm & Son, Ltd., Sheffield, England, 1945. 40 pp., illus. $9.95.
A short history of Sheffield cutlery and the House of Wostenholm.
How Knives are Made: The Encyclopedia of American Knives, Volume I, by Blackie Collins, The Benchmark Co., Rock Hill, SC, 1975. 175 pp., illus. $15.00.
Over 175 photos of knife making processes. Complete instructions for making a custom hunting knife and custom folding-knife.
How to Make Knives, by Richard W. Barney & Robert W. Loveless, Beinfield Publ., Inc., No. Hollywood, CA, 1977. 178 pp., illus. Paper covers. $9.95; Deluxe hardbound. $15.95.
A book filled with drawings, illustrations, diagrams, and 500 how-to-do-it photos.
The Indian Sword, by P. S. Rawson, Arco Pub. Co., Inc., NY, 1968. 108 pp., illus. $8.50.
The various types of Indian swords are accurately classified and the techniques and local styles of decoration are identified.
Introduction to Japanese Swords, by William M. Hawley, William M. Hawley, Hollywood, CA, 1973. 20 pp., illus. Paper covers. $2.00.
Clear concise details of construction that made Japanese swords the world's finest edged weapons.
Italian Fascist Daggers, by Frederick J. Stephens, Militaria Publ., Ltd., London, England, 1972. 24 pp., illus. Paper covers. $5.00.
Pictures and describes for the first time the daggers of Fascist Italy.
The I*XL Cutlery, reprinted by Americana/Reed, Louisville, KY, 1975. 53 pp., illus. Paper covers. $5.00.
A facsimile reprint of the first catalog issued by the firm of George Wostenholm & Son Ltd. in 1885.
I*XL Means I Excel, by William R. Williamson, Beinfeld, Publ., Inc., No. Hollywood, CA., 1973. 33 pp., illus. Paper covers. $5.00.
A short history of the I*XL Bowie Knife.
Japanese Polearms, by R. M. Knutsen, Holland Press, London, England, 1963. 271 pp., illus. $18.00.
The history and development of each category of spear from the Yayoi period to the Meiji Restoration.
Japanese Sword Blades, by Alfred Dobree, Arms and Armour Press, London, England, 1967. 39 pp., illus. Paper covers. $4.50.
A two-part monograph, reprinted from a notable work on Japanese blades.
Japanese Sword Fittings: The Naunton Collection, by Henri L. Joly, William M. Hawley, Hollywood, CA, 1973. 434 pp. and 88 plates. $50.00.
A reprint of the finest work ever done in English on the subject. 1300 fittings are shown in full size, and 66 schools are described in detail.
Japanese Sword-Mounts, by Helen C. Gunsaulus, Kraus Reprint Co., NY, 1968. 196 pp. plus 61 plates. Paper covers. $14.00.
A complete account of the world famous collection of Japanese sword mounts in the Chicago Field Museum of Natural History.
Japanese Swordsmiths, by William M. Hawley, William M. Hawley, Hollywood, CA, 1976. 2 volume set. Vol. 1, 512 pp.; Vol. 2, 256 pp. Flexible fabricoid covers. The 2 volumes. $25.00.
The first listing in any language of the 18,000 names used by 15,000 swordsmiths from the 8th to 20th century.
Ka-Bar Dependable Pocket Knives, reprinted by Ka-Bar Knives, Olean, NY, 1976. Unpaginated. Paper covers. $3.50.
A facsimile reprint of the 1925 Union Cutlery Co. catalog with many illustrations of old Ka-Bar knives.
Kentucky Knife-Traders Manual No. 5, by R. B. Ritchie, Hindman, KY, 1975. 103 pp., illus. Paper covers. $6.50.
A listing of pocketknives and razor values.
Robert Klaas Sword and Dagger Catalog, by Robert Klaas, reprinted by Herman A. Maeurer, College Point, NY, 1971. 16 pp., illus. Paper covers. $5.00.
Reprint of the original 1938 German catalog. A rare reference work.
Knife Album, by Col. Robert Mayes, Col. Robert Mayes, Middlesboro, KY, 1975. 554 pp., illus. $14.95.
Information pertaining to knives by the prominent makers.
The Knife Album Price Guide 1976 Edition, by Robert Mayes, Robert Mayes, Middlesboro, KY, 1976. 174 pp. Paper covers. $6.00.
The only book on identification and accurate pricing.
Knife Digest, First Annual Edition, edited by William L. Cassidy, Knife Digest Publ. Co., Berkeley, CA, 1974. 285 pp., illus. Paper covers. $5.95.
The first annual publication ever produced for the knife and edged weapon enthusiast and collector.
Knife Digest, Second Annual Edition, edited by William L. Cassidy, Knife Digest Publ. Co., Berkeley, CA, 1976. 178 pp., illus. Paper covers. $7.95; Cloth. $15.00.
The second annual edition of the internationally known book on blades.
Knife Fighting: Art of Self-Defense & Sport, by Geo. B. Wallace, Walmac Books, Los Angeles, CA, 1977. 36 pp., illus. Paper covers. $4.95.
Concerned only with the techniques of knife fighting and illustrates the various tactics of attack and defense.
Knife Handling for Self Defense, by Geo. B. Wallace, Walmac Books, Los Angeles, CA, 1973. 44 pp., illus. Paper covers. $2.50.
Step-by-step instructions on defense against clubs, chains, knives, etc.
Knife Throwing a Practical Guide, by Harry K. McEvoy, Charles E. Tuttle Co., Rutland, VT, 1973. 108 pp., illus. Paper covers. $3.25.
If you want to learn to throw a knife this is the "bible."
Knife Throwing in the Professional Style, by Harry K. McEvoy, The Tru-Bal Co., Grand Rapids, MI, 1969. 24 pp., illus. Paper covers. $1.95.
A brief handbook on the professional aspects of knife throwing.
Knifemakers of Old San Francisco, by Bernard R. Levine, Badger Books, San Francisco, CA, 1978. 240 pp., illus. $12.95.
The story about the knifemakers of San Francisco, the leading cutlers of the old West.
Knives, by Ken Warner, Winchester Press, NY, 1976. 224 pp., illus. $10.00.
All about knives for sport and utility.
Knives and Knifemakers, by Sid Latham, Winchester Press, NY, 1973. 152 pp., illus. $15.00.

Lists makers and suppliers of knife-making material and equipment.

Light But Efficient, by Albert N. Hardin, Jr. and Robert W. Hedden, Albert N. Hardin, Jr., Pennsauken, NJ, 1973. 103 pp., illus. $7.95.
A study of the M1880 Hunting and M1890 intrenching knives and scabbards.

The Modern Blacksmith, by Alexander G. Weygers, Van Nostrand Reinhold Co., NY, 1977. 96 pp., illus. $8.95.
Shows how to forge objects out of steel. Use of basic techniques and tools.

"Napanoch" a "White Man's" Knife with a "Red Man's" Name, by Rhett C. Stidham, Rhet C. Stidham, Belpre, OH 1976. 27 pp., illus. Paper covers. $5.00.
The history of the early 1900's Napanoch Knife Works, plus illustrations of the knives made by them.

Nathan Starr Arms Maker 1776-1845, by James E. Hicks, The Restoration Press, Phoenix, AZ, 1976. 166 pp., illus. $12.95.
Survey of the work of Nathan Starr of Middletown, CT, in producing edged weapons and pole arms for the U.S., 1799-1840, also some firearms.

Naval Swords, by P. G. W. Annis, Stackpole Books, Harrisburg, PA, 1970. 80 pp., illus. $5.50.
British and American naval edged weapons 1660-1815.

Naval Swords and Firearms, by Cmdr. W. E. May, R. N. and A. N. Kennard, Pendragon House, Palo Alto, CA, 1978. 22 pp., illus. Paper covers. $3.00.
British naval swords, dirks, pikes, etc. With an explanatory text.

Official Guide to Pocket Knives, by James F. Parker and J. Bruce Voyles, House of Collectibles, Florence, AL, 1976. 460 pp., illus. Paper covers. $5.95.
Price guide for buying and selling. Featuring Case, Winchester, Cattaraugus, Remington, Russell, and many more.

1000 Razors Priced and Illustrated, by William Schroeder, Collector Books, Paducah, KY, 1975. 71 pp., illus. Paper covers. $3.95.
Prices and illustrations of blade markings of 1000 straight razors.

Pictorial Price Guide Romance of Collecting Case Knives, by Mrs. Dewey P. Ferguson, Fairborn, OH, 1978. 208 pp., illus. Paper covers. $8.00.
The largest work on the subject yet written, and enthusiastically recommended by the Case factory.

Pocket Knife Book 1 & 2—Price Guide, by Roy Ehrhardt, Heart of America Press, Kansas City, MO, 1974. 96 pp., illus. Spiral bound stiff paper covers. $6.95.
Reprints from the pocket knife sections of early manufacturers and sporting goods catalogs.

Pocket Knife Book 3—Price Guide, by Roy and Larry Ehrhardt, Heart of America Press, Kansas City, MO, 1974. Spiral bound stiff paper covers. $6.95.
Compiled from sections of various product sales catalogs of both Winchester and Marble Co. dating from the '20s and '30s.

The Pocketknife Collector's Friend, by D. Hanby, Hanby Enterprises, Morgan City, AL, 1973. 12 pp. Paper covers. $3.50.
An alphabetical listing of makers with their locations and prices of their products in mint and used condition.

The Pocketknife Manual, by Blackie Collins, Blackie Collins, Rock Hill, SC, 1976. 102 pp., illus. Paper covers. $5.50.
Building, repairing and refinishing pocketknives.

Practical Blacksmithing, edited by J. Richardson, Outlet Books, NY, 1978. 4 volumes in one, illus. $7.98.
A reprint of the extremely rare, bible of the blacksmith. Covers every aspect of working with iron and steel, from ancient uses to modern.

Presenting America's Aristocracy of Fine Cutlery, reprinted by American Reprints, St. Louis, MO, n.d. 40 pp., illus. Paper covers. $3.50.
Reprint of a W. R. Case & Sons pocket knife catalog.

Price Guide to Romance of Knife Collecting, 1978 Edition, by Mrs. Dewey P. Ferguson, Fairborn, OH, 1978. 136 pp. Paper covers. $6.00.
The official guide to prices of Case knives.

A Primer of German Military Knives of the Two World Wars, by Gordon A. Hughes, Gordon A. Hughes, Sussex, England, 1976. 20 pp., illus. Paper covers. $4.00.
Detailed line drawings of some 40 trench combat knives of Imperial and Nazi Germany together with sheath variations.

A Primer of Military Knives: European & American, Combat, Trench & Utility Knives, by Gordon Hughes and Barry Jenkins, Brighton, England, 1973. 24 pp., illus. Paper covers. $5.00.
A primer of the knives used in the First and Second World Wars, with line drawings of the weapons and descriptive text.

A Primer of World Bayonets, by John Walter and Gordon Hughes, Brighton, England, 1969. In two volumes. Vol. I, 26 pp.; Vol. 2, 23 pp., illus. Paper covers. $6.50.
Vol. I, common knife and sabre bayonets. Vol. 2, further knife, sabre and socket bayonets.

Rapiers, by Eric Valentine, Stackpole Books, Harrisburg, PA, 1968. 76 pp., illus. $5.50.
A desirable monograph, first on its subject to be published in English.

Regulation Military Swords, by J. Wilkinson-Latham, Star Products, London, England, 1970. 32 pp., illus. Paper covers. $2.00.
A detailed comparison of the military swords used by Great Britain, the United States, France, Germany, Austria, Sweden and Russia.

Remington C-4 Catalog, reprinted by Parker-Frost Cutlery, Chattanooga, TN, 1978. 16 pp., illus. Paper covers. $3.50.
A facsimile reprint with knives pictured actual size.

Remington Cutlery, reprinted by American Reprints, St. Louis, MO, 1969. Unpaginated, illus. Paper covers. $2.50.
A facsimile reprint of a 1936 pocket knife catalog issued by Remington Arms Co.

Reproduction? Recognition!, by Frederick J. Stephens, Frederick J. Stephens, Bucks, England, 1976. 137 pp., illus. $15.50.
Frauds and reproductions of German Third Reich blades.

Rice's Trowel Bayonet, reprinted by Ray Riling Arms Books, Co., Phila., PA, 1968. 8 pp., illus. Paper covers. $3.00.
A facsimile reprint of a rare circular originally published by the U.S. Government in 1875 for the information of U.S. Troops.

Romance of Collecting Cattaraugus, Robeson, Russell, and Queen, by Mrs. Dewey P. Ferguson, Fairborn, OH, 1978. 220 pp., illus. Paper covers. $10.00.
Pictorial price guide. All companies listed with a history of their founding.

Romance of Knife Collecting, by Dewey P. Ferguson, Dewey P. Ferguson, Fairborn, OH, 4th ed., 1978. 176 pp., illus. Paper covers. $5.00.
A "must-have" by the modern master of pocketknife history.

Rules and Regulations for the Sword Exercise of the Cavalry, reprinted by Museum Restoration Service, Ontario, Canada, 1975. 160 pp., illus. Edition limited and numbered. $15.00.
A facsimile reprint originally printed for the War Office in London, in 1796.

Russell Green River Works Cutlery, reprinted by Dewey P. Ferguson, Fairborn, OH, 1970. 49 pp., illus. Paper covers. $5.00.
Facsimile reprint of an early pocketknife catalog with a modern pricing guide added.

Russian Military Swords 1801-1917, by E. Mollo, Historical Research Unit, London, England, 1973. 56 pp., illus. $12.50.
First book in English to examine and classify the various swords used by the Russian Army from Alexander I to the Revolution.

The Samurai Sword, by John M. Yumoto, Charles E. Tuttle Co., Rutland, VT, 1958. 191 pp., illus. $7.25.
A must for anyone interested in Japanese blades, and the first book on this subject written in English.

Schrade Pocket Knives and Price Guide, Catalog 'E' and Supplements, reprinted by A. G. Russell Knife Collectors Club, A. G. Russell, Springdale, AR, 1971. 123 pp., illus. Paper covers. $5.00.
Hundreds of illustrations of Schrade pocket knives with their values.

Scottish Swords from the Battlefield at Culloden, by Lord Archibald Campbell, The Mowbray Co., Providence, RI, 1973. 63 pp., illus. $5.00.
A modern reprint of an exceedingly rare 1894 privately printed edition.

Scottish Swords and Dirks, by John Wallace, Stackpole Books, Harrisburg, PA 1970. 80 pp., illus. $5.50.
An illustrated reference guide to Scottish edged weapons.

Secrets of Modern Knife Fighting, by David E. Steele, Phoenix Press, Arvada, CO, 1974. 149 pp., illus. Paper covers. $9.95; Cloth. $15.00.
Details every facet of employing the knife in combat, including underwater fighting.

The Sheffield Bowie & Pocket-Knife Makers 1825-1925, by Richard Washer, T. A. Vinall, Nottingham, England, 1974. 144 pp., illus. $14.50.
Alphabetical listing of all known makers with their various identification marks and their periods of manufacture.

Shosankenshu, by H. L. Joly, Holland Press, London, England, 1963. 241 pp., illus. $18.00.
Listing nearly 3000 names of Japanese artists and Kakihan found on sword furniture.

E. C. Simmons "Keen Kutter" Cutlery and Tools, reprinted by American Reprints Co., St. Louis, MO, 1970. 56 pp., illus. Paper covers. $3.50.
A facsimile reprint of a 1930 E. C. Simmons catalog.

Step-by-Step Knifemaking, by Davis Boye, Rodale Press, Emmous, PA, 1978. 288 pp., illus. $10.95.
Gives the fundamentals of knifemaking and shows how to make knives either as a hobby or as a business.

The Sword and Bayonet Makers of Imperial Germany 1871-1918, by John Walter, Arms and Armour Press, London, England, 1973. 120 pp., illus. $6.50.
Here for the first time is a comprehensive reference to the edged weapons producers of swords, sabres, sidearms, bayonets of Imperial Germany.

The Sword and the Centuries, by Alfred Hutton, Charles E. Tuttle Co., Rutland, VT, 1973. 392 pp., illus. $8.50.
A description of the various swords used in civilized Europe during the last five centuries, and of single combats which have been fought with them.

The Sword and Firearms Collection of the Society of the Cinncinnati, by John Brewer Brown, The Society of the Cinncinnati, Wash., DC, limited, numbered edition, 1965. 120 pp., illus. $10.00.
With biographical sketches of the original owners.

Sword, Lance and Bayonet, by Charles ffoulkes and E. C. Hopkinson, Arco Pub. Co., Inc., NY, 1967. 147 pp., illus. $7.50.
A facsimile of the first attempt at a consecutive account of the arms, both general and official use, since the discarding or armor.

The Sword and Same, by Arai Hakuseki and Inaba Tsurio, Holland Press, London, England, 1971. 256 pp., illus. $18.00.
This translation of a classic Japanese treatise on the sword was privately printed in an edition of only two hundred copies in 1913, and has been virtually unobtainable for many years.

Swords and Blades of the American Revolution, by George C. Neumann, A & W Books, NY, 1973. 288 pp., illus. $6.98.
Covers edged weapons in America, 1700-1783.

Swords of the British Army, by Brian Robson, Arms & Armour Press, London, England, 1975. 208 pp., illus. $19.95.
The regulation patterns, 1788-1914.

Swords and Daggers, by Eduard Wagner, Hamlyn, London, 1975. 253 pp., illus. $4.95.
Traces all types of European cut-and-thrust weapons from ancient times through their development to the twentieth century.

Swords for Sea Service, by Cmdr. W. E. May & P. G. W. Annis, Her Majesty's Stationery Office, London, England, 1970. A 2 volume set, 256; 398 pp., illus. $32.00.
A study based on the sword collection, which includes dirks and cutlasses, in the National Maritime Museum at Greenwich.

Things to Do With a Pocket Knife, by E. J. Tangerman, John M. Parker, Etowah, TN, 1976. 41 pp., illus. Paper covers. $3.00.
Reprint of a booklet published in 1934 by Remington Arms Co. Many items you can whittle with a pocket knife.

Third Reich Edged Weapon Accouterments, by Ltc. Thomas M. Johnson and Wilfrid Bradach, Ltc. Thomas M. Johnson, Alexandria, VA, 1977. 107 pp., illus. $10.00.
Factual information on the hangers, frogs, and knots accompanying the complete spectrum of edged weaponry of the Third Reich.

Tomahawks Illustrated, by Robert Kuck, Robert Kuck, New Knoxville, OH, 1977. 112 pp., illus. Paper covers. $8.50.
A pictorial record to provide a reference in selecting and evaluating tomahawks.

Tsubas in Southern California, compiled by W. M. Hawley, W. M. Hawley, Hollywood, CA, 1973. 302 pp., illus. $30.00.
A pictorial record of especially fine Japanese sword guards in the collections of members of the Nanka Token Kai.

Union Cutlery Company Catalog, reprinted by Ka-Bar Knives, Olean, NY, 1978. 40 pp., illus. Paper covers. $6.00.
Facsimile reprint of an original catalog *ca.* 1912-1923. An invaluable reference for the use of collectors of Ka-Bar knives.

U.S. Sword Bayonets 1847-1865, by Rollin V. Davis, Jr., M.D., Rollin V. Davis, Jr., M.D., Pittsburgh, PA, 1978. 50 pp., illus. Paper covers. $6.95.
A compilation of sword bayonets issued to the military services of the United States prior to and during the Civil War.

Voss Cutlery Co. Catalog, reprinted by Custom Cutlery Co., Dalton, GA, 1973. 72 pp., illus. Paper covers. $4.25.
A facsimile reprint of the Voss catalog showing patterns, pattern numbers, styles and unusual items as originally available.

Wearing the Edged Weapons of the Third Reich, by LTC Thomas M. Johnson, LTC Thomas M. Johnson, Columbia, SC, 1977. 50 pp., illus. $8.50.
An indispensible reference for every German edged weapon collector/researcher.

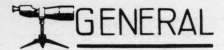

GENERAL

A.B.C. of Snap Shooting, by Horace Fletcher, Americana Archives Publ. Co., Topsfield, MA., 1971. 48 pp., illus. Paper, $3.00.
Authentic reproduction of a rare 1881 original.

Air Gun Batteries, by E. G. Wolff. Public Museum, Milwaukee, Wisc., 1964. 28 pp., illus., paperbound. 75¢.
Study of discharge mechanisms on reservoir air guns.

Air Gun Digest, by Robert Beeman & Jack Lewis, DBI Books, Inc., Northfield, IL, 1977. 224 pp., illus. Paper covers. $6.95.
Traces the first air, spring air, CO_2 and other types from prototype to current models.

The Album of Gunfighters, by J. Marvin Hunter and Noah H. Rose, Warren Hunter, Helotes, Texas, 1965. 4th printing. 236 pp., wonderfully illus., with spectacular oldtime photos. $19.50.
For the serious gunfighter fan there is nothing to equal this factual record of the men-behind-the-star and the human targets that they faced.

To All Sportsmen; and Particularly to Farmers and Gamekeepers, by Col. Geo. Hanger, Richmond Publ. Co., Richmond, England, 1971. 226 pp. $12.50.
Reprint of an 1814 work on hunting, guns, horses, veterinary techniques, etc.

Allied Pistols, Rifles and Grenades, by Peter Chamberlain and Terry Gander, Arco Publ. Co., NY, 1977. 64 pp., illus. Paper covers. $4.95.
Describes and illustrates the subject items used by the Allied forces in WW II.

American Artillery in the Mexican War 1846-47, by Lester R. Dillon, Jr., Presidial Press, Austin, TX, 1975. 120 pp., illus. $7.95.
An in depth critical analysis of the crucial role played by artillery in the United States' victory in the Mexican War.

The American B.B. Gun, by A. T. Dunathan, A. S. Barnes, S. Brunswick, NJ, 1971. 154 pp., illus. $10.00.
Identification reference and a price guide for B.B. guns, plus a brief history and advertising plates.

American Game Birds of Field and Forest, by F. C. Edminster, Book Sales, NY, 1972 490 pp. 99 plates. $6.95.
18 species; their origin, history, range, food, diseases, etc.

Americans and their Guns, compiled by Jas. B. Trefethen, ed. by Jas. E. Serven, Stackpole Books, Harrisburg, Pa., 1967. 320 pp., illus. $9.95.
The National Rifle Association of America story through nearly a century of service to the nation. More than a history—a chronical of help to novice and expert in the safe and proper use of firearms for defense and recreation, as well as a guide for the collector of arms.

America's Camping Book, by Paul Cardwell, Jr. C. Scribner's Sons, New York, NY 1st ed., 1969. 591 pp., well illus., in line and halftone. $10.00.
A fine illustrated guide to camping and woodcraft, with data on equipment, techniques, emergencies and nature study.

Anti-Aircraft Guns, by Peter Chamberlain and Terry Gander, Arco Publ. Co., NY, 1976. 64 pp., illus. Paper covers. $4.95.
Surface-to-air guns of all the major combatants, together with their components and complete listing of main data points.

Anti-Tank Weapons, by Peter Chamberlain and Terry Gander, Arco publ. Co., NY, 1974. 64 pp., illus. Paper covers. $4.95.
Covers anti-tank guns, rifles, mines and grenades, plus such recoilless weapons as the bazooka and the German Panzerfaust.

Archer's Digest, 2nd ed., ed. by Jack Lewis, DBI Books, Inc., Northfield, IL, 1977. 288 pp., illus. Paper covers. $7.95.
The latest technical data on compound bows plus essential chapters on equipment selection, tactics for bowhunting and fishing.

Archery: Its Theory and Practice, by H. A. Ford. Geo. Shumway, York, PA, 1971. 128 pp., illus. $6.00.
Reprint of the scarce 1856 ed.

Arco Gun Book, ed. by Larry Koller. Arco Publ. Co. Inc., NYC, 1962 397 pp., illus. $7.50.
A concise encyclopedia for arms collectors, shooters and hunters.

Armoured Fighting Vehicles, by Malcolm McGregor, Walker & Co., New York, 1967. 56 pp., illus. $15.00.
Describes 12 tanks and armored cars, representative of those used in the two World Wars. The illustrations in full-color are true scale drawn from actual models.

Armoured Forces, by R. M. Ogorkiewicz. Arco Pub. Co., NY, 1970. 475 pp., illus. Paper covers, $7.95.
A history of the armored forces and their vehicles.

Arms for Texas, by Michael J. Koury. The Old Army Press, Fort Collins, CO, 1973. 94 pp., illus. $7.50.
A study of the Republic of Texas guns.

Arms of the World: The 1911 Alfa Catalogue. Edited by Joseph J. Schroeder, Jr. Digest Books, Northfield, IL., 420 pp., Paper, $5.95.
Reprint in 4 languages of thousands of guns, cartridges, swords, helmets, tools, etc. Profusely illus., and priced the 1911 way.

The Art of Archerie, by Gervase Markham. A reprint of the 1634 original, publ. in London. Geo. Shumway, York, PA, 1968. 172 pp. $12.00.
This classic treatise, written to keep alive the art of archery in warfare, treats with the making of longbows and their use. A scholarly introduction to the new issue by S. V. Grancsay adds an enlightening historical perception.

The Art and Science of Taking to the Woods, by C. B. Colby and B. Angier, Stackpole Books, Harrisburg, Pa. 1970, 288 pp. illus. $7.95. Also in paper covers. $3.95.
Illustrated camper's manual covering all types of outdoor living and transportation, for novice and expert alike.

The Art of Survival, by C. Troebst. Doubleday & Co., Garden City, NY. 1965. 312 pp. illus. $6.95. Paper covers $3.50.
Narratives of devices of survival in difficult terrain or circumstances and evaluation of rescue and life-saving procedures.

The Art of the Decoy: American Bird Carvings, by Adele Earnest. Clarkson N. Potter, Inc., NYC, 1966. $10.00.
The origin of a lost art explained, plus some data on the most famous carvers. Over 106 black-and-white photos, 35 line drawings and an 8-page insert in full color.

Artillery of the World, by Christopher F. Foss, Ian Allan, London, 1974. 192 pp., illus. $8.95.
Covers all types of artillery from anti-tank guns to recoiless weapons.

Asian Fighting Arts, by D. F. Draeger and R. W. Smith. Kodansha Interna-

tional Ltd., Tokyo, Japan. 2nd printing, 1969. 207 pp., well illus., in line and halftone. $12.50.
A work of monumental research, interesting to all involved in the science of fighting techniques. Covers eleven Asian skills, ranging from Chinese T'ai-chi and Burmese Bando to Japanese Jujitsu and the lethal Pentjak-silak of Indonesia.

Author and Subject Index to the American Rifleman Magazine 1940-1950; 1951-1960; 1961-1970; 1971-1975, by W. R. Burrell, Galesburg, MI, 1973-75. 64 pp., Paper covers. Each index $6.50.
Alphabetical listing by author, title and subject of this famous arms publication.

Axis Pistols, Rifles and Grenades, by Peter Chamberlain and Terry Gander, Arco Publ. Co., NY, 1977. 64 pp., illus. Paper covers. $4.95.
Photographs and descriptions of those arms used by the axis powers during WW II.

Baron von Steuben and his Regulations, by Joseph R. Riling, Ray Riling Arms Books Co., Philadelphia, Penna., 1966. 207 pp., illus. $15.00.
A documented book on this great American Major General and the creation by him of the first official "Regulations." Includes the complete facsimile of these regulations.

Beginner's Guide to Guns and Shooting, by Clair F. Rees, DBI Books, Inc., Northfield, IL, 1978. 224 pp., illus. Paper covers. $6.95.
Indispensible to the beginner, and an enlightening review for the seasoned sportsman.

Being Your Own Wilderness Doctor, by Dr. E. Russel Kodet and Bradford Angier. Stackpole Books, Harrisburg, Pa., 1968. 127 pp., illus. In line drawings. $3.95.
Called the "outdoorsman's emergency manual" It offers security of knowing what to do best—in case of the worst.

Black Powder Gun Digest, 2nd ed., by Jack Lewis and Robert Springer, DBI Books, Inc., Northfield, IL, 1977. 288 pp., illus. Paper covers. $7.95.
A most comprehensive, authoritative book on black powder rifles, handguns, scatterguns and accessories.

Black Powder Guide 2nd ed., by George C. Nonte, Jr., Stoeger Publ. Co., So. Hackensack, NJ, 1976. 254 pp., illus. Paper covers. $6.95.
A complete guide to muzzle-loading rifles, pistols and shotguns—flintlock and percussion.

Black Powder Snapshots, by Herb Sherlock. Standard Publications. Huntington, W. VA, 50 pp., illus. $10.00.
Deluxe large volume containing 23 major Sherlock drawings and 95 punchy, marginal sketches.

The Book of the American West, ed. by Jay Monaghan. Julian Messner, New York, 1963. 608 pp., 200 illus. (many in color). $9.95.
A special chapter on frontier firearms is a feature of this massive work. 10 experts on Western hist. in as many fields of study contributed to the book. Illus. includ. works by the best contemporary artists.

The Book of the American Woodcock, by Wm. G. Sheldon, Ph.D. University of Mass. Press, Amherst, 1967. 227 pp., bibliography, appendices and index. $10.00

Bow & Arrow Archer's Digest, 2nd ed., ed. by Jack Lewis. DBI Books, Inc. Northfield, Ill., 1977. 320 pp., profusely illus. $7.95.
Comprehensive treatment of the art and science of archery. New 2nd edition.

Bowhunter's Digest, by C. R. Learn, DBI Books, Inc., Northfield, IL, 1974. 288 pp., illus. $6.95.
Covers large and small game bowhunting throughout the world. Many tips on camouflage, equipment and techniques to use.

Brassey's Artillery of the World, ed. by E. Bidwell, Brassey's, Ltd., London, England, 1977. 324 pp., over 300 illustrations. $49.50.
The design, characteristics, ammo, radar equipment, etc., of artillery throughout the world.

Brassey's Infantry Weapons of the World 1950-1975, edited by Maj. Gen. J. I. H. Owen, Bonanza Books, NY, 1977. 323 pp., illus. $7.98.
Infantry weapons and combat aids in current use by the regular and reserve forces of all nations.

Brassey's NATO Infantry and Its Weapons, ed. by J. I. H. Owen, Westview Press, Boulder, CO, 1976. 194 pp., illus. $14.50.
Man-portable weapons and equipment in service with the regular and reserve forces.

Brassey's Warsaw Pact Infantry and Its Weapons, edited by J. I. H. Owen, Brassey's Publishers Ltd., London, England, 1976. 112 pp., illus. $11.95.
Man-portable weapons and equipment in service with the regular and reserve forces of the Warsaw Pact Nations.

British and American Tanks of WW II, by P. Chamberlain and C. Ellis. Arco Pub. Co., New York., 1969 222 pp., illus. $9.95.
Complete, illus. history of American, British and Commonwealth tanks, 1939-1945. Photos, and precise specifications of each.

The British Code of Duel, Richmond Publ. Co., Richmond, England, 1971. 144 pp. Reprint of the 1824 ed. Reference on the laws of honour and the character of gentlemen. Together with **The Art of Duelling,** same publ., 1971. 70 pp. Reprint of the 1836 London ed. Both books $11.50.
Information useful to young Continental tourists.

Camper's Digest, 2nd ed. by Erwin and Peggy Bauer. Digest Books, Inc., Northfield, Ill. 60093, 1974. 288 pp., paper covers, $5.95.
Everything needed to be known about camping. Trails, tools, clothes, cooking. Articles by leading outdoor writers and campers.

Campground Cooking, edited by Charles and Kathleen Farmer, Digest Books Inc., Northfield, IL, 1974. 8½″X11″, 288 pp. Profusely illustrated. Paperbound. $6.95.
Covers cooking for campers, hunters, backpackers, boaters etc. with tips for game preparation, survival foods, favorite recipes.

The Camping Manual, compiled by Fred Sturges, Stackpole Books, Harrisburg, PA, 1967. 160 pp., illus. $3.95.
An excellent refresher on the fundamentals, with a digest of the newest methods and latest advice for those who want to enjoy camping more.

Carbine Handbook, by Paul Wahl. Arco Publ. Co., N.Y.C., 1964. 80 pp., illus. $6.00. Paperbound. $4.95.
A manual and guide to the U.S. Carbine, cal. .30, M1, with data on its history, operation, repair, ammunition, and shooting.

C.I.A. Special Weapons Supply Catalog, a facsimile reproduction by Paladin Press, Boulder, CO, 1975. 77 pp., illus. Paper covers $5.95.
A catalog listing over 1000 items available for use by various governmental organizations.

Clubs to Cannon, by Brigadier O. F. G. Hogg, Gerald Duckworth & Co. Ltd., London, (England), 1968. 264 pp., illus. $10.50.
Warfare and weapons before the introduction of gunpowder.

The Code of Honor; or Rules for the Government of Principals and Seconds in Duelling, by John Lyde Wilson, Ray Riling Arms Books Co., Phila., PA, 1971. 48 pp. Paper, $3.50.
Reprint of the rare 1858 edition.

The Complete Book of Game Conservation, by Chas. Coles, Barrie & Jenkins, London, 1971. 394 pp., $18.50.
Definitive work on the subject. 181 illustrations including color repro-

ductions of rare prints and original paintings.

The Complete Book of Trapping, by George Clawson, Winchester Press, NY, 1977. 256 pp., illus. $8.95.
All about fur trapping—from the earliest days to today's humane and profitable methods of harvesting pelts.

The Complete Book of Trick and Fancy Shooting, by Ernie Lind, Winchester Press, NY, 1972. 159 pp., illus. $6.95.
Step-by-step instructions for acquiring the whole range of shooting skills with rifle, pistol and shotgun; includes practical hints on developing your own shooting act.

The Complete Cannoneer, compiled by M. C. Switlik. Antique Ordnance Artificers, Jackson, MI, 1971. 106 pp., illus., paper covers. $4.50.
A must for the modern cannoneer. Compiled in two sections. Part first contains "School of the Piece" as orginally published in Artillery Drill by George S. Patton, in 1861. Part second contains current observations on the safe use of cannon.

Confederate Cannon Foundries, by Larry Daniel and Riley Gunter, Pioneer Press, Union City, TN, 1977. 114 pp., illus. $12.95.
Covers every known foundry in the South in detail, and is very well illustrated.

Conquering the Frontiers, by James E. Serven, The Foundation Press, Tucson, AZ, 1974. 256 pp., illus. $19.95.
Stories of American pioneers and the guns which helped them establish a new life.

Coping with Camp Cooking, by M. W. Stephens and G. S. Wells. Stackpole Books, Harrisburg, PA 1966. 94 pp., illus., decorated boards. $2.95.
Hints and recipes selected from the editors' writings appearing in *Camping Guide Magazine.*

Crossbow, From 35 Years with the Weapon, by George M. Stevens, Crossbow Books, Huntsville, AR, 1978. 170 pp., illus. Limited ed. $17.50.
A semi-technical work on the crossbow, from its origin through the workshop.

Crossbows, by Frank Bilson, Hippocrene Books, Edison, NJ, 1975. 148 pp., illus. $8.95.
The first book to be written on crossbows since the beginning of the century. Describes construction, design, etc.

The Crossbow, by Sir Ralph Payne-Gallwey, Holland Press Ltd., London, 1971. 375 pp., illus. $25.00.
New printing of the only work devoted to the crossbow and such related weapons as the siege engine, balistas, catapults, Turkish bows and the Chinese repeating crossbow.

Current American War Medals and Decorations, 1963-69, by E. E. Kerrigan. Medallic Publishing Co., Noroton Heights, CT 1st ed. 1969. Paper covers, 23 pp., illus. $3.00.
This supplement updates the author's *American War Medals and Decorations,* listing recently created awards and recipients.

Dead Aim, by Lee Echols, Acme Printing Co., San Diego, CA, a reprint, 1972. 116 pp., illus. $5.00.
Nostalgic antics of hell-raising pistol shooters of the 1930s.

Decoys of the Atlantic Flyway, by Geo. R. Starr, Jr., M.D., Winchester Press, NY, 1974. 308 pp., illus. with photographs by Geo. Dow. $17.95.
The art and history of decoy carving. Over 300 decoys illus. in color and b/w.

Decoys Simplified, by Paul W. Casson, Freshet Press, Rockville Centre, NY, 1972. 95 pp. plus 20 plans. $14.95.
How to make inexpensive cork decoys with only a small amount of equipment.

Description of U.S. Military Rifle Sights, by Edw. A. Tolosky, E. A. Tolosky, Publ., 1971. 117 pp. Paper, $8.50.
Covers period from 1861 to 1940. New and excellent work for collectors and fans of the U.S. Military. Definitive text, full-size line drawings.

The Details of the Rocket System, by Col. Wm. Congreve. Museum Restoration Service, Ottawa, Canada, 1970. 85 pp., illus. $10.00.
Reprint of the 1814 1st ed. with details, photos and plates of rockets and their launchers. Edition limited and numbered.

The Diary of Colonel Peter Hawker, by Col. P. Hawker, Richmond Publ. Co., Richmond, England. 1971. 759 pp., illus. $21.95.
Reprint of the 1893 ed. covers shooting in every way and how to outwit your opponent!

Dictionary of Weapons & Military Terms, by John Quick, McGraw-Hill, NY, 1973. 515 pp., illus. $25.00.
Describes the principal weapons and weapon systems from ancient times to present day.

Dixie Gun Works Muzzleloaders' Annual 1978, ed. by Russ Carpenter, Dixie Gun Works, Union City, TN, 1978. 102 pp., illus. Paper covers. $1.95.
Liberally spiced with color photographs and contains articles by eminent experts on muzzle-loading arms.

The Double-Armed Man, by Wm. Neade, Geo. Shumway, Publ., York, PA, 1971. 51 pp., 7 woodcuts. $8.00.
Facsimile ed. of a little book published in London in 1625. Describes use of the longbow in combination with the pike. Limited to 400 numbered copies.

Eat the Weeds, by B. C. Harris. Barre Publ., Barre, MA, 1968. 223 pp., illus., paper covers $3.95.
Practical directions for collecting and drying herbs, for using edible plants and fruits as food and for medical purposes or as substitutes for cultivated vegetables.

Encyclopedia of Continental Army Units; Battalions, Regiments and Independent Corps, by Fred A. Berg, Stackpole Books, Harrisburg, PA, 1972. 160 pp. $6.95.
The official and unofficial designations, organizational history, commanding officers and ethnic composition for every unit of the Continental Army for which these facts are known.

Encyclopedia of British, Provincial, and German Army Units 1775-1783, by P. R. Katcher. Stackpole Books, Harrisburg, PA, 1973. 160 pp., illus. $6.95.
Definitive study of America's opposing forces, meant for historians, buffs, and students; covers units, placement, commanders, arms, etc.

Encyclopedia of Modern Firearms, Vol. 1, compiled and publ. by Bob Brownell, Montezuma, IA, 1959. 1057 pp. plus index, illus. $27.50. Dist. by Bob Brownell, Montezuma, IA 50171.
Massive accumulation of basic information of nearly all modern arms pertaining to "parts and assembly." Replete with arms photographs, exploded drawings, manufacturers' lists of parts, etc.

Engines of War, by Henry Wilkinson, The Richmond Publishing Co., Surrey (England), a facsimile ed., 1973. 268 pp., illus. $10.95.
The history of projectile weapons together with metallurgical observations and gunpowder manufacture.

The English Bowman, by T. Roberts. George Shumway, York, PA, 1973. 347 pp. $6.
Facsimile of the original work of 1801, with a new intro. by E. G. Heath. The art and practice of archery, the techniques of shooting and the elements of toxophily are examined, with comments on an earlier and similar work by Roger Ascham, called *Toxophilus.*

The Experts Book of the Shooting Sports, ed. by D. E. Petzal. Simon and Schuster, NY, 1972. 320 pp., illus. $9.95.
America's foremost shooting and hunting experts disclose the secrets of their specialties.

Explosives and Bomb Disposal Guide, by Robt. R. Lenz. Chas. C. Thomas, Springfield, IL, 1971. 303 pp., illus. $14.00.
Course of instruction on handling clandestine and sabotage devices; now being taught to all military bomb disposal technicians.

Explosives and Demolitions, U.S. Field Manual 5-25, Normount Armament Co., Forest Grove, OR. 215 pp., illus., paperbound. $4.95.
A reprint of the Army FM dated 14 May 1959.

Explosives and Homemade Bombs, by Jos. Stoffel. Chas. C. Thomas, Springfield, IL, 1972. 304 pp., illus. $14.00.
Elementary text on design and manufacture of explosive devices, for use as a text in training bomb disposal personnel.

Falconry, by Gilbert Blaine, Neville Spearman, London, 1970. 253 pp., illus. $7.50.
Reprint of a 1936 classic on training, handling, types, furniture, etc., of hawks, plus a glossary and list.

Famous Guns that Won the West, by James Wycoff, Arco Publ., Inc., NY, 1975. 112 pp., illus. Paper covers. $2.
A story about the pioneer guns that won the West and which made the West famous at the same time.

Feasting Free on Wild Edibles, by Bradford Angier. Stackpole Books, Harrisburg, PA, 1972. 285 pp., illus. Paper covers. $4.95.
More than 500 ways to banquet on nature's bounty. A one-vol. issue combining Angier's *Free for the Eating* and *More Free for the Eating Wild Foods.*

Fighting Vehicles, by C. Ellis & P. Chamberlain. Hamlyn Publ., London, Eng., 1972. 96 pp. $3.95.
Illus. story of the tank, going back centuries. Covers mobile fortresses through Patton and W.W. II tanks to today's varied types.

Firearms Control, by Colin Greenwood, Routledge & Kegan Paul, London (England), 1972. 274 pp. $13.50.
A study of armed crime and firearms control in England and Wales.

The Firearms Dictionary, by R. A. Steindler, Paladin Press, Boulder, CO, 1976. 288 pp., illus. Paper covers, $6.95. Cloth, $12.50.
The basic illustrated reference encyclopedia of gun language. Defines over 1800 English and foreign terms relating to firearms, ammunition, accessories and gun repairing techniques.

Firearms Encyclopedia, by George C. Nonte, Jr., Outdoor Life/Harper & Row, NY, 1973. 341 pp., illus. $13.95.
A to Zed coverage of gun and shooting terms, plus a complete appendix of useful information and an index.

Firearm Silencers, by D. B. McLean. Anubus Press, Houston, TX, 1968. 123 pp., illus., paperbound. $5.95.
The history, design, and development of silencers for U.S. military firearms.

Firearms, Traps & Tools of the Mountain Men, by Carl P. Russell. A. A. Knopf, NY, 1967. 448 pp., illus. in line drawings. $17.50.
Detailed survey of fur traders' equipment in the early days of the west.

Flags & Standards of the Third Reich Army, Navy & Air Force, by Brian Leigh Davis, Arco Publ. Co., NY, 1975. 160 pp., illus. $15.00.
Describes and illus. the history and development of all the known flags and standards used by the armed forces of the Third Reich. Many in color.

Four Studies on the History of Arms, by Arne Hoff, et al. Tjhusmuseet, Copenhagen, 1964. 145 pp., illus., paperbound. $6.75.
A Danish museum publication containing in English text scholarly monographs on arms topics of historic interest.

Game and Bird Calling, by A. C. Becker, Jr., A. S. Barnes and Co., NY, 1972. 147 pp., illus. $4.95.
Discusses various types of calls and techniques used by hunters—tyros and professionals.

Game Bird Carving, by Bruce Burk. Winchester Press, NY, 1972. 256 pp. $12.50.
The first step-by-step book on bird carving techniques. Over 700 photographs and line drawings by the author.

Game Birds of North America, by Leonard Lee Rue and Douglas Allen, Jr., Outdoor Life-Harper & Row, NY, 1973. 490 pp., illus. $12.50.
Complete details on 75 species of American game birds. Profusely illustrated in color.

Game and Fish Cookbook, by H. and J. Barnett. Grossman Publ., New York, NY 1968, 162 pp., illus. $7.95.
Special culinary attention to fish and game, with interesting and different touches.

Game in the Kitchen, by B. Flood and W. C. Roux (eds.). Barre Publ., Barre, MA 1st ed., 1968, 234 pp., illus. $7.50.
A fish and game cookbook, with menus and information on preservation, cooking and serving.

German Army Uniforms and Insignia 1933-1945, by B. L. Davis. World Publ. Co., NY, 1972. 224 pp. $12.
Every aspect of the uniforms, insignias, and accoutrements of the Third Reich Army are covered in detail. Many illus. in full color.

German Artillery of World War Two, by Ian Hogg, Hippocrene Books, Inc., NY, 1975. 304 pp., illus. $22.50.
The most complete and comprehensive study of the subject ever published.

German Infantry Weapons, ed. by D. B. McLean. Normount Armament Co., Wickenburg, AZ, 1966. 191 pp., illus., paperbound. $3.50.
World War II German weapons described and illustrated, from military intelligence research.

German Infantry Weapons of World War II, by A. J. Barker. Arco Publ. Co., New York, NY 1969, 76 pp., illus. $3.50.
Historical and statistical data on all types of the subject weapons, ammunition, etc.

German Secret Weapons of World War II, by I. V. Hogg. Arco Pub. Co., NY, 1970. 80 pp., illus. $4.95.
Compact, comprehensive account of Germany's secret weapons, eccentric and brilliant. Includes plans and technical details.

The German Sniper, by Peter R. Senich and Howard Kyle, Normount Tech. Publ., Wickenburg, AZ, 1976. 165 pp., illus. Paper covers. $14.95; deluxe hardbound. $18.95.
A story of the man and his weapons.

German Tanks of World War II, by F. M. von Senger und Etterlin. Stackpole Books, Harrisburg, PA, 1969. 176 pp., nearly 300 photos and drawings. Large format. $11.95.
A fully illustrated and definitive history of German armoured fighting vehicles, 1926-1945. Written in English.

German Weapons-Uniforms-Insignia 1841-1918, by Maj. J. E. Hicks. J. E. Hicks & Son, La Canada, CA, 1958. 158 pp., illus. $6.00.
Originally published in 1937 as *Notes on German Ordnance 1841-1918,* this new edition offers the collector a wealth of information gathered from many authentic sources.

Gourmet Cooking for Free, by Bradford Angier. Stackpole Books. Harrisburg, PA 1970. 190 pp. illus. $4.95.
Cookery of large and small game, seafood and wild plants.
Grandi Incisioni Su Armi D'Oggi, by Mario Abbiatico, Gianoberto Lupi, and Franco Vacarri, Editoriale Olimpia, Brescia, Italy, 1977. 290 pp., illus. $35.00.
The work of forty Italian engravers is represented in this magnificent work on great gun engraving of today. **Italian text.**
The Great American Shooting Prints, selections and text by Robt. Elman. A. A. Knopf, NY, 1972. Large format. 72 full color plates. $25.
The hunting life in America as portrayed in paintings and lithographs from the 1820s to the present.
The Great Art of Artillery, by Casimir Simienowicz, with a new foreword by Brig. O. F. G. Hogg. S. R. Publi., Ltd., London, Eng., 1971. $15.00.
Facsimile of the original 1729 ed. Red-hot shot, chain shot and other incendiary "globes" are described in detail, and rockets are covered most extensively. Basically a work on fireworks—military and civil.
Guide to the Soviet Navy, by Siegfried Breyer, U.S. Naval Institute, Annapolis, MD, 1971. 353 pp. $10.00.
Compact, comprehensive, up-to-date view of organization, construction, weapons, equipment, forces, bases and ports. Over 100 photos, plans, tables and maps, specifications and profiles.
Guide to United States Machine Guns, by K. F. Schreier, Jr., Normount Armament Co., Wickenburg, AZ, 1971. 178 pp., illus. Paper, $4.95.
All machine guns procured by the U.S. Armed Forces and some of an experimental nature.
Gun Carriages: An Aide Memoire to the Military Sciences, 1846, by R. J. Nelson. Museum Restoration Service, Ottawa, Canada, 1972. 64 pp. Paper covers, $3.00.
Originally prepared in 1846 as a manual for the officers of the British Army. Illus. with detailed scaled drawings, plus tables of dimensions and weights.
Gun Control, by Robert J. Kukla, Stackpole Books, Harrisburg, PA, 1973. 448 pp., illus. Paper cover $4.95.
A written record of the efforts to eliminate the private possession of firearms in America.
Gun Digest 1979, 33rd Edition, edited by John T. Amber, DBI Books, Inc., Northfield, IL, 1978. 448 pp., illus. Paper covers. $9.95.
The world's greatest gun book in its 33rd annual edition.
Gun Digest Book of Modern Gun Values, 2nd ed., by Jack Lewis, DBI Books, Inc., Northfield, IL, 1978. 288 pp., illus. $7.95.
Invaluable guide for buying, selling, trading or identifying guns—handguns, rifles and shotguns are covered in separate sections. Feature articles relate to collecting and values.
Gun Digest Book of Exploded Firearms Drawings 2nd Edition, edited by Harold A. Murtz, DBI Books, Inc., Northfield, IL, 1978. 320 pp., illus. Paper covers. $7.95.
Hundreds of exploded drawings of modern and collector's firearms.
Gun Digest Treasury, 5th Edition, edited by John T. Amber, DBI Books, Inc., Northfield, IL, 1977. 288 pp., illus. Paper covers. $7.95.
The best articles from the first 30 years of Gun Digest.
Gundogs, Their Care and Training, by M. Brander. A. & C. Black, London, Eng., 1969. 97 pp., illus. $4.95.
Gun Fun with Safety, by G. E. Damon. Standard Publications, Huntington, W. VA, 1947. 206 pp., well illus. $6.00.
A long out-of-print work that is still much sought. A fine general coverage of arms and ammunition, old and new, with chapters on shooting, targets, etc., with safety always upper-most.
Gun Talk, edited by Dave Moreton. Winchester Press, NY, 1973. 256 pp., illus. $9.95.
A treasury of original writing by the top gun writers and editors in America. Practical advice about every aspect of the shooting sports.
The Gun That Made the Twenties Roar, by Wm. J. Helmer, rev. and enlarged by George C. Nonte, Jr., The Gun Room Press, Highland Park, NJ, 1977. Over 300 pp., illus. $16.95.
Historical account of John T. Thompson and his invention, the infamous "Tommy Gun."
The Gunfighter, Man or Myth? by Joseph G. Rosa, Oklahoma Press, Norman, OK, 1969. 229 pp., illus., (including weapons). $5.95.
A well-documented work on gunfights and gunfighters of the West and elsewhere. Great treat for all gunfighter buffs.
The Gunfighters, by Dale T. Schoenberger, The Caxton Printers, Ltd., Caldwell, ID, 1971. 207 pp., illus. $12.95.
Startling expose of our foremost Western folk heroes.
The Gun-Founders of England, by Charles ffoulkes, Geo. Shumway, York, PA, 1969. 133 pp., illus. $15.00.
Detailed study of cannon, casting. Describes preparation of moulds, castings, mfg. of powder and shot, etc.
The Gunner's Bible, by Bill Riviere. Doubleday, N.Y.C., 1965. 192 pp., illus. Paperbound. $2.50.
General Guide to modern sporting firearms and their accessories, for all shooters.
Guns, by Dudley Pope. Delacorte Press, N.Y.C., 1965. 256 pp., illus. $9.98.
Concise history of firearms, stressing early museum-quality weapons. Includes small arms as well as artillery, naval, and airborne types. Fine photographs, many in color.
Guns & Ammo 1978 Annual, edited by Rick L. Fines, Guns & Ammo magazine, Petersen Publ. Co., Los Angeles, CA, 1977. 320 pp., illus. Paper covers. $5.95.
Annual catalog of sporting firearms and accessories, with numerous articles for gun enthusiasts.
Guns & Ammo Guide to Guns of the Gunfighters, ed. by Garry James, Petersen Publ. Co., Los Angeles, CA, 1975. 224 pp., illus. Paper covers. $4.95.
The first detailed treatment of the men who used guns to build a reputation, whether good or bad.
Guns & Ammo Guide to Guns for Home Defense, by Elmer Keith, et al, Petersen Publ. Co., Los Angeles, CA, 1975. 176 pp., illus. Paper covers. $3.95.
How to select a gun for home defense, and learning how to use it.
Guns Illustrated 1979, 11th ed., ed. by Harold A. Murtz, DBI Books, Inc., Northfield, IL, 1978. 288 pp., illus. Paper covers. $7.95.
Technical articles for gun enthusiasts plus a complete illustrated catalog of all current guns, ammunition and accessories including specifications and prices.
Guns; An Illustrated History of Artillery, ed. by Jos. Jobe, New York Graphic Society, Greenwich, CT, 1971. 216 pp., illus. $17.98.
Traces the history and technology of artillery from its beginnings in the 14th century to its 20th century demise in the face of aerial bombs and guided missiles.
The Guns of Harpers Ferry, by S. E. Brown Jr. Virginia Book Co., Berryville, VA, 1968. 157 pp., illus. $12.50.
Catalog of all known firearms produced at the U.S. armory at Harpers

Ferry, 1798-1861, with descriptions, illustrations and a history of the operations there.
The Gunsmith in Colonial Virginia, by Harold B. Gill, Jr., University Press of Virginia, Charlottesville, VA, 1975. 200 pp., illus. Paper covers, $7.50; Cloth, $10.00.
The role of the gunsmith in colonial Virginia from the first landing at Jamestown through the Revolution is examined, with special attention to those who lived and worked in Williamsburg.
The Hall Carbine Affair; An Essay in Historiography, by R. Gordon Wasson, Privately Printed, Danbury, CT, 1971. 250 pp., illus. Deluxe slip-cased ed. of 250 copies. $75.00.
Based on the original work (limited to 100 copies) of 1941 and a 1948 revised ed. of only 750 copies. This issue, enlarged and re-researched, relates to sales and purchases of Hall carbines in the Civil War, in which J. Pierpont Morgan was involved.
Handbook for Hythe, by H. Busk, Richmond Pub. Co., Richmond, England, 1971. 194 pp., illus. $8.50.
Reprint of the 1860 ed. explaining laws of projectiles with an introduction to the system of musketry.
Handbook of Self-Defense for Law Enforcement Officers, by John Martone. Arco Publ. Co., New York, NY, 1968. 1st ed., 4th printing, 111 pp., $4.00.
A clearly-illustrated manual on offensive and defensive techniques recommended for the use of policemen.
The Handy Sportsman, by Loring D. Wilson, Winchester Press, NY, 1976. 256 pp., illus. $10.95.
29 inexpensive, easy-to-build sporting accessories for the hunter and fisherman.
Hatcher's Notebook, by Maj. Gen. J. S. Hatcher. Stackpole Books, Harrisburg, PA, 1952. 2nd ed. with four new chapters, 1957. 629 pp., illus. $12.95.
A dependable source of information for gunsmiths, ballisticians, historians, hunters, and collectors.
Heavy Artillery, by Peter Chamberlain and Terry Gander, Arco Publ. Co., NY, 1975. 64 pp., illus. Paper covers. $4.95.
The largest land weaponry of all the major powers from railway guns to coastal installations.
Helmets and Body Armor in Modern Warfare, by Bashford Dean, Americana Books & Gallery, Tuckahoe, NY, new edition, 1978. 470 pp., illus. $25.00.
A reprint of Dean's definitive 1919 work on helmets and body armor, plus the 1945 U.S. Ordnance Department publication, featuring helmets and body armor of WW II.
Hibbard, Spencer, Bartlett & Co. Catalog. American Reprints, St. Louis, MO, 1969. 92 pp., illus. Paper, $5.00.
Reprint of 1884 catalog on guns, rifles, revolvers, ammo, powder flasks, etc. Descriptions and contemporary prices.
A History of Firearms, by Major Hugh B. C. Pollard, Burt Franklin, NY, a facsimile ed. with a new introduction by Joseph R. Riling, 1973. 320 pp., illus. $25.50.
An excellent survey of the development of hand firearms. Lists over 2,000 American and foreign gunmakers.
A History of Marksmanship, by Charles Chenevix Trench, Follett Publ. Co., Chicago, IL, 1972. 319 pp., illus. $12.95.
A complete and wide-ranging survey of the marksman and his weapons, in peace and in war.
A History of War and Weapons, 449 to 1660, by A. V. B. Norman and D. Pottinger. Thomas Y. Crowell Co., NY, 1966. 224 pp., well illus. with sketches. $6.95.
An excellent work for the scholar on the evolution of war and weapons in England. Many sketches of arms and weapons of all sorts add importance.
The Hitler Albums, Vol. I, by Roger J. Bender, R. J. Bender Publ. Co., Mountain View, CA, 1970. 144 pp., $10.95.
Complete photographic study of Mussolini's state visit to Germany in September, 1937. 175 photos and illus..
Home Book of Taxidermy and Tanning, by G. J. Grantz, Stackpole Books, Harrisburg, PA, 1969, 160 pp., illus. $7.95.
Amateur's primer on mounting fish, birds, animals, and trophies.
Home Guide to Muzzle Loaders, by Geo. C. Nonte, Jr., Stackpole Books, Harrisburg, PA, 1974. 219 pp., illus. $6.95.
From the basics of muzzle loading, its ammo, to the differences between the modern and replica muzzle loader, plus how-to-make one.
Home in Your Pack, by Bradford Angier, Stackpole Books, Harrisburg, PA, 1965. 192 pp., illus. $4.50.
An outdoorsman's handbook on equipment, woodcraft, and camping techniques.
How to Build Your Home in the Woods, by Bradford Angier, Stackpole Books, Harrisburg, PA, 1967, 310 pp., illus. $7.95.
Detailed instructions on building cabins, shelters, etc., with natural materials. How to obtain food from nature, and how to live in the wilderness in comfort.
How to Cook His Goose (and other wild game), by Karen Green and Betty Black, Winchester Press, NY, 1973. 198 pp. Paper covers, $3.95; cloth, $6.95.
An informative and delightful guide to preparing and cooking game of all types.
How to Defend Yourself, your Family, and your Home, by Geo. Hunter. David McKay, N.Y.C., 1967, 307 pp., illus. $7.95.
The only book available for the public at large that advocates their ownership of firearms—including handguns. Covers laws of self-defense, setting up home protection, and much else.
How to Live in the Woods on Pennies a Day, by Bradford Angier, Stackpole Books, Harrisburg, PA, 1971. 192 pp., illus. $6.95.
New reprint on modern-day wilderness living in America, plus cooking and recipes.
How to Make Working Decoys, by George Ross Starr, Jr., M.D., Winchester Press, NY, 1978. 224 pp., illus. $12.50.
A carver's guide to making realistic decoys for the business of luring ducks.
The Identification and Registration of Firearms, by Vaclav "Jack" Krcma, C. C. Thomas, Springfield, IL, 1971. 173 pp., illus. $17.50.
Analysis of problems and improved techniques of recording firearms data accurately.
Improvised Modified Firearms, by J. David Truby and John Minnery. A two volume set, Paladin Press, Boulder, CO, 1975. Both books over 280 pages combined, with over 300 illus. The set $17.95.
A complete examination of improvised gunsmithing that explodes the myth of gun control.
Infantry Equipment 1875. A reprint of U.S. Ordnance Memoranda No. 19 by Francis Bannerman Sons, Blue Point, NY, 1969. 62 pp., plus 9 plates. $6.50.
A report covering materials, supplies, etc., to outfit troops in field and garrison.
Infantry, Mountain, and Airbourne Guns, by Peter Chamberlain and Terry Gander, Arco Publ. Co., NY, 1976. 64 pp., illus. Paper covers. $4.95.

Complete descriptions of light, portable weapons developed for use during WW II.
Instructions for Field Artillery, 1861 Edition, prepared by a Board of Artillery Officers, a facsimile reprint by Greenwood Press, NY, 1975. 348 pp., illus. $24.95.
A facsimile of the revised edition of 1861, the first wartime edition published during the Civil War.
Instructions for Use & Care of Gatling Guns, compiled by Commander J. D. Marvin, Fortress Publ., Stoney Creek, Ontario, Can., 1974. 43 pp. plus 5 folding plates, paper covers. $3.95.
A facsimile of the original 1875 manual on Naval Gatling Guns.
Instructions to Young Sportsmen: Guns and Shooting, by Col. P. Hawker, Richmond Publ. Co., Richmond, England, 1971. 507 pp., illus. $17.50. Deluxe ed., $35.00.
Reprint of the 1833 British work on guns, shooting and killing game.
The International Arms Review, edited by John Olson, A Jolex Publication, Paramus, NJ, 1977. 299 pp., illus. Paper covers. $6.95.
A new form of yearbook that combines the talents of an international team of distinguished firearms authorities whose writings explore all phases of firearms history and firearms development.
An Introduction to Tool Marks, Firearms and the Striagraph, by J. E. Davis. Chas. C. Thomas, Springfield, IL, 1st ed., 1958. 282 pp. $8.50.
Textbook on micro-contour analysis in criminalistics, with emphasis upon the striagraph in analysis of evidence.
Jane's Infantry Weapons 1975-76, ed. by F. W. A. Hobart, Jane's USA, NY, 1976. 843 pp., illus. with over 1500 photographs and diagrams. $72.50.
Deals with all weapons known to be in current service throughout the world.
Jane's Infantry Weapons 1977 ed., edited by Denis Archer, Jane's USA, NY, 1977. 700 pp., profusely illus. $72.50.
For everyone involved with the identification and analysis of weaponry and ammunition this is a reference work of unparalleled value.
Jane's Weapons Systems: 1975-76, by R. T. Pretty and D. H. R. Archer, Editors. Jane's Yearbooks, London, 1973. 606 pp. illus. $72.50.
Catalog of military hardware of the major nations.
Japanese Infantry Weapons, ed. by D. B. McLean. Normount Armament Co., Wickenburg, AZ, 1966. 241 pp., well illus., paperbound. $4.95.
Survey of World War II Japanese weapons, based on military intelligence research.
Kill or Get Killed, by Col. Rex Applegate, new rev. and enlarged ed., Paladin Press, Boulder, CO, 1976. 421 pp., illus. $15.95.
For police and military forces. Last word on mob control.
Know Your Antitank Rifles, by E. J. Hoffschmidt, Blacksmith Corp., Stamford, CT, 1977. 80 pp., illus. Paper covers. $3.95.
The antitank rifles of the major world powers.
Kuhlhoff on Guns, by Pete Kuhlhoff, Winchester Press, NY, 1970. 180 pp., illus. $5.95.
A selection of firearms articles by the late Gun Editor of *Argosy* Magazine.
Lewis Automatic Machine Gun, publ. originally by Savage Arms Co., Utica, NY. A reprint by L. A. Funk, Puyallup, WA, 1969. 47 pp., illus., paper covers. $3.00.
This facsimile covers the Model 1916 gun, explaining all features of operation, action, nomenclature, stripping and assembly.
Light and Medium Field Artillery, by Peter Chamberlain and Terry Gander, Arco Publ. Co., NY, 1975. 64 pp., illus. Paper covers. $4.95.
Describes and illustrates nearly every gun used by the various nations during WW II.
List of Changes in British War Material, in Relation to Edged Weapons, Firearms and Associated Ammunition and Accoutrements, Volume II, 1886-1900, compiled by Ian D. Skennerton, Margate, Australia, 1977. 200 pp., illus. $23.50.
Contains the original text for the introduction of articles into the British Service. The ultimate source of reference for collectors and students of British military weapons.
Lyman Muzzleloaders' Handbook, first ed., edited by C. Kenneth Ramage, Lyman Publ., Middlefield, CT, 1976. 248 pp., illus. Paper covers. $6.95.
A complete black powder catalog of all such rifles, pistols, shotguns, kits and accessories available today.
The Machine Gun, Vol., II, Part VII, by Lt. Col. G. M. Chinn. Paladin Press, Boulder, Col., n.d. 215 pp., illus. $15.00.
Reprint of a 1952 Navy publication of Soviet WW II rapid fire weapons.
Machine Guns, by Peter Chamberlain and Terry Gander, Arco Publ. Co., NY, 1974. 64 pp., illus. Paper covers. $5.95.
Covers arms used by the principle countries taking part in WW II. Each machine gun is described and illus.
Marksmanship: Secrets of High Scoring from a World Champ, by Gary L. Anderson. Simon & Schuster, NY, 1972. 79 pp. $5.95.
Illus. step-by-step guide to target shooting. Covers equipment, ammunition, breath control, arm position, etc.
Marlin Catalog of 1897. A reprint in facsimile by the Rocky Mountain Investment and Antique Co.; Cheyenne, WY, 1969. 192 pp. Well illus., paper covers, $4.00.
All models are covered, cartridges, sights, engraving, accessories, reloading tools, etc.
Marlin Catalog, 1905, Rocky Mountain Investment and Antique Co.; Cheyenne, WY, 1971. 128 pp. Paper, $4.00.
Reprint. Rifles, shotguns, pistols, tools, cartridge information, factory engraving and carving illustrated and described.
Mason Decoys, by Byron and Maureen Cheever, Hillcrest Publ., Inc., Spanish Fork, UT, 1974. 166 pp., illus. $12.95.
A well illustrated ready reference covering the decoys made by the Mason Decoy Factory of Detroit, Michigan.
Medicolegal Investigation of Gunshot Wounds, by Abdullah Fatteh, J. B. Lippincott Co., Phila., PA, 1977. 272 pp., illus. $18.50.
A much-needed work, clearly written and easily understood, dealing with all aspects of medicolegal investigation of gunshot wounds and deaths.
Mexican Military Arms, The Cartridge Period, by James B. Hughes, Jr. Deep River Armory, Inc., Houston, TX, 1967. 135 pp., photos and line drawings. $4.50.
An interesting and useful work, in imprinted wrappers, covering the period from 1866 to 1967.
Military Modelling, by Donald Featherstone, A. S. Barnes and Co., NY, 1971. 159 pp., illus. $6.95.
Describes the art of moulding and casting, soldering, glueing, painting and construction of small figures.
Military Small Arms of the Twentieth Century, by Ian V. Hogg and John Weeks, Arms and Armour Press, London, England, 1978. 304 pp., illus. $19.95.
A comprehensive illustrated encyclopedia of the world's small-caliber firearms, 1900-1977.
Military Uniforms, 1686-1918, by Rene North. Grosset & Dunlap, NY, 1970. 159 pp., illus. $3.95.
Concise survey of European and U.S. military dress and its history during the principal wars. Profusely illus., with some colored drawings.
Modern ABC's of Bow and Arrow, by G. H. Gillelan. Stackpole Books, Harrisburg, PA, 1967. 160 pp., illus. $4.95.
Survey of techniques for beginners and experts in target archery as well as bowhunting.
Modern ABC's of Guns, by R. A. Steindler. Stackpole Books, Harrisburg, PA, 1965. 191 pp., illus. $4.95.
Concise lexicon of today's sporting firearms, their components, ammunition, accessory equipment and use.
Modern Firearms, by Yves Cadiou and Alphonse Richard, William Morrow and Co., Inc., NY, 1977. 224 pp., illus. $19.95.
This excellently illustrated volume on the development of firearms concentrates on the evolution of modern handguns and rifles.
Mortars and Rockets, by Peter Chamberlain and Terry Gander, Arco Publ. Co., NY, 1975, 64 pp., illus. Paper covers. $4.95.
Mortars and rockets used by various nations during the period of 1939-1945.
The MP40 Submachine Gun, ed. by Fred L. Rexer, Fred L. Rexer & Associates, Inc., Houston, TX, 1976. 27 pp., illus. Paper covers. $3.50.
An English language manual on the use, maintenance, cleaning, loading and inspection of one of the most interesting weapons of WW II.
New England Militia Uniforms and Accoutrements, by J. O. Curtis and Wm. H. Guthman. Old Sturbridge Inc., Sturbridge, MA, 1971. 102 pp. Paper covers. $4.
An identification guide which illustrates uniforms, epaulettes, helmets, helmet plates, belt buckles and cartridge pouches.
New Principles of Gunnery, by Benjamin Robins. Richmond Publ. Co., London, 1972. 190 pp. $11.75.
Facsimile of the rare 1742 ed. For anyone, including libraries, interested in gunnery, military history and technology.
The New Way of the Wilderness, By Calvin Rutstrum. Macmillan Co., New York, NY 1st ed., 1966 [4th printing]. 276 pp., illus. in line. $4.95.
An outdoorsman's manual on traveling and living in the open, with chapters on transportation, equipment, food, hunting and fishing for food.
L. D. Nimschke, Firearms Engraver, by R. L. Wilson. John J. Malloy, publisher, Teaneck, NJ, 1965. Quarto, 107 pp., profusely illus. $30.00.
Showing a wide variety of designs, initials and monograms and ever-so-many portions of collectors' arms. A thoroughly interesting work for the collector and an inspiration to the engraver.
The 1951 Gun Digest Commemorative 5th Edition, edited by John T. Amber, DBI Books, Inc., Northfield, IL, 1977. 224 pp., illus. Paper covers. $6.95.
A reprint of the classic 5th edition, the first edition edited by John T. Amber.
No Second Place Winner, by Wm. H. Jordan, publ. by the author, Shreveport, LA (Box 4072), 1962. 114 pp., illus. $6.50.
Guns and gear of the peace officer, ably discussed by a U.S. Border Patrolman for over 30 years, and a first-class shooter with handgun, rifle, etc.
North American Ducks, Geese, and Swans, by Donald S. Heintzelman, Winchester Press, NY, 1978. 224 pp., illus. $15.00.
An illustrated guide to all the species that inhabit or regularly visit North America.
O.S.S. Special Weapons Catalog, a facsimile reproduction by Paladin Press, Boulder, CO, 1975. 100 pp., illus. Paper covers, $5.95.
Catalog of special weapons devices and equipment.
Outdoor Life Gun Data Book, by F. Philip Rice, Harper & Row Publ., Inc., NY, 1975. 480 pp., illus. $11.95.
Packed with formulas, data, and tips essential to the modern hunter, target shooter, gun collector, and all others interested in guns.
Outdoor Photographer's Digest, ed. by Erwin & Peggy Bauer, DBI Books, Inc., Northfield, IL, 1975. 288 pp., illus. $7.95.
Excellent guide to selection of equipment and techniques to use for the best in outdoor photography.
Outdoor Tips, by L. W. Johnson, Robt. Elman & Jerry Gibbs. Benjamin Co., NY, 1972. 190 pp., illus. Paper covers. $2.95.
Authoritative chapters on American hunting, fishing, camping, other outdoor activities.
Paradise Below Zero, by Calvin Rutstrum. Macmillan Co., New York, NY 1st ed., 1968. 244 pp., illus. in line and halftone. Paper covers. $2.95.
On the rewards and methods of camping and travel in Eskimo country, including check lists of provisions, tools, equipment, clothing and ways of getting about.
Pictorial History of Tanks of the World 1915-45, by P. Chamberlain & C. Ellis. Stackpole Books, Harrisburg, PA, 1972. 256 pp., illus. $9.98.
All tanks produced for military service are pictured, including many rarely seen experimental models and prototypes.
Picture Book of the Continental Soldier, by C. K. Wilbur. Stackpole Books, Harrisburg, PA, 1969. 96 pp., well illus. $5.95.
A wealth of detailed material in text and fine drawings, depicting Revolutionary War weapons, accouterments, field equipment, and the routine of the solder's life. Included are artillery, edged weapons, muskets, rifles, powder horns, etc.
The Plumber's Kitchen: The Secret Story of American Spy Weapons, ed. by Donald B. McLean, Anubus Press, Houston, TX, 1975. 282 pp., illus. Paper covers. $12.95.
Examines the development of unique weapons and devices essential to the profession of the modern spy.
Pocket Guide to Archery, by H. T. Sigler. Stackpole Co., Harrisburg, PA, 1960. 96 pp., illus. $2.95.
Useful introduction to the subject, covering equipment, shooting techniques, and bow hunting of small game and deer.
A Pocket History of Artillery: Light Field Guns, by Franz Kosar, Ian Allan, London, 1974. 248 pp., illus. $7.25.
Covers guns of the European countries and the non-European major powers, from the beginning of this century to the present.
Practical Wildlife Management, by Geo. V. Burger. Winchester Press, NY, 1973. 224 pp., illus. $10.00.
Anyone interested in wildlife will find this an invaluable reference as well as entertaining, informative reading.
Principles of Small Arms, by Major A. J. Barker, Paladin Press, Boulder, CO, 1977. 82 pp., illus. Paper covers. $4.00.
Covers stopping power of small arms bullets, construction and operation of automatic weapons; characteristics of pistols, rifles, and barrel, sights, ammunition design and development problems.
E. C. Prudhomme, Master Gun Engraver, A Retrospective Exhibition: 1946-1973, intro. by John T. Amber, The R. W. Norton Art Gallery, Shreveport, LA, 1973. 32 pp., illus., paper covers. $3.50.
Examples of master gun engraving by Jack Prudhomme.
The Pyrotechnists Treasury; The Complete Art of Firework Making, by Thomas Kentish, Paladin Press, Boulder, CO, 1977. 242 pp., illus. Paper covers. $9.95.

Originally published in 1905 at the height of the pyrotechnic art, every conceivable type, style and configuration of fireworks is described in detail.
Reading the Woods, by Vinson Brown. Stackpole Books, Harrisburg, PA, 1969. 160 pp. illus. $5.95.
Clues to the past, present and future development of wooded areas by observation of signs of change, decay, influences of water and wildlife, and the impact of man's presence.
Records of the Scottish Volunteer Force 1859-1908, by Lt. Gen. Sir James Moncrieff Grierson. Frederich Muller, Ltd., London, 1972. 372 pp. $29.50.
Limited reprint of the rare classic on the history and uniforms of the Scottish Volunteers before the re-organization of 1908. 47 full-color plates show 239 different uniforms.
Redbook of Used Gun Values, rev. 1978 ed., Publishers Dev. Corp., Skokie, IL, 1977. 130 pp. Paper covers. $5.00.
Today's values for commercial firearms, listed by manufacturer.
Remington Arms Revised Price-List, 1902. Arthur McKee, Northport, NY, n.d. 64 pp. Paper covers. $4.00.
Reprint, fully illustrated.
Remington Firearms, 1906 Catalog, Arthur McKee, Northport, NY, n.d., 48 pp., illus. Paper covers. $4.00.
Reprint. Guns, parts, ammo., prices, etc.
The Reverend Alexander John Forsyth, 1768-1843, by John Reid, Fortress Publ., Inc., Stoney Creek, Ontario, Can., 1976. 38 pp., illus. $2.75.
A reprint of 19th Century book about the life of this inventor.
Round Shot and Rammers, by Harold L. Peterson, Fortress Publ., Inc., Stoney Creek, Ontario, Canada, 1978. 128 pp., illus. $6.50.
Muzzle loading artillery in the United States.
Russian Infantry Weapons of World War II, by A. J. Barker and John Walter, Arco Publ. Co., NY, 1971. 80 pp., $4.95.
History and development of World War II infantry weapons used by the Red Army. Each weapon is fully described and illus..
Sam Colt: Genius, by Robt. F. Hudson, American Archives Publ. Co., Topsfield, MA, 1971. 160 pp., illus. Plastic spiral bound. $6.50.
Historical review of Colt's inventions, including facsimiles of patent papers and other Colt information.
Scloppetaria, by Capt. H. Beaufroy, Richmond Publ. Co., Richmond, England, 1971. 251 pp. $14.00.
Reprint of the 1808 edition written under the pseudonym "A Corporal of Rilfemen". Covers rifles and rifle shooting, the first such work in English.
Secret Fighting Arts of the World, by J. F. Gilbey. Tuttle, Rutland, VT 1963. 150 pp., illus. $6.50.
20 chapters on advanced techniques of unarmed combat, described in anecdotal form.
Secret Weapons of the Third Reich, by L. E. Simon, We, Inc., Old Greenwich, CT, 1971. 248 pp., illus. $8.95.
Review of German World War II military research and its products.
Shooter's Bible No. 69, 1978 ed., ed. by R. F. Scott, Stoeger Publ. Co., S. Hackensack, NJ, 1978. 575 pp., illus. Paper covers. $7.95.
An annually-published guide to firearms, ammunition and accessories.
Shooter's Bible Game Cook Book, by Geraldine Steindler. Follett Publ. Co., Chicago IL 1965. 224 pp., illus., cloth, $6.95; paper, $4.95.
Full information on preparing game for the table, including recipes and methods of field-dressing.
Shooter's Bible Treasury, 2nd edition, by Roger Barlow, Stoeger Publ. Co., So. Hackensack, NJ, 256 pp., illus. $3.95.
Compiled from the most interesting material to appear in Shooter's Bible. Shows famous old guns and shooting accessories.
The Shooter's Guide: or Complete Sportsman's Companion, by B. Thomas, Richmond Publ. Co., Richmond, England, 1971. 264 pp., illus. $12.00.
Reprint of an 1816 British handbook on hunting small game, game laws, dogs, guns and ammunition.
The Shooter's Workbench, by John A. Mosher, Winchester Press, NY, 1977. 256 pp., illus. $10.95.
Accessories the shooting sportsman can build for the range, for the shop, for transport and the field, and for the handloading bench.
Shooting the Muzzle-Loaders, ed. by R. A. Steindler, J. Philip O'Hara, Inc., Chicago, IL, 1975. 224 pp., illus. Paper covers. $6.95.
A complete treatise on the muzzle-loader written by experts. Covers rifle, shotgun and pistol.
The Shorebirds of North America, by Peter Matthiesen, ed. by Gordon Stout, with species accounts by R. S. Palmer. Viking Press, N.Y.C., 1967, 288 pp., 32 6-color plates, 10"x14", $22.50.
A magnificent book, probably the outstanding work on the shorebirds of the northern western world. 32 chapters cover 59 species. The illustrations are superb.
Silencers. Paladin Press, Boulder, CO, 1971 205 pp., illus. $11.95; paper covers. $8.95.
Reprint of Frankford Arsenal Report R-1896. The functional and physical details on foreign and domestic silencers, including patent drawings, engineering data, manufacture, etc.
Silencers for Hand Firearms, by Siegfried Huebner, Paladin Press, Boulder, CO, 1976. 100 pp., illus. Paper covers. $9.95.
Covers silencer principles, silencers in WW II, clandestine weapons, and five vital and intriguing other chapters.
Silencers, Snipers & Assassins, by J. David Truby, Paladin Press, Boulder, CO, 1972. 209 pp., illus. $15.95.
Traces development of silencers from their invention by Hiram Maxim in 1908 to American snipers' use during the Korean conflict.
Sketch Book 76: The American Soldier 1775-1781, by R. Klinger and R. A. Wilder, Pioneer Press Books, Union City, TN, 1967. 53 pp., illus. Paper covers. $2.75.
Sketches, notes, and patterns compiled from a study of clothing and equipment used by the American foot soldier in the Revolutionary War.
Skills for Taming the Wilds, by Bradford Angier, Stackpole Books, Harrisburg, PA, 1967. 320 pp., illus. $7.95.
A handbook of woodcraft wisdom, by a foremost authority, showing how to obtain maximum comfort from nature.
Small Arms Identification and Operation Guide—Eurasian Communist Countries, by Harold E. Johnson, Inco., 1972. 218 pp., illus. Paper covers. $4.00.
Reprint of 1970 U.S. Army manual FSTC-CW-07-03-70.
Small Arms Lexicon and Concise Encyclopedia, by Chester Mueller and John Olson. Stoeger Arms, So. Hackensack, NJ, 1968. 312 pp., 500 illus. $14.95; paper covers $5.95.
Definitions, explanations, and references on antiques, optics, ballistics, etc., from A to Z. Over 3,000 entries plus appendix.
Small Arms of the World, 11th Edition, a complete revision of W. H. B. Smith's firearms classic by Edward Clinton Ezell, Stackpole Books, Harrisburg, PA, 1977. 667 pp., illus. $20.00.
A complete revision of this firearms classic now brings all arms enthusiasts up to date on global weapons production and use.
The Social History of the Machine Gun, by John Ellis, Pantheon Press, NY, 1975. 186 pp., illus. Paper covers, $4.95. Cloth, $12.95.
A lavishly illustrated history of the machine gun which takes a dramatically new approach to the history of militarism in 19th and 20th century European and American society.
Sporting Arms of the World, by Ray Bearse, Outdoor Life/Harper & Row, N.Y., 1977. 500 pp., illus. $15.95.
A mammoth, up-to-the-minute guide to the sporting world's favorite rifles, shotguns, handguns.
The Sportsman's Eye, by James Gregg, Winchester Press, NY, 1971. 210 pp., illus. $6.95.
How to make better use of your eyes in the outdoors.
Stories of the Old Duck Hunters and Other Drivel, by Gordon MacQuarrie and compiled by Zack Taylor. Stackpole Books, Harrisburg, PA, 1967. 223 pp., illus. $6.95.
An off-beat relaxing and enjoyable group of 19 best-remembered outdoor stories, previously publ. in magazines.
The Story of the Guns, by Emerson Tennent. Richmond Publ. Co., Surrey, Eng., 1972. 364 pp. $11.50.
Reprint of the original 1864 London ed. Part I—The Rifled Musket, Part 2—Rifled Ordnance, Part 3—The Iron Navy.
Sub-Machine Guns and Automatic Rifles, by Peter Chamberlain and Terry Gander, Arco Publ. Co., N.Y. 1977. 64 pp., illus. Paper covers. $4.95.
Describes and illustrates the subject products used by the armed forces in WW II.
Submachine Guns Caliber .45, M3 and M3A1, U.S. FM23-41 and TM 9-1217. Normount Armament Co., Wickenburg, AZ, 1967. 141 pp., illus., paperbound. $3.95.
Reprint of two U.S. Army manuals on submachine guns.
The Survival Handbook, by W. K. Merrill. Winchester Press, NY, 1972. 320 pp., illus. $6.95.
How to stay out of trouble in all kinds of terrain and weather. Detailed advice on shelter, food and first aid for those caught unexpectedly in disaster situations.
Survival Guns, by Mel Tappan, The Janus Press, Inc., Los Angeles, CA, 1976. 458 pp., illus. Paper covers. $7.95.
A guide to the selection, modification and use of firearms and related devices for defense, food gathering, etc. under conditions of long term survival.
Tanks; An Illustrated History of Fighting Vehicles, by Armin Halle & Carlo Demand, New York Graphic Society, Greenwich, CT, 1971. 175 pp., illus. $16.98.
Comprehensively traces the development and technology of one of man's most complex and ingenious weapons.
Tanks and Other AFV's of the Blitzkrieg Era, 1939-1941, by B. T. White. The Macmillan Co., Riverside, NJ, 1973. 180 pp. $4.95.
Comprehensive, carefully illus. encyclopedia of the most important armored fighting vehicles developed by the principal countries at war.
Tear Gas Munitions. by T. F. Swearengen, Charles C. Thomas, Springfield, IL, 1966. 569 pp., illus. $34.50.
An analysis of commercial (riot) gas guns, tear gas projectiles, grenades, small arms ammunition, and related tear gas devices.
Technical Dictionary for Weapon Enthusiasts, Shooters and Hunters, by Gustav Sybertz. Publ. by J. Neumann-Neudamm, 3508 Melsungen, W. Germany, 1969, 164 pp., semi-soft covers. $7.50.
A German-English and English-German dictionary for the sportsman. An excellent handy work.
Tenting on the Plains, by Elizabeth Bacon Custer, Univ. of Oklahoma Press, Norman, OK, 1971. 706 pp. in 3 volumes, plus a 30-page intro. by Jane R. Stewart. Slip-cased. $8.85.
Deals with period after the Civil War when General Custer was stationed in Texas and Kansas.
Thompson Submachine Guns, compiled from original manuals by the publ. Anubus Press, Houston, TX, 1968. Over 230 pp., well illus., many exploded views. Paper wrappers. Paper Covers $8.95.
Five reprints in one book: Basic Field Manual, Cal. 45, M1928AI (U.S. Army); Cal. 45, Model 1928, (for British); Cal., 45 (U.S. Ordnance); Model M1, Cal., 45 (U.S. Ordnance) and Ultra Modern Automatic Arms (Auto-Ordnance Corp.).
Thompson Guns Models 1921-1923, a reprint by Americana Archives, Topsfield, MA, 1976. 24 pp., illus. Paper covers. $3.50.
A facsimile reprint of the 1924 Colt's Patent Fire Arms Mfg. Co. catalog of Thompson Guns.
Thompson Submachine Gun, Cal. 45, M1928A1, Paladin Press, Boulder, CO, 1976, 28 pp., illus., paper covers. $3.
A facsimile reprint of the War Department TM 9-1215.
The Tournament, its periods and phases, by R. C. Clephan. Frederick Ungar Co., NY, 1967. A reprint. 195 pp., illus. with contemporary pictures plus half-tones of armor and weapons used by contestants, $16.50.
A rare and eagerly-sought work, long out-of-print. A scholarly, historical and descriptive account of jousting.
Training Your Own Bird Dog, by Henry P. Davis, G. P. Putnam's Sons, New York, NY. New rev. ed., 1969, 168 pp., plus 10 pp. of field trial records. Illus. with photographs. $6.95.
The reappearance of a popular and practical book for the beginner starting his first bird dog—by an internationally recognized authority.
Treasure Hunter's Digest, by Jack Lewis, DBI Books, Inc., Northfield, IL, 1975. 288 pp., illus. $7.95.
Tells where to go, how to find it, etc. with articles on techniques, legendary treasures and laws.
A Treatise of Artillery 1780, by John Muller, Museum Restoration Service, Ontario, Canada, 1977. 214 pp., illus. Paper covers. $9.95.
A facsimile reprint of the most important artillery manual of the period, it introduced the theories upon which American artillery was based.
Treatise on Military Small Arms and Ammunition 1888, compiled by Col. J. Bond, R. A. Arms and Armour Press, London, Eng., 1971. 142 pp., illus. $10.00.
Facsimile of the original compiled in 1888 at the School of Musketry, Hythe, and accepted by the British Army as a definitive textbook.
Triggernometry, by Eugene Cunningham. Caxton Printers Lt., Caldwell, ID, 1970. 441 pp., illus. $9.95.
A classic study of famous outlaws and lawmen of the West—their stature as human beings, their exploits and skills in handling firearms. A reprint.
The True Book About Firearms, by R. H. Walton, Frederick Muller, Ltd., London, 1965. 143 pp., illus. $4.00.
How modern weapons work, are used and their effect on history.
Unconventional Warfare Devices and Techniques, a reprint of Army TM 31-200-1 234 pp., illus., paper covers. $10.00.
Published primarily for U.S. Army Special Forces. Deals with destructive techniques and their applications to targets in guerrilla warfare.
Uniforms, Organization and History of the Waffen SS, by R. J. Bender and H. P. Taylor. Borden Publ. Co., Alhambra, CA, 1969-1973. Various pagination. $10.95 each volume.
Detailed and intriguing study of Hitler's elite supermen.
United States Military Medals & Ribbons, by Philip K. Robles, Charles E. Tuttle Co., Rutland, VT, 1971. 187 pp., $14.00.

A definitive work; 139 plates in full color.
Walther, Volume II, by James L. Rankin, assisted by Gary Green, James L. Rankin, Coral Gables, FL, 1977. 136 pp., illus. $17.50.
Walther Models PP and PPK, especially engraved and presentation models.
Walther Models PP and PPK, 1929-1945, by James L. Rankin, assisted by Gary Green, James L. Rankin, Coral Gables, FL, 1974. 142 pp., illus. $14.00.
Complete coverage of the subject as to finish, proof marks and Nazi Party inscriptions.
L. T. Ward & Bro. Wildfowl Counterfeiters, by Byron and Maureen Cheever, Hillcrest Publ., Inc., Spanish Fork, UT, 1976. 99 pp., illus. $8.50.
The name Ward Bros. is synonomous with decoy making in the 20th Century. Included here are examples of their work.
Warriors' Weapons, by Walter Buehr. Crowell Co., NYC, 1963. 186 pp., illus. $5.95.
Illustrated history of pre-gunpowder arms, from stone ax to crossbow and catapult.

Waterfowl Studies, by Bruce Burk, Winchester Press, NY, 1976. 264 pp., illus. $15.
A book of study pictures for the decoy maker, collector, hunter, waterfowl artist and naturalist.
Weapons: A Pictorial History, by Edwin Tunis, World Publ. Co., NY, 1972. 151 pp., illus. $3.95.
Arms through the ages—from the first stone thrown by prehistoric man to the super bombs and atomic weapons of our own day.
Weapons of the American Revolution, and Accoutrements, by Warren Moore. A & W Books, NY, 1974. 225 pp., fine illus. $6.98.
Revolutionary era shoulder arms, pistols, edged weapons, and equipment are described and shown in fine drawings and photographs, some in color.
Weapons and Fighting Arts of the Indonesian Archipelago, by Donn F. Draeger. Chas. E. Tuttle Co., VT, 1972. 254 pp., illus. $12.50.
The varied combative forms of the islands, from empty-hand techniques to the use of spears, knives, the kris, etc.
Weapons and Tactics, Hastings to Berlin, by Jac Weller, St. Martin's Press, New York, 1966. 238 pp., illus. $6.00.
Primarily on the infantry weapons of today, with basic data on those of the past.

Weapons of War, by P. E. Cleator. Crowell Co., NYC, 1968. 224 pp., illus. $6.95.
A British survey of warfare from earliest times, as influenced by the weapons available for combat.
The Webley-Fosbery Automatic Revolver. A reprint of the original undated booklet pupl. by the British makers. Deep River Armory, Houston, TX, 1968. 16 pp., illus., paper. $3.00.
An instruction manual, parts list and sales brochure on this scarce military handgun.
Whitewings: The White-winged Dove, ed. by C. Cottam & J. B. Trefethen. D. Van Nostrand Co., Princeton, NJ, 1968. 348 pp. $7.50.
Compendium of research publications on an important game bird of Texas and Arizona, the Southwest, including Mexico. Excellent photographs.
Wild Game Cookbook, by L. E. Johnson. Benjamin Co., NYC, 1968. 160 pp. $2.95.
Recipes, sauces, and cooking hints for preparation of all types of game birds and animals.
Wild Sanctuaries . . ., by Robert Murphy. E. P. Dutton & Co., Inc., New York, NY, 1968, 288 pp., over 250 photographs in color and monochrome, plus 32 maps, including those of the flyways. $12.95.
Concerns America's national wildlife refuges. An all-encompassing treatise on its subject with fascinating pertinent text.
Wilderness Cookery, by Bradford Angier. Stackpole Books, Harrisburg, PA, 1969. 256 pp., illus. $4.95.
An excellent work, one that will be of big interest to hunters, fishermen, campers, et al.
The Wilderness Route Finder, by C. Rutstrum, Macmillan Co., NY, 1970. 214 pp. $4.95.
Complete guide to finding your way in the wilderness.
The Wildfowler's World, by Hanson Carroll and Nelson Bryant, Winchester Press, NY, 1973. 160 pp., illus. $12.95.
More than 100 breathtaking photographs, many in color, are included.
Wildlife Illustrated, by Ray Ovington, Digest Books, Inc., Northfield, IL. 1974. 8½"x11", 288 pp. Profusely illus. paperbound. $6.95.
Over 200 descriptions and sketches of North American game birds, animals and fishes. Covers lowland and upland game birds, small and large game animals, fresh- and saltwater fish with descriptions, habitat, and traits.

Wildwood Wisdom, by Ellsworth Jaeger. The Macmillan Company, New York, NY, 1964. 491 pp. well-illus. by author. $8.95.
An authoritative work, through many editions; about all there is to know about every detail for the outdoorsman.
Williams Blue Book of Gun Dealings 1977-78, publ. by Williams Gun Sight Co., Davison, MI, 1977. 111 pp., illus. Paper covers. $3.95.
Enlarged ed. of the modern guide to gun values.
The World of the Moose, by Joe Van Wormer. J. B. Lippincott Co., Phila., PA, 1972. 160 pp., illus. $7.95.
A record of the life style of these animals in their wild and remote habitats.
The World of the Ruffed Grouse, by Leonard Lee Rue, III. J. B. Lippincott, Phila., PA, 1973. 160 pp., illus. $7.95.
A year-round survey of the ruffed grouse and its environment, habitat, enemies, and relation to man.
The World of the White-Tailed Deer, by L. L. Rue III. J. B. Lippincott Co., Phila., 1967. A reprint. 137 pp., fine photos. $7.95.
An eminent naturalist-writer's account of the year-round activities of the white-tailed deer.
The World of the Wild Turkey, by J. C. Lewis. J. B. Lippincott Co., Phila., PA, 1973. 158 pp., illus. $7.95.
The author takes the reader into the wilderness world of the turkey's 6 surviving subspecies.
The World's Assault Rifles & Automatic Carbines, vol. 2, by Daniel D. Musgrave & Thomas B. Nelson, T. B. N. Enterprises, Alexandria, VA, 1977. 546 pp., illus. $17.50.
Data, history and photographs of over 200 weapons.
The World's Submachine Guns (Machine Pistols) vol. I, by Thomas B. Nelson and Hans B. Lockhoven, T. B. N. Enterprises, Alexandria, VA, 1977. 739 pp., illus. $19.95.
Containing data, history and photographs of over 300 weapons. With technical guide in 20 languages.
World's Machine Guns, vol. 2S, 1964-1977, by Thomas B. Nelson and Hans B. Lockhoven, T. B. N. Enterprises, Alexandria, VA, 1977. 600 pp., illus. $19.95.
Takes up where *World's Submachine Guns* ends and brings it up to the end of 1976. Over 550 illustrations.
Your First Gun, by Roderick Willet, Seeley, Service & Co., London, England, 1975. 88 pp., illus. $7.50.
A useful handbook for those about to start shooting, young or old.

Gunsmithing

The Art of Engraving, by James B. Meek, F. Brownell & Son, Montezuma, IA, 1973. 196 pp., illus. $19.95.
A complete, authoritative, imaginative and detailed study in training for gun engraving. The first book of its kind—and a great one.
Artistry in Arms. The R. W. Norton Gallery, Shreveport, LA., 1970. 42 pp., illus. Paper, $3.50.
The art of gunsmithing and engraving.
Black Powder Gunsmithing, by Ralph T. Walker, DBI Books, Inc., Northfield, IL, 1978. 288 pp., illus. Paper covers. $7.95.
An overview of the entire subject from replica building to the advanced, intricate art of restoration.
Building the Kentucky Pistol, by James R. Johnston, Golden Age Arms Co., Worthington, OH, 1974. 36 pp., illus. Paper covers. $4.00.
A step-by-step guide for building the Kentucky pistol. Illus. with full page line drawings.
Building the Kentucky Rifle, by J. R. Johnston. Golden Age Arms Co., Worthington, OH, 1972. 44 pp., illus. Paper covers. $5.
How to go about it, with text and drawings.
The Cape Gunsmith, by Barry M. Berkovitch, The Stellenbosch Museum, Stellenbosch, South Africa, 1976. 128 pp., illus. $13.75.
A history of gunsmiths and gun dealers at the Cape of Good Hope from 1795 to 1900, with particular references on their weapons.
Checkering and Carving of Gun Stocks, by Monte Kennedy. Stackpole Books, Harrisburg, PA, 1962. 175 pp., illus. $14.95.
Rev., enlarged clothbound ed. of a much sought-after, dependable work.
Complete Guide to Gunsmithing, by C. E. Chapel. Barnes & Co., NYC, 1962. 479 pp., illus. $9.95
2nd rev. edition, known earlier as *Gun Care and Repair*, of a comprehensive book on all details of gunsmithing for the hobbyist and professional.
The Complete Rehabilitation of the Flintlock Rifle and Other Works, by T. B. Tryon. Limbo Library, Taos, NM, 1972. 112 pp., illus. Paper covers. $6.95.
A series of articles which first appeared in various issues of the *American Rifleman* in the 1930s.
Firearms Blueing and Browning, by R. H. Angier. Stackpole Books, Harrisburg, PA, 151 pp., illus. $6.95.
A useful, concise text on chemical coloring methods for the gunsmith and mechanic.
Gun Care and Repair, by Monte Burch, Winchester Press, NY, 1978. 256 pp., illus. $10.95.
Everything the gun owner needs to know about home gunsmithing and firearms maintenance.
Gun Owner's Book of Care, Repair & Improvement, by Roy Dunlap, Outdoor Life-Harper & Row, NY, 1974. 336 pp., illus. $12.95.
A basic guide to repair and maintenance of guns, written for the average firearms owner.
Gunsmith Kinks, by F. R. (Bob) Brownell. F. Brownell & Son., Montezuma, I. 1st ed., 1969. 496 pp., well illus. $9.95.
A widely useful accumulation of shop kinks, short cuts, techniques and pertinent comments by practicing gunsmiths from all over the world.
The Gunsmith's Manual, by J. Stelle and W. Harrison, Rutgers Book Center, Highland Park, NJ, 1972. 376 pp., illus. $9.95.
Exact reprint of the original. For the American gunsmith in all branches of the trade.
Gunsmithing, by Roy F. Dunlap. Stackpole Books, Harrisburg, PA, 714 pp., illus. $14.95.
Comprehensive work on conventional techniques, incl. recent advances in the field. Valuable to rifle owners, shooters, and practicing gunsmiths.
Gunsmithing Simplified, by H. E. MacFarland. Washington, DC, 1950, A. S. Barnes, NYC, 1959. 303 pp., illus. $12.00.
A thorough dependable concise work with many helpful short-cuts.
Gunsmiths and Gunmakers of Vermont, by Warren R. Horn, The Horn Co., Burlington, VT, 1976. 76 pp., illus. Paper covers. $5.00.
A checklist for collectors, of over 200 craftsmen who lived and worked in Vermont up to and including 1900.
Hobby Gunsmithing, by Ralph Walker, Digest Books, Inc., Northfield, IL, 1972, 320 pp., illus. Paper, $6.95.
Kitchen table gunsmithing for the budding hobbyist.
Home Gun Care & Repair, by P. O. Ackley. Stackpole Books, Harrisburg, PA, 1969. 191 pp., illus. Paper covers. $3.95.
Basic reference for safe tinkering, fixing, and converting rifles, shotguns, handguns.
Home Gunsmithing Digest, 2nd ed., by Robt. Steindler, DBI Books, Inc., Northfield, IL, 1978, 288 pp., very well illus. within stiff decorated paper covers. $7.95.
An unusually beneficial assist for gun owners doing their own repairs, maintenance, etc. Many chapters on tools, techniques and theories.
HOW . . . by L. Cowher, W. Hunley, and L. Johnston. NMLR Assn., IN, 1961. 107 pp., illus. Paper covers. $2.95.
This 1961 rev. ed., enlarged by 3 chapters and additional illustrations, covers the building of a muzzle-loading rifle, target pistol, and powder horn, and tells how to make gunflints.
"How to Build Your Own Wheellock Rifle or Pistol", by Georg Lauber, The John Olson Co., Paramus, NJ, 1976. Paper covers. $6.95.
Complete instructions on building these arms.
"How to Build Your Own Flintlock Rifle or Pistol", by Georg Lauber, The John Olson Co., Paramus, NJ, 1976. Paper covers. $6.95.
The second in Mr. Lauber's three-volume series on the art and science of building muzzle-loading black powder firearms.
"How to Build Your Own Percussion Rifle or Pistol", by Georg Lauber, The John Olson Co., Paramus, NJ, 1976. Paper covers, $6.95.
The third and final volume of Lauber's set of books on the building of muzzle-loaders.
Lock, Stock and Barrel, by R. H. McCrory. Publ. by author at Bellmore, NY, 1966. Paper covers, 122 pp., illus. $4.00.
A handy and useful work for the collector or the professional with many helpful procedures shown and described on antique gun repair.
Master French Gunsmith's Designs of the 17th-18th Centuries, compiled by S. V. Grancsay. Winchester Press, New York, NY, 1970. A brand new work of 208 pp., beautifully illus. in facsimile. Numbered, limited issue of 1000 copies. $29.95.

Magnificient ornamentation of weapons taken from a superb collection of design books, gathered by a world authority. An inspiration and a must for the gunsmith-engraver.

The Modern Kentucky Rifle, How to Build Your Own, by R. H. McCrory. McCrory, Wantagh, NY, 1961. 68 pp., illus., paper bound. $4.00.
A workshop manual on how to fabricate a flintlock rifle. Also some information on pistols and percussion locks.

The NRA Firearms Assembly Guidebook to Shoulder Arms. National Rifle Assn., Wash., D.C., 1973. 203 pp. Paper covers. $4.
Text and illus. explaining the takedown of 96 rifles and shotguns, domestic and foreign.

The NRA Firearms Assembly Guidebook to Handguns. National Rifle Assn., Wash., D.C., 1973, 206 pp. Paper covers. $4.
Illus. articles on the takedown of 101 pistol and revolver models.

The NRA Gunsmithing Guide, National Rifle Association, Wash., DC, 1971. 336 pp., illus. Paper. $5.50.
Information of the past 15 years from the "American Rifleman," ranging from 03A3 Springfields to Model 92 Winchesters.

Pistolsmithing, by George C. Nonte, Jr., Stackpole Books, Harrisburg, PA, 1974. 560 pp., illus. $14.95.
A single source reference to handgun maintainence, repair, and modification at home, unequaled in value.

Professional Gunsmithing, by W. J. Howe, Stackpole Books, Harrisburg, PA, 1968 reprinting. 526 pp., illus. $14.95.
Textbook on repair and alteration of firearms, with detailed notes on equipment and commercial gunshop operation.

Recreating the American Rifle, by Wm. Buchel & Geo. Shumway, George Shumway, York, PA, 1973. 194 pp. illus. Paper $7.50.
A new edition with additional illustrations showing the workmanship of today's skilled rifle-makers.

Respectfully Yours H. M. Pope, compiled and edited by G. O. Kelver, Brighton, CO, 1976. 266 pp., illus. $16.50.
A compilation of letters from the files of the famous barrelmaker, Harry M. Pope.

Troubleshooting Your Handgun, by J. B. Wood, DBI Books, Inc., Northfield, IL, 1978. 192 pp., illus. Paper covers. $5.95.
A masterful guide on how to avoid trouble and how to operate guns with care.

Troubleshooting Your Rifle and Shotgun, by J. B. Wood, DBI Books, Inc., Northfield, IL, 1978. 192 pp., illus. Paper covers. $5.95.
A gunsmiths advice on how to keep your long guns shooting.

American Handgun Patents 1802-1924, by Jos. Macewicz, Museum Restoration Service, Ontario, Canada, 1978. 44 pp., illus. Paper covers. $4.95.
A must for the serious handgun collector.

American Pistol and Revolver Design and Performance, by L. R. Wallack, Winchester Press, NY, 1978. 224 pp., illus. $13.95.
How different types and models of pistols and revolvers work, from trigger pull to bullet impact.

handguns

Automatic Firearm Pistols, by Elmer Swanson, Wesmore Book Co., Weehawken, NJ. 1st (and only) ed. 1955, 210 pp., well illus. $20.00.
A veritable catalog exclusively on automatic handguns for collectors, with many line drawings and descriptions, plus then-market market values of each.

Book of Pistols & Revolvers, by W. H. B. Smith. Stackpole Books, Harrisburg, PA, 1968. 758 pp., profusely illus. $7.98.
Rev. and enlarged, this encyclopedic reference, first publ. in 1946, continues to be the best on its subject.

Browning Hi-Power Pistols. Anubus Press, Houston, TX, 1968. 48 pp., illus., paperbound. $3.00.
A handbook on all models of Browning Hi-Power Pistols, covering their use, maintenance and repair.

Colt Automatic Pistols, by Donald B. Bady, Borden Publ. Co., Alhambra, CA, 1974. 368 pp., illus. $12.50.
The rev. and enlarged ed. of a key work on a fascinating subject. Complete information on every automatic marked with Colt's name.

Combat Handgun Shooting, by James D. Mason, Charles C. Thomas, Springfield, IL, 1976. 256 pp., illus. $27.50.
Discusses in detail the human as well as the mechanical aspects of shooting.

Combat Shooting for Police, by Paul B. Weston. Charles C. Thomas, Springfield, IL, 1967. A reprint. 194 pp., illus. $12.50.
First publ. in 1960 this popular self-teaching manual gives basic concepts of defensive fire in every position.

Defensive Handgun Effectiveness, by Carroll E. Peters, Carroll E. Peters, Manchester, TN, 1977. 198 pp., charts and graphs. $10.00.
A systematic approach to the design, evaluation and selection of ammunition for the defensive handgun.

The Famous Automatic Pistols of Europe, compiled by John Olson, The John Olson Co., Paramus, NJ, 1976. 200 pp., illus. Paper covers. $6.95.
The inside story on thirty-three famous European automatic pistols.

Georgian Pistols; The Art and Craft of the Flintlock Pistol, 1715-1840, by Norman Dixon, Geo. Shumway, York, PA, 1971. 184 pp., illus. $18.00.
The art of the Georgian gunmaker, describing the evolution of the holster pistol and the duelling pistol, with the parallel changes in style of the turn-off pistol.

German Pistols and Revolvers 1871-1945, by Ian V. Hogg, A. & W. Books, NY, 1975. 160 pp., illus. $6.98.
Over 160 photos and drawings showing each gun, plus exploded views, markings, firms, patents, mfg. codes, etc.

Guns Annual Book of Handguns, ed. by Jerome Rakusan, Publishers' Dev. Corp., Skokie, IL, 1974. 98 pp., illus., paper covers. $2.00.
Complete catalog listing all latest models and articles dealing with handguns.

A Handbook on the Primary Identification of Revolvers & Semi-automatic Pistols, by John T. Millard, Charles C. Thomas, Springfield, IL, 1974. 156 pp., illus. $12.50.
A practical outline on the simple, basic phases of primary firearm identification with particular reference to revolvers and semi-automatic pistols.

The Handgun, by Geoffrey Boothroyd, Outlet Publ. Co., NY, 1978. 564 pp., illus. $10.98.
A comprehensive and detailed study of the handgun, from the earliest types to the revolvers and automatics of today.

Handgun Competition, by Maj. Geo. C. Nonte, Jr., Winchester Press, NY, 1978. 288 pp., illus. $12.95.
A comprehensive source-book covering all aspects of modern competitive pistol and revolver shooting.

Handguns Americana, by De Witt Sell. Borden Publ. Co., Alhambra, CA, 1972. 160 pp., illus. $8.50.
The pageantry of American enterprise in providing handguns suitable for both civilian needs and military purposes.

High Standard Automatic Pistols 1932-1950, by Charles E. Petty, American Ordnance Publ., Charlotte, NC, 1976. 124 pp., illus. $12.95.
A definitive source of information for the collector of High Standard pistols.

Home Gunsmithing the Colt Single Action Revolvers, by Loren W. Smith, Ray Riling Arms Books Co., Phila., PA, 1971. 119 pp., illus. $7.95.
Detailed, information on the operation and servicing of this famous and historic handgun.

The Inglis-Browing Hi-Power Pistol, by R. Blake Stevens, Museum Rest. Serv., Ottawa, Can., 1974. 28 pp., illus. Paper covers. $2.00.
The history of this scarce gun and its variations.

Japanese Hand Guns, by F. E. Leithe, Borden Publ. Co., Alhambra, CA, 1968. Unpaginated, well illus. $8.50.
Identification guide, covering models produced since the late 19th century. Brief text material gives history, descriptions, and markings.

Know Your 45 Auto Pistols—Models 1911 & A1, by E. J. Hoffschmidt, Blacksmith Corp., Stamford, CT, 1974. 58 pp., illus. Paper covers. $3.95.
A concise history of the gun with a wide variety of types and copies illus.

Know Your Walther P.38 Pistols, by E. J. Hoffschmidt, Blacksmith Corp., Stamford, CT, 1974. 77 pp., illus. Paper covers. $3.95.
Covers the Walther models, Armee, M.P., H.P., P-38—history and variations.

Know Your Walther P.P. & P.P.K. Pistols, by E. J. Hoffschmidt, Blacksmith Corp., Stamford, CT, 1975. 87 pp., illus. Paper covers. $3.95.
A concise history of the guns with a guide to the variety and types.

Law Enforcement Handgun Digest, New Revised Edition, by Dean A. Grennell, DBI Books, Inc., Northfield, IL, 1976. 320 pp., illus. Paper covers. $6.95.
The most comprehensive and up-to-date guide to arms and equipment for law enforcement.

The Luger Pistol (Pistole Parabellum), by F. A. Datig. Borden Publ. Co., Alhambra, CA, 1962. 328 pp., well illus. $9.50.
An enlarged, rev. ed. of an important reference on the arm, its history and development from 1893 to 1945.

Luger Variations, by Harry E. Jones, Harry E. Jones, Torrance, CA, 1975. 328 pp., 160 full page illus., many in color. $17.50.
A rev. ed. of the book known as "The Luger Collector's Bible."

Lugers at Random, by Charles Kenyon, Jr. Handgun Press, Chicago, IL. 1st ed., 1970. 416 pp., profusely illus. $17.50.
An impressive large side-opening book carrying throughout alternate facing-pages of descriptive text and clear photographs. A new boon to the Luger collector and/or shooter.

Lugers Unlimited, by F. G. Tilton, World-Wide Gun Reports, Inc., Aledo, IL, 1965. 49 pp., illus. Paper covers $2.00.
An excellent monograph about one of the most controversial pistols since the invention of hand firearms.

Mauser Pocket Pistols 1910-1946, by Roy G. Pender, Collectors Press, Houston, TX, 1971. 307 pp., $14.50.
Comprehensive work covering over 100 variations, including factory boxes and manuals. Over 300 photos. Limited, numbered ed.

The Mauser Self-Loading Pistol, by Belford & Dunlap. Borden Publ. Co., Alhambra, CA. Over 200 pp., 300 illus., large format. $12.50.
The long-awaited book on the "Broom Handles," covering their inception in 1894 to the end of production. Complete and in detail: pocket pistols, Chinese and Spanish copies, etc.

Mauser, Walther & Mannlicher Firearms, by W.H.B. Smith, with a intro. by John T. Amber. Stackpole Books, Harrisburg, PA, 1971. 673 pp., illus. $14.95.
W.H.B. Smith's three classics, now in one convenient volume.

Ed McGiverns' Book of Fast & Fancy Revolver Shooting, by Ed McGivern, Anniversary ed., Follett Publ. Co., Chicago, IL, 1975. 484 pp., illus. $10.00.
A facsimile of the much-sought-after classic by the dean of revolver shooters.

The Military Four, by Claude V. Holland. C. V. Holland, Bonita Springs, FL, 1972. 64 pp., illus. Paper covers. $3.50.
Technical data, photographs and history of the Luger, Colt, P-38 and Mauser broomhandle pistols.

Military Pistols and Revolvers, by I. V. Hogg. Arco Pub. Co., NY, 1970. 80 pp., illus. $3.50.
The handguns of the two World Wars shown in halftone illus., with brief historical and descriptive text.

The Modern Handgun, by Robert Hertzberg, A&W Books, NY, 1974. 112 pp., well illus. $3.50.
Pistols and revolvers of all types are traced from their beginnings. Data on modern marksmanship included.

The Official U.S. Army Pistol Marksmanship Guide, first authorized repro. of original U.S. Army work. J&A Publ., NY, 1972. 144 pp., illus. Paper covers. $6.50.
Every detail from sight alignment to International Pistol programs—technical and fundamental for championship shooting in easy-to-read illus. form.

The Original Mauser Automatic Pistol, Model 1930, a reprint by Harold C. Bruffett, Croswell, MI, 1973. 32 pp., illus., paper covers. $2.50.
Facsimile of the 1931 English-text export catalog on the "Broom Handle Mauser."

The "Parabellum" Automatic Pistol, Stoeger Publ. Co., S. Hackensack, NJ, 49 pp. plus three fold out tables. $2.00.
An exact reproduction of the instruction book issued in English by the original Luger manufacturer "Deutsche Waffen and Munitionsfabriken, Berlin."

The "Parabellum" Automatic Pistol, the English version of the official DWM handbook on Luger pistols. Normount Armament Co., Wickenburg, AZ, 1968. 42 pp., illus. Paper wrappers. $2.00.
A user's handbook, a reference work for collectors. A reprint of the ·iginal detailed instructions on use, disassembly and maintenance. Includes three folding plates.

Pistol and Revolver Digest, by Dean A. Grennell, DBI Books, Inc., Northfield, IL, 1976. 288 pp., illus. Paper covers. $7.95.
A comprehensive volume on all aspects of the handgun.

Pistol & Revolver Guide, 3rd Ed., by George C. Nonte, Follett Publ. Co., Chicago, IL, 1975. 224 pp., illus. Paper covers. $6.95.
A new and up-dated ed. of the standard reference work on military and sporting handguns.

Pistol Shooting as a Sport, by Hans Standl, Crown Publ., Inc., NY, 1976. 117 pp., illus. $5.95.
A guide to expert target shooting with special emphasis on Olympic requirements.

Pistolen Atlas, by Karl R. Pawlas, Nuremberg, Germany, 1970. Arranged alphabetically by maker and model in loose-leaf binding. Each vol. $15.00.

Carefully planned and researched for the "automatic arms buff," shooter and collector, depicts hundreds of auto. pistols of all nations and of all calibers with excellent illus. and descriptive text in English, French, German and Spanish. 13 volumes projected, of which vols. 1, 2, 3, 5, 6, 7 and 8 are now ready.

Pistols: A Modern Encyclopedia, by Henry M. Stebbins, Castle Books, NY, 1976. 380 pp., illus. $5.98.

Comprehensive coverage of handguns for every purpose, with material on selection, ammunition and marksmanship.

Pistols of the World, by Ian V. Hogg and John Weeks, Arms and Armour Press, London, England, 1978. 304 pp., illus. $22.50.

A comprehensive illustrated encyclopedia of the world's pistols and revolvers from 1870 to the present day.

Report of Board on Tests of Revolvers and Automatic Pistols. From The *Annual Report* of the Chief of Ordnance, 1907. Reprinted by J. C. Tillinghast, Marlow, NH, 1969. 34 pp., 7 plates, paper covers. $3.00.

A comparison of handguns, including Luger, Savage, Colt, Webley-Fosbery and other makes.

Saga of the Colt Six-Shooter, and the famous men who used it, by G. E. Virgines. Frederick Fell Co., New York, NY, 1969. 220 pp., well illus. $7.95.

History of the Colt Single action army revolver since 1873, with much information of interest to collectors and shooters.

Shooting to Live with the One-Hand Gun, by Wm. E. Fairbairn and Eric A. Sykes, Paladin Press, Boulder, CO, 1974. 96 pp., illus. $5.95.

Facsimile of the 1942 instruction manual on the use of the pistol for defense in police work.

System Mauser, a Pictorial History of the Model 1896 Self-Loading Pistol, by J. W. Breathed, Jr., and J. J. Schroeder, Jr. Handgun Press, Chicago, IL, 1967. 273 pp., well illus. 1st limited ed. hardbound. $15.00.

10 Shots Quick, by Daniel K. Stern. Globe Printing Co., San Jose, CA, 1967. 153 pp., photos. $8.50.

History of Savage-made automatic pistols, models of 1903-1917, with descriptive data for shooters and collectors.

Textbook of Automatic Pistols, by R. K. Wilson and Ian V. Hogg, Stackpole Books, Harrisburg, PA, 1975. 416 pp., illus. $17.95.

Complete history of automatic hand-held weaponry, from the origins in the 19th century to now.

United States Single Shot Martial Pistols, by C. W. Sawyer, WE, Inc., Old Greenwich, CT, 1971. 101 pp., illus. $5.00.

History of pistols used by the U.S. Armed Services 1776-1871.

U.S. Test Trials 1900 Luger, by Michael Reese II, Pioneer Press, Union City, TN, 1976. 130 pp., illus. Paper covers. $4.95.

Revised edition containing much additional material on the notable American Eagle test pieces. Rare illustrations.

The Walther P-38 Pistol, by Maj. Geo. C. Nonte, Paladin Press, Boulder, CO, 1975. 90 pp., illus. Paper covers. $5.00.

Covers all facets of the gun—development, history, variations, technical data, practical use, rebuilding, repair and conversion.

The Walther Pistols 1930-1945, by Warren H. Buxton, Warren H. Buxton, Los Alamos, NM, 1978. 350 pp., illus. $29.95.

Volume I of a projected 4 volume series "The P.38 Pistol." The histories, evolutions, and variations of the Walther P.38 and its predecessors.

hunting

The ABC of Shooting, ed. by Colin Willock, Andre Deutsch, Ltd., London, England, 1975. 351 pp., illus. $14.95.

A complete shotgun guide to game and rough shooting, wild fowling, pigeon shooting, deer stalking and clay pigeon shooting.

African Hunter, by James Mellon et al, Harcourt Brace Jovanovich, NY, 1975. 522 pp., illus. $39.95.

Hunting Africa's wild animals by a famous hunter and others. Trophies, weapons, best time to hunt and where.

African Rifles & Cartridges, by John Taylor, The Gun Room Press, Highland Park, NJ, 1977. 431 pp., illus. $16.95.

Experiences and opinions of a professional ivory hunter in Africa describing his knowledge of numerous arms and cartridges for big game. A reprint.

Alaskan Hunter, by Roy F. Chandler, Roy F. Chandler, Nokomis, FL, 1977. 281 pp., illus. $16.00.

Vividly told experiences, informative and entrancing.

All About Deer in America, ed. by Robert Elman, Winchester Press, NY, 1976. 256 pp., illus. $10.

Twenty of America's great hunters share the secrets of their hunting success.

All About Wildfowling in America, ed. by Jerome Knap, Winchester Press, NY, 1976. 256 pp., illus. $10.

More than a dozen top writers provide new and controversial ideas on how to and where to hunt wildfowl successfully.

All-Season Hunting, by Bob Gilsvik, Winchester Press, NY, 1976. 256 pp., illus. $9.95.

A guide to early-season, late-season and winter hunting in America.

All About Rifle Hunting and Shooting in America, by Steve Ferber, Winchester Press, NY, 1977. 263 pp., illus. $10.00.

Everything the rifle shooter would want to know from shooting the old muzzleloader to the newest cartridge guns.

All About Small-Game Hunting in America, ed. by Russell Tinsley, Winchester Press, NY, 1976. 308 pp., illus. $10.00.

Collected advice by the finest small-game experts in the country.

All About Wildfowling in America, by Jerome Knap, Winchester Press, NY, 1977. 256 pp., illus. $10.00.

More than a dozen top writers provide new and controversial ideas on how-to and where-to hunt wildfowl successfully.

The Art of Hunting Big Game in North America, by Jack O'Connor, Random House, NY, 1978. 418 pp., illus. $13.95.

A new revised and updated edition on technique, planning, skill, outfitting, etc.

Art of Small Game Hunting, by Francis Sell. Stackpole Books, Harrisburg, PA, 1973. 192 pp., illus. $3.95.

An invaluable primer and skill sharpener for any hunter.

Art of Successful Deer Hunting, by F. E. Sell, Stackpole Books, Harrisburg, PA, 1971. 192 pp., paper, $3.95.

Illus. re-issue of "The Deer Hunter's Guide." Western hunting lore for rifle and bow-hunter.

Asian Jungle, African Bush, by Charles Askins. Stackpole Books, Harrisburg, PA, 1959. 258 pp., illus. $10.00.

A where-to-go and how-to-do guide for game-rich Indo-China. The African section deals with game, the use of various arms and ammo on specific species.

The Best of Nash Buckingham, by Nash Buckingham, selected, edited and annotated by George Bird Evans. Winchester Press, NY, 1973. 320 pp. $10.

Thirty pieces that represent the very cream of Nash's output on his whole range of outdoor interests—upland shooting, duck hunting, even fishing.

The Big Game Animals of North America, by Jack O'Connor, Outdoor Life, NY, 1977, updated and revised edition. 238 pp., illus. $14.95.

A classic work on North American big game.

Big Game Hunter's Digest, by Tom Brakefield, DBI Books, Inc., Northfield, IL, 1977. 288 pp., illus. Paper covers. $7.95.

A truly complete reference to North American big game hunting.

Big Game Hunting Around the World, by Bert Klineburger and Vernon W. Hurst, Exposition Press, Jericho, NY, 1969. 376 pp., illus. $15.00.

The first book that takes you on a safari all over the world.

Big Game Hunting in North America, by Dave Petzal, Simon & Schuster, NY, 1977. 223 pp., illus. $10.95.

Expert advice on hunting America's top trophy game, such as antelope, bear, goat, caribou, elk, etc.

Big Game Hunting in the West, by Mike Cramond. Mitchell Press, Vancouver, B.C., Can., 1965. 164 pp., illus. $5.95.

Accounts of hunting many species of big game and predators are given plus a section on rifles, equipment, and useful tips for the field.

Big Game Hunting in New Zealand, by Gary Joll. Whitcombe & Tombs, Christchurch, NZ, 1971. 214 pp., illus. $10.00.

An experienced hunter's advice on various species of New Zealand game, guns, equipment, and other aspects of hunting.

The Big Shots; Edwardian Shooting Parties, by Jonathan Garnier Ruffer, Debrett's Peerage Ltd, London, England, 1978. 300 pp., illus. $17.95.

Reveals the secrets behind the Imperial, Royal and Nobel shooting parties that have been an integral part of upper class English life for so long.

Bird Hunting Know-How, by D. M. Duffey. Van Nostrand, Princeton, NJ, 1968. 192 pp., illus. $5.95.

Game-getting techniques and sound advice on all aspects of upland bird hunting, plus data on guns and loads.

Bobwhite Quail Hunting, by Charley Dickey, printed for Stoeger Publ. Co., So. Hackensack, NJ, 1974. 112 pp., illus., paper covers. $2.95.

Habits and habitats, techniques, gear, guns and dogs.

The Bobwhite Quail, its Life and Management, by Walter Rosene. Rutgers University Press, New Brunswick, NJ. 1st ed., 1969. 418 pp., photographs, maps and color plates. $27.50.

An exhaustive study of an important species which has diminished under the impact of changing agricultural and forestry practices.

Bow & Arrow Archer's Digest, by J. Lewis, Digest Books, Northfield, IL, 1971. 320 pp., illus. Paper, $5.95.

The encyclopedia for all archers, from picking a bow to varmint calling.

Bowhunter's Digest, by C. R. Learn, ed. by Jack Lewis, Digest Books, Inc., Northfield, IL. 1974. 8½"x11", 288 pp. Profusely illus. Paperbound. $6.95.

Large and small game bowhunting with much information on equipment, techniques and training.

Bowhunting, by M. R. James, The John Olson Co., Paramus, NJ, 1975. 224 pp., illus. $6.95.

Everything from bowhunting basics to advanced hunting techniques.

Bowhunting Big Game Records of North America, ed. by M. R. James, et al, Pope and Young Club, Milton, WI, 1975. 307 pp., illus. $17.50.

The official records book of bowhunting trophies of North American big game.

Bowhunting for Deer, by H. R. Wambold. Stackpole Books, Harrisburg, PA, 1964. 160 pp., illus. $5.95.

Useful tips on deer, their habits, anatomy, and how-when-where of hunting, plus selection and use of tackle.

Bowhunting the Whitetail Deer, by Dean Conatser, Winchester Press, NY, 1977. 224 pp., illus. $10.

A comprehensive, step-by-step guide for everyone who wants to hunt the wily whitetail with bow and arrow.

A Boy and His Gun, by Edward C. Janes. A. S. Barnes & Co., New York, NY. 207 pp., illus., $5.00.

Introduction to rifles, shooting and hunting techniques for young shooters with practical hints on game shooting with rifle or shotgun.

The Call of the Maneater, by Kenneth Anderson, George Allen & Unwin, Ltd., London, 1962. 274 pp., illus. $7.50.

True tales of tiger hunting in the jungles of India.

Calling All Game, by Bert Popowski. Stackpole Books, Harrisburg, PA, 1952, 306 pp. Illus. $7.50.

Practical methods of attracting game, from quail to moose, using artificial decoys and calls.

Charles Morgan on Retrievers, ed. by Ann Fowler and D. L. Walters. Abercrombie & Fitch, NYC, 1968, 168 pp., illus. $12.50.

Based on years of success in schooling hunting dogs, this work gives full details of an expert's proven methods to guide experienced trainers.

Complete Book of Bow and Arrow, by G. H. Gillelan, Stackpole Books, Harrisburg, PA, 1971. 320 pp., illus. $9.95.

Encyclopedic reference on archery, gear, rules, skill, etc.

The Complete Book of Deer Hunting, by Byron W. Dalrymple, Winchester Press, NY, 1973. 247 pp., illus. $8.95.

Practical "how-to" information. Covers the 20 odd North-American subspecies of deer.

Complete Book of Hunting, by Clyde Ormond. Harper & Bros., NYC, 1962. 467 pp., well-illus. $6.95.

Part I is on game animals, Part II is on birds. Guns and ammunition, game, habitats, clothing, equipment, etc. hunters' tips are discussed.

The Complete Book of the Wild Turkey, by Roger M. Latham, Stackpole Books, Harrisburg, PA, 1978. 228 pp., illus. $8.95.

A new revised edition of the classic on American wild turkey hunting.

The Complete Guide to Bird Dog Training, by John R. Falk, Winchester Press, NY, 1976. 256 pp., illus. $10.00.

How to choose, raise, train, and care for a bird dog.

Complete Guide to Hunting Across North America, by Byron Dalrymple. Outdoor Life, Harper & Row, NY, 1970. 848 pp., illus. with photos and 50 maps. $10.00.

A large reference work on hunting conditions, locating game, clothing, techniques, transportation, equipment for every region, etc.

The Complete Hunter's Catalog, by Norman Strung, J. B. Lippincott Co., Phila., PA, 1978. 438 pp., illus. $14.95.

Where and how to find the best buy on equipment for shooting sports, hunting, big game, waterfowl, archery and much more.

The Complete Wildfowler, by Grits Gresham, Winchester Press, NY, 1976. 304 pp., illus. $8.95.

A graduate course in wildfowling, this is a down-to-earth, step-by-step education in everything one needs to know on the subject.

Crow Shooting Secrets, by Dick Mermon. Winchester Press, New York, 1970. 149 pp., illus. $5.95.

An expert shares his secrets and touches all the bases.
Decoying Waterfowl, by A. C. Becker Jr. A. S. Barnes and Co., NY, 1973. 256 pp., illus. $12.
An in-depth study of decoy shape, paint finishes, and formations on the water, etc. Over 100 photos and drawings.
Deer Hunting, by R. Smith, Stackpole Books, Harrisburg, PA, 1978. 224 pp., illus. $9.95.
A professional guide leads the hunt for North America's most popular big game animal.
Deer Hunting Across North America, ed. by Nick Sisley, Freshet Press, Rockville Centre, NY, 1976. 200 pp., illus. $12.95.
Covers the physical characteristics and habits of all the North American deer species, tips, guns and cartridges to use, methods of hunting, etc.
Deer Hunting; Tactics and Guns for Hunting All North American Game, by Norman Sprung, J. B. Lippincott Co., Phila., PA, 1973. 237 pp., illus. $7.95.
A comprehensive guide to deer hunting, focusing on whitetailed and mule deer.
The Dove Shooter's Handbook, by Dan M. Russell, Winchester Press, NY, 1974. 256 pp., illus. $6.95.
A complete guide to America's top game bird—natural history, hunting methods, equipment, conservation and future prospects.
Dove Hunting, by Charley Dickey, Galahad Books, NY, 1976. 112 pp., illus. $3.98.
This indispensable guide for hunters deals with equipment, techniques, types of dove shooting, hunting dogs, etc.
The Duck Hunter's Handbook, by Bob Hinman, Winchester Press, NY, 1974. 252 pp., illus. $8.95.
Down-to-earth, practical advice on bagging ducks and geese.
Duck Hunting in Australia and New Zealand, by Jack Byrne, A. H. & A. W. Reed, Wellington, New Zealand, 1974. 241 pp., illus. $9.25.
Covers the various types of duck and how to identify them. How to build a mai-mai, shotgun safety, duck calling, etc.
Ducks of the Mississippi Flyway, ed. by John McKane. North Star Press, St. Cloud, MN, 1969. 54 pp., illus. Paper covers, $2.98.
A duck hunter's reference. Full color paintings of some 30 species, plus descriptive text.
The Education of a Bear Hunter, by Ralph Flowers, Winchester Press, NY, 1975. 288 pp., illus. $10.00.
Anyone who hunts bear will want this book for its wealth of hunting lore and woodcraft.
The Education of a Turkey Hunter, by Wm. F. Hanenkrat, Winchester Press, NY, 1974. 216 pp., illus. $8.95.
A complete course on how to hunt turkeys.
Elephant, by D. E. Blunt, Neville Spearman, London, 1971. 260 pp., illus. $12.50.
Reprint of a rare book, a hunter's account of the ways of an elephant.
Expert Advice on Gun Dog Training, ed. by David M. Duffey, Winchester Press, NY, 1977. 256 pp., illus. $10.
Eleven top pros talk shop, revealing the techniques and philosophies that account for their consistent success.
Game Animals in New Zealand, by Gordon Roberts. A. H. & A. W. Reed, Sydney, Australia, 1968. 112 pp., illus. $8.25.
Pictures of wild, live animals in their natural and often remote habitats.
Game Bird Hunting in the West, by Mike Cramond. Mitchell Press, Vancouver, B.C., Can., 1967. 246 pp., illus. $5.95.
Identification and hunting methods for each species of waterfowl and upland game birds, plus a section on shotgun types, equipment, and related subjects for the hunter.
Game and the Gunner, by Pierre Pulling, Winchester Press, NY, 1973. 233 pp., illus. $8.95.
Observations on same conservation and sport hunting.
Getting the Most out of Modern Waterfowling, by John O. Cartier, St. Martin's Press, NY, 1974. 396 pp., illus. $10.95.
The most comprehensive, up-to-date book on waterfowling imaginable.
Good Hunting, by Jas L. Clark, Univ. of Oklahoma Press, Norman, Okla., 1966. 242 pp., illus. $7.95.
Fifty years of collecting and preparing habitat groups for the American Museum.
A Good Keen Man, by Barry Crump. A. H. & A. W. Reed, Sydney, Australia, 1969. 192 pp., illus. $7.50.
A popular tale of deer hunting in the New Zealand back-country.
The Great Arc of the Wild Sheep, by J. L. Clark, Univ. of Oklahoma Press, Norman, Okla., 1978. 247 pp., illus. Paper covers. $8.95.
Every classified variety of wild sheep is discussed, as found in North America, Asia & Europe. Numerous hunting stories by experts are included.
Great Game Animals of the World, by Russell B. Aitken. Winchester Press, NY, 1969. 192 pp. profusely ills. in monochrome and color. $22.50.
Accounts of man's pursuit of big game in all parts of the world, told in many fine pictures.
Green Hills of Africa, by Ernest Hemingway. Charles Scribner's Sons, NY, 1963. 285 pp. illus. Paper covers, $3.45.
A famous narrative of African big-game hunting, first published in 1935.
Grizzly Country, by Andy Russell. A. A. Knopf, NYC, 1973, 302 pp., illus. $7.95.
Many-sided view of the grizzly bear and his world, by a noted guide, hunter and naturalist.
Grouse Feathers, by Burton L. Spiller. Crown Publ., NY, 1972. 207 pp., illus. $7.50.
Facsimile of the original Derrydale Press issue of 1935. How to hunt the ruffed grouse, with stories of the author's experiences with dogs and guns from boyhood. Illus. by Lynn Bogue Hunt.
Grouse and Grouse Hunting, by Frank Woolner. Crown Pub., Co., NY, 1970. 192 pp., illus. $7.50.
The history, habits, habitat and methods of hunting one of America's great game birds.
Gun Dog, by Richard A. Wolters, E. P. Dutton, New York, NY, 1969. 1st ed., 11th Printing. 150 pp., well illus. $5.95.
A popular manual for upland bird shooters who want to train their dogs to perfection in minimum time.
Gunning For Upland Birds and Wildlife, by Shirley E. Woods, Jr., Winchester Press, NY, 1976. 208 pp., illus. $10.00.
Practical field tested tips and techniques on two of America's most popular outdoor sports.
Handgun Hunting, by Maj. George C. Nonte, Jr. and Lee E. Jurras, Winchester Press, NY, 1975. 245 pp., illus. $8.95.
A book with emphasis on the hunting of readily available game in the U.S. with the handgun.
Highland Stage of Otago, by D. Bruce Banwell. A. H. & A. W. Reed, Sydney, Australia, 1968. 169 pp., illus. $9.75.
The romantic history of Otago's red deer. Trophy statistics, fully checked for accuracy, are given. An invaluable reference work.
Horns in the High Country, by Andy Russell, Alfred A. Knopf, NY, 1973. 259 pp., illus. $7.95.
A many-sided view of wild sheep and the natural world in which they live.
How to Hunt, by Dave Bowring, Winchester Press, NY, 1978. 256 pp., illus. $10.95.
A basic guide to hunting big game, small game, upland birds, and waterfowl.
How to Hunt American Game, by R. B. Vale. Stackpole Books, Harrisburg, PA. 5th printing, 1954. 199 pp., illus. $4.00.
Wildlife habits, conservation and the encouragement of hunting. Including the author's experiences in hunting game throughout America.
How to Hunt Small American Game, by L. A. Anderson. Funk and Wagnalls, New York, NY, 1969. 167 pp., well illus. $5.95.
A new basic guide for the small game hunter, similar to the author's 1959 *How to Hunt Deer and Small Game.* Written for beginner and expert, covers game, guns, equipment and game habits.
How to Hunt Whitetail Deer, L. A. Anderson. Funk & Wagnalls, NYC, 1968. 116 pp., illus. $5.95.
Useful reference for deer hunters, both novice and experienced, giving basic information and valuable pointers.
Hunt Close!, by Jerome B. Robinson, Winchester Press, NY, 1978. 224 pp., illus. $10.00.
A realistic guide to training close-working dogs for today's tight cover conditions.
Hunt the Far Mountain, by Keith Severinsen. A. H. & A. W. Reed, Wellington, N.Z., 1970. 182 pp., illus. $9.00.
An introduction to every hunting trophy New Zealand offers.
Hunter's Digest, edited by Erwin A. Bauer. Digest Books, Inc., Northfield, IL, 1973. 320 pp., illus. Paper covers. $6.95.
The best ways, times and places to hunt the most popular species of large and small game animals in North America.
The Hunter's Field Guide to Game Birds & Animals of North America, by Robt. Elman, Alfred A. Knopf, NY, 1974. 655 pp. Over 357 illus., including 116 in full color. $12.50.
A comprehensive book on strategy and facts on over 100 game animals, upland birds and waterfowl in North America.
A Hunter's Fireside Book, by Gene Hill Winchester Press, NY, 1972. 192 pp., illus. $7.95
An outdoor book that will appeal to every person who spends time in the field—or who wishes he could.
The Hunter's Game Cookbook, by Jacqueline E. Knight, Winchester Press, NY, 1978. 320 pp., illus. $10.95.
Everything you need to know about the preparation of game from the field to the table.
A Hunter's Wanderings in Africa, by Frederick C. Selous, Books of Rhodesia, Bulawayo, So. Africa, 1970. 455 pp., illus. $27.50.
A facsimile reproduction of the rare 1881 ed. A narrative of nine years spent among the game of the far interior of So. Africa.
The Hunter's World, by C. F. Waterman. Random House, NY, 1970. 250 pp., illus. $15.00.
A book for those who welcome an expert's guidance, one who understands the terrain, feed, cover, etc., of the game they hunt. Profusely illus. in color.
Hunting the American Wild Turkey, by Dave Harbour, Stackpole Books, Harrisburg, PA, 1975. 256 pp., illus. $8.95.
The techniques and tactics of hunting North America's largest, and most popular, woodland game bird.
Hunting America's Game Animals and Birds, by Robert Elman and George Peper, Winchester Press, NY, 1975. 368 pp., illus. $12.95.
A how-to, where-to, when-to guide—by 40 top experts—covering the continent's big, small, upland game and waterfowl.
Hunting Big-Game Trophies; A North America Guide, by Tom Brakefield, E. P. Dutton & Co., Inc., NY, 1976. 446 pp., illus. $10.95.
Where to go, when to go, camp savvy, animal lore, the hunt, etc.
Hunting with a Camera; A World Guide to Wildlife Photography, by Erwin A. Bauer, Winchester Press, NY, 1974. 324 pp., illus. $12.95.
A practical book which will help every amateur photographer to take better wildlife photos.
Hunting Dog Know-How, by D. M. Duffey, Van Nostrand, Princeton, NJ, 1965. 177 pp., illus. $6.95.
Covers selection, breeds, and training of hunting dogs, problems in hunting and field trials.
Hunting Hounds: How to Choose, Train and Handle America's Trail and Tree Hounds, by David Michael Duffey. Winchester Press, NY, 1972. 192 pp., illus. $6.95.
Origin, development, selection, care and usage of every breed and strain, with entertaining anecdotes and practical training tips.
Hunting for all Seasons, by Alex Kay, A & W Books, NY, 1976. 159 pp., illus. $5.95.
The complete how-to handbook on when and where to bag your quarry, how much gun to use on what game.
Hunting the Long-Tailed Bird, by Bob Bell, Freshet Press, Rockville Centre, NY, 1975. 115 pp., illus. $14.95.
A book about the ringneck pheasant and techniques for the successful hunting of it.
Hunting Moments of Truth, by Eric Peper and Jim Rikhoff, Winchester Press, NY, 1973. 208 pp., illus. $8.95.
The world's most experienced hunters recount 22 most memorable occasions.
Hunting with Bow and Arrow, by George Laycock and Erwin Bauer. Arco Publ. Co., Inc., NYC, 1966. $3.95.
A practical guide to archery as a present-day sport. Mentions equipment needed and how to select it. Illus. instructions on how to shoot with ease and accuracy.
Hunting Trophy Deer, by John Wootters, Winchester Press, NY, 1977. 288 pp., illus. $13.95.
One of America's most experienced and respected hunting writers provides all the specialized advice you need to succeed at bagging trophy deer.
Hunting Upland Birds, by Chas. F. Waterman. Winchester Press, NY, 1972. 320 pp., illus. $8.95.
Excellent treatment of game habits and habitat, hunting methods, and management techniques for each of the 18 major North American gamebird species.
Hunting the Uplands with Rifle and Shotgun, by Luther A. Anderson, Winchester Press, NY, 1977. 224 pp., illus. $10.
Solid, practical know-how to help make hunting deer and every major species of upland game bird easier and more satisfying.
Hunting Weapons, by Howard L. Blackmore. Walker & Co., NY, 1971. 401 pp., illus. $17.50.
Covers sporting arms from the Middle Ages to the present, by a prominent British expert on historical weapons.
Hunting in Westland, by Lew Sutherland. A. H. & A. W. Reed, Sydney, Australia, 1970. 95 pp., illus. Paper covers. $5.75.
Intended to assist parties of experienced hunters in planning an expedition.

Hunting Whitetail Deer, by Robert E. Donovan, Winchester Press, NY, 1978. 256 pp., illus. $12.50.
For beginners and experts alike, this book is the key to successful whitetail hunting.
The Imperial Collection of Audubon Animals, original text by John James Audubon and Rev. John Bachman, illus. by John James and John Woodhouse Audubon. A magnificent quarto reproduction of the rare original by Hammond, Inc., Maplewood, NJ, 1967. 307 pp., 150 animals pictured in full color. $7.95.
Each illus. accompanied by engaging text, as in the 1st ed. of 1848, including accounts of Audubon's exploring trips. A most useful work for hunters who want to know their game.
Jaybirds Go to Hell on Friday & Other Stories, by Havilah Babcock, Holt, Rinehart & Winston, NY, 1972. 149 pp. $6.95.
A sparkling collection of stories about hunting and fishing by the nation's number one quail hunter.
Living Off the Country, by B. Angier. Stackpole Books, Harrisburg, PA, 1959. 241 pp., illus. $6.95.
In a simple and entertaining manner the author explains how to live off nature when emergency arises and how to stay alive in the woods.
Man-Eaters & Jungle Killers, by Kenneth Anderson, George Allen & Unwin Ltd., London, 1970. 199 pp., illus. $10.00.
The author's methods and precautions in hunting the man-eaters of India.
Modern ABC's of Bird Hunting, by Dave Harbour, Stackpole Books, Harrisburg, PA, 1966. 192 pp., illus. $4.95.
From city's edge to wilderness this gives the occasional hunter the quickest way on how to increase his bag. Covers all game birds of the U.S. and Canada.
Modern Hunting with Indian Secrets, by Allan A. Macfarlan. Stackpole Books, Harrisburg, PA, 1971. 222 pp., $6.50.
How to acquire the new-old skills of the Redman, how to apply them to modern hunting.
Modern Turkey Hunting, by James F. Brady, Crown Publ., N.Y.C., NY, 1973. 160 pp., illus. $6.95.
A thorough guide to the habits, habitat, and methods of hunting America's largest game bird.
More Grouse Feathers, by Burton L. Spiller. Crown Publ., NY, 1972. 238 pp., illus. $7.50.
Facsimile of the original Derrydale Press issue of 1938. Guns and dogs, the habits and shooting of grouse, woodcook, ducks, etc. Illus. by Lynn Bogue Hunt.
Moss, Mallards & Mules and other Hunting and Fishing Stories, by Robert Brister, Winchester Press, NY, 1973. 216 pp., illus. $8.95.
A collection of 27 short stories on hunting and fishing.
Mostly Tailfeathers, by Gene Hill, Winchester Press, NY, 1975. 192 pp., illus. $8.95.
An interesting, general book about bird hunting with some stories on fishing.
My Health is Better in November, by Havilah Babcock,, Holt, Rinehart & Winston, NY, 1970. 284 pp., illus. $6.95.
A classic collection of 35 stories from an author just as versatile with pen as with rod and gun.
The New Hunter's Encyclopedia, edited by Leonard Miracle and James B. Trefethen, plus specialized articles by over 60 outstanding contributors. Stackpole Books, Harrisburg, PA, 1972. 1054 pp., with 2047 photos, diagrams, drawings and full-color plates. $14.95.
A massive work covering every detail of every sort of hunting in the U.S., Canada and Mexico.
Nine Centuries of Hunting Weapons, by L. G. Boccia, Editrice Edam, Firenze, Italy, 1967. 181 pp., illus. with many fine photos of superb museum quality in full color. $15.00.
In Italian text, a historical survey of hunting weapons of Italian origin and their makers.
North American Big Game, ed. by Wm. H. Nesbitt and Jack S. Parker, The Boone and Crockett Club and the National Rifle Association of America, Wash., DC, 7th ed., 1977. 367 pp., illus. $25.00.
The official records book for outstanding native North American big game trophies.
North American Big Game Hunting, by Byron W. Dalrymple, Winchester Press, NY, 1974. 383 pp., illus. $10.00.
A comprehensive, practical guide, with individual chapters devoted to all native species.
The North American Waterfowler, by Paul S. Bernsen. Superior Publ. Co., Seattle, WA, 1972. 206 pp. Paper covers, $4.95.
The complete inside and outside story of duck and goose shooting. Big and colorful, illus. by Les Kouba.
The Old Man and the Boy, by Robert Ruark, Holt, Rinehart and Winston, NY, 1974. 303 pp., illus. A reprint. $8.95.
The story of the author and his grandfather hunting and fishing in North Carolina, with the boy listening and learning. A classic.
On Your Own in the Wilderness, by Col. T. Whelen and B. Angier. Stackpole Books, Harrisburg, PA, 1958. 324 pp., illus. $5.00.
Two eminent authorities give complete, accurate, and useful data on all phases of camping and travel in primitive areas.
One Man's Wilderness, by Warren Page, Holt, Rinehart and Winston, NY, 1973. 256 pp., illus. $8.95.
A world-known writer and veteran sportsman recounts the joys of a lifetime of global hunting.
Outdoor Life's Deer Hunting Book, by Jack O'Connor, et al, Harper & Row Publ., Inc., NY, 1975. 224 pp., illus. $7.95.
A major new work on deer hunting. Covers every aspect of the sport.
The Outlaw Gunner, by Harry M. Walsh, Tidewater Publishers, Cambridge, MD, 1973. 178 pp., illus. $8.50.
A colorful story of market gunning in both its legal and illegal phases.
Pack and Rifle, by Philip Holden. A. H. & A. W. Reed, Sydney, Australia, 1971. 194 pp., illus. $9.75.
The hunting days of a New Zealand Forest Service professional shooter. Hunts after red deer, sika, rusa, and sambar.
The Part I Remember, by Chas. F. Waterman, Winchester Press, NY, 1974. 199 pp., illus. $8.95.
Stories—mostly funny, all true—of the outdoor life, by a master outdoorsman and incomparable storyteller.
Paw Prints; How to Identify Rare and Common Mammals by Their Tracks. O. C. Lempfert, NY, 1972. 71 pp., illus. with actual size prints. $7.50.
An authoritive manual for hunters and outdoorsmen.
The Practical Hunter's Dog Book, by John R. Falk, Winchester Press, NY, 1971. 314 pp., illus. $8.95.
Helps to choose, train and enjoy your gun dog.
Practical Pointer Training, by Sherman Webb, Winchester Press, NY 1976. 192 pp., illus. $6.95.
A good bird dog training book that fills the bill.
The Puma, Mysterious American Cat, by S. P. Young and E. A. Goldman, Dover Publ., NY, 1964. 358 pp., illus. Paper covers $3.50.
A two-part work: the first on the history, economic status and control: the second on classifications of the races of the puma.
Ranch Life and the Hunting Trail, by Theodore Roosevelt, Readex Microprint Corp., Dearborn, MI. 1966. 186 pp., With drawings by Frederic Remington. $10.
A facsimile reprint of the original 1899 Century Co. edition. One of the most fascinating books of the West of that day.
The Recollections of an Elephant Hunter, 1864-1875, by Wm. Finaughty, Books of Rhodesia, Bulawayo, So. Africa, 1973. 244 pp., illus. $25.00.
Facsimile reproduction of the rare 1916 ed. with additional illus. and new foreword and notes.
The Red Stags of the Rakaia, by D. Bruce Banwell. A. H. & A. W. Reed, Sydney, Australia, 1972. 165 pp., illus. $9.75.
An invaluable standard reference, and a lively, readable saga of a herd whose trophies have become world-famous.
Ringneck! Pheasants & Pheasant Hunting, by Ted Janes, Crown Publ., NY, 1975. 120 pp., illus. $8.95.
A thorough study of one of our more popular game birds.
Rowland Ward's Records of Big Game, 16th ed., comp. by G. A. Best, Rowland Ward Pub., Ltd., 1976. 438 pp., illus. $55.00.
New edition of the authoritive record of big game kills in Africa, by species.
Safari, by Elmer Keith. Safari Publ., La Jolla, CA, 1968. 166 pp., illus. $7.95.
Guide to big game hunting in Africa, with anecdote and expert advice on hunting many species of game. Information on guns, ammunition, equipment, and planning the safari is included. Fine photographs.
Safari by Jet, through Africa and Asia, by Sister Maria del Rey, Charles Scribner's Sons, New York, NY, 1962. 308 pp., profusely illus., with photos and line. $5.95.
Off-beat reading about an African-Asian grand tour, with tales of the land and the people of Tanganyika, Ceylon, the Philippines, Hong Kong, Taiwan, et al.
Safe Hunting, by Dick Pryce, Winchester Press, NY, 1974. 178 pp., illus. $7.95.
An introduction to hunting, guns, and gun safety.
Selected American Game Birds, by David Hagerbaumer and Sam Lehman, The Caxton Printers, Ltd., Caldwell, ID, 1972. The entire text of this book is executed in decorated calligraphy. $30.00.
Twenty-six of David Hagerbaumer's exquisite original watercolors, representing 29 bird species. A must for every book collector and art lover.
Sheep & Sheep Hunting, by Jack O'Connor, Winchester Press, NY, 1974. 308 pp., illus. $10.00.
Authentic detail about all varieties of wild sheep and how to hunt for them.
Shooting, A Complete Guide for Beginners, by John Marchington. Faber & Faber, London, Eng., 1972. 158 pp., illus. $9.75.
Guide to all aspects of shooting in the British manner, for all types of game.
Shooting Game, by Michael Kemp, A & C Black, London, England, 1972. 176 pp., illus. $8.95.
A step-by-step course to successful and enjoyable shooting.
Shooting for the Skipper, by Jack McNair. A. H. & A. W. Reed, Sydney, Australia, 1971. 153 pp., illus. $10.00.
Memories of a veteran New Zealand deer hunter.
Shooting Pictures, by A. B. Frost, with 24 pp. of text by Chas. D. Lanier. Winchester Press, NY, 1972. 12 color plates. Enclosed in a board portfolio. Ed. limited to 750 numbered copies. $50.
Frost's twelve superb 12" by 16" pictures have often been called the finest sporting prints published in the U.S. A facsimile of the 1895-6 edition printed on fine paper with superb color fidelity.
Small Game Hunting, by Clyde Ormond. Outdoor Life Books, NY, 1969. 126 pp., illus. $4.50.
Field-tested advice for increasing your take of chucks, squirrels, rabbits, crows, hawks, etc. Good information on guns, loads, field tips, etc.
A Sporting Chance . . ., by D. P. Mannix. E. P. Dutton & Co., NY, 1967. 248 pp., illus. with 50 photos. $1.98.
Unusual methods of hunting the exotic species from hounds to falcons. Inspiring reading for those desiring to get away from the commonplace.
The Sportsman's Companion, by Lee Wulff. Harper & Row, N.Y.C., 1968. 413 pp., illus. $11.95.
Compendium of writings by various experts on hunting and fishing for American game. A useful reference for the outdoorsman.
Sportman's Guide to Game Animals, by Leonard Lee Rue III. Harper & Row [Outdoor Life Books], New York, NY, 1st ed., 2nd printing, 1969. 635 pp., illus. with photographs and maps. $6.50.
Exhaustive and capable coverage of the behavior and habits of all North American game animals.
Squirrels and Squirrel Hunting, by Bob Gooch. Tidewater Publ., Cambridge, MD, 1973. 148 pp., illus. $6.
A complete book for the squirrel hunter, beginner or old hand. Details methods of hunting, squirrel habitat, management, proper clothing, care of the kill, cleaning and cooking.
The Standard Book of Hunting and Shooting, R. B. Stringfellow, ed. 1st ed., in 1950 by the Greystone Press, New York, NY, 564 pp., very well illus. $10.00.
An excellent anthology on hunting in America, giving meaningful information on all major species and on all types of guns, sights, ammunition, etc. An abridgement of the larger *Hunters Encyclopedia.*
Successful Waterfowling, by Zack Taylor, Crown Publ., NY, 1974. 276 pp., illus. $8.95.
The definitive guide to new ways of hunting ducks and geese.
Tales from the Indian Jungle, by Kenneth Anderson, George Allen & Unwin Ltd., London, 1970. 204 pp., illus. $11.95.
Adventures in the pursuit of man-eating tigers and leopards.
Timberdoodle, by Frank Woolner, Crown Publ., Inc., NY, 1974. 168 pp., illus. $7.95.
A thorough, practical guide to the American woodcock and to woodcock hunting.
Topflight; A Speed Index to Waterfowl, by J. A. Ruthven & Wm. Zimmerman, Moebius Prtg. Co., Milwaukee, WI, 1968. 112 pp. $7.50.
Rapid reference for specie identification. Marginal color band of book directs reader to proper section. 263 full color illustrations of body and feather configurations.
Tracks of an Intruder, by Gordon Young. Winchester Press, NY, 1970. 191 pp., illus. $5.95.
Fascinating, first hand account of how an American naturalist gained recognition as a master hunter from the Montagnard Lahu tribesmen of Southeast Asia.
Travel & Adventure in Southeast Africa, by F. C. Selous. A & F Press, N.Y.C., 1967. 522 pp., illus. $27.50.
New edition of a famous African hunting book, first published in 1893.
A Treasury of African Hunting, ed. by Peter Barrett. Winchester Press, NY, 1970. 251 pp., illus. $25.00.
Outstanding accounts by noted writers and experts on African hunting,

covering big game and small in many sections of the continent.
Trouble With Bird Dogs . . . and What to do About Them, by George Bird Evans, Winchester Press, NY, 1976. 288 pp., illus. $10.00.
How to custom-train your dog for specific kinds of hunting.
The Unnatural Enemy, by Vance Bourjaily. The Dial Press, 1963. 182 pp., illus. $2.49.
Beautifully written episodes of bird-hunting.
Upland Bird & Waterfowl Hunting, ed. by Dave Petzal, Simon & Schuster, NY, 1976. 315 pp., illus. $9.95.
A collection of stories by an outstanding panel of knowledgeable experts on the subject.
The Upland Game Hunter's Bible, by Dan Holland. Doubleday, N.Y.C., 1961. 192 pp., illus. paper covers. $2.50.
Hunter's manual on the principal species of American upland game birds and how to hunt them.
Varmint Hunter's Digest, by Jim Dougherty, DBI Books, Inc., Northfield, IL, 1977. 256 pp., illus. Paper covers. $6.95.
The how-to book for varminters.
Wanderings of an Elephant Hunter, by W. D. M. "Karamojo" Bell, K & S Arms Library, Edmond, OK, 1977. A new ed. 188 pp., illus. $11.
A noted elephant hunter's experiences in Africa.
Water Dog. by R. A. Wolters, E. P. Dutton & Co., NY, 1964. 179 pp., illus. $5.95.
Rapid training manual for working retrievers.
Waterfowl in the Marshes, by A. C. Becker Jr. A. S. Barnes and Co., New York, NY, 1969. 155 pp., photographs. $9.95.
A highly informative and practical guide to waterfowl hunting in America.
Wild Fowl Decoys, by Joel Barber. Dover Publ., N.Y.C., 1954. 156 pp., 134 illus., paperbound. $5.00.
A fine work on making, painting, care and use of decoys in hunting, recently reprinted. Full data on design and construction.
The Wild Sheep in Modern North America, a Boone & Crockett Club Book, Book & Crockett Club, Alexandria, VA, 1976. 302 pp., illus. Paper covers. $10.00.
The most comprehensive data on the past, present and future of these unique game animals.
The Wind on Your Cheek, by William J. Schaldach, Freshet Press, Rockville, NY, 1976. 157 pp., illus. $10.95.
Memories of the days spent upland shooting and trout fishing for almost 60 years.
The Young Shot, by Noel M. Sedgwick, A. & C. Black, London, Eng., 1976. 240 pp., illus. $8.95.
A revised and re-illustrated edition of Sedgwick's original work plus a preface and appendix dealing with changes in law since the first ed.

RIFLES

The Accurate Rifle, by Warren Page. Winchester Press, NY, 1973. 256 pp., illus. $8.95.
A masterly discussion. A must for the competitive shooter hoping to win, and highly useful to the practical hunter.
American Rifle Design and Performance, by L. R. Wallack, Winchester Press, NY, 1977. 288 pp., illus. $12.95.
An authoritative, comprehensive guide to how and why every kind of sporting rifle works.
The Bolt Action: A Design Analysis, by Stuart Otteson, Winchester Press, NY, 1976. 320 pp., illus. $12.95.
Precise and in-depth descriptions, illustrations, and comparisons of 16 bolt actions. A new approach.
Bolt Action Rifles, by Frank de Haas, ed. by John T. Amber, Editor of Gun Digest. DBI Books, Inc., Northfield, IL, 1971. 320 pp., illus. Paper, $7.95.
The definitive work, covering every major design since the Mauser of 1871.
The Book of the Garand, by Maj.-Gen. J. S. Hatcher, The Gun Room Press, Highland Park, NJ, 1977. 292 pp., illus. $11.95.
A new printing of the standard reference work on the U.S. Army M1 rifle.
The Book of Rifles, by W. H. B. Smith. Stackpole Books, Harrisburg, PA, 1963 (3rd ed.). 656 pp., profusely illus. $6.98.
An encyclopedic reference work on shoulder arms, recently up-dated. Includes rifles of all types, arranged by country of origin.
The Breech-Loading Single-Shot Match Rifle, by N. H. Roberts and K. L. Waters, D. Van Nostrand Co., Princeton, NJ, 1967. 293 pp., illus. $25.
Account of the Schuetzen rifle in America, with material on famous shooting gunsmiths, ammunition and related topics.
Browning Automatic Rifles, Normount Armament Co., Wickenburg, AZ, 81 pp., illus. Paper, $3.00.
Reprint of Ordnance Manual TM 9-1211, on all types of caliber 30's.
Carbines Cal. .30 M1, M1A1, M2 and M3, by D. B. McLean. Normount Armament Co., Wickenburg, AZ, 1964. 221 pp., well illus., paperbound. $5.95.
U.S. field manual reprints on these weapons, edited and reorganized.
Competitive Rifle Shooting, by James Sweet, Fortress Publ., Stoney Creek, Ontario, Canada, 1978. 120 pp., illus. Stiff card covers. $6.95.
The accepted textbook on target shooting and bedding of target rifles.
Description and Instructions for the Management of the Gallery-Practice Rifle Caliber .22—Model of 1903. Inco., 1972. 12 pp., 1 plate. Paper, $1.00.
Reprint of 1907 War Dept. pamphlet No. 1925.
Description of Telescopic Musket Sights, Inco, 1972. 10 pp., 4 plates. Paper, $1.00.
Reprint of 1917 War Dept. pamphlet No. 1957, first publ. in 1908.
The First Winchester, by John E. Parsons. Winchester Press, New York, NY, 1977. 207 pp., well illus., $14.95.
This new printing of *The Story of the 1866 Repeating Rifle* (1st publ. 1955) is revised, and additional illustrations included.
A Forgotten Heritage; The Story of a People and the Early American Rifle, by Harry P. Davis, The Gun Room Press, Highland Park, NJ, 1976. 199 pp., illus. $9.95.
Reprint of a very scarce history, originally published in 1941, the Kentucky rifle and the people who used it.
Garand Rifles M1, M1C, M1D, by Donald B. McLean. Normount Armament Co., Wickenburg, AZ, 1968. Over 160 pp., 175 illus., paper wrappers. $5.95.
Covers all facets of the arm: battlefield use, disassembly and maintenance, all details to complete lock-stock-and-barrel repair, plus variations, grenades, ammo., and accessories; plus a section on 7.62mm NATO conventions.
The Golden Age of Single-Shot Rifles, by James Edsall, Pioneer Press, Union City, TN, 1975. 33 pp., illus. Paper covers. $2.75.
A detailed look at all of the fine, high quality sporting single-shot rifles that were once the favorite of target shooters.
Guns Annual Book of Rifles, ed. by Jerome Rakusan, Publishers Development Corp., Skokie, IL, 1974. 102 pp., illus., paper covers. $2.00.
Complete catalog listing plus feature articles on benchrest rifles, reloading, etc.
How to Select and Use Your Big Game Rifle, by Henry M. Stebbins, Combat Forces Press, Washington, 1952. 237 pp., illus. $6.50.
Concise valuable data on rifles, old and new—slide action, lever, semi automatic, and single shot models are covered.
The Hunting Rifle, by Jack O'Connor. Winchester Press, NY, 1970. 352 pp., illus. $8.95.
An analysis, with wit and wisdom, of contemporary rifles, cartridges, accessories and hunting techniques.
The Improved American Rifle, by John R. Chapman, Beinfeld Publ., Inc., No. Hollywood, CA, 1976. 160 pp., illus. $5.95.
A facsimile reprint of the scarce 1848 edition, the earliest book on precision rifle shooting.
John Olson's Book of the Rifle, by John Olson, J. Philip O'Hara, Inc., Chicago, IL, 1974. 256 pp., illus. Paper covers. $6.95.
Rifle data "A to Z"—barrels, actions, stocks, calibers, cartidges, ballistics, scopes, mounts, metallic sights, handloading, gunsmithing, muzzleloading.
Know Your M1 Garand, by E. J. Hoffschmidt, Blacksmith Corp., Stamford, CT, 1975. 84 pp., illus. Paper Covers. $3.95.
Facts about America's most famous infantry weapon. Covers test and experimental models, Japanese and Italian copies, National Match models.
Maynard Catalog of 1880, a reprint in facsimile by the Rocky Mountain Investment and Antique Co.; Cheyenne, WY, 1969. 32 pp., illus., paper covers. $3.00.
All models, sights, cartridges, targets etc.
Modern Breech-Loaders, Sporting and Military, by W. W. Greener, with intro. by D. B. McLean. Normount Tech. Publ., Wickenburg, AZ, 1971. 256 pp., illus. Paper covers. $5.95.
Reprint of the 1870 ed. Covers rifles, carbines, and the "new" breechloading pistols.
Same title, this is a reprint of the 1871 ed. Lujac Publ., Pueblo, CO, 1972. 275 pp., illus. $5.95.
The Modern Rifle, by Jim Carmichel, Winchester Press, NY, 1975. 320 pp., illus. $12.95.
The most comprehensive, thorough, up-to-date book ever published on today's rifled sporting arms.
The Ninety-Nine, by Douglas P. Murray, Doug Murray, Westbury, Long Island, NY, 1977. 100 pp., illus. $15.
The first collectors reference book on the Savage 99. Detailed descriptions of all 28 versions.
100 Years of Shooters and Gunmakers of Single Shot Rifles, by Gerald O. Kelver, Brighton, CO, 1975. 212 pp., illus. Paper covers $7.50.
The Schuetzen rifle, targets and shooters, primers, match rifles, original loadings and much more. With chapters on famous gunsmiths like Harry Pope, Morgan L. Rood and others.
The Pennsylvania Rifle, by Samuel E. Dyke, Sutter House, Lititz, PA, 1975. 61 pp., illus. Paper covers. $3.00.
History and development, from the hunting rifle of the Germans who settled the area. Contains a full listing of all known Lancaster, PA gunsmiths from 1729 through 1815.
Pictorial History of the Rifle, By G. W. P. Swenson. Ian Allan Ltd., Shepperton, Surrey, England, 1971. 184 pp., illus. $9.50.
Essentially a picture book, with over 200 rifle illustrations. The text furnishes a concise history of the rifle and its development.
Position Rifle Shooting, by Bill Pullum and F. T. Hanenkrat. Winchester Press, NY, 1973. 256 pp., illus. $10.00.
The single most complete statement of rifle shooting principles and techniques, and the means of learning, teaching and using them, ever to appear in print.
The Revolving Rifles, by James Edsall, Pioneer Press, Union City, TN, 1975. 23 pp., illus. Paper covers. $2.50.
Valuable information on revolving cylinder rifles, from the earliest matchlock forms to the latest models of Colt and Remington.
The Rifle Book, by Jack O'Connor, Random House, NY, 1978. 337 pp., illus. $13.95.
The complete book of small game, varmint and big game rifles.
The Rifle: and How to Use it, by H. Busk, Richmond Publ. Co., Richmond, England, 1971. 225 pp., illus. $9.00.
Reprint of the 1859 ed. Covers mid-19th century military rifles.
Rifles AR15, M16, and M16A1, 5.56 mm, by D. B. McLean. Normount Armament Co., Wickenburg, AZ, 1968. Unpaginated, illus., paper covers. $5.95.
Descriptions, specifications and operation of subject models are set forth in text and picture.
Rifles: A Modern Encyclopedia, by Henry M. Stebbins, Castle Books, NY, 1976. 376 pp., illus. $5.98.
An excellently prepared work covering rifles for every use.
Schuetzen Rifles, History and Loading, by Gerald O. Kelver, Gerald O. Kelver, Publisher, Brighton, CO, 1972. Illus. $5.00.
Reference work on these rifles, their bullets, loading, telescopic sights, accuracy, etc. A limited, numbered ed.
Shooting the Percussion Rifle, by R. O. Ackerman. Publ. by the author, Albuquerque, N.M., 1966. 19 pp., illus. in line by the author. Paper wrappers, $1.50.
This well prepared work is Book No. 2 of a projected series. This one gives basic information on the use of the muzzle-loading rifle.
Single Shot Rifles and Actions, by Frank de Haas, ed. by John T. Amber, DBI Books, Northfield, IL, 1969. 352 pp., illus. $8.95.
The definitive book on over 60 single shot rifles and actions. Covers history, parts photos, design and construction, etc.
Sir Charles Ross and His Rifle, by Robt. Phillips and J. J. Knap, Museum Restoration Service, Ottawa, Canada., 1969. 32 pp., illus. Paper covers. $2.00.
The story of the man who invented the "Ross Model 1897 Magazine Sporting Rifle," the 1900 under the name of Bennett, and many others.
Small Bore Target Shooting, by H. G. B. Fuller. Herbert Jenkins, London, 1964. 264 pp., well illus. $10.00.
Authoritative English work, covering rifle types, buying hints, ammunition, accessories, and range technique.
Sniper Rifles of Two World Wars, by W. H. Tantum IV. Museum Restoration Service, Ottawa, Can., 1967. 32 pp., illus. $2.00.

Monograph on high-accuracy rifles used by troops in world wars I and II and in Korea. Paper wrappers.

The Target Rifle in Australia 1860-1900, by J. E. Corcoran, The Dolphin Press, Lane Cove, N.S.W., Australia, 1975. 223 pp., illus. $23.00.

The first book which attempts to gather together the history of Australian rifle shooting. Covers muzzle-loading and breech-loading rifles.

Target Rifle Shooting, by E. G. B. Reynolds & Robin Fulton. Barrie & Jenkins, London, Eng., 1972. 200 pp., illus. $9.50.

For the novice and intermediate shooter who wants to learn the basics needed to become a rifle marksman.

The .22 Rifle, by Dave Petzal. Winchester Press, NY, 1972. 244 pp., illus. $6.95.

All about the mechanics of the .22 rifle. How to choose the right one, how to choose a place to shoot, what makes a good shot, the basics of small-game hunting.

United States Rifle, Cal. .30, Model of 1917, a reprint of an official government booklet by Normount Publ. Co., Wickenburg, AZ, 1969. 80 pp., line illus., paper covers. $2.00.

A training manual issued by the War Department in 1918. A much-wanted and useful booklet.

United States Rifle 7.62 mm, M14 and M14E2, a reprint of an official government booklet by Anubus Press, Houston, TX, 1968. 50 pp., illus., paper covers. $3.00.

U.S. Army Field Manual 23-8, first published in 1965.

The Winchester 1873 Handbook, by George W. Stone, Frontier Press, Arvada, CO, 1973. 137 pp., illus., a limited numbered ed. $18.95.

A definitive study of the Model 1873 Winchester. Covers the technical, mechanical and historical aspects of the gun.

Winchester '73 & '76, the First Repeating Center-Fire Rifles, by D. F. Butler. Winchester Press, New York, NY, 1st ed., 1970. 95 pp., well and tastefully illus. in line, halftones and photos. Color frontispiece. $7.95.

A complete history of the subject arms and their then-new ammunition, plus details of their use on America's western frontiers.

Wonderful World of the .22, by John Lachuk, et al, Petersen Publ. Co., Los Angeles, CA, 1972. 192 pp., illus., paper covers. $3.95.

Complete cataloging of .22 rifles and handguns—prices, specifications.

shotguns

The American Shotgun, by David F. Butler. A & W Books, NY, 1973. 256 pp. Paper covers. $6.95.

Authoritive and profusely illus. Traces the entire evolution of the American shotgun and modern American shotshells.

American Shotgun Design and Performance, by L. R. Wallack, Winchester Press, NY, 1977. 184 pp., illus. $13.95.

An expert lucidly recounts the history and development of American shotguns and explains how they work.

The Art of Wing Shooting, by William Bruce Leffingwell, The Abercrombie & Fitch Library, Arno Press, NY, 1967. 190 pp., illus. $10.00.

A facsimile reprint first published in 1894. a Still regarded by experts as one of the few truly outstanding books in its field.

1909 Baker Gun Catalog, reprinted by Ronald Frodelius, Fayetteville, NY, 1976. 20 pp., illus. Paper covers. $2.95.

A facsimile reprint of a scarce old Baker Arms Co. catalog.

Clay Pigeon Marksmanship, by Percy Stanbury and G. L. Carlisle. Herbert Jenkins, London, 1964. 216 pp., illus. $7.50.

Handbook on learning the skills, with data on guns & equipment and competition shooting at all types of clay targets; by two eminent British writers.

1894 Parker Shotgun Catalog, originally published by Parker Bros., Meriden, CT, a reprint by Beinfeld Publ. Co., No. Hollywood, CA, 1976. 36 pp., illus. $27.95.

A limited ed. reprint of the most deluxe Parker shotgun catalog ever produced. Photographed from the only known original copy extant of this important reference.

The Fowler in Ireland, by Sir Ralph Payne-Gallwey, Richmond Publ. Co., Richmond, England, 1971. 503 pp., illus. $17.50.

Reprint of the 1882 work on wildfowling and wildlife in Ireland.

The Golden Age of Shotgunning, by Bob Hinman, Winchester Press, NY, 1971. 175 pp., illus. $8.95.

The story of American shotgun and wingshooting from 1870 to 1900.

Gough Thomas's Gun Book, by G. T. Garwood. A. & C. Black, London, England, 1969. 160 pp., illus. $8.95.

Excerpts of articles on the shotgun published in *Shooting Times,* by a noted British authority. Wide-ranging survey of every aspect on the shotgun, its use, behavior, care, and lore.

Gunning the Chesapeake, by Roy E. Walsh, Tidewater Publishers, Cambridge, MD, 1971. 117 pp., illus. $7.00.

Duck and goose shooting on the Eastern Shore.

High Pheasants, by Sir Ralph Payne-Gallwey, Richmond Publ. Co., Richmond, England, 1970. 79 pp. $9.90.

The first and last word on its subject.

History and Catalog of Holland & Holland Ltd., distributed by Service Armament Co., Ridgefield, NJ, 1977. 144 pp., illus. Paper covers. $24.95.

A folio containing a reprint of the Holland & Holland 72 page catalog of 1912, together with a 72-page book describing the Holland & Holland gun collection and the history of this famous firm of gunmakers.

How to be a Winner Shooting Skeet & Trap, by Tom Morton, Tom Morton, Knoxville, MD, 1974. 144 pp., illus. Paper covers. $8.95.

The author explains why championship shooting is more than a physical process.

John Olson's Book of the Shotgun, by John Olson, J. Philip O'Hara, Inc., Chicago, IL, 1975. 256 pp., illus. Paper covers. $6.95; cloth, $10.95.

Covers all phases, from design and manufacture to field use and performance.

The Mysteries of Shotgun Patterns, by Geo. G. Oberfell and Chas. E. Thompson, Oklahoma State University Press, Stillwater, OK, Xerox edition, 1978. 328 pp. Paper covers. $20.00.

Shotgun ballistics for the hunter in non-technical language, with information on improving effectiveness in the field.

New England Grouse Shooting, by W. H. Foster, Chas. Scribner's, NY, 193 pp., illus. $12.50.

Many interesting and helpful points on how to hunt grouse.

The New Wildfowler in the 1970's by N. M. Sedgwick, et al. Barrie & Jenkins, London, Eng., 1970. 375 pp., illus. $11.50.

A compendium of articles on wildfowling, hunting practices and conservation. An updated reprint.

Parker, America's Finest Shotgun, by P. H. Johnson. Outlet Book Co., Inc., NY, 1968. 260 pp., illus. $4.95.

An account of a great sporting arm—from post Civil War until 1947, when it was sold to Remington. Values, models, etc.

Parker Brother Gun Catalog, 1869. B. Palmer, Tyler, TX, 1972. 14 pp., illus. Paper covers. $4.

Facsimile of Charles Parker's first issued catalog on "Parker Breech-Loading Shot Guns."

Parker Guns Catalog 1930, a reprint, by Guns Unlimited, Salt Lake City, UT, 1973. 32 pp., illus., paper covers. $4.95.

Facsimile reprint showing all models, including the Parker single barrel trap gun.

A fundamental examination of the company, grades and types of guns as well as catalog photos, reloading tools, accessories and more than 100 photos of Parker guns.

The Parker Gun: An Immortal American Classic, Vol. 1, by Larry L. Baer, Beinfeld, Publ., Inc., North Hollywood, CA, 1974. 93 pp., illus. $12.95.

Primarily intended for the collector, and will aid him in buying, selling, and obtaining maximum satisfaction in owning and identifying Parkers.

The Parker Gun: An Immortal American Classic, Vol. 2, by Larry L. Baer, Beinfeld Publ., Inc., No. Hollywood, CA, 1977. 148 pp., illus. $15.95.

Beautifully printed and bound, this is primarily a photographic study with more than 150 Parker illus., several in full color.

Pigeon Shooting, by Archie Coates, Andre Deutsch Ltd., London, England, 1975. 142 pp., illus. $8.95.

Helpful and practical advice on every facet of the sport.

The Police Shotgun Manual, by Robert H. Robinson, Charles C. Thomas, Springfield, IL 1973. 153 pp., illus. $10.50.

A complete study and analysis of the most versatile and effective weapon in the police arsenal.

Rough Shooting, by G. A. Gratten & R. Willett. Faber & Faber, London, Eng., 1968. 242 pp., illus. $6.75.

The art of shooting, dogs and their training, games, rearing and their diseases, proof marks, etc.

Score Better at Skeet, by Fred Missildine, with Nick Karas. Winchester Press, NY, 1972. 160 pp., illus. $5.95. In paper covers, $2.95.

The long-awaited companion volume to *Score Better at Trap.*

Score Better at Trap, by Fred Missildine. Winchester Press, NY, 1971. 192 pp., illus. $5.95. In paper covers, $2.95.

Step-by-step instructions, fully illustrated, on mastering the game by one of the world's leading coaches.

Score Better at Trap and Skeet, by Fred Missildine, with Nick Karas, Winchester Press, NY, 1978. 352 pp., illus. $10.95.

It's like having personal trap and Skeet lessons from Fred Missildine himself.

75 Years with the Shotgun, by C. T. (Buck) Buckman, Valley Publ., Fresno, CA, 1974. 141 pp., illus. $5.95.

An expert hunter and trapshooter shares experiences of a lifetime.

The Shotgun, by T. D. S. & J. A. Purdey. A. & C. Black, London, Eng., 1969. 144 pp., illus. with Photos and diagrams. $7.50.

Reprinted 4th ed. of a well-known British work by two members of the notable gunsmith family. Covers the gun and its use in the field, at traps, and for skeet.

The Shotgun Book, by Jack O'Connor. Alfred A. Knopf, NY, 1965. 332 pp., plus index, illus. with line and photos. $15.00.

The definitive, authoritative book with up-to-date chapters on wild-fowling, upland gunning, trap and Skeet shooting. It includes practical advice on shotgun makes, models and functions, as well as data on actions.

Shotgun Digest, by Robert Stack, Digest Books, Inc., Northfield, IL. 1974. 8½"x11", 288 pp. Profusely illus. Paperbound. $6.95.

Movie star Robert Stack is a National Skeet Shooting Hall of Famer and an outstanding shotgunner. He covers all aspects of shotguns and shotgun shooting.

Shotgun and Shooter, by G. Carlisle and P. Stanbury, Barrie & Jenkins, London, 1970. 217 pp., illus. $7.95.

On guns, wildfowling, dog training, decoys, safety, etc.

Shotgun Marksmanship, by P. Stanbury & G. L. Carlisle. A. S. Barnes & Co., NY, 1969. 224 pp., illus. $8.95.

A new and revised edition for beginners, veterans, skeet shooters, hunters, etc. Valuable tips on improving marksmanship, etc.

The Shotgunner's Bible, by George Laycock. Doubleday & Co., Garden City, NY, 1969. 173 pp., illus., paper covers. $2.50.

Coverage of shotguns, ammunition, marksmanship, hunting of various types of game, care and safety, etc.

Shotgunning: The Art and the Science, by Bob Brister, Winchester Press, NY, 1976. 321 pp., illus. $10.

Hundreds of specific tips and truly novel techniques to improve the field and target shooting of every shotgunner.

Shotguns & Cartridges, by Gough Thomas. A. & C. Black, London, Eng., 1975. 254 pp., illus. $15.00.

A thoroughly revised and updated book on the understanding of modern guns and cartridges for clay pigeon and game shooting.

Shotguns and Shooting, by A. J. Barker, Paladin Press, Boulder, CO., 1973. 84 pp., illus., paper covers. $2.50.

All about shotguns and their use in shooting and hunting.

Shotguns & Shooting, by E. S. McCawley, Jr., Van Nostrand Reinhold Co., NY, 1965. 146 pp., illus. Paper covers. $4.95.

Covers the history and development, types of shotguns and ammunition, shotgun shooting, etc.

Skeet Shooting with D. Lee Braun, Robt. Campbell, ed. Grosset & Dunlap, NY, 1967. 160 pp., illus. Paper covers. $2.95.

Thorough instructions on the fine points of Skeet shooting.

L. C. Smith Shotguns, by Wm. S. Brophy, Beinfeld Publ., Inc., No. Hollywood, CA, 1977. 200 pp., illus. $24.95.

The first work ever on this important American gun and company. The original factory records form an authenticating basis for this comprehensive study.

Successful Shotgun Shooting, by A. A. Montague. Winchester Press, NY, 1970. 160 pp., illus. $6.95.

The work of a superb shot and a great teacher; even the experts can read with profit.

Trapshooting with D. Lee Braun and the Remington Pros., ed. by R. Campbell. Remington Arms Co., Bridgeport, CT, 1969. 157 pp., well illus., Paper covers. $3.95.

America's masters of the scattergun give the secrets of professional marksmanship.

Wing & Shot, by R. G. Wehle, Country Press, Scottsville, NY, 1967. 190 pp., illus. $8.50.

Step-by-step account on how to train a fine shooting dog.

Lightner Reprints

The following titles come from the Lightner Library Coll., Cocoa Beach, Fla. All have paper covers, all were publ. in 1973.

Baker Gun Catalog, 1915. 7 pp., illus. $2.00.
Facsimile showing all grades including deluxe.

Browning Arms Co. Catalog, 1935. 18 pp., illus. $4.00.
Facsimile reprint showing first superposed models and grades.

Charles Daly (Prussian) Catalog, ca. 1930. 24 pp., illus. $4.00.
Facsimile catalog showing Regent and Diamond grades, over-unders, 3-barrel trap models.

A. H. Fox (Original factory) Catalog, ca. 1910. 20 pp., illus. $4.00.
Facsimile of the first Fox catalog.

A. H. Fox Gun Co. Catalog, 1923. 40 pp., illus. $4.00.
Facsimile of the 1923 catalog. All models and grades including single barrel trap models, and information on the Fox-Kautsky single trigger.

A. H. Fox Gun Catalog, ca. 1936. 24 pp., illus. $4.95.
Facsimile showing all models and prices.

Ithaca Gun Co. Catalog, 1915. 25 pp., illus. $4.00.
Facsimile reprint of a large format catalog. Shows hammerless models.

D. M. Lefever (Bowling Green, Ohio) Catalog, 1905. 20 pp., illus. $4.00.
Facsimile of probably the rarest of all shotgun catalogs.

Lefever Arms Catalog, 1892. 32 pp., illus. $4.00.
Facsimile of a very rare catalog.

Lefever Arms Catalog, 1913. 32 pp., illus. $5.95.
Facsimile giving details on "Thousand Dollar Grade."

The Parker Gun Catalog, 1908. 32 pp., illus. $5.95.
Facsimile showing models A-1 Special through PH grades.

The Parker Gun Catalog, 1926. 32 pp., illus. $6.00.
Facsimile showing Invincible to Trojan, including P grades.

The Parker Gun Catalog, 1934. 15 pp., illus. $3.00.
Facsimile of the last catalog issued by the original Parker Bros. Company.

The Parker Gun Catalog, 1937. 34 pp., illus. $17.50.
Facsimile of the 1937 catalog, publ. by the Parker Gun Works, Remington Arms Co., Inc. Their largest, most beautiful and last regular catalog issued. The only one displaying all Parker trap and Skeet models.

The Parker Gun Dealer's Illustrated Price Catalog, 1940. 8 pp., illus. $3.00.
Last wholesale and retail price catalog issued by Parker Gun Works.

Remington Arms Co. Catalog, 1910. 62 pp., illus. $4.00.
Facsimile showing all double barreled models, including special 750 grade, autos, rifles, parts.

Remington Arms Co. Catalog, 1932. 32 pp., illus. $3.00.
Facsimile of first catalog showing the Model 32 over/under shotgun.

L.C. Smith (Hunter Arms Co.) Catalog, 1892. 24 pp., illus. $5.00.
Facsimile showing first hammerless models.

L.C. Smith (Hunter Arms Co.) Catalog, 1907. 34 pp., $5.95.
Facsimile of a large, beautifully illus. catalog. Shows early hammerless models, parts and prices.

L.C. Smith (Hunter Arms Co.) Catalog, 1918. 24 pp., illus. $4.95.
Facsimile reprint showing all hammerless models and prices.

Winchester Firearms Co. Catalog, 1933. 61 pp., illus. $3.00.
Facsimile showing first Model 21 double barrel shotguns, including Skeet and tournament trap grader.

Winchester Model 21 Catalog. 33 pp., illus. $4.95.
Facsimile of a special post-war catalog.

IMPORTANT NOTICE TO BOOK BUYERS

Books listed above may be bought from Ray Riling Arms Books Co., 6844 Gorsten St., P.O. Box 18925, Phila., PA, 19119. Joe Riling, the proprietor, is the researcher and compiler of "The Arms Library" and a seller of gun books for over 30 years.

The Riling stock includes the books classic and modern, many hard-to-find items, and many not obtainable elsewhere. The above pages list a portion of the current stock. They offer prompt, complete service, with delayed shipments occurring only on out-of-print or out-of-stock books.

NOTICE FOR ALL CUSTOMERS: Remittance in U.S. funds must accompany all orders. For U.S. add 50¢ per book with a minimum of $1.00 per order for postage and insurance. For UPS add 50% to mailing costs.

All foreign countries add 75¢ per book for postage and handling, plus $2.10 per 10-lb. package or under for safe delivery by registered mail. Parcels not registered are sent at the "buyers risk."

Payments in excess of order or for "Backorders" are credited or fully refunded at request. Books "As-Ordered" are not returnable except by permission and a handling charge on these of $1.00 per book is deducted from refund or credit. Only Pennsylvania customers must include current sales tax.

Full variety of arms books are also available from Rutgers Book Center, 127 Raritan Ave., Highland Park, NJ 08904.

R. H. DEVEREAUX
Stock is fancy screwbean mesquite, the 270 barrel by Douglas on a pre-'64 Model 70 action, all metal and wood work by RHD. With scope and sling, only 7 lbs. 2 oz.

WALTER S. ABE
This unusual rifle is a M2/22 LR Springfield stocked in California English walnut, fleur de lis and ribbon checkered. A '98 floorplate covers the rimfire magazine.

PERIODICAL PUBLICATIONS

Alaska Magazine
Alaska Northwest Pub. Co., Box 4-EEE, Anchorage, AK 99509. $15.00 yr. Hunting and fishing articles.

The American Blade*
Beinfeld Publishing, Inc., 13222 Saticoy St., No. Hollywood, CA 91605. $7.50 yr. Add $1 f. foreign subscription. A magazine for all enthusiasts of the edged blade.

American Field†
222 W. Adams St., Chicago, IL. 60606. $10.00 yr. Field dogs and trials, occasional gun and hunting articles.

American Firearms Industry
Nat'l. Assn. of Federally Licensed Firearms Dealers, 7001 No. Clark St., Chicago, IL 60626. $10 yr. For firearms dealers & distributors.

The American Handgunner
591 Camino de la Reina, San Diego, CA 92108. $9.95 yr. Articles for handgun enthusiasts, collectors and hunters.

The American Hunter (M)
Natl. Rifle Assn., 1600 Rhode Island Ave. N.W., Washington, DC 20036. $7.50 yr.

The American Rifleman (M)
National Rifle Assn., 1600 Rhode Island Ave., N.W., Wash., DC 20036. $15.00 yr. Firearms articles of all kinds.

The American Shotgunner
P.O. Box 3351, Reno, NV 89505. $12.00 yr. Shotgun articles of all kinds.

The American West*
Amer. West Publ. Co., 20380 Town Center Lane, Suite 160, Cupertino, CA 95014. $12.00 yr.

Arms Gazette
Beinfeld Publ., Inc., 13222 Saticoy St., No. Hollywood, CA 91605. $12.00 yr.; add $3 foreign subscr. Excellent brief articles for the collector of antique and modern firearms.

Australian Shooters' Journal
GPO Box 1064, Adelaide 5000, Australia. $12.00 yr. locally; $15.00 yr. overseas. Hunting and shooting articles.

Black Powder Times
P.O. Box 842, Mount Vernon, WA 98273. $8.00 for 12 issues.

Canada GunSport
P.O. Box 201, Willowdale, Ont., Canada M2N 2S9. $7 yr. Articles on guns, hunting, shooting, plus gun ads of all kinds.

Canadian Journal of Arms Collecting
Museums Restoration Service P.O. Drawer 390, Bloomfield, Ont., Canada KOK IGO. $5.00 yr.

Deer Unlimited*
P.O. Box 509, Clemson, SC 29631. $12.00 yr.

Deutsches Waffen Journal
Journal-Verlag Schwend GmbH, Postfach 340, D7170 Schwabisch Hall, Germany. DM48.00 yr. Antique and modern arms. German text.

Ducks Unlimited, Inc. (M)
P.O. Box 66300, Chicago, IL 60666.

Enforcement Journal (Q)
Natl. Police Officers Assn., 14600 S. Tamiami Trail, N.P., Venice, FL 33595. $6.00 yr.

The Field†
The Harmsworth Press Ltd., 8 Stratton St., London W.I., England. $40.80 yr. Hunting and shooting articles, and all country sports.

Field & Stream
CBS Publications, 383 Madison Ave., New York, N.Y. 10017. $7.95 yr. Articles on firearms plus hunting and fishing.

Fur-Fish-Game
A. R. Harding Pub. Co., 2878 E. Main St., Columbus, OH 43209. $5.00 yr. "Gun Rack" column by M. H. Decker.

Gray's Sporting Journal*
Gray's Sporting Journal Co., 7 Garden St., Marion, OH 43302. $18.00 f. 7 Issues. Hunting and fishing journals.

The Gun Report
World Wide Gun Report, Inc., Box 111, Aledo, IL 61231. $12.00 yr. For the gun collector.

The Gunrunner Newspaper
Kexco Publ. Co. Ltd., P.O. Box 565, Lethbridge, Alb., Canada T1J 3Z4. $5.00 yr. Gun ads of all kinds.

Gun Week
Amos Press, Inc., P.O. Box 150, Sidney, OH 45367. $9.00 yr. U.S. and possessions; $14.00 yr. other countries. Tabloid paper on guns, hunting, shooting.

Gun World
Gallant Publishing Co., 34249 Camino Capistrano, Capistrano Beach, CA 92624. $8.00 yr. For the hunting, reloading and shooting enthusiast.

Guns & Ammo
Petersen Pub. Co., 8490 Sunset Blvd., Los Angeles, CA 90069. $10.95 yr. Guns, shooting, and technical articles.

Guns
Guns Magazine, 591 Camino de la Reina, San Diego, CA 92108. $11.95 yr. Articles for gun collectors, hunters and shooters.

Guns Review
Ravenhill Pub. Co. Ltd., Standard House, Bonhill St., London E.C. 2A 4DA, England. $14.00 USA & Canada yr. For collectors and shooters.

The Handgunner (M)
U.S. Revolver Assn., 59 Alvin St., Springfield, MA 01104. $5.00 yr. General handgun and competition articles.

Handloader*
Wolfe Pub. Co. Inc., Box 3030, Prescott, AZ 86302 $7.75 yr. The journal of ammunition reloading.

Hobbies
Lightner Pub. Co., 1006 S. Michigan Ave., Chicago, IL 60605. $7.00 yr.; Canada $8.50; foreign $9.50. Collectors departments.

International Shooting Sport*
Union Internationale de Tir, 62 Wiesbaden, Webergasse 7, Germany. (Deutsche Mark) DM23.00 yr., p.p. For the International target shooter.

The Journal of the Arms & Armour Society (M)
F. Wilkinson (Secy.), 40 Great James St., Holborn, London WC1, N 3HB, England. $4.00 yr. Articles for the collector.

Journal of the Historial Breechloading Smallarms Assn.
Publ. annually, Imperial War Museum, Lambeth Road, London SE1 6HZ, England. $7 yr. Articles for the collector plus mailings of lecture transcripts, short articles on specific arms, reprints, etc.

Knife World
Knife World, Inc., P.O. Box 3395, Knoxville, TN 37917. $7.00 yr. The market place for knives.

Law and Order
Law and Order Magazine, 37 W. 38th St., New York, NY 10018. $9.00 yr. Articles on weapons for law enforcement, etc.

Muzzle Blasts (M)
National Muzzle Loading Rifle Assn. P.O. Box 67, Friendship, IN 47021. $10.00 yr. For the black powder shooter.

The Muzzleloader*
Rebel Publishing Co., Inc., P.O. Box 6072, Texarkana, TX 75501. $7.50 yr. The publication for black powder shooters.

National Parks & Conservation Magazine
Natl. Parks & Conservation Assn., 1701 18th St., NW, Washington, DC 20009. $12 yr.

National Rifle Assn. Journal (British)
Natl. Rifle Assn. (BR.), Bisley Camp, Brookwood, Woking, Surrey, England. GU24 OPB.

National Wildlife*
Natl. Wildlife Fed., 1412 16th St. N.W., Washington, DC 20036. $7.50 yr. (6 issues); *International Wildlife*, 6 issues, $7.50 yr. Both, $12.50 yr., plus membership benefits.

New Zealand Wildlife (Q)
New Zealand Deerstalkers Assoc. Inc., P.O. Box 6514, Wellington, N.Z. $2.00 U.S. and Canada, elsewhere on application. Hunting and shooting articles.

National Defense (M)*
American Defense Preparedness Assn., 819 Union First Bank, Wash., DC 20005. $12.00 yr. Articles on military-related topics, including weapons, materials, technology, management and policy.

Outdoor Life
Times Mirror Magazines, Inc., 380 Madison Ave., New York, NY 10017. $7.94 yr. Shooting columns by Jim Carmichel, and others.

Point Blank
Citizens Committee for the Right to Keep and Bear Arms (sent to contributors) 1601 114th S.E., Suite 151, Bellevue, WA 98004

The Police Marksman (Q)
200 South Hull St., Montgomery, AL 36140. $15.00 yr.

Police Times (M)
1100 N.E. 125th St., No. Miami, Fla. 33161.

Popular Mechanics
Hearst Corp., 224 W. 57th St., New York, NY 10019. $7.97 yr., $13.97 Canada and foreign. Hunting, shooting and camping articles.

Precision Shooting
Precision Shooting, Inc., Box 6, Athens, PA 18810. $6.00 yr. Journal of the International Benchrest Shooters and target shooting in general.

Rifle*
Wolfe Publishing Co. Inc., Box 3030, Prescott, AZ 86302. $7.75 yr. Journal of the NBRSA. The magazine for shooters.

Saga
Gambi Publ., 333 Johnson Ave., Brooklyn, N.Y. 11026. $6.00 yr. U.S.

Second Amendment Reporter
Second Amendment Fdn., Bellefield Off. Pk., 1601—114th St. SE, Suite 157, Bellevue, WA 98004. $15.00 yr. (non-contributors).

The Shooting Industry
Publisher's Dev. Corp., 591 Camino de la Reina, San Diego, CA 92108. $25.00 yr.

Shooting Magazine
59A Ilford Lane, Ilford, Essex, England. $15 for 12 issues. Journal catering exclusively for the shotgun enthusiast.

The Shooting Times & Country Magazine (England) †
Cordwallis Estate, Clivemont Rd., Maidenhead, Berksh., England. $30.00 yr. Game shooting, wild fowling, hunting and firearms articles.

Shooting Times
PJS Publications, News Plaza, P.O. Box 1790, Peoria, IL 61656. $9.00 yr. Guns, shooting, reloading; articles on every gun activity.

The Shotgun News‡
Snell Publishing Co., Box 669, Hastings, NB 68901. $7.50 yr. Sample copy $1.00. Gun ads of all kinds.

Shotgun West
2052 Broadway, Santa Monica, CA 90404. $8.00 yr. Trap, Skeet and international shooting, scores, articles, schedules.

The Skeet Shooting Review
National Skeet Shooting Assn., P.O. Box 28188, San Antonio, TX 78228. $12.00 yr. (Assn. membership of $15.00 includes mag.) Scores, averages, skeet and hunting articles.

Sporting Goods Business
Gralla Publications, 1515 Broadway, New York, NY 10036. Trade journal.

The Sporting Goods Dealer
1212 No. Lindbergh Blvd., St. Louis, Mo. 63166. $6.00 yr. The sporting goods trade journal.

Sports Afield
The Hearst Corp., 250 W. 55th St., New York, N.Y. 10019. $15.00 yr. Grits Gresham on firearms, hunting and fishing.

Sports Merchandiser
A.W.R.C. Smith Publication, 1760 Peachtree Rd. NW, Atlanta, GA 30357. Trade Journal.

Trap & Field
1100 Waterway Blvd., Indianapolis, IN 46202. $11.00 yr. Official publ. Amateur Trapshooting Assn. Scores, averages, trapshooting articles.

Turkey Call* (M)
Natl. Wild Turkey Federation, Inc., P.O. Box 467, Edgefield, SC 29824. $7.00 yr. ($10.00 w. membership)

Waterfowler's World*
P.O. Box 38306, Germantown, TN 38138. $5.50 yr.

Wisconsin Sportsman*
Wisconsin Sportsman, Inc., P.O. Box 1307, Oshkosh, WI 54901. $$4.95.

* Published bi-monthly † Published weekly ‡ Published twice per month. All others are published monthly.
M Membership requirements; write for details. Q Published Quarterly.

Shooting Sports Booklets & Pamphlets

Basic Pistol Marksmanship—Textbook for basic pistol courses. 25¢[2]

Basic Rifle Marksmanship—Textbook for basic rifle courses. 25¢ ea.[2]

The Elk—125-page report on the hunting and management of this game animal, more properly called *wapiti*. Extensive biblio. $1.00.[4]

Free Films—Brochure listing outdoor movies available to sportsmen's clubs. Free.[1]

The Gun Law Problem—Information about firearms Legislation. Free.[2]

How to be a Crack Shot—A 14-page booklet detailing everything necessary to becoming an outstanding shot. Free.[3]

Fundamentals of Claybird Shooting—A 39-page booklet explaining the basics of Skeet and trap in non-technical terms. Many diagrams. Free.[4]

Hunter Safety Instructor's Guide—How to conduct an NRA Hunter Safety Course. 25¢ ea.[2]

Hunting and Shooting Sportsmanship—A 4-page brochure defining the "true sportsman" and giving information on the outdoor field. 10¢[1]

Junior Rifle Handbook—Information about the NRA junior program with short instruction course. (25 copies issued to each new affiliated junior club without charge.) 25¢ ea.[2]

NRA Hunter Safety Handbook—Textbook for students. 10¢ ea[2]

National Shooting Preserve Directory—Up-to-date listing of small game preserves in the U.S. and Canada. Free with stamped envelope.[1]

Game, Gunners and Biology—A thumbnail history of American wildlife conservation. 50¢ ea.[4]

Shooting's Fun for Everyone—The why, when, where, and how of riflery for boys and girls. 20 pp. 25¢ ea.[1]

Trap or Skeet Fundamentals—Handbooks explaining fundamentals of these two sports, complete with explicit diagrams to start beginners off right. Free.[3]

25 Foot Shooting Program—Complete information on a short range shooting program with CO_2 and pneumatic rifles and pistols. 35¢[2]

When Your Youngster Wants a Gun—Straightforward answers to the 15 questions most frequently asked by parents. 8 pp. 25¢ ea.[1]

The Cottontail Rabbit—56-page rundown on America's most popular hunting target. Where to find him, how to hunt him, how to help him. Bibliography included. $1.00 ea.[4]

For the Young Hunter—A 32-page booklet giving fundamental information on the sport. Single copies free, 15¢ each in bulk.[4]

Gray and Fox Squirrels—112-page paperbound illustrated book giving full rundown on the squirrel families named. Extensive bibliography. $1.00 ea.[4]

The Mallard—80-page semi-technical report on this popular duck. Life cycle, laws and management, hunting—even politics as they affect this bird—are covered. Bibliography. $1.00 ea.[4]

NRA Booklets—Ranging from 12 to 36 pages, these are articles on specific arms or arms types. Titles available are: Sighting In; The 45 Automatic; The M1 Rifle; Telescopic Sights; Metallic Sights; Duck Hunting; U.S. Cal. 30 Carbine; Remodeling the 03A3; Remodeling the 303 Lee-Enfield; Remodeling the U.S. 1917 Rifle; M1903 Springfield Rifle; Military Rifles and Civil War Small Arms, 50¢ ea. Gun Cabinets, Racks, Cases & Pistol Boxes, 75¢. Deer Hunting, $1.00[2]

Under the heading of "Range Plans" are 15 booklets priced from 10¢ to $1.00. All are described in an order form pamphlet available from the NRA.

NRA Digest of the Federal Gun Control Act of 1968—A 12-page booklet clearly explaining the new law and its provisions. Free to NRA members.[2]

NRA Federal Firearms Laws—A 28-page booklet digesting the several U.S. gun laws affecting the citizen today. Free to NRA members.[2]

NRA Firearms & Ammunition Fact Book—352-page book of questions and answers, ballistic charts and tables, descriptions of firearms and ammunition. NRA, Washington, D.C., 1964. $2.00 ea. ($1.75 to NRA members).

NRA Firearms Assembly Handbook, Volumes I and II—Articles describing the assembly and disassembly of various arms. Vol. I. 160 pp., covers 77 guns, Vol. II, 176 pp., 87 guns. Illustrated with exploded-view and supplementary drawings. NRA, Washington, D.C., 1960 and 1964. $3.50 ea. ($2.50 to NRA members).

NRA Firearms Handling Handbook—21 major articles on the proper useage of most types of small arms available to civilians. Illus. NRA, Washington, D.C., 1962, 80 pp. $2.75 ($1.75 to NRA members).

NRA Gun Collectors Handbook—20 feature articles on all phases of gun collecting, plus a listing of all important museums. NRA, Washington, D.C., 1959. 48 pp., illus. $2.50 ($1.50 to NRA members).

NRA Handloader's Guide—Enlarged & Revised. A successor to the *NRA Illustrated Reloading Handbook,* this excellent new work covers all aspects of metallic-case and shotshell reloading. Washington, D.C., 1969, fully illus. $5.00 (NRA members, $4.00).

NRA Hunters Handbook—51 major pieces, 18 shorter ones. NRA, Washington, D.C., 1960. 72 pp., illus. $3.00 ($2.00 to NRA members).

NRA Illustrated International Shooting Handbook—18 major articles detailing shooting under ISU rules, training methods, etc. NRA, Washington, D.C., 1964. $2.50 ea. ($1.50 to NRA members).

NRA Illustrated Shotgun Handbook—50 articles covering every phase of smoothbore shooting, including exploded views of many shotguns. NRA, Washington, D.C., 1964. 128 pp. $3.00 ea. ($2.00 to NRA members).

NRA Questions and Answers Handbook—150 queries and replies on guns and shooting. NRA, Washington, D.C., 1959. 46 pp. with index, illus. $2.50 ($1.50 to NRA members).

NRA Shooters Guide—40 articles of high interest to shooters of all kinds. Over 340 illus. NRA, Washington, D.C., 1959. 72 pp., $3.00 ($2.00 to NRA members).

NRA Shooting Handbook—83 major articles plus 35 shorts on every phase of shooting. NRA, Washington, D.C., 1961. 224 pp., illus. $4.50 ($3.50 to NRA members).

Principles of Game Management—A 25-page booklet surveying in popular manner such subjects as hunting regulations, predator control, game refuges and habitat restoration. Single copies free, 15¢ each in bulk.[4]

The Ring-Necked Pheasant—Popular distillation of much of the technical literature on the "ringneck." 104-page paperbound book, appropriately illustrated. Bibliography included. $1.00 ea.[4]

Ruffed Grouse, by John Madson—108-page booklet on the life history, management and hunting of *Bonasa umbellus* in its numerous variations. Extensive biblio. $1.00.[4]

How To Start A Gun Club—All of the basic information needed to establish a club with clay bird shooting facilities. 24 pp. $1.00[1]

The White-Tailed Deer—History, management, hunting—a complete survey in this 108-page paperbound book. Full bibliography. $1.00 ea.[4]

Gun Club Booklets—Detailed 25-page booklets on gun club organization, operation and cashiering. Free.[3]

The Hunter and Conservation—An illustrated 25-page booklet that tells what the hunter has done for conservation and wildlife management. 25¢.[1]

Firearms Safety In The Home—A concise, handy reference covering everything you need to know about safe handling and storage of firearms, ammunition and reloading components. 25¢ ea.[1]

Handguns for Sport—A 20-page booklet with sections on selecting a handgun, learning to shoot, where to shoot and handgun hunting. 25¢.[1]

Gun Law Compilation—Includes the regulations issued under the GCA '68, a digest of the act and the complete text of the law. $1.00 ea.[1]

Firearms Prohibition—A logical examination of the arguments used to justify confiscation and the reasons why it won't control crime. 25¢ ea.[1]

Fact Pack II—Authoritative and complete study on gun use and ownership. This is a valuable 102-page reference. $2.00 ea.[1]

---

[1]National Shooting Sports Foundation, Inc. 1075 Post Road, Riverside, Conn. 06878

[2]National Rifle Association of America, 1600 Rhode Island Ave., Washington, D.C. 20036

[3]Remington Arms Company, Dept. C.—Bridgeport, Conn. 06602

[4]Olin Mathieson Conservation Dept., East Alton, Ill. 62024

[5]Winchester-Western, Shotgun Shooting Promotion, 275 Winchester Ave., New Haven, CT 06504

ARMS ASSOCIATIONS

IN

AMERICA AND ABROAD

UNITED STATES

ALABAMA

Alabama Gun Collectors Assn.
Dick Boyd, P.O. Box 5548, Tuscaloosa, AL 35401
North Alabama Gun Coll. Assn.
P.O. Box 564, Huntsville, AL 35804

ALASKA

Alaska Gun Collectors Assn.
Gene Coppedge, P.O. Box 4-1898, Anchorage, AK 99509

ARIZONA

Arizona Gun Collectors Assn., Inc.
Miles S. Vaughn, P.O. Box 1129, Tucson, AZ 85702

CALIFORNIA

Burbank Rifle & Revolver Club, Inc.
P.O. Box 6765, Burbank, CA 91510
Calif. Hunters & Gun Owners Assoc.
V. H. Wacker, 2309 Cipriani Blvd., Belmont, CA 94002
Greater Calif. Arms & Collectors Assn.
Donald L. Bullock, 8291 Carburton St., Long Beach, CA 90808
Los Angeles Gun & Ctg. Collectors Assn.
F. H. Ruffra, 20810 Amie Ave., Torrance, CA 90503
Southern California Arms Collectors Assn.
Chuck Schwartz, 6207 Lindenhurst Ave., Los Angeles, CA 90048

COLORADO

Pikes Peak Gun Collectors Guild
Charles Cell, 406 E. Uintah St., Colorado Springs, CO 80903

CONNECTICUT

Antique Arms Coll. Assn. of Conn.
T. N. Reiley, 17 Philip Rd., Manchester, CT 06040
Stratford Gun Collectors Assn., Inc.
P.O. Box 721, Stratford, CT 06497
Ye Conn. Gun Guild, Inc.
Robert L. Harris, P.O. Box 67, Cornwall Bridge, CT 06754

DELAWARE

Delaware Antique Arms Collectors
C. Landis, 2408 Duncan Rd., Wilmington, DE 19808

GEORGIA

Georgia Arms Collectors
Cecil W. Anderson, P.O. Box 218, Conley, GA 30027

HAWAII

Hawaii Historic Arms Assn.
Roy D. Warren, P.O. Box 1733, Honolulu, HI 96806

IDAHO

Idaho State Rifle and Pistol Assn.
Tom Price, 1621 Lost Ave., Coeur d'Alene, ID 83814

ILLINOIS

Central Illinois Gun Collectors Assn., Inc.
Donald E. Bryan, 20 Book Lane, Jacksonville, IL 62650
Fox Valley Arms Fellowship, Inc.
P.O. Box 301, Palatine, IL 60067
Illinois Deer Hunters Assn.
Terry Jenkins, P.O. Box 96, Girard, IL 62640
Illinois State Rifle Assn.
224 S. Michigan Ave., Room 200, Chicago, IL 60604
Illinois Gun Collectors Assn.
P.O. Box 1694, Kankakee, IL 60901
Little Fort Gun Collectors Assn.
Ernie Robinson, P.O. Box 194, Gurnee, IL 60031
Mississippi Valley Gun & Cartridge Coll. Assn.
Harold S. Parsons, R.R. No. 2, Alexis, IL 61412
Sauk Trail Gun Collectors
Gordell Matson, P.O. Box 645, Milan, IL 61264
Wabash Valley Gun Collectors Assn., Inc.
Mrs. Betty Baer, 1659 N. Franklin St., Danville, IL 61832

INDIANA

Indiana Sportsmen's Council—Legislative
Maurice Latimer, P.O. Box 93, Bloomington, IN 47401
Indiana State Rifle & Pistol Assn.
Thos. Glancy, P.O. Box 552, Chesterton, IN 46304
Northern Indiana Gun Collectors Assn.
James Orsculak, P.O. Box 2651, South Bend, IN 46680
Southern Indiana Gun Collectors Assn., Inc.
Harold M. McClary, 509 N. 3rd St., Boonville, IN 47601

IOWA

Central States Gun Collectors Assn.
Avery Giles, 1104 S. 1st Ave., Marshtown, IA 50158

KANSAS

Four State Collectors Assn.
M. G. Wilkinson, 915 E. 10th, Pittsburg, KS 66762
Kansas Cartridge Coll. Assn.
Bob Linder, Box 84, Plainville, KS 67663
Missouri Valley Arms Collectors Assn.
Chas. F. Samuel, Jr., Box 8204, Shawnee Mission, KS 66208

KENTUCKY

Kentuckiana Arms Coll. Assn.
Tony Wilson, Pres., Box 1776, Louisville, KY 40201
Kentucky Gun Collectors Assn., Inc.
J. A. Smith, Box 64, Owensboro, KY 42301

LOUISIANA

Bayou Gun Club
David J. Seibert, Jr., 2820 Ramsey Dr., New Orleans, LA 70114
Ft. Miro Muzzleloaders
Sandra Rushing, P.O. Box 256, Main St., Grayson, LA 71435.

MARYLAND

Baltimore Antique Arms Assn.
Stanley I. Kellert, R.D. 1, Box 256, Lutherville, MD 21093

MASSACHUSETTS

Bay Colony Weapons Collectors Inc.
Ronald B. Santurjian, 47 Homer Rd., Belmont, MA 02178
Massachusetts Arms Collectors
John J. Callan, Jr., P.O. Box 1001, Worcester, MA 01613

MICHIGAN

Royal Oak Historical Arms Collectors, Inc.
Dee Hamal, P.O. Box 202, Royal Oak, MI 48067

MINNESOTA

Minnesota Weapons Coll. Assn., Inc.
Box 662, Hopkins, MN 55343
Twin Ports Weapons Collectors
Jack Puglisi, 621 W. Central Entrance, Duluth, MN 55807

MISSISSIPPI

Mississippi Gun Collectors Assn.
Mrs. Jack E. Swinney, P.O. Box 1332, Hattiesburg, MS 39401

MISSOURI

Edwardsville, Ill. Gun Collectors
A. W. Stephensmeier, 1055 Warson Woods Dr., St. Louis, MO 63122
Mineral Belt Gun Coll. Assn.
D. F. Saunders, 1110 Cleveland Ave., Monett, MO 65708

MONTANA

Montana Arms Collectors Assn.
Lewis E. Yearout, 308 Riverview Dr. East, Great Falls, MT 59404
The Winchester Arms Coll. Assn.
Lewis E. Yearout, 308 Riverview Dr. East, Great Falls, MT 59404

NEBRASKA

Nebraska Gun & Cartridge Collectors
E. M. Zalud, 710 West 6th St., North Platte, NB 69101

NEW HAMPSHIRE

New Hampshire Arms Collectors Inc.
Frank H. Galeucia, Rte. 28, Box 44, Windham, NH 03087

NEW JERSEY

Englishtown Benchrest Shooters Assn.
Tony Hidalgo, 6 Capp St., Carteret, NJ 07008
Experimental Ballistics Associates
Ed Yard, 110 Kensington, Trenton, NJ 08618
Jersey Shore Antique Arms Collectors
Joe Sisia, P.O. Box 100, Bayville, NJ 08721
New Jersey Arms Collectors Club, Inc.
Angus Laidlaw, 230 Valley Rd., Montclair, NJ 07042

NEW MEXICO

New Mexico Gun Collectors Assn.
Jack Daniels, 3107 Central Ave., NE, Albuquerque, NM 87111

NEW YORK

Hudson-Mohawk Arms Collectors Assn., Inc.
Bennie S. Pisarz, 6 Lamberson St., Dolgeville, NY 13329
Iroquois Arms Collectors Assn.
Dennis Freeman, 12144 McNeeley Rd., Akron, NY 14001
Mid-State Arms Coll. & Shooters Club
Jack Ackerman, 24 S. Mountain Terr., Binghamton, NY 13903
Westchester Arms Collectors Club, Inc.
F. E. Falkenbury, Secy., 79 Hillcrest Rd., Hartsdale, NY 10530

NORTH CAROLINA

Carolina Gun Collectors Assn.
David Blalock, Jr., Rt. 1, Linden, NC 28356

OHIO

Central Ohio Gun and Indian Relic Coll. Assn.
Coyt Stookey, 134 E. Ohio Ave., Washington C.H., OH 43160
Maumee Valley Gun Collectors Assn.
A. Kowalka, 3203 Woodville Rd., Northwood, OH 43619
National Bench Rest Shooters Assn., Inc.
Bernice McMullen, 607 W. Line St., Minerva, OH 44657
Ohio Gun Collectors, Assn., Inc.
P.O. Box 300, Mount Gilead, OH 43338
The Stark Gun Collectors, Inc.
Russ McNary, 147 Miles Ave., N.W., Canton, OH 44708

OKLAHOMA

Indian Territory Gun Collectors Assn.
P.O. Box 4491, Tulsa, OK 74104

OREGON

Oregon Cartridge Coll. Assn.
John L. Heyman, 2101 West 10th St., Eugene, OR 97402
Oregon Arms Coll. Assn., Inc.
Ted Dowd, P.O. Box 25103, Portland, OR 97225

PENNSYLVANIA

Forks of the Delaware Weapons Assn., Inc.
John F. Scheid, 348 Bushkill St., Easton, PA 18042
Lancaster Muzzle Loading Assn.
James H. Frederick, Jr., R.D. #2, Box 402, Columbia, PA 17512
Presque Isle Gun Coll. Assn.
James Welch, 156 E. 37 St., Erie, PA 16506

SOUTH CAROLINA

Belton Gun Club Inc.
J. K. Phillips, P.O. Box 605, Belton SC 29627
South Carolina Arms Coll. Assn.
J. W. McNelley, 3215 Lincoln St., Columbia, SC 29201

SOUTH DAKOTA

Dakota Territory Gun Coll. Assn., Inc.
Curt Carter, Castlewood, SD 57223

TENNESSEE

Memphis Antique Weapons Assn.
Nelson T. Powers, 4672 Barfield Rd., TN 38117
Tennessee Gun Collectors Assn., Inc.
M. H. Parks, 3556 Pleasant Valley Rd., Nashville, TN 37204

TEXAS

Houston Gun Collectors Assn.
P.O. Box 37369, Houston, TX 77036
Texas State Rifle Assn.
Lafe R. Pfeifer, P.O. Drawer 34809, Dallas TX 75234

UTAH

Utah Gun Collectors Assn.
S. Gerald Keogh, 875 20th St., Ogden, UT 84401

VIRGINIA

Virginia Arms Collectors & Assn.
Clinton E. Jones, P.O. Box 333, Mechanicsville, VA 23111

WASHINGTON

Washington Arms Collectors, Inc.
J. Dennis Cook, P.O. Box 7335, Tacoma, WA 98407

WISCONSIN

Chippewa Valley Weapons Collectors
J. M. Sullivan, 504 Ferry St., Eau Claire, WI 54701
Great Lakes Arms Coll. Assn., Inc.
E. Warnke, 1811 N. 73rd St. Wauwatosa, WI 53213
Wisconsin Gun Collectors Assn., Inc.
Rob. Zellmer, P.O. Box 181, Sussex, WI 53089

WYOMING

Wyoming Gun Collectors
Bob Funk, Box 1805, Riverton, WY 82501

NATIONAL ORGANIZATIONS

Amateur Trap Shooting Assn.
P.O. Box 458, Vandalia, OH 45377
American Defense Preparedness Assn.
819 Union First Bank Bldg., Washington, DC 20005
The American Pistol Institute
Jeff Cooper, P.O. Box 401, Paulden, AZ 86334
American Police Pistol & Rifle Assn.
1100 N.E. 125th St., No. Miami, FL 33161
American Single Shot Rifle Assn.
L. B. Thompson, 318 Washington, Salem, OH 44460
American Society of Arms Collectors, Inc.
Robt. F. Rubendunst, 6550 Baywood Lane, Cincinnati, OH 45224
Armor & Arms Club
J. K. Watson, Jr., 25 Broadway, New York, NY 10004
Association of Firearm and Tool Mark Examiners
Invest. John S. Bates, N.Y. State Police, Scientific Lab., State Campus, Albany, NY 12226
Boone & Crockett Club
424 N. Washington St., Alexandria, VA 22314
Cast Bullet Assn., Inc.
Steve Myers, 2 Shepherd Rd., Franklin, MA 02038
Citizens Committee for the Right to Keep and Bear Arms
Natl. Hq.: Bellefield Office Park, 1601 114, S.E., Suite 151, Bellevue, WA 98004
Ducks Unlimited, Inc.
P.O. Box 66300, Chicago, IL 60666
Experimental Ballistics Assoc.
Ed Yard, 110 Kensington, Trenton, NJ 08618
International Benchrest Shooters
Evelyn Richards, 411 N. Wilbur Ave, Sayre, PA 18840
International Cartridge Coll. Assn., Inc.
Ellie Dodd, 1912 Sandra Ave., Metairie, LA 70003
Miniature Arms Collectors/Makers Society Ltd.
Joseph J. Macewicz, 104 White Sand Lane, Racine, WI 53402
National Assn. of Federally Licd. Firearms Dealers
Andrew Molchan, 7001 N. Clark St., Chicago, IL 60626
National Automatic Pistol Collectors Assn.
Tom Knox, P.O. Box 15738, Tower Grove Station, St. Louis, MO 63163
National Bench Rest Shooters Assn., Inc.
Stella Buchtel, 5735 Sherwood Forest Dr., Akron, OH 44139
National Deer Hunter Assn.
14958 Industrial Rd., Minnetoanka, MN 55343
National Muzzle Loading Rifle Assn.
Box 67, Friendship, IN 47021
National Police Officers Assn. of America
National Police Hall of Fame Bldg., 14600 S. Trail, N.P., Venice, FL 33595
National Reloading Mfrs. Assn., Inc.
1221 S.W. Yamhill St., Portland, OR 97205
National Rifle Assn.
1600 Rhode Island Ave., N.W., Washington, DC 20036

National Shooting Sports Fdtn., Inc.
Arnold H. Rohlfing, Exec. Director, 1075 Post Rd., Riverside, CT 06878
National Skeet Shooting Assn.
Carroll E. Bobo, P.O. Box 28188, San Antonio, TX 78228
National Wild Turkey Federation, Inc.
P.O. Box 467, Edgefield, SC 29824
North American Edged Weapon Collectors Assn.
John Cox, 2224 Wyandoge Dr., Oakville, Ont. L6L 2T5, Canada
North-South Skirmish Assn., Inc.
John L. Rawls, Rt. 2, Box 245A, Winchester, VA 22601
Ruger Collector's Assn., Inc.
Col. L. O. Friesz, P.O. Box 290, Southport, CT 06490
Second Amendment Foundation
Bellefield Office Park, 1601—114th S.E., Suite 157, Bellevue, WA 98004
Sporting Arms and Ammunition Mfrs. Inst., Inc.
420 Lexington Ave., New York, NY 10017

AUSTRALIA

Nat'l. Sporting Shooters' Assn. of Australia
Mrs. A. Brummell, P.O. Box 154, Punchbowl 2196, Australia

CANADA

ALBERTA

Canadian Historical Arms Society
P.O. Box 901, Edmonton, Alb., Canada T5J 2L8

ONTARIO

Oshawa Antique Gun Coll. Inc.
William A. Vaughan, Box 544, Whitby, Ont. L1N 5V3, Canada

QUEBEC

Lower Canada Arms Collectors Assn.
Jon Kirton, P.O. Box 564, Stock Exchange Tower, 800 Place Victoria, Montreal, Quebec, Can. H4Z 1S8

EUROPE

ENGLAND

Arms and Armour Society of London
F. Wilkinson, 40 Great James St., Holborn, London, WC1 N 3HB
British Cartridge Collectors Club
Peter F. McGowan, 15 Sandhurst Dr., Ruddington, Nottingham
Historical Breechloading Smallarms Assn.
D. J. Penn, M.A., Imperial War Museum, Lambeth Rd., London SE1 6HZ, England. Journal is $7 a yr.
Muzzle Loaders' Assn. of Great Britain
Membership Records, 12 Frances Rd., Baginton, Coventry, England
National Rifle Assn. (British)
Bisley Camp, Brookwood, Woking, Surrey, GU24 OPB, England

GERMANY (WEST)

Deutscher Schutzenbund
Klarenthaler Str., 6200 Wiesbaden-Klarenthal, West Germany

NEW ZEALAND

New Zealand Deerstalkers Assn.
J. M. Murphy, P.O. Box 6514, Wellington, New Zealand

SOUTH AFRICA

Historical Firearms Soc. of South Africa
"Minden" 11 Buchan Rd., Newlands 7700, Cape Town, South Africa
South African Reloaders Assn.
Box 27128, Sunnyside, Pretoria 0132, South Africa
U.S. Revolver Assn.
Stanley A. Sprague, 59 Alvin St., Springfield, MA 01104
United States Silueta Assn.
319 Thelma St., Nogales, AZ 85621

Directory of the Arms Trade

AMMUNITION (Commercial)

Alcan Shells, (See: Smith & Wesson Ammunition Co.)
Cascade Cartridge Inc., (See Omark)
DWM (see RWS)
Eastern Sports Intl., Inc., Savage Rd., Milford, NH 03055
Federal Cartridge Co., 2700 Foshay Tower, Minneapolis, MN 55402
Frontier Cartridge Co., Inc., Box 1848, Grand Island, NB 68801
H&H Cartridge Corp., P.O. Box 104, Greensburg, IN 47240 (Super Vel)
North American Arms Ammunition Co., Freedom, WY 83120
Omark-CCI, Inc., Box 856, Lewiston, Ida. 83501
Precision Prods. of Wash., Inc., N. 311 Walnut Rd., Spokane, WA 99206 (Exammo)
RWS (see Eastern Sports)
Remington Arms Co., Bridgeport, Conn. 06602
Service Armament, 689 Bergen Blvd., Ridgefield, N.J. 07657
Smith & Wesson Ammunition Co., 2399 Forman Rd., Rock Creek, OH 44084
Super Vel (see H&H Cartridge Corp.)
Weatherby's, 2781 E. Firestone Blvd., South Gate, Calif. 90280
Winchester-Western, East Alton, Ill. 62024

AMMUNITION (Custom)

Bill Ballard, 830 Miles Ave., Billings, MT 59101 (ctlg. 50¢)
Ballistek, Weapons Systems Div., Box 1813, Kearney, NE 68847
Beal's Bullets, 170 W. Marshall Rd., Lansdowne, PA 19050 (Auto Mag Specialists)
Bell's Gun & Sport Shop, 3309-19 Mannheim Rd., Franklin Park, IL 60131
Brass Extrusion Labs. Ltd., 800 W. Maple Lane, Bensenville, IL 60106
C. W. Cartridge Co., 71 Hackensack St., Wood-Ridge, NJ 07075
Russell Campbell, 219 Leisure Dr., San Antonio, Tex. 78201
Collectors Shotshell Arsenal, E. Tichy, 365 So. Moore, Lakewood, CO 80226
Crown City Arms, P.O. Box 1126, Cortland, NY 13045
Cumberland Arms, Rt. 1, Shafer Rd., Blantons Chapel, Manchester, TN 37355
E. W. Ellis Sport Shop, RFD 1, Box 315, Corinth, NY 12822
Ellwood Epps (Orillia) Ltd., Hwy. 11 North, Orillia, Ont., Canada
Ramon B. Gonzalez, P.O. Box 370, Monticello, NY 12701
Gussert Bullet & Cartridge Co., Inc., P.O. Box 3945, Green Bay, WI 54303
J-4, Inc., 1700 Via Burton, Anaheim, CA 92806 (custom bullets)
Jensen's Custom Ammunition, 5146 E. Pima, Tucson, AZ 85716
R. H. Keeler, 1304 S. Oak, Port Angeles, Wash. 98362
KTW Inc., 710 Foster Park Rd., Lorain, OH 44053 (bullets)
Dean Lincoln, P.O. Box 1886, Farmington, NM 87401
Lomont Precision Bullets, 4421 S. Wayne Ave., Ft. Wayne, IN 46807 (custom bullets)
Mansfield Gunshop, Box 83, New Boston, N.H. 03070
Numrich Arms Corp., 203 Broadway, W. Hurley, N.Y. 12491
Robert Pomeroy, Morison Ave., Corinth, ME 04427 (custom shells)
Precision Ammunition & Reloading, 122 Hildenboro Square, Agincourt, Ont. M1W 1Y3, Canada
Precision Prods. of Wash., Inc., N. 311 Walnut Rd., Spokane, WA 99206 (Exammo)
Anthony F. Sailer-Ammunition, Third St., P.O. Box L, Owen, WI 54460
Sanders Cust. Gun Serv., 2358 Tyler Lane, Louisville, Ky. 40205
Geo. Spence, P.O. Box 222, Steele, MO 63877 (box-primed cartridges)
The 3-D Company, Box 142, Doniphan, NB 68832 (reloaded police ammo)

AMMUNITION (Foreign)

Canadian Ind. Ltd. (C.I.L.), Ammo Div., Howard House, Brownsburg, Que., Canada, J0V 1A0
Eastern Sports International Inc., Savage Rd., Milford, NH 03055 (RWS; Geco)
Guilio Fiocchi S.p.A., 22053 Lecco-Belledo, Italy
Hirtenberger Patronen-, Zündhütchen- & Metallwarenfabrik, A.G., Leobersdorfer Str. 33, A2552 Hirtenberg, Austria
Hy-Score Arms Co., 200 Tillary, Brooklyn, N.Y. 11201
Paul Jaeger Inc., 211 Leedom St., Jenkintown, Pa. 19046
S. E. Laszlo, 200 Tillary, Brooklyn, N.Y. 11201
NORMA-Precision, Lansing, NY 14882
RWS (Rheinische-Westfälische Sprengstoff) see: Eastern

AMMUNITION COMPONENTS—BULLETS, POWDER, PRIMERS

Alcan, (see: Smith & Wesson Ammunition Co.)
Ammo-O-Mart, P.O. Box 543, Renfrew, Ont., Canada K7V-4B1 (Curry bullets)

Austin Powder Co. (see Red Diamond Dist. Co.)
Ballistic Research Inc., 935 E. Meadow Dr., Palo Alto, CA 94303 (BRI slug)
Barnes Bullets, P.O. Box 215, American Fork, UT 84003
B.E.L.L., Bell's Gun & Sport Shop, 3309-19 Mannheim Rd., Franklin Pk., IL 60131
Bitterroot Bullet Co., Box 412, Lewiston, Ida. 83501
Brass Extrusion Laboratories, Ltd., 800 W. Maple Lane, Bensenville, IL 60106
Centrix, 2116 N. 10th Ave., Tucson, Ariz. 85705
Kenneth E. Clark, 18738 Highway 99, Madera, CA 93637 (Bullets)
Curry Bullets Canada, P.O. Box 66, Hawkesbury, Ont., Canada
Division Lead, 7742 W. 61 Pl., Summit, Ill. 60502
DuPont, Explosives Dept., Wilmington, Del. 19898
Eastern Sports International, Inc., Savage Rd., Milford, NH 03055 (RWS percussion caps)
Elk Mountain Shooters Supply, 1719 Marie, Pasco, WA 99301 (Alaskan bullets)
Farmer Bros., 1102 Washington St., Eldora, IA 50627 (Lage wad)
Federal Cartridge Co., 2700 Foshay Tower, Minneapolis, MN 55402 (nickel cases)
Forty Five Ranch Enterprises, 119 S. Main, Miami, Okla. 74354
Godfrey Reloading Supply, Hi-Way 67-111, Brighton, IL 62012 (cast bullets)
Lynn Godfrey, see: Elk Mtn. Shooters Supply
Green Bay Bullets, 233 No. Ashland, Green Bay, Wis. 54303 (lead)
Gussert Bullet & Cartridge Co., Inc., P.O. Box 3945, Green Bay, WI 54303
Hardin Specialty Distr., P.O. Box 338, Radcliff, KY 40160 (empty, primed cases)
Hercules Powder Co., 910 Market St., Wilmington, Del. 19899
Herter's Inc., Waseca, Minn. 56093
Hodgdon Powder Co. Inc., 7710 W. 50th Hwy., Shawnee Mission, KS 66202
Hornady Mfg. Co., Box 1848, Grand Island, Neb. 68801
N. E. House Co., Middletown Rd., R.R. 4, Box 68, E. Hampton, CT 06424 (zinc bases only)
J-4, Inc., 1700 Via Burton, Anaheim, CA 92806 (custom bullets)
L. L. F. Die Shop, 1281 Highway 99 North, Eugene, Ore. 97402
Lage Uniwad Co., 1102 Washington St., Eldora, IA 50627
Ljutic Ind., Inc., Box 2117, Yakima, WA 98902 (Mono-wads)
Lomont Precision Bullets, 4421 S. Wayne Ave., Ft. Wayne, IN 46807 (custom bullets)
Lyman Products Corp., Rte. 147, Middlefield, CT 06455
Michael's Antiques, Box 233, Copiague, L.I., NY 11726 (Balle Blondeau)
Miller Trading Co., 20 S. Front St., Wilmington, N.C. 28401
Norma-Precision, Lansing, NY 14882
Nosler Bullets, P.O. Box 688, Beaverton, OR 97005
Robert Pomeroy, Morison Ave., East Corinth, ME 04427
Red Diamond Distributing Co., 1304 Snowdon Dr., Knoxville, TN 37912 (black powder)
Remington-Peters, Bridgeport, Conn. 06602
Sanderson's, 724 W. Edgewater, Portage, Wis. 53901 (cork wad)
Sierra Bullets Inc., 10532 Painter Ave., Santa Fe Springs, CA 90670
Smith & Wesson Ammunition Co., 2399 Forman Rd., Rock Creek, OH 44084
Speer Products Inc., Box 896, Lewiston, Ida. 83501
C. H. Stocking, Rte. 3, Box 195, Hutchinson, Minn. 55350 (17 cal. bullet jackets)
Taylor Bullets, P.O. Box 21254, San Antonio, TX 78221 (cast)
Vitt & Boos, 11 Sugarloaf Dr., Wilton, CT 06897 (shotgun slugs)
Winchester-Western, 275 Winchester Ave., New Haven, CT 06504
Wood Die Shop, Box 386, Florence, OR 97439 (17 cal.)
Xelex Ltd., P.O. Box 543, Renfrow, Ont. K7V 4B1, Canada (powder, Curry bullets)
Zero Bullet Co., P.O. Box 1012, Cullman, AL 35055
Wood Die Shop, Box 386, Florence, OR 97439 (17-cal. bullets)

ANTIQUE ARMS DEALERS

Robert Abels, P.O. Box 428, Hopewell Junction, NY 12533 (Catalog $1.00)
Wm. Boggs, 1243 Grandview Ave., Columbus, Ohio 43212
Ed's Gun House, Ed Kukowski, Rte. 1, Minnesota City, MN 55959
Ellwood Epps (Orillia) Ltd., Hwy. 11 North, Orillia, Ont., Canada
N. Flayderman & Co., Squash Hollow, New Milford, Conn. 06776
Fulmer's Antique Firearms, P.O. Box 792, Detroit Lakes, MN 56501
Herb Glass, Bullville, N.Y. 10915
Goergen's Gun Shop, 707 8th St. S.E., Box 499, Austin, MN 55912
Goodman's for Guns, 1002 Olive St., St. Louis, MO 63101

Griffin's Guns & Antiques, R.R. 4, Peterboro, Ont., Canada K9J 6X5
The Gun Shop, 6497 Pearl Rd., Cleveland, OH 44130
Hansen & Company, 244 Old Post Rd., Southport, CT 06490
Holbrook Arms Museum, 12953 Biscayne Blvd., N. Miami, Fla. 33161
Lew Horton Sports Shop, Inc., 450 Waverly St., Framingham, MA 01701
Jackson Arms, 6209 Hillcrest Ave., Dallas, Tex. 75205
Jerry's Gun Shop, 9220 Ogden Ave., Brookfield, Ill. 60513
Lever Arms Serv. Ltd., 771 Dunsmuir St., Vancouver, B.C., Canada V6C 1M9
Charles W. Moore, R.D. 2, Box 276, Schenevus, NY 12155
Museum of Historical Arms, 1038 Alton Rd., Miami Beach, FL 33139 (ctlg. $3)
National Gun Traders, Inc., 225 S.W. 22nd Ave., Miami, Fla. 33135
New Orleans Arms Co., Inc., P.O. Box 26087, New Orleans, LA 70186
Old West Gun Room, 3509 Carlson Blvd., El Cerrito, Cal. 94530 (write for list)
Pioneer Guns, 5228 Montgomery, (Cincinnati) Norwood, OH 45212
Pony Express Sport Shop, Inc., 17460 Ventura Blvd., Encino, CA 91316
Martin B. Retting Inc., 11029 Washington, Culver City, Calif. 90230
Ridge Guncraft, Inc., 234 N. Tulane Ave., Oak Ridge, Tenn. 37830
S.G. Intl., P.O. Box 702, Hermosa Beach, CA. 90254
San Francisco Gun Exch., 124 Second St., San Francisco, Calif. 94105
Santa Ana Gunroom, P.O. Box 1777, Santa Ana, Calif. 92701
Ward & Van Valkenburg, 114-32nd Ave. N., Fargo, ND 58102
M. C. Wiest, 234 N. Tulane Ave., Oak Ridge, Tenn. 37830
Yale's Gun Shop, 2618 Conowingo Rd., Bel Air, MD 21014
Lewis Yearout, 308 Riverview Dr. E., Great Falls, MT 59404

BOOKS (ARMS), Publishers and Dealers

Beinfeld Publishing, Inc., 13222 Saticoy St., No. Hollywood, CA 91605
DBI Books, Inc., 540 Frontage Rd., Northfield, IL 60093
EPCO Publ. Co., 75-24 64 St., Glendale, NY 11227
Fairfield Book Co., Inc., P.O. Box 289, Brookfield Center, CT 06805
Fortress Publications Inc., P.O. Box 241, Stoney Creek, Ont. L8G 3X9, Canada
Handgun Press, 5832 S. Green, Chicago, IL 60621
Jackson Arms, 6209 Hillcrest Ave., Dallas, TX 75205
Personal Firearms Record Book Co., P.O. Box 2800, Santa Fe, NM 87501
Ridge Guncraft Inc., M. C. Wiest, 234 N. Tulane Ave., Oak Ridge, TN 37830
Ray Riling Arms Books Co., 6844 Gorsten St., Philadelphia, PA 19119
Rutgers Book Center, Mark Aziz, 127 Raritan Ave., Highland Park, NJ 08904
James C. Tillinghast, Box 568, Marlow, NH 03456

BULLET & CASE LUBRICANTS

Birchwood-Casey Co., Inc., 7900 Fuller Rd., Eden Prairie, Minn. 55343 (Anderol)
Chopie Mfg. Inc., 531 Copeland, La Crosse, Wis. 54601 (Black-Solve)
Cooper-Woodward, Box 972, Riverside, Cal. 92502 (Perfect Lube)
D. R. Corbin Mfg. & Supply Inc., P.O. Box 758, Phoenix, OR 97535
Green Bay Bullets, 233 N. Ashland, Green Bay, Wis. 54303 (EZE-Size case lube)
Gussert Bullet & Cartridge Co., P.O. Box 3945, Green Bay, WI 54303 (Super Lube)
Herter's, Inc., Waseca, Minn. 56903 (Perfect Lubricant)
IPCO (Industrial Products Co.), Box 14, Bedford, MA 01730
Javelina Products, Box 337, San Bernardino, Cal. 92402 (Alox beeswax)
Jet-Aer Corp., 100 Sixth Ave., Paterson, N.J. 07524
LeClear Industries, P.O. Box 484, Royal Oak, MI 48068
Lenz Prod. Co., Box 1226, Sta. C, Canton, O. 44708 (Clenzoil)
Lyman Products Corp., Rte. 147, Middlefield, CT 06455 (Size-Ezy)
Marmel Prods., P.O. Box 97, Utica, MI 48087 (Marvelube, Marvelux)
Micro Shooter's Supply, Box 213, Las Cruces, N. Mex. 88001 (Micro-Lube)
Mirror Lube, P.O. Box 693, San Juan Capistrano, CA 92675
M&N Bullet Lube, Box 495, Jefferson St., Madras, OR 97741
Pacific Tool Co., P.O. Drawer 2048, Ordnance Plant Rd., Grand Island, NB 68801
Phelps Rel. Inc., Box 4004, E. Orange, N.J. 07019
Precision Ammunition & Rel., 122 Hildenboro Square, Agincourt, Ont. M1W 1Y3, Canada
RCBS, Inc., Box 1919, Oroville, Calif. 95965
SAECO Rel. Inc., P.O. Box 778, Carpinteria, CA 93103
Shooters Accessory Supply (SAS), see D. R. Corbin
Tamarack Prods., Inc., Box 224, Barrington, IL 60010 (Bullet lube)
Testing Systems, Inc., #5 Tenakill Pk., Cresskill, NJ 07626

BULLET SWAGE DIES AND TOOLS

Belmont Products, Rte. #1, Friendsville, TN 37737
C-H Tool & Die Corp., P.O. Box L, Owen, WI 54460
Clymer Mfg. Co., 14241 W. 11 Mile Rd., Oak Park, MI 48237
Lester Coats, 416 Simpson St., North Bend, OR 97459 (lead wire cutter)
D. R. Corbin Mfg. & Supply Inc., P.O. Box 758, Phoenix, OR 97535
Herter's Inc., Waseca, MN 56093
Hollywood, Whitney Sales Inc., P.O. Box 875, Reseda, CA 91335
Independent Machine & Gun Shop, 1416 N. Hayes, Pocatello, ID 83201 (TNT bullet dies)
L.L.F. Die Shop, 1281 Highway 99 North, Eugene, OR 97402
Rorschach Precision Products, P.O. Box 1613, Irving, TX 75060
SAS Dies, see: D. R. Corbin
Robert B. Simonson, Rte. 2, 2129 Vanderbilt Rd., Kalamazoo, MI 49002
TNT (see Ind. Mach. & Gun Shop)
Wood Die Shop, Box 386, Florence, OR 97439

CARTRIDGES FOR COLLECTORS

AD Hominem, R.R. 3, Orillia, Ont., Canada L3V 6H3
Antique Arsenal, 365 S. Moore, Lakewood, CO 80226
Peter Bigler, 291 Crestwood Dr., Milltown, N.J. 08850 (ctlg. $1.50)
Cameron's, 16690 W. 11th Ave., Golden, Colo. 80401
Centrefire Sports Dunedin, 41 Dowling St., Dunedin, New Zealand
Chas. E. Duffy, Williams Lane, West Hurley, N.Y. 12419
Tom M. Dunn, 1342 So. Poplar, Casper, Wyo. 82601
Ellwood Epps (Orillia) Ltd., Hwy. 11 North, Orillia, Ont., Canada
Idaho Ammunition Service, 410 21st Ave., Lewiston, ID 83501
George Kass, 30 Ivy Circle, West Haven, CT 06516 (ctlg. $1; rimfire cartridges)
San Francisco Gun Exchange, 124 Second St., San Francisco, CA 94105
Perry Spangler, 519 So. Lynch, Flint, Mich. 48503 (list 50¢)
Ernest Tichy, 365 So. Moore, Lakewood, CO 80226
James C. Tillinghast, Box 568, Marlow, N.H. 03456 (list 50¢)
Lewis Yearout, 308 Riverview Dr. E., Great Falls, MT 59404

CASES, CABINETS AND RACKS—GUN

Alco Carrying Cases, 601 W. 26th St., New York, N.Y. 10001
Allen Co., Inc., 2330 Midway Blvd., Broomfield, CO 80020
Morton Booth Co., Box 123, Joplin, Mo. 64801
Boyt Co., Div. of Welsh Sportg. Gds., Box 1108, Iowa Falls, Ia. 50126
Brenik, Inc., 925 W. Chicago Ave., Chicago, IL 60622
Browning, Rt. 4, Box 624-B, Arnold, MO 63010
Cap-Lex Gun Cases, Capitol Plastics of Ohio, Inc., 333 Van Camp Rd., Bowling Green, OH 43402
Challanger Mfg. Co., 118 Pearl St., Mt. Vernon, NY 10550
Dara-Ness Div., Nesci Enterprises, P.O. Box 119, East Hampton, CT 06424 (firearms security chests)
E & C Enterprises, 9582 Bickley Dr., Huntington Beach, CA 92646 (gun socks)
East-Tenn Mills, Inc., 2300 Buffalo Rd., Johnson City, TN 37601 (gun socks)
Ellwood Epps (Orillia) Ltd., Hwy. 11 North, Orillia, Ont., Canada (custom gun cases)
Norbert Ertel, Box 1150, Des Plaines, IL 60018 (cust. gun cases)
Flambeau Plastics Corp., 801 Lynn, Baraboo, Wis. 53913
Gun-Ho Case Mfg. Co., 110 East 10th St., St. Paul, Minn. 55101
Harbor House Gun Cabinets, 12508 Center St., South Gate, CA 90280
B. E. Hodgdon, Inc., 7710 W. 50 Hiway, Shawnee-Mission, Kans. 66202
Marvin Huey, Box 98, Reed's Spring, MO 65737 (handbuilt leath. cases)
Ithaca Gun Co., Terrace Hill, Ithaca, N.Y. 14850
Jumbo Sports Prods., P.O. Box 280-Airport Rd., Frederick, MD 21701
Kalispel Metal Prods. (KMP), Box 267, Cusick, WA 99119 (aluminum boxes)
Kolpin Mfg., Inc., Box 231, Berlin, WI 54923
Marble Arms Corp., 420 Industrial Park, Gladstone, Mich. 49837
Bill McGuire, 1600 No. Eastmont Ave., East Wenatchee, WA 98801 (custom cases)
W. A. Miller Co., Inc. (Wamco), Mingo Loop, Oguossoc, ME 04964 (wooden handgun cases)
National Sports Div., Medalist Ind., 19 E. McWilliams St., Fond du Lac, WI 54935
Nortex Co., 2821 Main St., Dallas, Tex. 75226 (automobile gun rack)
North Star Devices, Inc., P.O. Box 2095, North St., Paul, MN 55109 (Gun-Slinger portable rack)
P.T.C. Inc., 3411 East Kiest Blvd., Dallas, TX 75203 (carrying case)
Paul-Reed, Inc., P.O. Box 227, Charlevoix, Mich. 49720
Penguin Industries, Inc., Box 97, Parkesburg, Pa. 19365
Pistolsafe, Dr. L., N. Chili, NY 14514 (handgun safe)
Precise, 3 Chestnut, Suffern, NY 10901
Protecto Plastics, Inc., 201 Alpha Rd., Wind Gap, Pa. 18091 (carrying cases)
Provo Steel & Supply Co., P.O. Box 977, Provo, UT 84601 (steel gun cases)
Richland Arms Co., 321 W. Adrian, Blissfield, Mich. 49228
San Angelo Co. Inc., Box 984, San Angelo, TX 76901
Buddy Schoellkopf, 4949 Joseph Hardin Dr., Dallas, TX 75236
Security Gun Chest, Div. of Tread Corp., P.O. Box 13202, 1734 Granby St. N.E., Roanoke, VA 24012
Sile Distr., 7 Centre Market Pl., New York, N.Y. 10013 (leg o'mutton case)
Stearns Mfg. Co., P.O. Box 1498, St. Cloud, MN 56301
Tread Corp., P.O. Box 13207, 1734 Granby St. N.E., Roanoke, VA 24012 (security gun chest)
Trik Truk, P.O. Box 3760, Kent, WA 98031 (P.U. truck cases)
Vanguard Prods. Corp., 545 Cedar Lane, Box #10, Teaneck, NJ 07666 (Straight Shooter gun cases)
Woodstream Corp., Box 327, Lititz, Pa. 17543
Yield House, Inc., RFD, No. Conway, N.H. 03860

CHOKE DEVICES & RECOIL ABSORBERS

Arms Ingenuity Co., Box 1, Weatogue, Conn. 06089 (Jet-Away)
Contra-Jet, 7920 49th Ave. So., Seattle, Wash. 98118
Dahl's Gun Shop, 6947 King Ave., Route 4, Billings, MT 59102
Diverter Arms, Inc., P.O. Box 22084, Houston, TX 77027 (shotgun diverter)
Edwards Recoil Reducer, 269 Herbert St., Alton, Ill. 62002
Emsco Chokes, 101 Second Ave., S.E., Waseca, MN 56093
Herter's Inc., Waseca, Minn. 56093. (Vari-Choke)
J & K Enterprises, Rte. 1, B.O.B. 202-A, Scappoose, OR 97056 (Mercury recoil absorbers)
Lyman Products Corp., Rte. 147, Middlefield, CT 06455 (Cutts Comp.)
Mag-Na-Port Arms, Inc., 30016 S. River Rd., Mt. Clemens, MI 48043 (muzzle-brake system)

Pendleton Dekickers, 1210 S. W. Hailey Ave., Pendleton, Ore. 97801
Poly-Choke Co., Inc., Box 296, Hartford, Conn. 06101
Triple-S Development Co., Inc., 1450 E. 289th St., Wickliffe, OH 44092 (Choke-Matic)

CHRONOGRAPHS AND PRESSURE TOOLS

B-Square Co., Box 11281, Ft. Worth, Tex. 76110
Chronograph Specialists, P.O. Box 5005, Santa Ana, Calif. 92704
Custom Chronograph Co., 3518 1st Ave. N.W., Seattle, WA 98107
Diverter Arms, Inc., P.O. Box 22084, Houston, TX 77027 (press. tool)
Herter's, Waseca, Minn. 56093
Robert P. Medaris, 15412 Webster, Westminster, CA 92683
Oehler Research, P.O. Box 9135, Austin, Tex. 78756
Schmidt-Weston Co., Box 9, West Islip, NY 11795
Sundtek Co., P.O. Box 744, Springfield, Ore. 97477
Telepacific Electronics Co., Inc., P.O. Box 2210, Escondido, CA 92025
Vibra-Tek, 2807 N. Prospect St., Colorado Springs, CO 80907 (Krono-scope)
M. York, 19381 Keymar Way, Gaithersburg, MD 20760 (press. tool)

CLEANING & REFINISHING SUPPLIES

A 'n A Co., Box 571, King of Prussia, PA 19406 (Valet shotgun cleaner)
Armite Labs., 1845 Randolph St., Los Angeles, CA 90001 (pen oiler)
Armoloy Co. of Ft. Worth, 204 E. Daggett St., Ft. Worth, TX 76104
Birchwood-Casey, 7900 Fuller Rd., Eden Prairie, Minn. 55344 (Anderol, etc.)
Bisonite Co., Inc., P.O. Box 84, Kenmore Station, Buffalo, NY 14217
Blue and Gray Prods., Inc., 817 E. Main St., Bradford, PA 16701
Jim Brobst, 299 Poplar St., Hamburg, Pa. 19526 (J-B Compound)
GB Prods. Dept., H & R, Inc., Industrial Rowe, Gardner, MA 01440
Browning Arms, Rt. 4, Box 624-B, Arnold, Mo. 63010
J. M. Bucheimer Co., Airport Rd., Frederick, MD 21701
Burnishine Prod. Co., 8140 N. Ridgeway, Skokie, Ill. 60076 (Stock Glaze)
Caddie Products Corp., Div. of Jet-Aer, Paterson, NJ 07524 (the Cloth)
Chem-Pak Inc., Winchester, VA 22601 (Gun-Savr. protect. & lubricant)
Chopie Mfg. Inc., 531 Copeland, La Crosse, Wis. 54601 (Black-Solve)
Clenzoil Co., Box 1226, Sta. C, Canton, O. 44708
Clover Mfg. Co., 139 Woodward Ave., Norwalk, CT 06856 (Clover compound)
Dri-Slide, Inc., Industrial Park, 1210 Locust St., Fremont, MI 49412
Durango U.S.A., P.O. Box 1029, Durango, CO 81301 (cleaning rods)
Forty-Five Ranch Enterpr., 119 S. Main St., Miami, Okla. 74354
Gun-All Products, Box 244, Dowagiac, Mich. 49047
Frank C. Hoppe Div., P.O. Box 97, Parkesburg, Pa. 19365
J & G Rifle Ranch, Box S 80, Turner, MT 59542
Jet-Aer Corp., 100 Sixth Ave., Paterson, N.J. 07524 (blues & oils)
Kellog's Professional Prods., Inc., P.O. Box 1201, Sandusky, OH 44870
K.W. Kleinendorst, 48 Taylortown Rd., Montville, N.J. 07045 (rifle clg. cables)
LPS Res. Labs. Inc., 2050 Cotner Ave., Los Angeles, Calif. 90025
LEM Gun Spec., Box 31, College Park, Ga 30337 (Lewis Lead Remover)
Liquid Wrench, Box 10628, Charlotte, N.C. 28201 (pen. oil)
Loner Products, Inc., P.O. Box 219, Yorktown Heights, NY 10598
Lynx Line Gun Prods. Div., Protective Coatings, Inc., 20626 Fenkell Ave., Detroit, MI 48223
Marble Arms Co., 420 Industrial Pk., Gladstone, Mich. 49837
Micro Sight Co., 242 Harbor Blvd., Belmont, Ca. 94002 (bedding)
Mill Run Prod., 1360 W. 9th, Cleveland, O. 44113 (Brite-Bore Kits)
Mirror-Lube, P.O. Box 693, San Juan Capistrano, CA 92675
New Method Mfg. Co., Box 175, Bradford, Pa. 16701 (gun blue)
Northern Instruments, Inc., 6680 North Highway 49, Lino Lake, MN 55014 (Stor-Safe rust preventer)
Numrich Arms Co., West Hurley, N.Y. 12491 (44-40 gun blue)
Outers Laboratories, Box 37, Onalaska, Wis. 54650 (Gunslick kits)
Radiator Spec. Co., 1400 Independence Blvd., Charlotte, N.C. 28201 (liquid wrench)
Realist Inc., N. 93 W. 16288 Megal Dr., Menomonee Falls, Wis. 53051
Reardon Prod., 103 W. Market St., Morrison, IL 61270 (Dry-Lube)
Rice Gun Coatings, 1521-43rd St., West Palm Beach, FL 33407
Rig Products Co., Box 279, Oregon, Ill. 61061 (Rig Grease)
Rusteprufe Labs., Sparta, WI 54656
Saunders Sptg. Gds., 338 Somerset, No. Plainfield, NJ 07060 (Sav-Bore)
Schultea's Gun String, 67 Burress, Houston, TX 77022 (pocket-size rifle cleaning kit)
Service Armament, 689 Bergen Blvd., Ridgefield, N. J. 07657 (Parker-Hale)
Silicote Corp., Box 359, Oshkosh, Wis. 54901 (Silicone cloths)
Silver Dollar Guns, P.O. Box 475, 10 Frances St., Franklin, NH 03235 (Silicone oil)
Sportsmen's Labs., Inc., Box 732, Anoka, Minn. 55303 (Gun Life lube)
Taylor & Robbins, Box 164, Rixford, Pa. 16745 (Throat Saver)
Testing Systems, Inc., #5 Tenakill Pk., Cresskill NJ 07626 (gun lube)
Texas Platers Supply Co., 2453 W. Five Mile Parkway, Dallas, TX 75233 (plating kit)
Totally Dependable Prods., Inc., P.O. Box 277, Zieglerville, PA 19492
C. S. Van Gorden, 120 Tenth Ave., Eau Claire, Wis. 54701 (Instant Blue)
WD-40 Co., 1061 Cudahy Pl., San Diego, CA 92110
West Coast Secoa, 3915 U S Hwy. 98S, Lakeland, FL 33801 (Teflon coatings)
Williams Gun Sight, 7389 Lapeer Rd., Davison, Mich. 48423 (finish kit)
Winslow Arms Inc., P.O. Box 783, Camden, SC 29020 (refinishing kit)
Wisconsin Platers Supply Co., see: Texas Platers Supply Co.
Woodstream Corp., P.O. Box 327, Lititz, Pa. 17543 (Mask)
Zip Aerosol Prods., 21320 Deering Court, Canoga Park, CA 91304

CUSTOM GUNSMITHS

Walter Abe, Abe's Gun Shop, 5124 Huntington Dr., Los Angeles, CA 90032
Ahlman Cust. Gun Shop, R.R. 1, Box 20, Morristown, Minn. 55052
Amrine's Gun Shop, 937 Luna Ave., Ojai, CA 93023
Anderson's Guns, Jim Jares, 706 S. 23rd St., Laramie, WY 82070
Antique Arms, D. F. Saunders, 1110 Cleveland Ave., Monett, MO 65708 (Hawken copies)
R. J. Anton, 874 Olympic Dr., Waterloo, IA 50701
Dietrich Apel, P.O. Box 473, Star Rte., Newport, NH 03773
Atkinson Gun Co., P.O. Box 512, Prescott, AZ 86301
E. von Atzigen, The Custom Shop, 890 Cochrane Crescent, Peterborough, Ont., K94 5N3 Canada
Bacon Creek Gun Shop, Cumberland Falls Rd., Corbin, Ky. 40701
Bain and Davis Sptg. Gds., 599 W. Las Tunas Dr., San Gabriel, Calif. 41776
Joe J. Balickie, Rte. 2, Box 56-G, Apex, NC 27502
Wm. G. Bankard, 4211 Thorncliff Rd., Baltimore, MD 21236 (Kentuckys)
Barta's, Rte. 1, Box 129-A, Cato, Wis. 54206
Roy Bauer, c/o C-D Miller Guns, St. Onge, SD 57779
Bennett Gun Works, 561 Delaware Ave., Delmar, N.Y. 12054
Irvin L. Benson, Saganaga Lake, Pine Island Camp, Ontario, Canada (via Grand Marais, MN 55604)
Gordon Bess, 708 River St., Canon City, Colo. 81212
Bruce Betts Gunsmith Co., 100 W. Highway 72, Rolla, MO 65401
Al Biesen, W. 2039 Sinto Ave., Spokane, WA 99201
Roger Biesen, W. 2039 Sinto Ave., Spokane, WA 99201
John Bivins, Jr., 200 Wicklow Rd., Winston-Salem, NC 27106
Ralph Bone, 4118-19th St., Lubbock, TX 79407
Boone Mountain Trading Post, Averyville Rd., St. Marys, Pa. 15857
Victor Bortugno, Atlantic & Pacific Arms Co., 4859 Virginia Beach Blvd., Virginia Beach, VA 23462
Breckheimers, Rte. 69-A, Parish, NY 13131
John P. Brown, Jr., 3107 Elinore Ave., Rockford, IL 61103
L. H. Brown, Brown's Rifle Ranch, 1820 Airport Rd., Kalispell, MT 59901
Lenard M. Brownell, Box 25, Wyarno, WY 82845 (Custom rifles)
E. J. Bryant, 3154 Glen St., Eureka, CA 95501
David Budin, Main St., Margaretville, NY 12455
George Bunch, 7735 Garrison Rd., Hyattsville, Md. 20784
Samuel W. Burgess, 25 Squam Rd., Rockport, MA 01966 (bluing repairs)
Leo Bustani, P.O. Box 8125, W. Palm Beach, Fla. 33407
Cameron's Guns, 16690 W. 11th Ave., Golden, CO 80401
Carter Gun Works, 2211 Jefferson Pk. Ave., Charlottesville, VA 22903
Ralph L. Carter, Rt. 1, Box 92, Fountain, CO 80817
Cassell Gun Shop, 813 S. 12th, Worland, WY 82401
R. MacDonald Champlin, P.O. Box 74, Wentworth, NH 03282 (ML rifles and pistols)
Mark Chanlynn, Bighorn Trading Co., 1704-14th St., Boulder, CO 80302
N. C. Christakos, 2832 N. Austin, Chicago, IL 60634
Jim Clark, Custom Gun Shop, 5367 S. 1950 West, Roy, UT 84067
Kenneth E. Clark, 18738 Highway 99, Madera, Calif. 93637
Cloward's Gun Shop, J. K. Cloward, 4023 Aurora Ave. N., Seattle, WA 98102
Crest Carving Co., 14849 Dillow St., Westminster, Ca. 92683
Philip R. Crouthamel, 513 E. Baltimore, E. Lansdowne, PA 19050
Jim Cuthbert, 715 S. 5th St., Coos Bay, Ore. 97420
Dahl's Custom Stocks, Rt. 4, Box 187, Schofield Rd., Lake Geneva, WI 53147
Dahl's Gunshop, 6947 King Ave., Billings, MT 59102
Homer L. Dangler, Box 254, Addison, MI 49220 (Kentucky rifles)
Davis Gun Shop, 7213 Lee Highway, Falls Church, VA 22046
Dee Davis, 5658 So. Mayfield, Chicago, Ill. 60638
Jack Dever, 8520 N.W. 90, Okla. City, OK 73132
R. H. Devereaux, 475 Trucky St., St. Ignace, MI 49781
Dominic DiStefano, 4303 Friar Lane, Colorado Springs, CO 80907
Bill Dowtin, P.O. Box 72, Celina, TX 75009
Drumbore Gun Shop, 119 Center St., Lehigton, PA 18235
Drummond's Gun Shop, 123 E. 4th St., Williamsport, PA 17701
Charles Duffy, Williams Lane, W. Hurley, N.Y. 12491
John H. Eaton, 8516 James St., Upper Marlboro, MD 20870
Gerald D. Eisenhauer, Rte. #3, Twin Falls, Ida. 83301
Bob Emmons, 238 Robson Rd., Grafton, OH 44044
Bill English, 4411 S. W. 100th, Seattle, Wash. 98146
Ken Eyster, Heritage Gunsmiths Inc., 6441 Bishop Rd., Centerburg, O. 43011
N. B. Fashingbauer, Box 366, Lac Du Flambeau, Wis. 54538
Ted Fellowes, Beaver Lodge, 9245-16th Ave., S.W., Seattle, Wa. 98106 (muzzle loaders)
H. J. and L. A. Finn, 12565 Gratiot Ave., Detroit, MI 48205
Jack First, The Gunshop, Inc., 44633 Sierra Highway, Lancaster, CA 93534
Marshall F. Fish, Rt. 22 North, Westport, NY 12993
Jerry Fisher, 1244—4th Ave. West, Kalispell, Mont. 59901
Flynn's Cust. Gunsmithing, 3309 Elliott, Apt. B, Alexandria, LA 71301
Larry L. Forster, Box 212, Gwinner, ND 58040
Frazier's Custom Guns, Jay Frazier, Box 8644, Bird Creek, Alaska 99540
Clark K. Frazier/Matchmate, RFD 1, Rawson, OH 45881
Freeland's Scope Stands, 3737—14th Ave., Rock Island, Ill. 61201
Fred's Gunsmithing & Firearms Co., 214 Holly Ct., Darien, IL 60559
Fredrick Gun Shop, 10 Elson Drive, Riverside, R.I. 02915
R. L. Freshour, P.O. Box 2837, Texas City, TX 77590
Frontier Arms, Inc., 420 E. Riding Club Rd., Cheyenne, Wyo. 82001
Fuller Gunshop, Cooper Landing, Alas. 99572
Gentry's Bluing and Gun Shop, P.O. Box 984, Belgrade, MT 59714
Ed Gillman, Valley View Dr., R.R. 6, Hanover, PA 17331
Dale Goens, Box 224, Cedar Crest, NM 87008
A. R. Goode, Rte. 3, Box 139, Catoctin Furnace, Thurmont, MD 21788
Charles E. Grace, 10144 Elk Lake Rd., Williamsburg, MI 49690

George T. Gregory, Rt. 2, Box 8G, Plymouth, CA 95669 (saddle rifles)
Griffin & Howe, 589 Broadway, New York, N.Y. 10012
H. L. Grisel, 61400 S. Hwy. 97, Bend, OR 97701 (rifles)
Gun City, 504 Main Ave., Bismarck, ND 58501
H & R Custom Gun Serv., 68 Passaic Dr., Hewitt, N.J. 07421
Paul Haberly, 2364 N. Neva, Chicago, IL 60635
Martin Hagn, Kalmbachstr. 9, 8115 Kochel a. See, W. Germany (s.s. actions & rifles)
Chas. E. Hammans, Box 788, Stuttgart, AR 72160
Harkrader's Cust. Gun Shop, 825 Radford St., Christiansburg, VA 24073
Rob't W. Hart & Son Inc., 401 Montgomery St., Nescopeck, PA 18635 (actions, stocks)
Hal Hartley, 147 Blairs Fork Rd., Lenoir, NC 28645
Hartmann & Weiss KG, Rahlstedter Str. 139, 2000 Hamburg 73, W. Germany
Hubert J. Hecht, 55 Rose Mead Circle, Sacramento, CA 95831
Edw. O. Hefti, 300 Fairview, College Sta., Tex. 77840
Iver Henriksen, 1211 So. 2nd St. W., Missoula, MT 59801
Wm. Hobaugh, Box M, Philipsburg, MT 59858
Hodgson, Joseph & Assoc., 1800 Commerce St. 7S, Boulder, CO 80301
Richard Hodgson, 5589 Arapahoe, Unit 104, Boulder, CO 80301
Hoenig-Rodman, 6521 Morton Dr., Boise, ID 83705
Hollis Gun Shop, 917 Rex St., Carlsbad, N.M. 88220
Bill Holmes, 2405 Pump Sta. Rd., Springdale, AR 72764
Ernest Hurt's Specialty Gunsmithing, P.O. Box 1033, (820 E. Broadway), Muskogee, OK 74401 (bolts and breechblocks)
Hyper-Single Precision SS Rifles, 520 E. Beaver, Jenks, OK 74037
Independent Machine & Gun Shop, 1416 N. Hayes, Pocatello, Ida. 83201
Jackson's, Box 416, Selman City, TX 75689
Paul Jaeger, 211 Leedom St., P.O. Box 67, Jenkintown, PA 19046
J. J. Jenkins, 375 Pine Ave. No. 25, Goleta, CA 93017
Jerry's Gun Shop, 9220 Ogden Ave., Brookfield, Ill. 60513
Bruce Jones, 389 Calla Ave., Imperial Beach, CA 92032
Jos. Jurjevic, Gunshop, 605 Main St., Marble Falls, TX 78654
John Kaufield Small Arms Eng. Co., 7698 Garden Prairie Rd., Garden Prairie, IL 61038 (restorations)
Kennedy Gun Shop, Rt. 6, Clarksville, Tenn. 37040
Monte Kennedy, P.O. Box 214, Kalispell, MT 59901
Kennon's Custom Rifles, 5408 Biffle, Stone Mtn., Ga. 30083
Kerr Sport Shop, Inc., 9584 Wilshire Blvd., Beverly Hills, Calif. 90212
Kesselring Gun Shop, 400 Pacific Hiway 99 No., Burlington, Wash. 98233
Vern Kitzrow, 2504 N. Grant Blvd., Milwaukee, WI 53210 (single shots)
Don Klein Custom Guns, Box 277, Camp Douglas, WI 54618
K. W. Kleinendorst, 48 Taylortown Rd., Montville, NJ 07045
J. Korzinek, RD #2, Box R, Canton, PA 17724 (riflesmith)
L&W Casting Co., 5014 Freeman Rd. E., Puyallup, WA 98371
Sam Lair, 520 E. Beaver, Jenks, OK 74037
Maynard Lambert, Kamas, UT 84036
LanDav Custom Guns, 7213 Lee Highway, Falls Church, VA 22046
Alain Laquieze, P.O. Box 26087, New Orleans, LA 70186 (foreign long guns)
Harry Lawson Co., 3328 N. Richey Blvd., Tucson, Ariz. 85716
John G. Lawson, 1802 E. Columbia, Tacoma, Wa. 98404
Gene Lechner, 636 Jane N.E., Albuquerque, NM 87123
LeDel, Inc., Main and Commerce Sts., Cheswold, Del. 19936
Mark Lee, Ken's Metal Finishing, 2333 Emerson Ave. N., Minneapolis, MN 55411
Leer's Gun Barn, R.R. #3, Sycamore Hills, Elwood, IN 46036 (repairing and sight fitting)
Art LeFeuvre, 1003 Hazel Ave., Deerfield, Ill. 60015
LeFever Arms Co., R.D. 1, Lee Center Stroke, Lee Center, N.Y. 13363
Lenz Firearms Co., 1480 Elkay Dr., Eugene, OR 97404
Al Lind, 7821—76th Ave. S.W., Tacoma, WA 98498
Max J. Lindauer, R.R. 2, Box 27, Washington, MO 63090
Robt. L. Lindsay, 9416 Emory Grove Rd., Gaithersburg, Md. 20760 (services only)
Ljutic Ind., Box 2117, Yakima, WA 98902 (Mono-Wads)
Llanerch Gun Shop, 2800 Township Line, Upper Darby, Pa. 19083
Jim Lofland, 2275 Larkin Rd., Boothwyn, PA 19061 (SS rifles)
London Guns, 1528—20th St., Santa Monica, CA 90404
McCormick's Gun Bluing Service, 609 N.E. 104th Ave., Vancouver, WA 98664
Bill McGuire, 1600 N. Eastmont Ave., East Wenatchee, WA 98801
R. J. Maberry, 511 So. K, Midland, Tex. 79701
Harold E. MacFarland, Star Route, Box 84, Cottonwood, Ariz. 86326
Monte Mandarino, Box 26087, New Orleans, LA 70186 (Penn. rifles)
Marcos Gunsmithing, 547 Main St., Paterson, NJ 07501
Marquart Precision Co., P.O. Box 1740, Prescott, AZ 86301
Martel's Custom Handguns, 4038 S. Wisteria Way, Denver, CO 80237
E. H. Martin's Gun Shop, 937 S. Sheridan Blvd., Lakewood, CO 80226
Mashburn Arms Co., 1218 N. Pennsylvania, Oklahoma City, OK 73107
Seely Masker, Custom Rifles, 261 Washington Ave., Pleasantville, NY 10570
Mathews & Son, 10224 S. Paramount Blvd., Downey, Calif. 90241
Maurer Arms, 2366 Frederick Dr., Cuyahoga Falls, Ohio 44221 (muzzleloaders)
Eric Meitzner, Rte. 1, Northfield, MN 55057
Miller Custom Rifles, 655 Dutton Ave., San Leandro, CA 94577
Miller Gun Works, P.O. Box 7326, Tamuning, Guam 96911
C.D. Miller Guns, Purl St., St. Onge, SD 57779
Earl Milliron, 1249 N.E. 166th Ave., Portland, Ore. 97230
Mills (D.H.) Custom Stocks, 401 N. Ellsworth, San Mateo, Calif. 94401
Wm. Larkin Moore, 2890 Marlics St., Agoura, CA 91301
Larry Mrock, 4165 Middlebelt, Orchard Lake, MI 48033
Natl. Gun Traders, Inc., 225 S.W. 22nd Ave., Miami, Fla. 33135
Clayton N. Nelson, R.R. #3, Box 119, Enid, OK 73701
New England Custom Gun Serv., P.O. Box 473, Star Route, Newport, NH 03773

Newman Gunshop, 119 Miller Rd., Agency, Ia. 52530
Nu-Line Guns, Inc., 3727 Jennings Rd., St. Louis, Mo. 63121
O'Brien Rifle Co., 324 Tropicana No. 128, Las Vegas, Nev. 89109
Warren E. Offenberger, Star Route, Reno, Oh 45773 (ML)
Pachmayr Gun Works, 1220 S. Grand Ave., Los Angeles, Calif. 90015
Charles J. Parkinson, 116 Wharncliffe Rd. So., London, Ont., Canada N6J2K3
Byrd Pearson, 191 No. 2050 W., Provo, UT 84601
Bob Pease Accuracy, P.O. Box 787, New Braunfels, TX 78130 (benchrest)
John Pell, 410 College Ave., Trinidad, CO 81082
Pendleton Gunshop, 1210 S. W. Haley Ave., Pendleton, Ore. 97801
C. R. Pedersen & Son, Ludington, Mich. 49431
Al Petersen, Box 8, Riverhurst, Sask., Canada S0H3P0
A. W. Peterson Gun Shop, 1693 Old Hwy. 441, Mt. Dora, FL 32757 (ML rifles, also)
Phillip Pilkington, P.O. Box 2284, University Station, Enid, OK 73701
Ready Eddie's Gun Shop, 501 Van Spanje Ave., Michigan City, IN 46360
R. Neal Rice, Box 12172, Denver, CO 80212
Ridge Guncraft, Inc., 234 N. Tulane, Oak Ridge, Tenn. 37830
Rifle Ranch, Jim Wilkinson, Rte. 5, Prescott, AZ 86301
Riedl Rifles, 15124 Weststate St., Westminster, CA 92683
Rifle Shop, Box M, Philipsburg, MT 59858
W. Rodman, 6521 Morton Dr., Boise, ID 83705
Carl Roth, 4728 Pineridge Ave., Cheyenne, WY 82001 (rust bluing)
Royal Arms, Inc., 10064 Bert Acosta, Santee, Calif. 92071
Murray F. Ruffino, Rt. 2, Milford, ME 04461
Rush's Old Colonial Forge, 106 Wiltshire Rd., Baltimore, MD 21221 (Ky.-Pa. rifles)
Lewis B. Sanchez, Cumberland Knife & Gun Works, 5661 Bragg Blvd., Fayetteville, NC 28303
Sanders Custom Gun Serv., 2358 Tyler Lane, Louisville, Ky. 40205
Sandy's Custom Gunshop, Rte. #1, Rockport, Ill. 62370
Saratoga Arms Co., R.D. 3, Box 387, Pottstown, Pa. 19464
Roy V. Schaefer, 965 W. Hilliard Lane, Eugene, OR 97404
N.H. Schiffman Cust. Gun Serv., 963 Malibu, Pocatello, ID 83201
Schuetzen Gun Works, 624 Old Pacific Hwy. S.E., Olympia, WA 98503
Schumaker's Gun Shop, 208 W. 5th Ave., Colville, Wash 99114
Schwartz Custom Guns, 9621 Coleman Rd., Haslett, Mich. 48840
Schwarz's Gun Shop, 41-15th St., Wellsburg, W. Va. 26070
Shaw's, Rt. 4, Box 407-L, Escondido, CA 92025
Shell Shack, 113 E. Main, Laurel, MT 59044
George H. Sheldon, P.O. Box 489, Franklin, NH 03235 (45 autos & M-1 carbines only)
Shilen Rifles, Inc., 205 Metropark Blvd., Ennis, TX 75119
Harold H. Shockley, 204 E. Farmington Rd., Hanna City, IL 61536 (hot bluing & plating)
Walter Shultz, R.D. 3, Pottstown, Pa. 19464
Silver Dollar Guns, P.O. Box 475, 10 Frances St., Franklin, NH 03235 (45 autos & M-1 carbines only)
Simmons Gun Spec., 700 Rogers Rd., Olathe, Kans. 66061
Simms Hardward Co., 2801 J St., Sacramento, Calif. 95816
Fred Sinclair, 1200 Asbury Dr., Box 302, New Haven, IN 46774
Skinner's Gun Shop, Box 30, Juneau, Alaska 98801
Markus Skosples, c/o Ziffren Sptg. Gds., 124 E. Third St., Davenport, IA 52801
Jerome F. Slezak, 1290 Marlowe, Lakewood (Cleveland), OH 44107
Small Arms Eng., 7698 Garden Prairie Rd., Garden Prairie, IL 61038 (restorations)
John Smith, 912 Lincoln, Carpentersville, Ill. 60110
Smitty's Gunshop, 308 S. Washington, Lake City, Minn. 55041
Snapp's Gunshop, 6911 E. Washington Rd., Clare, Mich. 48617
R. Southgate, Rt. 2, Franklin, Tenn. 37064 (new Kentucky rifles)
Fred D. Speiser, 2229 Dearborn, Missoula, MT 59801
Sport Service Center, 2364 N. Neva, Chicago, IL 60635
Sportsmens Equip. Co., 915 W. Washington, San Diego, Calif. 92103
Sportsmen's Exchange & Western Gun Traders, Inc., P.O. Box 603, Oxnard, CA 93030
George B. Spring, 9 Pratt St., Essex, CT 06426
Jess L. Stark, 12051 Stroud, Houston, TX 77072
Keith Stegall, Box 696, Gunnison, Colo. 81230
Victor W. Strawbridge, 6 Pineview Dr., Dover Point, Dover, NH 03820 (antique arms restoring)
W. C. Strutz, Rte. 1, "Woodland", Eagle River, WI 54521
Suter's House of Guns, 332 N. Tejon, Colorado Springs, Colo. 80902
Swanson Custom Firearms, 1051 Broadway, Denver, Colo. 80203
A. D. Swenson's 45 Shop, P.O. Box 606, Fallbrook, CA 92028
T-P Shop, 212 E. Houghton, West Branch, Mich. 48661
Talmage Ent., 43197 E. Whittier, Hemet, CA 92343
Taylor & Robbins, Box 164, Rixford, Pa. 16745
Gordon Tibbitts, 1378 Lakewood Circle, Salt Lake City, UT 84117
Daniel Titus, 119 Morlyn Ave., Bryn Mawr, PA 19010
Tom's Gunshop, 4435 Central, Hot Springs, AR 71901
Trinko's Gun Serv., 1406 E. Main, Watertown, Wis. 53094
Herb. G. Troester's Accurizing Serv., 2292 W. 100 North, Vernal, UT 84078
Dennis A. "Doc" Ulrich, 2511 S. 57th Ave., Cicero, IL 60650
Brent Umberger, Sportsman's Haven, R.R. 4, Cambridge, OH 43725
Upper Missouri Trading Co., Inc., Box 181, Crofton, MO 68730
Roy Vail, R. 1, Box 8, Warwick, N.Y. 10990
Milton Van Epps, Rt. 69-A, Parish, NY 13131
VanHorn-Abe, 5124 Huntington Dr., Los Angeles, CA 90032
J. W. Van Patten, Box 145, Foster Hill, Milford, Pa. 18337
Vic's Gun Refinishing, 6 Pineview Dr., Dover, NH 03820 (antique arms restorations)
Walker Arms Co., R. 2, Box 73, Selma, AL 36701
Walker Arms Co., 127 N. Main St., Joplin, MO 64801
R. A. Wardrop, Box 245, 409 E. Marble St., Mechanicsburg, PA 17055

Weatherby's, 2781 Firestone Blvd., South Gate, Calif. 90280
Wells Sport Store, 110 N. Summit St., Prescott, Ariz. 86301
R. A. Wells, 3452 N. 1st, Racine, Wis. 53402
Robert G. West, 27211 Huey Ave., Eugene, OR 97402
Western Gunstocks Mfg. Co., 550 Valencia School Rd., Aptos, CA 95003
Duane Wiebe, 426 Creekside Rd., Pleasant Hill, CA 94563
M. C. Wiest, 234 N. Tulane Ave., Oak Ridge, Tenn. 37830
W. C. Wilber, 400 Lucerne Dr., Spartanburg, SC 29302
Williams Gun Sight Co., 7389 Lapeer Rd., Davison, Mich. 48423
Bob Williams, c/o Hermans-Atlas Custom Guns, 800 E St. N.W., Washington, DC 20004
Williamson-Pate Gunsmith Service, 6021 Camp Bowie Blvd., Ft. Worth, TX 76116
Wilson Gun Store Inc., R.D. 1, Rte. 225, Dauphin, Pa. 17018
Thomas E. Wilson, 644 Spruce St., Boulder, CO 80302 (restorations)
Robert M. Winter, Box 484, Menno, SD 57045
Lester Womack, Box 17210, Tucson, AZ 85710
Yale's Gun Shop, 2618 Conowingo Rd., Bel Air, MD 21014 (ML work)
Mike Yee, 4700-46th Ave. S.W., Seattle, WA 98116
York County Gun Works, RR 4, Tottenham, Ont., L0G 1W0 Canada (muzzleloaders)
Yukon Firearms Service, P.O. Box 36, Carcross, Yukon, Canada
Russ Zeeryp, 1601 Foard Dr., Lynn Ross Manor, Morristown, TN 37814

CUSTOM MELTALSMITHS

Ted Blackburn, 85 E. 700 South, Springfield, UT 84663 (precision metalwork)
Tom Burgess, 180 McMannamy Draw, Kalispell, MT 59901
Dave Cook, Dave's Gun Shop, 720 Hancock Ave., Hancock, MI 49930
Homer Culver, 1219 N. Stuart, Arlington, VA 22201
John H. Eaton, 8516 James St., Upper Marlboro, MD 20870
Geo. M. Fullmer, 2499 Mavis St., Oakland, CA 94601 (precise chambering —276 cals.)
Harkrader's Custom Gun Shop, 825 Radford St., Christiansburg, VA 24073
R. H. Lampert, Rt. 1, Box 61, Guthrie, MN 56451
Herman Waldron, Box 475, Pomeroy, WA 99347
Edward S. Welty, R.D. 2, Box 25, Cheswick, PA 15024
Dick Willis, 141 Shady Creek Rd., Rochester, NY 14623

DECOYS

Carry-Lite, Inc., 5203 W. Clinton Ave., Milwaukee, WI 53223
Deeks, Inc., P.O. Box 2309, Salt Lake City, UT 84114
G & H Decoy Mfg. Co., P.O. Box 937, Henryetta, OK 74437
Tex Wirtz Ent., Inc., 1925 Hubbard St., Chicago, IL 60622
Woodstream Corp., P.O. Box 327, Lititz, PA 17543

ENGRAVERS, ENGRAVING TOOLS

Alaska Original Engraving Inc., A. E. Scott, Box 4113, Kenai, AK 99611
Aurum Etchings, P.O. Box 401059, Garland, TX 75040 (acid engraving)
Austrian Gunworks Reg'd., P.O. Box 136, Eastman, Que., Canada, J0E 1P0
E. Averill, 60 Chestnut St., Cooperstown, NY 13326
BRPierce Engraving, Rt. 1, Box 27, Umatilla, OR 97882
Joseph C. Bayer, Sunset Ave., Sunset Hill, RD 1, Princeton, N.J. 08540
Sid Bell Originals, R.D. 2, Tully, NY 13159
Bergevin et Marechal, 69 rue du Bois-Saint-Martin, 77340 Pontault-Combault, France
Weldon Bledsoe, 6812 Park Place Dr., Fort Worth, Tex. 76118
Carl & Roger Bleile, Box 11285, Cincinnati, OH 45211
Henry "Hank" Bonham, 218 Franklin Ave., Seaside Heights, NJ 08751
Bryan Bridges, 6350 E. Paseo San Andres, Tucson, AZ 85710
Burgess Vibrocrafters (BVI), Rt. 83, Grayslake, Ill. 60030
Winston Churchill, Twenty Mile Stream Rd., Rt.1, Box 29B, Proctorsville, VT 05153
Tim Davis, 230 S. Main St., Eldorado, OH 45321
James R. DeMunck, 3012 English Rd., Rochester, NY 14616
Howard M. Dove, 402 Roanoke St., Blacksburg, VA 24060
Ernest Dumoulin-Deleye, 8 rue Florent Boclinville, 4410 Herstal (Vottem), Belgium
Bill Dyer, P.O. Box 75255, Oklahoma City, Okla. 73107
Wilton L. English, 12009-B Barksdale Dr., Omaha, NB 68123
Ken Eyster, Heritage Gunsmiths Inc., 6441 Bishop Rd., Centerburg, OH 43011
John Fanzoi, P.O. Box 25, Ferlach, Austria 9170
Jacqueline Favre, 3212-B Wynn Rd., Suite 214, Las Vegas, NV 89102
Armi FERLIB, 46 Via Costa, 25063 Gardone V.T. (Brescia), Italy
Lynn Fliger, 5036 Hughes Ave. NE, Fridley, MN 55421
H. H. Frank, Route #2, Whitefish, MT 59937
J. R. French, 2633 Quail Valley, Irving TX 75060
Ed F. Giles, 204 Tremont St., Rehoboth, MA 02769
Donald Glaser, 1520 West St., Emporia, Kans. 66801
Eric Gold, Box 1904, Flagstaff, AZ 86002
Daniel Goodwin, 26 Fairview Ave., RR 6, Marlborough, CT 06447
Howard V. Grant, P.O. Box 396, Lac Du Flambeau, WI 54538
John Gray, 3923 Richard Dr. NE, Cedar Rapids, IA 52402
Griffin & Howe, 589 Broadway, N.Y., N.Y. 10012
F. R. Gurney, Engraving Methods Ltd., #2301, 9925 Jasper Ave., Edmonton, Alberta, Can. T5J 2X4
Bryson J. Gwinnell, 3146 Brown St., Collins, NY 14034
Neil Hartliep, Box 733, Fairmont, Minn. 56031
Frank E. Hendricks, Inc., Rt. 2, Box 189J, San Antonio, TX 78229
Heide Hiptmayer, P.O. Box 136, Eastman, Que., Canada J0E 1P0
S. G. Hopper, 8221 Arapahoe, Boulder, CO 80303 (scrimshaw)

Steve Huff, 2217 W. Elizabeth, Apt. 208, Ft. Collins, CO 80521
Ken Hunt, c/o Trevallion, 3442 S. Post Rd., Indianapolis, IN 46239
Ralph W. Ingle, #4 Missing Link, Rossville, GA 30741
Paul Jaeger, 211 Leedom, Jenkintown, Pa. 19046
Bill Johns, 2217 No. 10th, McAllen, TX 78501
T. J. Kaye, 4745 Dellwood, Beaumont, TX 77706
Lance Kelly, 4226 Lamar St., Decatur, GA 30035
Jim Kelso, P.O. Box 518, Preston, WA 98050
Kleinguenther's, P.O. Box 1261, Seguin, TX 78155
E. J. Koevenig, Keystone, SD 57751
John Kudlas, 622-14th St. S.E., Rochester, MN 55901
Ben Lane, Jr., 2118 Lipscomb St., Amarillo, TX 79109
W. Neal Lewis, 6300 Mixon Rd., Palmetto, GA 30268
London Guns, 1528-20th St., Santa Monica, CA 90404
Ed. J. Machu, Jr., Sportsman's Bailiwick, 5306 Broadway, San Antonio, TX 78209
Lynton S.M. McKenzie, 5589 Arapahoe, Unit 104, Boulder, CO 80301
Wm. H. Mains, 3212 B. Wynn Rd., Suite 214, Las Vegas, NV 89102
Rudy Marek, Rt. 1, Box 1A, Banks, Ore. 97106
Franz Marktl, P.O. Box 716, Kalispell, MT 59901
Ray Mellen, Box 101, Winston, GA 30187
S. A. Miller, Miller Gun Works, P.O. Box 7326, Tamuning, Guam 96911
Frank Mittermeier, 3577 E. Tremont Ave., New York, N.Y. 10465
NgraveR Co., 879 Raymond Hill Rd., Oakdale, CT 06370 (engr. tool)
New Orleans Jewelers Supply, 206 Chartres St., New Orleans, LA 70130
Hans Obiltschnig, 12. November St. 7, 9170 Ferlach, Austria
Warren E. Offenberger, Star Route, Reno, OH 45773
Oker's Engraving, 280 Illinois St., Crystal Lake, IL 60014
Tom Overbey, 612 Azalea Ave., Richmond, VA 23227
Pachmayr Gun Works, Inc., 1220 S. Grand Ave., Los Angeles, Calif. 90015
Marcello Pedini, 48 Barnes Ave., Worcester, MA 01605
Hans Pfeiffer, 286 Illinois St., Elmhurst, IL 60126
Arthur Pitetti, Hawk Hollow Rd., Denver, NY 12421
Jeremy W. Potts, Box 85, Pine Bluff, WY 82082
Wayne E. Potts, 912 Poplar St., Denver, CO 80220
E. C. Prudhomme, 513 Ricou-Brewster Bldg., Shreveport, LA 71101
John and Hans Rohner, Sunshine Canyon, Boulder, Colo. 80302
Joe Rundall, 6198 Frances Rd., Clio, MI 48420
Robert P. Runge, 94 Grove St., Ilion, N.Y. 13357
Shaw-Leibowitz, Rt. 1, Box 421, New Cumberland, W.Va. 26047 (etchers)
George Sherwood, 1128 Page Rd., Sherwood, OR 97495
Ben Shostle, The Gun Room, 1201 Burlington Dr., Muncie, IN 47302
Ron Skaggs, 508 W. Central, Princeton, IL 61536
Russell J. Smith, 231 Springdale Rd., Westfield, Mass. 01085
George B. Spring, 9 Pratt St., Essex, CT 06424
Robt. Swartley, 2800 Pine St., Napa, Calif. 94559
George W. Thiewes, 1225 Prairie St., St. Charles, IL 60174
Robert Valade, Rte. 1, Box 30-A, Cove, OR 97824
John Vest, 6715 Shasta Way, Klamath Falls, OR 97601
Ray Viramontez, 4348 Newberry Ct., Dayton, OH 45432
Louis Vrancken, 30-rue sur le bois, 4531 Argenteau (Liege), Belgium
Vernon G. Wagoner, 12271 Chama Dr., Fountain Hills, AZ 85268
Floyd E. Warren, 1273 St. Rt. 305 N.E. Rt. #3, Cortland, OH 44410
John E. Warren, P.O. Box 72, Eastham, Mass. 02642
Mel Wood, 3901 Crestmont Dr., Santa Maria, CA 93454
Dwain Wright, 67168 Central, Bend, OR 97701

GAME CALLS

Black Duck, 1737 Davis, Whiting, Ind. 46394
Burnham Bros., Box 100-C, Marble Falls, Tex. 78654
Faulk's, 616 18th St., Lake Charles, La. 70601
Lohman Mfg. Co., 320 E. Spring, Neosho, Mo. 64850
Mallardtone Game Calls, 2901 16th St., Moline, IL 61265
Phil. S. Olt Co., Box 550, Pekin, Ill. 61554
Penn's Woods Products, Inc., 19 W. Pittsburgh St., Delmont, Pa. 15626
Sport-Lore, Inc., 1757 Cherry St., Denver, Colo. 80220
Johnny Stewart Wildlife Calls, Box 7954, Waco, Tex. 76710
Thomas Game Calls, P.O. Box 336, Winnsboro, TX 75494
Weems Wild Calls, 500 S. 7th, Fort Smith, AR 72901
Tex Wirtz Ent., Inc., 1925 W. Hubbard St., Chicago, Ill. 60622

GUN PARTS, U. S. AND FOREIGN

Badger Shooter's Supply, Box 397, Owen, WI 54460
Behlert Custom Guns, Inc., 725 Lehigh Ave., Union, NJ 07083 (handgun parts)
Philip R. Crouthamel, 513 E. Baltimore, E. Lansdowne, Pa. 19050
Charles E. Duffy, Williams Lane, West Hurley, N.Y. 12491
Federal Ordnance Inc., 9634 Alpaca St., So. El Monte, CA 91733
Fenwick's Gun Annex, P.O. Box 38, Weisberg Rd., Whitehall, MD 21161
Jack First, The Gunshop, Inc., 44633 Sierra Highway, Lancaster, CA 93534
Greg's Winchester Parts, P.O. Box 8125, W. Palm Beach, FL 33407
Hunter's Haven, Zero Prince St., Alexandria, Va. 22314
Walter H. Lodewick, 2816 N.E. Halsey, Portland, OR 97232
Numrich Arms Co., West Hurley, N.Y. 12491
Pacific Intl. Merch. Corp., 2215 "J" St., Sacramento, CA 95816 (Vega 45 Colt mag.)
Potomac Arms Corp. (see Hunter's Haven)
Martin B. Retting, Inc., 11029 Washington, Culver City, Cal. 90230
Sarco, Inc., 323 Union St., Stirling, NJ 07980
Sherwood Distr. Inc., 18714 Parthenia St., Northridge, CA 91324
Simms, 2801 J St., Sacramento, CA 95816
Clifford L. Smires, R.D., Box 39, Columbus, NJ 08022 (Mauser rifles)
N. F. Strebe Gunworks, 4926 Marlboro Pike, S.E., Washington, D.C. 20027
Triple-K Mfg. Co., 568-6th Ave., San Diego, CA 92101 (magazines, gun parts)

GUNS (Foreign)

American International, 103 Social Hall Ave., Salt Lake City, UT 84111
AYA (Aguirre y Aranzabal) see: IGI Domino or Wm. L. Moore (Spanish shotguns)
Pedro Arrizabalaga, Eibar, Spain
Armoury Inc., Rte. 202, New Preston, CT 06777
Armsport, Inc., 2811 N.W. 75th Ave., Miami, FL 33122
Beretta Arms Co., Inc., P.O. Box 697, Ridgefield, CT 06877
Blaser/Vinzenz Huber GmbH, P.O. Box 2245, D-7900 Ulm, W. Germany
Bretton, 21 Rue Clement Forissier, 42-St. Etienne, France
Browning, Rt. 4, Box 624-B, Arnold, Mo. 63010
Carlo Casartelli, 25062 Concesio (Brescia), Italy
Centennial Arms Corp., 3318 W. Devon, Chicago, (Lincolnwood) Ill. 60645
Century Arms Co., 3-5 Federal St., St. Albans, Vt. 05478
Champlin Firearms, Inc., Box 3191, Enid, OK 73701 (Gebruder Merkel)
Ets. Chapuis, 42380 St. Bonnet-le-Chateau, France
Clarex S.A., 11 rue Cornavin, 1201 Geneve, Switzerland (Chapuis)
Commercial Trading Imports, Inc., Marketing Serv. of Control Data, 8100 - 34th Ave. S., Bloomington, MN 55440 (Russian shotguns)
Connecticut Valley Arms Co., Saybrook Rd., Haddam, CT 06438 (CVA)
Continental Arms Corp., 697 Fifth Ave., New York, N.Y. 10022
Walter Craig, Inc., Box 927-A Selma, AL 36701
Creighton & Warren, P.O. Box 15723, Nashville, TN 37215 (Krieghoff combination guns)
Morton Cundy & Son, Ltd., P.O. Box 315, Lakeside, MT 59922
Davidson Firearms Co., 2703 High Pt. Rd., Greensboro, N.C. 27403 (shotguns)
Davis Gun Shop, 7213 Lee Highway, Falls Church, VA 22046 (Fanzoj, Ferlach; Spanish guns)
Diana Co., 842 Vallejo St., San Francisco, CA 94133 (Benelli, Breda shotguns)
Dixie Gun Works, Inc., Hwy 51, South, Union City, Tenn. 38261 ("Kentucky" rifles)
Ernest Dumoulin-Deleye, 8 rue Florent Boclinville, 4410 Herstal (Vottem), Belgium
Peter Dyson Ltd., 29-31 Church St., Honley, Huddersfield, Yorkshire HD7 2AH, England (accessories f. antique gun collectors)
Eastern Sports International, Inc., Savage Rd., Milford, NH 03055 (Rottweil; Geco)
Euroarms, Via Solferino 13/A, 25100 Brescia, Italy
Excam Inc., 4480 E. 11 Ave., P.O. Box 3483, Hialeah, FL 33013
Armi Fabbri, Casella 206, Brescia, Italy 25100
Armi Famars, Via Cinelli 33, Gardone V.T. (Brescia), Italy 25063
J. Fanzoj, P.O. Box 25, Ferlach, Austria 9170
F.E.T.E. Corp., 2867 W. 7th St., Los Angeles, CA 90005 (A. Zoli guns)
Armi FERLIB, 46 Via Costa, 25063 Gardone V.T. (Brescia), Italy
Ferlach (Austria) of North America, P.O. Box 430435, S. Miami, FL 33143
Firearms Center Inc. (FCI), 308 Leisure Lane, Victoria, TX 77901
Firearms Imp. & Exp. Co., 2470 N.W. 21st St., Miami, Fla. 33142
Flaig's Lodge, Millvale, Pa. 15209
Freeland's Scope Stands, Inc., 3737 14th Ave., Rock Island, Ill. 61201
J. L. Galef & Son, Inc., 85 Chambers, New York, N.Y. 10007
Renato Gamba, Fabbrica d'Armi, via Petrarca, 25060 Ponte Zanano di Sarezzo (Brescia), Italy
Armas Garbi, Fundidores 4, Urki #12-14, Eibar, Spain (shotguns)
Gastinne Renette, 39 Ave. F.D. Roosevelt, 75008 Paris, France
Golden Eagle Firearms, 5803 Sovereign, Suite 206, Houston, TX 77036
Georges Granger, 66 Cours Fauriel, 42 St. Etienne, France
Hawes National Corp., 15424 Cabrito Rd., Van Nuys, CA 91406
Healthways, Box 45055, Los Angeles, Calif. 90061
Gil Hebard Guns, Box 1, Knoxville, IL 61448 (Hammerli)
Heckler & Koch Inc., 933 N. Kenmore St., Suite 218, Arlington, VA 22201
A. D. Heller, Inc., Box 56, 2322 Grand Ave., Baldwin, NY 11510
Herter's, Waseca, Minn. 56093
Heym, Friedr. Wilh., Box 861, Bolton, Ont. L0P 1A0, Canada
IGI Domino, 200 Madison Ave., New York, NY 10016 (AYA)
Interarmco, see: Interarms (Walther)
Interarms Ltd., 10 Prince St., Alexandria, Va. 22313 (Mauser, Valmet M-62/S)
International Distr., Inc., 7290 S.W. 42nd St., Miami, FL 33155 (Taurus rev.)
Ithaca Gun Co., Terrace Hill, Ithaca, N.Y. 14850 (Perazzi)
Italguns, Via Leonardo da Vinci 169, 20090 Trezzano, (Milano), Italy
Paul Jaeger Inc., 211 Leedom St., Jenkintown, Pa. 19046
Jana Intl. Co., Box 1107, Denver, Colo. 80201 (Parker-Hale)
J. J. Jenkins, 375 Pine Ave. No. 25, Goleta, CA 93017
Kassnar Imports, 5480 Linglestown Rd., Harrisburg, PA 17110
Kerr's Sport Shop, Inc., 9584 Wilshire Blvd., Beverly Hills, CA 90212
Kimel Industries, P.O. Box 335, Matthews, NC 28105
Kleinguenther's, P.O. Box 1261, Seguin, TX 78155
Knight & Knight, 5930 S.W. 48 St., Miami, FL 33155 (made-to-order only)
Dr. Kortz Elko, 28 rue Ecole Moderne, 7400 Soignes, Belgium
L. A. Distributors, 4 Centre Market Pl., New York, N.Y. 10013
L.E.S., 3640 Dempster, Skokie, IL 60076 (Steyr, Mannlicher-Schönauer)
S. E. Laszlo, 200 Tillary St., Brooklyn, N.Y. 11201
Lever Arms Serv. Ltd., 771 Dunsmuir, Vancouver, B.C., Canada V6C 1M9
Liberty Arms Organization, Box 306, Montrose, Calif. 91020
McKeown's Guns, R.R. 1, Pekin, Ill. 61554
McQueen Sales Co. Ltd., 1760 W. 3rd Ave., Vancouver, B.C., Canada V6J 1K5
Mandall Shtg. Suppl. Corp., 3616 N. Scottsdale Rd., Scottsdale, AZ 85252
Manu-Arm, St. Etienne, France
Manufrance, 100-Cours Fauriel, 42 St. Etienne, France
Markwell Arms Co., 2414 W. Devon, Chicago, IL 60645
Mars Equipment Corp., 3318 W. Devon, Chicago, Ill. 60645
Mendi s. coop., P.O. Box 48, Eibar, Spain
Merkuria, P.O. Box 18, 17005 Prague, Czechoslovakia (BRNO)

Wm. Larkin Moore, 2890 Marlics St., Agoura, CA 91301 (AYA, Garbi)
Navy Arms Co., 689 Bergen Blvd., Ridgefield, N.J. 07657
Harry Owen, P.O. Box 774, Sunnyvale, Ca. 94088.
P.M. Air Services, Ltd., P.O. Box 1573, Costa Mesa, CA 92626
Pachmayr Gun Works, 1220 S. Grand Ave., Los Angeles, CA 90015
Pacific Intl. Merch. Corp., 2215 "J" St., Sacramento, CA 95816
Rob. Painter, 2901 Oakhurst Ave., Austin, TX 78703 (Chapuis)
Parker-Hale, Bisleyworks, Golden Hillock Rd., Sparbrook, Birmingham B11 2PZ, England
Ed Paul Sptg. Goods, 172 Flatbush Ave., Brooklyn, N.Y. 11217 (Premier)
Picard-Fayolle, 42-rue du Vernay, 42100 Saint Etienne, France
Precise, 3 Chestnut, Suffern, NY 10901
Premier Shotguns, 172 Flatbush Ave., Brooklyn N.Y. 11217
Leonard Puccinelli Co., P.O. Box 668, San Anselmo, CA 94960 (I.A.B., Rizzini of Italy)
RG Industries, Inc., 2485 N.W. 20th St., Miami, FL 33142 (Erma)
Richland Arms Co., 321 W. Adrian St., Blissfield, Mich. 49228
Rottweil, see: Eastern
SKB Sports Inc., 190 Shepard, Wheeling, IL 60090
Sanderson's, 724 W. Edgewater, Portage, Wis. 53901
Victor Sarasqueta, S.A., P.O. Box 25, 3 Victor Sarasqueta St., Eibar, Spain
Savage Arms Corp., Westfield, Mass. 01085 (Anschutz)
Security Arms Co., See: Heckler & Koch
Service Armament, 689 Bergen Blvd., Ridgefield, N.J. 07657 (Greener Harpoon Gun)
Sherwood Dist., Inc., 18714 Parthenia St., Northridge, CA 91324
Simmons Spec., Inc., 700 Rogers Rd., Olathe, Kans. 66061
Skinner's Gun Shop (see Alaskan Rifles)
Sloan's Sprtg. Goods, Inc., 10 South St., Ridgefield, CT 06877
Franz Sodia Jagdgewehrfabrik, Schulhausgasse 14, 9170 Ferlach, (Kärnten) Austria
Steyr-Daimler-Puch of America, Inc., 3560-64 Roger B. Chaffee Blvd., Grand Rapids, MI 49508
Stoeger Arms Co., 55 Ruta Ct., S. Hackensack, N.J. 07606
Tradewinds, Inc., P.O. Box 1191, Tacoma, Wash. 98401
Uberti, Aldo & Co., Via G. Carducci 41 or 39, Ponte Zanano (Brescia), Italy
Ignacio Ugartechea, Apartado 21, Eibar, Spain
Ultra-Hi Products Co., 150 Florence Ave., Hawthorne, NJ 07506 (ML)
Valor Imp. Corp., 5555 N.W. 36th Ave., Miami, FL 33142
Ventura Imports, P.O. Box 2782, Seal Beach, CA 90740 (European shotguns)
Verney-Carron, B.P. 88, 17 Cours Fauriel, 42010 St. Etienne Cedex, France
Waffen-Frankonia, Box 380, 87 Wurzburg, W. Germany
Weatherby's, 2781 Firestone Blvd., So. Gate, Calif. 90280 (Sauer)
Fabio Zanotti di Stefano, Casa fondata nel 1625, Via XXV Aprile 1, Gardone V.T. (Brescia) Italy
Zavodi Crvena Zastava, 29 Novembra St., No. 12, Belgrade, Yugosl.
Antonio Zoli & Co., 39 Via Zanardelli, 25063 Gardone V.T., Brescia, Italy

GUNS & GUN PARTS, REPLICA AND ANTIQUE

Antique Gun Parts, Inc., 1118 S. Braddock Ave., Pittsburgh, PA 15218 (ML)
Armoury Inc., Rte. 202, New Preston, CT 06777
Artistic Arms, Inc., Box 23, Hoagland, IN 46745 (Sharps-Borchardt replica)
Carter Gun Works, 2211 Jefferson Pk. Ave., Charlottesville, Va. 22903
Darr Tool Co., P.O. Box 778, Carpinteria, CA 93013 (S.S. items)
Dixie Gun Works, Inc., Hwy 51, South, Union City, Tenn. 38261
Federal Ordnance Inc., 9643 Alpaca St., So. El Monte, CA 91733
Fred Goodwin, Sherman Mills, ME 04776 (antique guns & parts)
Log Cabin Sport Shop, 8010 Lafayette Rd., Lodi, OH 44254
Lever Arms Service Ltd., 771 Dunsmuir, Vancouver, B.C., Canada V6C 1M9
Edw. E. Lucas, 32 Garfield Ave., East Brunswick, NY 08816 (45/70 Springfield parts)
Lyman Products Corp., Middlefield, CT 06455
Markwell Arms Co., 2414 W. Devon, Chicago, IL 60645
Numrich Arms Co., West Hurley, N.Y. 12491
Replica Models, Inc., 610 Franklin St., Alexandria, VA 22314
S&S Firearms, 88-21 Aubrey Ave., Glendale, N.Y. 11227
C. H. Stoppler, 1426 Walton Ave., New York, NY 10452 (miniature guns)
Upper Missouri Trading Co., 3rd & Harold Sts., Crofton, NB 68730
C. H. Weisz, Box 311, Arlington, VA 22210
W. H. Wescombe, P.O. Box 488, Glencoe, CA 95232 (Rem. R.B. parts)

GUNS (Pellet)

Air Rifle Hq., 247 Court St., Grantsville, W. Va. 26147
Beeman's Precision Airguns, 47 Paul Dr., Bldg. 6, San Rafael, CA 94903
Benjamin Air Rifle Co., 1525 So. 8th St., Louis, Mo. 63104
Continental Arms Corp., 697 5th Ave., New York, N.Y. 10022
Crosman Arms, 980 Turk Hill Rd., Fairport, NY 14450
Daisy Mfg. Co., Rogers, Ark. 72756 (also Feinwerkbau)
K. J. David & Co., P.O. Box 923, Oak Brook, IL 60521
Fanta Air Rifles, Box 8122, La Crescenta, Calif, 91214
J. L. Galef & Son, Inc., 85 Chambers St., New York, N.Y. 10007 (B.S.A.)
Great Lakes Airguns, S6175 So. Park Ave., Hamburg, NY 14075
Harrington & Richardson Arms Co., Industrial Rowe, Gardner, MA 01440 (Webley)
Healthways, Box 45055, Los Angeles, Calif. 90061
Gil Hebard Guns, Box 1, Knoxville, Ill. 61448
Hy-Score Arms Co., 200 Tillary St., Brooklyn, N.Y. 11201
Interarms, 10 Prince, Alexandria, Va. 22313 (Walther)
Paul Jaeger, Inc., 211 Leedom St., Jenkintown, PA 19046
LARC International, P.O. Box 34007, Coral Gables, FL 33134

Marksman Products, P.O. Box 2983, Torrance, CA 90509
Power Line (see: Daisy Mfg. Co.)
Precise, 3 Chestnut, Suffern, NY 10901
Service Armament, 689 Bergen Blvd., Ridgefield, N.J. 07657 (Webley)
Sheridan Products, Inc., 3205 Sheridan, Racine, Wis. 53403
Smith & Wesson, 2100 Roosevelt Ave., Springfield, MA 01104

GUNS, SURPLUS—PARTS AND AMMUNITION

Century Arms, Inc., 3-5 Federal St., St. Albans, Vt. 05478
Walter Craig, Inc., Box 927-A, Selma, AL 36701
Eastern Firearms Co., 790 S. Arroyo Pkwy., Pasadena, Calif. 91105
Hunter's Lodge, 200 S. Union, Alexandria, Va. 22313
Lever Arms Serv. Ltd., 771 Dunsmuir St., Vancouver, B.C., Canada V6C IM9
Mars Equipment Corp., 3318 W. Devon, Chicago, Ill. 60645
National Gun Traders, 225 S.W. 22nd, Miami, Fla. 33135
Pacific Intl. Merch. Corp., 2215 "J" St., Sacramento, CA 95816
Plainfield Ordnance Co., Box 447, Dunellen, N.J. 08812
Service Armament Co., 689 Bergen Blvd., Ridgefield, N.J. 07657
Sherwood Distrib. Inc., 18714 Parthenia St., Northridge, CA 91324

GUNS, U.S.-made

A.I.G. Corp., 7 Grasso Ave., North Haven, CT 06473
A-J Ordance, Inc., 1066 E. Edna Pl., Covina, CA 91722 (Thomas auto pistol)
AMT (Arcadia Machine & Tool), 11666 McBean Dr., El Monte, CA 91732
A. R. Sales Co., 9624 Alpaca St., South El Monte, CA 91733 (Mark IV sporter)
American Arms, 915 N.W. 72nd St., Miami, FL 33150
American Heritage Arms, Inc., Rte. 44, P.O. Box 95, West Willington, CT 06279 (ML)
ArmaLite, 118 E. 16th St., Costa Mesa, Calif. 92627
Artistic Arms, Inc., Box 23, Hoagland, IN 46745 (Sharps-Borchardt)
Auto-Ordnance Corp., Box ZG, West Hurley, NY 12491
Bauer Firearms, 34750 Klein Ave., Fraser, MI 48026
Brown Precision Co., 5869 Indian Ave., San Jose, CA 95123 (High Country rifle)
Challanger Mfg. Corp., 118 Pearl St., Mt. Vernon, NY 10550 (Hopkins & Allen)
Champlin Firearms, Inc., Box 3191, Enid, Okla. 73701
Charter Arms Corp., 430 Sniffens Ln., Stratford, CT 06497
Classic Arms Intl., Inc., 20 Wilbraham St., Palmer, MA 01069 (BP guns)
Clerke Products, 2219 Main St., Santa Monica, Ca. 90405
Colt, 150 Huyshope Ave., Hartford, CT 06102
Commando Arms, Inc., Box 10214, Knoxville, Tenn. 37919
Crown City Arms, P.O. Box 1126, Cortland, NY 13045 (45 auto handgun)
Cumberland Arms, Rt. 1, Shafer Rd., Blanton Chapel, Manchester, TN 37355
Day Arms Corp., 2412 S.W. Loop 410, San Antonio, TX 78227
Leonard Day & Co., 316 Burts Pits Rd., Northampton, MA 01060 (ML)
Detonics 45 Associates, 2500 Seattle Tower, Seattle, WA 98101 (auto pistol)
DuBiel Arms Co., 1724 Baker Rd., Denison, TX 75090
EE-DA-How Long Rifles, Inc., 3318 Camrose Lane, Boise, ID 83705
EMF Co. Inc., Box 1248, Studio City, CA 91604 (T.D.A. rev.)
FTL Marketing Corp., 11100 Cumpston St., No. Hollywood, CA 91601
Falling Block Works, P.O. Box 22, Troy, MI 48084
Firearms Imp. & Exp. Co., 2470 N.W. 21st St., Miami, FL 33142 (FIE)
Freshour Mfg. Co., 1914 - 15th Ave. N., Texas City, TX 77590 (Ranger rifle)
Golden Age Arms Co., 14 W. Winter St., Delaware, OH 43015
Franklin C. Green, Rte. 2, Box 114-A, Montrose, CA 81401 (free pistol)
Harrington & Richardson, Industrial Rowe, Gardner, MA 01440
A. D. Heller, Inc., Box 268, Grand Ave., Baldwin, NY 11510
High Standard Sporting Firearms, 31 Prestige Park Circle, East Hartford, CT 06108
Hopkins & Allen Arms, #1 Melnick Rd., Monsey, NY 10952
Hyper-Single Precision SS Rifles, 520 E. Beaver, Jenks, OK 74037
Ithaca Gun Co., Ithaca, N.Y. 14850
Iver Johnson Arms Inc., P.O. Box 251, Middlesex, NJ 08846
J & R carbine, (see: PJK Inc.)
Paul Jaeger, Inc., 211 Leedom St., Jenkintown, PA 19046
Ljutic Ind., Inc., P.O. Box 2117, Yakima, WA 98902 (Mono-Gun)
Marlin Firearms Co., 100 Kenna Dr., New Haven, Conn. 06473
Bob Meece Co., Inc., 1602 Stemmons, Suite C, Carrollton, TX 75006 (Snake Charmer)
Merrill Co. Inc., Box 187, Rockwell City, IA 50579
O. F. Mossberg & Sons, Inc., 7 Grasso St., No. Haven, Conn. 06473
Mowrey Gun Works, Box 28, Iowa Park TX 76367
Navy Arms Co., 689 Bergen Blvd., Ridgefield, N.J. 07657
North American Arms Co., P.O. Box 158, Freedom, WY 83120 (Casull handgun)
North Star Arms, R.2, Box 74A, Ortonville, MN 56278 (The Plainsman)
Numrich Arms Corp., W. Hurley, NY 12491
PJK, Inc., 1527 Royal Oak Dr., Bradbury, Ca 91010 (J&R Carbine)
Plainfield Machine Co., Inc., Box 447, Dunellen, N.J. 08812
Plainfield Inc., 292 Vail Ave., Piscataway, NJ 08854
R G Industries, 2485 N.W. 20th SE., Miami, FL 33142
Raven Arms, 1300 Bixby Dr., Industry, CA 91745
Remington Arms Co., Bridgeport, Conn. 06602
Riedl Rifles, 15124 Weststate St., Westminster, CA 92683 (S.S.)
Rocky Mountain Arms Corp., Box 224, Salt Lake City, UT 84110
Ruger (see: Sturm, Ruger & Co.)
Savage Arms Corp., Westfield, Mass. 01085

Sears, Roebuck & Co., 825 S. St. Louis, Chicago, Ill. 60607
Semmerling Corp., P.O. Box 400, Newton, MA 02160
Seventrees Ltd., 315 W. 39th St., New York, N.Y. 10018
Sharon Rifle Barrel Co., P.O. Box 1197, Kalispell, MT 59901
Sharps Rifle Co., 3428 Shakertown Rd., Dayton, OH 45430
Shiloh Products, 37 Potter St., Farmingdale, NY 11735 (Sharps)
Smith & Wesson, Inc., 2100 Roosevelt Ave., Springfield, MA 01101
Sporting Arms, Inc., 9643 Alpaca St., So. El Monte, CA 91733 (M-1 carbine)
Springfield Armory, 111 E. Exchange St., Geneseo, Ill 61254
Sterling Arms Corp., 4436 Prospect St., Gasport, NY 14067
Sturm, Ruger & Co., Southport, Conn. 06490
Thompson-Center Arms, Box 2405, Rochester, N.H. 03867
Trail Guns Armory, 2115 Lexington, Houston, TX 77006 (muzzleloaders)
Triple-S Development Co., Inc., 1450 E. 289th St., Wickliffe, OH 44092 (Wickliffe S.S. rifle)
United Sporting Arms, Inc., 35 Gilpin Ave., Hauppauge, L.I., NY 11787
United States Arms Corp., Doctors Path and Middle Road, Riverhead, NY 11901 (Abilene SA rev.)
Universal Firearms, 3740 E. 10th Ct., Hialeah, FL 33013
Unordco, P.O. Box 15723, Nashville, TN 37215
Ward's, 619 W. Chicago, Chicago, Ill. 60607 (Western Field brand)
Weatherby's, 2781 E. Firestone Blvd., South Gate, Calif. 90280
Dan Wesson Arms, 293 So. Main St., Monson, Mass. 01057
Wichita Eng. & Supply, Inc., P.O. Box 11371, Wichita, KS 67202
Wildey Firearms Co., Inc., P.O. Box 284, Cold Spring, NY 10516
Wilkinson Arms, 803 N. Glendora Ave., Covina, CA 91724 (Diane 25 ACP auto pistol)
Winchester Repeating Arms Co., New Haven, Conn. 06504
Winslow Arms Co., Inc., P.O. Box 783, Camden, SC 29020

GUNSMITHS, CUSTOM (see Custom Gunsmiths)
GUNSMITHS, HANDGUN (see Pistolsmiths)

GUNSMITH SCHOOLS

Colorado School of Trades, 1545 Hoyt, Lakewood, CO 80215
Lassen Community College, P.O. Box 3000, Susanville, CA 96130
North American School of Firearms, 4401 Birch St., Newport Beach, CA 92663 (correspondence)
Oregon Institute of Technology, Small Arms Dept., Klamath Falls, OR 97601
Penn. Gunsmith School, 812 Ohio River Blvd., Avalon, Pittsburgh, Pa. 15202
Trinidad State Junior College, Trinidad, Colo. 81082

GUNSMITH SUPPLIES, TOOLS, SERVICES

Albright Prod. Co., P.O. Box 1144, Portola, CA 96122 (trap buttplates)
Alley Supply Co., Carson Valley Industrial Park, Gardnerville, NV 89410
Ames Precision Machine Works, 5270 Geddes Rd., Ann Arbor, MI 48105 (portable hardness tester)
Anderson Mfg. Co., P.O. Box 3120, Yakima WA 98903 (tang safe)
Armite Labs., 1845 Randolph St., Los Angeles, Cal. 90001 (pen oiler)
B-Square Co., Box 11281, Ft. Worth, Tex. 76110
Jim Baiar, 490 Halfmoon Rd., Columbia Falls, MT 59912 (hex screws)
Behlert Custom Guns, Inc., 725 Lehigh Ave., Union, NJ 07083
Al Biesen, W. 2039 Sinto Ave., Spokane, WA 99201 (grip caps, buttplates)
Bonanza Sports Mfg. Co., 412 Western Ave., Faribault, Minn. 55021
Brookstone Co., 125 Vose Farm Rd., Peterborough, NH 03458
Bob Brownell's, Main & Third, Montezuma, Ia. 50171
W. E. Brownell, 1852 Alessandro Trail, Vista, Calif. 92083 (checkering tools)
Maynard P. Buehler, Inc., 17 Orinda Hwy., Orinda, Calif. 94563 (Rocol lube)
Burgess Vibrocrafters, Inc. (BVI), Rte. 83, Grayslake, Ill. 60030
M. H. Canjar, 500 E. 45th, Denver, Colo. 80216 (triggers, etc.)
Chapman Mfg. Co., Rte. 17 at Saw Mill Rd., Durham, CT 06422
Chase Chemical Corp., 3527 Smallman St., Pittsburgh, PA 15201 (Chubb Multigauge)
Chubb (see Chase Chem. Co.)
Chicago Wheel & Mfg. Co., 1101 W. Monroe St., Chicago, Ill. 60607 (Handee grinders)
Christy Gun Works, 875-57th St., Sacramento, Calif. 95819
Clover Mfg. Co., 139 Woodward Ave., Norwalk, CT 06856 (Clover compound)
Clymer Mfg. Co., 14241 W. 11 Mile Rd., Oak Park, Mich. 48237 (reamers)
Colbert Industries, 10107 Adella, South Gate, Calif. 90280 (Panavise)
A. Constantine & Son, Inc., 2050 Eastchester Rd., Bronx, N.Y. 10461 (wood)
Dave Cook, 720 Hancock Ave., Hancock, MI 49930 (metalsmithing only)
Cougar & Hunter, G 6398 W. Pierson Rd., Flushing, Mich. 48433 (scope jigs)
Alvin L. Davidson Prods. f. Shooters, 1215 Branson, Las Cruces, NM 88001 (action sleeves)
Dayton-Traister Co., P.O. Box 593, Oak Harbor, Wa. 98277 (triggers)
Dremel Mfg. Co., 4915-21st St., Racine, WI 53406 (grinders)
Chas. E. Duffy, Williams Lane, West Hurley, N.Y. 12491
Peter Dyson Ltd., 29-31 Church St., Honley, Huddersfield, Yorksh. HD7 2AH, England (accessories f. antique gun coll.)
E-Z Tool Co., P.O. Box 3186, 25 N.W. 44th Ave., Des Moines, Ia. 50313 (lathe taper attachment)
Edmund Scientific Co., 101 E. Glouster Pike, Barrington, N.J. 08007
F. K. Elliott, Box 785, Ramona, Calif. 92065 (reamers)
Forster Products, Inc., 82 E. Lanark Ave., Lanark, Ill. 61046
Keith Francis, P.O. Box 537, Talent, OR 97540 (reamers)

G. R. S. Corp., Box 1157, Boulder, Colo. 80302 (Gravermeister)
Gager Gage and Tool Co., 27509 Industrial Blvd., Hayward, CA 94545 (speedlock triggers f. Rem. 1100 & 870 pumps)
Gilmore Pattern Works, P.O. Box 50231, Tulsa, OK 74150
Gold Lode, Inc., 181 Gary Ave., Wheaton, IL 60187 (gold inlay kit)
Gopher Shooter's Supply, Box 278, Faribault, MN 55021 (screwdrivers, etc.)
Grace Metal Prod., 115 Ames St., Elk Rapids, MI 49629 (screw drivers, drifts)
Gunline Tools Inc., 719 No. East St., Anaheim, CA 92805
H. & M. 24062 Orchard Lake Rd., Box 258, Farmington, MI 48024 (reamers)
Half Moon Rifle Shop, 490 Halfmoon Rd., Columbia Falls, MT 59912 (hex screws)
Hartford Reamer Co., Box 134, Lathrup Village, Mich. 48075
Paul Jaeger Inc., 211 Leedom St., Jenkintown, PA. 19046
Jeffredo Gunsight Co., 1629 Via Monserate, Fallbrook, CA 92028 (trap buttplate)
Jerrow's Inletting Service, 452 5th Ave., E.N., Kalispell, MT 59901
Kasenite Co., Inc., 3 King St., Mahwah, N.J. 07430 (surface hrdng. comp.)
J. Korzinek, RD #2, Box R, Canton, PA 17724 (stainl. steel bluing)
LanDav Custom Guns, 7213 Lee Highway, Falls Church, VA 22046
John G. Lawson, 1802 E. Columbia Ave., Tacoma, WA 98404
Lea Mfg. Co., 237 E. Aurora St., Waterbury, Conn. 06720
Lightwood & Son Ltd., Britannia Rd., Banbury, Oxfordsh. OX1 68TD, England
Lock's Phila. Gun Exch., 6700 Rowland Ave., Philadelphia, Pa. 19149
Marker Machine Co., Box 426, Charleston, Ill. 61920
Michaels of Oregon Co., P.O. Box 13010, Portland, Ore. 97213
Viggo Miller, P.O. Box 4181, Omaha, Neb. 68104 (trigger attachment)
Miller Single Trigger Mfg. Co., R.D. on Rt. 209, Millersburg, PA 17061
Frank Mittermeier, 3577 E. Tremont, N.Y., N.Y. 10465
Moderntools Corp, Box 407, Dept. GD, Woodside, N.Y. 11377
N&J Sales, Lime Kiln Rd., Northford, Conn. 06472 (screwdrivers)
Karl A. Neise, Inc., 5602 Roosevelt Ave., Woodside, N.Y. 11377
Palmgren Prods., Chicago Tool & Eng. Co., 8383 South Chicago Ave., Chicago, IL 60167 (vises, etc.)
Panavise, Colbert Industries, 10107 Adelia Ave., South Gate, CA 90280
C. R. Pedersen & Son, Ludington, Mich. 49431
Ponderay Lab., 210 W. Prasch, Yakima, Wash. 98902 (epoxy glass bedding)
Redford Reamer Co., Box 40604, Redford Hts. Sta, Detroit, MI 48240
Richland Arms Co., 321 W. Adrian St., Blissfield, Mich. 49228
Riley's Supply Co., 121 No. Main St., Avilla, Ind. 46710 (Niedner buttplates, caps)
Ruhr-American Corp., So. Hwy #5, Glenwood, Minn. 56334
A. G. Russell, 1705 Hiway 71N, Springdale, AR 72764 (Arkansas oilstones)
Schaffner Mfg. Co., Emsworth, Pittsburgh, Pa. 15202 (polishing kits)
Schuetzen Gun Works, 624 Old Pacific Hwy. S.E., Olympia, WA 98503
Shaw's, Rt. 4, Box 407-L, Escondido, CA 92025
L. S. Starrett Co., Athol, Mass. 01331
Texas Platers Supply Co., 2453 W. Five Mile Parkway, Dallas, TX 75233 (plating kit)
Timney Mfg. Co., 2847 E. Siesta Lane, Phoenix, AZ 85024
Stan de Treville, Box 33021, San Diego, Calif. 92103 (checkering patterns)
Twin City Steel Treating Co., Inc., 1114 S. 3rd, Minneapolis, Minn. 55415 (heat treating)
Will-Burt Co., 169 So. Main, Orrville, OH 44667 (vises)
Williams Gun Sight Co., 7389 Lapeer Rd., Davison, Mich. 48423
Wilson Arms Co., 63 Leetes Island Rd., Branford, CT 06405
Wisconsin Platers Supply Co., see: Texas Platers
W. C. Wolff Co., Box 232, Ardmore, PA 19003 (springs)
Woodcraft Supply Corp., 313 Montvale, Woburn, MA 01801

HANDGUN ACCESSORIES

A. R. Sales Co., P.O. Box 3192, South El Monte, CA 91733
Baramie Corp., 6250 E. 7 Mile Rd., Detroit, MI 48234 (Hip-Grip)
Bar-Sto Precision Machine, 633 S. Victory Blvd., Burbank, CA 91502
Behlert Custom Guns, Inc., 725 Lehigh Ave., Union, NJ 07083
C'Arco, P.O. Box 308, Highland, CA 92346 (Ransom Rest)
Case Master, 4675 E. 10 Ave., Miami, Fla. 33013
Central Specialties Co., 6030 Northwest Hwy., Chicago, Ill. 60631
D&E Magazines Mgf., P.O. Box 4579, Downey, CA 90242 (clips)
Bill Dyer, 503 Midwest Bldg., Oklahoma City, Okla. 73102 (grip caps)
Essex Arms, Box 345, Phaerring St., Island Pond, VT 05846 (45 Auto frames)
R. S. Frielich, 396 Broome St., New York, N.Y. 10013 (cases)
Laka Tool Co., 62 Kinkel St., Westbury, L.I., NY 11590 (stainless steel 45 Auto parts)
Lee Custom Engineering, Inc., 46 E. Jackson St., Hartford, WI 53027
Lee Precision Inc., 4275 Hwy. U, Hartford, WI 53027 (pistol rest holders)
Los Gatos Grip & Specialty Co., P.O. Box 1850, Los Gatos, CA 95030 (custom-made)
Matich Loader, 10439 Rush St., South El Monte, CA 91733 (Quick Load)
W. A. Miller Co., Inc., Mingo Loop, Oguossoc, ME 04964 (cases)
No-Sho Mfg. Co., 10727 Glenfield Ct., Houston, TX 77096
Pachmayr, 1220 S. Grand, Los Angeles, Calif. 90015 (cases)
Pacific Intl. Mchdsg. Corp., 2215 "J" St., Sacramento, CA 95818 (Vega 45 Colt comb. mag.)
Pistolsafe, Dr. L., N. Chili, NY 14514 (handgun safe)
Platt Luggage, Inc., 2301 S. Prairie, Chicago, Ill. 60616 (cases)
Sportsmen's Equipment Co., 415 W. Washington, San Diego, Calif. 92103
M. Tyler, 1326 W. Britton, Oklahoma City, Okla. 73114 (grip adaptor)
Whitney Sales, Inc., P.O. Box 875, Reseda, CA 91335
Dave Woodruff, Box 5, Bear, DE 19701 (relining and conversions)

HANDGUN GRIPS

Crest Carving Co., 8091 Bolsa Ave., Midway City, CA 92655
Fitz, 653 N. Hagar St., San Fernando, CA 91340
Gateway Shooters' Supply, Inc., 10145-103rd St., Jacksonville, FL 32210 (Rogers grips)
Herrett's, Box 741, Twin Falls, Ida. 83301
Mershon Co., Inc., 1230 S. Grand Ave., Los Angeles, Calif. 90015
Mustang Custom Pistol Grips, 28715 Via Montezuma, Temecula, CA 92390
Robert H. Newell, 55 Coyote, Los Alamos, NM 87544 (custom)
Rogers Grips (see: Gateway Shooters' Supply)
Safety Grip Corp., Box 456, Riverside St., Miami, Fla. 33135
Jean St. Henri, 6525 Dume Dr., Malibu, CA 90265 (custom)
Schiermeier, Box 704, Twin Falls, ID 83301 (Thompson/Contender)
Sile Dist., 7 Centre Market Pl., New York, N.Y. 10013
Southern Gun Exchange, Inc., 4311 Northeast Expressway, Atlanta (Doraville), GA 30340 (Outrider brand)
Sports Inc., P.O. Box 683, Park Ridge, IL 60068 (Franzite)

HEARING PROTECTORS

AO Safety Prods., Div. of American Optical Corp., 14 Mechanic St., Southbridge, MA 01550 (ear valve)
Bausch & Lomb, 635 St. Paul St., Rochester, N.Y. 14602
Hodgdon, 7710 W. 50 Hiway, Shawnee Mission, Kans. 66202
Norton Co., Safety Prods. Div., 11320 Burbank Blvd., No. Hollywood, Ca. 91601 (Lee-Sonic ear valve)
Safety Direct, 23 Snider Way, Sparks, NV 89431 (Silencio)
Smith & Wesson, 2100 Roosevelt Ave., Springfield, MA 01101
Willson Safety Prods Div., P.O. Box 622, Reading, PA 19603 (Ray-O-Vac)

HOLSTERS & LEATHER GOODS

American Sales & Mfg. Co., P.O. Box 677, Laredo, Tex. 78040
Andy Anderson, P.O. Box 225, North Hollywood, CA 91603 (Gunfighter Custom Holsters)
Bianchi Holster Co., 100 Calle Cortez, Temecula, CA 92390
Boyt Co., Div. of Welch Sptg., Box 1108, Iowa Falls, Ia. 51026
Brauer Bros. Mfg. Co., 817 N. 17th, St. Louis, Mo. 63106
Browning, Rt. 4, Box 624-B, Arnold, MO 63010
J. M. Bucheimer Co., Airport Rd., Frederick, Md. 21701
Cathey Enterprises, Inc., 9516 Neils Thompson Dr., Austin, TX 78758
Chace Leather Prods., 507 Alden St., Fall River, MA 02722
Cobra Ltd., 878 Federal Rd., Brookfield, CT 06804
Colt's, 150 Huyshope Ave., Hartford, Conn. 06102
Daisy Mfg. Co., Rogers, Ark. 72756
Eugene DeMayo & Sons, Inc., 2795 Third Ave., Bronx, N.Y. 10455
El Dorado Leather Co., 1045 Vernon Way, El Cajon, CA 92020
Ellwood Epps (Orillia) Ltd., Hwy. 11 North, Orillia, Ont., Canada
The Eutaw Co., Box 608, U.S. Highway 176W, Holly Hill, SC 29059
Goerg Ent., 6543-140th Pl. N.E., Redmond, WA 98052
Gunfighter (See Anderson)
Hoyt Holster Co., P.O. Box 69, Coupeville, WA 98239
Don Hume, Box 351, Miami, Okla. 74354
The Hunter Co., 3300 W. 71st Ave., Westminster, CO 80030
Jackass Leather Co., 920 Waukegan Rd., Glenview, IL 60025
Jumbo Sports Prods., P.O. Box 280, Airport Rd., Frederick, MD 21701
George Lawrence Co., 306 S. W. First Ave., Portland, OR 97204
Leathercrafters, 710 S. Washington, Alexandria, VA 22314
S. D. Myres Saddle Co., 5530 E. Paisano, El Paso, TX 79905
Old West Inc. Leath. Prods., P.O. Box 2030, Chula Vista, CA 92012
Pancake Holsters, Roy Baker, Box 245, Magnolia, AR 71753
Pony Express Sport Shop Inc., 17460 Ventura Blvd., Encino, CA 91316
Ranger Leather Prods., Box 3198, East Camden, AR 71701
Red Head Brand Co., 4100 Platinum Way, Dallas, Tex. 75237
Rickenbacker's, P.O. Box 532, State Ave., Holly Hill, SC 29059
Roy's Custom Leather Goods, P.O. Box 852, Magnolia, AR 71753
Safariland Leather Products, 1941 Walker Ave., Monrovia, Calif. 91016
Safety Speed Holster, Inc., 910 So. Vail, Montebello, Calif. 90640
Buddy Schoellkopf Products Inc., 4949 Joseph Hardin Dr., Dallas, TX 75236
Seventrees, Ltd., 315 W. 39 St., New York, N.Y. 10018
Sile Distr., 7 Centre Market Pl., New York, N.Y. 10013
Smith & Wesson, 2100 Roosevelt Ave., Springfield, MA 01101
Torel, Inc., 1053 N. South St., Yoakum, TX 77995 (gun slings)
Triple-K Mfg. Co., 568 Sixth Ave., San Diego, CA 92101
Whitco, Box 1712, Brownsville, Tex. 78520 (Hide-A-Way)

HUNTING AND CAMP GEAR, CLOTHING, ETC.

Bob Allen Sportswear, P.O. Box 477, Des Moines, IA 50302
Eddie Bauer, 15010 NE 36th St., Redmond, WA 98052
L. L. Bean, Freeport, Me. 04032
Bear Archery Co., R.R. 1, Grayling, Mich. 49738 (Himalayan backpack)
Bell Fatigue Co., P.O. Box 3484, Augusta, GA 30904 (camouflage suits)
Bernzomatic Corp., 740 Driving Pk. Ave., Rochester, N.Y. 14613 (stoves & lanterns)
Big Beam, Teledyne Co., 290 E. Prairie St., Crystal Lake, Ill. 60014 (lamp)
Browning, Rte. 1, Morgan, Utah 84050
Camouflage Mfg. Co., P.O. Box 5437, Pine Bluff, AR 71601
Camp Trails, P.O. Box 14500, Phoenix, Ariz. 85031 (packs only)
Camp Ways, 12915 S. Spring St., Los Angeles, CA 90061
Challanger Mfg. Co., Box 550, Jamaica, N.Y. 11431 (glow safe)
Cobra, Box 167, Brady, TX 76825 (Cobra 3-in-1 light)
Coleman Co., Inc., 250 N. St. Francis, Wichita, Kans. 67201
Converse Rubber Co., 55 Fordham Rd., Wilmington, MA 01887 (boots)
Dana Safety Heater, J. L. Galef & Son, Inc., 85 Chamber St., N.Y. N.Y. 10007
DEER-ME Prod. Co., Box 345, Anoka, Minn. 55303 (tree steps)

Dunham's Footwear, RFD 3, Brattleboro, Vt. 05301 (boots)
Freeman Ind., Inc., 100 Marblehead Rd., Tuckahoe, N.Y. 10707 (Trak-Kit)
Game-Winner, Inc., 1900 Peachtree Cain Tower, 229 Peachtree, N.E., Atlanta, GA 30303 (camouflage suits)
Gander Mountain, Inc., Box 248, Wilmot, Wis. 53192
Gerry Mountain Sports, Inc. (see Colorado Sports)
Gokey, 94 E. 4th St., St. Paul, Minn. 55101
Gun Club Sportswear, Box 477, Des Moines, Ia. 50302
Gun-Ho Case Mfg. Co., 110 E. 10th St., St. Paul, Minn. 55101
Joseph M. Herman Shoe Co., Inc., Millis, MA 02054 (boots)
Herter's Inc., Waseca, Minn. 56093
Himalayan Industries, P.O. Box 5668, Pine Bluff, AR 71601
Bob Hinman Outfitters, 1217 W. Glen, Peoria, IL 61614
Kelty Pack, In., Box 3645, Glendale, Calif. 91201
Laacke & Joys, 1432 N. Water St., Milwaukee, WI 53202 (Wildwood prods.)
Peter Limmer & Sons Inc., Box 66, Intervale, NH 03845 (boots)
Marathon Rubber Prods. Co., 510 Sherman St., Wausau, WI 54401 (rain gear)
Marble Arms Corp., 420 Industrial Park, Gladstone, Mich. 49837
National Sports, 19 E. McWilliams St., Fond du Lac, WI 54935
Nimrod & Wayfarer Trailers, 500 Ford Blvd., Hamilton, O. 45011
Charles F. Orvis Co., Manchester, Vt. 05254 (fishing gear)
Paulin Infra-Red Prod. Co., 30520 Lakeland Blvd., Willowick, OH 44094
Ranger Mfg. Co., Inc., P.O. Box 3676, Augusta, GA 30904
Red Head Brand Co., 4100 Platinum Way, Dallas Tex. 75237
Red Wing Shoe Co., Rte. 2, Red Wing, Minn. 55066
Refrigiwear, Inc., 71 Inip Dr., Inwood, L.I., N.Y. 11696
Reliance Prod. Ltd., 1830 Dublin Ave., Winnipeg 21, Man., Can. (tent peg)
Royal Sporting Boots, Naugatuck, CT 06770
Royal Sports Clothing, Washington, IN 47501
W. R. Russell Moccasin Co., 285 S.W. Franklin, Berlin, WI 54923
Buddy Schoellkopf Prods Inc., 4949 Joseph Hardin Dr., Dallas, TX 75236
Servus Rubber Co., 1136 2nd St., Rock Island, Ill. 61201 (footwear)
The Ski Hut-Trailwise, 1615 University Ave., P.O. Box 309, Berkeley, CA 94701
Snow Lion Corp., P.O. Box 9056, Berkeley, CA 94709 (sleeping bags and parkas)
Stearns Mfg. Co., P.O. Box 1498, St. Cloud, MN 56301
Sterno Inc., 300 Park Ave., New York, NY 10022 (camp stoves)
Teledyne Co., Big Beam, 290 E. Prairie St., Crystal Lake, IL 60014
10-X Mfg. Co., 6185 Arapahoe, Boulder, CO 80303
Thermos Div., KST Co., Norwich, Conn. 06361 (Pop Tent)
Norm Thompson, 1805 N.W. Thurman St., Portland, Ore. 97209
Utica Duxbak Corp., 815 Noyes St., Utica, N.Y. 13502
Waffen-Frankonia, Box 380, 87 Wurzburg, W. Germany
Weinbrenner Shoe Corp., Polk St., Merrill, WI 54452
Wenzel Co., 1280 Research Blvd., St. Louis, MO 63132
Woods Bag & Canvas Co., Ltd., 90 River St., P.O. Box 118, Ogdensburg, NY 13669
Woodstream Corp., Box 327, Lititz, Pa. 17543 (Hunter Seat)
Woolrich Woolen Mills, Woolrich, Pa. 17779
Yankee Mechanics, Lacey Place, Southport, CT 06490 (hand winches)

KNIVES, AXES, HATCHETS, KNIFEMAKER'S SUPPLIES—HUNTING

E. R. Andrews, P.O. Box 126, Harrisonville, MO 64701 (custom knives)
Ballard Cutlery, P.O. Box 97, Golf, IL 60029 (folders)
Jack Barnett, 1496 E. Caley Ave., Littleton, CO 80121 (benchmade, custom knives)
Jack Barrett, 2122 Peach Orchard Rd., Augusta, GA 30906 (cust. knives)
O. M. Barringer, P.O. Box 1232, Port Richey, FL 33568 (scrimshander)
L. L. Bean, Freeport, Maine 04032
Bear Archery Co., R.R. 1, Grayling, MI 49738
Bone Knife Co., 4118-19th St., Lubbock, TX 79407
H. Gardner Bourne, 505 S. Huron, Columbus, OH 43204 (custom-knives)
Bowen Knife Co., P.O. Drawer 590, Blackshear, GA 31516
Floyd E. Brown, 1940 83rd Ave. S.W., Miami, FL 33155 (custom knives)
L. E. "Red" Brown, Diamond "B" Knife Co., 3203 Del Amo Blvd., Lakewood, CA 90712 (custom-knives)
Buck Knives, Inc., P.O. Box 1267, El Cajon, CA 92022
Busch Custom Knives, 418 Depre St., Mandeville, LA 70448
Camillus Cutlery Co., Main St., Camillus, NY 13031
Dick Campbell, 365 W. Oxford Ave., Englewood, CO 80110 (custom knives)
W. R. Case & Sons Cutlery Co., 20 Russell Blvd., Bradford, PA 16701
Centofante Knives, P.O. Box 17587, Tampa, FL 33682 (custom)
Challanger Mfg. Co., 118 Pearl St., Mt. Vernon, NY 10550
Charter Arms Corp., 430 Sniffens Lane, Stratford, CT 06497 (Skatchet)
Cheatham, 2930 W. Marlette, Phoenix, AZ 85017 (custom knives)
J. D. Clay, 4A Graysbranch Rd., Lloyd, KY 41156 (custom knives)
Collins Brothers Div. (belt-buckle knife), see: Bowen Knife Co.
Michael Collins, Rte. 4, Batesville Rd., Woodstock, GA 30188 (custom-knives, scrimshander)
Cooper Knives, P.O. Box 1423, Burbank, CA 91507 (custom, ctlg. 50¢)
Harold Corby, 1714 Brandonwood Dr., Johnson City, TN 37601 (custom knives)
Custom Knifemaker's Supply, P.O. Box 308, Emory, TX 75440 (ctlg. 50¢)
Dan-D Custom Knives, Box 2F, Del Norte, CA 81132 (ctlg. $1.00)
Davis Custom Knives, North 1405 Ash, Spokane, WA 99201
J. R. Dennard, 907 Greenwood Pl., Dalton, GA 30720 (custom-knives)
D'Holder Custom Knives, 6808 N. 30th Dr., Phoenix, AZ 85017
T. M. Dowell, 139 N.W., St. Helen's Pl., Bend, OR 97701 (TMD custom-knives, ctlg. $2)
Harvey Draper, 519 E. State Rd., American Fork, UT 84003 (cust. knives)
John Ek, Seminole Gun Shop, 1547 NW 119th St., No. Miami, FL 33167 (custom knives)
Ensign Co., Gunnison, UT 84634 (cust. knives)

Eze-Lap Diamond Prods., Box 2229, Westminster, CA 92683 (knife sharpeners)
Fischer Custom Knives, Rt. 1, Box 170-M, Victoria, TX 77901
Craig Floyd, Box 145, Bunker Hill, IN 46914 (sheathmaker)
H. H. Frank, Rte. #2, Whitefish, MT 59937 (custom-knives)
Mike Franklin, Rte. 41, Box 88, Aberdeen, OH 45101 (custom knives)
W. C. Frazier, 1029 Kavanaugh St., Mansfield, LA 71052 (scrimshander)
W. T. Fuller, 400 S. 8th St., East Gadsden, AL 35903 (custom-knives)
Gault Present. Knives, Rt. 1, Box 184, Lexington, TX 78947 (ctlg. 50¢)
Gerber Legendary Blades, 14200 S.W. 72nd St., Portland, OR 99223
Wayne Goddard, 473 Durham Ave., Eugene, OR 97404 (custom knives)
Rendon Griffin, 9706 Cedardale, Houston, TX 77055 (cust. knives)
Gutman Cutlery Co., Inc., 900 S. Columbus Ave., Mt. Vernon, NY 10550
H & B Forge Co., Rte. 2, Box 24, Shiloh, OH 44878 (tomahawks)
Lloyd A. Hale Handmade Knives, Rte. 2, Box 254-A, Lowell, AR 72745
Jim Hammond, Box 486, Arab, AL 35016 (cust. knives)
Don Haynes, P.O. Box 131, Murrells Inlet, SC 29576 (scrimshander)
J. A. Henckels Twinworks, 1 Westchester Plaza, Elmsford, NY 10523
Heritage Custom Knives, 2895 Seneca St., Buffalo, NY 14224
George Herron, 920 Murrah Ave., Aiken, SC 29801 (custom-knives, ctlg. $1)
Ron Hewitt, P.O. Box 632, Ludowici, GA 31316 (cust. knives)
Gene Hooper, Centreville, IN 47537 (scrimshander)
Jess Horn, Box 1274, Redding, CA 96001 (cust. knives)
Chubby Hueske, 4808 Tamarisk Dr., Bellaire, TX 77401 (custom-knives)
Imel Custom Knives, 1616 Bundy Ave., New Castle, IN 47362
Imperial Knife Assn. Co., Inc., 1776 Broadway, New York, NY 10019
Indian Ridge Traders, Box 869, Royal Oak, MI 48068
Jet-Aer Corp., 100 Sixth Ave., Paterson, NJ 07524 (G96 knives)
S. R. Jobs, 1513 Martin Chapel Rd., Murray, KY 42071 (cust. knives)
LaDow (Doc) Johnston, 2322 W. Country Club Parkway, Toledo, OH 43614 (custom-knives scrimshaw)
KA-BAR Cutlery, Inc., 5777 Grant Ave., Cleveland, OH 44105
KaBar Knives, Collectors Division, 434 No. 9th St., Olean, NY 14760
Lance Kelly, 4226 Lamar St., Decatur, GA 30035 (custom-Made)
Kershaw Cutlery Co., 500 Ridgeway, Lake Oswego, OR 97034
Jon W. Kirk, 800 N. Olive, Fayetteville, AR 72701 (custom-knives)
W. Kneubuhler, P.O. Box 327, Pioneer, OH 43554 (custom-knives)
Ron Lake, 38 Illini Dr., Taylorville, IL 62568 (custom knives)
Tommy Lee, Rt. 2, Box 463, Gaffey, SC 29340 (scrimshander)
Jimmy Lile Handmade Knives, Rte. 1, Box 56, Russellville, AR 72801
R. W. Loveless, P.O. Box 7836, Arlington Sta., Riverside, CA 92503 (custom-knives, ctlg. $2)
Robert L. Ludwig, 1028 Pecos Ave., Port Arthur, TX 77640 (custom-knives)
Marble Arms Corp., 420 Industrial Park, Gladstone, MI 49837
H. O. McBurnette, Jr., Rte. 4, Box 337, Piedmont, AL 36272 (custom knives)
Harry McEvoy, 2155 Tremont Blvd. N.W., Grand Rapids, MI 49504 (cust. knives)
John T. Mims, 620 S. 28th Ave., Apt. 327, Hattiesburg, MS 39401 (custom-knives)
Mitchell Custom Knives, 511 Ave. B, So. Houston, TX 77587
Wm. F. Moran, Jr., P.O. Box 68, Braddock Heights, MD 21744 (custom-knives, ctlg. 50¢)
Morseth Sports Equip. Co., 1705 Hiway 71N, Springdale, AR 72764 (custom-knives)
Naifeh Knives, Rte. 13, Box 380, Tulsa, OK 74107 (hand-crafted pocket knives)
Nolen Knives, Box 6216, Corpus Christi, TX 78411 (ctlg. 50¢)
Normark Corp., 1710 E. 78th St., Minneapolis, MN 55423
Ogg Custom Knives, Rt. 1, Box 230, Paris, AR 72855
Olsen Knife Co., Inc., 7 Joy St., Howard City, MI 49329
Melvin M. Pardue, P.O. Box 14357, Tampa, FL 33690 (cust. knives)
Leon Pittman, Rt. 1, Box 46, Pendergrass, GA 30567 (cust. knives)
Ramrod Knife & Gun Shop, Route 5, State Road 3 North, Newcastle, IN 47362 (custom-knives)
Randall-Made Knives, Box 1988, Orlando, FL 32802 (ctlg. 25¢)
Remote Survival Co., P.O. Box 523, New Haven, CT 06503 (custom knives)
Rigid Knives, P.O. Box 460, Santee, CA 92071 (custom-made)
Roman Eng. Prods. Co., 7727 W. Rascher Ave., Chicago, IL 60656 (cust. knives)
Ruana Knife Works, Box 574, Bonner, MT 59823 (ctlg. 50¢)
Joe Rundall, 6198 Frances Rd., Clio, MI 48420 (scrimshander)
A. G. Russell, 1705 Hiwy. 71 N., Springdale, AR 72764
Lewis B. Sanchez, Cumberland Knife & Gun Works, 5661 Bragg Blvd., Fayetteville, NC 28303
Sanders, 2358 Tyler Lane, Louisville, KY 40205 (Bahco)
Bob Schrimsher, Custom Knifemaker's Supply, P.O. Box 308, Emory, TX 75440
John J. Schwarz, 41 Fifteenth St., Wellsburg, WV 26070 (custom-knives)
N. H. Schiffman Custom Knives, 963 Malibu, Pocatello, ID 83201
Shaw-Leibowitz, Rt. 1, Box 421, New Cumberland, WV 26047 (blade etchings)
George Sherwood, Box 735, Winchester, OR 97495 (engraver, scrimshander)
Corbet R. Sigman, Rt. 1, Box 212-A, Liberty, WV 25124
Silver Fox Knives, 4714-44th St., Dickinson, TX 77539 (custom)
Ron Skaggs, 508 W. Central, Princeton, MI 48420 (scrimshander)
Skatchet, (see: Charter Arms)
Jim Small, 474 Foster St., Madison, GA 30650 (custom knives)
Smith & Wesson, 2100 Roosevelt Ave., Springfield, MA 01101
Jesse W. Smith Saddlery, E. 3024 Sprague, Spokane, WA 99201 (sheathmakers)
John T. Smith, 8404 Cedar Crest Dr., So. Haven, MS 38671 (custom-knives)
W. J. Sonneville, 1050 Chalet Dr. W., Mobile, AL 36608 (custom-knives)
Bernard Sparks, Box 32, Dingle, ID 83233 (custom-knives)

Glen Sterns, 224½ Huron St., Toledo, OH 43605 (scrimshander)
Stone Knives, 259 Arapaho Central Pk., Richardson, TX 75080 (custom knives)
Bill Thomason, 167 Lower Dawnville Rd. NE, Dalton, GA 30720 (cust. knives)
Thompson/Center, P.O. Box 2405, Rochester, NH 03867
Dwight L. Towell, Rt. 1, Midvale, ID 83645 (custom knives)
Track Knives, 126 N. Wisconsin Ave., Whitefish, MT 59937 (custom knives)
Tru-Balance Knife Co., 2115 Tremont Blvd., Grand Rapids, MI 49504
Unique Inventins, Inc., 3727 W. Alabama St., Houston, TX 77027 (throwing knife)
W-K Knives, P.O. Box 327, Pioneer, OH 43554
Western Cutlery Co., 1800 Pike Rd., Longmont, CO 80501
Walt Whinnery, 1947 Meadow Creek Dr., Louisville, KY 40281 (sheathmaker)
Horace Wiggins, P.O. Box 152, Mansfield, LA 71502 (custom knives)
W. C. Wilber, 400 Lucerne Dr., Spartanburg, SC 29302 (custom knives)
Ronnie Wilson, P.O. Box 2012, Weirton, WV 26062 (custom-knives)
Wyoming Knife Co., 115 Valley Dr., Casper, WY 82601
Ann Yancy, P.O. Box 943, Estes Park, CO 80517 (scrimshander)
Don Zaccagnino, P.O. Box Zack, Pahokee, FL 33476 (custom-knives)

LABELS, BOXES, CARTRIDGE HOLDERS

Milton Brynin, Box 162, Fleetwood Sta., Mount Vernon, NY 10552 (cartridge box labels)
E-Z Loader, Del Rey Products, P.O. Box 91561, Los Angeles, CA 90009
Jasco, J. A. Somers Co., P.O. Box 49751, Los Angeles, CA 90049 (cartridge box labels)
Peterson Label Co., P.O. Box 186, Redding Ridge, CT 06876 (cartridge box labels; Targ-Dots)
N. H. Schiffman, 963 Malibu, Pocatello, ID 83201 (cartridge carrier)

LOAD TESTING and PRODUCT TESTING, CHRONOGRAPHING, BALLISTIC STUDIES

Hutton Rifle Ranch, 1802 S. Oak Park Dr., Rolling Hills, Tucson, AZ 85710
Kent Lomont, 4421 S. Wayne Ave., Ft. Wayne, IN 46807 (handguns, handgun ammunition)
Kennon's, 5408 Biffle, Stone Mountain, Ga. 30083
Plum City Ballistics Range, Rte. 1, Box 29A, Plum City, WI 54761
H. P. White Lab., Box 331, Bel Air, Md. 21014

MISCELLANEOUS

Accurizing Service, Herbert G. Troester, 2292 W. 100 North, Vernal, UT 84078
Action Sleeves, Alvin L. Davidson, 1215 Branson, Las Cruces, NM 88001
Adapters, Sage Industries, P.O. Box 2248, Hemet, CA 92343 (12-ga. shotgun; 38 S&W blank)
Adhesive Flannel, Forest City Prod., 722 Bolivar, Cleveland, OH 44115
Ammo Pouch, Creed Enterprises, P.O. Box 159, Coeur d'Alene, ID 83814
Archery, Bear Co., R.R. 1, Grayling, Mich. 49738
Arms Restoration, J. J. Jenkins, 375 Pine Ave. No. 25, Goleta, CA 93017
Barrel Band Swivels, Phil Judd, 83 E. Park St., Butte, Mont. 59701
Bedding Kit, Bisonite Co., P.O. Box 84, Kenmore Station, Buffalo, NY 14217
Bedding Kit, Fenwal, Inc., Resin Systems Div., 400 Main St., Ashland, Mass. 01721
Belt Buckles, Adina Silversmiths, Ltd., 50 Churchville Lane, Churchville, PA 18966
Belt Buckles, Bergamot Brass Works, 42 N. Wisconsin, Darien, WI 53114
Belt Buckles, Just Brass Inc., 21 Filmore Place, Freeport, NY 11520 (ctgl. $2)
Belt Buckles, Sports Style Associates, 41 Jackson, Elmont, L.I., NY 11003
Belt Buckles, Pilgrim Pewter Inc., R.D. 2, Tully, NY 13159
Bootdryers, Baekgaard Ltd., 1855 Janke Dr., Northbrook, Ill. 60062
Bore Lamp, Spacetron, Inc., Box 84, Broadview, IL 60155 (Teenie-Genie)
Breech Plug Wrench, Swaine Machine, 195 O'Connell, Providence, R.I. 02905
Cannons, South Bend Replicas Inc., 61650 Oak Rd., S. Bend, IN 46614 (ctlg. $3)
Cannons, A & K Mfg. Co., Inc., 1651 N. Nancy Rose Ave., Tucson, AZ 85712 (replicas)
Case Gauge, Plum City Ballistics Range, Rte. 1, Box 29A, Plum City, WI 54761
Chrome Brl. Lining, Marker Mach. Co., Box 426, Charleston, Ill. 61920
Clips, D&E Magazines Mfg., P.O. Box 4579, Downey, CA 90242 (handgun and rifle)
Dryer, Thermo-Electric, Golden-Rod, Phinney-Hale, Inc., Box 5286, Oxnard, CA 93030
E-Z Loader, Del Rey Prod., P.O. Box 91561, Los Angeles, CA 90009
Ear-Valv, Sigma Eng. Co., 11320 Burbank Blvd., N. Hollywood, Cal. 91601 (Lee-Sonic)
Emergency Food, Chuck Wagon, Micro Dr., Woburn, Mass. 01801
Firearms Consultant, Shelley Braverman, Four Mile Point, Athens, NY 12015
Flares, Colt Industries, Huyshope Ave., Hartford, Conn. 06102
Flares, Intercontinental Arms, 2222 Barry Ave., Los Angeles, Ca. 90064 (MBA)
Flares, Smith & Wesson Chemical Co., 2399 Forman Rd., Rock Creek, OH 44084
Game Hoist, Cam Gear Ind., P.O. Box 1002, Kalispell, MT 59901 (Sportsmaster 500 pocket hoist)
Game Hoist, Precise, 3 Chestnut, Suffern, NY 10901
Game Scent, Buck Stop, Inc., 3015 Grow Rd., Stanton, Mi 48888

Game Scent, Pete Rickard, Box 1250, Cobleskill, NY 12043 (Indian Buck lure)
Gas Pistol, Penguin Ind., Inc., Box 97, Parkesburg, Pa. 19365
Golden-Rod, Buenger Enterprises, P.O. Box 5286, Oxnard, CA 93030 (Thermo-Electric Dryers)
Gun Bedding Kit, Resin Systems Div., Fenwal, Inc., 400 Main St., Ashland, Mass. 01721
Gun Jewelry, Sid Bell Originals, R.D. 2, Tully, NY 13159
Gun Jewelry, Pilgrim Pewter Inc., R.D. 2, Tully, NY 13159
Gun Jewelry, Al Popper, 614 Turnpike St., Stoughton, Mass. 02072
Gun Jewelry, Sports Style Assoc., 41 Jackson, Elmont, L.I., NY 11003
Gun Lock, E & C Enterprises, 9582 Bickley Dr., Huntington Beach, CA 92646
Gun Record Book, B. J. Co., Bridge St., Bluffton, SC 29910
Gun Sling, Kwikfire, Wayne Prods. Co., P.O. Box 247, Camp Hill, PA 17011
Gun Slings, Torel, Inc., 1053 N. South St., Yoakum, TX 77995
Hat Saver Co., Inc., P.O. Box 307, Rosenberg, TX 77471
Hollow Pointer, Goerg Ent., 6543-140th Pl. N.E., Redmond, WA 98052
Hugger Hooks, Roman Products, 15400 W. 44th Ave., Golden, CO 80401
Insect Repellent, Armor, Div. of Buck Stop, Inc., 3015 Grow Rd., Stanton, Mich. 48888
Insert Barrels, Sport Specialties, H. Owen, P.O. Box 774, Sunnyvale, Calif. 94088
Light Load, Jacob & Tiffin Inc., P.O. Box 547, Dept. R, Clanton, AL 35045
Locks, Gun, Bor-Lok Prods., 105 5th St., Arbuckle, CA 95912
Locks, Gun, Master Lock Co., 2600 N. 32nd St., Milwaukee, WI 53245
Military Museum, Lt. Col. E.H. Hoffman, 768 So. Main St., Woodstock, Va. 22664
Miniature Cannons, A & K Mfg. Co., 5146 E. Pima, Tucson, AZ 85712 (ctlg. $1)
Miniature Cannons, Karl J. Furr, 76 East-350 North, Orem, UT 84057 (replicas)
Miniature Guns, Charles H. Stoppler, 5 Minerva Place, New York, NY 10468
Monte Carlo Pad, Frank A. Hoppe Div., P.O. Box 97, Parkesburg, Pa. 19365
Muzzle-Top, Allen Assoc., 7502 Limekiln, Philadelphia, PA 19150 (plastic gun muzzle cap)
Patterning Data, Whits Shooting Stuff, P.O. Box 1340, Cody, WY 82414
Pell Remover, A. Edw. Terpening, 838 E. Darlington Rd., Tarpon Springs, FL 33589
Pockethoist, Cam-Gear Industries, Inc., P.O. Box 1002, Kalispell, MT 59901 (Sportsmaster 500)
Powder Storage Magazine, C & M Gunworks, 2603 41st St., Moline, IL 61265
Practice Ammunition, Hoffman Prods., P.O. Box 853, Lake Forest, IL 60045
Pressure Testg. Machine, M. York, 19381 Keymar Way, Gaithersburg, MD 20760
Ransom Handgun Rests, C'Arco, P.O. Box 308, Highland, CA 92346
Retriev-R-Trainer, Scientific Prods. Corp., 426 Swann Ave., Alexandria, VA 22301
Rifle Slings, Bianchi Leather Prods., 100 Calle Cortez, Temecula, CA 92390
RIG, NRA Scoring Plug, Rig Prod. Co., Box 279, Oregon, Ill. 60161
Rubber Cheekpiece, W. H. Lodewick, 2816 N. E. Halsey, Portland, Ore. 97232
Saddle Rings, Studs, Fred Goodwin, Sherman Mills, ME 04776
Safeties, Williams Gun Sight Co., 7389 Lapeer Rd., Davison, Mich. 48423
Salute Cannons, Naval Co., R.D. 2, 4747 Cold Spring Creamery Rd., Doylestown, PA 18901
Sav-Bore, Saunders Sptg. Gds., 338 Somerset St., N. Plainfield, NJ 07060
Scrimshaw Engraving, C. Milton Barringer, 217-2nd Isle N., Port Richey, FL 33568
Sharpening Stones, Russell's Arkansas Oilstones, 1705 Hiway 71N., Springdale, AR 72764
Shell Shrinker Mfg. Co., P.O. Box 462, Fillmore, CA 93015
Shooters Rubber Stamps, Craft Haven, 700 Sierra Dr., 70th & Vine, Lincoln, NB 68505
Shooting Coats, 10-X Mfg. Co., 6185 Arapahoe, Boulder, CO 80303
Shooting Glasses, Willson Safety Prods. Division, P.O. Box 622, Reading, PA 19603
Shooting Ranges, Kory Shooting Equipment, 233 S. Wacker, Sears Tower, Suite 7130, Chicago, IL 60606
Shotgun Sight, bi-ocular, Trius Prod., Box 25, Cleves, O. 45002
Shotshell Adapter, PC Co., 5942 Secor Rd., Toledo, OH 43623 (Plummer 410 converter)
Silver Grip Caps, Bill Dyer, P.O. Box 75255, Oklahoma City, Okla. 73107
Snap Caps, Dri-Fire Distributors, P.O. Box 1006, Redondo Beach, CA 90278 (shotgun)
Snap Caps, Frank's Mach. Shop, 11529 Tecumseh-Clinton Rd., Clinton, MI 49236
Springfield Safety Pin, B-Square Co., P.O. Box 11281, Ft. Worth, Tex. 76110
Springs, W. Wolff Co., Box 232, Ardmore, Pa. 19003
Supersound, Edmund Scientific Co., 101 E. Gloucester Pike, Barrington, NJ 08007 (safety device)
Swivels, Michaels, P.O. Box 13010, Portland, Ore. 97213
Swivels, Sile Dist., 7 Centre Market Pl., New York, N.Y. 10013
Swivels, Williams Gun Sight Co., 7389 Lapeer Rd., Davison, Mich. 48423
Tear Gas Pistol, Casady Eng. Associates, 560 Alaska Ave., Torrance, CA 90503
Trophies, Blackinton & Co., 140 Commonwealth, Attleboro Falls, Mass. 02763
Trophies, F. H. Noble & Co., 888 Tower Rd., Mundelein, IL 60060
Universal 3-shot Shotgun Plug, LanDav Custom Guns, 7213 Lee Highway, Falls Church, VA 22046

World Hunting Info., Jack Atcheson & Sons, Inc., 3210 Ottawa St., Butte, MT 59701
World Hunting Info., Jack Jonas Safaris, Inc., 800 E. Girard, Suite 118, Denver, CO 80231
World Hunting Info., Wayne Preston, Inc., 3444 Northhaven Rd., Dallas, TX 75229

MUZZLE-LOADING GUNS, BARRELS OR EQUIPMENT

A&K Mfg. C., Inc., 1651 N. Nancy Rose Ave., Tucson, AZ 85712 (ctlg. $1)
Luther Adkins, Box 281, Shelbyville, Ind. 47176 (breech plugs)
American Heritage Arms, Inc., Rt. 44, P.O. Box 95, West Willington, CT 06279 (rifles)
Anderson Mfg. Co., P.O. Box 3120, Yakima WA 98903
Armoury, Inc., Rte. 202, New Preston, CT 06777
Beaver Lodge, 9245 16th Ave. S.W., Seattle, WA 98106
John Bivins, Jr., 200 Wicklow Rd., Winston-Salem, NC 27106
Blue and Gray Prods., Inc., 817 E. Main St., Bradford, PA 16701
G. S. Bunch, 7735 Garrison, Hyattsville, Md. 20784 (flask repair)
Butler Creek Corp., Box GG, Jackson, WY 83001 (poly patch)
CAI, Conversion Arms, Inc., P.O. Box 449, Yuba City, CA 95991 (stainl. steel BP shotshell adaptors)
Cache La Poudre Rifleworks, 111 So. College, Ft. Collins, CO 80521 (custom muzzleloaders)
Challanger Mfg. Co., 118 Pearl St., Mt. Vernon, NY 10550
R. MacDonald Champlin, P.O. Box 74, Wentworth, NH 03282 (custom muzzleloaders)
Chopie Mfg. Inc., 531 Copeland Ave., LaCrosse, WI 54601 (nipple wrenches)
Classic Arms Intl., Inc., 20 Wilbraham St., Palmer, MA 01069 (BP guns and kits)
Connecticut Valley Arms Co. (CVA), Saybrook Rd., Haddam, CT 06438 (kits also)
Earl T. Cureton, Rte. 2, Box 388, Willoughby Rd., Bulls Gap, TN 37711 (powder horns)
DJ Inc., 1310 S. Park Rd., Fairdale, KY 40118
Leonard Day & Co., 316 Burt Pits Rd., Northampton, MA 10160
Dixie Gun Works, Inc., P.O. Box 130, Union City, TN 38261
EMF Co., Inc., Box 1248, Studio City, CA 91604
Eagle Arms Co., Riverview Dr., Mt. Washington, KY 40047
Euroarms of America, Inc., 14 W. Monmouth St., Winchester, VA 22601
The Eutaw Co., Box 608, U.S. Highway 176W, Holly Hill, SC 29059 (accessories)
Ted Fellowes, Beaver Lodge, 9245 16th Ave. S.W., Seattle, Wash. 98106
Firearms Imp. & Exp. Corp., 2470 N.W. 21st St., Miami, Fla. 33142
Marshall F. Fish, Rt. 22 N., Westport, NY 12993 (antique ML repairs)
Clark K. Frazier/Matchmate, RFD. 1, Rawson, OH 45881
C. R. & D. E. Getz, Box 88, Beavertown, PA 17813 (barrels)
Golden Age Arms Co., 14 W. Winter St., Delaware, OH 43015 (ctlg. $2)
A. R. Goode, Rte. 3, Box 139, Catoctin Furnace, Thurmont, MD 21788 (ML rifle bbls.)
Green River Forge, Ltd., P.O. Box 885, Springfield, OR 97477 (Forge-Fire flints)
Harper's Ferry Arms Co., 256 E. Broadway, Hopewell, VA 23860 (guns)
Hopkins & Allen Arms, #1 Melnick Rd., Monsey, NY 10952
International Arms, 23239 Doremus Ave., St. Clair Shores, MI 48080
JJJJ Ranch, Wm. Large, Rte. 1, Ironton, Ohio 45638
Art LeFeuvre, 1003 Hazel Ave., Deerfield, Ill. 60015 (antique gun restoring)
Les' Gun Shop (Les Bauska), Box 511, Kalispell, Mont. 59901
Lever Arms Serv. Ltd., 771 Dunsmuir, Vancouver 1, B.C., Canada
Log Cabin Sport Shop, 8010 Lafayette Rd., Lodi, OH 44254
Lyman Products Corp., Rte. 147, Middlefield, CT 06455
McKeown's Guns, R.R. 1, Pekin, IL 61554 (E-Z load rev. stand)
Judson E. Mariotti, Beauty Hill Rd., Barrington, NH 03825 (brass bullet mould)
Markwell Arms Co., 2414 W. Devon, Chicago, IL 60645
Maurer Arms, 2366 Frederick Dr., Cuyahoga Falls, OH 44221 (cust. muzzleloaders)
Mowrey Gun Works, Box 28, Iowa Park, TX 76367
Muzzleloaders Etc., Inc., Jim Westberg, 9901 Lyndale Ave. S., Bloomington, MN 55420
Numrich Corp., W. Hurley, N.Y. 12491 (powder flasks)
Ox-Yoke Originals, 130 Griffin Rd., West Suffield, CT 06093 (dry lubr. patches)
Penna. Rifle Works, 319 E. Main St., Ligonier, PA 15658 (ML guns, parts, ctlg. $1.50)
A. W. Peterson Gun Shop, 1693 Old Hwy. 441 N., Mt. Dora, FL 32757 (ML guns)
Richland Arms, 321 W. Adrian St., Blissfield, MI 49228
Rush's Old Colonial Forge, 106 Wiltshire Rd., Baltimore, MD 21221
Salish House, Inc., P.O. Box 27, Rollins, MT 59931
H. M. Schoeller, 569 So. Braddock Ave., Pittsburgh, Pa. 15221
Scott and Sons, P.O. Drawer "C", Nolanville, TX 76559
Sharon Rifle Barrel Co., P.O. Box 106, Kalispell, MT 59901
Shiloh Products, 37 Potter St., Farmingdale, NY 11735 (4-cavity mould)
C. E. Siler Locks, Rt. 6, Box 5, Candler, NC 28715 (flint locks)
Ken Steggles, 77 Lower Eastern Green Lane, Coventry, CV5 7DT, England (accessories)
Ultra-Hi Products Co., 150 Florence Ave., Hawthorne, NJ 07506
Upper Missouri Trading Co., 3rd and Harold Sts., Crofton, NB 68730
R. Watts, 826 Springdale Rd., Atlanta, GA 30306 (ML rifles)
W. H. Wescomb, P.O. Box 488, Glencoe, CA 95232 (parts)
Thos. F. White, 5801 Westchester Ct., Worthington, O. 43085 (powder horn)
Williamson-Pate Gunsmith Serv., 6021 Camp Bowie Blvd., Ft. Worth, TX 76116
York County Gun Works, R.R. #4, Tottenham, Ont. L0G 1W0, Canada (locks)

PISTOLSMITHS

Allen Assoc., 7502 Limekiln Pike, Philadelphia, PA 19150 (speed-cock lever for 45 ACP)
Bain and Davis Sptg. Gds., 559 W. Las Tunas Dr., San Gabriel, Cal. 91776
Bar-Sto Precision Machine, 633 So. Victory Blvd., Burbank, CA 91502 (S.S. bbls. f. 45 Acp)
Behlert Custom Guns, Inc., 725 Lehigh Ave., Union, NJ 07083 (short actions)
F. Bob Chow, Gun Shop, 3185 Mission, San Francisco, Calif. 94110
J.E. Clark, Rte. 2, Box 22A, Keithville, LA 71047
Custom Gun Shop, 725 Lehigh Ave., Union, NJ 07083
Day Arms Corp., 2412 S.W. Loop 410, San Antonio, TX 78227
Dominic DiStefano, 4303 Friar Lane, Colorado Springs, CO 80907 (accurizing)
Dan Dwyer, 915 W. Washington, San Diego, Calif. 92103
Ehresman Tool Co.; Inc., 5425 Planeview Dr., Ft. Wayne, IN 46805 (custom)
Giles' 45 Shop, Rt. 2, Box 847, Odessa, FL 33556
Gil Hebard Guns, Box 1, Knoxville, Ill. 61448
Innovation Inc., P.O. Box 43, Angola, IN 46703
Lee E. Jurras & Assoc., Inc., P.O. Drawer F, Hagerman, NM 88232
Kart Sptg. Arms Corp., RD 2, Box 929-Broad Ave., Riverhead, NY 11901 (handgun conversions)
Lenz Firearms Co., 1480 Elkay Dr., Eugene, OR 97404
Rudolf Marent, 9711 Tiltree, Houston, TX 77075 (Hammerli)
Nu-Line Guns, 3727 Jennings Rd., St. Louis, MO 63121
Pachmayr Gun Works, 1220 S. Grand Ave., Los Angeles, Calif. 90015
L. W. Seecamp Co., Inc., Box 255, New Haven, CT 06502 (DA Colt auto conversions)
R. L. Shockey Guns, Inc., 1614 S. Choctaw, E. Reno, Okla. 73036
Silver Dollar Guns, P.O. Box 475, 10 Frances St., Franklin, NH 03235 (45 ACP)
Sportsmens Equipmt. Co., 915 W. Washington, San Diego, Calif. 92103
Irving O. Stone, Jr., 633 S. Victory Blvd., Burbank, CA 91502
Victor W. Strawbridge, 6 Pineview Dr., Dover Pt., Dover, NH 03820
A. D. Swenson's 45 Shop, P.O. Box 606, Fallbrook, CA 92028
Dennis A. "Doc" Ulrich, 2511 S. 57th Ave., Cicero, IL 60650
Vic's Gun Refinishing, 6 Pineview Dr., Dover, NH 03820
Walters Industries, 6226 Park Lane, Dallas, TX 75225
Dave Woodruff, Box 5, Bear, DE 19701

REBORING AND RERIFLING

P.O. Ackley (see: Max B. Graff, Inc.)
Atkinson Gun Co., P.O. Box 512, Prescott, AZ 86301
Bain & Davis Sptg. Gds., 559 W. Las Tunas Dr., San Gabriel, Calif. 91776
Fuller Gun Shop, Cooper Landing, Alaska 99572
Max B. Graff, Inc., Rt. 1, Box 24, American Fork, UT 84003
Bruce Jones, 389 Calla Ave., Imperial Beach, CA 92032
Les' Gun Shop, (Les Bauska), Box 511, Kalispell, MT 59901
Morgan's Cust. Reboring, 707 Union Ave., Grants Pass, OR 97526
Nu-Line Guns, 3727 Jennings Rd., St. Louis, MO 63121 (handguns)
Al Petersen, Box 8, Riverhurst, Saskatchewan, Canada S0H3P0
Schuetzen Gun Works, 624 Old Pacific Hwy. S.E., Olympia, WA 98503
Siegrist Gun Shop, 2689 McLean Rd., Whittemore, MI 48770
Snapp's Gunshop, 6911 E. Washington Rd., Clare, Mich. 48617
R. Southgate, Rt. 2, Franklin, Tenn. 37064 (Muzzleloaders)
J. W. Van Patten, Box 145, Foster Hill, Milford, Pa. 18337
Robt. G. West, 27211 Huey Ave., Eugene, OR 97402

RELOADING TOOLS AND ACCESSORIES

Action LB, Box 100, Odessa, MO 64076 (spin wad)
Advance Car Mover Co., Inc., P.O. Box 1181, Appleton, WI 54911 (bottom pour lead casting ladles)
Advanced Mfg. Co., Inc., 18619 W. 7 Mile Rd., Detroit, MI 48219 (super fillerprimer tube)
American Wad Co., 125 W. Market St., Morrison, IL 61270 (12-ga. shot wad)
Anderson Mfg. Co., Royal, Ia. 51357 (Shotshell Trimmers)
Aurands, 229 E. 3rd St., Lewistown, Pa. 17044
B-Square Eng. Co., Box 11281, Ft. Worth, Tex. 76110
Bill Ballard, 830 Miles Ave., Billings, MT 59101 (ctlg. 50¢)
Bear Reloaders Inc., 807 Evans Ave., Akron, OH 44305
Belding & Mull, P.O. Box 428, Philipsburg, Pa. 16866
Berdon Co., P.O. Box 70131, Seattle, WA 98107 (metallic press)
Blackhawk SAA East, K2274 POB, Loves Park, Ill. 61111
Blackhawk SAA Mtn., 2117 S. Holly, Denver, CO 80222
Blackhawk SAA West, Box 285, Hiawatha, KS 66434
Bonanza Sports, Inc., 412 Western Ave., Faribault, Minn. 55021
Gene Bowlin, 3602 Hill Ave., Snyder, Tex. 79549 (arbor press)
Brown Precision Co., 5869 Indian Ave., San Jose, Calif. 95123 (Little Wiggler)
A. V. Bryant, 72 Whiting Rd., E. Hartford, CT 06118 (Nutmeg Universal Press)
C-H Tool & Die Corp., Box L, Owen, Wis. 54460
Camdex, Inc., 23880 Hoover Rd., Warren, MI 48089
Carbide Die & Mfg. Co., Box 226, Covina, CA 91724
Carter Gun Works, 2211 Jefferson Pk. Ave., Charlottesville, Va. 22903
Cascade Cartridge, Inc., (See Omark)
Catco-Ambush, Inc., P.O. Box 300, Corte Madera, CA 94926 (paper bullet patches)
Chevron Case Master, R.R. 1, Ottawa, IL 61350
Clymer Mfg. Co., 14241 W. 11 Mile Rd., Oak Park, MI 48237 (#4-jack. swaging dies)
Lester Coats, 416 Simpson St., No. Bend, Ore. 97459 (core cutter)

Container Development Corp., 424 Montgomery St., Watertown, WI 53094
Continental Kite & Key Co., Box 40, Broomall, PA 19008 (primer pocket cleaner)
Cooper-Woodward, Box 972, Riverside, Calif. 92502 (Perfect Lube)
D. R. Corbin Mfg. & Supply Inc., P.O. Box 758, Phoenix, OR 97535
J. Dewey Mfg. Co., 125 Fenn Rd., Middlebury, CT 06762
Diverter Arms, Inc., P.O. Box 22084, Houston, TX 77027 (bullet puller)
Division Lead Co., 7742 W. 61st Pl., Summit, Ill. 60502
Eagle Products Co., 1520 Adelia Ave., So. El Monte, Cal. 91733
Edmisten Co. Inc., P.O. Box 298, Boone, NC 28607
Efemes Enterprises, P.O. Box 122M, Bay Shore, NY 11706 (Berdan decapper)
W. H. English, 4411 S. W. 100th, Seattle, Wash. 98146 (Paktool)
Farmer Bros., 1102 Washington St., Eldora, IA 50627 (Lage)
Fitz, 653 N. Hagar St., San Fernando, CA 91340 (Fitz Flipper)
Flambeau Plastics, 801 Lynn, Baraboo, Wis. 53913
Forster Products Inc., 82 E. Lanark Ave., Lanark, Ill. 61046
Geo. M. Fullmer, 2499 Mavis St., Oakland, CA 94601 (seating die)
Gene's Gun Shop, 3602 Hill Ave., Snyder, Tex. 79549 (arbor press)
Goerg Enterprises, 6543-140th Pl. N.E., Redmond, WA 98052
Gopher Shooter's Supply, Box 278, Faribault, MN 55021
Griffin Mfg. Co., P.O. Box 935, Brownwood, TX 76801
The Gun Clinic, 81 Kale St., Mahtomedi, Minn. 55115
Hart Products, Rob. W. Hart & Son Inc., 401 Montgomery St., Nescopeck, PA 18635
Hensley & Gibbs, Box 10, Murphy, Ore. 97533
Herter's Inc., RR1, Waseca, Minn. 56093
Richard Hoch, The Gun Shop, Rte. 1, Box 507-B, Montrose, CO 81401 (custom schuetzen bullet moulds)
B. E. Hodgdon, Inc., 7710 W. 50 Hiway, Shawnee Mission, Kans. 66202
Hoffman Prods., P.O. Box 853, Lake Forest, IL 60045 (spl. gallery load press)
Hollywood Reloading, (see: Whitney Sales, Inc.)
Hornady (see: Pacific)
Hulme Firearm Serv., Box 83, Millbrae, Calif. 94030 (Star case feeder)
Independent Mach. & Gun Shop, 1416 N. Hayes, Pocatello, Ida. 83201
Ivy Armament, P.O. Box 10, Greendale, WI 53129
JASCO, Box 49751, Los Angeles, Calif. 90049
J & G Rifle Ranch, Box S80, Turner, MT 59542 (case tumblers)
Javelina Products, Box 337, San Bernardino, Cal. 92402 (Alox beeswax)
Neil Jones, 686 Baldwin St., Meadville, PA 16335 (decapping tool, dies)
Kexplore, 9450 Harwig #G, Houston, TX 77036
Kuharsky Bros. (see Modern Industries)
Lac-Cum Bullet Puller, Star Route, Box 242, Apollo, PA 15613
Lage Uniwad Co., 1102 N. Washington St., Eldora, IA 50627 (Universal Shotshell Wad)
LanDav, 7213 Lee Highway, Falls Church, VA 22046 (X-15 bullet puller)
Lee Custom Engineering, Inc., 46 E. Jackson St. Hartford, WI 53027
Lee Precision, Inc., 4275 Hwy. U, Hartford, WI 53027
Leon's Reloading Service, 3945 No. 11 St., Lincoln, Neb. 68521
Lewisystems, Menasha Corp., 426 Montgomery St., Watertown, WI 53094
L. F. Die Shop, 1281 Highway 99 N., Eugene, Ore. 97402
Dean Lincoln, P.O. Box 1886, Farmington, NM 87401 (mould)
Ljutic Industries, 918 N. 5th Ave., Yakima, Wash. 98902
Lock's Phila. Gun Exch., 6700 Rowland, Philadelphia, Pa. 19149
Lyman Products Corp., Rte. 147, Middlefield, CT 06455.
McKillen & Heyer, Box 627, Willoughby, O. 44094 (case gauge)
Paul McLean, 2670 Lakeshore Blvd., W., Toronto 14, Ont., Canada (Universal Cartridge Holder)
MEC, Inc. (see: Mayville Eng. Co.)
MTM Molded Prod., 5680 Webster St., Dayton, OH 45414
Magma Eng. Co., P.O. Box 881, Chandler, AZ 85224
Judson E. Mariotti, Beauty Hill Rd., Barrington, NH 03825 (brass bullet mould)
Marmel Prods., P.O. Box 97, Utica, MI 48087 (Marvelube, Marvelux)
Marquart Precision Co., Box 1740, Prescott, AZ 86301 (precision case-neck turning tool)
Mayville Eng. Co., 715 South St., Mayville, Wis. 53050 (shotshell loader)
Merit Gun Sight Co., P.O. Box 995, Sequim, Wash. 98382
Modern Industries, Inc., 613 W-11, Erie, PA 16501 (primer pocket cleaner)
Multi-Scale Charge Ltd., 3269 Niagara Falls Blvd., North Tonawanda, NY 14120
Murdock Lead/RSR Corp., P.O. Box 1695, Dallas, TX 75222
National Lead Co., Box 831, Perth Amboy, N.J. 08861
Normington Co., Box 6, Rathdrum, ID 83858 (powder baffles)
Ohaus Scale, (see: RCBS)
Ohio Thermal, Inc., 7030-A Huntley Rd., Columbus, OH 43229 (Pro-Melt lead castg. pot)
Omark-CCI, Inc., Box 856, Lewiston, Ida. 83501
Pacific Tool Co., P.O. Drawer 2048, Ordnance Plant Rd., Grand Island, NB 68801
Pak-Tool Co., 4411 S.W. 100th, Seattle, WA 98146
Perfection Die Co., 1614 S. Choctaw, El Reno, Okla. 73036
Personal Firearms Record Book, Box 201, Park Ridge, Ill. 60068
Ferris Pindell, R.R. 3, Box 205, Connersville, IN 47331 (bullet spinner)
Plum City Ballistics Range, Rte. 1, Box 29A, Plum City, WI 54761
Ponsness-Warren, Inc., P.O. Box 8, Rathdrum, ID 83858
Potter Eng. Co., 1410 Santa Ana Dr., Dunedin, FL 33528 (electric pots only)
Marian Powley, Petra Lane, R.R.I, Eldridge, IA 52748
Precise Alloys Inc., 69 Kinkel St., Westbury, NY 11590 (chilled lead shot; bullet wire)
Quaco Industries Ltd., St. Martins, St. John Co., New Brunswick, Canada E0G 2Z0 (Echo dies, etc.)
Quinetics Corp., Box 13237, San Antonio, TX 78213 (kinetic bullet puller)
RCBS, Inc., Box 1919, Oroville, Calif. 95965
Redding Inc., 114 Starr Rd., Cortland, NY 13045
Reloaders Equipment Co., 4680 High St., Ecorse, MI 48229 (bullet puller)
Remco, 1404 Whitesboro St., Utica, N.Y. 13502 (shot caps)

Republic Tool Mfg. Co., P.O. Box 112, Caldwell, NJ 07006 (port. rel. stand)
Rifle Ranch, Rte. 5, Prescott, Ariz, 86301
Rochester Lead Works, Rochester, N.Y. 14608 (leadwire)
Rorschach Precision Prods., P.O. Box 1613, Irving, Tex. 75060
Rotex Mfg. Co. (see Texan)
Ruhr-American Corp., So. East Hwy. 55, Glenwood, Minn. 56334
SAECO Rel. Inc., P.O. Box 778, Carpinteria, Calif. 93013
SSK Industries, Rt. 1, Della Drive, Bloomingdale, OH 43910 (primer tool)
Sandia Die & Cartridge Co., Rte. 5, Box 5400, Albuquerque, NM 87123
Shassere, P.O. Box 25218, Houston, TX 77005 (cartridge case caddy/ loading block)
Shiloh Products, 37 Potter St., Farmingdale, NY 11735 (4-cavity bullet mould)
Shooters Accessory Supply, see: D. R. Corbin
Sil's Gun Prod., 490 Sylvan Dr., Washington, Pa. 15301 (K-spinner)
Jerry Simmons, 713 Middlebury St., Goshen, Ind. 46526 (Pope de- & recapper)
Rob. B. Simonson, 13721 S. 5th St., Schoolcraft, MI 49087
Fred Sinclair, Sinclair, Inc., 1200 Asbury Dr., Box 302, New Haven, IN 46774
Smith & Wesson Ammunition Co., Inc., 2399 Forman Rd., Rock Creek, OH 44084
J. A. Somers Co., P.O. Box 49751, Los Angeles, CA 90049 (Jasco)
D. E. Stanley, P.O. Box 833, Ringold, OK 74754 (Kake-Kutter)
Star Machine, Inc., 418 10th Ave., San Diego, CA 92101
T.E.S., Inc., 2807 N. Prospect St., Colorado Springs, CO 80907 (Vibra-Tek)
T&T Products, Inc., 6330 Hwy. 14 East, Rochester, MN 55901 (Meyer shotgun slugs)
Texan Reloaders, Inc., 807 Evans Ave., Akron, OH 44305
Trico Plastics, 590 S. Vincent Ave., Azusa, CA 91702
WAMADET, Silver Springs, Goodleigh, Barnstaple, Devon, England
Walker Mfg. Inc., 8296 So. Channel, Harsen's Island, MI 48028 (Berdan decapper)
Wammes Guns Inc., 236 N. Hayes St., Bellefontaine, OH 43311 (Jim's powder baffles)
Weatherby, Inc., 2781 Firestone Blvd., South Gate, Calif. 90280
Webster Scale Mfg. Co., Box 188, Sebring, Fla. 33870
Whits Shooting Stuff, P.O. Box 1340, Cody, WY 82414
Whitney Sales, Inc., P.O. 875, Reseda, CA 91335 (Hollywood)
L. E. Wilson, Inc., P.O. Box 324, 404 Pioneer Ave., Cashmere, WA 98815
Xelex, Ltd., P.O. Box 543, Renfrow K7V 4B1, Canada (powder)
Zenith Enterprises, 361 Flagler Rd., Nordland, WA 98358

RESTS—BENCH, PORTABLE, ETC.

Bill Anderson, 551 Fletcher, Wayne, PA 19087
Bausch & Lomb, 635 St. Paul St., Rochester, NY 14602 (rifle rest)
Jim Brobst, 299 Poplar St., Hamburg, PA 19526 (bench rest pedestal)
C'Arco, P.O. Box 2043, San Bernardino, CA 92401 (Ransom handgun rest)
Cole's Acku-Rite Prod., Box 364, Ellington, NY 14732
Cravener's Gun Shop, 1627 - 5th Ave., Ford City, PA 16226 (portable)
Decker Shooting Products, 1729 Laguna Ave., Schofield, WI 54476 (rifle rests)
The Gun Case, 11035 Maplefield, El Monte, Cal. 91733
GVA Enterprises, P.O. Box 40725, Garland, TX 75040 (Rif-L-Vise)
Harris Engr., Inc., Barlow, KY 42024
Rob. W. Hart & Son, 401 Montgomery St., Nescopeck, Pa. 18635
Tony Hidalgo, 6 Capp St., Carteret, NJ 07008 (shooters stools)
North Star Devices, Inc., P.O. Box 2095, North St. Paul, MN 55109 (Gun Slinger)
Progressive Prods., Inc., P.O. Box 41, Holmen, WI 54636 (Sandbagger rifle rest)
Rec. Prods., Res., Inc., 158 Franklin Ave., Ridgewood, N.J. 07450 (Butts Pi-pod)
D. E. Stanley, P.O. Box 833, Ringold, OK 74754 (portable shooting rest)
Suter's, 332 Tejon, Colorado Springs, CO 80902
Tuller & Co., 29 Germania, Galeton, PA 16922 (Protector sandbags)
Wichita Eng. & Supply, Inc., P.O. Box 11371, Wichita, KS 67202

RIFLE BARREL MAKERS

P.O. Ackley Gun Barrels, Max B. Graff, Inc., Rt. 1, Box 24, American Fork, UT 84003
Atkinson Gun Co., P.O. Box 512, Prescott, AZ 86301
Ralph L. Carter, Rt. 1, Box 92, Fountain, CO 80817
Christy Gun Works, 875 57th St., Sacramento, Calif. 95819
Clerke Prods., 2219 Main St., Santa Monica, Calif. 90405
Cuthbert Gun Shop, 715 So. 5th, Coos Bay, Ore. 97420
B. W. Darr, Saeco-Darr Rifle Co., Ltd., P.O. Box 778, Carpinteria, CA 93013
Douglas Barrels, Inc., 5504 Big Tyler Rd., Charleston, W. Va. 25312
Douglas Jackalope Gun & Sport Shop, Inc., 1048 S. 5th St., Douglas, WY 82633
Federal Firearms Co., Inc., Box 145, 145 Thomas Run Rd., Oakdale, PA 15071
C. R. & D. E. Getz, Box 88, Beavertown, PA 17813
A. R. Goode, Rte. 3, Box 139, Catoctin Furnace, Thurmont, MD 21788
Hart Rifle Barrels, Inc., RD 2, Lafayette, N.Y. 13084
Wm. H. Hobaugh, Box M, Philipsburg, MT 59858
David R. Huntington, RFD #1, Box 23, Heber City, UT 83032
Kogot, John Pell, 410 College Ave., Trinidad, CO 81082 (custom)
Gene Lechner, 636 Jane N.E., Albuquerque, NM 87123
Les' Gun Shop, (Les Bauska), Box 511, Kalispell, MT 59901
Marquart Precision Co., Box 1740, Prescott, AZ 86301

Nu-Line Guns, Inc., 3727 Jennings Rd., St. Louis, Mo. 63121
Numrich Arms, W. Hurley, N.Y. 12491
Al Petersen, The Rifle Ranch, Box 8, Riverhurst, Sask., Canada SOH3PO
Sanders Cust. Gun Serv., 2358 Tyler Lane, Louisville, Ky. 40205
Sharon Rifle Barrel Co., P.O. Box 1197, Kalispell, MT 59901
Ed Shilen Rifles, Inc., 205 Metropark Blvd., Ennis, TX 75119
W. C. Strutz, Rte. 1, "Woodland", Eagle River, WI 54521
Titus Barrel & Gun Co., R.F.D. #1, Box 23, Heber City, UT 84032
Wilson Arms, 63 Leetes Island Rd., Branford, CT 06405

SCOPES, MOUNTS, ACCESSORIES, OPTICAL EQUIPMENT

Aimpoint U.S.A., 29351 Stonecrest Rd., Rancho Palos Verdes, CA 90274 (electronic sight)
Alley Supply Co., Carson Valley Industrial Park, Gardnerville, NV 89410 (Scope collimator)
American Import Co., 1167 Mission, San Francisco, Calif. 94103
Anderson Mfg. Co., P.O. Box 3120, Yakima, WA 98903 (lens cap)
Armsport, Inc., 2811 N.W. 75th Ave., Miami, FL 33122
B-Square Co., Box 11281, Ft. Worth, TX 76109 (Mini-14 mount)
Bausch & Lomb Inc., 635 St. Paul St., Rochester, N.Y. 14602
Bennett, 561 Delaware, Delmar, N.Y. 12054 (mounting wrench)
Browning Arms, Rt. 4, Box 624-B, Arnold, Mo. 63010
Maynard P. Buehler, Inc., 17 Orinda Highway, Orinda, Calif. 94563
Burris Co., 331 E. 8th St., Box 1747, Greeley, CO 80631
Bushnell Optical Co., 2828 E. Foothill Blvd., Pasadena, Calif. 91107
Butler Creek Corp., Box GG, Jackson Hole, WY 83001 (lens caps)
Kenneth Clark, 18738 Highway 99, Madera, Calif. 93637
Clearview Mfg. Co., Inc., 20821 Grand River Ave., Detroit, MI 48219 (mounts)
Clear View Sports Shields, P.O. Box 255, Wethersfield, CT 06107 (shooting/testing glasses)
Colt's, Hartford, Conn. 06102
Compass Instr. & Optical Co., Inc., 104 E 25th St., New York, N.Y. 10010
Conetrol Scope Mounts, Hwy 123 South, Seguin, TX 78155
Continental Arms Corp., 697-5th Ave., New York, N.Y. 10022 (Nickel)
Davis Optical Co., P.O. Box 6, Winchester, Ind. 47934
Del-Sports Inc., Main St., Margaretville, NY 12455 (Habicht, Swarovski)
M. B. Dinsmore, Box 21, Wyomissing, PA 19610 (shooting glasses)
Eder Instrument Co., 5115 N. Ravenswood, Chicago, IL 60640 (borescope)
Flaig's, Babcock Blvd., Millvale, Pa. 15209
Freeland's Scope Stands, Inc. 3734 14th, Rock Island, Ill. 61201
Griffin & Howe, Inc., 589 Broadway, New York, N.Y. 10012
H&H Assoc., P.O. Box 447, Strathmore, CA 93267 (target adj. knobs)
H. J. Hermann Leather Co., Rt. 1, Skiatook, OK 74070 (lens caps)
Herter's Inc., Waseca, Minn. 56093
J. B. Holden Co., 295 W. Pearl, Plymouth, MI 48170
The Hutson Corp., P.O. 1127, Arlington, Tex.76010
Hy-Score Arms Corp., 200 Tillary St., Brooklyn, N.Y. 11201
Interarms, 10 Prince St., Alexandria, VA 22313
Paul Jaeger, 211 Leedom St., Jenkintown, Pa. 19046 (Nickel)
Jana Intl. Co., Box 1107, Denver, Colo. 80201
Jason Empire Inc., 9200 Cody, Overland Park, KS 66214
Jeffredo Gunsight Co., 1629 Via Monserate, Fallbrook, CA 92028
Kesselring Gun Shop, 400 Pacific Hiway 99 No, Burlington, Wash. 98283
Kris Mounts, 108 Lehigh St., Johnstown, PA 15905
Kuharsky Bros. (see Modern Industries)
Kwik-Site, 5555 Treadwell, Wayne, MI 48185 (rings, mounts only)
LanDav, 7213 Lee Highway, Falls Church, VA 22046 (steel leverlock side mt.)
S. E. Laszlo House of Imports, 200 Tillary St., Brooklyn, NY 11201
L.E.S., 3640 Dempster, Skokie, IL 60076
Leatherwood Bros., Rte. 1, Box 111, Stephenville, TX 76401
T. K. Lee, 2830 S. 19th St., Off. #4, Birmingham, AL 35209 (reticles)
E. Leitz, Inc., Rockleigh, N.J. 07647
Leupold & Stevens Inc., P.O. Box 688, Beaverton, Ore. 97005
Jake Levin and Son, Inc., 9200 Cody, Overland Park, KS 66214
W. H. Lodewick, 2816 N.E. Halsey, Portland, OR 97232 (scope safeties)
Lyman Products Corp., Route 147, Middlefield, CT 06455
Mandall Shooting Supplies, 7150 E. 4th St., Scottsdale, AZ 85252
Marble Arms Co., 420 Industrial Park, Gladstone, MI 49837
Marlin Firearms Co., 100 Kenna Dr., New Haven, Conn. 06473
Modern Industries, Inc., 613 W-11, Erie, PA 16501
O. F. Mossberg & Sons, Inc., 7 Grasso Ave., North Haven, Conn. 06473
Normark Corp., 1710 E. 78th St., Minneapolis, Minn. 55423 (Singlepoint)
Numrich Arms, West Hurley, N.Y. 12491
Nydar, see: Swain Nelson Co.
PEM's Mounts, 6063 Waterloo, Atwater, PA 44201
PGS, Peters' Inc., 622 Gratiot Ave., Saginaw, Mich. 48602 (scope shields)
Pachmayr Gun Works, 1220 S. Grand Ave., Los Angeles, Calif. 90015
Pacific Tool Co., P.O. Drawer 2048, Ordnance Plant Rd., Grand Island, NB 68801
Precise, 3 Chestnut, Suffern, NY 10901
Ranging Inc., 90 N. Lincoln Rd., East Rochester, N.Y. 14445
Ray-O-Vac, Willson Prod. Div., P.O. Box 622, Reading, PA 19603 (shooting glasses)
Redfield Gun Sight Co., 5800 E. Jewell Ave., Denver, Colo. 80222
S & K Mfg. Co., Box 247, Pittsfield, Pa. 16340 (Insta-mount)
Sanders Cust. Gun Serv., 2358 Tyler Lane, Louisville, Ky. 40205 (MSW)
Savage Arms, Westfield, Mass. 01085
Sears, Roebuck & Co., 825 S. St. Louis, Chicago, Ill. 60607
Sherwood Distr., Inc., 18714 Parthenia St., Northridge, CA 91324 (mounts)
W. H. Siebert, 22720 S.E. 56th Pl., Issaquah, WA 98027
Singlepoint (see Normark)
Southern Precision Inst. Co., 3419 E. Commerce St., San Antonio, TX 78219
Spacetron Inc., Box 84, Broadview, IL 60155 (bore lamp)

Stoeger Arms Co., 55 Ruta Ct., S. Hackensack, N.J. 07606
Supreme Lens Covers, Box GG, Jackson Hole, WY 83001 (lens caps)
Swain Nelson Co., Box 45, 92 Park Dr., Glenview, Ill. 60025 (shotgun sight)
Swift Instruments, Inc., 952 Dorchester Ave., Boston, Mass. 02125
Tasco, 1075 N.W. 71st, Miami, Fla. 33138
Ted's Sight Aligner, Box 1073, Scottsdale, AZ 85252
Thompson-Center Arms, P.O. Box 2405, Rochester, N.H. 03867 (handgun scope)
Tradewinds, Inc., Box 1191, Tacoma, Wash. 98401
John Unertl Optical Co., 3551-5 East St., Pittsburgh, Pa. 15214
United Binocular Co., 9043 S. Western Ave., Chicago, Ill. 60620
Verano Corp., Box 270, Glendora, CA 91740
Vissing (see: Supreme Lens Covers)
Weatherby's, 2781 Firestone, South Gate, Calif. 90280
W. R. Weaver Co., 7125 Industrial Ave., El Paso, Tex. 79915
Williams Gun Sight Co., 7389 Lapeer Rd., Davison, Mich. 48423
Boyd Williams Inc., 8701-14 Mile Rd. (M-57), Cedar Springs, MI 49319 (BR)
Willrich Precision Instrument Co., 37-13 Broadway, Rte. 4, Fair Lawn, NJ 07410 (borescope)
Carl Zeiss Inc., 444 Fifth Ave., New York, N.Y. 10018 (Hensoldt)

SIGHTS, METALLIC

B-Square Eng. Co., Box 11281, Ft. Worth, Tex. 76110
Behlert Custom Sights, Inc., 725 Lehigh Ave., Union, NJ 07083
Bo-Mar Tool & Mfg. Co., Box 168, Carthage, Tex. 75633
Maynard P. Buehler, Inc., 17 Orinda Highway, Orinda, Calif. 94563
Christy Gun Works, 875 57th St., Sacramento, Calif. 95819
Jim Day, 902 N. Bownen Lane, Florence, SD 29501 (Chaba)
E-Z Mount, Ruelle Bros., P.O. Box 114, Ferndale, MT 48220
Firearms Dev. Lab., 360 Mt. Ida Rd., Oroville, CA 95965 (F. D. L. Wonder-sight)
Freeland's Scope Stands, Inc., 3734-14th Ave., Rock Island, Ill. 61201
Paul T. Haberly, 2364 N. Neva, Chicago, IL 60635
Paul Jaeger, Inc., 211 Leedom St., Jenkintown, PA 19046
Lee's Red Ramps, 34220 Cheseboro Rd., Space 19, Palmdale, CA 93550 (illuminated sights)
Jim Lofland, 2275 Larkin Rd., Boothwyn, PA 19061
Lyman Products Corp., Rte. 147, Middlefield, Conn. 06455
Marble Arms Corp., 420 Industrial Park, Gladstone, Mich. 49837
Merit Gunsight Co., P.O. Box 995, Sequim, Wash. 98382
Micro Sight Co., 242 Harbor Blvd., Belmont, Calif. 94002
Miniature Machine Co., 212 E. Spruce, Deming, N.M. 88030
Modern Industries, Inc., 613 W-11, Erie, PA 16501
C. R. Pedersen & Son, Ludington, Mich. 49431
Poly Choke Co., Inc., P.O. Box 296, Hartford, CT 06101
Redfield Gun Sight Co., 5800 E. Jewell St., Denver, Colo. 80222
Schwarz's Gun Shop, 41 - 15th St., Wellsburg, W. Va. 26070
Simmons Gun Specialties, Inc., 700 Rodgers Rd., Olathe, Kans. 66061
Slug Site Co., Whitetail Wilds, Lake Hubert, MN 56469
Sport Service Center, 2364 N. Neva, Chicago, IL 60635
Tradewinds, Inc., Box 1191, Tacoma, WA 98401
Williams Gun Sight Co., 7389 Lapeer Rd., Davison, Mich. 48423

STOCKS (Commercial and Custom)

Abe and VanHorn, 5124 Huntington Dr., Los Angeles, CA 90032
Adams Custom Gun Stocks, 13461 Quito Rd., Saratoga, CA 95070
Ahlman's Inc., R.R. 1, Box 20, Morristown, MN 55052
Don Allen, Rte. 1, Northfield, MN 55057 (blanks)
Anderson's Guns, Jim Jares, 706 S. 23rd St., Laramie, WY 82070
R. J. Anton, 874 Olympic Dr., Waterloo, IA 50701
Dietrich Apel, Star Route 2, Newport, NH 03773
Austrian Gunworks Reg'd., P.O. Box 136, Eastman, Que., Canada, J0E 1P0
Jim Baiar, 490 Halfmoon Rd., Columbia Falls, MT 59912
Joe J. Balickie, Custom Stocks, Rte. 2, Box 56-G, Apex, NC 27502
Bartas, Rte. 1, Box 129-A, Cato, Wis. 54206
John Bianchi, 100 Calle Cortez, Temecula, CA 92390 (U. S. carbines)
Al Biesen, West 2039 Sinto Ave., Spokane, Wash. 99201
Stephen L. Billeb, Rte. 3, Box 163, Bozeman, MT 59715
E. C. Bishop & Son Inc., Box 7, Warsaw, Mo. 65355
John M. Boltin, P.O. Box 1122, No. Myrtle Beach, SC 29582
Brown Precision Co., 5869 Indian Ave., San Jose, CA 95123
Lenard M. Brownell, Box 25, Wyarno, WY 82845
E. J. Bryant, 3154 Glen St., Eureka, CA 95501
Jack Burres, 10333 San Fernando Road, Pacoima, CA 91331 (English, Claro, Bastogne Paradox walnut blanks only)
Calico Hardwoods, Inc., 1648 Airport Blvd., Windsor, Calif. 95492 (blanks)
Dick Campbell, 365 W. Oxford Ave., Englewood, CO 80110
Winston Churchill, Twenty Mile Stream Rd., Rt.1, Box 29B, Proctorsville, VT 05153
Cloward's Gun Shop, Jim Cloward, 4023 Aurora Ave. N., Seattle, WA 98102
Crane Creek Gun Stock Co., 25 Shephard Terr., Madison, WI 53705
Crest Carving Co., 8091 Bolsa Ave., Midway City, CA 92655
Custom Gunstocks, Dick Campbell, 365 W. Oxford Ave., Englewood, CO 80110
Dahl's Custom Stocks, Rt. 4, Box 187, Schofield Rd., Lake Geneva, WI 53147 (Martin Dahl)
Jack Dever, 8520 N.W. 90, Oklahoma City, OK 73132
Charles De Veto, 1087 Irene Rd., Lyndhurst, O. 44124
Bill Dowtin, P.O. Box 72, Celina, TX 75009
Reinhart Fajen, Box 338, Warsaw, Mo. 65355
N. B. Fashingbauer, Box 366, Lac Du Flambeau, Wis. 54538
Ted Fellowes, Beaver Lodge, 9245 16th Ave. S. W., Seattle, Wash. 98106